Frommer's 96

Caribbean

by Darwin Porter
Assisted by Danforth Prince

Macmillan • USA

MACMILLAN TRAVEL

A Simon & Schuster Macmillan Company
1633 Broadway
New York, NY 10019

ISBN 0-02-860645-0
ISSN 1044-2375

Cover by
Design by Michele Laseau
Digital Cartography by John Decamillis, Ortelius Design

SPECIAL SALES

Bulk purchases (10+ copies) of Frommer's travel guides are available to corporations at special discounts. The Special Sales Department can produce custom editions to be used as premiums and/or for sales promotion to suit individual needs. Existing editions can be produced with custom cover imprints such as corporate logos. For more information write to Special Sales, Simon & Schuster, 1230 Avenue of the Americas, New York, NY 10020.

Manufactured in the United States of America

Contents

List of Maps

INVITATION TO THE READER

In researching this book, I discovered many wonderful places—hotels, restaurants, shops, and more. I'm sure you'll find others. Please tell us about them, so we can share the information with your fellow travelers in upcoming editions. If you were disappointed with a recommendation, we'd love to know that, too. Please write to:

Darwin Porter
Frommer's Caribbean '96
Macmillan Travel
1633 Broadway
New York, NY 10019

AN ADDITIONAL NOTE

Please be advised that travel information is subject to change at any time—and this is especially true of prices. We therefore suggest that you write or call ahead for confirmation when making your travel plans. The authors, editors, and publisher cannot be held responsible for the experiences of readers while traveling. Your safety is important to us, however, so we encourage you to stay alert and be aware of your surroundings. Keep a close eye on cameras, purses, and wallets, all favorite targets of thieves and pickpockets.

WHAT THE SYMBOLS MEAN

✪ Frommer's Favorites

Hotels, restaurants, attractions, and entertainments you should not miss.

Ⓢ Super-Special Values

Hotels and restaurants that offer great value for your money.

The following abbreviations are used for credit cards:

AE American Express	EU Eurocard
CB Carte Blanche	JCB Japan Credit Bank
DC Diners Club	MC MasterCard
DISC Discover	V Visa
ER enRoute	

The Best of the Caribbean

The Caribbean dream of days spent lolling on palm-tree-shaded beaches or snorkeling in crystalline waters is only a few hours by plane from North America. Dubbed the "Eighth Continent of the World," the Caribbean islands have a variety of exotic, rich cultures. The terrain includes thick rain forests, black-sand beaches, and haunting volcanoes. Visitors can hike through national parks, dive along underwater mountains, and engage in all kinds of other outdoor activities. But perhaps you'd rather plunk yourself down by the pool with a frosted drink in hand. The island you choose will depend on who you are and what you like to do.

Whether you want a veranda with a view of the sea or a plantation house set in a field of sugarcane, this chapter will help you choose the island that best suits your needs. The best choices for all kinds of lodgings, including most romantic, most escapist, and most family oriented, are detailed. If you're looking for a rum-and-reggae cruise or an utterly quiet evening, the "Best of the Caribbean" will provide you with expert advice.

For a thumbnail portrait of each island, see "Islands in Brief," in Chapter 2.

1 The Best Beaches

Good beaches can be found on virtually every island of the Caribbean, with the possible exceptions of Saba (where residents swim off rocky shores) and Dominica (where the limited number of beaches are lined with sands that are dramatically black and highly reflective of the hot sun).

- **Cane Garden Bay,** Tortola, British Virgin Islands. One of the more spectacular stretches of beach, Cane Garden Bay extends for 1¹/₂ miles of white sand. A jogger's favorite, the beach is the rival of the Magens Bay beach on St. Thomas.
- **Magens Bay Beach,** St. Thomas, U.S. Virgin Islands. Known for its half-mile-long loop of brilliant white sand, and for its clear and calm waters, this public beach is the most popular in the U.S. archipelago. Two peninsulas protect the beach, and its flat, sandy bottom make it safe for children.
- **Seven Mile Beach,** Grand Cayman. It's really about 5¹/₂ miles, but the label of "seven mile" has stuck. Lined with condos and

plush resorts, this beach is known for its array of water sports and its translucent aquamarine waters. Australian pines dot the background, and the average winter temperature of the water is 80°F.

- **Playa Grande,** Dominican Republic. One of the Caribbean's least crowded beaches, but one of the best, Playa Grande lies along the north shore. The long stretch of sand is powdery, and farther west is another beautiful beach at Sosúa, with calm waters and lots of tourist facilities.

- **Negril Beach,** Jamaica. In the northwestern section of the island, this beach stretches for 7 miles along the sea and in the backdrop lie some of the most hedonistic resorts in the Caribbean, such as the appropriately named Hedonism II. Not for the conservative, the beach also contains some nudist "patches" along with bare-all Booby Island offshore. The nude beach areas are sectioned off, but some new oceanfront resorts have views of these areas.

- **Luquillo Beach,** Puerto Rico. This crescent-shaped public beach, 30 miles east of San Juan, is the local favorite. Much photographed because of its white sands and coconut palms, it also has tent sites and picnic facilities. These often-fierce Atlantic waters are subdued by the coral reefs protecting the crystal-clear lagoon.

- **Trunk Bay,** St. John, U.S. Virgin Islands. Protected by the U.S. National Park Service, this beach is one of the Caribbean's most popular. A favorite with cruise-ship passengers, it's known for its underwater trail, where markers guide beachcombers along the reef just off the white sandy beach.

- **Shoal Bay,** Anguilla. Often so empty it has been called "paradise" or "Eden," this silvery beach helped put Anguilla on the map. Divers are drawn to the schools of iridescent fish that dart among the coral gardens offshore.

- **St. Jean,** St. Barthélemy, French West Indies. A somewhat narrow, golden sandy beach, St. Jean is the gem of this French-held island with a Swedish heritage. In spite of its French connection, however, nudity is not permitted. Nevertheless, this is most often compared to a beach on France's Côte d'Azur. The beach strip is protected by reefs, making it ideal for swimming.

- **Le Diamant,** Martinique, French West Indies. This bright white sandy beach stretches for about 6¹/₂ miles, much of it undeveloped. It faces a rocky offshore island, Diamond Rock, which has uninhabited shores.

2 The Best Honeymoon Resorts

As wedding ceremonies have become increasingly expensive and complicated, more and more couples are exchanging their vows in the Caribbean. Many resorts will arrange everything from the preacher to the flowers, so I've included in the following list some resorts that provide wedding services. For more information about the various options and the legal requirements for marriages on some of the more popular Caribbean islands, see Chapter 3, "Planning a Trip to the Caribbean."

- **Sandals** (☎ **800/SANDALS**). There are half a dozen members of this resort chain in Jamaica alone, and at least two others scattered through the English-speaking islands of the Lesser Antilles. Each resort in the chain prides itself on providing an all-inclusive (cash-free) environment where meals are provided in abundance to any couple. Enthusiastic members of the staff bring heroic amounts of community spirit to whatever knot-tying rituals happen to be celebrated on-site. Sandals will provide everything from a preacher to petunias (as well as champagne, a cake, and all the legalities) for you to get hitched on-site. Any of these resorts can provide a suitable setting, but one of the most appealing is Sandals Royal Caribbean, outside Montego Bay, Jamaica.

- Bolongo Beach Resorts Club Everything, St. Thomas, U.S. Virgin Islands. This is probably the most popular choice for honeymooners of all the offshore islands under U.S. jurisdiction. Scattered over three well-accessorized sites (which are interconnected by free minivan transfers), it welcomes newlyweds with a passion, and plans such special features as a carnival-night buffet, Sunday brunches (where the happy couple's recent knot-tying ceremony might be announced to the dining room), and a chilled bottle of champagne upon arrival. Lots of the usual sporting activities are included as additional diversions.

- **The Buccaneer,** St. Croix, U.S. Virgin Islands. Imbued with a discreet kind of posh, this resort boasts some of the most extensive vacation facilities on St. Croix. These include three beaches, eight tennis courts, a spa and fitness center, an 18-hole golf course, and 2 miles of carefully maintained jogging trails. The accommodations include beachside rooms with fieldstone terraces leading toward the sea. Although there are many charming aspects to this resort, one of the most alluring is the stone sugar mill (originally built in 1658), which is one of the most popular sites for weddings and visiting honeymooners on all of St. Croix.

- **Biras Creek Hotel,** Virgin Gorda, British Virgin Islands. If you're eager to escape your in-laws and bridesmaids after a wedding ceremony, this is the place. It's a quintessential mariner's hideaway, reachable only after a boat ride of several miles across the open sea. Perched on a narrow promontory jutting into the Caribbean Sea, it's a 150-acre intensely private retreat with a crisscrossing network of signposted nature trails. Honeymooners get better acquainted within the spacious open-air walled showers that occupy each bathroom.

- **Hyatt Regency Grand Cayman,** Cayman Islands. It reigns without contest as the most glamorous and best-landscaped resort in the Cayman Islands. Honeymooners can buy a package that includes champagne and wine, a room with an oversize bed, a one-day Jeep rental, a romantic sundowner sail on a 65-foot catamaran, and discounts at clothing stores, in-house restaurants, and a golf course. As a souvenir of your time in the Caymans, they'll even contribute a honeymoon memento for your home.

- **Four Seasons,** Nevis. Though not as historic as some of Nevis's plantation-style inns, the Four Seasons rules without peer as the most spectacular, best-financed, and best-accessorized hotel on the island. Set in a palm grove adjacent to the island's finest beach, it has the atmosphere of a supremely indulgent country club. The Four Seasons can offer you a four-day wedding package with a choice of wedding venues (in a church, on a beach; with a judge or with a civil magistrate). Your wedding cake will be individually designed by the resort's pastry chef, and music, photographs, flowers, legalities, and virtually anything else you might need or want can be arranged by the resort's hardworking staff. Obviously, there's plenty of room to house family and friends who might want to attend your wedding.

- **Sandy Lane,** Barbados. A satisfying sense of ritual pervades this venerable British-inspired hotel. Four-day honeymoon packages begin at $650 per night and include a bottle of champagne, a breakfast, tennis, a lunch or dinner cruise, and a candlelit dinner, among other things.

- **El Conquistador,** Puerto Rico. A richly accessorized complex of hotels set on a forested bluff overlooking the sea, this is one of the most lavish resorts ever built in the Caribbean. The architecture incorporates Moorish gardens and Andalusian fortresses. You'll find hammocks for two on the resort's offshore private island, as well as about a dozen private Jacuzzis artfully concealed by vegetation at romantically strategic points throughout the grounds. The language of love is, indeed, Spanish, and it's probably spoken better at El Conquistador than anywhere else in the Caribbean.

- **Hyatt Regency St. John,** St. John, U.S. Virgin Islands. The gardens here are among the most lavish on the island. The swimming pool features the kind of waterfall you'd have expected in a tropical rain forest. Honeymooners receive a bottle of champagne, a basket of fruit, one breakfast, one dinner, a sunset sail, and a massage for two, among other complimentary perks. A 7-night honeymoon package for two begins at $1,891.

- **St. James's Club,** Antigua. It's posh, it's British, and a list of the clientele reads like a Who's Who from the London society page. The creation of this resort required transplanting entire forests of palm trees and the installation of hundreds of tons of sand. There are enough diversionary pastimes to keep a honeymoon couple up and about for weeks. There is a wide choice of accommodations, each of which is well-upholstered and very comfortable. Honeymoon packages include daily breakfast and dinner, a bottle of champagne, a sunset cruise, and a horseback ride, among other treats. Seven-night packages cost $3,290 per couple in high-season, $2,520 in off-season.

3   The Best Family Vacations

- **Sapphire Beach Resort & Marina,** St. Thomas, U.S. Virgin Islands. More than any other hotel on St. Thomas, this well-designed resort caters to the needs of both adults and children. There are supervised activities for preteens at the Little Gems Kids Klub, and a toddler program for one- to three-year-olds. Other activities can include the entire family. Also, the white sandy beaches are among the safest and most desirable on the island.

- **Bolongo Beach Resorts Club Everything,** St. Thomas, U.S. Virgin Islands. Lots of family activities are provided by a relentlessly enthusiastic staff, including scavenger hunts, ball games, puppet shows, and arts and crafts. When booking, ask about the plan where children can stay and eat free. This is a carefully monitored safe haven on an island that has had occasional bouts of violence against visitors.

- **The Buccaneer,** St. Croix, U.S. Virgin Islands. Posh, upscale, and offering extremely good service, this hotel is a well-established favorite that occupies a 300-acre former sugar estate. In addition to activities for adults, it features kids' programs that include a half-day sailing excursion to Buck Island Reef and guided nature walks through groves of trees and shrubs. (Kids from urban areas seem especially eager to touch, smell, and taste tropical fruit.) The program caters to children and preteens aged 5 through 12.

- **Chenay Bay Beach Resort,** St. Croix, U.S. Virgin Islands. The owners of this West Indian cottage colony designed a "Cruzan Kids" program whose activities were based on the experiences of their own children. Programs are generally sports oriented, such as tennis, swimming, and kayaking, and are most heavily featured during midsummer and again at Christmastime.

- **El Conquistador,** Puerto Rico. Adults love its combination of Moorish/Andalusian design with tropical gardens and state-of-the-art American technology. But children aren't forgotten amid the glamour and hoopla. Camp Coquí provides for children 3 to 12, every day between 9am and 3pm, at a price of $38 per child per day. Activities include fishing, sailing, arts and crafts, and nature treks. Babysitting services are available, and children under 12 stay free in a room with their parents.

- **Four Seasons,** Nevis. The staff of the Kids for All Seasons day camp are kindly, matronly souls who work well with children. During the adult cocktail hour, when parents might opt for a romantic sundowner *à deux,* kids attend a supervised "children's hour" that resembles a really good birthday bash. Other activities include tennis lessons, water sports, and story telling.

- **Boscobel Beach,** Ocho Rios, Jamaica. This well-accessorized, all-inclusive hotel (complete with a petting zoo!) is one of the few anywhere that specifically markets itself to parents with young children. A vast array of activities are planned for children under 14, including painting classes, computer fun, and parties.

- **FDR,** Runaway Bay, Jamaica. In some hotels, they'll give you a room; FDR gives you a suite with its own kitchen, and a "Girl Friday" whose duties include babysitting. There are two restaurants. Neither its beach nor its pool is the most appealing on Jamaica, but the price is right—and the babysitting is part of the all-inclusive price. Programs for children include dress-up parties, donkey rides, basketball, tennis, and snorkeling.

- **Sandy Beach,** Barbados. Set amid lots of fast-food and family-style restaurants on the southwest coast, this family-oriented hotel offers one- and two-bedroom suites. Each unit has a kitchen for the preparation of economical meals. The beach is a few steps away, and the ambience is informal. If you bring the kids, they'll have plenty of playmates.

- **Hyatt Regency Aruba,** Aruba. Designed like a luxurious hacienda, with award-winning gardens, this resort is the most upscale on Aruba. There are supervised activities for children 3 to 12, and for teenagers 13 to 17. These include excursions by Jeep through the lunar landscapes of Aruba, snorkeling trips to offshore reefs where marine life is abundant, "Rock Out" barbecue parties, sunset sails, and a wide array of things to do for the little ones.

4 The Best Places to Get Away from It All

Activity and a fast pace might be the last thing you're seeking in the Caribbean. You may just plain want to escape from the world. Assuming that you don't feel any urgent need to visit a casino or disco, here is a list of practically perfect options:

- **Ottley's Plantation Inn,** St. Kitts. As you approach it, its dignified verandas appear majestically at the crest of 35 acres of impeccably maintained lawns and gardens. It's one of the most charming plantation house inns anywhere in the world, maintained with style, humor, and goodwill by its expatriate American owners. The food is the best on the island, and the setting will probably soothe your tired nerves within a few hours after your arrival.

- **Biras Creek,** Virgin Gorda, British Virgin Islands. The only access to this resort is by private launch. Whiffs of sea air and views over islets, cays, and deep blue waters will relax you in your charming hotel room. The nautical atmosphere will quickly remove all thoughts of the nine-to-five job you left behind.

- **Guana Island Club,** Guana Island, British Virgin Islands. One of the most secluded hideaways in the entire Caribbean, this resort occupies a privately owned 850-acre bird sanctuary with nature trails. Despite its role as an unspoiled outpost, Guana Island is the sixth-largest island in the British Virgin Islands, with several excellent uncrowded beaches. Head here for views of rare plant and animal life, but be warned that there's a complete lack of nightlife options.

- **Jumby Bay,** Antigua. With 300 acres, this retreat is less than half the size of Guana Island (above), but its amenities are much more luxurious. Buildings are designed with white stucco and terra-cotta roofs in the Spanish style, and children under eight are not admitted. A private island with a 200-year history of plantation life, Jumby Bay is exclusive, expensive, and eminently able to help you forget any rat race worries.

- **Little Cayman Beach Resort,** Cayman Islands. The only way to reach the 10-square-mile island that contains this resort is by boat or airplane. Snorkelers will marvel at some of the most spectacular and colorful marine life in the Caribbean. This relatively new (1992–93) resort has the most complete water sports facilities on the island. Bicycles are available for excursions to the island's distant end.

5 The Friendliest Islands

Open-minded visitors with a sense of humor will almost always have a good rapport with locals regardless of which destination they choose. Remember, though, that islands known for friendliness are usually the smaller ones that don't have much tourism.

Some of the most idyllic islands can be plagued with racial tensions and violent crime. Also, innumerable small but embarrassing interpersonal incidents can mar your holiday.

In particular, Jamaica's portside cities (especially Ocho Rios, Kingston, and Montego Bay) are known for crowds of hawkers and peddlers who aggressively pressure tourists to buy unwanted souvenirs.

On the hostility chart, St. Thomas and St. Croix probably lead the pack. That doesn't mean that those islands aren't filled with friendly, hospitable people. But St. Thomas and St. Croix, to everyone's regret, are the most crime-prone islands in the Caribbean, much of it drug-related.

Last, both Puerto Rico and the Dominican Republic are large enough in population to have an urban atmosphere where some visitors might feel anonymous. Locals can show a detached attitude about the welfare of tourists.

So, with these warnings expressed (however regretfully), let us proceed to friendlier oases.

- **Virgin Gorda,** British Virgin Islands. Vandalism doesn't exist, and home or hotel break-ins are very rare. Many locals leave their houses and cars unlocked. However, as friendly as Virgin Gorda is, I don't recommend that you become *that* casual. But it's the lazy, peaceful life here. Visitors are welcomed into most places with a smile.

- **St. John,** U.S. Virgin Islands. Crimes against tourists, especially violent crimes, are rare here. Pickpockets, however, prey on cruise-ship passengers at Trunk Bay, the island's best beach. But, for the most part, St. John remains an unspoiled and relatively safe destination. The people aren't as jaded to the arrival of tourists as they are on St. Thomas, and in most places you'll receive a genuine welcome. Many places appreciate your business and want you to return, so they make you feel welcome.
- **Bonaire,** Dutch Leewards. Bonaire's desert climate and infertile soil have helped make its population one of the smallest in the Caribbean (only 11,000). The result is a small-town setting with a pace slow enough for the most diehard escapist. Residents are usually moderately curious about off-islanders, and even extend friendly courtesies.
- **Saba,** Dutch Windwards in the Leewards. The residents here refer to their island as the "Unspoiled Caribbean Queen." This is because there are no beaches, casinos, or large hotels, and only a handful of bars, and very little nightlife. There's almost no crime. The population of 1,200 shy, cautiously friendly residents follows traditions that were established by hardy Dutch settlers who first arrived in the 1600s. Saba's somewhat clannish society is known for lacemaking, fishing, and boatbuilding. You'll be very safe here, but will be expected to behave with dignity and respect for island traditions.
- **Nevis,** British Leewards. After sugarcane was introduced to Nevis in 1640, the economy boomed in ways that became the envy of the entire British Empire. Today, it's a small-scale society of charming and historic inns, with a British tradition of good manners. The island's only large-scale resort (the Four Seasons) is as classy and low-key as you'll find anywhere.
- **Montserrat,** British Leewards. The residents here seem to have retained the long-ago cultural influence of the British, who still consider Montserrat a member of their Commonwealth. The churchgoing people of this underpopulated, lush island have good manners and clipped British accents. Yes, it's friendly too.
- **Grenada/St. Vincent/The Grenadines,** British Windwards. The islands of the southern Caribbean are English-speaking, music-loving outposts positioned near the South American mainland. For generations, islanders have devoted themselves to the spice trade, farming, churchgoing, rum making, and fishing. Despite the eviction of Cuban forces from Grenada in the 1980s (or perhaps because of it), North Americans are viewed as helpmates, and locals can be warm and welcoming.

6 The Best Romantic Getaways

- **Anse Chastanet Beach Hotel,** St. Lucia. Offering panoramic views of mountains and jungle, this hotel is a winner with romantics. With its small size, it offers a lot of privacy and rustic charm.
- **Rawlins Plantation,** St. Kitts. Surrounded by 25 acres of carefully clipped lawns and tropical shrubbery, and set on a panoramic hillock about 350 feet above sea level, this hotel evokes a 19th-century plantation. You'll be separated from the rest of the island by hundreds of acres of sugarcane, and there are few phones and no televisions. The style of the house includes mahogany floors, carpets made locally of woven rushes, and carved four-poster beds. Drinks and dinner are served in a brick-sided room originally designed for boiling sugarcane.

- **Horned Dorset Primavera,** Puerto Rico. This resort occupies a site on the western edge of Puerto Rico where steep hillsides slope down to a narrow sandy beach. The main clubhouse is reminiscent of an Iberian villa. Great care is lavished on a sophisticated continental/Californian cuisine, and drinks are consumed in a well-stocked library. (A caged myna bird, with a bilingual vocabulary, keeps you company.) The accommodations are comfortable and dignified, and contain oversize mahogany beds and large private verandas with views of lushly planted hillsides sloping down to the sea.
- **The Golden Lemon,** St. Kitts. It started its life as a French manor house during the 17th century, but by the time its present owners began restoring it, it was decidedly less glamorous. It required the refined tastes of Arthur Leaman, a former editor at *House & Garden,* to bring it to its full potential. Today the Golden Lemon is an authentic Antillean retreat—luxurious, laid-back, and romantic—set in an isolated fishing village loaded with charm.
- **Jumby Bay,** Antigua. This small-scale pocket of luxury is set on a privately owned coral cay, a 12-minute boat ride from the northern coast of Antigua. Other than the staff and about 70 other guests, you'll share the island with sea birds and flocks of wild sheep. The comfortably discreet accommodations are separated by verdant lawns and shrubbery. Beach hammocks are scattered amid the island's groves of sea grape trees.
- **Peter Island,** British Virgin Islands. Romantics appreciate its isolation as an 1,800-acre private landfall south of Tortola and east of St. John. (Reaching it requires a 30-minute waterborne transfer, which many urban refugees consider part of the fun.) Conceived during the 1960s as a prestigious private retreat by a Norwegian shipowner, it has been continually improved since its original conception, and today is a discreet and well-managed garden of very laid-back repose. Bring a companion and/or a good book, and enjoy the comings and goings of yachts at the island's private marina.
- **Petit Saint Vincent (PSV) Resort,** Grenadines. Although the Caribbean contains other resorts on privately owned islands, the sheer distance of PSV from the North American mainland adds an additional splash of romance. It's probably the most secluded and discreet of the Caribbean's luxury hideaways. The artfully built clubhouses and bungalows were crafted from tropical woods and local stone. The resort is simultaneously rustic and lavish. Your bungalow is designed in such a way that if you don't put on any clothes until dinnertime, no one will see you *au naturel* except your companion.
- **Cap Juluca,** Anguilla. One of the boldest and most imaginative resorts in the Caribbean, it combined millions of dollars worth of 1980s stock-market profits with a thrillingly beautiful beach and the skills of some of the most sophisticated postmodern architects. The result looks like a Saharan casbah whose domed villas seem to float against the scrubland and azure sky. You'll always have the feeling that someone very famous is enjoying a romantic off-the-record tryst behind the sheltering walls of this extremely stylish resort.
- **Castelets,** St. Barthélemy. Set on a semi-arid hilltop, and ringed with a forest of pines, this resort is like a stone-sided manor house you might find in Provence. Windows are positioned to provide sweeping views of the sea (whose beaches and bikinis are a short drive away). There are only about a dozen accommodations here, most of them airy and discreetly lavish suites some of whose occupants have had very famous names.

- **Cotton House,** Mustique, The Grenadines. Cosmopolitan, and infused with a vivid sense of fashionable London, this hotel was built during the 18th century as a warehouse for the island's ample supplies of—you guessed it—cotton. Richly overhauled in the 1970s by one of Britain's most tasteful designers, it houses 27 airy accommodations. Although part of the glamour of this hotel has tarnished in recent years after many management changes and the demise of its most illustrious guests, the Cotton House is still undeniably romantic.

7 The Best Inns

- **Ocean View Hotel,** Barbados. Shortly after the turn of the century, this hotel was the island's most fashionable. Today, stripped of much of its original gingerbread, it seems unadorned compared to the dozens of newer hotels that sprawl nearby. With its English country house quality, the Ocean View maintains worthy accommodations. Dorothy Lamour and Isabella Rossellini have both, during their respective eras, stayed here.
- **Frangipani Hotel,** Bequia, Grenadines. This is the century-old homestead of the Mitchell family, whose most famous scion later became prime minister of St. Vincent. Today the premises functions as a small, very relaxed inn. It's fun to watch the yachts making their seaward forays from the nearby marina.
- **Avila Beach Hotel,** Curaçao. This hotel's historic core, built in 1780 as the "country house" of the island's governor, retains its dignity and lack of excess ornamentation. Although it has functioned as a hotel since the end of World War II, in the early 1990s a new owner added 40 bedrooms in motel-like outbuildings and upgraded the sports and dining facilities. Today the Avila provides a sandy beach and easy access to the shops and distractions of nearby Willemstad.
- **Hermitage Plantation,** Nevis. Here, guests are housed in clapboard-sided cottages separated by carefully maintained landscape of bougainvillea and grasslands. The beach is a short drive away, but the sense of 19th-century plantation life (and candlelit dinners amid the antiques and polished silver of the main house) create holidays that are decidedly romantic.
- **Villa Madeleine,** St. Croix. This recently built, almost perfect re-creation of a 19th-century Great House occupies the summit of a scrub-covered ridge. The food is among the best on St. Croix. Accommodations include richly furnished hideaway suites with sweeping high-altitude views over the coastline.
- **Spice Island Inn,** Grenada. Each of this hotel's 56 accommodations is a suite (with Jacuzzi) either beside the beach (one of Grenada's best) or near a swimming pool. Friday nights feature live music from the island's most popular bands.
- **François Plantation,** St. Barthélemy. About a dozen pastel-colored bungalows are scattered within the dense thicket of what's probably the lushest garden on St. Barts. The mood is discreet, permissive, and—to the extent it doesn't bother anybody else—fun. Food is French-inspired and served on a wide veranda decorated in a whimsical, colonial style.
- **The Admiral's Inn,** Antigua. The most historically evocative corner of Antigua is Nelson's Dockyard, which was originally built in the 1700s to repair His Majesty's ships. The brick-and-stone inn that flourishes there today was once a warehouse for turpentine and pitch. In the late 1960s it was transformed into a well-designed and very charming hotel. (If you're trying to escape from urban

pressures, you might be bothered by the sometimes-raucous activities in the hotel's bar and restaurant.) The Admiral's Inn is unique, and an ideal choice for a two- or three-night stopover.

- **Trident Villas and Hotel,** Jamaica. Here, high-ceilinged villas are outfitted in an unashamedly English aesthetic. The dining room staff wears white gloves, and some of the very posh guests often dress with understated elegance at dinner. Overall, the resort's allegiance to the formal customs of colonial Jamaica is one of its most endearing virtues. It can rain a lot here during certain off-seasons, which accentuates the drama of its rocky seafront setting.

- **Drake's Anchorage Inn,** Mosquito Island, British Virgin Islands. Set off the northeastern coast of Virgin Gorda, this simple, austere 12-room inn is the only establishment of any kind on Mosquito Island. Guests can enjoy the island's 126 acres of forest and scrubland. Snorkeling opportunities abound offshore. There's a restaurant, a bar frequented by yachtspeople, and a kind of roguish charm that many escapists find endearing. Don't expect luxurious amenities— everything is almost aggressively simple here. But if you want an insight into the way the Caribbean used to be, this is the place.

8 The Best Destinations for Serious Shoppers

Since the American government allows U.S. citizens to take (or send) back home greater numbers of goods duty-free from the U.S. Virgins than from other ports of call, the U.S. Virgin Islands remain the shopping bazaar of the Caribbean. U.S. citizens are allowed to carry home $1,200 worth of goods untaxed, as opposed to only $400 worth of goods from most islands in the Caribbean. (The only exception to this rule is Puerto Rico, where any purchase, regardless of the amount, can be carried tax-free back to the U.S. mainland. For more on this, see below.)

- **St. Thomas.** Many of its busiest shops are in restored warehouses that were originally built in the 1700s. Charlotte Amalie, the capital, is a shopper's town. However, despite all the fanfare, real bargains are hard to come by. Regardless, the island attracts hordes of cruise-ship passengers on a sometimes-frantic hunt for bargains, real or imagined. The number of stores in Charlotte Amalie is staggering—they are stocked with more merchandise than anywhere else in the entire Caribbean. Look for two local publications, *This Week* and *Best Buys;* either might steer you to the type of merchandise you're seeking. If at all possible, try to avoid shopping when more than one cruise ship is in port: The shopping district is a madhouse on those days.

- **St. Croix.** Compared to St. Thomas, this is like a poor stepchild. Nevertheless, there is much to interest the "born-to-shop" visitor here, and merchandise has never been more wide-ranging than it is today. Even though most cruise ships call at Frederiksted, a colorful but isolated town near the island's western tip, the majority of shops are found in Christiansted, the island's capital. The U.S. Virgins share many of the same merchants. You'll see many of the same shops and chains on St. Croix that you find on St. Thomas, including such omnipresent establishments as Little Switzerland and Java Wraps. Prices are about the same as in St. Thomas.

- **Aruba.** The wisest shoppers on Aruba are cost-conscious souls who have carefully checked prices of comparable goods before leaving home. Duty on things sold on Aruba is relatively low (only 3.3%). Much of the European china, jewelry, perfumes, wristwatches, and crystal have a disconcerting habit of reappearing at shopping malls and hotel boutiques throughout Aruba, so after you determine exactly which brand of watch or china you want, you might scan as many retail outlets as possible for the best bargain.

- **Barbados.** Bajan shops seem to specialize in all the niceties of a well-bred life in England. Merchandise includes bone china from British and Irish manufacturers, china, wristwatches, jewelry, and perfumes. (There's also a wide array of other goods.) Bridgetown's Broad Street is the shopping headquarters of the island, although some of the stores represented there maintain boutiques (with similar prices but with a less extensive range of merchandise) at many of the island's hotels and in shopping malls along the congested southwestern coast. Except for cigarettes and tobacco, duty-free items can be hauled off by any buyer as soon as they're paid for. Duty-free status is extended to anyone showing a passport or ID and an airline ticket with a date of departure from Barbados.

- **Curaçao.** Curaçao has been a mercantile center since the 1700s. There's something about the tidy and prosperous orderliness of Willemstad, the island's capital, which encourages an acquisitive urge, and hundreds of merchants will be only too happy to cater to your needs. A handful of malls lie on Willemstad's outskirts, but the majority of shops are clustered within a few blocks of the capital's Dutch-inspired core. During seasonal sales, goods might be up to 50% less than comparable prices in the States, whereas throughout most months of the year, you'll find luxury goods (porcelain, crystal, watches, and gemstones) priced at about 25% less than in the States. Technically, you'll pay import duties on virtually everything you buy, but rates are so low you might not even notice.

- **Dominican Republic.** The island's best buys include handcrafts, amber from Dominican mines, and the distinctive pale-blue semiprecious gemstone known as larimar. Be aware that the amber you buy from a streetside vendor might be nothing more than orange-colored transparent plastic—buy only from well-established shops if your investment is a large one. Other charming souvenirs might include a Dominican rocking chair (remember the one JFK used to sit in?), which is sold boxed, in pieces. Shopping malls and souvenir stands abound in Santo Domingo, in Puerto Plata, and along the country's northern coast.

- **Jamaica.** The shopping was better in the good old days before new taxes added a 10% surcharge. Despite that, Jamaica offers a wealth of desirable goods, the most obvious of which include flavored rums; Jamaican coffees; handcrafts such as woodcarvings, woven baskets, and sandals; original paintings and sculpture; and cameras, wristwatches, and VCRs. Unless you're a glutton for handmade souvenirs (which will make themselves available to you on virtually every beach and streetcorner), you'd be wise to limit most of your purchases to bonafide merchants and stores.

- **Puerto Rico.** For U.S. citizens, there's no duty on anything (yes, anything) you buy in Puerto Rico. That doesn't guarantee that prices will be particularly low. Jewelry and watches abound, often at competitive prices, especially in the island's best-stocked area, Old San Juan. Also of great interest are such Puerto Rican handcrafts as charming folkloric papier-mâché carnival masks.

- **Sint Maarten/St. Martin.** Although there's no duty on any purchases you'll make on either side of the island's Dutch/French border, goods are not especially cheap. Merchants have been suspected of fixing prices on both sides of the border, and after a few days, you might grow exceedingly tired of displays of electronic gadgets. It's best to arrive on the island as a well-educated consumer, with a firm grip on what is and what isn't a favorable price for whatever you really need. Phillipsburg, capital of the island's Dutch side, has a broader selection of merchandise, and a greater number of stores, than anywhere else on either side of the island.

- **Cayman Islands.** Goods are sold tax free from a daunting collection of malls and minimalls throughout Grand Cayman. Most of these are along the highway that parallels Seven Mile Beach; you'll need a car to go from one to another. There are also lots of stores in George Town, which you can explore by foot, poking in and out of some large emporiums in your search for bargains.

9 The Best Nightlife

It's sleepy time on the following islands: The British Virgins, Montserrat, Nevis, Anguilla, St. Eustatius, Saba, St. Barthélemy, Dominica, Bonaire, St. Vincent, and all of the Grenadines. The serious partier will probably want to avoid those tranquil havens and seek out the nighttime action of the following islands:

- **Puerto Rico.** Puerto Rico contains all the raw ingredients for great nightlife, including casinos, endless rows of bars and bodegas, cabaret shows with girls and glitter, and discos that feature everything from New York imports to some of the best salsa and merengue anywhere. If you're a really serious partier, know that you'll have lots of company in Puerto Rico. Be prepared to stay out very late; perhaps you'll recover from your Bacardi hangover near the soothing waves of a palm-fringed beach.

- **St. Thomas.** The Virgin Islands' most active nightlife is found here. Don't expect glitzy shows like those in San Juan's Condado area, or any kind of casino. The resort with the strongest emphasis on music is Marriott's Frenchman's Reef, while the Hard Rock Café in Charlotte Amalie is best for nightly rock 'n' roll. Nearby, the Greenhouse Restaurant features recorded music, live concerts, and golden-oldies nights.

- **St. Croix.** It's very similar to St. Thomas, although the list of nightlife options is smaller. A consistently good choice is the Buccaneer Hotel, which stages limbo/folkloric shows, reggae players, and concerts by such local stars as Jimmy Hamilton, who played with Duke Ellington's orchestra. The Cormorant Beach Club features steel bands on Thursday and Sunday, and jazz on Friday. Otherwise, the idiosyncratic clubs and hole-in-the-wall bars of Christiansted dominate the nightscape.

- **Aruba.** This island contains 10 casinos, each with its own unique decor, and each with a coterie of devoted gamblers. Some offer their own cabaret or comedy shows, dance floors with live or recorded music, restaurants of all degrees of formality, and bars.

- **Barbados.** Bridgetown is home to at least two disco boats (the *Bajan Queen* and the *Jolly Roger*), which embark at sundown for rum-and-reggae cruises, as well as oversize music bars like the Warehouse and Harbour Lights. Otherwise, a host of bars, British-inspired pubs, dozens of restaurants, and discos (both within and outside of large hotels) beckon from St. Lawrence Gap or the crowded south-west coast.

- **Dominican Republic.** Large resort hotels in the Dominican Republic evoke a Latino version of Las Vegas in ways that haven't been seen since the days of Batista's Cuba. And if cabaret shows aren't your thing, there are casinos, and enough discos to keep a soca or hip-hop enthusiast busy for weeks. In Santo Domingo, you should be alert to the dangers of late-night strolls. At the end of your evening, get a cab to bring you back to your hotel room.

- **Jamaica.** Repeat visitors are usually motivated by a love for the island's distinct musical forms. Foremost among these are reggae and soca, both of which are performed at hotels, resorts, and raffish dives throughout the island. Hotels often stage folkloric shows that include entertainers who sing, dance, swallow torches, and walk on broken glass. There are also plenty of indoor/outdoor bars where you might actually be able to talk to people. Local tourist boards in Negril and Montego Bay sometimes organize weekly beach parties called "Boonoonoonoos."

- **Sint Maarten/St. Martin.** This island contains what's probably the densest concentration of restaurants in the Caribbean, each with its own bar. Discos are often indoor/outdoor affairs. Throughout the nightlife scene there's a sense of internationalism. Hotel casinos abound, and if you're addicted to the jingle of slot machines and roulette wheels, you won't lack for company.

10 The Best Gambling

Here is a list of islands that simply wouldn't be the same without their glittering casinos:

- **Aruba.** By day, visitors play at the beach. After dark, they throng to the island's 10 casinos. The casinos are big, they're splashy, they're colorful, and, yes, people even occasionally win. Drinks are usually free while you play; visitors under 18 aren't admitted. Conveniently, the legal tender in most of Aruba's casinos is the U.S. dollar.

- **Curaçao.** The canny merchants of Curaçao have known how to make a guilder since the early colonial days. There are at least a dozen casinos beckoning from strategic points throughout the island.

- **Dominican Republic.** The tourist areas of Puerto Plata and Santo Domingo are sprinkled with casinos, and the island's ever-developing north shore contains its share of jingle-jangle too. My favorite is the casino in the Jaragua Hotel in Santo Domingo, which offers floor shows, live merengue concerts, a wraparound bar, and at least five different restaurants.

- **Puerto Rico.** The country's gaming headquarters lies along the Condado in San Juan, though there are also casinos in mega-hotels scattered throughout the island. The casinos here are probably the most fun in the Caribbean, and also some of the most spectacular. Each contains lots of sideshows (restaurants, merengue bars, art galleries, piano bars, shops) that can distract you from the roulette and slots. Puerto Ricans take pride in dressing well at their local casinos, which enhances an evening's glamour. No drinking is permitted at the tables, and tight controls are exerted by U.S. gaming authorities.

- **Sint Maarten.** Gambling is illegal on the island's French side (St. Martin), so the casinos are the exclusive domain of the Dutch. The gaming halls have an atmosphere of nonchalance, which might appeal to you if you dislike gaming halls with high stakes and lots of intensity. There are about seven casinos in Sint Maarten, usually in large resort hotels. Hotels on the French side sometimes arrange gambling junkets to the Dutch side.

11 The Best Dive Sites

All the major islands offer diving trips, lessons, and equipment. Intermediate and advanced divers can also take advantage of night dives.

- **Virgin Gorda.** Many divers plan their entire vacations around exploring the famed wreck of the RMS *Rhône,* off Salt Island. This royal mail steamer, which went down in 1867, is the most celebrated dive site in the Caribbean.
- **Grand Cayman.** This island has been called "the best known dive destination in the Caribbean—if not the world," by *Skin Diver* magazine. There are 34 dive operations on Grand Cayman, 5 on Little Cayman, and 3 on Cayman Brac. A full range of professional dive services is available, including equipment sales, rentals, and repairs; instruction at all levels; underwater photography; and video schools.
- **Bonaire.** The highly accessible reefs that surround Bonaire have never suffered from poaching or pollution, and the island's environmentally conscious dive industry will ensure that they never do. Diving is possible 24 hours a day throughout the year. Created from volcanic eruptions, the island is an underwater mountain. As such, fringe reefs await right off the beach of every hotel on any part of the island.
- **St. Croix.** Increasingly known as a top diving destination, St. Croix hasn't overtaken Grand Cayman yet, but it has a lot going for it. Beach dives, reef dives, wreck dives, nighttime dives, wall dives—they're all here. But none can compete with the underwater trails of the national park at Buck Island, off St. Croix's mainland. Other desirable sites include the drop-offs and coral canyons at Cane Bay and Salt River. Davis Bay is the location of the 12,000-foot-deep Puerto Rico Trench, the fifth-deepest body of water on earth.
- **Saba.** Islanders can't brag about its beaches, but Saba is blessed with some of the Caribbean's richest marine life. It's considered one of the premier diving locations in the Caribbean, with 38 official dive sites. The unusual setting includes underwater lava flows, black sand, large strands of black coral, millions of fish, and underwater mountaintops submerged under 90 feet of water.

12 The Best Snorkeling

A reader's poll of *Scuba Diving* magazine confirmed what Virgin Islanders knew all along: The islands of St. Croix, St. John, and St. Thomas are among the top five favorite places to snorkel in the Caribbean. The waters off the Virgin Islands abound in rich flora and fauna.

- **Buck Island Reef National Monument,** St. Croix. More than 250 species of fish, as well as a variety of sponges, corals, and crustaceans, have been found at this 850-acre island and reef system, 2 miles off St. Croix's north shore. The reef is strictly protected by the National Park Service.

- **Trunk Bay,** St. John. This self-guided 225-yard-long trail has large under-water signs that identify species of coral and other items of interest. There are showers, changing rooms, equipment rentals, and a lifeguard.
- **Magens Bay,** St. Thomas. On the north shore, Coki Point offers year-round snorkeling, especially around the coral ledges near Coral World's underwater tower, a favorite with cruise-ship passengers.
- **Leinster Bay,** St. John. With easy access from land or sea, Leinster Bay offers calm, clear, and uncrowded waters, with an abundance of sea life.
- **Haulover Bay,** St. John. A favorite with locals, this small bay is rougher than Leinster and often deserted. The snorkeling is dramatic, with ledges, walls, nooks, and sandy areas set close together. At this spot, only about 200 yards separate the Atlantic Ocean from the Caribbean Sea.
- **Cane Bay,** St. Croix. One of the island's best diving and snorkeling sites is off this breezy north-shore beach. On a clear day, you can swim out 150 yards and see the Cane Bay Wall that drops off dramatically to deep waters below. Multicolored fish and elkhorn and brain coral are in abundance here.
- **Bonaire.** All the attributes that make Bonaire a world-class dive destination (see above) apply to snorkeling. Snorkelers can wade from the shores by their hotels to the reefs and view an array of coral and a range of colorful fish. The reefs just off Klein Bonaire and Washington/Slagbaai Park receive especially rave reviews.
- **Grand Cayman.** Stingray City has been called the best 12-foot dive (or snor-kel) site in the world.
- **Tobago.** The shallow, sun-flooded waters off the South American coastline boast enormous colonies of marine life. Buccoo Reef on Tobago offers many opportunities for snorkeling, and many local entrepreneurs take snorkeling enthusiasts out for junkets.
- **Curaçao Underwater Park,** Curaçao. In contrast to Curaçao's sterile terrain, the marine life that rings the island is rich and spectacular. The best-known snorkeling sites stretch for 12^1/$_2$ miles along Curaçao's southern coastline (the Curaçao Underwater Park), though there are many other highly desirable sites. Sunken ships, gardens of hard and soft coral, and millions of fish are a snorkeler's treat.

13 The Best Golfing Destinations

Some of the world's most famous golf architects, including Robert Trent Jones (both Junior and Senior), Pete Dye, Gary Player, and others, have designed chal-lenging courses in the Caribbean.

- **Casa de Campo,** Dominican Republic. Hispaniola's most challenging golf course, named "Teeth of the Dog," is considered one of designer Pete Dye's masterpieces. Seven holes are set adjacent to the sea, while the other 11 are con-foundedly labyrinthine. The resort also has a second golf course, "The Links," which some claim is even more difficult.
- **Golf de St-François,** Guadeloupe. Six of its 18 holes are ringed with water traps, the winds are devilishly unpredictable, and the par is a sweat-inducing 71. This fearsome course displays the wit and skill of its designer, Robert Trent Jones, Sr. Most of the staff are multilingual, and because it's owned by the local municipality, it's a lot less snobby than you might expect.

- **Tryall,** Montego Bay, Jamaica. This is the finest golf course on an island known for its tricky breezes. The site was once the home of one of Jamaica's best-known sugar plantations; the only remnant is a ruined waterwheel. The promoters of Johnny Walker Scotch, who know a lot about golfing, selected this place for their most prestigious competition. During the winter season, the course is usually open only to guests of Tryall.
- **El Conquistador,** Puerto Rico. Its fairways meander over the rolling hills that surround one of Puerto Rico's most fabled resorts. The par-72 layout was designed by Robert Von Hagge in 1967, and redesigned by Arthur Hills & Associates (who flattened some of the more obnoxious slopes). Golfers, who must be guests of El Conquistador, enjoy sweeping views of the sea. The winds are tricky and change frequently, adding to the challenge.
- **Hyatt Dorado Beach,** Puerto Rico. This resort maintains two golf courses, both set on what were originally citrus and coconut plantations. Both courses were designed by Robert Trent Jones, Sr. No one can agree on which of the two courses is the more interesting, but the elegance of both is breathtaking. If you're an absolute golf glutton, the Hyatt's companion resort, the Cerromar, a short drive down the coastal road, offers an additional pair of golf courses.
- **Palmas del Mar,** Puerto Rico. Designed by Gary Player, this par-72 golf course near Humacao is considered by most experts as one of the most noteworthy anywhere. Its botanical highlights include thousands of mature palm trees and carefully maintained sections of tropical rain forest. The course is considered so good that many golf-playing retirees have bought homes adjacent to the fairways. The most challenging holes? Probably nos. 11 through 16, although many beginners have lost their tempers over no. 18 as well. Lessons are offered to players of all different levels.
- **The Four Seasons,** Nevis. I consider this my personal favorite in all the Caribbean. It was carved out of a coconut plantation and tropical rain forest in the 1980s, and its undulating beauty is virtually unequaled. Designed by Robert Trent Jones, Jr., the course begins at sea level, rises to a point midway up the slopes of Mount Nevis, then slants gracefully back down near the beachfront clubhouse. Electric carts carry golfers through a labyrinth of well-groomed paths, some of which skirt steep ravines.

14 The Best Tennis Facilities

When you're booking your holiday, ask about a "tennis package," which some resorts offer; it usually includes rooms and often meals at discounted rates.

- **Buccaneer,** St. Croix. Hailed as having the best tennis facilities in the Virgin Islands, this resort is the venue for several tournaments every year. There are eight all-weather Laykold courts, two of which are illuminated at night. There's also a pro shop. Nonguests can play here for a charge.
- **Sugar Bay Plantation,** St. Thomas. Some tennis buffs are deserting Buccaneer for this new challenger at Estate Smith Bay. The resort offers the U.S.V.I.'s first stadium tennis court, with a capacity of 220 spectators. In addition, it offers about half a dozen Laykold courts, each of which is lit for night play. There's an on-site pro shop and lessons are available.
- **Curtain Bluff,** Antigua. It's small, select, and carefully run by people who love tennis. It's also the annual site of a well-known spring tournament. The courts are set in a low-lying valley.

- **Casa de Campo,** Dominican Republic. There are so many facilities at this 7,000-acre resort that tennis might come as an afterthought. But if you're a tennis devotee, the facilities include 13 clay courts (half are lighted, and two are ringed with stadium seating), four all-weather Laykold courts, a resident pro, ball machines, and in-house tennis buffs who are usually available to play with guests. During midwinter, residents and clients of Casa de Campo have first crack at court time.
- **Half Moon Club,** Montego Bay, Jamaica. This resort sprawls over hundreds of acres; amid the expanse are about a dozen tennis courts and at least four squash and/or racquetball courts. Jamaica has a strong, British-based affinity for tennis, and Half Moon keeps the tradition alive.
- **El Conquistador,** Puerto Rico. Facilities here include seven Har-Tru tennis courts, a resident pro, and a clubhouse with its own bar. If you're looking for a partner, the hotel will find one for you. Only guests of the hotel can use the courts, some of which are illuminated for night play.
- **Hyatt Regency Cerromar Beach/Hyatt Dorado Beach,** Puerto Rico. These twin beachfront resorts are within a 15-minute walk of one another. There are 20 Laykold tennis courts, some lit, some ringed with stadium seats; all are administered by a tennis pro who gives lessons. If you want pointers on improving your serve or strokes, someone will be on hand to videotape you.

15 The Best Sailing

Virtually any large-scale hotel in the Caribbean will provide small sailboats (especially Sunfish, Sailfish, and small, one-masted catamarans) for their guests. Also widely available are the smallest sailing craft of all, windsurfers. For larger craft, The Virgin Islands and The Grenadines come instantly to mind for their almost ideal sailing conditions. These two regions offer many options for dropping anchor at secluded coves surrounded by relatively calm waters. Both areas are spectacular, but whereas the Virgin Islands offer more dramatic, mountainous terrain, the Grenadines offer insights into island cultures little touched by the modern world.

Other sailing venues in the Caribbean include Antigua, Barbados, St. Martin, and the French-speaking islands. But if you plan on doing a lot of sailing, know in advance that the strongest currents (and biggest waves) usually occur on the northern and eastern sides of most islands—the Atlantic, as opposed to the Caribbean side.

- **The Virgin Islands** Perhaps because of their well-developed marine facilities (and those of the nearby United States), the Virgin Islands receive the lion's share of really devoted yachting enthusiasts. The reigning capital for sailing is Tortola, the largest island of the British Virgins. On site are about 300 well-maintained sailing craft available for bareboat rentals, and perhaps 100 charter yachts.

  The largest of the Caribbean's yacht chartering services is The Moorings (☎ **809/494-2331, 813/530-9747** in southern Florida, or **800/535-7289** in the U.S.). Run by Ginny and Charlie Cary, this yachting charter center will be described more fully in Chapter 7, "The British Virgin Islands." If you'd like sailing lessons, consider Steve Colgate's Offshore Sailing School (☎ **800/221-4326** for more information) or Tortola's Treasure Isle Hotel, which offers courses in seamanship year round. (One of their teaching offerings is designed exclusively for operators of catamarans.) On Virgin Gorda, one of the best bets for rentals of both boats and hotel accommodations is the Bitter End Yacht Club (☎ 809/494-2746).

Some of the biggest charter business in the Caribbean is conducted on St. Thomas, especially at the Ramada Yacht Haven Marina, on the eastern outskirts of Charlotte Amalie, and on St. Thomas's eastern tip, the Red Hook Marina. Other reliable rental agents include the American Yacht Harbor, at Red Hook (☎ 809/775-6454); Club Nautico, also at Red Hook (☎ 809/779-2555); and Charteryacht League, at Flagship (☎ 809/774-3944).

On St. Croix, boating is less a factor in the local economy than it is on St. Thomas or in the British Virgins. A well-recommended choice there, however, is Caribbean Sea Adventures (☎ 809/778-7004).

- **The Grenadines** Boating is a way of life in the Grenadines, partly because access to many of the remote islands is difficult or impossible by airplane. Although boats that belong to a yacht charterer might be scattered at any of several ports (Union Island, Bequia, Mayreau, or Mustique), the corporate entity that actually owns the boats is often located on nearby St. Vincent. One of the most visible of these is Nicholson Yacht Charters (☎ 809/460-1530 in St. Vincent, or **800/662-6066** in the U.S.). On Bequia, Mustique, Petit St. Vincent, and Union Island, the limited number of hotels are well aware of the names of local entrepreneurs who rent sailing craft.

16 The Best Hiking

- **St. John,** U.S. Virgin Islands. Much of St. John's land area is devoted to a national park. There are sudden changes of altitude, sweeping views, lush greenery, and ample opportunities for snorkeling. The island's trails, which are kept in tiptop condition by the U.S. National Park Service, are among the best marked in the Caribbean.
- **St. Croix,** U.S. Virgin Islands. One district on the island's northwestern edge, called "The Rain Forest," contains many little-used roads that double as hiking paths. Buck Island, legendary throughout the Caribbean for its underwater life, also offers a network of hiking trails (and snorkeling in its offshore reefs).
- **Tortola,** British Virgin Islands. The highest peak in the Virgins (Mount Sage) rises almost 1,800 feet from a verdantly forested location northwest of Road Town. It's ringed by about 100 acres of hillside richly woven with plant and bird life. Most visitors combine their explorations of the park with a picnic lunch.
- **Guadeloupe,** French West Indies. The mountainous terrain of Basse-Terre island is considered some of the most beautiful in the entire Caribbean. Although the coastline of Basse-Terre is lined with beach resorts and fishing villages, the mountainous interior is a sparsely inhabited region devoted almost completely to a French national forest, *Le Parc Naturel de Guadeloupe.* Near the park's southernmost boundary stands the 4,812-foot volcanic peak, La Soufrière. The park contains more than 200 miles of hiking trails, allowing physically fit hikers to visit a wealth of gorges, ravines, rivers, and (at points north of La Soufrière) some of the highest waterfalls in the Caribbean.
- **Martinique,** French West Indies. The French Forestry Service (Office National des Forêts) maintains a network of hiking trails to the top of Mt. Pelée, which rises 4,575 feet above sea level.

17 The Best Offbeat Experiences

- **Seeing the Wreck of the *Rhône*.** You can only experience this deep-sea adventure if you're a certified scuba diver. One of the world's most unusual dive sites is the wreck of the *Rhône*. A 310-foot steel-hulled steamship, it was built in Britain in 1865 and sank during a violent storm in 1867. Today the ruined hulk rests on a steep slope off the western coast of Salt Island, southwest of Tortola. Divers visit either the bow of the sunken wreck (80 feet underwater) or the stern (20 feet underwater), but in either case the experience is eerie, and sometimes mystical. Many of the most evocative shots of *The Deep,* a film with Jacqueline Bissett, were shot here.

- **Two Unspoiled Islands.** Marie-Galante (named by Columbus in 1493) and the Iles des Saintes are rarely visited islands near the coast of Guadeloupe—they're among the least-known outposts in the Caribbean. Never having attained the stylish elegance of, say, their French-speaking cousin, St. Barthélemy, they preserve a raffish, seafaring atmosphere you might have found in Marseille during the 1930s. There's very little to do but sunbathe, bicycle, and savor the seclusion.

- **Carib Indian Reservation,** Dominica. The only community of Carib Indians left in the Caribbean is located along the eastern coast of the rarely visited island of Dominica. The Caribs once dominated the region (and even gave it its name). Reviled by Spanish invaders because of their cannibalism, the Caribs now live peacefully in half a dozen villages, the largest of which are Bataka, Sineku, and Salybia. Local affairs are administered by tribal chiefs; the populace speaks a combination of English and Créole patois. Souvenir kiosks sell remarkable baskets and straw mats woven by Carib artisans.

- **Jamaica's People to People.** Almost 700 Jamaican families are registered to spend a few hours (or a few days) with off-island visitors. Tell the Jamaican tourist board what your interests are (butterflies, reggae, Bible studies, sailing, etc.) and they'll pair you up with respectable Jamaicans who will, without fuss or bother, include you in the normal routine of their lives (eating at table, going to the beach, visiting grandma, or whatever). No overnight accommodations are included in this program, but there are no costs involved other than your offering a small gift as a gesture of appreciation. Many lasting friendships have formed as a result of this program.

  If you're going to Grenada, it has an almost-identical People to People program.

Which Island Is for You?	Vacation Costs	All-Inclusive Resorts	Beaches	Above-Average Food	Campgrounds	Casinos	Condo/Villa Rentals	Family-Friendly	Cruise-Ship Port	Deluxe Resorts
Anguilla	$$$$	✔	✔	✔			✔			✔
Antigua	$$$	✔	✔	✔		✔		✔	✔	✔
Aruba	$$	✔	✔	✔		✔	✔	✔	✔	✔
Barbados	$$$	✔	✔	✔			✔	✔	✔	✔
Barbuda	$$$$		✔	✔						✔
Bonaire	$$		✔							
Cayman Islands	$$$	✔	✔	✔			✔	✔	✔	✔
Curaçao	$$		✔			✔			✔	✔
Dominica	$									
Dominican Republic	$	✔	✔			✔		✔	✔	✔
Grenada	$$		✔					✔	✔	✔
The Grenadines	$$	✔	✔							✔
Guadeloupe	$$	✔	✔	✔	✔	✔			✔	
Ile des Saintes/M. Galante	$$		✔	✔						
Jamaica	$$	✔	✔	✔	✔		✔	✔	✔	✔
Martinique	$$$	✔	✔	✔	✔	✔			✔	✔
Montserrat	$$		✔				✔			
Nevis	$$$		✔	✔						✔
Puerto Rico	$		✔	✔	✔	✔	✔	✔	✔	✔
Saba	$									
St. Barthélemy	$$$$		✔	✔			✔			✔
St. Croix	$$		✔	✔			✔	✔	✔	✔
St. Eustatius	$		✔							
St. John	$$$		✔	✔	✔		✔	✔		✔
St. Kitts	$$	✔	✔			✔		✔		✔
St. Lucia	$$	✔	✔					✔	✔	✔
St. Martin/Sint Maarten	$$$	✔	✔	✔		✔	✔	✔	✔	✔
St. Thomas	$$	✔	✔	✔			✔	✔	✔	✔
St. Vincent	$		✔							
Tobago	$$		✔							✔
Tortola	$$		✔		✔		✔	✔	✔	✔
Trinidad	$		✔							
Virgin Gorda	$$$	✔	✔	✔	✔			✔		✔

	Hiking	Historic Sites	Mountainous Terrain	Music/Entertainment/Nightlife	Nonstop Flights from U.S.	Public Transport	Rain Forest	Romantic Getaways	Sailing	Scenic Beauty	Scuba Diving/Snorkeling	Secret Hideaways	Shopping	Verdant & Lush Terrain	Very Dry Climate
								✔			✔	✔			✔
✔	✔	✔			✔			✔	✔	✔	✔	✔			
✔				✔	✔	✔					✔		✔		✔
✔	✔	✔		✔	✔	✔			✔	✔		✔			
		✔						✔			✔	✔			✔
	✔				✔							✔			✔
✔				✔	✔	✔			✔		✔		✔		
	✔	✔		✔	✔	✔					✔		✔		✔
	✔	✔	✔			✔	✔			✔		✔		✔	
✔	✔	✔	✔	✔		✔				✔		✔	✔	✔	
✔	✔	✔	✔		✔	✔	✔	✔	✔	✔	✔	✔		✔	
								✔	✔	✔		✔			✔
✔	✔		✔		✔		✔	✔	✔	✔	✔			✔	
												✔			✔
✔	✔	✔	✔	✔	✔	✔	✔	✔	✔	✔	✔	✔	✔	✔	
	✔	✔	✔							✔	✔	✔		✔	
✔								✔	✔	✔		✔		✔	
✔	✔	✔		✔		✔	✔		✔	✔	✔		✔	✔	
		✔													
	✔	✔	✔					✔	✔	✔	✔	✔		✔	
✔	✔	✔						✔		✔		✔			
✔	✔		✔		✔		✔	✔		✔		✔		✔	
✔				✔	✔	✔			✔				✔		✔
✔		✔	✔	✔	✔	✔			✔				✔		
	✔		✔						✔					✔	
✔							✔					✔	✔	✔	
	✔		✔			✔			✔	✔	✔	✔		✔	
	✔			✔	✔	✔	✔			✔				✔	
	✔		✔			✔		✔	✔	✔	✔	✔		✔	

2 Getting to Know the Caribbean

The Caribbean Sea is ringed by the Greater Antilles on the north; the Lesser Antilles on the east; the coasts of Venezuela, Colombia, and Panama on the south; and Central America and the Mexican Yucatán on the west. It spans one million square miles. The amazing variety of the islands—which stretch from 10° north of the Equator almost to the Tropic of Cancer—is reflected in their size, topography, and depths of the sea around them.

The Greater Antilles includes Cuba, Jamaica, Hispaniola (Haiti and the Dominican Republic), Puerto Rico, and the Cayman Islands. The name Lesser Antilles was given to the remainder of the chain of islands: the Leeward Islands curving from Anguilla in the north to Dominica in the south, and the Windward Islands from Martinique to Grenada, but not including Barbados. There is also a little island chain paralleling the South American coast embracing three of the six islands today called the Netherlands Antilles.

1 The Islands in Brief

ANGUILLA (British Leewards)   Although it's rapidly developing as sunseekers discover its 12 miles of arid but spectacular beaches, Anguilla is still quiet, sleepy, and relatively free of racial tensions. A flat, coral-based island whose elongated shape caused the Spaniards to dub it "the eel" (Anguilla), it maintains a maritime tradition of proud fisherfolk who, until the recent tourist-related boom, eked out a living from the sea. Although some low-cost accommodations are still available, Anguilla is increasingly known as home to some of the most glamorous and expensive resorts in the Caribbean.

ANTIGUA (British Leewards)   During the 1700s, most of the surface of this largest of the Leeward Islands (108 square miles) was blanketed in sugarcane. Formed by coral deposits millions of years ago, low-slung Antigua is famous for having a different beach for each day of the year, and links to British tradition that remain a nostalgic memory despite the nation's relatively recent independence in 1981. (It's one of the three or four Caribbean nations most devoted to the English sport of cricket, and has produced many champions.) The island has a population of 80,000, mostly descended from the African slaves of plantation owners. The island boasts isolated pockets of highly conservative glamour, horribly maintained highways, and some of the most interesting historic naval sites in the British maritime world. Antigua (pronounced An-*tee*-gah) is politically linked to the sparsely inhabited and largely undeveloped island of Barbuda (not to be confused with Barbados), which lies about 30 miles to Antigua's north.

ARUBA (Dutch Leewards)   Until the value of its beaches were recognized by a new generation of sunseekers in the late 1970s, Aruba was an almost-forgotten outpost of Holland, mostly valued for its oil refineries and salt factories. Today it's favored for the lunar landscapes of its desertlike terrain, spectacular beaches whose sands are almost never marred by rain, and its almost complete lack of racial tensions. Its population of 70,000 is among the most culturally diverse anywhere, with roots in Holland, Portugal, Spain, Venezuela, India/Pakistan, and Africa. A building boom in the 1980s has transformed this gambling-conscious island into a pale version of Las Vegas and created some of the most aggressive marketing campaigns in Caribbean history.

BARBADOS   For generations, this Atlantic outpost was one of the most staunchly loyal members of the British Commonwealth. Originally devoted to a plantation economy which made its aristocracy rich, the island is the most easterly in the Caribbean, floating in the mid-Atlantic like a great coral reef ringed with beige-sand beaches. Cosmopolitan and international, Barbados has the densest population of any island in the Caribbean, a sports tradition which avidly pursues cricket, and a loyal group of return visitors who appreciate its many stylish, medium-size hotels. Service is usually extremely good, a by-product of a touristic infrastructure based on British mores, which has flourished since the turn of the century. Topography varies from rolling hills and savage waves on the eastern (Atlantic) coast, to densely populated flatlands, rows of hotels and apartments, and sheltered beaches in the southwest.

BONAIRE   Its strongest historic and cultural links are to Holland, and although it has always been considered a poor relation of nearby Curaçao, Bonaire boasts better scuba diving and better bird life than any of its larger and richer neighbors. The terrain is as dry and inhospitable as anything you'll find in the Caribbean, a desert landscape whose sparseness is offset by a wealth of marine life above the island's miles of offshore reefs. The architecture is a rather dusty hybrid based on Dutch and Hispanic models, with lots of recent investments by residents of nearby Venezuela. The island's capital bears the difficult-to-pronounce name of Kralendijk.

BRITISH VIRGIN ISLANDS   Still a British Crown Colony, this lushly forested subdivision of the Caribbean chain contains about 50 mountainous islands (depending on how many rocks, cays, and uninhabited islets you want to include). Superb as a venue for sailing, the BVI is less densely populated and less developed, and has fewer social problems than its neighors in the U.S. Virgin Islands a short boat ride to the west. Tortola (whose capital is the sprawling settlement of Road Town) is the main island, followed by Virgin Gorda, which boasts some of the poshest hotels in the West Indies, including some developed by Laurence Rockefeller. Anegada, a coral atoll geologically different from the other members of the BVI, attracts mainly a clientele that arrives by private yacht.

CAYMAN ISLANDS   This is a trio of islands set improbably close to the southern coastline of Cuba. Flat and prosperous, this tiny nation is dependent on Britain for its economic survival and attracts millionaire expatriates from virtually

The Caribbean Islands

FLORIDA

Gulf of Mexico

• Miami

Straits of Florida

THE BAHAMAS

Havana •

Cuba

Little Cayman

Grand Cayman —

Cayman Brac

CAYMAN ISLANDS

Montego Bay

JAMAICA

Kingston

Hai

Port-au-Prince •

GREATER

C a r i b b e a n   S e a

COLOMBIA

9859

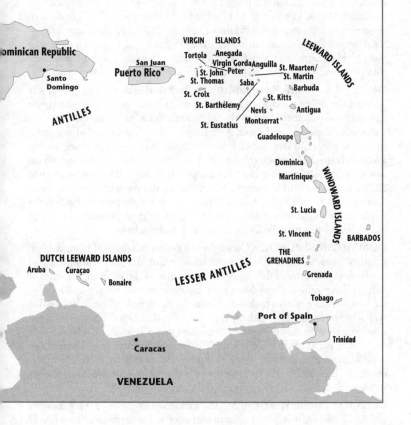

Atlantic

Ocean

TURKS AND CAICOS ISLANDS

ominican Republic

Santo
Domingo

San Juan
Puerto Rico

ANTILLES

VIRGIN   ISLANDS

Tortola   Anegada
          Virgin Gorda Anguilla
          Peter
St. John
St. Thomas

St. Croix
St. Barthélemy

St. Eustatius

Saba

Nevis
Montserrat

St. Kitts

LEEWARD ISLANDS

St. Maarten/
St. Martin

Barbuda

Antigua

Guadeloupe

Dominica

Martinique

St. Lucia

St. Vincent

WINDWARD ISLANDS

BARBADOS

DUTCH LEEWARD ISLANDS

Aruba   Curaçao

Bonaire

LESSER ANTILLES

THE
GRENADINES

Grenada

Tobago

Port of Spain

Caracas

Trinidad

VENEZUELA

0   200 mi
           320 km

N

everywhere because of its lenient tax and banking laws. Relatively unattractive, these islands are covered with scrubland and swamp, but boast more than their share of upscale (and horrendously expensive) private homes and condominiums. Until recently, Grand Cayman enjoyed one of the most closely knit social fabrics in the Caribbean, although with recent prosperity, some of it is beginning to unravel. Because of the marine life above the offshore reefs, scuba divers seek out the Caymans almost as avidly as tax exiles. Greater numbers of hotels have begun lining the sands of the nation's most famous sunspot, Seven Mile Beach.

CURAÇAO (Dutch Leewards)　It was originally settled in 1634 by a scraggly group of settlers from Holland, who battled with Spaniards several times throughout the first century of the island's history. Realizing the lack of fertility of the soil (much of the island's surface is an arid desert that grows only cactus), the canny Dutch quickly developed Curaçao into one of the Dutch Empire's busiest trading posts. (Its foremost commodities included slaves, salt, fish, and, beginning in 1915, oil.) During World War II, the island's population soared as the island's vast refineries transformed Venezuelan crude into products for the European war effort. Until the postwar collapse of the oil refineries, Curaçao was a thriving mercantile society in its own right, with a capital (Willemstad) that somewhat resembled Amsterdam and a population with a curious mixture of bloodlines (including Dutch, Venezuelan, and Pakistani). Much attention has been devoted to developing tourism as a new industry during the 1980s, and many new hotels—usually in the Dutch colonial style—have been built. Overall, Curaçao is more than just a hotel industry: It's a well-defined society in its own right with a distinctively colored liqueur—blue Curaçao—that the island proudly calls its own.

DOMINICA (British Windwards)　An English-speaking island set midway between Guadeloupe and Martinique, Dominica (Doh-mi-*nee*-kah), the largest and most mountainous island of the Windwards, is not to be confused with the Dominican Republic (see below). A mysterious, rarely visited land of waterfalls, rushing streams, and rain forests, it is not favored for its beaches, which are few and mainly lined with black volcanic sand. But for many devotees of the offbeat and unusual, it's the lushest and most fascinating island in the Caribbean. Some 82,000 people live here, including 2,000 remaining descendants of the once-fierce Carib Indians. The capital is Roseau. Dominica is one of the poorest islands in the Caribbean with the ironic misfortune of lying directly in the path of many of the hurricanes that periodically devastate the Caribbean basin.

DOMINICAN REPUBLIC　Occupying the eastern two-thirds of Hispaniola, an island shared with Haiti, the mountainous Dominican Republic is the second-largest country of the Caribbean. Long-time victim of an endless series of military dictatorships, it now has a more favorable political climate and some of the least expensive options for holidaymaking in the entire Caribbean. Its crowded capital is Santo Domingo, with a population of two million. The island enjoyed a building boom in the 16th century, but it isn't particularly safe for solo midnight strolls. The island offers lots of Hispanic color, wonderful merengue music, and many opportunities to dance, drink, and party your cares away. Here, more than on many other islands, the contrast between the comparative wealth of foreign holidaymakers and local poverty is especially obvious.

GRENADA (British Windwards)　The southernmost nation of the Windward Islands, Grenada (Gre-*nay*-dah) is one of the lushest in the Caribbean. Extravagantly fertile, and without the forbidding mountains of some of its neighbors to the north, it's one of the largest producers of spices in the western hemisphere, a result of a gentle climate, volcanic soil, and a corps of good-natured islanders who make cultivating nutmeg and cloves their primary source of income. There's a lot of very appealing local color on Grenada, particularly since the political troubles of the 1980s seem—at least for the moment—to have ended. The beaches are white and sandy, and the populace (a mixture of English expatriates and islanders of African descent) is friendly. Once a British Crown Colony but now independent, the island nation also incorporates two smaller islands—Carriacou and Petit Martinique, neither of which has many tourist facilities. Grenada's capital, St. Georges, is one of the most raffishly charming in the Caribbean.

GUADELOUPE (French West Indies)   It isn't as sophisticated or cosmopolitan as the two outlying islands over which it holds administrative authority (Saint Barthélemy and the French section of St. Martin). Despite that, there are a lot of unusual contrasts and rampant natural beauty in this *département* of mainland France. With a relatively low population density (only 340,000 people live here, mostly along the coast), butterfly-shaped Guadeloupe is actually two distinctly different volcanic islands separated by a narrow saltwater strait, the Rivière Salée. It's ideal for scenic drives and Créole color, offering any francophile an unusual insight into the French colonial world. At its worst, Guadeloupe can combine the least attractive aspects of mainland France with some of the worst apathy in the Caribbean. At its best, it can be absolutely charming.

JAMAICA   A favorite of North American honeymooners, Jamaica is a mountainous island rising abruptly from the sea 90 miles south of Cuba and about 100 miles west of Haiti. One of the most densely populated nations in the Caribbean, with a vivid sense of its own identity, Jamaica has an evocative history rooted in the plantation economy, and some of the most turbulent and impassioned politics in the western hemisphere. Despite a regrettable increase in crime and harassment of tourists by vendors in such resorts as Ocho Rios, Jamaica is one of the most successful black democracies in the world. The island is large enough to allow the more or less peaceful coexistence of all kinds of people within its beach-lined borders, including everything from expatriate English aristocrats to dyed-in-the-wool Rastafarians. Overall, and despite its long history of social unrest and increasing crime, Jamaica is a fascinating island.

MARTINIQUE (French West Indies)   This is one of the most exotic French-speaking destinations in the Caribbean, the birthplace of Napoleon's first wife, Joséphine, and the site of one of the few settlements ever completely demolished by volcanic activity (St. Pierre, now only a pale shadow of a once-thriving city). Like Guadeloupe and St. Barts, Martinique is legally and culturally French, although many Créole customs and traditions continue to flourish. The beaches are beautiful, the Créole cuisine is well prepared, and despite driving patterns that resemble those on the French mainland, the island has lots of tropical charm.

MONTSERRAT (British Leewards)   This tiny pear-shaped "Emerald Isle" (only 11 miles long and 7 miles wide), lies 27 miles southeast of Antigua. It's a British Crown Colony with a deep-rooted respect for conservative church-going values. Long a favorite with holidaymaking British rock stars (who seem to be gracefully accepted by the island's infrastructure), Montserrat has fertile volcanic soil, beaches of both black and white sand, and a distinct sense of lying off the main thoroughfares of Caribbean tourism. Its population numbers only 12,500 residents, most of African descent. Unless you rent one of the island's private villas, tourist facilities are limited, although clean and tidy.

PUERTO RICO   The smallest and easternmost of the Greater Antilles, 110 by 35 miles, the Commonwealth of Puerto Rico is under the jurisdiction of the United States. It's home to 3.3 million people whose primary language is Spanish. It's one of the most urbanized islands of the Caribbean with lots of traffic, glittering casinos, a relatively high crime rate, and a more-or-less comfortable juxtaposition of Latin culture with imports from the U.S. mainland. The island's interior is filled with ancient volcanic mountains; the coastline is ringed with sandy beaches. The commonwealth also includes a trio of small, offshore islands: Culebra, Mona, and Vieques (the last has the most tourist facilities). San Juan, the island's 16th-century capital, has some of the most extensive and best-preserved Spanish colonial neighborhoods in the New World, lots of things to see and do, and a steady flow of cruise-ship passengers who keep the stores and casinos filled throughout much of the year.

SABA (Dutch Windwards in the Leewards)   Saba is a cone-shaped extinct volcano that rises abruptly and steeply from the watery depths of the Caribbean. There are no beaches to speak of, but the local Dutch- and English-speaking populace has traditionally made a living from fishing, trade, and needlework rather than from tourism. Hotel choices are limited, and are often designed in the traditional Saban style of stone foundations terraced into sloping hillsides with white walls and red roofs. The thrifty and frugal seafaring folk of Saba can offer insights into the old-fashioned aspects of the Antilles. There's only one road on the island, and unless you opt to hike away from its edges, all island traffic proceeds along its narrow, winding route.

ST. BARTHÉLEMY (also called St. Barts or St. Barths; French West Indies)   Part of the French *département* of Guadeloupe, lying 15 miles from Sint Maarten, St. Barts is a small, hilly island with a population of 3,500 people who live on 13 square miles of verdant terrain ringed by pleasant white sand beaches. A small number of African descendants live harmoniously on this chic Caribbean island with descendants of Norman and Breton mariners and a colony of more recent expatriates from Europe's mainland. Considered an expensive and exclusive stamping ground of the rich and famous, with a distinctive seafaring tradition, St. Barts has a "storybook" capital at Gustavia, which is named after a Swedish king. Sweden was ceded St. Barts in 1785 in exchange for granting the French trading rights in the Baltic. About a century later it was ceded back to the French, whose influence permeates the island today.

SINT EUSTATIUS (known as Statia; Dutch Windwards in the Leewards)   During the 1700s this Dutch-controlled island ("The Golden Rock") was one of the most important trading posts in the Caribbean. Assisted by Dutch neutrality, it boasted more than a mile of seafront warehouses which stored and redistributed contraband goods imported from both hemispheres of the globe. During the U.S. War of Independence, a brisk arms trade helped the local economy too. The glamour ended in 1781, when British Admiral Romney sacked the port, hauled off most of the island's wealth, and propelled Sint Eustatius onto a path of sleepy obscurity, where, until the advent of tourism, it remained for almost 200 years. Today the island is among the poorest in the Caribbean, with 8 square miles of arid landscape, beaches that have strong and sometimes-dangerous undertows, a population of around 1,700 people, and a sleepy capital whose name is Oranjestad. The island is very committed to maintaining its political and fiscal links to the Netherlands.

ST. KITTS & NEVIS (British Leewards)   Richly permeated with a sense of British maritime history, these two islands form a single nation despite their separation by a 2-mile strait. St. Kitts (also known as St. Christopher, with 68 square miles) and Nevis (with 36 square miles) both enjoyed some of the richest sugarcane economies of the plantation age, and the boiling rooms and Great Houses have in many cases been transformed into quaint inns. Both islands lie somewhat off the beaten track of Caribbean tourism, and both have very appealing small-scale charm.

ST. LUCIA (British Windwards)   St. Lucia (*Loo*-sha), 24 miles south of Martinique, is the second-largest of the Windward Islands. Although in 1803 Britain eventually won a prolonged struggle to control it, the years of French influence are still evident in the widespread use of a Créole dialect. A volcanic island with lots of rainfall and great natural beauty, it has both white and black sand beaches, bubbling sulfur springs, and some of the most panoramic mountain scenery in the West Indies. Although its population is only around 150,000, St. Lucia is the most populous island in the Windwards. Most of the onslaught of modern tourism has occurred in the island's northwestern tip, near the capital (Castries), but the arrival of up to 200,000 visitors a year has inevitably altered many of the island's isolated and agrarian lifestyles.

SINT MAARTEN/ST. MARTIN (Dutch Windwards in the Leewards/French West Indies)   Lying 144 miles east of Puerto Rico, this island of 37 scrub-covered square miles has been divided between the Dutch (Sint Maarten) and the French (St. Martin) since 1648. Regardless of how you spell it, it's the same island, although both sides of the unguarded border are quite different. The Dutch side contains the island's more important airport, greater numbers of shops, and more tourist facilities; whereas St. Martin, whose capital is Marigot, has some of the poshest hotels on either side of the island. (The French side also has some of the best food on the island.) There's a lot to do on this island, especially dining and drinking options, as the recent tourist boom proves. Both sides of the island are modern, urbanized, and proudly international in their flair. Both of them suffer from such modern problems as traffic jams, a lack of parking space in the capitals, tourist-industry burnout (especially on the Dutch side), and a disturbing increase in recent years in the incidence of crime.

ST. VINCENT & THE GRENADINES (British Windwards)   Despite its natural beauty and its population of 105,000 people (of mostly African descent), this mini-archipelago has only recently emerged from the obscurity that was cast upon it by its better-known neighbors. Its allure, however, has always been known to divers and yachtspeople, who considered its north-to-south string of cays and coral islets one of the most magnificent sailing regions in the world. (Only the Virgin Islands competes with the Grenadines for the numbers of private yachts that explore its relatively undeveloped seascapes.) St. Vincent is by far the largest and most fertile island in the country, 18 miles long and 11 miles wide. Its capital is the sleepy, somewhat-dilapidated town of Kingstown. (This is not to be confused with Kingston, Jamaica, which is enormous in comparison.) Stretching like a pearl necklace to the south of St. Vincent are some 32 neighbor islands called the Grena-dines. These include the charming boatbuilding community of Bequia and chic Mustique where Princess Margaret has a home (which she often rents out to any-one who can afford it). Less densely populated islands in the chain include the tiny outposts of Mayreau, Canouan, Palm Island, and Petit St. Vincent, whose sunblasted surfaces were for the most part covered with scrub until around the late 1960s, when hardworking hotel owners planted much-needed groves of palms and hardwood trees.

TRINIDAD & TOBAGO   The southernmost of the West Indies, this two-island nation lies just 7 miles off the coast of Venezuela. Both islands once had plantation economies, and both enjoyed fantastic wealth from sugarcane during the 18th century. Trinidad is probably the most industrialized island in the Caribbean, with oil deposits and a polyglot population derived from India, Pakistan, Venezuela, Africa, and each of the European powers that at one time competed for its ownership. Known for its calypso music and carnivals, Trinidad is one of the most culturally distinctive nations in the Caribbean, with a land-mass of over 1,800 square miles, a rich artistic tradition, a bustling capital (Port-of-Spain), and an impressive variety of exotic flora and fauna.

About 20 miles northeast of Trinidad, tiny Tobago (9 miles wide and 26 miles long) is calmer and less heavily forested, with a rather dull capital (Scarborough) and a spectacular array of white-sand beaches. Whereas Trinidad seems to consider tourism as only one of many viable industries, Tobago is absolutely dependent on it.

U.S. VIRGIN ISLANDS   Formerly Danish possessions, they became part of the U.S. in 1917 when a need was perceived for a stronger U.S. presence within the Caribbean basin. Originally based on a plantation economy, St. Croix is the largest and flattest of the U.S. Virgins, whereas St. Thomas and St. John are more moun-tainous and a bit smaller. St. Thomas and, to a lesser degree, St. Croix possess all the diversions, facilities, and amusements you'd find on the U.S. mainland, includ-ing bars, restaurants, and lots of modern resort hotels. St. Thomas is sometimes referred to as the shopping mall of the Caribbean, a result of its deep harbor and frequent arrival of cruise-ship passengers. Much of the surface of St. John is devoted to a national park, the result of the generous Laurance Rockefeller, who donated many of his holdings to the National Park System. All three islands present countless opportunities for sailing and snorkeling, unspoiled vistas, and lots of U.S.–inspired activities. Crime is on the increase, however, an unfortunate fly in the ointment of what would otherwise be considered a U.S.–owned corner of paradise.

2 Music

Calypso, reggae, and the beat of voodoo drums spring to mind when the music of the Caribbean is mentioned. The gutsy, aggressive beat of African music was brought in with the slave ships—it drowned out the harpsichord music wafting from the master's house soon enough.

The best way to enjoy the music and dancing of the Caribbean is at **carnival** time. On islands with strong Roman Catholic ties, this is similar to Mardi Gras in New Orleans. For some islands, carnival lasts from Epiphany (January 6) to Ash Wednesday, with parades and dancing in the streets, especially on each Sunday before Lent. On other islands, festivals, fiestas, and special days (many held in summer) take the place of carnival. For example, Barbados holds a festival celebrating the end of the sugarcane harvest.

The carnivals and festivals are marked by flamboyant masqueraders, folkloric music and dance, and feasting on local specialties. If you can't visit during a carnival, you might still enjoy a taste of it as many nightclubs present abbreviated versions by folkloric groups.

Offering radically different types of music, the major "music islands" of the Caribbean are Jamaica and Puerto Rico, and to a lesser extent the Dominican Republic, Trinidad, and Barbados.

At least some of the **instruments** used in traditional Puerto Rican music had their origins with the Taíno peoples. Most noteworthy is the *guicharo,* or *guiro,* a notched, hollowed-out gourd whose form was almost directly adapted from pre-Columbian days. At least four different stringed instruments were adapted from the six-string Spanish classical guitar: the *requinto,* the *bordonua,* the *cuatro,* and the *tiple,* each of which produces a unique tone and pitch. The most popular of these, and the one for which the greatest number of adaptations and compositions have been written, is the cuatro, a guitarlike instrument with 10 strings (arranged into five different pairs).

Also in wide circulation on the island are such percussion instruments as *tambours* (hollowed tree trunks covered with stretched-out animal skin), *maracas* (gourds filled with pebbles or dried beans and mounted on handles), and a host of different drums whose original designs were brought from Africa by the island's slaves. All these instruments have a place in a rich variety of folk music with roots in the cultural melting pot of the island's Spanish, African, and native Taíno traditions.

The major music coming out of Puerto Rico now is **salsa.** Its name is literally translated as the "sauce" that makes parties happen. Originally developed in the Puerto Rican community of New York, it draws heavily on the musical roots of the Cuban and the African-Caribbean experience. Highly danceable, its rhythms are hot, urban, rhythmically sophisticated, and very compelling. Salsa bands employ a huge array of percussion instruments, including maracas, bongos, timbales, conga drums, and claves—and, to add the jíbaro (hillbilly) touch, a clanging cow bell. Of course, it also takes a bass, a horn section, a chorus, and a lead vocalist to get the combination right.

The roots of Jamaica's unique **reggae** music can be found in an early form of Jamaican music called *mento.* This music was brought to the island from Africa by slaves. Played by forced laborers to help forget their anguish, mento is reminiscent of the rhythm and blues that in the mid-20th century swept across North America. It was usually accompanied by hip-rolling dances known as dubbing, with highly suggestive lyrics to match. Famous Jamaican mento groups reaching their prime in the 1950s included the Pork Chops Rhumba Box Band of Montego Bay and the Ticklers.

In the late 1950s Jamaican musicians combined boogie-woogie with rhythm and blues to form a short-lived but vibrant music named ska. It was the politicization of ska by Rastafarians that led to the creation of reggae.

Sometimes referred to as the heartbeat of Jamaica, reggae is the island's most distinctive musical form, as closely linked to Jamaica as soul is to Detroit, jazz to New Orleans, and blues to Chicago. The term *reggae* is best defined as "coming from the people." It has influenced the music of international stars like the Rolling Stones, Eric Clapton, and Paul Simon. Most notably, it propelled onto the world scene a street-smart kid from Kingston named Bob Marley. Today the recording studios of Kingston, sometimes called "The Nashville of the Third World," churn out hundreds of reggae albums every year, many snapped up by "dance-aholics" in Los Angeles, Italy, and Japan.

One of the most recent adaptations of reggae is **soca,** which is more upbeat and less politicized. Aficionados say that reggae makes you think, while soca makes you dance. The music is fun, infectious, and spontaneous, perfect for partying, and often imbued with the humor and wry attitudes of Jamaican urban dwellers.

After 1965, the influx of Jamaican immigrants to the potboiling pressures of North America's ghettos had a profound influence on popular music. Such Jamaican-born stars as Clive Campbell, combining the Jamaican gift for the spoken word with reggae rhythms and high electronic amplification, developed the roots of what eventually became known as **rap.** This genre is known for its rhyming, street-smart lyrics.

Some purists point out that **calypso** music is really a product of Trinidad, though it remains very popular in Jamaica (and also Barbados). Calypso, which originated on Trinidad, is a mixture—basically African but with African-Spanish rhythms, English verses, and traces of French structure. The words to calypso tunes were originally (and sometimes still are) spontaneous improvisations based on all sorts of subjects—love, sex, politics, whatever.

3 A Guide to Island Cuisine

FOOD

Hotel chefs prepare a presentable American and continental cuisine, but in recent years hotels have placed a greater emphasis on local dishes. Even so, it's still better to order a $15 meal at a local restaurant than it is to have a $50 dinner in a so-called gourmet restaurant at some deluxe resort.

FRUITS, VEGETABLES & SIDE DISHES   The abundance of fruit in the islands is obvious; at breakfast you'll usually find freshly sliced fruit. Coconut is used in everything from breads to soups. Soursop ice cream appears on some menus, and guava might turn up in anything from juice to cheese. Papaya is called paw paw, and it will most often be your melon choice at breakfast. Mango is ubiquitous, used not only in chutney but also in drinks and desserts. The avocado, most often called "pears," is used in fresh seafood salads and often stuffed with fresh crabmeat.

By now most visitors know that plantain (which is similar to a banana but red in color) is not eaten raw. It's usually served as a cooked side dish, the way we might present french fries. Puerto Ricans eat dried plantains, called tostones, instead of potato chips. Plantains can also be served mashed or boiled, and they turn up in many desserts, especially when mixed with coconut and pineapple.

Two staples of the Caribbean islands have always been rice and pigeon peas. Balls of cornmeal, called fungi, often accompany a salt-pork main dish known as mauffay. Sometimes these cornmeal concoctions will appear on the menus of local restaurants as coo coo. Roast suckling pig is nowhere better than on Puerto Rico and in the Dominican Republic. Everything that appears unattractive and less desirable in the pig usually turns up in souse, including the head, tail, and feet. It's usually served with black pudding.

One of the most common vegetables in the islands is christophine (sometimes called foo foo), a green, prickly gourd that tastes somewhat like zucchini. Breadfruit, introduced to the islands by Captain Bligh (of *Bounty* fame) is green and round and used like a potato. Potatoes and yams are also local favorites. The leaflike callaloo is one of the best-known vegetables in the West Indies. It's like spinach and is often served with crab, salt pork, and fresh fish with floating fungi as a garnish.

In a true local restaurant in the Caribbean, you'll see hot peppers placed on the table. Be sparing. A selection of hot pepper pastes is called sambal.

SEAFOOD Throughout the islands, warm-water lobster is the king of the sea and the most sought after—and most expensive—main course to order. The "catch of the day" is most likely to be red snapper or grouper, but could also be shark or barracuda.

Caution is urged in eating barracuda, which have been known to contain copper deposits. Fish caught north of Antigua and also along the Cayman Islands and Cuba are said to be at risk. The barracuda in south-lying Barbados are fine and usually very healthy.

Dolphin may also appear on the menu, but—never fear—this dolphin is a fish and not the playful mammal we usually associate with the term.

DRINKS Since the late 16th century, rum has been associated with slavery, Yankee traders, pirates, and bootlegging. A whole series of rum barons arose, with names that became famous around the world: Bacardi, Gonzalez, Myers, and Barcelo, to name only a few. "Kill-devil," as rum was once called, is of course the established drink of the islands.

Distilled easily from sugarcane, rum played a major role in the history of the West Indies. Today the rusted machinery and tumbledown ruins of distilleries are tourist stopovers on dozens of Caribbean islands. The enormous crushing devices were powered by wind, water, or steam. The resulting mash was fermented in open vats and then distilled through long lengths of copper tubing. While planter's punch is the most popular drink in the islands, the average bar in the Caribbean is likely to offer a bewildering array of rum-based drinks.

Don't think that the only beer you'll be able to find will be imported from Milwaukee or Holland. Of course, Heineken is ubiquitous, as is Amstel, especially in the Dutch islands, but Red Stripe from Jamaica is the most famous.

A Word of Caution: Be alert to your limits, especially if you're driving. The pastel-colored drinks can make visitors very drunk on very short notice because of their elevated sugar content, as well as the hot climate.

Water is generally safe throughout the islands, but many tourists get sick from drinking it simply because it's different from the water they're accustomed to. If it's available, order bottled water.

SPECIALTIES OF THE ISLANDS

ANGUILLA Order spiny lobsters if you can get them—they're very good and invariably fresh. Seafood lovers will also enjoy the crayfish, whelk, yellowtail, and red snapper. Some local restaurants serve some of the most elegant continental fare in the West Indies, although they are generally forced to work with frozen ingredients imported from elsewhere, often Miami.

ANTIGUA & BARBUDA   At most restaurants and in most resorts catering to tourists, you get typical American or continental fare. A host of French restaurants have opened in the past few years, as well, on Antigua. Local food, when it's available on either island, tends to be spicy, with sauces often based on Créole recipes or even on East Indian curry dishes. That means pepperpot stew, spare ribs, curried goat, and the like. A British heritage lingers in some of the island's blander dishes. If fresh seafood is on the menu, go for it.

ARUBA   A few of Aruba's restaurants serve *rijstaffel,* the Indonesian "rice table," or *nasi goreng,* a minirijstaffel. In addition, many Chinese restaurants operate in Oranjestad. More and more Aruban specialties are beginning to appear on menus. Although not always suited to the tropics, these include *keshi yena,* Edam cheese filled with a mixture of chicken or beef and flavored with onions, pickles, tomatoes, olives, and raisins. *Sopito de pisca* is a savory fish chowder made with a bouquet of spices. *Funchi,* like a cornmeal pudding of the Deep South, accompanies many regional dishes. *Pastechi* is a meat-stuffed turnover, and *cala* is a bean fritter. The French repertoire is the cuisine of choice for many of the island's top chefs.

BARBADOS   The famous flying fish appears on every menu, and when prepared right, it's a delicacy—moist and succulent, nutlike in flavor, approaching the subtlety of brook trout. Bajans boil it, steam it, bake it, stew it, fry it, and stuff it.

Try the sea urchin, or *oursin,* which you may have already sampled on Martinique and Guadeloupe. Bajans often call these urchins "sea eggs." Crab-in-the-back is another specialty, as is *langouste,* the Barbadian lobster. Dolphin and salt fish cakes are other popular items. Yams, sweet potatoes, and eddoes (similar to yams) are typical vegetables. Luscious Barbadian fruits include papaya, passionfruit, and mango.

If you hear that any hotel or restaurant is having a *cohobblopot* (or more commonly, a Bajan buffet), call for a reservation. This is a Barbadian term that means to "cook up," and it inevitably will produce an array of local dishes.

At Christmas, roast ham or turkey is served with *jug-jug,* a rich casserole of Scottish derivation that includes salt beef, ground corn flour, pigeon peas, and spices. *Cou-cou,* a side dish made from okra and cornmeal, accompanies fish.

BONAIRE   Bonaire's food is generally acceptable. Nearly everything has to be imported, of course. Your best bet is fresh-caught fish and an occasional *rijstaffel,* the traditional Indonesian "rice table," or try the local dishes. Popular foods are conch cutlet or stew, pickled conch, red snapper, tuna, wahoo, dolphin, fungi (a thick cornmeal pudding), rice, beans, *sate* (marinated meat with curried mayonnaise), goat stew, and Dutch cheeses.

BRITISH VIRGIN ISLANDS   Food is relatively simple and straightforward, with fresh fish the best item on the menu. Most of the other produce, including meat and poultry, is shipped in frozen. In most major restaurants and hotels, an American or continental cuisine prevails. For a "taste of the islands," seek out the local dives (several of which will be recommended later). Locals give colorful names to the various fish brought home for dinner, everything from "ole wife" to "doctors." "Porgies and grunts," along with yellowtail, kingfish, and bonito, show up on many tables. Fish is usually boiled in a lime-flavored brew seasoned with hot peppers and herbs, and is commonly served with a Créole sauce of peppers, tomatoes, and onions, among other ingredients. Salt fish and rice is another low-cost dish, the fish flavored with onion, tomatoes, shortening, garlic, and green pepper.

Conch Créole is a tasty brew, flavored with onions, garlic, spices, hot peppers, and salt pork. A favorite local dish is chicken and rice, made with Spanish peppers. Curried goat, the longtime "classic" West Indian dinner, is made with herbs, including cardamon pods and onions.

The famous johnnycakes that accompany many of these fish and meat dishes are fried in deep fat or baked. Indians may have made johnnycakes with ground corn, baked on hot coals.

CAYMAN ISLANDS   American and continental cooking predominate, although there is also a cuisine known as Caymanian, which features specialties made from turtle. (Environmental groups in the States consider this species to be endangered; however, in the Cayman Islands it is bred for food, as opposed to being caught in the wild at sea.) Fresh fish is the star, and conch is used in many ways. Local lobster is in season from late summer through January. Since most dining places have to rely on imported ingredients, prices tend to be high.

CURAÇAO   The basic cuisine is Dutch, but there are many specialty items, particularly Latin American and Indonesian. The cuisine strikes many visitors as heavy for the tropics, so you may want to have a light lunch and order the more filling concoctions, such as *rijstaffel*, in the evening. You'll want to finish your meals with Curaçao, the orange-based liqueur that made the island famous.

Ertwensoep, the well-known Dutch pea soup, is a popular dish, as is *keshi yena,* which is Edam cheese stuffed with meat and then baked. *Funchi,* a Caribbean tortilla, accompanies many local dishes. *Sopito,* fish soup often made with coconut water, is an especially good local dish, and conch is featured in curries and many other dishes.

DOMINICA   The local delicacy is the fine flesh of the *crapaud* (a frog), called "mountain chicken." Freshwater crayfish is another specialty, as is *tee-tee-ree,* fried cakes made from tiny fish. Stuffed crab back is usually a delight—the backs of red and black land crabs are stuffed with delicate crabmeat and Créole seasonings. The fresh fruit juices of the island are divine nectar, and no one spends a day without at least one rum punch.

DOMINICAN REPUBLIC   The national dish is *sancocho,* a thick stew made with meats (maybe seven kinds), vegetables, and herbs, especially marjoram. Another national favorite is *chicharrones de pollo,* pieces of fried chicken and fried green bananas flavored with pungent spices. One of the most typical dishes is *la bandera* (the flag), made with red beans, white rice, and stewed meat. Johnnycakes and *mangu,* the latter a plaintain-like dish inherited from people called Cocolos who came to the Dominican Republic from the Windward and Leeward Islands, are frequently eaten. Johnnycakes can be bought on the street corner or at the beach, but you must ask for them as *vaniqueques.*

A good local beer is called Presidente. Wines are imported, so prices tend to run high. Dominican coffee compares favorably with that of Colombia and Brazil.

GRENADA   I've found food on Grenada better than on the other British Windward Islands. Many of the chefs are European or European-trained, and local cooks are also on hand to prepare Grenadian specialties, such as conch (called *lambi* here), lobster, callaloo soup (with greens and crab), and soursop or avocado ice cream. Turtle steaks appear on many menus, although this is an endangered species. The national dish, called "oil down," consists of breadfruit and salt pork covered with dasheen leaves and steamed in coconut milk (it's not the favorite of every visitor). Some 22 kinds of fish, including fresh tuna, dolphin, and barracuda, are caught off the island's shores, and most are good for eating. Naturally, the spices of the island, such as nutmeg, are used plentifully. Meals are often served family style in an open-air setting with a view of the sea.

GUADELOUPE   The Créole cuisine of Guadeloupe is similar to Martinique's. The food served here, at least in my opinion, is the best in the Caribbean. The island's chefs have been called "seasoned sorcerers." Having African roots, Créole cooking is based on seafood. Out in the country, every cook has his or her own herb garden, since the cuisine makes great use of herbs and spices. Except in the major hotels, most restaurants are family run, offering real homemade cooking. Best of all, you usually get to dine al fresco.

Stuffed, stewed, skewered, or broiled spiny lobsters, as well as clams, conch, oysters, and octopus are presented to you with French taste and subtlety. Every good chef knows how to make *colombo,* a spicy rich stew of poultry, pork, or beef served with rice, herbs, sauces, and a variety of seeds. Another Créole favorite is calalou (callaloo in English), a soup flavored with savory herbs. Yet another traditional French Caribbean dish is *blaff,* fresh seafood poached in clear stock and usually seasoned with hot peppers.

JAMAICA   There is great emphasis on seafood. Rock lobster appears on every menu—grilled, thermidor, cold, hot. *Saltfish and ackee,* the national dish, is a concoction of salt cod and a brightly colored vegetable that tastes something like scrambled eggs. *Escovitch* (marinated fish) is usually fried and then simmered in vinegar with onions and peppers. Curried mutton and goat are popular, as is pepperpot stew, all highly seasoned.

Jerk pork is found in country areas, where it's barbecued slowly over wood fires until crisp and brown. Rice and peas (really red beans) are usually served with onions, spices, and salt pork. Vegetables are exotic: breadfruit, imported by Captain Bligh in 1723; callaloo, rather like spinach, used in pepperpot soup; *cho-cho,* served boiled or stuffed; and green bananas and plantains, fried or boiled and served with almost everything. Then there's pumpkin, which goes into a soup or is served on the side, boiled and mashed with butter. Sweet potatoes appear with main courses, but there is also a sweet-potato pudding made with sugar and coconut milk, flavored with cinnamon, nutmeg, and vanilla.

You'll come across dishes with really odd names: *stamp and go* are saltfish cakes eaten as appetizers; *dip and fall back* is a salty stew with bananas and dumplings; and *rundown* is mackerel cooked in coconut milk, often eaten for breakfast. For the really adventurous, *manish water,* a soup made from goat offal and tripe, is said to increase virility. *Patties* (meat pies)—the best on the island are at Montego Bay—are another staple snack. Boiled corn, roast yams, roast saltfish, fried fish, soups, and fruits are all sold at roadside stands.

Tea is used to describe any nonalcoholic drink in Jamaica, a tradition dating back to plantation days. *Fish tea* is actually a bowl of hot soup made from freshly caught fish. *Skyjuice,* a favorite with Jamaicans on hot afternoons, is sold by street vendors from not-always-sanitary carts. It consists of shaved ice with sugar-laden fruit syrup and is sold in small plastic bags with a straw. Coconut water is a refreshing drink, especially when you stop by the road to have a local vendor chop open a fresh coconut.

Rum punches are everywhere, and the local beer is Red Stripe. The island produces many liqueurs, the most famous being Tía Maria, made from coffee beans. Rumona is another good one to take home with you. *Bellywash,* the local name for limeade, will supply the extra liquid you may need to counteract the heat. Blue Mountain coffee is the best, but tea, cocoa, and milk are usually available to round off a meal.

MARTINIQUE See Guadeloupe, above.

MONTSERRAT Some of the best fruits and vegetables in the Caribbean are grown in the rich, volcanic soil of Montserrat. The island is known for its tomatoes, carrots, and mangoes. *Goat water* (a mutton stew) is the most popular local dish. Another island specialty is *mountain chicken,* otherwise known as frogs' legs.

PUERTO RICO Although Puerto Rican cooking has similarities to Cuban, Spanish, and Mexican cuisine, it has its own unique style, using such indigenous seasonings and ingredients as cilantro, papaya, cacao, nispero, apio, plantains, and yampee.

Cocina Criola (Créole cooking) was initiated by the Arawaks and Taínos, the original inhabitants of the island. Long before Columbus arrived, these peaceful people thrived on diets of corn, tropical fruits, and seafood. When Ponce de León arrived with Columbus in 1508, the Spanish added beef, pork, rice, wheat, and olive oil to the island's foodstuffs. Soon after, the Spanish began planting sugarcane and importing slaves from Africa, who brought with them okra and taro, known in Puerto Rico as *yauita.* The mingling of flavors and ingredients from different ethnic groups created Puerto Rican cuisine.

Lunch and dinner generally begin with sizzling hot appetizers such as *bacalaitos* (crunchy cod fritters), *surullitos* (sweet, plump cornmeal fingers), and *empanadillas* (crescent-shaped turnovers filled with lobster, crab, conch, or beef). Next, a bowl of steaming *asopao* (a hearty gumbo soup with rice and chicken or shellfish) may be followed by *lechón asado* (roast suckling pig), *pollo en vino dulce* (succulent chicken in wine), or *bacalao* (dried salted cod mixed with various roots and tubers and fried). No matter the selection, main dishes are served with salted *tostones* (deep-fried plantains or green bananas) and plentiful portions of rice and beans.

The aroma that wafts from kitchens throughout Puerto Rico comes from adobo and sofrito—blends of herbs and spices that give many of the native foods their distinctive taste and color. *Adobo,* made from peppercorns, oregano, garlic, salt, olive oil, and lime juice or vinegar, is rubbed into meats before they are roasted. *Sofrito,* a potpourri of onions, garlic, and peppers browned in olive oil or lard and colored with *achiote* (annatto seeds), imparts a bright-yellow color to the island's rice, soups, and stews.

Dessert is usually *flan* (custard) or perhaps *nisperos de batata* (sweet-potato balls made with coconut, cloves, and cinnamon), or guava jelly and *queso blanco* (white cheese).

Finish your meal with Puerto Rican coffee—strong, black, and aromatic. Rum is the national drink, and you can buy it in almost any shade. On Puerto Rico it's quite proper to order a cold beer before even looking at the menu; one local choice is India, famous for its pure water. However, most Puerto Ricans drink a golden brew known as Medalla.

SABA   At this Dutch island, no one visits for the food. Caribbean and continental dishes prevail, and there is no really outstanding restaurant. Most of the food is imported.

ST. BARTS   This is one of the few islands in the Caribbean where haute cuisine prevails. Perhaps it's somewhat incongruous in a tropical setting, but some excellent continental cuisine is served. There are almost no local dishes, except fresh fish and lobster. Sometimes, however, dishes are given Caribbean flavor, as in chicken breast served with mango sauce or perhaps pan-fried prawns Créole style. Antillean stuffed crab is a regular feature, as is a *colombo* of lamb (stew flavored with curry and roasted bananas). But chances are the chef will serve you sole with champagne sauce or filet of beef in pepper sauce, as in France.

ST. EUSTATIUS   Often called Statia, this Dutch island is not written up in gourmet cookbooks. Most of the food is imported, and restaurants are adequate, not exciting. Some restaurants make a stab at preparing a French cuisine with generally frozen ingredients. Local bistros serve some regional cooking such as stewed conch, salt fish with johnnycakes, or curried goat.

ST. KITTS & NEVIS   On St. Kitts, most guests eat at their hotels; however, St. Kitts has a scattering of good restaurants where you are likely to have spiny lobster, crab back, pepperpot stew, breadfruit, and curried conch. The drink of the island is CSR (Cane Spirit Rothschild), a pure sugarcane liqueur developed by Baron Edmond de Rothschild. Islanders mix it with Ting, a bubbly grapefruit soda.

On Nevis, the local food is good. Suckling pig is roasted with many spices, and eggplant is used in a number of tasty ways, as is avocado. (You may see turtle on some menus, but remember that this is an endangered species.)

ST. LUCIA   Try to break free of your hotel and dine in one of St. Lucia's little character-loaded restaurants. The local food is excellent and reflects the years of French and British occupation. St. Lucia's marketplace offers the ingredients for local dishes, including callaloo soup (fresh greens, dumplings, and salted beef), *pouile dudon* (a sweet, zesty chicken dish), and breadfruit cooked on open hot coals. Pumpkin soup, flying fish, lobster, and *tablette* (a coconut sugar candy that resembles white coral) round out the menu choices.

SINT MAARTEN/ST. MARTIN   This island, part Dutch, part French, has a truly excellent cuisine, in spite of its heavy reliance on imported ingredients. Here you'll find classic French cuisine, as well as American and continental, with a touch of West Indian spice and flavors. All the French classics are served, including frogs' legs and escargots, but Caribbean offerings, inspired by Martinique, include *crabes farcis* (stuffed crab), *blaff* (seafood poached and seasoned with peppers), and curried *colombo* (a stew with chicken, mutton, or goat).

Nearby Anguilla supplies a never-ending basket of spiny lobsters, the most delectable dish on the island. Dutch specialties are rare, although there's plenty of tasty Dutch beer. A lot of good French wine, served either by the bottle or carafe, is also shipped into the island.

ST. VINCENT & THE GRENADINES   Most dining takes place in the hotels, although there is a scattering of local bistros serving such West Indian food as local fish Créole style and callaloo soup. But mostly locals try to serve what they've heard foreigners like, including frozen steak flown in from Chicago, frozen shrimp from South America, and frozen french fries from who-knows-where. What is served often doesn't matter after diners have had a few rum punches before dinner. Local bartenders take pride in the variety of their rum punches as well as their lethal effects.

TRINIDAD & TOBAGO The food on these islands is as varied and cosmopolitan as the islanders themselves. Although this was a British colony for years, English cuisine never made much of an impression. Red-hot curries testify to Trinidad's strong East Indian influence, and some Chinese dishes are about as good here as any you'll find in Hong Kong. Créole and Spanish fare, as well as French, are also to be enjoyed.

A typical savory offering is a rôti, a king-size crêpe, highly spiced and filled with chicken, shellfish, or meat. Of course, you may prefer to skip such local delicacies as opossum stew and fried armadillo. Naturally, your fresh rum punch will have a dash of Angostura Bitters. In Trinidad there is a tendency to deep-fry everything—you can avoid this by careful menu selections. Tobago has fewer dining choices than Trinidad. In Tobago your best bet is local fish dishes, such as stuffed kingfish in Créole sauce. Local crayfish is also good, and lobster appears on some menus, perhaps stuffed into a crêpe. One island favorite that appears frequently is seafood casserole with ginger wine. Some typical Tobago dishes include baby shark marinated in lime and rum and conch stewed with coconut and rum.

U.S. VIRGIN ISLANDS Although a lot of the food is imported and frozen (often from Miami or Puerto Rico), St. Thomas, and to a lesser extent St. Croix and St. John, serve some of the finest American and continental cuisine in the Caribbean. Very experienced chefs, especially from Europe, are often brought in during the winter season to tempt your tastebuds. A whole range of ethnic restaurants exist too, including Chinese and Mexican. Italian food is commonplace.

The most famous soup of the islands is kallaloo, or *callaloo,* made in an infinite number of ways from a leafy green vegetable similar to spinach. This soup is flavored with salt beef, pig mouth, pig tail, ham bone, fresh fish, crabs, or perhaps conch, along with okra, onions, and spices. Many soups are sweetened with sugar, and putting fruits in soups is common. The classic *red-bean soup* made with pork or ham, various spices, and tomatoes, is sugared to taste. Tannia soup is made from the root of the so-called "Purple Elephant Ear." Salt-fat meat and ham, along with tomatoes, onions, and spices, are added to the tannias.

Souse is an old-time favorite made with the feet, head, and tongue of the pig, and flavored with a lime-based sauce and various spices. Salt-fish salad is traditionally served on Holy Thursday or Good Friday, as well as at other times. It's made with boneless salt fish, potatoes, onions, boiled eggs, and an oil-and-vinegar dressing.

Herring gundy is an old-time island favorite made with salt herring, potatoes, onions, sweet and hot green peppers, olives, diced beets, raw carrots, herbs, and boiled eggs. Seasoned rice is popular with Virgin Islanders, who often serve several starches at one meal. Most often rice is flavored with ham or salt pork, tomatoes, garlic, onion, and shortening. *Fungi* is a simple cornmeal dumpling that can be made more interesting with the addition of various ingredients, such as okra. Sweet fungi becomes a dessert, with sugar, milk, cinnamon, and raisins.

Okra (often spelled ochroe in the islands) is a mainstay vegetable, often accompanying beef, fish, or chicken. It's fried in an iron skillet after being flavored with hot pepper, tomatoes, onions, garlic, and bacon fat or butter. *Accra,* another popular dish, is made with okra, black-eyed peas, salt, and pepper. It's dropped into boiling fat and fried until golden brown.

The classic vegetable dish—some families serve it every night—is peas and rice, made with pigeon peas flavored with ham or salt meat, onion, tomatoes, herbs, and sometimes slices of pumpkins.

For dessert, *sweet-potato pone* is a classic, made with sugar, eggs, butter, milk, salt, cinnamon, raisins, and chopped almonds. The exotic fruits of the islands lend themselves to various homemade ice creams, including mango. Orange-rose sherbet is made by pounding rose petals into a paste and flavoring it with sugar and orange juice. Guava ice cream is a delectable flavor, as are soursop, banana, and papaya. Sometimes dumplings are served for dessert, made with guava, peach, plum, gooseberry, or cherry, and certainly apple.

Planning a Trip to the Caribbean

3

This chapter is devoted to the where, when, and how of your Caribbean trip—the advance-planning issues that need resolving before you leave home. It explains how to get there, what it will cost, when to go, what health precautions to take, what insurance coverage is necessary, where to obtain more information, and more.

Before we begin, I'd like to make a recommendation: Since the islands are so culturally and ethnically diverse, I encourage you to island-hop rather than to stay in one place. It's easy to fly within the region, and island-hopping will enrich your Caribbean vacation.

1 Information, Entry Requirements, Customs & Money

INFORMATION

All the major islands have tourist representatives whom you can contact to obtain information before you go (see "Fast Facts" under the individual island listings). The **Caribbean Tourism Organization,** 20 E. 46th St., New York, NY 10017 (☎ **212/682-0435**), can also provide general information.

You may also want to contact the U.S. State Department for background bulletins. Contact the Superintendent of Documents, **U.S. Government Printing Office,** Washington, DC 20402 (☎ **202/783-3238**).

Other useful sources are **newspapers and magazines.** To find the latest articles published about the destination, go to your library and ask for the *Reader's Guide to Periodical Literature* and look under the island/country for listings.

A good **travel agent** can also provide information, but make sure the agent is a member of the American Society of Travel Agents (ASTA). If you have a complaint, write to **ASTA Consumer Affairs,** 1101 King St., Alexandria, VA 22314 (☎ **703/739-2851**).

ENTRY REQUIREMENTS

Even though the Caribbean islands are, for the most part, independent nations and thereby classified as international destinations, passports are not generally required. You do, however, have to have identity documents, and a passport is the best form of identification and will speed you through Customs and Immigration. Other acceptable documents include an ongoing or return ticket, plus a current voter registration card or a birth certificate (the original or a copy that has been certified by the U.S. Department of Health). You will also need some photo ID, such as a driver's license or an expired passport; however, driver's licenses are not acceptable as a sole form of ID. Visas are usually not required, but some countries may require you to fill out a tourist card (see the individual island chapters for details).

Before leaving home, make two copies of your documents, including your passport and your driver's license; your airline ticket; and any hotel vouchers. If you're on medication, you should also make copies of prescriptions.

CUSTOMS

Each island has specific requirements. Generally, you are permitted to bring in items intended for your personal use, including tobacco, cameras, film, and a limited supply of liquor—usually 40 ounces.

U.S. CUSTOMS   The U.S. government generously allows U.S. citizens $1,200 worth of duty-free imports every 30 days from the U.S. Virgin Islands; those who go over their exemption are taxed at 5% rather than the usual 10%. The limit is $400 for such international destinations as the French islands of Guadeloupe and Martinique, and $600 for many other islands. If you visit only Puerto Rico, you don't have to go through Customs at all because of its status as an American commonwealth.

Joint Customs declarations are possible for members of a family traveling together. For instance, if you are a husband and wife with two children, your exemptions in the U.S. Virgin Islands become duty free up to $4,800! Unsolicited gifts can be sent to friends and relatives at the rate of $100 per day from the U.S. Virgin Islands (or $50 a day from the other islands). U.S. citizens, or returning residents 21 years of age, traveling directly or indirectly from American Samoa, Guam, or the U.S. Virgin Islands are allowed to bring in free of duty 1,000 cigarettes, 5 liters of alcohol, and 100 cigars (but not Cuban). Duty-free limitations on articles from other countries are generally 1 liter of alcohol, 200 cigarettes, and 200 cigars.

Collect receipts for all purchases made abroad. Sometimes merchants suggest a false receipt to undervalue your purchase, but be aware that you could be involved in a "sting" operation—the merchant might be an informer to U.S. Customs. You must also declare on your Customs form the nature and value of all gifts received during your stay abroad. It's prudent to carry proof that you purchased expensive cameras or jewelry on the U.S. mainland. If you purchased such an item during an earlier trip abroad, you should carry proof that you have previously paid Customs duty on the item.

If you use any medication containing controlled substances or requiring injection, carry an original prescription or note from your doctor.

For more specific guidance, write to the U.S. Customs Service, P.O. Box 7407, Washington, DC 20044, and request the free pamphlet "Know Before You Go."

CANADIAN CUSTOMS   For total clarification, write for the booklet "I Declare," issued by Revenue Canada, 875 Heron Rd., Ottawa, ON K1A 0L5. Canada allows its citizens a $300 exemption, and they are permitted to bring back duty free 200 cigarettes, 2.2 pounds of tobacco, 40 Imperial ounces of liquor, and 50 cigars. In addition, they are allowed to mail gifts to Canada from abroad at the rate of $60 (Canadian) a day, provided the gifts are unsolicited and aren't alcohol or tobacco (write on the package: "Unsolicited gift, under $60 value"). All valuables should be declared on the Y-38 Form before departure from Canada, including serial numbers (for example, expensive foreign cameras you already own). You should note that the $300 exemption can be used only once a year and only after an absence of seven days.

BRITISH CUSTOMS   On returning from the Caribbean, British subjects who either arrive directly in the U.K. or arrive via a port in another EC country where they did not pass through Customs controls with all their baggage, must go through U.K. Customs and declare any goods in excess of the allowances, which are: 200 cigarettes or 100 cigarillos or 50 cigars or 250 gms of tobacco; 2 liters of still table wine and 1 liter of spirits or strong liqueurs over 22% volume, or 2 liters of fortified or sparkling wine or other liqueurs, or 2 liters of additional still table wine; 60cc/ml of perfume; 250cc/ml of toilet water; and £136 worth of all other goods, including gifts and souvenirs. (No one under 17 years of age is entitled to a tobacco or drinks allowance.) Only go through the Green "nothing to declare" channel if you're sure that you have no more than the Customs allowances and no prohibited or restricted goods. For further details on U.K. Customs, contact HM Customs and Excise Office, New King's Beam House, 22 Upper Ground, London SE1 9PJ (☎ 0171/382-5468).

Money

CASH/CURRENCY   The U.S. dollar is widely accepted on many of the islands, and is the legal currency of the U.S. Virgin Islands, the British Virgin Islands, and Puerto Rico. Many islands use the Eastern Caribbean dollar, even though your hotel bill will most likely be presented in U.S. dollars. French islands use the French franc, although many hotels often quote their prices in U.S. dollars.

For details, see "Fast Facts" in the individual island chapters.

TRAVELER'S CHECKS   Before leaving home, purchase traveler's checks and arrange to carry some ready cash (usually about $250, depending on your habits and needs). In the event of theft, if the checks are properly documented, the value of your checks will be refunded. Most large banks sell traveler's checks, charging fees averaging between 1% and 2% of the value of the checks you buy, although some out-of-the-way banks, in rare instances, have charged as much as 7%. If your bank wants more than a 2% commission, it sometimes pays to call the traveler's check issuers directly for the address of outlets where this commission will be less.

American Express (☎ **800/221-7282** in the U.S. and Canada) is one of the largest and most immediately recognized issuers of traveler's checks. No commission is charged to members of the American Automobile Association and to holders of certain types of American Express cards. The company issues checks denominated in U.S. dollars, Canadian dollars, British pounds, Swiss francs, French francs, German marks, Japanese yen, and Dutch guilders. The vast majority of checks sold in North America are denominated in U.S. dollars. For questions or problems arising outside the United States or Canada, contact any of the company's many regional representatives.

Citicorp (☎ **800/645-6556** in the U.S. and Canada, or **813/623-1709**, collect, from other parts of the world), issues checks in U.S. dollars, British pounds, German marks, Japanese yen, and Australian dollars.

Thomas Cook (☎ **800/223-7373** in the U.S. and Canada, or **609/987-7300**, collect, from other parts of the world) issues MasterCard traveler's checks denominated

The U.S. Dollar & the British Pound

The U.S. dollar is commonly used throughout the Caribbean, except on the French islands of Martinique and Guadeloupe. It is widely accepted even on islands that print their own currency. However, the pound sterling should be converted into dollars, even for use on islands that are British Crown Colonies.

International exchange rates fluctuate from time to time depending on complicated political and economic factors. Thus the rates given in the table below—based on £1 = $1.58 U.S.—may not be the same when you travel to the Caribbean, and so this table should be used only as a guide.

U.S.$	U.K.£	U.S.$	U.K.£
.25	.16	15	9.49
.50	.32	20	12.66
.75	.47	25	15.82
1.00	.63	50	31.65
2.00	1.27	75	47.47
3.00	1.90	100	63.29
4.00	2.53	150	94.94
5.00	3.16	200	126.58
6.00	3.80	250	158.23
7.00	4.43	300	189.87
8.00	5.06	350	221.52
9.00	5.70	400	253.16
10.00	6.33	500	316.46

in U.S. dollars, Canadian dollars, French francs, British pounds, German marks, Dutch guilders, Spanish pesetas, Australian dollars, and Japanese yen. Depending on individual banking laws in each of the various states, some of the above-mentioned currencies might not be available at every outlet.

Interpayment Services (☎ **800/221-2426** in the U.S. and Canada, or **212/858-8500,** collect, from other parts of the world) sells Visa checks issued by a consortium of member banks and the Thomas Cook organization. Traveler's checks are denominated in U.S. or Canadian dollars, British pounds, and German marks.

CREDIT & CHARGE CARDS   Credit and charge cards are widely used in the Caribbean. Visa and MasterCard are the major cards used, although American Express and, to a lesser extent, Diners Club, are also popular.

2 When to Go

THE "SEASON"

More and more, the Caribbean is becoming a year-round destination. The "season" runs roughly from mid-December to mid-April. Hotels charge their highest prices during the peak winter period, which is generally the driest season; however, it can be a wet time in mountainous areas, and you can expect showers especially in December and January on Martinique, Guadeloupe, Dominica, St. Lucia, on the north coast of the Dominican Republic, and in Jamaica's northeast section.

For a winter vacation, make reservations two to three months in advance— or earlier for trips at Christmas and in February. The mails are unreliable, so book through one of the many Stateside representatives all major and many minor hotels use, or through a travel agent. You can also telephone or fax the hotel of your choice.

The temperature variations in the Caribbean are surprisingly slight, averaging between 75° and 85° Fahrenheit in both winter and summer, although it can get really chilly, especially in the early morning and at night. The Caribbean winter is usually like a perpetual May.

THE "OFF-SEASON"

The fabled Caribbean weather is balmy all year, with temperatures varying little more than 5° between winter and summer. The mid-80s prevail throughout most of the region, and trade winds make for comfortable days and nights, even without air conditioning.

Dollar for dollar, you'll spend less money by renting a summer house or self-sufficient unit in the Caribbean than you would on Cape Cod, Fire Island, Laguna Beach, or the coast of Maine. Sailing and water sports are better too, because the West Indies are protected from the Atlantic on their western shores, which border the calm Caribbean Sea.

20% to 60% Reductions

The off-season in the Caribbean—roughly from mid-April to mid-December (although this varies from hotel to hotel)—amounts to a summer sale. In most cases, hotel rates are slashed a startling 20% to 60%.

Other Off-Season Advantages

- After the winter hordes have left, a less-hurried way of life prevails. You'll have a better chance to appreciate the food, the culture, and the local customs.
- Swimming pools and beaches are less crowded—perhaps not crowded at all.
- Year-round resort facilities are offered, often at reduced rates, and are likely to include snorkeling, boating, and scuba diving.
- To survive, resort boutiques often feature summer sales, hoping to clear the merchandise they didn't sell in February to accommodate stock they've ordered for the coming winter. Duty-free items in free-port shopping are draws all year too.
- You can often walk in unannounced at a top restaurant and get a seat for dinner, and since the waiters are less hurried, you'll get better service.
- No waiting for a rented car (only to be told none is available); no long tee-up for golf; more immediate access to the tennis courts and water sports.
- The atmosphere is more cosmopolitan because of the influx of Europeans; you'll no longer feel as if you're at a Canadian or American outpost.
- Some package-tour fares are as much as 20% lower, and individual excursion fares are also reduced between 5% and 10%.
- All accommodations, including airline seats and hotel rooms, are much easier to obtain.

The Hurricane Season

The curse of Caribbean weather, the "hurricane season" lasts—officially, at least—from June 1 to November 30. But there's no cause for panic. Satellite forecasts give adequate warnings so that precautions can be taken. Of course, there is always prayer: U.S. Virgin Islanders actually have a legal holiday in the third week of July, called Supplication Day, when prayers that the Virgin Islands will be spared another hurricane are said in churches islandwide. In late October, at the end of the season of danger, a supplemental Thanksgiving Day is celebrated.

To get a weather report before you go, call your nearest branch of the National Weather Service, listed in your phone directory under the "U.S. Department of Commerce." You can also call Weather Trak; for the telephone number for your particular area, dial **900/370-8725** (a taped message gives you the three-digit access code for the place you're interested in; the call costs 75¢ for the first minute and 50¢ for each additional minute).

3 Tips for the Disabled

Hotels rarely give much publicity to what facilities, if any, they offer the disabled, so it's always better to contact the hotel directly, in advance. Tourist offices rarely have good data about such matters.

There are many agencies that provide advance data to help you plan your trip. One is the **Travel Information Service,** MossRehab Hospital (☎ **215/ 456-9603**), which provides information to telephone callers only.

You can obtain a free copy of **"Air Transportation of Handicapped Persons,"** published by the U.S. Department of Transportation. Write for Free Advisory Circular No. AC12032, Distribution Unit, U.S. Department of Transportation, Publications Division, M-4332, Washington, DC 20590.

For names and addresses of operators of tours specifically for disabled visitors, contact the **Society for the Advancement of Travel for the Handicapped,** 347 Fifth Ave., Suite 610, New York, NY 10016 (☎ 212/447-7284). Yearly membership dues in the society are $45, $25 for senior citizens and students. Send a self-addressed, stamped envelope.

You might also consider the **Federation of the Handicapped (FEDCAP),** 154 W. 14th St., New York, NY 10011 (☎ 212/727-4200), which offers summer tours for its members, who pay a yearly membership fee of $4.

The **Information Center for Individuals with Disabilities,** Fort Point Place, 27–43 Wormwood St., Boston, MA 02210 (☎ 617/727-5540), is another good source. It has lists of travel agents who specialize in tours for the disabled.

For the blind or visually impaired, the best source is the **American Foundation for the Blind,** 15 W. 16th St., New York, NY 10011 (☎ 212/620-2147, or 800/ 232-5463 to order information kits and supplies). It offers information on travel and various requirements for the transport and border formalities for seeing-eye dogs. It also issues identification cards to those who are legally blind.

One of the best organizations serving the needs of the disabled (wheelchairs and walkers) is **Flying Wheels Travel,** 143 W. Bridge St. (P.O. Box 382), Owatoona, MN 55060 (☎ 507/451-5005, or 800/535-6790). It offers various escorted international tours and cruises.

For a $20 annual fee, consider joining **Mobility International USA,** P.O. Box 10767, Eugene, OR 97440 (☎ 503/343-1284). It answers questions on various destinations and also offers discounts on its programs, videos, and publications.

Finally, a bimonthly publication, **Handicapped Travel Newsletter,** keeps you current on world-wide, accessible sights for the disabled. To order an annual subscription for $15, call **903/677-1260.**

TIPS FOR DISABLED BRITISH TRAVELERS   The **Royal Association for Disability and Rehabilitation (RADAR),** Unit 12, City Forum, 250 City Rd., London EC1V 8AF (☎ **0171/250-3222**), publishes two annual holiday guides for the disabled. "Holidays and Travel Abroad" costs £5, while "Holidays in the British Isles" costs £7. RADAR (whose patroness is Elizabeth, the Queen Mother), also provides a number of fact sheets on such subjects as sports and outdoor holidays, insurance, financial arrangements for the disabled, and accommodations in nursing-care units for groups or for the elderly. Each of these fact sheets is available for 75p. Fact sheets or the above-mentioned holiday guides can be mailed outside the U.K. for a nominal mailing fee.

Another good service is the **Holiday Care Service,** 2 Old Bank Chambers, Station Road, Horley, Surrey RH6 9HW (☎ **01293/774-535;** fax 01293/784-647), a national charity that advises on accommodations for elderly and disabled people. Annual membership costs £25. Members receive a newsletter and access to a free reservations network for hotels throughout Britain and, to a lesser degree, Europe and the rest of the world.

4 Alternative/Adventure Travel

EDUCATIONAL TRAVEL

The best information is available from the **Council on International Educational Exchange (CIEE),** 205 E. 42nd St., New York, NY 10017 (☎ **212/661-1450**). Request a copy of the 606-page *Work, Study, Travel Abroad: The Whole World Handbook* ($14.45 by mail), with more than 1,000 study opportunities abroad.

Elderhostel, 75 Federal St., Boston, MA 02110-1941 (☎ **617/426-7788**), established in 1975, maintains an array of postretirement study programs, several of which are in the Caribbean. Most courses last two or three weeks and are a good value, considering that hotel accommodations in student dormitories or modest inns, all meals, and tuition are included. Courses involve no homework, are ungraded, and center mostly on the liberal arts. Participants must be age 60 or older. However, if two members go as a couple, only one member needs to be 60 or over. Write for their free newsletter and a list of upcoming courses and destinations.

A series of international programs combining travel and learning for people over 50 years of age is offered by **Interhostel,** developed by the University of New Hampshire. Each program lasts two weeks and is escorted by a university faculty or staff member, and arranged in conjunction with a host college, university, or cultural institution. Participants can stay beyond two weeks if they wish. For information, contact the University of New Hampshire, Division of Continuing Education, 6 Garrison Ave., Durham, NH 03824 (☎ **603/826-1147,** or **800/ 733-9753** in the U.S.).

GARDEN TOURS

Although the seascapes of the Caribbean exert a powerful allure, many visitors search out the lush and verdant gardens for which the region is praised. If you're interested in knowing more about tropical gardens, you might consider contacting the tour operator recommended by the American Horticultural Society, the

Leonard Haertter Travel Company, 7922 Bonhomme Ave., St. Louis, MO 63105 (☎ **314/721-6200,** or **800/942-6666**). Founded in 1964, it operates at least four garden tours a year to such island clusters as the Leewards, the Windwards, the U.S. and British Virgin Islands, and the Lower Caribbean. Each of the tours is aboard some kind of oceangoing yacht. (In 1994 it was the M/V *Yorktown Clipper.*)

ADVENTURE TOURS

Unlike many of its neighboring islands, Jamaica offers landscapes which include mountain peaks of up to 7,400 feet. The flora, fauna, waterfalls, and panoramas of those peaks have attracted increasing numbers of hikers and hillclimbers, each determined to experience the natural beauty of the island firsthand. One outfit that caters to these needs is the **Jamaica Alternative Tourism Camping and Hiking Association,** whose membership includes at least three separate tour operators well versed in the wealth of Jamaica's ecological wonders. Foremost among these is **SENSE Adventures Ltd.,** P.O. Box 216, Kingston 7, Jamaica (☎ **809/927-2097;** fax 809/929-6967), whose owner, Peter Bentley, offers individually designed backpacking tours of the Blue Mountains and canoe trips along its rivers. His organization's crew of Jamaican guides can accompany hillclimbers on expeditions ranging from one to several days. Most of these expeditions use the Maya Lodge, a rustic but clean and comfortable 15-acre base from which hiking tours depart for explorations of the mountain regions to the north and east. Frequently ravaged by hurricane damage since its original construction in 1981, the site contains a café, laundry facilities, one simply built five-sided cabin, an even simpler dormitory facility, and ample space for campsites. Most important, a team of trained guides is on hand for guided exploration of the Blue Mountains. The cost for one of these guides is between $50 and $100 a day, depending on the guide's level of

---

In Search of the Big Wahoo

Some of the world's premier fishing grounds are found in the Caribbean—they're teeming with a spectacular variety of deep-sea game fish, including wahoo, sailfish, tuna, marlin, and dolphin (the fish, not the mammal). Among the shallow-water fish are tarpon, bonefish, pompano, and barracuda.

Spring through autumn is the best time to fish, although the sport is practiced during the winter.

Puerto Rico is virtually the fishing capital of the Caribbean—some 30 world records have been set there. Charters are plentiful in San Juan and Palmas del Mar.

Some of the other best fishing grounds are in the Cayman Islands, whose offshore waters are filled with tuna, yellowtail, marlin, and other catches; and the Dominican Republic, which attracts anglers in pursuit of sailfish, marlin, and bonito. Those in search of marlin head for the north coast of Jamaica from September to April, whereas the south coast is favored in winter. Port Antonio is Jamaica's major fishing center.

The U.S. Virgin Islands are popular with vacationers pursuing Allison tuna, bonito, marlin, and wahoo. Red Hook on St. Thomas is the major charter center, although St. John and St. Croix lure anglers as well.

expertise, plus tips, food, and accommodation for the guide. Camping gear can be rented. Many participants opt for all-inclusive packages priced at $55 to $90 U.S. per person per day, depending on the number of participants. A handful of other accommodations, scattered throughout the Blue Mountains and the rest of Jamaica, are also available for daily or weekly rentals.

Arawak Expeditions, Cruz Bay, St. John (☎ **809/693-8312,** or **800/ 238-8687** in the U.S.), is the only outfitter in the Virgin Islands offering multiday sea-kayaking/island-camping excursions. Full- and half-day trips are also available. You cruise through the islands somewhat as the Arawaks did—except that they used dugout canoes. Today's vessels are two-person fiberglass kayaks complete with a foot-controlled rudder. The outfit provides all the kayaking gear, healthful meals, camping equipment, and two experienced guides. The cost of a full-day trip is $55, a half-day trip is $30, and multiday excursions range in price from $750 to $1,195.

HOME EXCHANGES

House swapping keeps costs low if you don't mind a stranger living in your mainland home or apartment, and sometimes the exchange includes use of the family car.

Many home-exchange directories are published, but there's no guarantee that you'll find a house or apartment in the area you're seeking.

The Invented City, 41 Sutter St., Suite 1090, San Francisco, CA 94104 (☎ **415/673-0347**), is an international home-exchange agency. Home-exchange listings are published three times a year, in February, May, and November. A membership fee of $50 allows you to list your home, and you can also give your preferred time to travel, your occupation, and your hobbies.

Intervac U.S., P.O. Box 590504, San Francisco, CA 94119 (☎ **415/ 435-3497,** or **800/756-HOME** in the U.S.), is part of the largest worldwide home-exchange network. It publishes four catalogs a year, containing more than 9,400 homes in more than 36 countries. Members contact each other directly. The $65 cost, plus postage, includes the purchase of three of the company's catalogs (which will be mailed to you), plus the inclusion of your own listing in whichever one of the three catalogs you select. If you want to publish a photograph of your home, it costs $11 extra. Hospitality and rentals are also available.

TOURS FOR WOMEN SAILORS

A program for women of all ages and levels of nautical expertise is offered by **Womanship, Inc.,** The Boat House, 410 Severn Ave., Annapolis, MD 21403 (☎ **410/267-6661,** or **800/342-9295** in the U.S.). It offers expert sailing instruction by women for a maximum of six students with two instructors. Participants sleep aboard the sailing vessel. Tortola is the primary port of departure for the Caribbean trips, and sailing instruction is taught in the British Virgin Islands. Most courses last a full week.

5 Getting There by Plane

All the biggest islands have air links to North America with regularly scheduled service, and the smaller islands are tied into this vast network through their own carriers. For details of how to reach each island, see the "Getting There" sections in the individual island chapters.

REGULAR FARES

Always shop around to secure the lowest airfare, and keep calling the airlines. Sometimes you can purchase a ticket that is lower in price at the very last minute—if the flight is not fully booked, an airline will discount tickets to try to fill it up.

If you fly in summer, spring, and fall, you'll see substantial reductions on airfares to the Caribbean. You can also ask about the cost-conscious APEX (Advance Purchase Excursion) fare and find out if it's cheaper to fly Monday through Thursday. Also, consider air-and-land packages, which offer considerably reduced rates.

OTHER GOOD-VALUE CHOICES

Proceed with caution through the next grab bag of suggestions. What constitutes good value keeps changing in the airline industry, and it's hard to keep up, even if you're a travel agent.

BUCKET SHOPS (CONSOLIDATORS)   The name originated in the 1960s in Britain, where the airlines gave that (then-pejorative) name to resellers of blocks of unsold tickets consigned to them by major carriers. "Bucket shop" has stuck as a label, but it might be more polite to refer to them as "consolidators." They exist in many shapes and forms. In its purest sense, a bucket shop acts as a clearinghouse for blocks of tickets that airlines discount and consign during normally slow periods of air travel. In the case of the Caribbean, that usually means from mid-April to mid-December.

Charter operators (see below) and bucket shops used to perform separate functions, but their offerings in many cases have been blurred in recent times. Many outfits perform both functions.

Tickets are sometimes—but not always—discounted 20% to 35%. Terms of payment can vary, from anywhere from 45 days prior to departure to the last minute. Discounted tickets can also be purchased through regular travel agents, who usually mark up the ticket 8% to 10%, maybe more, thereby greatly reducing your discount.

A survey conducted of flyers who use consolidator tickets voiced only one major complaint: You can't arrange for an advance seat assignment, so you're likely to be assigned a "poor seat." The survey revealed that most flyers received a savings off the regular price. But—and here's the hitch—many flyers reported no savings at all, as the airlines will sometimes match the consolidator ticket with a promotional fare. The situation is a bit tricky and calls for some careful investigation on your part to determine just how much you are saving.

Bucket shops abound from coast to coast. Look for their ads in your local newspaper's travel section; they're usually very small and a single column in width.

One of the biggest U.S. consolidators is **Travac,** 989 Sixth Ave., New York, NY 10018 (☎ **212/563-3303,** or **800/TRAV-800** in the U.S.), which offers discounted seats throughout the United States on airlines that include TWA, United, and Delta. Another Travac office is at 2601 E. Jefferson St., Orlando, FL 32803 (☎ **407/896-0014**).

In New York try **TFI Tours International,** 34 W. 32nd St., 12th Floor, New York, NY 10001 (☎ **212/736-1140,** or **800/745-8000** outside New York State). This tour company offers services to 177 cities worldwide.

For the Middle West, explore the possibilities of **Travel Avenue,** 10 S. Riverside Plaza, Suite 1404, Chicago, IL 60606 (☎ **800/333-3335** in the U.S.). Its tickets are often cheaper than most shops, and it charges the customer only a $25 fee on international tickets, rather than taking the usual 10% commission from an airline. Travel Avenue rebates most of that back to the customers—hence, the lower fares.

In New England, a possibility is **TMI (Travel Management International)**, 39 JFK St. (Harvard Square), 3rd Floor, Cambridge, MA 02138 (☎ **800/ 245-3672** in the U.S.), which offers a wide variety of discounts, including youth fares, student fares, and access to other kinds of air-related discounts as well.

CHARTER FLIGHTS   Charter flights allow you to travel at rates lower than on regularly scheduled flights. Many of the major carriers offer charter flights at rates that are sometimes 30% (or more) off the regular airfare.

There are some drawbacks, however. Advance booking of up to 45 days or more may be required, and there are hefty cancellation penalties, although you can take out insurance against emergency cancellations. Also, you must depart and return on your scheduled dates or you will lose your money. It will do no good to call the airline and tell them you're on Trinidad with yellow fever! If you're not on the plane, you can kiss your money good-bye.

Since charter flights are so complicated, it's best to ask a good travel agent to explain the problems and advantages. Sometimes charters require ground arrangements, such as the prebooking of hotel rooms.

One reliable charter-flight operator is **Council Charter,** run by the Council on International Educational Exchange (CIEE), 205 E. 42nd St., New York, NY 10017 (☎ **212/661-0311,** or **800/800-8222** in the U.S.), which arranges charter seats on regularly scheduled aircraft.

One of the biggest New York charter operators is **Travac,** 989 Sixth Ave., New York, NY 10018 (☎ **212/563-3303,** or **800/TRAV-800** in the U.S.). Other Travac offices are at 2601 E. Jefferson St., Orlando, FL 32803 (☎ **407/ 896-0014**).

REBATORS   To confuse the situation even more, rebators have also begun to compete in the low-airfare market. These outfits pass along to the passenger part of their commission, although many of them assess a fee for their services. They are not the same as travel agents, but they sometimes offer roughly similar services, such as discounted land arrangements, including hotels and car rentals. Most rebators offer discounts averaging anywhere from 10% to 25% (but this could vary from place to place), plus a $25 handling charge.

Specializing in clients in the Middle West, **Travel Avenue,** 10 S. Riverside Plaza, Suite 1404, Chicago, IL 60606 (☎ **312/876-1116,** or **800/333-3335** in the U.S.), is said to be one of the oldest agencies of its kind. It offers up-front cash rebates on every airline ticket over $300 it sells. In a style similar to a discount brokerage firm, they pride themselves on *not* offering travel counseling. Instead, they sell airline tickets to independent travelers who have already worked out their travel plans. Also available are tour and cruise fares, plus hotel reservations, usually at prices lower than if you have reserved them on your own.

Another major rebator is **The Smart Traveller,** 3111 SW 27th Ave. (P.O. Box 330010), Miami, FL 33133 (☎ **305/448-3338,** or **800/448-3338** in the U.S.). The agency also offers discounts on package tours.

TRAVEL CLUBS   Travel clubs supply an unsold inventory of tickets offering discounts in the usual range of 20% to 60%. After you pay an annual fee, you are given a "hotline" number to call to find out what discounts are available. Some discounts become available a few days in advance of actual departure, some a week in advance, and some as much as a month. Of course, you're limited to what's available, so you have to be flexible. Some of the best of these clubs include:

Moment's Notice, 425 Madison Ave., New York, NY 10017 (☎ **212/486-0500**), charges $25 per year for membership, which allows spur-of-the-moment participation in dozens of tours. Each is geared for impulse purchases and last-minute getaways, and each features air and land packages which sometimes represent substantial savings over what you'd have paid through more conventional channels. Although membership is required for participation in the tours, anyone can call the company's hotline (☎ **212/750-9111**) to learn what options are available. Most of the company's best-valued tours depart from New Jersey's Newark airport.

Sears Discount Travel Club, 3033 S. Parker Rd., Suite 900, Aurora, CO 80014 (☎ **800/255-1487** in the U.S.), offers members a catalog (issued four times a year), maps, discounts at select hotels, and a limited guarantee that equivalent packages will not be undersold by any other travel organization. Membership costs $50. It also offers a 5% rebate on the value of all airline tickets, tours, hotel accommodations, and car rentals that are purchased through them. (To collect this rebate, participants are required to fill out some forms and photocopy their receipts and itineraries.)

6 Cruises & Chartered Boats

CRUISES

Vacations to Go, 2411 Fountain View, Houston, TX 77057 (☎ **800/338-4962** in the U.S.), provides catalogs and information on discount cruises through the Atlantic, the Caribbean, and the Mediterranean. Annual membership costs $19.95 per family.

Here's a rundown of some of the major cruise lines serving the Caribbean; pick up a copy of *Frommer's Cruises* for more detailed information.

Carnival Cruise Lines (☎ **305/599-2600,** or **800/327-9501**). Operating from such ports as Miami, San Juan, St. Thomas, and Grand Cayman, this enormous company operates seven ships. Cruises range from three to seven nights, and tend to feature lots of partying. Many single passengers opt for this line; the average passenger is 42.

Celebrity Cruises (☎ **305/262-6677,** or **800/437-3111**). It maintains three newly built, medium-size ships, each offering cruises of between 5 and 11 nights. Ports of call usually include Key West, San Juan, Grand Cayman, Ocho Rios, St. Thomas, Antigua, and St. Barts. Accommodations are roomy and well equipped, and many passengers compare their vessels to well-equipped all-inclusive resorts.

Club Med Cruises (☎ **602/948-9190,** or **800/258-2633**). The ship that is associated with the France-based chain of all-inclusive resorts is small and clublike. Destinations in the Lesser Antilles include such offbeat hideaways as Dominica, Marie Galante, the Tobago Cays, Bequia, Mayreau Island, Iles des Saintes, and Carriacou.

Commodore Cruise Line (☎ **305/444-4600,** or **800/227-4759**). Although the ships might be a bit old-fashioned and worn, many clients like this company because of its reasonable prices. Cruises range from 7 to 14 days, and ports include Grand Cayman, the largest ports of Puerto Rico, St. Croix, Antigua, Martinique, and ports along the Mexican coast. There's a share of families with children on board, as well as lots of couples who don't care about the ships' relative lack of state-of-the-art facilities.

Costa Cruise Lines (☎ **305/358-7325,** or **800/462-6782**). Its ships are relatively large and relatively new, and hold around 1,300 passengers each. Ports of call include Nassau, San Juan, St. Thomas, St. Martin, and Key West. Cruises range from 7 to 11 nights at sea. There's an Italian atmosphere here, with entertainment like Carnival in Venice.

Crystal Cruises (☎ **310/785-9300,** or **800/446-6620**). Most of the itinerary of this line's premier ship, the *Crystal Harmony*, revolves around the ports of Florida and the beaches of Mexico and Belize, although stopovers in Jamaica are often included. This medium-size ship offers lots of exercise activities and one of the best dining experiences.

Cunard (☎ **800/221-4770**). Some visitors remember Cunard fondly from transatlantic journeys they've taken in the past on the line's very British flagship, the *QE2*. The company is one of the premier cruise lines in the world, with an undeniable flair that extends even to its less expensive vessels. Ports of call include San Juan, St. Thomas, St. Kitts, Barbados, and, in some cases, isolated ports in the southern Caribbean.

Diamond Cruise Lines (☎ **305/776-6123,** or **800/333-3333**). Its only ship, the *Radisson Diamond*, is small and engineered with twin hulls like a catamaran. Cruises last four to seven nights, and often originate in either St. Thomas, Barbados, or San Juan. En route, the ship stops at such off-the-beaten-track places as Jost van Dyke and certain islands in the Grenadines. The ship is in some ways a lot like a large floating hotel. (This vision is encouraged by Radisson, the giant hotel chain that helps manage it.)

Dolphin Cruise Line (☎ **305/358-2111,** or **800/222-1003**). Its trio of ships are among the oldest in the industry. Each has been refurbished, and today they ply the waters between the ports of southern Florida, Nassau, and San Juan. Less frequently, it travels to other ports farther south that include Dominica, Martinique, and Curaçao. Nothing is particularly fancy, but no one seems to mind in view of the good values.

Fantasy Cruise Lines (☎ **305/262-6677,** or **800/423-2100**). Its two ships are refurbished older models; each has a distinctive personality, a quality sometimes missing from newer ships. The line is known for serving extremely good food for such a cost-conscious company. Each of its cruises specializes in relatively inexpensive seven-day cruises originating in either San Juan or Miami. The clientele tends to be senior citizens, families, students, and anyone else traveling on a budget. There's lots to do on board, including organized group games and trivia contests. Maritime stopovers include ports as far south as Curaçao and Grenada, and as far north and west as Key West and Mexico.

Holland America Line (☎ **206/281-3535**). Its seven vessels represent one of the great maritime nations of Europe (the Netherlands), and the crew and staff are as cosmopolitan as anything you're likely to find on the high seas. The company was founded in 1873, and has accumulated really wonderful pieces of cruising memorabilia. (Many of these grace the public areas of the ships.) Tours range from 7 to 17 days, and the ships cruise to such places as Nassau, Key West, the coast of Mexico, Grand Cayman, Dominica, and St. John. Passengers tend to be some-what older than the usual mix.

Majesty Cruise Line (☎ 305/536-0000, or 800/532-7788). This is a com-pany whose U.S. port of embarkation is almost always Miami, and whose one ship (the *Royal Majesty*) was specifically built in 1992 for continuous three- or four-day circuits whose outer limits are usually Nassau, Key West, and the coastal resorts of Mexico. Majesty is usually considered the upscale twin of the less glamorous (and less expensive) Dolphin Cruise lines; both are owned by the same company.

Norwegian Cruise Line (☎ 305/447-9660, or 800/327-7030). Marked by a policy of appealing to all ages and income levels, this line features Scandinavian officers, an international staff, and a pervasive theme of sailing with modern-age Vikings into the land of the Midnight Sun. The company's five ships usually cruise for between three and seven days, stopping at Nassau, Key West, the beaches of Mexico, St. Thomas, Aruba, Tortola, and a Bahamian island that is wholly owned by NCL. The company's largest ship and corporate symbol (the *Norway*) offers what's usually considered the best amenities and services; its smallest (the *Starward*) cruises to the southern Caribbean.

Premier Cruise Lines (☎ 800/473-3262). The company has three ships, the *Atlantic,* the *Oceanic,* and the *Majestic,* each of which has an on-board program that makes great efforts to cater to children. Some of the company's routes begin and end in Miami and head for Nassau, Port Lucaya, and the beaches of Mexico.

Princess Cruises (☎ 310/553-1770, or 800/568-3262). It owns nine ships, at least four of which sail in Caribbean and Bahamian waters. The company is one of the very few in the world offering luxury accommodations and upscale service on its mega-ships. These usually carry a smaller complement of passengers than similarly sized vessels at less elegant lines. Cruises last 7 to 10 days each, and in-corporate both major and minor islands, as well as off-the-beaten-track places. The clientele is upscale, with an average passenger age of 55 or over. Much of the staff is British, and service is often extremely good.

Regal Cruise Lines (☎ 201/934-3753 in New Jersey or 813/867-1300 in Florida). It owns just one ship, the 23,000-ton *Regal Empress,* which offers two-day quickies and seven-day cruises which usually originate from Port Manatee, Florida. Regular ports of call include Jamaica, Key West, Grand Cayman, and Mexico.

Regency Cruises (☎ 212/972-4499). Most of this company's flotilla of ships were originally designed as transatlantic ocean liners and, as such, seem unusually solid. Four ships depart from ports in Florida, Jamaica, Puerto Rico, and Mexico on cruises that last four to seven nights. Ships touch down in such ports as the Vir-gin Islands, Aruba, Grenada, and Belize. The cruises are relatively inexpensive, but not luxurious.

Renaissance Cruises (☎ 305/463-0982, or 800/525-5350). Only one of its vessels, the small and elegant *Renaissance III,* plies the Caribbean. Cruises usually last about a week.

Royal Caribbean Cruise Line (☎ 305/539-6000). This company led the industry in the development of mega-ships, and three of its six vessels are among the largest anywhere. A houseparty theme tends to permeate the on-board ambience of these ships. There are enough on-board activities to suit any taste and age level. Though accommodations are more than adequate, they are not upscale.

Royal Cruise Line (☎ 415/956-7200). The ships of this line that venture into Caribbean waters are small compared to those of its competitors. The company offers some of the best-accessorized and most upscale cruises on the market, with a high percentage of repeat passengers. Cruises usually last 7 to 10 days, and begin in such U.S. ports as Fort Lauderdale and New Orleans. Service from the mostly Greek-born staff is usually excellent. Cruises tend to be stylish and tasteful without a lot of glitter.

Royal Viking Cruise Line (☎ **305/447-9660,** or **800/327-7030**). It owns only two ships, but the company is almost always viewed as a well-managed, hardworking chain with appealing itineraries, excellent service, and some of the best on-board cuisine of any cruise line in the world. Clients tend to be a bit more sedate and well mannered than on many other cruises. Itineraries include Barbados, St. Barts, Key West, Virgin Gorda, San Juan, and selected ports in the Virgin Islands.

Seabourn Cruise Line (☎ **415/391-7444**). The upscale and expensive *Seabourne Pride* offers cruises of 10 to 14 days. Stops include the islands of St. Thomas, Jost van Dyke, Virgin Gorda, and the French side of St. Martin. There is a great array of activities, a surprising amount of on-board space per passenger, and French-inspired food. The emphasis is on prestige, good service, and luxury.

Seawind Cruises (☎ **305/854-7800,** or **800/258-8006**). It operates only one ship, the *Seawind Crown*. Although it's a large ship, it carries only 624 passengers, allowing lots of room to wander and relax. Most of its cruises last seven nights. Ports of call include Fort Lauderdale, Casa de Campo (Dominican Republic), St. Lucia, Martinique, Barbados, and Antigua.

Silversea Cruises (☎ **305/522-4477**). This company's Caribbean itineraries are for the most part aboard the *Silver Cloud,* which sails to such ports as La Romana, Antigua, Barbados, and Virgin Gorda. Most cruises begin in Fort Lauderdale. The ship was launched in 1994 and was designed in a format midway between a very large yacht and a very small ocean liner. Many visitors prefer it because of the extra amenities and facilities that are available. Also appealing is the added stability during rough seas, and the on-board sense of luxury and enhanced service. There's a big emphasis here on water sports during port stops.

Sun Line Cruises (☎ **212/397-6400,** or **800/872-6400**). Its only ship, the *Stella Solaris,* usually makes runs of 10 to 12 days from ports like Galveston, Texas, and Fort Lauderdale. Ports of call include Nassau, Grand Cayman, St. Lucia, and St. Martin.

Windstar Cruises (☎ **206/281-3535,** or **800/626-9900**). Many passengers consider these sailing yachts some of the most appealing anywhere. Although both the *Wind Star* and the *Wind Spirit* are equipped with motors, part of their mobility comes from the wind—sails hang from four masts. Although the amenities are suitably 20th century, passengers get a vivid sense of the bygone clipper ship.

CHARTERED BOATS

Experienced sailors and navigators can charter "bareboat," a term meaning a rental with a fully equipped boat but with no captain or crew. You're on your own, and you'll have to prove your qualifications before you're allowed to rent such a craft. Even an experienced skipper may want to take along someone familiar with local waters—waters that may in some places be tricky.

You can also charter a boat with a skipper and crew. Charter yachts, varying from 50 to more than 100 feet, can accommodate four to a dozen people.

Most yachts are rented on a weekly basis, with a fully stocked bar, plus equipment for fishing and water sports. However, more and more bareboat charterers are learning that they can save money and select menus more suited to their tastes by doing their own provisioning. The average charter carries four to six passengers, and usually is reserved for a week. In summer, when business tends to be slow, you might be able to charter a boat for four or five days.

The Moorings, 19345 U.S. North, Suite 402, Clearwater, FL 34624 (☎ **813/535-1446,** or **800/535-7289** in the U.S. and Canada), operates one of the biggest boat-charter operations in the Caribbean, with its main branch located in the British Virgin Islands, cruise capital of the world. Charlie and Ginny Cary started the venture in 1969, and today preside over a mini-empire of seven Caribbean and Bahamian branches, each bristling with a regatta of yachts, some of which are available for chartering. Depending on their size, yachts are rented to up to four couples at a time in comfort and style. Arrangements can be made either for bareboating (qualified sailors only) or for rental of yachts with a full crew and cook. Depending on circumstances, boats come equipped with barbecue, snorkeling gear, dinghy, and linens, and boats are serviced by an experienced staff of mechanics, electricians, riggers, and cleaners. If you're going out on your own, you'll get a thorough briefing about Caribbean waters, reefs, and anchorages.

Windjammer Barefoot Cruises Ltd., P.O. Box 120, Miami Beach, FL 33119 (☎ **305/534-7447,** or **800/327-2601** in the U.S.), offers 6- and 13-day sailing adventures on classic tall ships through the Caribbean. The *Flying Cloud* island-hops the British Virgins, the *Yankee Clipper* sails the Grenadines, the *Polynesia* and *Fantôme* sail through the West Indies, and the *Mandalay* takes a leisurely 13-day cruise through the West Indies and Grenadines. The supply ship *Amazing Grace* carries 96 passengers from Freeport to Grenada and on to Trinidad. Rates start at $650. Air-sea package deals are offered.

Nicholson Yacht Charters, 432 Columbia St., Suite 21A, Cambridge MA 02141-1043 (☎ **617/225-0555,** or **800/662-6066** in the U.S.), or P.O. Box 103, St. John's, Antigua, West Indies—one of the best in the business—handles charter yachts for use throughout the Caribbean basin, particularly the route between Dutch-held Sint Maarten and Grenada and the routes around the U.S. and British Virgin Islands and Puerto Rico. Specializing in boats of all sizes, it can arrange rentals of motor or sailing yachts up to 298 feet long. Especially popular are arrangements where two or more yachts, each sleeping eight guests in four equal double cabins, race each other from island to island during the day, anchoring near each other in secluded coves or at berths in Caribbean capitals at night. Nicholson's offers a series of possibilities. The price for renting a yacht depends on the number in your party, the size of the vessel, and the time of the year. Rates range from $3,500 weekly up to something in the neighborhood of $50,000. You can get a really nice vessel for $12,000 to $25,000 weekly.

Sunsail, 3347 NW 55th St., Fort Lauderdale, FL 33309 (☎ **800/327-2276** in the U.S.), specializes in yacht chartering from its bases in the British Virgin Islands, St. Lucia, the French West Indies, and The Bahamas. Bareboat and crewed yachts between 30 and 56 feet are available for cruising these waters. The company usually requires a deposit of 25% of the total rental fee; arrangements should be made four to six months in advance. Clients with flexible schedules need only reserve a month in advance.

7 Package Tours

To save time comparing the price and value of all the package tours out there, consider hiring the services of **TourScan Inc.**, P.O. Box 2367, Darien, CT 06820 (☎ **203/655-8091,** or **800/962-2080**). Every season, the company gathers and computerizes the contents of about 200 brochures containing 10,000 different vacations in the Caribbean, The Bahamas, and Bermuda. TourScan selects the best value at each hotel and condo. Two catalogs are printed each year. Each lists a broad-based choice of hotels on most of the islands of the Caribbean, in all price ranges. (The scope of the islands and resort hotels is amazing.) Catalogs cost $4 each, the price of which is credited to any TourScan vacation.

Another good deal might be a combined land-and-air package offered by one of the major U.S. carriers. Call their toll-free numbers: **American Airlines Fly-Away Vacations** (☎ **800/321-2121**), and **Delta's Dream Vacations** (☎ **800/872-7786**). **TWA Getaway Vacations** (☎ **800/GETAWAY**) specializes only in cruises, and **United Airlines Vacations** (☎ **800/328-6877**) only fly to San Juan.

Other tour operators include the following:

Caribbean Concepts Corp., 575 Underhill Blvd., Syosset, NY 11791 (☎ **516/496-9800,** or **800/423-4433** in the U.S.), offers low-cost air-and-land packages to the islands, including apartments, hotels, villas, or condo rentals.

Clothing-optional tours are arranged through **Caribbean Travel Naturally,** P.O. Box 897, Lutz, FL 33549 (☎ **813/948-1303,** or **800/462-6833** in the U.S.). Both nudist resorts and cruises through the West Indies are offered.

The best diving cruises are packaged by **Oceanic Society Expeditions,** Fort Mason Center, Building E, San Francisco, CA 94123 (☎ **415/441-1106,** or **800/326-7491** in the U.S.). Whale-watching jaunts and some research-oriented trips are also a feature. Another specialist in this field is **Tropical Adventures,** 111 Second Ave. N., Seattle, WA 98109 (☎ **206/441-3483,** or **800/247-3483** in the U.S.). Its packages to Saba are a particular delight.

AIB Tours, 2500 NW 79th Ave., Suite 211, Miami, FL 33122 (☎ **305/715-0056,** or **800/242-8687** outside Florida), offers tours to Aruba, Bonaire, and Curaçao.

If you're seeking just general independent packages, consider **Domenico Tours,** 751 Broadway, Bayonne, NJ 07002 (☎ **800/554-8687** in the U.S.), with packages to Puerto Rico, Sint Maarten/St. Martin, St. Thomas, Aruba, and Jamaica. Included are airfare, airport transfers, accommodations, and car rentals. **Sunbrella Vacations,** 2655 Lejeune Rd., Suite 400, Coral Gables, FL 33134 (☎ **800/874-0027** in the U.S.), offers deals to Ocho Rios, Jamaica, St. Thomas, and Grenada. **Horizon Tours,** 1010 Vermont Ave. NW, Suite 202, Washington, DC 20005 (☎ **202/393-8390,** or **800/395-0025** in the U.S.), specializes in all-inclusive resorts on the islands of The Bahamas, Jamaica, Aruba, and Puerto Rico.

Club Med, Club Med Sales, P.O. Box 4460, Scottsdale, AZ 85258 (☎ **800/258-2633** in the U.S.), has various all-inclusive options throughout the Caribbean and The Bahamas.

Finally, advertising more packages to The Bahamas and the Caribbean than any other agency is **Liberty Travel** (☎ **800/216-9776**), with offices in many states.

FOR BRITISH TRAVELERS

Package tours can be booked through **British Virgin Islands Holidays,** a division of Wingjet Travel Ltd., 11–13 Hockerill St., Bishop's Stortford, Herts. CM23 2DW (☎ **01279/656111**). This company is the major booking agent for all the important hotels in the BVI. Stays can be arranged in more than one hotel if you'd like to visit more than one island. The company also offers staffed yacht charters and bareboat charters.

Caribbean Connection, Concorde House, Forest Street, Chester CH1 1QR (☎ **01244/341131**), offers all-inclusive packages (airfare and hotel) to the Caribbean. It publishes a 100-page catalog of Caribbean offerings.

Other Caribbean specialists operating out of England include **Tradewinds Faraway Holidays,** Station House, 81–83 Fulham High St., London SW6 3JP (☎ **0171/731-8000**), and **Kuoni House,** Kuoni Travel, Dorking, Surrey RH5 4AZ (☎ **01306/742-2220**). **Caribtours,** 161 Fulham Rd., London SW3 6SN (☎ **0171/581-3517**), also specializes in Caribbean travel.

8 Tips on Accommodations

Few travel destinations in the world offer such a wide range of accommodations: a tropical villa on St. Thomas, a millionaire's estate on Jamaica, a 17th-century Great House on St. Kitts, a 200-year-old sugar warehouse on St. Vincent, or a beachfront apartel (an efficiency apartment for short-term rental) on Puerto Rico. All guest units have private bathrooms unless otherwise noted.

HOTELS & RESORTS   There is no rigid classification of Caribbean hotels. The word "deluxe" is often used—or misused—when "first class" might have been a more appropriate term. "First class," itself, often isn't. I've presented fairly detailed descriptions of the properties so that you'll get an idea of what to expect once you're there. However, even in the deluxe and first-class properties, don't expect top-rate service and efficiency. Life in the tropics has its disadvantages. When you go to turn on the shower, sometimes you get water and sometimes you don't. You may even experience island power failures.

THE WEST INDIAN GUESTHOUSE   An entirely different type of accommodation is the guesthouse, where most of the Antilleans themselves stay when they travel. In the Caribbean, the term *guesthouse* can mean anything. Sometimes so-called guesthouses are really like simple motels built around swimming pools. Others are small individual cottages, with their own kitchenettes, constructed around a main building in which you'll often find a bar and a restaurant serving local food. Some are surprisingly comfortable, often with private baths and swimming pools. You may or may not have air conditioning.

For value, the guesthouse can't be topped. You can always journey over to a big beach resort and use its seaside facilities for only a small charge, perhaps no more than $4. Although bereft of frills, the guesthouses I've recommended are clean and safe for families or single women. The cheapest ones are not places where you'd want to spend time, because of their simple, modest furnishings.

SELF-CATERING HOLIDAYS   Particularly if you're a family or a group of friends, a housekeeping holiday can be one of the least expensive ways of vacationing in the Caribbean. Self-catering accommodations are now available on nearly all the islands. Some are individual cottages you can rent, others are housed in one building, and some are private homes rented when the owners are away. All have small kitchens or kitchenettes, so you can do your own cooking. Most self-catering places have maid service included in the rental, and you're given fresh linen as well.

CONDOS & VILLAS   Even Princess Margaret rents out her private villa on Mustique in the Grenadines, providing you have "the proper references." Throughout the Caribbean you can secure good deals by renting privately owned villas and condos.

Many villas have a staff, or at least a maid who comes in a few days a week, and they also provide the essentials for home life, including bed linen and cooking paraphernalia. Condos usually come with a reception desk and are often comparable to life in a suite in a big resort hotel. Nearly all condo complexes have swimming pools (some more than one).

Agencies specializing in these rentals include the following:

Villas of Distinction, P.O. Box 55, Armonk, NY 10504 (☎ **914/273-3331,** or **800/289-0900** in the U.S.) is one of the best offering "complete vacations," including airfare, rental car, and domestic help. Some private villas have one or two bedrooms, and almost every villa has a swimming pool. Islands on which you can rent villas include St. Martin, Mustique, Barbados, the U.S. Virgins, the Cayman Islands, St. Lucia, and Antigua, among others.

At Home Abroad, 405 E. 56th St., Suite 6-H, New York, NY 10022-2466 (☎ **212/421-9165**), has a roster of private homes for rent in the Caribbean, all with maid service included.

Caribbean Connection Plus Ltd., P.O. Box 261, Trumbull, CT 06611 (☎ **203/261-8603**), offers many apartments and villas in the Caribbean, especially on St. Kitts, Nevis, and Montserrat, but also on some of the more obscure islands such as St. Eustatius, Tobago, St. Vincent, Dominica, and Nevis. This is one of the few reservations services whose staff has actually been on the islands, so members can talk to people from experience and not from a computer screen.

VHR, Worldwide, 235 Kensington Ave., Norwood, NJ 07648 (☎ **201/767-9393,** or **800/NEED-A-VILLA** in the U.S.), offers the most comprehensive

---

What the Abbreviations Mean

Travelers to the Caribbean may at first be confused by classifications on rate sheets. I've used these same classifications in this guide:

MAP (Modified American Plan) usually means room, breakfast, and dinner, unless the room rate has been quoted separately, and then it means only breakfast and dinner.

CP (Continental Plan) includes room and a light breakfast.

EP (European Plan) means room only.

AP (American Plan) is the most expensive rate of all because it includes your room plus three meals a day.

portfolio of luxury villas, condominiums, resort suites, and apartments for rent not only in the Caribbean, but also in The Bahamas, Mexico, the United States, and Europe.

Hideaways International, 767 Islington St. (P.O. Box 4433), Portsmouth, NH 03801-4433 (☎ **603/430-4433,** or **800/843-4433** in the U.S.), publishes *Hideaways Guide,* a 140-page pictorial directory of home rentals throughout the Caribbean with full descriptions so you know what you're renting. Rentals range from cottages to staffed villas to whole islands! On most rentals you deal directly with owners. At condos and small resorts Hideaways offers member discounts. Other services include yacht charters, airline ticketing, car rentals, and hotel reservations. Annual membership is $99; a four-month trial membership is $39.95.

Heart of the Caribbean Ltd., 17485 Peinbrook Dr., Brookfield, WI 53045 (☎ **414/783-5303,** or **800/231-5303** in the U.S.), is a villa wholesale company offering travelers a wide range of private villas and condos on several islands, including Sint Maarten/St. Martin, Tortola, St. John, Anguilla, and the Cayman Islands. Accommodations range from one to six bedrooms, and the establishment offers modest villas and condos, as well as palatial estates. Homes have complete kitchens.

Rent-a-Home International, 7200 34th Ave. NW, Seattle, WA 98117 (☎ **206/789-9377**), specializes in condos and villas. It arranges weekly or longer bookings.

Sometimes local tourist offices will also advise you on vacation-home rentals if you write or call them directly.

PRIVATE APARTMENTS & COTTAGES   Private apartments can be rented, either with or without maid service. This is more of a no-frills option than the villas and condos. The apartments may not be in buildings with swimming pools, and they may not have a front desk to help you. Cottages are the most free-wheeling way to live in these four major categories of vacation homes. Most of them are fairly simple; many open onto a beach, while others may be clustered around a communal swimming pool. Many contain no more than a simple bedroom with a small kitchen and bath. For the peak winter season, reservations should be made at least five or six months in advance.

Dozens of agents throughout the United States and Canada offer these types of rentals. You can also write to local tourist offices.

Travel experts agree that savings, especially for a family of three to six people or two or three couples, can range from 50% to 60% of what a hotel would cost. If there are only two in your party, these savings don't apply. However, groceries are sometimes priced 35% to 60% higher than the average on the U.S. mainland because nearly all foodstuffs have to be imported. Even so, preparing your own food will be a lot cheaper than dining at restaurants.

9 Getting Married in the Caribbean

In recent years, the high cost of traditional weddings and the greater incidence of second or third marriages has led to an increased demand for less showy (and less expensive) weddings in warm-weather settings. If you yearn to tie the knot on a sun-dappled island, here are some wedding basics on the islands where most weddings occur:

ANGUILLA   Couples need to be on Anguilla for 48 hours prior to applying for a wedding license, which is granted immediately after presentation of a passport or a birth certificate and photo I.D. If applicable, proof of divorce must be shown. The fee for the license is $284. A local wedding service, Sunshine Lady Productions, Box 85, The Valley, Anguilla, Leeward Islands, B.W.I. (☎ **809/497-2911**), will make the arrangements.

ANTIGUA   Either the bride or the prospective groom must have been on Antigua for at least three days prior to the ceremony. Wedding hopefuls must present passports or birth certificates, and, if applicable, a divorce or death certificate for either party's previous spouse(s). The wedding license costs $100.

ARUBA   Aruba welcomes honeymooners, but the island magistrates prefer that they say "I do" somewhere else. To be married on Aruba, one of the partners must have been a resident of the island for at least a year prior to the ceremony.

BARBADOS   Spend $12.50 for wedding taxes, and enlist your hotel in procuring the services of a local clergyman. After four days of residency on Barbados, apply for a license at the island's Ministry of Home Affairs. Bring either a passport or photo I.D., $50 in fees, plus proof, if applicable, of pertinent deaths or divorces of former spouse(s).

BONAIRE   See "Aruba," above. The same conditions apply.

BRITISH VIRGIN ISLANDS   There is no requirement of island residency, but the paperwork (whether you mail it yourself from off-island or whether you apply in person) usually takes about three days to process. Present a passport or birth certificate, plus certified proof of your marital status, plus any divorce or death certificates that apply to former spouse(s). The fee ranges from $35 to $110, depending on the site you select for your marriage ceremony. Marriages can be performed by the local registrar or by the officiant of your choice. Contact the Registrar's Office, P.O. Box 418, Road Town, Tortola, B.V.I. (☎ **809/494-3701** or **809/494-3492**).

CAYMAN ISLANDS   Both participants must be on-island for the application process. There is no waiting period. Present a birth certificate plus the embarkation/disembarkation cards issued by the island's immigration authorities, divorce decrees (if applicable), and a license fee of $200.

CURAÇAO   See "Aruba," above. The same conditions apply.

JAMAICA   In high season, some Jamaican resorts witness several weddings a day. Many of the larger Jamaican resorts can arrange for an officiant, a photographer, and even the wedding cake and champagne. Some resorts, however, will even throw in your wedding with the cost of your honeymoon at the hotel. Both the Jamaican Tourist Board and your hotel, perhaps one of the many Sandals resorts in Jamaica, will assist you with the paperwork. Participants must reside on Jamaica for 24 hours before the ceremony. Bring birth certificates and affidavits saying you've never been married before, or, if you've been divorced, bring copies of your divorce papers. The cost of the formalities and the ceremony ranges from $50 to $200, depending on how much legwork you want to do yourself.

PUERTO RICO   There are no residency requirements. You'll need parental consent if either party is under 18. Blood tests are required, although a test conducted within 10 days of the ceremony on the U.S. mainland will suffice. A doctor must sign the license after an examination of the bride and groom. For complete details, contact the Commonwealth of Puerto Rico Health Department, Demographic Register, 26 Fernandez Juncos (P.O. Box 9342), San Juan, PR 00908 (☎ **809/ 728-7980**).

ST. LUCIA   Both parties must have remained on the island for 48 hours prior to the ceremony. Present your passport or birth certificate, plus (if either participant has been widowed or divorced) proof of death or divorce from the former spouse(s). Before the ceremony, it usually takes about four days to process all the paperwork. Fees usually run around $150 for a lawyer (one is usually needed for the application to the governor-general), $25 for the registrar to perform the ceremony, and $103.50 for the stamp duty and the license.

U.S. VIRGIN ISLANDS   No blood tests or physical examinations are necessary, but there is a $25 license fee, a notarized application, and an eight-day waiting period, which is sometimes waived, depending on circumstances. Civil ceremonies before a judge of the territorial court cost $200 each; religious ceremonies by a clergy are equally valid. Fees and schedules for church weddings must be negotiated directly with the officiant. Your wedding in the Virgin Islands can be planned by any number of services, including Virgin Island Wedding Consultants, P.O. Box 1192, St. Thomas, USVI 00801 (☎ **809/775-9203,** or **800/843-3566**). You can also contact Weddings the Island Way, P.O. Box 11694, St. Thomas, USVI 00801 (☎ **809/776-4455**). Weddings for cruise passengers and hotel guests on St. Thomas or St. John can also be arranged by Weddings by IPS, Dept. MB, P.O. Box 9979, St. Thomas, USVI (☎ **800/937-1346**).

The guide "Getting Married in the U.S. Virgin Islands" is distributed by U.S.V.I. tourism offices; it gives information on all three islands, including wedding planners, places of worship, florists, and limousine services. The guide also provides a listing of island accommodations that offer in-house wedding services.

Couples can apply for a marriage license for St. Thomas/St. John by contacting the Territorial Court of the Virgin Islands, P.O. Box 70, St. Thomas USVI 00804 (☎ **809/774-6680**). For weddings on St. Croix, applications are available by contacting the Territorial Court of the Virgin Islands, Family Division, P.O. Box 929, Christiansted, St. Croix, USVI 00821 (☎ **809/778-9750**).

Some of the all-inclusive hotel chains are more involved with weddings than others. Club Med (☎ **800/CLUB-MED**) and Sandals (☎ **800/SANDALS**) are two chains that have helped tie the knot for many couples.

The Cayman Islands 4

Columbus first sighted the Cayman Islands in 1503. He called them Las Tortugas, or "the turtles." The name Cayman comes from a Spanish-Carib word, *caymanas*, or "crocodiles." The crocodiles, island historians believe, were not those animals at all, but were iguanas that used to live in the Caymans. The first colonists were a motley crew—bands of shipwrecked sailors and buccaneers, including the rollicking 17th-century Welshman, Sir Henry Morgan. Later, Scottish fishermen arrived and forged a quiet, peaceful settlement that today is a tranquil oasis at the western edge of the Caribbean.

Don't go to the Cayman Islands expecting fast-paced excitement. Island life focuses on the sea. Snorkelers will find a paradise; beach lovers will relish the powdery sands of Seven Mile Beach.

The Caymans, 480 miles due south of Miami, consist of three islands—Grand Cayman, Cayman Brac, and Little Cayman. Despite its name, Grand Cayman is only 22 miles long and 8 miles across at its widest point. The other islands are considerably smaller, of course, and contain very limited tourist facilities, in contrast to well-developed Grand Cayman. George Town on Grand Cayman is the capital, and is therefore the hub of government, banking, and shopping.

English is the official language of the islands, although it's often spoken with an English slur mixed with an American southern drawl and a lilting Welsh accent.

GETTING THERE

The Cayman Islands are easily accessible by air. Flying time from Miami is 1 hour 20 minutes; from Houston, $2^3/_4$ hours; from Tampa, 1 hour 40 minutes, and from Atlanta 3 hours 35 minutes. Only a handful of nonstop flights are available from the heartland of North America to Grand Cayman, so many visitors use Miami as their gateway.

Cayman Airways (☎ 800/422-9626) offers the most frequent service to Grand Cayman, with two to four daily flights from Miami, three nonstop flights a week from Tampa (with a stopover in Atlanta), and three nonstop flights a week from Houston. Once in the Caymans, the airline's subsidiary, **Island Air Ltd.,** operates frequent flights between Grand Cayman and Little Cayman and

Cayman Brac. Round-trip fares between Grand Cayman and Cayman Brac begin at $94.

Many visitors also opt for flights to Grand Cayman on **American Airlines** (☎ **800/433-7300**), which operates daily nonstop flights from Miami to Grand Cayman.

Northwest Airlines (☎ **800/447-4747**) flies to Grand Cayman from Detroit, Minneapolis, and Memphis via Miami.

USAir (☎ **800/428-4322**) operates regular service to Grand Cayman from Tampa and from Charlotte, N. C.

FAST FACTS: THE CAYMAN ISLANDS

Area Code   To call the Cayman Islands from the mainland, dial 809, then the seven-digit number. This area code is not needed once you're in the Caymans.

Business Hours   Normally, **banks** are open Monday through Thursday from 9am to 2:30pm and on Friday from 9am to 1pm and 2:30 to 4:30pm. **Shops** are usually open Monday through Saturday from 9am to 5pm. Most **other businesses,** including government offices, operate Monday through Friday from 9am to 5pm.

Currency   The legal tender is the **Cayman Islands (C.I.) dollar,** currently valued at $1.25 U.S. ($1 U.S. equals 80¢ C.I.). Canadian, U.S., and British currencies are accepted throughout the Cayman Islands, but it's estimated that you'll save money if you exchange your U.S. dollars for Cayman Islands dollars. The Cayman dollar breaks down into 100 cents. Coins come in 1¢, 5¢, 10¢, and 25¢. Bills come in denominations of $1, $5, $10, $25, $50, and $100 (note that there is no $20 C.I. bill). Most hotels quote rates in U.S. dollars. However, many restaurants quote prices in Cayman Islands dollars, which leads you to think that food is much cheaper. Unless otherwise noted, quotations in this chapter are in U.S. dollars, rounded off. The cost of living in the Cayman Islands is about 20% higher than in the United States.

Documents   No passports are required for U.S. or Canadian citizens, but proof of citizenship (voter registration card or birth certificate) and a return ticket are.

Drugs   The Cayman Islands has strict laws on the use of marijuana and other drugs, and large fines and prison terms are imposed on offenders.

Electricity   It's 110 volts A.C., 60 cycles, so American and Canadian appliances will not need adapters or transformers.

Emergencies   For medical emergencies, dial **555**. Call **911** to summon the police.

Holidays   Official holidays include New Year's Day, Ash Wednesday, Good Friday, Easter Monday, the third Monday in May, the Monday following the Saturday appointed as the official birthday of the reigning sovereign of the United Kingdom, the first Monday in July (Constitution Day), the Monday after Remembrance Sunday (in November), and Christmas Day.

Hospitals   On Grand Cayman, the only hospital is George Town Hospital, Hospital Road (☎ **809/949-8600**). On Cayman Brac, the only hospital is the 18-bed Faith Hospital (☎ **809/948-2243**).

Information The **Cayman Islands Department of Tourism** has the following offices in the United States: 9525 W. Bryn Mawr, Suite 160, Rosemont, IL 60018 (☎ **708/678-6446**); Two Memorial City Plaza, 820 Gessner, Suite 170, Houston, TX 77024 (☎ **713/461-1317**); 3440 Wilshire Blvd., Suite 1202, Los Angeles, CA 90010 (☎ **213/738-1968**); 6100 Blue Lagoon Dr., Suite 150, Miami, FL 33126 (☎ **305/266-2300**); and 420 Lexington Ave., Suite 2733, New York, NY 10170 (☎ **212/682-5582**). In Canada, contact Earl B. Smith, Travel Marketing Consultants, 234 Eglinton Ave. E., Suite 306, Toronto, ON M4P 1K5 (☎ **416/485-1550**). In the United Kingdom, the contact is Trevor House, 100 Brompton Rd., Knightsbridge, London SW3 1EX (☎ **0171/581-9960**).

Taxes A government tourist tax of 6% is added to your hotel bill. Also, a departure tax of $8 C.I. ($10) is collected when you leave the Caymans.

Telegraph and Telex The Cable and Wireless, Anderson Square, George Town, on Grand Cayman (☎ **809/949-7800**), is open from 8:15am to 5pm Monday through Friday, to 1pm on Saturday, and to 11am on Sunday.

Telephone A modern automatic telephone system enables Cayman operators to dial numbers worldwide 24 hours; international direct dialing is also possible. Local calls now require the use of all 7 digits, unlike the 5 necessary in the past.

Time Eastern standard time is in effect all year—daylight saving time is not observed. Therefore, when Miami is on daylight saving time and it's noon there, it's still 11am in the nearby Cayman Islands.

Tipping Many restaurants add a 10% to 15% charge in lieu of tipping. Hotels also add a 10% service charge to your bill.

1 Grand Cayman

Shipwrecked sailors, marooned mariners, and buccaneers founded Grand Cayman, once called "the island that time forgot." Today the largest of the three islands, a diving mecca, is one of the hottest tourist destinations in the Caribbean. With more than 500 banks, its capital, George Town, is the offshore banking center of the Caribbean. Retirees are drawn to the peace and tranquility of this British Crown Colony, site of a major condominium development. Almost all the Cayman Islands' population of 29,000 live on Grand Cayman. The civil manners of the locals reflect their British heritage.

ORIENTATION
GETTING AROUND

BY TAXI All arriving flights are met by taxis. The rates are fixed by the director of civil aviation (☎ **809/949-7811**); typical one-way fares from the airport to Seven Mile Beach range from $10 to $12. Taxis (which can hold five people) will also take visitors on around-the-island tours. **Cayman Cab Team** (☎ **809/947-1173**) and **Holiday Inn Taxi Stand** (☎ **809/947-4491**) offer 24-hour service.

BY RENTAL CAR Several car-rental companies operate on the island: **Cico Avis** (☎ **809/949-2468** on Grand Cayman, or **800/228-0668** in the U.S.), **Budget** (☎ **809/949-5605** on Grand Cayman, or **800/527-0700** in the U.S.), and

Ace Hertz (☎ **809/949-2280** on Grand Cayman, or **800/654-3131** in the U.S.). Each will issue the mandatory Cayman Islands driving permit, for $5 (U.S.). All three require that reservations be made between 6 and 36 hours before pickup. Avis and Hertz require that drivers be at least 18 and 25 years old, respectively, and Budget requires that drivers be between 25 and 65 years old. All three require the presentation of a valid driver's license and either a valid credit or charge card or a large cash deposit.

It pays to call around for the lowest rate; however, count on paying about $35 to $55 per day, depending on the type of vehicle desired.

An optional collision-damage waiver will eliminate any financial responsibility you might have if you damage your car. (Check the coverage provided with your credit/charge card; you *may* already have adequate coverage.) All three rental companies maintain kiosks within walking distance of the airport, although most visitors find it easier to take a taxi to their hotels and then arrange for the cars to be brought to their hotels.

Remember to drive on the left and to reserve your car as far in advance as possible, especially in midwinter.

BY MOTORCYCLE OR BICYCLE   Try **Bicycles Cayman,** North Church Street, in George Town (☎ **809/949-5572**), located at Ashton's Scuba View. Bicycles are available at $10 daily. **Soto Scooters Ltd.,** Seven Mile Beach (☎ **809/947-4363**), located at Coconut Place, offers Honda Elite scooters for $25 daily, or bicycles for $15 daily.

ESSENTIALS

The **Department of Tourism** is in the Pavilion Building, Cricket Lane (P.O. Box 67), George Town, Grand Cayman, B.W.I. ((☎ **809/949-0623**). The best-located **pharmacy** is Cayman Drug, Kirk Freeport Centre, Panton Street (☎ **809/949-2597**) in George Town, open Monday through Saturday from 8:30am to 5:30pm. Another well-located drugstore is Island Pharmacy, West Shore Centre, West Bay Road (☎ **809/949-8987**), open Monday through Saturday from 9am to 10pm and on Sunday from noon to 6pm. Also in George Town, the **post office and Philatelic Bureau** is on Edward Street (☎ **809/949-2474**), open Monday through Friday from 8:30am to 5pm and on Saturday from 8:30am to noon. There is also a counter at the Seven Mile Beach Post Office, open the same hours.

WHERE TO STAY

True budget travelers will rent an apartment or condominium (shared with friends or families), so they can cut costs by cooking their own meals. Divers will want to find hotels or small resorts that include a half day's dive in their tariffs. Hotels, unlike many Caymanian restaurants, generally quote prices to you in U.S. dollars.

VERY EXPENSIVE

Caribbean Club

West Bay Rd. (P.O. Box 30499), Grand Cayman, B.W.I. ☎ **809/947-4099.** Fax 809/947-4443. 18 villas. A/C TV TEL. Winter, $260–$310 one-bedroom villa for one or two; $310–$425 two-bedroom villa for four. Off-season, $160–$270 one-bedroom villa for one or two; $190–$295 two-bedroom villa for four. AE, MC, V. Free parking.

The Caribbean Club is an exclusive compound of well-furnished one- and two-bedroom villas, each with a full-size living room, dining area, patio, and kitchen, but when the owners are away the units are rented to guests. The pink villas are 3 miles north of George Town, either on or just off the beach; ocean-front units are always more expensive, of course. In winter, children under age 11 are not accepted. At the core of the colony, the club center rises two stories with tall, graceful arches and picture windows that look out onto the grounds planted with palm trees and flowering shrubs.

Dining/Entertainment: Latanas, the dining room, is open for lunch and dinner (see "Where to Dine," below).

Services: Room service (during open hours of Latanas—breakfast is not available).

Facilities: Tennis court.

Hyatt Regency Grand Cayman

West Bay Rd. (P.O. Box 1698), Grand Cayman, B.W.I. ☎ **809/949-1234,** or 800/553-1300. Fax 809/949-8528. 236 rms, 40 villas. A/C MINIBAR TV TEL. Winter, $295–$415 single or double; $500 Regency Club double; $470 one-bedroom villa for two; $595–$720 two-bedroom villa for four. Off-season, $180–$300 single or double; $370 Regency Club double; $300 one-bedroom villa for two; $425–$550 two-bedroom villa for four. Breakfast $13 extra. AE, DC, MC, V. Free parking.

This is the best managed and most stylish hotel in the Cayman Islands. Two miles north of George Town, the hotel is a major component in the 90-acre Britannia Resort community, which includes the Britannia Golf Course. Two acres front Seven Mile Beach. The hotel's design combines neoclassicism with modern art and a sort of British colonial airiness. Dozens of Doric arcades are festooned with flowering vines whose tendrils cascade beneath reflecting pools and comfortable teakwood settees. Low-rise buildings surround a large landscaped courtyard that contains gardens, waterfalls, and the swimming pool.

The Hyatt offers luxury rooms with private verandas. Two buildings and 43 rooms are devoted to the Regency Club, which has 24-hour concierge service. The hotel also offers one- and two-bedroom luxury villas along the Britannia Golf Course or waterway, which have fully equipped kitchens and easy access to the resort's many facilities. Guests in the villas have their own private pool, whirlpool, cabaña, and patio area.

👥 Family-Friendly Accommodations

Holiday Inn Grand Cayman *(see p. 68)* Here, triples and quads cost the same as double rooms—a great bargain for families of three or four. After a swim, kids flock to the Sweet Tooth, which offers ice cream and yogurt treats.

Hyatt Regency Grand Cayman *(see p. 67)* With gardens, waterfalls, and a swimming pool, this is definitely the choice for kids with well-heeled parents. A wide range of accommodations is offered, designed to meet the needs of families of almost any size.

Silver Sands *(see p. 73)* Most units here are suitable for four to six guests. You can save money by preparing your meals in your own fully equipped kitchen. All units are grouped around a freshwater pool.

Sleep Inn Hotel *(see p. 70)* Children 12 and under stay free in their parents' room at this 1992 hotel, which lies only 200 feet from the beach and a mile from the center of George Town. The resort is built around a large freshwater pool, and barbecues are featured in the courtyard.

Dining/Entertainment: The resort offers several dining choices, including the Garden Loggia Café, which serves breakfast, lunch, and dinner (a buffet champagne brunch on Sunday is a special feature). An Oriental and Italian cuisine is featured. There's a seafood restaurant, Hemingway's (see "Where to Dine," below), and you can also have lunch daily at the Britannia Golf Club and Grille, a few steps away from the first tee.

Services: Room service, babysitting, laundry.

Facilities: The most complete array of water sports in the Caymans (see "Sports Outdoor Activities," below, for more information on the Hyatt's Red Sail Sports facility and its offerings), a one-third-acre swimming pool (with a whirlpool and swim-up bar), the Britannia golf course, tennis courts, croquet.

EXPENSIVE

Holiday Inn Grand Cayman

West Bay Rd. (P.O. Box 904), Grand Cayman, B.W.I. ☎ **809/947-4444**, or 800/421-9999 in the U.S. Fax 809/947-4213. 215 rms. A/C TV TEL. Winter, $208–$298 single, double, triple, or quad. Off-season, $158–$228 single, double, triple, or quad. Breakfast $10 extra. AE, MC, V. Free parking.

Some 3 miles north of George Town and 5 miles from the airport, this modern beachfront hotel boasts bedrooms with bright, tropical flair, done in floral prints. Most have sitting areas, and all have baths with dressing rooms. Each unit has a southern-style balcony whose white balustrades overlook a garden courtyard planted with palms and shrubs. Ocean-view and oceanfront rooms are more expensive, of course. This is an ideal choice for families, since rooms can house three to four guests at no extra charge for the third or fourth occupant.

Dining/Entertainment: A breakfast buffet is served in the Verandah Dining Room, lunch is offered at the Cabaña Grill, and dinner is served back at the Verandah, where different theme buffets are presented. The Sweet Tooth is an ice cream and yogurt parlor, and the Ten Sails Pub contains swashbuckling murals and serves English pub–style meals such as steak-and-kidney pie along with draft beer.

Services: Room service, babysitting, laundry.

Facilities: Lagoonlike swimming pool with arched bridges and poolside cocktails available, fully equipped dive shop, four tennis courts (lit at night), sailing, snorkeling, waterskiing, and deep-sea fishing available.

Indies Suites

Foster Dr., off West Bay Rd. (P.O. Box 2070), Grand Cayman, B.W.I. ☎ **809/947-5025**, or 800/654-3130 in the U.S. and Canada. Fax 809/947-5024. 38 one-bedroom suites, 2 two-bedroom suites. A/C TV TEL. Winter, $240 one-bedroom suite; $290 two-bedroom suite. Off-season, $160 one-bedroom suite, $190 two-bedroom suite. (Includes continental breakfast.) AE, MC, V. Free parking.

Built in 1990 and set about two blocks from the sea, this establishment offers some of the most comfortable accommodations on the island. The two-story motel-like units surround a landscaped swimming pool. Each unit contains a kitchen and a decor of pastel colors. On the premises are coin-operated laundry facilities, hotel-type maid service, a freshwater pool and Jacuzzi, a scuba facility (Indies Divers), a *bohío*-style poolside bar, and a gift shop. The hotel does not contain a restaurant, although a wide choice of eateries is within a short drive away, and many of the (sometimes) long-term guests prefer to prepare their own meals anyway. On Wednesday night there's a barbecue with live music around the pool.

The Cayman Islands

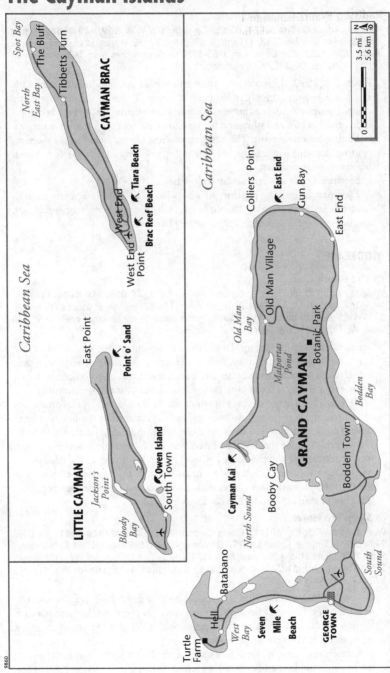

Airport ✈ Beach ☚

Radisson Resort Grand Cayman

West Bay Rd. (P.O. Box 30371), Grand Cayman, B.W.I. ☎ **809/949-0088**, or 800/ 333-3333. Fax 809/949-0288. 311 rms. 4 suites. A/C TV TEL. Winter, $245–$390 single or double; from $650 suite. Off-season, $155–$250 single or double; from $425 suite. Breakfast $11 extra. AE, DC, MC, V. Free parking.

Opened in 1990, this hotel rises from an enviable position beside Seven Mile Beach, a five-minute drive (2 miles) north of George Town. Its red-roofed, vaguely colonial design resembles a cluster of balconied town houses. Each of the bedrooms is decorated in blue and white and has views over the ocean or a garden courtyard.

Dining/Entertainment: The hotel has two restaurants, including the more expensive Regency Grill and the less formal Brighton Beach Club. Poolside sunset buffets are often featured.

Services: Room service, laundry, babysitting.

Facilities: Swimming pool ringed with a beach bar/cabaña and sun parasols (located a few steps from the famous beach), fully equipped dive shop, whirlpool, spa, beauty shop, health club, full range of water sports.

MODERATE

⑤ The Beach Club

West Bay Rd. (P.O. Box 903G), Grand Cayman, B.W.I. ☎ **809/949-8100.** Fax 809/ 947-5167. 41 rms. A/C MINIBAR TV TEL. Winter, $178–$265 single or double. Off-season, $125–$185 single or double. MAP $50 per person extra. Scuba packages available for $50 a day. AE, DC, MC, V. Free parking.

Set 3 miles north of George Town, the Beach Club is one of the oldest and best-located hotels on the island. Built in the early 1960s along Seven Mile Beach, it established a scuba-diving center and has since attracted a loyal clientele. When cruise-ship passengers are in port, however, the beach space is overcrowded.

Designed like a large colonial plantation villa, it has a formal Doric portico, lots of lattices, and a popular bar that separates the hotel from the beach. There, calypso music and rum flow freely for a clientele who seem to be dressed in bathing suits throughout the day. The divers who opt for week-long scuba packages usually take one of the tile-floored villas clustered amid trees at the edge of the beach. Otherwise, most accommodations are simple but comfortable bedrooms in the main hotel. Each unit comes with a veranda and furniture ranging from Caribbean rattan to reproductions of English Sheraton.

⑤ Sleep Inn Hotel

West Bay Rd. (P.O. Box 30111), Grand Cayman, B.W.I. ☎ **809/949-9111.** Fax 809/ 949-6699. 115 rms, 6 suites. A/C TV TEL. Winter, $135–$165 single; $160–$175 double; $180–$190 triple; $195–$205 quad; from $175 suite for two. Off-season, $95–$130 single; $105–$145 double; $125–$160 triple; $135–$175 quad; $185 suite for two. AE, DC, MC, V. Free parking.

Opened in 1992, the Sleep Inn is the closest hotel on Seven Mile Beach to the center of George Town. It lies only a short walk from the beaches and about a five-minute drive from the international airport. It's considered one of the more reasonably priced hotels on the island.

A franchise of Choice Hotels International, the largest hotel chain in the world, it offers both smoking and no-smoking rooms. Superior single rooms contain one queen-size bed, whereas superior double rooms contain two queen-size beds. Some units are suitable for the handicapped. Rooms have modern tropical furnishings and TVs with built-in radios and clocks equipped with alarms. Each room has a small safe for valuables.

Features include the Dive Shop, with a full-service dive and water-sports program, a swimming pool and Jacuzzi, a pool bar, and a pool grill, where barbecues are regularly held.

Spanish Bay Reef

West Bay Rd. (P.O. Box 30867), Grand Cayman, B.W.I. ☎ **809/949-3765,** or 800/ 223-6510 in the U.S., 800/424-5500 in Canada. 48 rms. A/C TV TEL. $178–$265 single or double. Breakfast $10 extra. All-inclusive four-day/three-night package $591–$678 per person. Children 6–15 sharing a room with two adults $85 per night; one child under 6 stays free in room with two adults. AE, MC, V. Free parking.

A small, intimate resort set in an isolated position amid the scrublands of the northwestern tip of Grand Cayman, this is the island's only all-inclusive establishment. Rather informally run, it draws a clientele of divers who appreciate the marine life of the offshore reefs. The casual furnishings are in a Caribbean motif. Accommodations have balconies or patios with garden or ocean views.

The package rates quoted above include all meals and beverages, island sightseeing, entertainment, use of bicycles, introductory scuba and snorkeling lessons, unlimited snorkeling or scuba diving from the shore (including tanks and weight belt), round-trip transfers, taxes, and service. If you're a diver, ask about Certified Divers Packages when making your reservations. Facilities include a private coral beach, freshwater pool, and Jacuzzi. Guests lounge around Calico Jack's Poolside Bar, and later enjoy an array of food (with lots of fish) in the Spanish Main Restaurant. There is also a disco.

INEXPENSIVE

⑤ Cayman Diving Lodge

East End (P.O. Box 11), Grand Cayman, B.W.I. ☎ **809/947-7555,** or 800/852-3483. 12 rms. $651 single for three nights, $1,125 for five nights, $1,599 for seven nights; $547 per person double for three nights, $951 for five nights, $1,355 for seven nights. (Rates all-inclusive.) AE, MC, V. Free parking.

In the southeast corner of the island, 20 miles east of George Town (take the A2) and 19 miles east of the airport, is a friendly, informal, laid-back place for divers. The horseshoe-shaped lodge is a two-story half-timbered building set amid tropical trees on a private coral-sand beach with a live coral barrier reef just offshore. Diving and snorkeling equipment are available for unlimited shore diving. Scuba and snorkeling trips can be arranged.

Ocean-view rooms are simple, yet modern and pleasant. Caymanian chefs serve abundant meals and specialize in fish dishes. Vegetarian food is available. There are laundry facilities.

CONDOS

Colonial Club

West Bay Rd. (P.O. Box 320W), Grand Cayman, B.W.I. ☎ **809/947-4660.** Fax 809/ 947-4839. 24 units. A/C TEL. Winter, $350–$400 apartment for one or two; $400–$450 apartment for three or four; $450–$500 apartment for five or six. Minimum stay five nights Dec 16–Apr 5. Off-season, $230–$280 apartment for one or two; $280–$330 apartment for three or four; $330–$380 apartment for five or six. AE, MC, V. Free parking.

Although smaller than the hostelries flanking it on three sides, the pastel-pink Colonial Club (evocative of Bermuda) occupies a highly desirable stretch of the famous beach. Built in 1985, it's a three-story condominium about 4 miles north of George Town and some 10 minutes from the airport. First-class maintenance, service, and accommodations are provided in the apartments, all with kitchen fans, maid service, and laundry facilities.

Usually only 10 of the 24 apartments are available for rent—the rest are privately owned and occupied. You have a choice of units with two bedrooms and three baths or units with three bedrooms and three baths. Facilities include tennis courts (lit at night), a Jacuzzi, and a freshwater pool.

Harbour Heights

West Bay Rd. (P.O. Box 30624), Grand Cayman, B.W.I. ☎ **809/947-4295.** Fax 809/947-4522. 18 units. A/C TV TEL. Winter, $275 apartment for two; $285 apartment for three; $295 apartment for four. Off-season, $185 apartment for two; $195 apartment for three; $205 apartment for four. Additional person $15 C.I. ($18.80) extra. Minimum stay 10 days in winter. AE, MC, V. Free parking.

You can stay in style and comfort by the day, week, or month in this beachfront complex 6 miles north of George Town. You're on your own for meals, but there's a good-sized recreation area and a large free-form swimming pool with a surrounding tile terrace filled with white lounge furniture. The apartments are of generous size and can accommodate one to four guests. Each has a living room and dinette, an attractive and complete kitchen, two bedrooms, two baths, ample closet space, and its own balcony or patio. The furnishings are all in white tropical designs with decorative fabrics and accent rugs. Daily maid service is included.

London House

Seven Mile Beach, Grand Cayman, B.W.I. ☎ **809/947-4060.** Fax 809/947-4087. 21 units. A/C TV TEL. Winter, $295 one-bedroom apartment for two; $334 one-bedroom mini-penthouse for two; $315–$345 two-bedroom apartment for four; $750 three-bedroom penthouse for six. Off-season, $235 one-bedroom apartment for two; $265 one-bedroom mini-penthouse for two; $245–$275 two-bedroom apartment for four; $500 three-bedroom apartment for six. AE, MC, V. Free parking.

At the more tranquil northern end of Seven Mile Beach, this hotel is an enduring favorite for those seeking apartment living in the Caymans. Units have fully equipped kitchens, spacious living and dining areas, and private patios or balconies overlooking the water. Florid prints and airy rattan set the decorating note in most of the units. Ceiling fans supplement the air conditioning. Daily maid service is available. The complex has its own seaside swimming pool. Sometimes house parties are staged on the patio. Many restaurants are nearby, although there is a stone barbecue for private poolside cookouts.

Morrit's Tortuga Club

East End (P.O. Box 496GT), Grand Cayman, B.W.I. ☎ **809/947-7449,** or 800/447-0309. Fax 809/947-7669. 72 units. A/C TV. Winter, $175–$195 apartment for one or two; $230–$295 apartment for three or four. Off-season, $145 apartment for one or two, $160–$185 apartment for three or four. AE, DC, MC, V. Free parking.

Set on the grounds of the famed Tortuga Club, which was destroyed in 1989 by Hurricane Hugo, this condo cluster was built in the Antillean plantation style from the wreckage of the former hotel. The property sits on 8 beachfront acres on the East End, known for some of the island's best diving. Profiting from its position near offshore reefs teeming with marine life, it's the site of Cay-man Windsurfing, which offers snorkeling, windsurfing, and the rental of sailing craft and catamarans. Tortuga Divers, also on the premises, offers resort courses.

About a 26-mile drive from the airport, the club is composed of clusters of three-story beachfront condos opening onto the water. There's also a swim-up bar around a swimming pool. Each of the comfortably furnished one- and two-bedroom apartments has a fully equipped kitchen, although many clients opt instead for meals in the complex's restaurant.

Pan-Cayman

West Bay Rd. (P.O. Box 440GT), Grand Cayman, B.W.I. ☎ **809/947-4002.** Fax 809/ 947-4002. 10 units. A/C TEL. Winter, $290 two-bedroom unit for two to four; $370 three-bedroom unit for six. Off-season, $155–$175 two-bedroom unit for two to four; $235 three-bedroom unit for six. Additional person $35–$40 extra. MC, V. Free parking.

The Georgian-style facade of this popular beachfront choice 4 miles north of George Town was attractively altered to suit its Caribbean setting. Each apartment has its own fully equipped kitchen, a private balcony or patio with an unrestricted view of the sea, and comfortable summer furniture. Hotel-type maid service is provided. This place is popular in winter, so reserve well in advance.

Silver Sands

West Bay Rd. (P.O. Box 205GT), Grand Cayman, B.W.I. ☎ **809/949-3343,** or 800/ 223-6510 in the U.S., 800/424-5500 in Canada. Fax 809/949-1223. 19 units. A/C TV. Winter, $310–$320 two-bedroom unit for one to four; $380 three-bedroom unit for one to six. Off-season, $195–$205 two-bedroom unit for one to four; $250 three-bedroom unit for one to six. Additional person $20 extra. Children under 11 stay free in parents' unit. AE, MC, V. Free parking.

This modern eight-building complex is arranged horseshoe fashion on the beach 7 miles north of George Town. The apartments are grouped around a freshwater pool. The eight apartment blocks contain either two-bedroom/two-bath or three-bedroom/three-bath units. The two-bedroom unit can hold up to six people, and the three-bedroom unit can house up to eight guests. Each apartment comes with a balcony, a fully equipped kitchen, and maid service. The resident manager will point out the twin tennis courts and two utility rooms with washer-dryers.

WHERE TO DINE

Make sure you understand which currency the menu is printed in. If it's not written on the menu, ask the waiter if the prices are in U.S. dollars or Cayman Island dollars. It will make a difference when you get your final bill.

EXPENSIVE

✪ Chef Tell's Grand Old House

Petra Plantation, S. Church St. ☎ **809/949-9333.** Reservations required. Appetizers $4.25– $6.95 C.I. ($5.30–$8.70); main courses $17.95–$28 C.I. ($22.40–$35). AE, MC, V. Lunch Mon–Fri 11:45am–2:30pm; dinner daily 6–10pm. Closed Sun June–Nov. AMERICAN/ CARIBBEAN/PACIFIC RIM.

This beautiful white mansion is a former plantation house constructed at the turn of the century by a Bostonian coconut merchant. It lies amid venerable trees 1 mile south of George Town past Jackson Point. Built on bedrock near the edge of the sea, it stands on 129 ironwood posts that support the main house and a bevy of gazebos. The Grand Old House is the island's premier caterer and hosts everything from lavish weddings and political functions to informal family celebrations.

German-born chef Tell Erhardt specializes in conch fritters, Swedish gravlax, and Cajun popcorn shrimp with sherry remoulade. One of the favorite appetizers is spicy fried coconut shrimp with an apricot-mustard sauce. Many dishes reflect chef Tell's origins, including coffee-lacquered duck or schweinepfeffer (thin strips of pork sautéed, then finished with a cream and demi-glace sauce).

✪ Hemingway's

In the Hyatt Regency Grand Cayman, West Bay Rd. ☎ **809/949-1234.** Reservations recommended. Appetizers $4.75–$5.50 C.I. ($5.90–$6.90) at lunch, $3.50–$7.25 C.I. ($4.40–$9.10) at dinner; main courses $8.95–$14.50 C.I. ($11.20–$18.10) at lunch, $16–$34 C.I. ($20–$42.50) at dinner. AE, MC, V. Lunch daily 11:30am–2:30pm; dinner daily 6–10pm. SEAFOOD/INTERNATIONAL.

Perhaps the finest seafood on the island can be found 2 miles north of George Town at Hemingway's, which is named after the novelist and inspired by Key West, his residence. You can dine in the open air with a view of the sea. The menu is among the more imaginative on the island, including some appetizers that might be a first for you, like the turtle-and-vegetable eggroll. Other appetizers include pepperpot soup—a reputed favorite of Hemingway—and gazpacho served with a black-bean relish. The catch of the day, perhaps snapper or wahoo, emerges from the grill to your liking. You can also order conch steak with lime butter or roast rack of lamb with red lentil chili. The signature dish of the Caymans, turtle steak, is served here with brown rice. More imaginative might be such dishes as grouper stuffed with crabmeat, macadamia-crusted pork with mango mousse, and coconut-almond shrimp.

✪ Latanas

In the Caribbean Club, West Bay Rd. ☎ **809/947-5595.** Reservations required. Appetizers $4–$8 C.I. ($5–$10) at lunch, $5–$8.50 C.I. ($6.30–$10.60) at dinner; main courses $9.50–$18 C.I. ($11.90–$22.50) at lunch, $12.50–$29 C.I. ($15.60–$36.30) at dinner. AE, MC, V. Lunch Mon–Fri 11:30am–2pm; dinner daily 5:30–10pm. CARIBBEAN/AMERICAN.

In the middle of Seven Mile Beach, 4 miles north of George Town, is one of the best dining choices on Grand Cayman. The restaurant is named for the tiny lantana flower, whose pink and orange petals grow not only in the arid Cayman Islands but also in the American Southwest. The menu is arguably the most imaginative on the island. Begin, for example, with barbecued lobster, guacamole, and roasted red bell pepper in sour cream. The fish dishes are generally excellent, as exemplified by blackened or grilled dolphin with pepper Alfredo. The kitchen will even prepare an island-style jerk pork tenderloin with rice, black beans, plantains, and mango salsa. About the only indication that chef Fred Schrock is Austrian is his Viennese apple strudel for dessert. The upstairs, where lunch is served, has a view of Seven Mile Beach, and the downstairs, where dinner is offered, has a southwestern decor.

✪ Ottmar's Restaurant & Lounge

West Bay Rd. ☎ **809/947-5879.** Reservations recommended. Appetizers $4.50–$7.50 C.I. ($5.60–$9.40); main courses $13.95–$20 C.I. ($17.40–$25); Sun brunch $30 C.I. ($37.50). AE, MC, V. Lunch Mon–Sat 11:30am–3pm; dinner daily 5–11pm; brunch Sun 11:30am–3:30pm. INTERNATIONAL.

One of the island's top restaurants, Ottmar's is outfitted in a French Empire motif with lots of paneling, rich upholstery, and plenty of space between tables. There's a formal bar/lounge area decorated with deep-sea fishing trophies. At table, you can order such dishes as Bavarian cucumber soup, bouillabaisse, French pepper steak, an Indonesian rijstaffel (rice table with many condiments), wienerschnitzel, veal Oscar with asparagus and hollandaise sauce, and an array of sophisticated desserts. Lunch is served at the Waterfront Café. The entrance to Ottmar's is adjacent to the rear entrance of the Clarion Grand Pavilion.

Ristorante Pappagallo

At Villas Pappagallo, Palmetto Dr., Conch Point, Barkers. ☎ **809/949-1119.** Reservations required. Appetizers $4–$8.50 C.I. ($5–$10.60); main courses $14.95–$25.50 C.I. ($18.70–$31.90). AE, MC, V. Dinner only, daily 6–10:30pm. NORTHERN ITALIAN/SEAFOOD.

One of the island's most whimsical and memorable restaurants is near the northern terminus of West Bay Road and Spanish Cove, 8 miles north of George Town. It lies on a 14-acre bird sanctuary overlooking a natural lagoon. Its designers incorporated Caymanian and Aztec weaving techniques in its thatched roof. Glass doors, black marble, and polished brass mix a kind of Edwardian opulence with an otherwise Tahitian decor. You dine on black tagiolini with lobster sauce, fresh crab ravioli with asparagus sauce, lobster in brandy sauce, or perhaps Italian-style veal and chicken dishes. Good, too, for a nightcap.

MODERATE

The Almond Tree

North Church St., near the corner of Eastern Ave. ☎ **809/949-2893.** Reservations recommended. Appetizers $4.50–$5.50 C.I. ($5.60–$6.90); main courses $14.95–$19.95 C.I. ($18.70–$24.90). AE, MC, V. Dinner only, Mon–Sat 5:30–10pm. SEAFOOD/INTERNATIONAL.

Likeable and unpretentious, this restaurant is in a high-ceilinged re-creation of the kind of houses built on the island of Yap in the South Pacific. Supported by poles and branches, and lined with reeds and thatch rising into a peak, it contains a bar area accented with Trader Vic's–style artifacts and a garden lined with palmettos and flowering shrubs. (Many guests prefer the garden; others like a table in the building's interior.) Operated by a team of female entrepreneurs from Alaska who escaped to sunnier climes, the place serves uncomplicated and straightforward cuisine, including such dishes as braised turtle steak, mango chicken, conch steak, catch of the day, lobster, and filet mignon.

Benjamin's Roof

Coconut Place, off West Bay Rd. ☎ **809/947-4080.** Reservations required. Appetizers $3.50–$7.50 C.I. ($4.40–$9.40); main courses $11.95–$27.50 C.I. ($14.90–$34.40). AE, MC, V. Dinner only, daily 5:30–10:30pm. AMERICAN/INTERNATIONAL.

Set on the upper floor of a shopping center off West Bay Road, this restaurant is decorated like the interior of a greenhouse, with a wealth of verdant plants. There's a bar set up in the corner of the place, and an accommodating staff serves food and drink to the accompaniment of live piano music. Menu items might include blackened alligator tail, oysters wrapped in bacon with garlic butter, lobster bisque, a mixed grill of seafood, Austrian-style wienerschnitzel, lobster fettuccine, blackened shrimp, and grilled lamb with herbs.

❸ Crow's Nest Restaurant

South Sound. ☎ **809/949-9366.** Reservations recommended. Appetizers $2.25–$7.95 C.I. ($2.80–$9.90); main courses $9.75–$16.95 C.I. ($12.20–$21.20); lunch specials $4.95–$7.50 C.I. ($6.20–$9.40). AE, MC, V. Lunch Mon–Sat 11:30am–2pm; dinner daily 5:30–10pm. CARIBBEAN.

With a boardwalk and terrace jutting onto the sands, with a view of both Sand Cay and a nearby lighthouse, this informal restaurant on the southwesternmost tip of the island, a four-minute drive from George Town, is one of those places that evoke the Caribbean "the way it used to be." There's no pretense here. What you get is good, honest Caribbean cookery featuring grilled seafood. Try one of the daily specials or perhaps sweet, tender lobster. Other dishes might include grilled tuna steak with ackee or Jamaican chicken curry with roast coconut. For dessert, try the key lime mousse pie, if it's available.

⑤ Hog Sty Bay Café and Pub

N. Church St. ☎ 809/949-6163. Reservations recommended in winter. Appetizers $4.95–$7.95 C.I. ($6.20–$9.90); main courses $14.50–$18.95 C.I. ($18.10–$23.70); breakfast from $5.95 C.I. ($7.40). AE, MC, V. Breakfast daily 8:30–11:15am; lunch daily 11:30am–5:30pm; dinner daily 5:30–10pm (last order). CARIBBEAN/ENGLISH.

On a stony plot of seafront land near the beginning of West Bay Road, the Hog Sty Bay Café and Pub has developed a loyal clientele. In a low-slung cottage whose verandas are vivid shades of pink, blue, and yellow, it's the creative statement of Pennsylvania-born Tom Keagy. The place divides its time and attention between an amusingly decorated pub and a Caribbean-inspired dining room open to a view of the harbor.

In the pub, you can order such British staples as fish and chips or cottage pie, and such drinks as a Snake Bite (composed of equal parts of hard English cider and English lager). Also available are all the foamy tropical drinks you'd expect.

Dining choices include a Caesar salad topped with marinated conch or Cajun chicken, grilled filet of shark served with a sauce made from scotch bonnet (a form of very hot pepper), and smoked and barbecued alligator ribs. Smoked, unpeeled shrimp is available by the quarter or half pound. Don't overlook this as a possible site for breakfast.

Lobster Pot

N. Church St. ☎ 809/949-2736. Reservations required in winter. Appetizers $3–$6.95 C.I. ($3.80–$8.70); main courses $10.50–$25 C.I. ($13.10–$31.30). AE, MC, V. Lunch Mon–Fri 11:30am–2:30pm; dinner daily 5:30–10pm. SEAFOOD.

One of the island's best-known restaurants overlooks the water from its second-floor perch at the western perimeter of George Town near what used to be Fort George. True to its name, it offers lobster prepared in many different ways: Cayman style, bisque, and salad. Conch schnitzel and seafood curry are on the menu, together with turtle steak grown for food at Cayman Island kraals. The place is also known for its prime beef steaks. For lunch, you might like the English fish and chips or perhaps a seafood basket of fried oysters and shrimp. The Lobster Pot's pub is a pleasant place for a drink—you may find someone for a game of darts, too.

The Wharf

West Bay Rd. ☎ 809/949-2231. Reservations recommended. Appetizers $4–$8 C.I. ($5–$10); main courses $15–$26 C.I. ($18.80–$32.50). AE, MC, V. Lunch Mon–Fri noon–2:30pm; dinner daily 6–10pm. CARIBBEAN/CONTINENTAL.

About 2 miles north of George Town, the Wharf has been everything from a dinner theater to a nightclub. In 1989 it became a leading restaurant on the island. It's decorated in soft pastels and offers dining inside, out on an elevated veranda, or on a beachside terrace. The sound of the surf mingles with music from visiting calypso bands and the convivial chatter from the Ports of Call Bar located on the premises. Many diners begin with a Wharf salad of seasonal greens; others prefer the homemade black-bean soup or the home-smoked salmon. The main dishes are divided into "From the Sea" or the "From the Land," featuring everything from Cayman green turtle steak (when available) to peppersteak Madagascar (with a green peppercorn sauce).

INEXPENSIVE

Ⓢ Big Daddy's Restaurant and Sports Bar

West Bay Rd. ☎ **809/949-8511.** Reservations recommended at dinner. Appetizers $2.75–$6.95 C.I. ($3.40–$8.70); main courses $4.95–$14.50 C.I. ($6.20–$18.10); breakfast from $5.50 C.I. ($6.90). AE, MC, V. Breakfast Mon–Sat 8–11am; lunch Mon–Sat noon–4pm; dinner daily 5–10pm. INTERNATIONAL.

Set on the upper level of a building whose ground floor is devoted to a liquor store under the same management, this is a bustling, big-windowed emporium of food and drink. One area is devoted to a woodsy, nautically decorated bar area, where TV screens broadcast either CNN or whatever sports events might be of interest to an informal clientele. Three separate dining areas, more or less isolated from the activities at the bar, serve well-prepared food. Menu items include deli sandwiches, half-pound burgers, garlic shrimp, T-bone steaks, barbecued ribs, fresh catch of the day, and pasta dishes.

Ⓢ Island Taste

S. Church St. ☎ **809/949-4945.** Reservations recommended. Appetizers $3–$6.95 C.I. ($3.80–$8.70); main courses $9–$21.50 C.I. ($11.30–$26.90). AE, MC, V. Lunch Mon–Sat 10:30am–4:30pm; dinner Mon–Sat 6–10pm. CARIBBEAN/MEDITERRANEAN.

Set beside the harborfront in George Town, this restaurant sits across from the headquarters of the *Atlantis* submarine. There's an indoor and outdoor bar area and a scattering of indoor tables, but by far the most popular seating area is on the wraparound veranda, one floor above street level. The restaurant has one of the largest "starter" selections on the island. Soups include both white conch chowder and turtle soup. Appetizers feature fresh oysters, Mexican ceviche, and calamari Vesuvio. At least seven pasta dishes are on the dinner menu, including linguine with small clams. You can also order T-bone steak and chicken parmigiana. However, most of the menu is devoted to seafood dishes. Dolphin is served in different ways and perennial favorites include the turtle steak and spiny lobster. Every night the chef offers all-you-can-eat deep-fried shrimp for only $15.75 C.I. ($19.70) per person.

Whitehall Bay

The Waterfront, N. Church St. ☎ **809/949-8670.** Reservations recommended Sat–Sun. Appetizers $1.95–$9 C.I. ($2.40–$11.30) at lunch, $2–$12 C.I. ($2.50–$15) at dinner; main courses $6.50–$12.95 C.I. ($8.10–$16.20) at lunch, $9.50–$21.50 C.I. ($11.90–$26.90) at dinner. AE, MC, V. Daily 11am–10pm. CARIBBEAN.

Most of this restaurant's dining tables overlook the coral reef and piers that jut out into the sea, a short walk north of George Town's center. An inner room provides additional tables, a bar, and an unusual collection of photographs depicting an earlier generation of Cayman Islanders. Menu items include salads, sandwiches, marinated conch, catch of the day, crab backs, curried chicken, steaks, turtle stew, and Cayman-style lobster.

WHAT TO SEE & DO

The capital, **George Town,** can easily be explored in an afternoon; it's visited for its restaurants and shops (and banks!)—not sights. The town does offer a clock monument to King George V and the oldest government building in use in the

Caymans today, the post office on Edward Street. Stamps sold here are sought by collectors.

The island's premier museum, the **Cayman Islands National Museum,** Harbor Drive, in George Town (☎ **809/949-8368**), is in a much-restored clapboard-sided antique building directly on the water. (The veranda-fronted building served until recently as the island's courthouse.) The formal exhibits include a collection of Caymanian artifacts collected by Ira Thompson, beginning in the 1930s. Today the museum incorporates a gift shop, theater, café, and more than 2,000 items portraying the natural, social, and cultural history of the Caymans. Admission is $5 C.I. ($6.30) for adults and $2 C.I. ($2.50) for children under 12 and senior citizens. It's open Monday through Friday from 9am to 5pm and on Saturday from 10am to 2pm (last admission is half an hour prior to closing).

The **Treasury Discovery Centre & Museum,** West Bay Road (☎ **809/ 947-5033**), near the Hyatt Regency in the George Town Building, offers a wide assortment of displays, some relating to the discovery of the New World by Columbus. Other items concern sunken treasure and the "lore 'n legends" of pirates. Admission is $5 for adults, $3 for children 5 to 12, and free for children under 5. It's open Monday through Saturday from 9am to 5pm. There's also a gift shop.

Elsewhere on the island, you might **go to Hell!** That's at the north end of West Bay Beach, a jagged piece of rock named Hell by a former commissioner. There the postmistress will stamp "Hell, Grand Cayman" on your postcard to send back to the States.

The ✪ **Cayman Turtle Farm,** Northwest Point (☎ **809/949-3894**), is the only green-sea-turtle farm of its kind in the world, and is also, with some 250,000 visitors annually, the most popular land-based tourist attraction in the Caymans. Once the islands had a multitude of turtles in the surrounding waters (which is why Columbus called the islands "Las Tortugas"), but today these creatures are sadly few in number (practically extinct elsewhere in the Caribbean) and the green sea turtle has been designated an endangered species. You cannot bring turtle products into the United States. The turtle farm has a twofold purpose: to provide the local market with edible turtle meat and to replenish the waters with hatchling and yearling turtles. Visitors today can look at 100 circular concrete tanks in which these sea creatures can be observed in every stage of development; the hope is that one day their population in the sea will regain its former status. Turtles here range in size from 6 ounces to 600 pounds. At a snack bar and restaurant, you can sample turtle dishes. The turtle farm is open daily from 9am to 5pm. Admission is $5 for adults, $2.50 for children 6 to 12, free for children under 6.

At **Botabano,** on the North Sound, fishermen tie up with their catch, much to the delight of photographers. You can buy lobster (in season), fresh fish, even conch. A large barrier reef protects the sound, which is surrounded on three sides by the island and is a mecca for diving and sports fishing.

If you're driving, you might want to go along **South Sound Road,** which is lined with pines and, in places, old wooden Caymanian houses. After leaving the houses behind, you'll find good spots for a picnic. On the road again, you reach **Bodden Town,** once the largest settlement on the island. At Gun Square, two cannons commanded the channel through the reef. They are now stuck muzzle-first into the ground.

On the way to the **East End,** just before Old Isaac Village, you'll see the on-shore sprays of water shooting up like geysers. These are called "blowholes," and they sound like the roar of a lion. Later, you'll spot the fluke of an anchor stick-ing up from the ocean floor. As the story goes, this is a relic of the famous "Wreck of the Ten Sails" in 1788. A modern wreck can also be seen—the *Ridgefield*, a 7,500-ton Liberty ship from New England, which struck the reef in 1943.

Old Man Bay is reached by a road that opened in 1983. Head back to town along the cross-island road through savannah country, where royal palms sway in the breeze. You might even spot the green Cayman parrot. At Old Man Bay, you can travel along the north shore of the island to **Rum Point,** which has a good beach and is as fine a place as any to end the tour.

The offshore waters of Grand Cayman are home to one of the most unusual (and ephemeral) underwater attractions in the world, **Stingray City.** Set in the sun-flooded, 12-foot-deep waters of North Sound, about 2 miles east of the island's northwestern tip, the site originated in the mid-1980s when local fishermen cleaned their catch and dumped the offal overboard. They quickly noticed scores of stingrays (which usually eat marine crabs) feeding on the debris, a phenomenon that quickly attracted local divers and marine zoologists. Today, between 30 and 50 relatively tame stingrays hover in the waters around the site for daily handouts of squid and ballyhoo from increasing hordes of amateur snorkelers and scuba enthusiasts.

Interestingly, most of the stingrays that feed here are females, the males prefer-ring to remain in deeper waters offshore. To capitalize on the phenomenon, about half a dozen entrepreneurs lead expeditions from points along Seven Mile Beach, traveling around the land mass of Conch Point to the feeding grounds. One well-known outfit is **Treasure Island Divers** (☎ **809/949-4456**), which charges divers $45 or snorkelers $25.

Be warned that stingrays possess deeply penetrating and viciously barbed stingers capable of inflicting painful damage to anyone who mistreats them. (Above all, the divers say, never try to grab one by the tail.) Despite the dangers, divers and snorkelers seem adept at feeding and petting the velvet surfaces of these creatures without incident.

An annual event, **Cayman Islands Pirates' Week,** is held in late October. It's a national festival with cutlass-bearing pirates and sassy wenches storming George Town, capturing the governor, thronging the streets, and staging a costume parade. The celebration, which is held throughout the islands, pays tribute to the nation's past and its cultural heritage. For the exact dates, contact the Pirates Week Festival Administration, P.O. Box 51, Grand Cayman, B.W.I. (☎ **809/949-5078**).

On 60 acres of rugged wooded land off Frank Sound Road, in the East End, the **Queen Elizabeth II Botanic Park** (☎ **809/947-9462**), offers visitors a half-hour walk through wetland, swamp, dry thicket, and mahogany trees. The trail is eight-tenths of a mile long and took more than a year to create; it was mostly the work of volunteers. By early 1993 the rough trail had been carved, and some 200 endemic plants identified, including orchids and bromeliads. Likely to be spot-ted are hickatees, the freshwater turtles found only on the Caymans. Occasionally you'll spot the rare Grand Cayman parrot; if not that, perhaps the anole lizard with a cobalt-blue throat pouch. Even rarer is the endangered blue iguana. There are six rest stations along the trail with detailed information about the park. The park can be visited Tuesday through Sunday from 7:30am to 5:30pm. Admission is $3 for adults, $1.25 for children.

SPORTS & OUTDOOR ACTIVITIES

What they lack in nightlife, the Caymans make up in water sports—the fishing, swimming, waterskiing, and diving are among the finest in the Caribbean. *Skin Diver* magazine has written that "Grand Cayman has become the largest single island in the Caribbean for dive tourism." Coral reefs and coral formations encircle the islands and are filled with lots of marine life—which scuba divers are banned from taking.

It's easy to dive close to shore, so boats aren't necessary—but there are plenty of boats and scuba facilities available. On certain excursions I recommend a trip with a qualified divemaster. For rentals, the island maintains many "dive shops," but they will not rent scuba gear or supply air to a diver unless he or she has a card from one of the national diving schools, such as NAUI or PADI. Hotels also rent diving equipment to their guests, as well as arrange snorkeling and scuba-diving trips.

Universally regarded as the most up-to-date and best-equipped water-sports facility in the Cayman Islands, **Red Sail Sports,** in the Hyatt Regency Grand Cayman, West Bay Road (P.O. Box 1588), Grand Cayman, B.W.I. (☎ **809/ 947-5965,** or **800/266-6425**), has its headquarters in a gaily painted wooden house beside the beach.

Their deep-sea fishing excursions in search of tuna, marlin, and wahoo are arranged on a variety of air-conditioned vessels with an experienced crew. Tours depart at 7:30am and 12:30pm, last half a day, and cost $500 (a full day costs $700). The fee can be split among eight people.

Red Sail also rents 16-foot Hobie cats for $33 per hour, depending on the time of day. One of the best-designed sailing catamarans in the Caribbean is berthed in a canal a short walk from the water-sports center. Some 65 feet in length, with an aluminum mast 75 feet tall, it's fast, stable, and exhilarating. A sail to "Stingray City," with snorkeling equipment and lunch included in the price of $55 per person, leaves once daily. A sunset sail from 5 to 7pm, with hors d'oeuvres, costs $25 per person. A romantic $3\frac{1}{2}$-hour dinner sail costs $56.25.

Red Sail offers beginners' scuba diving as well as excursions for longtime aficionados of the deep. A two-tank morning dive includes exploration of two different dive sites at depths ranging from 50 to 100 feet, lasts a full morning, and costs $60. Beginners can take advantage of a resort course offered daily and costing $100 per person. A full certification course, requiring a maximum of five days, costs $440.

Waterskiing can be arranged for $50 per half hour, and the cost can be divided among several people. Red Sail also offers parasailing at $40 per ride.

BEACHES   One of the finest in the Caribbean, Grand Cayman's ✪ **Seven Mile Beach,** which begins north of George Town, has sparkling white sands with Australian pines in the background. Beaches on the **east and north coasts** are also fine, as they are protected by an offshore barrier reef. In winter the average water temperature is 80°; it rises to 85° in summer.

FISHING   Grouper and snapper are most plentiful for those who bottom-fish along the reef. Deeper waters turn up barracuda and bonito. The flats on Little Cayman are said to offer the best bonefishing in the world. Sports people from all over the world come to the Caymans for the big ones—tuna, wahoo, and marlin. Most hotels can make arrangements for charter boats and experienced guides are also available.

GOLF The major golf course on Grand Cayman is at the **Britannia Golf Club,** next to the Hyatt Regency on West Bay Road (☎ **809/949-8020**). The course, the first of its kind in the world, was designed by Jack Nicklaus and is unique in that it incorporates three different courses in one: a 9-hole championship layout, an 18-hole executive setup, and an 18-hole Cayman course. The last was designed for play with the Cayman ball, which goes about half the distance of a regulation ball. The Britannia charges $50 to $80 for greens fees, depending on the configuration of the course you intend to play. Cart rentals cost $15 to $25; club rentals, $25. Britannia guests can reserve 48 hours in advance, but everyone else, including Hyatt guests, can reserve no more than 24 hours in advance. Guests of the Hyatt and Britannia receive a discount off the above-mentioned rates.

SCUBA DIVING Established in the 1940s, the best-known dive operation in the Cayman Islands is **Bob Soto's Diving Ltd.,** P.O. Box 1801, Grand Cayman, B.W.I. (☎ **809/949-2022,** or **800/262-7686** to make reservations). Owned by Ron Kipp, the operation has grown to include full-service dive shops at the Holiday Inn on Seven Mile Beach, the SCUBA Centre on North Church Street, the Cayman Islander Hotel, and Soto's Coconut in the Coconut Place Shopping Centre. A resort course, designed to teach the fundamentals of scuba to beginners who know how to swim, costs $90. This requires a full day: The morning is spent in the pool and the afternoon is a one-tank dive from a boat. All necessary equipment is included. Certified divers can choose from a wide range of one-tank ($40 to $45) and two-tank ($65) boat dives daily on the west, north, and south walls, plus shore diving from the SCUBA Centre. Nondivers can take advantage of daily snorkel trips ($25). The staff is helpful and highly professional.

✪ SUBMARINE DIVES On Grand Cayman, you can explore the ocean depths two ways: by taking the *Atlantis* reef dive, which takes you deeper than any resort diver can go, or by going on the *Atlantis* deep dive, which takes you beyond the limits of scuba diving to 800 feet.

One of the island's most popular attractions is the ***Atlantis XI,*** Goring Avenue (P.O. Box 1043), Grand Cayman, B.W.I. (☎ **809/949-8296,** or **800/253-0493**), a tourist submersible that's 65 feet long, weighs 80 tons, and was built at a cost of $3 million to carry 46 passengers. You can view the reefs and colorful tropical fish through the 26 large viewpoints 2 feet in diameter, 13 on each side of the submarine, as it cruises at a depth of 100 feet through the maze of coral gardens at a speed of $1^{1}/_{2}$ knots; a guide keeps you informed. There are three types of dives. The premier dive, Coral Odyssey Plus, features such high-tech extras as divers communicating with submarine passengers by wireless underwater phone and moving about on underwater scooters. This dive, operated both day and night, costs $79. On the Coral Odyssey dive you'll experience the reef and see the famous Cayman Wall; this dive lasts 55 minutes and costs $69. The Reef Express, costing $55, lasts 40 minutes and introduces viewers to the marine life of the Caymans. Children 4 to 12 are charged half price (no children under 4 allowed). *Atlantis XI* dives Monday through Saturday, and reservations are recommended 24 hours in advance.

Atlantis also operates two deep-diving research submersibles, each of which carries two passengers and one pilot at a time. The submarines go as deep as 800 feet, though their limit is 1,000 feet. Grand Cayman is the top of an underwater mountain, whose side—known as the Cayman Wall—plummets straight down for 500 feet before becoming a steep slope falling away for 6,000 feet to the bottom of the ocean. These trips last just more than an hour and allow passengers to see the variety of sea life at different levels of the dive. Weather permitting, each dive goes down to the wreck of the *Kirk Pride*, a cargo ship that sank in 1976 and was lodged on a rock ledge at 780 feet. These deep dives cost $275 per person, and are available to anyone over the age of 8. Reservations should be made as early as possible, as availability is severely limited.

SAVVY SHOPPING

The free-port shopping in George Town encompasses silver, china, crystal, Irish linen, British woolen goods, and such local crafts as black-coral jewelry. However, I have found the prices on many items to be similar to U.S. prices.

Don't purchase turtle products—they cannot be brought into the United States.

Artifacts Ltd.
Harbour Dr., George Town. ☎ **809/949-2442.**

Generally recognized as the premier outlet on the island for back issues of some of the rare stamps issued by the Caymanian government, this shop is managed by Charles Adams, one of the country's philatelic authorities. Stamps range in price from 20¢ to $900, and inventory includes the rare War Tax Stamp issued during World War II. Other items for sale include antique Dutch and Spanish coins unearthed from underwater shipwrecks, enamelled boxes, and antique prints and maps. The shop lies on the harborfront of George Town, across from the landing dock for cruise-ship tenders.

Black Coral and . . .
Fort St., George Town. ☎ **809/949-0123.**

Connoisseurs of unusual fine jewelry and unique objets d'art are drawn to the stunning black-coral creations of an internationally acclaimed sculptor, Bernard K. Passman, displayed here. In the past two decades, the Iowa-born artist has created pieces of exquisite black-coral and gold jewelry and sculpture. He produced the royal wedding gift from the Cayman Islands to the now-estranged Prince Charles and Lady Diana—a 97-piece cutlery set of sterling silver with black-coral handles. Another commission for the Cayman Islands was the creation of a black-coral horse and corgi dogs for Queen Elizabeth II and Prince Philip. Passman is credited with elevating the use of black coral from simple souvenirs to a prized art form in the Caribbean. The gallery on Fort Street is a sightseeing attraction. Signed, limited-edition pieces are considered excellent investments.

Caymandicraft
S. Church St., George Town. ☎ **809/949-2405.**

Less than a five-minute walk south of the center of George Town, this shop is probably the best established on the island for the fabrication and distribution of locally made gifts. The staff makes sewing kits, pincushions, handkerchief sets, stuffed animals, and decorative bookcovers. Also for sale are stylish fabrics, sold by the yard, from Liberty of London, as well as linens from Ireland and men's silk neckties.

English Shoppe
Harbour Dr., George Town. ☎ **809/949-2457.**

Watches, black- and pink-coral jewelry, 14K and 18K jewelry, Irish crystal, and collectors' items are the offerings here, all with prices quoted in U.S. dollars. T-shirts and souvenirs are also sold. The shop is in front of the cruise-ship landing.

Kennedy Gallery
West Shore Centre., George Town. ☎ **809/949-8077.**

This gallery opened in 1993 in a shopping center on Seven Mile Beach. Specializing in watercolors by local artists (including Joanne Sibley and Lois Brezinski) as well as copies and originals of works by the establishment's founder, Robert Kennedy, it sells artworks ranging from $15 to as much as $7,000.

Kirk Freeport Plaza
Cardinal Ave. and Panton St., George Town. ☎ **809/949-7477.**

The largest store of its kind in the Caymans, Kirk Freeport Plaza contains a treasure trove of gold jewelry, watches, china, crystal, perfumes, and cosmetics. The store holds a Gucci franchise for the island and has handbags, valises, and perfumes priced 15% to 35% below suggested retail prices Stateside. Also stocked are crystal and porcelain priced 30% to 50% less than recommended retail prices Stateside, from such manufacturers as Wedgwood, Royal Doulton, Waterford, Lladró, Baccarat, Herend, Hummel, and Daum.

The Jewelry Centre
Fort St., George Town. ☎ **809/949-0070.**

This is one of the largest and most amply stocked jewelry stores in the Caymans. It is, in fact, a virtual department store of jewelry. In a two-story building in the center of town, it contains six departments specializing in loose or set diamonds, gold (sold as chains or as ornaments, including coins found in shipwrecks offshore), black coral, colored gemstones, and caymanite, the pinkish-brown striated rock found only on the Caymans.

Sunflower Boutique
S. Church St., George Town. ☎ **809/949-4090.**

The largest establishment of its type in the Cayman Islands, this is an unusual boutique. Established some quarter of a century ago in a two-story building beside the waterfront, it sells hand-painted skirts and blouses; T-shirts and shorts for men and women; jewelry fashioned from black, pink, and white coral; an assortment of gift items; and Caribbean paintings. You'll find it directly on the waterfront in the center of George Town.

GRAND CAYMAN AFTER DARK

PUBS & CLUBS

Lone Star Bar & Grill
West Bay Rd. ☎ **809/947-5175.**

Everything about it represents a corner of the Texas Panhandle. You can enjoy juicy hamburgers beneath the heavy trusses of the smoke-filled dining room, unless you prefer to head immediately for the bar in back. There, beneath murals of Lone Star beauties, you can watch several sports events simultaneously on 15 different TV screens. The house specialty drinks are lime and strawberry margaritas. Most guests order fajitas or Texas-style cheese steaks (hot chile peppers cost extra). Meals cost $4.95 to $15.95 C.I. ($6.20 to $19.90). Monday through Thursday are all-you-can-eat fajitas night, costing $10.99 C.I. ($13.70) per person. It's open Monday through Saturday from 11:30am to 1pm and on Sunday from 11:30am to noon.

Long John Silver's

In the Treasure Island Resort, West Bay Rd. ☎ **809/949-7777.** Cover $5 C.I. ($6.30) Mon, Wed, and Fri–Sat.; free Tues and Thurs. Always free for hotel guests.

This popular nightclub is reached through the lobby of the previously recommended hotel. Designed with a recording studio on its upper balcony, Silver's uses the same acoustic principles as the Grand Ole Opry in Nashville. At least 90% of its entertainment comes from live local bands, whose music usually begins punctually at 9pm. Decorated in Caribbean-inspired colors, Silver's has two large bars and a dance floor. Beer costs $3.25 C.I. ($4.10) and up. Open Monday through Friday from 8pm to 1am and on Saturday from 8pm to midnight.

Rumhead's Disco

West Bay Rd. ☎ **809/949-7169.** Cover $3 C.I. ($3.80) Tues–Thurs, $5 C.I. ($6.30) Fri–Sat.

About a block inland from West Bay Road, this dance club is adjacent to the island's only cinema. It's the most popular and animated disco on the island, and is set in a large and echoing room that is sometimes crowded with island residents, usually in the 18 to 36 age range. A large bar stands in the center, with a dance floor nearby. Live bands usually alternate with recorded dance and rock music. For Monday-night football, there is no admission fee. Open Sunday through Friday from 8pm to 1am and on Saturday from 8pm to midnight.

Ten Sails Pub and Coconuts Comedy Club

In the Holiday Inn Grand Cayman, West Bay Rd. ☎ **809/947-4444.** Pub, free during the day; comedy club, $10 C.I. ($12.50), plus a two-drink minimum.

During the day, this place functions as an English-inspired pub. Several nights a week, however, the premises are transformed into the comedy club Coconuts, with comedic talents imported from all over the world. After the show, you can try your talents at a karaoke platform. Murals of swashbuckling pirates and their treasure adorn the walls. A few steps from the pub's entrance, beside the hotel pool, a local musician and his band play island music throughout the evening. Drinks begin at $3.50 C.I. ($4.40). The pub is open daily from 11am to 8pm; the comedy club has performances on Tuesday, Wednesday, Friday, Saturday, and Sunday at 9pm.

2 Cayman Brac

The "middle" island of the Caymans is Cayman Brac, 12 miles long and a mile wide, about 89 miles east-northeast of Grand Cayman. It was given the name Brac (Gaelic for bluff) by 17th-century Scottish fishermen who settled here. The bluff for which the island was named is a towering limestone plateau rising to 140 feet above the sea, covering the eastern half of Cayman Brac. Caymanians refer to the island simply as Brac, and its 1,400 inhabitants, a hospitable bunch of people, are called Brackers.

The big attraction of the bluff today isn't new. There are more than 170 caves honeycombing its limestone height. In the early 18th century the Caymans were occupied by pirates, and Edward Teach, the infamous Blackbeard, is supposed to have spent quite a bit of time around Cayman Brac. Some of the caves are at the bluff's foot while others can be reached only by climbing over jagged limestone rock. One of the biggest of them is Great Cave, with a number of chambers. Harmless fruit bats cling to the roofs of the caverns.

On the south side of the bluff you won't see many people, and the only sounds are the sea crashing against the lavalike shore. The island's herons and wild green parrots are seen here. Most of the Brackers live on the north side, many in traditional wooden seaside cottages, some built by the island's pioneers. The islanders must all have green thumbs, as attested to by the variety of flowers, shrubs, and fruit trees in many of the yards. On Cayman Brac you'll see poinciana trees, bougainvillea, Cayman orchids, croton, hibiscus, aloe, sea grapes, cactus, and coconut and cabbage palms. The gardeners grow cassava, pumpkins, breadfruit, yamsa, and sweet potatoes.

There are no actual towns on the island—only settlements, such as Stake Bay (the "capital"), Spot Bay, the Creek, Tibbitt's Turn, the Bight, and West End, where the airport is located.

GETTING THERE

Flights from Grand Cayman to Cayman Brac are operated on **Cayman Airways** (☎ **809/949-2311,** or **800/422-9626** in the U.S.). The airline uses relatively large 737 jets carrying 122 passengers each. There is an evening flight there, plus a morning return. The cost is $94 round-trip.

WHERE TO STAY & DINE

Brac Reef Beach Resort

P.O. Box 56, Cayman Brac, B.W.I. ☎ **809/948-1323,** or 800/327-3835 in the U.S. and Canada. 40 rms. A/C TV TEL. Winter, $592 single for divers, $442 single for nondivers; $452 per person double for divers, $302 per person double for nondivers. Off-season, $532 single for divers, $397 single for nondivers; $407 per person double for divers, $272 per person double for nondivers. (Rates for three-night packages include MAP and two days of diving.) AE, MC, V. Free parking.

On a sandy plot of land on the south shore 2 miles east of the airport, near some of the best snorkeling in the region, this resort contains motel-style units comfortably furnished with carpeting, ceiling fans, and modern baths. Once the location was little more than a maze of sea grapes, a few of whose venerable trunks still rise amid the picnic tables, hammocks, and boardwalks. On the premises are the rusted remains of a Russian lighthouse tower that was retrieved several years ago from a Cuban-made trawler.

Dining/Entertainment: A hideaway no guest should miss is the thatch-roofed two-story bar whose stout wooden columns rise from above the surf. Perfect for a moonlit tryst, it has a breezy interior where nightcaps are served. Lunches are informal affairs, while dinners are most often served buffet style under the stars.

Services: Laundry, maid service.

Facilities: Pool, Jacuzzi, Reef Divers (a full-service operation with instruction for both beginning and advanced divers, and the use of all rental gear, including masks, snorkels, fins, regulators, and weight belts).

Divi Tiara Beach Resort

P.O. Box 238, Cayman Brac, B.W.I. ☎ **809/948-1553,** or 800/801-5550 in the U.S. and Canada. Fax 809/948-7564. 46 rms, 13 suites. A/C TV TEL. Winter, $180 single or double;

$200 suite. Off-season, $95–$125 single or double; $140 suite. MAP $38 per person extra. AE, MC, V. Free parking.

Part of the Divi Divi hotel chain, the Tiara, about 2 miles east of the airport, attracts divers and honeymooners. Many newcomers respond at once to the landscaping, which incorporates croton, bougainvillea, and palms. All accommodations are housed in motel-like outbuildings; 13 of the units are luxury suites, each with an ocean view, Jacuzzi, and king-size bed.

Dining/Entertainment: On piers on the beach is a Tahitian-style thatch-roofed bar where guests can gaze out to sea while sipping their drinks before heading to the Poseidon dining room to enjoy a Caribbean and American cuisine. There is entertainment at the hotel twice weekly.

Services: Laundry.

Facilities: An excellent Peter Hughes Dive Tiara operation; a swimming pool raised above a white sand beach where boardwalks run beneath groves of palms.

WHAT TO SEE & DO

The **Brack Museum,** in the former Government Administration Building, Stake Bay (☎ **809/948-4222**), has an interesting collection of Caymanian antiques, including pieces rescued after shipwrecks and items from the 18th century. The museum is open Monday through Friday from 9am to 4pm and on Saturday and Sunday from 1 to 5pm. Admission is free.

Of course, the biggest lure to Cayman Brac is the variety of **water sports**—swimming, fishing, snorkeling, and some of the world's best diving and exploration of coral reefs. There are undersea walls on both the north and south sides of the island, with stunning specimens lining their sides. The best dive center is **Peter Hughes Dive Tiara** at the Divi Tiara Beach Resort (see "Where to Stay & Dine," above).

3 Little Cayman

The smallest of the Cayman Islands, Little Cayman is 10 miles long and about a mile across at its widest point. It lies about 75 miles northeast of Grand Cayman and some 5 miles from Cayman Brac. The cigar-shaped island, which today has only about 40 permanent inhabitants, was first colonized in the 17th century by European adventurers. However, the settlers soon became the target of pirate raids and the little island was abandoned. With the stifling of pirate enterprise, settlers from Grand Cayman moved to Little Cayman in 1833, and it has been home to a few people ever since, although economic endeavors, including turtling and co-conut growing, were not successful. It is believed that there may still be pirate treasure buried on the island, but it's in the dense interior of what is now the largest bird sanctuary in the Caribbean.

Little Cayman is home to a unique species of lizard that predates the iguana. It's the oldest species of New World reptile, and there are only 50 specimens in the world. The entire island is coral and sand. Any rocks here were brought in from elsewhere, probably used as ballast in pirate ships.

The islands of the Caymans are mountaintops of the long-submerged Sierra Maestra Range, which runs north and into Cuba. The peaks were slowly built on by living corals after the submersion of the mountains, thus forming the islands of today. Little Cayman's Bloody Bay offers one of the mountain's walls nearest the surface—a stunning sight for snorkelers and scuba divers.

The island seems to have come into its own now that fishing and diving have been recognized as its main resources; this is a near-perfect place for such pursuits. The waters around the little island were hailed by the late Philippe Cousteau as one of the three finest diving spots in the world. Fine bonefishing is available just offshore, and a brackish inland pool can be fished for tarpon. Even if you don't dive or fish, you can row 200 yards off Little Cayman to isolated and uninhabited Owen Island, where you can swim at the sandy beach and picnic by a blue lagoon.

Blossom Village, the island's "capital," is on the southwest coast.

GETTING THERE

Most visitors fly from Grand Cayman to Little Cayman. Cayman Airways (☎ 809/949-2311 on Grand Cayman, or 800/422-9626 in the U.S.) is the reservations agent for **Island Air,** a charter company that charges $122 round-trip. You can also call Island Air directly (☎ 809/922-949-5252, or 800/922-9626).

WHERE TO STAY & DINE

Little Cayman Beach Resort

Blossom Village, Little Cayman, Cayman Islands, B.W.I. ☎ **809/948-4533,** or 800/327-3835 in the U.S. and Canada. Fax 809/948-4533. 32 rms. A/C TV. $648–$729 single for divers, $498–$579 single for nondivers; $475–$526 per person double for divers, $325–$376 per person double for nondivers. Off-season, $631 single for divers, $481 single for nondivers; $473 per person double for divers, $323 per person double for nondivers. (Rates for three-night packages include MAP.) AE, MC, V.

The governor of the Cayman Islands flew in to open this largest-ever resort on Little Cayman. The first part opened in 1992, the second half in 1993. Lying on the south coast, the resort is close to many diving and sporting attractions of the island, including bonefishing in the South Hole Sound Lagoon. Attracted to the resort are fisherfolk, divers, birdwatchers, and what has been called "soft adventure"–oriented travelers. The hotel, owned by the Tibbetts family, lies only three-quarters of a mile from the Edward Bodden Airport (really a grass airstrip), and it has a white sand beach fringing a reef-protected shallow bay. No-smoking units are available, and the rooms have ceiling fans and air conditioning. They are divided into two pastel coral two-story buildings, reflecting traditional Caymanian architecture with gingerbread trim. The hotel has a swimming pool overlooking the sea and a Jacuzzi, along with complete water-sports facilities including a dive shop. Its bar and restaurant are among the most popular on the island.

Pirates Point Resort Ltd.

Little Cayman, Cayman Islands, B.W.I. ☎ **809/948-1010.** Fax 809/948-1011. 10 rms. A/C. Winter, $240 single for divers $180 single for nondivers; $200 per person double for divers, $140 per person double for nondivers; $180 per person triple for divers, $130 per person triple for nondivers. Off-season, $220 single for divers, $165 single for nondivers; $180 per person double for divers. $125 per person double for nondivers; $160 per person triple for divers, $115 per person triple for nondivers. (Rates all-inclusive.) MC, V. Free parking.

For water activities or just relaxing, this resort directly west of the airstrip, toward West End Point, offers a family environment with gourmet cuisine. The owner and manager, Gladys Howard, is a graduate of Cordon Bleu in Paris, has studied with such stars of the kitchen as Julia Child and James Beard, and has written several cookbooks. In her menus, she uses fresh fruits and vegetables grown locally, as well as the bounty from the sea.

The place has six remodeled furnished rooms, usually rented by one to three guests (the third is often a child). In addition, it has four recently built seaside cottages, with balconies overlooking Preston Bay. The resort offers package holidays including room, three excellent meals per day with appropriate wines and all alcoholic beverages, plus two-tank boat dives daily featuring the Bloody Bay Wall, the Cayman trench, and Jackson Reef. Nondiving activities include snorkeling, birdwatching, and exploring. Bonefishing, tarpon fishing, and an Owen Island picnic are available for an additional charge. Prince Charles himself, sailing by on his yacht, selected Owen Island for a picnic.

Puerto Rico 5

If Castro and Communism had never descended on Cuba, the island would probably still be a bustling center for gambling casinos, glittering Las Vegas–style revues, and swanky hotels and resorts. But dark days enveloped Cuba, and Puerto Rico took its place.

Today Puerto Rico is the fun island of the Caribbean, with more going on here than anywhere else. It has hundreds of beaches, almost all water sports available, acres of golf courses, miles of tennis courts, and casinos galore. It has more discos than any other place in the Caribbean, and shopping bargains to equal St. Thomas.

Accommodations have also been greatly improved, even in some of the smaller cities such as Ponce and Mayagüez. *Paradores*—government-sponsored inns—are sprinkled across the island for visitors who want a more intimate experience than that provided by the deluxe hotels of San Juan.

There are 79 towns and cities on Puerto Rico, each with a unique charm and flavor. Puerto Rico has a rich countryside with centuries-old coffee plantations, sugar estates still in use, foreboding caves and enormous boulders with mysterious petroglyphs carved by the Taíno peoples (the original settlers), and meandering mountain trails leading out to tropical settings.

It was on Columbus's second voyage to the New World in 1493 that he sighted the island he called San Juan (for St. John the Baptist); it was later renamed Puerto Rico. The island's government has undergone many changes since the days of its first governor, Ponce de León, to its present status as an American commonwealth.

Lush, verdant Puerto Rico is only half the size of New Jersey and is located some 1,000 miles southeast of the tip of Florida. With 272 miles of Atlantic and Caribbean coastline, and a culture dating back 2,000 years, Puerto Rico is a formidable attraction. Old San Juan is its greatest historic center, with 500 years of history, as reflected in its restored Spanish colonial architecture.

San Juan is the world's second-largest home port for cruise-ship passengers. The old port of San Juan recently underwent a $90-million restoration. The beauty and charm of the island have remained since the first navigators called it "the island of enchantment."

GETTING THERE

Puerto Rico is by far the most accessible of the Caribbean islands, as it receives more incoming flights, with greater numbers of passengers, than many major cities on the U.S. mainland. Much of the credit for this goes to **American Airlines** (☎ 800/433-7300), which designated San Juan as its hub for the entire Caribbean, and one of the most important cogs in its international network. American offers nonstop daily flights to San Juan from New York (JFK), Newark, Boston, Miami, Dallas–Fort Worth, Washington (Dulles), Orlando, Tampa, Chicago, Baltimore, Hartford, Philadelphia, and Raleigh-Durham, and flights to San Juan from both Montréal and Toronto with changes in Chicago and Raleigh/Durham. There are also two daily flights from Los Angeles to San Juan that touch down in Dallas. In all, the carrier now offers more than 42 daily nonstop flights to Puerto Rico, far more than any of its competitors.

American, because of its wholly owned subsidiary, **American Eagle,** also is the undisputed leader among the short-haul local commuter flights of the Caribbean. It specializes in short-haul commuter services, usually in propeller planes carrying between 19 and 64 passengers. American Eagle links Puerto Rico with almost 100 daily incoming flights from nearly 40 destinations throughout the Caribbean.

Delta (☎ 800/221-1212) has four daily nonstop flights from Atlanta Monday through Friday, eight nonstop on Saturday, and six nonstop on Sunday. It also offers one daily nonstop flight to San Juan from Orlando. Flights into Atlanta from around the world are frequent, with excellent connections from points throughout Delta's network in the South and Southwest.

United Airlines (☎ 800/538-2929), also a potent force in international air travel, has two daily nonstop flights from Chicago to San Juan and two daily nonstop flights from Miami. United offers connecting service from most major U.S. cities.

Northwest (☎ 800/447-4747) has one weekly nonstop flight in winter from Boston to San Juan and one daily nonstop flight from Detroit. Delta offers connecting service through Detroit from cities nationwide.

TWA (☎ 800/892-4141) has four daily nonstop flights from New York to San Juan and one daily nonstop flight from Miami. On Saturday and Sunday it offers a nonstop flight from St. Louis to San Juan. TWA, like United, also offers connecting service from most major U.S. cities.

USAir (☎ 800/428-4322) also competes, with one weekly nonstop flight from Baltimore to San Juan, one daily nonstop flight from Charlotte (N.C.) to San Juan, and one daily nonstop flight from Philadelphia to San Juan. The airline has connecting service from most major U.S. cities.

Smaller airlines competing include **Carnival** (☎ 800/824-7386), a Florida-based airline wholly owned by the Carnival Group of cruise-line fame. It has one daily nonstop flight from New York to Aguadilla and Ponce, one daily nonstop flight from Newark to San Juan, one daily nonstop flight from Newark to Aguadilla and Ponce, and one daily nonstop flight from Miami to San Juan.

Another smaller airline competing is **Kiwi** (☎ 800/538-5494), with two weekly nonstop flights from Atlanta to San Juan, two weekly nonstop flights from Chicago to San Juan, one daily nonstop flight from Newark to San Juan, and five weekly nonstop flights from Orlando to San Juan.

Tower (☎ 800/221-2500) has a Saturday-morning flight from New York to San Juan.

British wanting to visit San Juan can take a **BA** (☎ 800/247-9297) weekly flight direct from London to San Juan; **Lufthansa** (☎ 800/645-3880) passengers can fly three times weekly from Frankfurt to San Juan, and **Iberia** (☎ 800/772-4642) has two weekly flights from Madrid to San Juan.

GETTING AROUND

BY PLANE

American Eagle (☎ 809/749-1747) flies from Luís Muñoz International Airport to Mayagüez, which can be your gateway to the west of Puerto Rico. Most one-way fares are $54, or $65 to $75 round-trip, depending on advance notice. For information about air connections to the offshore islands of Vieques and Culebra, see Sections 9 and 10, respectively, below.

BY PUBLIC TRANSPORTATION

Públicos are cars or minibuses that provide low-cost transportation and are designated with the letters P or PD following the numbers on their license plates. They run to all the main towns of Puerto Rico, including Mayagüez and Ponce. Passengers are dropped off and picked up along the way. Rates are set by the Public Service Commission. Públicos usually operate during daylight hours and depart from the main plaza (central square) of a town.

Information about público routes between San Juan and Mayagüez is available from **Lineas Sultana,** calle Esteban González 898, Urbanización Santa Rita, Rio Piedras (☎ 809/765-9377). Information about público routes between San Juan and Ponce is available from **Choferes Unidos de Ponce** (☎ 809/764-0540). Fares vary according to whether or not the público will make a detour to pick up or drop off a passenger at a specific locale. (If you want to deviate from the predetermined routes, you'll pay more than if you wait for a público beside the main highway.) Fares from San Juan to Mayagüez range from $8 to $20; from San Juan to Ponce, from $5 to $14. Be warned that although prices of públicos are admittedly low, the routes are slow, with frequent stops, an often erratic routing, and lots of inconvenience.

BY RENTAL CAR

Some local rental-car agencies may tempt you with slashed prices, but if you're planning to tour the island, you won't find any local branches should you run into car trouble. And some of the agencies advertising low-cost deals don't take credit or charge cards and want cash in advance. You also have to watch out for "hidden" extras and the difficulties connected with regulating insurance claims which sometimes proliferate among the smaller and not-very-well-known firms.

If you're planning to do much touring on the island, it's best to stick to the old reliables: **Avis** (☎ 809/791-2500, or 800/331-2112), **Budget** (☎ 809/791-3685, or 800/527-0700), or **Hertz** (☎ 809/791-0840, or 800/654-3001). At press time, Budget offered many of the most reasonable rates from a fleet of well-maintained cars: A small but peppy Nissan Sentra with air conditioning and automatic transmission rented for $180 per week, with unlimited mileage included. A more substantial midsize car, a Ford Tempo (also with automatic transmission and air conditioning) rented for not very much more, about $240 per week with unlimited mileage. These prices, like those at the competition, can and almost certainly will change during the lifetime of this edition, although discounts are sometimes offered for members of organizations such as the AAA, depending on the policies of the individual rental company.

All three of the companies preferred that renters be at least 25 years old, although Budget allows drivers aged 21 to 25 to rent if they pay a small supplemental charge. In all cases, if a valid credit or charge card is not presented at the time of rental, a substantial cash deposit is required in advance.

Each of the companies offers an optional loss/damage waiver priced at $12 to $13 a day. Its purchase eliminates most or all of the financial responsibility faced by a renter in the event of an accident. (Without it, a renter would be liable for up to the full value of the car in the event it was damaged.) Paying for the rental with certain types of credit or charge cards sometimes eliminates the need to buy this extra insurance, although prospective renters should check these policies directly with the card issuers.

Each of the "big three" companies offers minivan transport to its office and car depot. Added security comes from an antitheft double-locking mechanism that has been installed in most of the rental cars available on Puerto Rico. Car theft is high on Puerto Rico, so caution is always needed.

Distances are often posted in kilometers rather than miles (a kilometer is 0.62 miles), but speed limits are in miles per hour.

BY SIGHTSEEING TOUR

Castillo Watersports & Tours, calle Don Tella 27, Punta La Marias, Santurce, PR 00913 (☎ **809/791-6195** or **809/726-5752**), maintains offices at some of the capital's best-known hotels, including the San Juan Hilton, the El San Juan, and the Holiday Inn (Santurce). Using either its own vehicle (a 29-passenger van) or that of a subcontractor, it operates bus tours that pick up passengers at their hotels as an added convenience.

One of the most popular half-day tours departs most days of the week between 8:30 and 9am, lasts between four and five hours, and costs $35 per person. Departing from San Juan, it tours along the northeastern part of the island to El Yunque rain forest.

The company also offers a city tour of San Juan which departs daily at 1 or 1:30pm. The four-hour trip costs $25 per person, and includes a stopover at the Bacardi rum factory, where you're treated to a complimentary rum drink.

For a day sea excursion to the best islands, beaches, reefs, and snorkeling in the area, contact **Capt. Jack Becker,** Villa Marina Yachting, Fajardo (☎ **809/860-0861**). Captain Jack, a long-ago native of Washington, D.C., and a long-time resident of Puerto Rico, takes four to six passengers at a time on his sailboat. Participants appreciate the sun, the reefs, and the marine life such a tour makes visible. Before departure, guests are directed to a nearby delicatessen, where they can buy drinks and a package lunch. The price for a swimfest is $50 per person and it lasts from 10am to 3:30pm. Reservations can be made any evening after 6pm.

ECO-TOURS   Puerto Rico's varied and often hard-to-reach natural treasures have been conveniently packaged into a series of eco-tours, operated by **Tropix Wellness Tours** (call **809/268-2173,** or **800/582-0613,** for complete data). Four major tours are offered, including the exploration of sea turtles' nesting sites in Culebra, the phosphorescent bay in Vieques, the Río Camuy cave system in Camuy, and the dry, desertlike forest in Guanica.

The **Happy Turtle Tour** on Culebra includes a half-day kayaking/snorkeling expedition and a visit to the sea turtles' nesting sites during the spring/summer season. Culebra, one of Puerto Rico's offshore islands, is ideally situated off the southeastern coast of the mainland. Boasting good snorkeling, it's home to the National Wildlife Refuge, which protects the habitats of the island's wildlife. The Happy

Puerto Rico

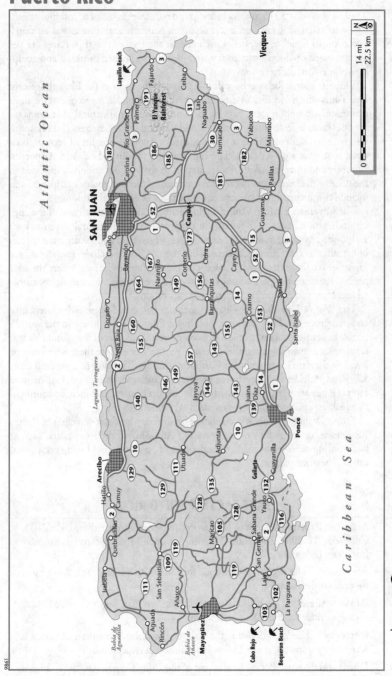

Airport ✈   Beach ☈

Turtle Tour costs $315 and includes four days/three nights of accommodations. The tour starts at Rivas Dominici Airport in Miramar and inter-island air transportation to Culebra Airport is included in the cost of the trip. Rates are per person, based on double occupancy, and include continental breakfast and equipment for escorted expeditions.

Vieques, Puerto Rico's other offshore island, is the focus of the **Phosphorescent Bay Tour,** which includes an expedition to the Isla Nena, home to one of the most panoramic phosphorescent bays in the world. Additional natural attractions on Vieques include reefs, bird sanctuaries, and deserted sandy beaches. The Phosphorescent Bay Tour costs $325 and includes four days/three nights of accommodations at the Casa del Francés. The tour starts at the Rivas Dominici Airport in Miramar and inter-island air transportation to the Vieques airport is included in the price of the tour. Rates quoted are per person, based on double occupancy, and include continental breakfast and equipment for escorted expeditions.

The **Caveman Tour** in Camuy includes an expedition through one of the largest underground cave river systems in the world. Miles of natural waterways are surrounded by stalagmites, stalactites, sunless vegetation, and 20 different species of marsupials. The Camuy Caveman Tour costs $275 and includes four days/three nights of accommodations at the Costa Dorado Hotel in Isabela, where the tour begins. Rates are per person, based on double occupancy, and include continental breakfast and equipment for escorted expeditions.

The **Wet & Dry Tour** in Guanica includes two expeditions: a dry forest hike and mangrove kayaking at sunset. Southwest Puerto Rico is home to the world's largest remaining tract of tropical dry coast forest. This part of the island also features miles of mangrove channel systems. Visitors can explore these waterways by kayak as they are led to secluded Caribbean beaches. The Wet & Dry Tour costs $275 and includes four days/three nights of accommodations at the Copamarina Hotel. Rates are per person, based on double occupancy, and include continental breakfast and equipment for escorted expeditions.

Tropix Wellness Tours will customize an itinerary for those traveling to Puerto Rico alone, or for groups of six or more. "Add-ons" to the fixed tours, such as body-rafting expeditions through underground cave rivers and hiking excursions, can also be arranged.

FAST FACTS: PUERTO RICO

American Express   American Express–related services are at Ashford Ave. 1035, Condado (☎ **809/725-0960**). The office is open Monday through Saturday from 9am to 5pm.

Area Code   The telephone area code for Puerto Rico is 809. You don't use it for calls on the island.

Banks   All major U.S. banks have branches in San Juan, and are open Monday through Friday from 8:30am to 2:30pm.

Currency   The U.S. dollar is the coin of the realm. Canadian currency is accepted by some big hotels in San Juan, although reluctantly.

Documents   Since Puerto Rico is part of the United States, American citizens do not need a passport or visa. Canadians, however, should carry some form of identification, such as a birth certificate. Citizens of the United Kingdom should have a passport.

Electricity   The electricity is 110 volts A.C., as it is in the continental United States and Canada.

Emergencies   In an emergency, call the local police (☎ **809/343-2020**), fire department (☎ **809/343-2330**), ambulance (☎ **809/343-2550**), or medical assistance (☎ **809/754-3535**).

Holidays   Puerto Rico has many public holidays when stores, offices, and schools are closed. They include New Year's Day, January 6 (Three Kings' Day), Washington's Birthday, Good Friday, Memorial Day, July 4, Labor Day, Thanksgiving, Veterans' Day, and Christmas Day, plus such local holidays as July 25 (Constitution Day) and November 19 (Discovery Day).

Information   Out in the island, it's best to go to the local city hall for tourist data. Ask for a copy of *Qué Pasa,* the official visitors' guide containing much useful information.

   For information before you leave home, contact one of the following **Puerto Rico Tourism Company** offices: 575 Fifth Ave., New York, NY 10017 (☎ **212/599-6262,** or **800/223-6530**); 3575 W. Cahuenga Blvd., Suite 560, Los Angeles, CA 90068 (☎ **213/874-5991**); or 901 Ponce de Leon Blvd., Suite 604, Coral Gables, FL 33134 (☎ **305/445-9112**). In Canada you can only phone for information (☎ **416/969-9025**).

Language   English is understood at the big resorts and in most of San Juan. Out in the island, Spanish is still *numero uno*.

Newspaper   The *San Juan Star,* an English-language newspaper, is published daily.

Safety   Use common sense and take precautions. Muggings have been reported on the Condado and Isla Verde beaches in San Juan, so you might want to confine your moonlit-beach nights to the fenced-in and guarded areas around some of the major hotels. The countryside of Puerto Rico is safer than San Juan, but caution is always the rule. Avoid small and narrow little country roads and isolated beaches, either night or day.

Taxes and Tips   In addition to the government tax of 7% in regular hotels or 10% in hotels with casinos, some hotels add a 10% service charge to your bill. If they don't, you are expected to tip for services rendered. Tip as you would in the United States. There is no airport departure tax.

Time   Puerto Rico is on Atlantic standard time year round, making it one hour ahead of eastern standard time. In winter, when it's noon in Miami, it's 1pm in San Juan. But from April until late October (during daylight saving time on the East Coast), Puerto Rico and the East Coast keep the same time.

Weather   Puerto Rico's temperature is lower than that typical of the region as the island is cooled by trade winds blowing in from the northeast. Sea, land, and mountain breezes also help keep the temperatures at a comfortable level. The climate is fairly stable all year, with an average temperature of 76° Fahrenheit. The only variants are found in the mountain regions, where the temperature fluctuates between 66° and 76°, and on the north coast, where the temperature ranges from 70° to 80°.

1 San Juan

San Juan, the capital of Puerto Rico, is an urban sprawl with one municipality flowing into another to form a great metropolitan area. San Juan introduces you to Puerto Rico, and the look of this old city ranges from decaying ruins that recall the Spanish empire to modern beachfront hotels that evoke Miami Beach.

San Juan breaks down into several divisions: San Juan Island, containing the city center and the old walled city (Old San Juan); Santurce, a large peninsula that's linked to San Juan Island by causeway; Condado, a narrow peninsula that stretches between San Juan Island and Santurce; Puerto de Tierra, the section east of old San Juan that contains many government buildings; Miramar, a lagoonfront section south of Condado; and Isla Verde, which is detached from the rest of San Juan by an isthmus.

Getting Around

BY FERRY   The *Agua Expreso* connects the old town of San Juan with the industrial and residential communities of Hato Rey and Cataño, across the bay. Ferries depart daily every 30 minutes from 6am to 9pm. The one-way fare is 75¢ to Hato Rey, 50¢ to Cataño. Departures are from the San Juan Terminal at the pier in Old San Juan. However, avoid rush hours, as locals who work in town use this ferry connection by the hundreds. Rides last about 20 minutes. For more information, call **809/751-7055.**

BY TAXI   Taxis, operated by the Public Service Commission, are metered in San Juan—or should be. The initial charge is $1, plus 10¢ for each one-tenth of a mile and 50¢ for every suitcase. A minimum fare is $3. Various taxi companies are listed in the *Yellow Pages* of the phone book under "Taxis," or you can call the PSC (☎ **809/756-1919**) to request information or report any irregularities.

BY TROLLEY   The best way to save your feet in Old San Juan is to board one of the free open-air trolleys that slowly make their way through the narrow, often cobbled, old streets. You can board a trolley at any point along its route, or go to the marina or La Puntilla for departures.

BY BUS   The Metropolitan Bus Authority operates buses in the greater San Juan area. Bus stops are marked by upright metal signs or yellow posts, reading PARADA. Bus terminals in San Juan are in the dock area and at plaza de Colón. A typical fare is 25¢ to 50¢. For more information about routes and schedules, call **809/767-7979.**

BY MINIVAN OR LIMOUSINE   Be alert to the fact that a wide variety of vehicles at the San Juan airport might refer to themselves as *limosinas* (their Spanish name). One outfit with a sign-up desk in the arrivals hall of the International Airport, near the American Airlines arrival facilities, is the **Airport Limousine Service** (☎ **809/791-4745**). It offers minivan transport from the airport to various neighborhoods of San Juan for prices that are lower than for similar routings offered by taxis. Whenever 8 to 10 passengers can be accumulated, the fare for transport, with luggage, to any hotel in Isla Verde is $3.50 to $4.50 per person; to the Condado, $4 to $5 per person; and to Old San Juan, $4.50 to $5.70 per person. Obviously, you'll share the van with other passengers.

For conventional limousine service, **Bracero Limousine** (☎ **809/740-0444**) offers upholstered cars with drivers to meet you and your entourage at the arrivals terminal of the airport for luxurious and strictly private transport to your hotel. Transport anywhere in San Juan ranges from $85 to $145, depending on your destination and should be arranged in advance of your arrival.

ESSENTIALS

TOURIST INFORMATION   Tourist information is available at the **Luís Muñoz Marín Airport** (☎ **809/791-1014**). Another office is at **La Casita,** Pier 1, Old San Juan (☎ **809/722-1709**).

FAST FACTS   One of the most centrally located **drugstores** is the Puerto Rico Drug Co., calle San Francisco 157 (☎ **809/725-2202**), in Old San Juan; it's open Monday through Saturday from 7:15am to 9:30pm and on Sunday from 8:30am to 8:30pm. Walgreen's, Ashford Ave. 1130, Condado (☎ **809/725-1510**), is a 24-hour pharmacy. In a **medical emergency,** call **809/721-2116.** Maintaining 24-hour emergency rooms are Ashford Memorial Community Hospital, Ashford Ave. 1451 (☎ **809/721-2160**), and the San Juan Health Center, De Diego Ave. 200 (☎ **809/725-0202**).

WHERE TO STAY

All hotel rooms on Puerto Rico are subject to a 7% to 9% tax, which is *not* included in the rates listed in this chapter. Most hotels also impose a 10% service charge.

IN OLD SAN JUAN

✪ Casa San José

Calle San José 159, San Juan, PR 00901. ☎ **809/723-1212.** Fax 809/723-7620. 4 rms, 5 suites. A/C TEL. Bus A7, T1, or 2. Winter, $205–$225 single; $225–$245 double; $345–$600 suite. Off-season, $160–$180 single; $180–$200 double; $270–$500 suite. (Includes continental breakfast.) AE, DC, MC, V. Free parking.

By anyone's estimate, this is the most stylish hotel in the historic heart of San Juan. Set midway between calle San Francisco and calle Luna, near plaza de Armas, it was originally designed as a private house more than 300 years ago. Shortly before a $1.5-million restoration in 1991 by members of the Mehta family, it suffered the indignity of functioning as a run-down pension, a supermarket, and a variety store. Since the restoration, it has been hailed as one of the best renovations in Puerto Rico.

Today the three-story facade opens to reveal an interior with beamed ceilings, exposed brick, gray-and-white marble floors, and an eclectic collection of European antiques. An interior patio filled with flowering plants brings light into the establishment's remote corners. Children under 12 are not welcomed.

Dining/Entertainment: Other than breakfast, no meals are served. Drinks are served daily between 7 and 10:30pm in the second-floor Salón Grande.

Services: 24-hour room service (for drinks and light snacks), laundry, a staff that can arrange almost anything.

⑤ Galería San Juan

Calle Norzagaray 204-206, San Juan, PR 00901. ☎ **809/722-1808.** Fax 809/724-7360. 7 rms (5 with bath), 3 suites. TEL. Bus A7, T1, or 21. $85–$95 single or double; $150–$175 suite. (Includes continental breakfast.) AE, MC, V. Three free parking spaces; other parking available on street.

Set on a hilltop in the old town, across the street from a sweeping view of the sea, this unusual hotel contains a maze of verdant courtyards. In the 1700s the premises were built as the headquarters of an aristocratic Spanish family. Today the place is one of the most whimsically bohemian hotels in the Caribbean. The guesthouse is run by its Connecticut-born owner, Jan D'Esopo, a noted painter, sculptor, and silk-screen artist. She is assisted by her husband, Manuco Gandís. Breakfast is the only meal served. All courtyards and rooms are adorned with hundreds of sculptures, silkscreens, or original paintings, usually for sale.

IN PUERTO DE TIERRA

Caribe Hilton

Calle Los Rosales, San Juan, PR 00902. ☎ **809/721-0303,** or 800/HILTONS in the U.S., 800/268-9275 in Canada. Fax 809/725-8849. 616 rms, 52 suites. A/C MINIBAR TV TEL. Bus A7. Winter, $295–$399 single; $320–$439 double. Off-season, $195–$285 single; $220–$320 double. Year round, $495–$1,200 suite. Children stay free in their parents' room. Continental breakfast $9.50 extra. AE, DC, MC, V. Parking $5.

The Hilton stands near the old Fort San Jerónimo, which has been incorporated into its complex. With Old San Juan at its doorstep and San Juan Bay at its backyard, the Hilton is conveniently close to the walled city of San Juan. Built in 1949 in a 17-acre tropical park, it recently underwent a major $40-million renovation. You can walk to the 16th-century fort or spend the day on a tour of Old San Juan, then come back and enjoy the beach and swimming cove. Some of the rooms are in the 20-story tower added in 1972. The bedrooms have been given fresh, modern styling and pastel-colored shades.

Dining/Entertainment: The Caribe Terrace restaurant complex features an international cuisine with a different menu each night. Other restaurants and entertainment facilities include El Batey del Pescador, a fish restaurant; La Rôtisserie, devoted to northern Italian cuisine; the Peacock Paradise Chinese Restaurant; and the Caribe Terrace Bar, with huge windows. The 12,400-square-foot casino, adjacent to the lobby atrium area, is open daily from noon to 4am, featuring blackjack, craps, baccarat, roulette, and slot machines.

Services: Room service (6:30am to 11pm), laundry/valet, babysitting.

Facilities: Spa Caribe, two freshwater swimming pools, health club, six lighted tennis courts, business center.

Radisson Normandie

Avenida Muñoz-Rivera (at the corner of calle Los Rosales), San Juan, PR 00902. ☎ **809/729-2929,** or 800/333-3333 in the U.S. Fax 809/729-3083. 174 rms, 6 suites. A/C MINIBAR TV TEL. Bus A7. Winter, $200–$230 single; $210–$240 double; $490 suite. Off-season, $155–$185 single; $165–$195 double; $450 suite. Continental breakfast $9.50 extra. AE, DC, MC, V. Parking $5.

Geared to the upscale business traveler, but also a haven for vacationers, the Normandie first opened in 1939 and reopened in 1989 after a $20-million renovation and reconstruction. Built in the shape of the famous French oceanliner, the *Normandie,* it's a monument to art deco. Adorned with columns, cornices, and countless decorations, it was originally built for a Parisian cancan dancer (who was married to a building tycoon). Next door to the Caribe Hilton, the hotel lies only five minutes from Old San Juan, and its beachside setting adjoins the noted Sixto Escobar Stadium. The elegant and elaborate rooms are well furnished with all the amenities. The more expensive units are executive rooms.

Dining/Entertainment: A continental menu with tableside cookery is served in the elegant Normandie Restaurant. The Atrium Lounge is set in a swirl of greenery.

Services: Room service (to 11pm), laundry, concierge desk, babysitting.

Facilities: Freshwater swimming pool with a bar, hair salon.

CONDADO

Once this area was devoted to residences for the very wealthy, but with the construction of El Centro, the Puerto Rico Convention Center, all that changed. Private villas were torn down to make way for high-rise hotel blocks, restaurants, and nightclubs. The Condado shopping area, along Ashford Avenue and Magdalena Avenue, became the center of an extraordinary number of boutiques. There are bus connections into Old San Juan, or you can take a taxi.

Very Expensive

✪ Condado Plaza Hotel & Casino

999 Ashford Ave., San Juan, PR 00907. ☎ **809/721-1000,** or 800/624-0420 in the U.S. Fax 809/253-0178. 540 rms, 15 suites. A/C MINIBAR TV TEL. Bus A7. Winter, $265–$375 single; $285–$395 double; $355–$1,150 suite. Off-season, $195–$325 single; $215–$345 double; $305–$750 suite. Continental breakfast $12 extra. AE, DC, MC, V. Parking $5.

This is one of the busiest hotels in Puerto Rico, with enough facilities, restaurants, and distractions to keep a holiday-maker busy for weeks. Although not the most intimate of San Juan's hotels, it is the most visible, set on a strip of beachfront at the beginning of the Condado. The original buff-colored structure is linked by an elevated passageway above Ashford Avenue to its annex, the Laguna Wing. This structure has its own lobby with direct access from the street. All accommodations have a private terrace. The complex's most deluxe section, the Plaza Club, contains 75 units, five duplex suites, a VIP lounge reserved exclusively for the use of its guests, and private check-in/check-out service.

The hotel is owned by the same consortium that owns the somewhat more upscale El San Juan Hotel & Casino. Use of the facilities at one hotel can be charged to a room at the other. It also maintains a shuttle-bus service, which runs frequently between the two hostelries.

👪 Family-Friendly Accommodations

El San Juan Hotel & Casino   *(see p. 102)* This hotel, although expensive, has more activities for children than any other hotel on Puerto Rico. Its supervised Kids Klub has daily activities ranging from face painting to swimming lessons—all for children 5 to 12 years old.

Caribe Hilton   *(see p. 98)* Children under 16 stay free in their parents' room at this deluxe hotel, which has two swimming pools and is set in a 17-acre tropical park.

Hyatt's Resorts   *(see p. 125–126)* These offer "family getaway" packages at Camp Coquí, the Puerto Rican version of Camp Hyatt, featuring professionally supervised day and evening programs for children three to five. Children also receive a 50% discount on meals.

Palmas del Mar Resorts   *(see p. 130)* This resort complex offers an activities program for children 5 to 14 in June and July, with supervised activities including swimming, handcrafts, and aquatic polo. Kids delight in the 3 miles of beaches, too.

El Conquistador   *(see p. 127)* A special activities area and games room are just for kids. Camp Coquí provides for children 3 to 12 daily for $38 per day (9am to 3pm). Activities may include such educational and fun possibilities as fishing, sailing, or arts and crafts. Children under 12 stay free in a room with their parents. Babysitting services are available.

Dining/Entertainment: The Lotus Flower is one of the island's premier Chinese restaurants (see "Where to Dine," below). The Capriccio has northern Italian seafood as well as a collection of other classic Italian dishes. Las Palmas and Tony Roma's are other dining choices. La Posada, open 24 hours a day, is known for its prime beef and seafood; attracting tired gamblers, it's set adjacent to the casino. For nighttime entertainment, La Fiesta offers live Latin music.

Services: 24-hour room service, chaise longues and towels provided free at beach and pools, laundry.

Facilities: Five swimming pools, water sports, fitness center in the Laguna Wing, two lit Laykold tennis courts.

Radisson Ambassador Hotel & Casino

1369 Ashford Ave., San Juan, PR 00907. ☎ **809/721-7300,** or 800/468-8512 in the U.S. Fax 809/723-6151. 146 rms. 87 suites. A/C TV TEL. Bus A7. Winter, $210–$240 single; $220–$250 double; from $270 suite. Off-season, $175–$230 single; $185–$240 double; from $225 suite. Breakfast $10 extra. AE, DC, MC, V. Parking $5.

Although it had always enjoyed an enviable spot in the heart of the Condado, the Ambassador emerged as a star-studded hotel after entrepreneur Eugene Romano poured more than $40 million into its restoration in 1990. The hotel offers theatrical drama and big-time pizzazz, with Czech and Murano chandeliers; hand-blown wall sconces; Turkish, Greek, and Italian marble; and yards of exotic hardwoods.

Accommodations are in a pair of high-rise towers, one of which is devoted to suites. Decors include inspirations from 18th-century Versailles, 19th-century London, Imperial China, and art deco California. Each unit has pay-for-view movies and a balcony with outdoor furniture.

Dining/Entertainment: The developers took care not to diminish from what might be the most famous Howard Johnson restaurant in the chain and the only one that caters to late-night gamblers. More intriguing is La Scala's northern Italian restaurant, the hotel's culinary highlight. The Jade Beach Chinese restaurant offers Szechuan and Cantonese cuisine. The casino has a higher percentage of slot machines than any other casino on the Condado, and a resident singer/pianist performs from a quiet corner bar. There are also four different bar/lounges.

Services: 24-hour concierge, VIP floors with extra amenities and enhanced services, a social programmer who offers a changing array of daily activities, room service (6:30am to midnight), babysitting, laundry.

Facilities: Penthouse-level fitness and health club, beauty salon, rooftop swimming pool, Jacuzzi, business center (staffed with typists, translators, guides, and stenographers).

Expensive

The Condado Beach Trio

1061 Ashford Ave., Condado, San Juan, PR 00907. ☎ **809/721-6090,** or 800/468-2775 in the U.S. Fax 809/468-2775. 241 rms, 4 suites (Condado Beach Hotel); 219 rms, 17 suites (La Concha Hotel). A/C TV TEL. Bus T1. Condado Beach Hotel: Winter, $185–$210 single; $195–$220 double; $225–$250 triple; $240–$435 suite. Off-season, $140–$160 single; $155–$175 double; $185–$205 triple; $215–$340 suite. La Concha Hotel: Winter, $155–$190 single; $165–$195 double; $190–$220 triple; $280–$750 suite. Off-season, $135–$155 single; $145–$165 double; $170–$190 triple; $455–$600 suite. Breakfast $8–$12 extra. AE, DC, MC, V. Parking $5.

In 1991, Carnival Cruise Lines and other investors bought a sprawling trio of Condado properties and incorporated them into a coherent whole, after a renovation. Among them are El Centro (built in the 1970s as the largest convention center in the Caribbean), and two famous hotels, La Concha and the Condado Beach Hotel.

Each of the three parts that form the trio has a distinct identity that can still be recognized. The Condado Beach Hotel was built in 1919 by the Vanderbilts as the first hotel along what is now the heavily congested Condado. Although its once-elaborate gardens were long ago swallowed up by the neighborhood around it, it retains its colonial facade. A favorite hotel for weddings and catered celebrations of local families, it retains some of its dignified grandeur and a legendary double staircase in the lobby. Most of the hotel's bedrooms are in a rambling modern wing (invisible from the street). The hotel's clients have included Ted Kennedy, Plácido Domingo, and Michael Bolton.

La Concha Hotel, also on the Condado and separated from its more glamorous neighbor by the convention center, was originally built in 1959. Most of its bedrooms are in a concrete-sided wing, where each of the comfortably spacious bedrooms has an ocean view. Rooms in La Concha, usually priced 15% to 20% less than those in the Condado Beach Hotel, are functionally comfortable and decorated in tropical colors.

Dining/Entertainment: Both hotels share the small-scale but elegant casino on the lobby level of the Condado Beach Hotel. Restaurants on the premises include Vivas (recommended separately in "Where to Dine," below) and the Café del Arte (in the Condado Beach Hotel), and an Italian restaurant (Adagio) in La Concha. Cabaret shows—some of the best on the island—are often presented at El Teatro in the Convention Center. Also recommended is Sirena's (in La Concha), the most architecturally interesting nightclub on the island.

Services: Room service (7am to 11pm), same-day laundry service, babysitting, sports and activities desk; access to tour operators and rental-car agents nearby.

Facilities: Guests of either hotel have free use of all the facilities within the trio. Both hotels have their own freshwater pools, bars, and well-accessorized sun decks; two beaches (the one at La Concha is sandier and wider); an array of water-sports options; and two tennis courts. An open-air seaside promenade interconnects the two hotels, away from the traffic congestion of Ashford Avenue.

Moderate

Condado Lagoon Hotel

Calle Clemenceau 6 (P.O. Box 13145), San Juan, PR 00907. ☎ **809/721-0170.** Fax 809/724-4356. 46 rms, 2 suites. A/C MINIBAR TV TEL. Bus A7. Winter $95 single; $110 double; $150 suite. Off-season, $75 single; $85 double; $130 suite. (Includes continental breakfast.) AE, MC, V. Free parking.

In the Condado at the corner of calle Joffre, this hotel is small and personal. If you're booking from the States, allow plenty of lead time (two or three weeks will do) since rooms go fast both in- and off-season. All the rooms, suitably furnished, have refrigerators, and guests are free to use the hotel's swimming pool. Meals can be enjoyed at the Ajili Mojili restaurant—it's named after a garlic-and-onion sauce invented at the hotel. Although the hotel isn't on the beach, the sands are only a short walk away; it's a block from the main street of the Condado. Babysitting is available, and room service is offered from 7am to 10pm.

Ⓢ El Canario by the Lagoon Hotel

Calle Clemenceau 4, San Juan, PR 00907. ☎ **809/722-5058,** or 800/533-2649 in the U.S. Fax 809/723-8590. 40 rms. A/C TV TEL. Bus A7 or 2. Winter, $85–$95 single; $95–$105 double. Off-season, $65–$75 single; $75–$85 double. (Includes continental breakfast and morning newspaper.) AE, DC, MC, V. Free parking.

A European-style hotel operated by the Olsons, El Canario is in a quiet residential neighborhood just a short block from Condado Beach. The attractive but small rooms all have their own balconies, and the hotel has a guest laundry and an in-house tour desk. A relaxing, informal atmosphere prevails.

Budget

ⓢ El Canario Inn

1317 Ashford Ave., San Juan, PR 00907. ☎ **809/722-3861,** or 800/443-0266 in the U.S. Fax 809/722-0391. 25 rms. A/C TV TEL. Bus M3 or M7. Winter, $75 single; $85 double. Off-season, $60 single; $70 double. (Includes continental breakfast and morning newspaper.) AE, DC, MC, V.

This inn offers one of the best bed-and-breakfast values in San Juan. You'll recognize the building by its arched veranda and the porte-cochère, which covers a side yard filled with plants, a fountain, and a gazebo. Keith and Jude Olson are the accommodating owners. The hotel, completely remodeled in 1988 and partially rejuvenated in 1994, consists of a main house and two nearby sets of servants' quarters, all linked by a terrace. On the premises are an outdoor breakfast bar and lots of quiet corners. Rooms contain two double beds, two twin beds, or one double bed. There's a communal kitchen, but many restaurants are nearby. The beach is a short block away, and a tour desk is available in the lobby. Note that no parking is available.

Casablanca

Calle Caribe 57, San Juan, PR 00907. ☎ **809/722-7139.** Fax 809/722-7139. 7 rms. Bus T1, A7, or 2. Winter $50–$65 single; $60–$75 double. Off-season, $35–$50 single; $45–$60 double. (Includes continental breakfast.) AE, MC, V.

This informal guesthouse occupies a valuable plot of land in the Condado. Originally built as a guesthouse in the 1940s, it was expanded by a former resident of Massachusetts, Alex Leighton. You'll find it behind a wraparound veranda, a wall, and a garden near Ashford Avenue. Inside, the small and simple guest rooms have ceiling fans (four rooms are air-conditioned) and movie posters on the walls. The front porch is a social center for guests. You shouldn't expect the Ritz, but you'll benefit from the management's advice and knowledge of the Condado. Street parking is available.

ISLA VERDE

Beach-bordering Isla Verde is closer to the airport than the other sections of San Juan. Hotels here lie farther from the old town than do those in Miramar, the Condado, and Ocean Park. However, a few of these establishments are among the deluxe showcases of the Caribbean. If you don't mind the isolation and want access to the fairly good beaches, then consider one of the following hotels.

Very Expensive

❁ El San Juan Hotel & Casino

Isla Verde Ave. (Rte. 37; P.O. Box 2872), San Juan, PR 00902. ☎ **809/791-1000,** or 800/468-2818. Fax 809/253-0178. 372 rms, 20 suites. A/C MINIBAR TV TEL. Bus A7, M7, or T1. Winter, $285–$405 single; $305–$425 double; from $520 suite. Off-season, $215–$335 single; $235–$355 double; from $750 suite. Breakfast buffet $13 extra. AE, DC, MC, V. Parking $8.

For dozens of reasons, this is considered the best hotel on Puerto Rico, and some say the best in the entire Caribbean basin. Built in the 1950s, it was restored with the infusion of $45 million. The hotel is surrounded by 350 palms, century-old banyans, and gardens. Its 700-yard sandy beach is probably the finest in the San Juan area. At the hotel's river pool, currents, cascades, and lagoons evoke a jungle stream. The hotel's lobby is perhaps the most opulent and memorable in the Caribbean. Entirely sheathed in red marble and hand-carved mahogany paneling, the public rooms stretch on almost endlessly.

The accommodations have intriguing touches of high-tech and are decorated in turquoise and pink. Each contains dressing rooms, three phones, and VCRs. A few feature Jacuzzis. About 150 of the accommodations, designed as comfortable bungalows, are in the outer reaches of the garden. Known as casitas, they include Roman tubs, atrium showers, and access to the fern-lined paths of a tropical jungle a few steps away.

Dining/Entertainment: La Veranda Restaurant, near the sands, is open 24 hours. Dar Tiffany, a steak-and-seafood restaurant, is open nightly; or you might prefer Don Juan, an upmarket restaurant serving a nouvelle Caribbean cuisine. Good Italian food is served for lunch and dinner at La Piccola Fontane. Or you can promenade down a re-creation of a Hong Kong waterfront street to a Chinese restaurant, Back Street Hong Kong. The in-house casino is open daily from noon to 4am.

Services: 24-hour room service, dry cleaning, babysitting, massage service.

Facilities: Rooftop health club, two swimming pools, water sports, steam room, sauna.

Sands Hotel & Casino Beach Resort

187 Isla Verde Ave., Isla Verde, PR 00913. ☎ **809/791-6100**, or 800/443-2009 in the U.S. Fax 809/791-8525. 397 rms, 17 suites. A/C TV TEL. Bus A7, M7, or T1. Winter, $265–$325 single; $285–$345 double; from $340 suite. Off-season, $195–$240 single; $210–$255 double; from $340 suite. Breakfast $11.50 extra. AE, DC, MC, V. Parking $5.

Originally built around 40 years ago as the Americana, this hotel received a new lease on life in 1987, when it was overhauled into a Caribbean version of the Sands Hotel in Atlantic City. Today, amid verdant plantings, pink marble floors, and a somewhat stripped-down version of its 1987 remake, it enjoys a high occupancy rate and the attentions of many different tour operators from around the Americas. The bedrooms are comfortable but simple, often with sea views and (unstocked) refrigerators. The most desirable are in the Plaza Club, a minihotel within the hotel. It sports a private entrance, concierge service, complimentary food and beverage buffets, and private spa and beach facilities.

Dining/Entertainment: The hotel's most upscale restaurant is Giuseppe, serving a northern Italian cuisine. Equally appealing is Ruth Chris Steak House, and Tucano's, a tropical theme restaurant serving seafood and Caribbean cuisine. Simple beachfront dining is offered in the Boardwalk Grill. The in-house nightclub offers revue-style spoofs of Hollywood legends and glittery Vegas-inspired revues, depending on bookings. The in-house casino is also popular.

Services: 24-hour room service, babysitting, laundry, limousine service, massage service.

Facilities: The resort boasts what is said to be the Caribbean's largest free-form swimming pool, complete with waterfalls, rockscapes, and a swim-up bar; other facilities include a business center and scuba diving.

Expensive

Holiday Inn Crowne Plaza Hotel & Tropical Casino

Rte. 187 km 1.5, San Juan PR 00937. ☎ **809/253-2929,** or 800/HOLIDAY in the U.S. and Canada. Fax 809/253-0079. 222 rms, 32 suites. A/C TV TEL. Bus T1. Winter, $185.50–$225.50 single; $205.50–$245.50 double; $265.50–$365.50 suite. Off-season, $165.50–$205.50 single; $175.50–$215.50 double; from $240.50 suite. Breakfast $12.25 extra. AE, DC, MC, V. Valet parking $10, self-parking $6.

This is the easternmost of the grand modern hotels of San Juan, and the leading Caribbean showcase of the Holiday Inn chain. Set on a landscaped plot of seafront close to the airport, the hotel incorporates tropical themes and colors into its decor. Rising 12 soundproof stories above a beach, the resort has gathered a loyal clientele from North America and the Caribbean since it opened in 1991.

You register in a large but simple lobby sheathed with beige marble. The bedrooms each offer some kind of ocean view and are decorated in pastel shades of peach or mint green. The bathrooms, which contain both marble and tile, have hairdryers and a phone. Each accommodation is double-insulated against noises from the nearby airport.

Dining/Entertainment: The premier dining outlet is Windows on the Sea, an oceanfront emporium serving international and Puerto Rican food. Cascades Pool Bar & Grill offers light lunches, and Tex-Mex specializes in the typical dinner dishes from northern Mexico and the southwestern part of the United States. El Tropical Lounge offers drinking and dancing every evening. The hotel also contains a large casino, El Tropical.

Services: Room service (6:30am to 11pm daily), babysitting, laundry. On floors devoted to enhanced facilities and services, a concierge staff provides free continental breakfasts and complimentary early-evening hors d'oeuvres.

Facilities: A large free-form swimming pool with swim-up bar, a sandy beachfront studded with palm trees and sea grapes, car-rental facilities, a tour desk, children's games room, children's pool, fitness center, an in-house gift shop, and both a sports club and a beach club devoted to land and water sports.

Moderate

Empress Oceanfront Hotel

2 Amapola St., Isla Verde, PR 00913. ☎ **809/791-3083,** or 800/678-0757 in the U.S. Fax 809/791-1423. 30 rms. A/C TV TEL. Bus T1. Winter, $128 single; $148–$168 double. Off-season, $68 single; $88–$128 double. Breakfast from $5.25 extra. AE, DC, MC, V. Free parking.

Set on $2^1/2$ acres of rocky headlands jutting out from the coastline of a quiet neighborhood in Isla Verde, this four-story pink-sided hotel, built on the site of a former private home, is efficiently run by a local Anglo-Latino family who immigrated to Puerto Rico from Brooklyn. From its enclosed swimming-pool terrace, you'll enjoy one of the most sweeping views anywhere of the high-rise hotels and valuable real estate nearby.

On the premises is a popular night bar, the Blue Dolphin, and a likeable restaurant, Sonny's Oceanfront Place for Ribs. A Jacuzzi is near the pool; the pleasantly airy decor is inspired by the tropics.

Travelodge

Avenida Isla Verde (P.O. Box 6007, Loiza Station), Santurce, PR 00914. ☎ **809/728-1300,** or 800/468-2028. Fax 809/268-0637. 85 rms, 6 suites. A/C TV TEL. Winter, $120 single;

$135 double; $175 suite. Off-season, $83 single; $91 double; $150 suite. Breakfast $6 extra. AE, MC, V.

Rising eight stories above the busy traffic of Isla Verde, this salmon-colored member of a national hotel chain offers simply furnished and comfortable bedrooms outfitted with blandly modern furniture. Many guests carry a tote bag to the beach across the street, then patronize the bars, restaurants, and swimming facilities of the nearby expensive hotels. There's only one restaurant (the Country Kitchen) and one bar (the Escort Lounge) at Travelodge. Don't expect too personalized a contact with the desk personnel or staff.

WHERE TO DINE

OLD SAN JUAN

Expensive

✪ La Chaumière

Calle Tetuán 367. ☎ **809/722-3330.** Reservations recommended. Bus A7, T1, or 2. Appetizers $5.50–$12.50; main courses $21.50–$36.50. AE, DC, MC, V. Dinner only, Mon–Sat 6pm–midnight. Closed July–Aug. FRENCH.

Behind the Tapía Theater, La Chaumière is decorated like a provincial French inn, with heavy ceiling beams, black-and-white checkerboard floors, and large rows of wine racks. The place is known for its classic French dishes. Menu items include liver and country pâté, rack of baby lamb provençal; chateaubriand for two, and daily specials, such as fish soup. Veal Oscar and oysters Rockefeller also appear on the menu.

Yukiyu

Calle Recinto Sur 311. ☎ **809/721-0653.** Reservations recommended. Bus A7, T1, or 2. Appetizers $5.75–$7.95; main courses $14–$19; fixed-price teppanyaki dinners $19–$36; sushi $2.50–$2.75 apiece. AE, MC, V. Lunch Mon–Sat noon–2:20pm; dinner Mon–Fri 5–11pm, Sat 7–11pm. JAPANESE.

Traditional Japanese and Oriental cooking techniques are combined in this restaurant in the old town. Its sushi bar is acclaimed as the best in the Caribbean, although tabs mount quickly. Sushi is available at both lunch and dinner, although the teppanyaki grill at the front, where your own personal chef will attend to you, is offered only for dinner. The dining room itself is postmodern and monochromatic.

Against this backdrop, the various chefs tempt you with hibatchi chicken or chicken with scallops and sesame seeds. You might begin with miso soup or steamed pork dumplings, then go on to a shrimp-and-vegetable tempura, perhaps filet of sole with capers. Fresh yellowfin tuna with teriyaki is a favorite, as is the chicken teriyaki. The sushi bar is extensive.

Moderate

Al Dente

Calle Recinto Sur 309. ☎ **809/723-7303.** Reservations recommended. Bus A7, T1, or 2. Appetizers $4.50–$8; main courses $11–$24. AE, MC, V. Mon–Sat noon–10pm. SICILIAN.

Located in the heart of Old San Juan, this restaurant has a decor that might remind you of the trattoria you enjoyed in Palermo. Both the dress code and the ambience are relaxing and casual. You might begin with a selection of seafood antipasti, followed by gnocchi with pesto, fettuccine maestro, ravioli, well-seasoned calamari, a savory version of roast goat, or a choice from a traditional array of veal and chicken dishes. Brochettes of fresh tuna laced with pepper and Mediterranean herbs is an excellent choice.

◐ Amadeus

Calle San Sebastián 106. ☎ **809/722-8635.** Reservations recommended. Bus M2, M3, or T1. Appetizers $2.75–$7.50; main courses $7.50–$18. AE, MC, V. Tues–Sun noon–2am (kitchen closes at 12:30am). CARIBBEAN.

Housed in a brick-and-stone building that was constructed in the 18th century by a wealthy merchant, Amadeus offers Caribbean ingredients with a nouvelle twist. You might enjoy an appetizer of fried green plantains with caviar and fish mousse, fried dumplings in guava sauce, a cassoulet of shrimp with black beans and sausages, grilled mahi mahi, or rabbit with prunes and red-wine sauce. The establishment lies in the heart of the old city, across from the Iglesia de San José.

El Patio de Sam

Calle San Sebastián 102. ☎ **809/723-1149.** Reservations not required. Bus A7, T1, or 2. Appetizers $2.50–$9.75; main courses $8.95–$20.95. AE, DC, MC, V. Sun–Thurs 11am–midnight, Fri–Sat 11am–1:30am. AMERICAN/PUERTO RICAN.

Located across from the Iglesia de San José, the oldest building on the island faces the statue of Ponce de León, the island's first governor. This is a popular gathering spot for American expatriates, newspeople, and shopkeepers, and is known for having the best hamburgers in San Juan. Even though the dining room is not outdoors, it has been transformed into a patio. You'll swear you're dining al fresco: Every table is placed near a cluster of potted plants, and canvas panels and awnings cover the skylight. For a satisfying lunch, try the black-bean soup, followed by the burger platter, and topped with a key lime tart. Other main dishes include various steaks, barbecued ribs, and filet of sole stuffed with crab.

La Tasca del Callejón

Calle Fortaleza 317. ☎ **809/721-1689.** Reservations recommended. Bus A7, T1, or 2. Tapas $3.50–$14.95; main courses $14.95–$25. AE, DC, MC, V. Sun–Thurs noon–11pm, Fri–Sat noon–2am, Sun 5–11pm. SPANISH.

This is a restaurant with singing waiters. In a large brick-sided room reminiscent of old Iberia, a battalion of attractive waiters and waitresses will interrupt their service to sing, dance, or play the guitar to an enthusiastic crowd.

The specialty here is tapas, an array of hot or cold appetizers. Dishes include cannelloni stuffed with pâté, octopus in vinaigrette, fabada asturiana (the bean dish of northern Spain), a hearty potato-and-kale soup called caldo gallego, grilled New York sirloin, and paella. No one will mind if you order a single dish of tapas and drink the night away. The waiters begin singing at 7pm and continue, with breaks, until closing. In the beginning of the day, from 11am to 6pm daily, only the front section (the pub) is open, serving drinks and sandwiches costing $2.75 to $5.50.

Inexpensive

⑤ Butterfly People Café

Calle Fortaleza 152. ☎ **809/723-2432.** Reservations not required. Bus A7, T1, or 2. Appetizers $3.25–$4.50; main courses $8.50–$10. AE, DC, MC, V. Lunch only, Mon–Sat 11am–5pm. CONTINENTAL/AMERICAN.

This restaurant is on the second floor of a restored mansion in Old San Juan. Next to the world's largest gallery devoted to butterflies, you can dine in the café, which overlooks a patio and has 15 tables inside. The cuisine is tropical and light European fare made with fresh ingredients. You might begin with gazpacho or vichyssoise, follow with quiche or one of the daily specials, and finish with chocolate mousse or the tantalizing raspberry chiffon pie with fresh raspberry sauce. A full bar offers tropical specialties featuring piña coladas, fresh-squeezed Puerto Rican orange juice, and Fantasias—a frappe of seven fresh fruits. Wherever you look, framed butterflies will delight you.

Hard Rock Café

Calle Recinto Sur 253. ☎ **809/724-7625.** Reservations not required. Bus A7, T1, or 2. Appetizers $3.50–$7.25; main courses $8.95–$16.95. AE, MC, V. Daily 11am–midnight. (Bar, daily 11am–2am.) AMERICAN.

Filled with rock 'n' roll memorabilia, this café lies in a historic district of the old town. Serving a "classic" American cuisine against a backdrop of loud rock music, it is firmly entrenched. Between drinks and burgers, diners look at the collection of artifacts from the rock 'n' roll hall of fame, ranging from a wig worn by Elton John to a jacket worn by John Lennon. There's also Pink Floyd's guitar and Phil Collins's drumsticks. Throughout the day well-stuffed sandwiches and juicy burgers are served, although many prefer to make the café their dinner venue, filling up on fajitas, barbecued chicken, pork ribs, or even the catch of the day. The chili will set you ablaze. This is probably the most frequented dining spot in the old town. There's a gift shop selling such merchandise as Hard Rock T-shirts.

⑤ La Bombonera

Calle San Francisco 259. ☎ **809/722-0658.** Reservations recommended. Bus M2, M3, or T1. Main courses $5.50–$11. AE, MC, V. Daily 7:30am–8:30pm. PUERTO RICAN.

This favorite was established in 1902, and ever since it has been offering homemade pastries and endless cups of coffee in a traditional colonial decor. Its sandwiches are considered some of the best in town. For decades it was a rendezvous for the island's literati and for old San Juan families, but now it has been discovered by foreign visitors. The food is authentic and inexpensive. The regional dishes include rice with squid, roast leg of pork, and seafood asopao. For dessert, you might select an apple, pineapple, or prune pie, or one of many types of flan. Service is polite, if a bit rushed, and the place fills up quickly at lunchtime.

⑤ La Mallorquina

Calle San Justo 207. ☎ **809/722-3261.** Reservations not accepted at lunch, recommended at dinner. Bus A7, T1, or 2. Appetizers $3.25–$8.95 at lunch, $3.25–$8.95 at dinner; main courses $13.95–$29.95 at dinner. AE, MC, V. Lunch Mon–Sat 11:30am–4pm; dinner Mon–Sat 4–10pm. PUERTO RICAN.

San Juan's oldest restaurant was founded in 1848. It's in a three-story, glassed-in courtyard with arches and antique wall clocks. Even if you've already eaten, you might want to have a drink at the old-fashioned wooden bar. The chef specializes in the most typical Puerto Rican rice dish—asopao. You can have it with either chicken, shrimp, or lobster and shrimp. Arroz con pollo is almost as popular. Begin with garlic soup or gazpacho. Other recommended main dishes are grilled pork chop with fried plantain, beef tenderloin Puerto Rican style, and assorted seafood stewed in wine. Lunch is busy; dinners are sometimes quiet.

CONDADO

Very Expensive

La Scala

In the Radisson Ambassador Plaza Hotel & Casino, 1369 Ashford Ave. ☎ **809/721-7300.** Reservations recommended. Bus A7. Appetizers $5–$10.50; main courses $20–$34.

AE, MC, V. Lunch Mon–Fri noon–3pm; dinner Mon–Fri 5–11:30pm, Sat–Sun 5pm–midnight. NORTHERN ITALIAN.

One of the most sophisticated Italian restaurants in San Juan caters to discerning diners who appreciate the nuances of fine cuisine and service. The decor includes neutral colors, stucco arches, and murals. The menu lists just about the entire repertoire of northern Italian cuisine. You'll find a specialty version of Caesar salad, fresh mushrooms in garlic sauce, a succulent half-melted version of fresh mozzarella in carozza and many different preparations of seafood, veal, chicken, and beef. The fresh fish and seafood are flown in from New York and Boston.

Los Faisanes

Avenida Magdalena 1108. ☎ **809/725-2801.** Reservations recommended. Bus A7, T1, or 2. Appetizers $6–$12; main courses $17–$38. AE, DC, MC, V. Lunch Sun–Fri noon–3pm; dinner Mon–Thurs 6:30–11pm, Fri–Sat 6:30–11:30pm, Sun 6–10pm. INTERNATIONAL.

On a relatively quiet corner of the Condado, Los Faisanes is considered one of the finest and most discreetly elegant restaurants in San Juan. Amid a restrained decor that reminds some visitors of a comfortably sedate private home, you'll be offered an array of wines and a selection of dishes inspired by the cuisines of France, Italy, and the Hispanic world. Several different preparations of pheasant are usually available, as well as a changing selection of chicken, beef, veal, and seafood dishes, several of them prepared at your table. Fresh filet of tuna is prepared Hemingway style, with onions, chardonnay, lemon juice, and olive oil.

✪ Ramiro's

Avenida Magdalena 1106. ☎ **809/721-9049.** Reservations recommended. Bus A7, T1, or 2. Appetizers $7–$15; main courses $23–$35; five-course fixed-price meal $55. AE, DC, MC, V. Lunch Mon–Fri noon–3pm, Sun noon–3:30pm; dinner Mon–Thurs 6:30–10:30pm, Fri–Sat 6:30–11pm, Sun 6–10pm. SPANISH/INTERNATIONAL.

In a half-century-old building near La Concha Hotel, you'll find a refined cuisine and a touch of Old Spain. One of the most distinguished dining places in Puerto Rico, this restaurant prepares "New Créole" cooking, a style pioneered by owner and chef Jesús Ramiro. You might begin with breadfruit "Mille Feuille" with local crabmeat and avocado. For your main course, any fresh fish or meat can be charcoal-grilled for you on request. Rack of lamb is one of the specialties; you can also have fresh filet of grouper. Among the many homemade desserts are caramelized mango on puff pastry with strawberry-and-guava sauce, and "four seasons" chocolate.

Expensive

Chart House

1214 Ashford Ave. ☎ **809/724-0110.** Reservations recommended Mon–Fri, required Sat–Sun. Bus A7, T1, or 2. Appetizers $4.95–$8.95; main courses $16.95–$47. AE, DC, MC, V. Dinner only, Mon–Thurs 6–11:15pm, Fri–Sat 6pm–12:15am, Sun 6–10:15pm. (Bar, Mon–Fri 5pm–1am, Sat–Sun 5–11pm.) STEAK/SEAFOOD.

Chart House, one of the best restaurants on the island, attracts literally hundreds of locals on any night. It's housed in a lattice-trimmed villa built in 1910. Today the heavy ceiling beams have been exposed, track lighting installed, and paintings added to create a warm ambience. The food is well prepared, and prime rib is a specialty. You can also order New England clam chowder, top sirloin, shrimp teriyaki, Australian lobster, Alaskan king crab, and a copious salad. The special dessert is called "mud pie." The Chart House is part of a chain of restaurants based in California.

✪ Compostela

Avenida Condado 106. ☎ **809/724-6088.** Reservations recommended. Bus 2. Appetizers $8–$15; main courses $16–$30. AE, DC, MC, V. Lunch Mon–Fri noon–3pm; dinner Mon–Sat 6:30–10:30pm. SPANISH/PUERTO RICAN.

Set in a comfortably unpretentious pine-trimmed decor, much of this restaurant's formality is derived from the battalion of formally dressed waiters whose manners evoke Old Spain. Established by a Galician-born family, who named it after their native region's most famous religious shrine (Santiago de Compostela, in northern Spain), the restaurant has gained an image as one of the best in the capital.

Specialties include roasted peppers stuffed with a salmon mousse, brochettes of filet studded with truffles, grilled shellfish with brandy sauce, rack of lamb, duck with kiwi sauce, lobster au gratin, and two different versions of paella. The wine list is appropriately international.

Scotch & Sirloin

In La Rada Hotel, 1020 Ashford Ave. ☎ **809/722-3640.** Reservations recommended. Bus A7, T1, or 2. Appetizers $3.50–$9; main courses $18.95–$39; dinner special (5:30–7:30pm) $17.95. AE, DC, MC, V. Dinner only, daily 5:30pm–midnight. STEAK/SEAFOOD.

It's probably the most famous independent restaurant on the Condado, long affiliated with names from show biz and the nearby casinos. The restaurant offers seating on a covered, open-air terrace near a swimming pool overlooking the lagoon. Despite the view outside, I prefer a table in the restaurant's interior, where evocative paintings complement the soothing lighting and colors.

Menu specialties include ale-battered shrimp, prime aged beef, broiled fresh salmon steak, barbecued pork ribs and chicken or sirloin teriyaki. All main courses include complimentary access to a well-stocked salad bar offering banana bread and a soup of the day.

✪ Vivas

In the Condado Beach Trio, Ashford Ave. ☎ **809/721-6090.** Reservations recommended. Bus T1. Buffets $14.50–$32.95; Sun brunch $27.95. AE, DC, MC, V. Dinner daily 6:30–10:30pm; brunch Sun 11:30am–4pm. INTERNATIONAL.

Open since 1992, this restaurant is in the most important landmark hotel on the Condado. You can begin your evening listening to the music in Vivas Lounge, and sampling fine champagnes and sparkling wines from around the world, among other drinks. A series of buffets is featured, the most reasonable of which is an Italian buffet offered nightly at $14.50. Feast on spaghetti, ravioli, tortellini, ziti, or your favorite pasta dish. The most expensive buffet, costing $32.95, is offered on Friday—a seafood buffet with fresh clams, oysters, shrimp, and more from the raw bar, along with the catch of the day. The big draw is all the lobster you can eat. On Saturday a "Here's the Beef" buffet is offered, featuring a choice of juicy mixed grills, steak, lamb chops, veal, chicken, and spicy sausages served with hot soup or a Caesar's salad. On Sunday night a Chinese dinner is offered, with a buffet of dim sum, stir-fries, steamed dishes, fried rice, and lots more. The Sunday brunch features exotic fruits, fresh salads, a raw bar, and both Puerto Rican and continental dishes, plus all the champagne you can drink.

Moderate

Lotus Flower

In the Laguna Wing of the Condado Plaza Hotel & Casino, 999 Ashford Ave. ☎ **809/ 722-0940.** Reservations required. Bus A7, T1, or 2. Appetizers $3–$14; main courses $15– $35. AE, DC, MC, V. Lunch Mon–Fri noon–3pm; dinner Mon–Sat 6–11:30pm, Sun 1–11:30pm. CHINESE.

One of the finest Chinese restaurants in the Caribbean overlooks the Condado Lagoon. The chef is equally at home in turning out Hunan, Szechuan, or Cantonese cookery. Specialties include lemon chicken, beef with scallops and shrimp in a hot sauce, and Szechuan Phoenix, made with prime beef and chicken in a hot sauce. Start your meal with the noodles in sesame sauce, a delectable dish.

Martino's

In the Dutch Inn Hotel & Casino, avenida Condado 55. ☎ **809/722-5256.** Reservations recommended. Bus A7. Appetizers $7.95–$11.75; main courses $15.95–$34.50. AE, DC, MC, V. Dinner only, daily 5:30pm–midnight. NORTHERN ITALIAN.

Under a steel-and-glass canopy on the 13th (top) floor of this well-known hotel and casino, Martino's offers not only some of the finest service on the Condado, but also a classic Italian cuisine. It is the domain of chef and owner Martin Acosta. His picture windows open onto views of the Atlantic and the night lights of the Condado. Appetizers include hot seafood antipasti and Caesar and spinach salads. You can order one of the homemade pasta dishes for a main course or else roam the menu, finding such dishes as seafood suprême, vitello Martino (with shrimp), gnocchi with cream sauce and parmesan, and filet mignon Monnalisa, which is flambéed at your table. In fact, almost any dish can receive a tableside flambé if that's your dining wish. Good and reasonably priced wines add to the dining pleasure.

Inexpensive

ⓢ Oasis

1043 Ashford Ave. ☎ **809/724-2005.** Reservations not required. Bus A7, T1, or 2. Appetizers $2.50–$12.95; main courses $6.50–$32. AE, DC, MC, V. Lunch daily noon–3pm; dinner daily 6–11pm. CUBAN/INTERNATIONAL.

This lone budget eatery manages to hold its own along an expensive Condado beachfront strip where prices are sometimes lethal in the better-known establishments. Most dishes here are very reasonable in price, except shellfish (especially lobster). The family-style dining room has a large array of "Cuban Créole" dishes, along with international specialties and Puerto Rican selections. The tables in back open onto views of the ocean.

Caldo Gallego, that richly flavored soup of beans and greens, with meat and sausage, is a hearty opener, followed by any number of main courses, perhaps stuffed Cornish game hen, oxtails in a Créole sauce, breaded red snapper filet, or lobster asopao. Paella is another specialty, although at least two diners must order this dish. Good value, good food (and plenty of it), and an informal, relaxed atmosphere keep this place going year after year.

Tony Roma's

In the Condado Plaza Hotel, 999 Ashford Ave. ☎ **809/721-1000,** ext. 2123. Reservations not accepted. Bus A7. Appetizers $3.95–$6; main courses $7.50–$19. AE, DC, MC, V. Daily noon–midnight. BARBECUE.

Efficient and unpretentious, this is Puerto Rico's busiest branch of a chain of eat-eries that now maintains outlets throughout North America. It's probably one of the least expensive restaurants in the Condado, and as such, is well appreciated for its spicy barbecued food. (The honey barbecue is not as spicy.) Menu items include a wide range of barbecued dishes, such as chicken and several different varieties of ribs, as well as hamburgers and large loaves of onion rings.

SANTURCE

✪ La Casona

Calle San Jorge 609, at the corner of Fernández Juncos. ☎ **809/727-2717.** Reservations required. Bus 1. Appetizers $6–$12; main courses $17–$35. AE, DC, MC, V. Mon–Fri noon–11pm, Sat 6–11pm. SPANISH/INTERNATIONAL.

One of the finest dining rooms in Puerto Rico offers the kind of dining usually found in Madrid, complete with a strolling guitarist. Since 1972 the chefs here have dispensed their special blend of Spanish and international dishes in a turn-of-the-century mansion surrounded by gardens. The much-renovated but still charming place draws some of the most fashionable diners in Puerto Rico. Paella marinara, prepared for two or more, is a specialty, as is zarzuela de mariscos (sea-food medley). Or you might select filet of grouper in Basque sauce, octopus vinaigrette, rabbit stew, or a rack of lamb.

ISLA VERDE

Very Expensive

✪ Dar Tiffany

In El San Juan Hotel & Casino, Isla Verde Ave. ☎ **809/791-7272.** Reservations required. Bus M4 or T1. Appetizers $4.95–$15.95; main courses $21.95–$30. AE, DC, MC, V. Dinner only, daily 6:30–11:30pm. SEAFOOD/AMERICAN.

One of the best choices in San Juan for a taste of the good life, Dar Tiffany is usu-ally jammed, especially on weekends, with the island's beautiful people, like Joan Rivers and Eddie Murphy. On the ground floor of Puerto Rico's most glamorous hotel, it provides considerate service and an elegant decor in a multilevel room, with lots of plants and tropical furniture. The wine list is actually more extensive than the food menu, which offers prime rib, filet mignon, veal chops, sea scallops, and filet of fresh Norwegian salmon. Prime dry-aged steaks are a specialty, as are live Maine lobsters and the fresh fish of the day. Salads are superb, especially the Caesar salad and spinach salad.

Expensive

Back Street Hong Kong

In El Juan Hotel & Casino, Isla Verde Ave. ☎ **809/791-1224.** Reservations recommended. Bus M4 or T1. Appetizers $5–$10; main courses $16–$26. AE, MC, V. Dinner only, Mon–Sat 6pm–midnight, Sun noon–midnight. MANDARIN/SZECHUAN/HUNAN.

To reach this restaurant, you head down a re-creation of a backwater street in Hong Kong. Disassembled from its original home at the 1964 New York World's Fair, it was rebuilt with the exposed electrical meters and lopsided facades of its original design intact. A few steps later you enter one of the best Chinese res-taurants in the Caribbean. Beneath a soaring redwood ceiling, you can enjoy pineapple fried rice served in a real pineapple, a version of scallops with orange sauce, Szechuan beef with chicken, or a Dragon and Phoenix (lobster mixed with shrimp).

La Piccola Fontana

In El San Juan Hotel & Casino, Isla Verde Ave. ☎ **809/791-1000, ext. 1271.** Reservations required. Bus T1. Appetizers $5.95–$12.95; main courses $19–$36. AE, MC, V. Dinner only, daily 6pm–midnight. ITALIAN.

Right off the luxurious Palm Court in this previously recommended hotel, this restaurant arguably serves the finest classic northern Italian cuisine in Puerto Rico. From its white linen to its classically formal service, it enjoys a worldwide reputation. Small and intimate, it's an octagonal neo-Palladian room with lattices and crystal chandeliers. Look for the daily specials, such as fish of the day (depending on the catch), or try one of the eight classic veal dishes. From the sea come such main courses as hot seafood suprême or calamari marinara. Many diners prefer one of the pasta dishes as a main course, perhaps the homemade manicotti or baked ziti. For openers, there are such temptations as hot seafood antipasti and a Caesar salad. The chocolate cheesecake, a chef's specialty, is a smooth finish.

Inexpensive

Howard Johnson's

In the Radisson Ambassador Plaza Hotel & Casino, 1369 Ashford Ave. ☎ **809/721-7300.** Reservations not required. Appetizers $3.50–$6; main courses $9–$16; full American breakfast $6–$12. AE, DC, MC, V. Daily 8am–11:30pm. AMERICAN.

On the lobby level of one of the best-recommended hotels of the Condado is this comfortable and cozy eatery, which reigns supreme as the most famous Howard Johnson's in the Caribbean. Despite its down-home image, it attracts some of the most prestigious politicians and financiers on Puerto Rico to its booths and tables. (Many of these luminaries live nearby and consider it their neighborhood diner.) In addition, it's the only Howard Johnson's in the world that caters, during the wee hours, almost exclusively to a clientele of gamblers.

Depending on the time of day, you can order pancakes, omelets, muffins, hash-brown potatoes, and sausages; or you can order lunch and dinner foods such as fish fries, teriyaki steaks, the famous Hojo clam platters, and an array of sandwiches and burgers. Don't overlook the many varieties of ice cream.

Sonny's Oceanfront Place for Ribs

In the Empress Oceanfront Hotel, 2 Amapola St. ☎ **809/791-3083.** Reservations not required. Bus T1. Appetizers $3.75–$5.95; main courses $7.95–$16.50. AE, DC, MC, V. Daily 8am–11pm. AMERICAN.

Located at street level in this previously recommended Isla Verde hotel, this restaurant overlooks the sea and the hotel's terraced swimming pool. The cuisine is unpretentious and guaranteed to satisfy hunger pangs that only a return to the U.S. mainland might otherwise satisfy. Menu items include hamburgers, several different types of barbecued ribs, pastas, at least four different preparations of chicken, four kinds of omelets, and steaks, including filet mignon.

WHAT TO SEE & DO

The streets are narrow and teeming with traffic, but a walk through Old San Juan (in Spanish, El Viejo San Juan) is like a stroll through five centuries of history. You can do it in less than a day. In a seven-square-block historic landmark area in the westernmost part of the city you can see many of Puerto Rico's chief historical sightseeing attractions, and do some shopping along the way.

The Spanish moved to Old San Juan in 1521, and the city played an important role as Spain's bastion of defense in the Caribbean. Once the city was called Puerto Rico (Rich Port), as the whole island was once called San Juan.

While I have outlined a walking tour of Old San Juan farther on in this section, here is an introduction to the sights you'll come across on it, as well as others you may wish to seek out yourself.

CHURCHES

Capilla de Cristo

Calle del Cristo. Admission free. Open Tues 10am–4pm. Bus T1.

Cristo Chapel was built to commemorate what legend says was a miracle. Horse racing down calle del Cristo was the highlight of the fiestas on St. John's Day, the patron saint of the city. In 1753 a young rider lost control of his horse and plunged over the precipice. Moved by the accident, the secretary of the city, Don Mateo Pratts, invoked Christ to save the youth, and had the chapel built. Today it's a landmark in the old city and one of its best-known historical monuments. The chapel's Campèche paintings and gold and silver altar can be seen through its glass doors.

Since the chapel is open only one day a week, most visitors have to settle for a view of its exterior. The chapel lies directly west of paseo de la Princesa.

Catedral de San Juan

Calle del Cristo 153, at caleta San Juan. ☎ **809/722-0861.** Admission free. Open daily 8:30am–4pm. Bus T1.

San Juan Cathedral was begun in 1540 and has had a rough life. Restoration today has been extensive, so it hardly resembles the thatch-roofed structure that stood here until 1529, when it was wiped out by a hurricane. Hampered by lack of funds, the cathedral slowly added a circular staircase and two adjoining vaulted Gothic chambers. But along came the earl of Cumberland in 1598 to loot it, and a hurricane in 1615 to blow off its roof. In 1908 the body of Ponce de León was brought here. After he'd died from an arrow wound in Florida, his body had originally been taken to the Iglesia de San José. The cathedral faces plaza de las Monjas (or the Nuns' Square), a tree-shaded spot where you can rest and cool off.

Convento de los Dominicos

In plaza de San José, calle Norzagaray 98. ☎ **809/724-0700.** Admission free. Chapel museum, Wed–Sun 9am–noon and 1–4:30pm; arts museum, Mon–Sat 9:15am–4:15pm. Bus T1.

This convent was started by Dominican friars in 1523, shortly after the city itself was founded. It was the first convent on Puerto Rico, and women and children often hid here during Carib attacks. The friars lived here until 1838, when the Crown closed down the monasteries and turned this building into an army barracks. The American army used it as its headquarters until 1966. Gregorian chants help re-create the long-ago atmosphere. There are two small museums on the premises

Iglesia de San José

In plaza de San José, calle del Cristo. ☎ **809/725-7501.** Admission free. Church, Mon–Sat 8:30am–3:30pm; Chapel of Belém, Mon–Fri 10am–4pm, Sun 11:30am–4pm. Bus T1.

This church stands right next to the Convento de los Dominicos. Initial plans were drawn in 1523 and work, supervised by Dominican friars, began in 1532. Before going into the church, look for the statue of Ponce de León on the adjoining plaza. It was made from British cannons captured during Sir Ralph Abercromby's unsuccessful attack on San Juan in 1797.

Both the church and its monastery were closed by decree in 1838, and the property was confiscated by the royal treasury. Later, the Crown turned the convent into a military barracks. The Jesuits restored the badly damaged church. This was the place of worship for Ponce de León's descendants, who are buried here under the family's coat-of-arms. And the conquistador was interred here until his removal to the Catedral de San Juan in 1908.

Although badly looted, the church still has some treasures, including *Christ of the Ponces,* a carved crucifix presented to Ponce de León. Packed in a crate, the image survived a terrible shipwreck outside San Juan Harbor. The church has four oils by José Campèche and two large works by Francisco Oller. Many miracles have been attributed to a painting in the Chapel of Belém, a 15th-century Flemish work called *The Virgin of Bethlehem.*

FORTS

Fort San Cristóbal
Northeast corner of Old San Juan, calle Norzagaray uphill from Plaza de Colón. ☎ **809/729-6960.** Admission free. Open daily 9am–5pm. Bus T1.

This fort, begun in 1634 and redesigned 200 years ago, is one of the largest defenses ever built in the Americas. Its walls rise more than 100 feet above the sea, a marvel of military engineering. San Cristóbal protected San Juan against attackers coming by land, a partner to El Morro, to which it is joined by half a mile of massive walls filled with cannon-firing positions. Tunnels and dry moats connect the center of San Cristóbal to its "outworks"—trenches, traps, bunkers, and bastions arranged defensively, layer after layer, over a 27-acre site. You'll get the idea if you look at a scale model on display. Like El Morro, this fort is protected by the National Park Service. Museum exhibits show what a soldier's life was like in the late 18th century. A video in English and Spanish is shown. Because of the steep hillside and enormous 18th-century walls, only a small number of spaces to park cars are available.

✪ Castillo San Felipe del Morro
At the end of calle Norzagaray. ☎ **809/729-6960.** Admission free. Open daily 9:15am–6pm. Bus T1.

Called El Morro, this fort stands on a rocky promontory dominating the entrance to San Juan Bay. Ordered built in 1540, the original fort was a round tower, which can still be seen deep inside the lower levels of the castle. More walls and cannon-firing positions were added, and by 1787 the fortification attained the complex design we see today. This fortress was attacked repeatedly by both the English and the Dutch. The National Park Service protects the fortifications of Old San Juan, which have been declared a World Heritage Site by the United Nations. With some of the most dramatic views in the Caribbean, you'll find El Morro to be an intriguing labyrinth of dungeons, barracks, vaults, lookouts, and ramps. A video in English and Spanish is shown. The nearest parking to the historic fort is the underground facility beneath the Quincentennial Plaza at the Ballajá barracks (Cuartel de Ballajá) on calle Norzagaray.

Fort San Jerónimo

East of the Caribe Hilton, at the entrance to Condado Bay. ☎ **809/724-5949.** Admission free. Open Wed–Sun 9:30am–noon and 1:30–4:30pm. Bus T1.

Completed in 1788, this fort was damaged in the English assault of 1797. Reconstructed in the closing year of the 18th century, it has now been taken over by the Institute of Puerto Rican Culture.

HISTORIC SIGHTS

San Juan Gate, calle San Francisco and calle Recinto Oeste, built around 1635, just north of La Fortaleza, was the main gate and entry point into San Juan—that is, if you came by ship in the 18th century. The gate is the only one remaining of the several entries to the old walled city. Bus T1.

Plazuela de la Rogativa, caleta de las Monjas, basks in legend. In 1797 the British across San Juan Bay at Santurce held the old town under siege. However, that same year they mysteriously sailed away. Later, the commander claimed he feared that the enemy was well prepared behind those walls—he apparently saw many lights and believed them to be reinforcements. Some people believe that those lights were torches carried by women in a *rogativa,* or religious procession, as they followed their bishop. A handsome statue of a bishop, trailed by a trio of torch-bearing women, was donated to the city on its 450th anniversary. Bus T1.

The **City Walls** around San Juan were built in 1630 to protect the town against both European invaders and Caribbean pirates. The thickness of the walls averages 20 feet at the base and 12 feet at the top, with an average height of 40 feet. Between Fort San Cristóbal and El Morro, bastions were erected at frequent intervals. You can start seeing the walls from your approach from San Cristóbal on your way to El Morro. Bus T1.

El Arsenal

La Puntilla, ☎ **809/724-5949.** Admission free. Open Wed–Sun 9am–4:30pm. Bus T1.

The Spaniards used a shallow craft to patrol lagoons and mangroves in and around San Juan. Needing a base for these vessels, they constructed El Arsenal at the turn of the century, and it was at this same base that they, so to speak, staged their last stand, flying the Spanish colors until the final Spaniard was removed in 1898, at the end of the Spanish-American War. Exhibitions are held in the building's three galleries.

La Casa del Libro

Calle del Cristo 255. ☎ **809/723-0354.** Admission free. Open Tues–Sat 11am–4:30pm. Bus T1.

This restored 19th-century house shelters a library and museum devoted to the arts of printing and bookmaking, with examples of fine printing dating back five centuries, as well as some medieval illuminated manuscripts.

La Fortaleza

Calle Fortaleza, overlooking San Juan Harbor. ☎ **809/721-7000,** ext. 2211. Admission free. Tours of the gardens (conducted in English and Spanish) given Mon–Fri, every hour 9am–4pm. Bus T1.

The office and residence of the governor of Puerto Rico is the oldest executive mansion in continuous use in the western hemisphere, and it has served as the island's seat of government for more than three centuries. Yet its history goes back farther, to 1533 when construction began for a fortress to protect San Juan's Spanish settlers during raids by Carib tribesmen and pirates. The original medieval towers remain, but as the edifice was subsequently enlarged into a palace, other modes of architecture and ornamentation were also incorporated, including baroque, Gothic, neoclassical, and Arabian. La Fortaleza has been designated a national historic site by the U.S. government. Informal but proper attire is required.

Alcaldía (City Hall)

Calle San Francisco. ☎ **809/724-1227.** Admission free. Tours by appointment Mon–Sat 8am–3pm. Closed holidays. Bus T1.

The City Hall, with its double arcade blanked by two towers resembling Madrid's City Hall, was constructed in stages from 1604 to 1789. Still in use, this building is more than a historical site, it is a unique place full of monuments and legends.

Casa Blanca

Calle San Sebastián 1. ☎ **809/724-4102.** Admission free. Wed–Sun 9am–noon and 1–4:30pm. Bus T1.

Ponce de León never lived here, although construction of the house (built in 1521) is sometimes attributed to him. The house was erected two years after the explorer's death, and work was ordered by his son-in-law, Juan García Troche. The parcel of land was given to Ponce de León as a reward for services rendered to the Crown. Descendants of the explorer lived in the house for about $2^1/2$ centuries until the Spanish government took it over in 1779 for use as a residence for military commanders. The U.S. government as well used it as a home for army commanders. This historic residence now houses two museums. On the first floor, the Juan Ponce de León Museum is furnished with antiques, paintings, and artifacts from the 16th through the 18th century which illustrate the various uses of the house.

The Search for Life in Space

Dubbed "an ear to heaven," Arecibo Observatory contains the world's largest and most sensitive radar/radiotelescope. The telescope features a 20-acre dish or radio mirror set in an ancient sinkhole. It's 1,000 feet in diameter and 167 feet deep, and allows scientists to examine the ionosphere, the planets, and the moon with powerful radar signals and to monitor natural radio emissions from distant galaxies, pulsars, and quasars. It's being used by scientists as part of the Search for Extraterrestrial Intelligence (SETI). This research effort speculates that advanced civilizations elsewhere in the universe might also communicate via radio waves. The 10-year, $100-million search for life in space was launched on October 12, 1992, the anniversary of the New World's discovery by Columbus.

Unusually lush vegetation flourishes under the giant dish—ferns, wild orchids, and begonias. Assorted creatures like mongooses, lizards, and dragonflies have also taken refuge there. Suspended in outlandish fashion above the dish is a 600-ton platform that resembles a space station.

Self-guided tours are available at the observatory (☎ 809/878-2612) Tuesday through Friday from 2 to 3pm and on Sunday from 1 to 4:30pm. There is a souvenir shop on the grounds. The observatory lies west of San Juan, outside the town of Arecibo. It's a 35-minute drive via Routes 129, 134, 635, and 625 (the site is signposted).

On the second floor, the Taíno Indian Ethno-Historic Exhibit opens with a series of 16th-century European maps of the known world, reproductions of famous paintings of Columbus, and charts of his voyage. The Taíno Indian life is depicted through artifacts, ceremonial objects, everyday articles, and a model of an Indian village.

Casa de los Contrafuertes (House of the Buttresses)

Plaza de San José, calle San Sebastián 101. ☎ **809/724-5477.** Admission free. Open Wed–Sun 9am–4:30pm. Bus T1.

Adjacent to the Museo de Pablo Casals, this building, which has thick buttresses, is believed to be the oldest residence remaining in El Viejo San Juan. The complex also contains a Pharmacy Museum, which existed in the 19th century in the town of Cayey. If you go upstairs, you'll find a Graphic Arts Museum, displaying an exhibition of prints and paintings by local artists.

MUSEUMS

Museo de Pablo Casals

Plaza de San José, calle San Sebastián 101. ☎ **809/723-9185.** Admission $1 adults, 50¢ children. Open Tues–Sat 9:30am–5:30pm, Sun 1–5pm. Bus T1.

Adjacent to the Iglesia de San José, at the corner of plaza de San José, this museum is devoted to the memorabilia left by the artist to the people of Puerto Rico. The maestro's cello is here, along with a library of videotapes (played upon request) of some of his festival concerts. This small 18th-century house also contains manuscripts and photographs of Casals. Born in 1876, the maestro achieved fame as a cellist and also won glory as a conductor and composer. His annual Casals Festival draws worldwide interest and attracts some of the greatest performing artists; it's still held during the first two weeks of June.

Museo de Arte e Historia de San Juan

Calle Norzagaray 150. ☎ **809/724-1875.** Admission free. Open Mon–Sat 9am–noon and 1–4pm. Bus T1 to Old San Juan terminal; then a trolley car from the terminal to the museum.

Located in a Spanish colonial building at the corner of calle MacArthur, this is today a contemporary cultural center. In the mid-19th century, it was the city's main marketplace. Local art is displayed in the east and west galleries, and audiovisual materials reveal the history of the city. Sometimes major cultural events are staged in the museum's large courtyard. English- and Spanish-language audiovisual shows are presented Monday through Friday every hour on the hour from 9am to 4pm.

Museum of the University of Puerto Rico

Avenida Ponce de León, Recinto de Río Piedras. ☎ **809/764-0000,** ext. 2452. Admission free. Open Mon–Wed and Fri 9am–4:30pm, Thurs 9am–9pm, Sat 9am–3pm. Take the bus marked "Río Piedras" from plaza de Colón in Old San Juan to stop 36.

Here you'll find good collections of paintings by Puerto Rican artists, including Francisco Oller and José Campèche, the first important artist of the country (18th century). There is also a large collection of pre-Columbian Puerto Rican native artifacts from the Ingeri, sub-Taíno, and Taíno civilizations. In the museum's temporary exhibition hall you can see the work of contemporary Puerto Rican artists, retrospectives of important aspects of Puerto Rican art, and exhibits of the work of other Puerto Rican and U.S. artists.

SHOPPING

Puerto Rico has the same tariff barriers as the U.S. mainland. That's why U.S. citizens don't pay duty on items brought back to the United States. Nevertheless, you can still find great bargains on Puerto Rico, where the competition among shopkeepers is fierce. Even though the U.S. Virgin Islands are duty free, many readers report finding far lower prices on many items in San Juan than on St. Thomas.

The streets of the **old town,** such as calle San Francisco and calle del Cristo, are the major venues for shopping. Note, however, that most stores in Old San Juan are closed on Sunday.

Native handcrafts can be good buys. Look for *santos* (hand-carved wooden religious figures), needlework (women no longer get 3¢ an hour for it!), straw work, ceramics, hammocks, guayabera shirts for men, papier-mâché fruit and vegetables, and paintings and sculptures by Puerto Rican artists.

The biggest and most up-to-date shopping plaza in the Caribbean Basin is **Plaza Las Americas,** which lies in the financial district of Hato Rey, right off the Las Americas Expressway. The complex, with its fountains and advanced architecture, has more than 200 shops, most of them upmarket. Open Monday through Thursday and on Saturday from 9:30am to 6pm, and on Friday from 9:30am to 9:30pm.

ANTIQUES

José E. Alegria & Associates
Calle del Cristo 152–154. ☎ **809/721-8091.**

Opposite the Gran Hotel Convento, this shop is housed in an adjacent pair of old Spanish buildings dating from the 1520s, with rooms opening onto patios and courtyards. It sells antique furniture and paintings, with an emphasis on the 18th century, and the collection is considered the finest in San Juan. A collection of furniture from modern Spain is also for sale. Intermingled are the paintings of contemporary artists who live on Puerto Rico or elsewhere. Prices are not low, but the quality is very high. There is a wine boutique in the old cellar.

ART

Galería Botello
Calle del Cristo 208. ☎ **809/723-2879.**

A contemporary Latin American art gallery, Galería Botello is a living tribute to the late Angel Botello, considered one of the most outstanding artists on Puerto Rico, who died in 1986. Born in a small village in Galicia, Spain, he fled after the Spanish Civil War to the Caribbean and spent a 12-year period in the art-conscious country of Haiti. His paintings and bronze sculptures, evocative of his colorful background, are done in a style uniquely his own. This *galería* is his former home, and he restored the colonial mansion himself. It is today a setting to display his paintings and sculptures, and it also offers a large collection of Puerto Rican antique santos.

BOOKSTORES

The Book Store
Calle San José 255. ☎ **809/724-1815.**

This is the leading bookstore in the old town, with the largest selection of titles. It sells a number of books on Puerto Rican culture and also sells good touring maps of the island. You can ship purchases back to the States.

BUTTERFLIES [MOUNTED]

Butterfly People
Calle Fortaleza 152. ☎ **809/723-2432.**

Butterfly People is a gallery and café in a handsomely restored building in Old San Juan. Butterflies, sold here in artfully arranged boxes, range from $20 for a single mounting to many thousands of dollars for whole-wall murals. The butterflies are preserved and will last forever. The dimensional artwork is sold in limited editions and can be shipped worldwide. The majority of these butterflies come from farms around the world, some of the most beautiful coming from Indonesia, Malaysia, and New Guinea.

CLOTHING

London Fog Factory Outlet
Calle del Cristo 156. ☎ **809/722-4334.**

London Fog often has discount sales on men's wear, including a wide selection of raincoats (which today are often made in Korea) and casual-wear winter jackets. Items for women are on the ground floor.

Nono Maldonado
1051 Ashford Ave. ☎ **809/721-0456.**

Named after its owner, a Puerto Rico–born designer who worked for many years as the New York–based fashion editor of *Esquire* magazine, this is one of the most fashionable and upscale haberdashers in the Caribbean. Selling both men's and women's clothing, it contains everything from socks to dinner jackets, as well as ready-to-wear versions of Maldonado's twice-a-year collections. Both ready-to-wear and couture are available here. Although this is the main store for the designer (midway between the Condado Plaza and the Condado Beach Trio), the establishment also maintains a boutique in the El San Juan Hotel in Isla Verde.

Polo Ralph Lauren Factory Store
Calle del Cristo 201. ☎ **809/722-2136.**

This is one of the best shops in the old town if you're looking for sportswear for men, women, or children. Sometimes discounts of 40% to 50% are offered.

W. H. Smith
In the Condado Plaza Hotel, 999 Ashford Ave. ☎ **809/721-1000,** ext. 2094.

This outlet sells mostly women's clothing, everything from bathing suits and beach attire to jogging suits. For men, there are shorts, bathing suits, and jogging suits. There's also a good selection of books and maps.

GIFTS & HANDICRAFTS

Bared & Sons
Calle Fortaleza 265, at the corner of calle San Justo. ☎ **809/724-3215.**

This store sells Lladro figurines and hand-embroidered tablecloths at something like 25% to 30% off Stateside prices. It also offers a good selection of jewelry and watches.

Olé

Calle Fortaleza 105. ☎ **809/724-2445.**

Even if you don't buy anything, you can still learn a lot about the crafts displayed here. Practically everything that isn't made on Puerto Rico comes from South America, and all is artistically displayed in a high-ceilinged room decorated clear to the top. If you want a straw hat from Ecuador, hand-beaten Chilean silver, Christmas ornaments, or Puerto Rican santos, this is the place to buy them.

Puerto Rican Arts & Crafts

Calle Fortaleza 204. ☎ **809/725-5596.**

In a colonial building is this unique store, which is probably the premier outlet on the island for authentic artifacts from Puerto Rico. From modern contemporary ceramics to traditional crafts such as hand-carved santos you'll experience Puerto Rico in a special way. Of particular interest are the papier-mâché carnival masks from the south-coast town of Ponce, whose grotesque and colorful features were originally made to chase away evil spirits.

JEWELRY

Barrachina's

Calle Fortaleza 104, between calle del Cristo and calle San José. ☎ **809/725-7912.**

The birthplace, in 1963, of the piña colada, Barrachina's is a favorite of cruise-ship passengers, offering one of the largest selections of jewelry, perfume, and gifts in San Juan. There's a patio for drinks where you can order a piña colada. There is also a Bacardi rum outlet, a costume-jewelry department, a gift shop, and a section for authentic silver jewelry. Watches by Raymond Weil, Movado, Bulova, and Rado are sold.

Riviera

Calle La Cruz 205. ☎ **809/725-4000.**

This fine jewelry store specializes in first-class gemstones and excellent watches by Rolex and Patek Philippe. The third-generation owner, Julio Abislaiman, and his staff will respond to your needs. They don't sell costume jewelry.

200 Fortaleza

Calle Fortaleza 200, at the corner of calle La Cruz. ☎ **809/723-1989.**

Known as a leading place to buy fine jewelry in Old San Juan, this shop has famous-name watches; you also can purchase Italian 14-karat-gold chains and bracelets which are measured, fitted, and sold by weight and priced according to the gold market. You can buy your diamond initials pendant set in 14-karat white-and-yellow gold. 200 Fortaleza Jewelry Center has always carried the most recent designs in Italian jewelry.

Yas Mar

Calle Fortaleza 205. ☎ **809/724-1377.**

This shop sells convincingly glittering fake diamonds for those afraid or unwilling to wear the real thing. It also stocks real diamond chips, emeralds, sapphires, and rubies.

LEATHER

Leather & Pearls

Calle del Cristo 202. ☎ **809/724-8185.**

Majorca pearls and fine leather garments, bags, and accessories (including Mark Cross, Fendi, and Paloma Picasso) are sold here. There is also a collection of Lladró figurines. The shop is located one block from the cathedral.

SAN JUAN AFTER DARK

✪ THE LELOLAI VIP PROGRAM

For $10, the cost of membership in Puerto Rico's LeLoLai VIP (Value in Puerto Rico), visitors to the island can enjoy the equivalent of up to $250 in travel benefits. Admission to folkloric shows and discounts on guided tours of historic sites and natural attractions, as well as on lodgings, meals, shopping, sports activities, and more add up to significant savings.

The *paradores puertorriqueños,* the island's modestly priced network of country inns, give lower room rates for cardholders by 20% Monday through Thursday. Discounts of 10% to 15% are offered at many restaurants, from San Juan's toniest hotels to several *mesones gastronómicos,* government-sanctioned restaurants out on the island serving Puerto Rican fare. Shopping discounts are offered at many stores and boutiques and, best yet, 10% to 50% discounts at many island attractions.

The folkloric shows alone are worth the card's membership price. Showcasing Puerto Rico's musical traditions are three different evening shows at leading San Juan hotels and an afternoon performance at Casa Blanca, the island's "white house," predating Washington's version by almost 300 years.

Fantasia . . . Puerto Rico on Sunday evening at 9pm at the Convention Center features the Taller de Voces Ballet with musical selections from traditional 19th-century Puerto Rican classics to modern compositions.

My Island Sings for You, on Monday at 9pm at the Condado Plaza Hotel & Casino, features music of contemporary Puerto Rican composers performed by the popular Perla del Sur dance company.

The traditional jíbaro music and dancing from the mountains of Puerto Rico enliven Wednesday evening beginning at 8:30pm at the Caribe Hilton International's Caribe Terrace.

Discounted guided tours under the LeLoLai VIP program include:

• Half-day tours on Monday of Fort San Cristóbal and El Morro Castle, the fortifications of Old San Juan.
• Full-day walking tours of historic sites in Old San Juan on Tuesday; full-day tours of the Rio Camuy Cave Park on Wednesday; a full-day tour of Ponce, Puerto Rico's second city, on the southern coast, including the Ponce Museum of Art, Serralles Castle, the famed 19th-century Parque de Bombas red-and-black firehouse, Tibes Indian Ceremonial Park, and more than 500 restored 19th-century buildings; and full-day tours to El Yunque rain forest and the east coast, including the historic El Faro lighthouse and Cabezas de San Juan Nature Reserve.

For information and show reservations, call the LeLoLai office (☎ **809/723-3135**).

THE PERFORMING ARTS

Qué Pasa, the official visitor's guide to Puerto Rico, lists cultural events, including music, dance, theater, film, and art exhibits. It's distributed free by the tourist office.

Centro de Bellas Artes

Avenida Ponce de León 22. ☎ **809/724-4747.** Tickets, $12–$35 (prices are determined by the producers of the various shows and can vary).

Built in 1981, in the heart of Santurce, the Performing Arts Center is a six-minute taxi jaunt from most of the hotels on Condado Beach. Costing $18 million (relatively modest for such a complex), the center contains 1,883 seats in the Festival Hall, 760 in the Drama Hall, and 210 in the Experimental Theater. Some of the events here will be of interest only to those who speak Spanish, while others attract an international audience.

El Teatro

In El Centro, at the Condado Beach Trio, Ashford Ave. ☎ **809/721-6090.** Admission $28 (but the price can vary, depending on the show or special event).

In San Juan's convention center, part of the previously recommended Condado Beach Trio complex of hotels and restaurants, this room is known for having the most spectacular show revues in San Juan. Usually these are in the *Olé Latino* style, with colorful costumes, Latin music, and dancing. A "taste of the tropics" is promised and ultimately delivered. However, the room is also used for special events, so call to find out what's happening at the time of your visit. Show time is either 9 or 11pm (sometimes both). Bus A7.

Teatro Tapía

Avenida Ponce de León. ☎ **809/722-0407.** Tickets, $10–$30 (prices are determined by the producers of the various shows).

The Tapía Theater was paid for by taxes on bread and imported liquor. Standing across from plaza de Colón, it's one of the oldest theaters in the western hemisphere, built about 1832. In 1976 a restoration returned the theater to its original look. Much of Puerto Rican theater history is connected with the Tapía, named after the island's first prominent playwright, Alejandro Tapía y Rivera (1826–82). Adelina Patti (1843–1919), the most popular and highly paid singer of her day, made her operatic debut here when she was barely 14.

Various productions—some musical—are staged here throughout the year and include drama, dances, and cultural events. You'll have to call the box office (open Monday through Friday from 9am to 4pm). Sunday matinees, when performed at all, always begin at 3:30pm, and evening performances, when featured, always begin at 8:30pm.

THE CLUB & MUSIC SCENE

Amadeus Disco

In the El San Juan Hotel & Casino, Isla Verde Ave., Isla Verde. ☎ **809/791-1000.** Cover (including one drink) free Tues–Wed and Sun, $10 Thurs–Sat.

Its conservative art deco interior welcomes a widely divergent collection of the rich and beautiful, the merely rich, and the gaggle of onlookers pretending to be both. The Amadeus Disco is in the most exciting hotel in San Juan (see "Where to Stay," above), so a visit here could be combined with exploring the adjacent casino and the best-decorated lobby on Puerto Rico. The duplex area has one of the best sound systems in the Caribbean. The club is open Tuesday through Sunday from 9:30pm to 4am.

Copa

In the Sands Hotel & Casino, Isla Verde Ave., Isla Verde. ☎ **809/791-6100.** Cover (including two drinks) $28, but the price could vary.

This is one of the major showrooms for revues along the San Juan beachfront strip. Although I can't predict what show is likely to be featured at the time of your visit, one previous revue was *Hollywood Legends,* with impersonators appearing as Liza, Cher, and Tina Turner. The show might also feature a major Las Vegas–type headliner from the mainland. Performances are given Friday through Wednesday at 10:30pm. Bus A7, T1, or 2.

La Laguna Night Club

Calle Barranquitas 53, Condado. Cover (including first drink) Mon free, Tues–Sun $5.

This is one of the best-known gay nightlife centers in San Juan, which is unofficially recognized as the gay capital of the Caribbean. Happy hour is nightly from 9 to 10pm, when drink prices are reduced. The club is open seven nights a week from 9pm "until whenever." There's dancing every night.

Peggy Sue

Avenida Roberto H. Todd 1. ☎ **809/722-4750.** Cover (including one or two drinks) $5–$10, depending on the night of the week and the time you arrive.

This is one of the busiest nightclubs for young, upwardly mobile singles. There's a dance floor well worn by years of boogeying feet, although many visitors come only for drinks at the long and very accommodating bar. The decor is inspired by 1950s retro-chic, the music embraces most of the major musical movements since the 1960s, and people can usually meet and mingle without hindrance.

There's live music every Friday and Saturday night. The club is on two floors: one devoted to disco, the other to Latin music. No jeans are allowed. Its transformation from a bar into a crowded disco usually occurs around 9pm. Open Wednesday through Sunday from 5pm to 6am.

THE BAR SCENE

Fiesta Bar

In the Condado Plaza Hotel & Casino, 999 Ashford Ave. ☎ **809/721-1000.**

This bar succeeds at attracting a healthy mixture of local residents who mingle happily with hotel guests. The margaritas are appropriately salty, the rhythms are hot and appropriately Latin, and the free admission usually helps you forget any losses you might have suffered in the nearby casinos. Drinks begin at $5; beer costs $4 to $5. It's open on Monday and Tuesday from 5pm to 1am on Wednesday and Thursday from 5pm to 2am, on Friday from 5pm to 3am, and on Saturday and Sunday from noon to 3am. Happy hour is from 5 to 7pm, when drinks are half price.

Palm Court

In the El San Juan Hotel & Casino, Isla Verde Ave., Isla Verde. ☎ **809/791-1000.**

Many of its aficionados consider this the most beautiful bar on the island—perhaps in the entire Caribbean. Set amid the hotel's russet-colored marble and burnished Italian mahogany, and designed in an oval wrapping around a sunken bar area, it offers a view of one of the world's largest chandeliers and an undeniable sense of style. After 9pm Monday through Saturday, live music emanates from an adjoining room (El Chico Bar). The rest of the time, clients content themselves with a view of one of the most animated lobbies on the island. Drinks run $5 to $5.50. Open daily from noon to 4am.

Shannon's Irish Pub

Calle Loiza 1503, Santurce. ☎ **809/728-6103.**

The allure of Ireland and its ales gets tropicalized at this pub with a Latin accent which has seven TV monitors. It's the regular watering hole of many of the island's university students, a constant supplier of high-energy rock 'n' roll, and the after-hours hangout of the staff at many of the city's restaurants. Happy hours occur twice daily, from noon to 2pm and 4 to 9pm, when drinks are reduced in price. There are pool tables, and a simple café serves inexpensive lunches daily from noon to 2pm. Beer costs $2.75, except during happy hour when you get two for $3.50. Light lunches begin at $10 each. Open Sunday through Thursday from 11:30am to 3:30am and on Friday and Saturday from noon to 4:30am.

Tiffany's Salon

Calle del Cristo 213.

Many young guests have wandered into this popular spot expecting a quick piña colada or daiquiri, only to stay all evening. Tropical drinks and frappes are also popular. The establishment is on one of the main streets of Old San Juan. Hard drinks start at $3.50. Open daily from 11am to 3am.

Violeta's

Calle Fortaleza 56. ☎ **809/723-6804.**

Stylish, comfortable, and urbanized, Violeta's occupies the ground floor of a 200-year-old beamed house two blocks from the landmark Gran Hotel Convento. Sometimes a pianist performs at the oversize grand piano. An open courtyard in back provides additional seating. Margaritas, at $4, are probably the most popular drink. Open daily from 4pm to 3am.

CASINOS

These are one of the island's biggest draws. Many visitors come here on package deals and stay at one of the posh hotels at the Condado or Isla Verde, with just one intent—to gamble.

You can try your luck at the **Caribe Hilton** (one of the better ones), the **Condado Beach Trio, El San Juan Hotel & Casino** on Isla Verde Avenue in Isla Verde, and the **Condado Plaza Hotel & Casino.** There are no passports to flash, admissions to pay, or whatever, as there often is in European gambling casinos. The **Radisson Ambassador Plaza Hotel and Casino** is another deluxe hotel noted for its casino action. There is yet another casino at the **Dutch Inn Hotel & Casino,** avenida Condado 55. One of the latest casinos to open on the island is at the previously recommended **Holiday Inn Crowne Plaza Hotel and Tropical Casino** on Route 187.

The largest casino on the island is the **Sands Casino** at the Sands Hotel & Casino Beach Resort, on Isla Verde Avenue in Isla Verde. Open from noon to 4am daily, this 10,000-square-foot gaming facility is an elegant rendezvous. One of its Murano chandeliers is longer than a bowling alley. The casino offers 207 slot machines, 16 blackjack tables, three dice tables, four roulette wheels, and a minibaccarat table. Puerto Rican law provides that a percentage of gaming revenues be set aside for education funding.

The best casinos "out in the island" are those at the **Hyatt Regency Cerromar Beach** and **Hyatt Dorado Beach.** In fact, you can drive to either of these from San Juan to enjoy their nighttime diversions. There is also a casino at **Palmas del**

Mar and yet another at the **Mayagüez Hilton** in western Puerto Rico. Puerto Rico's "second city," Ponce, now has a major casino following the opening of the **Ponce Hilton and Casino.**

Most casinos are open daily from 1 to 4pm and again from 8pm to 4am. Jackets for men are sometimes requested, as the commonwealth is trying to keep a "dignified, refined atmosphere."

2   Dorado

The name itself evokes a kind of magic. Along the north shore of Puerto Rico, about a 40-minute drive (22 miles) west of the capital, a world of luxury resorts and villa complexes unfolds. The big properties of the Hyatt Dorado Beach Hotel and Hyatt Regency Cerromar Beach Hotel sit on the choice white sandy beaches here.

Many clients book into one of these hotels, and only pass through San Juan on arrival and departure. Others, particularly first-timers, may want to spend a day or so sightseeing and shopping in San Juan before heading for one of these complete resort properties, since, chances are, once at the resort they'll never leave the grounds. The hotels are self-contained, with beach, swimming, golf, tennis, dining, and nightlife activities.

If you don't have a car and need to use public transportation, call **Dorado Transport Corp.** (☎ **809/796-1214**) in San Juan. It offers shuttle service to the area from the airport daily from 11am to 9pm. The charge is only $15 per passenger, but a minimum of three must take the trip.

WHERE TO STAY

✪ Hyatt Dorado Beach Hotel

Dorado, PR 00646. ☎ **809/796-1234,** or 800/233-1234 in the U.S. Fax 809/796-2022. 298 rms, 17 casitas. A/C MINIBAR TV TEL.. Winter, $465–$610 single or double; from $730 casita. Off-season, $155–$230 single or double; from $350 casita. MAP $60 per person extra. AE, DC, MC, V. Free parking.

The Hyatt sprawls across a plantation filled with palms, pine trees, and purple bougainvillea, and a 2-mile stretch of sandy ocean beach. Located 22 miles west of San Juan, the Dorado Beach is a low-rise building and is the more tranquil of the two Hyatts here. Two side-by-side 18-hole championship golf courses, designed by Robert Trent Jones, Sr., are its big draw (see "Sports & Outdoor Activities Around the Island," later in this chapter). The present hotel, originally a Rockefeller playground, opened in 1958, and many repeat guests, including celebrities, have been coming back ever since.

Hyatt Hotels Corporation has spent millions on improvements. The renovated bedrooms have marble baths and terra-cotta flooring throughout. Rooms are available on the beach or in villas tucked in and around the lushly planted grounds. The casitas are a series of private beach or poolside houses.

Dining/Entertainment: Breakfast can be taken on your private balcony and lunch on an outdoor ocean terrace. Dinner is served in a three-tiered main dining room where you can watch the surf. Hyatt Dorado chefs have won many awards, and the food at the hotel restaurants and Su Casa Restaurant (not included in the MAP) is considered among the finest in the Caribbean. And don't forget the casino.

Services: 24-hour room service, babysitting, laundry/dry cleaning.

Facilities: Two 18-hole golf courses; seven all-weather tennis courts; two swimming pools; a children's camp; a private airfield; one of the best windsurfing schools in Puerto Rico, the Lisa Penfield Windsurfing School (see "Sports & Outdoor Activities Around the Island," later in this chapter).

✪ Hyatt Regency Cerromar Beach Hotel

Dorado, PR 00646. ☎ **809/796-1234,** or 800/233-1234. Fax 809/796-4647. 504 rms, 43 suites. A/C MINIBAR TV TEL. Winter, $205–$295 single or double; from $660 suite. Off-season, $160–$265 single or double; from $350 suite. MAP $62 per person extra. AE, DC, MC, V. Free parking.

Near the elegant Hyatt Dorado Beach Hotel, this Hyatt stands on its own beach. The high-rise Cerromar is a combination of two words—*cerro* (mountain) and *mar* (sea)—and true to its name, you're surrounded by mountains and ocean. Approximately 22 miles west of San Juan, the Cerromar shares the 1,000-acre former Livingston estate with the Dorado, so guests can enjoy the Robert Trent Jones, Sr., golf courses as well as the other facilities at the next-door hotel; a shuttle bus runs back and forth between the two resorts every half hour.

All rooms have first-class appointments and are well maintained; the majority have private balconies. Floors throughout are tile and furnishings are casual tropical, in soft colors and pastels. All rooms have honor bars and in-room safes.

Dining/Entertainment: The outdoor Swan Café has three levels connected by a dramatic staircase; some tables overlook a lake populated by swans and flamingos. Other dining choices include Sushi Wong's and the Chi Chi Steakhouse, both winter offerings, and the hotel's pride and joy, Medici's. The Flamingo bar offers a wide, open-air expanse overlooking the sea and the water playground.

Services: 24-hour room service, laundry/dry cleaning, babysitting.

Facilities: The water playground contains the world's longest freshwater swimming pool—a 1,776-foot-long fantasy pool inaugurated in 1986, with a current like a river because of differing heights in five connected free-form pools. It takes 15 minutes to float from one end of the pool to the other. There are also 14 waterfalls, tropical landscaping, a subterranean Jacuzzi, water slides, walks, bridges, and a children's pool. A full-service spa and health club provides services for both body and skin care, including Swedish massages and a "Powercise" machine that "talks" to you. In addition to 21 tennis courts, there is also a children's day camp for guests 3 through 13, open year round and known as Camp Coquí.

WHERE TO DINE

El Malecón

Rte. 693, km 8.2. ☎ **809/796-1645.** Reservations not required. Appetizers $3–$8.95; main courses $9–$31. AE, MC, V. Sun–Thurs 11am–10pm. Fri–Sat 11am–11pm. PUERTO RICAN.

If you'd like to discover an unpretentious local place serving a good Puerto Rican cuisine, then head for El Malecón, a simple concrete structure set in a small shopping center. Established around 1985, it has a cozy family ambience and is especially popular on weekends. Some members of the staff speak English, and the chef is best with fresh seafood, which most diners seem to order. The chef can also prepare, if the ingredients are available, a variety of items not listed on the menu.

Medici's

In the Hyatt Regency Cerromar. ☎ **809/796-1234, ext. 3047.** Reservations required. Appetizers $6.50–$12; main courses $22–$32. AE, DC, MC, V. Dinner only, daily 6:30–9:30pm. INTERNATIONAL.

Medici's is an elegant 340-seat dining room. Tables sit on tiers at several levels, each of which has been angled for views of one of the gardens. The staff sets the mood of relaxed formality, the music is "upbeat classical," and the wine cellar is diversified. Guests can take their pick—from steak to "spa cuisine," from osso buco to Caribbean flavors. The kitchen also turns out a light Italian cuisine, and most items, including pastas, are available as appetizers or main or side dishes. Try grilled salmon on spinach with a dill sauce. Herb granita (Italian ice) is served between courses.

✪ Su Casa

In the Hyatt Dorado Beach Hotel. ☎ **809/796-1234.** Reservations required. Appetizers $6.50–$19; main courses $27–$36. AE, DC, MC, V. Dinner only, daily 7–9:30pm. SPANISH/ CONTINENTAL.

Su Casa is the 19th-century Livingston family plantation home on the resort property. The Spanish colonial building with tile courtyards has been a favorite dining place for the rich and famous since the Rockefellers entertained guests at their posh Dorado Beach hideaway. Diners sit at candlelit tables and enjoy the serenade of strolling entertainers as they partake of Spanish and classical European dishes. The chef produces an innovative cuisine, using Puerto Rican fruits and vegetables whenever possible, including plantain, spinach, and eggplant. Specialties include pastel de langosta (lobster fried in a corn tortilla with tomato-and-cilantro sauce), filete de res "Carlos V" (filet mignon with a Spanish brandy sauce on eggplant), rack of lamb, paella mixta (a very special blend of fresh seafood and spices), and a house special dessert, Bien me sabe, made with Caribbean coconut and biscuit. Don't plan to rush through a meal at Su Casa—allow yourself enough time to enjoy your dinner.

3 Las Croabas

From San Juan, head east on Route 3 toward Fajardo a distance of 31 miles to Las Croabas. At the intersection, cut northeast on Route 195 and continue to the intersection with Route 987, at which point you head north.

WHERE TO STAY

✪ El Conquistador Resort & Country Club

Las Croabas, PR 00738 (or P.O. Box 70001, Fajardo, PR 00738). ☎ **809/863-1000,** or 800/ 468-5228 in the U.S. Fax 809/860-3280. 802 rms, 122 suites. A/C MINIBAR TV TEL. Transportation: Limousine from the San Juan airport ($25). Winter, $315–$460 single or double; from $920 suite. Off-season, $275–$390 single or double; from $870 suite. Children under 12 stay free in parents' room. Additional bed for third or fourth occupant $40 extra. Breakfast $13.75 extra. MAP $75 extra per adult, $40 extra per child under 12. AE, DC, MC, V. Parking $5–$10.

One of the most impressive hostelries anywhere in the tropics, El Conquistador is considered a destination unto itself. Rebuilt in 1993 at a cost of $250 million by Kumagai/Mitsubishi, it incorporates a million dollars' worth of art, and five hotels into 500 acres of forested hills whose edge slopes down to the sea. The architecture drew its inspiration from Mediterranean models. Each of the far-flung elements of the resort is interconnected with serpentine, landscaped walkways, and with a railroad-style funicular that makes frequent trips up and down the hillside. Throughout, gardens mingle with murals, paintings, and sculptures. The accommodations are outfitted with comfortable and stylish furniture, soft tropical colors, and about half a dozen unexpected amenities (such as bathrobes and ironing boards).

Dining/Entertainment: The resort contains nine different restaurants, one of which is a 24-hour tropical deli; others are highlighted in "Where to Dine," below. The Exotica Café, beside the resort's marina, is the purveyor of ice creams, pastries, and hot chocolates. A casino offers gambling as well as live music from a nearby piano bar. The array of bars and nightlife include Drake's Library, outfitted with books, mahogany, and a billiards table, and the Amigos Bar and Lounge, with live merengue and salsa.

Services: Room service, babysitting, men's and women's beauty salon, laundry/dry cleaning, massages, spa services.

Facilities: The hotel is sole owner of a "fantasy island" (Palomino Island), with caverns, nature trails, and a wide choice of such water sports as scuba diving, windsurfing, and snorkeling. About half a mile offshore, the island is connected by private ferries to the main hotel at frequent intervals. There's also a 35-slip marina where some of the boats are for rent, six swimming pools, many different Jacuzzi tubs, and some of the largest and most up-to-date conference facilities in the world. Tennis courts are lit for night play, and there's an 18-hole championship golf course designed by Arthur Hills with "unbelievable views"; greens fees are $95 per person. An arcade of shops includes branches of W. H. Smith bookstores and Reinhold Jewelers.

WHERE TO DINE

✪ Isabela's

In El Conquistador Resort. ☎ **809/863-1000.** Reservations recommended. Appetizers $5.50–$12; main courses $24–$45; Sun buffet lunch $40 per person. AE, DC, MC, V. Lunch buffet Sun noon–3pm; dinner daily 6pm–midnight. SPANISH/INTERNATIONAL.

Of all the restaurants in El Conquistador Resort, this is considered the premier. The severe Spanish baroque room was inspired by an aristocratic monastery in Spain. The massive gates, among the most spectacular pieces of wrought iron on Puerto Rico, were created in the 19th century in Provence. There's additional seating on an open-sided terrace for diners who want exposure to the sea and the trade winds. The service is impeccable—and the food is among the finest on the island.

Menu items might include roast lamb with Dijon sauce, grilled filet of beef with red-wine sauce and exotic mushrooms, roast chicken with natural juices (or fresh ginger sauce), and baked Caribbean lobster tail with drawn butter. Among the appetizers is black-bean soup.

Los Gauchos

In El Conquistador Resort. ☎ **809/863-1000.** Reservations required. Appetizers $5–$28; main courses $12–$32. AE, DC, MC, V. Dinner only, daily 6:30pm–midnight. ARGENTINEAN.

This is the name given to the Argentinean prairie riders whose lifestyles resemble that of the American cowboy. The meat is grilled in an authentic Argentinean tradition. Located at Las Olvas Village, it has many house specialties, including an Argentine tableside grill with various traditional meats as well as the popular grilled Argentine "skirt steak." Seafood is also served, including mahi mahi broiled with olive oil, garlic, and parsley. A surf-and-turf *parrillada* (called Mar y Tierra) is also offered.

Otello's

In El Conquistador Resort. ☎ **809/863-1000.** Reservations required. Appetizers $5.50–$12.50; main courses $19–$37. AE, DC, MC, V. Dinner only, daily 6pm–midnight. NORTHERN ITALIAN.

Here you can dine by candlelight in the old-world tradition, with a choice of both indoor and outdoor seating. The cuisine is authentic northern Italian and the decor is neo-Palladian. You might begin with one of the soups, perhaps pasta fagioli, or select one of the zesty Italian appetizers, such as clams Areganata. Pastas can be ordered as a half-portion appetizer or as a main dish, and they include the likes of homemade manicotti or spaghetti carbonara. The chef is known for veal dishes, coming in nine different ways. A selection of poultry and vegetarian food is offered nightly, along with several shrimp and clam dishes.

4 Palmas del Mar

Called the "Caribbean side of Puerto Rico," the residential resort community of Palmas del Mar lies on the island's southeastern shore, 45 miles from San Juan, outside the town of Humacao. It's about an hour's drive from the San Juan airport.

You'll find plenty to do: golf, tennis, scuba diving, sailing, deep-sea fishing, horseback riding, whatever. Hiking on the resort's grounds is another favorite activity. There is a forest preserve with giant ferns, orchids, and hanging vines. There's even a casino.

In fact, the resort has one of the most action-packed sports programs in the Caribbean (see "Sports & Outdoor Activities Around the Island," later in this chapter, for more details).

The Humacao Regional Airport is 3 miles from the northern boundary of Palmas del Mar. Its 2,300-foot strip will accommodate private planes; no regularly scheduled airline currently serves the Humacao Airport.

Palmas del Mar will arrange minivan or bus transport from Humacao to the San Juan airport for $16 each way. Call the resort if you want to be met at the airport.

The Lighthouse

Las Cabezas de San Juan Nature Reserve is better known as El Faro or "The Lighthouse." In the northeast corner of Puerto Rico, north of Fajardo off Route 987, this is one of the most beautiful and important areas of the island—a number of different ecosystems flourish in the vicinity.

Surrounded on three sides by the Atlantic Ocean, the 316-acre site encompasses forestland, mangroves, lagoons, beaches, cliffs, offshore cays, and coral reefs. El Faro serves as a research center for the scientific community. It's home to a vast array of flora and fauna (such as sea turtles and other endangered species).

The nature reserve is open Friday through Sunday; reservations are required, so call before going. For reservations throughout the week, call **809/722-5882;** for reservations on Saturday and Sunday, call **809/860-2560** (reservations on weekends can be made only on the day of your intended visit). Admission is $4 for adults, $1 for children under 12. Guided tours are conducted at 9:30am, 10:30am, and 1:30pm.

WHERE TO STAY

Lying on 2,700 acres, **Palmas del Mar,** P.O. Box 2020, Humacao, PR 00791 (☎ **809/852-6000,** or **800/468-3331** in the U.S.), is a former coconut plantation that includes a stretch of the Caribbean coastline. Guests are housed in villas built around a marina, the beach, a tennis complex, and a championship golf course. You have a choice of either rooms or villas, depending on your space needs. In the same complex are some privately owned condominium homes that the owners make available to guests when they're not living in them. In addition to the villas, guests can stay at the luxurious Palmas Inn or the Candelero Hotel. Most guests book in Palmas del Mar on a package plan, such as a golf package. Most packages are for seven days/six nights in winter and four days/three nights in summer.

Once you arrive at Palmas del Mar, you can depend on free hotel shuttle service to get you to the properties recommended below.

Candelero Hotel

Palmas del Mar (P.O. Box 2020), Humacao, PR 00791. ☎ **809/852-6000,** or 800/468-3331 in the U.S. Fax 809/850-4445. 101 rms. A/C TV TEL. Winter, $185–$205 single or double. Off-season, $140 single or double. MAP $68 per person extra in winter, $55 extra off-season. AE, DC, MC, V. Free parking.

Rooms here come in a variety of sizes, some with king-size beds. High cathedral ceilings accentuate the roominess that is further extended by patios on the ground floor. Some of the superior and deluxe accommodations have private balconies. The main dining spot, Las Garzas, is previewed under "Where to Dine," below. The beach and golf course are near at hand.

Palmas Inn

Palmas del Mar (P.O. Box 2020), Humacao, PR 00661. ☎ **809/852-6000,** or 800/468-3331 in the U.S. Fax 809/852-6330. 23 junior suites. A/C TV TEL. Winter, $293–$325 suite for two. Off-season, $190 suite for two. MAP $65 per person extra in winter, $55 extra off-season. (Includes continental breakfast.) AE, DC, MC, V. Free parking.

This gem contains only deluxe junior suites, each with a panoramic vista of sea and mountains. The decor here evokes that of a Mediterranean villa, with a spacious, airy feeling; accommodations are decorated in a Spanish antique style. The inn also houses the Palm Terrace Restaurant, previewed in "Where to Dine," below.

Villa Suites

Palmas del Mar (P.O. Box 2020), Humacao, PR 00661. ☎ **809/852-6000,** or 800/468-3331 in the U.S. Fax 809/852-2230. 10 studios, 135 villa suites. A/C TV TEL. Winter, $220 studio; $288–$430 one-bedroom villa; $389–$565 two-bedroom villa; $508–$710 three-bedroom villa. Off-season, $190 studio; $265 one-bedroom villa; $340–$370 two-bedroom villa; $420–$460 three-bedroom villa. MAP $68 per person extra in winter, $55 extra off-season. Three-day minimum booking in winter. AE, DC, MC, V. Free parking.

Adjacent to the Candelero Hotel, this complex of red-roofed, white-walled, Iberian-inspired villas would be a suitable vacation headquarters for a family. Each of the villas, furnished and decorated according to the taste of its absentee owner, contains a full working kitchen and enough privacy to allow a feeling of relaxed well-being. Prices in each category of villa depend on the building's proximity to either the beachfront or the golf course; an additional handful built against a steep hillside overlook the tennis courts.

WHERE TO DINE

Moods for dining in Palmas del Mar come in a wide variety, depending on which "village" you're staying in. The Palm Terrace Restaurant is arguably the best, serving continental food, but the choice is vast. Currently, MAP guests can select from a choice of six specialty restaurants on the grounds, as well as five restaurants off the property. They can also enjoy five theme nights, including a western night and a Mexican night.

All the restaurants are open during the winter season; however, in summer only three or four may be fully functioning.

Chez Daniel/Le Grill

Marina de Palmas del Mar. ☎ **809/850-3838.** Reservations required. Appetizers $6.50–$8.50; main courses $21.50–$26.50. AE, MC, V. Lunch Fri–Sat only, noon–3pm; dinner Wed–Mon 6:30–10pm. Closed June. FRENCH.

It's French, it's nautical, it's fun, and it's the preferred dining area for occupants of the yachts that moor at its adjacent pier. Daniel Vasse, the executive chef, presents a menu that might begin with fish soup or stuffed mussels, followed by such main courses as bouillinade (a traditional Catalan-style bouillabaisse) or lobster and chicken sautéed with butter in tarragon-and-lemon sauce. Filet mignon in a roquefort sauce is another delectable dish, as are filet of salmon or roast rack of lamb. For dessert, you can order a soufflé Cointreau.

Las Garzas

In the Candelero Hotel. ☎ **809/852-6000, ext. 50.** Reservations required only for groups of six or more. Appetizers $3.75–$7.50; main courses $10.95–$31. AE, DC, MC, V. Breakfast daily 7–11am; lunch daily noon–3pm; dinner daily 6–10:30pm. INTERNATIONAL.

Cooled by trade winds, this restaurant overlooks a courtyard and swimming pool and is an ideal choice for any meal. Lunch always includes sandwiches and burgers galore; if you want heartier fare, ask for the Puerto Rican specialty of the day, perhaps red snapper in garlic butter, preceded by black-bean soup. Dinner is more elaborate. Begin with a chilled papaya bisque served in half a coconut, followed by Caribbean lobster, New York sirloin, paella, or catch of the day. Every night is a virtual theme night here, ranging from an Italian festival on Monday to a Puerto Rican night on Saturday.

Palm Terrace Restaurant

In the Palmas Inn. ☎ **809/852-6000, ext. 52.** Reservations recommended. Appetizers $5.50–$9.50; main courses $16.95–$28. AE, MC, V. Dinner only, daily 6–11pm. CARIBBEAN/CONTINENTAL.

In the Palmas Inn near the casino, this restaurant offers a hilltop vantage point for views of Candelero Beach and the Caribbean Sea. It is acclaimed for providing what many consider the finest dining among the wide selection of offerings in and around this sprawling resort. The chefs feel equally at home wandering the Caribbean Sea or the continent of Europe. A zarzuela (mixed medley) of shellfish might tempt you, as would the Caribbean lobster or perhaps baked island wahoo. Meat fanciers can order such dishes as medallions of beef tenderloin. For an appetizer you can sample the likes of fried conch, squid flavored with garlic, or black-bean soup. The restaurant has an Iberian colonial decor, with wide expanses of glass to absorb the view.

PALMAS DEL MAR AFTER DARK

The hot nightspot in Palmas del Mar is the **Palm Terrace Restaurant & Lounge,** near the casino. Here guests can drink and dance to the latest rhythms Wednesday through Sunday from 8pm to 2am (perhaps later on Friday and Saturday). The $7 minimum includes your first drink.

The **casino** (☎ **809/852-6000, ext. 13513**) in the Palmas del Mar complex, near the Palmas Inn, is in the Culebra Room on the second floor. The casino has nine blackjack tables, two roulette wheels, a craps table, and dozens of slot machines. The place is open from 6pm to 3am daily. However, in summer it closes on Monday and Tuesday. Guests are requested to dress with "casual elegance." Under Puerto Rican law, drinks cannot be served in a casino, but you can enjoy one in the Palm Terrace Lounge.

5 Rincón

At the westernmost point of the island, Rincón, 6 miles north of Mayagüez, has one of the most exotic beaches on the island, which draws surfers from around the world. In and around this small fishing village are some unique accommodations.

If you choose to rent a car at the San Juan airport, it will take approximately 2½ hours to drive to the hotel via the busy northern Route 2, or 3 hours via the scenic mountain route (no. 52) to the south. I recommend the southern route through Ponce.

In addition, there are five daily flights from San Juan to Mayagüez on **American Eagle** (☎ **800/433-7300**). These flights take 45 minutes. From the Mayagüez airport, Rincón is a 30-minute drive to the north on Route 2 (go left or west at the intersection with Route 115). Round-trip fares range from $60 to $100 per person.

WHERE TO STAY

✪ Horned Dorset Primavera Hotel

P.O. Box 1132, Rincón, PR 00677. ☎ **809/823-4030.** Fax 809/823-5580. 24 suites. A/C. Directions: From the Mayagüez airport, take Route 2 north half a mile to the Anasco intersection; turn left onto Route 115 toward Rincón for 4 miles; after El Coche Restaurant, take a sharp left onto Route 429 and go about a mile; the hotel is on the left, at distance marker km 3. Winter, $245 single; $325–$440 double. Off-season, $135 single; $190–$210 double. MAP $62.25 per person extra. AE, DC, MC, V. Free parking.

Many consider this the most sophisticated hotel on Puerto Rico, and (among the smaller properties) one of the most exclusive and elegant anywhere in the Caribbean. Established in 1987, it was built on the massive breakwaters and seawalls erected by a local railroad many years ago, and was named after a successful hotel (the Horned Dorset), which its owners still maintain in upstate New York.

The hacienda evokes an aristocratic Spanish villa, with wicker armchairs, hand-painted tiles, ceiling fans, seaside terraces, and cascades of flowers. Management does not allow children under 12, most pets, radios, or televisions. Accommodations are in a series of suites that ramble uphill amid lush gardens. The decoration is tasteful, with four-poster beds and brass-footed tubs in marble-sheathed bathrooms.

Dining/Entertainment: The hotel's restaurant is one of the finest in the Caribbean (see "Where to Dine," below). There's a bar open throughout the day that serves some of the most delectable rum punches on the island. Guitarists and singers often perform during cocktail and dinner hours.

Services: Room service, concierge, laundry, massage, limousine and touring services.

Facilities: Probably the best hotel library on Puerto Rico (books on art, music, comparative literature, and poetry), swimming pool, secluded semiprivate beach, tennis courts, deep-sea fishing, golf; scuba diving available nearby.

Parador Villa Antonio

Route. 115, km 12.3 (P.O. Box 68), Rincón, PR 00677. ☎ **809/823-2645**, or 800/443-0266 in the U.S. Fax 809/823-3380. 55 apartments. A/C TV. Head north from Mayagüez along Route 2, then turn left (or west) at the junction with Route 115. $69.55–$101.65 one-bedroom apartment; $90.95–$107 two-bedroom apartment. AE, DC, MC, V. Free parking.

Ilia and Hector Ruíz offer apartments by the sea with a littered beach at your doorstep. The most sensible way to get here is by way of Mayagüez airport, just 25 minutes away by car. Facilities include a children's playground, two tennis courts, and a swimming pool. Surfing and fishing can be enjoyed just outside your front door, and you can bring your catch right into your cottage and prepare a fresh seafood dinner in your own kitchenette. There is no restaurant. Be aware that the air conditioning doesn't work properly here, and in general better maintenance is needed.

WHERE TO DINE

✪ Horned Dorset Primavera

Rincón. ☎ **809/823-4030.** Reservations recommended. Appetizers $11–$16; main courses $24–$30; lunch from $18; fixed-price dinner $45. AE, MC, V. Lunch daily noon–2:30pm; dinner daily, with seatings at 7, 8, and 9pm. CLASSICAL FRENCH.

This place reigns without equal as the finest restaurant in western Puerto Rico, 6$^{1}/_{2}$ miles northwest of Mayagüez, and is so alluring that diners sometimes journey out from San Juan for an intimate dinner. In the previously recommended hotel (see "Where to Stay," above), it's the counterpart of an award-winning restaurant in Leonardsville, New York, the Horned Dorset. Meals are served beneath soaring ceilings. A masonry staircase sweeps from the garden to reach the second-floor precincts.

Menu specialties might include medallions of lobster in an orange-flavored beurre-blanc sauce, grilled breast of duckling with bay leaves and raspberry sauce, and dorado (mahi mahi) grilled and served with a ginger-cream sauce and served on a bed of braised Chinese cabbage. The famous desserts include Martinique cake.

6 Mayagüez

Puerto Ricans have nicknamed their third-largest city the "Sultan of the West." This port city, not architecturally remarkable, was once considered the needlework capital of the island. There are still craftspeople who do fine embroidery.

Mayagüez is the honeymoon capital of Puerto Rico. The tradition dates from the 16th century when, it is said, local fathers needed husbands for their daughters (because of the scarcity of eligible young men), so they kidnapped young Spanish sailors who stopped here for provisions en route to South America.

GETTING THERE

American Eagle (☎ 800/433-7300) flies five times daily from San Juan to Mayagüez (flight time: 45 min.). Depending on restrictions, round-trip passage ranges from $60 to $100 per person.

If you rent a **car** at the San Juan airport, it will take approximately 2¹/₂ hours to drive to Mayagüez via the busy northern Route 2, or 3 hours via the scenic mountain Route 52 to the south. The southern route via Ponce is easier.

WHERE TO STAY

Holiday Inn

2701 Rte. 2, km 149.9, Mayagüez, PR 00680-6328. ☎ **809/833-1100,** or 800/ HOLIDAY in the U.S. and Canada. Fax 809/933-1300. 147 rms, 5 suites. A/C TV TEL. $111– $141 single; $121–$151 double; $220 suite. Breakfast $8 extra. AE, DC, MC, V. Free parking.

Set 2 miles north of the city center, behind a parking lot and a well-maintained lawn, this six-story hotel opened in 1993. Clean, contemporary, and comfortable, it has a marble-floored, high-ceilinged lobby and a small swimming pool which offers a bit of breathing space for motorists traveling through Mayagüez. The bedrooms are functionally furnished in an international style, and there's a bar and restaurant, Holly's, on the premises.

Hotel Parador El Sol

Calle Santiago Riera Palmer, 9 Este, Mayagüez, PR 00680. ☎ **809/834-0303.** Fax 809/ 265-7567. 52 rms. A/C TV TEL. $44 single; $65 double. Breakfast $6 extra. AE, MC, V. Free parking.

This hotel provides some of the most reasonable and hospitable accommodations in this part of Puerto Rico, although it's far more geared to the commercial traveler than to the tourist. Furnishings are in the "no-frills style." Central to the shopping district and to all western-region transportation and highways, two blocks from the landmark plaza del Mercado in the heart of the city, the seven-floor restored hotel offers up-to-date facilities that include cable TV, a restaurant, and a swimming pool.

Mayagüez Hilton and Casino

Rte. 104 (P.O. Box 3629), Mayagüez, PR 00709. ☎ **809/831-7575,** or 800/HILTONS in the U.S. and Canada. Fax 809/834-3475. 141 rms, 4 suites. A/C MINIBAR TV TEL. $144–$156 single; $156–$220 double; from $300 suite. Breakfast $11.50 extra. AE, DC, MC, V. Parking $4.50.

This country club–style hotel is set on 20 acres of tropical gardens at the northern approach to the city, 3 miles from the airport. Its grounds have been designated an adjunct to the nearby Mayagüez Institute of Tropical Agriculture by the U.S. Department of Agriculture. There are no fewer than five species of palm trees, including the royal palm (native to Puerto Rico), eight kinds of bougainvillea, and numerous species of rare flora. The institute has the largest collection of tropical plants in the western hemisphere.

The hotel was built in 1964 and has been completely refurbished. The well-appointed rooms open onto the swimming pool, and many units contain private balconies. The year-round rates depend on whether you take a standard, superior, or a deluxe accommodation.

Dining/Entertainment: The Rôtisserie Dining Room serves a blend of Puerto Rican and international specialties, and buffets are presented four times a week. In the corner of the restaurant is the Chef's Corner, a small gourmet restaurant. The Hilton is also the entertainment center of the city. The casino, established in 1987, has free entrance and is open daily from noon to 4am. You can dance to the latest hits at the Baccus Music Club from 9:30pm to 3am or later Tuesday through Saturday; entrance is free for hotel guests, but nonresidents pay $8.

Services: Room service, laundry, babysitting.

Facilities: Olympic-size swimming pool, Jacuzzi, minigym, three tennis courts; deep-sea fishing, skin-diving, surfing, and scuba diving can be arranged. An 18-hole golf course is at Borinquen Field, a former SAC airbase, about 30 minutes from the Hilton.

WHERE TO DINE

La Rôtisserie

In the Mayagüez Hilton and Casino, Rte. 104. ☎ **809/831-7575.** Reservations recommended. Appetizers $7.50–$11.25; main courses $15.50–$32.50. Wed-night all-you-can-eat Italian buffet $21.50; breakfast buffet $11.25; lunch buffet Mon–Fri $15.95; Sun brunch buffet $21. AE, DC, MC, V. Breakfast daily 6:30–11am; lunch Mon–Sat 11:30am–2:30pm, Sun noon–3pm; dinner daily 6:30–10:30pm. INTERNATIONAL.

Considered the most elegant dining room in Mayagüez, it contains all the accoutrements (richly grained paneling, a formally dressed staff) of a fine European restaurant. Menu specialties, changing with the seasons, might include such dishes as spinach tortellini with smoked salmon and cream sauce, asopao of shrimp, several different kinds of steaks and grilled meats, fish such as salmon or red snapper, and a trio of dishes prepared flambé-style at your table from steak, shrimp, or lobster. Desserts are appropriately dramatic and caloric, and a full array of wines might complement any of your meals.

WHAT TO SEE & DO

The chief sight is the **Tropical Agriculture Research Station** (☎ 809/831-3435). At the administration office, ask for a free map of the tropical gardens, which contain one of the largest collections of tropical species useful to people, including cacao, fruit trees, spices, timbers, and ornamentals. The location is on Route 65, between Post Street and Route 108, adjacent to the University of Puerto Rico at Mayagüez campus and across the street from the **Parque de los Próceres** (Patriots' Park). The grounds are open free, Monday through Friday from 7am to 4pm.

Mayagüez might also be the jumping-off point for a visit to **Mona Island,** "the Galapagos of the Caribbean," which enjoys many legends of pirate treasure and is known for its white sand beaches and marine life. Accessible only by private boat or plane, the island is virtually uninhabited, except for two policemen and a director of the institute of natural resources. The island attracts hunters seeking pigs and wild goats, along with big-game fishers. But mostly it's intriguing to anyone who wants to escape civilization. Playa Sardinera on Mona Island was a nesting ground of pirates. On one side of the island, Playa de Pajaros, there are caves where the Taíno people left their mysterious hieroglyphs.

7 Ponce

Puerto Rico's second-largest city, Ponce—called "The Pearl of the South"—was named after Loíza Ponce de León, grandson of Ponce de León. Founded in 1692, it is today Puerto Rico's principal shipping port on the Caribbean Sea. The city is well kept and attractive, as reflected by its many plazas, parks, and public buildings. There is something in its lingering air that suggests a provincial Mediterranean town. Look for the *rejas* (framed balconies) of the handsome colonial mansions.

Maps and information can be found at the **tourist office,** on the second floor of the Citibank Building on plaza de las Delicias (☎ **809/841-8160**).

GETTING THERE

Ponce lies 75 miles southwest of San Juan and is reached by Route 52. There is no bus service between the two cities.

American Eagle (☎ 800/433-7300) flies twice a day between San Juan and Ponce (flight time: 40 min.) for $60 to $90 round-trip, depending on the ticket.

WHERE TO STAY

Meliá

Calle Cristina 2, Ponce, PR 00731. ☎ **809/842-0260.** Fax 809/841-3602. 74 rms. A/C TV TEL. $65–$80 single; $70–$85 double. (Includes continental breakfast.) AE, DC, MC, V. Parking $3.

A city hotel with southern hospitality, the Meliá—which has no connection with other hotels in the world bearing the same name—often attracts businesspeople. The location is a few steps away from Our Lady of Guadalupe Cathedral and from the Parque de Bombas (the red-and-black firehouse). The lobby floor and all stairs are covered with Spanish tiles of Moorish design. The desk clerks are well versed in English. The rooms are comfortably furnished and pleasant enough, and most have a balcony facing either busy calle Cristina or the old plaza. Breakfast is served on a rooftop terrace with a good view of Ponce, and the Hotel Meliá Restaurant serves some of the best cuisine in town. You can park your car in the lot nearby.

✪ Ponce Hilton and Casino

Avenida Santiago de los Caballeros 14 (P.O. Box 7419), Ponce, PR 00732. ☎ **809/259-7676,** or 800/HILTONS in the U.S. and Canada. Fax 809/259-7674. 148 rms, 8 suites. A/C MINIBAR TV TEL. $140 single; $160 double; $300 suite. Additional person $30 extra. Breakfast $9–$11 extra. AE, DC, MC, V. Parking $4.50.

Opened in 1993 on an 80-acre tract of land at the western end of avenida Santiago de los Caballeros, about a five-minute drive (7 miles) from the center of Ponce, this is the best-accessorized and most glamorous hotel in southern Puerto Rico. Designed like a miniature village, with turquoise-blue roofs, white walls, and lots of open-sided exposure to tropical plants, ornamental waterfalls, and gardens, it welcomes conventioneers and individual tourists alike. Accommodations contain tropically inspired furnishings, ceiling fans, terraces or balconies, and several luxurious extra amenities.

Dining/Entertainment: The most glamorous of the hotel's three restaurants is La Hacienda (recommended separately in "Where to Dine," below). Other choices include Terrazza, overlooking the sea, and a less formal selection for hamburgers and snacks, El Bohío. There's also a casino open daily from noon to 4am. Breakfasts, served from an elaborate buffet, are the best in Ponce.

Services: Room service, laundry, babysitting (if arranged in advance).

Facilities: A lagoon-shaped pool ringed with gardens, a business center with a supply of personal computers, a fitness center, a video arcade, a summer camp for children; water sports available.

WHERE TO DINE

El Ancla

Avenida Hostos Final 9, Playa Ponce. ☎ **809/840-2450.** Reservations not required. Appetizers $3–$10; main courses $9–$25. AE, DC, MC, V. Sun–Thurs 11am–10pm, Fri–Sat 11am–midnight. PUERTO RICAN/SEAFOOD.

Established by members of the Lugo family in 1978, this is considered among the best restaurants of Ponce. Much of its allure derives from its position south of the city on soaring piers that extend from the rocky coastline out over the surf. As you dine, the sound of the sea rises literally from beneath your feet.

Specialties, made with the catch of the day, might include red snapper served with a pumpkin flan, dorado in a tomato-brandy sauce, seafood casserole, and broiled lobster. Steak, veal, and chicken dishes are also available.

✪ La Hacienda/La Cava de la Hacienda

In the Ponce Hilton, avenida Santiago de los Caballeros 14. ☎ **809/259-7676.** Reservations recommended. Appetizers $6.50–$9.50; main courses $20–$25. AE, DC, MC, V. Dinner only, daily 6:30–10:30pm. INTERNATIONAL.

Set in the Ponce Hilton, these restaurants are the most elegant and stylish dining rooms in Ponce. Designed like a network of interconnected rooms in a 19th-century coffee plantation, they offer impeccable service and a dignified sense of formality. The menu at both restaurants is the same—only the ambience is different. La Hacienda is a high-ceilinged octagon, with plenty of room between tables and lots of exposed paneling. La Cava de la Hacienda resembles an underground wine cellar. There's also a pair of private dining rooms for groups of 6 to 10 diners.

Menu items change every two weeks, but might include snails in a pinot noir sauce, cheese fondue for two, a paillard of salmon with sorrel sauce, veal medallions, minted lamb chops, and lobster-stuffed ravioli. Desserts might include a flamed baked Alaska, crème brûlée, or apple beignets with honey-vanilla sauce.

La Montserrate

Sector Las Cucharas, Rte. 82. ☎ **809/841-2740.** Reservations not required. Appetizers $1.50–$6.95; main courses $14–$21. AE, DC, MC, V. Daily 10am–10pm. PUERTO RICAN/ SEAFOOD.

Beside the seafront, in a residential neighborhood about 4 miles west of the town center, this restaurant draws a loyal clientele from the surrounding houses. Considered a culinary institution in Ponce, it occupies a large, airy, modern building divided into two different dining areas. The first of these is slightly more formal than the next. Most visitors, however, head for the large room in back, where windows on three sides encompass a view of some offshore islands. Specialties, concocted from the catch of the day, might include octopus salad, four different kinds of asopao, a whole red snapper in Créole sauce, or a selection of different steaks and grills.

WHAT TO SEE & DO

IN PONCE

A $40-million restoration project is restoring more than 1,000 buildings to their original turn-of-the-century charm. Here architectural styles combine neoclassical with "Ponce Créole" and later art deco to give Ponce its distinctive ambience.

Any of the Ponceños will direct you to their ✪ **Museo de Arte de Ponce,** avenida Las Americas 25 (☎ **809/848-0505**). This excellent museum was donated to the people of Puerto Rico by Luís A. Ferré, a former governor. The building was designed by Edward Durell Stone (the designer of the New York Cultural Center), and it has been called the "Parthenon of the Caribbean." In spite of such a fanciful label, its collection represents principal schools of American and European art of the past five centuries. It's open daily from 10am to 5pm. Adults pay $3; children under 12, $2; and students, $1.

Most visitors head for the **Parque de Bombas,** plaza de las Delicias (☎ **809/ 840-4146, ext. 342**), the main plaza of Ponce. This old firehouse is fantastic— painted black and red. It was built for a fair in 1883. It's open Wednesday through Monday from 9:30am to 6pm.

Around from the firehouse, the trail will lead to the **Cathedral of Our Lady of Guadalupe,** calle Concordia/calle Union (☎ **809/842-0134**). Designed by architects Francisco Porrato Doría and Francisco Trublard in 1931, featuring a pipe organ installed in 1934, it remains an important place for prayer for many of Ponce's citizens. The cathedral, named after a famous holy shrine in Mexico, is probably the most famous church in southern Puerto Rico. A church has stood on this site since around 1600. It's open daily from 8am to noon and 3 to 6pm.

El Museo Castillo Serrallés, El Vigía 17 (☎ **809/259-1774**), is the largest and most imposing building in Ponce, built high on a hilltop above town by the Serrallés family (owners of a local rum distillery) during the 1930s. This is considered one of the architectural gems of Puerto Rico and probably the best evidence of the wealth produced by the turn-of-the-century sugar boom. Guides will escort you through the Spanish Revival house, where Moorish and Andalusian details include panoramic courtyards, a baronial dining room, a small café and souvenir shop, and a series of photographs showing the tons of earth that was brought in for the construction of the terraced gardens. It's open Tuesday through Sunday from 10am to 5pm. Admission is $3 for adults, $2 for senior citizens over 65, and $1.50 for children under 12 and students.

NEARBY

The oldest cemetery in the Antilles, excavated in 1975, is on Route 503 at km 2.7. The **Tibes Indian Ceremonial Center** (☎ **809/840-2255**) contains some 186 skeletons, dating from A.D. 300, as well as pre-Taíno plazas from A.D. 700. Bordered by the Portugues River, the museum is open Tuesday through Sunday from 9am to 4pm. Admission is $2 for adults and $1 for children. Guided tours in English and Spanish are conducted through the grounds. Shaded by trees are seven rectangular ball courts and two dance grounds. The arrangements of stone points on the dance grounds, in line with the solstices and equinoxes, suggest a pre-Columbian Stonehenge. A re-created Taíno village includes not only the museum but also an exhibition hall where you can see a documentary about Tibes; you can also visit the cafeteria and souvenir shop.

The **Hacienda Buena Vista,** Route 10, km 16.8 (☎ **809/284-7020**), lies a 30-minute drive north of Ponce. Built in 1833, it preserves an old way of life, with its whirring waterwheels and artifacts of 19th-century farm production. Once it was one of the most successful plantations on Puerto Rico, producing coffee, corn, and citrus. It was a working coffee plantation until the 1950s, and 86 of the original 500 acres are still part of the estate. The rooms of the hacienda have been furnished with authentic pieces from the 1850s. Tours, lasting two hours, are conducted Friday through Sunday at 8:30am, 11:30am, 1:30pm, and 3:30pm. Reservations are required; contact the Conservation Trust of Puerto Rico (☎ **809/ 722-5882** Monday through Friday; otherwise, call the hacienda directly). Tours cost $5 for adults, $2 for children. The hacienda lies in the small town of Barrio Magüeyes, on Route 10 from Ponce to Adjuntas.

8 Sports & Outdoor Activities Around the Island

Dorado Beach, Cerromar Beach, and Palmas del Mar are the chief centers for those seeking the golf, tennis, and beach life. San Juan's hotels on the Condado/Isla Verde coast also have, for the most part, complete water sports.

BEACHES   With some 300 miles of coastline, both Atlantic and Caribbean, Puerto Rico obviously has plenty of beaches in addition to the ones mentioned above. Some, such as Luquillo, are overcrowded, especially on Saturday and Sunday. Others are practically deserted. If you find that secluded, hidden beach of your dreams, proceed with caution. On unguarded beaches you'll have no way to protect yourself or your valuables should you be approached by a robber or mugger, which has been known to happen. For more information about the island's many beaches, call the **Department of Sports and Recreation** (☎ **809/722-1551**).

Beaches on Puerto Rico are open to the public, although you will be charged for parking and for use of *balneario* facilities, such as lockers and showers. The public beaches on the north shore of San Juan at **Ocean Park** and **Park Barbosa** are good, and can be reached by bus. **Luquillo,** on the north coast, is some 30 miles east of San Juan. Public beaches shut down on Monday; if Monday is a holiday, the beaches are open for the holiday but close the next day, Tuesday. Beach hours are 9am to 5pm in winter, to 6pm off-season.

Along the western coastal roads of Route 2, to the north of Mayagüez, lie what are reputed to be the best surfing beaches in the Caribbean. Surfers from as far away as New Zealand are attracted to these beaches. The most outstanding of all, comparable to the finest surfing spots in the world according to competitors in the 1988 World Surfing Championship held there, is at **Punta Higuero,** on Route 413 near the town of Rincón. In the winter months especially, uninterrupted Atlantic swells with perfectly formed waves averaging 5 to 6 feet in height roll shoreward, and rideable swells sometimes reach 15 to 25 feet.

DEEP-SEA FISHING   It's top-notch! Allison tuna, white and blue marlin, sailfish, wahoo, dolphin, mackerel, and bonito are some of the fish that can be caught in Puerto Rican waters, where 30 world records have been broken. Charter arrangements can be made through most major hotels and resorts.

It is said in deep-sea fishing circles that **Capt. Mike Benitez,** who has chartered out of San Juan for 42 years, sets the standard by which to judge other captains. In 1993, the *Sports Fishing Tournament Guide* listed him as one of the 15 most qualified sport-fishing captains in the world. Past clients have included, among others, ex-President Carter. Benitez Fishing Charters can be contacted directly at P.O. Box 5722, Puerto de Tierra, San Juan, PR 00906 (☎ **809/723-2292** until 6pm). The captain offers two boats, one a 45-foot air-conditioned deluxe Hateras, the *Sea Born,* and the other a 61-foot Davis (*Sea Born II*). Depending on the boat, fishing tours for parties of up to six cost $390 to $625 for a half-day excursion and $690 to $1,200 for a full day, with all equipment included.

Some of the best year-round fishing in the Caribbean is found in the waters just off Palmas del Mar, the resort complex on the southeast coast of Puerto Rico. There, **Capt. Bill Burleson,** P.O. Box 8270, Humacao, PR 00792 (☎ **809/850-7442**), operates charters on his fully customized 48-foot sport-fisherman, *Karolette,* which is electronically equipped for successful fishing. Burleson prefers to take fishing groups to Grappler Banks, 18 nautical miles away. The banks are two sea mounts, rising to about 240 feet below the surface and surrounded by deeps of 6,000 to

A Tropical Rain Forest

Some 25 miles east of San Juan lies El Yunque, the only tropical forest in the U.S. National Forest system. It was given national park status by President Theodore Roosevelt. With 28,000 acres, it's said to contain some 240 tree species (only half a dozen of which are found on the mainland United States). In this world of cedars and satinwood (draped in tangles of vines), you'll hear chirping birds, see wild orchids, and perhaps hear the song of the tree frog, the coquí. The entire forest is a bird sanctuary and may be the last retreat of the rare Puerto Rican parrot.

El Yunque is situated high above sea level, and the peak of El Toro rises to 3,532 feet. You can be fairly sure you'll be showered upon, as more than 100 billion gallons of rain falls here annually. But the showers are brief, and there are lots of shelters.

El Yunque offers a number of walking and hiking trails. One such trail is the rugged "El Toro," which passes through four different forest systems en route to the 3,523-foot Pico El Toro, the highest peak in the forest. El Yunque Trail leads to three of the recreation area's most spectacular lookouts, and Big Tree Trail is an easy walk to panoramic La Mina Falls. Just off the main road is La Coca Falls, a sheet of water cascading down mossy cliffs.

Nearby, the Sierra Palm Interpretive Service Center offers maps and information and arranges for guided tours of the forest. In the same vicinity is the popular El Yunque Restaurant, where visitors can take a break within earshot of the thunderous La Mina River.

A 45-minute drive from San Juan (Route 3 connecting with Route 191), El Yunque is a popular half-day or full-day outing. Major hotels provide guided tours. For more information about the park, call the rangers' office (☎ **809/887-2875**).

8,000 feet. They lie in the migratory paths of the wahoo, tuna, and marlin. A maximum of six people are taken out, costing $450 for four hours, $600 for six hours, and $800 for nine hours. He also offers snorkeling expeditions to Vieques at $75 per person for a five-hour trip.

GOLF   Among the major **tournaments** held in Puerto Rico is the Hyatt Senior Tour Championship in which the top 30 golfers of the Senior PGA Tour compete for a $1-million prize. The tournament is scheduled each December at the Hyatt Dorado Beach resort. Rums of Puerto Rico sponsors an annual Rums of Puerto Rico National Club Pro Am at the Hyatt Regency Cerromar Beach in November.

A golfer's dream, Puerto Rico has some splendid courses, and eight major ones—too many for me to document them fully here. Costs vary widely, depending on the course and the season, ranging from $15 to $95 for 18 holes. The **Hyatt Resorts Puerto Rico** at Dorado (☎ **809/796-1234**), with 72 holes of golf, constitutes the greatest concentration of the sport in the Caribbean. The 18-hole Robert Trent Jones, Sr., courses at the Hyatt Regency Cerromar and the Hyatt Dorado Beach match the finest anywhere.

The **Club de Golf,** at Palmas del Mar in Humacao (☎ **809/852-6000**), is one of the leading golf courses in Puerto Rico. On the southeast coast, it has a par-72,

6,690-yard layout designed by Gary Player. Crack golfers consider holes 11 through 15 the toughest five successive holes in the Caribbean.

The **Mayagüez Hilton** at Mayagüez (☎ **809/831-7575**) makes arrangements for guests to play at a 9-hole course at a nearby country club. **Punta Borinquén Golf Club** (☎ **809/890-2987**), at Aguadilla, the former Ramey Air Force Base, has an 18-hole public course, open daily from 7am to 7pm.

HORSEBACK RIDING   The equestrian center at **Palmas del Mar** (☎ **809/852-6000**) has 42 horses, including English hunters for jumping, plus a variety of trail rides and instruction at all levels of ability (see Section 4, above). The land set aside for equestrian pursuits abuts the resort's airstrip and is bounded on one side by a stream. Trail rides skirt this creek and follow paths through the coconut plantation and jungle, and along the beach. A trail ride lasts one hour and costs $20 per person.

HORSE RACING   Great thoroughbreds and outstanding jockeys compete all year at **El Comandante,** avenida 65 de Infanteria, Route 3, km 15.3 at Canovanas (☎ **809/724-6060**), Puerto Rico's only racetrack, a 20-minute drive east of the center of San Juan. Post time is at 2:15pm on Monday, Wednesday, Friday, and Sunday. A restaurant is open on race days from 12:30 to 4:30pm. Entrance to the clubhouse costs $3 per person, although there is no admission charged for the grandstand. Telephone for luncheon reservations; most credit and charge cards are accepted.

SCUBA/SNORKELING   The continental shelf, which surrounds Puerto Rico on three sides, contributes to an abundance of coral reefs, caves, sea walls, and trenches for scuba diving and snorkeling.

In San Juan, one of the best-recommended possibilities for underwater diving is **Karen Vega's Carib Aquatic Adventures,** P.O. Box 2470, San Juan Station, San Juan, PR 00902 (☎ **809/729-2929, ext. 240**). Most of its activities revolve around its main office in the rear lobby of the Radisson Normandie Hotel. The company offers diving certification from both PADI and NAUI as part of 40-hour

Spelunking, Anyone?

Río Camuy Cave Park contains the third-largest underground river in the world. It runs through a network of caves, canyons, and sinkholes that have been cut through the island's limestone base over the course of millions of years. Known to the pre-Columbian Taíno peoples, the caves came to the attention of speleologists in the 1950s. They were opened to the public in 1987.

Visitors first see a short film about the caves, then descend in open-air trolleys to the caverns. The trip takes you through a 200-foot-deep sinkhole and a chasm where tropical trees, ferns, and flowers flourish, along with birds and butterflies. The trolley then goes to the entrance of Empalme Cave, one of 16 in the Camuy caves network, where visitors begin a 45-minute walk, viewing the majestic series of rooms rich in stalagmites, stalactites, and huge sculptures formed over the centuries.

The caves are open Wednesday through Sunday from 8am to 4pm. Tickets are $6 for adults, $4 for children 2 to 12; senior citizens pay $3. Parking is $1. For more information, phone the park (☎ **809/898-3100**).

The site lies 2$^{1}/_{2}$ hours west of San Juan on Route 129, at km. 18.9.

courses priced at $330 each. A resort course for first-time divers costs $90. Also offered are kayak rentals (single or double) at $15 or $30 per hour, windsurfing (see below), and a choice of full-day diving expeditions to various reefs off the east coast of Puerto Rico or in San Juan. Private charter cruises start at $55 per person, with a maximum boat capacity of 35 persons on a 60-foot yacht, *San Antonio*.

Away from San Juan, several other companies offer scuba and snorkeling instruction.

Coral Head Divers & Water Sports Center, P.O. Box 10246, Humacao, PR 00792 (☎ **809/850-7208,** or **800/635-4529** in the U.S.), operates out of a building on the harbor at Palmas del Mar Resort. The dive center owns two fully equipped boats, measuring 26 and 38 feet. The center offers daily two-tank open-water dives for certified divers, plus snorkeling trips to Monkey Island and Vieques (see Section 9, below). The two-tank dive includes tanks, weights, and computer at $75. A snorkeling trip to Monkey Island includes use of equipment and beverage at $45 per person. A scuba resort lesson costs $40.

TENNIS   Again, the twin resorts of **Dorado** and **Cerromar** (☎ **809/796-1234**) have the monopoly on this game, with a total of 21 courts between them. The charge is $15 an hour, rising to $18 from 6 to 8pm. Lessons are available for $50 per hour.

In San Juan, the **Caribe Hilton & Casino** and the **Condado Plaza Hotel & Casino** have tennis courts. Also there's a **public court** at the old navy base, Isla Grande, Miramar. The entrance is from avenida Fernández Juncos at Stop 11.

The **Tennis Center** at Palmas del Mar in Humacao, the largest on Puerto Rico, features 20 courts. Court fees for hotel guests are $16 per hour during the day and $20 at night. Special tennis packages are available, including accommodations. Call **809/852-6000, ext. 51,** for more information.

WINDSURFING   Windsurfing is another water sport popular in Puerto Rico, with the sheltered waters of the Condado Lagoon in San Juan a favorite spot. Other sites include Ocean Park, Ensenada, Boquerón, Honda Beach, and Culebra. Throughout the island, many of the companies offering snorkeling and scuba diving also offer windsurfing equipment and instruction, and dozens of hotels offer the facility on their own premises.

One of the best places in San Juan to go windsurfing is at **Karen Vega's Carib Aquatic Adventures,** with its main branch in the rear lobby of San Juan's Radisson Normandie Hotel (☎ **809/729-2929, ext. 240**). Rentals cost $25 per hour, with a lesson costing $40.

One of the best places on the island's north shore is along the carefully maintained beachfront of the Hyatt Dorado Beach Hotel. Here the **Lisa Penfield Windsurfing School** (☎ **809/796-1234, ext. 3760,** or 809/796-2188) offers 90-minute lessons for $55 each; board rentals cost $45 per half day. Well supplied with a wide array of windsurfers, including some designed specifically for beginners and children, the school benefits from the almost uninterrupted flow of the north shore's strong, steady winds and an experienced crew of instructors.

The U.S. Virgin Islands

6

All three U.S. Virgin Islands are known for their sugar-white beaches, which are considered among the finest in the world. The most developed island in the chain is St. Thomas, with the largest concentration of shopping in the Caribbean at its capital, Charlotte Amalie. With a population of some 50,000, tiny St. Thomas isn't exactly a tropical retreat; you'll hardly have its beaches to yourself. The place abounds in bars and restaurants, including fast-food joints, and has a vast selection of hotels in all price ranges.

St. Croix is bigger, but more tranquil. A favorite with cruise-ship passengers (as is St. Thomas), St. Croix touts its shopping and has more stores than most islands in the Caribbean, especially in and around Christiansted, although it's not the shopping mecca Charlotte Amalie is. Its major attraction is Ruck Island, a national park that lies offshore. The place is peppered with inns and hotels and is "condo heaven."

St. John, the smallest of the three islands, is also the most beautiful and the least developed. Lying a few miles east of St. Thomas, it has only two big hotels. Some two-thirds of the island is a national park. Even if you visit only for the day while based on St. Thomas, you'll want to sample the "dream beach," Trunk Bay.

The U.S. Virgin Islands lie in two bodies of water: St. John is entirely in the Atlantic Ocean, St. Croix is entirely in the Caribbean Sea, and St. Thomas separates the Atlantic and the Caribbean. These islands enjoy one of the most perfect year-round climates in the world. They lie directly in the belt of the subtropical, easterly trade winds. At the eastern end of the Greater Antilles and the northern tip of the Lesser Antilles, the U.S. Virgins are some 60 miles east of Puerto Rico and 1,100 miles southeast of Miami.

GETTING THERE

Nonstop flights to the U.S. Virgin Islands from either New York or Atlanta usually take $3^3/_4$ and $3^1/_2$ hours, respectively. The flight time between St. Thomas and St. Croix is only 20 minutes. Flying to San Juan from mainland cities and changing planes may save you money over the APEX nonstop fare.

American Airlines (☎ **800/433-7300**) offers one of the easiest and most comprehensive routes into St. Thomas and St. Croix from the U.S. mainland. A daily nonstop flight departs from New York at 9:15am every day and arrives on St. Thomas at 2pm. Passengers originating in other parts of the world are usually routed to St. Thomas through American's hubs in Miami, San Juan, and Raleigh-Durham, all of which offer nonstop service (often several times a day) to St. Thomas. Connections from Los Angeles or San Francisco to either St. Thomas or St. Croix are usually made either through New York, San Juan, or Miami.

American's tour desk can arrange discount air passage if a hotel reservation is made through American at the same time. American's lowest fare to St. Thomas requires a 14-day advance payment, and a delay of between 3 and 30 days before activating the return portion. A penalty will be imposed if you make any changes before departure from North America. APEX fares vary with the season, and travel in both directions on Monday through Thursday usually saves money. Requesting a change of aircraft at American's hub in Puerto Rico, or opting for an early-morning or late-night flight might also save you money. Flights from Puerto Rico to the U.S. Virgin Islands are usually on American's partner, **American Eagle** (☎ **800/433-7300**).

Delta (☎ **800/221-1212**) offers two daily nonstop flights between New York's Kennedy International Airport and St. Thomas and a third nonstop flight from Atlanta to St. Thomas. Additionally, one of the New York flights provides connections to St. Croix.

TWA (☎ **800/221-2000**) does not fly nonstop into any of the Virgin Islands, but instead offers connections on other carriers through San Juan, Puerto Rico. TWA flies into San Juan twice daily nonstop from New York's JFK, once daily nonstop from Miami, and once daily from St. Louis, with a touchdown in Miami.

Travelers from the South and Midwest have better access to St. Thomas and St. Croix since **United Airlines** (☎ **800/241-6522**) formed an alliance with **Sunaire Express Airlines** (☎ **800/495-2840** for more information). Sunaire Express is a St. Croix–based commuter airline. The two companies agreed to a code-share that lists Sunaire flights from Puerto Rico to the U.S. Virgin Islands as connecting United Airlines flights. Passengers flying from Chicago, Miami, and other United Airlines points of origin to Puerto Rico are able to board any of 18 flights to St. Croix and St. Thomas via Sunaire. Under the agreement, the carriers coordinate their schedules and provide quick transfers of passengers and luggage.

Virgin Islands Paradise Airways (☎ **800/299-USVI** for more information) flies daily to St. Thomas and St. Croix, with nonstop flights originating in Miami and Newark. A professional crew, clad in island-style clothing, serves local cuisine, including pâtés and Cruzan rum, to guests aboard the 727-200s. Caribbean music serenades passengers, while a TV screen provides previews of places to see and things to do on St. Thomas, St. John, and St. Croix.

FAST FACTS: The U.S. Virgin Islands

Area Code   It's 809 for the U.S. Virgin Islands, and you don't need it for calls within the islands.

Banks   Several major banks are represented in the U.S. Virgins, although hours vary. They're usually open Monday through Thursday from 9am to 2:30pm and on Friday from 9am to 2pm and 3:30 to 5pm.

Customs   Every U.S. resident can bring home $1,200 worth of duty-free purchases, including a gallon of alcoholic beverages per adult. If you go over the $1,200 limit, you pay a flat 5% duty, up to an additional $1,000. You can also mail home an unlimited amount in gifts valued at up to $100 per day, which you don't have to declare. (At other spots in the Caribbean, U.S. citizens are limited to $400 or $600 worth of merchandise and a single bottle of liquor.)

Driving   Remember to *drive on the left.* This comes as a surprise to many visitors, who expect that U.S. driving practices will hold here. Of course, obey speed laws, which are 20 m.p.h. in towns, 35 m.p.h. outside.

Electricity   It's the same as on the mainland: 120 volts A.C., 60 cycles. No transformer, adapter, or converter is needed.

Holidays   In addition to the standard legal holidays observed in the United States, the islanders also observe the following: January 6 (Three Kings' Day), March 31 (Transfer Day—transfer of the Danish Virgin Islands to the Americans), June 20 (Organic Act Day—in lieu of a constitution, they have an "Organic Act"), July 3 (Emancipation Day, commemorating the freeing of the slaves by the Danes in 1848), July 25 (hurricane supplication day), October 17 (hurricane thanksgiving day), November 1 (Liberty Day), and December 26 (Boxing Day to the British but called Christmas Second Day in the U.S. Virgins). The islands also celebrate two carnival days on the last Friday and Saturday in April: Children's Carnival Parade and Grand Carnival (adults') Parade.

Information   Before you go, contact the **U.S. Virgin Islands Division of Tourism,** 1270 Ave. of the Americas, New York, NY 10020 (☎ **212/332-2222**). Branch offices are at 225 Peachtree St. NE, Suite 260, Atlanta, GA 30303 (☎ **404/688-0906**); 500 N. Michigan Ave., Suite 2030, Chicago, IL 60611 (☎ **312/670-8784**); 2655 Le Jeune Rd., Coral Gables, FL 33134 (☎ **305/442-7200**); 3460 Wilshire Blvd., Suite 412, Los Angeles, CA 90010 (☎ **213/739-0138**); and 900 17th St. NW, Suite 500, Washington, DC 20006 (☎ **202/293-3707**). Other offices outside the United States are found at 33 Niagara St., Toronto, ON M5V 1C2, Canada (☎ **416/362-8784**), and at 2 Cinnamon Row, Plantation Wharf, York Place, London SW11 3TW, England (☎ **0171/978-5262**).

Mail   The Virgin Islands are part of the U.S. Postal System, so postage rates are the same as on the mainland.

Newspapers   Daily newspapers from the mainland are flown to St. Thomas and St. Croix every day, and local papers such as the *Virgin Island Daily News* also carry the latest news. St. Croix has its own daily newspaper, the *St. Croix Avis.*

Safety   The U.S. Virgin Islands have more than their share of crime. St. John is safer than St. Thomas or St. Croix. But even on St. John there is crime, usually stolen possessions that were left unattended. Travelers should exercise extreme caution both day and night when wandering the backstreets of Charlotte Amalie on St. Thomas and both Christiansted and Frederiksted on St. Croix—muggings are commonplace in those districts. Avoid night strolls or drives along quiet roads. Never go walking on the beaches at night.

Time   The U.S. Virgins are on Atlantic standard time year round, which places the islands an hour ahead of eastern standard time. When it's 6am in the Virgin

Islands, it's still 5am in Florida. When the East Coast goes on daylight saving time, Virgin Island clocks and those on the mainland record the same time.

Tipping   As a general rule, it's customary to tip 15%. Some hotels add a 10% to 15% surcharge to cover service. When in doubt, ask.

Water   There is ample water for showers and bathing in the Virgin Islands, but you are asked to conserve. Hotels will supply you with all your drinking water. Many visitors drink the local tap water with no harmful after-affects. Others, more prudent or with more delicate stomachs, should stick to bottled water.

Weather   From November through February, temperatures average about 77° Fahrenheit. The average temperature divergence is 5° to 7°. Sometimes in August the temperature peaks in the high 80s, but the subtropical breezes keep it comfortably cool in the shade. The temperature in winter may drop into the low 60s, but this happens rarely.

1 St. Thomas

The busiest cruise-ship harbor in the West Indies, St. Thomas is the second largest of the U.S. Virgins, about 40 miles north of larger St. Croix. St. Thomas, with the U.S. Virgins' capital at Charlotte Amalie, is about 12 miles long and 3 miles wide. The capital is also the shopping center of the Caribbean (see "Savvy Shopping," below).

Hotels on the north side of St. Thomas face the Atlantic, and those on the south side front the calmer Caribbean. It's possible for the sun to shine in the south as the north experiences showers.

Holiday makers discovered St. Thomas right after World War II, and they've been flocking back in increasing numbers ever since. Shopping, sights, and sun prove a potent lure. Tourism has raised the standard of living here; it's now one of the highest in the Caribbean. Condominium apartments have grown up over the debris of bulldozed shacks.

St. Thomas is a boon for cruise-ship shoppers, who flood Main Street, the shopping center, basically three to four blocks long in the center of town. However, this center, which gets very crowded, is away from all beaches, major hotels, most restaurants, and entertainment facilities. At a hotel "out on the island," you can still find the seclusion you may be seeking.

If you're visiting in August, make sure you carry along mosquito repellent.

ORIENTATION
GETTING AROUND

BY BUS   St. Thomas has the best public transportation of any island in the U.S. chain. Administered by the government, they are called **Vitran buses,** and, depending on their route, service Charlotte Amalie, its outlying neighborhoods, and the countryside as far away as Red Hook. Vitran stops are found at reasonable intervals beside each of the most important traffic arteries on St. Thomas. Among the most visible are those that line the edges of Veteran's Drive in the capital. You rarely have to wait more than 30 minutes during the day, and they run between 6am and 9pm. A one-way ride costs 75¢ within Charlotte Amalie, $1 for rides from Charlotte Amalie to outer neighborhoods, and $3 for rides from Charlotte Amalie to other communities such as Red Hook, site of ferryboat departures to

St. Thomas

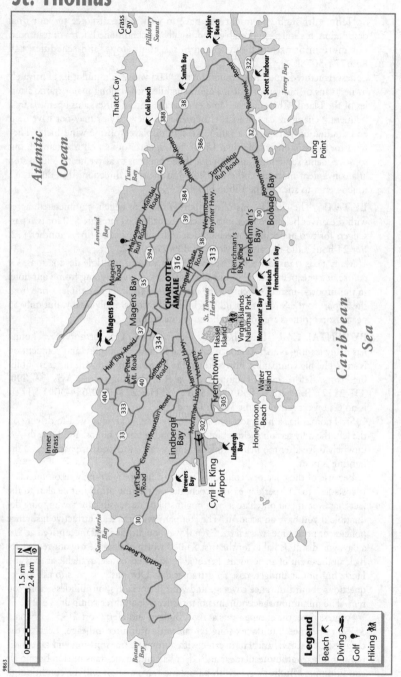

Legend

Beach ↖
Diving ⟋
Golf ⛳
Hiking 🚶

Atlantic Ocean

Caribbean Sea

Grass Cay

Pillsbury Sound

Sapphire Beach

Smith Bay

Secret Harbour

Coki Beach

Redhook Road

Thatch Cay

Jersey Bay

322

388

38

386

32

Tutu Bay

42

Turpentine Run Road

Long Point

Loveland Bay

Mandal Road

Smith Bay Road

384

39

Weymouth Rhymer Hwy.

Bolongo Bay

Magens Road

394

38

Frenchman's Bay Road

Gowen Road

30

Magens Bay

35

313

Frenchman's Bay

Mahogany Run Road

CHARLOTTE AMALIE

316

Sugar Estate Road

Frenchman's Bay

Magens Bay

37

Limetree Beach

Morningstar Bay

Frenchman's Bay

Half Bay Road

334

St. Thomas Harbor

Virgin Islands National Park

St. Peter Mt. Road

Solberg Road

Hassel Island

40

Harwood Hwy.

Veterans Dr.

404

Crown Mountain Road

Moravian Hwy.

Frenchtown

Water Island

Honeymoon Beach

333

Inner Brass

33

305

West End Road

Lindbergh Bay

302

Lindbergh Bay

Brewers Bay

Cyril E. King Airport

Santa Maria Bay

30

Fortuna Road

Botany Bay

N

0   1.5 mi
0   2.4 km

9863

St. John. Although you might still have to walk some distance to your final destination, it's still a comfortable (and usually air-conditioned) form of transport. For more information about Vitran buses, their stops, and schedules, call **809/774-5678.**

Less structured, and more erratic, are the **"taxi vans,"** a miniflotilla of privately owned vans or minibuses that make unscheduled stops along major traffic arteries of the island. Charging the same rates as the Vitran buses, and operated by a frequently changing cast of local entrepreneurs, they may or may not have their end destination written on a cardboard sign displayed on the windshield. They tend to be less comfortable than Vitran buses, and not as well maintained, but some residents sometimes opt for a ride if one happens to arrive near a Vitran stop at a convenient moment and if it's headed in the right direction. If in doubt, it's much better to stick to the Vitran buses.

BY TAXI   The chief means of transport is the taxi, which is unmetered; agree with the driver before you get into the car. Actually, taxi fares are $30 for two passengers for two hours of sightseeing; each additional passenger pays another $12. For 24-hour radio-dispatch service, call **809/774-7457.**

Many taxis transport 8 to 12 passengers in vans to multiple destinations. Of course, it's cheaper to travel in one of these—say, if you're going from your hotel to the airport—instead of renting the taxi all to yourself. For example, a ride from the airport to the Stouffer Grand Beach Resort costs $9 individually, but only $6 per person if others are going in the same direction.

BY RENTAL CAR   Partly because of its status as a U.S. territory, St. Thomas has many leading North American car-rental firms at the airport, and competition is stiff. The big companies, however, tend to be easier to deal with in cases of billing errors. Before you go, compare the rates of the "big three": **Avis** (☎ **800/331-2112**), **Budget** (☎ **800/626-4516**), and **Hertz** (☎ **800/654-3001**). There is no tax on car rentals in the Virgin Islands.

St. Thomas has a high accident rate: Many visitors are not used to driving on the left, the hilly terrain shelters blind curves and entrance ramps, and some drivers unwisely drive after too many drinks. In many cases, the roads are narrow and the lighting is poor.

Because of these factors, collision-damage insurance is strongly recommended. It costs $10 to $13 per day extra, depending on the fine print, but be alert to the fact that even if you purchase it, you might still be responsible for a whopping deductible if you have an accident. The company with the least attractive insurance policies, at press time, was Hertz. Even if you bought the insurance, priced at $13 a day, you'd still be liable for the first $3,000 worth of damage to your rented vehicle in the event of an accident. Personal accident insurance, available at Avis and Hertz but not at Budget, cost $3 extra per day. Obviously, it pays to ask lots of questions about insurance coverage and your financial responsibilities before you rent. The minimum age requirements for drivers at all three companies is 25.

At press time, the cheapest cars at Avis, Budget, and Hertz cost $193, $199, and $177, respectively, for week-long rentals with unlimited mileage. Each of the cheapest cars at Avis and Hertz came with automatic transmission and air conditioning, whereas the cheapest car at Budget had automatic transmission but no air conditioning. (Budget's cars with automatic transmission and air conditioning rented for a minimum of $219 per week, with unlimited mileage.) Each of the companies also offered larger cars, usually Mazdas, Suzukis, or Mitsubishis.

BY BOAT   If you're getting around by private boat, then you may want to get the *Yachtsman's Guide to the Virgin Islands,* available at major marine outlets, bookstores, book departments of major yachting publications, or direct from Tropic Isle Publishers, Inc., P.O. Box 610938, North Miami, FL 33261-0938 (☎ **305/ 893-4277**). The guide, revised annually, is supplemented by sketch charts, photographs, and landfall sketches and chartlets showing harbors and harbor entrances, anchorages, channels, and landmarks, plus information on preparations necessary for cruising the islands.

ESSENTIALS

American Express is represented on St. Thomas by the **Caribbean Travel Agency, Inc./Tropic Tours,** 9716 Estate Thomas, Suite 1 (☎ **809/774-1855**). It lies a five-minute drive east of Charlotte Amalie's center, opposite the entrance to the Havensight Shopping Mall. **St. Thomas Hospital,** the largest on the island with probably the best-equipped emergency room, is at 48 Sugar Estate, Charlotte Amalie (☎ **809/776-8311**), a five-minute drive east of the town's commercial center. **Radio weather reports** can be heard at 8:30am and 7:30pm on 99.5 FM.

WHERE TO STAY

Nearly every beach has its own hostelry. You may want to stay in the capital, Charlotte Amalie, or at any of the far points of St. Thomas. St. Thomas may have more quaint inns than any place else in the Caribbean. There is a 8% government hotel tax.

If you're interested in a condo rental, contact **Property Management Caribbean, Inc.,** 6222 Estate Nazareth, Suite 8, St. Thomas, USVI 00802 (☎ **809/ 775-6220,** or **800/524-2038**), which currently represents six condo complexes. Rental units range from studio apartments to four-bedroom villas suitable for up to eight people. Each has a fully equipped kitchen. Although no food is provided, a coffee starter set is. A minimum stay of three days is required in any season, seven nights around Christmas.

Ocean Property Management, Inc., P.O. Box 8529, St. Thomas, USVI 00801 (☎ **809/775-5901,** or **800/775-5901**), enjoys a repeat business of some 60%. Among other offerings, it rents accommodation at Secret Harbourview Villas, on a hillside in a garden setting. These are condo suites featuring private balconies with ocean views, lying a short walk from the beach. Several other St. Thomas locations with condo suites are also available for vacationers.

VERY EXPENSIVE

Bolongo Elysian Beach Resort

50 Estate Bolongo, Cowpet Bay (P.O. Box 7337), St. Thomas, USVI 00801. ☎ **809/ 779-2844,** or 800/524-4746. Fax 809/775-3208. 120 rms, 1 loft suite. A/C MINIBAR TV TEL. Winter, $285–$425 single or double; $690 two-bedroom loft suite for six. Off-season, $205– $275 single or double; $475 two-bedroom loft suite for six. (Includes continental breakfast.) AE, DC, MC, V. Free parking. Transportation: Hotel-owned open-air shuttle.

This elegant resort opened in 1989 on Cowpet Bay between a pair of upscale condo complexes in the East End. This resort has a Europeanized kind of glamour, and it's within a 20-minute drive of Charlotte Amalie. The thoughtfully planned bedrooms have balconies, and some offer sleeping lofts reached by a spiral staircase. The decor is tropical, with white ceramic-tile floors, rattan and bamboo furnishings, and natural-wood ceilings. The rooms are in a bevy of four-story buildings connected to landscaped gardens.

Facilities: Fitness center, swimming pool, snorkel gear, canoes, Sunfish, tennis court. A complementary shuttle service allows Elysian guests also to enjoy Bolongo's inclusive beach resort, Club Everything (see below), connecting them with a choice of three beaches, four pools, eight tennis courts, seven restaurants, five shops, and a full variety of nightly entertainment.

✪ Grand Palazzo

Great Bay, St. Thomas, USVI 00802. ☎ **809/775-3333**, or 800/545-0509. Fax 809/775-5635. 150 suites. A/C MINIBAR TV. Dec 20–Apr 2, $475–$865 suite for two; Apr 3–May and Nov 21–30, $350–$650 suite for two; June–Nov 20 and Dec 1–19, $250–$475 suite for two. MAP $65 per person extra. AE, DC, MC, V. Free parking.

The recent procurement of one of the last large tracts of seafront land on the island (15 acres with a panoramic view of St. John) was viewed as a minor triumph in its own right. Shortly after its acquisition, the developers of this luxury hotel hired some of the best architects, decorators, and landscape experts for the construction of what today is probably the most upscale and desirable hotel on St. Thomas. Set near Red Hook, it lies about 4½ miles southeast of Charlotte Amalie.

Opened in August 1992, the accommodations are in half a dozen three-story villas designed with motifs of the Italian Renaissance and Mediterranean colors like ocher yellow and burnt sienna. These encircle a freshwater pond (home to a colony of Bahamian ducks) whose boundaries were respected as part of the ecology-conscious theme. Guests register in the "reception palazzo," whose arches and accessories were inspired by a palace in Venice, before heading to bedrooms whose themes evoke Europe. These contain all the electronic amenities you'd expect (including a digital safe) and marble bathrooms. Public rooms carry nautical themes.

Dining/Entertainment: The Palm Terrace, set beneath rows of arcades, is the more formal of the hotel's two restaurants. Equally appealing is the Café Vecchio, whose murals depict the botanical diversity of a latter-day garden of Babylon. On the premises are a trio of bars, one of which has live piano music (in winter only).

Services: Concierge, 24-hour room service, top-notch tennis instructors, massage.

Facilities: Air-conditioned health club/gym, free use of Hobie cats and Sunfish, a 53-foot catamaran (*The Lady Lynsey*) for cocktail sails, four tennis courts, a swimming pool designed so that its water appears like an extension of the sea stretching toward St. John.

✪ Marriott's Morning Star Beach Resort

Frenchman's Reef Beach Resort, Flamboyant Point, Charlotte Amalie, St. Thomas, USVI 00802. ☎ **809/776-8500**, or 800/524-2000. Fax 809/776-3054. 96 rms. A/C MINIBAR TV TEL. Winter, $315–$395 single or double. Off-season, $195–$270 single or double. MAP $52 per person extra. AE, DC, MC, V. Free parking. Transportation: Water or land taxi from Charlotte Amalie.

Both its public areas and its plushly outfitted accommodations are among the most desirable on the island. They were built on the landscaped flatlands near the beach of the well-known Marriott's Frenchman's Reef Beach Resort (see below). The resort has five buildings, each containing between 16 and 24 units. Guests have the amenities and attractions of the large hotel nearby, yet maintain the privacy of an exclusive enclave. Each accommodation has rattan furniture; a color scheme of lilac, plum, and red mahogany; and views of the garden or beach. Swimming can be supplemented with a wide array of water sports.

Dining/Entertainment: Tavern on the Beach, the hotel's premier restaurant, is one of the most outstanding on the island (see my separate recommendation in "Where to Dine," below). Caesar's Ristorante, located on Morning Star Beach, serves lunch and dinner. The Oriental Terrace offers a Japanese cuisine. The Sand Bar is an ideal spot for sunset cocktails, and a variety of restaurants and bars are also available at the adjoining Marriott's Frenchman's Reef Beach Resort.

Services: Room service, babysitting, valet, plus all the services provided by Frenchman's Reef next door.

Facilities: The two giant swimming pools, four tennis courts, water-sports program including parasailing, diveshop, Jacuzzi, and private beach offered by Frenchman's Reef are shared by Morning Star.

Point Pleasant Resort

Estate Smith Bay No. 4, St. Thomas, USVI 00802. ☎ **809/775-7200**, or 800/524-2300. Fax 809/776-5694. 134 rms. A/C MINIBAR TV TEL. Winter, $275–$295 double. Off-season, $200–$265 double. Breakfast $10 extra. AE, MC, V. Free parking. Transportation: Taxi.

This all-suite private, unique resort on Water Bay sits on the far northeastern tip of St. Thomas. From your living room you look out on Tortola, St. John, and Jost Van Dyke. The complex is set on a 15-acre bluff with flowering shrubbery, frangipani trees, secluded nature trails, and lookout points. The hotel offers villa-style accommodations, based on double occupancy, all with kitchens. These are a series of condo units rented when the owners are away. The furnishings are light and airy, mostly rattan and floral fabrics.

Dining/Entertainment: The Agave Terrace is one of the finest restaurants on the island and offers three meals a day. The menu is a blend of nouvelle American dishes with Caribbean specialties.

Services: Complimentary use of a car four hours a day; shopping and dinner shuttle available.

Facilities: Three freshwater swimming pools, night-lit tennis courts, snorkeling equipment, Sunfish sailboats.

✪ Sapphire Beach Resort & Marina

Rte. 36, Smith Bay Rd. (P.O. Box 8088), St. Thomas, USVI 00801. ☎ **809/775-6100,** or 800/524-2090 in the U.S. Fax 809/775-4024. 171 suites and villas. A/C MINIBAR TV TEL. Winter, $295–$335 suite for two; $355–$395 villa for two. Off-season, $190–$225 suite for two; $235–$265 villa for two. Additional person $35 extra. Children 12 and under eat free if staying in parents' room. MAP $60 per person extra. AE, MC, V. Free parking. Transportation: Vitran bus.

One of the finest modern luxury resorts in the Caribbean is this secluded retreat in the East End. Guests can arrive by yacht and occupy a berth in the 67-slip marina or else take a suite or villa. The accommodations open onto a bay with one of St. Thomas's best beaches, and exude casual elegance. The beaches are two crescents broken by the coral-reef peninsula of Prettyklip Point. The suites have fully equipped kitchens and microwaves, bedroom areas, living/dining rooms with queen-size sofa beds, and large, fully tiled outdoor galleries with lounge furniture. Villas are on two levels: The main one contains the same amenities as the suites, while the upper level includes a second full bath, a bedroom and sitting area with a queen-size sofa bed, and a sun deck with outdoor furniture. Suites accommodate one to four guests, whereas villas are suitable for up to six guests.

Dining/Entertainment: Meals are served at the beach bar, and at night you can dine at the Seagrape, along the seashore, one of the island's finest eating places. Sometimes a five-piece band is brought in for dancing under the stars. For casual dining, the Sailfish Café features such standard fare as hamburgers but also Mexican dishes.

Services: Beach towels, daily chamber service, guest-services desk, babysitting.

Facilities: A 1-acre freshwater pool, snorkeling equipment, Sunfish sailboats, windsurfing boards, four all-weather tennis courts, waterfront pavilion with snack bar, complete diving center.

Stouffer Grand Beach Resort

Rte. 38, Smith Bay Rd. (P.O. Box 8267), St. Thomas, USVI 00801. ☎ **809/775-1510,** or 800/468-3571 in the U.S. Fax 809/775-2185. 254 rms, 36 suites. A/C MINIBAR TV TEL. Winter, $315–$435 single or double; from $895 suite for six. Off-season, $215–$355 single or double; from $550 suite for six. MAP $55 per person extra. AE, DC, MC, V. Free parking. Transportation: Vitran bus.

Seven miles northeast of Charlotte Amalie, perched on a steep hillside above a small beach, this resort occupies 34 acres on the northeast shore of St. Thomas. Accommodations are in two separate areas: poolside and hillside. The two-story town-house suites and one-bedroom suites have whirlpool spas, and all units are stylishly outfitted. Each accommodation has satellite color TV with HBO and Spectravision, a hairdryer, a robe, a safe, and an open balcony or patio.

Dining/Entertainment: You can enjoy beachfront breakfast, lunch, and dinner at Baywinds, which features continental and Caribbean cuisine. Dinner and Sunday brunch are served in Smugglers Bar and Grill. Lighter fare is offered at the poolside snack bar. For drinks, live entertainment, and dancing, there's the Baywinds Lounge.

Services: Concierge, daily children's program, round-the-clock babysitting, laundry service, tropical garden tour, 23-hour room service, twice-daily chamber service, newspaper and coffee with wake-up call.

ⓘ Family-Friendly Accommodations

Sapphire Beach Resort & Marina   *(see p. 151)* This resort does more for kids than most hotels on the island, and it even has supervised activities at the Little Gems Kids Klub. Children under 12 stay and eat free when accompanied by their parents.

Stouffer Grand Beach Resort   *(see p. 152)* This big resort offers a daily year-round children's program free for guests 3 to 14. The program is directed by counselor-supervised trained personnel. There's also a kiddie pool.

Bolongo Beach Resorts Club   *(see p. 153)* Ideal for families, this resort offers a free children's program called the Kid's Corner. Activities for ages 3 to 12 range from hermit crab races to tennis lessons and water aerobics.

Hyatt Regency St. John   *(see p. 179)* This hotel has a supervised activities program for ages 3 to 15 during the summer months, winter weekends, and certain holiday periods. A special children's menu is available in the restaurants.

Maho Bay   *(see p. 184)* The tents in this laid-back hideaway are really like small canvas houses, with kitchen areas and sun decks.

Facilities: Two swimming pools; daily scuba and snorkel lessons; free Sunfish sailboats, kayaks, windsurfers, snorkel equipment; on-site full-service dive shop; water-sports center, where you can arrange for day sails, deep-sea fishing, and other island excursions; six lit tennis courts; exercise facility; newsstand; gift shop, beauty salon. There's an 18-hole golf course 10 minutes away.

EXPENSIVE

Bluebeard's Castle

Bluebeard's Hill (P.O. Box 7480), Charlotte Amalie, St. Thomas, USVI 00801. ☎ **809/774-1600**, or 800/524-6599 in the U.S. Fax 809/774-5134. 170 rms. A/C TV TEL. Winter, $195–$235 single or double. Off-season, $150–$185 single or double. Additional person $30 extra. Breakfast $10 extra. MAP $50 per person extra. AE, DC, MC, V. Free parking.

Bluebeard's is a popular resort lying on one side of the bay overlooking Charlotte Amalie at the east end of the main street. The history of this spot dates from 1665. In the 1930s, the U.S. government turned what had been a private home into a hotel which, on one occasion, attracted Franklin D. Roosevelt.

The hill surrounding the hotel is now heavily built up with everything from offices to time-shares. Many guests prefer the rooms in the old tower, especially no. 139 or 140. Some 50 rooms in the newer unit, which also includes meeting rooms, have less charm. The guest rooms come in a wide variety of shapes and sizes—all pleasantly decorated. Transportation to the beach is provided by the hotel.

Dining/Entertainment: The Terrace Restaurant commands a panoramic view and offers many American and Caribbean specialties, open-air brunch, lunch, and late-night dining. The hotel also has another open-air restaurant, Entre Nous, which serves an international cuisine (see my recommendations in "Where to Dine," below).

Services: Free transportation to famous Magens Bay Beach.

Facilities: Freshwater swimming pool, two whirlpools, championship tennis courts.

Bolongo Beach Resorts Club Everything

50 Bolongo Estate, St. Thomas, USVI 00802. ☎ **809/779-2844**, or 800/524-4746 in the U.S. Fax 809/775-3208. 161 rms, 40 suites. A/C MINIBAR TV TEL. Winter, $235–$245 double; $260 suite for two. Off-season, $190–$205 double; $215 suite for two. (Includes all meals.) AE, DC, MC, V. Free parking. Transportation: Vitran bus.

The long-established Bolongo Beach Resorts has combined three of its four widely scattered hostelries into one sprawling complex that has welcomed more honeymooners than any other place on the island. It also operates the Bolongo Elysian Beach Resort (see above). This resort complex with its beachside location is called "Club Everything" because of the wide choice of activities it offers, ranging from scuba lessons to fitness centers to sports, especially tennis. The original Bolongo Villas and Bolongo Bay Beach are side by side on the same beach; a section originally known as "Limetree" is farther along the shoreline and is connected by minivan shuttles. This resort is a family affair, run by Dick and Joyce Doumeng, aided by their children. Club Everything offers handsomely furnished rooms and suites, set either beside beaches or in gardens, all with beachfront or ocean views along two palm-lined beaches.

Dining/Entertainment: The five restaurants include Viola's Calypso Kitchen, with West Indian food; Lord Rumbottom's, serving giant-cut prime ribs with a large salad bar; the Caribbean Lobster House; Coconut Henry's Family Restaurant, with a sundae bar; and Iggies Sing-along and Sports Bar.

Services: Open-air shuttle to town, babysitting.

Facilities: "Kid's Korner" program with a full range of challenging recreational activities for children 3 to 21, six tennis courts, three swimming pools with swim-up bars, scuba-diving club; fleet of private boats, spa and fitness center (with fully equipped weight room, outdoor aerobics deck, massage therapy, and herbal wraps).

Marriott's Frenchman's Reef Beach Resort

Flamboyant Point (P.O. Box 7100), Charlotte Amalie, St. Thomas, USVI 00801. ☎ **809/776-8500,** or 800/524-2000 in the U.S. Fax 809/776-3054. 421 rms, 18 suites. A/C MINIBAR TV TEL. Winter, $260–$295 single or double; from $428 suite. Off-season, $165–$190 single or double; from $248 suite. MAP $52 per person extra. AE, DC, MC, V. Free parking. Transportation: Water or land taxi from Charlotte Amalie.

Frenchman's Reef, lying 3 miles east of Charlotte Amalie, has a winning southern position on a projection of land overlooking both the harbor at Charlotte Amalie and the Caribbean. Everywhere you look are facilities devoted to the good life. To reach the private beach, you take a glass-enclosed elevator. The bedrooms vary greatly, but are generally traditionally furnished in quite good taste.

Dining/Entertainment: Seafood with a continental flair is served in Windows on the Harbour, which resembles the inside of a cruise ship and has a view of the harbor. The Lighthouse Bar was once an actual lighthouse. Caesar's offers an Italian cuisine at surfside. The Oriental Terrace features Japanese exhibition cooking on the teppanyaki grill. The Raw Bar offers fresh seafood appetizers and light meals daily from 11am to 11pm. In the evening, the Top of the Reef, a supper club, offers entertainment, or you can go to La Terraza lounge.

Services: Room service (7am to 10:30pm), laundry, babysitting.

Facilities: Two swimming pools with poolside bar, tennis courts, water sports (snorkeling, scuba diving, sailing, deep-sea fishing).

Pavilions & Pools

6400 Estate Smith Bay, St. Thomas, USVI 00802. ☎ **809/775-6110,** or 800/524-2001. Fax 809/775-6110. 25 villas. A/C TV TEL. Winter, $235–$255 single or double. Off-season, $175–$195 single or double. (Includes continental breakfast.) AE, DC, MC, V. Free parking. Transportation: Taxi.

Ideal for a honeymoon, this place offers your own villa, with floor-to-ceiling glass doors opening directly onto your own private swimming pool. The resort is a string of condominium units. After checking in, you don't have to see another soul until you check out. The fence and gate are high, and your space opens onto greenery. Around your own swimming pool is an encircling deck. Inside, a high room divider screens a kitchen. Each bedroom has plenty of closets behind louvered doors. The bath has a garden shower where you can bathe surrounded by greenery, yet you are protected from Peeping Toms.

Dining/Entertainment: A small bar and barbecue area is set against a wall on the reception terrace, where rum parties and cookouts are held. Informal, simple meals are served nightly. Occasionally a musician or singer entertains.

Services: A helpful front desk provides bookings for guided tours, day sails, and restaurant reservations.

Facilities: Free snorkeling gear, tennis courts.

Sugar Bay Plantation Resort

6500 Estate Smith Bay, St. Thomas, USVI 00802. ☎ **809/777-7100,** or 800/927-7100 in the U.S. Fax 809/777-3269. 294 rms, 6 suites. A/C TV TEL. Winter, $270–$370 single or double; $550–$795 suite. Off-season, $180–$280 single or double; $450–$595 suite. MAP $35 per person extra. AE, DC, MC, V. Free parking.

This hotel lies on the East End, a five-minute ride from Red Hook, adjacent to the Stouffer Grand Beach Resort. It was built in 1992 as an upscale branch of the Holiday Inn chain. It contains a central core where visitors register, and at least six pale-green and white-sided outbuildings, each with three or five stories, that contain the accommodations. About 90% of these have balconies and ocean views, and each contains a wall safe, a coffee maker, a hairdryer, and an unstocked refrigerator. Decors include rattan furniture and pastel color schemes inspired by the tropics.

Dining/Entertainment: The resort has several food and beverage outlets, the most glamorous of which is the Manor, serving American food in a re-creation of a colonial plantation house. The Ocean Club Bar, near the hotel lobby, evokes a lounge in a cruise ship, complete with big windows and a sweeping view over the sea. Also available is a poolside bar and snack bar.

Services: Room service, babysitting, tour desk.

Facilities: Three swimming pools, sandy beach, health club, availability of snorkeling equipment. Its tennis facilities are the finest on the island, containing the first stadium tennis court, with a seating capacity of 220, plus six additional Laykold courts, lit at night, and a pro shop.

MODERATE

Ⓢ Blackbeard's Castle

Blackbeard's Hill (P.O. Box 6041), Charlotte Amalie, St. Thomas, USVI 00801. ☎ 809/776-1234, or 800/344-5771 in the U.S. Fax 809/776-4321. 18 rms, 3 junior suites, 3 full suites. A/C TV TEL. Winter, $110 single; $140 double; $170 junior suite for two; $190 full suite for two. Off-season, $75 single; $95 double; $120 junior suite for two; $145 full suite for two. (Includes continental breakfast.) AE, MC, V. Free parking. Directions: From the airport, turn right onto Route 30; when you get to Route 35, take a left turn and travel for half a mile until you see the sign pointing left to the hotel.

An Illinois businessman, Bob Harrington, and his Brazilian partner, Henrique Konzen, transformed what had been a private residence into a genuinely charming inn that enjoys one of the finest views of Charlotte Amalie and the harbor, thanks to its perch high on a hillside above the town. In 1679 the Danish governor erected a soaring tower of chiseled stone here as a lookout for unfriendly ships. Legend says that Blackbeard himself lived in the tower half a century later. Each bedroom has a semisecluded veranda, a flat-weave Turkish kilim, terra-cotta floors, simple furniture, and a private bath. Guests enjoy use of a swimming pool, and the establishment's social center is the stylish bar and restaurant (see "Where to Dine," below). Live jazz is presented in the lounge Tuesday through Sunday.

Ⓢ Hotel 1829

Kongens Gade (P.O. Box 1567), Charlotte Amalie, St. Thomas, USVI 00804. ☎ **809/776-1829,** or 800/524-2002 in the U.S. Fax 809/776-4313. 13 rms, 2 suites. A/C MINIBAR TV TEL. Winter, $70–$160 single; $80–$170 double; from $220 suite. Off-season, $50–$110 single; $60–$120 double; from $155 suite. (Includes continental breakfast.) AE, MC, V. Free parking.

Built by a French sea captain for his bride, this place was designed by an Italian architect in a Spanish motif. Danish and African labor completed the structure in 1829—hence the name. After a major renaissance, this once-decaying historical site has become one of the leading small hotels of character in the Caribbean. Right in the heart of town, it stands about three minutes from Government House and was built on a hillside with many levels and many steps (no elevator)—it's reached by a climb. The 1829 has actually been a hotel since the 19th century and has entertained King Carol of Rumania (and his mistress, Madame Lupescu), Edna St. Vincent Millay, and Mikhail Baryshnikov.

Amid a cascade of flowering bougainvillea are the upper rooms, which overlook a central courtyard with a miniature swimming pool. The rooms, some of which are boxlike and small, are well designed, comfortable, and attractive; most face the sea. During the restoration, the old was preserved wherever possible, and some rooms have antiques. The hotel lies a 15-minute ride from the beach.

⑤ Villa Blanca

4 Raphune Hill, Rte. 38, Charlotte Amalie, St. Thomas USVI 00801. ☎ **809/776-0749.** Fax 809/779-2661. 12 rms. TV. Winter, $115–$125 single; $125–$135 double. Off-season, $75–$85 single; $85–$95 double. AE, DC, MC, V. Free parking.

Small, intimate, and charming, this small-scale hotel lies 1 1/2 miles east of Charlotte Amalie on 3 secluded acres of hilltop land, which connoisseurs claim is some of the most panoramic on the island. Originally built in 1953 as the private home of Christine Cromwell, heiress to the Dodge fortune, its main building served as the private home of its present owner, Blanca Terrasa Smith, between 1973 and 1985. After the death of her husband, Mrs. Smith added a 12-bedroom annex in her garden and opened her grounds to paying guests.

Each of the rooms contains a ceiling fan and/or air conditioning, a well-equipped kitchenette, and a private balcony or terrace with sweeping views either eastward to St. John or westward to Puerto Rico and the harbor of Charlotte Amalie. No meals of any kind are served on the premises, but nonetheless a home-like and caring ambience prevails. On the premises are a freshwater swimming pool and a large covered patio.

⑤ Windward Passage Hotel

Veterans Dr. (P.O. Box 640), St. Thomas, USVI 00804. ☎ **809/774-5200,** or 800/524-7389 in the U.S. Fax 809/774-1231. 140 rms. 11 junior suites. A/C TV TEL. Winter, $125–$150 single; $135–$160 double; $180–$230 junior suite. Off-season, $90–$125 single; $100–$135 double; $140–$180 junior suite. (Includes continental breakfast.) AE, DC, MC, V. Free parking. Transportation: Vitran bus.

One of the best choices if you'd like to be in the center of Charlotte Amalie, only a 10-minute taxi ride east of the airport, this many-balconied hotel enjoys one of the highest rates of repeat reservations on the island. Built in 1968 and last renovated in 1992, its rooms are arranged around a massive central atrium, which contains a soaring concrete fountain, the On the Bay restaurant serving an Italian cuisine, a bar with a devoted local clientele, a rectangular swimming pool, and a variety of facilities for children. There is no beach nearby, but there are frequent shuttle buses to and from Magens Bay, Morningstar Beach, and Sapphire Beach. Although the 54 harborfront rooms have views of some of the world's largest cruise ships, and are also subject to street noise, many frequent visitors request a bedroom overlooking the adjacent Emile Griffith Park, where baseball games provide the entertainment. The bedrooms are pastel colored and comfortably modern, with marble-trimmed bathrooms.

INEXPENSIVE

The Admiral's Inn

Villa Olga (P.O. Box 6162), Frenchtown, Charlotte Amalie, St. Thomas, USVI 00802. ☎ **809/774-1376,** or 800/544-0493 in the U.S. 16 rms. A/C TV TEL. Winter, $99–$159 single or double. Off-season, $89–$129 single or double. Children under 12 stay free in parents' room. (Includes continental breakfast.) AE, MC, V. Free parking. Transportation: Vitran bus.

Set on a peninsula in Frenchtown near the western entrance to Charlotte Amalie's harbor, this beachfront hotel, which attracts yachtspeople and divers, provides modern lodging in a relaxed setting with both harbor and oceanfront views. The secluded yet central location is just a short walk to town. The rooms sit on a landscaped hillside, each refurbished in 1992. The freshwater pool was terraced into the slope and has a large sun deck and flowering borders. The saltwater beach and sea pool lie a few paces from the lanai-style ocean-view rooms. Full breakfasts and light lunches are available, and the poolside bar remains open for guests throughout the morning and afternoon. Dinner is served in the on-site Chart House Restaurant (see "Where to Dine," below).

Bunkers' Hill Hotel

7 Commandant Gade, Charlotte Amalie, St. Thomas, USVI 00802. ☎ **809/774-8056.** Fax 809/774-3172. 11 rms, 4 suites. A/C TV TEL. Winter, $70 single; $80 double; $90 suite. Off-season, $59 single; $69 double; $79 suite. (Includes continental breakfast.) MC, V. Free parking.

This clean and centrally situated guest lodge is suitable for anyone on an economy budget who doesn't want to sacrifice comfort and safety, and doesn't mind putting up with some street noise. Some of the accommodations share a small kitchenette, and 10 of them contain balconies, some with a view of the city and sea. In 1990 the hotel was upgraded with a new lobby and improved furnishings. The management prepares meals for guests with advance notice.

Galleon House

Government Hill (P.O. Box 6577), Charlotte Amalie, St. Thomas, USVI 00804. ☎ **809/774-6952,** or 800/524-2052 in the U.S. Fax 809/774-6952. 14 rms (13 with bath). A/C TV TEL. Winter, $59 single without bath, $109 single with bath; $69 double without bath, $119 double with bath. Off-season, $49 single without bath, $69 single with bath; $59 double without bath, $79 double with bath. (Includes continental breakfast.) AE, MC, V. Free parking.

The main attraction of this place is its location, at the east end of Main Street, next to the Hotel 1829 on Government Hill, about one block from the main shopping section of St. Thomas. You'll walk up a long flight of stairs past a neighboring restaurant's veranda to reach the concrete terrace that doubles as this hotel's reception area.

The rooms are scattered in several hillside buildings, and each contains a ceiling fan and a cable TV with HBO. Some rooms have private balconies and refrigerators. There's also a small freshwater pool and sun deck. Breakfast consists of a variety of freshly prepared items such as waffles and assorted muffins, and is served on a veranda overlooking the harbor.

Ⓢ Heritage Manor

1A Snegle Gade (P.O. Box 90), Charlotte Amalie, St. Thomas, USVI 00804. ☎ **809/774-3003,** or 800/828-0757 in the U.S. Fax 809/776-9585. 8 rms (4 with bath), 2 apartments. A/C. Winter (including continental breakfast), $70 single or double without bath; $95 double with bath; $115–$130 apartment. Off-season, $55 single or double without bath; $75 double with bath; $85–$95 apartment. AE, MC, V. Free parking.

This 150-year-old restored Danish merchant's town house is located in the historic district of Charlotte Amalie, about four blocks from the sea. Intimate and personal, it offers well-furnished, comfortable bedrooms and two apartments with kitchens. The rooms contain many extras, including fans, hairdryers, and refrigerators. Most of the accommodations have a view of the harbor. The small inn has a freshwater pool installed in a former Danish bakery complete with a chimney. A taxi, van, or bus will take you to the nearest beaches. Be careful walking back to the guesthouse at night through the back streets of Charlotte Amalie.

Island View Guesthouse

11-C Contant (P.O. Box 1903), St. Thomas, USVI 00803. ☎ **809/774-4270,** or, for reservations only, 800/524-2023. Fax 809/774-6167. 15 rms (13 with bath). TV TEL. Winter, $60 single without bath, $94 single with bath; $65 double without bath, $99–$119 double with bath. Off-season, $40 single without bath, $68 single with bath; $45 double without bath, $73–$93 double with bath. (Includes continental breakfast.) AE, DC, MC, V. Free parking. Directions: From the airport, turn right to Route 30; then cut left and continue to the unmarked Scott Free Road where you go left and look for the sign.

The Island View is located in a steeply inclined neighborhood of private homes and villas about a seven-minute drive west of Charlotte Amalie. Set 545 feet up Crown Mountain, it has sweeping views over Charlotte Amalie and the harbor. Family owned and managed, it was originally built in the 1960s as a private home. Enlarged in 1989, it contains main-floor rooms (two without private bath) and some poolside rooms, plus six units in a recent addition (three with kitchens and all with balconies). The bedrooms are cooled by breezes and fans, and the newer ones have optional air conditioning. A self-service open-air bar on the gallery operates on the honor system.

WHERE TO DINE

The cuisine on St. Thomas is among the top in the entire West Indies. Prices, unfortunately, are high, and many of the best spots can only be reached by taxi. With a few exceptions, the finest and most charming restaurants aren't in Charlotte Amalie, but are out on the island.

IN CHARLOTTE AMALIE

Blackbeard's Castle

Blackbeard's Hill. ☎ **809/776-1234.** Reservations recommended for dinner. Appetizers $5–$10.75; main courses $17.50–$27.50; Sun brunch from $12. AE, MC, V. Lunch Mon–Fri 11:30am–2:30pm; dinner daily 6:30–9:30pm; brunch Sun 11am–3pm. AMERICAN/CARIBBEAN.

This previously recommended hotel above the town offers an elegant dining room, with one of the best harbor views of the island, featuring a contemporary American cuisine with a Caribbean flair. Awarded three gold meals for ambience, Caribbean dishes, and overall food in local contests, owners Bob Harrington and Henrique Konzen offer one of the best Sunday brunches on the island.

Guests have a wide choice of appetizers, including sautéed escargots with sun-dried tomatoes or pan-seared langostino cakes with a roasted red-pepper sauce. There is also the chef's daily selection of hot or chilled soups, plus an array of salads including the classic Caesar's. Pastas, such as cheese tortellini with smoked chicken breast, are available in half portions as appetizers. Main courses are likely to feature veal chop stuffed with fresh vegetables, Black Forest ham, and mozzarella; grilled swordfish steak with a tropical salsa; or pan-seared red snapper filet with a fresh-fruit/butter sauce. The dessert menu, a treat unto itself, is likely to feature everything from Bailey's Irish Cream cheesecake to frozen peanut-butter pie with a chocolate drizzle. Lunches are slightly less elaborate and are about one-third the price. In winter, live jazz is presented Tuesday through Saturday from 8pm to midnight.

Entre Nous

In Bluebeard's Castle, Bluebeard's Hill. ☎ **809/776-4050.** Reservations recommended. Appetizers $7–$15; main courses $19–$38. AE, MC, V. Dinner only, Mon–Sat 6:30–9:30pm. Closed Sept. FRENCH/ITALIAN.

This long-established restaurant operates under independent management in one of the most famous hotels of St. Thomas (see "Where to Stay," above), and serves some of the island's best cuisine. An open-air restaurant, it offers dinners by candlelight and a sweeping view of the faraway harbor. Caesar salad will be prepared at your table, followed by Caribbean lobster prepared any way you like, perhaps Fra Diavolo style, or more simply with garlic butter. Also appealing are pepper-crusted filet of venison with lingonberry sauce, seafood melange with garlic-butter sauce, chateaubriand with herbs, and roast duckling with onions, fresh thyme, and olives. Dessert might be baked Alaska or bananas Foster prepared at your table. Wines derive from France, Italy, California, and Australia.

Hard Rock Café

In International Plaza, The Waterfront, Queen's Quarter. ☎ **809/777-5555.** Reservations not accepted. Appetizers $5.95–$7.95; main dishes $8.95–$13. AE, MC, V. Tues–Thurs and Sun 11am–10pm, Fri–Sat 11am–midnight. AMERICAN.

Occupying the second floor of a pink-sided mall whose big windows overlook the ships moored in Charlotte Amalie's harbor, this restaurant is a member of the international chain that defines itself as the Smithsonian of Rock 'n' Roll. Entire walls are devoted to the memorabilia of such artists as John Lennon, Eric Clapton, and Bob Marley. Throughout most of the day the place functions as a restaurant, serving barbecued meats, salads, sandwiches, burgers, fresh fish, and steaks. On Friday and Saturday nights a live band performs.

Hotel 1829

Kongens Gade. ☎ **809/776-1829.** Reservations recommended, but not accepted more than one day in advance. Appetizers $7.50–$11.50; main courses $21–$40. AE, DC, MC, V. Dinner only, Mon–Sat 6–10pm. Closed Sun May–Nov. CONTINENTAL.

At the east end of Main Street, the Hotel 1829 is graceful and historic (see "Where to Stay," above), and its restaurant serves some of the finest food on St. Thomas. Guests head for the attractive bar for a before-dinner drink. Dining is on a terrace or in the main room, whose walls are made from ships' ballast. The floor is made of Moroccan tiles, two centuries old. The cuisine has a distinctively European twist, with many dishes prepared and served from trolleys beside your table. For an appetizer, try assorted seafood cocktail, cold cucumber soup, or lobster bisque. Fish and meat dishes are usually excellent and might include yellowtail, snapper amandine, roast rack of lamb with rosemary hollandaise, or pasta paella. The chateaubriand for two is a house specialty. Dessert might be an array of soufflés, such as chocolate, amaretto, and raspberry.

Virgilio's

18 Dronningens Gade. ☎ **809/776-4920.** Reservations recommended. Appetizers $8.95–$11.95; main dishes $12–$25. AE, MC, V. Lunch Mon–Sat 11:30am–4pm; dinner Mon–Sat 4–10:30pm. ITALIAN.

Considered one of the best Italian restaurants in the Virgin Islands, this restaurant is sheltered under heavy ceiling beams and brick vaulting which remains the way it was originally designed 200 years ago. Be alert to the position of its entrance, set on a narrow alleyway running between Main Street and Back Street. A well-trained staff attends to only 12 tables at one of the smallest and most intimate restaurants on St. Thomas. Menu specialties include the full repertoire of northern Italy, including homemade pastas, elegant salads, such seafood dishes as red snapper l'amatriciana, cioppino (a savory seafood stew), and veal chop celestino (stuffed with prosciutto, mozzarella, and mushrooms), and an extensive array of desserts, many of them flambéed.

AT COMPASS POINT

For the Birds

Scott Beach, near Compass Point. ☎ **809/775-6431.** Reservations not required. Appetizers $3.50–$12; main courses $10–$20. AE, MC, V. Lunch daily 11am–3pm; dinner daily 6–10:30pm. TEX-MEX.

Set in a low-slung bungalow whose green roof matches the growth around it, this restaurant east of Charlotte Amalie offers reasonably priced, well-prepared food in gargantuan helpings. The surf and a sandy beach are a few steps away. Select heaps of nachos or an entire loaf of deep-fried onion rings, a plate of the best baby back ribs on the island, filet mignon, or southern fried catfish. Shrimp "in the rough" which you peel yourself is another popular item. There's also a selection of such Mexican specialties as beef or chicken enchiladas, chimichangas, and burritos. Margaritas are huge—46 ounces. A DJ plays music nightly.

Raffles

In Compass Point Marina. ☎ **809/775-6004.** Reservations required. Appetizers $5–$8; main courses $12–$25. AE, MC, V. Dinner only. Tues–Sun 6:30–10:30pm. Transportation: Taxi. CONTINENTAL/SEAFOOD.

Named after the legendary hotel in Singapore, this establishment is filled with tropical accents more evocative of the South Pacific than of the Caribbean. The furnishings include peacock chairs, lots of wicker, and ceiling fans. In honor of the Australian homeland of its owners, Sandy and Peter Englesberger, the restaurant sports a Christmas tree that hangs upside down throughout the year. You can choose from fresh seafood, beef, veal, lamb, chicken, and marinated two-day duck. The fish of the day is freshly caught and well prepared with tasty sauces. Or you might try Maryland softshell crabs; sautéed conch with garlic, white wine, and shallots; or grilled quail with juniperberries. Raffles nestles beside the lagoon at Compass Point, east of Charlotte Amalie. Established in 1977, this was the first of the many restaurants that later sprang up in Compass Point.

Windjammer Restaurant

In Compass Point Marina, off Rte. 32. ☎ **809/775-6194.** Reservations recommended. Appetizers $3.75–$7.75; main dishes $7.75–$18.75. MC, V. Lunch Mon–Sat 11:30am–5pm; dinner Mon–Sat 5–10pm. Closed Sept. Transportation: Taxi. AMERICAN/GERMAN.

The paneling and smoothly finished bar of this cozy place are crafted largely from thick slabs of mahogany. After dark, oil lamps add a nautically romantic glow to a relaxed atmosphere with traces of tropical *gemütlichkeit*. The restaurant is in a seaport village a mile west of Red Hook, near the easternmost tip of the island.

The extensive menu features more than 40 main dishes, many reflecting the restaurant's German heritage. These might include red snapper Adlon (boneless filet of snapper topped with shrimp and mushrooms), rahmschnitzel (veal medallions in a richly flavored cream sauce), chicken à la Bremen (casserole of boneless chicken breast with mussels, peas, mushrooms, shrimp, and asparagus), and jagertopf (filet mignon served with strips of veal, onions, mushrooms, and a red-wine-and-cream sauce). Appetizers include escargots in garlic butter and veal soup. The classic desserts—key lime pie, a light and creamy cheesecake, chocolate rum cake (made with aged local rum), and apple strudel—are all homemade.

AT FRENCHTOWN

Alexander's

Rue de St. Barthélemy. ☎ **809/776-4211.** Reservations recommended. Appetizers $5.25–$8.50; main courses $12–$20. AE, MC, V. Lunch Mon–Fri 11am–5pm, Sat 11am–3pm; dinner daily 5:30–10pm. Transportation: Vitran bus. AUSTRIAN/GERMAN.

Alexander's, west of town, will accommodate you at one of its 12 tables in air-conditioned comfort with picture windows overlooking the harbor. It's named for its Austrian-born owner, Alexander Treml. There's a heavy emphasis on seafood, including conch schnitzel. Other dishes include a mouth-watering wienerschnitzel, Nürnberger rostbraten, goulash, and homemade pâté. For dessert, try the homemade strudel, either apple or cheese, or the Schwartzwald torte. Lunch consists of a variety of crêpes, quiches, and a daily chef's special. At both lunch and dinner, the menu offers a selection of at least 15 different pasta dishes. The establishment's bar keeps the same hours as the restaurant.

⑤ Café Normandie

Rue de St. Barthélemy. ☎ **809/774-1622.** Reservations recommended. Appetizers $5.50–$14.50; fixed-price dinner $29.50–$38.50. AE, MC, V. Dinner only, 6–10pm. Closed Mon in summer. Transportation: Vitran bus. FRENCH.

The fixed-price meal offered here is one of the best dining values on the island: It begins with soup, although you have a choice of ordering an à la carte appetizer. Then you're served a salad and sorbet before your main course, which you select from specialties ranging from lobster mornay to the poached catch of the day in white wine. The dessert special (not featured on the fixed-price meal) is their original chocolate-fudge pie, and the chef definitely will not divulge the recipe. The restaurant is air-conditioned, and the glow of candlelight makes it quite elegant. The service is excellent. There is also a relaxed informality about the dress code, but you shouldn't show up in a bathing suit.

Chart House Restaurant

In the Admiral's Inn, Villa Olga, Frenchtown. ☎ **809/774-4262.** Reservations recommended. Appetizers $4.95–$8.95; main courses $16.95–$29.95; fixed-price dinner (until 6:30pm) $14.95. AE, DC, MC, V. Dinner only, Sun–Thurs 5–10pm, Fri–Sat 5–11pm. STEAK/SEAFOOD.

The restaurant is on the same property as this previously recommended hotel (the site of the Russian consulate in the 19th century), but is run separately. The dining gallery is a large open terrace fronting the sea. Cocktail service starts at 5pm daily, and the bartender will make you his special drink, called a Bailey's banana colada. The restaurant features the best salad bar on the island, with a choice of 30 items, which comes with the dinner. Steaks are a specialty, but menu choices range from chicken teriyaki to Australian lobster tail. Of course, this chain is known for serving the finest cut of prime rib anywhere. For dessert, order the famous Chart House "mud pie."

● Provence

Rue de St. Barthélemy. ☎ **809/777-5600.** Reservations recommended. Appetizers $4.50–$12; main dishes $13–$18.50. AE, MC, V. Dinner only, daily 6–10:30pm. Closed Sun off-season. PROVENÇAL/MEDITERRANEAN.

Established in 1993, this is a well-managed French bistro owned by a Paris-trained Cordon Bleu chef who works hard to keep the quality high and the prices moderate. Set on the second floor of a clapboard-sided building in Frenchtown, it's decorated with murals of agricultural scenes in Provence and a donkey cart loaded with fresh flowers, vegetables, and loaves of bread. A wine bar in the corner dispenses 20 kinds of French and Italian wines by the glass, priced at $4 to $7 each, depending on the vintage. Patricia LeCorte serves dishes that might include salmon carpaccio with a tapenade of black olives, romaine salad with roasted anchovies and garlic dressing, roast goat cheese salad, braised lamb shank with al dente vegetables and orzo pasta, roast free-range garlic chicken with mashed potatoes, a traditional steak au poivre, a selection of fresh seafood which arrives according to market conditions, and at least three kinds of dessert soufflés. Many guests appreciate the elegant array of Mediterranean antipasti which are displayed as a before-dinner tempter.

FLAMBOYANT POINT

● Tavern on the Beach

In Marriott's Morningstar Beach Resort, Flamboyant Point. ☎ **809/776-8500.** Reservations recommended in winter. Appetizers $5.25–$11.95; main dishes $17.95–$34.50. AE, DC, MC, V. Dinner Tues–Sat 6pm–10:30pm. Transportation: Water or land taxi from Charlotte Amalie. INTERNATIONAL/CARIBBEAN.

One of Florida's best known chefs, German-born Eddie Hale, runs this hot spot set on the ocean at this previously recommended hotel. His courses, divided into first, second, and third "plates," reflect both Caribbean and international influences. Sample dishes include Thai-flavored pork satay with crispy-noodle salad and lemon-grass/coconut dipping sauce; sautéed local snapper with a Cruzan rum/brown butter, sweet-potato salad, and braised endives; and jerk marinated roast rack of lamb with mashed yams, tannia, and mango chutney. Desserts include cashew-caramel tart with a vanilla-bean/banana sundae, and lemon-drop flan with ginger- and herb-flavored exotic fruit salsa.

ON THE NORTH COAST

● Eunice's Terrace

66–67 Smith Bay, Rte. 38. ☎ **809/775-3975.** Reservations recommended for dinner. Appetizers $2.50–$7.95 at lunch, $7–$11 at dinner; main dishes $4–$7.95 at lunch, $9.95–$26 at dinner. AE, MC, V. Lunch Mon–Sat 11am–3:30pm; dinner Mon–Sat 6–10pm. Transportation: Red Hook bus. WEST INDIAN/AMERICAN.

A 30-minute taxi ride east of the airport, just east of the Coral World turnoff, is one of the best-known local restaurants, which went from a simple shack to a modern building. A collection of West Indian locals and tourists from nearby Stouffer's Grand Beach crowd into its confines for savory platters of island food served in generous proportions. A popular concoction called a Queen Mary (tropical fruits laced with dark rum) is a favorite. Dinner specialties include conch fritters, broiled or fried fish (especially dolphin), sweet-potato pie, and a number of specials usually served with fungi, rice, or plantain. On the lunch menu are fishburgers, sandwiches, and such daily specials as Virgin Islands doved pork or mutton. (Doving, pronounced "*dough*-ving," involves baking sliced meat while basting with a combination of its own juices, tomato paste, Kitchen Bouquet, and island herbs.) Key lime pie is a favorite dessert.

✪ Romano's Restaurant

97 Smith Bay Rd. ☎ **809/775-0045.** Reservations recommended. Appetizers $7.95–$10.95; main dishes $22.95–$26.95; pastas $15.95–$18.95. AE, MC, V. Dinner only, Mon–Sat 6:30–10:30pm. Closed one week in Apr for Carnival. Transportation: Vitran bus. ITALIAN.

Located on the sandy-bottomed flatlands near Coral World, this chef-owned creation of New Jersey–born Tony Romano is skillfully decorated with exposed brick and well-stocked wine racks. Considered the best Italian restaurant on St. Thomas, it specializes in the flavorful and herb-laden cuisine that some diners yearn for after a constant diet of Caribbean cooking. Specialties include linguine con pesto, a four-cheese lasagne, osso buco, scaloppine marsala, and broiled salmon. All desserts are made on the premises. In spite of the fact that Tony doesn't advertise, his place always seems full of happy diners.

RED HOOK

East Coast

In Red Hook Plaza, Rte. 38. ☎ **809/775-1919.** Reservations not required. Appetizers $2.50–$4.75; main courses $6.75–$18.75; Sun brunch $15. AE, MC, V. Dinner daily 5:30–11pm; brunch Sun noon–4pm. (Bar, daily 4:30pm–4am.) Transportation: Red Hook bus. CARIBBEAN.

Across the street from Red Hook Plaza, East Coast packs a Stateside and local crowd of sports fans into its pine-sheathed interior nightly to cheer their favorites playing on TV. What is not readily apparent is that the adjacent restaurant serves very good meals. Put your name on the list and enjoy a beer at the bar while waiting for a table. You can dine in a denlike haven or on an outdoor terrace in back. A different fish of the day is prepared according to the way you like it: grilled, baked, or broiled. The selections might include tuna, wahoo, dolphin, swordfish, or snapper. The latter is best in a garlic-cream sauce. The kitchen also turns out such items as Cajun shrimp and their famous "Coast burgers." Live bands sometimes entertain in the Shark Room from 8:30pm to 2am, but call first to check that.

⑤ Piccola Marina Ristorante

6300 Smith Bay, Red Hook, Rte. 38. ☎ **809/775-6250.** Reservations required for dinner. Appetizers $5–$8.25; main dishes $13–$24; lunch platters $4.50–$13.50; pizza $9.50–$12.50. AE, MC, V. Lunch Mon–Sat 11am–3pm; dinner Sun–Thurs 6–10pm, Fri–Sat 5:30–11pm; brunch Sun 11am–3pm. Transportation: Red Hook bus. ITALIAN.

A popular eatery, with an open veranda offering a view of the yachts moored at this marina, the Piccola offers lunch with various salads from Caesar to Greek, a fresh antipasto primavera, and an assortment of sandwiches, plus charcoal-broiled hamburgers. All the food is homemade with only fresh ingredients. Fresh pasta dishes, such as Alfredo, carbonara, and pesto, and fresh fish, steak, chicken, and shrimp are on the dinner menu. Pasta with clams is especially popular. Desserts include a homemade brownie specialty on Sunday and award-winning cheesecakes. The kitchen doesn't turn out magic, but it's acceptable standard fare.

NEAR THE SUB BASE

⑤ Victor's Hide Out

32A Sub Base, off Rte. 30. ☎ **809/776-9379.** Reservations recommended. Appetizers $5–$7.95; main dishes $9.95–$50. AE, MC, V. Lunch Mon–Sat 11:30am–3:30pm; dinner daily 5:30–10pm. Transportation: Taxi. WEST INDIAN/AMERICAN.

Victor's is operated by Victor Sydney, who comes from Montserrat. You never know who's going to show up here—maybe Bill Cosby, perhaps José Feliciano. Victor's has some of the best local dishes on the island, but first you must find it, as it's truly a place to hide out. If you're driving, call for directions; otherwise, take a taxi. On a hilltop perch, the large, airy restaurant serves fresh lobster prepared Montserrat style (that is, in a creamy sauce) or grilled in the shell. You might also ask for a plate of juicy barbecued ribs. For dessert, try the coconut, custard, or apple pie.

WHAT TO SEE & DO

IN CHARLOTTE AMALIE

The color and charm of a real Caribbean waterfront town come vividly to life in the capital of St. Thomas, Charlotte Amalie, where most visitors begin their sightseeing on the small island. In days of yore, seafarers from all over the globe flocked to this old-world Danish town, as did pirates and members of the Confederacy, who used the port during the American Civil War. St. Thomas was also the biggest slave market in the world.

The old warehouses once used for storing pirate goods still stand and, for the most part, house today's shops. In fact, the main streets (called "Gade" here in honor of their Danish heritage) are now a virtual shopping mall and are usually packed. Sandwiched among these shops are a few historic buildings, most of which can be covered on foot in about two hours (see the walking tour, below). Before starting your tour, stop off in the so-called Grand Hotel, near Emancipation Park. No longer a hotel, it contains, along with shops, a **visitor center** (☎ 809/774-8784).

Seven Arches Museum, Government Hill (☎ 809/774-9295), is a two-century-old Danish house, completely restored to its original condition and furnished with antiques. You can walk through the yellow ballast arches and visit the great room with its view of the busiest harbor in the Caribbean. You can also view the original separate stone Danish kitchen above the cistern. The admission of $7.50 includes a cold tropical drink served in a walled garden filled with flowers. It's open Tuesday through Sunday from 10am to 3pm.

NEARBY

West of Charlotte Amalie, Route 30 (Veteran's Drive) will take you to **Frenchtown** (turn left at the sign to the Admirals Inn). This was settled by a French-speaking people who were uprooted when the Swedes invaded and took over their homeland in St. Barts. They were known for wearing *cha-chas,* or straw hats. Many of the people who live here today are the direct descendants of those long-ago immigrants.

This colorful village, many of whose residents engage in fishing, contains several interesting restaurants and taverns. Now that Charlotte Amalie has been deemed a dangerous place to be at night, Frenchtown has picked up the business, and it's the best choice for nighttime dancing, entertainment, and drinking.

The number-one tourist attraction of St. Thomas is a 20-minute drive from downtown off route 38. The ✪ **Coral World Marine Park & Underwater Observatory,** 6450 Coki Point, (☎ 809/775-1555), a marine complex that features a three-story underwater observation tower 100 feet offshore. Through windows you'll see sponges, fish, and coral—underwater life in its natural state.

In the Marine Gardens Aquarium, saltwater tanks display everything from sea horses to sea urchins. Another attraction is an 80,000-gallon reef tank featuring exotic marine life of the Caribbean; another tank is devoted to sea predators, with circling sharks and giant moray eels, among other creatures. Entrance is through a waterfall of cascading water.

The latest addition to the park is a semi-submarine that lets you enjoy the panoramic view and the "down under" feeling of a submarine without ever leaving the ocean's surface. Coral World's guests can take advantage of adjacent Coki Beach for snorkel rental, scuba lessons, or simply swimming and relaxing. Lockers and showers are available.

Also included in the marine park are the Tropical Terrace Restaurant, duty-free shops, and a tropical nature trail. Activities include daily fish and shark feedings and exotic bird shows. The complex is open daily from 9am to 6pm. Admission is $16 for adults and $10 for children.

A popular attraction in the 1970s, the **Paradise Point Tramway** resumed operation in the summer of 1994, taking visitors for a dramatic view of Charlotte Amalie harbor with a gondola ride to a 697-foot peak. Paradise Point Gondolas operates six cars, each with a 12-person capacity, and carries up to 600 people an hour, on the $3^{1}/_{2}$-minute ride.

The gondolas, similar to those used at ski resorts, hauls customers from the Havensight area to Paradise Point, where riders disembark to visit Paradise Point retail shops and the popular restaurant and bar.

The Paradise Point Gondolas run daily from 9am to 9pm, costing $10 per person round-trip. The $2.8-million tramway line is supported by seven towers and specifically engineered to withstand all types of weather conditions.

The **Estate St. Peter Greathouse Botanical Gardens,** at the corner of Route 40 (St. Peter Mountain Road) and Barrett Hill Road (☎ **809/774-4999**), decorates 11 lushly planted acres of grounds at the volcanic peaks on the northern rim of the island. It's the creation of Howard Lawson DeWolfe, a Mayflower descendant who with his wife, Sylvie, bought the estate in 1987 and set about transforming it into a tropical paradise. Damaged by Hurricane Hugo in 1989, the property was reopened again in 1992. A virtual Garden of Eden, it's riddled with self-guided nature walks that will acquaint you with some 200 varieties of West Indian plants and trees, including an umbrella plant from Madagascar. Making it a true Eden are such delights as a rain forest, an orchid jungle, a monkey habitat, waterfalls, and reflecting ponds. From a panoramic deck you can see some 20 of the Virgin Islands, including Hans Lollick, an uninhabited island between Thatched Cay and Madahl Point. The house itself is worth a visit, its interior filled with art by locals. It's open daily from 9am to 5pm, charging an admission of $8 for adults and $4 for children.

SPORTS & OUTDOOR ACTIVITIES
BEACHES

Chances are, your hotel will be right on the beach, or very close to one, and this is where you'll anchor for most of your stay. All the beaches in the Virgin Islands are public, and most lie anywhere from 2 to 5 miles from Charlotte Amalie.

THE NORTH SIDE I've already extolled the glory of **Magens Bay,** 3 miles north of the capital. Named one of the world's 10 most beautiful beaches, it charges $1 for adults and 25¢ for children under 12. Changing facilities are available, and snorkeling gear and lounge chairs can be rented. Administered by the government, this beach is less than a mile long and lies between two mountains. There is no public transportation to reach it. From Charlotte Amalie, take Route 35 north all the way. The gates to the beach are open daily from 6am to 6pm (after 4 o'clock you'll need insect repellent).

In the northeast near Coral World, **Coki Beach** is good, but should be avoided when cruise ships are in port as it becomes overcrowded. Snorkelers are attracted here, as are pickpockets—so protect your valuables. Lockers can be rented at Coral World, next door. An East End bus runs to Smith Bay and lets you off at the gate to Coral World and Coki.

Also on the north side is **Stouffer Grand Beach,** one of the island's most beautiful, with the previously recommended hotel in the background. Many water sports are available at this beach, which opens onto Smith Bay and is in the vicinity of Coral World. The beach lies right off Route 38.

THE SOUTH SIDE   On the south side near Marriott's Frenchman's Reef Beach Resort, **Morningstar** lies about 2 miles east of Charlotte Amalie. This is where you can wear your most daring swimwear. Or you can rent sailboats, snorkeling equipment, and lounge chairs. The beach can easily be reached by a cliff-front elevator at Frenchman's Reef.

At the **Bolongo Beach Resorts Club Everything,** Limetree Beach has been called a classic, and lures those who like a serene spread of sand. You can feed hibiscus blossoms to iguanas, and rent snorkeling gear and lounge chairs. There is no public transportation, but the beach can easily be reached by taxi from Charlotte Amalie.

One of the most popular beaches, **Brewer's** lies in the southwest near the University of the Virgin Islands and can be reached by the public bus marked "Fortuna" heading west from Charlotte Amalie Road.

Near the airport, **Lindberg Beach** has a lifeguard, toilet facilities, and a bathhouse. It, too, lies on the Fortuna bus route heading west from Charlotte Amalie.

THE EAST END   Small and special, **Secret Harbour** lies near a collection of condos whose owners you'll meet on the beach. With its white sand and coconut palms, it's a cliché of Caribbean charm. No public transportation stops here, but it's an easy taxi ride east of Charlotte Amalie heading toward Red Hook.

One of the finest on St. Thomas, ✪ **Sapphire Beach** is set against the backdrop of the desirable Sapphire Beach Resort & Marina complex, where you can lunch or order drinks. Windsurfers like it a lot, and snorkeling gear and lounge chairs can be rented. A large reef is found close to the shore, and there are good views of offshore cays and St. John. The beach of fine white coral sand opens onto beautiful views of the bay. To reach it, you can take the East End bus from Charlotte Amalie, going via Red Hook. Ask to be let off at the entrance to Sapphire Bay; it's not too far to walk from there toward the water.

BOATING

The biggest charter business in the Caribbean is done by Virgin Islanders. On St. Thomas most of the business centers around the Red Hook and Yacht Haven marinas.

Perhaps the easiest way to go to sea is to charter "your yacht for the day" from **Yacht** *Nightwind,* Red Hook (☎ **809/775-4110,** 24 hours a day) for only $85 per person. You're granted a full-day sail starting with breakfast and including a champagne buffet lunch and an open bar aboard this 50-foot yawl. You're also given free snorkeling equipment and instruction and you visit St. John and the outer islands. Operators Stephen and June March have taken visitors out since 1977. If you're interested, ask them about two- or three-bedroom villas for rent on the beach.

New Horizons, 6501 Red Hook Plaza, Suite 16, Red Hook (☎ 809/775-1171), offers windborne excursions amid the cays and reefs of the Virgin Islands. This two-masted 60-foot ketch was built in 1969 in Vancouver. It has circumnavigated the globe and has been used as a design prototype for other boats.

Owned and operated by Canadian Tim Krygsveld, it contains a hot-water shower, serves a specialty drink called a New Horizons Nooner (with a melon-liqueur base), and carries a complete line of snorkeling equipment for adults and children. A full-day excursion, with a "hot buffet Italian al fresco" and an open bar, costs $85 per person. Children 2 to 12, when accompanied by an adult, are charged $42.50. Excursions depart daily, weather permitting, from the Sapphire Beach Club Marina. Call ahead for reservations and information.

True Love (☎ 809/775-6547) is a sleek 54-foot Malabar schooner, used during the filming of *High Society* starring Bing Crosby, Frank Sinatra, and Grace Kelly. It sails at 9:30am from the Sapphire Beach Club Marina and costs $85 per person. Bill and Sue Beer have sailed it since 1965. You can join one of the captain's snorkeling classes and later enjoy one of Sue's gourmet lunches with champagne.

Of course, if you want something more elaborate, you can go bareboating—that is, you can rent a craft where you're the captain. However, you must prove you're able to handle the craft before you're allowed to go out in it alone. On the other hand, if you'd like everything done for you, a fully crewed yacht with a captain at your service is the way to go on a charter plan. Either type of charter rental is available through Avery's Marina, P.O. Box 5248, Veterans Drive Station, St. Thomas, USVI 00803 (☎ 809/776-0113 during the day, 809/775-2773 at night).

DEEP-SEA FISHING

It's very good in the U.S. Virgins, and 19 world records have been set in recent years (eight for blue marlin). Sports fishing is offered on the *Fish Hawk* (☎ 809/775-9058). Captain Al Petrosky of New Jersey sails from Fish Hawk Marina Lagoon at the East End on his 48-foot diesel-powered craft, which is fully equipped with rods and reels. All equipment (but no lunch) is included in the rate of $400 per half day for up to six passengers. A full-day excursion, depending on how far the boat goes out, ranges from $700 to $800.

GOLF

On the north shore, Mahogany Run, at the Mahogany Run Golf & Tennis Resort, Mahogany Run Road (☎ 809/775-5000, or 800/253-7103), is an 18-hole, par-70 course. Designed by Tom and George Fazio, this is considered one of the most beautiful courses in the West Indies, rising and dropping like a roller coaster on its journey to the sea where cliffs and crashing sea waves are the ultimate hazards at the 13th and 14th holes. Greens fees December through April are $70 for 18 holes and $35 for 9 holes. After 2pm, you get the twilight rate: $55 for 18 holes. Off-season, greens fees are $50 for 18 holes or $25 for 9 holes, reduced to $35 for 18 holes after 2pm. A cart is mandatory, costing $15 for 18 holes or $10 for 9 holes.

SCUBA & SNORKELING

With 30 spectacular reefs just off St. Thomas, the U.S. Virgins are rated as one of the "most beautiful areas in the world" by *Skin Diver* magazine.

St. Thomas Diving Club, Bolongo Beach Resorts, 7147 Bolongo Bay (☎ **809/776-2381,** or **800/538-7348**), is a full-service PADI five-star IDC center, considered the best on the island. If you're a guest at this resort, you get such extras as a sail to St. John and a harbor cruise on the resort's 52-foot *Heavenly Daze.* An open-water certification course, including four scuba dives, costs $330. An advanced open-water certification course, including five dives that can be accomplished in two days, goes for $275. Every Thursday participants are taken on an all-day scuba excursion that includes a two-tank dive to the wreck of the RMS *Rhône* in the British Virgin Islands, costing $110. You can also enjoy local snorkeling for $22.

Dive In, in the Sapphire Beach Resort & Marina, Smith Bay Road, Route 36 (☎ **809/775-6100**), is a well-recommended and complete diving center offering some of the finest diving services in the U.S. Virgin Islands, including professional instruction (beginner to advanced), daily beach and boat dives, custom dive packages, underwater photography and videotapes, snorkeling trips, and a full-service PADI dive center. An introductory course costs $55, a one-boat dive goes for $50, and two-boat dives run $140. An open-water certification course with four dives over a period of three days costs $350, and a six-dive pass can be had for $185. It's especially convenient for those staying at hotels on the East Side.

TENNIS

The best tennis on the island is at **Sugar Bay Plantation Resort,** 6500 Estate Smith Bay (☎ **809/777-7100**), which has the Virgin Island's first stadium tennis court, seating 220, plus six additional Laykold courts lit at night. There's also a pro shop.

Another good resort for tennis is the **Bolongo Bay Beach and Tennis Club,** Bolongo Bay (☎ **809/779-2844**), which has four courts, two of which are lit until 10pm. It's free to members and hotel guests, except for lessons, which cost $18 per hour and are available to anyone.

At **Marriott's Frenchman's Reef Tennis Courts,** Flamboyant Point (☎ **809/776-8500,** ext. 444), four courts are available, and nonresidents are charged $8 a half hour per court. Lights stay on until 10pm.

At the famous **Bluebeard's Castle,** Bluebeard's Hill (☎ **809/774-1600**), nonguests are charged $4 per hour to play on its two courts.

WINDSURFING

This increasingly popular sport is available at the major resort hotels and at some public beaches, including Brewers Bay, Morningstar Beach, and Limetree Beach. **Stouffer Grand Beach Resort,** Smith Bay Road, Route 38 (☎ **809/775-1510**), is the major hotel offering windsurfing. Stouffer guests are granted a lesson for $25 and use of the equipment for free. If you're a nonresident, the cost goes up to $35 per hour.

SHOPPING

Shoppers not only have the benefits of St. Thomas's liberal duty-free allowances (Customs regulations are outlined in "Fast Facts: The U.S. Virgin Islands," at the beginning of this chapter), but they also will find well-known brand names at savings of up to 40% off Stateside prices. However, to find true value, you often have to plow through a lot of junk. Many items offered for sale—binoculars, stereos, watches, cameras—can be matched in price at your hometown discount store. Therefore, you need to know the prices back home to determine if you're in fact making a savings.

Most of the shops, some of which occupy former pirate warehouses, are open Monday through Saturday from 9am to 5pm, regular business hours, and some stay open later. Nearly all stores close on Sunday and major holidays—unless a cruise ship is in port. Friday is the biggest cruise-ship visiting day at Charlotte Amalie (one day I counted eight at one time)—so try to avoid shopping then.

If you want to combine a little history with shopping, go into the courtyard of the old **Pissarro Building,** entered through an archway off Main Street. The impressionist painter lived here as a child, and the old apartments have been turned into a warren of interesting shops.

Recently, the town leaders ordained that it was illegal for most street vendors to ply their trades outside a designated area called **Vendors Plaza,** at the corner of Veterans Drive and Tolbod Gade. Hundreds converge at 7:30am, remaining there usually no later than 5:30pm, Monday through Saturday. (Very few remain in place on Sunday, unless a cruise ship is scheduled to arrive.) Their protection from the elements usually derives from oversize parasols. The only exception to this strictly maintained ordinance are food vendors, who are permitted to sell on sidewalks outside Vendors Plaza.

A. H. Riise Gift & Liquor Stores
At A. H. Riise Gift & Liquor Mall, 37 Main St. ☎ **809/776-2303.**

A wide selection of imported merchandise is displayed in a restored 18th-century Danish warehouse that extends from Main Street to the waterfront. Special attention is paid to the collection of jewelry and watches from Europe. Featured among the many name brands in the china and crystal department are Waterford, Lalique, Daum, Baccarat, and Wedgwood. A. H. Riise Gift & Liquor Stores also has a large selection of fragrances for men and women, and cosmetics, and carries a large choice of liquors, wines, cordials, and tobacco. Every purchase is backed by a 60-day unconditional guarantee. For a brochure and toll-free shop-by-phone service, call **800/524-2037** Monday through Saturday from 9am to 5pm and on Sunday from 9am to 1pm Atlantic standard time; closed major holidays.

Blue Carib Gems and Rocks
2 Back St. ☎ **809/774-8525.**

For a decade, the owners prospected for gemstones in the Caribbean, and these stones have been brought direct from the mine to you in this store behind Little Switzerland. The raw stones are cut, polished, and then fashioned into jewelry by the lost-wax process. On one side of the premises you can see the craftspeople at work, and on the other side view their finished products. A lifetime guarantee is given on all handcrafted jewelry. Since the items are locally made, they are duty free and not included in the $1,200 exemption. Incidentally, this establishment also provides emergency eyeglass repair.

Camille Pissarro Art Gallery
14 Dronningens Gade. ☎ **809/777-5511.**

On the second floor of the Camille Pissarro building, overlooking the courtyard, this art gallery has a central in-town location from Main Street and Back Street. Two high-ceilinged, airy rooms display a variety of original and fine art from local and regional artists. The gallery honors Camille Pissarro, dean of French impressionists, who was born at this address on July 10, 1830.

Cardow Jewelers

39 Main St. ☎ **809/776-1140.**

Often called the Tiffany's of the Caribbean, Cardow Jewelers boasts the largest selection of fine jewelry in the world. This fabulous shop, where more than 20,000 rings are displayed, offers savings because of its worldwide direct buying, large turnover, and duty-free prices. Unusual and traditional designs are offered in diamonds, emeralds, rubies, sapphires, and Brazilian stones, as well as pearls. Cardow has a whole wall of Italian gold chains, and also features antique-coin jewelry. The Treasure Cove has cases of fine gold jewelry all priced under $200.

Caribbean Marketplace

Havensight Mall (Building III). ☎ **809/776-5400.**

One of the best selections of Caribbean handcrafts is found here, including Sunny Caribbee products—a vast array of condiments (ranging from spicy peppercorns to nutmeg mustard). There's also a wide selection of Sunny Caribbee's botanical products such as foaming rosemary bath gel plus natural beauty soaps made from such concoctions as chamomile or coconut. Other items range from steel-pan drums from Trinidad to wooden Jamaican jigsaw puzzles, from Indonesian batiks to bikinis from the Cayman Islands.

Coki of St. Thomas

Compass Point Marina. ☎ **809/775-6560.**

Some $1^{1}/_{2}$ miles from Charlotte Amalie in the East End, Coki is set in the midst of a little "restaurant row." An American, George McBride, employs island women who sew and stitch together pieces of canvas and hand-woven Madras cotton into the kind of resortwear suitable for yachting, beaching, or "hanging out." In winter, the shop is open Wednesday through Monday from 9am to 9pm; off-season hours are shorter.

Colombian Emeralds International

Havensight Mall. ☎ **809/774-2442.**

The Colombian Emerald stores are renowned throughout the Caribbean for offering the finest collection of Colombian emeralds, both set and unset. In addition to jewelry, the shop stocks some of the world's finest watches, including Raymond Weil and Seiko. There's another outlet on Main Street.

Cosmopolitan, Inc.

Drakes Passage and the waterfront. ☎ **809/776-2040.**

Since 1973 this store has drawn a lot of repeat business. Its shoe salon features Bally of Switzerland and handmade A. Testoni of Bologna, Italy. In swimwear, it offers one of the best selections of Gottex of Israel for women and Gottex, Hom, Lahco of Switzerland, and Fila for men. A men's wear section offers Paul & Shark from Italy, Metzger shirts from Switzerland, and Burma Bibas sports shirts. Tennis wear is also featured. The outlet also features ties of Gianni Versace and Pencaldi of Italy (in both instances these ties are at least 30% less than the Stateside price). It also carries an array of Nautica sportswear for men.

Dockside Bookshop

Havensight Mall (Building VI). ☎ **809/774-4937.**

The best supply of books is found at this store near the cruise-ship dock, east of Charlotte Amalie. The shop has a selection of books on island lore, as well as numerous light and serious reading selections, everything from photo books to plants and animals.

Down Island Traders
At the waterfront. ☎ **809/776-4641.**

The aroma of spices will lead you to these original native markets, which have an attractive array of spices, teas, seasoning, candies, jellies, jams, and condiments, most of which are packaged from natural Caribbean products. The owner carries a line of local cookbooks, as well as silk-screened T-shirts and bags, Haitian metal sculpture, handmade jewelry, Caribbean folk art, and children's gifts.

H. Stern Jewellers
Havensight Mall. ☎ **809/776-1939,** or 800/524-2024.

Colorful gem and jewel creations are offered at Stern's locations in St. Thomas—three on Main Street, this one at the Havensight Mall, and branches at Stouffer Grand Beach Resort and Marriott's Frenchman's Reef. Stern gives worldwide guaranteed service, including a one-year exchange privilege.

Irmela's Jewel Studio
In the Old Grand Hotel, at the beginning of Main St. ☎ **809/774-5875,** or 800/524-2047.

Irmela's has made a name for itself in the highly competitive jewelry business on St. Thomas. Here the jewelry is unique, custom-designed by Irmela, and hand-made by her studio or imported from around the world. Irmela has the largest selection of cultured pearls in the Caribbean, including freshwater Biwa, South Sea, and natural color black Tahitian pearls. Choose from hundreds of clasps and pearl necklaces. Irmela has a large selection of unset stones, such as rubies, sapphires, emeralds, tanzanite, and alexandrite. Diamonds range from pear-shaped to emerald cut, marquis, even heart-shaped, in sizes from tiny two-pointers to several carats.

Java Wraps
American Yacht Harbor, Red Hook. ☎ **809/777-3450.**

From the East Indies to the West Indies, Java Wraps is known for hand-batiked women's, men's, and children's resortwear. A kaleidoscope of colors and prints dazzle the eye. Every day the store evokes the celluloid image of Dorothy Lamour as local salespeople demonstrate wrapping and tying Java Wraps beach pareos and sarongs. The men's shirts come in a wide array of tropical and flamboyant prints, and there's also a collection of clothing for children.

Java Wraps Home Store
American Yacht Harbor, Red Hook. ☎ **809/775-6407.**

Enter the world of Java Wraps. Textiles for the home cascade from antique Dutch colonial chests, and old teak tables are laden with hand-drawn batik tablecloths, napkins, and card placements. In addition, intricately patterned hand-batik quilted bedcovers are also sold. Mahogany hand-carved desk accessories are also elegant. A collection of island-inspired hand-painted fish plates are also featured, as are large banana-leaf trays, coral reef salad bowls, and other tropical tablewear.

✪ Jim Tillett Gallery
Tillett Gardens, Tutu. ☎ **809/775-1929.**

A visit to the art gallery and craft studios of Jim Tillett is a sightseeing expedition. The Tillett compound was converted from a Danish farm called Tutu. The Tillett name conjures up high-fashion silk-screen printing by the famous Tillett brothers, who for years had their exquisite fabrics used by top designers and featured in such magazines as *Vogue* and *Harper's Bazaar*. Jim Tillett settled on St. Thomas after creating a big splash in Mexico, where his work was featured in *Life* magazine. You can visit the adjoining workshop to see silk-screening in progress. Upstairs is an art gallery with an abundance of maps, paintings, sculpture, and graphics by local artists. Mr. Tillett created a series of maps on fine cotton canvas that are best-selling items.

The Leather Shop, Inc.

1 Main St. ☎ **809/776-0290.**

Here you'll find a good selection from these Italian designers—Fendi, Bottega Veneta, De Vecchi, Prima Classe, Furla, and II Bisonte. There are many styles of handbags, belts, wallets, briefcases, and attaché cases, as well as all-leather luggage from Land. The traditional Indian molas of Colombia and Panama, which are still stitched entirely by hand, have been incorporated into leather handbags. There's also a branch at the Havensight Mall.

The Linen House

7A Royal Dane Mall. ☎ **809/774-8117.**

The Linen House is considered to be one of the best stores for linen in the West Indies. You'll find a wide selection of placemats, decorative tablecloths, and many hand-embroidered goods. There are many high-fashion styles. Other branches are at A. H. Riise Mall (☎ **809/774-0469**) and Havensight Mall (☎ **809/774-0868**).

Lion in the Sun

A. H. Riise Alley. ☎ **809/766-4203.**

This is one of the most upscale sportswear outlet stores on the island. Patrons shop here for the collection of designer casual apparel and accessories. Whether it's tanks, Ts, shorts, pants, or skirts, this store is likely to have what you're looking for. It has a men's department as well. The owner is firm about prices as marked— no bargaining here.

Little Switzerland

5 Main St. ☎ **809/776-2010.**

Little Switzerland, with a branch on the dock at Havensight Mall, sells fine watches, a wide selection of jewelry from Europe and Asia, and the best in crystal and china. They also maintain the official outlets for Hummel, Lladró, and Swarovski figurines.

Louis Vuitton

24 Main St. at Palm Passage. ☎ **809/774-3644.**

For fine leather goods, you can't beat Louis Vuitton, where the complete line by the world-famous French designer is available. Suitcases, handbags, wallets, and other accessories are carried here.

Mountain Top

Rte. 33. ☎ **809/774-2400.**

Set near the center of the island, this modern shopping mall contains only about a dozen shops, but many clients come as much for the view as for the merchandise. You'll be faced with a choice from boutiques selling everything from beachwear to island-inspired prints and engravings, as well as jams, jellies, and local crafts. There's an aquarium and aviary on the premises, a snack bar, and an observation platform with a view over the rest of the island.

Polo/Ralph Lauren Factory Store
2 Garden St./2A–2C Commandant Gade. ☎ **809/774-3806.**

Buying the sportswear of the famous designer at this factory outlet allows you discounts of around 30% from what you'd have paid at a retail outlet Stateside. A full range of the designer's most popular items for both men and women are for sale here. Business is brisk at what appears to be one of the city's most popular shops.

Royal Caribbean
33 Main St. ☎ **809/776-4110.**

This is the largest camera and electronics store in the Caribbean, and has been since 1977. These outlets carry Nikon, Minolta, Pentax, Canon, Olympus, Samsung, Aiwa, Sony, and Panasonic products. It's also a good source for watches, including such brand names as Seiko, Movado, Baume & Mercier, Corum, Fendi, Tissot, Paolo Gucci, Concord, and Swatch. They also have a complete collection of Philippe Charriol watches, jewelry, and leather bags. In addition, there's a wide selection of Mikimoto pearls, 14K and 18K jewelry, and Lladró figurines.

There are additional branches at 23 Main St. (☎ **809/776-5449**) and Havensight Mall (☎ **809/776-8890**).

Tropicana Perfume Shoppes
2 and 14 Main St. ☎ **809/774-0010,** or 800/233-7948.

These two stores stand at the beginning of Main Street near the Emancipation Park post office. The first is billed as the largest perfumery in the world, and it offers all the famous names in perfumes and cosmetics, including Nina Ricci and Chanel for women and men. Men will also find Europe's best colognes and aftershave lotions here. When you return home, you can mail-order all these same fragrances by taking advantage of Tropicana's toll-free number.

ST. THOMAS AFTER DARK

St. Thomas has more nightlife than any other island in the Virgin Islands, either U.S. or British, but it's not as extensive as you might think. The big hotels seem to offer the most varied programs.

THE CLUB & MUSIC SCENE

Andiamo Ristorante/Club Z
41 Contant Rd., Rte. 33. ☎ **809/776-4655.** Admission free, but every Friday, from 6 to 8pm, a $10 admission charge provides a limitless array of bar drinks and access to a buffet of hors d'oeuvres.

This famous nightspot lies a five-minute drive west of Charlotte Amalie. Profiting from a panoramic view over the capital, the former Great House on Contant Hill attracts a young, urban crowd. Patrons come here to dine or to enjoy after-dinner dancing. An Italian-American cuisine is served in either the bistro or the main dining room. Only dinner is served, Monday through Saturday from 6:30 to 11pm. Appetizers range from $4.50 to $9 and main courses cost $12 to $19, making for moderately priced meals consisting of pizzas, pastas, and veal, chicken, and beef dishes.

Club Z is open Monday through Saturday from 9pm to 3:30am, attracting a crowd usually aged 18 to 30. The DJ changes the focus of the music from reggae to Latin to rock 'n' roll, depending on the tastes of the crowd. Drinks cost $3 and up.

Barnacle Bill's

At the Crown Bay Marina, in the Sub Base. ☎ **809/774-7444.** Admission free, except on "Limelight Mondays" when several different bands, everyone from local amateurs to imported pros, are featured in rapid succession; then there's a cover charge of $3 per person.

The enormous plastic lobster that perches on this establishment's roof was originally designed as part of a float that adorned a local parade. Today the pastel-colored building functions as a restaurant throughout the day and as one of the most desirable nightclubs on St. Thomas throughout the evening. Beginning around 9pm, a parade of local and imported musical talent plays to full houses until at least 1am. Although the bar is open nightly, live music is presented every night except Tuesday and Sunday. Beer ranges from $2.25 to $2.75.

Epernay

Rue de St. Barthélemy, Frenchtown. ☎ **809/774-5348.**

Adjacent to Alexander's Restaurant, this stylish watering hole adds a touch of Europe to the neighborhood of Frenchtown. You can order glasses of at least six different brands of champagne, and vintage wines by the glass. No main courses are served, but appetizers, costing $6 to $10, include sushi and caviar. You can also order tempting desserts. Wines and champagnes cost $4 to $10 a glass. Open Monday through Saturday from 4:30pm to 1am.

Fat Tuesday

26A Royal Dane Mall, on the waterfront in downtown Charlotte Amalie. ☎ **809/777-8676.** Admission free.

This nightspot specializes in frozen concoctions served up from a bank of slurpee machines that dominates the interior. In the partylike atmosphere of Fat Tuesday, patrons enjoy such specialties as the Tropical Itch (a frozen punch made with bourbon and 151 rum) or the Moko Jumbi Juice (made with vodka, bourbon, 151 rum, and banana and cocoa liqueurs). Also among the selections is a wide variety of beer, highballs, and shooters including the Head Butt which contains Jagermeister, Bailey's, and amaretto. Every night this bar sponsors a special event such as Monday Night Football or T.G.I.F. Night. A light lunch is served from 11am to 4pm daily. Fat Tuesday is open daily from 10am to midnight or 1am (later on Friday and Saturday if the crowd warrants it). Drinks range from $2 to $9.25.

Greenhouse

Veterans Dr. ☎ **809/774-7998.** Admission free Thurs–Tues, $5 Wed (including the first drink).

Set directly on the waterfront, this bar and restaurant is one of the few nightlife venues recommended in Charlotte Amalie. You can park nearby and walk to the entrance. Each night a different entertainment is featured, ranging from oldies night to rock 'n' roll. Wednesday night is the "big blast." Beer costs $3.50, with meals from $15. Open daily from 7am to 2am.

Iggies

At the Bolongo Beach Resorts Club Everything, Frenchman's Bay Rd., Frenchman's Bay. ☎ **809/779-2844.** Admission free.

During the day, Iggies functions as an informal open-air bistro. After dark, however, it turns into a popular center of lighthearted fun and comedy. Iggies' karaoke machine entices even the most stage-frightened patrons with hundreds of singable pop songs. Urged on by a talented and affable master of ceremonies and encouraged by an outgoing staff, members of the audience have the chance to become the star they always wanted to be. Tropical drinks help to lubricate the participants' vocal cords. Drinks begin at $4. Open Monday, Tuesday, and Thursday from 8am to midnight and on Friday and Saturday from 8am to 1am.

Paradise Club Disco & Caribbean Lobster House

In Bolongo's Limetree Beach Resort, Frenchman's Bay Rd., Frenchman's Bay. ☎ **809/776-4770.** Admission $12.

Located on an elevated terrace near the lobby of the Bolongo Beach Resort Hotel, this restaurant and nightclub are separated by a quasi-soundproof glass wall. Guests move freely from one area to another. The Paradise Club is a disco with live local bands playing a combination of reggae, soca, calypso, and contemporary sounds, or a DJ for your listening pleasure. The Caribbean Lobster House is a full-service seafood restaurant offering fresh local seafood prepared to tantalize your palate and refreshing breezes wafting in from the patio. Drinks and sea breezes flow, conversation grows, and the combination of fine dining and entertainment contribute to a good time. Drinks begin at $4. The club is open Tuesday, Friday, and Saturday from 10pm to 2am.

The Top of the Reef

In Marriott's Frenchman's Reef Beach Resort, Flamboyant Point. ☎ **809/776-8500.** Admission $20 adults, $10 children 10 and under.

Set in a dining room with a professional stage in a previously recommended hotel, this is the island's only dinner theater. The list of comedies, dramas, and musicals changes every five to six weeks, but has included performances by local and visiting theatrical troupes. Performances begin at 8pm, with restaurant service from 6pm. Main courses on an à la carte menu in the restaurant range from $13 to $25. Open Monday through Saturday from 6 to 10:30pm.

Turtle Rock Bar

In the Mangrove Restaurant at the Sugar Bay Resort, 6500 Estate Smith Bay. ☎ **809/777-7100.** Admission free.

Set a few minute's drive west of Red Hook, this is a popular bar where live music, steel-pan bands, and karoake provide diversions from the beach life nearby. Although there's lots of space on the premises if anyone should get the urge to dance, very few clients ever seem to take the opportunity, preferring instead to listen to the steel-pan bands (which play from 2pm to closing every night), or the more elaborate bands which play on Tuesday, Sunday, and on assorted other nights according to availability. Thursday night is karoake, when anyone can be a star. If you're hungry, burgers, salads, steaks, and grilled fish are available at the Mangrove Restaurant a few steps away. Entrance to the complex is free, and each happy hour (when most drinks are half price) is from 4 to 6pm every night. Open daily from 2pm to midnight. Drinks cost $4.

EASY EXCURSIONS
WATER ISLAND

The fourth-largest of the U.S. Virgins, with 500 acres of land, Water Island is only half a mile long and about a half a mile to a mile wide; its nearest point is less than half a mile from St. Thomas. The highest elevation is only 300 feet above sea level, and the Arawak peoples were the first to inhabit it. Originally the island had freshwater ponds from which sailing vessels replenished their casks. The army used Fort Segarra as a base in World War I.

Visitors head for Water Island to spend the day on **Honeymoon Beach,** where they swim, snorkel, sail, waterski, or just sunbathe on the palm-shaded beach and order lunch or a drink from the beach bar.

Water Island is often visited via private boat from the St. Thomas mainland as a kind of escapist holiday for Virgin Islanders, but if you're not lucky enough to have access to a private yacht, you can take one of the public ferryboats maintained by Launch with Larry. Priced at $3 per person each way ($5 each way for evening passages), it runs between the Crown Bay Marina (part of St. Thomas's submarine base) from a pier opposite Tickles Restaurant. It departs from St. Thomas every day at 7, 8, and 11am, noon, and 2, 4, 5, and 6pm, with a return to St. Thomas scheduled for approximately 30 minutes later. On Tuesday, Friday, and Saturday nights there are additional departures from St. Thomas at 9 and 10pm, with a return from Water Island to St. Thomas 30 minutes later.

If you happen to miss any of these departures, the ferryboat operator will sometimes schedule private departures for a minimum price of $20 for up to four passengers. Getting information about departure times of the individual boats is somewhat awkward (leave a beeper message with Launch with Larry at either **809/775-8071** or **809/779-6807** and hope for a return call.) Although not associated with the ferryboat, the reception staff at the Limestone Reef, Water Island's only hotel (☎ **800/872-8784**), can also provide data and information about ferryboat transit to and from Water Island from St. Thomas.

UNDER THE SEA

A major attraction is the ✪ **Atlantis submarine,** which takes you on a one-hour voyage to depths of 150 feet, unfolding a world of exotic marine life. You'll gaze on coral reefs and sponge gardens through 2-foot windows on the air-conditioned 65-foot-long sub, which carries 46 passengers. You take a surface boat from the West Indies Dock, right outside Charlotte Amalie, to the submarine, which lies near Buck Island (the St. Thomas version, not the more famous Buck Island near St. Croix). Divers swim with the fish and bring them close to the windows for photos. The fare is $68 per person; children 4 to 12 pay $25 (ages under 4 not permitted). The *Atlantis* operates daily from November through April and Tuesday through Saturday from May through October. Reservations are imperative. For tickets, go to the Havensight Shopping Mall, Building 6, or call **809/776-5650** for reservations.

2 St. John

About 3 to 5 miles east of St. Thomas, depending on where you measure, St. John lies just across Pillsbury Sound. The island is about 7 miles long and 3 miles wide, with a total land area of some 20 square miles.

The smallest and least populated of the three main U.S. Virgins, St. John has more than half its land mass, as well as its shoreline waters, set aside as the Virgin Islands National Park, dedicated in 1956. Once it was slated for big development when it was under Danish control, but a slave rebellion and a decline of the sugarcane plantations ended that idea.

Ringed by a rocky coastline formed into crescent-shaped bays and white sand beaches, St. John hosts an array of birdlife and wildlife that's the envy of ornithologists and zoologists around the world. Its miles of serpentine hiking trails are dotted with spectacular views and ruins of 18th-century Danish plantations. Mysterious geometric petroglyphs incised into boulders and cliffs will be pointed out by island guides; of unknown age and origin, the figures have never been deciphered.

The boating world seeks out its dozens of sheltered coves for anchorages, swimming, and extended holidays. The hundreds of coral gardens that surround St. John's perimeter are protected as rigorously as the land surface by the National Park Service. Any attempt to damage or remove coral from these waters is punishable by large and strictly enforced fines.

ORIENTATION

GETTING THERE

BY BOAT   The easiest and most frequented way to get to St. John is by **ferryboat,** which leaves from the Red Hook landing pier on St. Thomas's eastern tip; the trip takes about 20 minutes each way. Beginning at 6:30am, boats depart more or less every hour, with minor exceptions throughout the day. The last ferry back to Red Hook departs from St. John's Cruz Bay at 11:15pm. Because of such frequent departures, even cruise-ship passengers temporarily anchored in Charlotte Amalie for only a short visit can visit St. John for a quickie island tour. The one-way fare is $3 for adults, $1 for children under 11. Schedules can change without notice, so call in advance (☎ **809/776-6282**) before your intended departure.

To reach the ferry, take the Vitran bus from a point near Market Square (in Charlotte Amalie) directly to Red Hook. The cost is $3 per person each way. In addition, dozens of privately owned taxis will probably be willing to negotiate a price to carry you from virtually anywhere to the docks at Red Hook.

It's also possible to board a **boat** for St. John directly at the Charlotte Amalie waterfront for a cost of $7 each way. The ride takes 45 minutes. The ferryboat departs from Charlotte Amalie at 9am and continues at intervals of between one and two hours until the last boat departs around 7pm. (The last boat to leave St. John's Cruz Bay for Charlotte Amalie departs at 5:15.)

Also, a **launch service** departs once daily from the dock at Caneel Bay (on St. John) and heads for the national park dock at Red Hook on St. Thomas. It departs from Caneel Bay at 10:30am, returning at 11:10am. The one-way fare is $9 per person. In some instances the national park boat will continue from Red Hook on to Charlotte Amalie, in which event the one-way fare from Caneel Bay to Charlotte Amalie is $12. For information, call **809/776-6111.**

Should you ever get stranded, you can call a privately operated **launch service,** suitable for up to four passengers, whose hours and priorities are less rigid than those of the publicly operated ferryboats. (Because of their expense, these are usually an option only if all else fails.) The cost is $56 per trip during daylight hours, and $95 per trip after midnight.

GETTING AROUND

BY PUBLIC TRANSPORTATION   The most popular way to get around is by **surrey-style taxi.** Typical fares are $3 to Trunk Bay, $3.50 to Cinnamon Bay, or $7 to Mahoe Bay. Between midnight and 6am fares are increased by 40%.

It's also possible to use the **bus** service, which runs from Cruz Bay to Maho Bay and stops at Caneel and Cinnamon Bays. The one-way bus fare is $3.50.

BY CAR OR JEEP   The extensive stretches of St. John's National Park have kept the edges of the island's roads undeveloped and uncluttered, with some of the most panoramic vistas anywhere. Because of these views, many visitors opt to rent a vehicle (sometimes with four-wheel drive) to tour the island. Unless you have luggage, which should probably be locked away in a concealed trunk, you might consider one of the open-sided Jeep-like vehicles; sturdy and endlessly ventilated, with manual transmissions, they are arguably among the most fun of the island's relatively limited facilities. Most renters need a car for only a day or two. During the busiest periods of midwinter, there's sometimes a shortage of cars, so try to reserve early, if possible.

Gasoline is almost never included in the price of a rental. You're likely to be delivered a car with an almost-empty tank, just enough to get you to one of the island's two gas stations. (At press time, a third gas station on the island dispensed gas only to government vehicles.) Because of the distance between gas stations, it's never a good idea to drive around St. John with less than half a tank of gas.

The two largest car-rental agencies on St. John are Hertz and Avis (Budget is not represented). **Hertz** (☎ **809/776-6412,** or 800/654-3001) rents four types of vehicles, some of which feature four-wheel drive. Depending on the models, costs range from $65 to $80 a day, with a collision-damage waiver priced at around $10 extra per day. If you don't buy the waiver, you might be liable for up to the full value of the car in the event of damage to the vehicle. Use of certain credit or charge cards sometimes eliminates the need for extra insurance, but the fine print of every card issuer varies widely from card to card, so check! Drivers must be at least 25 years old, and must present a valid credit or charge card at the time of rental.

Also available on St. John are the services of **Avis Rent-a-Car** (☎ **809/776-6374,** or **800/331-2112**), at Cruz Bay. Avis charges between $45 and $75 a day, depending on the model. In winter, Avis tends to be fully booked many weeks in advance, although that situation might change. Drivers must be 25 or older, and present a valid credit or charge card at the time of rental. A collision-damage waiver costs $11.95 a day, which eliminates any financial responsibility in the event of an accident.

If you want a local firm, try **St. John Car Rental, Inc.,** across from the post office in Cruz Bay (☎ **809/776-6103**). It offers daily or weekly rentals in airconditioned four-door sedans, Suzuki jeepsters, eight-passenger safaris, and seven-passenger minivans. Sedans cost $50 to $60 per day.

BY SIGHTSEEING TOUR   The **St. John Taxi Association** (☎ **809/776-6060**) conducts a two-hour tour of St. John, including swimming at Trunk Bay and a visit to the Caneel Bay resort, at a cost ranging from $40 to $45 for one or two people. Depending on demand, tours depart Cruz Bay daily.

ESSENTIALS

In an emergency, call **915** for the **police, 921** to report a **fire,** or **922** for a **medical emergency;** Otherwise, go to **St. John Myrah Keating Smith Community Health Clinic,** 3B Sussanaberg (☎ **809/693-8900**). A leading drugstore is **St. John Drugcenter, Inc.,** in the Boulon Shopping Center, Cruz Bay (☎ **809/776-6353**), which also sells film.

The **St. John Tourist Office** (☎ **809/776-6450**) is located near the Battery, a 1735 fort that's a short walk from where the ferry from St. Thomas docks.

St. John

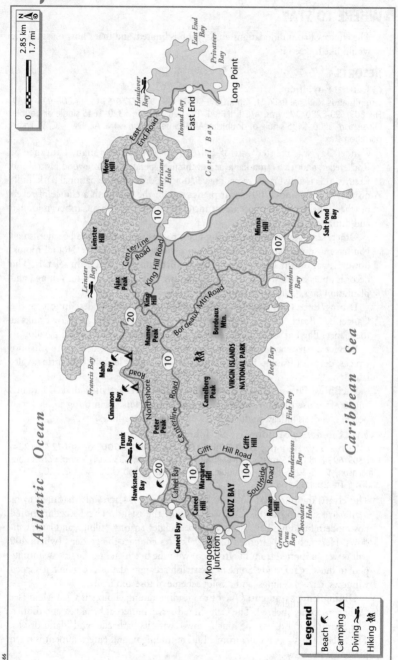

Legend
- Beach
- Camping
- Diving
- Hiking

WHERE TO STAY

The choice of accommodations on St. John is limited, and that's how most people would like to keep it.

RESORTS

✪ Caneel Bay, Inc.

Virgin Islands National Park, St. John, USVI 00831. ☎ **809/776-6111,** or 800/928-8889. Fax 809/693-8280. 171 rms. A/C MINIBAR TV. Dec 20–Mar, $320–$645 single or double. Off-season, $200–$495 single or double. MAP $65 per person extra. AE, DC, MC, V. Transportation: Taxi.

Caneel Bay was created out of a dream of an idealistic man, Laurance S. Rockefeller, and it's a remarkable achievement. Operated by Rosewood Hotels and Resorts, this is a luxurious resort on a 170-acre portion of the national park, built on the site of a mid-1700s sugar plantation on the bay, with a choice of seven beaches. The main buildings are strung along the bays, with a Caribbean lounge and dining room at the core.

Other, separate buildings housing guest rooms stand along the beaches, so all you have to do is step from your private veranda onto the sands. Not all rooms, however, are on the beaches; some are set back on low cliffs or headlands. The decor is understated, with rich woods, hand-woven fabrics, elegant furnishings, and plantation fans. Gardens surround all buildings.

Dining/Entertainment: See "Where to Dine," below, for descriptions of the Caneel Bay Beach Terrace Dining Room and Equators. You can enjoy drinks at the Caneel Bay Bar, beneath the soaring ceiling of a stone-and-timber pavilion.

Services: An array of scheduled garden tours, diving excursions to offshore wrecks, deep-sea fishing, free snorkeling lessons, tennis lessons, babysitting, valet laundry.

Facilities: Full-service dive shop and water-sports activities desk, 11 tennis courts, free use of Sunfish sailboats and windsurfers, swimming pool, seven beaches, endless hideaways for solitary or romantic interludes.

✪ Hyatt Regency St. John

Great Cruz Bay, St. John, USVI 00831. ☎ **809/693-8000,** or 800/233-1234. Fax 809/693-8888. 285 rms. A/C MINIBAR TV TEL. Winter, $330–$515 single or double. Off-season, $195–$295 single or double. MAP $62 per person extra. AE, DC, MC, V. Free parking. Transportation: Taxi.

The Hyatt, the splashiest hotel on St. John, sits on 34 acres of what used to be mangrove swamp on the southwest side of the island. The 13 cedar-roofed postmodern buildings have ziggurat-shaped angles, soaring ceilings, and large windows. Herringbone-patterned brick walkways connect the gardens (where 400 palms were imported from Puerto Rico) with the beach and the largest swimming pool in the Virgin Islands. Some of the stylish accommodations contain fan-shaped windows, curved ceilings, and a color scheme of rose and mauve.

Dining/Entertainment: One of the leading dining choices is Ciao Mein (see "Where to Dine," below). The Café Grand serves buffets at breakfast and dinner. The Spanish Grill draws the lunch crowd, with its barbecues and island drinks. The Splash Bar is open daily from 11am to midnight, and entertainment is often presented in season.

Services: Round-trip transfers from St. Thomas airport, supervised activities program for children, babysitting, laundry, room service.

Facilities: 11,000-square-foot swimming pool, six lit tennis courts, 1,200-foot beach, water sports, fitness center.

HOUSEKEEPING UNITS

Villa vacations are on the rise on St. John, a home away from home. Offering large measures of freedom, private homes and condos deliver spaciousness and comfort, as well as privacy, and come with fully equipped kitchens, dining areas, bedrooms, and such amenities as VCRs and patio grills. Rentals go from large multiroom resort homes to simply decorated one-bedroom condos. Villa rentals typically average about $1,200 to $2,000 per week year round, an affordable option for multiple couples or families looking for a large house. Condos generally range from $105 to $360 per night per unit. For information on privately owned villas and condos on St. John, call **800/USVI-INFO.**

Ⓢ Caribbean Villas & Resort Management Co., Inc.

P.O. Box 458, St. John, USVI 00831. ☎ **809/776-6152**, or 800/338-0987 in the U.S. A/C. Most less than $200 per night (a Cruz View two-bedroom unit for four costs $220 in winter, $150 off-season). Private homes more expensive. Children under 6 stay free. No credit cards. Free parking. Transportation: Taxi.

Caribbean Villas & Resorts, the island's biggest company, is your best bet if you're seeking a villa or a condo on St. John. This well-run outfit, directed by Richard Clark, offers 74 private villas and condos.

For vacationers to St. John, this has become an alternative vacation lifestyle. There are actually more villa and condo beds available for rent on St. John than there are hotel beds. For babyboomers who now have their own babies, spending a week in a hotel room with two or three kids can be stressful, but not in a three-bedroom, 3,500-square-foot, $600,000 private luxury home which might be yours for the same price you'd pay for a hotel room. Villa rentals can be an economical yet comfortable and luxurious option for honeymooners, couples, families, or groups of friends who wish to vacation on St. John. Private homes range from two to six bedrooms, renting for around $200 to $1,500 (although prices vary) per night with swimming pools, Jacuzzi, and views.

Estate Concordia

P.O. Box 310, Cruz Bay, St. John, USVI 00831. ☎ **212/472-9453** in New York City, or 800/ 392-9004 in the U.S. and Canada. Fax 212/861-6210 in New York City. 9 studios. Winter, $135–$190 studio for two. Off-season, $95–$150 studio for two. Additional person $25 extra. Seven nights minimum stay in winter. No credit cards. Free parking.

Opened in 1993, this development project was widely praised for its adherence to sustainable development and integration with the local ecosystem. Elevated modular structures were designed to coexist with the stunning but fragile landscapes of the dry southern edge of St. John. Nestled on a low cliff above a salt pond, surrounded by hundreds of acres of pristine national park, the secluded location is recommended for those who arrange for their own rental vehicle. Each building was sited to protect mature trees, and is interconnected to its neighbors with raised boardwalks, under which the utility and electrical lines are concealed. Their developer was Stanley Selengut, a New York–based entrepreneur whose pioneer work in ecological preservation has achieved fame throughout the region.

The nine units are contained in six postmodern cottages capped with ventilation stacks which cool by means of natural convection. Each comes with kitchen, bathroom, sleeping beds, balcony, ceiling fan, tile floors, and more. Each floor plan features a large airy space usually without dividing walls, and contains either a kitchenette or a full kitchen and, in some cases, high peaked ceilings. Some units have an extra bedroom or a larger-than-expected private bathroom.

Estate Concordia also features a private deep-water swimming pool and guest laundry facilities. On-site management assists with activity suggestions and ideas for touring the several sights of natural beauty nearby.

Harmony

P.O. Box 310, Cruz Bay, St. John, USVI 00831. ☎ **212/472-9453** in New York City, or 800/ 392-9004 in the U.S. and Canada. Fax 212/861-6210 in New York City. 12 studios. Winter, $150–$170 double. Off-season, $95–$125 double. Additional person $25 extra. Seven nights minimum stay in winter. No credit cards. Free parking.

Built on a hillside above the well-recommended and well-established Maho Bay Campground, this is a small-scale cluster of 12 luxury units in six two-story houses with views sweeping down to the sea. Designed to combine both ecological technology and comfort, it's one of the few resorts in the Caribbean to operate exclusively on sun and wind power. Its construction guidelines are among the most ecologically sensitive anywhere, and were adopted as part of the U.S. National Park Service "Handbook for Sustainable Design." Most of the building materials are derived from recycled materials, including reconstituted plastic and glass containers, newsprint, old tires, and scrap lumber. The managers and staff are committed to offering educational experiences as well as the services of a small-scale resort. Guests are asked to share their experience of living in an ecologically sensitive resort. They are taught to operate a user-friendly computer telling them how their unit's energy is being spent, and to give their assessments of the establishment's experimental appliances, furnishings, and supplies.

Units contain queen-size sofabeds and/or twin beds, tile bathrooms, kitchenettes, dining areas, and outdoor terraces. Guests can walk a short distance downhill to use the restaurant, grocery store, and water-sports facilities at the Maho Bay campground.

Lavender Hill Estates

P.O. Box 8306, Cruz Bay, St. John, USVI 00831-8306. ☎ **809/776-6969.** Fax 809/ 776-6969. 10 condo apartments. TV TEL. Winter, $210 one-bedroom unit; $265 two-bedroom unit. Summer, $135 one-bedroom unit; $160 two-bedroom unit. MC, V. Free parking. Transportation: Taxi.

The outfit offers some of the best condominium values on the island, with a swimming pool with lounging deck and a tropical setting. It's a short walk to the shops, markets, restaurants, and safari buses of Cruz Bay. The rates are midway between the campgrounds and inns and the upscale properties of Virgin Grand and Caneel Bay. The units, built in 1984, overlook Cruz Bay Harbor, and each one has a spacious central living/dining area opening onto a tiled deck, along with a fully equipped kitchen and one or two bedrooms. Laundry facilities are available. Units are furnished in a modern Caribbean style.

Villa Portfolio Management

P.O. Box 618, Cruz Bay, St. John, USVI 00831. ☎ **809/693-9100,** or 800/858-7989. A/C. Winter, $195–$295 per night, $1,365–$1,675 per week, for one or two occupants. Summer, $105–$125 per night, $875–$966 per week, for one or two occupants. No credit cards. Free parking. Transportation: Taxi.

This agency offers about a dozen condominium apartments which many renters accept for time periods of a week or more. (The names of the individual building complexes include the Battery Hill Condominiums and the Villa Caribe Condominiums.) Each has its own self-contained kitchen, as well as views over either the town and harbor of Cruz Bay or the faraway coastline of St. Thomas. Units include one- and two-bedroom town houses, often on more than one level, and usually with verandas, terraces, ceiling fans, and patios. Each is individually furnished in off-whites and pastel colors, and all units under the management of this company are a short walk south of Cruz Bay.

GUESTHOUSES

Let's face it. Except for the campgrounds recommended next, the tabs at most of the establishments on St. John are far beyond the pocketbook of the average traveler. If you'll settle for just the minimum necessities, the following places will provide a low-cost holiday on St. John. These are places merely "to bunk."

⑤ The Cruz Inn

P.O. Box 566, Cruz Bay, St. John, USVI 00831. ☎ **809/693-8688,** or 800/666-7688 in the U.S. Fax 809/693-8688. 14 rms (5 with bath and kitchen). Winter, $55 double without bath; $65–$95 efficiency for two. Off-season, $50 double without bath; $65–$85 efficiency for two. Additional person $15 extra. (Includes continental breakfast.) Three-day minimum stay in housekeeping units. AE, MC, V. Free parking.

Seven of the guest rooms are in the main building and share two baths; each has an overhead fan and either a double bed or twin beds. Other accommodations are efficiencies and apartments in the complex. Five of the units have cooking facilities. Overlooking Enighed Pond, the inn also has a convivial bar and offers weekly entertainment. Tennis courts are available nearby. A food service allows you to order a full breakfast if you want to, as well as a take-out lunch or a simple dinner.

⑤ Raintree Inn

P.O. Box 566, Cruz Bay, St. John, USVI 00831. ☎ **809/693-8590,** or 800/666-7449. Fax 809/693-8590. 8 rms, 3 efficiencies. A/C TEL. Winter, $70 double; $95 efficiency. Summer, $50 double; $75 efficiency. Three-day minimum stay in efficiencies. AE, MC, V. Free parking.

One block from the ferry stop, next to the Catholic church, the Raintree Inn has simple no-smoking double rooms, some with high ceilings. Linen, towels, and soap are supplied upon request. The three efficiencies have full kitchens, and two twins are in a carpeted loft. A small deck is attached. The inn adjoins a reasonably priced restaurant next door, the Fish Trap (see "Where to Dine," below). Laundry service is available on the premises.

CAMPGROUNDS

Cinnamon Bay Campground

P.O. Box 720, Cruz Bay, St. John, USVI 00831. ☎ **809/776-6330,** or 800/539-9998 in the U.S. Fax 809/776-6458. 126 units (none with bath). Winter, $86–$95 cottage for two; $67 tent; $15 bare site. Off-season, $59–$61 cottage for two; $44 tent; $15 bare site (five-day minimum). $18.50 per person extra. AE, MC, V. Free parking. Transportation: Safari bus from Cruz Bay.

Established by the National Park Service in 1964, this is the most complete campground in the Caribbean. The site is directly on the beach, and thousands of acres of tropical vegetation surround you. Life is simple here, and you have a choice of three different ways of sleeping: tents, cottages, and bare sites. At the bare camp-sites, nothing is provided except general facilities. Canvas tents are 10 by 14 feet with floor, and a number of facilities are offered, including all cooking equipment. Even your linen is changed weekly. Cottages are 15 by 15 feet, a screened room with two concrete walls and two screen walls. They contain four twin beds, and two cots can be added; cooking facilities are also supplied. Lavatories and show-ers are in separate buildings nearby. Camping is limited to a two-week period in any given year. Near the road is a camp center office, with a grocery and a cafeteria (dinners for $15).

✪ Maho Bay

P.O. Box 310, Cruz Bay, St. John, USVI 00831. ☎ **809/776-6226** or 212/472-9453 in New York City, or 800/392-9004. Fax 212/816-6210 in New York City. 114 tent-cottages (none with bath). Mid-Dec to Apr, $90 tent-cottage for two (minimum stay of seven nights re-quired). May to mid-Dec, $60 tent-cottage for two (no minimum stay required). Additional occupant $12 extra for those over 16, $10 extra for each children 15 and younger. No credit cards. Free parking. Transportation: Maho Bay shuttle.

Maho Bay is an interesting concept in ecology vacationing, where you camp close to nature, but with considerable comfort. Defined as a deluxe campground, an 8-mile drive northeast from Cruz Bay, it's set on a hillside above the beach sur-rounded by the Virgin Islands National Park. To preserve the existing ground cover, all 114 tent-cottages are on platforms above a thickly wooded slope. Utility lines and pipes are hidden under wooden boardwalks and stairs.

The tent-cottages are covered with canvas and screens. Each unit has two movable twin beds, a couch, electric lamps and outlets, a dining table, chairs, a pro-pane stove, and an ice chest (cooler). That's not all—you're furnished linen, towels, and cooking and eating utensils. There's a store where you can buy supplies. You can do your own cooking or eat at the camp's outdoor restaurant. Guests share communal bathhouses.

Maho Bay has an open-air Pavilion Restaurant, which always serves breakfast and dinner. Lunches are offered in winter, and the international dinner menu is changed nightly depending on what food is fresh. Both meat and vegetarian selections are offered. The Pavilion also functions as an amphitheater and com-munity center where various programs are featured. The camp has an excellent water-sports program.

WHERE TO DINE
VERY EXPENSIVE
Caneel Bay Beach Terrace Dining Room

In the Caneel Bay Hotel. ☎ **809/776-6111.** Reservations required for dinner. Appetizers $6.50–$12.50; main courses $28–$38; fixed-price dinner $55; lunch buffet $22. AE, DC, MC, V. Lunch daily 11:30am–2:30pm; dinner daily 7–9pm. Transportation: Taxi. INTERNATIONAL/SEAFOOD.

Right below the Equators (see below) is an elegant choice with open-air tables overlooking the beach. The self-service buffet luncheon is one of the best in the Virgin Islands. Appetizers might include papaya with prosciutto. Salads are good, including the marinated green bean or the tossed garden greens mimosa. Main dishes are likely to include baked filet of red snapper or roast prime rib of blue-ribbon beef carved to order with natural juices. For dessert, try strawberry cheesecake or Boston cream pie. Menus change nightly. On Monday the chef offers surf and turf on the grill.

EXPENSIVE

Ciao Mein

In the Hyatt Regency St. John, Great Cruz Bay. ☎ **809/693-8000.** Reservations recommended. Appetizers $5.75–$10.25; main courses $20–$26.75. AE, DC, MC, V. Dinner only, daily 6–9:30pm. Transportation: Taxi. ASIAN/ITALIAN.

Hypermodern marble tables are placed one floor above the most dramatic lobby in the Caribbean, with views down an atrium to an architectural design, inspired by the ziggurats of ancient Egypt or Mesopotamia. Piano music filters from a spot-lit dais to the lobby below as scents from the hotel's gardens filter upward. You can dine transculturally here, first going Oriental with an order of Thai spring rolls or perhaps shredded duck salad. Of course, if it's Italian, it might be antipasto or zuppe minestrone. Chinese specialties include a fried whole fish with a julienne of vegetables or perhaps crispy duck with Chinese barbecue sauce. Main dishes on the Italian side feature chicken breast baked with mozzarella and Parmesan in a marinara sauce or pan-seared veal Norman with eggplant.

Ellington's

Gallows Point, Cruz Bay. ☎ **809/776-7166.** Reservations required for upstairs seating only. Appetizers $6–$10; main dishes $13–$30. AE, MC, V. Breakfast daily 8–11am; dinner daily 6–10pm. CONTINENTAL.

Ellington's is set near the neocolonial villas of Gallows Point, to the right after you disembark from the ferry. Its putty-colored exterior has the same kind of double staircase, fan windows, louvers, and low-slung hip roof found in an 18th-century Danish manor house. Drop in for a drink on the panoramic upper deck where an unsurpassed view of St. Thomas and neighboring cays unfolds with a backdrop of sunsets. The establishment is named after a local radio announcer ("The Fat Man"), raconteur, and mystery writer whose real estate developments helped transform St. John into a stylish enclave for the American literati of the 1950s and 1960s. Named Richard "Duke" Ellington (not to be confused with the great musician), he entertained his friends, martini in hand, around a frequently photographed table painted with a map of St. John. The tabletop today is a centerpiece at the sunset lounge.

The dinner menu changes often to accommodate the freshest offerings of the sea—sometimes wahoo or mahi mahi with Cajun spices. Some other favorites include conch fritters, swordfish scampi, coconut shrimp with passionfruit dipping sauce, chilled mango soup, chicken Martinique, baked scallops à la Duke, and blackened beef tips Bolongo.

✪ Equators

In the Caneel Bay Hotel, Caneel Bay. ☎ **809/776-6111.** Reservations recommended. Appetizers $6–$10; main courses $13.50–$30. AE, MC, V. Dinner only, Tues–Sun 6:30–10pm. CARIBBEAN/LATIN/THAI.

This restaurant lies behind the bougainvillea-laden tower of an 18th-century sugar mill, where ponds with water lilies fill former crystallization pits for hot molasses. A flight of stairs leads to a monumental circular dining room, with a wraparound veranda and sweeping views of a park. In the center rises the stone column that horses and mules once circumambulated to crush sugarcane stalks.

Entrées include teriyaki tuna with a picked lobster hand roll and tempura vegetables; pepper-cured tandoori lamb with Egyptian couscous; and wok-fried catfish with Polynesian ponzu and fried rice.

Le Château de Bordeaux

Junction 10, Centerline Rd., Bordeaux Mountain. ☎ **809/776-6611.** Reservations recommended. Appetizers $5.95–$7.95; main dishes $17.95–$26.95. DC, MC, V. Dinner only, Mon–Sat with two nightly seatings, 5:30–6:30pm and 7:45–8:45pm. Transportation: Taxi. CONTINENTAL/CARIBBEAN.

Set 5 miles east of Cruz Bay near the geographical center of the island, close to one of its highest points at an elevation of 1,300 feet, this restaurant is known for its eastward-facing vistas and some of the best high-altitude views on St. John. Although an ice-cream kiosk sells sundaes and milkshakes throughout the day, most visitors patronize the place for its evening allure. Then, amid a Victorian decor with lace tablecloths, you can enjoy such dishes as banana-papaya conch fritters, saffron-flavored pastas, West Indian seafood chowder, smoked salmon, filet mignon, wild game specials, roast rack of lamb, and a changing array of cheesecakes, among other desserts. The specialty drink is a passionfruit daiquiri.

✪ Paradiso

Mongoose Junction. ☎ **809/776-8806.** Reservations recommended. Appetizers $3.50–$7.95; main courses $15–$26.50. AE, MC, V. Dinner only, Tues–Sun 6–10pm. (Bar, daily 4:30pm–midnight.) ITALIAN/AMERICAN.

The most talked-about restaurant on St. John, and the only one that's air-conditioned, is located among the catwalks and lattices of the island's most interesting shopping center, Mongoose Junction. The decor includes lots of brass, glowing hardwoods, and nautical antiques. Paradiso has what might be the most beautiful bar on the island—it's crafted from mahogany, purpleheart, and angelique.

Menu items include pastas, Caesar salads, a platter of smoked seafood, baked stuffed sole with a lobster-cream sauce, lobster Fra Diavolo (with seafood and red chiles), and a selection of daily specials whose availability depends on their arrival that day from the U.S. mainland. The house drink is Paradiso Punch, the bartender's version of plantation punch.

MODERATE

⑤ Café Roma

Cruz Bay. ☎ **809/776-6524.** Reservations not required. Appetizers $2.75–$8; main courses $12–$15.50. AE, MC, V. Dinner only, daily 5–10pm. ITALIAN.

Diners climb a flight of steps to reach this restaurant in the center of Cruz Bay. You might arrive early and have a strawberry colada, then enjoy a pasta, veal, seafood, or chicken dish. Ask for their "white pizza," made without the red sauce. Different specialties are featured every night. Italian wines are sold by the glass or bottle, and you can end the evening with an espresso.

INEXPENSIVE

Don Carlos Mexican Seafood Cantina

10–19 Estate Carolina, Coral Bay. ☎ **809/776-6866.** Reservations required during winter. Appetizers $5.95–$8.95; main courses $9.95–$17.95. AE, MC, V. Daily 11am–9 or 10pm. (Bar, daily 11am–10:30pm.) MEXICAN.

An open-sided pavilion at the edge of the sea overlooking Coral Bay, this establishment is one of the best Mexican restaurants in the Virgin Islands, a branch of an award-winning chain of Stateside restaurants known for their fajitas and foaming margaritas. Amid a decor of Mexican weavings and a prominent bar, you can order such food items as Mexican-style conch fritters served with avocado slices and salsa ranchero, at least four kinds of what the owners claim are the most famous fajitas north of the Mexican border, and swordfish Vera Cruz, charcoal-grilled with beans, rice, and a tomato-onion salsa. The most popular drink? A jumbo, 36-ounce margarita concocted for two, priced at $14 each.

The Fish Trap

In the Raintree Inn, Cruz Bay. ☎ **809/693-9994.** Reservations required only for parties of six or more. Appetizers $2.95–$8.95; main dishes $15.95–$22.95; pastas and burgers $8.95–$17.95. AE, MC, V. Dinner only. Tues–Sun 4:30–9:30pm. SEAFOOD.

In this previously recommended inn standing in the center of the island's capital, the Fish Trap enjoys both local and foreign patronage. It's known for its wide selection of seafood, but it also caters to the vegetarian and burger crowd. In the midst of coconut palms and banana trees, most diners begin with the conch fritters or the Fish Trap chowder. They might try a tasty seafood combo, blackened sea scallops, or shrimp Palermo (with olive oil, garlic, and parsley). All desserts are prepared fresh in the kitchen daily.

Mongoose Restaurant, Café, and Bar

Mongoose Junction. ☎ **809/776-7586.** Reservations required during winter. Appetizers $3–$8 at lunch, $3–$10 at dinner; main dishes $8–$20; Salads, burgers, and sandwiches $5–$9. AE, DC, MC, V. Breakfast daily 8:30–11:30am; lunch Mon–Sat 11:30am–5pm; dinner daily 5–10pm; brunch Sun 11:30am–5pm. (Bar, daily 11am–10pm.) CARIBBEAN.

Some visitors compare the soaring interior design here to a large Japanese birdcage, because of the strong vertical lines and the 25-foot ceiling. Set among trees and built above a stream, it's a lot like a structure you might find in northern California. Some guests perch at the open-centered bar for a drink and sandwich, while others sit on an adjacent deck where a canopy of trees filters the tropical sunlight. The bar offers more than 20 varieties of frothy island-inspired libations.

Lunches include soups, well-stuffed sandwiches, salad platters, burgers, and pastas. Dinner is more formal, with such specialties as grilled steaks, fresh catch of the day, surf and turf, seafood Créole, and island fish cakes. This establishment's Sunday brunch is mobbed with St. Johnians, who make eggs Benedict the most popular dish.

Pusser's

Wharfside Village, Cruz Bay. ☎ **809/693-8489.** Reservations recommended. Appetizers $4.95–$8.95; main courses $12.95–$24.95. AE, MC, V. Lunch daily 11am–3pm; dinner daily 6–10pm. INTERNATIONAL/CARIBBEAN.

A double-decker air-conditioned store and pub in Cruz Bay, Pusser's overlooks the harbor and is near the ferry dock. These stores are unique in the Caribbean, and they serve Pusser's Rum, a blend of five West Indian rums that the Royal Navy has served to its men for three centuries. Here you can enjoy traditional English fare, including steak and ale. Other dishes are Cajun barbecued chicken, crab ravioli, lobster medallions, and New York strip steak. Finish with Pusser's famous "mud pie." If you're in your bathing suit and want only a hamburger or some such fast food for lunch, try Pusser's Beach Bar.

Ⓢ Shipwreck Landing

34 Freeman's Ground, Rte. 107, Coral Bay. ☎ **809/693-5640.** Reservations not required. Appetizers $3.50–$8.50; main courses $11.25–$17.50. MC, V. Daily 11am–10pm. (Bar, daily 11am–11pm.) SEAFOOD/CONTINENTAL.

Eight miles east of Cruz Bay on the road to Salt Pond Beach, Shipwreck Landing is run by Pat and Dennis Rizzo. You dine amid palms and tropical plants on a veranda overlooking the sea. The intimate bar specializes in tropical frozen drinks. The menu includes conch fritters and scungilli salad, blackened red snapper, and surf and turf, along with daily seafood specials. Vegetarian dishes and pasta are a special feature. There's likely to be music featured on Tuesday, Thursday, and Sunday night in winter.

WHAT TO SEE & DO

Many visitors like to spend a lot of time at **Cruz Bay,** where the ferry docks. In this West Indian village there are interesting bars, restaurants, boutiques, and pastel-painted houses. It's pretty sleepy, but it's relaxing after the fast pace of St. Thomas. The **Elaine Ione Sprauve Museum** (☎ **809/776-6359**) at Cruz Bay isn't big, but it does contain some local artifacts, and it will teach you some of the history of the island. It's at the public library and can be visited Monday through Friday from 9am to 5pm; admission is free.

Most cruise-ship passengers dart through Cruz Bay and head for the island's biggest attraction, the ✪ **Virgin Islands National Park** (☎ **809/776-6201**). But before going to the park, you may want to stop at the visitor center at Cruz Bay, which is open daily from 8am to 4:30pm. There you'll see some exhibits and learn more about what you can see in the park.

Established in 1956 to preserve significant natural and cultural values, the park totals 12,624 acres, including submerged lands and water adjacent to St. John. The park has more than 20 miles of biking trails to explore.

If time is limited, try to visit the **Annaberg Ruins,** Leinster Bay Road, where the Danes maintained a thriving plantation and sugar mill after 1718. It's located off North Shore Road east of Trunk Bay on the north shore. On certain days of the week (dates vary) guided walks of the area are given by park rangers.

Trunk Bay is considered one of the world's most beautiful beaches. It's also the site of one of the world's first marked underwater trails (bring your mask, snorkel, and fins). It lies to the east of Cruz Bay along North Shore Road. Beware of pickpockets.

Fort Berg (also called Fortsberg), at Coral Bay, dating from 1717, played a disastrous role during the 1733 slave revolt. The fort may be restored as a historic monument.

NATIONAL PARK ACTIVITIES   The National Park Service provides a number of free ranger-led activities in the park. One of the most popular is the 2 1/2-mile Reef Bay hike. A park ranger leads the hike down the Reef Bay Trail interpreting the natural and cultural history along the way. Included is a stop at the only known petroglyphs on the island and a tour of the sugar mill ruins. Reservations are required for this hike and can be made by calling **809/776-6330.** Visitors are encouraged to stop by the Cruz Bay Visitor Center upon their arrival on the island. At the visitor center you can pick up the park brochure, which includes a map of the park, and the *Virgin Islands National Park News,* which has the latest information on activities in the park.

NATURE NOTES   St. John's status as the home of the largest U.S. National Park in the Caribbean guarantees a wide choice of clearly marked **walking paths.** At least 20 of these originate from various clearly marked points along either North Shore Road (Route 20) or from points along the island's main east-west artery, Centerline Road (Route 10). Each is marked at its origin with what a hiker might expect to find at the final destination, and each presents a pre-planned itinerary which usually lasts 10 minutes to two hours.

Another series of **hikes** traversing the more arid eastern section of St. John originate at clearly marked points along the island's southeastern tip, at points leading off Route 107. Regardless of their locations, many of the trails traverse the grounds of 18th-century plantations, often circumnavigating ruined schoolhouses, rum distilleries, molasses factories, and Great Houses, many of them verdantly overgrown with encroaching vines and trees.

Because of the island's semiwild state, with terrain ranging from arid and dry (in the east) to moist and semitropical in the northwest, many hikers and trekkers consider a visit here among the most rewarding in the Virgin Islands. The island boasts more than 800 species of plants, 160 species of birds, and more than 20 hiking trails maintained in fine form by the island's crew of park rangers.

Maps of the island's hiking trails are readily available from the national park headquarters at Cruz Bay, but one of my favorite tours requires only about a half-mile stroll (about 30 minutes, round-trip, not including stops to admire the views) and departs from clearly marked points along the island's north coast, near the junction of Routes 10 and 20. Identified by the National Park Service as **Trail no. 10 (the Annaberg Historic Trail)**, it's a self-guided tour which includes the partially restored ruins of a manor house built during the 1700s overlooking the island's north coast. Signs along the way give historical and botanical data.

If you want to prolong your experience, **Trail no. 11 (the Leinster Bay Trail)** begins near the point where Trail no. 10 ends. Following the edge of Watermelon Bay, it leads past mangrove swamps and coral inlets rich with plant and marine life, often with markers identifying some of the plants and animals.

SPORTS & OUTDOOR ACTIVITIES

Don't visit St. John expecting to play golf. Rather, anticipate some of the best snorkeling, scuba diving, swimming, fishing, hiking, sailing, and underwater photography in the Caribbean. The island is known for its coral-sand beaches, winding mountain roads, trails past old, bush-covered sugarcane plantations, and hidden coves.

BEACHES

The lure is ✪ **Trunk Bay,** already endorsed under "What to See and Do." It's the biggest attraction on St. John and a beach collector's find. To miss its great white sweep would be like touring Europe and skipping Paris. Trouble is, even though it's a beautiful stretch of sand, the word is out. It's likely to be overcrowded, and there are pickpockets. The beach has lifeguards and offers rentals, such as snorkel gear. Beginning snorkelers in particular are attracted to its underwater trail near the shore. Both taxis and "safari buses" to Trunk Bay meet the ferry as it docks at Cruz Bay from Red Hook on St. Thomas.

As mentioned, **Caneel Bay,** the stamping ground of the rich and famous, has seven beautiful beaches on its 170 acres—but only one open to the public. That's **Hawksnest Beach,** a little gem of white sand, beloved by St. Johnians. The beach is a bit narrow and windy, but beautiful, as filmmakers long ago discovered. Close to the road are barbecue grills, and there are portable toilets. Safari buses and taxis from Cruz Bay will take you along North Shore Road.

The campgrounds of **Cinnamon Bay** and **Maho Bay** (see "Where to Stay," above) have their own beaches where forest rangers sometimes have to remind visitors to put their swimming trunks back on. Snorkelers find good reefs here, and changing rooms and showers are available.

Salt Pond Bay is known to locals but often missed by visitors. The bay here is tranquil and there are no facilities. The Ram Head Trail beginning here and winding for a mile leads to a panoramic belvedere overlooking the bay.

HIKING

Hiking is the big thing here, and a network of trails covers the national park. However, I suggest a tour by Jeep first, just to get your bearings. At the visitor center at Cruz Bay, ask for a free trail map of the park. It's best to set out with someone experienced in the mysteries of the island. Both Maho Bay and Cinnamon Bay conduct nature walks (see "Campgrounds" in "Where to Stay," above).

TENNIS

Caneel Bay (☎ 809/776-6111) has seven courts and a pro shop, but these courts aren't lit at night and are used exclusively by guests. There are two public courts at Cruz Bay, however. The **Hyatt Regency St. John,** Great Cruz Bay (☎ 809/693-8000), has six tennis courts, all lit at night.

WATER SPORTS

The most complete line of water sports available on St. John is offered at the **Cinnamon Bay Watersports Center** on Cinnamon Bay Beach (☎ 809/776-6330). For the adventurous, there is windsurfing, kayaking, sailing, and bicycling.

The windsurfing here is some of the best anywhere, for either the beginner or the expert. High-quality equipment is available for all levels, even for kids. You can rent a board at $12 an hour; a two-hour introductory lesson costs $40.

Want to paddle to a secluded beach, explore a nearby island with an old Danish ruin, or jump overboard anytime you like for snorkeling or splashing? Then try a sit-on-top kayak; one- and two-person kayaks are available for rent at $10 to $17 per hour.

You can also sail away in a 12- or 14-foot Hobie monohull sailboat, renting for $20 to $30 per hour. Bicycles, at $10 per hour, are also on the sports menu. While St. John's steep hills and off-road trails can challenge the best of riders, more moderate rides are to visit the ruins at Annaberg or the beaches at Maho, Francis, Leinster, or Watermelon Bay.

You can also take half- and full-day **boat charters,** including trips to the Baths at Virgin Gorda on Tuesday. The cost of this full-day adventure is $65 per person. An "Around St. John Snorkel Excursion" costs $40 per person, and a sunset cocktail cruise also goes for $40 per person. Call Capt. Robert Conn (☎ 809/776-6462 or 809/771-3996) for more details.

You can obtain snorkeling equipment from the Watersports Beach Shop for $4. Divers can ask about scuba packages at **Low Key Watersports,** Wharfside Village (☎ 809/693-8999, or 800/835-7718). All wreck dives are two-tank/two-location dives. A one-tank dive costs $45 per person, with night dives going for $55. Snorkel tours are also available at $25 per person. The center uses its own custom-built dive boats and also offers and specializes in water-sports gear, including masks, fins, snorkels, and "dive skins." It also arranges day sailing charters and deep-sea sportfishing.

Cruz Bay Watersports, Cruz Bay (☎ 809/776-6234), is a PADI and NAUI five-star diving center on St. John. Certifications can be arranged through a divemaster, costing $350 to $495. It operates four custom dive boats every day of the year with a staff of 10 instructors. Certification classes start daily, as well as two-tank reef dives with all the dive gear for $70 to $78. Beginner scuba lessons start at $65, and wreck dives (Wednesday and Friday), night dives, and dive packages are available at accommodations that range from budget to first class.

SHOPPING

Compared to St. Thomas, it isn't much, but what's here is interesting. The boutiques and shops of Cruz Bay are individualized and quite special. Most of the shops are clustered at **Mongoose Junction,** in a woodsy area beside the roadway, about a five-minute walk from the ferry dock. I've already recommended restaurants in this complex (see "Where to Dine," above), and it also contains shops of merit.

Before you set sail for St. Thomas, you'll want to visit **Wharfside Village,** just a few steps from the ferry-departure point on the waterfront, opening onto Cruz Bay. Here in this complex of courtyards, alleys, and shady patios is a mishmash of all sorts of boutiques, along with some restaurants, fast-food joints, and bars.

Bamboula

Mongoose Junction. ☎ **809/693-8699.**

Bamboula has an unusual and very appealing collection of gifts from such destinations as Guatemala, Haiti, India, Indonesia, and Central Africa. Its exoticism is unexpected and very pleasant.

The Canvas Factory

Cruz Bay. ☎ **809/776-6196.**

The Canvas Factory produces its own handmade, rugged, and colorful canvas bags in the "factory" at Mongoose Junction. Their products range from sailing hats to handsome luggage to an extensive line of island-made 100% cotton clothing.

The Clothing Studio

Mongoose Junction. ☎ **809/776-6585.**

The Caribbean's oldest hand-painted–clothing studio has been in operation since 1978. You can watch talented artists create original designs on fine tropical clothing, including swimwear, and daytime and evening clothing, for babies, women, and men.

Donald Schnell Studio

Mongoose Junction. ☎ **809/776-6420.**

In this working studio and gallery, Mr. Schnell and his assistants feature one of the finest collections of handmade pottery, sculpture, and blown glass in the Caribbean. The staff can be seen working daily and are especially noted for their rough-textured coral work. Water fountains are a specialty item, as are house signs. The coral pottery dinnerware is unique and popular. The studio will mail works all over the world. Go in and discuss any particular design you may have in mind—they enjoy designing to please customers.

Fabric Mill

Mongoose Junction. ☎ **809/776-6194.**

This shop features silk-screened and batik fabrics from around the world. Vibrant rugs and bed, bath, and table linens add the perfect touch to your home. Whimsical soft sculpture, sarongs, scarves, and handbags are also made in this studio shop.

Pusser's of the West Indies

Wharfside Village, Cruz Bay. ☎ **809/693-8489.**

This link in a famous chain was previously recommended for food and drink. The store offers a large collection of classically designed old-world travel and adventure clothing along with unusual accessories. It's a unique shopping trip for the island. Clothing for women, men, and children is displayed, along with T-shirts carrying Pusser's emblem. Nautical paintings and antiques from "all over" are also displayed.

R and I Patton Goldsmithing

Cruz Bay. ☎ **809/776-6548.**

On the island since 1973, this is one of the oldest tourist businesses here. Next to the entrance to Mongoose Junction, it has a large selection of island-designed jewelry in sterling silver, gold, and precious stones.

3 St. Croix

The largest of the U.S. Virgin Islands, 84 square miles, St. Croix was a stop for Columbus on November 14, 1493, but the reception committee of Carib tribesmen was far from friendly. He anchored his ship off Salt River Point, on the north shore of St. Croix, before the Caribs drove him away. However, before leaving he named the island Santa Cruz (Spanish for Holy Cross). The cannibalistic Caribs made later colonizing parties less than eager to settle on St. Croix.

The Dutch, the English, the Spanish, and the French all claimed St. Croix at one time or another, but the Danes purchased the island in 1773, attracted to the site because of its slave labor and sugarcane fields. This marked the golden era for both planters and pirates. However, the sugar boom ended with eventual slave uprisings, the introduction of the sugar beet in Europe, and the emancipation of 1848. Even though seven different flags have flown over St. Croix, it's the nearly 2^1/$_2$ centuries of Danish influence that still permeates the island and its architecture.

At the east end of St. Croix, which, incidentally, is the easternmost point of the United States, the terrain is rocky and arid. The west end is lusher, with a rain forest of mango and mahogany, tree ferns, and dangling lianas. Rolling hills and upland pastures characterize the area lying between the two extremes. African tulips are just some of the flowers that add a splash of color to the landscape, which is dotted with stately towers that once supported grinding mills.

St. Croix has some of the best beaches in the Virgin Islands, and ideal weather. It doesn't have the nightlife of St. Thomas, nor would its permanent residents want that.

ORIENTATION

GETTING AROUND

BY BUS   Air-conditioned buses run between Christiansted and Frederiksted about every 40 minutes daily between the hours of 6am and 9pm. Beginning at Tide Village, to the east of Christiansted, buses go along Route 75 to the Golden Rock Shopping Center. Then they make their way to Route 70, with stopovers at the Sunny Isle Shopping Center, La Reine Shopping Center, St. George Village Botanical Garden, and Whim Plantation Museum, before reaching Frederiksted.

Bus service is also available from the airport to each of the two towns. Fares are $1. For more information, call **809/773-7746.**

BY TAXI At Alexander Hamilton Airport you'll find official taxi rates posted. Per-person rates require a minimum of two passengers; a single person pays double the posted fares. Expect to pay about $10 for one or two riders from the airport to Christiansted and about $8.50 for one or two from the airport to Frederiksted. As the cabs are unmetered, agree on the rate before you get in.

The **St. Croix Taxicab Associations** (☎ **809/778-1088**) offer door-to-door service.

Taxi tours are the ideal way to explore the island. For one or two passengers, the cost is often $35 for two hours or $45 for three hours, but all fares have to be negotiated.

BY RENTAL CAR This is a suitable means of exploring for some, but know that if you're going into "bush country," the roads are often disastrous. Sometimes the government smooths them out before the big season begins.

Car-rental rates on St. Croix are reasonable. However, because of the island's higher-than-usual accident rate (which is partly because many tourists aren't used to driving on the left), insurance costs might be higher than on the mainland.

Budget (☎ **809/778-9636,** or **800/472-3325**), **Hertz** (☎ **809/778-1402,** or **800/654-3001**), and **Avis** (☎ **809/778-9365,** or **800/331-2112**) all maintain their headquarters at the island's airport, with kiosks near the baggage-claim areas.

Each of the big-three companies offer such vehicles as Suzuki Swifts, Suzuki Esteems, and Ford Escorts, usually with automatic transmission and air conditioning. Rates vary from company to company. A spot check revealed Budget offering cars for $198 to $270 for five or six days; Hertz, $240 to $370 weekly; and Avis, $189 to $269 weekly.

Renters at all three companies must be older than 25 and, in some cases, not older than 70, and present a valid driver's license and a credit or charge card at the time of rental.

Collision-damage insurance can be arranged for an additional fee of $9.95 to $11.95 per day, depending on the company. It's a wise investment, especially since without it you're liable for up to the full value of the car in the event of an accident. However, your credit-or charge-card issuer might cover collision-damage protection; check with the card issuer directly to find out.

ESSENTIALS

The **American Express representative** is Southerland, Chandler's Wharf, Gallows Bay (☎ **809/773-9500**). For medical care, try the **St. Croix Hospital,** 6 Diamond Bay, Christiansted (☎ **809/778-6311**).

WHERE TO STAY

All rooms are subject to a 8% hotel room tax, which is *not* included in the rates given below.

If you're interested in a villa or condo rental, contact **Island Villas,** Property Management Rentals, 14A Caravelle Arcade, Christiansted (☎ **809/773-8821,** or **800/626-4512**), which offers some of the best properties on St. Croix. The outfit specializes in villa and condo rentals, really private residences with pools; many are on the beach. The range goes from one-bedroom units to six-bedroom villas, with prices of $1,200 to $5,000 per week.

VERY EXPENSIVE

✪ Buccaneer

Rte. 82 (P.O. Box 25200), Gallows Bay, St. Croix, USVI 00824. ☎ **809/773-2100,** or 800/255-3881 in the U.S. Fax 809/773-0010. 150 rms. A/C TEL. Winter, $175–$320 single; $195–$340 double. Off-season, $145–$215 single; $165–$235 double. (Includes continental breakfast.) AE, DC, MC, V. Free parking.

A large, luxury, family-owned resort in operation since 1948, the Buccaneer is 2 miles east of Christiansted, and its 240 acres contain three of the island's best beaches. The property was once a cattle ranch and a sugar plantation, and its first estate house, dating from the mid-17th century, stands near a freshwater swimming pool. Pink and patrician, the hotel offers a choice of accommodations in its main building or in one of the beachside properties. The baronially arched main building has a lobby opening toward drinking or viewing terraces, with a sea vista on two sides and Christiansted to the west. The accommodations effectively use modern construction materials and tropical furnishings to provide fresh, comfortable bedrooms, which range from "standard" to "deluxe."

Dining/Entertainment: Breakfast and dinner are served at the Terrace Dining Room and at the Little Mermaid Restaurant. Lunch is also served at the Mermaid and the Grotto, where hamburgers and hot dogs are available. The hotel's gourmet restaurant, the Brass Parrot, is recommended in "Where to Dine," below. There is entertainment nightly at the Terrace Lounge, with a variety of music ranging from Jimmy Hamilton's jazz to island steel drums.

Services: Best sports program on St. Croix; trips arranged to Buck Island.

Facilities: Swimming pool, eight championship tennis courts, fitness center and health spa, 18-hole golf course, 2-mile jogging trail.

Carambola Beach Resort

P.O. Box 3031, Kingshill, St. Croix, USVI 00851. ☎ **809/778-3800,** or 800/333-3333 in the U.S. and Canada. Fax 809/778-1682. 153 rms. A/C TV TEL. Winter, $205–$345 single or double. Off-season, $178–$280 single or double. Breakfast $12 extra. AE, MC, V. Free parking.

Set on 28 acres above Davis Bay, on the island's sparsely populated north shore, a 30-minute drive from Christiansted, this hotel reopened in 1993 after renovations and an ill-fated three-year closing. It had originally opened with much fanfare in 1987, but was done in by Hurricane Hugo. Today it's owned by the Kentucky-based Sargasso Corporation and is operated as a Radisson. The island's only chain hotel, and one of the largest hostelries on St. Croix, it's adjacent to the golf course designed by Robert Trent Jones.

Guests are housed in red-roofed, two-story outbuildings, each of which contains six units. The accommodations are furnished in rattan and wicker, with pastel colors and a balcony partially concealed from outside view, overlooking either the garden or sea.

Dining/Entertainment: Diners face a trio of choices, and the rooms are open to nonresidents. The Saman Room offers breakfast and lunch daily, with dinner served only on Sunday, Monday, and Wednesday night. In the air-conditioned Mahogany Room, dinner is served on Tuesday, Thursday, and Saturday night. Sandwiches and salads are offered daily in the New York Deli, and the hotel's Sunday brunch (11am to 2pm) is already an island tradition. Friday night is a pirate's buffet from 7 to 9pm.

St. Croix

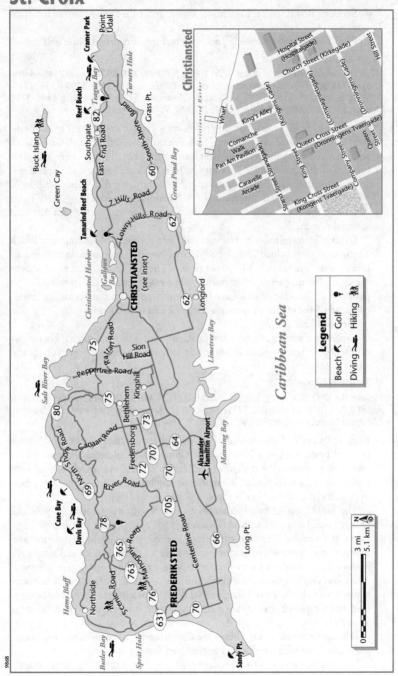

Christiansted

Hospital Street (Hospitalgade)
Church Street (Kirkegade)
Hill Street
King's Alley
Wharf
(Kongens Gade)
Queen Cross Street (Dronningens Tvaergade)
(Dronningens Gade)
King Street
(Companiegade)
Company Street
Comanche Walk
Pan Am Pavilion
Queen Street
Christiansted Harbor
Caravelle Arcade
King Cross Street (Kongens Tvaergade)
Strand Street (Strandgade)
Company Street (Kongens Tvaergade)

Cramer Park
Point Udall
Buck Island
Green Cay
Turners Hole
Reef Beach
Teague Bay
Southgate
East End Road
Grass Pt.
82
60
South Shore Road
Great Pond Bay
Tamarind Reef Beach
7 Hills Road
Lowry Hills Road
62
Christiansted Harbor
Gallows Bay
CHRISTIANSTED
(see inset)
62
Longford
Limetree Bay
75
Ratan Road
Sion Hill Road
Peppertree Road
Kingshill
75
Bethlehem
73
Canaan Road
Fredensborg
707
72
64
River Road
70
Alexander Hamilton Airport
Manning Bay
69
705
Cane Bay
Davis Bay
78
66
North Shore Road
765
Mahogany Road
Long Pt.
Salt River Bay
80
763
Scenic Road
Centerline Road
76
Northside
FREDERIKSTED
631
70
Hams Bluff
Butler Bay
Sprat Hole
Sandy Pt.

Caribbean Sea

Legend

Beach	Golf
Diving	Hiking

N

0   3 mi
0   5.1 km

9868

Services: Room service, babysitting, concierge for the arrangement of tours, car rentals.

Facilities: A large swimming pool, four turf tennis courts, 18-hole golf course.

Cormorant Beach Club

4126 La Grande Princesse, St. Croix, USVI 00820. ☎ **809/778-8920**, or 800/548-4460 in the U.S. Fax 809/778-9218. 34 rms, 4 suites. A/C TV TEL. Winter, $185–$200 single; $210–$230 double; $245–$265 triple; $295 suite. Off-season, $120–$160 single; $140–$190 double; $165–$230 triple; $300 suite. AE, DC, MC, V. Free parking.

The setting, amid a colony of king palms on a 12-acre site about 3 miles northwest of Christiansted along Route 75 on Pelican Cove, strikes a balance between seclusion and accessibility. Long Reef, one of the better-known zoological playgrounds of the Caribbean, is a few hundred feet from the hotel's sandy beachfront. In winter, parents are politely discouraged from bringing their children under 5, which many vacationers appreciate. In well-maintained outbuildings, each room contains a spacious bath lined with coral blocks, cane and wicker furniture, and seasonal flowers.

Dining/Entertainment: You can stay here on the CBC (Comorant Beach Club) meal plan, which includes a gourmet breakfast, complete lunch, and all drinks until 5pm for only $37.50 per person. The AIP (all-inclusive plan) adds to the CBC plan an open dinner menu and all beverages until closing, totaling $77.50 per person. Thursday night is Caribbean Grill Night, with a buffet and entertainment, and Sunday brunch is rated among the best on the island.

Services: Laundry.

Facilities: Freshwater swimming pool, two tennis courts, croquet, library just off the lobby; arrangements can be made for golf, horseback riding, sailing, and scuba diving.

Villa Madeleine

Gallows Bay (P.O. Box 3109), St. Croix, USVI 00822. ☎ **809/778-7377**, or 800/548-4461. Fax 809/773-7515. 43 villas. A/C TV TEL. Winter, $425 two-bedroom villa for four. Off-season, $300 two-bedroom villa for four. AE, DC, MC, V. Free parking.

Eight miles east of Christiansted, Villa Madeleine was built in 1990 on $6^1/2$ acres. Its focal point is a Great House whose Chippendale balconies and four-square proportions emulate the designs of the Danish colonial era. Inside, a splendidly conceived decor incorporates the masses of English chintz and mahogany paneling you'd expect to find in the pages of *Architectural Digest*.

The hotel rents 43 two-bedroom villas, each with its own privacy wall and plunge pool. Decorated with style, each unit has a four-poster bed, marble bathroom, and kitchen. The villas comprising the resort are individually owned, and different management companies handle some of them. Service and standards, it should be noted, can vary greatly depending on the villa you're assigned. Therefore, don't expect the standards and service tradition of a typical Caribbean luxury resort. Beach-lovers willingly travel the third of a mile to the nearest beaches, Reef and Grapevine. Parents are discouraged from bringing their children under 12 years of age.

Dining/Entertainment: There's the Café Madeleine, a continental restaurant, and a piano bar with nautical accessories. No breakfast is served.

Services: Concierge, maid service every three days, babysitting (with advance notice).

Facilities: Small library with writing tables, mini-boutique, games room for cards and billiards, laundry room; access to nearby tennis courts.

MODERATE

Anchor Inn

58 King St., Christiansted, St. Croix, USVI 00820. ☎ **809/773-4000,** or 800/524-2030 in the U.S. Fax 809/773-4408. 31 rms. A/C MINIBAR TV TEL. Winter, $95–$125 single; $115–$145 double; $135–$165 triple. Off-season, $80–$95 single; $90–$105 double; $110–$125 triple. Additional person $20 extra. Breakfast $6 extra. AE, DC, MC, V. Free parking.

One of the few hotels in town directly on the waterfront is set in a courtyard near Government House and the Old Danish Customs House, right in the heart of the national historic district and shopping belt, on the main street of town. The space is so compact and intimate that you might not believe it holds 31 comfortably furnished rooms, each with refrigerator, radio, bath, and a small porch. A few rooms (without porches) have king- and queen-size beds and dressing rooms.

Directly on the waterfront is a sun deck and small swimming pool, as well as the Anchor Inn's own boardwalk, where catamarans and glass-bottom boats operate daily to Buck Island. There are also deep-sea fishing boats, a scuba-dive shop, and honeymoon and family package tours. Dining is at Antoine's on the harbor (see "Where to Dine," below).

Caravelle Hotel

44A Queen Cross St., Christiansted, St. Croix, USVI 00820. ☎ **809/773-0687,** or 800/524-0410 in the U.S. Fax 809/778-7004. 43 rms. A/C TV TEL. Winter, $115–$125 single; $125–$135 double. Off-season, $85–$95 single; $95–$105 double. Breakfast $6 extra. AE, DC, MC, V. Free parking.

Biggest of the downtown hotels, located between Church Street and King Cross Street, the Caravelle usually caters to a business clientele. There's a tile fountain in the lobby. Many resort activities, such as sailing, deep-sea fishing, snorkeling, scuba, golf, and tennis, can be arranged at the reception desk. A swimming pool and sun deck face the water, and all the shopping and activities of the town are close at hand. Rooms are priced according to their view.

⊙ King Christian Hotel

59 King's Wharf (P.O. Box 3619), Christiansted, St. Croix, USVI 00822. ☎ **809/773-2285,** or 800/524-2012 in the U.S. Fax 809/773-9411. 39 rms. A/C TV TEL. Winter, $90 economy single, $120 superior single; $95 economy double, $130 superior double. Off-season, $85 economy single, $95 superior single; $85 economy double, $102 superior double. AE, DC, MC, V.

This hotel is right in the heart of everything, directly on the waterfront. All its front rooms have two double beds, bathroom, cable color TV, refrigerator, room safe, and private balcony overlooking the harbor. No-frills economy-wing rooms have two single beds or one double and a bath, but no view or balcony.

On the premises is the Chart House, one of the best restaurants on St. Croix. You can relax on the sun deck or shaded patio, or in the freshwater pool. The staff will make arrangements for golf, tennis, horseback riding, and sightseeing tours, and there's a beach just a few hundred yards across the harbor, reached by ferry. Mile Mark Charters water-sports center offers daily trips to Buck Island's famous snorkeling trail as well as a complete line of water sports. You can park in a public lot off King Street.

⑤ Pink Fancy

27 Prince St., Christiansted, St. Croix, USVI 00820. ☎ **809/773-8460,** or 800/524-2045 in the U.S. Fax 809/773-6448. 12 rms. A/C TV TEL. Winter, $75–$90 single; $90–$120 double. Off-season, $65–$75 single; $75–$90 double. (Includes continental breakfast.) Children under 12 stay free in parents' room. MC, V.

The Pink Fancy was restored and turned into this small, unique private hotel located one block from the Annapolis Sailing School. The oldest part of the four-building complex is a 1780 Danish town house, now one of the historic places of St. Croix. Years ago the building was a private club for wealthy planters. Fame came when Jane Gottlieb, the Ziegfeld Follies star, opened it as a hotel in 1948. In the 1950s the hotel became a mecca for writers and artists, including, among others, Noel Coward. The efficiency rooms, with ceiling fans, are in four buildings clustered around the swimming pool. Other than the complimentary breakfast and a 24-hour complimentary bar, you're on your own for meals.

INEXPENSIVE

Danish Manor Hotel

2 Company St., Christiansted, St. Croix, USVI 00820. ☎ **809/773-1377,** or 800/524-2609 in the U.S. Fax 809/773-1913. 34 rms, 2 suites. A/C TV. Winter, $59–$85 single; $69–$95 double; $95–$130 suite. Off-season, $49–$85 single; $59–$85 double; $85–$100 suite. (Includes continental breakfast.) AE, DC, MC, V.

Built around an old Danish courtyard and a freshwater pool, right in the heart of town between King Street and Queen Street, this compound combines the very old and the very new. The hotel was erected on the site of a Danish West Indies Company's counting house. An L-shaped three-story addition stands in the rear, with spacious rooms with air conditioning, ceiling fans, and cable TV with HBO. All rooms overlook the courtyard dominated by an ancient mahogany tree. The entrance to the courtyard is through old arches. You can park in a public lot off King Street. The hotel has a courtyard for guests where cool drinks and wine coolers are available, and the popular Italian/seafood restaurant, Tutto Bene (see "Where to Dine," below), fronts the hotel. Guests can swim at the beach in Christiansted Harbor, about a five-minute ferry ride from the hotel.

The Frederiksted

20 Strand St., Frederiksted, St. Croix, USVI 00840. ☎ **809/772-0500,** or 800/524-2025 in the U.S. Fax 809/778-4009. 40 rms. AC/TV TEL. Winter, $85–$95 single; $95–$105 double. Off-season, $75–$85 single; $85–$95 double. Breakfast $4–$7 extra. AE, DC, MC, V. Free parking.

For those who'd like to stay in the "second city" of St. Croix, historic Frederiksted, this contemporary four-story inn is the answer. The location is about a 10-minute ride from the airport in the center of Frederiksted. Much of the activity takes place in the outdoor tiled courtyard, where guests enjoy drinks and listen to live music on Friday and Saturday nights. There's also a small swimming pool here. The bedrooms are done in a tropical motif of pastels and are equipped with small refrigerators for drinks as well as a "wet bar." The best bedrooms—and the most expensive—are those with an ocean view. A full breakfast is served at the poolside patio, and the bar is popular in the evening, as guests order rum punches.

CONDOS

In general, condominiums are rented at half or a third the going hotel rates, and if you wait until after April 15, prices are lowered even more.

Cane Bay Reef Club

P.O. Box 1407, Kingshill, St. Croix, USVI 00851. ☎ **809/778-2966,** or 800/253-8534 in the U.S. 9 suites. Winter, $125–$165 suite for one or two. Off-season, $85–$110 suite for one or two. Additional person $15 extra. MC, V. Free parking.

Since 1975 Carl Seiffer has run one of the little gems of the island, offering nine large suites, each with a living room, a full kitchen, a bedroom, a bath, and a balcony overlooking the water. Trade winds make air conditioning unnecessary, although two units contain it, and the decor is breezy tropical, with cathedral ceilings, overhead fans, and Chilean tiles. The location is on the north shore of St. Croix, about a 20-minute taxi ride from Christiansted, fronting a rocky beach near the Waves at Cane Bay (see below). Guests enjoy the pool, and local rum drinks are served at the patio bar. The hotel's dining choice is the No Name Bar & Grille, where a sample dinner menu always includes grilled fresh fish (perhaps dolphin, wahoo, swordfish, halibut, or tuna). Other dishes might include an old-fashioned pot roast or various stir-fries.

Chenay Bay Beach Resort

Rte. 82, East End Rd. (P.O. Box 24600), St. Croix, USVI 00824. ☎ **809/773-2918,** or 800/548-4457 in the U.S. Fax 809/773-2918. 50 cottages. A/C TV TEL. Winter, $180–$225 cottage for one or two. Off-season, $130–$165 cottage for one or two. Additional person $25 extra. AE, MC, V. Free parking.

With a quiet and "barefoot-casual" ambience, these West Indian–style cottages, new or newly renovated, are nestled on a 30-acre beach, with an open-air swimming pool. With one of the island's finest beaches for swimming, snorkeling, and windsurfing, Chenay Bay is just 3 miles east of Christiansted. Each cottage contains a fully equipped kitchenette, private bath, and ceiling fan. The Beach Bar and Grille is open for Caribbean dining daily from 9am to 9pm. The hotel has a popular Tuesday West Indian buffet and pig roast and a Saturday-night "Caribbean kaleidoscope" with a melange of West Indian cuisine and entertainment. The resort also has one of the best children's programs on the islands, in effect in summer and during holiday periods.

Colony Cove

3221 Estate Golden Rock, St. Croix, USVI 00820. ☎ **809/773-1965,** or 800/828-0746 in the U.S. Fax 809/773-5397. 60 apartments. A/C TV TEL. Winter, $185–$210 apartment for one or two. Off-season, $125–$150 apartment for one or two. Additional person $20 extra. AE, MC, V. Free parking. Directions: Travel east on Rte. 75 going toward Christiansted as far as Five Corners, and then turn left and pass Mill Harbor; Colony Cove is the next driveway to the left.

Of all the condo complexes on St. Croix, Colony Cove is perhaps the most like a full-fledged hotel. About a mile west of Christiansted next to a palm-dotted beach, it's composed of four three-story buildings that ring a swimming pool. Each apartment contains its own washer and dryer (rare for St. Croix), a kitchen, an enclosed veranda or gallery, two air-conditioned bedrooms, and a pair of bathrooms.

Sugar Beach Condominiums

3245 Estate Golden Rock, St. Croix, USVI 00820. ☎ **809/773-5345,** or 800/524-2049 in the U.S. Fax 809/773-1359. 46 studios and apartments. A/C TV TEL. Winter, $180 studio; $225 one-bedroom apartment; $275 two-bedroom apartment; $350 three-bedroom apartment. Off-season, $121 studio; $160 one-bedroom apartment; $200 two-bedroom apartment; $275 three-bedroom apartment. Maid service extra. AE, MC, V. Free parking.

This row of modernized studios and one-, two-, and three-bedroom apartments is strung along 500 feet of sandy beach on the north coast off North Shore Road.

Its location, however, near a housing development, is a turn-off for some visitors. When you tire of the sand, you can swim in the free-form freshwater pool nestled beside a sugar mill where rum was made three centuries ago. Under red-tile roofs, the apartments with enclosed balconies are staggered to provide privacy. All apartments open toward the sea, are tastefully decorated, and have completely equipped kitchens. The property has two Laykold tennis courts, and the Carambola golf course is minutes away.

The Waves at Cane Bay

Cane Bay (P.O. Box 1749, Kingshill), St. Croix, USVI 00851. ☎ **809/778-1805,** or 800/545-0603 in the U.S. Fax 809/778-1805. 12 rms. A/C TV. Winter, $130–$195 single or double. Off-season, $85–$125 single or double. Additional person $20 extra. AE, MC, V. Free parking. Directions: From the airport, go left on Route 64 for 1 mile, turn right on Route 70 for 1 mile, go left at the junction with Route 75 for 2 miles, and then drive left at the junction with Route 80 for 5 miles.

This intimate and tasteful property run by Suzanne and Kevin Ryan is about 8 miles from the airport, midway between the island's two biggest towns on a well-landscaped plot of oceanfront property on Cane Bay, the heart of the best scuba and snorkeling. There's a PADI dive shop on the property. Accommodations are in two-story units with screened-in verandas, all directly on the ocean. The Ryans host cocktail parties on the oceanside terrace and add many homelike touches. Units are high-ceilinged, with fresh flowers, well-stocked kitchens, private libraries, and thick towels. A two-room villa next to the main building has a large oceanside deck. The social center is a beachside bar ringed with stone and coral. A restaurant on the premises is open two nights a week, featuring an all-you-can-eat barbecue one night plus a seafood night.

WHERE TO DINE

The island's independently owned restaurants are among the best in the Caribbean.

IN CHRISTIANSTED

Expensive

Antoine's

58A King St. ☎ **809/773-0263.** Reservations required in winter. Appetizers $3.75–$6; main courses $13–$20. AE, MC, V. Lunch daily 11am–2:30pm; dinner daily 6:30–9:30pm. GERMAN/ITALIAN/CARIBBEAN.

Set directly on King's Wharf, on the second floor of a building overlooking Christiansted's harbor and marina, this is a large, well-established enclave of food and drink. Many visitors arrive just for the bar, which dispenses more than 35 different kinds of frozen blender drinks, and the island's largest selection of beer. In addition to the covered terrace, there's a satellite bar in back (the Aqua Lounge) decorated with a windsurfer suspended from the ceiling, and a cubbyhole Italian restaurant (Pico Bello) serving dinner only, Thursday through Sunday. Regardless of where you decide to consume your meal, a range of pastas and veal dishes is available, as well as such Teutonic specialties as gulasch, knockwurst salad, roulade of beef, and wienerschnitzel, as well as local dishes like fish chowder, lobster, and a choice of seafood.

The Chart House

59 King's Wharf. ☎ **809/773-7718.** Reservations recommended on weekends. Appetizers $5–$9; main courses $12.95–$37.95. AE, DC, MC, V. Dinner only, daily 6–10pm. (Bar, daily 5–10pm.) STEAK/SEAFOOD.

Set at the edge of the boardwalk just a few paces from the edge of the harbor, adjacent to the King Christian Hotel, this nautically decorated restaurant offers thick steaks, well-prepared seafood, wicker chairs, Oriental carpets, and lots of nautical accessories. It's a member of a California-based restaurant chain whose staff is known for its positive outlook about the restaurant industry and about life in general. It also has one of the best salad bars on the island and generously portioned versions of prime rib, twice-baked potatoes, and mud pie that are justifiably celebrated.

❂ Indies

55–56 Company St. ☎ **809/692-9440.** Reservations recommended. Appetizers $6.50–$8.50; main courses $16–$21; lunch platters $6–$9.50. AE, MC, V. Lunch Mon–Fri 11:30am–2:30pm; dinner daily 6–9:30pm. CARIBBEAN/INTERNATIONAL.

Set in a 19th-century courtyard ringed with multicolored gingerbread and antique cobblestones, this is one of the most noteworthy restaurants of St. Croix. Its creative vision comes from San Francisco–born Catherine Plav-Driggers, who is assisted by her husband, Curtis. She prepares an island-inspired menu of fresh ingredients and keeps her prices reasonable. The dinner menu changes nightly to reflect the bounty of the tropics. You'll dine adjacent to a carriage and cookhouse from the 1850s, in a sheltered courtyard protected from the noise of the street outside. Menu items include spring rolls, spicy Caribbean chicken, grouper (cooked in coconut milk, shrimp, scallions, tomato, and ginger), and grilled tenderloin of beef with corn-based custard and fried-onion chutney. Dessert might be a key lime pie or coconut mousse. The wine list, mostly California vintages, is especially attractive.

❂ Kendricks

52 King St. ☎ **809/773-9199.** Reservations recommended. Appetizers $4–$9; main courses $14–$26. AE, MC. V. Dinner only. Mon–Sat 6–10pm. Closed June. CONTINENTAL.

Kendricks is a fine restaurant in an old brick building in the heart of the town. Climb a flight of brick stairs to the second-floor dining room, which has a view of old Christiansted and the distant sea peeking out from above the rooftops. Appetizers might include artichoke hearts filled with scallops on a bed of lemon-cream sauce or one of the soups, perhaps chilled pear and watercress. There's always a selection of pastas, including homemade stuffed manicotti. Main dishes might be homemade ravioli stuffed with spinach, porcini mushrooms, and feta cheese, with fresh oregano/scallion-cream sauce; seared scallops and sweet-potato pancakes with a tomato-garlic coulis and an avocado/red-onion salsa; Kendricks' Cordon Bleu, which combines chicken breasts stuffed with lobster, mango, and Monterey jack cheese with a chardonnay-and-rosemary sauce; or grilled filet mignon laced with glazed onions, thyme, sautéed bananas, and served with a spicy Cruzan rum demiglace.

Top Hat

52 Company St., opposite Market Sq. ☎ **809/773-2346.** Reservations recommended. Appetizers $5.50–$10; main courses $14.50–$30; three-course fixed-price meal $20. AE, DC, MC, V. Lunch Tues–Fri 11:30am–2pm; dinner Mon–Sat 6–10pm. Closed May–June. CONTINENTAL/DANISH.

Set on the second floor of an 18th-century merchant's house, two blocks inland from Christiansted's wharves, this is the only Danish restaurant in the Virgin Islands. Operated since 1970 by Bent and Hanne Rasmussen, two Scandinavians, it offers well-prepared versions of such dishes as crisp roast duck prepared in the

Danish style with apples, prunes, red cabbage, sugar-brown Irish potatoes, and demiglace sauce; gravlax, herring, chilled cucumber soup, local dolphin simply sautéed with butter and lime; and an excellent version of wienerschnitzel.

Moderate

Tivoli Gardens

39 Strand, upstairs over the Pan Am Pavilion. ☎ **809/773-6782.** Reservations recommended for dinner. Appetizers $3.50–$7; main courses $13–$19. AE, MC, V. Lunch Mon–Fri 11:15am–2:30pm; dinner daily 6–9:30pm. INTERNATIONAL.

From this large second-floor porch festooned in lights you get the same view of Christiansted Harbor that a sea captain might. White beams hold up the porch of this favorite local rendezvous, and trellises and hanging plants add to the decor. The menu has everything from lobster-stuffed mushroom caps to a goulash inspired by a recipe concocted in the days of the Austro-Hungarian Empire. The Thai curry is also excellent. Save room for the wicked chocolate velvet cake. Often there is dancing from 7pm.

Tutto Bene

2 Company St. ☎ **809/773-5229.** Reservations recommended for parties of five or more. Appetizers $4.95–$8; main courses $10.95–$18.95. AE. Dinner only, daily 6–10pm. Closed Mon off-season. ITALIAN.

Set on the street level of a building in the heart of town, this restaurant evokes a cozy and colorful village inn on the Mediterranean. If you don't feel like eating, there's a large mahogany bar in back which does a brisk business of its own. You'll dine on wooden tables covered with painted tablecloths, amid warm colors and, often, lots of carefully controlled hubbub. Menu items are written on a pair of oversize mirrors against one wall, and include a full range of pastas, and fish prepared parmigiana, seafood Genovese (mussels, clams, shrimp, and white-wine/pesto sauce over linguini), and chicken alla Napoli, with sausages and peppers of different degrees of spiciness.

Inexpensive

Ⓢ Camille's Café

At Queen Cross St. and Company St. ☎ **809/773-2985.** Reservations not required. Appetizers $3.50–$4; main courses $9.95–$19.95; fixed-price dinner $13.95; sandwiches $3.95–$8.95. No credit cards. Daily 7:30am–10pm. INTERNATIONAL.

Across from Government House, Camille's serves New York deli–type food, along with a selection of international dishes. It's one of the best dining values in town, especially its fixed-price dinner. Fresh salads are featured, or you might begin with a homemade soup. Sandwiches are also available for lunch. The menu includes such dishes as fresh fish, filet mignon, lobster, and chicken. The place is a neighborhood enclave of convivial locals. Its brick walls and beamed ceilings were originally part of an 18th-century guesthouse.

Comanche Club

1 Strand St. ☎ **809/773-2665.** Reservations recommended. Appetizers $3.50–$10.75; main courses $7.75–$14.75. AE, MC, V. Breakfast daily 7–10am; lunch daily 11:30am–2:30pm; dinner daily 6–11pm. Closed for breakfast June–Oct. WEST INDIAN/CONTINENTAL.

Although relaxed, the Comanche is quietly elegant and one of the best-liked restaurants on the island. A block from King Street, it's a very busy place. Salads and a cold buffet are traditionally featured, and Comanche curries have their devotees here. Island fish might be sautéed with lemon butter and capers, and a typical West

Indian dish would be conch Créole with fungi. Fish cakes with seasoned rice is the Friday-night specialty, and the most popular desserts are Comanche cheesecake and key lime pie.

Dino's

4C Hospital St. ☎ **809/778-8005.** Reservations required. Appetizers $4.50–$10; main courses $13–$19. AE. Dinner only, Mon–Sat 6–10pm. ITALIAN.

This Mediterranean-style bistro is housed in a 200-year-old brick building, and has two different sections: an air-conditioned interior and an open-air terrace. Begin with one of the homemade pasta dishes, such as ravioli stuffed with eggplant or sweet potato. Veal is a specialty and it's prepared in at least three different ways, including saltimbocca. The local fish du jour is prepared Caribbean style—sautéed with tropical fruits, tomato, ginger, and cilantro. But Dino's is mainly for pastas, including all the classics such as fettuccine Alfredo, but also a list of original creations. One of these, for example, is fettuccine Caribbean with chicken, rum, black beans, ginger, cilantro, and sweet and hot peppers. The list of homemade desserts changes daily.

AROUND THE ISLAND

The Brass Parrot

In the Buccaneer, Gallows Bay. ☎ **809/773-2100.** Reservations recommended. Appetizers $5.50–$9.50; main courses $19–$24. AE, DC, MC, V. Dinner only, Thurs–Mon 6:30–9:30pm. INTERNATIONAL.

Two miles east of Christiansted along the coastal road, and already previewed as one of the island's leading resorts (see "Where to Stay," above), the Buccaneer is home to the most formal and one of the best restaurants on the island, and it remains popular with locals and visitors alike. Named after the brass parrot that perches in the apéritif lounge, this air-conditioned, glassed-in cocoon is set in the pink Great House of the hotel. Views open onto the sea, as well as onto the lights of Christiansted.

The chef specializes in seafood, but there are plenty of other choices on the menu, backed up by an extensive and reasonably priced wine list. The menu changes with the season but dishes tend to be innovative, offering products native to the Caribbean Basin, as exemplified by the sweet-potato soup topped with fresh ginger whipped cream. Try such other appetizers as Caribbean-style saltfish wontons with a pineapple dipping sauce, and smoked black-bean soup topped with grilled tender strips of marinated chicken. Main dishes might include grilled Jamaican jerk, Cornish hen, or cinnamon-crusted seared tuna over crisp rice noodles with a red-pepper sauce. The best steaks and chops are flown down from Chicago. No smoking is allowed inside the restaurant, and slacks and collared shirts are required for men.

Duggan's Reef

East End Rd., Teague Bay. ☎ **809/773-9800.** Reservations required for dinner. Appetizers $3.50–$9.50; main courses $14.50–$29; pastas $16.50–$24. AE, MC, V. Lunch daily noon–3pm; dinner daily 6–9:30pm. (Bar, daily 11am–11:30pm.) CONTINENTAL/CARIBBEAN.

Set only 10 feet from the still waters of Reef Beach, and open to the sea breezes, Duggan's Reef is an ideal perch for watching the windsurfers and Hobie cats careening through the nearby waters. The restaurant, owned for more than a decade by Boston-born Frank Duggan, is considered the most popular on St. Croix—all visitors seemingly dine here at least once during their stay on the island.

At lunch, a simple array of salads, crêpes, and sandwiches is offered. At night a more elaborate menu contains the popular house specialty—Duggan's Caribbean lobster pasta and Irish whiskey lobster. The local seafood is fresh and depends on the day's catch—in other words, fresh fish or no fish. That catch of the day can be baked, grilled, or blackened in the Cajun style. It also can be served island style (with tomato, pepper, and onion sauce). Begin with fried calamari or a conch chowder before sampling a pasta dish such as seafood Diavolo. Main dishes include New York strip or veal piccata.

The Galleon

East End Rd., Green Cay Marina, 50 Estate Southgate. ☎ **809/773-9949.** Reservations recommended. Appetizers $5–$8.50; main courses $13.50–$29. AE, MC, V. Dinner only, daily 6–10pm. Closed Sun–Mon in summer. Directions: Proceed east on Route 82 from Christiansted for five minutes: after going a mile past the Buccaneer, turn left into Green Cay Marina. FRENCH/ITALIAN.

Overlooking the ocean, the Galleon is a local favorite—and deservedly so. The best cooking in Europe is found in northern Italy and France, and that's what's offered here, including osso buco, just as good as that served in Milan. Freshly baked bread, two fresh vegetables, and rice or potatoes accompany main dishes. The menu always includes at least one local fish, such as wahoo, tuna, swordfish, or dolphin, even fresh Caribbean lobster. Or you might order a perfectly done rack of lamb carved at your table. An extensive listing of wines is sold by the glass. Music from a baby grand accompanies your dinner.

⑤ Oskar's Bar and Restaurant

4A La Grande Princess, Rte. 75. ☎ **809/773-4060.** Reservations not required. Soups $2.50 each; main courses $8–$13. No credit cards. Lunch Mon–Sat 11am–2:30pm; dinner Mon–Sat 5:30–9pm. Transportation: Taxi. CONTINENTAL.

Just outside Christiansted is a good, inexpensive restaurant. This Swiss-run place is often filled when other, better-known (and more expensive) establishments are empty. Meals, tasty and big ones, cost only $17. Try the special of the day, which might be roast pork with gravy, accompanied by mashed potatoes and corn. Or you may prefer bratwurst with sauerkraut, wienerschnitzel, beef roulade, or even filet mignon. To finish your repast, why not Swiss chocolate cake?

Sprat Hall Beach Restaurant

Rte. 63. ☎ **809/772-5855.** Reservations not required. Lunch $3.50–$15. No credit cards. Wed–Sun 9am–4pm (hot food 11:30am–2:30pm). CARIBBEAN.

One mile north of Frederiksted, this is an informal spot on the western coast of St. Croix near Sprat Hall Plantation. It's about the best place on the island to combine lunch and a swim. For a "taste of St. Croix," stop off here at this spot in business since 1948, feeding both locals and the ever-changing array of foreign visitors. Try such local dishes as conch chowder, pumpkin fritters, tannia soup, and the fried fish of the day. If you'd like more standard fare, they also do salads and burgers. The bread is home-baked daily. The place is directed by Cruzan born Joyce Merwin Hurd and her husband, Jim, who charge $2 for use of the showers and changing rooms.

WHAT TO SEE & DO

IN CHRISTIANSTED

The picture-book harbor town of the Caribbean, Christiansted is an old Danish port, handsomely restored (or at least in the process of being restored). On the northeastern shore of the island, on a coral-bound bay, the town is filled with

Danish buildings erected by prosperous merchants in the booming 18th century. These red-roofed structures are often washed in pink, ocher, or yellow. Arcades over the sidewalks make ideal shaded colonnades for shoppers. Government House—in fact, the whole area around the harborfront—has been designated a historic site and is looked after by the National Park Service.

If you're an independent type of traveler, consider our walking and driving tours below. However, if you'd like guidance, you can take a walking tour of both Christiansted and Frederiksted from **Take-a-Hike.** Guided one-hour walks of both towns are possible, with tours leaving Monday and Thursday at 10am from the Visitors' Bureau in Christiansted. Call **809/778-6997** for all the details. The Christiansted tour costs $5.50; the Frederiksted tour, $6.50. Children are charged $3.50 for either tour. Take-a-Hike also conducts nature hikes; inquire about them if you're interested.

IN FREDERIKSTED

This old Danish town at the western end of the island, about 17 miles from Christiansted, is a sleepy port town that comes to life only when a cruise ship docks at its shoreline.

In 1994, a 1,500-foot pier opened to accommodate the largest cruise ships (the old pier had suffered damage from Hurricane Hugo in 1989). The pier facility is designed to accommodate two large cruise vessels and two mini-cruise ships simultaneously.

Frederiksted was destroyed by a fire in 1879, and the citizens rebuilt it with wood frames and clapboards on top of the old Danish stone and yellow-brick foundations.

Most visitors begin their tour at russet-colored **Fort Frederick,** next to the pier. Some historians claim that this was the first fort to sound a foreign salute to the U.S. flag, in 1776. It was here on July 3, 1848, that Gov.-Gen. Peter von Schohen emancipated the slaves in the Danish West Indies. The fort, at the northern end of Frederiksted, has been restored to its 1840 look. You can explore the courtyard and stables, and an exhibit area has been installed in what was once the Garrison Room.

Just south of the fort, the **Customs House** is an 18th-century building with a 19th-century two-story gallery. Here you can go into the **visitors' bureau** and pick up a free map of the town.

Nearby, privately owned **Victoria House,** on Market Street, is a gingerbread-trimmed structure built after the fire of 1879. In the rebuilding, some of the original 1803 structure was preserved.

Along the waterfront Strand is the **Bellhouse,** once the Frederiksted Public Library. One of its owners, G. A. Bell, ornamented the steps with bells. The house today is an arts-and-crafts center and a nursery. Sometimes a local theater group presents dramas here.

The **Danish School,** on Prince Street, was adapted in the 1830s into a building designed by Hingelberg, a well-known Danish architect. Today it's the police station and Welfare Department.

Two churches are of interest: **St. Paul's Anglican Church,** 28 Prince St., was founded outside the port in the late 18th century; the present building dates from 1812. **St. Patrick's Catholic Church,** 5 Prince St. was built in the 1840s.

On the waterfront in Frederiksted you can visit the pint-sized but interesting **St. Croix Aquarium,** housing some 40 species of marine animals and more than 100 species of invertebrates. With constant rotation, each creature can adjust easily back to its natural habitat, as hundreds of species pass through the tanks each year. A touch pond features starfish, sea cucumbers, brittle stars, and pencil urchins. The aquarium is not just a place to view marine life, but also to become familiar with it before scuba diving or snorkeling. It's open Wednesday through Sunday from 11am to 4pm, charging an admission of $3 for adults or $1.50 for children.

AROUND THE ISLAND

North of Frederiksted you can drop in at **Sprat Hall,** the island's oldest planta-tion, or else continue along to the rain forest, which covers about 15 acres, includ-ing the 150-foot-high **Creque Dam.** The terrain is private property, but the owner lets visitors go inside to explore. Most visitors come here to see the jagged estuary of the northern coastline's **Salt River.** Salt River was where Columbus landed on November 14, 1493, the only known site where the explorer landed on what is now U.S. territory during any of his four expeditions. Marking the 500th anniversary of Columbus's arrival, then-President George Bush signed a bill cre-ating the 912-acre **Salt River Bay National Historical Park and Ecological Preserve.** The land mass includes the site of the original Carib village explored by Columbus and his men, including the only ceremonial ball court ever discovered in the Lesser Antilles.

The park contains the largest mangrove forest in the Virgin Islands, sheltering many endangered animals and plants, plus an underwater canyon attracting scuba divers from around the world.

The park today is virtually in a natural state, with a plaque indicating what it is. Plans call for a visitor center and a museum.

At the Carib settlement, the men of Columbus liberated several Taíno women and children held as slaves. On the way back to their vessels, the Spaniards faced a canoe filled with hostile Caribs, armed with poison arrows. One Spanish soldier was killed, and perhaps six Caribs were either slain or captured. This is the first documented case of hostility between invading Europeans and the Native Americans. Sailing away, Columbus named this part of St. Croix "Cape of the Arrows."

The St. Croix Environmental Association conducts tours of the area and can be called at **809/773-1989** for details.

St. George Village Botanical Garden of St. Croix

127 Estate St., Kingshill. ☎ **809/772-3874**. Admission $5 adults, $1 children 12 and under; donations welcome. Dec–Apr, daily 9am–5pm; May–Nov, Tues–Sat 9am–4pm. Transportation: Taxi.

Just north of Centerline Road, 4 miles east of Frederiksted at Estate St. George, is a veritable Eden of tropical trees, shrubs, vines, and flowers. Built around the ruins of a 19th-century sugarcane workers' village, the garden is a feast for the eye and the camera—from the entrance drive bordered by royal palms and bougain-villea to the towering kapok and tamarind trees. Restoration of the ruins is a continuing project. Two sets of workers' cottages provide space for a gift shop, restrooms, a kitchen, and an office; these have been joined together with a Great Hall, which is used by the St. Croix community for various functions. Other completed projects include the superintendent's house, the blacksmith's shop, and various smaller buildings used for a library, a plant nursery, workshops, and storehouses.

Self-guided walking-tour maps are available at the entrance to the Great Hall.

St. Croix **207**

Cruzan Rum Factory
W. Airport Rd., Rte. 64. ☎ **809/772-0280**. Admission $2. Tours Mon–Fri 8:30–11:30am and 1–4:15pm.

This factory distills the famous Virgin Islands rum, which is considered by residents to be the finest in the world. Guided tours depart from the visitors' pavilion; call for reservations and information.

Estate Whim Plantation Museum
Centerline Rd. ☎ **809/772-0598**. Admission $5 adults, $1 children. Daily 10am–4pm.

About 2 miles east of Frederiksted, this museum was restored by the St. Croix Landmarks Society and is unique among the many sugar plantations whose ruins dot the island of St. Croix. This Great House is different from most in that it's composed of only three rooms. With 3-foot-thick walls made of stone, coral, and molasses, the house is said by some to resemble a luxurious European château.

In 1992 a division of Baker Furniture Company, Milling Road, used the Whim Plantation's collection of models for one of its most successful lines of reproductions, the "Whim Museum–West Indies Collection." A showroom in the museum offers these reproductions for sale, including pineapple-capped four-poster beds, cane-bottomed planters' chairs with built-in leg rests, and Caribbean adaptations of Empire-era chairs with cane-bottomed seats.

Also on the museum's premises is a woodworking shop which features tools and techniques from the 18th century, the estate's original kitchen, a gift shop, and a reproduction of a typical town apothecary. The ruins of the plantation's sugar-processing plant, complete with a restored windmill, remain.

EXPLORING THE RAIN FOREST

Unlike the rest of St. Croix, a verdant parcel in the island's western district is covered with dense forest, a botanical landscape very different from the scrub-covered hills covering other parts of the island. Set amid the sparsely populated terrain of the island's northwestern corner, north of Frederickstad, the area grows thick with mahogany trees, kapok (silk-cotton) trees, turpentine (red birch) trees, samaan (rain) trees, and all kinds of ferns and vines. In many cases, sweet limes, mangoes, hog plums, and breadfruit trees, which have sown themselves in the wild since the days of the district's plantations, intersperse themselves among the forest's larger trees. Birdlife includes crested hummingbirds, pearly-eyed thrashers, green-throated caribs, yellow warblers, and perky but drably camouflaged banana quits.

Although technically the district is not a tropical rain forest, it's known by virtually everyone as the Rain Forest. How best to experience its botanical charms? Some visitors opt to drive along Route 76 (which is also known as Mahogany Road, and which is arguably the most mysterious road on St. Croix), stopping their car beside any of the footpaths that meander off the highway into dry riverbeds and glens on either side. (It's advisable to stick to the best-worn of the foot trails to avoid losing your way, and retrace your steps after a few moments of admiring the local botany.)

Equally feasible is a hike beside those highways of the island's western sector where few cars ever venture. Three of the most viable include the Creque Dam Road (Routes 58/78), the Scenic Road (Route 78), and the Western Scenic Road (Routes 63/78). Consider beginning your trek near the junction of Creque Dam Road and Scenic Road. (Though passable by cars, it's likely you'll see only a few along these roads during your entire walking tour.)

Your trek will cover a broad triangular swath, beginning at the above-mentioned junction, heading north and then west along Scenic Road. First the road will rise, then descend toward the coastal lighthouse of the island's extreme northwestern tip, Hamm's Bluff. Most trekkers will decide to retrace their steps after about 45 minutes of northwesterly walking, returning to their parked cars after admiring the land and seascapes. Real diehards, however, will continue trekking all the way to the coastline, then head south along the coastal road (Butler Bay Road), then head east along Creque Dam Road to their parked car at the junction of Creque Dam Road and Scenic Road. Embark on this longer expedition only if you're really prepared for a prolonged trek (about five hours) and some serious nature-watching.

SPORTS & OUTDOOR ACTIVITIES

BEACHES

Beaches are the big attraction. The drawback is that getting to them from Christiansted, center of most of the hotels, isn't always easy. It can also be expensive, especially if you want to go back and forth every day of your stay. Of course, you can always rent one of those housekeeping condos right on the water.

In Christiansted, if you want to beach it, head for the **Hotel on the Cay.** You'll have to take a ferry to this palm-shaded island.

Cramer Park, at the northeastern end of the island, is a special public park operated by the Department of Agriculture. Lined with sea-grape trees, the beach also has a picnic area, a restaurant, and a bar.

I highly recommend **Davis Bay** and **Cane Bay** as the type of beaches you'd expect to find on a Caribbean island—palms, white sand, and good swimming and snorkeling. Cane Bay adjoins Route 80 on the north shore. Snorkelers and divers are attracted to this beach, with its rolling waves, coral gardens, and dropoff wall. No reefs guard the approach to Davis Beach, which draws bodysurfers but doesn't have changing facilities. It's off the South Shore Road (Route 60), in the vicinity of the Carambola Beach Resort.

Windsurfers like **Reef Beach,** which opens onto Teague Bay along Route 82, East End Road, a half-hour ride from Christiansted. Food can be ordered at Duggan's Reef. On Route 63, a short ride north of Frederiksted, **Rainbow Beach** invites with its white sand and ideal snorkeling conditions. In the vicinity, also on Route 63, about five minutes north of Frederiksted, **La Grange** is another good beach. Lounge chairs can be rented, and there's a bar nearby.

At the ✪ **Cormorant Beach Club** (see "Where to Stay," above), about 5 miles west of Christiansted, some 1,200 feet of white sands are shaded by palm trees. Since a living reef lies just off the shore, snorkeling conditions are ideal. **Grapetree Beach** offers about the same footage of clean white sand on the eastern tip of the island (Route 60). Follow the South Shore Road to reach it. Water sports are popular here.

Two more beaches on St. Croix include **Buccaneer Beach,** 2 miles west of Christiansted, and **Sandy Point,** directly south of Frederiksted, the largest beach in all the U.S. Virgin Islands. Its waters are shallow and calm, perfect for swimming. Jutting out from southwestern St. Croix like a small peninsula, Sandy Point is reached by taking the Melvin Evans Highway (Route 66) west from the Alexander Hamilton Airport.

FISHING

The fishing grounds at **Lang Bank** are about 10 miles from St. Croix. Here you'll find kingfish, dolphin, and wahoo. Using light-tackle boats along the reef, the catch is likely to turn up jack or bonefish. At Clover Crest, in Frederiksted, Cruzan anglers fish right from the rocks.

Serious sports fishers can board the *Shenanigans,* a 42-foot Hatteras convertible, available for half- or full-day charters with bait and tackle included. It's anchored at the St. Croix Marina, Gallows Bay. Reservations can be made by calling **809/773-7165** during the day or **809/773-4141** at night.

GOLF

St. Croix has the best golfing in the U.S. Virgins. In fact, guests staying on St. John and St. Thomas often fly over for a day's round on the island's two 18-hole and one 9-hole golf courses.

The ✪ **Carambola Golf Course** (☎ **809/778-5638**), on the northeast side of St. Croix, was designed by Robert Trent Jones, who called it "the loveliest course I ever designed." The course, formerly the Fountain Valley and the site of "Shell's Wonderful World of Golf," has been likened to a botanical garden. Its collection of par-3 holes is known to golfing authorities as the best in the tropics. Carambola's course record of 66 was set by Tom Kite in 1987. Greens fees are $55 per person for a day, which allows you to play as many holes as you like. Rental of a golf cart is mandatory at $18 per 18 holes.

The other major course, at the **Buccaneer** (☎ **809/773-2100, ext. 738**), 2 miles east of Christiansted (see "Where to Stay," above), is a challenging 6,200-yard, 18-hole course with panoramic vistas that allows the player to knock the ball over rolling hills right to the edge of the Caribbean. Nonguests who reserve pay greens fees of $30, and carts rent for $13. A golf pro is available for lessons, and there's a pro shop.

A final course is the **Reef,** at Teague Bay (☎ **809/773-8844**), a 3,100-yard, 9-hole course, charging greens fees of $14, with carts renting for $8. On the east end of the island, its longest hole is a 579-yard par 5.

HORSEBACK RIDING

Specializing in nature tours, **Paul and Jill's Equestrian Stables,** Sprat Hall Plantation, Route 58 (☎ **809/722-2880**), is the largest equestrian stable in the Virgin Islands. Set on the sprawling grounds of the island's oldest plantation Great House, it's operated by Paul Wojcie and his wife, Jull Hurd, one of the daughters of the establishment's original founders. The stables are known throughout the Caribbean for the quality of the horses and the scenic trail rides through the forests, past ruins of abandoned 18th-century plantations and sugar mills, to the tops of the hills of St. Croix's western end. All tours are accompanied by the operators, who give running commentaries on island fauna, history, and riding techniques. Beginners and experienced riders alike are welcome.

A two-hour trail ride costs $50 per person. Tours usually depart daily in winter at 10am and 4pm and off-season at 5pm, with slight variations according to demand. Reservations at least a day in advance are important.

TENNIS

Some authorities rate the tennis at the **Buccaneer** (☎ **809/773-2100, ext. 736**) as the best in the West Indies. This hotel (see "Where to Stay," above) offers a choice of eight courts, two lit for night games, all open to the public. Nonguests pay $10 per person per hour; however, you must call to reserve a court. A tennis pro is available for lessons, and there is also a pro shop.

A notable selection of courts is also found at the **Carambola Golf Club** (☎ **809/778-0797**), which has five clay courts, two of which are lit for night games. Open to the public, it charges $23 per hour for nonguests, around $30 at night. You must call to reserve. Both a pro shop and a tennis pro for lessons are available.

WATER SPORTS

Sponge life, black-coral trees (considered the finest in the West Indies), and steep dropoffs into water near the shoreline have made St. Croix a diver's goal.

Buck Island, with an underwater visibility of more than 100 feet, is the site of the nature trail of the underwater national monument, and it's the major diving target (see "An Excursion to Buck Island" at the end of this chapter). All the minor and major agencies offer scuba and snorkeling tours to Buck Island. Divers also like to go to **Pillar Coral,** with its columns of coral spiraling up to 25 feet; **North Cut,** one of the tallest, largest coral pinnacles in the West Indies; **Salt River Dropoff,** plunging to well over 1,000 feet deep; and **Davis Bay Dropoff,** with its unique coral and rock mound structures in grotesque shapes.

Dive St. Croix, 59 King's Wharf (☎ **809/773-3434,** or 800/523-DIVE in the U.S.), operates the 46-foot dive boat *Betty Ann.* The staff offers complete instructions from resort courses through full certification, as well as night dives. A resort course, including all equipment and a one-boat dive, is $65. A two-tank boat dive for certified divers goes for $75.

V.I. Divers Ltd., Pan Am Pavilion, 1102 Strand St., Christiansted (☎ **809/773-6045,** or **800/544-5911**), is a PADI five-star dive center established in 1971. *Skin Diver* magazine called its offerings one of the "10 top dives in the Caribbean." An introductory resort course costs $85, with a two-dive boat tour going for $70.

WINDSURFING

The best place for this increasingly popular sport is the **Tradewindsurfing Water Sports Center** (☎ **809/773-2035**), located on a small offshore island in Christiansted Harbor and part of the Hotel on the Cay. They give lessons and are open daily from 10am to 5pm. Renting a sailboat costs $60 for two hours.

SHOPPING

IN CHRISTIANSTED

In Christiansted, where the core of my shopping recommendations are found, the emphasis is on hole-in-the-wall boutiques selling one-of-a-kind merchandise; handmade items are strong. Of course the same duty-free stipulations, as outlined earlier, apply to your shopping selections on St. Croix.

Knowing that it can't compete with Charlotte Amalie, Christiansted has forged its own creative statement in its shops and has now become the "chic spot for merchandise" in the Caribbean. All the shops are easily compressed into half a mile or so. Most shops are open Monday through Saturday from 9am to 5pm.

American West India Company

1 Strand St. ☎ **809/773-7325.**

Occupying the two floors of a 1733 town house in the center of Christiansted, the American West India Company offers a broad collection of luxury products actually made in the Caribbean. Included are artwork from Haiti, gourmet foods, limited-production rums and liqueurs, Sea Island cotton clothing, T-shirts with unique Caribbean designs, ceramic figurines, island-made jewelry, and much more.

Colombian Emeralds

43 Queen Cross St. ☎ **809/773-1928.**

Along with stunning emeralds, called "the rarest gemstone in the world," rubies and diamonds also dazzle here. Other gemstones are ametrine, blue topaz, opals, and amethyst. The staff will show you their large range of 14-karat-gold jewelry, along with the best buys in watches, including Seiko quartz.

Down Island Clothing

In the West Indian Townhouse, King St. ☎ **809/773-9235.**

For a fashionable island look, head here for one-of-a-kind dresses, sandals, accessories, casuals, and swimwear. Atop the Bombay Club, it captures the light, laidback spirit of St. Croix resort fashion more than any other place on the island.

Folk Art Traders

1B Queen Cross St. ☎ **809/773-1900.**

Since 1985, the operators of this store have traveled throughout the Caribbean ("in the bush") to acquire a unique collection of local art and folk-art treasures, not only carnival masks, pottery, ceramics, and original paintings, but also hand-wrought jewelry. The assortment is wide-ranging, including batiks from Barbados and high-quality iron sculpture from Haiti. For the serious Caribbeanist, there's nothing like it in the Virgin Islands.

Java Wraps

In the Pan Am Pavilion, Strand St. ☎ **809/773-3770.**

Known for resortwear for women, men, and children, this shop is a kaleidoscope of colors and prints. You expect Dorothy Lamour, star of all those "Road" pictures (such as *The Road To Bali*, with Bob Hope and Bing Crosby), to appear at any minute. In fact, today's Dorothy (actually a local salesperson) demonstrates how to wrap and tie beach pareos and sarongs. Men's shirts are a collection of tropical and ethnic prints, and there's also a children's selection.

Java Wraps Home Store

51 Company St. ☎ **809/773-2920.**

In this world of Java Wraps, textiles for the home cascade from antique Dutch colonial chests, and old teak tables are laden with hand-drawn batik tablecloths, napkins, and card placements. There's also a collection of intricately patterned, hand-batiked quilted bedcovers. Wood carvings make unusual gifts. Other merchandise includes island-inspired hand-painted fish plates, large banana-leaf trays, coral-reef salad bowls, and other tropical tableware.

Land of Oz

2126 Company St. ☎ **809/773-4610.**

This is the most enchanting store for children in the Caribbean. However, owner Marsha Feehan says, "The store is for children of all ages." Variety is the keynote of this establishment, with emphasis on unusual items from around the world. An example is games, ranging from Wahree, one of the world's oldest games, to the latest advertised on TV. Some 3,000 different items are in stock. Shipping is available.

Little Switzerland

1108 King St. ☎ **809/773-1976.**

This is one of the best sources on the island for crystal, figurines, watches, china, perfume, flatware, and lots of fine jewelry. It specializes in all the big names, such as Paloma Picasso leather goods. For that luxury item, the Rolex watch, the Omega, and for heirloom crystal such as Lalique, Swarovski, and Baccarat, this is the place. Some items—at least a few—are said to sell for up to 30% less than on the U.S. mainland.

Many Hands

In the Pan Am Pavillion, Strand St. ☎ **809/773-1990.**

Many Hands is devoted exclusively to Virgin Islands handcrafts. The merchandise includes West Indian spices and teas, shellwork, stained glass, hand-painted china, pottery, and handmade jewelry. Be sure to see their collection of local paintings and their year-round "Christmas tree."

Only in Paradise

5 Company St. ☎ **809/773-0331.**

In this spacious air-conditioned store there's a choice assortment of gifts, such as art glass, linens, fine and costume jewelry, and decorative items, as well as pearls however you want them—cultured, freshwater, or baroque. Its boutique, around back in a secluded courtyard, offers leather goods and cotton lingerie.

Pegasus Jewelers

58 Company St. ☎ **809/773-6926.**

Both a retail outlet and a jewelry workshop, Pegasus specializes in diamonds, gold, and gemstones, and can be trusted. In their undulating showcase they offer earrings, pendants, bracelets, and many one-of-a-kind pieces. Tariffs are based on the fluctuating price of gold. They also have a varied selection of handcrafted black coral and pearl jewelry.

The Royal Poinciana

Strand St. ☎ **809/773-9892.**

This is probably the most interesting gift shop on St. Croix, the creative statement of Carl Brown and Jack Rahn. In what looks like an antique apothecary shop, you'll find such Caribbean-inspired items as hot sauces, seasoning blends for gumbos, island herbal teas, Antillean coffees, a scented array of soaps, toiletries, lotions, and shampoos, and museum-reproduction greeting cards and calendars.

Simply Cotton

36C Strand St. ☎ **809/773-6860.**

Selling items made of 100% cotton, this store is ideal for casual fashion for both women and children. The makings of a tropical wardrobe are all here, including skirts, washable tops, shorts, jackets, and pants. They even sell reasonably priced and casual nighttime wear.

Violette Boutique

In the Caravelle Arcade, 38 Strand St. ☎ **809/773-2148.**

A small department store with many boutique areas carrying lines known worldwide, Violette includes many exclusive fragrances and hard-to-find bath lines. It also has the latest in Cartier, Fendi, Pequignet, and Gucci. A wide selection of famous cosmetic names are featured, and Fendi has its own area for bags and accessories.

Woolworth's

In the Sunny Island Shopping Center, Centerline Rd. ☎ **809/778-5466.**

Although this is primarily a department store, this retail outlet at a major shopping center contains the largest supply of discounted liquor on the island. The liquor is duty free. Cruzan rum is in plentiful supply, along with a vast array of other brand-name liquors and liqueurs.

AROUND THE ISLAND

St. Croix Leap

Mahogany Rd., Rte. 76. ☎ **809/772-0421.**

On your tour of the island, especially if you're on western St. Croix near Frederiksted, you might want to stop off at St. Croix Leap for an adventure. In this open-air shop, you can see stacks of rare and beautiful wood being fashioned into tasteful objects. It's a St. Croix Life and Environmental Arts Project, dedicated to the natural environment through manual work, conservation, and self-development. The end result is a fine collection of Cruzan mahogany serving boards, tables, wall hangings, clocks, and sections of unusual pieces crafted into functional objects. They become a form of naturalistic art.

St. Croix Leap is 15 miles from Christiansted, 2 miles up Mahogany Road from the beach north of Frederiksted. Large mahogany signs and sculptures flank the driveway. Visitors should bear to the right to reach the woodworking area and gift shop. The site is open daily but keeps no set hours—"not too early, not too late." For inquiries, write to Leap, P.O. Box 245, Frederiksted, USVI 00841-0245.

Whim Gift Shop

In the Estate Whim Plantation Museum, east of Frederiksted on Centerline Rd. ☎ **809/772-0598.**

Offering a good selection of gifts and appealing to a wide age spectrum, the Whim Gift Shop has many imported items, but also many that are Cruzan made. Some were personally made for the Whim shop. And if you buy something, it all goes to a worthy cause: the upkeep of the museum and the grounds.

ST. CROIX AFTER DARK

St. Croix doesn't have the nightlife of St. Thomas, so to find the action, you might have to hotel- or bar-hop or consult *St. Croix This Week.*

If he's playing, the one man to seek out is **Jimmy Hamilton,** Duke Ellington's "Mr. Sax." He and his quartet are a regular feature of St. Croix nightlife. Ask at your hotel if he's appearing locally at the time of your visit.

Also try to catch a performance of the **Quadrille Dancers,** the cultural treat of St. Croix. Their dances are little changed since plantation days; the women wear long dresses, white gloves, and turbans, and the men are attired in flamboyant shirts, sashes, and tight black trousers. When you've learned their steps, you're invited to join the dancers on the floor. Ask at your hotel if and where they are performing.

THE CLUB & MUSIC SCENE

Hondo's Nightclub

53 King St. ☎ **809/778-8103.** Admission $3 women, $5 men.

Simply called "Hondo's" by its habitués, this is a late-night hot spot with either live or recorded music. No one's exactly sure what will be happening around here on any given night. Be careful going through the streets late at night. Drinks begin at $3, but are reduced to $1.75 at happy hour from 9 to 10pm. The club is open on Wednesday and Thursday from 9pm to 2am and on Friday and Saturday from 9pm to 4am.

The Terrace Lounge

In the Buccaneer, Rte. 82, Estate Shoys. ☎ **809/773-2100.** Admission $8 for those who aren't staying in the hotel.

Every night this lounge off the main dining room of one of St. Croix's up-scale hotels welcomes some of the Caribbean's finest entertainers, including Jimmy Hamilton or a "down-island" steel band. Drinks cost $4 to $5. Open daily from 8 to 11pm.

The Wreck Bar

5 A-B Hospital St., Christiansted. ☎ **809/773-6092.**

It's had only three owners in its 16-year history, and a chain of command that has always maintained the same name and a reputation for margaritas that are "absolutely habit-forming." The decor is inspired directly by the TV series "Gilligan's Island," with a retractable awning that extends over the open-air dance floor whenever it rains, and an indoor-outdoor space that uses ample amounts of bamboo and thatch. Bill and Penny are the married entrepreneurs who maintain the place's sense of irreverent fun. Margaritas start at $3 each, and the club is open Monday through Saturday from 4pm to at least 1:30am.

AN EXCURSION TO BUCK ISLAND

The crystal-clear water and the white coral sand of Buck Island, a satellite of St. Croix, are legendary. Slithering through its undergrowth in days of yore, you'd likely have run into Morgan, LaFitte, Blackbeard, or even Captain Kidd. Now the National Park Service has marked an underwater snorkeling trail. The park covers about 850 acres, including the land area, which has a sandy beach with picnic tables set out and pits for having your own barbecues, as well as restrooms and a small changing room. There are two major underwater trails for snorkeling on the reef, plus many other labyrinths and grottoes for more serious divers. You can also take a hiking trail through the tropical vegetation that covers the island.

Only a third of a mile wide and a mile long, Buck Island lies only 1 1/2 miles off the northeastern coast of St. Croix. A barrier reef shelters many reef fish, including queen angelfish and the smooth trunkfish. The attempt to return the presently uninhabited Buck Island to nature has been successful—even the endangered brown pelicans are producing young here.

Small boats run between St. Croix and Buck Island. Snorkeling equipment is furnished. You head out in the morning, and nearly all charters allow 1 1/2 hours of snorkeling and swimming.

A WALKING TOUR

A radically different kind of walking tour than that through the rain forest (see above) encompasses Buck Island, a sun-blasted, low-lying stretch of sand and coral rock off the island's northeastern coast. Here the climate is considerably dryer than in the rain forest, although most of the interest on this walk involves the marine life in the sun-flooded and shallow waters off the rocky coastline of this long and narrow offshore island.

During the 19th century, goats overgrazed the island's surface, reducing the land to the barren condition you'll find today. Despite that, the island is eminently suitable for pedestrian hikes. Bring something to protect you from too constant an exposure to the sun's sometimes-merciless rays. Even more important, don't rush to touch every plant you see. The island's western edge has groves of poisonous machineel trees, whose leaves, bark, and fruit contain toxins that cause extreme irritation if they come into contact with human skin.

Although most visitors to Buck Island come for its beaches and its offshore snorkeling, a circumnavigation of the island on foot will take about two hours. Despite the fact that access to Buck Island is only via chartered tours and boat trips (see below), the numbers of visitors here make this one of the most-visited rock spits in the Caribbean.

Managed and protected from environmental assaults by the National Park Service, Buck Island has a trail meandering from several points along its coastline to its sun-flooded summit, affording views over nearby St. Croix.

A Snorkeling Tour

Of (arguably) greater interest on Buck Island is the underwater snorkeling trail, which rings part of the island. With a face mask, swim fins, and a snorkel, you'll be treated to some of the most spectacular underwater views in the Caribbean. Plan on spending at least two-thirds of a day at this extremely famous ecological site.

Mile Mark Watersports, in the King Christian Hotel, 59 King's Wharf, Christiansted (☎ **809/773-2628,** or 800/524-2012), offers twice-daily tours to the aquatic wonders of Buck Island. They offer two ways to reach the reefs. One is a half-day tour aboard a glass-bottom boat departing from in front of the King Christian Hotel. Tours are daily from 9:30am to 1pm and 1:30 to 5pm, and cost $35 per person; all snorkeling equipment is included. A more romantic journey is aboard one of the company's wind-powered sailboats, which, for $40 per person, offers the sea breezes and the thrill of wind power to reach the reef. A full-day tour, offered daily from 10am to 4pm on the company's 40-foot catamaran, can take up to 20 participants to Buck Island's reefs. Included in the tour are a West Indian barbecue picnic on the isolated sands of Buck Island's beaches, complimentary rum punches, and plenty of opportunities for snorkeling. The cost is $40 for adults and $25 for children under 14.

Captain Heinz, (☎ **809/773-3161** or **809/773-4041**) is an Austrian-born skipper with some 20 years of sailing experience. His trimaran, *Teroro II,* leaves Green Cay Marina "H" Dock at 9am and 2pm, never filled with more than 24 passengers, who pay $40 per person. All gear and safety equipment are provided. The captain sailed the first *Teroro* across the Atlantic, and he's not only a skilled sailor but is also a considerate host. He will even take you around the outer reef, which the other guides do not, for an unforgettable underwater experience.

7

The British Virgin Islands

With its small bays and hidden coves, once havens for pirates, the British Virgin Islands are considered among the world's loveliest cruising grounds by the yachting set. Strung over the northeastern corner of the Caribbean, about 60 miles east of Puerto Rico, are some 40 islands, although skeptics might consider many of these rocks, perhaps cays, and in some cases, "spits of land." Only a trio of the British Virgins are of any significant size: Virgin Gorda (the "Fat Virgin"), Tortola ("dove of peace"), and Jost Van Dyke. Other islands have such names as Fallen Jerusalem and Ginger. Norman Island is said to have been the prototype for Robert Louis Stevenson's *Treasure Island*. On Deadman Bay, a rocky cay, Blackbeard marooned 15 pirates and a bottle of rum, which gave rise to the ditty.

Columbus came this way in 1493, but the British Virgins apparently made little impression on him. Although the Spanish and Dutch contested it, Tortola was officially annexed by the English in 1672. Today the British Virgin Islands are a British colony, with their own elected government and a population of about 11,000.

The vegetation is varied and depends on the rainfall. In some parts, palms and mangoes grow in profusion, while other places are arid and studded with cactus.

There are predictions that mass tourism is on the way, but so far the British Virgins are still a paradise for escapists. According to a report I once read, the British Home Office listed them as "the least important place in the British Empire."

GETTING THERE
BY PLANE

There are no direct flights from New York to the British Virgin Islands, but you can make good connections from San Juan and St. Thomas to Beef Island/Tortola. (See Chapter 5 on Puerto Rico and Chapter 6 on the U.S. Virgin Islands for information on transportation to these islands.)

Your best bet to reach Beef Island/Tortola is to take **American Eagle** (☎ 800/433-7300 in the U.S.), which is probably viewed as the most reliable airline in the Caribbean and operates at least four daily trips from San Juan to Beef Island/Tortola.

Another choice, if you're on one of Tortola's neighboring islands, is **Leeward Islands Air Transport (LIAT)** (☎ 809/462-0701).

This Caribbean carrier flies to Tortola from St. Kitts, Antigua, St. Maarten, St. Thomas, and San Juan, in small planes not known for their frequency or careful scheduling. Reservations are made through travel agents or through the larger U.S.–based airlines that connect with LIAT hubs. The flying time to Beef Island/Tortola from San Juan is 35 minutes; from St. Thomas, 25 minutes; and from the most distant of the LIAT hubs (Antigua), 90 minutes, including stopovers in St. Kitts and one other island.

Beef Island, the site of the main airport for passengers arriving in the British Virgins, is connected to Tortola by the one-lane Queen Elizabeth Bridge.

BY BOAT

You can travel from Charlotte Amalie (St. Thomas) by public ferry to West End and Road Town on Tortola, a 45-minute voyage along Drake's Channel through the islands. Services making this run include **Native Son** (☎ **809/495-4617**), **Smith's Ferry Service** (☎ **809/495-4495**), and **Inter-Island Boat Services** (☎ **809/776-6597**). The last specializes in a somewhat obscure routing—that is, from St. John to the West End on Tortola. This routing offer three trips a day, and four on Friday.

FAST FACTS: The British Virgin Islands

Area Code   The area code for the British Virgin Islands is 809. (Also see "Telephone," below.)

Business Hours   Generally, **banks** are open Monday through Thursday from 9am to 2:30pm and on Friday from 9am to 2:30pm and 4:30 to 6pm. Most **offices** are open Monday through Friday from 9am to 5pm; **government offices** are open from 8:30am to 4:30pm. **Shops** are generally open Monday through Friday from 9am to 5pm and on Saturday from 9am to 1pm.

Currency   The **U.S. dollar** is the legal currency, much to the surprise of arriving Britishers who find no one willing to accept their pounds. Thus all prices in this chapter are given in U.S. dollars.

Documents   U.S. and Canadian citizens need produce only an authenticated birth certificate or a voter registration card to enter the British Virgin Islands for a stay of up to six months, but they must possess return or ongoing tickets and show evidence of adequate means of support and prearranged accommodations during their stay. British citizens need a passport.

Electricity   Your U.S.–made appliances can be used here, as the electricity is 110 volts AC, 60 cycles.

Holidays   The B.V.I. celebrates the following holidays: January 1 (New Year's Day); Commonwealth Day (in March; dates vary); Easter Monday; Whit Monday; the Sovereign's Birthday (in June; the actual day of observance can vary); July 1 (Territory Day); Festival Monday, Festival Tuesday, and Festival Wednesday (in August); October 21 (St. Ursula's Day); November 14 (birthday of the heir to the throne); and December 25 and 26 (Christmas Day and Boxing Day).

Information   For more information on the British Virgin Islands, contact the **British Virgin Islands Tourist Board,** 370 Lexington Ave., Suite 313, New York, NY 10017 (☎ **212/696-0400,** or 800/835-8530 in the U.S.). On the West Coast, contact the B.V.I. Tourist Board, 1686 Union St., San Francisco,

CA 94123 (☎ **415/775-0344,** or 800/835-8530 in the U.S.). In the United Kingdom, contact FCB Travel/Marketing, 110 St. Martin's Lane, London, WC2N 4DY (☎ **0171/240-4259).**

Language English is spoken in this British colony.

Medical Care Thirteen doctors practice on Tortola, and there is a hospital, Peebles Hospital, Porter Road, Road Town (☎ **809/494-3497**), with x-ray and laboratory facilities. One doctor practices on Virgin Gorda. If you need them, your hotel will put you in touch with the islands' medical staff.

Prohibitions Unlike some parts of the Caribbean, nudity is an offense punishable by law in the B.V.I. Drugs, their use or sale, are also strictly prohibited.

Safety Crime is rare here: In fact, the B.V.I. is one of the safest places in the Caribbean. But crime does exist, and you should take all the usual precautions you would anywhere. Don't leave items unattended on the beach.

Taxes A government tax of 7% is imposed on all hotel rooms. There is no sales tax. A $5 departure tax is collected from everyone leaving by air, $4 for those departing by sea.

Telephone Each phone number in the islands begins with 49. However, once you are here, omit both the 809 and the 49 to make local calls; dial only the last five digits of the numbers given in this chapter.

Time The islands operate on Atlantic standard time year round. In the peak winter season, when it's 6am in the British Virgins, it's only 5am in Florida. However, when Florida and the rest of the East Coast goes on daylight saving time, the clocks are the same.

Weather The islands, covering about 59 square miles, have a perfect year-round climate, with temperatures of 75° to 85° Fahrenheit, and the prevailing trade winds keep the islands from being too humid. Rainfall is infrequent, and even during the rainy season in early autumn, precipitation is generally heavy for only about 10 or 15 minutes and stops just as abruptly as it began.

1 Anegada

The most northerly and isolated of the British Virgins, 30 miles east of Tortola, Anegada has a population of about 250, none of whom has found the legendary treasure from the more than 500 wrecks lying off its notorious Horseshoe Reef. It's different from the other British Virgins in that it's a coral-and-limestone atoll, flat, with a 2,500-foot airstrip. Its highest point reaches 28 feet, and it hardly appears on the horizon if you're sailing to it.

At the northern and western ends of the island are some good beaches, which might be your only reason for coming here. This is a remote little corner of the Caribbean: Don't expect one frill, and be prepared to put up with some hardships, such as mosquitoes.

Most of the island has been declared off-limits to settlement and reserved for birds and other wildlife. The BVI National Parks Trust has established a flamingo colony in a bird sanctuary, which is also the protected home of several different varieties of heron as well as ospreys and terns. It has also designated much of the interior of the island as a preserved habitat for Anegada's animal population of some 2,000 wild goats, donkeys, and cattle. Among the endangered species being given a new lease on life here is the rock iguana, a fierce-looking but quite

The British Virgin Islands

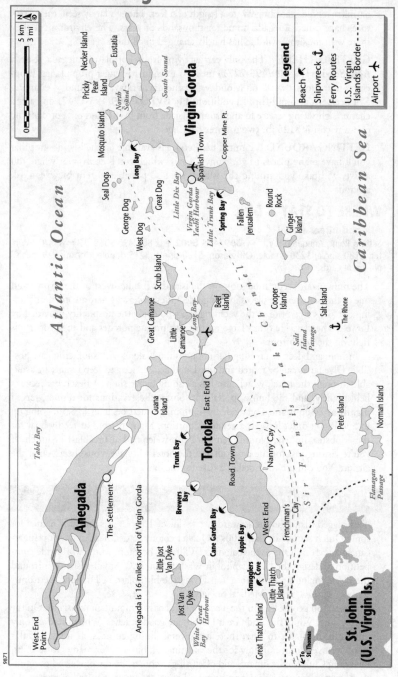

Atlantic Ocean

Caribbean Sea

5 km
3 mi

N

Legend

Beach
Shipwreck
Ferry Routes
U.S. Virgin Islands Border
Airport

Necker Island
Eustatia
Prickly Pear Island
Mosquito Island
South Sound
North Sound
Virgin Gorda
Seal Dogs
George Dog
West Dog
Great Dog
Long Bay
Little Dix Bay
Spanish Town
Copper Mine Pt.
Virgin Gorda Yacht Harbour
Little Trunk Bay
Spring Bay
Fallen Jerusalem
Round Rock
Ginger Island
Scrub Island
Great Camanoe
Little Camanoe
Long Bay
Beef Island
Cooper Island
Salt Island
The Rhone
Guana Island
East End
D r a k e   C h a n n e l
Salt Island Passage
Trunk Bay
Tortola
Road Town
Nanny Cay
S i r   F r a n c i s
Peter Island
Norman Island
Brewers Bay
Cane Garden Bay
Apple Bay
West End
Frenchman's Cay
Smugglers Cove
Little Thatch Island
Great Thatch Island
Jost Van Dyke
White Bay
Great Harbour
Little Jost Van Dyke
Flanagan Passage
St. John (U.S. Virgin Is.)
←To St. Thomas

Anegada
Table Bay
West End Point
The Settlement
Anegada is 16 miles north of Virgin Gorda

9871

harmless reptile that can grow to a length of 5 feet. Though rarely seen, these creatures have called Anegada home for thousands of years. The environment they share with the other wildlife has hardly changed in all those years.

GETTING THERE   The only carrier flying from Tortola to Anegada, **Gorda Aero Service** (☎ 809/495-2271) uses six- to eight-passenger prop planes. It operates four times a week, on Monday, Wednesday, Friday, and Sunday, charging $54 per person round-trip. In addition, **Fly BVI** (☎ 809/495-1747) operates a charter/sightseeing service to and from Anegada from Beef Island off Tortola. The one-way cost is $125 for two to three passengers.

GETTING AROUND   Limited **taxi** service is available on the island—not that you'll have many places to go. Tony's Taxis, which you'll easily spot when you arrive, will take you around the island. It's also possible to rent bicycles—ask around.

WHERE TO STAY & DINE

Anegada Reef Hotel
Setting Point, Anegada, B.V.I. ☎ **809/495-8002.** Fax 809/495-9362. 12 rms. A/C. Winter, $180 single; $230 double. Off-season, $160 single; $215 double. (Includes all meals.) No credit cards.

The only major accommodation on the island is 3 miles west of the airport and one of the most remote places in this guide. Guests who stay here are in effect "hiding out." It's a favorite of the yachting set, who enjoy the hospitality provided by Lowell Wheatley. He offers large rooms with private porches and the property is right on the beachfront.

Inshore and deep-sea fishing (also bonefishing), along with snorkeling, are possible. Dive tanks can be rented and filled, and taxi service and Jeep rentals are available through the hotel, which also has a fishing tackle shop. A beach barbecue is held nightly, and the house specialty is lobster. Reservations for dinner, served nightly at 7:30pm, must be made by 4:30pm. Dinners begin at $16.50, going up to $30 if you order lobster, a generous portion. Many patrons arrive by boat for these lobster dinners. Nonresidents are also welcomed at breakfast or lunch. If you're visiting just for the day, call and the hotel will have a bus meet you at the airport. You can use the hotel as a base for the day.

2 Jost Van Dyke

This rugged island, on the seaward (west) side of Tortola, was probably named for some Dutch settler. In the 1700s a Quaker colony settled here to develop sugarcane plantations. One of the colonists, William Thornton, won a worldwide competition to design the U.S. Capitol in Washington, D.C. Smaller islands surround the place, including Little Jost Van Dyke, the birthplace of Dr. John Lettsome, founder of the London Medical Society.

About 130 people live on the 4 square miles of this mountainous island. On the south shore, White Bay and Great Harbor are good beaches. While there are only a handful of places to stay, there are several dining choices, as it's a popular stopping-over point not only for the yachting set, but also for many cruise ships, including Club Med, Cunard, and often all-gay cruises. So the peace and tranquility of yesteryear often aren't to be found anymore unless you're here when the cruise ships aren't.

GETTING THERE   Guests heading for any point on Jost Van Dyke usually opt for ferryboat transit from either St. Thomas or Tortola. (Be warned that departure times can vary widely throughout the year, and at times don't adhere very closely to whatever happens to be printed in the timetables.) Ferryboats from St. Thomas depart from Red Hook three days a week (Friday, Saturday, and Sunday) about twice a day. More convenient (and more frequent) are the daily ferryboat shuttles that head for Jost Van Dyke from Tortola's isolated West End. From there, ferryboats depart three times a day, travel for 25 minutes each way, and cost $8 each way, or $14 round-trip. Call the **Jost Van Dyke Ferryboat service** (☎ **809/494-2997**) for information about departures from any of the above-mentioned points. Of course, if all else fails, there are a handful of privately operated **water taxis** that will, for a carefully negotiated fee, transport you, your entourage, and your luggage to Jost Van Dyke.

WHERE TO STAY

Sandcastle Hotel
White Bay, Jost Van Dyke, B.V.I ☎ **809/775-5262.** Fax 809/775-3590. 4 cottages. Jan 15–May 14, $255 single; $325 double. May 15–Jan 14, $175–$195 single; $225–$265 double. Additional person $75–$95 extra. (Includes meals.) MC, V. Transportation: Private motor launch from Tortola, a 20-minute trip.

A retreat for escapists, these cottages are surrounded by flowering shrubbery and bougainvillea and take advantage of the view. The small, personalized hotel caters to only a handful of guests. You mix your own drinks at the beachside bar, the Soggy Dollar, and you keep your own tab. Visiting boaters often drop in to enjoy the beachside informality and order a drink called a "Painkiller." In the guest book you'll read: "I thought places like this only existed in the movies."

For reservations and information, call or write the Sandcastle, Suite 201, Red Hook Plaza, St. Thomas, USVI 00802-1306 (☎ **809/775-5262**). Don't send mail to Jost Van Dyke, as it could take months to reach there, and if you call the Jost Van Dyke phone number above, you'll get only an answering machine.

Sandy Ground
East End (mailing address: P.O. Box 594, West End, Tortola, B.V.I.). ☎ **809/494-3391.** Fax 809/495-9379. 8 villas. Winter, $1,200 per week villa for two. Off-season, $780 per week villa for two. Additional person $150 extra in winter, $100 extra off-season. MC, V. Transportation: Private water taxi from Tortola.

On a 17-acre hill site on the eastern part of Jost Van Dyke are self-sufficient housekeeping units. The complex rents two- and three-bedroom villas. One of my favorites was constructed on a cliff that seems to hang about 80 or so feet over a good beach. If you've come all this way to reach this tiny outpost you might as well stay a week, which is the way the rates are quoted. The airy villas, each privately owned, are fully equipped with refrigerators and stoves. The managers help guests with boat rentals and water sports.

WHERE TO DINE

Abe's by the Sea
Little Harbour. ☎ **809/495-9329.** Reservations recommended for groups of five or more. Appetizers $3–$5; main courses $12–$30. MC, V. Lunch daily noon–3pm; dinner daily 7–10pm. WEST INDIAN. Transportation: Take a private motor launch or boat from Tortola; as you approach the east side of the harbor you'll see Abe's on your right.

In this local bar and restaurant, sailors are satisfied with a menu of fish, lobster, conch, and chicken. Prices are low too, and it's money well spent, especially when a fungi band entertains you with its music and plays for dancing. For the price of the main course, you get peas and rice, along with coleslaw, plus dessert. On Wednesday night in season, Abe's has a festive pig roast. Friday is barbecue night, costing $18 per person.

⊙ Rudy's Mariner's Rendezvous

Great Harbour. ☎ **809/495-9282.** Reservations required by 6:30pm. Dinner $10–$22.50. AE, MC, V. Dinner only, daily 7pm–midnight. WEST INDIAN.

Rudy's, at the western end of Great Harbour, serves good West Indian food and plenty of it in a place that looks and feels like a private home with a waterfront terrace for visiting diners. A welcoming drink awaits sailors and landlubbers alike, and the food that follows is simply prepared and inexpensive. Conch always seems to be available, and a catch of the day is featured.

3 Marina Cay

Near Beef Island, Marina Cay is a private 6-acre islet. Its only claim to fame was as the setting of the Robb White 1958 book *Our Virgin Isle*, which was filmed with Sidney Poitier and John Cassavetes. The island lies five minutes away by launch from Trellis Bay, adjacent to Beef Island International Airport. There are no cars on the island. I only mention the tiny cay at all because of the Marina Cay Hotel.

WHERE TO STAY

Marina Cay Hotel

Marina Cay (mailing address: P.O. Box 76, Road Town, Tortola), B.V.I. ☎ **809/494-2174.** Fax 809/494-4775. 4 rms, 2 villas. Winter, $95–$125 double; $300 villa. Off-season, $60–$75 double; $195 villa. (Includes breakfast.) AE, MC, V. Transportation: Private launch from Beef Island.

This small cottage hotel, opened in 1960 and extensively renovated, attracts the sailing crowd. It houses guests in double rooms with king-size beds, all over-looking a reef and Sir Francis Drake Channel, dotted with islands. Marina Cay is a tropical garden.

Dining is casual, with a cuisine featuring continental and West Indian dishes. Activities include snorkeling, windsurfers, scuba diving (with certification courses taught by a resident divemaster), castaway picnics on secluded beaches, kayaking, underwater safaris, and deep-sea fishing.

4 Peter Island

Most of this island, with its good marina and docking facilities, is devoted to the yacht club described below. The other part is deserted. Beach facilities are found at palm-fringed Deadman Bay, which faces the Atlantic but is protected by a reef. All goods and services are at the hotel. The island is so private that about the only creature a guest will encounter is an iguana or a wild cat, whose ancestors were abandoned generations ago by shippers (the cats are said to have virtually elimi-nated the rodent population).

GETTING THERE   A complimentary hotel-operated ferry, **Peter Island Boat** (☎ **809/495-2271**), picks up any overnight guest who arrives at the Beef Island airport. It departs from the pier at Trellis Bay, near the airport, and requires a 30-minute crossing. Other boats depart eight or nine times a day from the CSY Dock in Road Town, for a 20- to 30-minute crossing. Passengers must communicate their needs to the hotel in advance of their arrival or departure.

WHERE TO STAY & DINE

✪ Peter Island Resort and Yacht Harbour

Peter Island (mailing address: P.O. Box 211, Road Town, Tortola), B.V.I. ☎ **809/494-2561**, or 800/346-4451. Fax 809/494-2313. 50 rms, 3 villas. A/C MINIBAR TEL. Transportation: See above. Winter, $395–$525 double; $675–$875 Hawk's Nest two-bedroom villa for two; $3,220 Crow's Nest four–bedroom villa for up to eight. Off-season, $275–$385 double; $475–$675 Hawk's Nest two-bedroom villa for two; $1,230–$3,220 Crow's Nest four-bedroom villa for up to eight. MAP $65 per person extra. AE, MC, V.

This tropical island, comprising 1,800 acres, is solely dedicated to Peter Island Resort guests and yacht owners who moor their craft here. After damage by the 1989 hurricane, the facilities and marina were restored and reopened in 1991. The island's tropical gardens and hillside are bordered by five private beaches.

The resort contains 30 rooms facing Sprat Bay and Sir Francis Drake Channel (ocean-view or garden rooms), and 20 larger rooms on Deadman Bay Beach (beachfront). Designed with a blend of casual elegance, they have a balcony or terrace, ceiling fan, coffee maker, clock radio, and hairdryer. The Crow's Nest, a luxurious four-bedroom villa, overlooks the harbor and Deadman Bay and features a private swimming pool, full kitchen, maid, gardener, personal steward, and island vehicle. The Hawk's Nest villas are two two-bedroom villas situated on a tropical hillside. The rates for the Crow's Nest villa include all meals.

Dining/Entertainment: The Tradewinds Restaurant serves breakfast and dinner throughout the year in fine Caribbean tradition. For a more casual setting, the Deadman's Beach Bar and Grill serves sandwiches and salads beside the ocean. The main bar, Drakes Channel Lounge, is also open throughout the day and evening.

Services: Room service (breakfast only), laundry, massage, babysitting, guest launch transport to/from Beef Island airport.

Facilities: Fitness center, gift shop, freshwater pool, four tennis courts (two lit for night play), scuba-diving base, library, spa, conference facility, basketball, mountain bikes; complete yacht marina with complimentary use of Sunfish, snorkeling gear, sea kayaks, windsurfers, and 19-foot Squib day-sailers.

5 Tortola

On the southern shore of this 24-square-mile island, Road Town is the capital of the British Virgin Islands, the seat of Government House and other administrative buildings, but it seems more like a village. The landfill at Wickhams Cay, a 70-acre town center development and marina in the harbor, has brought in a massive yacht-chartering business and has transformed the sleepy capital into more of a bustling center.

The entire southern coast, including Road Town, is characterized by rugged mountain peaks. On the northern coast are white sandy beaches, banana trees, mangoes, and clusters of palms.

Close to Tortola's eastern end, **Beef Island** is the site of the main airport for passengers arriving in the British Virgins. The airstrip is 3,600 feet long and can accommodate the Avro 748 turbo-jet 48-seaters. The tiny island is connected to Tortola by the Queen Elizabeth Bridge, which the queen dedicated in 1966. The one-lane bridge spans the 300-foot channel that divides the little island from its bigger neighbor, Tortola. On the north shore of Beef Island is a good beach, Long Bay.

Because Tortola is the gateway to the British Virgin Islands, the information on how to get there is covered at the beginning of this chapter.

ORIENTATION
GETTING AROUND

BY TAXI   Taxis meet every arriving flight. Your hotel can also call a taxi. The fare from the Beef Island airport to Road Town is $15 for one to three passengers. A tour lasting 2^1/$_2$ hours costs $45 for one to three people. To call a taxi in Road Town, dial **809/494-2322;** on Beef Island, **809/495-2378.**

BY RENTAL CAR   Because of the volume of tourism to Tortola, it's recommended that you reserve your rental car in advance, especially in winter. A handful of local companies rent cars, but because of the more lenient refund policies in case of billing errors, damage disputes, or insurance claims, I recommend using one of the U.S.–based giants, even if the cost is slightly higher. On Tortola, the well-recommended **Budget** is at 1 Wickhams Cay, Road Town (☎ **809/ 494-5150, or 800/527-0700** in the U.S.). **Avis** maintains offices opposite the police headquarters in Road Town (☎ **809/494-3322, or 800/331-2112** in the U.S.). **Hertz** (☎ **809/495-4405, or 800/654-3001** in the U.S.) has offices outside Road Town, on the island's West End, near the ferryboat landing dock. Government regulations prohibit anyone from renting a car at the airport—visitors must take a taxi to their hotels. Rental companies will usually deliver cars to a client's hotel.

All three companies require that renters be at least 25 years old. They also require presentation of a valid driver's license and purchase of a temporary B.V.I. driver's license, which the car-rental company can sell you; the cost is $10, and it's valid for three months.

At press time, Budget charged $210 per week for its least expensive car, a Nissan Sentra with manual transmission suitable for four passengers—in a pinch, up to five. For an extra $18 a week, the same model was available with automatic transmission. A collision-damage waiver (CDW), eliminating all but $600 worth of financial responsibility in the event of an accident, costs an additional $8 per day. If you opt not to buy the CDW, you'll be asked to leave either the imprint of a valid credit or charge card or a substantial cash deposit. A 5% government tax is extra. Rates at the other two companies are competitive.

The rates will almost certainly change before your departure. Call the companies for last-minute price adjustments at least 36 business hours before your intended pickup.

Remember to *drive on the left*. Because the island roads are notoriously under-illuminated, with few, if any, lines marking the shoulder of the sinuous and narrow roads, nighttime driving can be disturbing. It's a good idea to hire a taxi to take you to that difficult-to-find restaurant or nightspot.

BY BUS   **Scato's Bus Service** (☎ **809/494-2365**) operates from the north end of the island to the west end, picking up passengers who hail it down. Fares for a trek across the island are $1 to $3.

ESSENTIALS

To **cash traveler's checks,** try the Bank of Nova Scotia, Wickhams Cay (☎ 809/ 494-2526), or Barclays Bank, Wickhams Cay (☎ 809/494-2171), both near Road Town. The local **American Express representative** is Travel Plan Ltd., Waterfront Drive (☎ 809/494-2347).

The best place for **photographic needs** is Bolo's Brothers Department Store, Wickhams Cay (☎ 809/494-2867). It has some of the best supplies on the island (stock up here on film if you're going to one of the other islands) and features one-hour developing service. If you need a **drugstore,** try J. R. O'Neal Ltd., Main Street, Road Town (☎ 809/494-2292); it's closed Sunday. Stock up here on any prescribed medicines or other supplies you'll need if you're planning visits to the other islands.

WHERE TO STAY

None of the island's hotels is as big, splashy, and all-encompassing as the hotels in the U.S. Virgin Islands, although many of the island's repeat clients seem to like that just fine. All rates given in this unit are subject to a 10% service charge and a 7% government tax on the room.

EXPENSIVE

Frenchman's Cay Resort Hotel

West End (P.O. Box 1054), Tortola, B.V.I. ☎ **809/495-4844,** or 800/235-4077 in the U.S., 800/463-0199 in Canada. Fax 809/495-4056. 9 villas. A/C. Winter, $195 one-bedroom villa for two; $295 two-bedroom villa for four. Off-season, $115–$135 one-bedroom villa for two; $170–$200 two-bedroom villa for four. MAP $45 per person extra. AE, MC, V. Free parking. From Tortola, cross the bridge to Frenchman's Cay, turn left, and follow the road to the eastern tip of the cay.

This intimate all-villa resort is tucked away at the windward side of Frenchman's Cay, that little island connected by bridge to Tortola. The 12-acre landscaped estate enjoys year-round cooling breezes and views of Sir Francis Drake Channel and the outer Virgins. The individual one- and two-bedroom villas are well furnished, each with a shady terrace, full kitchen, dining room, and sitting room. The two-bedroom villas have two full baths.

Dining/Entertainment: The Clubhouse Restaurant and lounge bar is located in the main pavillion. The menu features a continental and Caribbean cuisine.

Facilities: Beach with snorkeling, freshwater swimming pool, tennis court, Sunfish sailboats, kayaks, windsurfers; day-sail trips, horseback riding, scuba diving, island tours, and car rentals can be arranged.

✪ Long Bay Beach Resort

Tortola, B.V.I. ☎ **809/495-4252,** or 800/729-9599 in the U.S. and Canada, 0800/898-379 in Britain. Fax 914/833-3318 in Larchmont, N.Y. 62 rms, 20 villas. A/C. Winter, $175–$265 single; $195–$295 double; from $600 two-bedroom villa for four. Off-season, $55–$120 single; $110–$180 double; from $425 two-bedroom villa for four. MAP $37.50 per person extra. AE, MC, V. Free parking. Transportation: Taxi.

On the north shore, about 10 minutes from the West End, is a low-rise hotel resort complex set in a 52-acre estate with a mile-long white sand beach. Available in a wide range of styles, shapes, and sizes, the accommodations include hillside rooms and studios as well as beachfront deluxe rooms and beachfront cabañas. In addition the resort offers two- and three-bedroom villas complete with kitchen, living area, and a large deck with a gas grill. Beachfront deluxe rooms and villas have cable television. Hillside rooms, studios, and villas offer ocean views. Beachfront deluxe rooms and cabañas are set at the edge of the white sands overlooking the ocean with either balconies or patios.

Dining/Entertainment: The Beach Restaurant offers breakfast and lunch as well as informal à la carte suppers. In the ruins of an old sugar mill the restaurant offers regular evening buffets with live entertainment. The Garden Restaurant serves dinner by reservation only, and the food is of excellent quality.

Services: Daily maid service, laundry, babysitting, car rental; chef available on request for villa renters.

Facilities: Oceanside freshwater swimming pool, tennis court, beach bar, shops.

The Sugar Mill

Apple Bay (P.O. Box 425, Road Town), Tortola, B.V.I. ☎ **809/495-4355,** or 800/ 462-8834. Fax 809/495-4696. 20 units. 1 villa. Winter, $235 single; $250 double; $265 triple; $280 quad; $575 two-bedroom villa. Off-season, $160–$175 single; $175 double; $190 triple; $220 quad; $390–$450 two-bedroom villa. Breakfast $9 extra. AE, MC, V. Free parking. Closed Aug–Sept. Transportation: Taxi.

Set in lush foliage on the site of a 300-year-old sugar mill on the north side of Tortola, this cottage colony sweeps down the hillside to its own little beach, with flowers and fruits brightening the grounds. The estate is owned by Jeff and Jinx Morgan, formerly of San Francisco, who are travel, food, and wine writers.

Comfortable apartments climb up the hillside. At the center is a circular swimming pool for those who don't want to go down to the beach. The accommodations are contemporary and well planned, ranging from suites and cottages to studio apartments, all self-contained with kitchenettes, private terraces with views, and ceiling fans. Four of the units are suitable for families of four.

Lunch or dinner is served down by the beach at the Islands, which offers dinner from 6:30 to 9pm Tuesday through Saturday January to May, featuring Caribbean specialties along with burgers and salads. Dinner is also offered in the old Sugar Mill Restaurant (see "Where to Dine," below). Breakfast is served on the terrace. The bars are open all day, and you can use the free snorkeling equipment.

MODERATE

The Moorings/Mariner Inn

Wickhams Cay (P.O. Box 139, Road Town), Tortola, B.V.I. ☎ **809/494-2332,** or 800/ 334-2435 in the U.S. for reservations. Fax 809/494-2226. 39 rms, 2 suites. A/C TV TEL. Winter, $150 single; $165 double; $230 suite. Off-season, $80 single; $90 double; $125 suite. Additional person $15 extra. Breakfast $7–$15 extra. AE, MC, V. Free parking. Transportation: Taxi.

The Caribbean's only complete yachting resort is outfitted with at least 100 sailing yachts, some worth around $500,000 or more. On an 8-acre resort, the inn was obviously designed with the yachting crowd in mind, offering not only support facilities and service but also shoreside accommodations (suites and lanai hotel rooms), a dockside restaurant, Mariner Bar, swimming pool, tennis court, beach club, gift shop, and dive shop that has underwater video cameras available for rent. The rooms are spacious and all have kitchenettes.

Nanny Cay Resort & Marina

P.O. Box 281, Road Town, Tortola, B.V.I. ☎ **809/494-2512,** or 800/786-4753 in the U.S. Fax 809/494-0555. 42 studios. A/C TV TEL. Winter, $140–$255 studio for one or two. Off-season, $45–$195 studio for one or two. Additional person $20 extra, children under 12 stay free in their parents' room. Breakfast $10 extra. Special diving, sailing, and windsurfing packages available. AE, MC, V. Free parking. Transportation: Taxi.

On a 25-acre inlet adjoining a 180-slip marina, Nanny Cay is located 3 miles from the center of Road Town and 10 miles from the airport. All accommodations are studios with fully equipped kitchenettes. Standard studios have two double beds; deluxe studios are larger, with a sitting area and two queen-size beds. Units have ceiling fans along with private balconies opening onto a view of the water, marina, or gardens. The decor is West Indian.

Dining/Entertainment: The hotel's Pegleg Landing Restaurant serves both lunch and dinner daily, featuring international dishes with a Caribbean flair. More casual food is offered at the Plaza Café.

Prospect Reef Resort

Western end of Road Town (P.O. Box 104, Road Town), Tortola, B.V.I. ☎ **809/494-3311,** or 800/356-8937 in the U.S., 800/463-3608 in Canada. Fax 809/494-5595. 131 units. TEL. Winter, $147–$190 single or double; $410 two-bedroom villa for four. Off-season, $88–$117 single or double; $274 two-bedroom villa for four. Continental breakfast $6 extra. AE, MC, V. Free parking. Transportation: Taxi.

Built by a consortium of British investors in 1979, this is the largest resort in the B.V.I. It's in a series of two-story concrete buildings scattered over a steeply sloping 15-acre, landscaped terrain. It rises above a small, private harbor. Views from the bedrooms encompass one of the most panoramic anywhere of the Sir Francis Drake Channel. Each of the resort's buildings is painted in hibiscus-inspired shades of pink, peach, purple, or aquamarine. (Each building contains up to 10 individual accommodations.) Initially designed as condominiums, there are unique studios, town houses, and villas, in addition to guest rooms. All include private balconies or patios; larger units have kitchenettes, good size living and dining areas, plus separate bedrooms or sleeping lofts. Thirty-nine rooms are air-conditioned, while others are cooled by ceiling fans and the constant trade winds. All rooms are wired for TVs, which can be rented if anyone asks. Food at the hotel's Upstairs Restaurant, offering a combination of continental specialties and island favorites, was praised by *Gourmet* magazine. Count on spending about $30 per person at dinner, more if you order wine and lobster. Light meals are served on the terrace of the Scuttlebutt Café or around the Seapool Bar and Grill. There's a pool to swim in, another to dive in, plus sand-terraced sea pools for snorkeling. Six tennis courts are available. The hotel has a health and fitness center and a pitch-and-putt course. Guest services can fill you in on what's available from the harbor—day sailing, snorkeling, scuba diving, and sportfishing.

Ⓢ Treasure Isle Hotel

Pasea Estate, east end of Road Town (P.O. Box 68, Road Town), Tortola, B.V.I. ☎ **809/494-2501,** or 800/334-2435 in the U.S. for reservations. Fax 809/494-2507. 39 rms, 2 suites. A/C TV TEL. Winter, $150 single; $165 double; $230 suite. Off-season, $80 single; $90 double; $125 suite. Additional person $15 extra. Breakfast $10–$12 extra. AE, MC, V. Free parking. Transportation: Taxi.

The most complete and central resort on Tortola was built at the edge of the capital on 15 acres of hillside overlooking a marina. The core of the hotel is a rather splashy and colorful lounge and swimming-pool area. The rooms are on two levels along the hillside terraces; a third level is occupied by suites.

Adjoining the lounge and pool area is a covered open-air dining room overlooking the harbor. The cuisine is respected here, with barbecue and full à la carte menus offered at dinner, 6:30 to 9pm Thursday through Tuesday. On Wednesday a West Indian "grill out" is served, and entertainment and dancing are part of the fun. The hotel has a fully equipped dive facility that handles beginning instruction up to full certification courses.

WHERE TO DINE
EXPENSIVE

✪ Brandywine Bay Restaurant
Brandywine Estate. ☎ **809/495-2301.** Reservations required. Appetizers $6–$13; main courses $21–$27. AE, MC, V. Dinner only, Mon–Sat 6:30–9:30pm. Closed Aug–Oct. Drive 3 miles east of Road Town (toward the airport) on South Shore Road. ITALIAN.

On the south shore, 3 miles from the center of Road Town overlooking Sir Francis Drake Channel, this restaurant is set on a cobblestone garden terrace. Davide Pugliese, the chef de cuisine, and his wife, Cele McLachlan, the hostess, have earned a reputation on Tortola for their outstanding Florentine food. Once a fashion photographer, Davide changes his menu daily based on the availability of fresh produce. Typical dishes include beef carpaccio, homemade pasta, his own special calves' liver dish (the recipe is a secret), pheasant, venison, the typical bistecca alla fiorentina, and homemade mozzarella with fresh basil and tomatoes.

The Cloud Room
Ridge Rd. ☎ **809/494-4429.** Reservations required. Fixed-price meals $22–$30. AE, MC, V. Dinner only, Mon–Sat 7:30–10pm. Closed June–Oct. Transportation: Private pickup from your hotel. CONTINENTAL.

A unique dining experience, this restaurant and bar, the second-highest restaurant on the island—converted from a former private home—sits at the top of Butu Mountain, overlooking Road Town half a mile to the south. When weather permits, which is practically every day of the year, the roof slides back and you dine under the stars. The road to the restaurant is bad and there's no place to park, so the owner, Paul Wattley, prefers to arrange to pick you up when you make your reservation. You'll get a selection of juicy sirloin steaks, fresh fish in season, shish kebab (the house specialty), and shrimp in Créole sauce.

✪ Skyworld
Ridge Rd. ☎ **809/494-3567.** Reservations recommended. Appetizers $5.60–$7; main courses $22–$28; fixed-price six-course meal $34–$40. AE, MC, V. Lunch daily 11:30am–3pm; dinner daily 6:30–9pm. Closed Sept. INTERNATIONAL.

Skyworld is all the rage, and is certainly the worthiest excursion on the island. On one of the loftiest peaks on the island, at a breezy 1,337 feet, it offers views

---

Family-Friendly Accommodations

Guavaberry Spring Bay Vacation Homes *(see p. 237)* Staying in one of these hexagonal redwood houses on stilts is like living in a tree house. Each has two bedrooms.

Frenchman's Cay Resort Hotel *(see p. 225)* Families can stay in one-or two-bedroom detached villas and enjoy the most active sports Program on the island.

Prospect Reef Resort *(see p. 227)* These units come in a wide array of sizes and styles to fit most families, some of whom tuck the kids in sleeping lofts. There's an activity-filled sports program.

of both the U.S. and the British Virgins. The french fries and onion rings have been praised by *Gourmet* magazine. You might try the conch fritters, which are considered the best on the island. On the classic French-inspired menu, main dishes include scallops, lamb, lobster ravioli, and fresh fish grilled to order. You can finish with a dish of homemade tropical ice cream.

Sugar Mill Restaurant

Apple Bay. ☎ **809/495-4355.** Reservations required. Appetizers $5–$7; main dishes $16–$28. AE, MC, V. Lunch daily noon–2pm; dinner daily 7–8:30pm. From Road Town, drive west for about 7 miles, take a right turn over Zion Hill going north, and then at the T-junction opposite Sebastians, turn right; Sugar Mill lies about half a mile down the road. CALIFOR-NIAN/CARIBBEAN.

You'll dine in an informal room that was transformed from a three-century-old sugar mill (see "Where to Stay," above). Works by Haitian painters hang on the old stone walls of the dining room, and big copper basins once used in distilling rum have been planted with tropical flowers. Before going to the dining room, once part of the old boiling house, I suggest a visit to the open-air bar.

Your hosts, the Morgans, know a lot about food and wine. Jinx Morgan super-vises the dining room and is an imaginative cook herself. One of their most popular creations, published in *Bon Appétit,* is a curried-banana soup. They are likely to prepare delectable chicken breasts, seafood Créole, lobster crêpes, and a cold rum soufflé. Everything is homemade, and the Morgans have a vegetable and herb garden. Lunch can be ordered by the beach at the second restaurant, Islands, where dinner is also served Tuesday through Saturday from 6:30 to 9pm from January through May and features Caribbean specialties. Try "jerk" ribs or stuffed crabs.

MODERATE

The Apple

Zion Hill, Little Apple Bay. ☎ **809/495-4437.** Reservations recommended. Appetizers $3.25–$8; main courses $14–$30. Lunch $6–$10. AE, MC, V. Lunch daily 11am–2:30pm; dinner daily 6:30–9:30pm. Closed Sept–Oct. Transportation: Taxi. WEST INDIAN.

The Apple continues to please readers. You get West Indian fare with flair at this point about a 25-minute drive from Road Town on the northwest coast of Tortola where it opens onto Little Apple Bay at the bottom of Zion Hill. Diners can begin with a Virgin "souppy" made with soursop juice (from the famous Carib-bean fruit) and rum, among other ingredients. Then they select from seafood dishes, including whelks (large marine snails) in garlic butter, conch B.V.I. style, or the catch of the day steamed and served with a Créole sauce. Curried chicken and steaks can be ordered, and vegetarian meals are also offered. Lunch features chicken or vegetable rôtis.

Mrs. Scatliffe's Restaurant

Carrot Bay. ☎ **809/495-4556.** Reservations required for dinner (call before 5:30pm). Fixed-price meal $20–$27. No credit cards. Dinner only, daily 7–8pm (no later). Transpor-tation: Taxi. WEST INDIAN.

For the best and most authentic West Indian cuisine (with a touch of the inter-national kitchen), check out Mrs. Scatliffe's Restaurant. She offers meals on the deck of her island home, and some of the vegetables come right from her garden. You can begin with one of the best daiquiris on the island, made from fresh tropi-cal fruit. Then you'll be served soup (maybe spicy papaya), which will be followed by curried goat, "old wife" fish, or perhaps chicken in a coconut shell. After dinner your hostess and her family will entertain you with a fungi-band performance (Monday through Saturday only). If not that, maybe some gospel songs.

Be alert that part of your experience at this place might be an exposure to the gentle and often humorous form of Christian fundamentalism that affects many aspects of Mrs. Scatliffe's life. A Bible reading and a heartfelt rendition of a gospel song might follow your meal after the dessert is served. Advance reservations are absolutely essential before you head out on the rather arduous road toward this restaurant.

Pusser's Landing

Frenchman's Cay, West End. ☎ **809/495-4554.** Reservations recommended. Appetizers $4–$9; main courses $13–$25; lunch $6–$8.75. AE, MC, V. Lunch daily 11am–3pm; dinner daily 6–10pm. Transportation: Taxi. CARIBBEAN/ENGLISH PUB/MEXICAN.

This second Pusser's (see below for the first) is even more desirably located in the West End, opening onto the water. Here you can choose a well-prepared dinner, including fresh grilled fish, or select some English-inspired dishes, perhaps a classic shepherd's pie with a potato crust. In a nautical setting, begin with a hearty bowl of fresh soup with seasonal ingredients and follow it with filet mignon, West Indian roast chicken, or a filet of swordfish. "Mud pie" is the classic dessert. Happy hour is daily from 4 to 6pm.

INEXPENSIVE

Pusser's Ltd.

Main St., Road Town. ☎ **809/494-3897.** Reservations not accepted. Appetizers $3–$7.95; main courses $7–$13.95. AE, MC, V. Daily 9am–10pm. CARIBBEAN/ENGLISH PUB/MEXICAN.

Standing on the waterfront across from the ferry dock, Pusser's serves Caribbean fare, English pub grub, and good pizzas. The complete lunch and dinner menu includes English shepherd's pies and New York deli–style sandwiches. *Gourmet* magazine asked for the recipe for its chicken-and-asparagus pie. John Courage ale is on draft, but the drink to have here is the famous Pusser's Rum, the same blend of five West Indian rums that the Royal Navy has served to its men for more than 300 years.

WHAT TO SEE & DO

No visit to Tortola is complete without a trip to ✪ **Mount Sage,** a national park rising 1,780 feet. Here you'll find traces of a primeval rain forest and you can enjoy a picnic while overlooking neighboring islets and cays. The mountain is reached by heading west from Road Town.

Before you head out, go by the tourist office and pick up a brochure called "Sage Mountain National Park." It has a location map, directions to the forest (where there is a parking lot), and an outline of the main trails through the park.

Covering 92 acres, the park was established in 1964 to protect the remnants of Tortola's original forests not burned or cleared during the island's plantation era. From the parking lot, a trail leads to the main entrance to the park. The two main trails are the Rain Forest Trail and the Mahogany Forest Trail.

An organized tour may be your best way to see Tortola. **Travel Plan Tours,** Waterfront Plaza, Road Town (☎ 809/494-2872), will pick you up at your hotel and take one to three people on a 2¹/₂-hour tour of the island for about $50 to $60.

A **taxi tour** lasting 2¹/₂ hours costs $45 for up to three people. To call a taxi in Road Town, dial **809/494-2322;** on Beef Island, **809/495-2378.**

SPORTS & OUTDOOR ACTIVITIES

Tortola boasts the largest fleet of bareboat sailing charters in the world. It also offers some of the finest offshore diving areas anywhere.

BEACHES

Beaches are rarely crowded on Tortola unless a cruise ship is docked. You can rent a car or a Jeep to reach these beaches, or else take a taxi (but arrange for it to return at an appointed time to pick you up). There is no public transportation.

The finest beach is **Cane Garden Bay** (see "An Excursion to Cane Garden Bay," below), which some aficionados have compared favorably to the famous Magens Bay Beach on the north shore of St. Thomas. It's directly west of Road Town, up and down some steep hills, but it's worth the effort.

Surfers like **Apple Bay,** west of Road Town. A hotel here, Sebastians, caters to a surfing crowd. January and February are the ideal time for visits.

Brewers Bay, site of a campground, is northwest of Road Town. Both snorkelers and surfers are attracted to this beach.

Smugglers Cove is at the extreme western end of Tortola, opposite the offshore island of Great Thatch and very close to the American island of St. John, directly to the south. Snorkelers also like this beach, sometimes known as Lower Belmont Bay.

Long Bay Beach is on Beef Island, east of Tortola and the site of the major airport. This mile-long stretch of white sandy beach is reached by taking the Queen Elizabeth Bridge. Long Bay is approached by going along a dirt road to the left before you come to the airport. From Long Bay you'll have a good view of Little Camanoe, one of the rocky offshore islands around Tortola.

BOATING

The best place for this is **The Moorings,** Wickhams Cay (P.O. Box 139, Road Town), B.V.I. (☎ 809/494-2332, or 800/535-7289 in the U.S.), whose 8-acre waterside resort is also recommended in "Where to Stay," above. This place, along with a handful of others, makes the British Virgins the cruising capital of the world. Charlie and Ginny Cary started the first charter service in the B.V.I. You can choose from their fleet of sailing yachts, which can accommodate up to four couples in comfort and style. Depending on your skill and inclination, you can arrange a bareboat rental (with no crew); a fully crewed rental with a skipper, a staff, and a cook; or any variation in between. Boats usually come equipped with a portable barbecue, snorkeling gear, dinghy, linens, and galley equipment.

The Moorings has an experienced staff of mechanics, electricians, riggers, and cleaners. In addition, if you're going out on your own, you'll get a thorough briefing session about Virgin Island waters and anchorages.

HORSEBACK RIDING

Shadow's Ranch, Todman's Estate (☎ 809/494-2262), offers horseback rides through Mount Sage National Park or down to the shores of Cane Gardens Bay. Call for details Monday through Saturday from 9am to 4pm. The cost is $25 per hour.

SCUBA & SNORKELING

The one dive site in the British Virgin Islands that lures them over from St. Thomas is the wreckage of the **RMS *Rhône,*** which sank in 1867 near the western point of Salt Island. *Skin Diver* magazine called this "the world's most fantastic shipwreck dive." It teems with marine life and coral formations and was featured in the motion picture *The Deep*.

For the entry-level diver to those more experienced, **Baskin in the Sun,** a PADI five-star facility (☎ **809/494-5854, or 800/233-7938** in the U.S.), is a good choice on Tortola. Baskin in the Sun has three locations: Prospect Reef Resort, near Road Town; Sopher's Hole, at Tortola's West End; and Villa Cay Marina, at Road Town. Baskin offers a "Discover Scuba Diving" experience for $95, including a guided reef tour to give beginners a taste of diving under supervision. Daily trips are scheduled to such sites as the RMS *Rhône,* Painted Walls, and the Indians.

Underwater Safaris (☎ **809/494-3235, or 800/537-7032** in the U.S.) takes you to all of the best sites, including the RMS *Rhône,* "Spyglass Wall," and "Alice in Wonderland." Its offices, "Safari Base," are located in Road Town and its "Safari Cay" office lies on Cooper Island. Get complete directions and information when you call. The center, connected with the Moorings, offers a complete PADI and NAUI training facility. An introductory resort course and one dive costs $95, and an open-water certification, with four days of instruction and four open-water dives, goes for $385.

If you plan on snorkeling by yourself, exercise due caution and consider driving to Marina Cay or Cooper Island. **Marina Cay,** off Tortola's East End, is known for its good snorkeling beach, and I also recommend the one at **Cooper Island,** across Drake's Channel. Underwater Safaris (see above) leads dives and snorkel expeditions to both sites, weather permitting.

SHOPPING

Most of the shops are on Main Street, Road Town, but know that the British Virgins have no duty-free-port shopping. British goods are imported without duty, and the wise shopper will be able to find some good buys among these imported items, especially in English china. In general, store hours are 9am to 4pm Monday through Friday and 9am to 1pm on Saturday.

Bonker's Gallery
Main St., Road Town. ☎ **809/494-2535.**

Located next to a bakery, this is a shop for women's fashion, carrying, among other items, Java Wrap sarongs (although there is a much larger collection of these on St. Thomas and St. Croix). Bathing suits and accessories for women, including cotton and washable silk tops and bottoms, are the main feature, but there are also some shirts and pants for men as well.

Caribbean Fine Arts Ltd.
Main St., Road Town. ☎ **809/494-4240.**

This store has one of the most unusual collections of art from the West Indies. Not only does it sell original watercolors and oils, but also offers limited-edition serigraphs and sepia photographs from the dawn of the century. It also sells pottery and primitives.

Caribbean Handprints
Main St., Road Town. ☎ **809/494-3717.**

This store features island hand-prints, all hand-done by local craftspeople on Tortola. It also sells colorful fabric by the yard.

Flamboyance

Soper's Hole. ☎ **809/495-4699.**

This is the best place to shop for duty-free perfume. Fendi purses are also sold here.

J. R. O'Neal

Upper Main St., Road Town. ☎ **809/494-2292.**

Across from the Methodist church, this is a decorative and home accessories store, with the most extensive collection of items on the island. You'll find terra-cotta pottery, wicker and rattan home furnishings, Mexican glassware, Dhurrie rugs, baskets, and ceramics. There's also a collection of fine crystal and China, including Royal Worcester.

Kids in de Sun

Main St., Road Town. ☎ **809/494-3343.**

In the Abbot Building, this outlet carries the best collection of tropical wear for children, including T-shirts, shorts, and swimsuits, among other items.

Little Denmark

Main St., Road Town. ☎ **809/494-2455.**

Little Denmark is your best bet for famous names in gold and silver jewelry and china: Spode and Royal Copenhagen. Here you'll find many of the well-known designs from Scandinavian countries. It also offers jewelry made in the B.V.I., and there's a collection of watches. The outlet also offers a large selection of fishing equipment.

Pusser's Company Store

Main St., Road Town. ☎ **809/494-3897.**

There's a long, mahogany-trimmed bar accented with many fine nautical artifacts and a Pusser's Store selling a proprietary line of Pusser's sports and travel clothing and upmarket gift items. Pusser's Rum is one of the best-selling items here, or perhaps you'd prefer a Pusser's ceramic flask as a memento of your visit.

Sunny Caribbee Herb and Spice Company

Main St., Road Town. ☎ **809/494-2178.**

This old West Indian building was the first hotel on Tortola, and its shop specializes in Caribbean spices, seasonings, teas, condiments, and handcrafts. You can buy two world-famous specialties here: West Indian hangover cure and Arawak love potion. A Caribbean cosmetics collection, Sunsations, is also available and includes herbal bath gels, island perfume, and sunshine lotions. Most of the products are blended and packaged in an adjacent factory behind the retail store. With its aroma of spices permeating the air throughout the entire neighborhood, this factory is an attraction in itself. There's a daily sampling of island products, something different every day—perhaps tea, coffee, sauces, or dips. In the Sunny Caribbee Art Gallery, adjacent to the spice shop, you'll find an extensive collection of original art, prints, metal sculpture, and many other Caribbean crafts.

TORTOLA AFTER DARK

Ask around to find out which hotel might have entertainment on any given evening. Steel bands and fungi or scratch bands (African-Caribbean musicians who improvise on locally available instruments) appear regularly, and nonresidents are usually welcome. Pick up a copy of *Limin' Times,* an entertainment magazine listing "what's happening" locally that's usually available at your hotel.

Bomba's Surfside Shack, Cappoon's Bay (☎ 809/495-4148), is the oldest, most memorable, and most uninhibited nightlife venue on the island and sits on a 20-foot-wide strip of unpromising coastline near the West End. By anyone's standards this is the "junk palace" of the island; it's covered with Day-Glo graffiti and laced into a semblance of coherence with wire and rejected odds and ends of plywood, driftwood, and abandoned rubber tires. Despite its makeshift appearance, the shack has the electronic amplification systems to create a really great party. The place is at its wildest on Wednesday and Sunday nights, when there's live music and an all-you-can-eat barbecue. A Bomba punch costs $3.50, and beer goes for $2. The Sunday barbecue is $8 per person. Open daily from 10am to midnight (or later, depending on business).

AN EXCURSION TO CANE GARDEN BAY

If you've decided to risk everything and navigate the roller-coaster hills of the B.V.I., then you need a destination. Cane Garden Bay is one of the choicest pieces of real estate on the island, long ago discovered by the sailing crowd. Its white sandy beach is a cliché of Caribbean charm, with sheltering palms.

Rhymer's, Cane Garden Bay (☎ 809/495-4639), is the place to go for food and entertainment. Skippers of any kind of craft are likely to stock up on supplies here, but you can also order cold beer and refreshing rum drinks. If you're hungry, try the conch or whelk, or the barbecued spareribs. The beach bar and restaurant is open daily from 8am to 9pm and serves breakfast, lunch, and dinner. Appetizers range from $4 to $6, with main courses costing $12 to $20. On some nights a steel-drum band entertains the mariners. Ice and freshwater showers are available (and you can rent towels). Ask about renting Sunfish and windsurfers. American Express, MasterCard, and Visa are accepted.

6 Virgin Gorda

The second-largest island in the cluster of British Virgins, Virgin Gorda is 10 miles long and 2 miles wide, with a population of some 1,400. It is 12 miles east of Road Town and 26 miles from St. Thomas.

In 1493, on his second voyage to the New World, Columbus named the island Virgin Gorda or "fat virgin" (the mountain that frames the island looks like a protruding stomach).

The island was a fairly desolate agricultural community until Laurance S. Rockefeller established the resort of the Little Dix Bay Hotel in the early 1960s, following his success with St. John and Caneel Bay in the 1950s. He envisioned a "wilderness beach," where privacy and solitude reign, and he literally put Virgin Gorda on the map. Other major hotels followed in the wake of Little Dix, but privacy and solitude still reign supreme among visitors to the island.

In 1971 the Virgin Gorda Yacht Harbour opened. Operated by the Little Dix Bay Hotel, it accommodates 120 yachts.

GETTING THERE

BY PLANE   Air St. Thomas (☎ 809/495-5935) flies to Virgin Gorda daily from San Juan.

BY BOAT   Speedy's Fantasy (☎ 809/495-5240) operates a ferry service between Road Town and Virgin Gorda. Three ferries a day leave from Road Town Monday through Saturday, reduced to two on Sunday. The cost is $10 one way or $19 round-trip. From St. Thomas to Virgin Gorda, there is service three times a week (Tuesday, Thursday, and Saturday), costing $25 one way or $45 round-trip.

ESSENTIALS

The local **American Express representative** is Travel Plan Ltd., Virgin Gorda Yacht Harbour (☎ **809/495-5586**).

WHERE TO STAY
VERY EXPENSIVE

✪ Biras Creek Estate

North Sound (P.O. Box 54), Virgin Gorda, B.V.I. ☎ **809/494-3555**, or 800/223-1108 in the U.S. Fax 809/494-3557. 32 suites, 16 cottages. Winter, $465–$685 suite for two; $840 cottage for two; $998 cottage for four. Off-season, $340–$550 suite for two; $575 cottage for two; $710 cottage for four. (Includes all meals.) AE, MC, V. Transportation: Hotel's private motor launch from Beef Island airport.

A private and romantic resort stands at the northern end of Virgin Gorda like a hilltop fortress. On a 150-acre estate with its own marina, it occupies a narrow neck of land flanked by the sea on three sides. To create their Caribbean hideaway, Norwegian shipping interests carved out this resort in a wilderness, but wisely protected the natural terrain. The greenhouse on the grounds keeps the resort supplied with foliage and flowers. Cooled by ceiling fans, units have well-furnished bedrooms and divan beds with a sitting room and private patio, plus a refrigerator.

Dining/Entertainment: The food has won high praise, and the wine cellar is also good. The dining rooms and drinking lounge are quietly elegant, and there's always a table with a view. A barbecued lunch is often served on the beach.

Services: Laundry, babysitting, taxi service for guests arriving in Virgin Gorda to the hotel's motor launch, free trips to nearby islands.

Facilities: Swimming pool, snorkeling, Sunfish, paddleboards, tennis courts.

✪ The Bitter End Yacht Club

John O'Point, North Sound (P.O. Box 46), Virgin Gorda, B.V.I. ☎ **809/494-2746**, or 800/872-2392 in the U.S. for reservations. Fax 809/494-4756. 92 rms, 6 suites. Winter, $380–$470 single; $480–$570 double; from $950 suite. Off-season, $280–$370 single; $380–$470 double; from $495 suite. (Includes meals.) AE, DC, MV, V. Free parking.

This rendezvous point for the yachting set has hosted treasure hunter Mel Fisher and Jean-Michel Cousteau. The Bitter End offers an informal yet elegant life, as guests settle into one of the hillside chalets or well-appointed beachfront and hill-side villas overlooking the sound and yachts at anchor. Forty rooms are air-conditioned. For something novel, you can stay aboard one of the 30-foot yachts, yours to sail, with dockage and including daily maid service, meals in the Yacht Club dining room, and overnight provisions.

Dining/Entertainment: Dining is in the Clubhouse Steak and Seafood Grille or the English Carvery. The social hub of the place is the bar.

Services: Babysitting, laundry, free trips to nearby islands, taxi service for guests arriving in Virgin Gorda to the hotel's motor launch.

Facilities: Unlimited use of Lasers, Sunfish, Rhodes 19s, J-24s, windsurfers, and outboard skiffs in sheltered waters; reef snorkeling; scuba diving; sportfishing; expeditions to neighboring cays; marine science participation; swimming pool.

❶ Little Dix Bay Hotel

On the northwest corner of the island (P.O. Box 70), Virgin Gorda, B.V.I. ☎ **809/495-5555,** or 800/928-3000 in the U.S. Fax 809/495-5661. 98 rms, 4 suites. TEL. Winter, $450–$790 single or double; $1,200 suite. Off-season, $225–$560 single or double; $750–$930 suite. Third person in room $65 extra. (Includes breakfast.) All meals $70 extra. AE, DC, MC, V. Free parking. Transportation: Private ferry service between Beef Island Airport and the resort.

Completely renovated in 1993, this hotel is now run by the Dallas-based chain of ultra-luxurious hotels, Rosewood Hotels. An embodiment of understated luxury, the Little Dix Bay Hotel is a resort discreetly scattered along a crescent-shaped private bay on a 500-acre preserve. It has the same quiet elegance as Caneel Bay on St. John in the U.S. Virgins. All rooms, built in woods, have private terraces with views of the sea or of gardens. Trade winds come through louvers and screens, and the units are further cooled by ceiling fans. Some units are two-story rondavels raised on stilts to form their own breezeways. All the guest rooms have been renovated with new furnishings and fabrics. Telephones have been added to each room, providing guests with the option to reach out to the world or leave it at bay. Forty-four of the rooms contain air conditioning.

Dining/Entertainment: Four interconnected pyramids that face the sea comprise the roof of the Pavilion, venue for lunch buffets, afternoon teas, and candlelit dinners. The cuisine is international, with Caribbean specialties using fresh seafood. For drinks, guests sit on the restaurant's terrace where a band performs nightly. The Sugar Mill is elegant but casual, specializing in fresh grilled fish, lobster, and steaks. On the edge of the beach, the Beach Grill serves breakfast, light lunches, and dinners.

Services: Unequalled service with a staff-to-guest ratio of one-to-one.

Facilities: Seven all-weather outdoor tennis courts, Sunfish sailboats, windsurfers, snorkeling, scuba diving, waterskiing, boat rentals, deep-sea fishing, diving excursions, and the Virgin Gorda Yacht Harbor, half a mile from the resort (owned and operated by Little Dix Bay).

MODERATE

❸ Fischers Cove Beach Hotel

The Valley (P.O. Box 60), Virgin Gorda, B.V.I. ☎ **809/495-5252.** Fax 809/495-5820. 12 rms. 8 cottages. A/C. Winter, $125–$130 single; $145–$150 double; $170–$180 one-bedroom cottage. Off-season, $90 single; $100 double; $125–$135 one-bedroom cottage. MAP $40 per person extra. AE, MC, V. Free parking. Transportation: Taxi.

There's swimming at your doorstep in this group of units nestled near the beach of St. Thomas Bay. Erected of native stone, each cottage is self-contained, with one or two bedrooms and a combination living and dining room with a kitchenette. At a food store near the grounds you can stock up on your provisions if you're doing your own cooking. There are 12 pleasant but simple rooms with views of Drake Channel. Each has its own private bath (hot and cold showers) and private balcony.

Lunch (daily from 11am to 3:30pm) costs $7 to $15 and dinner (daily from 6 to 10:30pm) runs $14 to $32. Special features include a beach buffet, occasional reggae band, and an all-Caribbean dinner.

❸ The Olde Yard Inn

The Valley (P.O. Box 26), Virgin Gorda, B.V.I. ☎ **809/495-5544,** or 800/633-7411. Fax 809/495-5986. 14 rms. Winter, $130 single; $180 double; $205 triple; $230 quad. Off-season, $80 single; $95 double; $120 triple; $140 quad. MAP $45 per person extra. AE, MC, V.

This little charmer is 1 mile from the airport. Near the main house are two long bungalows with large renovated bedrooms, each with its own bath and patio. Scattered about are a few antiques and special accessories.

You can go for a sail on a yacht or a snorkeling adventure at one of 16 beaches, with a picnic lunch provided.

Dining/Entertainment: Served under a cedarwood roof, the French-accented meals are one of the reasons for coming over. You can enjoy lunch from noon to 2pm for $10 and up. Dinners, from 6:30 to 9pm, begin at $18 but could run up to $30 if you want lobster. Among the recent improvements are a huge pool and Jacuzzi, a poolside bar and grill, and a health club with the most modern equipment—all complimentary to hotel guests. There is live entertainment twice a week in the dining room.

Facilities: Tennis courts, sailboat rentals, pool.

INEXPENSIVE

Guavaberry Spring Bay Vacation Homes

Spring Bay (P.O. Box 20), Virgin Gorda, B.V.I. ☎ **809/495-5227.** Fax 809/495-5283. 16 houses. Winter, $135 one-bedroom house for two; $200 two-bedroom house for four. Off-season, $90 one-bedroom house for two; $140 two-bedroom house for four. Additional person $20 extra. No credit cards. Free parking. Closed three weeks in Sept.

Staying in one of these hexagonal white-roofed redwood houses built on stilts is like living in a treehouse, with screened and louvered walls to let in sea breezes. Each home, available for daily or weekly rental, has one or two bedrooms, and all have a private bath, small kitchenette, and dining area. The hosts will show you to one of their unique vacation homes, each with its own elevated sun deck overlooking Sir Francis Drake Passage. Within a few minutes of the cottage colony is the beach at Spring Bay, and the Yacht Harbour Shopping Centre is 1 mile away. It's also possible to explore "The Baths" nearby.

The owners provide a complete commissary for guests, and tropical fruits can be picked in season or bought at local shops. They will make arrangements for day charters for scuba diving or fishing, and will also arrange for island Jeep tours and sailing.

WHERE TO DINE

Bath and Turtle Pub

Virgin Gorda Yacht Harbour, Spanish Town. ☎ **809/495-5239.** Reservations recommended. Appetizers $6; main courses $16–$25; snacks, sandwiches, salads, and platters $5–$25; tropical drinks $3–$6.50. AE, MC, V. Daily 7am–midnight. INTERNATIONAL.

At the end of the waterfront shopping plaza in Spanish Town, this is the most popular bar and pub on Virgin Gorda, with an active local trade whose interest is enhanced by its twice-daily happy hours (from 10:30 to 11:30am and again from 4 to 6pm). Even if you don't care about food, you might join the regulars over midmorning guava coladas or peach daiquiris. There's live music every Wednesday and Sunday from 8pm to midnight (no cover charge). From its handful of indoor and courtyard tables, you can order fried fish fingers, nachos, very spicy chili, pizzas, reubens or tuna melts, steak, lobster, and daily seafood specials such as conch fritters.

Chez Michelle

The Valley. ☎ **809/495-5510.** Reservations recommended. Appetizers $6–$7.50; main courses $16–$28. MC, V. Dinner only, daily 6:30–9:30pm. Closed Sept. CONTINENTAL.

Chez Michelle lies beside the main road, a short walk north of the Yacht Harbour at Spanish Town. On the ground floor of a clean and modern breeze-filled house, it is considered the most competent and urbanized of the privately owned restaurants on the island. Menu specialties might include lobster Rémy (flambéed with a sauce of cognac, cream, and tomatoes), pasta (such as fettuccine with chicken, burgundy wine, tomatoes, spinach, and mushrooms), and steaks. Desserts are considered one of the high points of a meal here.

⑤ Teacher Ilma's

The Valley. ☎ **809/495-5355.** Reservations required for dinner (call before 3pm). Full meals $18–$25. No credit cards. Lunch daily 12:30–2pm; dinner daily 7–8:30pm. WEST INDIAN. At Spanish Town, turn left at the main road past the entrance to the Fischers Cove Hotel; the sign to Teacher Ilma's is about two minutes ahead and to the right.

Mrs. Ilma O'Neal, who taught youngsters in the island's public school for 43 years, began her restaurant by cooking privately for visitors and island construction workers. Main courses, which include appetizers, might be chicken, local goat meat, lobster, conch, pork, or fish (your choice of grouper, snapper, tuna, dolphin, swordfish, or triggerfish), followed by such desserts as homemade coconut, pineapple, or guava pies. Teacher Ilma emphasizes that her cuisine is not Créole but local in its origins and flavors.

WHAT TO SEE & DO

The northern side of Virgin Gorda is mountainous, with one peak reaching 1,370 feet. However, the southern half is flat, with large boulders appearing at every turn. The best **beaches** are the Baths, where giant boulders form a series of panoramic pools and grottoes flooded with sea water (nearby snorkeling is excellent). Neighboring the Baths is Spring Bay, one of the best of the island's beaches, with white sand, clear water, and good snorkeling. Trunk Bay is a wide sand beach reachable by boat or along a rough path from Spring Bay. Savannah Bay is a sandy beach north of the yacht harbour, and Mahoe Bay, at the Mango Bay Resort, has a gently curving beach with vivid blue water.

Among the places of interest, **Coppermine Point** is the site of an abandoned copper mine and smelter. Because of loose rock formations, it can be dangerous, and you should exercise caution if you explore it. Legend has it that the Spanish worked these mines in the 1600s; however, the only authenticated document reveals that the English sank the shafts in 1838 to mine copper.

You'll find ✪ **The Baths** on every visitor's list, and the area is known for its snorkeling. Equipment can be rented on the beach. These are a phenomenon of tranquil pools and caves formed by gigantic house-size boulders. As these boulders toppled over one another, they formed saltwater grottoes, suitable for exploring. The pools around the Baths are excellent for swimming.

Devil's Bay National Park can be reached by a trail from the Baths roundabout. The walk to the secluded coral-sand beach takes about 15 minutes through a natural setting of boulders and dry coastal vegetation.

The Baths and surrounding areas are part of a proposed system of parks and protected areas for the B.V.I. The protected area encompasses 682 acres of land, including sites at Little Fort, Spring Bay, the Baths, and Devil's Bay on the east coast.

The best way to see the island if you're over for a day trip is to call Andy Flax at the Fischers Cove Beach Hotel (☎ **809/495-5252**). He runs the **Virgin Gorda Tours Association,** which will give you a tour of the island for about $50 for one to three people. The tour leaves twice daily. You can be picked up at the ferry dock.

Kilbrides Underwater Tours (☎ 809/495-9638, or 800/932-4286 in the U.S.) is located at the Bitter End Resort at North Sound. Today Kilbrides offers the best diving in the B.V.I. at 15 to 20 dive sites, including the wreck of the ill-fated RMS *Rhône*. Prices range from $80 to $90 for a two-tank dive on one of the coral reefs. Tanks and weighted belts are supplied at no charge, and videos of your dives are available.

7 Mosquito Island (North Sound)

The sandy, 125-acre Mosquito (also spelled Moskito) Island just north of Virgin Gorda wasn't named for those pesky insects—it took its name from the Mosquito (or Moskito) tribe, who were the only known inhabitants of the small land mass before the arrival of the Spanish conquistadors in the 15th century. Archeological relics of these peaceful people and their agricultural pursuits have been found here.

GETTING THERE   Getting here requires taking a plane to the Virgin Gorda airport and Speedy's Taxi from there to Leverick Bay Dock. The taxi driver will radio ahead, and a boat will be sent from Drake's to take you on the five-minute ride from the dock to the resort.

WHERE TO STAY

Drake's Anchorage Resort Inn
North Sound (P.O. Box 2510, Virgin Gorda), B.V.I. ☎ **809/494-2254**, 617/969-9913 in Massachusetts, or 800/624-6651. 8 rms, 2 suites, 2 villas. Winter, $218 single; $412–$423 double; $485 suite; $595 villa. Off-season, $218 single; $311–$338 double; $343–$373 suite; $490–$515 villa. (Includes all meals.) AE, MC, V.

Today the privately owned island is uninhabited except for Drake's Anchorage Resort Inn, which many patrons consider their favorite retreat in the British Virgins. The hotel has comfortable rooms and suites with private baths and sea-view verandas. The resort's restaurant, attractively tropical in design, faces the water and offers a cuisine featuring local and continental dishes, including lobster and a fresh fish of the day.

Guests have free use of windsurfers, snorkeling equipment, and bicycles. For additional fees, you can go scuba diving, deep-sea fishing, sailing, or to the Baths on Virgin Gorda. The snorkeling and scuba here are considered so good that members of the Cousteau Society spend a month each year exploring local waters. There are four beaches on the island, each with different wave and water conditions.

8 Guana Island

This 850-acre island, a nature sanctuary, is one of the most private hideaways in the Caribbean. Don't come here seeking resort action; rather, consider vacationing here if you want to retreat from the world. Lying right off the coast of Tortola, this small island offers seven virgin beaches and nature trails ideal for hiking, and abounds in unusual species of plant and animal life. Its highest point is Sugarloaf Mountain at 806 feet, from which a panoramic view is possible. Arawak relics have been found on the island. It is said that the name of the island came from a jutting rock that resembled the head of an iguana.

GETTING THERE   The Guana Island Club will send a boat to meet arriving guests at Beef Island airport (trip time: 10 min.).

WHERE TO STAY

Guana Island

P.O. Box 32, Road Town, Tortola, B.V.I. ☎ **809/494-2354,** or 800/544-8262 in the U.S. 15 rms, 1 cottage. For reservations, write or call the Guana Island Reservations Office, 10 Timber Trail, Rye, NY 10580 (☎ **914/967-6050,** or 800/544-8262 in the U.S.; fax 914/967-8048). Nov–Dec 15, $435 double; $660 cottage. Dec 16–Mar, $595 double; $890 cottage. Apr–Aug, $435 double; $660 cottage. (Includes all meals.) No credit cards. Closed Sept–Oct. Transportation: Private launch from Tortola.

Guana Island, the sixth or seventh largest of the British Virgin Islands, was bought in 1974 by Henry and Gloria Jarecki, dedicated conservationists who also run this resort. After your arrival on the island, a Landrover will transport you up one of the most scenic hills in the region, in the northeast of Guana. You arrive at a cluster of white cottages that were built as a private club in the 1930s on the foundations of a Quaker homestead. The stone cottages never hold more than 30 guests (and only two telephones), and since the dwellings are staggered along a flower-dotted hillside, the sense of privacy is almost absolute. Although water is scarce on the island, each airy accommodation has a shower. The decor is of rattan and wicker and each unit has a ceiling fan. The panoramic sweep from the terraces is spectacular, particularly at sunset.

Dining/Entertainment: Guests will find a convivial atmosphere at the rattan-furnished clubhouse. Casually elegant dinners by candlelight are served on the veranda, with menus that include home-grown vegetables and continental and Stateside specialties. A buffet lunch is served every day. The self-service bars operate on the honor system.

Services: Laundry.

Facilities: Seven beaches (some of which require a boat to reach), two tennis courts (one clay and one all-weather), fishing, snorkeling.

The Dominican Republic

8

Called "the fairest land under heaven," the Dominican Republic attracts visitors to its white sandy beaches, its colonial heritage, and its mountain resorts. It is among the fastest-growing tourist destinations in the Caribbean.

It may be a fair land, but there is also grinding poverty here, and crime, especially muggings and robbery of tourists, is on the rise, yet the island holds such compelling fascination that visitors are often repeat customers.

Canadians are especially fond of the island because their dollar (less valuable than the U.S. dollar) buys more in the Dominican Republic than on any other island in the Caribbean. Incidentally, the island is not "just another poorer Puerto Rico." It has its own distinctive cuisine and culture.

Five centuries of culture and tradition converge in the mountainous Dominican Republic. The 54-mile-wide Mona Passage separates the Republica Dominicana from Puerto Rico, and many poverty-stricken citizens risk their lives across this channel every day hoping to slip into Puerto Rico and then illegally go on to the U.S. mainland. Some never make it. In the Dominican interior, the fertile Valley of Cibao (rich sugarcane country) ends its upward sweep at Pico Duarte, formerly Pico Trujillo, the highest mountain peak in the West Indies which soars to 10,417 feet.

Nestled amid Cuba, Jamaica, and Puerto Rico, the island of Hispaniola (Little Spain) consists of Haiti, on the westernmost third of the island, and the Dominican Republic, which has a lush land mass equal to that of Vermont and New Hampshire combined.

Columbus sighted the coral-edged Caribbean coastline on his first voyage to the New World—"There is no more beautiful island in the world." The first permanent European settlement in the New World was founded here on November 7, 1493, and its ruins still remain near Montecristi in the northeast. Primitive native tribes called the island Quisqueya, "Mother Earth," before the Spaniards arrived to butcher them.

Much of what Columbus first saw still remains in a natural, unspoiled condition, but that may change: The country is building and expanding rapidly.

In the heart of the Caribbean archipelago, the country has an 870-mile coastline, about a third of which is given to magnificent beach. The average temperature is 77° Fahrenheit. August is the warmest month and January the coolest, although even then it's still warm enough to swim and enjoy the tropical sun. So why did it take so long for the Dominican Republic to be discovered by visitors? The answer is largely political. The country has been steeped in misery and bloodshed almost from the beginning, and it climaxed with the infamous reign of Rafael Trujillo and the civil wars that followed.

Today the Dominican Republic is rebuilt and restored, and it offers visitors a chance to enjoy the sun and sea as well as to learn about the history and politics of a developing society.

GETTING THERE

The airline offering the most frequent service to the Dominican Republic is **American Airlines** (☎ **800/433-7300** in the U.S.). From New York's JFK Airport, the Miami International Airport, and San Juan's Luís Muñoz Marin Airport, American offers about a dozen daily flights to either Santo Domingo or Puerto Plata; some are nonstop and some require connections. Many other flights on American Eagle depart every day from San Juan and Mayagüez, Puerto Rico for airports in Santo Domingo, Puerto Plata, La Romana, and Punta Cana.

Continental Airlines (☎ **800/525-0280** in the U.S.) flies daily from New Jersey's Newark airport to Santo Domingo.

Flights are also available to the Dominican Republic with **Air Dominicana** (☎ **212/765-7310** in New York City). Some readers, however, have complained that contacting this carrier by phone is difficult.

The Dominican Republic is geared to mass tourism and offers all-inclusive packages for however many days you specify. These packages almost always save money over what you would have paid if you had booked your airfare and hotel accommodations separately. Call your travel agent or a major airline to hear what's currently available. American might be your best bet for this type of package.

A Traveler's Advisory   Arriving at Santo Domingo's Las Américas International Airport is confusing and chaotic. Customs officials tend to be rude and overworked, and give you a very thorough check! In addition, many readers have reported loss of luggage here to thieves. Beware of "porters" who offer to help. Hold on to your possessions carefully. Arrival at La Unión International Airport, 23 miles east of Puerto Plata on the north coast, is generally much easier, but it, too, requires caution.

For information on flights into Casa de Campo/La Romana, see Section 2 of this chapter.

GETTING AROUND

This is not always easy if your hotel is remote. The most convenient means of transport is provided by taxis, rental cars, *públicos* (multipassenger taxis), and *guaguas* (public buses).

BY TAXI   Taxis aren't metered, and determining the cost in advance (which you should do) may be difficult if you and your driver have a language problem (the official language is Spanish). Taxis can be hailed in the streets, and you'll definitely find them at the major hotels and outside the airport as you emerge from Customs. The minimum fare within Santo Domingo is $6 but most drivers try to get more. Don't get into an unmarked street taxi. Many visitors, particularly in Santo Domingo, have been assaulted and robbed by doing just that.

BY RENTAL CAR   The best way to see the Dominican Republic is by car; Island buses tend to be erratic, hot, and overcrowded; there's no rail transportation; and chartering a small plane is sometimes an expensive option. It's a very good idea to assure in advance that the car being proposed for your use has functioning safety belts.

Your Canadian or American driver's license is suitable documentation, along with a valid credit or charge card or a substantial cash deposit. And unlike many places in the Caribbean, you *drive on the right.*

Be aware, however, that although the major highways are relatively clear of obstacles, the country's secondary roads, especially those in the east, are disturbingly potholed and rutted. Plan a generous amount of transit time between destinations, drive carefully, and avoid alcohol.

At least three U.S.–based car-rental firms maintain branches in the Dominican Republic, usually at Puerto Plata and Santo Domingo.

The high accident and theft rate in recent years has helped to raise the price of car rentals substantially. Prices are always changing, so call around for last-minute quotations. You should fully understand your insurance coverage (or lack thereof) and drive very, very carefully. Your credit- or charge-card issuer may already provide you with this insurance; contact the issuer. Know before you rent that roads are potholed, badly lit, and badly marked in both the city and the countryside. In addition, a policeman often flags you down alleging (often wrongly) that you committed some infraction. Many locals give the policeman $5 "for your children" and then are allowed to go on their way. In the Dominican Republic low-paid policemen supplement their income by this form of *regalo* or gift.

For reservations and more information, call the rental companies at least a week before your departure: **Avis** (☎ **800/331-1084** in the U.S.), **Budget** (☎ **800/527-0700** in the U.S.), and **Hertz** (☎ **800/654-3001** in the U.S.).

BY PUBLIC TRANSPORTATION   *Públicos* are a kind of unmetered multi-passenger taxi that travels on main thoroughfares and stops to pick up people waving from the side of the street. You must tell the driver your destination when you're picked up to make sure the público is going to your destination. Watch for cars with a white seal on the car's front door.

Public buses, often in the form of minivans or panel trucks, are called **guaguas.** They provide the same service as públicos, but they are more crowded. Larger buses provide service outside the towns. Fares are dirt-cheap, but beware of pickpockets.

BY SIGHTSEEING TOUR   One of the leading tour operators is **Prieto Tours,** avenida Francia 125 (☎ **809/685-0102**), which will arrange a number of sightseeing excursions for you in and around Santo Domingo. A tour of the Colonial Zone costs $25, and a day at Casa de Campo and Atlas de Chavón goes for $30. They also offer a full-day sailing excursion to the Isla Saona, located close to La Romana, which costs $70 per person and includes the transportation from Santo Domingo, lunch, soft drinks, and sailing on a large catamaran.

FAST FACTS: The Dominican Republic

Area Code   It's 809, and you don't need it for intra-island calls.

Currency   The Dominican monetary unit is the **peso (RD$),** made up of 100 **centavos.** Coin denominations are 5, 10, 25, and 50 centavos, and 1 peso. Bill denominations are RD$5, RD$10, RD$20, RD$50, RD$100, RD$500, and RD$1,000. Price quotations in this chapter appear sometimes in American and sometimes in Dominican currency, depending on the policy of the establishment—the use of any currency other than Dominican pesos is technically illegal, but few seem to bother with this mandate. As of this writing, you get about RD$12.90 to $1 U.S. Check with your bank or the tourist office before planning your budget for the Dominican Republic. Bank booths at the international airports and major hotels will change your currency into Dominican pesos at the rate of exchange prevailing in the free market. You will be given a receipt for the amount of foreign currency you have exchanged. If you don't spend all your Dominican currency, you can present the receipt with the remaining pesos at the Banco de Reservas booth at the airport and receive the equivalent in American dollars to take out of the country.

Documents   To enter the Dominican Republic, citizens of the United States and Canada need only proof of citizenship, such as a passport or an original birth certificate. However, citizens may have trouble returning home without a passport—a reproduced birth certificate is not acceptable. Upon your arrival at the airport, you must purchase a tourist card for $10 U.S. To avoid waiting in line in the Dominican Republic, purchase this at the airport counter when you check in at your point of embarkation for your flight south.

Electricity   The country generally uses 110 volts A.C., 60 cycles, so adapters and transformers are usually not necessary for U.S. appliances. You might want to check with your hotel to be on the safe side.

Embassies   All embassies are in Santo Domingo, the national capital. The **U.S. Embassy** is on calle Cesar Nicholas Penson (☎ **809/221-2171**); the **British Embassy** is at Independencia 506 (☎ **809/540-3132**), and the **Canadian Embassy** is at avenida Máximo Gómez 30 (☎ **809/685-1136**).

Holidays   The Dominican Republic celebrates the usual holidays, such as Christmas and New Year's, but also has some of its own: January 21 (Our Lady of La Altagracia), January 26 (Duarte's Birthday), February 27 (National Independence Day), Movable Feast (60 days after Good Friday, a Corpus Christi holiday), August 16 (Restoration Day), and September 24 (Our Lady of Las Mercedes).

Information   Before your trip, contact any of the following **Dominican Republic Tourist Information Centers:** 1 Times Square Plaza, New York, NY 10036 (☎ 212/579-4966); 2355 Salzedo St., Coral Gables, FL 33134 (☎ 305/444-4592); and 1650 de Maisonneuve West, Suite 302, Montréal, PQ H3H 2N4, Canada (☎ 514/499-1918). At the **information hotline** (☎ 800/752-1151 in the U.S., Monday through Friday from 8am to 5pm Atlantic standard time), operators can field questions on a wide range of subjects, including travel tips, tourist regions, beaches, traveling around the country, sports, money matters, sightseeing, festivals, and special events.

Language   The official language is Spanish, but English is making inroads in the Dominican Republic.

Safety   Once you've cleared the airports (see "Getting There," above), the Dominican Republic has more than its fair share of crime. Avoid unmarked street

The Dominican Republic

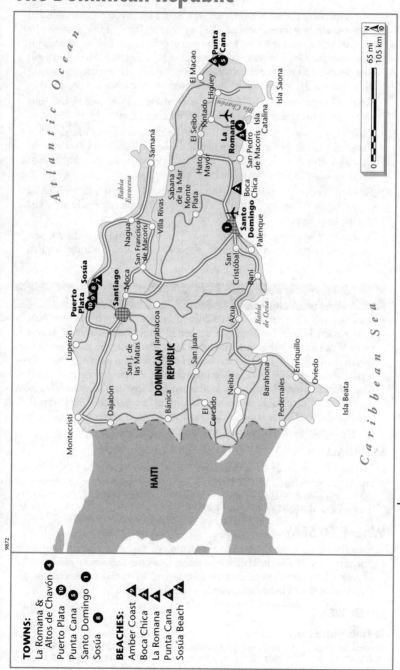

TOWNS:

La Romana &
Altos de Chavón ❹
Puerto Plata ❿
Punta Cana ❺
Santo Domingo ❶
Sosúa ❽

BEACHES:

Amber Coast ⓐ
Boca Chica ⓑ
La Romana ③
Punta Cana ⑥
Sosúa Beach ⑦

Airport ✈

9872

taxis, especially in Santo Domingo; you could be targeted for assault and robbery. While strolling around the city, you are likely to be accosted by hustlers selling various wares, and you can also be mugged. Pickpocketing is commonplace. Don't go walking in Santo Domingo after dark. Many locals will offer their services as a guide, and sometimes a loud refusal is not enough to shake their presence. Hiring an official guide from the tourist office can prevent this.

Taxes   A departure tax of $10 U.S. is assessed and must be paid in U.S. currency. The government imposes a 13% tax on hotel rooms.

Time   It's Atlantic standard time throughout the country year round. When New York and Miami are on eastern standard time and it's 6am, it's 7am in Santo Domingo. However, during daylight saving time, when it's noon on the East Coast mainland, it's the same time in Santo Domingo.

Tips and Service   In most restaurants and hotels, a 10% service charge is added to your check. Most people usually add 5% to 10% more, especially if the service has been good.

Weather   The average temperature is 77° Fahrenheit. August is the warmest month and January the coolest month, although even then it's warm enough to swim.

1 Santo Domingo

Bartholomeo Columbus, brother of Christopher, founded the city of New Isabella (later renamed Santo Domingo) on the banks of the Ozama River on August 4, 1496, which makes it the oldest city in the New World. On the southeastern Caribbean coast, Santo Domingo—known as Ciudad Trujillo from 1936 to 1961—is the capital of the Dominican Republic. It has had a long, sometimes glorious, more often sad, history. At the peak of its power, Diego de Valásquez sailed from here to settle Cuba, Ponce de León went forth to discover and settle Puerto Rico and Florida, and Cortés was launched toward Mexico. The city today still reflects its long history—French, Haitian, and especially Spanish.

ESSENTIALS

In Santo Domingo, 24-hour **drugstore** service is provided by San Judas Tadeo, avenida Independencia 57 (☎ 809/689-2851). An **emergency room** operates at the Centro Médico Universidad, avenida Máximo Gómez 68 (☎ 809/221-0171). To summon the **police,** phone **911.**

WHERE TO STAY

Even the highest-priced hotels in Santo Domingo might be classified as medium priced in most of the Caribbean. Remember that taxes and service will be added to your bill, which will make the rates 23% higher. When making reservations, ask if they are included in the rates quoted—usually they aren't.

EXPENSIVE

El Embajador Hotel Casino

Avenida Sarasota 65, Santo Domingo, Dominican Republic. ☎ **809/221-2131**, or 800/457-0067. Fax 809/532-5306. 280 rms, 20 suites. A/C MINIBAR TEL. $135–$160 single or double; from $210 suite. American breakfast $12 extra. AE, DC, MC, V. Free parking.

Trujillo had a luxury penthouse for his own use installed in this concrete-and-glass deluxe hotel. It was built 3 miles southwest of the city center on the grounds of a horse-racing track, but today modern high-rise buildings have encroached on the land where, in the Trujillo era, playboy Porfirio Rubirosa and El Jefe's son, Ramfis Trujillo, once played polo. The seven-story building, which still has the aura of its 1950s heyday, has bedrooms done in French provincial style, with both king- and queen-size beds, walk-in closets, and private terraces. The last remodeling was completed in 1995.

Dining/Entertainment: Among the best restaurants in Santo Domingo are the Jade Garden, featuring Chinese cuisine, and the Embassy Club, a deluxe restaurant and nightclub with an international cuisine known for its flambé dishes. La Terraza is an informal eatery. You can drink and dance in La Fontana lounge. The casino is described in "Evening Entertainment," below.

Services: Room service, laundry, babysitting.

Facilities: Eight tennis courts, undulating swimming pool with waterside terrace for refreshments, sauna and massage facilities.

✪ Hotel Santo Domingo

Avenida Independencia (at the corner of Abraham Lincoln), Santo Domingo, Dominican Republic. ☎ **809/221-1511.** Fax 809/535-4050. 220 rms, 5 suites. A/C MINIBAR TV TEL. Transportation: Taxi. $115 single or double; $135 Excel Club single or double; $105–$600 suite. MAP $30 per person extra. AE, MC, V. Free parking.

Run by Premier Resorts & Hotels, the Santo Domingo has a tasteful extravagance created by William Cox and the Dominican haute couturier, Oscar de la Renta. Their flair has made this ocher stucco structure, 15 minutes from the downtown area, a prestigious address that often attracts presidents of other Latin American countries. Opening onto the sea, this deluxe hotel stands on 14 acres of tropical landscaped grounds.

The fair-sized rooms are in two structures, three stories tall and framing latticework loggias, one dedicated to orange trees. Most of the rooms open onto views of the water, but some face the garden, which isn't bad either. Excel Club rooms offer ocean-view balconies, complimentary breakfast, and other benefits.

Dining/Entertainment: Guests enjoy dinner at El Alcázar (see "Where to Dine," below). The hotel's gourmet restaurant is El Cafetal, and you can also enjoy a poolside lunch at Las Brisas. The piano bar, Las Palmas, draws a lively crowd at night.

Services: Room service (7am to 1am), laundry, babysitting.

Facilities: Three professional tennis courts (lit at night), Olympic-size swimming pool, sauna.

✪ Jaragua Renaissance Resort & Casino

Avenida George Washington 367, Santo Domingo, Dominican Republic. ☎ **809/221-2222,** or 800/228-9898 in the U.S. and Canada. Fax 809/686-0528. 289 rms, 11 suites. A/C MINIBAR TV TEL. Winter, $190–$230 single or double; from $585 suite. Off-season, $110–$140 single or double; from $415 suite. MAP $52 per person extra. AE, DC, MC, V. Free parking.

"The pride of the Dominican Republic" was built on the 14-acre site of the old Jaragua (Ha-*ra*-gua), popular in Trujillo's day. Officially opened in 1988, the hotel is a splashy waterfront palace. Located off the Malecón, convenient to the major attractions and shops of Santo Domingo, the hotel spreads its accommodations across two separate buildings: the 10-story Jaragua Tower (where there's butler service on the deluxe floors) and the two-level Jaragua Gardens Estate.

Seemingly no expense was spared in the luxuriously appointed rooms, as reflected by marble bathrooms with large makeup mirrors and hairdryers, three phones, refrigerators, and computerized door locks. And all this luxury is comparatively inexpensive, especially off-season.

Dining/Entertainment: The Jaragua boasts the largest casino in the Caribbean and a 1,000-seat Las Vegas–style showroom. Guests are also entertained at its cabaret theater, La Fiesta. For its restaurants—the Manhattan Grill, Figaro, and Latino—see "Where to Dine," below. In addition, Lotus is a Chinese restaurant with unusual specialties, including seafood.

Services: 24-hour room service and butler service on the deluxe floors of the Jaragua Tower, laundry and dry cleaning, doctor on 24-hour call, special children's programs.

Facilities: Swimming pool with 12 private cabañas, snack bar, and outdoor bar; one of the best tennis centers in Santo Domingo, with four clay courts (lit at night) and a pro shop; beauty parlor and barber. The hotel's Spa and Health Club is the finest in the Dominican Republic, open Monday through Friday from 7am to 8pm and on Saturday and Sunday from 9am to 9pm.

MODERATE

Gran Hotel Lina

Avenidas Máximo Gómez and 27 de Febrero, Santo Domingo, Dominican Republic. ☎ **809/686-5000.** Fax 809/686-5521. 221 rms. A/C MINIBAR TV TEL. $65 single; $70 double. (Includes breakfast.) AE, DC, MC, V. Free parking. Transportation: Taxi.

Rising 15 floors in a sterile cinderblock design in the heart of the capital, the Lina offers a wide range of services and facilities. All the rather plain rooms contain refrigerators and full-size beds; at least 30% of the accommodations overlook the Caribbean. The best rooms are on the 11th floor. The hotel has attracted everybody from Julio Iglesias to David Rockefeller to Latin American presidents.

Dining/Entertainment: The hotel boasts one of the best-known restaurants in the Caribbean (see "Where to Dine," below), a cafeteria and snack bar, and a nightclub.

Service: 24-hour room service, laundry.

Facilities: Swimming pool, Jacuzzi, solarium, gym, sauna, shopping arcade.

⑤ Sheraton Santo Domingo & Casino

Avenida George Washington 365, Santo Domingo, Dominican Republic. ☎ **809/221-6666,** or 800/325-3535 in the U.S. Fax 809/687-8150. 260 rms. A/C TV TEL. Winter, $90–$120 single; $100–$130 double. Off-season, $75–$100 single; $90–$110 double. Breakfast from $8 extra. AE, DC, MC, V. Free parking.

The Sheraton is a high-rise set back from the Malecón. You travel along a tree-lined drive until you arrive at a vast lobby that's really a solarium. The fair-sized bedrooms are equipped with hairdryers, and except for those on the third floor, all have ocean views. Service appears a bit helter-skelter.

Dining/Entertainment: The plant-filled Petit Café overlooks the lobby, and Yarey's Lounge is a piano bar with entertainment. Dining is at Antoine's (see "Where to Dine," below), an elegant continental place. Breakfast, lunch, and dinner are available at La Terraza coffeehouse, which has a terrace surrounding a large pool that opens onto views of the sea. Other additions to the hotel are La Canasta, featuring Dominican food, the Omni Disco, and a casino.

Services: 24-hour room service, babysitting, laundry, dry cleaning.

Facilities: Complete business center, health club, facilities for the disabled.

BUDGET

⑤ Hostal Nicolás de Ovando

Calle Las Damas 55 (at calle Las Mercedes), Santo Domingo, Dominican Republic. ☎ **809/686-5720.** Fax 809/221-4167. 45 rms. A/C TEL. $60 single or double. AE, DC, MC, V. Free parking.

In the shop-studded area of La Atarazana, in the old town, two 15th-century mansions have been converted into a hostal and named after the governor of Hispaniola, who lived here from 1502 to 1509. The structure is an example of a fortified house, with its own observation tower overlooking the Ozama River. Lying in the colonial zone, the palacio is said to be the oldest hotel in the New World. This hotel is not for resort lovers; however, for those interested in being in the heart of the old city, this is the best choice. Its spartan bedrooms are small and unpretentious, although clean. The public rooms have heraldic tapestries, bronze mirrors, and colonial furnishings. Even if you don't stay here, stop in for lunch at the Extramadura Restaurant, open from 9am to 10pm daily. Main courses cost RD$125 to RD$210 ($9.60 to $16.20).

WHERE TO DINE

Santo Domingo has a host of restaurants serving good food, and most stretch along the seaside-bordering avenida George Washington, popularly known as the Malecón.

Most places will accept casual dress, although shorts are frowned upon at the first-class places. Many Dominicans prefer to dress up when dining out—that is, put on a little show. Some of the best restaurants are in hotels. It's safer to take a taxi to places at night and not wander alone on the often-dark streets, where muggings are frequent.

EXPENSIVE

Antoine's

In the Sheraton Santo Domingo Hotel & Casino, avenida George Washington 361. ☎ **809/221-6666.** Reservations recommended. Appetizers RD$40–RD$55 ($3.10–$4.20); main courses RD$150–RD$350 ($11.60–$27); lunch buffet RD$80–RD$120 ($6.20–$9.20). AE, DC, MC, V. Lunch daily noon–3pm; dinner daily 8pm–midnight. INTERNATIONAL.

This is where the well-dressed Dominican family goes to celebrate a special occasion. Of course, the well-run restaurant also draws the international crowd staying in this previously recommended hotel set back from the Malecón. Unusual appetizers include squid in garlic dressing. The waiters often suggest the lobster thermidor, but I've found the red snapper Basque style more interesting, and it costs less. If you don't want fish, try the tournedos Rossini. For dessert, you might like baked Alaska.

✪ Figaro

In the Jaragua Renaissance Resort & Casino, avenida George Washington 367. ☎ **809/221-2222.** Reservations recommended. Appetizers $6–$8; main courses $15–$25. AE, DC, MC, V. Dinner only, Tues–Sun 6:30pm–midnight. ITALIAN.

Homemade pasta, including vegetable lasagne, may attract you to Figaro, which features northern and southern Italian fare, along with delectable pastries and cappuccino. Set on the lobby level of this previously recommended hotel, Figaro is now acclaimed as one of the best Italian restaurants in Santo Domingo.

Cured ham with fresh mozzarella is one of the best dishes. Other chef's special-ties include lobster Fra Diavolo, eggplant parmigiana, and sirloin steak. The atmosphere is that of an Italian trattoria, with an open kitchen, bright tiles, and hanging cheese.

✪ Lina Restaurant

In the Gran Hotel Lina, avenida Máximo Gómez. ☎ **809/686-5000.** Reservations required. Transportation: Taxi. Appetizers $4–$11.50; main courses $12.50–$24. AE, DC, MC, V. Lunch daily noon–4:30pm; dinner daily 6:30pm–midnight. INTERNATIONAL.

The Lina is one of the most prestigious restaurants in the Caribbean, lying one floor above street level in this previously recommended hotel. Spanish-born Lina Aguado originally came to Santo Domingo when it was Ciudad Trujillo; her culinary fame was so great in Madrid that she was hired as the personal chef de cuisine of the dictator Trujillo. She served El Jefe (as Trujillo was called) well until she left to open her own restaurant. It was a small place, but its fame grew, and she became the number-one restauratrice in the Dominican Republic.

Today this modern hotel and restaurant has nothing to do with the old place, except that Dona Lina taught the cooks her secret recipes. Four master chefs now rule in the kitchen. The cuisine is international with an emphasis on Spanish dishes, and the service is first-rate. Try the paella valenciana or sea bass flambéed with brandy, or perhaps mixed seafood au Pernod cooked in a casserole—the repertoire is vast.

Reina de España

Avenida Cervantes 103. ☎ **809/685-2588.** Reservations required Fri–Sat. Appetizers RD$55–RD$95 ($4.20–$7.30); main courses RD$100–RD$300 ($7.70–$23.10). AE, MC, V. Daily noon–midnight. SPANISH/CREOLE/INTERNATIONAL.

One of the best independent restaurants in Santo Domingo, Reina de España lies in a once-private villa said to have belonged to an intimate friend of Trujillo. The chef features frogs' legs Romana, quail stew with herbs, roast suckling pig, and roast duck with mango sauce. Lobster is prepared almost any way you like it, and most fish dishes are excellent, including the seafood casserole. Local dishes aren't ne-glected; you might ask for a Dominican shrimp soup. Meals here are among the most expensive in the capital, but patrons are usually satisfied, knowing they are getting quality ingredients handled by master chefs. Imported meat is used. The restaurant is near the Hotel Sheraton Santo Domingo.

Vesuvio I

Avenida George Washington 521. ☎ **809/221-3333.** Reservations recommended Fri–Sat. Appetizers RD$40–RD$110 ($3.10–$8.50); main courses RD$100–RD$220 ($7.70–$16.90). AE, DC, MC, V. Daily 11am–midnight. ITALIAN.

Along the Malecón, the most famous Italian restaurant in the Dominican Republic draws crowds of visitors and local businesspeople. What to order? That's always a problem here, as the Neapolitan owners, the Bonarelli family, have worked since 1954 to perfect and enlarge their menu. Their homemade soups are excellent. The restaurant prepares fresh red snapper, sea bass, and oysters in interesting ways. Crayfish specialties include à la Vesuvio, which is topped with garlic and bacon. The broiled seafood platter is a sample of all their seafood, and the veal comes from the Bonarellis' own herd. A favorite dessert is tortelloni al vodka, but you may pre-fer a recent creation, choccolat fettuccine à la parra, a real chocolate pasta, only instead of sugar they've added salt.

The owner claims to be the pioneer of pizza in the Dominican Republic, and he makes a unique one next door in **Pizzeria Vesuvio**—a yard-long pizza pie! If you want to try their other Italian place, go to **Vesuvio II,** avenida Tiradentes 17 (☎ **809/562-6060**).

MODERATE

El Alcázar

In the Hotel Santo Domingo, avenida Independencia at avenida Abraham Lincoln. ☎ **809/221-1511.** Reservations required. Fixed-price lunch buffet RD$142 ($10.90). AE, DC, MC, V. Lunch only, daily noon–3pm. INTERNATIONAL. Transportation: Taxi (a 15-minute ride from the center).

Dominican designer Oscar de la Renta created El Alcázar in a Moroccan motif, with aged mother-of-pearl, small mirrors, and lots of fabric. Dishes are always good, and sometimes excellent; well-made sauces add zest to the meals. The menu is likely to be Chinese one day, Mexican another day, Italian the next, although Monday is usually devoted to Dominican food. The presentation of the food and the service are two more reasons to dine here. The international lunch buffets provide one of the best food buys in the city. At present only lunch is offered.

⑤ La Banía

Avenida George Washington 1. ☎ **809/682-4022.** Reservations not required. Appetizers RD$75–RD$145 ($5.80–$11.20); main courses RD$110–RD$235 ($8.50–$18.10). AE, MC, V. Daily 9am–2am. SEAFOOD.

You'd never know that this unprepossessing place right on the Malecón serves some of the best, and freshest, seafood in the Dominican Republic. One predawn morning as I passed by, fishermen were waiting outside to sell the chef their latest catch. Rarely in the Caribbean will you find a restaurant with such a diversity of seafood offerings. For your appetizer, you might prefer ceviche, sea bass marinated in lime juice, or lobster cocktail. Soups are likely to contain big chunks of lobster as well as shrimp. Specialties include kingfish in coconut sauce, sea bass Ukrainian style, baked red snapper, and seafood in the pot. Conch is a special favorite with the chef. Desserts are superfluous, and the restaurant will stay open until the last customer departs.

Jardín de Jade

In the Hotel Embajador, avenida Sarasota 65. ☎ **809/221-2131.** Reservations recommended. Appetizers RD$65–RD$145 ($5–$11.20); main courses RD$130–RD$275 ($10–$21.20). AE, DC, MC, V. Lunch daily noon–3pm; dinner daily 7:30–11:30pm. CHINESE.

Jade Garden, 3 miles southwest of the center of town, is clearly in the front rank in Santo Domingo's Chinese cookery. The management even sent its cooks to Hong Kong to learn some of the secret methods of Peking and northern Chinese cuisine, and they returned to please customers with an array of delectables, such as minced pigeon, soya-bean chicken, sweet-corn soup (superb), lemon duck (even better!), sweet-and-sour pork, deep-fried fish, and fortune chicken, finished off with a toffee banana. The pièce de résistance is the Peking duck, which the chef roasts in an open-fire stove.

Restaurant/Bar Jai-Alai

Avenida Independencia 411, at the corner of Jose Joaquin Pérez. ☎ **809/685-2409.** Reservations not required. Appetizers RD$65–RD$200 ($5–$15.40); main courses RD$95–RD$225 ($7.30–$17.30). AE, MC, V. Lunch daily 11:30am–4pm; dinner daily 6:30pm–midnight. INTERNATIONAL.

The original owner of this cosmopolitan restaurant behind the Sheraton left his home in Bilbao, Spain, when he was 18. After running a successful eatery in Lima, Peru, he came to Santo Domingo and set up this restaurant named after the favorite sport of his Basque ancestors. Today the staff welcomes guests with a smile and a fluency in several languages. Shellfish is famous here, with such offerings as lobster Créole, shrimp Jai-Alai, seafood casserole, and oysters in red sauce. Other dishes include octopus Créole, garlic soup, Spanish-style pork chops, rabbit in garlic sauce, and sea bass. You might enjoy a glass of the Peruvian pick-me-up called pisco.

INEXPENSIVE

⑤ Café St. Michel

Avenida Lope de Vega 24. ☎ **809/562-4141.** Reservations recommended. Appetizers RD$52–RD$135 ($4–$10.40); main courses RD$75–RD$235 ($5.80–$18.10). AE, DC, MC, V. Daily noon–midnight. CARIBBEAN. Transportation: Taxi.

On a busy street in a north-central section of town called Naco is a popular restaurant that may have its finest hour daily at lunch, when the place is filled with local businesspeople. The interior is done in light-grained wood and stone trim, and there is an Italian-marble and wood bar. The chef calls the cuisine "Caribbean Transcultural," and much of its emphasis is placed on the use of local ingredients. Menu items include beefsteak, red snapper, green plantain vichyssoise, and chicken breast dishes. For dessert, try the chocolate soufflé or chocolate-nut tarts.

⑤ Fonda La Atarazana

Calle Atarazana 5. ☎ **809/689-2900.** Reservations not required. Appetizers $2–$8; main courses $5–$12. AE, DC, MC, V. Daily 10am–1am. CREOLE/INTERNATIONAL.

For regional food in a colonial atmosphere, with night music for dancing as well, this patio restaurant often has folklore festivals. Just across from the Alcázar, it's a convenient stop as you're shopping and sightseeing in the old city. A cheap, good dish is chicharrones de pollo, which is tasty fried bits of Dominican chicken. Or you might try curried baby goat in a sherry sauce. Sometimes the chef cooks lobster thermidor and Galician-style octopus. If you don't mind waiting half an hour, you can order the sopa de ajo (garlic soup). Many fans come here especially for the fricasséed pork chops.

WHAT TO SEE & DO

Santo Domingo, a treasure trove, is part of a major government-sponsored restoration. The old town is still partially enclosed by remnants of its original city wall. Its narrow streets, old stone buildings, and forts are like nothing else in the Caribbean, except Old San Juan. The only thing missing is the clank of the conquistadors' armor.

Old and modern Santo Domingo meet at the **Parque Independencia,** a big city square whose most prominent feature is its Altar de la Patria, a shrine dedicated to Duarte, Sanchez, and Mella, who are all buried here. These men led the country's fight for freedom from Haiti in 1844. As in provincial Spanish cities, the square is a popular family gathering point on Sunday afternoon. El Conde Gate stands at the entrance to the plaza and was named in 1955 for Count (El Conde) de Penalva, the governor who resisted the forces of Admiral Penn, the leader of a British invasion. It was also the site of the March for Independence in 1844, and holds a special place in the hearts of Dominicans.

In the shadow of the Alcázar, **La Atarazana** is a fully restored section that centered around one of the New World's finest arsenals, serving the conquistadors. It extends for a city block, catacombed with shops, art galleries (both Haitian and Dominican paintings), boutiques, and some good regional and international restaurants.

Just behind river moorings, the oldest street in the New World is called **calle Las Damas** (Street of the Ladies). Some visitors assume that this was a bordello district, but actually it wasn't. Rather, the elegant ladies of the viceregal court used to promenade here in the evening. It's lined with colonial buildings.

Just north is the chapel of **Our Lady of Remedies,** where the first inhabitants of the city used to attend mass before the cathedral was erected.

Try also to see the **Puerta de la Misericorda.** Part of the original city wall, this "Gate of Mercy" was once a refuge for colonists fleeing hurricanes and earthquakes. To reach it, head four blocks west along calle Padre Billini and turn left onto calle Palo Hincado.

The **Monastery of San Francisco** is but a mere ruin, lit at night. That any part of it still is standing is a miracle; it was destroyed by earthquakes, pillaged by Drake, and bombarded by French artillery. To reach the ruins, go along calle Hostos and across calle Emiliano Tejera. Continue up the hill and about midway along you'll see the ruins.

In total contrast to the colonial city, modern Santo Domingo dates from the Trujillo era. A city of broad, palm-shaded avenues, its seaside drive is called **avenida George Washington,** more popularly known as the **Malecón.** This boulevard is filled with restaurants, as well as hotels and nightclubs. Be aware that you should proceed with caution at night—there are pickpockets galore.

I also suggest a visit to **paseo de los Indios,** a sprawling 5-mile park with a restaurant, fountain displays, and a lake.

About a 20-minute drive from the heart of the city, off the autopista de las Américas on the way to the airport and the beach at Boca Chica, is **Los Tres Ojos** or "three eyes," which stare at you across the Ozama River from Old Santo Domingo. There is a trio of lagoons set in scenic caverns, with lots of stalactites and stalagmites. One lagoon is 40 feet deep, another 20 feet, and yet a third—known as "Ladies Bath"—only 5 feet deep. A Dominican Tarzan will sometimes dive off the walls of the cavern into the deepest lagoon. The area is equipped with walkways.

The monumental **El Faro a Colón** (Columbus Lighthouse), avenida España, lies on the water side of Los Tres Ojos near the airport in the Sans Souci district. Built in the shape of a pyramid cross, the towering monument is both a sightseeing attraction and a cultural center. In the heart of the structure is a chapel containing the Columbus tomb, and perhaps his mortal remains. The "bones" of Columbus were moved here from the Cathedral of Santa María la Menor (see below). (It should be pointed out that other locations, including the Cathedral of Seville, also claim to possess the remains of the explorer.) Adjacent to the chapel is a series of museums representing more than 20 countries, plus a museum dedicated to the history of Columbus and the lighthouse itself. The most outstanding and unique feature is the lighting system composed of 149 xenon Skytrack searchlights and a 70-kilowatt beam that circles out for nearly 44 miles. When illuminated, on Friday and weekends, the lights project a gigantic cross in the sky which can be seen for miles beyond, even as far as Puerto Rico.

While the concept of the memorial dates back 140 years, the first stones were not laid until 1986 following the same design submitted in 1929 by J. L. Gleave, the winner of the worldwide contest held to choose an architect. The monumental lighthouse was inaugurated on October 6, 1992, the day Columbus's "remains" were transferred from the Santo Domingo Cathedral, the oldest in the Americas. The multi-million-dollar monument stands 688 feet tall (taller than the Washington Monument) and 131 feet wide with sloping sides from 56 feet at the top to 109 feet at the bottom. The complex is open Tuesday through Sunday from 9am to 4pm, charging an admission of RD$5 (40¢) for adults, RD$1 (10¢) for children under 12.

You'll see a microcosm of Dominican life as you head east along calle El Conde from the Parque Independencia to Columbus Square, which has a large bronze statue honoring the discoverer. The statue was made in 1882 by a French sculptor. On the south side of the plaza, the ✪ **Catedral de Santa María la Menor,** calle Arzobispo Meriño (☎ **809/689-1920**), begun in 1514 and completed in 1540, is the oldest cathedral in the Americas. Characterized by a gold coral limestone facade, it's a stunning example of the Spanish Renaissance style, with elements of gothic and baroque. The cathedral, visited by Pope John Paul II in 1979 and again in 1984, was the axis for celebration of the 500th anniversary of the European Discovery of America marked in 1992. An excellent art collection of retables, ancient wood carvings, furnishings, funerary monuments, and silver and jewelry of the Treasury of the cathedral can be seen Monday through Saturday from 9am to 4pm. On Sunday masses begin at 6am. Admission is free.

✪ Alcázar de Colón

Calle Emiliano Tejera, at the foot of calle Las Damas. ☎ **809/687-5361.** Admission RD$10 (80¢). Mon and Wed–Fri 9am–5pm, Sat 9am–4pm, Sun 9am–1pm.

The most outstanding structure in the old city is the Alcázar, a palace built for the son of Columbus, Diego, and his wife, the niece of Ferdinand, king of Spain. Diego became the colony's governor in 1509, and Santo Domingo rose as the hub of Spanish commerce and culture in America. Constructed of native coral limestone, it stands on the bluffs of the Ozama River. For more than 60 years it was the center of the Spanish court and entertained such distinguished visitors as Cortés, Ponce de León, and Balboa. After its heyday, it experienced two disastrous centuries as invaders pillaged it. By 1835 it lay in virtual ruins, and it was not until 1957, in Trujillo's day, that the Dominican government finally restored it to its former splendor. The nearly two dozen rooms and open-air loggias are decorated with paintings and period tapestries, as well as 16th-century antiques.

Casa del Cordón [Cord House]

At the corner of calles Emiliano Tejera and Isabel la Católica. Admission free. Tues–Sun 8:30am–4:30pm.

Near the Alcázar de Colón, the Cord House was named for the cord of the Franciscan order, which is carved above the door. Francisco de Garay, who came to Hispaniola with Columbus, built the casa in 1503–04, which makes it the oldest stone house in the western hemisphere. It once lodged the first Royal Audience of the New World, which performed as the Supreme Court of Justice for the island and the rest of the West Indies. On another occasion, in January 1586, the noble ladies of Santo Domingo gathered here to donate their jewelry as ransom demanded by Sir Francis Drake in return for his promise to leave the city.

The restoration of this historical manor was financed by the Banco Popular Dominicano, where its executive offices are found.

Jardín Botánico
Avenida de los Proceres. Admission RD$5 (40¢). Daily 10am–6pm.

In the northern sector of Arroyo Hondo, the 445-acre Botanical Gardens are the biggest in all of Latin American and contain flowers and lush vegetation of the Dominican Republic. Seek out, in particular, the Japanese Park, the Great Ravine, and the floral clock. You can also tour the grounds by horse carriage or take a boat.

Museo de Arte Moderno
Plaza de la Cultura, calle Pedro Henríquez Ureña. ☎ **809/685-2153.** Admission RD$10 (80¢). Tues–Sat 10am–10pm.

The former site of the Trujillo mansion, plaza de la Cultura has been turned into a park and contains the Museum of Modern Art, which displays national and international works (the emphasis is, of course, on native-born talent).

Also in the center are the **National Library** and the **National Theater** (☎ **809/687-3191**), which sponsors, among other events, folkloric dances, opera, outdoor jazz concerts, traveling art exhibits, classical ballet, and music concerts.

Museo de las Casas Reales (Museum of the Royal Houses)
Calle Las Damas, at corner of calle Las Mercedes. ☎ **809/682-4202.** Admission RD$10 (80¢). Tues–Sat 9am–5pm, Sun 10am–1pm.

Through artifacts, tapestries, maps, and re-created halls, including a courtroom, this museum traces Santo Domingo's history from 1492 to 1821. Gilded furniture, arms and armor, and other colonial artifacts, all inspected by King Juan Carlos of Spain in 1976, make it the most interesting of all museums of Old Santo Domingo. It contains replicas of the three ships commanded by Columbus, and one exhibit is said to hold part of the ashes of the famed explorer. You can see, in addition to pre-Columbian art, the main artifacts of two galleons sunk in 1724 on their way from Spain to Mexico, along with remnants of another 18th-century Spanish ship, the *Concepción.*

SPORTS & OUTDOOR ACTIVITIES

BASEBALL   The national sport is baseball, and many of the country's native-born sons have gone on to the U.S. major leagues. From October through February, games are played at stadiums in Santo Domingo and elsewhere. Check the local newspaper for schedules and locations of the nearest game.

BEACHES   The Dominican Republic may have some great beaches, but they aren't in Santo Domingo. The principal beach resort near the capital is at Boca Chica, less than 2 miles east of the international airport and about 19 miles from Santo Domingo. Clear, shallow blue water laves the fine white sand beach and a natural coral reef that protects the area from big fish. The east side of the beach, known as "St. Tropez," is popular with Europeans.

The great beaches are at **Puerto Plata,** but that's a rough, three-hour drive or an easy flight from the capital, and at **La Romana,** a two-hour drive to the east (see Sections 4 and 2, respectively, later in this chapter).

Most of the major Santo Domingo hotels have swimming pools.

GOLF   Serious golfers head for **Casa de Campo** with three 18-hole Pete Dye courses or the course that Robert Trent Jones designed at **Playa Dorada,** near Puerto Plata.

A Tour of Goat Island

With more than two dozen national parks and seven reserves, the Dominican Republic is a nature's lover's Eden. It's estimated that there are more than 300 varieties of orchids alone on the island of Hispaniola. There are some 254 native and exotic birds on the island.

To the west of Santo Domingo, close to the Haitian border, lies the saltwater lake, Lago Enriquillo, at 144 feet below sea level, the lowest place in the West Indies. It's the habitat of a large reserve of American crocodiles. In the center of the 21-mile-long lake is a 5-mile-long island, Isla Cabrito or "Goat Island," with a research station offering information about the region and its geology. Feeding along the lake and on Goat Island are flamingos, terns, sandpipers, herons, and even roseate spoonbills.

It's not possible to visit the island unguided, but Ecoturisa (☎ **809/ 221-4104** in Santo Domingo) offers a two-hour tour of the lake with an overnight stay in a mountain resort for $160 per person.

Golf is available in the capital at the **Santo Domingo Country Club,** an 18-hole course that grants privileges to guests of most of the major hotels (the hotel staff has to make the arrangements for you). The rule here is members first, which means it's impossible for weekend games.

HORSE RACING Santo Domingo's race track, **Hipódromo Peria Antillana,** on avenida San Cristóbal (☎ 809/565-2353), schedules races on Tuesday, Thursday, and Saturday at 3pm. You can spend the day here and have lunch at the track's restaurant. Admission is free.

POLO Made so famous during Trujillo's day, polo is still a popular sport. Polo fields are in Santo Domingo at **Sierra Prieta,** where games are played on weekends, and in La Romana at **Casa de Campo,** where there are four fields.

TENNIS The major hotels have very good courts, especially the **Santo Domingo Sheraton, Embajador,** and **Gran Hotel Lina.** Guests at the **Jaragua Renaissance Resort & Casino** and **Hotel Santo Domingo** will find excellent courts set aside for residents. Some of these courts are lit for night games.

SHOPPING

The best buys are in handcrafted native items, especially **amber** jewelry, the national gem, a petrified fossil resin millions of years old. The pine the resin came from disappeared from the earth long ago. The origins of amber were a mystery until the beginning of the 19th century when scientists determined the source of the gem.

Look for pieces of amber with trapped objects, such as insects and spiders, inside the enveloping material. Colors range from a bright yellow to black, but most of the gems are golden in tone. Amber deposits in the Dominican Republic were only discovered in modern times. Fine-quality amber jewelry, along with lots of plastic fakes, is sold throughout the country.

A semiprecious stone of light blue (sometimes a dark-blue color), **larimar** is the Dominican turquoise. It often makes striking jewelry, and is sometimes mounted with wild boar's teeth.

Ever since the Dominicans presented John F. Kennedy with what became his favorite rocker, visitors have wanted to take home a **rocking chair.** To simplify transport, these rockers are often sold unassembled.

Other good buys include Dominican rum, hand-knit articles, macramé, ceramics, and crafts in native mahogany. Always haggle over the price, particularly in the open-air markets; no stallkeeper expects you to pay the first price asked. The **best shopping streets** are El Conde, the oldest and most traditional shop-flanked avenue, and avenida Mella.

In the colonial section, **La Atarazana** is filled with galleries and gift and jewelry stores, charging inflated prices. Duty-free shops are found at the airport, in the capital at the **Centro de los Héroes,** and at both the Hotel Santo Domingo and the Hotel Embajador. Shopping hours are generally 9am to 12:30pm and 2 to 5pm Monday through Saturday.

Ambar Marie

Caonabo 9, Gazcue. ☎ **809/682-7539.**

In case you're worried that the piece of amber you like may be plastic, you can be assured of the real thing at Ambar Marie, where you can even design your own setting for your choice gem. Look especially for the beautiful amber necklaces, as well as the earrings and pins. The shop is in a residential area and is open during regular business hours, Monday through Friday.

Ambar Tres

La Atarazana 3. ☎ **809/688-0474.**

In the colonial section of the old city, Ambar Tres sells jewelry made from amber, black coral, mahogany carvings, watercolors, oil paintings, and other Dominican products. The shop is open daily, but it closes at noon on Sunday.

✪ El Mercado Modelo

Avenida Mella.

Head first for the National Market, filled with stall after stall of crafts and spices, fruits, and vegetables. The merchants will be most eager to sell, and you can easily get lost in the crush. Remember to bargain. You'll see a lot of tortoise-shell work here, but exercise caution, since many species, especially the hawksbill, are on the endangered-species list and could be impounded by U.S. Customs if discovered in your luggage. Rockers are for sale here, as are mahogany ware, sandals, baskets, hats, clay braziers for grilling fish, and so on.

Galería de Arte Nader

At Lupero and Duarte. ☎ **809/687-6674.**

In the center of the most historical section of town is a well-known gallery that sells so many Dominican and Haitian paintings that they're sometimes stacked in rows against the walls. Don't miss the ancient courtyard in back if you want a glimpse of how things looked in the Spanish colonies hundreds of years ago.

Novo Atarazana

La Atarazana 21. ☎ **809/689-0582.**

Although the name would imply that it's new, this is actually one of the best-established shops in town. You can purchase pieces of amber, black coral, leather goods, wood carvings, and Haitian paintings. It's open seven days a week.

Plaza Criolla

At the corner of avenidas 27 de Febrero and Anacaona.

Plaza Criolla is a modern shopping complex with a distinguished design theme. Shops are set in gardens with tropical shrubbery and flowers, facing the Olympic Center. The architecture makes generous use of natural woods, and a covered wooden walkway links the stalls together.

Tu Espacio
Avenida Cervantes 102. ☎ **809/686-6006.**

One of the most charming shops in the capital is crammed with all sorts of goodies, including Taíno art (hand-carved reproductions, of course), Dominican and European antiques, monumental bamboo furniture, and odds and ends that Victorians used to clutter their homes with. If you're looking for that special trinket, you're likely to find it here. The merchandise is always changing.

SANTO DOMINGO AFTER DARK
CASINOS

Santo Domingo has several major casinos. The most spectacular is the **Jaragua Renaissance Resort & Casino,** avenida George Washington 367 (☎ **809/221-2222**), whose brightly flashing sign is the most dazzling light along the Malecón at night. The most glamorous casino in the country is fittingly housed in the capital's poshest hotel. Action—blackjack, baccarat, roulette, slot machines—is from 4pm to 4am Sunday through Thursday, 4pm to 5am on Friday and Saturday, depending on business. You can gamble in either Dominican pesos or U.S. dollars.

Other casinos include **El Embajador Casino,** avenida Sarasota 65 (☎ **809/221-2131**), where the popular games of blackjack, craps, and roulette are offered daily from 4pm to 5am. In between gaming sessions, you can have a drink at La Fontana, their casual bar where hors d'oeuvres are served.

Another casino is at the **Hispaniola Hotel,** avenida Independencia (☎ **809/221-7111**), open daily from 4pm to 5am.

One of the most stylish casinos is the **Omni Casino,** in the Sheraton Santo Domingo Hotel & Casino, avenida George Washington 361 (☎ **809/221-6666**). Its bilingual staff will help you play blackjack, craps, baccarat, and keno, among other games. There is also a piano bar. It's open daily from 3pm to 7am.

2 La Romana & Altos de Chavón

On the southeast coast of the Dominican Republic, La Romana was once a sleepy sugarcane town that also specialized in cattle raising, and unless one had business here with either industry, no tourist bothered with it. But when Gulf + Western opened (and later sold) a tropical paradise resort of refinement and luxury, the Casa de Campo, on its outskirts, La Romana soon became known among the jet-set travelers. Just east of Casa de Campo is Altos de Chavón, a village built specially for artists.

GETTING THERE

BY PLANE   The easiest air routing to Casa de Campo from almost anywhere in North America is through San Juan, Puerto Rico (see "Getting There" in Chapter 5, "Puerto Rico"). **American Eagle** (☎ toll free **800/433-7300** in the U.S.) operates three daily nonstop flights to Casa de Campo/La Romana every day from San Juan. Each is a turboprop plane, carrying between 32 and 64 passengers, requires just over an hour of flight time, and departs late enough in the day to permit transfers from other flights. For passengers who reserve their tickets at least three days in advance, round-trip passage from San Juan costs $150.

BY CAR   If you're already in Santo Domingo, you can drive here in about an hour and 20 minutes from the international airport, along Las Américas Highway. (Allow another hour if you're in the center of the city.) Of course, everything depends on traffic conditions. (Watch for speed traps—low-paid police officers openly solicit bribes whether you were speeding or not.)

LA ROMANA
WHERE TO STAY

✪ Casa de Campo
La Romana, Dominican Republic. ☎ **809/523-3333,** or 800/877-3643 in the U.S., Canada, Puerto Rico, and the Virgin Islands. Fax 809/523-8548. 300 casitas, 150 villas. A/C MINIBAR TV TEL. Winter, $175–$225 casita for one or two; $400–$600 two-bedroom villa for up to four. Off-season, $130 casita for one or two; $240 two-bedroom villa for up to four. MAP $45 per person extra. AE, MC, V. Free parking.

Translated as "House in the Country," Casa de Campo is the greatest resort in the entire Caribbean area—and the competition is stiff. It brings a whole new dimension to a holiday. Gulf + Western took a vast hunk of coastal land, more than 7,000 acres in all, and carved out this chic resort, today owned and operated by Premier Resorts & Hotels. Ubiquitous Miami architect William Cox helped create it, and Oscar de la Renta provided the style and flair. Tiles, Dominican paintings, louvered doors, and flamboyant fabrics decorate the interior.

The resort divides its accommodations into red-roofed, two-story casitas near the main building and more upscale villas that dot the edges of the golf courses, the gardens near the tennis courts, and the shores of the Atlantic. Some, within La Terrazza, are clustered in a semiprivate hilltop compound with views overlooking the meadows, the cane, and the fairways down to the distant sea.

Dining/Entertainment: At the core of everything is a wonderland swimming pool—four, in fact, each on a different level—with thatch huts on stilts to provide beverages and light meals. Perched over the pool is La Caña, the two-level bar and lounge, with a thatch roof but no walls. Dinner is on a rustic roofed terrace where you'll find some of the best food in the Dominican Republic. Perhaps they'll throw a roast suckling pig barbecue right on the beach. Most of the beef used is grown right on the plains of La Romana. Other dining choices include El Patio, which is like a glamorized coffee shop with substantial daily specials, and the Lago Grill, serving breakfast daily from 7 to 11am and lunch daily from noon to 4pm. See "Where to Dine," below, for Tropicana.

Services: 24-hour room service, laundry, babysitting.

Facilities: One of the most complete fitness centers on the island, with weight and exercise machines, whirlpool and sauna, aerobics classes, and masseuses. See "Sports & Outdoor Activities," below, for the golf, water-sports, fishing, and polo and horseback-riding facilities.

WHERE TO DINE

Tropicana
In Casa de Campo. ☎ **809/523-3333, ext. 3000.** Reservations required. Appetizers RD$50–RD$185 ($3.90–$14.20); main courses RD$120–RD$195 ($9.20–$15). AE, MC, V. Dinner only, daily 6–11pm. CARIBBEAN.

One of the most glamorous restaurants in the complex, the Tropicana is a breezy pavilion known for its innovative "Caribbean flair" and a wide range of seafood and exotic West Indian dishes. Lying behind the main lobby area, it sometimes offers a seafood bar in winter.

SPORTS & OUTDOOR ACTIVITIES

At La Romana, on 7,000 acres of lush turf, you'll find three Pete Dye golf courses, a stable of horses with thrice-weekly polo, a private marina with deep-sea and river trips, snorkeling on live reefs, a fitness center (at Casa de Campo, above), and 13 tennis courts.

BEACHES A large, palm-fringed sandy crescent, **Bayahibe** is a 20-minute launch trip or a 30-minute drive from La Romana. In addition, **La Minitas** is a tiny, but nice, immaculate beach and lagoon. Transportation is provided on the bus, or you can rent a horse-drawn buckboard. Finally, **Catalina** is a turquoise beach on a deserted island just 45 minutes away by motor boat.

GOLF The **Casa de Campo** courses are known to dedicated golfers every-where—in fact, *Golf* magazine called it "the finest golf resort in the world." The course Teeth of the Dog has also been called "a thing of almighty beauty," and it is. The ruggedly natural terrain has seven holes skirting the ocean. Opened in 1977, the Links is the inland course, built on sandy soil away from the beach. A golf professional will answer your questions (dial extension 8115). Most golf passes are sold as three-day memberships, priced at $135, and seven-day memberships, at $265. These allow unlimited golf playing. Extra days cost $45 each. Rentals of golf carts are $13 per person per round. If anyone wants to play a mere 18 holes, the cost is $80 for Teeth of the Dog, or $56 for the Links. These prices include the use of a golf cart. Hours are 7am to 7pm daily.

POLO & HORSEBACK RIDING Ever since the grand days when Domini-can playboy Porfirio Rubirosa mounted some of the finest horses in the world, the Dominican Republic has been a polo-playing mecca. Today **Casa de Campo** is the best place in the Caribbean for playing, learning, and watching the fabled sport of kings and princes. On the premises are three full-size polo fields (one a prac-tice field), a horse-breeding farm, and scores of polo ponies, as well as a small army of veterinarians, grooms, and polo-related employees. If during your visit you hear that a polo match will be played, by all means go.

Most serious polo players arrive with their own equipment, but beginners learn by watching more experienced players and participating in trail rides (which last one to three hours), as well as taking riding lessons at the resort's dude ranch. If polo players are present, they can play polo for $44 per player per match per chukker. Since most people aren't polo players, horseback riding might be a more viable option. Trail rides cost $18 for one hour or $32 for two hours, and riding lessons go for $45 per hour.

TENNIS A total of 13 clay courts at **Casa de Campo** are lit for night play. The courts are available daily from 7am to 10pm. Charges are RD$180 ($13.90) during the day or RD$200 ($15.40) at night.

WATER SPORTS & FISHING Casa de Campo (☎ **809/523-3333**) has one of the most complete water-sports facilities in the Dominican Republic. Reserva-tions and information on any seaside activity can be arranged through the resort's concierge. You can charter a boat for snorkeling or deep-sea fishing. The resort maintains eight charter vessels, with a minimum of eight people required per outing. Only four can fish at a time. Patrons interested in river fishing on the Chavón can arrange trips there through the hotel as well. Some of the biggest snook ever recorded have been caught here. Wednesday through Monday, snorkeling trips to Isla Catalina cost RD$375 ($28.90) for a full day and a full-day tour to Isla Saona goes for RD$625 ($48.10) per snorkeler. Deep-sea fishing costs RD$3,500 ($269.50) for four hours or RD$5,500 ($423.50) for eight hours.

ALTOS DE CHAVÓN

In 1976, a plateau—100 miles east of Santo Domingo—was selected by Charles G. Bluhdorn, then chairman of Gulf & Western Industries, as the site for a remarkable project. Dominican stone cutters, woodworkers, and ironsmiths began the task that would produce Altos de Chavón, today a flourishing Caribbean art center set above the canyon of the River Chavón and the Caribbean Sea.

A walk down one of the cobblestone paths of Altos de Chavón reveals at every turn architecture reminiscent of another era. Coral block and terra-cotta brick buildings house artists' studios, craft workshops, galleries, stores, and restaurants. Mosaics of black river pebbles, sun-bleached coral, and red sandstone spread out to the plazas. The **Church of St. Stanislaus** is centered on the main plaza, with its fountain of the four lions, colonnade of obelisks, and panoramic views.

The **School of Design** at Altos de Chavón has offered a two-year Associate in Applied Science degree, in the areas of communication, fashion, environmental studies, product design, and fine arts/illustration since its inauguration in 1982. The school is affiliated with the Parsons School of Design in New York and Paris, providing local and international graduates with the opportunity to acquire the advanced skills needed for placement in design careers.

From around the world come artists-in-residence, the established and the aspiring. Altos de Chavón provides them with lodging, studio space, and a group exhibition at the culmination of their three-month stay.

The **galleries** at Altos de Chavón offer a varied and engaging mix of exhibits. In three distinct spaces, the Principal Gallery, the Rincón Gallery, and the Loggia, the work of well-known and emerging Dominican and international artists is showcased. The gallery has a consignment space where finely crafted silk-screen and other multiple works are available for sale.

Altos de Chavón's *talleres* are craft ateliers, where local artisans have been trained to produce ceramic, silk-screen, and woven fiber products. From the clay apothecary jars with carnival devil lids to the colored tapestries of Dominican houses, the richness of island myth and legend, folklore, and handcraft tradition is much in evidence. The posters, note cards, and printed T-shirts that come from the silk-screen workshops are among the most sophisticated in the Caribbean. All the products of Altos de Chavón's *talleres* are sold at **La Tienda,** the foundation village store.

Thousands of visitors annually view the Altos de Chavón **Regional Museum of Archeology,** which houses the objects of Samuel Pion, an amateur archeologist and collector of treasures from the vanished Taíno tribes, the island's first settlers. The timeless quality of some of the museum's objects makes them seem strangely contemporary in design—one discovers sculptural forms that recall the work of Brancusi or Arp. The museum is open daily from 9am to 9pm.

At the heart of the village's performing-arts complex is the 5,000-seat open-air **amphitheater.** Since its inauguration over a decade ago by Frank Sinatra and Carlos Santana, the amphitheater has hosted renowned concerts, symphonies, theater, and festivals, including concerts by Julio Iglesias and Gloria Estefan. The annual Heineken Jazz Festival has brought together such diverse talents as Dizzy Gillespie, Toots Thielmans, Tania Maria, and Randy Brecker.

WHERE TO DINE

Café de Sol

Altos de Chavón. ☎ **809/523-3333, ext. 2346.** Reservations not required. Appetizers RD$50–RD$125 ($3.90–$9.60); main courses RD$105–RD$140 ($8.10–$10.80). AE, MC, V. Daily 11am–11pm. PIZZA/AMERICAN.

If you want a pizza after your exploration of the village, you'll probably enjoy this stone-floored indoor/outdoor café. To reach it, you climb a flight of exterior stone steps to the rooftop of a building whose ground floor houses a jewelry shop. Salads and bar drinks also attract patrons.

✪ Casa del Río

Altos de Chavón. ☎ **809/523-3333, ext. 2345.** Reservations required. Appetizers RD$130–RD$220 ($10–$16.90); main courses RD$220–RD$300 ($16.90–$23.10). AE, MC, V. Dinner only, daily 6–11pm. FRENCH.

The most glamorous restaurant at Altos de Chavón occupies the basement of an Iberian-style house whose towers, turrets, tiles, and massive stairs are entwined with strands of bougainvillea. Inside, brick arches support oversize chandeliers, suspended racing sculls, and filled wine racks. Piano music might accompany your meal. You could begin with an unusual presentation of escargots and gnocchi, or a soup, perhaps hearts of palm vichyssoise. Main courses are likely to include honey-flavored breast of duck or lobster lasagne.

3 Punta Cana

Continuing east from La Romana, you reach Punta Cana, site of several major tourist developments, including Club Med, and more are projected at the easternmost tip of Hispaniola. This perhaps will one day become a formidable rival of Puerto Plata.

The area, known for its white sand beaches and clear waters, is an escapist's retreat, although resorts compete to have enough activities around the clock to keep guests on the premises.

When white sand bores you, head inland to the typical Dominican city of **Higüey,** 27 miles from Punta Cana, which hasn't been made pretty for tourists. There, you can see the **Basilica Nuestra Señora de la Altagracia,** with the largest carillon in the Americas. The founders of the church conceived the basilica to honor Our Lady of Altagracia, the patron saint of the Dominican Republic. The church is said to represent the best modern architecture on the island and is reputedly the site of miracles.

Higüey was founded in 1494 by the conqueror of Jamaica, Juan de Esquivel, with immigrants brought in between 1502 and 1508 by Ponce de León to populate the land. It was from the castle he built here that the tireless seeker of the Fountain of Youth set out in 1509 to conquer Puerto Rico and in 1513 to check out Florida.

Toward the southern coast is **Saona Island,** where some 1,000 people live on 80 square miles of land, surviving primarily by fishing and hunting for pigeons and wild hogs—it must be a healthy way to live, for Saona has the lowest mortality rate in the Dominican Republic.

GETTING THERE

American Eagle (☎ **800/433-7300** in the U.S.) maintains one or two daily non-stop flights to Punta Cana from San Juan, Puerto Rico; flight time is an hour and 10 minutes. Flights depart late enough in the day (1:45pm) to connect with dozens of flights to San Juan. The turboprop planes hold no more than 36 passengers. At press time, year-round one-way fares to Punta Cana from San Juan are around $185 for passengers who paid for their tickets at least three days in advance. You can also opt for one of American Eagle's two or three daily flights from San Juan to La Romana, which is a 90-minute drive from Punta Cana.

WHERE TO STAY & DINE

Bavaro Beach Resort Complex

Apdo. Postal 1, Punta Cana, Higüey, Dominican Republic. ☎ **809/876-6612,** or 800/876-6612 in the U.S. Fax 809/539-1160. 1,955 rms, 64 junior suites. A/C TV TEL. Winter, $175 single; $200 double. Off-season, $123 single; $140 double. Suite $8–$12 per person extra. (Rates include MAP.) MAP $27 for children 2–11 occupying parents' room. Minimum stay three days. AE, DC, MC, V. Free parking.

This massive resort colony, conceived as a village unto itself and the largest in the Dominican Republic, sits on one of the best beaches in the Caribbean, with 26 miles of fine white sand stretching in both directions. Arranged in the shape of a horseshoe, it contains five different low-rise sections, most of which lie parallel to the beachfront for a maximum exposure to the sea. Families often stay in the cluster of one-bedroom apartments with small kitchenettes, which lies in the establishment's gardens (not directly on the beach). Each accommodation is equipped with a terrace, a safety-deposit box, and either two double beds or one double and one single bed. Clients appreciate their unrestricted access to the many bars, restaurants, swimming pools, and entertainment facilities of the resort's different sections. Most rooms are booked and fully paid for in advance through a travel agent.

   Dining/Entertainment: The resort contains 15 restaurants (some of which participate in the hotel's MAP program) and at least 15 different bars. Every evening, two of these are transformed into nightclubs, one specializing in disco, the other in Latin music where someone always seems to be on hand to teach you the merengue. The resort has one of the largest casinos in the region, which opens every evening around 5pm and remains open till the last casino chip hits the roulette table.

🔵 Family-Friendly Accommodations

Casa de Campo *(see p. 259)* In summer, children's programs include full-day camping with horseback riding, aerobics, swimming, sack races, and treasure hunts. Depending on their ages, kids become either "pirates" or "conquistadors."

Club Mediterranée–Punta Cana *(see p. 264)* This is a family-oriented type of Club Med. Children under 11 can stay free in their parents' room during most weeks of the summer, and there's a mini-club for juniors.

Jack Tar Village *(see p. 266)* This all-inclusive resort makes family-discount offers to children staying in rooms with their parents. Its Kids Klub offers an activity-filled agenda.

Services: Laundry, babysitting, massage.

Facilities: Four swimming pools, 18-hole golf course, daily aerobics sessions, scuba diving, snorkeling, sailing, windsurfing, waterskiing, deep-sea fishing, tennis, horseback riding, beauty salon, medical facilities, on-site bank.

Club Mediterranée–Punta Cana

Apdo. Postal 106, Province La Altagracia, Dominican Republic. ☎ **809/687-2767**, or 212/750-1670 in New York, or 800/CLUB-MED in the U.S. Fax 809-687-2896. 334 rms. A/C. Christmas and New Year's holiday, $1,839 per person per week double. Midsummer, $700 per person per week double. (Includes all meals.) Rates at other times vary between these figures, depending on the particular week. Children under 11, $1,312 per week in winter, free during certain weeks of summer, when staying in parents' room. AE, MC, V. Free parking.

Some 145 miles east of Santo Domingo, Club Med opened in 1981 and put the far-eastern tip of the island of Hispaniola on the tourist map. The village lies along a reef-protected white sandy beach, which offers some of the best diving areas on the islands. It was here that the crews of the *Nina, Pinta,* and *Santa Maria* are believed by some to have put ashore. Three-story clusters of bungalows are strung along the beach, contain twin beds, and open either on the sea or onto a coconut grove. Each room has a private safe. Note that there is no such thing as a guaranteed single room. The staff mixes and matches single clients into double configurations. Every guest is asked to pay an annual membership fee of $50 per adult and $20 per child, and also to pay a one-time initiation fee of $30.

Dining/Entertainment: The heart of the village is a combined dining room/bar/dance floor and theater complex facing the sea. Three restaurants and a disco are located beside the sea. You get the usual Club Med activities here, including picnics, boat rides, nightly dancing, shows, and optional excursions.

Services: Laundry.

Facilities: Sailing, windsurfing, snorkeling, waterskiing, swimming, archery, 10 tennis courts (4 lit at night); Mini-Club for juniors 2 to 11, highlighting circus training and other activities.

Meliá Bávaro

Playa El Cortecito, Punta Cana, Higüey, Dominican Republic. ☎ **809/221-2311**, or 800/336-3542. Fax 809/686-5427. 504 suites. A/C MINIBAR TV TEL. Winter, $94–$202 junior suite for one or two. Off-season, $79–$102 junior suite for one or two. Additional person $30 extra. MAP $20–$30 per person extra. AE, DC, MC, V. Free parking.

The most glamorous addition to the hotels at Punta Cana opened in 1992. The Spanish-born architect who designed it (Alvaro Sanz) did everything he could to create an oasis for both vacationers and the hundreds of species of birds that call the resort their home. Most of the palms and many of the mangrove clusters on the property were retained, and freshwater reservoirs were incorporated into the landscaping in an attempt to attract birds. Owned by Meliá Hotels, the Spain-based giant, this resort drew at least part of its architectural inspiration from Meliá's successful hostelry in Bali, Indonesia.

Each of the accommodations is a suite that lies within earshot of the resort's mile-long private beach of sugar-fine sands. All but about a hundred of the units are in a compound of two-story bungalows, and the rest sit adjacent to the resort's headquarters—a high-ceilinged, open-air pavilion.

Dining/Entertainment: An international restaurant, El Licey sits on a pier jutting above a freshwater lake, adjacent to an open-air disco. A seafood restaurant, El Trapiche, is on an island in the middle of one of the swimming pools. The resort's main restaurant serves an array of buffets. All these are supplemented by a handful of bars, one of them a soundproof music pub/disco floating atop the waters of the lake, another a swim-up bar in the pool.

Services: 24-hour room service, concierge, babysitting.

Facilities: Two swimming pools, complete array of land and water sports, shopping arcade, four lit tennis courts.

4 Puerto Plata

Originally it was Columbus's intention to found America's first city at Puerto Plata and name it La Isabela. But a tempest detained him, and it wasn't until 1502 that Nicolás de Ovando founded Puerto Plata, or "port of silver," which lies 130 miles northwest of Santo Domingo. The port became the last stop for ships going back to Europe, their holds laden with treasures taken from the New World.

Puerto Plata appeals to a market that may shun more expensive resorts, and some hotels boast a nearly full occupancy rate almost all year. It's already casting a shadow on business at longer-established resorts throughout the Caribbean, especially in Puerto Rico.

Most of the hotels are not actually in Puerto Plata itself but are in a special tourist zone called **Playa Dorada.** The backers of this usually sun-drenched spot have poured vast amounts of money into a flat area between a pond and the curved and verdant shoreline. (It rains a lot in Puerto Plata during the winter, while the south and Punta Cana are drier.) There are major hotels, a scattering of secluded condominiums and villas, a Robert Trent Jones–designed golf course, and a riding stable with horses for each of the major properties.

ORIENTATION
GETTING THERE

BY PLANE   The international airport is actually not in Puerto Plata but is east of Playa Dorado on the road to Sosúa. For information about flights from North America, see "Getting There" at the beginning of this chapter.

BY CAR   From Santo Domingo, the $3^{1}/_{2}$-hour drive directly north on autopista Duarte passes through the lush Cibao Valley, home of the tobacco industry and Bermudez rum, and through Santiago de los Caballeros, the second-largest city in the country, 90 miles north of Santo Domingo.

GETTING AROUND

For information on renting a car, see "Getting Around" at the beginning of this chapter. You might find that a motor scooter will be suitable for transportation in Puerto Plata or Sosúa, although the roads are potholed.

BY TAXI   Make an agreement with the driver on the fare before your trip starts, as the vehicles are not metered. You'll find taxis on Central Park at Puerto Plata. At night it's wise to hire your cab for a round-trip. If you go in the daytime by taxi to any of the other beach resorts or villages, check on reserving a vehicle for your return trip.

BY MOTOCONCHO   The cheapest way of getting around is on a motoconcho, found at the major corners of Puerto Plata and Sosúa. This motorcycle "concho," or taxi, offers a ride to practically anywhere in town. You can also go from Puerto Plata to Playa Dorada (site of most of the hotels). Fares range from RD$15 to RD$25 ($1.20 to $1.90).

BY MINIVAN   Minivans are another means of transport, especially if you're traveling outside town. They leave from Puerto Plata's Central Park and will take you all the way to Sosúa. Determine the fare before getting in. Vans operate Monday through Saturday from 6am to 5pm and on Sunday from 6am to midnight.

ESSENTIALS

Round-the-clock **drugstore** service is offered by Farmacía Deleyte, avenida John F. Kennedy 89 (☎ 809/586-2583). Emergency **medical service** is provided by Clinica Dr. Brugal, calle José del Carmen Ariza 15 (☎ 809/586-2519). Phone 809/586-2331 to summon the **police** in Puerto Plata.

WHERE TO STAY

EXPENSIVE

Jack Tar Village

Playa Dorada (Apdo. Postal 368), Puerto Plata, Dominican Republic. ☎ **809/320-3800,** or 800/999-9182 in the U.S. Fax 809/320-4161. 283 rms, 3 suites. A/C TV TEL. Winter, $170–$200 single; $300–$340 double; $100 extra for one-bedroom suite; $300 extra for three-bedroom suite. Off-season, $80–$110 single; $190–$250 double; $75 extra for one-bedroom suite; $250 extra for three-bedroom suite. Children 6–11 sharing their parents' room $85 in winter, $50 off-season; children under 6, free. (Rates all-inclusive.) AE, MC, V. Free parking.

Owned by an investment group from Texas, this all-inclusive resort east of the airport is set at the edge of the sea and clustered around two swimming pools. The facility offers drinks, all meals, most water sports, and entertainment as part of its standard package, so you never have to leave the grounds. In the center of the resort, you'll find dozens of adults and children playing shuffleboard, cards, table tennis, and volleyball. If you prefer to linger beside one of the indoor/outdoor bars, where all your drinks are free, you'll have plenty of company. If you're more energetic, many water and land sports are offered, most of them included in the overall price of your accommodation.

Dining/Entertainment: In 1990 the resort opened a large, plush casino, one of the largest in the country, and a disco. Two nights a week, dinners are sit-down affairs in a high-ceilinged dining room with frequent musical entertainment. The rest of the time, and often at lunch, meals are buffet style. Drinks are free at the indoor and outdoor bars.

Services: Laundry.

Facilities: Two swimming pools, sailing, windsurfing, horseback riding, Robert Trent Jones–designed golf course.

MODERATE

Caribbean Village Club on the Green

Playa Dorada, Puerto Plata, Dominican Republic. ☎ **809/320-1111.** Fax 809/320-5386. 336 rms, 144 suites. A/C TV TEL. $90 single; $160 double; from $270 suite for two. (Rates all-inclusive.) AE, MC, V. Free parking.

Bought and, to some degree, upgraded in 1992 by a chain of hotels with other properties in the Dominican Republic and in Mexico, this hostelry is a modern low-rise hotel set near a cluster of competitors east of the airport. The hotel offers comfortable but simple bedrooms, and includes three meals a day, all beverages, and some water sports in the all-inclusive prices.

Dining/Entertainment: Dominican and international food is offered at El Pilon, Italian pastas at Firenze, and fresh fish and seafood and local beef on the continental menu at La Condesa. At that last restaurant you may want to sample some of the excellent Chilean vintages, all at reasonable prices.

Services: Laundry, babysitting.

Facilities: Water sports, seven all-weather tennis courts, gym, swimming pool with swim-up bar.

Dorado Naco

Playa Dorada (Apdo. Postal 162), Puerto Plata, Dominican Republic. ☎ **809/320-2019,** or 800/322-2388 in the U.S. Fax 809/320-3608. 150 suites. A/C TV TEL. Winter, $100 one-bedroom suite; $140 two-bedroom suite; $115 one-bedroom penthouse. Off-season, $75–$80 one-bedroom suite; $100–$110 two-bedroom suite; $95 one-bedroom penthouse. (Includes breakfast.) Children under 12 stay free in parents' room. AE, DC, MC, V. Free parking.

When the Dorado Naco was built east of the airport in 1982, there was only one other hotel in the entire Playa Dorada area. After registering, you'll be ushered past the poolside bar and restaurant complex, down a series of flowered walkways into your room. Each suite contains comfortable furniture, a kitchen, and a creative arrangement of interior space. You can spend some of your evenings en famille, cooking at home. Many of the units are clustered along parapets or around well-planted atriums, and some of the larger ones include duplex floor plans and enough spacious luxury to satisfy any vacationer. One-bedroom suites accommodate one or two, and two-bedroom suites and the penthouse can sleep up to four.

Dining/Entertainment: A wide array of entertainment is available, and a full range of activities is planned throughout the week in season. A beach bar and grill lie a short walk from every room. A nightly buffet is spread under a portico near the pool, and à la carte meals are available in the Flamingo Gourmet Restaurant and Valentino's Italian restaurant. Consider the Flamingo for dining even if you're not a resident of the hotel. It's one of the best in the area, serving a continental menu. The hotel has live music every night and live shows twice weekly.

Services: Room service (7am to 11pm), laundry, babysitting.

Facilities: Swimming pool, tennis court, water sports center (for scuba diving, snorkeling, waterskiing, and sailing).

Playa Dorada Hotel & Casino

Playa Dorada (Apdo. Postal 272), Puerto Plata, Dominican Republic. ☎ **809/586-3988,** or 800/423-6902 in the U.S. Fax 809/320-1190. 344 rms. A/C TV TEL. $190 single or double. Additional person $10 extra. MAP $20 per person extra. AE, DC, MC, V. Free parking.

This theatrically designed hotel east of the airport is one of the few in all the Caribbean that can boast nearly full occupancy during most of the year. The reception area is an air-conditioned oasis of Victorian latticework set beneath the soaring ceiling. The bedrooms are arranged along rambling corridors. More than two-thirds of the hotel's units are set into red-roofed wings that face the $1^1/2$-mile-long beach. The hotel also has specially designed rooms for disabled patrons. A sports package is included in the rates, so all the facilities are free.

Dining/Entertainment: In addition to La Palma restaurant, the many bars and entertainment facilities include a cocktail lounge. Las Brisas and Mar Azul are two other restaurants. Around the swimming pool, the management hosts barbecues, buffet suppers, and weekly entertainment, including singers and dancers known throughout the Spanish-speaking world.

Services: Babysitting, laundry, valet.

Facilities: Boating, water sports, golf, three tennis courts (lit at night), swimming pool.

Villas Doradas Beach Resort

Playa Dorada (Apdo. Postal 1370), Puerto Plata, Dominican Republic. ☎ **809/586-3000.** Fax 809/320-4790. 239 rms. A/C TV TEL. $115 single; $180 double. (Rates include meals.) AE, MC, V. Free parking.

This collection of town houses east of the airport is arranged in landscaped clusters, usually around a courtyard. There's no beachfront here. Each unit is pleasantly furnished with louvered doors and windows.

Dining/Entertainment: A focal point of the resort is the restaurant Las Garzas, where a musical trio entertains guests every evening beneath the soaring pine ceiling. The management also features barbecues around the pool area, where a net is sometimes set up for volleyball games. Of course, it would be tempting never to leave the shade of the cone-shaped thatch-roofed pool bar, which is one of the most popular parts of the whole resort. El Pescador is a fish restaurant open for dinner beside the beach, and Pancho serves Mexican dishes.

Services: Laundry, babysitting.

Facilities: Swimming pool, tennis, horseback riding, kiddie pool; sand beaches and golf facilities within walking distance.

BUDGET

⑤ Montemar

Avenida Las Hermanas Mirabal (Apdo. Postal 382), Puerto Plata, Dominican Republic. ☎ **809/586-2800.** Fax 809/586-2009. 94 rms. A/C MINIBAR TV TEL. $80 single; $120 double. (Rates all-inclusive.) AE, DC, MC, V. Free parking.

The Montemar complex east of the airport plays a double role: It's one of the pioneer resorts in the area, and it houses the local hotel school. The lobby is one of the most distinctive in the area, with large bamboo chandeliers and a naturalistic mural behind the reception desk. Most of the accommodations have views of palms and the sea. Some of the rooms are air-conditioned. Your needs will be cared for by a battalion of students.

A lounge nearby engages a merengue band, which plays every night beside the illuminated palms. There are two tennis courts. Laundry, babysitting, and room service are provided. Three times a day a shuttle bus from the hotel takes guests to the beach, where they can drink free at a private beach bar, as part of the hotel's all-inclusive plan.

WHERE TO DINE

EXPENSIVE

El Fogón

Avenida Antera Mota 23, Puerto Playa. ☎ **809/586-3418.** Reservations recommended. Appetizers $2–$5; main courses $10–$30. AE, DC, MC, V. Daily noon–midnight. INTERNATIONAL.

Perhaps the most distinguished restaurant in Puerto Plata is El Fogón which originally gained fame as De Armando. In this elegant setting, you can select an appetizer such as escargots bourguignons or perhaps lobster bisque. The kitchen serves excellent fresh fish dishes. For that Dominican flavor, there's more concho, rice, and black beans served with pork fritters. Desserts are freshly made, and a trio entertains at night.

MODERATE

Jardín de Jade

In the Villas Doradas Beach Resort, Playa Dorada. ☎ **809/586-3000.** Reservations recommended. Appetizers RD$25–RD$100 ($1.90–$7.70); main courses RD$100–RD$230 ($7.70–$17.70). AE, DC, MC, V. Dinner only, daily 6–11pm. CHINESE.

A high-ceilinged, airy, modern restaurant, the Jardín de Jade offers the finest Chinese food in the area. It's one of the best dining values at the resort. Typical menu items include barbecued Peking duck, sautéed diced chicken in chile sauce, and fried crab claws. The chefs specialize in Cantonese and Szechuan cuisine.

INEXPENSIVE

⑤ Porto Fino

Avenida Las Hermanas Mirabal. ☎ **809/586-2858.** Reservations not required. Appetizers RD$15–RD$35 ($1.20–$2.70); main courses RD$50–RD$175 ($3.90–$13.50). AE, MC, V. Daily 11am–11pm. ITALIAN.

In this popular Italian restaurant just across from the entrance of the Hotel Montemar in Puerto Plata, parmesan breast of chicken, eggplant parmesan, ravioli, and pizzas are served in generous helpings. You'll get off cheap if you order only pizza. Locals and visitors mingle freely here.

⑤ Roma II

Calle Beiler at Emilio Prud'homme. ☎ **809/586-3904.** Reservations not required. Appetizers RD$35–RD$125 ($2.70–$9.60); main courses RD$100–RD$250 ($7.70–$19.30). AE, MC, V. Daily 11am–midnight. INTERNATIONAL.

This air-conditioned restaurant in the center of town is staffed by an engaging crew of well-mannered young employees who work hard to converse in English. You can order from a selection of 13 varieties of pizza, topped with tempting combinations of cheese, shrimp, and garlic. Seafood dishes include paella, seafood casserole, several preparations of lobster, sea bass, and octopus prepared Créole style or with vinaigrette; beef dishes include Stroganoff or tenderloin.

Valentino's

In the Dorado Naco Resort Hotel, Playa Dorada. ☎ **809/320-2019.** Reservations required. Appetizers RD$35–RD$85 ($2.70–$6.50); main courses RD$85–RD$225 ($6.50–$17.30). AE, DC, MC, V. Daily noon–1am. ITALIAN.

The specialties of this ristorante and pizzeria east of the airport are homemade pasta, such as lasagne verdi al forno, and brick-oven pizza. Against an elegant backdrop, with fountains and pink marble, it serves a savory cuisine. Have a drink on the terrace, perhaps the bartender's special called a Bloody Mary antipasto; then follow with one of the main dishes, such as risotto primavera with grilled chicken Venetian style.

WHAT TO SEE & DO

Fort San Felipe, considered the oldest fort in the New World, is a popular attraction. Philip II of Spain ordered its construction in 1564, a task that took 33 years to complete. Built with 8-foot-thick walls, the fort was virtually impenetrable, and the moat surrounding it was treacherous. The Spaniards sharpened swords and embedded them in coral below the surface of the water to discourage use of the moat for entrance or exit purposes. The doors of the fort are only 4 feet high, another deterrent to swift passage. During Trujillo's rule, Fort San Felipe was used as a prison. Standing at the end of the Malecón, the fort was restored in the early

1970s. Admission is RD$10 (80¢). It's open Friday through Wednesday from 9am to noon and 3 to 5pm.

Isabel de Torres, a tower with a fort built when Trujillo was in power, affords a panoramic view of the Amber Coast from a point near the top, 2,595 feet above sea level. You reach the observation point by cable car (*teleférico*), a seven-minute ascent. Once there, you are also treated to 7 acres of botanical gardens. The round-trip costs RD$20 ($1.50). The aerial ride is operated on Tuesday and Thursday though Sunday from 8am to 5pm. Be warned that there's often a long wait in line for the cable car, and at certain times it's likely to be closed for repairs, so check at your hotel before going there.

You can see a collection of rare amber specimens at the **Museum of Dominican Amber,** calle Duarte 61 (☎ **809/586-2848**). The museum, open Monday through Saturday from 9am to 5pm, is near Puerto Plata's Central Park. Guided tours in English are offered. Admission is RD$15 ($1.20).

The neoclassical house sheltering the Amber Museum also contains the densest collection of boutiques in Puerto Plata. Merchandise is literally packed into seven competing establishments. A generous percentage of the paintings is from neighboring Haiti, but the amber, larimar, and mahogany wood carvings are from the Dominican Republic. On the premises is a patio bar.

SPORTS & OUTDOOR ACTIVITIES

The north coast is a water-sports scene, although the sea here tends to be rough. Snorkeling is popular, and the windsurfing is among the best in the Caribbean. The resort of **Cabarete,** east of Puerto Plata, hosts an annual windsurfing tournament.

BEACHES   You'll find superb beaches to the east and west of Puerto Plata. Among the better known are Playa Dorada, Sosúa, Long Beach, Cofresi, Jack Tar, and Cabarete.

GOLF   Robert Trent Jones, Jr., designed the par-72, 18-hole **Playa Dorada championship golf course** (☎ **809/320-4340**), which surrounds the resorts and runs along the coast. Even nongolfers can stop at the clubhouse for a drink or a snack to enjoy the views. It's best to make arrangements at the activities desk of your hotel. Greens fees are RD$400 ($30.80) for 18 holes.

TENNIS   Nearly all the major resort hotels have tennis courts. If yours doesn't, there are seven all-weather tennis courts at the **Caribbean Village Club on the Green** (see the previous recommendation), although guests at the resort come first, of course.

SHOPPING

Unless otherwise cited, shops are open Monday through Saturday from 9am to 6pm.

Centro Artesanal
Calle J. F. Kennedy 3. ☎ **809/586-3724.**

This is a nonprofit school for the training of future Dominican craftspeople, and it's also a promotion center for local crafts and jewelry. Selected student projects are for sale. Open Monday through Friday from 8am to noon and 2 to 5pm.

Harrison's
Plaza Isabel, Playa Dorada. ☎ **809/586-3933.**

This is the best-established jewelry store in the Dominican Republic, having begun as a single-store operation in 1980, launched by Robert Harrison. Today he not only has 15 stores across the island, but celebrities wearing his jewelry include Madonna, Keith Richards of the Rolling Stones, and actor Patrick Swayze. Harrison flew to Bangkok to launch Michael Jackson's 1993 world tour. The singer's ancient-coin pendant from Harrison's was mounted with the replica of a leopard and an emerald. The coin, an 8 *reale*, was retrieved from the shipwreck *Concepción*, which went down off the north coast of the Dominican Republic in 1620. The store offers the largest selection of platinum jewelry in the Caribbean. Harrison's is also found in the Playa Dorada Shopping Plaza in the Playa Dorado Hotel complex.

Plaza Isabela
Playa Dorada.

About 500 yards from the entrance to the Playa Dorada hotel complex, this collection of small specialty shops is constructed in the Victorian gingerbread style, but has a Spanish flair unique in the islands.

Plaza Turisol Complex
Plaza Turisol.

The largest shopping center on the north coast has a multicolored roof and about 80 different outlets. Each week, or so it seems, a new store opens. You may want to head here to get a sampling of the merchandise available in Puerto Plata before going to any specific recommendation. The plaza lies about five minutes from the centers of Puerto Plata and Playa Dorada, on the main road heading east.

PUERTO PLATA AFTER DARK
CASINOS

Jack Tar Village
Playa Dorada. ☎ **809/320-3800.**

Jack Tar joins the gaming flock with a casino and disco, along with a European-style restaurant. It's built in Spanish Mediterranean colonial style with a terra-cotta roof. Between bouts at the games tables, guests quench their thirst at one of five bars. No shorts or bathing suits are allowed in the casino. There is also an entertainment center that includes a 90-seat restaurant and a disco for 250 dancers. The casino is open daily from 4pm to 4am.

Playa Dorada Casino
In the Playa Dorada Hotel, Playa Dorada. ☎ **809/586-3988.**

The casino's entrance is flanked by columns and leads to an airy garden courtyard. Inside, mahogany gaming tables are reflected in the silver ceiling and ringed with mauve and pink walls. No shorts are permitted inside the premises after 7pm, and beach attire is never allowed. Open daily from 4pm to 4am.

Puerto Plata Beach Resort & Casino
Avenida Malecón. ☎ **809/586-4243.**

This was the first casino in Puerto Plata, and it's still one of the most charming, with high ceilings and tall French windows. Guests find craps tables, blackjack setups, roulette wheels, and two "big six" layouts. Gamblers can play in either pesos or U.S. dollars. Open daily from 4pm to 4am.

5   Sosúa

About 15 miles east of Puerto Plata is one of the finest beaches in the Dominican Republic, Sosúa Beach, a strip of white sand more than half a mile wide in a cove sheltered by coral cliffs. The beach connects two communities, which together make up the town known as Sosúa. But, regrettably, you may not be allowed to enjoy a day on the beach in peace, as vendors, and often beggars, frequently annoy visitors.

At one end of the beach is **El Batey,** an area with residential streets, gardens, restaurants, shops, and hotels that can be visited by those who can tear themselves away from the beach. Real-estate transactions have been booming in El Batey and its environs, where many streets have been paved and villas constructed.

At the other end of Sosúa Beach lies **Los Charamicos,** a sharp contrast to El Batey. Here you'll find tin-roofed shacks, vegetable stands, chickens scrabbling in the rubbish, and warm, friendly people. This community is a typical Latin American village, recognizable through the smells, sights, and sounds in the narrow, rambling streets.

Sosúa was founded in 1940 by European Jews seeking refuge from Hitler, when Trujillo invited 100,000 of them to settle in his country on a banana plantation. Actually, only 600 or so Jews were allowed to immigrate, and of those, only about a dozen or so remained. However, there are some 20 Jewish families living in Sosúa today, and for the most part they are engaged in the dairy and smoked-meat industry the refugees began during the war. There is a local one-room synagogue, where biweekly services are held. Many of the Jews intermarried with Dominicans, and the town has taken on an increasingly Spanish flavor; women of the town are often seen wearing both the Star of David and the Virgin de Altagracia. Nowadays many German expatriates are also found in the town.

GETTING THERE   Taxis, charter buses, and públicos from Puerto Plata and Playa Dorada let passengers off at the stairs leading down from the highway to Sosúa beach. Take the autopista east for about 30 minutes from Puerto Playa. If you venture off the main highway, anticipate potholes that fall all the way to China.

WHERE TO STAY

Ⓢ Hotel Sosúa

Calle Dr. Alejo Martínez, El Batey, Sosúa, Dominican Republic. ☎ **809/571-2683.** Fax 809/571-2180. 40 rms. A/C TEL. Winter, $30 single; $40 double. Off-season, $25 single; $35 double. (Rates include continental breakfast.) AE, MC, V. Free parking.

Although this has been one of the best and most likely choices for cost-conscious accommodations in Sosúa for at least a decade, it was made even better in 1994 after the owners completely renovated the interior. It lies within a suburban community about a two-minute drive from the center of town. Its simple and attractive layout includes a reception area designed to conceal a flagstone-rimmed pool from the street. The bedrooms are strung along a wing extending beside the pool, and contain simple furniture ceiling fans, a minifridge, and an occasional balcony. On the premises is a restaurant (La Tortuga, recommended separately), a mini-gym, a bar, and a boutique.

Hotel Yaroa

El Batey, Sosúa, Dominican Republic. ☎ **809/571-2651.** Fax 809/571-3814. 24 rms. A/C. Winter, $50 single or double. Off-season, $28 single or double. Breakfast $5 extra. AE, MC, V. Free parking.

The Yaroa is named after a long-ago native village. Opened in 1986, it encompasses views of dozens of leafy trees that ring its foundations. Inside you'll find an atrium illuminated by a skylight, lots of exposed wood and stone, and a well-designed garden ringing a sheltered swimming pool. Each bedroom has a Spanish-style mirador (sheltered balcony) with a planter filled with local ferns, pine louvers for privacy, terra-cotta floors, and lots of airy space. Two of the accommodations are designed like private cabañas at poolside. Breakfast, light lunches, and dinners featuring French cuisine are served in the dining room, Verena (see "Where to Dine," below).

Sand Castle Beach Resort

Puerto Chiquito, Sosúa, Dominican Republic. ☎ **809/571-2420,** or 800/446-5963 in the U.S. Fax 809/571-2000. 240 rms, 80 suites. A/C MINIBAR TV TEL. Winter, $85–$113 single or double; from $125 suite. Off-season, $65–$93 single or double; from $105 suite. MAP $35 per person extra. AE, MC, V. Free parking.

One of the most luxurious accommodations along the north shore opens onto views of the Atlantic and Puerto Chiquito Beach. The multilevel apartment-hotel was inaugurated in 1989. Created for an upmarket clientele as a "place to remember," it was constructed on a strip of land between the ocean and a saltwater pond. It offers two swimming pools and a Jacuzzi. The expensive decor includes stained glass, detailed mahogany work, and 10-foot-long full-length mirrors in every bath. Dining choices include the Sahara Gourmet (the best) and the Guarapo which is more informal, serving buffets. The hotel is known for the many facilities included as part of a stay here: horseback riding, windsurfing, snorkeling, tennis, bicycling, a daily program of entertainment, nightly shows, sailing, and entrance to the disco.

Sosúa by the Sea

Sosúa Beach, Sosúa (Apdo. Postal 361, Puerto Plata), Dominican Republic. ☎ **809/571-3222.** Fax 809/571-3020. 81 studios, 30 apartments. A/C MINIBAR TV TEL. Winter, $75–$85 studio for one or two; $125 apartment. Off-season, $50 studio for one, $60–$70 studio for two; $90 apartment. AE, MC, V. Free parking.

The blue-and-white main building here is softened with inviting wooden lattices. The pool area opens onto Sosúa Bay, and the resort stands on a coral cliff above the beach. From the open-air rooftop lounge you have a view of Mount Isabel de Torres. Accommodations lie along meandering paths through tropical gardens. Reached by elevator, the airy bedrooms are either studios or one-bedroom apartments, all with safes. A formal restaurant serves both Dominican specialties and an international cuisine, and you can have lunch at the poolside bar and grill. The hotel has many amenities, including a massage parlor and a beauty salon.

Villas Los Coralillos

Alejo Martínex, Sosúa (Apdo. Postal 851, Puerto Plata), Dominican Republic. ☎ **809/571-2645.** Fax 809/571-2095. 25 rms, 27 villas. A/C TEL. Winter, $50 single; $60 double; from $125 villa. Off-season, $30 single; $45 double; from $100 villa. (MAP rates.) AE, DC, MC, V. Free parking.

The well-furnished accommodations here lie in a series of terra-cotta–tiled Iberian villas cantilevered over a bougainvillea-draped hillside. The action centers around the pool and main restaurant overlooking Sosúa Bay. Guests can request one- or two-bedroom villas, and the views from some of the villas are among the most panoramic in Sosúa. Each standard unit has twin beds and a small veranda. Dining is at the hotel's El Coral Restaurant (see "Where to Dine," below). The hotel has added yet another restaurant, La Bahía, serving pizzas, and it's open daily from 8am to 3am. Los Coralillos is the only hotel in town with direct access to the main Sosúa beach; if you tire of the pool, you can stroll to the sea through century-old mahogany and almond trees.

WHERE TO DINE

El Coral

El Batey. ☎ **809/571-2645.** Reservations recommended. Appetizers RD$40–RD$100 ($3.10–$7.70); main courses RD$100–RD$300 ($7.70–$23.10). AE, DC, MC, V. Daily 7am–10:30pm. CARIBBEAN.

The best and arguably the most pleasant restaurant in town is El Coral, in a Spanish-style building roofed with red tiles and set at the bottom of the garden near the end of the Sosúa beach. It offers a spacious area with terra-cotta tiles, wooden accents, and stark-white walls opening onto a panoramic view of the ocean. If you look out over the rear garden from one of the flowered terraces or through one of the big windows, you see a pool midway down the hill leading to the ocean. There's a bar in a room adjoining the dining room. The specialties include conch or octopus Créole style, pork chops with pineapple, and shrimp with garlic.

Morua Mai

Pedro Clisante 5, El Batey. ☎ **809/571-2503.** Reservations not required. Appetizers RD$25–RD$90 ($1.90–$6.90); main courses RD$90–RD$285 ($6.90–$21.90). AE, MC, V. Daily 8am–midnight. CONTINENTAL/DOMINICAN.

The patio here, which faces a popular intersection in the center of town, is the closest thing to a European sidewalk café in town. Inside, where occasional live entertainment is an important attraction, is a high-ceilinged, double-decked, and stylish space filled with touches of neo-Victorian gingerbread, upholstered banquettes, and wicker furniture. Consider this place for a sun-washed drink or cup of afternoon tea in the side courtyard, where a cabaña bar serves drinks from beneath a palm-thatched roof. Pasta, pizzas, and sandwiches, along with light meals, are served at lunch. Full dinners include such dishes as charcoal-grilled lobster, seafood platters, and lots of locally caught fish. An excellent paella is filled with lobster and shrimp, and one of the most popular dishes is surf and turf. All meats and seafood are specially selected by the owner for freshness.

Sunset Place Restaurant

At Sosúa by the Sea, Sosúa. ☎ **809/571-3222.** Reservations not required. Appetizers RD$25–RD$55 ($1.90–$4.20); main courses RD$120–RD$250 ($9.20–$19.30). AE, MC, V. Breakfast daily 7:30–11am; lunch daily 11am–4pm; dinner daily 6:30–10:30pm. INTERNATIONAL/DOMINICAN.

Rooftop gourmet dining is a feature of this previously recommended hotel with a continental chef. Open to nonresidents, the restaurant serves soups, salads, and both hot and cold dishes at lunch, although it is at dinner that the chef's particular talents are realized more fully. After watching the sun go down, follow that act with a selection of appetizers that might include soup, pâté of the house, or perhaps vol-au-vent seafood pastry shell or a Caesar salad. Main dishes usually feature grilled lobster or perhaps tuna fish with bacon and mushrooms. You might also try the pepper steak, spaghetti carbonara, or chicken with pineapple. A selection of freshly made pastries is featured, and you can also order such continental favorites as crêpes Suzette or sabayon.

La Tortuga

In the Hotel Sosúa, calle Dr. Alejo Martinez, El Batey, Sosúa. ☎ **809/571-2683.** Reservations not required. Appetizers RD$20–RD$160 ($1.50–$12.30); main courses RD$70–RD$160 ($5.40–$12.30). AE, MC, V. Lunch daily noon–2pm; dinner daily 7:30–11pm. DOMINICAN/ITALIAN.

Always known as a pleasant eatery, the restaurant in the Hotel Sosúa benefitted from a radical upgrade in 1994. The result is La Tortuga (The Tortoise), whose dining room overlooks a swimming pool and a small but pleasant garden. Set within a residential neighborhood a short walk from the resort's center, it serves a medley of inexpensive Italian wines that go well with such dishes as tortellino, spaghetti (with either meat or shellfish sauce), paella (for two diners only), and veal parmigiana. Main courses include four different preparations of chicken and beef.

Ⓢ Restaurant Verena

In the Hotel Yaroa, El Batey. ☎ **809/571-2651.** Reservations recommended. Appetizers RD$25–RD$80 ($1.90–$6.20); main courses RD$100–RD$210 ($7.70–$16.20). AE, MC, V. Daily 8am–11pm. DOMINICAN/INTERNATIONAL.

Verena has a good-quality menu, not overly large but select, with well-chosen ingredients and fine service. There's an emphasis on freshly prepared cuisine. You might try poached kingfish in a white-butter sauce, or filet steak with roquefort. For dessert, the crêpes Suzette are an experience.

9

The British Leeward Islands

A string of islands that form a crescent, the British Leewards consist of Antigua and Barbuda, Montserrat, the twin state of St. Kitts and Nevis, and little Anguilla. Of them all, Antigua, with its many beaches and resort hotels, is the best equipped for mass tourism and is a good base for going almost anywhere in the Caribbean. However, the opening of more hotels and the addition of modern tourist facilities are drawing thousands to Montserrat, Nevis, and to more remote Anguilla, which has become a chic address.

1 Antigua & Barbuda

Antigua boasts of a different beach for every day of the year, which is a bit of an exaggeration. Most of these beaches are protected by coral reefs, and the sand is often sugar-white. For most visitors, these beaches are reason enough to visit, but Antigua is also known for its sailing facilities centered at English Harbour. The principal "tourist zone" lies north of the capital of St. John in the northwest. Here you'll find some of the best hotels (but not *the* best) and an array of restaurants, beach bars, and water-sports facilities.

Antigua, Barbuda, and Redonda form the independent nation of Antigua and Barbuda, within the Commonwealth of Nations. (Redonda is an uninhabited rocky islet of less than a square mile located 20 miles southwest of Antigua. Sparsely populated Barbuda is covered at the end of this section.) Since its independence in 1981, this small state has had a British-style parliamentary government administered by a Cabinet of Ministers headed by a prime minister.

FAST FACTS: Antigua & Barbuda

Area Code   When calling from overseas, the telephone area code for Antigua and Barbuda is **809** (also, see "Telephone," below).

Banking Hours   Banks are usually open Monday through Thursday from 8am to 1pm and on Friday from 8am to 1pm and 3 to 5pm.

Currency   The **Eastern Caribbean dollar (EC$)** is used on these islands. However, nearly all hotels bill you in U.S. dollars, and only certain tiny restaurants present their prices in EC dollars. Make sure you know which dollars are referred to when you inquire about a price. The EC dollar is worth about 37¢ in U.S. currency

(EC$2.70 = $1 U.S.). Unless otherwise specified, rates quoted in this chapter are given in U.S. dollars.

Customs Arriving visitors are allowed to bring in 200 cigarettes and one quart of liquor, plus 6 ounces of perfume.

Documents A valid passport is preferred when U.S. and Canadian nationals are visiting the island. However, an original birth certificate accompanied by a photo identification is also acceptable. Citizens of the United Kingdom need a passport, and all visitors must be in possession of an onward-going ticket, usually air.

Electricity Most of the island's electricity is 220 volts A.C., 60 cycles. However, the Hodges Bay area and some hotels are supplied with 110 volts A.C., 60 cycles.

Embassy The **U.S. Embassy** is on Queen Elizabeth Highway, St. John's, Antigua, W.I. (☎ **809/462-3505**).

Emergencies In an emergency, contact the police (☎ **809/462-0125**), the fire department (☎ **462-0044**), or an ambulance (☎ **809/462-0251**).

Information Contact the **Antigua and Barbuda Department of Tourism,** 610 Fifth Ave., Suite 311, New York, NY 10020 (☎ **212/541-4117**); or 25 SE Second Ave., Suite 300, Miami, FL 33131 (☎ **305/381-6762**). In Canada, contact the **Antigua and Barbuda Department of Tourism & Trade,** 60 St. Clair Ave. E., Suite 304, Toronto, ON M4T 1N5 (☎ **416/961-3085**). In the United Kingdom, information is available at **Antigua House,** 15 Thayer St., London W1M 5LD (☎ **0171/486-7073**).

Language The official language is English.

Taxes and Service A departure tax of $10 U.S. is imposed, and a 7% government tax is added to all hotel bills. Most hotels also add a 10% service charge.

Telephone Each phone number on the islands begins with 46. Once you are here, omit the 809 area code but dial the full seven-digit number. A 24-hour-a-day telephone service links Antigua to all parts of the world.

Time Antigua is on Atlantic standard time year round, so it's one hour ahead of eastern standard time. When daylight saving time takes over in the States, then Antigua's time is the same as in the eastern United States.

Water Water generally is safe to drink here, but many visitors prefer the bottled variety.

Weather The average year-round temperature ranges from 75° to 85° Fahrenheit.

ANTIGUA

From a poverty-stricken sugar island, Antigua has risen to become a 20th-century vacation haven. American millionaires seeking British serenity under a tropical sun turned Antigua into a citadel of elegance around the exclusive Mill Reef Club, where you will be accepted only if recommended by a member. The island has now developed a broader base of tourism and attracts not just the rich, but also the middle- and even lower-income voyager.

Rolling, rustic Antigua (An-*tee*-gah) has as its highest point Boggy Peak, 1,360 feet above sea level. Stone towers, once sugar mills, dot the landscape; however, its inland scenery isn't as dramatic as on St. Kitts. But, oh, those beaches!

Discovered by Columbus on his second voyage in 1493, Antigua has a population of about 67,000 and an area of 108 square miles.

Independence has come, but Antigua is still British in many of its traditions. English planters settled Antigua in 1623. In 1666 the French occupied the island, but Antigua was ceded to England the following year by the Treaty of Breda.

The **summer carnival** takes place on the first Monday and Tuesday in August and the preceding week. Included in this festival are a beauty competition and calypso and steel-band competitions. Carnival envelops the streets in exotic costumes that recall the people's African heritage. The spring highlight is Antigua's annual **sailing week** in late April or May.

The capital is **St. John's,** a large, neatly laid-out town, 6 miles from the airport and less than a mile from Deep Water Harbour Terminal. The port is the focal point of commerce and industry, as well as the seat of government and visitor shopping. Trade winds keep the streets fairly cool, as they were built wide just for that purpose. Protected in the throat of a narrow bay, the port city consists of cobblestone sidewalks, weather-beaten wooden houses, corrugated iron roofs, and louvered Caribbean verandas.

ORIENTATION
Getting There

The major airline flying to Antigua's V. C. Bird Airport is **American Airlines** (☎ **800/433-7300** in the U.S.), which offers three daily nonstop flights to Antigua departing from San Juan, Puerto Rico; flight time is about 1 1/2 hours. Each of these flights departs late enough in the day to allow easy transfers from other flights. One of these flights from San Juan is the continuation of a nonstop flight from New York's JFK, a fact that allows passengers originating in New York to remain on the same aircraft during the flight's brief touchdown on Puerto Rico. Most vacations in Antigua will cost less if you book your air transport simultaneously with a hotel reservation; American's tour desk will provide these arrangements for you.

Passengers originating in England sometimes prefer to take advantage of the **British Airways** (☎ **800/247-9297** in the U.S.) four-times-per-week flights between London's Gatwick Airport and Antigua.

Air Canada (☎ **800/363-5440** in Canada, **800/776-3000** in the U.S.) offers regularly scheduled flights from Toronto on Wednesday and Sunday in winter.

BWIA (☎ **800/327-7401** in the U.S.) is an increasingly popular means of reaching Antigua. It offers twice-weekly nonstop service from Miami to Antigua, and service Wednesday through Monday from Kingston to Antigua. Two flights arrive weekly from London, and one flight weekly from Frankfurt, Germany. There are also several flights weekly from Toronto to Antigua.

Getting Around

BY TAXI Transportation isn't hard to find. Taxis meet every airplane, and drivers wait outside the major hotels. In fact, if you're going to be on Antigua for a few days, you may find that a particular driver has "adopted" you. The typical one-way fare from the airport to St. John's is $12, but to English Harbour it's $25 and up. The government of Antigua fixes the rates, and the taxis have no meters.

While it's costly, the best way to see Antigua is by private taxi as the drivers are also guides. Most taxi tours cost $40 for one to four passengers.

Antigua

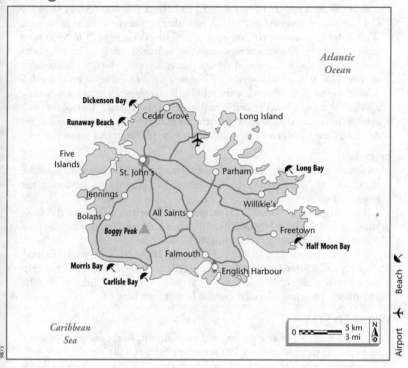

Atlantic Ocean

Dickenson Bay

Runaway Beach

Cedar Grove

Long Island

Five Islands

St. John's

Parham

Long Bay

Jennings

All Saints

Willikie's

Bolans

Boggy Peak

Freetown

Half Moon Bay

Morris Bay

Falmouth

Carlisle Bay

English Harbour

Caribbean Sea

0   5 km   3 mi

N

Beach

Airport

BY BUS   Buses are not recommended for the average visitor, although they do exist and are cheap. Service seems erratic and undependable along impossibly bumpy roads. Officially, buses operate between St. John's and the villages daily from 5:30am to 6pm, but don't count on it. In St. John's, buses leave from the West Bus Station for Falmouth and English Harbour, and from the East Bus Station to other parts of the island. Most fares are $1.

BY RENTAL CAR   Newly arrived drivers quickly (and ruefully) learn that the island's roads are among the worst, most potholed, and most badly marked in the Caribbean. Many visitors will prefer to hire one of the island's taxis whenever they want to go somewhere. (Hotels and restaurants on the island summon taxis for patrons.) Considering the need to *drive on the left* (a holdover from the British tradition), and the temptation to have one piña colada too many, renting a car on Antigua is usually not worth it.

If you insist on driving, you must obtain an Antiguan driver's license, which costs $12. To obtain one, you must produce a valid driver's license from home. Most car-rental firms are authorized to issue you an Antiguan license, which they usually do without a surcharge.

Several different car-rental agencies operate on Antigua, although they are sometimes precariously financed local operations with cars best described as "battered." The best of them are affiliated with major car-rental companies in the United States.

Avis (☎ **800/331-2112** in the U.S.) and **Hertz** (☎ **800/654-3131** in the U.S.) are both represented on Antigua, each offering pickup service at the airport. With a two-day advance reservation, the companies charge $270 to $300 for a week's rental of their cheapest cars, including unlimited mileage. The companies charge $10 per day for a collision-damage waiver; however, you'll still be liable for the first $1,000 worth of damage. (Without it you'll be liable for up to the full value of any accidental damage to the vehicle.) Both companies require a minimum age of 21 (if a major credit or charge card is presented at pickup). Each of the companies offers occasional discounts to members of certain organizations, such as the AAA. All these factors and prices could change, so phone around before you go.

Essentials

Antigua is generally safe, but that doesn't mean you should go wandering alone at night on the practically deserted streets of St. John's. Don't leave valuables unguarded on the beach.

The **Antigua and Barbuda Department of Tourism,** at Thames and Long Streets in St. John's (☎ **809/462-0480**), is open Monday through Thursday from 8:30am to 4:30pm and on Friday from 8:30am to 3pm.

The principal medical facility is **Holberton Hospital,** on Queen Elizabeth Highway (☎ **809/462-0251**). **Telephone calls** can be made from hotels or from the office of Cable & Wireless, 42–44 St. Mary's St., in St. John's (☎ **809/462-0840**). Faxes and telegrams can also be sent from here.

WHERE TO STAY

Antigua's hotels are among the best and most plentiful in the eastern Caribbean, and generally they are small—a 100-room hotel is rare on the island. Check summer closings, which often depend on the caprice of the owners, who may decide to shut down if business isn't good. Incidentally, air conditioning, except in first-class hotels, isn't as common as some visitors think it should be. Chances are, your hotel will be on a beach. You can also rent an apartment or cottage if you want to cook for yourself.

Reminder: A 7% government tax and 10% service charge are added to your hotel bill, which makes quite a difference in your final tab.

Very Expensive

✪ Curtain Bluff

Old Road (P.O. Box 288, St. John's), Antigua, W.I. ☎ **809/462-8400,** or 212/289-8888 in New York. Fax 809/462-8409. 51 rms, 12 suites. Dec 19–Apr 14, $495–$675 single; $595–$775 double; $855–$1,550 suite for two. Apr 15–May 14 and Oct 12–Dec 18, $395–$575 single; $495–$675 double; $755–$1,350 suite for two. (Rates include all meals.) AE. Free parking. Closed May 15–Oct 11.

Opened in 1961, this oasis of serenity and comfort is the home of Sailing Week and is one of the island's premier resorts. It lies on the southwest shore 15 miles from the airport, in the village of Old Road, in the most tropical-looking section of the resort-studded island. Once a pilot for Texaco, founder Howard W. Hulford discovered his Shangri-La back in the 1950s while flying over it.

In a setting like a subtropical forest, the resort offers beautifully furnished accommodations, including superior units with king-size beds, deluxe rooms with king-size beds, a terrace room with a king-size four-poster bed, plus suites. Ceiling fans and trade winds keep the rooms cool, and individual terraces open onto the water. Thoughtful amenities include wall safes, marble or tile floors, terry-cloth robes, bidets, tubs and showers, and fresh flowers daily (there's a plant nursery on the grounds). Rates include all meals (superb ones, at that), wine by the glass, soft drinks, tennis, water sports, laundry, and postage.

Dining/Entertainment: One reason guests check in here is for the food. Swiss-born Ruedi Portmann keeps his continental menu limited, so that all the food will be freshly prepared and artistically arranged. Curtain Bluff boasts the most extensive wine selection in the Caribbean, including all major red bordeaux. After dinner, guests can dance under the stars to a live band. Men are requested to wear slacks and collared shirts after 7pm. Once a week the resort hires a steel band to entertain guests down at the beach with a buffet. Dinner on Sunday night is served at the Beach Club and features some Antiguan recipes. Local entertainers are featured on Sunday night.

Services: Room service (8am to 9pm), babysitting.

Facilities: Sailing, waterskiing, skin diving, scuba diving (for certified divers only), tennis (four championship courts plus a pro shop and a full-time pro), squash, exercise room, aerobics classes—all at no extra charge.

Galley Bay

Five Islands (P.O. Box 305, St. John's), Antigua, W.I. ☎ **809/462-0302**, or 800/424-5550. Fax 809/462-4551. 30 rms. Winter, Gauguin cottages, $340 single, $445 double, $625 triple; deluxe beachfront rooms, $380 single, $485 double, $665 triple; executive rooms, $420 single, $525 double; $705 triple. Off-season, Gauguin cottages, $205 single; $340 double; $485 triple; beachfront rooms, $265 single; $380 double; $525 triple; executive rooms, $315 single; $420 double; $565 triple. (Includes all meals, drinks, service, and tax.) AE, DC, MC, V. Free parking. Directions: Leave St. John's on the harbor road south, pass through Five Islands Village, and turn right onto Galley Bay Road; it's a distance of 5 miles.

A retreat set on 40 acres of grounds, along half a mile of palm-fringed beach, Galley Bay offers a variety of accommodations. Gauguin Village, with 12 units, is 150 feet off the beach and built around a salt pond in a coconut grove. Each of its units consists of two grass-roofed cottages—one the bedroom and the other the bath and dressing room. Directly on the beach are the other units, built in a more conventional style, and, as advertised, "only four seconds from bed to sea." Galley Bay operates on an all-inclusive rate covering meals, drinks, and most sports.

Dining/Entertainment: There's a beachside bar, and the restaurant specializes in West Indian cuisine made with fresh local produce, including seafood.

Services: Laundry, babysitting.

Facilities: Water sports (such as windsurfing, snorkeling, and Sunfish sailing), tennis.

Jumby Bay

Long Island (P.O. Box 243, St. John's), Antigua, W.I. ☎ **809/462-6000**, or 800/421-9016 in the U.S. Fax 809/462-6020. 38 suites, 12 two- or three-bedroom villas. Winter, $875 junior suite for one; $975 junior suite for two. Off-season, $675 junior suite for one, $775 junior suite for two. Year round, $1,195–$1,525 villa. (Rates include all meals, with a selection of house wines, unlimited drinks, a weekly sunset champagne cruise, use of sporting equipment and facilities, snorkeling, tennis, sailing, bicycles, airport transfers, and mailing service.) AE, MC, V. Transportation: Taxi to "Beachcomber Dock" on the northeast coast of Antigua (northeast of the airport); then board the hotel's private launch to Jumby Bay Island.

This exclusive little island resort, which opened in 1982 on 300 acres off the eastern coast of Antigua, is reached after a 12-minute launch ride. Boats depart from the Antiguan "mainland" every hour between 10am to 10pm. On the Antiguan side, there's a facility for preregistration. The site was selected for its white sandy beaches along a coastline protected by coral reefs. The grounds have been handsomely landscaped with loblolly and white cedar trees. It's the site of the former private home of a sugarcane plantation owner.

Guests are housed in deluxe resort suites, each with an oversize master bedroom. All have private terraces, and most feature private shower courtyards and ocean views. These resort suites are found in a 14-unit Spanish-style villa, 12 rondavels, and 12 cottages. These breezy accommodations are open to the tradewinds. There are also 12 luxury villas, either two or three bedrooms.

As an ecological sideline, the Jumby Bay is engaged in an ongoing project to protect the endangered hawksbill sea turtle. Guests who are interested are encouraged to participate in the program by joining nightly patrols to tag, measure, and photograph the turtles.

Dining/Entertainment: A gourmet cuisine is artfully presented by a master chef. Dinner is served at the Estate House, a 230-year-old plantation manor that's the property's centerpiece. A jazz ensemble performs on Saturday evening, and on Wednesday night a bountiful buffet is presented on the main beach. Guests eat while enjoying the rhythms of a calypso band. Breakfast and lunch are served al fresco at the Beach Pavilion.

Service: Room service (7 to 10am), laundry.

Facilities: Snorkeling, scuba, tennis courts, fishing, sailing, waterskiing, nature trails, bicycling, croquet courts, putting green.

Pineapple Beach Club

Long Bay, St. John's, Antigua, W.I. ☎ **809/463-2452,** or 800/345-0356. Fax 809/463-2452. 131 rms. A/C. Winter, $330–$400 single; $390–$460 double; $530–$570 quad. Off-season, $260–$330 single; $320–$390 double; $460–$500 quad. (Rates all-inclusive.) AE, MC, V. Free parking.

This resort prides itself on offering a low-cost alternative to larger, more anonymous all-inclusive resorts that have recently appeared throughout the Caribbean. It's a low-slung colony of two-story, red-roofed buildings built on 25 acres of sandy, palm-dotted flatlands beside the beach. About 90% of the clientele arrives as members of couples, sometimes with children, although very young children (under six) are not admitted. Included in the rates are all meals, drinks, water sports, and access to the evening's live entertainment.

Standard and garden-view rooms don't include any sea view at all; waterside and beachfront rooms feature views (and sometimes direct access) to the beach. Each accommodation has either a balcony or a terrace, big windows, and simple (often rattan) furniture. The local entrepreneurs who own this resort pride themselves on their lack of electronic amenities (rooms are air-conditioned but do not include TV or phone), and their firm commitment to closing down the resort's main bar and stopping the in-house entertainment just before midnight. (If you're committed to all-night partying, this is probably not the place for you; otherwise, you might appreciate the opportunity of going to bed relatively early.)

Facilities: Freshwater swimming pool, four tennis courts, nightly entertainment, water-sports facilities, fitness center, in-house shopping boutique, an electronic casino (slot machines only), and a hilltop eyrie (the Outhouse) that operates as a bar and snack restaurant.

✪ St. James's Club

Mamora Bay (P.O. Box 63, St. John's), Antigua, W.I. ☎ **809/460-5000,** 212/486-2575 in New York City, or 800/274-0008 in the U.S. Fax 809/460-3015. 85 rms, 20 suites, 73 two-bedroom villas. A/C TV TEL. Winter, $340–$790 single or double; $540–$590 suite;

$690–$790 villa. Off-season, $210–$610 single or double; $360–$410 suite; $510–$610 villa. Additional person $20 per day extra. MAP $65 per person extra. AE, DC, MC, V. Free parking. Closed June–Sept. Transportation: Taxi.

The St. James's Club, a luxurious resort on Mamora Bay, offers elegant ocean-view rooms and suites complete with radios. Pricey villas and hillside homes are also rented. The resort's leisure facilities are among the best in the Caribbean.

Dining/Entertainment: The best of local and international dishes, freshly caught seafood, salads, barbecue grills, and tropical fruit are accompanied by cool white wine or dark rum cocktails. You can relax in elegant surroundings in the Rainbow Garden Restaurant or eat al fresco by candlelight at the Docksider Café overlooking Mamora Bay, enjoying lobster, barbecued chicken, or ribs. Pisces is a hillside restaurant featuring a continental cuisine with views of the sunset over the bay. Lunch at the poolside Reef Deck is a social occasion and offers salads, burgers, and local delicacies. The Jacaranda nightclub will top off an evening for more active guests. Many enjoy gambling in the high-ceilinged but small European-style casino, whose walls are covered in a combination of Italian art deco columns and vertical stripes.

Services: Room service, laundry, babysitting.

Facilities: Water sports, including sailboats (Sunfish and Hobie cats), sailboards, aqua bikes, deep-sea fishing, waterskiing, snorkeling, scuba diving (with a scuba certification school offering American and European certification); seven hard tennis courts (two lit for night play), with a center court for tournaments; stables with Texas quarterhorses and hillside trails; complete Universal-equipped gymnasium; Jacuzzi; massage facility; beauty salon; croquet court; three swimming pools; two beaches; a playground and playhouse for children.

Expensive

Blue Waters

Soldier Bay (P.O. Box 256, St. John's), Antigua, W.I. ☎ **809/462-0292,** or 800/491-2121 in the U.S. Fax 809/462-0293. 46 rms, 8 villas. A/C MINIBAR TEL. Winter, $205–$255 single; $245–$295 double; from $380 villa. Off-season, $125–$150 single; $147–$185 double; from $240 villa. MAP $47 per person extra. AE, DC, MC, V. Free parking.

Blue Waters curves around a private sandy beach where you can lie in a hammock as a waiter serves you a rum punch. It's 4 miles (about a 15-minute drive) from St. John's, a 13-minute taxi ride south of the airport. All rooms, housed in rather plain buildings, are beachfront, surrounded by coconut palms on the extensive grounds. Eight two- and three-bedroom villas were added in 1986.

Dining/Entertainment: The hotel's premier dining room is the Cacubi Room, cooled by ceiling fans, where you may want to dine even if you're not a guest at Blue Waters. The restaurant is known for its well-prepared continental dishes, which are topped by dessert flambéed at your table. Reservations are requested. The Sunday brunch at poolside is popular and includes entertainment by a steel band. There are also outdoor buffets and barbecues.

Services: Shuttle service to St. John's ($5), laundry, babysitting, breakfast room service.

Facilities: Water sports, tennis, sailing, fishing, small beach (only so-so for swimming).

✪ The Copper and Lumber Store

Nelson's Dockyard, English Harbour (P.O. Box 184, St. John's), Antigua, W.I. ☎ **809/ 460-1058.** Fax 809/460-1529. 3 rms, 11 suites. Winter, $160–$180 single; $195–$275 double; $215–$325 suite. Off-season, $80–$90 single; $85–$145 double; $215–$325 suite.

Family-Friendly Accommodations

St. James's Club   *(see p. 282)* There are activity programs for children lasting one to three hours daily. Afternoon donkey rides are sponsored three times a week for all walking, toilet-trained kids. A children's playhouse and playground are also available.

Falmouth Harbour Beach Apartments   *(see p. 287)* Near the famous English Harbour, this outlet rents 28 double studio apartments, each with a complete kitchen. Children under 16 sharing an apartment with their parents are charged $15. The beach is sheltered, making it suitable for kids.

Jack Tar Village St. Kitts Beach Resort & Casino   *(see p. 317)* Kids get greatly reduced discounts when staying in a room with two parents, and an array of activities is geared directly to them.

Four Seasons Resort Nevis   *(see p. 336)* Complimentary accommodations for children (maximum of two) staying in the same room as a parent or guardian, as well as enrollment in the Kids for All Seasons youth program. There's a supervised children's hour at 6pm daily in the Grill Room.

Continental breakfast $5 extra. AE, MC, V. Free parking. Directions: From St. John's, follow the signs southeast to English Harbour.

This 18th-century building was originally occupied by purveyors of wood and sheet copper for building and repairing the British sailing ships that plied the waters of the Caribbean. The store and its adjacent harbor structures were built of brick brought from England in the holds of ships as ballast. These bricks imbue the building with 18th-century English charm and sometimes serve to conceal its necessary modern amenities.

Each of the brick-lined period units has its own design and is filled with fine Chippendale and Queen Anne reproductions, antiques, brass chandeliers, hardwood paneling, and hand-stenciled floors. Even the showers look like cabinetry in a sailing vessel, lined with thick paneled slabs of mahogany accented with polished brass fittings. All suites have kitchens, private baths (with showers only), and ceiling fans.

Dining/Entertainment: A traditional English pub adjoins the hotel and offers food daily from 10:30am to 9:30pm. The Wardroom serves dinner nightly except Wednesday.

Services: Room service, laundry, babysitting.

Hawksbill Beach Resort

Five Islands (P.O. Box 108, St. John's), Antigua, W.I. ☎ **809/462-0301,** or 800/223-6510 in the U.S. Fax 809/462-1515. 99 units, 1 suite. Winter, $287 single; $300–$437 double; $325–$512 cottage; $1,650 suite for three to six. Off-season, $131 single; $168–$206 double; $173–$278 cottage; $797 suite for three to six. MAP $25 per person extra. (Rates include breakfast.) AE, MC, V. Free parking.

Taking its name from an offshore rock that locals say resembles a hawksbill turtle, this 37-acre resort has a former sugar mill, now turned into a boutique. The resort is 10 miles west of the airport and 4 miles southwest of St. John's. Set on four brown sandy beaches (one reserved for those who want to go home *sans* tan lines), it's a magnet for the sporting set, and also popular for weddings and honeymoons. The hotel revolves around an open-air, breezy central core and offers comfortably furnished although rather small bedrooms with ceiling fans and showers. The most expensive unit is the deluxe suite, while the least costly accommodations open onto a garden. Rooms are without phones, TV sets, or air conditioning. In the Great House is a three-bedroom suite suitable for three to six occupants.

Dining/Entertainment: There are two restaurants (one on the beach) and two bars. It's usually lively here if the crowd is right, with entertainment, such as limbo dancers and calypso singers, in season.

Services: Room service, laundry, babysitting.

Facilities: Swimming pool, tennis court, Sunfish sailing, windsurfing, snorkeling, waterskiing (for a nominal charge).

The Inn at English Harbour

English Harbour (P.O. Box 187, St. John's), Antigua, W.I. ☎ **809/460-1014.** Fax 809/460-1603. 28 rms. TEL. Winter, $190–$230 single; $250–$360 double or twin. Off-season, $90–$120 single; $120–$190 double or twin. MAP $50 per person extra. AE, MC, V. Free parking. Directions: From St. John's, head south, through All Saints and Liberta, until you reach the south coast.

In a corner of Freeman's Bay, this small hotel offers guests a choice of pleasantly furnished rooms either on the beach or in hillside cottages. Rooms are available as singles, doubles, or twins. Amenities include hairdryers, wall safes, direct-dial phones, and small refrigerators. The inn occupies one of the finest sites on Antigua, with views over Nelson's Dockyard and English Harbour from the terrace.

Dining/Entertainment: Have a before-dinner drink in the old-style English Bar, with its stone walls and low overhead beams. Lunch is served both at the beach house and in the main dining room. The inn is known for the quality of its cooking.

Services: Room service, laundry, babysitting.

Facilities: Complimentary water sports (including Sunfish sailing, windsurfing, snorkeling, and rowing), daytime water taxi to Nelson's Dockyard; tennis courts (lit) nearby; waterskiing and day sailing available at an extra cost. Deep-sea fishing, scuba diving, golf, and horseback riding can be arranged.

Long Bay Hotel

Long Bay (P.O. Box 442, St. Johns), Antigua, W.I. ☎ **809/463-2005,** or 800/225-4255 in the U.S. Fax 809/463-2439. 20 rms, 6 cottages. Winter, $270–$285 single MAP; $350–$375 double MAP; $220–$420 cottage for one or two (no meals). Off-season, $170–$185 single MAP; $250–$275 double MAP; $165–$395 cottage for one or two (no meals). AE, MC, V. Free parking.

Lying on a spit of land between the open sea and a sheltered lagoon, Long Bay is on the eastern shore 1 mile beyond the hamlet of Willikie's. It faces one of the best beaches on the island, as well as the waters of a reef-free lagoon that's considered safe for water sports. Owned and operated by the Lafaurie family since 1966, it's more an inn than a large-scale hotel. It features breeze-filled rooms as well as six furnished cottages for more reclusive guests.

Dining/Entertainment: The resort is centered around a hip-roofed clubhouse with the stone-walled Turtle Restaurant. The bar provides a relaxing environment. The hotel has a library and games room, plus a beach house restaurant and bar.

Services: Room service, laundry, babysitting, special dinner seating for children.

Facilities: Championship tennis court, complete scuba facilities, sailboats, windsurfers, snorkeling; golf nearby. Fishing can be arranged.

Rex Halcyon Cove

Dickenson Bay (P.O. Box 251, St. John's), Antigua, W.I. ☎ **809/462-0256.** Fax 809/462-0271. 194 rms, 17 suites. TEL. Winter, $180–$300 single or double; from $360 suite.

Off-season, $120–$240 single or double; from $300 suite. MAP $50 per person extra. AE, DC, MC, V. Free parking.

Halcyon Cove is 1^1/$_2$ miles west of the airport and 7 miles north of St. John's, about a 15-minute taxi ride. It's a favorite with the packaged-tour crowd, not only from the United States but from Europe. So many of your fellow guests will be staying here at discount rates, perhaps cheaper than you unless you, too, booked in on a "deal." Most of the bedrooms have a balcony or terrace; the majority of the units are set at beach level. Rooms range from garden rooms to superior rooms to poolside deluxe. The most expensive are called "oceanfront deluxe" and "ocean-front suites," the latter with color TV, mini-refrigerator, and a separate bedroom, living room, sitting area, and dressing area. Some of the units are air-conditioned.

Dining/Entertainment: The Arawak Terrace, the hotel's main dining room, is open for breakfast and dinner. You can also lunch or dine on the elongated Warri Pier, which stands on stilts 200 feet from the shore. There's also a beach barbecue for lunch. Frostie's Deli offers a coffee-shop menu.

Services: Room service (at breakfast), laundry, babysitting.

Facilities: Half-mile beach (often filled with aggressive vendors), water-sports program (including a freshwater swimming pool, snorkeling, windsurfing, pedal boats, waterskiing, volleyball, sailing, and scuba diving), four all-weather tennis courts (lit for night play).

Sandals Antigua

Dickenson Bay, St. John's, Antigua, W.I. ☎ **809/462-0267,** or 800/SCANDALS in the U.S. and Canada. Fax 809/462-4135. 219 rms, 32 junior suites, 17 rondaval suites, 12 honeymoon suites. A/C TV TEL. Winter, $1,760–$2,150 per person standard double; $2,275 per person junior suite; $2,435 per person rondaval suite; $2,550 per person honeymoon suite. Off-season, $1,660–$2,045 per person standard double; $2,160 per person junior suite; $2,315 per person rondaval suite; $2,425 per person honeymoon suite. (Rates all-inclusive seven-night stay.) AE, MC, V. Free parking.

This is one of the latest manifestations of the chain of resorts founded in Jamaica for male-female couples in love. The resort caters only to twosomes, and a large percentage of the clientele are honeymooners. Set on the island's northwestern coast, a 15-minute drive from St. John's, it occupies the site of an older hotel whose architectural configurations were altered for its new role. Most accommodations are in two-story motel-like units, many facing the beach. Most desirable are a series of 17 one-room rondavals, circular buildings containing only one accommodation. Each unit offers a balcony or patio, a king-size bed, hairdryer, and safety-deposit box.

Dining/Entertainment: There are three restaurants, devoted to international, Caribbean, and Asian food, respectively; four bars (including one swim-up bar in the pool and a beach bar); a disco bar, and an extroverted staff who actively encourage guests to participate in group activities.

Services: Organized tours to island attractions.

Facilities: Four pools, sandy beach, complete array of land and water sports (most included in the all-inclusive price), fitness center, saunas, four tennis courts, volleyball, four Jacuzzis.

Moderate

Admiral's Inn

English Harbour (P.O. Box 713, St. John's), Antigua, W.I. ☎ **809/460-1027,** or 800/ 223-5695 in the U.S. Fax 809/460-1534. 14 rms, 1 suite. Winter, $84–$96 single; $104–$128 double; $140–$152 suite. Off-season, $60–$68 single; $72–$86 double; $104–$110 suite.

MAP $44 per person extra. AE, MC, V. Free parking. Closed Sept to mid-Oct. Directions: Take the road southeast from St. John's, following the signs to English Harbour.

Designed in 1785, the year Nelson sailed into the harbor as captain of the HMS *Boreas*, and completed in 1788, the building once used to house dockyard services. Today it's one of the most atmospheric inns in Antigua. In the heart of Nelson's Dockyard, and loaded with West Indian charm, the hostelry is constructed of weathered brick brought from England as ships' ballast and has a terrace opening onto a centuries-old garden. The ground floor, with brick walls, giant ship beams, and island-made furniture, has a tavern atmosphere, with decorative copper, boat lanterns, old oil paintings, and wrought-iron chandeliers.

There are three types of character-filled accommodations. The highest tariffs are charged for some ground-floor rooms in a tiny brick building—on the site of a provisions warehouse for Nelson's troops—across the courtyard from the main structure. Each of these spacious rooms has a little patio and a garden entry as well as optional air conditioning. The same superior rate applies to front rooms on the first floor of the main building with views of the lawn and harbor. A medium rate applies to the back rooms on this floor, all of which have air conditioning. The lowest rate is for smaller chambers on the top floor, which may get warm during the day in summer but are quiet, with dormer-window views over the yacht-filled harbor. All rooms have twin beds and ceiling fans. The Joiner's Loft is an upstairs suite adjacent to the annex rooms of the inn, with a large living room looking out over the water, there are two bedrooms, two baths, and a full kitchen. Reservations are recommended.

Dining/Entertainment: For the inn's restaurant, see "Where to Dine," below. On Saturday night a steel band plays.

Services: Room service, laundry, babysitting, free transportation to two nearby beaches.

Facilities: Snorkeling equipment, Sunfish craft.

Ⓢ Falmouth Harbour Beach Apartments

English Harbour Village, Yacht Club Rd. (P.O. Box 713, St. John's), Antigua, W.I. ☎ **809/460-1094.** Fax 809/460-1534. 28 studios. Winter, $94–$98 studio for one; $118–$130 studio for two; $142–$154 studio for three. Off-season, $64–$68 studio for one; $82–$86 studio for two; $106–$110 studio for three. AE, MC, V. Free parking. Directions: Take the road southeast from St. John's and follow the signs to English Harbour.

This relatively simple place might be what you're looking for if you'd like to be near historic English Harbour. On, or just above, a small sandy beach, it offers an informal Antiguan atmosphere and rents twin-bedded studio apartments. Each unit has a ceiling fan, electric stove, refrigerator, oven, and terrace overlooking the water. A dozen studios are directly on the beach, while the others lie on a hillside just behind. You can dine at the nearby Admiral's Inn (see "Where to Dine," below). There are also other restaurants nearby, along with a supermarket, bank, post office, boutiques, and galleries, all within half a mile. Temo Sports, with tennis and squash facilities, is just next door, and there is a dive operation in the dockyard, with many sailing and fishing boat charters. Bus service runs daily to and from St. John's, so it's possible to be self-sufficient without having to go to the expense of renting a car.

Inexpensive

Ⓢ Barrymore Hotel

Old Fort Rd. (P.O. Box 1574, St. John's), Antigua, W.I. ☎ **809/462-1055.** Fax 809/462-4062. 36 rms. TV TEL. Winter, $70 single; $80 double; $90 triple. Off-season, $55 single; $65 double; $75 triple. Breakfast $7 extra. AE, MC, V. Free parking.

The Barrymore has its special niche on resort-crowded Antigua. It's a good bargain and offers a holiday in an unpretentious setting. A bungalow colony with a freshwater swimming pool, it stands on 3 acres of private grounds 1 mile north of St. John's and about a mile from the nearest beach. Rooms and efficiencies are in modern, white bungalows scattered about the grounds, bordered by flowering shrubbery. The bedrooms have motel-style modern appointments, along with patios; some are air-conditioned. A restaurant, Palms, on the premises, serves three meals a day, featuring French, English, American, and local Caribbean dishes. There's also a children's games room.

Lord Nelson Beach Hotel

Dutchman's Bay (P.O. Box 155, St. John's), Antigua, W.I. ☎ **809/462-3094.** Fax 809/462-0751. 16 rms. Winter, $80 single; $100 double. Off-season, $60 single; $70 double. Third person in room $20 in winter, $15 off-season. Breakfast $4–$10 extra. AE, MC, V. Free parking.Transportation: Taxi.

Originally built just before World War II on Antigua's northeast coast 5 miles east of St. John's as a single-story wood-sided beach club for American army officers, this establishment was acquired by the Fuller family in 1949. Today it's a more substantial concrete structure, with a dining room capped with timbers that were salvaged from warehouses destroyed during the hurricanes of 1950. Later a bar was added, using local stone and glass salvaged from an offshore lighthouse, as well as an annex containing two floors of simply furnished guest bedrooms. Today the place functions as a family-managed inn, set close to a white-sand beach and waters that are protected from ocean swells with a man-made reef.

Condos and Villas

Antigua Village

Dickenson Bay (P.O. Box 649, St. John's), Antigua, W.I. ☎ **809/462-2930,** or 800/223-1588 in the U.S. Fax 809/462-0375. 65 studies or apartments. A/C. Winter, $170–$275 studio or one-bedroom apartment; from $300 two-bedroom apartment. Off-season, $75–$160 studio or one-bedroom apartment; from $190 two-bedroom apartment. AE, MC, V. Free parking.

On a peninsula stretching out into turquoise waters, 2 miles north of St. John's, Antigua Village is more of a self-contained condominium community than a holiday resort. A freshwater pool and a minimarket are on the premises. You can use the neighboring tennis court, and there's an 18-hole golf course nearby, plus comprehensive water-sports facilities. The apartments all have kitchenettes, patios or balconies, twin beds, and sofa beds in the living rooms.

Siboney Beach Club

Dickenson Bay (P.O. Box 222, St. John's), Antigua, W.I. ☎ **809/462-0806,** or 800/533-0234 in the U.S. Fax 809/462-3356. 13 suites. Winter, $200–$270 suite for one; $230–$290 suite for two. Off-season, $110–$150 suite for one; $130–$170 suite for two. Additional person $30 extra for adults, $20 extra for children under 12. Tree house negotiable. AE, MC, V. Free parking.

Owned by Australia-born Tony Johnson and his wife, Ann, the Siboney Beach Club is named after the Amerindian tribe predating the Arawaks. Set north of St. John's, on a thickly foliated acre of beachfront fronting the mile-long white sandy beach of Dickenson Bay, it's shielded on the inland side by what may be the tallest and most verdant hedge on the island. The club's social center is the Coconut Grove restaurant (see "Where to Dine," below). The comfortable suites are in a three-story balconied building draped with bougainvillea and other vines. Suites have optional air conditioning, fans, and louvered windows for natural ventilation, and televisions are available. All units have separate bedrooms, living rooms, and balconies or patios, plus tiny kitchens behind moveable shutters. There's also a tree house—a single room with a king-size bed and jungle decor perched high in a *ficus Benjamina* tree.

WHERE TO DINE

In St. John's

Big Banana Holding Company

Redcliffe Quay. ☎ **809/462-2621.** Reservations not required. Main courses $6.50–$13. AE, DC, MC, V. Mon–Sat 8:30am–midnight, Sun 4–10pm. PIZZA.

Some of the best pizza in the eastern Caribbean is served in what used to be slave quarters, now amid the most stylish shopping and dining emporiums in town, a few steps from the Heritage Quay Jetty. With its ceiling fans and laid-back atmosphere, you almost expect Sydney Greenstreet to stop in for a drink (called "dwinks" on the menu). The frothy libations, coconut or banana crush, are practically desserts. In addition to the zesty pizza, you can order overstuffed baked potatoes, fresh-fruit salad, or conch salad. Beer costs $2.50.

Chez Pascal

4 Tanner St., at Cross St. ☎ **809/462-3232.** Reservations recommended. Appetizers $7.70–$11.60; main courses $22–$29. AE, DC, MC, V. Dinner only, 6:30–10pm. FRENCH.

This is the most stylish independent restaurant on Antigua. Owned and managed by French-born chef Pascal Milliat, its menus reflect the classical French cuisine of the chef's hometown of Lyon, the gastronomic center of France. Previously he was chef at one of the most exclusive resorts in the French Caribbean, La Samana, on St. Martin. The restaurant is in a low-slung, restored 150-year-old colonial house at the northern edge of St. John's. Its candlelit dining room is outfitted in tones of mauve, and its walled-in, vine-strewn garden provides additional seating.

   Dinners are intricate and might include a croissant of snails, a chicken-liver mousse, lobster thermidor, and scallops in a chablis sauce with steamed leeks, even chateaubriand with a béarnaise sauce. Dessert might be a classical tarte des demoiselles Tatin, an apple turnover once described as "cooked on the wrong side and served on the right side." The wine list is extensive.

⑤ Hemingway's

St. Mary's St. ☎ **809/462-2763.** Reservations not required. Appetizers $2.50–$6; main courses $8–$15. AE, MC, V. Mon–Sat 8:30am–11pm. WEST INDIAN/INTERNATIONAL.

Set on the second floor of a building in the heart of St. John's, and accented with intricate gingerbread painted in bright tropical colors, this is a charming and bustling café which attracts a crowd of shoppers and sightseers. It's very busy when a cruise ship docks. From its upper verandas, you can enjoy a sight of pedestrian traffic in the street below, and of the landing dock where tenders are unloaded from the cruise ships anchored offshore. Menu items include salads, sandwiches, burgers, sautéed filets of fish, pastries, ice creams, and an array of brightly colored tropical drinks.

Around the Island

⑤ Admiral's Inn

In Nelson's Dockyard, English Harbour. ☎ **809/460-1027.** Reservations recommended, especially for dinner in high season. Appetizers $2–$7; main courses $10.50–$25.

AE, MC, V. Breakfast daily 7:30–10am; lunch daily noon–2:30pm; dinner daily 7–9:30pm. Sept to mid-Oct. AMERICAN/CREOLE.

This historic building has already been recommended as a hotel (see "Where to Stay," above). In a 17th-century setting, lobster, seafood, and steaks are served. The favorite appetizer is pumpkin soup, which is followed by a choice of four or five main courses daily—perhaps local red snapper, grilled steak, or lobster. Before dinner, have a drink in the bar, where you can read the names of sailors carved in wood more than a century ago. The service is agreeable and the setting is heavy on atmosphere.

Coconut Grove

In the Siboney Beach Club, Dickenson Bay. ☎ **809/462-1538.** Reservations recommended, especially for dinner. Appetizers $5.50–$10.50; main courses $16–$28. AE, DC, MC, V. Lunch daily 11:30am–3pm; dinner daily 6:30–10pm. INTERNATIONAL/SEAFOOD.

Right on the beach are simple tables set on a flagstone floor beneath a thatch roof. North of St. John's, in a coconut grove (of course) and cooled by sea breezes, the restaurant is one of the best on the island. Each day a soup is prepared fresh from local ingredients. One appetizer is a seafood delight—scallops, shrimp, crab, lobster, and local fish with a mango-and-lime dressing. Lobster and shrimp dishes are strongly featured, and there's a catch of the day and a vegetarian specialty of the day. T-bone steak is regularly featured, as is Cajun chicken. Lighter fare is served at lunch.

Colombo's Restaurant

In the Galleon Beach Club, English Harbour. ☎ **809/463-1452.** Reservations recommended. Appetizers $6–$14; main courses $22–$32. AE, DC, MC, V. Lunch daily 12:30–2:30pm; dinner daily 7–10pm. Sept–Oct 5. ITALIAN.

Colombo's serves up Italian food—the best on the island—on a Polynesian-style open-air terrace sheltered by a ceiling crafted from woven palm fronds. It's only a few steps across the flat sands to the water. Lunches in this sprawling place might include spaghetti marinara, lobster salad, and sandwiches. Dinners are more elaborate and include daily specials from a classic Italian inventory of veal scaloppine, veal pizzaiola, and lobster mornay. These can be accompanied by a wide assortment of French or Italian wines. Live music, including reggae, rock 'n' roll, jazz, and calypso, is presented on Wednesday night when there is no cover charge, although a two-drink minimum is imposed.

✪ Jaws Restaurant/Barracuda Pub

Five Islands Village. ☎ **809/462-2428.** Reservations recommended. Appetizers $6–$12; main courses $16–$25; "shark" drinks from $5 each. AE, MC, V. Dinner only, daily 5:30–10pm. CARIBBEAN/INTERNATIONAL.

Set above one of the most spectacular panoramas on Antigua, on a hillside above the Royal Antiguan Hotel, this American-owned restaurant has received excellent recommendations from many readers. Barry Rubinson owns and operates this place, a pink stucco pavilion built in 1989 whose walls are open to the views of the coves and hills below. The pub area occupies one side of the area, and specializes in rum-based drinks with appropriate names like the killer shark, the happy shark, the sexy shark, and (for children) the nurse shark. Menu items in the nearby restaurant include lobster cocktails, chicken "Deep Bay" (stuffed with lobster and served with onions and mushrooms on a bed of spinach), chicken à l'orange banana (with fruit slices), avocados stuffed with shrimp salad, conch fritters, pumpkin or callaloo soup, and an array of fresh fish of the day including (what else?) filet of shark, and filets of snapper, grouper, wahoo, and kingfish, usually pan-fried with garlic butter.

◯ La Perruche

Midway between English Harbour and Falmouth Harbour. ☎ **809/460-3013.** Reservations recommended. Appetizers EC$12–EC$34 ($4.40–$12.60); main courses EC$42–EC$70 ($15.50–$25.90). AE, MC, V. Dinner only, Mon–Sat 5:30–10:30pm. CARIBBEAN/INTERNATIONAL.

Set in a sheltered patio whose edges are almost completely concealed by masses of potted palms and green and white trim, this is an al fresco, garden-style restaurant which has won respect throughout the island since its establishment by French-trained David Wallach and his partner, Swedish-born Mona Frisell. Menu items include avocado mousse with sweet-potato wafers, a filet of South American white-fish served with polenta and lobster bordelaise sauce, filet of tenderloin with cognac-cream sauce, red snapper with citrus and herbs, and an artful use of tropical fruits combined into visually elegant desserts.

◯ Le Bistro

Hodges Bay. ☎ **809/462-3881.** Reservations required, especially in high season. Appetizers EC$20–EC$35 ($7.40–$13); main courses EC$65–EC$75 ($24.10–$27.80). AE, MC, V. Dinner only, Tues–Sun 6:30–10:30pm. FRENCH.

This authentic bistro is one of the best on the island. Raffaele and Philippa Esposito run this little enclave of French cuisine on the north shore, 2 miles west of the airport on the road to Hodges Bay. Recognized for its superb fare by many international magazines, including *Gourmet,* it has a French chef, who named the maccheroni ziti Raffaele, made with cream, parmesan, and mushrooms, after one of the owners. Interesting appetizers include a panache of sea scallops in a mornay sauce with brandy and linguine alla caprese in a picón sauce with fresh basil and anchovies. One of the most successful main courses is a whole local snapper baked in white-wine sauce, black olives, and various herbs. Another good dish is a côté de boeuf, a double rib of beef carved at the table and served with a béarnaise or bordelaise sauce.

Pascal's

At the St. James's Club, Mamora Bay. ☎ **809/460-5000, ext. 571.** Reservations required. Appetizers $8–$13; main courses $22–$29. AE, DC, MC, V. Dinner only, Mon–Sat 6:30–10pm. FRENCH.

One of the best and most innovative restaurants along the south coast is Pascal's, which is operated by Florence and Pascal Milliat; they also run the successful Chez Pascal near St. John's (see above). Since 1985, at one location or another, Lyon-born Pascal has been pleasing some of the most exacting gastronomes to visit Antigua. Pascal's at this deluxe hotel opened in 1994, and both residents and non-residents can enjoy a refined French cuisine in a candlelit atmosphere. Try, for an appetizer, escargots Paçon Guérard, which is snails in a fresh tomato concasse. Many other classic French dishes appear regularly on the menu. The chef's specialty is a rack of lamb cooked in its own juice. There is also an extensive wine list.

Shirley Heights Lookout

Shirley Heights. ☎ **809/463-1785.** Reservations not required. Appetizers $5.25–$7.75; main courses $15.75–$27. AE, MC, V. Daily 9am–10pm. AMERICAN/SEAFOOD.

In the 1790s this was the lookout station for unfriendly ships heading toward English Harbour. To strengthen Britain's position in this strategic spot, Nelson ordered the construction of a powder magazine. Today the panoramic spot, directly east of English Harbour, is one of the most romantic on Antigua. Visitors some-times prefer to be served on the stone battlements below the restaurant, though I'd rather dine under the angled rafters of the upstairs restaurant, where large, old-fashioned windows surround the room on all sides.

Specialties include pumpkin soup, grilled lobster in lime butter, garlic-flavored shrimp, and good desserts, such as banana flambé and carrot cake. Less expensive hamburgers and sandwiches are available in the pub downstairs. A tradition with residents and visitors alike is Sunday at the Heights. The "end of the week" bar-becue that begins at 3pm features six hours of nonstop entertainment, with a steel-band concert from 3 to 6pm and a reggae band from 6 to 9pm. However, avoid it when cruise-ship passengers take over. It's best at lunch.

WHAT TO SEE & DO
St. John's

In the southern part of St. John's, the **market** is colorful and interesting, especially on Saturday morning. Vendors busy selling their fruits and vegetables bargain and gossip. The semi-open-air market lies at the lower end of Market Street.

Also in town, **St. John's Cathedral** (☎ 809/461-0082), the Anglican cathe-dral, between Long Street and Newgate Street at Church Lane, has had a disas-trous history. Originally built in 1683, it was replaced by a stone building in 1745. That, however, was destroyed by an earthquake in 1843. The present pitch-pine interior dates from 1847. The interior was being restored when, in 1973, the twin towers and structure were badly damaged by another earthquake. The towers and the southern section have been restored, but restoring the northern part is esti-mated to cost thousands of dollars, for which contributions are gratefully received. At the entrance, iron gates were erected by the vestry in 1789. The figures of St. John the Baptist and St. John the Divine, at the south gate, were said to have been taken from one of the Napoleonic ships and brought to Antigua by a Brit-ish man-of-war.

The **Museum of Antigua and Barbuda,** at Long and Market streets (☎ 809/462-1469), traces the history of the two-island nation—from geological birth to the present day. Housed in the old Court House building from 1750, exhibits in-clude a wattle-and-daub house model, African-Caribbean pottery, and utilitarian objects of daily life. It's open Monday through Thursday from 8:30am to 4:30pm, on Friday from 8:30am to 3pm, and on Saturday from 10am to 2pm. Admission is a $2 minimum donation.

The **Antigua and Barbuda Botanical Gardens,** at the corner of Nevis and Temple streets (☎ 809/462-1007), at St. John's, was established in 1893 in the Green Belt of St. John's. As you enter the gardens you are captured by the unfold-ing majesty of the 80-year-old ficus tree, contrasted by the rolling lawns. The me-lodic sounds of tree frogs and birds emanate from the hollow, filled with lianas draped from branches of trees in the rain forest. Tropical blossoms, herbal plants, ferns, dripping philodendrons, rare bromeliads, and a colorful carpet of flowers await the visitor. Open daily from 9am to 6pm. Admission is by a minimum donation of $2.

Around the Island

After leaving St. John's, most visitors head southeast for 11 miles to ✪ **Nelson's Dockyard National Park** (☎ 809/460-1053), one of the biggest attractions of the eastern Caribbean. The dockyard is the only existing example of a Georgian naval dockyard in the world today, and is the centerpiece of the national park. One of the safest landlocked harbors in the world, the restored dockyard was used by Admirals Nelson, Rodney, and Hood, and was the home of the British fleet at the time of the Napoleonic Wars. From 1784 Nelson was the commander of the British navy in the Leeward Islands, and he made his headquarters at English Harbour. English ships used the harbor as early as 1671, finding it a refuge from hurricanes. The era of privateers, pirates, and great sea battles in the 18th century revolved around the dockyard.

Restored by the Friends of English Harbour, the dockyard is sometimes known as a Caribbean Williamsburg. Its colonial naval buildings stand now as they did when Nelson was here (1784–87). However, Nelson never lived at Admiral House—it was built in 1855. The house has been turned into a museum of nautical memorabilia. (For accommodations at English Harbour, see "Where to Stay," above.)

The park itself is worth exploring, filled with sandy beaches and much tropical vegetation, including various species of cactus along with mangroves. The latter provides shelter for a migrating colony of African cattle egrets. The park is further enhanced by archeological sites dating well before the time of Christ. Nature trails have been cut through the park to expose the vegetation and coastal scenery. Tours of the dockyard are given, lasting 15 to 20 minutes, and tours along nature trails can last anywhere from 30 minutes to five hours. Boat cruises, lasting from 30 minutes to three hours, are also given. The cost is $2.50 per person to tour the dockyard; children under 13 are admitted free. The dockyard and its museum are open daily from 8am to 6pm.

Another major attraction is the **Dow's Hill Interpretation Center,** just 2¹/₂ miles from the dockyard. The only one of its kind in the Caribbean, it offers multimedia presentations—a journey through six periods of the island's history, including the Amerindian hunters, the British military, and the struggles connected with slavery. A belvedere opens onto a panoramic view of the park. Admission to the center, including the multimedia show, is $5 for adults, or $3 for children under 16. The center is open daily from 9am to 5pm.

A footpath leads to **Fort Barclay,** the fort at the entrance to English Harbour. The path starts just outside the dockyard gate, and the fort is about half a mile away. The interesting fort is a fine specimen of old-time military engineering.

If you're at English Harbour at sunset, head for **Shirley Heights** directly to the east, named after General Shirley, governor of the Leeward Islands in 1781, who fortified the hills guarding the harbor. Still standing are Palladian arches, once part of the barracks. The Block House, one of the main buildings, was put up as a stronghold in case of siege. The nearby Victorian cemetery contains an obelisk monument to the officers and men of the 54th Regiment.

On a low hill overlooking Nelson's Dockyard, **Clarence House** was built by English stonemasons to accommodate Prince William Henry, later known as the duke of Clarence, and even later known as King William IV. The future king stayed here when he was in command of the *Pegasus* in 1787. At present it's the country home of the governor of Antigua and Barbuda and is open to visitors when His Excellency is not in residence. A caretaker will show you through (it's customary to tip, of course), and you'll see many pieces of furniture on loan from the National Trust. Princess Margaret and Lord Snowdon stayed here on their honeymoon.

On the way back, take ✪ **Fig Tree Drive,** a 20-some-mile circular drive across the main mountain range. It passes through lush tropical hills and fishing villages along the southern coast. You can pick up the road just outside Liberta, north of Falmouth. Winding through a rain forest, it passes thatched villages, and every hamlet has a church and lots of goats and children running about. However, don't expect fig trees—*fig* is an Antiguan name for bananas.

About half a mile before reaching St. John's you come to **Fort James,** which was begun in 1704 as a main lookout post for the port. It was named after James II in whose reign efforts were made to build the fort on the point known as St. John's.

Other places on the island worth seeking out include the following:

Parham Church, overlooking Parham Town, was erected in 1840 in the Italian style. Richly adorned with stucco work, it was damaged by an earthquake in 1843. Much of the ceiling was destroyed and very little of the stucco work remains, but the octagonal structure is still worth a visit.

Potworks Dam, holding back the largest artificial lake on Antigua, is surrounded by an area of natural beauty. The dam has a capacity of a billion gallons of water and provides protection for Antigua in case of a drought.

Indian Town, one of Antigua's national parks, is at a northeastern point on the island. Over the centuries Atlantic breakers have lashed the rocks and carved a natural bridge known as Devil's Bridge. It's surrounded by numerous blowholes spouting surf.

Megaliths, at Greencastle Hill, reached by a long climb, are said to have been set up by human hands for the worship of a sun god and a moon goddess. Some experts believe, however, that the arrangement is an unusual geological formation, a volcanic rockfall.

The **Antigua Rum Distillery,** at Rat Island (☎ **809/462-1072**), turns out fine Cavalier rum. Check at the tourist office about arranging a visit. Established in 1932, the plant is next to Deep Water Harbour. Its annual production rate is in excess of 250,000 Imperial gallons.

SPORTS & OUTDOOR ACTIVITIES

BEACHES   Beaches, beaches, and more beaches—Antigua has some 365 of them. However, because of crime it's unwise to have your fun in the sun at what appears to be a deserted beach. You could be the victim of a mugging in such a lonely setting. Some are superior, and all are public. There's a lovely beach at **Pigeon Point,** in Falmouth Harbour, about a four-minute drive from Admiral's Inn. The beach at **Dickenson Bay,** near the Halcyon Cove Hotel, is also superior and a center for water sports; for a break, you can enjoy meals and drinks on the hotel's Warri Pier, built on stilts in the water. Chances are, however, you'll swim at your own hotel.

Other beaches are at the Curtain Bluff resort, with its long, sandy white **Carlisle Beach** set against a backdrop of coconut palms, and **Morris Bay,** which, in addition to its sandy strip of white sands, has waters attracting snorkelers, among others. The beach at **Long Bay** is on the somewhat-remote eastern coast, but the beach here is beautiful, and most visitors consider it worth the effort to reach it. **Half Moon Bay** is famous in the Caribbean and attracts what used to be called "blue bloods" to a stretch of sand that goes on for almost a mile. Site of such hotels as the Barrymore Beach, **Runaway Beach** is probably one of the most popular on Antigua, but because of its white sands it's worth fighting the crowds. **Five Islands** is actually a quartet of remote beaches with brown sands and coral reefs located near the Hawksbill Hotel.

Increasingly, readers complain of vendors hustling everything from jewelry to T-shirts, disrupting their time on the beach. The beaches are open to all and hotels can't restrain beach use—so be duly warned.

GOLF   Antigua doesn't have the facilities of some of the other islands, but what it has is good. The 18-hole, par-70 **Cedar Valley Golf Club,** Friar's Hill Road (☎ **809/462-0161**), is 3 miles east of St. John's, near the airport. The island's largest, with panoramic views of Antigua's northern coast, it was designed by the late Richard Aldridge to fit the contours of the area. Daily greens fees are $30 for 18 holes.

PARASAILING   This sport is gaining in popularity on Antigua. Facilities are available during the day Monday through Saturday on the beach at **Dickenson Bay.** There are also facilities at the **Royal Antiguan Hotel.**

SAILING   All major hotel desks can book a day cruise on the 108-foot "pirate ship," the *Jolly Roger,* Redcliffe Quay (☎ **809/462-2064**). For $50 you are taken sightseeing on a fun-filled day, with drinks and a barbecued steak, chicken, or lobster. The *Jolly Roger* is the largest sailing ship in Antiguan waters. Lunch is combined with a snorkel trip. Dancing is on the poop deck, and members of the crew teach passengers how to dance calypso.

SCUBA DIVING & OTHER WATER SPORTS   Scuba diving is best arranged through **Dive Antigua,** at the Rex Halcyon Cove, Dickenson Bay (☎ **809/462-3483**), Antigua's longest-established and most experienced dive operation. For $75 per person you can have instruction and a boat dive with all equipment provided.

The **Long Bay Hotel** (☎ **809/463-2005**), on the northeastern coast of the island at Long Bay, is a good location for various water sports—swimming, sailing, waterskiing, and windsurfing. The hotel also has complete scuba facilities. Both beginning snorkelers and experienced divers are welcomed, though Long Bay doesn't offer scuba courses for beginners. You're taken on snorkel trips by boat to Green Island and Great Bird Island (minimum of four). The shallow side of the double reef across Long Bay is ideal for the neophyte, and the whole area on the northeastern tip has many reefs of varying depths.

The **Blue Waters Beach Hotel,** Soldiers Bay (☎ **809/462-0290**), has one of the best water-sports programs on the island. Waterskiing is available at about $12 per person per 15 minutes. In addition, they offer snorkeling gear, fishing rods, windsurfers, pedaloes, Sunfish, Hobie cats, and canoeing, all complimentary to Blue Waters guests.

TENNIS   Tennis buffs will find courts at most of the major hotels, and some are lit for night games. I don't recommend playing tennis at noon—it's just too hot! If your hotel doesn't have a court, you can find them available at the **Rex Halcyon Cove,** the **Cedar Valley Golf Club,** and the **Royal Antiguan Hotel** (the last two have eight courts each). If you're not a guest, you'll have to book a court and pay charges that vary from hotel to hotel. Residents of a hotel usually play free.

WINDSURFING   Located at the Lord Nelson Beach Hotel, on Dutchman's Bay, **Windsurfing Antigua** (☎ **809/462-9463**) offers windsurfing for the absolute beginner, the intermediate sailor, and the advanced athlete. The outlet guarantees to get a neophyte up and enjoying the sport after a two-hour introductory lesson. A lesson costs $45, including free use of training equipment. There's another branch at the Rex Halcyon Cove (☎ **809/462-0256**).

Another center for intermediate and advanced windsurfers is operated at the **Lord Nelson Beach Hotel,** Dutchman's Bay (☎ **809/462-9463**). Onshore wind speeds vary from 12 to 25 knots, with a 2- to 3-foot chop off a quarter of a mile of white sandy beach. Instruction in jibing and other advanced windsurfer techniques is offered. Classes are offered daily from 10am to noon and 2 to 4pm.

SHOPPING

Most of the shops are clustered on St. Mary's Street or High Street in St. John's. Some shops are open Monday through Saturday from 8:30am to noon and 1 to 4pm, but this rule varies greatly from store to store—Antiguan shopkeepers are an independent lot. Many of them close at noon on Thursday.

There are many duty-free items for sale, including English woolens and linens, and you can also purchase several specialized items made in Antigua, such as original pottery, local straw work, Antigua rum, and silk-screened, hand-printed local designs on fabrics, as well as mammy bags, floppy foldable hats, and shell curios.

If you want an island-made bead necklace, don't bother to go shopping; just lie on the beach—anywhere—and some "bead lady" will find you.

If you're in St. John's on a Saturday morning, you can attend the **fruit and vegetable market** at the West Bus Station. Handcrafts made locally are also offered for sale. One visitor said that "the incredibly sweet and juicy Antiguan black pineapple is worth the trip into town itself."

Caribelle Batik
Redcliffe St., St. John's. ☎ **809/462-2972.**

This shop is an outlet for the Romney Manor workshop on St. Kitts. The Caribelle label consists of batik and tie-dye items such as beach wraps, scarves, and a range of casual wear for both women and men. The Sensual Silk label is also found here—these items are 100% silk in Caribbean colors, ranging from dresses and separates to accessories such as jewelry and scarves.

Harmony Hall
In Brown's Bay Mill, near Freetown. ☎ **809/460-4120.**

Overlooking Nonsuch Bay, this old plantation-site house and sugar mill dates back to 1843—but now is much restored and an ideal luncheon stopover or a shopping expedition. Dinner is served here Thursday through Saturday, but only from November through May; reservations are imperative. It displays an excellent selection of Caribbean arts and crafts, and in November plays host to the annual Caribbean Craft Fair. Lunch is served daily from noon to 4pm, featuring Green Island lobster, flying fish, and other specialties. Sunday is barbecue day. The entire complex is open daily from 10am to 6pm. To get there, follow the signs along the road to Freetown and Half Moon Bay.

Island Hopper
Jardine Court, St. Mary's St., St. John's. ☎ **809/462-2972.**

This shop has a range of gifts and clothing, specializing in products made in the Caribbean. The owner goes to some trouble to provide items not readily available elsewhere. The range is wide—T-shirts, spices, coffees, handcrafts, and casual wear.

Quin Farara's Liquor Store
Long St. and Corn Alley, St. John's. ☎ **809/462-0463.**

Antigua has some of the lowest liquor prices in the Caribbean, and this has one of the largest collections of wines and liquors on the island. Often you'll save up to 50% on what you'd pay in the States. The staff will show you how to take home a "gallon," pay the duty, and still save. Don Diego (originally Cuban) cigars are also on sale.

The Scent Shop
Lower High St., St. John's. ☎ **809/462-0303.**

This shop stocks some 100 brands of perfume, along with such collector items as Hummel figurines, Cartier watches, leather goods, and Baccarat, Lalique, and Waterford crystal.

Shoul's Chief Store
St. Mary's St., St. John's. ☎ **809/462-1139.**

Opposite Barclays Bank is a cave of treasures. The store sells household items and appliances, a wide range of local and imported souvenirs, Antigua T-shirts, and fabrics of all colors, designs, and textures.

Shopping Centers

HERITAGE QUAY   Antigua's first shopping-and-entertainment complex is a multi-million-dollar center featuring some 40 duty-free shops and a vendors' arcade in which local artists and craftspeople display their wares. Restaurants in Heritage Quay offer a range of cuisine and views of St. John's Harbour, while a "food court" serves visitors who prefer to feast on local specialties in an informal setting. You could start your shopping with any of these leading shops:

   Colombian Emeralds (☎ **809/462-3462**) is the largest retailer of Colombian emeralds in the world, with some 24 branches in the Caribbean and The Bahamas. It offers an excellent variety of emeralds along with jewelry made from other precious stones, including sapphires, diamonds, rubies, topaz, and pearls.

   Little Switzerland (☎ **809/462-3108**) is a name familiar to frequent travelers to the Caribbean. It sells the best selections of Swiss-made watches in Antigua, such as Rolex, Omega, Cartier, and Audemars Piquet. It also displays china and crystal made by Royal Doulton and Baccarat. Little Switzerland has opened a perfume shop in Heritage Quay called La Perfumery by Little Switzerland.

   "Sunsneakers," 13 Heritage Quay (☎ **809/462-4523**), was established in 1989 when duty-free shopping was introduced on a large scale on Antigua. The outlet possibly has one of the largest selections of swimwear available in the Caribbean. It accommodates size D or clients who are seeking everything from a double D to a size 26.

   Island Arts, Upstairs, Heritage Quay (☎ **809/462-2787**), was founded by Nick Maley, a makeup artist who worked on *Star Wars* and *The Empire Strikes Back.* You can purchase one of his own fine-art reproductions, including the provocative *Windkissed & Sunswept.* Visitors are free to browse through everything from low-cost prints to works by artists exhibited in New York's Museum of Modern Art. Other outlets are found at the Royal Antiguan Hotel and the St. James's Club.

REDCLIFFE QUAY   This historic complex is one of the best centers for shopping (or dining) in St. John's. Once, Redcliffe Quay was a slave-trading quarter, but after the abolition of slavery the quay was filled with grog shops and merchants peddling various wares. Now it has been redeveloped and contains a number of the most interesting shops in town, some in former warehouses.

   A Thousand Flowers (☎ **809/462-4264**) sells Indonesia batiks, crafted on the island into sundresses, knock-'em-dead shirts, sarongs, rompers, and various accessories such as necklaces and earrings. Many of the garments are designed in a one-size-fits-all motif of knots and flowing expanses of cloth appropriate for the tropics.

Jacaranda (☎ **809/462-1888**) might tempt you with the art of John Woodland or placemats and prints by Jill Walker. The shop also stocks local clothing, the works of local artists, and herbs and spices as well as gels, soaps, and salts for the bath.

Base (☎ **809/462-0920**), the brainchild of Steven Giles, an English designer, is one of the best-known companies in the Caribbean. It carries an intriguing line of casual comfort clothing in stripes, colors, and prints, all made at the company's world headquarters at Redcliffe Quay. The cotton and Lycra beachwear is eagerly sought out.

The Goldsmitty (☎ **809/462-4601**) presents the designs of Hans Smit in precious stones and gold. The jewelry is all designed and made on the premises. Buyers can select from many one-of-a-kind creations. Black opal, imperial topaz, and other exotic gemstones are set in exquisite creations of 14- and 18-karat gold. Closed in September.

ANTIGUA AFTER DARK

Most nightlife revolves around the hotels, unless you want to roam Antigua at night looking for that "hot native club." If you're going out for the night, make arrangements to have a taxi pick you up—otherwise you could be stranded in the wilds somewhere. Antigua has some of the best steel bands in the Caribbean.

The Royal Casino
In the Royal Antiguan Hotel, Deep Bay. ☎ **809/462-3733.** Admission free.

This 6,000-square-foot international casino has American games, including blackjack, baccarat, roulette, craps, and slot machines. Open daily from 9pm "until."

BARBUDA

Known by the Spanish as Dulcina, sparsely populated Barbuda, part of the independent nation of Antigua and Barbuda, is considered the last frontier of the Caribbean. Charted by Columbus in 1493, the island lies 26 miles to the north of Antigua, and is about 15 miles long by 5 miles wide with a population of some 1,200 hardy souls, most of whom live around the unattractive village of **Codrington.**

Don't come here seeking lush, tropical scenery, as flat Barbuda consists of coral rock. There are no paved roads, few hotel rooms, only a handful of restaurants, and pastel-colored beaches, the most famous of which stretches for more than 17 miles.

The main town is named after Christopher Codrington, who was once the governor of the Leeward Islands. He is believed to have deliberately wrecked ships on the reefs circling Barbuda. What *is* known is that he used the island, which he'd received in 1691 from the Crown, for the purposes of breeding slaves. He was given the island in return for "one fat pig per year, if asked."

Barbuda has a temperature that seldom falls below an average of 75° Fahrenheit.

ORIENTATION

GETTING THERE   The island is a 15-minute flight from Antigua's V. C. Bird Airport. Barbuda has two airfields: one at Codrington; the other a private facility,

Barbuda

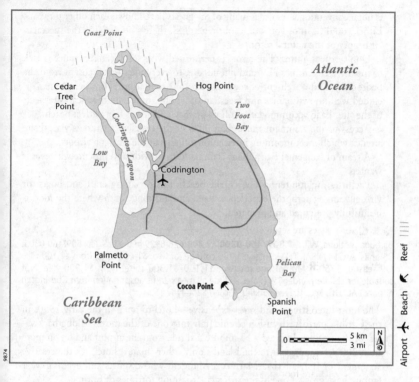

Reef |||

Beach 📍

Airport ✈

the Coco Point Airstrip, which lies some 8 miles from Codrington at Coco Point Lodge.

To reach Barbuda from Antigua, you can contact **LIAT** (☎ 809/462-0701), which operates two daily flights (usually around 8am and again around 4pm) from Antigua to Barbuda's Codrington Airport.

GETTING AROUND   Many locals rent small Suzuki four-wheel-drive **Jeeps,** which are the best way to get around the island. They meet incoming flights at Codrington Airport. Prices are negotiable. An Antiguan driver's license (see above) is needed if you plan to drive.

WHERE TO STAY & DINE

Coco Point Lodge

(Mailing address: P.O. Box 90, St. John's, Antigua, W.I.). ☎ **809/462-3816.** For reservations, contact Coco Point Lodge Reservations Office, 275 Madison Ave., Suite 1901, New York, NY 10016 (☎ **212/986-1416;** fax 212/986-0901). 34 rms. Winter, $600–$1,000 single; $700–$1,100 double. Off-season, $500–$900 single; $650–$1,000 double. Additional occupant of double room $175–$200 extra. (Rates all-inclusive.) No credit cards. Free parking.

This is one of the most isolated and upscale hotels in the Caribbean, an escapist haven whose access requires formidable amounts of advance planning. In the 1960s the Kelly family acquired a flat, sandy peninsula (164 acres). Ever since, they've devoted their time, funds, and energy to building up a club that was so private that yacht owners who dropped in for a drink were often barred from the facilities. This is not a conventional resort, as many of the guests have known each other for years. Either you'll fit in or you won't, but regardless, there's no denying the spectacular beauty of the natural setting.

Don't expect glitter: The resort is permeated with solid Yankee values, a lack of intrusive electronics (TV and phones are, to everyone's relief, absent from the bedrooms), and a well-entrenched disdain for ostentation. The clientele has included well-known names and faces, all of whom appreciate the escapist aspects of the site. Each accommodation offers privacy and access to a perfect beach.

Access to the resort for more than 90% of the overseas visitors is via private aircraft which meet incoming international flights at the Antigua airport.

A team of congenial Barbudians is on hand to provide and procure whatever is wanted.

Facilities include tennis courts, the beach, lots of sailing craft and boats for virtually any waterborne experience, bars, and a dining room where the food is beautifully presented and prepared.

✪ K-Club

Barbuda, Antigua, W.I. ☎ **809/460-0300,** or 800/628-8929 in the U.S. Fax 809/460-0305. 35 units. A/C MINIBAR TEL. Winter, $1,100 cottage for two; $1,600 suite; from $2,100 villa. Off-season, $750–$900 cottage for two; $1,100–$1,300 suite; from $1,900 villa. Not suitable for children under 12. (Rates include all meals and transportation from Codrington airport.) AE, DC, MC, V. Free parking. Closed Sept–Nov 15.

The most interesting—and *super*-expensive—hotel to open in the early 1990s in the Caribbean, this is a fusion of chic Italy into one of the most farflung backwaters of the Antilles. Located a 15-minute taxi ride from the airport and set on more than 200 acres, adjacent to the island's only other (major) hotel, it's the creative statement of Italy's Krizia Mariuccia Mandelli whose sports and evening-wear empire have grossed one of the spectacular fashion fortunes of Europe.

The resort's architectural style, conceived by Italian architect Gianni Gamondi, consists of bungalows and a main clubhouse whose roof is supported by a forest of white columns. The resort's dominant color scheme is in the teal-blue and white that are the designer's trademark. The furnishings include lots of Hamptons-style wicker and a stylish insouciance. The resort was inaugurated in 1990 when a planeload of glitterati—spearheaded by Giorgio Armani—headed en masse for Barbuda.

Dining/Entertainment: The all-inclusive rates provide for all meals (but no drinks or wine). The cuisine is fashioned after the Mediterranean kitchen, with an emphasis on Italian specialties and fresh pasta.

Services: Transportation from Codrington Airport.

Facilities: Two tennis courts, seawater swimming pool, waterskiing, snorkeling, Sunfish sailing, windsurfing, deep-sea fishing.

WHAT TO SEE & DO

Hunters, anglers, and just plain beachcombers are attracted to the island, as it has some fallow deer, guinea fowl, pigeons, and wild pigs. Those interested in fishing for bonefish and tarpon can negotiate with the owners of small boats who hire them out.

Trippers over just for the day usually head for **Wa'Omoni Beach Park,** where they can visit the frigate bird sanctuary, snorkel for lobster, and eat barbecue.

Indeed, the most impressive sight on Barbuda is the **frigate bird sanctuary,** one of the largest in the world, where visitors can see the birds, *Fregata magnificens,* sitting on their eggs in the mangrove bushes. The mangroves stretch for miles in a long lagoon accessible only by a small motorboat. Tours to the sanctuary can be arranged on Antigua at various hotels and resorts. Besides the frigate bird, the island attracts some 150 species of birds, including pelicans, herons, and tropical mockingbirds.

Other curiosities of the island include a **"Dividing Wall,"** which once separated the Codrington family from the black people, and the **Martello Tower,** which predates the known history of the island. Tours also cover interesting underground **caves** on the island. Stamp collectors might want to call at the **Philatelic Bureau** in Codrington.

2 Montserrat

To see "the way the Caribbean used to be," visit Montserrat. Vacationers often fly to the volcanic island just for the day and then wish they could spend more time here. Called the "Emerald Isle of the Caribbean," Montserrat is some 27 miles southwest of Antigua, between Guadeloupe and Nevis. The pear-shaped island is mountainous with lush green forests, much tropical vegetation, and some licorice-colored beaches of volcanic sand that are powdery but black.

In the northwest (see below) are some beaches of lighter colored sand, but great beaches are not the reason visitors fly to Montserrat. It attracts climbers and hikers, but mostly it's a place where people seek the uncommercialized, laidback life of the Caribbean. That, in part, explains its appeal to senior citizens.

Celebrities ranging from Elton John to Paul McCartney often descend here as well. In the 1980s the hills were alive with music, even that of Sting and Stevie Wonder, but the glory days of Air Studios, a state-of-the-art recording studio in the north, ended in 1989 when Hurricane Hugo hit a sour note.

Montserrat was sighted by Columbus in 1493 and named after the famous sawtoothed mountain near Barcelona. However, it wasn't until 1632 that Irish settlers colonized the island, when Oliver Cromwell, it is believed, shipped out a band of reluctant colonists who had been captured after a rebellion. By 1648 Montserrat had also become home to 1,000 Irish families who fled their new homes on St. Kitts because of religious persecution. The Irish influence is shown in place names on the island and in the surnames of present-day residents.

The flag of Montserrat is the British Union Jack, but the official badge is the very Irish "Lady with the Harp." The shamrock is on the center gable of Government House, and it's also on the stamp that Montserrat immigration people stamp in your passport. The island even marks March 17 as a public holiday, but this is because the slaves in the early days staged a rebellion on St. Patrick's Day. Today Montserrat's more than 11,000 hardworking, friendly people, most of whom were descended from African slaves, often speak with an Irish brogue.

The island was captured by the French in 1664, restored to England in 1668, and retaken by the French in 1782, who ceded it to Britain in 1783. Today the officials have elected to remain a British Crown Colony, as they don't have the financial wherewithal to go it alone. The island is politically stable and is popular with retirees. The capital, **Plymouth,** is reputed to be one of the cleanest in the

Caribbean; it's best viewed during market day on Saturday, when gossip is traded along with fruit.

ORIENTATION
GETTING THERE

At least 80% of passengers flying into Montserrat do so via transfers through Antigua. (For information on getting to Antigua, see "Getting There" in the Antigua section of this chapter.) From Antigua, two different airlines run a flotilla of small planes. **LIAT** operates daily flights to Montserrat on planes holding between 19 and 37 passengers. For information about these flights, call LIAT on Antigua (☎ **809/462-0700**), or call LIAT's Montserrat-based sales representative, Montserrat Aviation (☎ **809/491-2533**). The fare for the 20-minute flight is $36 each way. LIAT has a total of six daily (Monday through Thursday) flights: five 10- to 20-minute trips to Montserrat from Antigua, and one hour-long flight from St. Maarten, which stops on St. Kitts. There are five flights Friday through Sunday: four from Antigua and one from St. Maarten.

LIAT's main competitor on this route is **Montserrat Airways** (☎ **809/491-6494**), a smaller carrier that operates about a dozen flights per day from Antigua on planes carrying no more than nine passengers per flight. This is a non-scheduled airline, flying only when they have passengers. Montserrat Airways is also amenable to arranging charters to and from any of the Caribbean's neighboring islands. For information about Montserrat Airways, call either their sales representative, Carib World Travel, Parliament Street, in Plymouth (☎ **809/491-2714**), or contact the airline directly.

Windward Islands Airways International N.V., or **Winair** (☎ **599/5-44230** on St. Maarten), offers 40-minute service twice daily to/from Montserrat. Flight 101 leaves St. Maarten at 8am and arrives in Montserrat at 8:40am; Flight 102 returns from Montserrat at 8:50am, arriving on St. Maarten at 9:30am. The late-afternoon Flight 111 leaves St. Maarten at 4pm and arrives on Montserrat at 4:40pm; Flight 112 leaves for St. Maarten at 4:50pm, arriving at 5:30pm.

Most passengers coming from the North American mainland find it cheaper and more convenient to allow larger carriers, such as **American** (☎ **800/433-7300**) or **BWIA** (☎ **800/327-7401**), to make bookings into Montserrat on either of the above-mentioned airlines as part of ongoing flights through Antigua from the North American mainland.

GETTING AROUND

BY TAXI AND BUS   There are 15 miles of surfaced roads, and taxis and buses are the most popular means of transport. Taxi drivers meet every plane. The typical fare from the airport to Plymouth are EC$30 ($11.10) each way. Sightseeing tours cost about $25 per hour.

Buses run between Plymouth and Salem and to most areas at fares ranging from EC$1.50 to EC$3 (60¢ to $1.10).

BY RENTAL CAR   None of the major U.S.–based car-rental companies offers outlets on Montserrat, although you'll find a handful of private outfits. One of the most recommendable is **Pauline's Car Rentals,** Church Road, in Plymouth (☎ **809/491-2345**). Operated by one of the island's most active entrepreneurs, the hardworking Pauline Jeffers, the company maintains about half a dozen Toyotas, Jeeps, and Daihatsus. They rent for $35 to $50 a day, or $25 to $45 per day for a two- to four-day rental. A collision-damage waiver costs $8 to $10 per

Montserrat

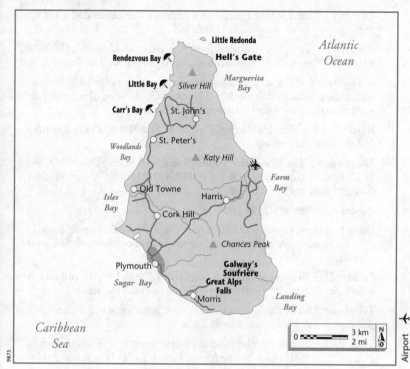

Little Redonda

Hell's Gate

Rendezvous Bay

Atlantic
Ocean

Little Bay

Silver Hill

Marguerita
Bay

Carr's Bay

St. John's

St. Peter's

Woodlands
Bay

Katy Hill

Farm
Bay

Old Towne

Harris

Isles
Bay

Cork Hill

Chances Peak

Plymouth

Galway's
Soufrière
Great Alps
Falls

Sugar Bay

Morris

Landing
Bay

Caribbean
Sea

0   3 km
     2 mi

N

Airport

9875

day, but even if you buy it, you'll still be liable for up to the first $1,000 worth of damage in the event of an accident. The office lies about half a mile north of Plymouth, although an employee will drop the car off either at the airport for your arrival or at your hotel after you check in. American Express, MasterCard, and Visa are accepted.

To rent a car, you'll need a valid U.S. or Canadian license and to pay $12. Most of the time, visitors can obtain these from the police officers at the Immigration Department at the island's airport.

There are only about five gas stations (referred to as "petrol" stations) on the island, so it's usually a good idea to drive with at least half a tank of gas. Two of the most visible outlets are the Texaco station on the northern outskirts of Plymouth, and the N & B Servicentre, opposite the public market in the heart of town.

BY BIKE   Island Bikes, Harney Street (☎ **809/491-4696**), offers a mobile way to see the lush scenery of Montserrat. You can ride on your own or ask Island Bikes to arrange a guide. Either way, you'll see Montserrat from a different perspective. The cost is $25 per day.

FAST FACTS: Montserrat

Area Code   To call Montserrat from mainland North America, dial the Caribbean area code of 809, then 491 (the prefix for all phone numbers on the island), then the four-digit local number. For information on dialing numbers on the island, see "Telephone," below.

Currency Most Leeward Islands use the **Eastern Caribbean dollar (EC$)**, although most prices are given in U.S. dollars.

Drugstores Try Lee's Pharmacy, Evergreen Drive, in Plymouth (☎ 809/491-3274). The pharmacy is open Monday through Saturday from 9am to 7pm.

Electricity You'll need an electrical transformer and adapter for all U.S.–made appliances, as the island supplies 220–230 volts A.C., 60 cycles. Check with your hotel, though, to see if they've converted their circuitry.

Hospitals The Glendon Hospital, Plymouth (☎ 809/491-2552), operates a 24-hour emergency room.

Information The **Montserrat Tourist Board** is on Marine Drive (P.O. Box 7), Plymouth, Montserrat, B.W.I. (☎ 809/491-2230). It is open Monday through Friday from 8am to 4pm.

Police Call **809/491-2555**.

Safety As in the Caymans and the British Virgins, crime is rare here. It would be wise, however, to take the usual precautions about safeguarding your valuables.

Taxes The government charges a hotel tax of 7% to 10%. In addition, it imposes an EC$25 ($9.30) departure tax when you leave the island.

Telephone When dialing a number once you're on the island, omit the 809 area code and dial only the last seven digits.

Time Montserrat is on Atlantic standard time year round: When it's 6am in Plymouth, it's 5am in New York or Miami. However, island clocks match those of the eastern standard zone on the mainland when summer's daylight saving time is in effect in the United States.

Tips and Service Hotels and restaurants add a 10% surcharge to your final tab to cover tips. If they don't, it's customary to tip 10% to 15%.

Weather The mean temperature of the island ranges from a high of 86.5° to a low of 73.5° Fahrenheit.

WHERE TO STAY

Don't forget that the government imposes a 7% to 10% room tax on hotels, and a 10% service charge is also added. Ask about these charges when you make your reservation.

HOTELS

ⓢ Flora Fountain Hotel

Lower Dagenham Rd. (P.O. Box 373), Plymouth, Montserrat, B.W.I. ☎ **809/491-6092.** Fax 809/491-2568. 16 rms. A/C TEL. Winter, $60 single; $85 double. Off-season, $50 single; $70 double. Breakfast $7 extra. AE, MC, V. Free parking.

Popular with business travelers who appreciate its central location in Plymouth, this 1983 hotel is built around a circular courtyard centered on a fountain whose illumination is computerized. There isn't much of a view, but each unit has its own balcony nonetheless, along with a private bath.

Try to catch the Saturday-morning West Indian buffet breakfast, when you can feast on such local dishes as saltfish, bananas, breadfruit, souse, and blood pudding—or bacon and eggs. Lunch is pizzas and sandwiches and dinner is fixed price at EC$18 to EC$25 ($6.70 to $9.30) for a full meal.

✪ Vue Pointe Hotel

P.O. Box 65, Old Towne, Montserrat, B.W.I. ☎ **809/491-5210,** or 800/235-0709 in the U.S. Fax 809/491-4813. 40 rms. TV TEL. Winter, $109–$150 single; $126–$166 double; $200 triple. Off-season, $70–$90 single; $80–$105 double; $125 triple. MAP $40 per person extra. AE, MC, V. Free parking.

This family-run cottage colony 4 miles north of Plymouth consists of hexagonal, shingle-roofed villas, plus some interconnected rooms. They're set on 5 acres of sloping land near a black sand beach just 11 miles from the Montserrat airport and about two minutes from the challenging seaside Montserrat Golf Club.

Most of the accommodations are constructed with natural lumber with open-beamed ceilings, and they're furnished with bamboo and modern pieces. Each has a private bath, a small refrigerator, a sitting-room area, and twin beds. A natural breeze sweeps through accommodations in lieu of air conditioning. The staff members are unobtrusive and well trained.

Dining/Entertainment: The cuisine is the best on the island, and everybody shows up for the West Indian barbecue on Wednesday night. There are two attractive bars: one at the rambling main house; the other, called the Nest, at water's edge. Dress is informal. Sometimes there's music and dancing to a steel band.

Services: Room service, laundry, babysitting.

Facilities: Freshwater swimming pool, dive shop, two tennis courts; fishing, sailing, and snorkeling can be arranged.

CONDOS & VILLAS

Belham Valley Hotel

P.O. Box 409, Old Towne, Montserrat, B.W.I. ☎ **809/491-5553.** 3 apartments. TV TEL. Winter, $400 per week Jasmine studio; $525 per week Frangipani studio; $525 per week Mignonette unit. Off-season, $300 per week Jasmine studio; $375 per week Frangipani studio; $475 per week Mignonette unit. AE, MC, V. Free parking.

Despite its designation as a hotel, this establishment maintains and operates three apartment units, each with kitchen, which are rented on a weekly basis to temporary visitors. These apartments lie on a hillside 4 miles north of Plymouth, overlooking Belham Valley, its river, and the golf course. The beach is about a seven-minute walk, and you can also stroll over in the evening to the Vue Pointe Hotel. The Frangipani studio cottage, surrounded by tropical shrubs and coconut palm, can accommodate two guests and consists of a bedroom, living area, fully equipped kitchen, private bath, and a balcony facing the golf course and the sea. The Jasmine studio apartment also accommodates two and contains a large bed-sitting room, a small dinette, a private bath, a fully equipped kitchen, and a small private patio with views of the sea or mountains. Another apartment, the Mignonette, accommodates four guests and has two bedrooms, a bath, and a living area with kitchen, plus a big patio facing the golf course and sea.

Lime Court Apartments

P.O. Box 250, Plymouth, Montserrat, B.W.I. ☎ **809/491-3656.** Fax 809/491-5069. 8 studios and apartments. $25 studio; $30 one-bedroom apartment; $45 penthouse; $40 two-bedroom apartment. AE, MC, V. Free parking.

Right in the center of town, a 15-minute taxi ride north of the airport, this colonial-style apartment colony is a short walk from the beach, shops, and restaurants. Furnished apartments are available with kitchens and electric cooking, although some units need refurbishing. Each unit has a hot-water shower, and all utilities and maid service are included; several have a phone and TV. The best unit is no. 9, a penthouse apartment offering a view of the harbor and a private patio. The simplest and cheapest way to live here is in a studio, although they may be dark and not well ventilated. The year-round rates quoted above are for single or double occupancy. The manager advises that in winter all bookings should be made at least two months in advance.

Montserrat Springs Hotel

P.O. Box 259, Plymouth, Montserrat, B.W.I. ☎ **809/491-2481.** Fax 809/491-4070. 34 rms, 6 suites. A/C TV TEL. Winter, $115–$140 single; $145–$165 double; $205–$215 one-bedroom suite; $320–$335 two-bedroom suite for four. Off-season, $85–$110 single; $130–$150 double; $150–$160 one-bedroom suite; $220–$245 two-bedroom suite for four. MAP $40 per person extra. Children under 12 stay free in parents' room. AE, MC. Free parking.

Bouncing back after Hurricane Hugo, this hotel clusters accommodations into a series of interconnected, black-roofed town houses set a 25-minute taxi ride north-west of the airport on steeply sloping land. Some are closer to the sea than others, but all are ringed with landscaping. Each accommodation contains wicker furniture, private bath, and balcony. The suites contain kitchenettes and washing machines and are air-conditioned. Built on the site of natural springs, the premises contain a covered pair of circular hot and cold baths, a 70-foot swimming pool, tennis courts, access to the sands of Jumbee Bay, a beach bar and a pool bar, and a dining room.

Shamrock Villas

P.O. Box 58, Plymouth, Montserrat, B.W.I. ☎ **809/491-2431.** Fax 809/491-4660. 20 apartments, 15 villas. Winter, $540 per week one-bedroom apartment for two; $695 per week two-bedroom apartment for four; $1,000–$2,170 per week villa. Off-season, $420 per week one-bedroom apartment for two; $480 per week two-bedroom apartment for four; $685–$1,200 villa. No credit cards. Free parking.

A condominium and villa hillside colony at Plymouth, near the Montserrat Springs Hotel, Shamrock Villas suggests an Iberian village of white, balcony-studded houses. Owners have arranged for their condo units to be rented in their absence. All accommodations have views of the sea, the black sand beaches, and Plymouth. Linen and cutlery are included, even for short-term rentals. Maid service is available two days a week. Services are close by. Bread comes fresh from the baker, and at the local market you can sample the produce grown on the island, especially the tomatoes, carrots, and pineapples. A beach and tennis court are adjacent. The condos are in a white-walled and balconied complex, and the villas are properties set in widely scattered neighborhoods throughout the island. Most of the villas have their own swimming pool, and the condos have a communal pool in their center.

A GUEST HOUSE

⑤ Providence Estate House

St. Peter's, Montserrat, W.I. ☎ **809/491-6476.** Fax 809/491-8476. 2 rms. TV. Winter, $55–$65 single; $70–$85 double. Off-season, $40–$50 single; $60–$80 double. (Rates include breakfast.) MC, V.

This B&B guesthouse is part of a turn-of-the-century plantation in the quiet countryside about 20 minutes north of the capital, Plymouth. Several acres of gardens can be viewed from the large veranda that encloses the swimming pool. From the veranda, at an elevation of 500 feet, there's a panoramic 180° view of the Caribbean, including the islands of Nevis and Redonda as well as much of the northern coastline of Montserrat. A full breakfast is served against this backdrop. The house became locally famous when Paul McCartney and his family rented it for several months some time ago. The guest rooms feature the original thick stone walls, heavy timbered ceilings, and tile floors. A kitchen is available on the veranda for drinks, snacks, and warm-up meals. Evening meals can be arranged with advance notice.

WHERE TO DINE

Many guests dine at their hotels. But since there are so few hotels and since many visitors rent condos and villas, a number of independent eateries exist, mainly cafés. Some of these are tiny local spots with a following. Often the appearance is a bit ramshackle, but good, simple food is served.

MODERATE

✪ Belham Valley Restaurant

Old Towne. ☎ **809/491-5553.** Reservations recommended, especially for dinner. Appetizers EC$8.50–EC$15 ($3.10–$5.60); main courses EC$35–EC$75 ($13–$27.80). AE, MC, V. Lunch Tues–Sun noon–2pm; dinner Tues–Sun 6:30–11pm. FRENCH/AMERICAN.

Near the Vue Pointe Hotel, 4 miles north of Plymouth, is the premier restaurant of Montserrat. You can enjoy a local creamy pumpkin soup, prime steaks, fettuccine with seafood, Montserrat conch fritters, or a combination of seafood served in a rich vermouth sauce. The kitchen always prepares Montserrat "mountain chicken" (frogs' legs). Desserts are likely to include coconut-cream cheesecake, mango mousse, and fresh coconut pie. The setting is tropical, and the restaurant occupies a former private home on a hillside overlooking the Belham River and its valley. It's convenient for guests at the Montserrat Golf Course. In winter, live entertainment is offered Thursday through Saturday night and Chinese food is featured every Thursday evening.

❾ Blue Dolphin Restaurant

Parsons. ☎ **809/491-3263.** Reservations required. Main courses EC$25–EC$60 ($9.30–$22.20). No credit cards. Lunch Mon–Sat noon–2pm; dinner Mon–Sat 6pm–midnight. CARIBBEAN.

Serviced by a kind-hearted staff, the Blue Dolphin is on the side of a steep hillside near the medical school amid a lush landscape. Direct your eye to the view of the town and harbor, not to the utterly plain decor with its Naugahyde chairs and chalkboard menu. Main dishes, which are served with soup, include lobster, kingfish, "mountain chicken," pork chops, tenderloin steaks, and breaded boneless breast of chicken. Coconut-cream pie with ice cream is one of the desserts.

Emerald Café

Wapping Rd., Wapping. ☎ **809/491-3821.** Reservations recommended. Appetizers EC$7–EC$14 ($2.60–$5.20); main courses EC$26–EC$55 ($9.60–$20.40). AE, MC, V. Mon–Sat 8am–midnight, Sun 3pm–midnight. INTERNATIONAL.

Set in a green-and-white concrete-sided house about 150 feet from the water's edge, this is an unpretentious restaurant owned by island-born Alvin Greenaway. Tables are ringed with plants and flowers, and lie beneath parasols on an outdoor patio as well as inside, near a bar. Menu items change with the availability of the ingredients, but are likely to include boneless breast of chicken with spicy tomato sauce and cheese, at least three different preparations of red snapper (grilled, broiled, or pan-fried with herbs), lobster, and such desserts as soursop mousse and coconut-meringue cream pie. Established in 1988, this has proven one of the most enduring restaurants on the island. Entertainment is likely to be offered on weekends.

✪ Niggy's Bistro

Kinsale, Plymouth, Montserrat, B.W.I. ☎ **809/491-7489.** Fax 809/491-3599. Reservations recommended. Appetizers EC$7–EC$15 ($2.60–$5.60); main courses EC$22–EC$45 ($8.10–$16.70). MC, V. Dinner only, Tues–Sat 7–10pm. INTERNATIONAL.

Set in a century-old clapboard house in the village of Kinsale, three-quarters of a mile south of Plymouth, this is one of the most appealing food and music emporiums in Montserrat. Operated by English-born Anthony Overman and his Chicago-born wife, Niggy, it offers well-prepared food, a dose of humor and goodwill, and live jazz and calypso performances from 8pm to midnight nightly in winter when Niggy herself performs. As you enter, you'll see a prominent bar—actually an old fishing boat—likely to be patronized by His Excellency, the governor of Montserrat, the local police commissioner, or varied members of the British/American expatriate community. Menu items might include beef tenderloin bordelaise, shrimp scampi with garlic sauce, filet mignon with garlic butter, lamb chops with real mint sauce, or snapper provençal. Dessert might be a chocolate mousse or zabaglione.

The ground level of the main house contains two clean pension-style bedrooms, with simple furniture, shared bathrooms, and almost no amenities. One room has only a single bed; the other offers three beds. Charges are $15 single, $20 double, or $25 triple if all three beds are used. Breakfast costs $2.60 to $4.40 extra, depending on what you order.

Vue Pointe Restaurant

In the Vue Pointe Hotel, Old Towne. ☎ **809/491-5211.** Reservations recommended if you're not a hotel guest. Appetizers $5–$10; main courses $13–$23; fixed-price dinner $25. AE, MC, V. Lunch daily noon–3pm; dinner daily 7–10pm. FRENCH/CARIBBEAN.

Graciously elegant, and surrounded by the lawns and shrubbery of this previously recommended hotel 4 miles north of Plymouth, this is one of the best-run restaurants on the island. Fixed-price dinners are available, or you can order à la carte. The Wednesday-night barbecue, an island event, is enlivened by a steel band. The kitchen turns out "mountain chicken," filet of kingfish, Créole-style red snapper, West Indian curried chicken with condiments, and filet of sole. Dessert might be lime cheesecake or a tropical fruit salad. A Sunday luncheon buffet contains barbecued spareribs, fresh fish, and chicken.

INEXPENSIVE

Brattenmuce

Belham Bridge. ☎ **809/491-7564.** Reservations required. Main courses EC$25–EC$45 ($9.30–$16.70). MC, V. Dinner only, Wed–Sat 7–9pm. Aug–Sept. INTERNATIONAL.

Set about 3 miles north of Plymouth, a short walk south of Old Towne, this restaurant is named after an acronym for the two Canadian-born owners, Bruce Munro and Matt Hawthorne. Set beside the highway, in a simple house with a bright-yellow facade, the restaurant serves platters of uncomplicated food. It's important to phone in advance, because if there aren't enough reservations on any given night, the restaurant might shut down. You'll dine either in the bistro-inspired interior or on the patio, depending on your mood and the weather. Main platters might include meatloaf, wienerschnitzel, fried fish, or barbecued steak, and the menu for the night of your arrival might be recited to you orally over the phone at the time of your call. No appetizers are served, and salad, bread, and butter are included in the price of the meal. Some nights are theme nights—for example, varied pasta dishes are offered on Wednesday, fish on Friday (ocean perch, sole, flounder, flying fish, sea trout, and others), and barbecued steak on Saturday. Dessert, usually key lime pie or cheesecake, made fresh on the premises, costs extra.

WHAT TO SEE & DO

The island is small, only 11 miles long and 7 miles across at its widest point. Its gently rolling hills and mountains reach their zenith at **Chances Peak,** which rises to 3,000 feet. From its vantage point, a panoramic vista over the island unfolds. To climb the mountain, even serious hikers need a guide, which your hotel can arrange.

Galway's Soufrière, in the south-central region of the island, is a crater that bubbles and steams with sulfur smoke. A mountain road lined with tree ferns allows you to drive to within a 15-minute walk of the vents. Yellow sulfur spills over the side in stark contrast to the forest's green. Look also for the exotic incense tree. Again, you should have your hotel arrange a mountain guide.

On the way there, stop to explore **Galway's Plantation,** an archeological project directed by the Montserrat National Trust. In the 1660s David Galway, an Irishman from Cork, settled the land with Irish indentured servants who were later replaced by African slaves. He established a sugar plantation which reached its peak a century later; however, the plantation declined after the slaves were freed. The ruins remain today and include the old sugar-boiling house and the sugar mill.

On the outskirts of Plymouth, St. Anthony's Church—the main Anglican church on the island—was built between 1632 and 1666, and then rebuilt in 1730. Freed slaves, upon their emancipation, donated the two beautiful silver chalices on display.

About a 15-minute drive from town, the ruined **Fort St. George** dates from the 18th century. The fort is 1,184 feet above sea level and offers panoramic views.

At yet another fortification, **Bransby Point,** you can see restored cannons. The early earthworks date from 1640 to 1660. In 1693 a gun battery was built on this site, but it was destroyed by the French in 1712. In 1734 the British constructed a gun platform. By 1983 the restoration had been completed, after 200 years of destruction.

The **Montserrat Museum,** housed in an old sugar mill at Richmond Hill in Plymouth, displays a collection of Montserratian artifacts, including pictures of island life at the turn of the century. Some of the artifacts relate to the island's pre-Columbian history. The featured exhibit is a small replica of a wind-driven sugar mill. Admission is free, but donations maintain the museum. Hours are 2:30 to 5pm on Wednesday and Sunday.

SPORTS & OUTDOOR ACTIVITIES

BEACHES If you demand that your beaches on a Caribbean island be either white or pink sands, you'll have to look elsewhere. Perhaps you'll be drawn to the black sandy beaches (the soil is of volcanic origin) on the northern rim of the island. If you prefer your beaches in beige tones, head for the northwest coast where you'll find the most frequented beaches: **Carr's Bay, Little Bay,** and **Rendezvous Bay.** The Vue Pointe Hotel can arrange day sails to these beaches.

GOLF   The **Montserrat Golf Club,** Old Town (☎ **809/491-5220**), laid out in 1965, with 11 holes on some 100 acres in Belham Valley, is considered one of the finest in the eastern Caribbean. Greens fees are EC$60 ($22.20) per person per day. The second hole, the best known, is about 600 yards across two branches of the Belham River. Rental clubs and pull carts are available, and you can visit the clubhouse and bar.

TENNIS   Tennis buffs will find two asphalt courts at the previously recommended **Vue Pointe Hotel,** Old Towne. Residents play free, but nonresidents are charged EC$10 ($3.70) per hour. Two tennis courts are also available at the **Montserrat Golf Club** (see above) for those who pay court rental. There are also floodlit courts at the Montserrat Springs Hotel.

SCUBA DIVING   Beginning divers (or experienced divers on a second shallow dive) should try **Colbys,** a dive site with rare, elkhorn corals and fingerlike pillar corals projecting through the water, said to resemble supermarket aisles. The area is large enough for several dives; the maximum depth is about 45 feet.

With shallow and deep water, **O'Garros,** off the southern tip of the island, is ideal for those at all diving levels. A short, shallow shelf separates the shore from the Guadeloupe trench. There is a sharp dropoff which is a focal point for corals and large fish, such as barracuda and shark. Turtles and rays also frequent this spot.

Pinnacle is considered the island's best dive site—but it's for experienced divers only. The sea bed rises to a maximum shallow point of 65 feet, and then drops to 300 feet. There are lots of fish, since this area is not accessible for spearfishing. Colorful sponges grow from the sand in between huge brain corals, and cavernous basket sponges, large enough to conceal a fully equipped diver, are abundant.

Aquatic Discoveries, at the Vue Pointe Hotel, Old Road Bay in Old Towne (☎ **809/491-3474**), is a full-service scuba-diving facility which also offers snorkeling, equipment rentals, repair, and tank fills. Deep-sea-fishing charters can also be arranged, as can PADI certification. Boat dives are available at $70 for a two-tank dive, including equipment, and dive packages are also offered. Dives range from the very shallow to the deep. The diver will see not only elkhorn corals, pillar corals, basket sponges, and huge brain corals, but a variety of large fish and sea turtles.

SHOPPING

There is no duty-free shopping, but some interesting locally made handcrafts are for sale. Straw goods and small ceramic souvenirs predominate, along with Sea Island cotton fabrics. Most shops are open Monday through Saturday from 8am to noon and 1 to 4pm, but they usually close at 12:30pm on Wednesday.

Carol's Corner, in a public room of the Vue Pointe Hotel, Old Towne (☎ **809/491-5210**), offers one of the most concentrated collections of Montserrat-related memorabilia on the island. They sell the famous stamps of Montserrat and copies of the difficult-to-obtain flag. There's also a collection of road maps, top-quality T-shirts, a selection of local jams and honey, and cosmetics and sundries as well.

Liquor Locker/Montserrat Shirts, Strand Street (☎ **809/491-3256**), is opposite one of Plymouth's busiest piers. This is the largest and best-stocked

Where the Sidewalk Ends

Montserrat, a lush and verdant island whose interior is only rarely visited by outsiders, offers the opportunity for several hillclimbs and hikes. The two most interesting of these are easy enough to be negotiated by novice climbers who are reasonably mobile. Both lie in the island's south-central district and are relatively easy; they can both be visited in one day.

The **Galway Soufrière Hike** offers insights into the volcanic forces that shaped the earth's crust. Head south from Plymouth, along the unnamed coastal road. En route you'll drive through the villages of Trials, Kinsale, and Jingoes. After about 15 minutes, turn left (inland) at the sign pointing to Galway Soufrière. On the way you'll pass the ruins of Galway Plantation (described in "What to See and Do," below). Continue inland for about half a mile until signs indicate the parking lot for Galway Soufrière. Park your car and set out on foot, taking care not to stray from the gravel-covered trail that skirts the pits of fumaroles whose bubbling waters are hot enough to cook an egg. This is an easy 20-minute ramble along trails that are maintained by the Montserrat government.

To visit another natural wonder, retrace your car's route back to the coastal highway, then turn left (south) and pass through the village of St. Patrick. About three-quarters of a mile later, just before the end of the road, notice the signs for the **Great Alps Falls,** and head inland a short distance until you reach a parking lot marked GREAT ALPS FALLS. There, about half a dozen government guides will accompany you on the 45-minute climb to the falls. (For more information on this, contact the Montserrat Tour Guides Association at **809/491-3160.**) Hikers climb up the bottom of a gorge, crossing several times over a stream, the White River, lined with tropical vegetation. Near the gorge's end, a stream of water cascades 70 feet down a fern-covered cliff. It's recommended that you hire a government guide for this climb because of the sometimes-unclear path of the official trail. The cost recommended by the island's tourist office is $10 (U.S.) per person.

liquor store on the island, run by a couple from California. One side of the shop is devoted to an outlet of Montserrat Shirts (see below).

The Montserrat Sea Island Cotton Company sales outlet, at the corner of George and Strand streets (☎ **809/491-7009**), offers exclusive locally hand-woven West Indian Sea Island cotton products. The outlet is open from 8am, and closes at 4pm on Monday, Tuesday, Thursday, and Friday, and from 8am to noon on Wednesday and Saturday.

Montserrat Shirts, Parliament Street (☎ **809/491-2892**), is one of the premier souvenir outlets on the island, stocked with flamboyant shirts, T-shirts, gift items, and clothing, often in original designs.

Paradise Shirts, Church Road (☎ **809/491-4661**), offers a selection of unique T-shirts in original designs, often hand-painted using combinations of stencils and spray guns. Also available are souvenirs and gift items.

Tapestries of Montserrat (The John Bull Shop), Parliament Street, Plymouth (☎ **809/491-2520**), sells handcrafted rugs, wall hangings, and tote bags with Caribbean designs. Products are handmade by skilled artisans, whom you can watch at work.

MONTSERRAT AFTER DARK

Montserrat may be sleepy during the day, but it gets even quieter at night. The most activity is at the **Vue Pointe Hotel,** Old Towne (☎ **809/491-5210**), where a steel band plays every Wednesday night, when you can order a barbecue dinner for EC$66 ($24.40) per person. There is also nightly entertainment by local musicians in season.

The Village Place, Salem (☎ **809/491-5202**), is for nostalgic rock buffs. If you weren't looking for it, you might think that its encircling hibiscus fences concealed a private house. Set north of Plymouth and directly east of Old Towne, it's one of the most popular night bars and most enduring restaurants on Montserrat. Serving endless rounds of beer, and a lethal version of rum punch concocted by owner Andy Lawrence, it enjoys some of the best-entrenched rock-related legends on the island. (Legend says that Elton John proposed to his wife here, and that Eric Clapton, Sting, members of Dire Straits and Deep Purple, and Mick Jagger have all enjoyed its raffish and occasionally rowdy charms.) Many visitors come just to drink, but if you want a meal, excellent versions of fried chicken and barbecued spareribs are served by Andy's hardworking wife, Sonia. It's open Tuesday through Sunday from 6pm to very late. Beer costs EC$5 ($1.90) a bottle; a three-course meal, around EC$50 ($18.50).

The Nest Beach Bar, Old Road Bay, Old Towne (☎ **809/491-5834**), is set near the beach, downhill from the Vue Pointe Hotel (on whose land it sits). This is one of the island's busiest gossip and rumor mills for the British expatriate community as well as locals. English-owned, and near the windsurfing playground of Sting and Paul Young (who lost his Rolex in the surf and had it shortly thereafter returned by a local lad), it defines itself as an open-air bar that happens to serve lunches and snacks. Two of the rum-based drinks invented here include the Green Flash and the Sandslide, although no one will mind if you order the establishment's perennial favorite, beer. Food items range from EC$4 to EC$16 ($1.50 to $5.90), and include a pub-inspired assortment of Caesar salads, liver pâté with toast, ploughman's lunches, BLTs, and hot dogs. It's open Tuesday through Sunday from 11am to 11pm. Drinks cost EC$5 to EC$10 ($1.90 to $3.70).

3 St. Kitts

The volcanic island of the British Leewards (although it's no longer British), St. Kitts has become a resort mecca in recent years. Its major crop is sugar, a tradition dating from the 17th century. But beach tourism may overwhelm it in the years to come, as its southeastern peninsula, site of the best white sand beaches, has been set aside for massive hotel and resort development. Most of the island's other beaches are of gray or black volcanic sand.

Far more active and lively than Nevis, its companion island, St. Kitts is still fairly sleepy itself. But go now before its inherent Caribbean character changes forever.

At some point during your visit you should eat sugar directly from the cane. Any farmer will sell you a huge stalk, and there are sugarcane plantations all over the island—just ask your taxi driver to take you to one. You strip off the hard exterior of the stalk, bite into it, chew on the tasty reeds, and swallow the juice. It's best with a glass of rum.

The Caribs, the early settlers, called St. Kitts Liamuiga, or "fertile isle." Its mountain ranges reach up to nearly 4,000 feet, and in its interior are virgin rain

St. Kitts

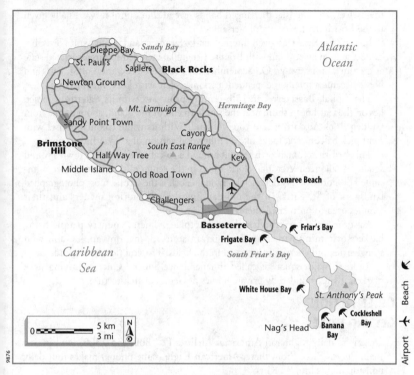

forests, alive with hummingbirds and wild green vervet monkeys. The monkeys were brought in as pets by the early French settlers and were turned loose in the forests when the island became British in 1783. These native African animals have proliferated and can be seen at the Estridge Estate Behavioral Research Institute. Another import, this one British, is the mongoose, brought in from India as an enemy of rats in the sugarcane fields. However, the mongooses and rats operate on different time cycles—the rats ravage while the mongooses sleep. Wild deer are found in the mountains.

Sugarcane climbs right up the slopes, and there are palm-lined beaches around the island. As you travel around St. Kitts, you'll notice ruins of old mills and plantation houses. You'll also see an island rich in trees and vegetation.

St. Kitts, 23 miles long and 6 1/2 miles wide, rides the crest of that arc of islands known as the northerly Leeward group of the Lesser Antilles. It's separated from the associated state of Nevis by a 2-mile-wide strait, and its administrative capital is Basseterre.

On his second voyage in 1493, Columbus spotted St. Kitts and named it Saint Christopher, but the English later changed the name to St. Kitts. In 1623 Sir Thomas Warner landed with his wife and son and a party of 14 farmers, and made St. Kitts the first British colony in the West Indies. When the island later sent out parties of settlers to neighboring islands, St. Kitts became known as the "mother colony of the West Indies."

Shortly after their arrival, the English were joined by the French. In 1627 they divided the island between them and, united, they withstood attacks from the Caribs and the Spanish. But in time the British and French fought among themselves, and the island changed hands several times until it was finally given to the British by the Treaty of Versailles.

In 1967 St. Kitts was given internal self-government and, along with Nevis, became a state in association with Britain. (Anguilla, included in this associated state at the time, broke away.) On September 19, 1983, the Federation of St. Kitts and Nevis became a totally independent nation, replete with U.N. membership.

The capital, **Basseterre,** an 18th-century-print port with its waterfront intact, lies on the Caribbean shore near the southern end of the island, about a mile from Golden Rock Airport, where you will land. With its white colonial houses with toothpick balconies, it looks like a Hollywood version of a West Indian port.

This British colonial town is built around a so-called Circus, the town's round square. A tall green Victorian clock stands in the center of the Circus. After Brimstone Hill Fortress, this Berkeley Memorial Clock is the second most photographed landmark of St. Kitts. In the old days, wealthy plantation owners and their families used to promenade here.

At some point, try to visit the marketplace. There, country people bring baskets brimming with mangoes, guavas, soursop, mammy apples, and wild strawberries and cherries just picked in the fields. Tropical flowers abound.

Another major square is called Independence Square. Once a thriving slave market, it's surrounded by private homes of Georgian architecture.

ORIENTATION
GETTING THERE

Dozens of daily flights on **American Airlines** (☎ 800/433-7300) land in San Juan, Puerto Rico. From there, **American Eagle** (same phone) makes four daily nonstop flights into St. Kitts.

If you're already on St. Maarten and want to visit St. Kitts (with perhaps a side trip to Nevis), you can do so aboard one of the most remarkable little airlines in the Caribbean. Known by its nickname, **Winair (Windward Islands Airways International)** (☎ 809/465-2186), it makes several flights a week from St. Maarten to St. Kitts, with easy connections to or from such other Dutch islands as Saba, St. Eustatius, and about a dozen other destinations throughout the Caribbean.

Another possibility involves transfers into St. Kitts or Nevis through Antigua, St. Maarten, or San Juan on the Antigua-based carrier, **LIAT** (☎ 809/465-2286). LIAT's one-way fares from each of those destinations to St. Kitts are $52, $56, and $105, respectively.

Reservations for ongoing flights from any of the above-mentioned hubs can most easily be made through the telephone networks of many of the U.S.–based carriers.

GETTING AROUND

BY PLANE   Most visitors to St. Kitts or Nevis like to spend at least one day on the neighbor island. **LIAT** provides three daily flights to and from Nevis at a cost of $21 per person one way. Make reservations at the LIAT office on Front Street in Basseterre (☎ 809/465-2286) instead of at the airport.

BY FERRY   The government passenger ferry M.V. *Caribe Queen* departs from each island between 7 and 8:30am on Monday, Tuesday, Wednesday, Friday, and Saturday, returning at 4 and 6pm (check the time at your hotel or the tourist office). The cost is $4 each way. A more modern vessel, *Spirit of Mount Nevis*

(☎ **809/469-9373**), makes the run twice daily, carrying 110 passengers and charging $6 each way.

BY TAXI   Since most taxi drivers are also guides, this is the best means of getting around. You don't even have to find a driver at the airport—one will find you. Drivers also wait outside the major hotels. Before heading out, however, you must agree on the price—taxis aren't metered. Also, ask if the rates quoted to you are in U.S. dollars or the Eastern Caribbean dollar. To go from Golden Rock Airport to Basseterre costs about EC$16 ($5.90); to Sandy Point, EC$36 ($13.30) and up.

You can negotiate with a taxi driver to take you on a tour of the island for about $50 for a three-hour trip, and most drivers are well versed in the lore of the island. Lunch can be arranged either at the Rawlins Plantation Inn or the Golden Lemon.

BY RENTAL CAR   The only U.S.–based car-rental firm maintaining a representative on St. Kitts is **Avis,** South Independence Square (☎ **809/465-6507,** or toll free **800/331-2112** in the U.S.). They charge $38 to $45 per day, $228 to $270 per week. Five-seat station wagons are available at $55 per day, $330 per week. Tax is 5% extra, and a week's rental allows a seventh day for free. The company offers free delivery service to either the airport or to any of the island's hotels. Drivers must be between ages 25 and 75.

Delisle Walwyn & Co., Liverpool Row, Basseterre (☎ **809/465-8449**), is a local company offering cars and Jeeps. Daily charges range from $28 to $50. This might be your best deal on the island.

Reflecting British tradition, *driving is on the left!* You'll need a local driver's license, which can be obtained at the Traffic Department, on Cayon Street in Basseterre, for EC$30 ($12). Usually a member of the staff at your car-rental agency will drive you to the Traffic Department to get one.

FAST FACTS: St. Kitts

Area Code   To call St. Kitts from the North American mainland, dial the 809 area code, then the local number. You don't need the area code once you're on the island.

Banking Hours   If you want to exchange your dollars into Eastern Caribbean dollars, you'll find banks open Monday through Friday from 8am to noon and also on Friday from 3 to 5pm.

Currency   The local currency is the **Eastern Caribbean dollar (EC$),** exchanged at about $2.70 to the U.S. dollar. Many bills, however, including those of hotels, are quoted in U.S. dollars. Always determine which "dollar" locals are talking about.

Customs   You are allowed in duty free with your personal belongings. Sometimes luggage is subjected to a drug check.

Drugstores   The Skeritt's Drug Store, Fort Street, Basseterre (☎ **809/ 465-2008**), is open Monday through Friday from 8am to 8pm (to 6pm on Thursday) and on Saturday from 8am to 6pm. When the pharmacy is closed, you can call for 24-hour prescription service.

Electricity   St. Kitt's electricity is 230 volts A.C., 60 cycles, so you'll need an adapter and a transformer for U.S.–made appliances.

Emergencies   Telephone **99** from Basseterre main exchanges and **999** from all other exchanges.

Entry Requirements   U.S. and Canadian citizens can enter with proof of citizenship, such as a voter registration card or birth certificate. British subjects need a passport, but not a visa.

Hospital   In Basseterre, there's a 24-hour emergency room at Joseph N. France General Hospital, Buckley Site (☎ **809/465-2551**).

Information   Tourist information is available from the tourist board's Stateside offices at 414 E. 75th St., New York, NY 10021 (☎ **212/535-1234**); 1464 Whippoorwill Way, Mountainside, NJ 07092 (☎ **908/232-6701**); and Presidents' Plaza II, 8700 W. Bryn Mawr, Suite 800-S, Chicago, IL 60631. In Canada, an office is at 11 Yorkville Ave., Suite 508, Toronto, ON M4W 1L3 (☎ **416/921-7717**), and in the United Kingdom at 10 Kensington Court, London W8 5DL (☎ **0171/376-0881**).

Language   English is the language of the island, and is spoken with a decided West Indian patois.

Police   Call **99** in Basseterre and **999** elsewhere.

Safety   This is still a fairly safe place to travel. Most crimes against tourists—and there aren't a lot—are robberies on Conaree Beach, so exercise the usual precautions. It would be wise to safeguard your valuables. Women should not go jogging along deserted roads.

Taxes   The government imposes a 7% tax on rooms and meals, plus another EC$20 ($8) airport departure tax (but not to go to Nevis).

Telecommunications   Telegrams and Telexes can be sent from Skantel, Cayon Street, Basseterre (☎ **809/465-2219**), Monday through Friday from 8am to 6pm, on Saturday from 8am to 2pm, and on Sunday and public holidays from 6 to 8pm. International telephone calls, including collect calls, can also be made from this office.

Time   St. Kitts is on Atlantic standard time all year. This means that in winter when it's 6am in Basseterre, it's 5am in Miami or New York. When the U.S. goes on daylight saving time, St. Kitts and the East Coast mainland are on the same time.

Tipping   Most hotels and restaurants add a service charge of 10% to cover tipping. If not, tip 10% to 15%.

Water   The water on St. Kitts and Nevis is so good that Baron de Rothschild's chemists selected St. Kitts as their only site in the Caribbean to distill and produce CSR (Cane Sugar Rothschild), a pure sugarcane liqueur.

Weather   St. Kitts lies in the tropics, and its warm climate is tempered by the trade winds. The average air temperature is 79° Fahrenheit and the average water temperature is 80°. Average rainfall is 55 inches. Dry, mild weather is usually experienced from November to April; May through October it's hotter and rainier.

WHERE TO STAY
VERY EXPENSIVE

✪ Golden Lemon
Dieppe Bay, St. Kitts, W.I. ☎ **809/465-7260,** or 800/633-7411 in the U.S. Fax 809/465-4019. 7 rms. 15 suites. A/C. Winter. $225–$325 single; $350–$395 double or twin; from $495 suite. Off-season, $175–$250 single; $280–$320 double or twin; from $400 suite.

Four-night minimum stay required in winter. Honeymoon and Eco packages available. Children under 16 not accepted. (MAP rates.) AE, DC, MC, V. Free parking.

Arthur Leaman, one-time decorating editor of *House & Garden* magazine, has used his taste and background to create a tiny oasis that's a citadel of charm in this once-busy French shipping port. The 1610 French manor house with an 18th-century Georgian upper story is set back from a coconut grove and a black volcanic-sand beach beyond St. Paul's on the northwest coast of St. Kitts. Flanking the Great House are the Lemon Court and Lemon Grove Condominiums, where you can rent luxuriously furnished suites surrounded by manicured gardens. Most have private pools. The spacious rooms are furnished with antiques and always contain fresh flowers. "Sophisticated" and "elegant" describe the Golden Lemon and its clientele.

Dining/Entertainment: The Golden Lemon Restaurant serves a continental and Caribbean cuisine (see "Where to Dine," below).

Services: Massage, laundry, duty-free shopping.

Facilities: Swimming pool, tennis, snorkeling, rain-forest trips. Spa facilities include a blend of fitness, nutrition, and privacy. The maximum number of participants at any one time is only 20. Spa meals are provided from fresh, organically grown ingredients. Seven-night packages are marketed, including the spa and three meals daily, as well as exercise sessions, morning walks, water aerobics, Thallassotherapy, breathing exercises, seminars, a facial, three body massages, a manicure, and a pedicure. Many other treatments are available as well, including reflexology massages, body scrubs and wraps, waxing, and electrolysis. Based on double occupancy and depending on the time of the year, per person weekly inclusive rates range from $1,810 to $2,750.

Jack Tar Village St. Kitts Beach Resort & Casino

Frigate Bay (P.O. Box 406), St. Kitts, W.I. ☎ **809/465-8651**, or 800/999-9182 in the U.S. Fax 809/465-1031. 241 rms, 3 suites. A/C TV TEL. Winter, $200 single; $340 double. $100 children 5-11 sharing parents' room. Off-season, $150–$185 single; $260–$330 double. Suites $100–$150 per person supplement year round. Children 5–12 sharing parents' room $100 extra in winter, $90 extra off-season. (Rates include meals, golf fees, drinks, and most water sports.) AE, MC, V. Free parking.

The largest hotel on St. Kitts, and certainly the showcase hotel of the much-touted Frigate Bay development, is 1 1/2 miles east of the airport on a flat, sandy isthmus between the sea and a saltwater lagoon. It seems a lot like a private country club, and the resort is almost completely self-contained. Each of the regular units has a patio or balcony and tropical furniture. Most visitors prefer the second-floor rooms because of the higher ceilings. When you check in, ID tags are issued in an effort to help you get acquainted with your fellow guests.

Dining/Entertainment: The resort has two restaurants, a number of bars, and the island's only casino. Organized activities include Scrabble and shuffleboard tournaments, scuba lessons, and toga contests.

Services: Laundry, babysitting.

Facilities: Two swimming pool areas (one for quiet reading, another for active sports), four tennis courts (lit at night); golf course nearby.

Rawlins Plantation

P.O. Box 340, Mount Pleasant, St. Kitts, W.I. ☎ **809/465-6221**, 0171/730-7144 in London, or 800/346-5358 in the U.S. Fax 809/465-4954. 10 rms. Winter, $260 single; $390 double. Off-season, $180 single; $265 double. (MAP rates.) No credit cards. Free parking. Closed Sept–Oct.

Among the remains of a muscovado sugar factory, near Dieppe Bay just outside St. Paul's on the northeast coast, 16 miles from Basseterre, this former plantation is 350 feet above sea level and enjoys cooling breezes from both ocean and mountains. Behind the grounds the land rises to a rain forest and Mount Liamuiga. A 17th-century windmill has been converted into a charming accommodation, complete with private bath and sitting room; and the boiling houses, formerly housing a caldron of molasses, have been turned into a cool courtyard where guests dine amid flowers and tropical birds. A $25 West Indian buffet lunch is served daily. One critic called the food here "a mix of Kittitian, serious Cordon Bleu, and love and inspiration." In the evening elegant dinners are offered at a fixed price of $40, and reservations are needed. Accommodations are rented in the main house, as well as in pleasantly decorated cottages equipped with modern facilities. There is no air conditioning, but ceiling fans and cross ventilation keep it cool. Laundry and afternoon tea are included in the rates, and facilities offered are a spring-fed swimming pool, a grass tennis court, and a croquet lawn.

The White House

P.O. Box 436, St. Peter's, St. Kitts, W.I. ☎ **809/465-8162,** or 800/223-1108 in the U.S. and Canada. Fax 809/465-8275. 8 rms. Winter, $275 single; $375 double. Off-season, $175 single; $275 double. (Rates include MAP and afternoon tea.) AE, MC, V. Free parking. Closed July–Aug.

Small and special, the White House boasts a plantation Great House ambience at the foot of Monkey Hill overlooking Basseterre, directly west of Golden Rock Airport. Set in stone cottages, the guest rooms are bright and airy, with four-poster beds and Laura Ashley fabrics. Each one is individually decorated.

Dining/Entertainment: The dining room serves an excellent cuisine with many unusual dishes, such as chilled and zesty watermelon soup with citrus flavoring, and "drunken" beef made with rum.

Services: Room service, laundry, shuttle to the beach (15 minutes away).

Facilities: Grass tennis court, swimming pool.

EXPENSIVE

✪ Ottley's Plantation Inn

Ottley's (P.O. Box 345, Basseterre), St. Kitts, W.I. ☎ **809/465-7234,** or 800/772-3039 in the U.S. Fax 809/465-4760. 15 rms. A/C. Winter, $160–$250 single; $180–$295 double. Off-season, $115–$175 single; $135–$195 double. Wedding, honeymoon, and other packages available. Children under 10 not accepted. MAP $50 per person extra. AE, MC, V. Free parking.

North of Basseterre on the east coast, beyond Hermitage Bay, 6 miles north of the airport, Ottley's became one of the most desirable places to stay on the island shortly after it opened in 1989. For those seeking charm and tranquility, it occupies an unbeatable 35-acre site on a former West Indian plantation founded in the 18th century, near a rain forest. Nine rooms are in an 1832 Great House and six are divided among three cottages, with air conditioning and overhead fans. One structure is called English cottage, in memory of a visit by Princess Margaret.

The innkeepers are Ruth and Art Keusch, who operated a chain of bookstores in the Northeast, and Nancy and Marty Lowell. The Great House contains a sitting room and library with an extensive collection of classic books and videos.

Dining/Entertainment: The plantation operates one of the best restaurants on the island, the Royal Palm (see "Where to Dine," below). The chef prepares classic and contemporary dishes, many light in sauce and texture, along with local favorites. There is a Sunday champagne brunch. With a day's advance notice, the kitchen will prepare a box lunch with directions as to how to reach one of many secluded beaches on the southeastern peninsula.

Services: Room service for continental breakfast, laundry, babysitting, massage; daily shuttle to the beach, tennis, shops, golf course.

Facilities: Spring-fed, granite-tiled, 65-foot swimming pool in an old sugar factory; extensive tropical gardens and an on-site rain-forest ravine with walking trails.

MODERATE

Bird Rock Beach Hotel

P.O. Box 227, Basseterre, St. Kitts, W.I. ☎ **809/465-8914,** or 800/621-1270 in the U.S. Fax 809/465-1675. 26 rms, 12 suites. A/C TV TEL. Winter, $120–$140 single or double; from $220 suite. Off-season, $75–$80 single or double; from $125 suite. Additional person $15 extra. Breakfast $7 extra. AE, MC, V. Free parking.

Set 2 miles southeast of Basseterre, on a secluded, half-moon-shaped beach, this small, white-sided resort is clean, uncomplicated, and easy-going. Views from the balconies of most of the bedrooms are either of the Bay of Basseterre and the capital, or of the ocean stretching toward Nevis. Each of the suites contains a kitchen; all the units have private patios or balconies, cable color TV, clock radio, and blandly international furniture inspired by the tropics. There's a swimming pool with its own swim-up bar, a tennis court, a beachfront snack bar with a well-attended happy hour, and an evening restaurant (the Lighthouse) with well-prepared cuisine.

Colony's Timothy Beach Resort

Frigate Bay (P.O. Box 81, Basseterre), St. Kitts, W.I. ☎ **809/465-8597,** or 800/858-5375 in the U.S. Fax 809/465-7723. 60 rms and studios. Winter, $150–$190 single or double; $200–$380 studio. Off-season, $105–$140 single or double; $150–$295 studio. AE, MC, V. Free parking.

Located on a beach at the foot of a green mountain, this resort—a family favorite—is the only hotel on Caribbean Beach at Frigate Bay. This is one of the finest beaches on St. Kitts, lying 3 miles east of Basseterre. Naturally the most sought-after units in this one- and two-bedroom condo complex are those opening directly onto the beach, with swimming, sailing, and water sports at your doorstep. There's also a swimming pool, and you're just a short drive from an 18-hole golf course.

The various units can be turned into combinations housing one or two people, or else studios (which are really junior suites). Groups or families can take over more space, housing up to six guests. Rooms are furnished in a Caribbean motif, and the larger accommodations have kitchens.

Guests are booked in on the EP (no meals), but they can patronize the increasingly popular Coconut Café, which features informal beachfront dining. Dinners at the café are particularly restful, and fresh grilled seafood is a specialty.

Frigate Bay Resort

P.O. Box 137, Frigate Bay, St. Kitts, W.I. ☎ **809/465-8935,** or 800/223-9815 in the U.S. Fax 809/465-7050. 40 rms, 24 suites. A/C TEL. Winter, $119–$169 single or double; $259 one-bedroom suite; $369 two-bedroom suite. Off-season, $75–$107 single or double; $170 one-bedroom suite; $215 two-bedroom suite. MAP $35 per person extra. Honeymoon, dive, and golf packages available. AE, MC, V. Free parking.

On a verdant hillside east of Basseterre, Frigate Bay has standard rooms and condominium suites administered as hotel units for their absentee owners. The central core of the resort contains a large swimming pool and a cabaña bar where you can enjoy a drink while partially immersed. An 18-hole golf course and tennis courts are within walking distance. Rooms are nicely furnished to the taste of the owner and painted in an array of pastel colors. They have cool tile floors, air conditioning and ceiling fans, and private balconies. Many rooms have fully equipped kitchens with breakfast bars.

⑤ Ocean Terrace Inn

P.O. Box 65, Fortlands, St. Kitts, W.I. ☎ **809/465-2754,** 0181/367-5175 in London, or 800/524-0512 in the U.S., 800/267-7600 in Canada. Fax 809/465-1057. 53 rms, efficiencies, and apartments. A/C TV TEL. Winter, $93–$215 single; $116–$326 double; $165 efficiency for two; $242–$346 one- or two-bedroom luxury apartment. Off-season, $76–$178 single; $101–$264 double; $138 efficiency for two; $177–$235 one- or two-bedroom apartment. Continental breakfast $6.50 extra. AE, DC, MC, V. Free parking. Directions: Go west along Basseterre Bay Road past Cenotaph.

The Ocean Terrace Inn is affectionately known as the "O.T.I." If you want to be near Basseterre, it's the best hotel around the port. The O.T.I. commands a view of the harbor and the capital, with oceanfront verandas. It's so compact that a stay here is like a house party on a great liner. Terraced into a well-landscaped hillside above the edge of Basseterre, the hotel has well-landscaped gardens and grounds.

All the handsomely decorated bedrooms have a light, tropical feeling and overlook a well-planted terrace. In addition to its stylish rooms in the hillside buildings, the hotel offers the Fisherman's Wharf and Village, a few steps from the nearby harbor. These wooden apartments are filled with most of the comforts of home.

Dining/Entertainment: The flagstone-edged swimming pool has a row of underwater stools where you'll be served well-made drinks while still immersed. My favorite of the four bars is in the shadow of an elaborate aviary. For further details on the cuisine here, see "Where to Dine," below.

Services: Room service, laundry, babysitting.

Facilities: Two pools, Jacuzzi, complimentary water sports, scuba diving. Rain-forest safaris, historic-plantation tours, deep-sea fishing, snorkeling adventures, and island tours available through the hotel reception.

WHERE TO DINE
EXPENSIVE

✪ The Golden Lemon

Dieppe Bay. ☎ **809/465-7260.** Reservations required. Fixed-price dinner $25–$50; lunch appetizers $2.50–$4; lunch main courses $8.50–$35; Sun brunch $24. AE, DC, MC, V. Lunch daily noon–3pm; dinner daily 7–10:30pm; brunch Sun noon–3pm. CONTINENTAL/CREOLE.

If you're touring St. Kitts, the best luncheon stop is at the Golden Lemon, a 17th-century house converted into a hotel (see "Where to Stay," above), on the northern coast beyond St. Paul's. Enjoy your lunch either on the hotel's gallery or in the garden. The food is very good and the service is polite. Dinner is served in an elegant, candlelit dining room. The cuisine features Créole, continental, and American dishes, with locally grown produce. The menu changes daily, but is likely to include baked Cornish hen with ginger, fresh fish of the day, and Créole sirloin steak with a spicy rum sauce. Dress is casual chic.

The Patio

Frigate Bay Beach. ☎ **809/465-8666.** Reservations required. Appetizers $6–$10; main courses $26–$30. MC, V. Dinner only, Mon–Sat 7–9pm. Closed May 31–Dec 15. CARIBBEAN/INTERNATIONAL.

The Patio is at the private home of a Kittitian family, the Mallalieus, six minutes southwest of the airport. Complimentary drinks are served in the flower garden just a few feet from the house. The family's high-ceilinged modern living room is transformed with antique furniture, tablecloths, and kerosene lanterns into a dining room. Meals include home-grown vegetables and a fresh seafood menu that changes nightly. Fresh lobster, Black Angus beef, Long Island duckling with an orange-rum sauce, and plantation roast loin of pork with ginger sauce are often featured. If you have any special menu requests, Peter Mallalieu will probably follow them; each dish is prepared to order. Dress is casual elegant—no shorts, please.

✪ The Royal Palm

In Ottley's Plantation Inn, Ottley's. ☎ **809/465-7234.** Reservations required. Appetizers $4.95–$9.95; main courses $20.95–$31.50; fixed-price four-course dinner from $42; Sun champagne brunch $20. AE, MC, V. Lunch daily noon–3pm; dinner seatings daily 7:30–8:30pm; brunch Sun noon–2pm. CARIBBEAN/INTERNATIONAL.

Lying on the grounds of this previously recommended inn, the Royal Palm is an island favorite. Panoramic vistas are viewed through the ancient stone arches opening onto the ocean on one side and Mount Liamuiga and the inn's Great House on the other.

The restaurant is set beside the pool, and many diners prefer to visit it at night. The menu is changed daily. Perhaps you'll start with Brazilian gingered chicken soup or chilied shrimp corn cakes. Lobster quesadillas with local lobster is a favorite, as is an Antillean seafood salad with lobster and shrimp. You might also enjoy Carib-beer-batter-dipped flying fish or Jamaican jerk rubbed grilled chicken. The dinner menu, which wanders the globe for its inspiration, is more elaborate, beginning perhaps with a white-cheddar and green-chili bisque or "galloping horses," a traditional Thai appetizer of thinly sliced pork tenderloin with an array of spices and ingredients. Main dishes are likely to include French roast rack of lamb, or breast of chicken Molyneux with almonds, country ham, mozzarella, and mushroom stuffing. A selection of housemade desserts is always available.

MODERATE

The Anchorage

Frigate Bay. ☎ **809/465-8235.** Reservations not required. Sandwiches $1.75–$4.75; salads $8–$19; main courses $10–$22. AE, MC, V. Daily 8am–11pm. WEST INDIAN/CONTINENTAL.

This isolated beachfront no-smoking restaurant on the rolling acres of Frigate Bay sits in the shadow of an enormous leafy tree. A roof shelters its concrete-slab floor from sudden showers. The owners prepare rum-based drinks and seafood, with a menu that offers four or five salads (lobster is the most expensive), broiled or thermidor lobster, sirloin, spareribs, hamburgers, a dozen kinds of sandwiches, fresh fish, and ice cream. If you're looking for an unspoiled beach with a casual restaurant, you may want to head here.

Ballahoo Restaurant

The Circus. ☎ **809/465-4197.** Reservations recommended. Appetizers $2.50–$5.50; main courses $10–$21.15. AE, MC, V. Mon–Sat 6:30am–10pm. CARIBBEAN.

Overlooking the town center Circus Clock and entered from Fort Street, the Ballahoo is about a block from the sea on the second story of a traditional stone building. Its open-air dining area is one of the coolest places in town on a hot afternoon, thanks to the sea breezes and the high ceilings. Meals include fresh Blue

Parrot fish filet, chili, seafood platters with a coconut salad and rice, chicken in red wine, or baby back ribs. For dessert, try the rum-and-banana toasted sandwich with ice cream.

Fisherman's Wharf Seafood Restaurant and Bar

Fortlands, Basseterre. ☎ **809/465-2754.** Reservations not required. Appetizers $2–$2.45; main courses $14.50–$21. AE, MC, V. Dinner only, daily 6pm–midnight. SEAFOOD/ CARIBBEAN.

At the west end of Basseterre Bay Road, the Fisherman's Wharf is between the sea and the white picket fence surrounding the Ocean Terrace Inn. Its heart and soul lie near the busy buffet grill, where hardworking chefs prepare fresh seafood. An employee will take your drink order, but you personally place your food orders at the buffet grill. Specialties are grilled lobster, shrimp in garlic sauce, grilled swordfish steak, and grilled catch of the day. The fish is caught locally and grilled to order over St. Kitts chosha coals.

⑤ Ocean Terrace Inn

Fortlands. ☎ **809/465-2754.** Reservations recommended. Appetizers $3–$8; main courses $15–$20; fixed-price three-course lunch $14; fixed-price four-course dinner $35. AE, DC, MC, V. Lunch daily noon–2pm; dinner daily 7:30–10:30pm. Directions: Drive west on Basseterre Bay Road to Fortlands. CARIBBEAN/INTERNATIONAL.

Some of the finest cuisine in Basseterre is found here, along with one of the best views, especially at night when the harbor is lit up. Your dinner might begin with curried chicken broth, followed by sliced hard-boiled eggs in a mushroom sauce served on the half shell. Then comes an order of tasty fish cakes, accompanied by breaded carrot slices, creamed spinach, a stuffed potato, johnnycake, a cornmeal dumpling, and a green banana in a lime-butter sauce, topped off by a tropical fruit pie and coffee! The kitchen also prepares French or English dishes along with some flambé specialties, including Arawak chicken, chateaubriand, steak Diane, and veal Fantasia. Some form of entertainment is often presented. Dining is on an open-air veranda.

O.T.I. Turtle Beach Bar & Grill

Southeastern Peninsula. ☎ **809/469-9086.** Reservations recommended. Appetizers $4; main courses $8.50–$18.50; Sun buffet $18. AE, MC, V. Lunch daily noon–5pm; dinner Sat 7:30–10pm. Directions: Follow the Kennedy Simmonds Highway over Basseterre's Southeastern Peninsula, then follow the signs to the O.T.I. Turtle Beach Bar. SEAFOOD.

Set directly on the sands above Turtle Beach, this airy and sun-flooded restaurant is part of the Ocean Terrace Inn (see "Where to Stay," above). Many clients spend the hour before their meal swimming or snorkeling beside the offshore reef; others simply relax beneath the verandas or shade trees (hammocks are available), perhaps with a drink in hand. Scuba diving, ocean kayaking, windsurfing, and volleyball are possible, and a flotilla of rental sailboats moor nearby. Menu specialties might be stuffed broiled lobster, conch fritters, barbecued swordfish steak, prawn salads, and barbecued honey-mustard spareribs. The hotel runs a shuttle service between the restaurant and the hotel's reception area. On Sunday a West Indian buffet with a steel band is presented.

INEXPENSIVE

Pisces Restaurant & Bar

Cayon St., Basseterre. ☎ **809/465-5032.** Reservations recommended for dinner. Breakfast EC$16.05 ($5.90); sandwiches from EC$6.50 ($2.40); dinner EC$16.05–EC$39.45 ($5.90–$14.60). No credit cards. Daily 7am–2am. CARIBBEAN.

An immediate local favorite since it opened in 1993, Pisces lies on Cayon Street at the back of the Glimbara Guest House in Basseterre. It likes to think of itself as "your home away from home." The restaurant is owned and operated by Nerita Godfrey, or "Rita," as she's affectionately known on the island. She specializes in seafood such as lobster, shrimp, and whelk. Each day she prepares some local dish, perhaps bullfoot soup with dinner rolls or a "cookup" (saltfish, pigtail, pig snout, chicken, and red pea), which is traditionally served on Tuesday. Her barbecued spareribs and conch stew are justly praised. On Saturday locals visit to sample her "goatwater." Lamp chops, pork chops, shrimp fried rice, and her special chicken are favorites of those who don't want to go too local. Throughout the day you can order breakfast, sandwiches, and several forms of burger, ranging from cheese to fish to veggie.

WHAT TO SEE & DO

The ✪ **Brimstone Hill Fortress** (☎ **809/465-6211**), 9 miles west of Basseterre, is the major stop on any tour of St. Kitts. This historic monument, among the largest and best preserved in the Caribbean, is a complex of bastions, barracks, and other structures ingeniously adapted to the top and upper slopes of a steep-sided 800-foot hill.

The fortress dates from 1690 when the British armed the hill to aid in the recapture from the French of their Fort Charles below. In 1782 an invading force of 8,000 French troops bombarded the fortress for a month before its small garrison, supplemented by local militia, surrendered. The fortress was restored to the British the following year, and they thereupon embarked on an intense program of building and reconstruction that resulted in the imposing military complex that came to be known as "The Gibraltar of the West Indies."

Today the fortress is the centerpiece of a national park of nature trails and a diverse range of plant and animal life, including the green vervet monkey. It's also a photographer's paradise, with views of mountains, fields, and the Caribbean Sea. On a clear day, six neighboring islands can be seen.

Visitors will enjoy self-directed tours among the many ruined or restored structures, including the barrack rooms at Fort George, which comprise an interesting museum. At the gift shop, prints of rare maps and paintings of the Caribbean can be purchased. Admission is $5, half price for children. The Brimstone Hill Fortress National Park is open every day from 9:30am to 5:30pm.

At the hamlet of **Half-Way Tree,** a large tamarind marked the boundary in the old days between the British-held sector and the French half.

It was near the hamlet of **Old Road Town** that Sir Thomas Warner landed with the first band of settlers and established the first permanent colony to the northwest at Sandy Point. Sir Thomas's grave is in the cemetery of St. Thomas Church.

A sign in the middle of Old Road Town points the way to **Carib Rock Drawings,** all the evidence that remains of the former inhabitants. The markings are on black boulders, and the pictographs date back to prehistoric days.

Two commercial tours might interest you. Get your driver to take you to the **Sugar Factory,** which is best visited February through July, when you can see raw cane processed into bulk sugar. As mentioned, a very light liqueur, CSR, is now being produced at the factory, and it's enjoyed with a local grapefruit drink, "Ting." You don't need a reservation.

Guests are also allowed to visit the **Carib Beer Plant,** an English lager beer-processing house. Carib Beer is considered the best in the West Indies, if sales

Into the Volcano

Mount Liamuiga was dubbed "Mount Misery" long ago, but it sputtered its last gasp around 1692. On the northeast coast, the dormant volcano is today one of the major goals for hikers on St. Kitts. Lava boulders blown from the volcano have given the area around the blow-hole the name "Black Rocks." A round-trip takes about four hours. The peak of the mountain often lies under a cloud cover.

The ascent to the volcano is usually made from the north end of St. Kitts at Belmont Estate. The trail winds through a rain forest and travels along deep ravines up to the rim of the crater at 2,625 feet. The actual peak is at 3,792 feet. Figure on about 2 1/2 hours to ascend and about 1 1/2 hours to descend.

The caldera itself has a depth of some 400 feet from its rim to the crater floor. Many hikers climb—or crawl—down into the dormant volcano. However, the trail is steep and slippery. At the crater floor is a tiny lake along with volcanic rocks and various vegetation. Although many hikers go to the crater rim without a guide, it's absolutely necessary to have a guide to go into the volcano.

Greg's Safaris (☎ **809/465-4121**) offers guided hikes to the crater for $50 per person (a minimum of four needed), including breakfast and a picnic at the crater's rim. The same outfit also offers half-day rain-forest explorations, also with a picnic, for $40 per person.

are any indication. At the end of the tour through the plant, visitors are given a cold Carib in the lounge. Check before heading there to see if it's open.

SPORTS & OUTDOOR ACTIVITIES

BEACHES   Beaches are the primary concern of most visitors, who find the swimming best at the twin beaches of **Banana Bay** and **Cockleshell Bay, Conaree Beach** (2 miles from Basseterre), talcum-powder-fine **Frigate Bay** (north of Banana Bay), and **Friar's Bay** (a peninsula beach that opens onto both the Atlantic and the Caribbean). The narrow peninsula in the southeast that contains the island's salt ponds also boasts the best white sand beaches. All beaches, even those that border hotels, are open to the public. However, if you use the beach facilities of a hotel, you must obtain permission first and will probably be assessed a fee.

GOLF   At Frigate Bay is the **Royal St. Kitts Golf Club** (☎ **809/465-8339**), with an 18-hole championship golf course designed by Peter Thomas. Greens fees are $35 per 18 holes.

TENNIS   Daytime tennis is available for guests of the **Ocean Terrace Inn** (see "Where to Stay," above). Also downtown, at the **St. Kitts Lawn Tennis Club,** you can arrange for a temporary membership. Call **809/465-2938** for details.

WATER SPORTS   Some of the best diving spots include **Nagshead,** at the south tip of St. Kitts. This is an excellent shallow-water dive starting at 10 feet and extending to 70 feet. A variety of tropical fish, eaglerays, and lobster are found here. The site is ideal for certified divers. Another good spot for diving is **Booby Shoals,** lying between Cow 'n Calf Rocks and Booby Island, off the coast of St. Kitts. Booby Shoals has abundant sea life, including nurse sharks, lobster, and stingrays. Dives—ideal for both certified and resort divers—are up to 30 feet in depth.

A variety of activities is offered by **Pro-Divers,** at the Ocean Terrace Inn's Turtle Beach (☎ **809/465-3223**). You can swim, sail, float, paddle, or go on scuba-diving and snorkeling expeditions from there. Snorkeling equipment, and ocean kayaks are offered free to the O.T.I.'s guests. At Turtle Beach, you can also charter a boat for deep-sea fishing. A two-tank dive costs $50 with your own equipment or $60 without equipment. Night dives are $50. A PADI certification is available for $300, and a resort course costs $75.

SHOPPING

The good buys here are in local handcrafts, including leather items made from goatskin, baskets, and coconut shells. Some good values are also to be found in clothing and fabrics, especially Sea Island cottons. Store hours vary, but are likely to be 8am to noon and 1 to 4pm Monday through Saturday.

If your time is limited on the island, head first for the **Pelican Shopping Mall,** containing some two dozen shops. Opened in 1991, it also offers banking services, a restaurant, and a philatelic bureau. Some major retail outlets in the Caribbean, including Little Switzerland, have branches at this mall. But don't confine all your shopping to the mall. Check out the offerings along the quaintly named **Liverpool Row,** which has some unusual merchandise. Fort Street is also worth traversing.

Cameron Gallery
10 N. Independence Sq. ☎ **809/465-1617.**

In this gallery in the center of Basseterre, Britisher Rosey Cameron-Smith produces watercolors and limited-edition prints of scenes from St. Kitts and Nevis. She makes an effort to reproduce in art some of the essence of true West Indian life. Rosey is well known on the island for her paintings of Kittitian Carnival clowns. She also produces greeting cards, postcards, and calendars, as well as first-day covers of the Christmas stamps of Carnival clowns and masqueraders she painted for the government. She also displays the works of some 20 other artists.

✪ Caribelle Batik
Romney Manor, Old Road, Basseterre. ☎ **809/465-6253.**

This place qualifies as a sightseeing attraction as well as a shopping expedition. Its studios and sales areas are in the most romantic setting of any shopping recommendation in this guide. Romney Manor stands on 5 acres of well-landscaped grounds. Established in the 17th century, the grounds offer 30 varieties of hibiscus, rare orchids, and huge ferns, climaxed by a huge 250-year-old saman tree.

As you leave the village of Old Road, and if you're on a taxi tour, ask your driver to show you the Carib petroglyphs. You then pass through the ruins of an old sugar estate, formerly waterpowered as confirmed by the still-intact aqueducts, finally through rain forests to the gardens of Romney Manor.

Inside Caribelle's workshop, island artists demonstrate and produce true batik in the methods used for centuries. A full explanation is given and questions are answered. Caribelle offers a full range of distinctive clothing and wall hangings. The fabric is 100% Sea Island cotton, the colors are flamboyant, and the styles wide ranging. All items are duty free. The management welcomes visitors to stay and picnic on the grounds. Romney Manor is open Monday through Friday from 8:30am to 4pm.

Craftshouse

Plaza Treasury Pier. ☎ **809/465-8086.**

Craftshouse is an outlet for the handcrafts of St. Kitts and Nevis made by craftspeople working through the National Handicraft and Cottage Industries Development Board. They offer items in copper, wood, coir (a coarse fiber made from the outside of a coconut), and coconut, including furniture. The shops, found at the Golden Rock International Airport and the shoreline Plaza Treasury Pier (Bay Road), are open during regular business hours.

Island Hopper

The Circus, Basseterre. ☎ **809/465-1640.**

In the Circus, below the popular Ballahoo Restaurant, Island Hopper is one of St. Kitt's most patronized retail attractions. This store is worth a visit just to see the West Indian interior, and the owner goes to great lengths to provide items unavailable elsewhere. Island Hopper is the town outlet for Caribelle batik, selling everything from silks to pottery, from T-shirts to high fashion.

Lemonaid

At the Golden Lemon, Dieppe Bay. ☎ **809/465-7260.**

This bazaarlike shop at the Golden Lemon (see "Where to Stay," above) specializes in local antiques crafts, and artwork, jewelry, and silverware, and carries a full line of duty-free fragrances, plus spa products and skin-care lotions. Island clothes are from John Warden's Island to Island collection, and the shop also sells Kisha batik fashions from Bali.

The Palms

In the Palms Arcade, Basseterre. ☎ **809/465-2599.**

The Palms specializes in island "things": handcrafts; larimar, sea opal, and amber jewelry; West Indies spices, teas, and perfumes; tropical clothes by Canadian designer John Warden; and Bali batiks by Kisha.

Plantation Picture House

Mount Pleasant. ☎ **809/465-7740.**

Set in an impeccably restored West Indian house, on a hillside below the Rawlins Plantation (see "Where to Stay," above), this is considered the finest art gallery on St. Kitts. Virtually all the paintings on display are by Kate Spencer from England, whose work is well known throughout North America and Europe. Her still-lifes, portraits, and paintings of island scenes range in price from $200 to $3,000, and have received critical acclaim from several different sources. Also for sale are a series of Ms. Spencer's silk-screened scarves, each crafted from extra-heavy stone-washed silk, priced at $84 to $125 each.

A Slice of the Lemon

The Circus, Basseterre. ☎ **809/465-2889.**

The island's oldest and most complete perfumery, this duty-free gift shop now offers skin-care and cosmetic lines at competitive prices, 14-karat gemstone and silver and gold baubles, fun watches, and the latest in costume jewelry. There's a self-contained Portmeirion Pottery Shop featuring all aspects of this highly collectible line which is exclusive to this shop.

ST. KITTS AFTER DARK

Ocean Terrace Inn's (O.T.I.) Fisherman's Wharf, Fortlands (see "Where to Stay," above), has a live band every Friday night from 8 to 10pm and a disc jockey from 10pm. O.T.I.'s **Turtle Beach Bar and Grill,** on the southeast peninsula, has a popular seafood buffet on Sunday with a live steel band from 12:30 to 3pm; on Saturday it's beach disco time. There's no cover charge at the Inn's Fisherman's Wharf or Turtle Beach Bar and Grill. Drinks cost $1.80 to $3.80.

If you're in the mood to gamble, St. Kitts's only casino is at the **Jack Tar Village,** Frigate Bay (☎ **809/465-8651**). It's open to all visitors, who can try their luck at roulette, blackjack, craps, and slot machines. The casino is open daily from 10:30am to 2am. There's no cover charge.

4   Nevis

A local once said that the best reason to go to Nevis was to practice the fine art of *limin'.* To him, that meant doing nothing in particular. Limin' might still be the best reason to venture over to Nevis, a small volcanic island. Once there, if you don't elect to stay at the major hotel on the island, the Four Seasons, you can find lodging in one of the old plantation houses, now converted to inns, and experience the regal calm that is still found on Nevis. If you want to go to the beach, head for reef-protected Pinney's Beach, a 3-mile strip of dark-gold sand set against a backdrop of palm trees, with panoramic views of St. Kitts.

Two miles south of St. Kitts, Nevis (*Nee*-vis) was sighted by Columbus in 1493. He called it Las Nieves, Spanish for "snows," because its cloud-capped mountains reminded him of the snow-capped range in the Pyrenees. When viewed from St. Kitts, the island appears like a perfect cone, rising gradually to a height of 3,232 feet. A saddle joins the mountain to two smaller peaks, Saddle Hill (1,250 feet) in the south and Hurricane Hill (only 250 feet) in the north. Coral reefs rim the shoreline, and there is mile after mile of palm-shaded white sandy beaches.

Settled by the British in 1628, the volcanic island is famous as the birthplace of Alexander Hamilton, the American statesman who wrote many of the articles contained in the *Federalist Papers* and was Washington's secretary of the Treasury. He was killed by Aaron Burr in a duel.

Nevis is also the island on which Admiral Horatio Lord Nelson married a local woman, Frances Nisbet, in 1787. The historical facts are romanticized, but are nontheless accurate, in the chapter "A Wedding on Nevis," which appeared in James Michener's bestseller *Caribbean.*

In the 18th century, Nevis, the "Queen of the Caribees," was the leading spa of the West Indies, made so by its hot mineral springs.

Once Nevis was peppered with prosperous sugarcane estates, but they are gone now—many have been converted into some of the most intriguing character hotels in the Caribbean. Sea Island cotton is the chief crop today.

As you drive around the nostalgic island, through tiny villages such as Gingerland (named for the spice it used to export), you'll reach the heavily wooded slopes of Nevis Peak, which offers views of the neighboring islands. Nevis is an island of beauty and has remained relatively unspoiled. Its people, in the main, are descendants of African slaves.

On the Caribbean side, Charlestown, the capital of Nevis, was fashionable in the 18th century, when sugar planters were carried around in carriages and sedan chairs. Houses are of locally quarried volcanic stone, encircled by West Indian fretted verandas. A town of wide, quiet streets, this port only gets busy when its major link to the world, the ferry from St. Kitts, docks at the harbor.

ORIENTATION
GETTING THERE

BY PLANE   You can fly to Nevis on **LIAT** (☎ 809/469-9333), which offers scheduled service to the island. Flights from St. Kitts and Antigua are usually non-stop, while flights from St. Thomas, St. Croix, San Juan, Barbados, and Caracas, Venezuela, usually require at least one stop before reaching Nevis. The cost of taking one of LIAT's several daily flights between St. Kitts and Nevis—a seven-minute trip—is $42 round-trip.

Any of North America's larger carriers, including **American Airlines** (☎ 800/433-7300), can arrange ongoing passage to Nevis on LIAT through such hubs as Antigua, San Juan, or St. Maarten, as part of through passage from virtually any major airport in North America.

The airport lies half a mile from Newcastle in the northern part of the island.

BY FERRY   You can also use the inter-island ferry service from St. Kitts to Charlestown on Nevis aboard the government passenger ferry M.V. *Caribe Queen*. The *Spirit of Mount Nevis* also makes the run twice daily except Monday and Wednesday. For information on these services, see "Getting Around" in Section 3 on St. Kitts.

GETTING AROUND

BY TAXI   Taxi drivers double as guides, and you'll find them waiting at the airport at the arrival of every plane. A taxi ride between Charlestown and Newcastle Airport costs EC$30 ($11.10); between Charlestown and Old Manor Estate, EC$26 ($9.60); and from Charlestown to Pinney's Beach, EC$10 ($3.70). Between 10pm and 6am, 10% is added to the prices for Charlestown trips. A 3¹/₂-hour sightseeing tour around the island will cost $75; the average taxi holds up to four people, so when the cost is sliced per passenger, it's a reasonable investment. No sightseeing bus companies operate on Nevis, but a number of individuals own buses that they use for taxi service.

BY RENTAL CAR   If you're prepared to face the winding, rocky, potholed roads of Nevis, you can arrange for a rental car from a local firm through your hotel. Or you can check with **Skeete's Car Rental,** Newcastle Village, near the airport (☎ 809/469-9458). Prices range from $35 per day.

To drive on Nevis you must obtain a permit from the Traffic Department, which costs EC$30 ($11.10) and is valid for a year. Remember, *drive on the left side of the road.*

FAST FACTS: Nevis

Language, currency, and entry requirements have already been discussed in the St. Kitts section, earlier in this chapter. Most visitors will clear Customs on St. Kitts, so arrival on Nevis should not be complicated.

Area Code   To call Nevis from the mainland, dial area code 809 and then the local number. Once on the island, you don't need the area code.

Banking Hours   Banks are open Monday through Saturday from 8am to noon and most are also open on Friday from 3:30 to 5:30pm.

Drugstores   Try Evelyn's Drugstore, Charlestown (☎ 809/469-5278), open Monday through Friday from 8am to 5pm, on Saturday from 8am to 7pm, and on Sunday only one hour, from 7 to 8pm, to serve emergency needs.

Nevis

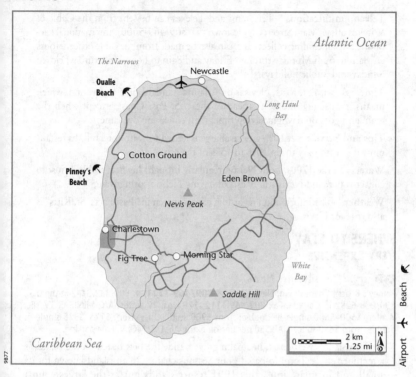

Electricity As on St. Kitts, an electrical transformer and adapter will be needed for most U.S. and Canadian appliances as the electricity is 230 volts A.C., 60 cycles. However, check with your hotel to see if they have converted their voltage and outlets.

Emergencies For the police, call **911**.

Hospitals A 24-hour emergency room operates at Alexandra Hospital in Charlestown (☎ **809/469-5473**).

Information The best source is the **Tourist Bureau** on Main Street in Charlestown (☎ **809/469-1042**). For information before you go, refer to "Fast Facts: St. Kitts," in Section 3, earlier in this chapter.

Language English is the language of the island and is often accented with a lilting West Indian patois.

Post Office The post office, on Main Street in Charlestown, is open Monday through Wednesday and on Friday from 8am to 3:30pm, and on Thursday from 8 to 11:30am.

Safety Although crime is rare here, protect your valuables and never leave them unguarded on the beach.

Taxes The government imposes a 7% tax on hotel bills, plus a departure tax of EC$27 ($10) per person. You don't have to pay the departure tax in Nevis if you're returning to St. Kitts.

Telecommunications   Telegrams and Telexes can be sent from the Cable & Wireless office, Main Street, Charlestown (☎ **809/469-5000**). International telephone calls, including collect calls, can also be made from the cable office. Hours are 8am to 6pm Monday through Friday and 8am to noon on Saturday; closed Sunday and public holidays.

Time   As with St. Kitts, Nevis is on Atlantic standard time year round, which means it's usually one hour ahead of the U.S. East Coast, except when the mainland goes on daylight saving time; then clocks are the same.

Tips and Service   A 10% service charge is added to your hotel bill. In restaurants it's customary to tip 10% to 15% of the tab.

Water   In the 1700s, Lord Nelson regularly brought his fleet to Nevis just to collect water, and Nevis still boasts of having Nelson spring water.

Weather   The information regarding climate given in "Fast Facts: St. Kitts" is also true for Nevis.

WHERE TO STAY
VERY EXPENSIVE

✪ Four Seasons Resort Nevis
Pinney's Beach, Charlestown, Nevis, W.I. ☎ **809/469-1111,** or 800/332-3442 in the U.S., 800/268-6282 in Canada. Fax 809/469-1112. 179 rms. 17 suites. A/C MINIBAR TV TEL. Winter, $500–$600 single or double; from $900 suite. Off-season, $175–$375 single or double; from $650 suite. MAP $80 per person extra. AE, DC, MC, V. Free parking.

On the island's west coast, in a palm grove beside the best beach on the island, is a member of the Toronto-based Four Seasons chain. On an island known for its small and intimate inns, this 1991 resort stands out as the largest, most accessorized, and best financed on Nevis. Designed in low-rise harmony with the surrounding landscapes, the accommodations offer rich but conservative mahogany furniture, touches of marble, carpeting, and wide patios or verandas overlooking the beach, the golf course, or Mount Nevis. Each contains all the amenities you'd expect in an urban hotel (including hairdryers and bathrooms with double sinks). The public areas contain rooms inspired by paneled libraries in London, complete with one of the few working fireplaces on Nevis. You'll also find broad, airy spaces below cathedral ceilings.

   Dining/Entertainment: Guests are faced with the largest choice of drinking and dining facilities on Nevis. The resort's centerpiece is the plantation-inspired great house, which contains the most formal restaurant of all, the Dining Room (see "Where to Dine," below). Satellite restaurants include the Grill Room (for steaks and barbecues), the Tap Room (similar to a British pub), the Pool Cabaña (poolside sandwiches and salads), the Ocean Terrace (drinks and light fare), the Sports Pavilion (adjacent to both the tennis courts and the golf course), and what is perhaps the most opulent watering hole on Nevis, the Library Bar.

   Services: 24-hour room service, laundry, babysitting. Employees will arrange for diving, deep-sea fishing, boating, hiking, or shopping excursions. A flotilla of hypermodern yachts is on hand to ferry hotel clients to and from the international airport on St. Kitts.

   Facilities: Carved into the surrounding hills and valleys is an 18-hole Robert Trent Jones, Jr.–designed golf course, considered spectacular by its aficionados. The resort also boasts direct access to one of the finest beaches in the Caribbean, 10 tennis courts with three different surfaces, an on-site scuba department, massage facilities, health club, sauna, whirlpool, beauty salon, two swimming pools, and one of the most carefully planned children's programs in the Caribbean.

Montpelier Plantation Inn

St. John Figtree (P.O. Box 474), Montpelier, Nevis, W.I. ☎ **809/469-3462,** 416/484-4864 in Canada, 0181/367-5175 in England, or 212/599-8280 in the U.S. Fax 809/469-2932. 17 rms. TEL. Winter, $225 single; $280 double. Off-season, $150 single; $180 double. (Rates include breakfast.) MC, V. Free parking. Closed July 25–Sept 11.

One of the Plantation Inns of Nevis, the Montpelier stands 700 feet up in the hills, above the sandfly level at night, with grandstand views of the ocean. It's owner managed, and a house-party atmosphere prevails. Diana, Princess of Wales, made the inn her choice during a 1993 visit. Everything is done with style and grace. The 18th-century plantation is in the center of its own 100-acre estate, which contains 10 acres of ornamental gardens as a setting for the cottage rooms. Accommodations have either one king-size bed or two double beds, direct-dial phones, ceiling fans, and a bathroom with tub and shower. Guests make use of the complimentary transport to the inn's own private beach.

Dining/Entertainment: Montpelier focuses on the standard of its food, wine, and service. Much use is made of fresh local produce (see "Where to Dine," below). Breakfast is served in the garden room and dinner on a covered terrace overlooking the garden. In season, a steel or string band is brought in about every 10 days.

Services: Laundry, babysitting (evenings), room service (only for continental breakfast).

Facilities: Huge swimming pool with pool bar, hard tennis court, private beach, windsurfing, horseback riding, hiking, "eco rambles."

✪ Nisbet Plantation Beach Club

Newcastle, St. James' Parish, Nevis, W.I. ☎ **809/469-9325,** or 800/742-6008 in the U.S. and Canada. Fax 809/469-9864. 26 rms, 12 suites. Winter, $251–$326 single; $326 double; from $435 suite. Off-season, $180–$255 single; $240 double; from $340 suite. (MAP rates.) AE, MC, V. Free parking. Directions: Turn left out of the airport and go 1 mile.

In this gracious estate house on a coconut plantation, a respect for fine living prevails. This is the former home of Frances Nisbet, who married Lord Nelson at the age of 22. Although enamored of Miss Nisbet when he married her, Lord Nelson later fell in love with Lady Hamilton, and Frances Nisbet died a bitter old woman in England.

The present main building on the 30-acre plantation was rebuilt on the foundations of the original 18th-century Great House. The ruins of a circular sugar mill stand at the entrance, covered with bougainvillea, hibiscus, and poinciana. Set in the palm grove are guest cottages consisting of superior and deluxe rooms with showers and covered verandas, and a series of premier junior suites with private baths. All rooms come with king-size beds and are brightly decorated and beautifully appointed. Among the complimentary extras are afternoon tea and a rum-punch party.

Dining/Entertainment: Breakfast and lunch are served at the Coconuts Beach and Poolside Restaurant, where occasional barbecues and even dinners are sometimes served. Dinner is served on the veranda of the Great House. Local fish and lobster are featured, along with a continental and American cuisine.

Services: Laundry.

Facilities: Swimming pool, tennis court, snorkeling opportunities off the beach, 3 miles of beachcombing right in front of the hotel, scuba diving, sports fishing, sailing, horseback riding, eco-rambles, and mountain hiking; golf can be arranged at the Four Seasons.

EXPENSIVE

Golden Rock Estate

P.O. Box 493, Gingerland, Nevis, W.I. ☎ **809/469-3346.** Fax 809/469-2113. 15 rms. 1 suite. Winter, $200 single; $245 double; $315 suite. Off-season, $125 single; $170 double; $260 suite. Children under 2 stay free in parents' room. (MAP rates.) AE, MC, V. Free parking.

A sugar estate built in 1815 high in the hills of Nevis, a 15-minute drive east of Charlestown, has been turned into one of the most charming and atmospheric inns of the Caribbean. You walk through a 25-acre garden in a tropical setting of about 100 acres. The original windmill, a stone tower, has been turned into a duplex honeymoon suite (or accommodations for a family of four or five), with an elaborate four-poster bed. Rooms are scattered about the garden, and each villa has four-poster king-size beds made of bamboo. Fabrics are island made, with tropical flower designs. In addition, the rooms have large porches with views of the sea. The owner-manager is Pam Barry, who is known for her interest in helping guests observe the wild African green monkeys. The hotel also lies at the beginning of a rain-forest walk, taking three to four hours to follow a trail round-trip (the hotel provides map).

Dining/Entertainment: Dinner is likely to be a West Indian meal served at the 175-year-old "long house." Saturday night from December through June there's a West Indian buffet, served plantation style, while a string band plays outside under the stars. Before dinner you can enjoy a drink in the hotel's bar. A separate facility at Pinney's Beach, the Carousel Bar, serves lobster, shrimp, grilled fish, and hamburgers with coconut-husk flavor; it's open daily during the winter season. Picnic lunches can be prepared in the hotel's kitchen.

Services: Laundry, babysitting, free round-trip shuttles to both beaches (with stops in Charlestown if requested).

Facilities: Freshwater swimming pool with a shady terrace (where tropical rum punches are served), tennis court, hiking through a rain forest, access to one beach on the leeward side (part of Pinney's Beach) and another beach on the windward side (where there's surfing).

Hermitage Plantation

Hermitage Village, St. John's Parish, Nevis, W.I. ☎ **809/469-3477,** or 800/682-4025 in the U.S. Fax 809/469-2481. 15 rms. 1 manor house. Winter, $215–$315 single; $285–$385 double. Off-season, $120–$200 single; $190–$270 double. Year round, $690 manor house. (MAP rates.) AE, MC, V. Free parking. Directions: Proceed on the main island road 4 miles from Charlestown.

This much-photographed, frequently copied historians' delight is said to be the oldest all-wood house in the Antilles and was built amid the high-altitude plantations of Gingerland in 1740. Here, former Philadelphian Richard Lupinacci and his wife, Maureen, have assembled one of the best collections of antiques on Nevis. Wide-plank floors, intricate latticework, and high ceilings add to the beauty of this hotel. Accommodations are in nine glamorous outbuildings designed like small plantation houses. Many contain huge four-poster beds, antique accessories, and colonial louvered windows. Gently sloping land inland from the sea, the property is protected by parallel rows of dry retaining walls. The most luxurious and expensive accommodation is a yellow manor house on a half acre of private gardens with its own ceramic-tile pool, two large bedrooms furnished with antique canopy beds, and oversize baths with dressing rooms, a comfortable living room, dining room, full kitchen, and laundry.

Services: Laundry.

Facilities: Swimming pool, tennis court, thoroughbred stables.

Mount Nevis Hotel & Beach Club

Newcastle (P.O. Box 494), Charlestown, Nevis, W.I. ☎ **809/469-9373,** 212/874-4276 in New York City, or 800/75-NEVIS in the U.S. and Canada. Fax 809/469-9375. 16 rms, 16 studios and suites. Winter, $170–$195 single or double; $245 studio; $415–$440 suite. Off-season, $120–$140 single or double; $175 studio; $295–$315 suite. Additional person $35 extra. (Rates include continental breakfast.) AE, MC, V. Free parking.

On the slopes of Mount Nevis a five-minute drive southwest of Newcastle Airport, is a family-owned and -run resort dating from 1989. It's known for the quality of its accommodations, for its panoramic views, and for serving some of the best food on Nevis. Near the historic fishing village of Newcastle, it offers deluxe rooms, suites, and studios, the latter with fully equipped kitchens and space enough to accommodate at least four guests comfortably, making it an ideal family favorite. Rooms have such amenities as color TVs and VCRs, and are furnished in a tropical motif, with wicker and colorful island prints.

Dining/Entertainment: The hotel's main restaurant is recommended separately (see "Where to Dine," below). Just minutes from the hotel, the Mount Nevis Beach Club offers a site on Newcastle Bay and features a beach pavilion, bar, and restaurant. It virtually introduced pizza to the island. The club is open daily from 10am to 10pm November through June. Occasional entertainment is offered.

Services: Beach shuttle, room service (during mealtimes).

Facilities: Outdoor 60-foot swimming pool, water-sports program (with windsurfing, waterskiing, snorkeling, and deep-sea fishing at the beach club).

ⓢ Old Manor Estate

P.O. Box 70, Gingerland, Nevis, W.I. ☎ **809/469-3445,** or 800/223-9815 or 800/892-7093 in the U.S., 800/468-0023 in Canada. Fax 809/469-3388. 14 rms. Winter, $130 single; $175 double. Off-season, $130 single; $175 double. Breakfast $8 extra. AE, MC, V. Free parking.

East of Charlestown and north of Gingerland, at a cool and comfortable elevation of 800 feet, the Old Manor Estate has an old-world grace. When Nevis was originally colonized, the forested plot of land on which the hotel sits was granted to the Croney family in 1690 by the king of England. The estate thrived as a working sugar plantation until 1936. Today the stately ruins of its Great House, once dubbed by British historians as "the best example of Georgian domestic architecture in the Caribbean," complement the hotel's outbuildings. Scattered around the property are the rusted flywheels of cane-crushing machines whose bases are engraved "GLASGOW—1859–1861." The former smokehouse and jail were replaced by a rambling villa called the Overseer's Building.

Each of the accommodations contains wide-plank floors of tropical hardwoods, reproduction furniture, and high ceilings.

Dining/Entertainment: A big part of the success of Croney's is the culinary inspiration of Mrs. Knorr. Her Cooperage dining room (see "Where to Dine," below) is among the finest on the island. Lunch is in the raftered dining room or beside an unusual swimming pool chiseled from fitted blocks of black volcanic rock. You serve yourself from a buffet table and a century-old grill in the plantation's colonial kitchens. Every Friday night there's a popular barbecue-and-buffet party.

Services: Beach and town shuttle.
Facilities: Swimming pool.

INEXPENSIVE

Hurricane Cove Bungalows

Oualie Beach, Nevis, W.I. ☎ **809/469-9462.** Fax 809/469-9462. 9 bungalows, 1 villa. Winter, $145 one-bedroom bungalow; $235–$275 two-bedroom bungalow; $395 three-bedroom villa. Off-season, $95–$110 one-bedroom bungalow; $165–$230 two-bedroom bungalow; $225 three-bedroom villa. MC, V. Free parking.

This cluster of self-catering bungalows is set on a hillside with a world-class view on the northernmost point of Nevis, a five-minute drive west of the airport. Each bungalow is wood-sided and vaguely Scandinavian in design, with a tile roof and a massive foundation which anchors it into the rocky hillside. No meals are served. Each bungalow contains a full kitchen; guests can dine out every night or prepare meals in their own kitchens or at a poolside barbecue grill. Each bungalow contains a queen-size bed, covered porch, private bath, ceiling fan, and kitchen. A freshwater pool was built into the foundation of a 250-year-old fortification, and the beach lies at the bottom of the steep hillside. On the grounds is a three-bedroom villa with its own small but private pool.

Oualie Beach Club

Oualie Bay, Nevis, W.I. ☎ **809/469-9735.** Fax 809/469-9176. 20 rms, 2 suites. TEL. Winter, $135–$155 single; $175–$195 double; $215–$255 suite. Off-season, $100–$115 single; $140–$155 double; $165–$205 suite. (Rates include breakfast.) AE, MC, V. Free parking.

Set on low-lying flatlands adjacent to the white sands of the island's second-most-famous beach (Oualie Beach), this hotel contains four concrete outbuildings, which offer a total of 22 accommodations. Each unit is clean and simple, with tiled floors, and is often fully booked several months in advance by European sun-lovers. Four rooms are air-conditioned, and many contain small, unstocked refrigerators; 16 offer a TV. A limited number contain kitchenettes. Set 5 miles east of Charlestown, on the island's relatively unpopulated north coast, the hotel was built in 1989. The resort's centerpiece is its well-recommended restaurant and bar, where sliding glass doors open directly onto a view of the beach. (See my separate recommendation in "Where to Dine," below.)

WHERE TO DINE
VERY EXPENSIVE

The Dining Room

In the Four Seasons Resort Nevis, Pinney's Beach. ☎ **809/469-1111.** Reservations recommended. Appetizers $6.50–$12; main courses $25–$42. AE, DC, MC, V. Dinner only. Tues–Sun 6:30–10pm. INTERNATIONAL/WEST INDIAN/ASIAN.

Set beneath a soaring, elaborately trussed ceiling in the largest and most formal dining room on Nevis, this is one of the island's best restaurants. Decorated in a Caribbean interpretation of French Empire designs, it offers rows of beveled-glass windows on three sides, massive bouquets of flowers, hurricane lamps with candles, a fireplace, a collection of unusual paintings, and impeccable service. Some of the food items served are low in fat and calories. Examples include seafood gumbo, Cuban black-bean soup with applewood-smoked bacon, pan-seared salmon with spinach and curried-fruit relish, grilled mahi mahi with a wasabi-mango sauce, and a vegetarian main course of vegetable cannelloni gratiné with a purple basil–tomato sauce. Dessert might be a flaming meringue "Mount Nevis."

✪ Miss June's

Jones Bay. ☎ **809/469-5330.** Reservations required. Fixed-price meal $65 per person, including drinks. MC, V. Three to five evenings a week, depending on business, beginning around 7:30pm. CARIBBEAN.

This charming dining venue is located in the private home of June Mestier, a Trinidad-born grande dame whose late husband (a New Orleans–educated sugar chemist) was distantly related to Frances Nesbit, first wife of Horatio Lord Nelson. A dinner in her home requires advance reservations, which are made by some visitors before they even depart from their home countries.

The setting is midway between the Four Seasons Resort and the island's airport, in a house adorned with lattice work and Victorian gingerbread. Guests at these dinner parties assemble in an airy living room for canapés and drinks, then sit down for soup and sherry. Fish and wine follow. All of this is followed with samples of about 20 buffet dishes that hail from Trinidad, New Orleans, India, and the French isles. Ms. Mestier's comments on the food are considered one of the evening's most delightful aspects.

Ms. Mestier is assisted by four helpers and by her son Darrell. Seating is at tables holding 2 to 10 diners, and silver and porcelain is quaintly elegant (and charmingly mismatched). After the buffet, guests retire to a lounge for dessert and port. Many visitors find the meal to be one of the highlights of their visit to Nevis.

EXPENSIVE

Hermitage Plantation

Hermitage Village, St. John's Parish. ☎ **809/469-3477.** Reservations required. Lunch $6–$15; dinner $40–$45. AE, MC, V. Lunch daily noon–2:30pm; dinner daily at 8pm. Directions: Proceed south on the main island road from Charlestown. INTERNATIONAL.

You can combine an excellent dinner with a visit to the oldest house on Nevis, now one of the island's most unusual hotels (see "Where to Stay," above). Meals are served on the latticed porch of the main house, amid candles and good cheer. Maureen Lupinacci, who runs the place with her husband, Richard, sees to combining continental recipes with local ingredients. Have a before-dinner drink in the colonial-style living room before you enjoy the likes of snapper steamed in banana leaves, carrot-and-tarragon soup, brown-bread ice cream, and a delectable version of rum soufflé. Nonresidents are accepted as dinner guests. Many turn up on Wednesday for the roast-pig dinner.

Montpelier Plantation Inn

Montpelier. ☎ **809/469-3462.** Reservations recommended for lunch, required for dinner. Lunch buffet $20; fixed-price three-course dinner $45. MC, V. Lunch daily 12:30–2pm; dinner daily at 8:15pm. Closed July 25–Sept 11. INTERNATIONAL.

The previously recommended hotel (see "Where to Stay," above), a mile off the main island road toward Gingerland, provides some of the finest dining. You dine by candlelight on the verandas of this grand old West Indian mansion overlooking the floodlit gardens, the lights of Charlestown, and the ocean. Lobster and fish are served the day the catch comes in. The three foreign and three Nevisian chefs conspire to produce delectable tropical dishes. Menus might include Cajun prawns, fresh tuna salad, mussels provençal, curried ackee, suckling pig, and soursop-and-orange mousse for dessert. There is one seating for dinner, so try to show up on time. A buffet or à la carte lunch is offered daily. An excellent and well-balanced wine list is available.

✪ Mount Nevis Beach Club

Newcastle. ☎ **809/469-9373.** Reservations recommended for dinner. Appetizers $3–$6 at lunch, $5–$9 at dinner; main courses $7–$14 at lunch, $19.50–$25 at dinner. AE, MC, V. Lunch daily 11:30am–2:30pm; dinner Tues–Sun 6–9pm. CARIBBEAN/CONTINENTAL.

In this previously recommended hotel, this relatively unheralded restaurant is a discovery, serving some of the finest cuisine on Nevis with menus that change every night. Just steps above the pool, the restaurant offers vistas of palm groves and the Caribbean Sea from its bar and dining terrace. You never know what's likely to be featured, perhaps gazpacho (made with lobster) as an appetizer or calamari stuffed with shrimp-and-lobster mousse. Main dishes are likely to include grilled pork tenderloin with tannia pancakes, grilled lobster tails with couscous, linguine with shrimp pesto and calamari, or perhaps something more familiar—filet mignon with mushroom sauce. At lunch the menu is more limited, ranging from a Mount Nevis lobster club sandwich to a Créole chicken sandwich with Nevis salsa.

MODERATE

✪ The Cooperage

In the Old Manor Estate, Gingerland. ☎ **809/469-3445.** Reservations recommended, especially for those not staying in the hotel. Appetizers $2.50–$3.50; main courses $11.95–$20. AE, MC, V. Daily 7am–9pm. INTERNATIONAL/CARIBBEAN.

Directly east of Charlestown and north of Gingerland, the Cooperage is the previously recommended hotel's dining room, in a reconstructed 17th-century building where coopers once made barrels for the sugar mill. Under the guidance of Ohio-born Vicki Knorr, the dining room has a high, raftered ceiling and stone walls. Lunch includes spinach salad, stuffed Caribbean lobster, and fruit desserts. At dinner, you might choose shrimp with green-pepper soup, Jamaican jerk chicken, local fish bought fresh each morning, or a succulent variety of local shrimp. Grilled swordfish steak seasoned with lime and butter is often featured, as is grilled local wahoo prepared the same way.

ⓢ Oualie Beach Club

Oualie Bay. ☎ **809/469-9735.** Reservations recommended for dinner. Appetizers EC$6–EC$10 ($2.20–$3.70); main courses EC$22–EC$40 ($8.10–$14.80). AE, MC, V. Daily 6am–11pm. INTERNATIONAL.

This restaurant is the centerpiece of the only hotel that lies adjacent to the second-most-famous swimming spot on Nevis, Oualie Beach. An airy, open-sided building with a pleasant staff and a setting a few steps from the ocean, it contains a bar area, a screened-in veranda, and a chalkboard menu containing such dishes as broiled wahoo, several preparations of lobster, Créole conch stew, pastas, and spinach-stuffed chicken breast. Any of an array of brightly colored rum drinks are available to accompany your meal.

INEXPENSIVE

Eddy's

Main St., Charlestown. ☎ **809/496-5958.** Reservations not required. Appetizers EC$8–EC$15 ($3–$5.60); main courses EC$12–EC$35 ($4.40–$13). AE, MC, V. Lunch daily 11:45am–3pm; dinner daily 7–10pm. INTERNATIONAL.

Set on the upper floor of a plank-sided Nevisian house in the center of Charlestown, this local restaurant is open on three sides to the prevailing winds and offers an eagle's-eye view of street life in the island's capital. Its balcony juts out over the pedestrian traffic below, and the clean and airy interior contains a tuckaway bar, lattices and gingerbread, and lots of tropical color. Menu items are posted on one of several signs, and are among the best prepared in Charlestown. They might include split-pea soup, conch fritters, stir-fried or curried chicken, club sandwiches, and fresh filets of fish. No one will mind if you arrive only for a drink at the corner bar. Some nights are devoted to theme evenings, featuring, for example, Italian, Caribbean, or Mexican cuisine.

Muriel's Cuisine

Upper Happyhill Dr., Charlestown. ☎ **809/469-5920.** Reservations recommended. Soups EC$3–EC$5 ($1.10–$1.90); platters EC$12–EC$18 ($4.40–$6.70). AE, MC, V. Mon–Sat 8am–10pm. WEST INDIAN.

This Nevis-owned restaurant occupies the back of a concrete building whose front is devoted to a store. It lies within a six-minute walk from Charlestown's waterfront, in an outlying neighborhood of low-rise commercial buildings. Head here for an insight into island life, and for a West Indian cuisine that might include three kinds of curries (goat, chicken, or lobster), chicken or seafood rôtis, lobster Créole, several preparations of conch (stewed or curried), saltfish, jerk pork or chicken, steamed fish, and (on Saturday night only) goatwater stew.

WHAT TO SEE & DO

When you arrive at the airport, negotiate with a taxi driver to take you around Nevis. The distance is only 20 miles, but you may find yourself taking a long time if you stop to see specific sights and talk to all the people who will want to talk to you.

The major attraction is the **Museum of Nevis History** at the Birthplace of Alexander Hamilton, on Main Street in Charlestown (☎ **809/469-5786**), overlooking the bay. Mr. Hamilton was the illegitimate son of a Scotsman, James Hamilton, and Rachel Fawcett, a Nevisian of Huguenot ancestry. The family immigrated to St. Croix and from there Alexander made his way to the North American colonies where he became the first secretary of the U.S. Treasury. His picture appears on the U.S. $10 bill. The lava-stone house by the shore has been restored and a museum dedicated to the history and culture has been established. The Archives of Nevis are housed here. The museum is open Monday through Friday from 8am to 4pm and on Saturday from 10am to noon. Admission is $2 for adults, $1 for children.

At Bath Village, about half a mile from Charlestown, stands the **Bath Hotel,** in serious disrepair, and its **Bath House,** which has been restored to use as a police garrison. Shortly after the Bath Hotel was completed on Nevis in 1778, its thermal baths attracted the elite from the United States, Canada, and Europe, who came to "take the waters." Temperatures rose as high as 108°. They also drank and gambled in its casino with wealthy local residents who frequented the site. Some say the Bath Hotel also housed a brothel for a short time. There are legends of entire plantation estates changing hands in the casino, as well as a fair share of bloody duels of honor.

Today the baths are in a stone and wood-sided outbuilding, a dim reminder of the site's earlier glamour. If you're interested in sampling the reputed health benefits of the waters, you'll be ushered down a flight of rough-sawn wooden steps to the reservoirs. There, behind thin-walled partitions, five concrete-bottomed holding tanks contain shallow pools of the famous waters. No soap is allowed in the holding tanks, and no more than about 15 minutes of immersion is recommended, as serious health problems have resulted from too much time in the waters. The baths are open Monday through Friday from 8am to 5pm. Admission is free, although use of the baths costs $2.

Nearby, **St. John's Church** stands in the midst of a sprawling graveyard in Fig Tree Village. It is said to have been the parish church of Lady Nelson, wife of Horatio Lord Nelson. An 18th-century church of gray stone, it contains the record of Nelson's marriage to Frances Nisbet in the church register.

At Bellevue, Bath Plain, just beyond the Bath Hotel and next to Government House, stands the **Horatio Nelson Museum** (☎ **809/469-0408**). The vast collection of Nelson memorabilia gathered by Robert Abrahams, a Philadelphia lawyer, was given to the Nevis Historical and Conservation Society. A museum was opened on March 11, 1992, the 205th anniversary of the wedding of Nelson to Nevisian Frances Nisbet. The exhibition, entitled "Nevis in the Time of Nelson," is the backdrop for the display of one of the largest collections of Horatio Nelson memorabilia in the western hemisphere. Fanny's Shoppe features Nelson memorabilia, island crafts, and books for both adults and children. The museum is open Monday through Friday from 9am to 4pm and on Saturday from 10am to 1pm. Admission is $2 for adults, $1 for children.

Fort Ashby, which overlooks what is thought to be the site of Jamestown, a settlement that slid into the sea around 1640, is now overgrown, but it was once used by Lord Nelson to guard his ships in Nevis while they took on fresh water and supplies. Nearby is **Nelson's Spring,** near Cotton Ground Village. In the 18th century, Nelson is said to have watered his ships here before they left to fight in the American Revolution. The fort, in sad disrepair, overlooks the site of Jamestown, an early settlement that was devastated by a 1680 tidal wave.

The **Eden Brown Estate,** about a mile and a half from New River, is said to be haunted. Once it was the home of a wealthy planter, whose daughter was to be married, but her husband-to-be was killed in a duel at the prenuptial feast. The mansion was then closed forever and left to the ravages of nature. A gray solid stone still stands. Only the most adventurous come here on a moonlit night.

Outside the center of Charlestown, the **Jewish Cemetery** was restored in part by an American, Robert D. Abrahams, the Philadelphia lawyer already mentioned. At the lower end of Government Road, it was the resting place of many of the early shopkeepers of Nevis. At one time, Sephardic Jews who came from Brazil made up a quarter of the island's population. It is believed that Jews introduced sugar production into the Leewards. Most of the tombstones date from between 1690 and 1710.

An archeological team from the United States believes that an old stone building in partial ruin on Nevis is probably the oldest **Jewish synagogue** in the Caribbean, according to historian Dr. Vincent K. Hubbar, a resident of the island and author of *Swords, Ships, and Sugar: A History of Nevis to 1900*. Preliminary findings in 1993 traced the building's history to one of the two oldest Jewish settlements in the West Indies, Hubbard noted, and current work at the site plus historic documents in England establish its existence prior to 1650.

The original function of the building site, located adjacent to the government administration building in Charlestown, had been forgotten perhaps as much as 150 or more years ago. However, because of Nevis's relatively large Jewish population in the 17th century and its well-known **Jewish cemetery,** many scholars and historians believed that a synagogue must have existed but didn't know exactly where.

SPORTS & OUTDOOR ACTIVITIES

BEACHES   The best beach on Nevis—in fact, one of the best beaches in the Caribbean—is the reef-protected **Pinney's Beach,** which has clear water, golden sands, and gradual slope, and is just north of Charlestown on the west coast. You'll have 3 miles of sand (often virtually to yourself) that culminates in a sleepy lagoon. It's best to bring your own sports equipment; while hotels are stocked with limited gear, it may be in use by other guests when you want it. You can go snorkeling or scuba diving among damselfish, tangs, grunts, blue-headed wrasses, and parrotfish, among other species.

GOLF   The **Four Seasons Golf Course,** Pinney's Beach (☎ 809/469-1111), has one of the most challenging and visually dramatic golf courses in the world. Designed by Robert Trent Jones, Jr. (who called it "the most scenic golf course I've ever designed"), this 18-hole championship golf course wraps around the resort and offers panoramic ocean and mountain views at every turn. From the first tee (which begins just steps from one of the most accessorized Sports Pavilions in the Caribbean) through the 660-yard, par-5, to the 18th green at the ocean's edge, the course is, in the words of one avid golfer, "reason enough to go to Nevis." Greens fees are $95 to $110.

HORSEBACK RIDING   Horseback riding is available at the **Nisbet Plantation Beach Club,** Newcastle (☎ 809/469-9325), discussed earlier. You can ride English saddle, and the cost is $40 per person for $1^1/_2$ hours. With a guide, you're taken along mountain trails to visit sites of long-forgotten plantations.

The **Nevis Jockey Club** organizes and sponsors thoroughbred races every month. Local horses as well as some brought over from other islands fill out a typical five-race card. If you want to have a glimpse at what horse racing must have been like a century or more ago, you'll find the Nevis races a memorable experience. For information, contact Richard Lupinacci, a Jockey Club officer and owner and operator of the Hermitage Plantation (☎ 809/469-3477).

MOUNTAIN CLIMBING   This is strenuous, and is recommended only to the stout of heart. Ask your hotel to pack a picnic lunch and arrange a guide (who will probably charge about $30 to $35 per person). Hikers can climb **Mount Nevis,** 3,232 feet up to the extinct volcanic crater, and enjoy a trek to the rain forest to watch for wild monkeys. The hike takes about $2^1/_2$ hours and once at the summit you'll be rewarded with views of Antigua, Saba, Statia, St. Kitts, Guadeloupe, and Montserrat. Of course, you've got to reach that summit, which means near-vertical sections of the trail requiring handholds on not-always-reliable vines and roots. It's definitely not for acrophobes! Guides can usually be found at the Nevis Historical and Conservation Society (☎ 809/469-5786), based at the Museum of Nevis History on Main Street in Charlestown.

TENNIS   Most of the major hotels have tennis courts.

WATER SPORTS & FISHING   For **snorkeling,** head for Pinney's Beach. You might also try the waters of Fort Ashby, where the settlement of Jamestown is said to have slid into the sea; legend has it that the church bells can still be heard and the undersea town can still be seen when conditions are just right. So far, no diver, to my knowledge, has ever found the conditions "just right."

For scuba divers, some of the best sites on Nevis include **Monkey Shoals,** 2 miles west of the Four Seasons. This is a beautiful reef starting at 40 feet, with dives up to 100 feet in depth. Angelfish, turtles, nurse sharks, and extensive soft coral can be found here. **The Caves** are on the south tip of Nevis, a 20-minute boat ride from the Four Seasons resort. A series of coral grottos with numerous squirrelfish, turtles, and needlefish make this an ideal dive for both certified and resort divers. **Champagne Garden,** a five-minute boat ride from the Four Seasons, gets its name from bubbles created from an underwater sulfur vent. Because of the warm water temperature, large numbers of tropical fish are found here. Finally, **Coral Garden,** 2 miles west of the Four Seasons, is another beautiful coral reef with schools of Atlantic spadefish and large seafans. The reef is at a maximum of 70 feet and is suitable for both certified and resort divers.

   Scuba Safaris Ltd., Oualie Beach (☎ **809/469-9518**), on the island's north end, offers scuba diving and snorkeling in an area rich in dive sites. They also offer resort and certification courses, dive packages, and equipment rental. A one-tank scuba dive costs $50; a two-tank dive, $90. Full certification courses cost $300 per person. Glass-bottom-boat and snorkeling trips take you from Nevis across the narrows to St. Kitts. The 30-foot glass-bottom boat goes at a leisurely pace, and masks, fins, snorkels, snorkel vests, rum punch, and drinks are provided during the 2^{1}/$_{2}$-hour cruise. Boat charters to Basseterre, Banana Bay, Cockleshell Bay, and other beaches are offered, as well as deep-sea fishing trips on request. Scuba Safaris operates on the premises of the Oualie Beach Club (☎ **809/ 469-9735**), to which it has no financial or managerial links.

SHOPPING

Normal store hours are Monday through Friday from 8am to noon and 1 to 4pm, but on Thursday some places close in the afternoon and on Saturday some stay open to 8pm. Most are closed Sunday.

Island Hopper

In the T.D.C. Shopping Mall, Main St., Charlestown. ☎ **809/469-5430.**

Hand-painted or tie-dyed cotton along with batik clothing are featured at this chain shop which also has locations in St. Kitts and Antigua. From beach wraps to souvenirs, a wide selection of products is available, although most shoppers are here to look at the batiks.

Nevis Handicraft Cooperative Society Ltd.

Cotton House, Charlestown. ☎ **809/469-1746.**

In a stone building about 200 feet from the wharf, near the marketplace, this handcraft shop contains locally made gift items, including unusual objects of goatskin, local wines made from a variety of fruits grown on the island, hot-pepper sauce, guava cheese, jams, and jellies. Open Monday through Friday from 8:30am to 12:30pm and 1:30 to 4pm, and on Saturday from 8:30am to 12:30pm.

Nevis Philatelic Bureau

Head Post Office, Market St., Charlestown. ☎ **809/469-5535.**

Those interested in stamp collecting can come here to see the wide range of colorful stamps. The postage stamps feature butterflies, shells, birds, and fish. It lies next to the public market. Open Monday through Friday from 8am to 4pm.

The Sandbox Tree

Parkview Plaza, Charlestown. ☎ **809/469-5662.**

Housed in a clapboard house which was originally built in 1836, probably for a local doctor, this is one of the most appealing gift shops in Nevis. Maintained by a Nevisian-American partnership of Henry Loomis and Patricia Thompson, it contains a collection of artworks from Haiti and Nevis, books for adults and for children, hand-painted clothing, sheets, napkins, several pieces of antique furniture, and such culinary aids as spices, relishes, and exotic chutneys.

5 Anguilla

It's small, serene, secluded, and special, and if you look like Tom Cruise or Demi Moore and have millions in the bank, this place is for you. The most northerly of the Leeward Islands in the eastern Caribbean, 5 miles north of St. Maarten, Anguilla (rhymes with "vanilla") is only 16 miles long, with 35 square miles in land area. Columbus may have spotted the island, and may have called it *anguilla* (Spanish for "eel") because of its elongated shape. Anguilla has very little rainfall so the soil is unproductive, with mainly low foliage and sparse scrub vegetation, but the beaches of white coral sand around the island are outstanding. Some 30 stretches of sand shaded by sea grapes encircle Anguilla.

The little island has a population of some 9,000 people, predominantly of African descent but also some of European, particularly Irish. Most of the locals work in the tourist industry or in lobster fishing.

First colonized by the British in 1650, the island was subjected to sporadic raids by Irish and French freebooters. Attempted invasions by the French in 1745 and 1796 were repulsed, the latter by heroic Anguillans who fed their cannons with lead balls from their sprat nets. Once part of the federation with St. Kitts and Nevis, Anguilla gained its independence from that association in 1980 and has since been a self-governing British possession.

Anguilla used to be for the adventurous explorers attracted to its unspoiled nature. However, with the opening of some super-deluxe (and super-expensive) hotels in the 1980s, Anguilla was suddenly "discovered," and has become one of the most chic targets in the Caribbean. Recently some hotels have opened that are aimed at the "mid-market" price range. Not wanting to be "spoiled," Anguilla has controlled development so most operations are small and informal.

ORIENTATION

GETTING THERE

BY PLANE   Various airlines maintain more than 50 scheduled flights per week into Anguilla, not counting the many charter flights. Because there are no nonstop flights to Anguilla from mainland North America, visitors usually transfer through either San Juan, Puerto Rico, or nearby St. Maarten. Some visitors also come in from St. Kitts, Antigua, and St. Thomas.

One of the most reliable services into Anguilla is offered by **American Eagle** (☎ **800/433-7300** in the U.S.), the commuter partner of American Airlines, which offers three nonstop flights daily to Anguilla from its hub in San Juan. Carrying 44 to 46 passengers, flights leave at different times based on the seasons. Because schedules are subject to change, check with the airline or your travel agent.

From Dutch St. Maarten, **Winair** (Windward Islands Airways International) (☎ **809/775-0183** on Anguilla, **599/5-44230** on St. Maarten, or **800/813-4264**) offers three scheduled flights to Anguilla daily, plus one daily flight from St. Thomas to Anguilla, usually on Twin Otters.

LIAT (☎ 809/465-2286)—not the most on-time airline—flies daily from Antigua to Anguilla and daily from St. Kitts to Anguilla. On some days it might operate two or three flights from either Antigua or St. Kitts to Anguilla. **Air Anguilla** (☎ 809/497-2643) operates one scheduled flight daily from St. Thomas to Anguilla. It also operates charter flights from St. Maarten, Tortola (B.V.I.), and San Juan to Anguilla.

Tyden Air (☎ 809/497-2719) offers one daily flight between St. Maarten and Anguilla, and also operates a charter service between San Juan and Anguilla. It maintains a kiosk at the St. Maarten airport.

Flying time from St. Maarten to Anguilla is 7 minutes; from San Juan and Antigua, 50 minutes; from St. Thomas, 30 minutes; and from St. Kitts, also 30 minutes.

GETTING AROUND

BY TAXI The best way to get an overview of the island is on a taxi tour. In about 2¹/₂ hours, a local driver (all of them are guides) will show you everything for $40 to $45. If you're visiting just for the day (as most sightseers do), you can be let off at your favorite beach after a look around, and then be picked up and returned to the airport in time to catch your flight back to wherever. Typical taxi fares are as follows: from the airport to Cap Juluca, $18; to the Fountain Beach Hotel, $12; and to the Malliouhana Hotel, $14.

BY FERRY Ferries run between the ports of Marigot Bay, French St. Martin, and Blowing Point, Anguilla, at approximately 30-minute intervals daily. The first ferry leaves St. Martin at 8am and the last at 6:40pm; from Blowing Point, the first ferry leaves at 7:30am and the last at 6:15pm. A night ferry departs Blowing Point on Anguilla at 10:15pm nightly; there is also a night ferry departing from Marigot Bay on French St. Martin nightly at 10:45pm. The one-way fare for a day ferry is $9; for a night ferry, $12. There's a $2.20 departure tax for those leaving by boat. No reservations are necessary.

BY RENTAL CAR To explore the island in any detail, it's best to rent a car. Several rental agencies on the island can issue the mandatory Anguillian driver's licenses, which are valid for three months. These are also issued at police headquarters in the Valley and at ports of entry. You'll need a valid driver's license from your home country, and pay a one-time fee of $6. Remember to *drive on the left!*

Most experienced visitors to Anguilla pay a taxi to carry them from the island's airport to their hotel, and then, the following day, arrange for a rental car to be delivered to wherever they're staying. Each of the island's car-rental companies delivers vehicles to anywhere on Anguilla for no extra charge, and each offers slight discounts for rentals of seven days or more.

Three of North America's largest car-rental firms are represented on Anguilla, although with the local branch of **Avis** (☎ 800/331-2112 in the U.S.), rental terms are so rigid that many visitors opt instead for rentals at either **Budget** (☎ 800/527-0700 in the U.S.) or **Hertz** (☎ 800/654-3001 in the U.S.). Most attractive of the three is Hertz, where the cheapest car, with automatic transmission and air conditioning, rents for $216 per week, including taxes and unlimited mileage. An optional collision-damage waiver costs $6.95 to $9.95 per day, although even with its purchase renters are still liable for up to $100 to $600 worth of damage in the event of an accident. Hertz is represented locally by Triple K Car Rentals (☎ 809/497-2934).

Anguilla

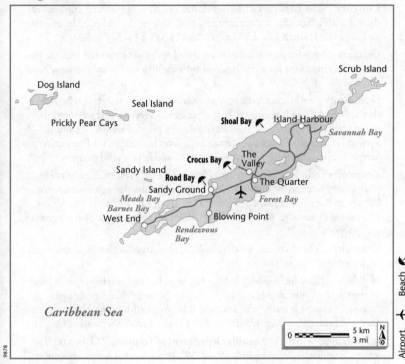

Dog Island

Seal Island

Prickly Pear Cays

Scrub Island

Shoal Bay Island Harbour

Savannah Bay

Crocus Bay The Valley

Sandy Island The Quarter

Road Bay

Sandy Ground

Meads Bay *Forest Bay*

Barnes Bay

West End Blowing Point

Rendezvous Bay

Caribbean Sea

0 ⸻ 5 km / 3 mi N

Beach ⚓ ✈ Airport

Budget charges $330 per week, with unlimited mileage, plus 6% tax, for a Ford Escort reserved 14 business days in advance, with modest discounts for rentals reserved and prepaid two weeks in advance. A collision-damage waiver costs $8 per day, and renters are still liable for $900 worth of damage in the event of an accident. Drivers between 21 and 24 (inclusive) pay a $10-per-day surcharge. Renters must be 21 to 65 years old. For information locally, call **809/497-2217.**

Less convenient than either of its competitors is Avis. You can request a car in Anguilla through Avis's toll-free number within two weeks to a month of the anticipated pickup of your car. Rentals begin at $270 per week, plus tax. The collision-damage waiver is mandatory and costs $7 extra per day. Even with its purchase, a renter's liability is $600. Also, a deposit of $20 is taken in advance for use of gas. Renters must be 25 and up. If you're interested, contact Bennie & Sons, Blowing Point, Anguilla, B.W.I. (☎ **809/497-2788**).

You can also rent an automatic- or standard-shift car or Jeep from **Connor's Car Rental,** c/o Maurice Connor, P.O. Box 65, South Hill, Anguilla, B.W.I. (☎ **809/497-6433**). Daily rates begin at $40. Mileage is unlimited, but gas is extra.

FAST FACTS: Anguilla

Area Code   Calls can be made directly from the U.S. by dialing the area code, 809, then 497 plus four digits. Don't use the area code when you're on the island.

Banking Hours   Banks are open Monday through Thursday from 8am to 3pm and on Friday from 8am to 5pm.

Currency   The **Eastern Caribbean dollar (EC$)** is the official currency of Anguilla, although U.S. dollars are the actual "coin of the realm." The official exchange rate is about EC$2.70 to each $1 U.S. (EC$1 = 37¢ U.S.).

Customs   Even for tourists, duties are levied on goods imported into the island at varying rates: from 5% on foodstuffs to 30% on luxury goods, wines, and liquors.

Documents   All visitors must have an onward or return ticket. It is preferred that U.S. and Canadian citizens have a passport, even one that's expired (but not more than five years ago). In lieu of a passport, proof of identity is required—a photo ID with an original birth certificate, a voter registration card, or a driver's license. Citizens from the United Kingdom should have a valid passport.

Drugstores   Go to the Government Pharmacy at the Princess Alexandra Hospital, Stoney Ground (☎ 809/497-2551), open Monday through Saturday from 8:30am to 8pm and on Sunday from 8:30 to 10am and 2 to 8pm. In addition, Paramount Pharmacy, Waterswamp (☎ 809/497-2366), has a 24-hour emergency service.

Electricity   The electricity is 110 volts A.C., so no transformers or adapters are necessary for U.S. appliances.

Holidays   These include May 1, May 30 (Anguilla Day), a celebration in June of the Queen's birthday (dates vary), August Monday (the first Monday in August), August Thursday (the Thursday after August Monday), Constitution Day (the Friday after August Monday), and December 19 (Separation Day).

Information   Go to the **Anguilla Department of Tourism,** P.O. Box 60, The Valley, Anguilla, B.W.I. (☎ 809/497-2759). In the United Kingdom, contact the Anguilla Tourism Office, 3 Epirus Rd., London SW6 7UI (☎ 0171/937-7725).

Language   English is spoken here, often with a West Indian accent.

Medical Care   For medical services, there is the Princess Alexandra Hospital, Stoney Ground (☎ 809/497-2551), plus several district clinics.

Police   You can reach the police at their headquarters in the Valley (☎ 809/497-2333) or the substation at Sandy Ground (☎ 809/497-2354).

Post Office   The main post office is in the Valley (☎ 809/497-2528). Collectors consider Anguilla's stamps valuable, and the post office also operates a philatelic bureau. It's open Monday through Friday from 8am to 3:30pm.

Radio   A daily broadcast service is provided by Radio Anguilla, which operates on a frequency of 1505 kHz (200m) with a power of 1,000 watts.

Safety   Although crime is rare here, secure your valuables; never leave them in a parked car or unguarded on the beach. Anguilla is one of the safest destinations in the Caribbean, but you should take the usual discreet precautions advised anywhere.

Taxes   The government collects an 8% tax on rooms and a departure tax of $7 U.S. if you leave the island by air.

Telecommunications   Telephone, cable, and Telex services are offered by Cable & Wireless Ltd., Wallblake Road (☎ 809/497-3100), open Monday through Friday from 8am to 6pm and on Saturday from 9am to 1pm.

Time   Anguilla is on Atlantic standard time year round, which means it's usually one hour ahead of the U.S. East Coast. When the mainland goes on daylight saving time, the clocks are the same.

Weather   The hottest months in Anguilla are July to October; the coolest, December to February. The mean monthly temperature is about 80° Fahrenheit.

WHERE TO STAY

Don't forget than an 8% government tax will be added to your hotel bill, plus 10% for service.

VERY EXPENSIVE

✪ Cap Juluca

Maunday's Bay (P.O. Box 240), Anguilla, B.W.I. ☎ **809/497-6666**, 212/425-4684 in New York City, or 800/323-0139 in the U.S. Fax 809/497-6617. 85 rms, 13 suites. A/C MINIBAR TEL. Winter, $435–$700 single or double; $1,010–$1,630 one-bedroom suite. Off-season, $275–$515 single or double; from $530 one-bedroom suite. MAP $65 per person extra. AE. Free parking.

Cap Juluca is one of the most boldly conceived, most luxurious, and most pampering oases in the Caribbean. Named after the rain god (Juluca) of the island's long-ago inhabitants, the Arawaks, and occupying a rolling 179-acre site along the southwestern coast on one of the island's best beaches, Cap Juluca was the brainchild of half a dozen original investors who each achieved a measure of fame for their investment savvy on Wall Street. In their wake has followed a constant stream of Hollywood stars and financial barons.

The architects were given free rein to create a Moorish fantasy with white walls, palms, and bougainvillea. Accommodations are in villas evocative of Marrakesh, Morocco. Most have soaring domes, walled courtyards, labyrinthine staircases, and concealed swimming pools ringed with thick walls. Inside, a mixture of elegantly comfortable wicker furniture is offset with Moroccan accessories. Each unit faces one of the world's most perfect beaches, whose coral sands sprawl seaward toward a view of the blue-tinged mountains of French St. Martin. Most units can be expanded from deluxe doubles into one- or two-bedroom suites.

Expected amenities include safety-deposit boxes, ice makers, king-size beds, marbled and mirrored bathrooms, and plenty of space.

Dining/Entertainment: A continental breakfast is served daily on your terrace. On the premises are two interconnected restaurants: the less formal Italian terrace, Chatterton's, and the richly formal French/Caribbean restaurant, Pimms (see "Where to Dine," below). Midway along the beach, the Pool Terrace Grill is a casual dining alternative for three meals a day. At dinner, fresh lobster, whole grilled fish en papillotte, seafood and chicken brochettes, along with grilled sirloin, are served buffet style from an outdoor grill. Platters of antipasti, a variety of salads, and West Indian specialties are also served. Live music is presented several times a week.

Services: Laundry, massage, concierge, shuttle buses from the guest rooms to the hotel's restaurants and bars.

Facilities: Water sports (including waterskiing, fishing, windsurfing, Sunfish sailing, and snorkeling), championship tennis court, large pool, fitness center. A 32-foot excursion boat, *Lynbar,* a luxurious power cruiser accommodating up to

16 passengers, offers half- or full-day excursions to nearby cays, bays, and to out islands; the vessel also goes out on sunset cruises.

Casablanca Resort

Rendezvous Bay West (P.O. Box 444), Anguilla, B.W.I. ☎ **809/497-6999**, or 800/654-1337 or 800/231-1945 in the U.S. Fax 809/497-6899. 95 rms, 16 suites. A/C MINIBAR TV TEL. Dec 16–Apr 14, $400–$450 single; $600–$750 double; $700–$1,400 suite for two. Apr 15–Dec 15, $455 single; $700 double; $520–$1,000 suite. AE, MC, V. Free parking.

Set at the edge of one of the longest strips of beachfront in the Caribbean (more than 3 miles), with views overlooking the nearby mountains of St. Martin, this 40-acre development is gaudy, glitzy, and a lot of fun. Outfitted in a Moorish theme, which reflects its ownership by a consortium of Middle Eastern investors, the resort is unified with green-glazed roof tiles and a decorative theme that evokes the palaces of Imperial Morocco. Accommodations are scattered among five two-story buildings set either along the beach or in the garden. Each room contains Italian marble, a private patio, 10-foot ceilings with spinning ceiling fans, a safety-deposit box, and an opulent decor with lots of handcrafted ceramic mosaics. To create the Moorish motifs, teams of Moroccan artisans spent months on embellishments that accompany the dozens of artifacts imported from the Moroccan sub-Sahara.

Dining/Entertainment: French cuisine is served with views of the mountains of nearby St. Martin at the Casablanca Signature Restaurant. A player piano (appropriately named "Sam") and tall drinks are the theme at Rick's Café Américain. Beside the pool, the Blue Parrot serves midday grills, pizzas from a brick oven, and evening cocktails. An additional bar lies beside the beach.

Services: Massage, 24-hour room service, babysitting, valet, twice-daily maid service.

Facilities: Large and beautifully engineered swimming pool, well-equipped health club whose exercise machines overlook a view of the sea, two lit tennis courts, library, games room, communal wide-screen TV with feature movies every night, wide array of land and water sports (some of them complimentary).

Coccoloba

Barnes Bay (P.O. Box 332), Anguilla, B.W.I. ☎ **809/497-6871**, or 800/833-3559 in the U.S. Fax 809/497-6332. 12 suites, 42 villas. A/C MINIBAR TV TEL. Winter, $375–$575 suite for one or two; $475–$950 villa. Off-season, $225–$370 suite for one or two; $275–$735 villa. Additional person $90 extra. Packages available. (Rates include American breakfast.) AE, MC, V. Free parking.

One of the island's most solidly comfortable resorts is built on a rocky headland which juts seaward between two of the island's excellent beaches, 7 miles west of the airport. Originally built on 30 acres of seaside scrubland by expatriate investors during the 1980s, it reminds many newcomers of a chic resort in the Mediterranean. Gaily striped parasols and awnings, an interconnected series of swimming pools, and a swim-up bar contribute to the holiday flavor. The resort's reception lies under a soaring A-frame building. Accommodations ramble along a low-rise bluff above the sea, and most are in simple cottages with verandas and summer-inspired furniture.

Dining/Entertainment: The resort is justly proud of the Caribbean/Créole and French/American cuisine served in its major restaurant, the Pavilion (see "Where to Dine," below). A pair of bars operates beside the pool and the beach.

Services: Room service (for continental breakfast only), laundry, massage, island tours.

Facilities: Freshwater pool and swim-up bar, two tennis courts (lit at night); deep-sea fishing, sunset-cruise trips, and waterskiing can be arranged.

Cove Castles Villa Resort

Shoal Bay West (P.O. Box 248), Anguilla, B.W.I. ☎ **809/497-6801,** or 800/348-4716 in the U.S. Fax 809/497-6051. 12 beach houses and villas. TV TEL. Winter, $590 beach house for one or two; $790 beach house for three or four; $790 villa for two; $990 villa for three to six. Off-season, $350 beach house for one or two; $450 beach house for three or four; $450 villa for two; $650 villa for three to six. AE. Free parking. Closed Sept.

This resort defines itself as something midway between a collection of private residences and a luxury hotel. Praised by *Architectural Digest,* it features modern structures originally designed in 1985 by award-winning architect Myron Goldfinger. Later enlarged in 1988, the resort contains only a dozen units cooled by ceiling fans (not air conditioning). These include an interconnected row of town house–style beach houses and a handful of larger, fully detached villas. The elemental design combines traditional elements from North Africa, the Caribbean, and the futuristic theories of Le Corbusier.

Set amid the dunes and scrublands of the island's southwestern coast at the edge of a white sandy beach, each of the deliberately stark buildings was constructed parallel to its neighbor to maximize views of the sea. Each contains louvered doors and windows crafted from Brazilian walnut, terra-cotta tiles from the Dominican Republic, comfortably oversize rattan furniture, fully equipped kitchens, and hammocks.

Dining/Entertainment: Candlelit dinners, prepared by the resort's French chef, are served overlooking the beach in an intimate private dining room. At breakfast and lunch, meals are brought into the beach villa, upon request.

Services: Concierge, massage, babysitting.

Facilities: Complimentary use of snorkeling gear, Sunfish sailboats, bicycles, lit tennis court, car rental, boutique.

✪ Malliouhana

Meads Bay (P.O. Box 173), Anguilla, B.W.I. ☎ **809/497-6111,** or 800/835-0796 in the U.S. Fax 809/497-6011. 34 rms, 17 suites. MINIBAR TEL. Winter, $480–$550 single or double; from $660 suite for two. Off-season, $240–$265 single or double; from $360 suite for two. Seven-night minimum stay required Dec 18–Mar. Breakfast $12.50 extra. No credit cards. Free parking.

Malliouhana is the Carib word for Anguilla, but this is all that's primitive about this deluxe and glamorous hotel, one of the most discreetly elegant in the Caribbean. Established in 1984 by the Anglo-French Roydon family, it occupies a rocky bluff jutting seaward between sandy beaches, in the southwest corner of the island beyond Long Bay, 8 miles northwest of the airport. Privacy plays a pivotal role at Malliouhana, where thick walls and shrubbery provide anonymity. The entire complex occupies 25 acres of sloping scrubland whose central core is landscaped into terraces and banks of flowers, pools, and fountains. At its edges sprawl almost 2 miles of white sand beaches.

Public and private areas enjoy open-air themes with plants and sea or garden views. A fine assemblage of Haitian art and the rest of the decorations were chosen by the famed "Boston Brahmin" decorator, Lawrence Carleton Peabody II. The spacious bedrooms and suites are distributed among the main buildings and outlying villas. Each room has tropical furnishings and wide private verandas, and the villas can be rented as a single unit or subdivided into three comfortable accommodations.

Dining/Entertainment: The resort's restaurant is considered one of the most prestigious in the Caribbean (see "Where to Dine," below). Scattered over the premises are a handful of bars for drinking and snacking throughout the day.

Services: Room service (7am to 11pm), concierge, laundry, massage, tennis lessons from a qualified pro.

Facilities: Beauty salon, boutiques, TV room, library, water-sports center with instruction in practically everything, four tennis courts (three lit for night play), gym with resident instructor, swimming pools, state-of-the-art children's playground on Meads Bay Beach.

EXPENSIVE

Cinnamon Reef Resort

Little Harbour, Anguilla, B.W.I. ☎ **809/497-2727,** or 800/346-7084 in the U.S. Fax 809/497-3727. 14 suites, 8 villas. MINIBAR TEL. Winter, $250–$350 suite for one or two; $550 two-bedroom villa for four. Off-season, $150–$250 suite for one or two; $450 two-bedroom villa for four. Additional person $60 extra. MAP $50 per person extra. (Rates include continental breakfast.) AE, MC, V. Free parking. Closed Sept–Oct.

This small and intimate hotel lies 2 miles west of the airport on the southern coast, astride a circular cove whose calm waters are said to be the best on the island for windsurfing. The resort's Mediterranean-inspired 7-acre core is set on 30 acres of rolling scrubland. Because of its limited size, guests have the feeling of living in a pleasantly informal private estate. Accommodations are in white stucco villas and garden suites, where large archways lead onto private terraces. Each unit contains well-appointed bedrooms and dressing areas, ceiling fans, and spacious living rooms.

Dining/Entertainment: The Palm Court Restaurant and the bar area are the focal points (see "Where to Dine," below). The views over the veranda are of the reef-sheltered harbor. Some entertainment and occasional dancing is offered at night.

Services: Room service (during meal hours), laundry.

Facilities: Freshwater pool, hot tub and Jacuzzi, two championship tennis courts, beach sheltered by a reef; free sailboats, paddleboats, windsurfers, and snorkeling and fishing equipment; scuba diving can be arranged.

All-Inclusive Resorts

The Mariners

Road Bay (P.O. Box 139), Sandy Ground, Anguilla, B.W.I. ☎ **809/497-2671,** or 800/848-7938 in the U.S. Fax 809/497-2901. 43 rms. 19 suites. TEL. Winter, $250–$260 single; $420–$430 double; from $560 suite for two. Off-season, $225–$235 single; $300–$310 double; from $380 suite. (Rates all-inclusive.) AE, MC, V. Free parking.

This all-inclusive resort west of the airport occupies a flat sandy area beside an isolated beach whose access road winds between flowering shrubs and hillocks. Accommodations are in three two-story buildings and cottages delightfully embellished with West Indian gingerbread. All rooms have ceiling fans (some are air-conditioned) and a decor reminiscent of New England summer cottages in the 1930s. It's also possible to book in here on EP rates (no meals), although most guests find the all-inclusive terms more favorable. The staff is very laidback.

Services: Room service, laundry.

Facilities: Swimming pool, tennis court, two Jacuzzis.

Pineapple Beach Club

The Valley (P.O. Box 157), Anguilla, B.W.I. ☎ **809/497-6061,** in Florida 407/994-5640, or 800/345-0356 in the U.S. outside Florida. 27 rms. Winter, $340–$360 single; $400–$440 double. Off-season, $260–$280 single; $330–$360 double. Three-night minimum stay in winter. (Rates all-inclusive.) AE, MC, V. Free parking.

Set on the white sands of Rendezvous Bay, near Anguilla's southernmost tip, this Anguillan-owned property is one of the few all-inclusive resorts on the island. Designed around a central garden/courtyard whose open end is exposed to a view of the beach, the resort offers accommodations in colonial-inspired single-story wings whose front verandas are interconnected to their neighbors like the wings of an old-fashioned plantation house. You get ceiling fans instead of air conditioning. Most of the resort's social life revolves around an open-sided bar and restaurant where all food and beverages are included in the all-inclusive price. On the premises is a freshwater swimming pool. A water-sports program includes windsurfing, reef fishing, kayaking, snorkeling, and sailing.

MODERATE

Fountain Beach Hotel

Shoal Bay Beach, Anguilla, B.W.I. ☎ **809/497-3491,** or 800/342-3491 in the U.S. Fax 809/497-3493. 10 units. Winter, $150 single or double; $245 junior studio; $280 one-bedroom suite; $365 two-bedroom suite. Off-season, $100 single or double; $170 junior studio; $200 one-bedroom suite; $285 two-bedroom suite. MAP $35 per person extra. AE, MC, V. Free parking.

Built in 1989 right on the beach, this coral-colored resort was inspired by Mediterranean architecture. Surrounded by 5 acres of sloping and forested land on the island's underpopulated north coast, it's simple, with few amenities but with ample opportunities for reading, sunbathing, or doing nothing. The bedrooms are large and airy, with ceramic-tile floors, sliding glass windows, and pastel-toned color schemes. Each unit has an unstocked refrigerator, and some have kitchenettes. On the premises, in an annex at the edge of one of the island's most noteworthy beaches, is a restaurant serving Italian cuisine and seafood.

La Sirena

Meads Bay (P.O. Box 200), Anguilla, B.W.I. ☎ **809/497-6827,** or 800/331-9358 in the U.S., 800/223-9815 in Canada. Fax 809/497-6829. 20 rms, 5 villas. MINIBAR TV. Winter, $160 single; $210–$280 double; from $280 villa for up to four. Off-season, $100 single; $130–$180 double; from $180 villa for up to four. Breakfast $8 extra. AE, MC, V. Free parking.

Built in 1989 on 3 acres of sandy soil, this resort is pleasant, intimate, and small-scale. At least 80% of its clientele derives from the German-speaking world (Switzerland and Germany), thanks to its Swiss ownership and its European marketing drives. Arranged in bougainvilla-draped wings, each with two stories, the accommodations are large and airy, with rattan and wicker furnishings similar to those in some of the island's more expensive hostelries. Some have air conditioning; all have ceiling fans and hairdryers. Although the hotel is not beside the beach, guests walk down through the garden and a sandy footpath to reach it. On the beach are beach hats, umbrellas, and lounge chairs laid out for guests.

Dining/Entertainment: The Top of the Palms restaurant, open only for dinner, is recommended separately (see "Where to Dine," below). Less formal is the

Coconuts Café, site of breakfast and lunch, specializing in pastas, sandwiches, and ice creams.

Services: Babysitting, laundry.

Facilities: Freshwater swimming pool.

CONDOS & VILLAS

Anguilla is increasingly riddled with vacation villas, which absentee owners rent out when they're off the island. Several rental agencies have listings of these villas, which come in a vast range of different prices. One of the best is **Anguilla Connection** (☎ **809/497-4403**, or **800/648-1405** in the U.S.; fax 809/497-4402). It's the only agency that offers 24-hour personalized service. Choices range from luxury in a secluded hideaway to condo-style living.

⑤ Carimar Beach Club

Meads Bay (P.O. Box 327), Anguilla, B.W.I. ☎ **809/497-6881**, or 800/235-8667. Fax 809/497-6071. 23 apartments. Winter, $300–$350 one-bedroom apartment; $400–$440 two-bedroom apartment; $630 three-bedroom apartment. Off-season, $130–$160 one-bedroom apartment; $200–$230 two-bedroom apartment; $325 three-bedroom apartment. AE, MC, V. Free parking.

Opening onto Meads Bay, this is considered the best of the small apartment hotels on the island, where you get the privacy of an apartment yet some of the comforts of a hotel. The well-appointed units are in two-story Mediterranean-style villas, each with a large living room, dining area, and patio or balcony overlooking mile-long Meads Bay Beach. For dinner, if you want to splurge, you can go to the nearby super-priced Malliouhana, or next door to Blanchards Restaurant. The hotel is west of the airport beyond Long Bay.

WHERE TO DINE
VERY EXPENSIVE

✪ Malliouhana Restaurant

Meads Bay. ☎ **809/497-6111.** Reservations required. Appetizers $12–$20 at lunch, $14–$27 at dinner; main courses $11–$30 at lunch, $25–$37 at dinner. AE, MC, V. Lunch daily 12:30–3:30pm; dinner daily 7–10:30pm. FRENCH/CARIBBEAN.

Eight miles northwest of the airport, the most Europeanized restaurant on Anguilla offers the most intensely structured service rituals, some of the finest food, and a clientele whose somewhat self-conscious glamour is perhaps the most theatrical on the island. Michel Rostang, the successful son of the legendary Jo Rostang, one of the most famous chefs of southern France, is often in charge. You'll dine in an open-sided pavilion built atop a rocky promontory jutting seaward. There's lots of space between tables, an ocean view, a superb wine list, and a splashing fountain.

The hors d'oeuvres selection is perhaps the finest on the island, including fresh goat-cheese terrine with sweet red peppers, and potted minced goose with mixed green salad with cornbread. There's also lobster ravioli with carrots in lobster juice, or lemon-flavored fettuccine with a caviar cream. Main courses are likely to range from saddle of lamb with Sisteron flavored with shallots and garlic to Bresse chicken roasted on a spit and served with a potato gratin. The fish dishes are outstanding, including grilled snapper with baby leeks in a soya sauce, filet of salmon grilled with fennel, or more simply the grilled catch of the day.

EXPENSIVE

Barrel Stay Beach Bar & Restaurant

Sandy Ground. ☎ **809/497-2831.** Reservations recommended. Appetizers $7–$21; main courses $20–$40. AE, MC, V. Lunch daily 11am–2:30pm; dinner daily 6:30–9:30pm. FRENCH/CREOLE.

This restaurant's walls, screens, tables, chairs, and bars are fashioned from barrels and disassembled barrel stays. The establishment sits beside the beach and has ample space for dining or drinking—there's an outdoor drink terrace and a smaller inner bar that sees most of its activity at night. A favorite here is fish soup served in the French fashion, the conch Créole, or the island fish with garlic sauce. You can also order barbecued lobster, steak au poivre, stuffed crab, or veal kidneys in the provençal style. A selection of French wines is offered at reasonable prices, along with rum drinks and beer.

Hibernia

Island Harbour. ☎ **809/497-4290.** Reservations required. Appetizers $6–$9; main courses $17–$30. AE, MC, V. Lunch Tues–Sun noon–2pm; dinner Tues–Sun 7–9pm. Closed Sept–Oct and lunch Apr–Christmas. FRENCH/ASIAN.

Hibernia is a lovely little spot in a West Indian–style house with a veranda overlooking Scilly Cay, on the northeast corner of the island. Small and intimate, it contains only 10 tables. It's the personal statement of a French chef, Raoul Rodríguez, and Irish-born Mary Pat O'Hanlon. Local ingredients are used in the specialties, which sometimes have an Asian influence. For a starter, try perhaps Vietnamese spring rolls with crab and chicken or slices of smoked duck breast. Fish soup is served with accompaniments. Main courses are likely to include a hot-and-sour Thai broth with a variety of Caribbean fish or perhaps a fricassée of lobster with ginger and black mushrooms. A Burmese coconut-and-noodle casserole is served with crayfish. The kitchen makes its own bread and ice cream.

Palm Court Restaurant

In the Cinnamon Reef Resort, Little Harbour. ☎ **809/497-2727.** Reservations recommended. Appetizers $6–$7 at lunch, $7–$10 at dinner; salads and main courses $12–$18 at lunch, main courses $20–$28 at dinner; sandwiches $10–$12. AE, MC, V. Lunch daily noon–2:30pm; dinner daily 7–9:30pm. CARIBBEAN.

In one of the finest small hotels on Anguilla, this restaurant has earned an excellent reputation. Tables are scattered before a sweeping view of a circular bay whose waters are sheltered by an offshore reef. Lunches are informal and feature Anguillan lobster or chicken salads; succulent soups; seafood pasta made with grilled snapper, cream, and herbs; and sandwiches such as lobster clubs.

The real allure of the cuisine, however, appears at dinner, with some tempting creations like grilled loin of yellowfin tuna with bok choy, or perhaps grilled Anguilla lobster (the last always at the daily market price). If you don't like one of the dishes from the "new Caribbean cuisine," you can always order such classics as rack of lamb baked en croûte or pan-seared scallops.

Paradise Café

Shoal Bay West End. ☎ **809/497-6010.** Reservations recommended. Appetizers $4.95–$9 at lunch, $5.50–$9 at dinner; main courses $8.50–$13.50 at lunch, $9.95–$25 at dinner. AE, MC, V. Lunch Tues–Sun noon–2:30pm; dinner Tues–Sun 7–9:30pm. MEDITERRANEAN/CARIBBEAN.

This restaurant is set right on the beach at Shoal Bay West End, and the breeze from the Caribbean caresses the many windchimes decorating the dining room.

Attracting a clientele of movie stars, singers, politicians, the rich and famous, and a scattering of ordinary folks, it lies between Blue Waters Resort and CoveCastles Resort with a panoramic view of the islands of St. Martin and Saba.

On the lunch menu, you can order such selections as fish soup, tempura calamari, or a stir-fried scallop salad along with more ordinary selections such as a grilled hamburger. The dinner menu is more elaborate, featuring various versions of focaccia or a quesadilla as an appetizer. Pastas are regularly featured at night, including one made with local crayfish medallions. You can also order such selections as a red Thai curry or grilled tenderloin with an onion confit.

Pavilion Restaurant

In the Coccoloba Hotel, Barnes Bay. ☎ **809/497-6871.** Reservations required. Appetizers $8–$12; main courses $20–$24. AE, MC, V. Lunch daily 12:30–2:30pm; dinner daily 7–9:30pm. INTERNATIONAL.

The Coccoloba Hotel's main dining room is open to visitors who call in advance. Seven miles west of the airport, it offers tables exposed to the sea breezes on two sides and whimsically elegant Caribbean style. Lunches are informal, often a poolside buffet, with chilled lobster soup, avocado and grapefruit salads, and sandwiches made from fresh salmon and tuna. Dinners are more elaborate and might include freshly marinated suprême of salmon, grilled catch of the day, or steamed lobster. Dessert might be Black Forest or coconut cake.

✪ Pimms/Chatterton's

In the Cap Juluca, Maunday's Bay. ☎ **809/497-6666.** Reservations required. Appetizers $7–$24; main courses $25–$33. AE. Lunch daily noon–2:30pm; dinner daily 6:30–9:30pm. FRENCH/CARIBBEAN.

Pimms, open only for dinner, is one of the most elegant restaurants on Anguilla and one of the finest in the Caribbean. Set among the archways and domes of Anguilla's most spectacular resort, Cap Juluca, it blends the finest culinary standards of the Old and New Worlds with fresh and exotic ingredients flown in regularly. Tables overlook the island's most spectacular beach and are lit with flickering candlelight.

Adjoining the restaurant is Chatterton's, which serves both lunch and dinner in a low-slung oceanside pavilion. It's elegant and informal, a lighthearted alternative to the main restaurant, Pimms. You'll dine with a view of one of Anguilla's best beaches. The menu is frequently changed, but for an appetizer you might be offered a selection of soups, perhaps a familiar one with a different culinary twist— gazpacho with spicy avocado and fresh goat cheese. Hors d'oeuvres are likely to feature lobster ravioli in a light cream sauce or even lobster risotto with curry-and-pumpkin sauce. Main-dish selections range from the fresh local fish with garlic and a bouillabaisse sauce to steamed filet of snapper with crunchy cabbage, soya, and sesame-oil sauce. Shrimp couscous in a spicy sauce is also served, or you may prefer the more classic roast rack of lamb, with black olives and a rosemary sauce.

Top of the Palms

In La Sirena Hotel, Meads Bay. ☎ **809/497-6827.** Reservations recommended. Appetizers $5–$11.50; main courses $15.50–$36. AE, MC, V. Dinner only, daily 7–9:30pm. FRENCH.

On the second floor of a previously recommended hotel, with open access to ocean breezes, this restaurant offers views over Meads Bay and the surrounding treetops. Menu specialties are prepared by a well-trained Swiss chef, Stephan Peterer. You might begin with conch fritters or quesadillas, then follow with filet of beef grilled to your specifications, or perhaps a choice of two types of fondue: bourguignonne or chinoise. If you want the fondues you must call by 5pm. Many fish dishes are regularly featured, including even a fondue Neptune. You cook for yourself small pieces of lobster, fish, and shrimp in a hot fish stock. The local lobster is grilled every night, and pan-fried grouper or steamed snapper regularly appear. The snapper might be served with a touch of tarragon-and-lemongrass sauce. Homemade tropical fruit sorbets provide a smooth finish to a meal.

MODERATE
La Fontana

In the Fountain Beach Hotel, Shoal Bay Beach. ☎ **809/497-3492.** Reservations recommended for dinner. Appetizers $7–$10; main courses $15–$35. AE, MC, V. Lunch daily noon–3pm; dinner daily 6–10pm. ITALIAN.

Contained in this previously recommended hotel on the northern side of the island, this restaurant looks out over the western end of Shoal Bay Beach. Sheltered from the direct rays of the sun, but open to breezes at the sides, the restaurant combines ingredients from both Italy and the Caribbean. Italian wines, freshly baked breads, and an undeniable flair are part of the experience here. Menu items are likely to include soup made from porcini mushrooms; pasta with lobster, shrimp, and calamari; lobster marinated with fresh herbs and sautéed in white wine; or perhaps steak fiorentina. Most courses are moderately priced—unless you order lobster.

Lucy's Harbour View and Restaurant

South Hill. ☎ **809/497-6253.** Reservations recommended. Appetizers $5–$9; main courses $14–$28. AE, MC, V. Lunch Mon–Sat 11:30am–3:30pm; dinner Mon–Sat 7–10pm. Closed late Aug to late Oct. CARIBBEAN/INTERNATIONAL.

Not only does it boast the most attractive view on the island, but Lucy's also offers imaginatively prepared food. What makes it special is its owner, Lucy Halley, who lived in the French part of St. Martin and learned many secrets of the cuisine there. The 40-seat restaurant is in a converted home at the top of a steep hillside overlooking the salt ponds and houses of Sandy Ground. When you call (or after you arrive spontaneously), ask Lucy what she has in the larder, or tell her what kind of food you like. The menu usually contains homemade pumpkin soup, lobster salad, fresh Anguillan lobster (split and grilled), conch fritters, curried goat, kingfish, and T-bone steaks. Dishes are usually served with fresh vegetables and bread pudding. This is a lively, fun, and very informal spot, painted in the signature green and white known throughout Anguilla as Lucy's trademark colors. Live entertainment is offered on Tuesday.

✪ Mango's

Barnes Bay. ☎ **809/497-6479.** Reservations required for dinner as far in advance as possible. Appetizers $4.50–$7.25; main courses $11.95–$32. AE, MC, V. Dinner only, Wed–Mon at 6:30–7pm and 8:30–9pm. Closed Aug–Oct. NEW AMERICAN.

In a pavilion set a few steps from the edge of the sea on the northwestern part of the island, this is probably the most alluring independent restaurant on Anguilla. The restaurant specializes in serving the freshest obtainable fish, meat, and produce, all cooked on the grill with the absolute minimum of added fats or calories. All the breads and desserts, including the ice cream and sorbet, are made fresh daily on the premises. You might start with lobster cakes with a homemade tartar sauce or Mango's red chicken soup with a taste of curry. For a main course, grilled local lobster is featured, as is spicy whole snapper. "Simply grilled" fish with lemon-and-herb butter seems to be the preferred main dish.

Smuggler's Grill

Forest Bay. ☎ **809/497-3728.** Reservations not required. Appetizers $5–$8.75; main courses $14–$35.50. AE, MC, V. Dinner only, daily 6:30–9:45pm (last order). Closed Aug–Sept. INTERNATIONAL/CONTINENTAL.

Set atop pilings sunk deep into the waters of Forest Bay, east of the airport, this is probably the most deliberately nautical restaurant in all of Anguilla. In the establishment's center, a re-created sailing ship (complete with masts and spars) juts upward from the plank floor. Best of all, sweeping views of the ocean unfold on all sides.

You can stop here just for a drink (the rum punches and the views are memorable), but if you're hungry, you might opt for lobster soup, seafood quiche, lobster or shrimp brochettes, filet of snapper with tartar sauce, or a 25-ounce porterhouse steak. The restaurant also has a diverse salad bar.

INEXPENSIVE

Ⓢ Ferryboat Inn

Cul de Sac Rd., Blowing Point (P.O. Box 189), Anguilla, B.W.I. ☎ **809/497-6613.** Reservations recommended. Appetizers $5.50–$16; main courses $6.50–$35. AE, MC, V. Lunch Mon–Sat noon–3pm; dinner Mon–Sat 7:30–10pm. Closed Tues in summer. Directions: Turn right just before the Blowing Point Ferry Terminal and travel 150 yards before making a left turn. CARIBBEAN/FRENCH.

Established by English-born John McClean with his Anguillan wife, Marjorie, and set directly on the beach a short walk from the Blowing Point ferry pier, this restaurant comes well recommended. Specialties are French onion soup, black-bean soup, some of the best lobster thermidor on the island (liberally laced with brandy, cream, and both parmesan and gouda cheese), and scallop of veal Savoyard (with white wine and fresh cream). Don't miss the house's special planter's punch.

The McCleans also rent nine simple but comfortable apartments, which represent good value. Single or double occupancy costs $125 to $225 per day, EP; off-season, these prices are reduced to $70 to $125.

Smitty's Restaurant

Island Harbour. ☎ **809/497-4300.** Reservations not required. Burgers and sandwiches $5–$8; platters $10–$22. No credit cards. Daily 10am–11pm. SEAFOOD/WEST INDIAN.

Set directly on the sands of a beach near Anguilla's northern tip, beneath sea grapes, palms, and a rickety lattice, this is a raffish hangout where the food is slowly prepared in the Caribbean style. No one will mind if you spend an hour or two drinking rum-based drinks at one of the battered wooden tables, but if you want something to eat, Smitty, the extroverted owner, or Seal, his assistant, and wife, will prepare platters of ribs, chicken, fish, conch, steak, or lobster. Don't expect luxury or anything other than open-air informality and recorded reggae. The food is simple but savory, tasting its best when washed down with a beer or two. There's usually live music presented every Thursday from 7:30pm till very late.

WHAT TO SEE & DO

Boat trips can be arranged to **Sombrero Island,** 38 miles northwest of Anguilla. This mysterious island, with its lone lighthouse, is 400 yards wide at its broadest point, three-quarters of a mile in length. Phosphate miners abandoned it in 1890; and limestone rocks, now eroded, rise in cliffs around the island. The treeless, waterless terrain evokes a moonscape. Adventure seekers can sometimes arrange to go over on the supply boat serving the island on the 1st and the 16th of the month. A boat leaves Anguilla at 6am, returning at noon. Call Errol Carty (☎ 809/ 497-2564) if you'd like to arrange such a trip.

One of Anguilla's most festive, and certainly most colorful, annual festivals is **Carnival,** held jointly under the auspices of the Ministries of Culture and of Tourism. Boat races are Anguilla's national sport, and during Carnival they form 60% of the celebration. The island's people display the culture, drama, creativity, and love of their land. The festival begins on the Friday before the first Monday in August and lasts a week. Carnival harks back to Emancipation Day, or "August Monday" as it's called, when all enslaved Africans were freed.

SPORTS & OUTDOOR ACTIVITIES

BEACHES   One of the most popular beaches is **Road Bay,** framed by the crescent-shaped village of Sandy Ground (the capital) and a large salt pond. **Sandy Isle,** with a few palms, is a tiny little islet surrounded by a coral reef. It lies offshore from Road Bay. Once there, you'll find a beach bar and restaurant, plus free use of snorkeling gear and underwater cameras. Sandy Island Enterprises (☎ 809/ 497-5643) has daily trips from the pier by Johnno's Beach Bar at Sandy Ground. The cost of a round-trip is $8, and the first boat leaves at 10am. The last boat back (don't miss it) departs at 4pm. You can also go farther out to Prickly Pear Cay, which stretches like a sweeping arc all the way to a sand spit populated by sea birds and pelicans.

Other good beaches include ✪ **Shoal Bay,** which apart from its silver sands boasts some of Anguilla's best coral gardens, the habitat of hundreds of tiny iridescent fish. This 2-mile beach with its talcum-powder-soft sand is not only the best beach on Anguilla, but one of the best in the entire Caribbean Basin. Crocus Bay is a long, golden beach, where a fisherman might take you out in search of snapper or grouper, or ferry you to such wee islands as Little Scrub.

FISHING   Fishing excursions can be made with the local fishermen. Your hotel can make the arrangements for you, but you should bring your own tackle. Agree on the cost before setting out, however, as some misunderstandings have been reported.

Malliouhana, Meads Bay (☎ 809/497-6111), has a 34-foot fishing cruiser, *Kyra,* that holds up to eight passengers at a time. It can be chartered for fishing parties. The cost is $400 for up to four hours, with a surcharge of another $100 for each additional hour. A box lunch can be packed for an additional charge, but all fishing gear is included.

SCUBA DIVING   Most of the coastline of Anguilla is fringed by coral reefs, and the island's waters are rich in marine life; off the shore are sunken coral gardens and brilliantly colored fish. Conditions for scuba diving and snorkeling on the island are ideal. In addition, the government of Anguilla has systematically created artificial enlargements of the existing reef system, a first for the Caribbean. Never before have so many battered and outmoded ships been deliberately sunk in carefully designated places in efforts to enlarge the island's marine ecosystem. These artificial reefs act as nurseries for fish and lobster populations, and also provide new sites for divers.

Tamariain Watersports Ltd., Sandy Ground (☎ 809/497-2020), is a five-star PADI international training center and offers a complete line of PADI certification courses. They carry several lines of scuba equipment for sale or rental. A two-tank dive costs $70.

TENNIS   Most of the resorts have their own tennis courts (see "Where to Stay," above). **Malliouhana,** Meads Bay (☎ **809/497-6111**) has four championship Laykold tennis courts with a year-round professional coach, Peter Burwash, and shop. Three courts are lit for night games. There are also two courts at **Cinnamon Reef,** Little Harbour (☎ **809/497-2727**).

WINDSURFING   Many hotel and villa properties offer windsurfing to guests: Cap Juluca, Cinnamon Reef Beach Club, Coccoloba, Fountain Beach, La Sirena, Malliouhana, the Mariners, Pineapple Beach Club, Shoal Bay Villas, and Rendez-vous Bay. Water-sports facilities also offer windsurfing. The Mariners has windsurfing or Sunfish sailboats at $15 per half-hour rental or lessons, and $25 per hour rental or lessons.

SHOPPING

Anguillan handcrafts are simple. Handcrafted mats are quite beautiful, and table-cloths and bedspreads are woven into spidery lace designs—but many of these are grabbed up by shops on neighboring islands and sold there at high prices. Baskets and mats are made from stripped corn husks and sisal rope. Model schooners and small pond boats are also for sale, as are gifts made of shells and wooden dolls.

Stamp collectors should head to the Valley Post Office (☎ **809/497-2528**), where they'll find unusual stamps from Anguilla.

The Boutique

In the Malliouhana Hotel, Meads Bay. ☎ **809/497-6111.**

Probably the most interesting and upscale boutique on Anguilla lies in one of the island's premier hotels. Here you'll find jewelry, sportswear and casual beachwear for men and women, evening dresses, gift items, and bathing suits from La Perla, Gottex, and Canovas, plus Kaminsky Rafia hats.

Cheddie's Carving Shop

The Cove. ☎ **809/497-6027.**

Just down the road from Coccoloba, this outlet showcases the work of Anguilla-born Cheddie Richardson—a self-taught carver. His unique carvings have become some of the most unusual sculptures for collectors of Caribbean art. Using mostly natural wood—mahogany, walnut, and driftwood—Cheddie also utilizes other Anguillian resources including alabaster and coral. He makes bronze castings, too. The artwork, which he's been creating since age nine, mostly por-trays wildlife—fish, dolphins, or birds. Occasionally it characterizes people. He combs the pristine beaches for perfect pieces of wood, letting their natural forms inspire him to develop a particular image. Cheddie then spends long hours add-ing fine detail to the sculpture, sometimes using stains, oils, and wax to enhance the natural wood. Each piece usually takes a week or so to complete, depending on size and amount of detail. The gallery is open Monday through Saturday from 10am to 6pm.

Cotton Gin Art Gallery

The Valley. ☎ **809/497-2949.**

This gallery offers paintings by Anguillian, Caribbean, and international artists. The gallery also features the work of well-known proprietor-artist Courtney

Devonish. The Devonish Gallery is housed in a historic Anguillian building, a reminder of a time when Anguilla grew cotton. The machinery for ginning cotton remains on view to all callers. Visitors might witness hand-made pottery production on Saturday.

New World Gallery
Old Factory Plaza, The Valley. ☎ **809/497-5950.**

This gallery features fine art, including exquisite pastels, paintings, and prints by Anguilla's Penny Slinger; paintings by New York expressionist master Peter Dean; and paintings and etchings by St. Croix's Maria Henle. New World also stocks an impressive range of exotic collectibles, artifacts, textiles, and jewelry from around the globe. For expert collectors and investors, the New World Gallery offers special opportunities. It's open daily from 10am to 6pm.

Sunshine Shop
In South Hill. ☎ **809/497-6964.**

Opposite Connor's car-rental agency, this is easily identifiable by the "I-95 sign," as it is on I-95 West at the Blowing Point expressway exit. The shop stocks fine cotton wear, art, jewelry, and packable gift items. For men, there are unusual batik shirts and bathing briefs. The shop also sells shoes, belts, and hats. Look for a classic line of women's sportswear in linen and wrinkle-free fabrics.

ANGUILLA AFTER DARK

Nightlife on Anguilla consists mainly of entertainment at the various hotels (in winter, mostly). These take the form of barbecues, West Indian parties, or singers and musicians. Calypso combo groups and others with musical talent, both local and imported, are hired by the hotels.

The most intriguing cultural treat is a performance of the **Mayoumba Folkloric Theater,** playing at La Sirena on Meads Bay on Thursday night. Call **809/ 497-6827** for details before going. African drums and a string band will give you an insight into Antillean culture.

Johnno's Beach Bar, Sandy Ground (☎ **809/497-2728**), is a favorite of Michael J. Fox and other Hollywood types when they visit Anguilla. Open-air, with sunlight and sea winds wafting into its unpretentious premises, the club is open Tuesday through Sunday from 11am to 1am. You can order Beck's beer on the beach as well as barbecued spareribs, grilled chicken, or fresh fish. Meals cost $10 to $22. You can try Johnno's popular drink of rum, crème de cacao, Guavaberry liqueur, and guava nectar, for $5. Live entertainment is presented on Wednesday, Friday, and Saturday from 8pm to 1am and also on Sunday from 3 to 9pm. A big Sunday barbecue begins at 11am and lasts "until the food runs out."

10 | The Dutch Windwards in the Leewards

Sint Maarten, Sint Eustatius (called "Statia"), and Saba—no more than dots on the map—have long been dubbed "The Dutch Windwards." This is confusing to the visitor, but it makes sense in the Netherlands. The Dutch-associated islands of Aruba, Bonaire, and Curaçao, just off the coast of South America, go by the name of "The Dutch Leewards" (covered in Chapter 16). The three Windward Islands, along with Bonaire and Curaçao, form the Netherlands Antilles (Aruba is now a separate entity).

The Dutch Windwards were once inhabited by the fierce Carib peoples, who believed that one acquired and assimilated the strength of one's slain enemy by eating his flesh! Columbus, on his second voyage to America, is said to have sighted the group of small islands on the name day of San Martino (St. Martin of Tours), hence the present name of Sint ("Saint") Maarten.

Cooled by trade winds, the Windwards are comfortable to visit year round.

1 St. Maarten

It's small, only 37 square miles, about half the area of the District of Columbia. A split-personality island, St. Maarten is the Dutch half. The other half, St. Martin, is French (For more information on St. Martin, see Chapter 12).

Returning visitors who have been "off island" for a long time are often surprised and shocked at the St. Maarten greeting them today. No longer a sleepy Caribbean backwater, it has expanded like a boomtown in recent years, with a vast urban sprawl filled with overcommercialized condos, glittering hotels, and casinos.

The 36 beaches of white sand are still there, and the clear turquoise waters are still there to entice. In fact, you can live far more luxuriously on St. Maarten than you ever could before, and the rows of restaurants are also better than ever. The 100% duty-free shopping has turned the island into a virtual shoppers' mall, and the capital, Philipsburg, is bustling with cruise-ship passengers who often arrive by the hordes. The sunshine is virtually guaranteed year round, making all sorts of water sports and sailing possible. The nightlife is among the best in the Caribbean.

But much has been lost to the bulldozer as well. This is obviously not an island for people who don't like people—lots of them—so if "getting away from it all" is your aim, better head over to the nearby Dutch islands of Statia and Saba (see below). Nevertheless, in spite of its problems, including crime, traffic congestion, and corruption, St. Maarten continues to attract massive numbers of visitors. Increasingly, St. Maarten is more for those who like their Caribbean island Las Vegas in style.

The divided island is considered the smallest territory in the world shared by two sovereign states. The only way you know you're crossing an international border is when you see the sign BIENVENUE, PARTIE, FRANÇAISE—attesting to the peaceful coexistence between the two nations on the island. The island was divided in 1648, and visitors still ascend Mount Concordia, near the border, where agreement was reached. Even so, St. Maarten changed hands 16 times before it became permanently Dutch. Legend has it that a gin-drinking Dutchman and a wine-guzzling Frenchman walked around the island to see how much territory each could earmark for his side in one day; the Frenchman outwalked the Dutchman, but the canny Dutchman got the more valuable piece of property.

St. Maarten lies 144 miles southeast of Puerto Rico. A lush island, rimmed with bays and beaches, it has a year-round temperature of 80° Fahrenheit. The Dutch capital, **Philipsburg,** curves like a toy village along Great Bay. The town lies on a narrow sand isthmus separating Great Bay and Great Salt Pond. The capital was founded in 1763 by Commander John Philips, a Scot in Dutch employ. To protect Great Bay, Fort Amsterdam was built in 1737.

The main thoroughfare is the busy Front Street, which stretches for about a mile and is lined with stores selling international merchandise, such as French designer fashions and Swedish crystal. More shops are along the little lanes, known as *steegijes*, that connect Front Street with Back Street, another shoppers' mart.

ORIENTATION
GETTING THERE

St. Maarten's **Queen Juliana International Airport** is the second busiest in the Caribbean, topped only by San Juan, Puerto Rico.

American Airlines (☎ 800/433-7300 in the U.S.) offers more options and more frequent service into St. Maarten than any other airline. Daily nonstop flights travel to the island from New York's JFK (one per day) and Miami (one per day). Several additional nonstop daily flights are offered into St. Maarten on either American Airlines or **American Eagle** (same toll-free number) from San Juan, Puerto Rico. Ask for one of the airline's tour operators, because you can usually save money by booking your air travel and hotel accommodation at the same time.

Continental Airlines (☎ 800/525-0280 in the U.S.) flies daily to St. Maarten from its hub in Newark, New Jersey.

In winter, **Northwest** (☎ 800/447-4747 in the U.S.) offers Saturday-only service from both Boston and Minneapolis.

ALM Antillean Airlines (☎ 800/327-7230 in the U.S.) offers nonstop and some direct daily service to St. Maarten from the airline's home base on Curaçao.

GETTING AROUND

BY TAXI Taxis are unmetered, but St. Maarten law requires drivers to have a list that details fares to major destinations on the island. The typical fare, say, from Juliana Airport to the Mullet Bay Resort and Casino, is $5; from Philipsburg to Juliana Airport it's $10. There are minimum fares for two passengers, and each additional passenger pays another $2. Passengers are entitled to two pieces of luggage free, and each additional piece is assessed 50¢ extra. Fares are 25% higher between 10pm and midnight, and 50% higher between midnight and 6am. Even if you're renting a car, taxi regulations require you to take a cab to your hotel, where your car will be delivered. For late-night cab service, call 599/5-22359.

BY MINIBUS   This is a reasonable means of transport on St. Maarten if you don't mind inconveniences, and at times overcrowding. Buses run daily from 7am to midnight and serve most of the major locations on St. Maarten. The most popular run is from Philipsburg to Marigot on the French side. Privately owned and operated, minibuses tend to follow specific routes, with fares ranging from $1.15 to $2, depending on where you're going.

BY RENTAL CAR   Because of the island's size and diversity, car rentals on St. Maarten are practical, particularly if you want to experience both the Dutch and the French sides of the island. The taxi drivers' union strictly enforces a law that forbids anyone from picking up a car at the airport. As a result, every rental agency on the island is well equipped to deliver cars to a client's hotel, where an employee will complete all the necessary paperwork on the spot. If you prefer to rent your car upon arrival, head for one of the tiny rental kiosks that lie across the road from the airport, or take a taxi the short distance to where each company warehouses its cars.

Experienced visitors, however, reserve their car in the United States in advance (especially important in winter) and head immediately to their hotel by taxi, thereby bypassing the long lines at the car-rental kiosks near the airport, the numerous local car-rental hucksters, and the hassle of island navigation.

The twin nationality of the island also causes complication in some rentals. In years gone by, some rental companies, depending on their in-house policies, preferred not to rent a car on the Dutch side to a client staying on the French side. In recent years, this injunction has been relaxed considerably and now depends on the individual discretion of the various companies. Bear in mind that Avis, Budget, and Hertz each maintains an office on the French side as well as on the Dutch side. Although prices tend to be roughly equivalent for rentals of equivalent cars from each company, you might find that the increased competition works to your advantage, at least in terms of convenience.

All three major car-rental agencies require that renters be at least 25 years old to rent. Among the "big three" companies, currently **Budget** (☎ **599/5-54030,** or **800/527-0700** in the U.S.) and **Hertz** (☎ **599/5-54314, or 800/654-3131** in the U.S.) charge $240 and $222, respectively, for their least expensive vehicles. **Avis** (☎ **599/5-44316, or 800/331-2112** in the U.S.) charges $270 per week, plus tax, for its least expensive vehicle, although clients who agree to prepay their rentals several weeks or months in advance of their arrival on St. Maarten are offered a lower rate for the same car, also with unlimited mileage. These prices will almost certainly change before your visit, and might be discounted by your membership in such organizations as the AAA. An optional collision-damage waiver costs $9.50 to $15 extra per day at each of the three companies, but even if you purchase the waiver, you might, depending on the company, still be responsible for up to $600 of repairs to your car in the event of an accident, particularly if you went for the cheaper policy. Your credit- or charge-card issuer may provide this coverage; check directly with the company before your trip.

St. Maarten

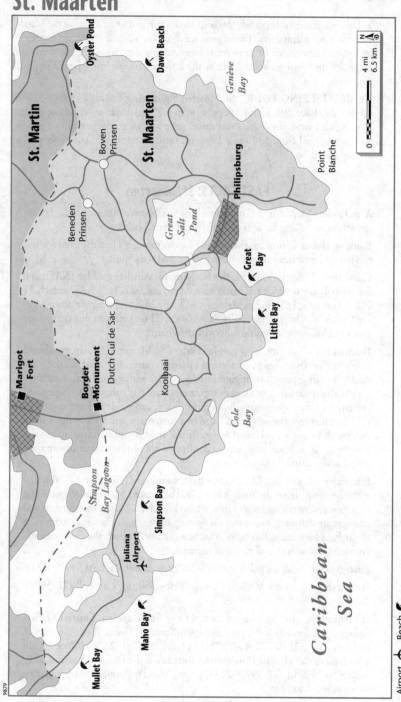

St. Martin

St. Maarten

Oyster Pond

Dawn Beach

Genève Bay

Boven Prinsen

Beneden Prinsen

Great Salt Pond

Philipsburg

Point Blanche

Great Bay

Little Bay

Marigot Fort

Border Monument

Dutch Cul de Sac

Koolbaai

Cole Bay

Simpson Bay Lagoon

Mullet Bay

Maho Bay

Juliana Airport

Simpson Bay

Caribbean Sea

Airport ✈   Beach ⛱

N

0   4 mi
    6.5 km

9879

Drive on the right-hand side (on both the French and Dutch sides of the island), and don't drink and drive. Traffic jams are common near the island's major settlements, so be prepared to be patient. International road signs are observed, and there are no Customs formalities at the border between the island's political divisions.

BY SIGHTSEEING TOUR   St. Maarten Sightseeing Tours (☎ 599/5-52646) offers a 2¹/₂ hour tour for $13 per person in a 29-passenger air-conditioned bus. You can also arrange to have a taxi driver serve as your guide; one or two passengers are charged from $30 for a 2¹/₂ hour tour, an additional passenger paying around $7.50.

FAST FACTS: St. Maarten

Area Code   St. Maarten is not part of the Caribbean's 809 area code. For information on calling St. Maarten, see "Telephone," below.

Banking Hours   Most banks are open Monday through Thursday from 8:30am to 1pm and on Friday from 8:30am to 1pm and 4 to 5pm.

Currency   The legal tender is the **Netherlands Antilles guilder (NAf)**, and the official rate at which the banks accept U.S. dollars is 1.77 NAf for each $1 U.S. Regardless, U.S. dollars are easily, willingly, and often eagerly accepted in the Dutch Windwards, especially St. Maarten. Thus, prices in this chapter are given in U.S. currency unless otherwise designated.

Documents   To enter the Dutch-held side of St. Maarten, U.S. citizens should have proof of citizenship in the form of a passport (preferably valid but not more than five years expired), an original birth certificate with a raised seal or a photocopy with a notary seal, or a voter's registration card with photo ID. Naturalized citizens may show their naturalization certificate, and resident aliens must provide the alien registration "green" card or a temporary card which allows them to leave and reenter the United States. British and Canadian visitors need valid passports. All visitors must have a confirmed room reservation before their arrival and a return or ongoing ticket.

Electricity   Dutch Sint Maarten uses the same voltage (110 volts A.C., 60 cycles) with the same electrical configurations as the United States, so adapters and transformers are not necessary However, on French St. Martin transformers and adapters are definitely necessary. To simplify things, many hotels on both sides of the island have installed built-in sockets suitable for both the European and North American forms of electrical currents.

Emergencies   Call the police at 599/5-22222 or an ambulance at 599/5-22111.

Hospitals   Go to the Medical Center, Welegen Road, Cay Hill (☎ 599/5-31111).

Information   Before you go, contact the **St. Maarten Tourist Office,** Robinson, Yesawich + Pepperdine, 1900 Summit Tower Blvd., Suite 600, Orlando, FL 32810 (☎ **407/871-1111,** or 800/786-2278). Once on the island, go to the **Tourist Information Bureau,** in the Imperial Building at 23 Walter Nisbeth Rd. (☎ 599/5-22337), open Monday through Friday from 8am to noon and 1 to 5pm.

Language   The language is officially Dutch, but most people speak English.

Safety   Crime is on the rise on St. Maarten and, in fact, has become quite serious. If possible, avoid night driving—it's particularly unwise to drive on remote, usually unlit, back roads at night. Also, let that deserted, isolated beach remain so. It's safer in a crowd, although under no circumstances should you ever leave anything unguarded on the beach.

Taxes and Service   A $5 departure tax is charged when you're leaving the island for St. Eustatius or Saba, and $10 is charged for international flights. A 5% government tax is added to hotel bills, and in general, hotels also add a 10% or 15% service charge. If service has not been added (unlikely), it's customary to tip around 15% in restaurants.

Telephone   Neither Dutch St. Maarten nor French St. Martin is part of the 809 area code that applies to most of the Caribbean. To call Dutch St. Maarten from the United States, if your long-distance telephone company is equipped to handle international direct dialing, dial 011 (the international access code), then 599 (the country code for the Netherlands Antilles), and finally 5 (the area code for all of St. Maarten) and the local number. If you cannot direct-dial internationally, dial 0 ("zero," for the operator) and tell the operator you wish to make an international call; once you are transferred to the international operator, state the 599 country code and then the area code and local number, and the operator will dial the call for you.

To make a call within St. Maarten you need only the five-digit local number. If you are calling "long distance" to the French side of the island, dial 06 and the six-digit French number; to call Dutch St. Maarten from the French side, dial 93 and then 5 (the area code) and the five-digit local number.

Time   St. Maarten operates on Atlantic standard time year-round. Thus in winter, when the United States is on standard time, if it's 6pm in Philipsburg it's 5pm in New York. During daylight saving time in the United States, the island and the U.S. East Coast are on the same time.

Weather   The island has a year-round temperature of about 80° Fahrenheit.

WHERE TO STAY

Remember, a government tax of 5% and a 10% to 15% service charge are added to your hotel bill. Ask about this when you book a room to save yourself a shock when you check out. See Chapter 12 on the French West Indies for my accommodations recommendations on French St. Martin.

VERY EXPENSIVE

✪ Sheraton Port de Plaisance

Union Rd., Cole Bay (P.O. Box 2089), Philipsburg, St. Maarten, N.A. ☎ **599/5-45222**, or 800/732-9479 in the U.S. Fax 599/5-42315. 88 suites. A/C TV TEL. Winter, $340 junior suite for one or two; $455–$555 one-bedroom suite for up to four; $600 two-bedroom suite for up to six. Off-season, $220 junior suite for one or two; $290–$360 one-bedroom suite for up to four; $385 two-bedroom suite for up to six. Breakfast $16 extra. AE, DC, MC, V. Free parking.

Unlike virtually every other hotel on St. Maarten, this one is sited at the edge of the island's saltwater lagoon, a locale famous as one of the safest anchorages in the Caribbean. That means it's not on the beach, although a shuttle will carry you to the sands. Set on 200 acres of sun-flooded flatlands near the French border, it includes a privately owned island linked to the mainland by an arched footbridge, and clusters of low-rise buildings rising amid gardens on the mainland. Designed and built by ITT Sheraton, the resort contains only suites, each spacious and comfortably furnished, with European-style bathrooms and fully equipped kitchens. Each has views over the surrounding islands, coves, and keys. A marina rings the edges of the island, allowing residents a view over some of the most expensive yachts in the hemisphere.

Dining/Entertainment: See separate recommendations for the hotel's casino and its major dining choice, La Terrasse. Other dining choices include L'Espadon Bar & Grill, where al fresco dining combines with a seafood menu with everything from Caribbean lobster to Atlantic salmon. The Pool and Cascade Café offers grilled burgers, Antillean-style chicken, sandwiches, and tropical drinks. Adjacent to one of the swimming pools is a veranda-style bar capped with a lookout tower which offers a 360° view of the surrounding land and seascapes.

Services: Room service, laundry, babysitting. There are also daily boat excursions, both to sandy beaches on the open sea, about 20 minutes away, and to the shops and restaurants of Marigot, capital of the French-speaking section of the island.

Facilities: The Tennis Center is among the most advanced of its kind on St. Maarten, with seven illuminated courts and a resident tennis pro for instruction. The Spa offers massages, keep-fit regimes, pedicures, beauty treatments, skin and muscle treatments, and aerobic exercise classes for enhancement of fitness and well-being. The resort contains two swimming pools, one specifically designed for lap swimming, another centered around a waterfall, and outdoor Jacuzzis. There's also a water-sports center.

EXPENSIVE

Belair Beach Hotel

Little Bay (P.O. Box 940, Philipsburg), St. Maarten, N.A. ☎ **599/5-23362**, or 800/622-7836 in the U.S. Fax 599/5-25295. 72 suites. A/C TV TEL. Winter, $185–$375 one-bedroom suite for one or two; $240–$440 two-bedroom suite for three. Off-season, $165–$185 one-bedroom suite for one or two; $220–$240 two-bedroom suite for three. Additional person (up to a maximum of six in a unit) $30 extra. Family plan available under "Kids under 18 Stay Free" (subject to availability). Breakfast from $8 extra. AE, DC, MC, V. Free parking.

One of the most surprising things about this breezy, oceanfront hotel right on Little Bay Beach, a 10-minute taxi ride east of the airport, is the size of the accommodations—they're all suites. Each contains a spacious bedroom, two full bathrooms with a tub and shower, a fully equipped kitchen, a 21-foot terrace with a sweeping view of the sea, and many extras. The suites were recently renovated. Although the Belair Beach is expensive, many visitors to St. Maarten consider this a good value, considering the many amenities offered.

Dining/Entertainment: The Sugar Bird Café serves breakfast, lunch, and dinner in a casual atmosphere. A grocery is on the premises. For vacationers who want more activities, the Little Bay Resort and Casino is a short walk down the beach.

Services: Laundry, babysitting, car-rental desk, activities desk.

Facilities: Beach with a seafront freshwater pool, two tennis courts, water sports.

Divi Little Bay Beach Resort and Casino

Little Bay (P.O. Box 961, Philipsburg), St. Maarten, N.A. ☎ **599/5-22333**, or 800/367-3484 in the U.S. Fax 599/5-23911. 130 rms, 3 suites. A/C TV TEL. Winter, $160–$230 single or double; $215–$350 one-bedroom suite. Off-season, $110–$130 single or double; $150–$205 one-bedroom suite. MAP $45 per person extra. AE, MC, V. Free parking.

Set close to two other resorts along a strip of beachfront a 10-minute drive east of the airport, this hotel was one of the island's first resorts. It opened in 1955 with only 20 rooms. The Netherlands' Queen Juliana and her husband, Prince Bernhard, were among the first guests, followed in later years by Queen Beatrix. Today, much altered and enlarged, and catering to a mass-market clientele of families, the resort occupies a series of buildings, none higher than three stories. Each accommodation has a veranda or patio and comfortable tropical-inspired furnishings.

Dining/Entertainment: The Café Divine offers informally elegant dining by candlelight with soft musical accompaniment.

Services: Laundry, babysitting.

Facilities: Water sports, three freshwater pools, three tennis courts (lit at night).

Great Bay Beach Hotel and Casino

Front St. (P.O. Box 310), Philipsburg, St. Maarten, N.A. ☎ **599/5-22446**, or 800/223-0757. Fax 599/5-23859. 285 rms, 10 suites. A/C MINIBAR TV TEL. Winter (all-inclusive), $200–$220 single; $320–$360 double; $260–$280 triple; $290–$405 suite for two. Off-season (EP), $85–$140 single; $90–$150 double; $125–$180 triple; $140–$205 suite for two. AE, DC, MC, V. Free parking.

This deluxe all-inclusive resort at the southwestern corner of Great Bay lies within walking distance of Philipsburg, ideal for shopping trips. The hotel was given a complete $10-million renovation; all guest rooms have been refurbished, and contain designer furniture, a terrace or patio, and a king-size bed or two full-size beds. The corner ocean rooms are the most expensive. Bathrooms have Valentino-designed tiles.

Dining/Entertainment: The hotel has a casino and disco, plus two restaurants, including a gourmet French dining room and a grill open nightly until 11pm.

Services: Laundry, babysitting.

Facilities: One all-weather tennis court; two freshwater pools, which are infinitely preferred to the polluted water at the beach.

La Vista

Pelican Key Estates (P.O. Box 2086, Philipsburg), St. Maarten, N.A. ☎ **599/5-43005**, 212/251-1800 in New York City. Fax 599/5-43010. 24 suites and cottages. A/C TV TEL. Winter, $217 junior suite for two; $270–$345 suite or cottage. Off-season, $110 junior suite for two; $130–$160 suite or cottage. Continental breakfast $5–$10 extra. AE, DC, MC, V. Free parking.

La Vista, although not well known, offers large and handsomely furnished time-share junior suites and Antillean cottages. Each accommodation opens onto a sea view and contains an equipped kitchenette, a generous living and dining area, and a good-sized balcony. The resort is about a 10-minute drive west of Philipsburg, longer with traffic.

Dining/Entertainment: The complex features a lounge area, as well as an open-air restaurant, the Hideaway.

Services: Room service, laundry, babysitting.

Facilities: Freshwater swimming pool. Guests have use of the facilities at the adjacent Pelican Resort.

Maho Beach Hotel and Casino

Maho Bay, Philipsburg, St. Maarten, N.A. ☎ **599/5-52115**, 212/969-9220 in New York City, or 800/223-0757 in the U.S. Fax 599/5-53180. 624 rms, 35 suites. A/C TV TEL. Winter, $195–$270 single; $215–$295 double; $$335–$590 suite. Off-season, $140–$210 single; $155–$220 double; $240–$460 suite. MAP $26 per person extra. AE, DC, MC, V. Free parking.

Separated into three distinct sections, each built over an eight-year period beginning in the mid-1980s, this is the largest hotel on the island. Set along the busy coastal road adjacent to a crescent-shaped beach, the hotel is unified by its trademark color scheme of pink and white. About a third of the rooms contain microwaves and refrigerators, and each has wicker furniture, Italian tiles, and plush upholstery. The hotel's only drawback is its very large scale and the thundering noise of the aircraft that land at the nearby airport several times a day.

Dining/Entertainment: Because of its large size, the hotel contains 10 restaurants, more than any other hotel on the island. About half a dozen of these are independently operated, and lie in arcades lining each side of the main entrance. The trio operated by the hotel include the Ocean Terrace and the Palms, for international food and seafood, and the Ristorante Roma, for Italian cuisine. Across the busy coastal road from the hotel is the largest casino on the island, the Casino Royale. In addition, the open-air disco, La Luna, is considered an island hot spot.

Services: Laundry, babysitting.

Facilities: Four tennis courts, two outdoor swimming pools with a view of Maho Bay, health club spa, duty-free shopping (70 boutiques), a sandy beach with water sports (at the bottom of the hill).

Mullet Bay Resort and Casino

Mullet Bay (P.O. Box 909, Philipsburg), St. Maarten, N.A. ☎ **599/5-52801,** or 800/ 4-MULLET in the U.S. Fax 599/5-54281. 300 rms. 300 suites. A/C TV TEL. Winter, $275–$325 single or double; $370–$510 one-bedroom suite; $590–$1,350 two-bedroom suite. Off-season, $160–$195 single or double; $245–$310 one-bedroom suite; $385–$830 two-bedroom suite. Third person $35 extra; children under 12 stay free in parents' room. MAP $60 per person extra. Golf, honeymoon, and other packages available. AE, DC, MC, V. Free parking.

Mullet Bay sprawls over 172 acres whose terrain is bisected by one of St. Maarten's major roads. Located on a narrow isthmus of flat and sandy land midway between the open sea and a saltwater lagoon, a five-minute drive west of Juliana Airport, the resort was established in the late 1960s as one of the first of the Caribbean mega-resorts.

None of its architecture rises more than two stories. A series of semidetached town houses and fully detached villas lie scattered across the palm-studded grounds. All accommodations have refrigerators and are spacious and comfortably furnished.

Dining/Entertainment: The Shipwreck on the Beach serves breakfast and lunch, and Little Italy overlooking Simpson Bay Lagoon offers three meals a day. On Mullet Bay Beach, the Little Ocean Reef features open-grill specialties, including fresh seafood. The Frigate, a lagoonside restaurant, offers steaks and salads, and

---

🅘. Family-Friendly Accommodations

Mullet Bay Resort and Casino   *(see p. 366)* Kids under 12 stay free in their parents' room, and the resort has lots of amusements for the children.

Belair Beach Hotel   *(see p. 364)* Special parent-children packages are offered here at summer vacation time, and families can save money by preparing their own meals in fully equipped kitchens.

Town House Villas   *(see p. 369)* This group of apartments is ideal for families. Each unit has two large bedrooms, plus a fully equipped kitchen. Prices are reasonable, too.

the Bamboo Garden serves a cuisine from four regions of China. After dark, there's gambling plus live musical entertainment at the Grand Casino.

Services: Concierge, babysitting.

Facilities: The island's only golf course, (a championship 18-hole layout designed by Joseph Lee), 14 tennis courts (two lit at night), water sports (including windsurfing, snorkeling, parasailing, and waterskiing), fitness center, two swimming pools, food market, shopping arcade with more than 20 shops.

Pelican Resort & Casino

Simpson Bay (P.O. Box 431, Philipsburg), St. Maarten, N.A. ☎ **599/5-42503**, or 800/ 626-9637 in the U.S. Fax 599/5-42133. 540 suites. A/C TV TEL. Winter, $215 junior suite for two, $270 junior suite for four; $275 one-bedroom suite for two, $340 one-bedroom suite for four; $445 two-bedroom suite for four. Off-season, $120 junior suite for two, $160 junior suite for four; $175 one-bedroom suite for two, $225 one-bedroom suite for four; $350 two-bedroom suite for four. Seven-night minimum stay usually required in winter. AE, DC, MC, V. Free parking.

The Pelican, built in 1979 on 12 acres of land near the airport, is the largest time-share facility on St. Maarten. It's set on one of the biggest tracts of land under the ownership of a single hotel on the Dutch side. Although many of the suites are leased for predesignated periods throughout the year, others are rented as they become available by the on-site managers. Accommodations contain full kitchens, and are arranged into village-style clusters carefully separated from other units with lattices, hibiscus hedges, and bougainvillea. Furnishings are blandly international, in pastel colors, and usually contain patios or verandas. Scattered around the property are a lily pond, many small waterways, and an orchid garden.

Dining/Entertainment: The Pelican Reef Restaurant (see "Where to Dine," below) is one of the island's best steak-and-seafood restaurants, with a waterfront ambience. The Crocodile Café is a casual dinery open late and offering live entertainment. The Italian Connection, a pasta house and pizzeria, offers casual waterfront Italian dining, with pizzas made from scratch. The Brazilian Bar is the resort's waterfront gathering spot for sunsets and long, long happy hours. The hotel's casino is a nightlife mecca.

Services: Laundry, babysitting.

Facilities: Six tennis courts; six swimming pools; 1,400 feet of ocean-front marina; L'Aqualigne, a unique health and beauty center (see "Revitalization Center" in "Sports & Outdoor Activities," below). Water sports can be arranged.

✪ Oyster Pond Beach Hotel

Oyster Pond (P.O. Box 239, Philipsburg), St. Maarten, N.A. ☎ **599/5-22206,** or 800/839-3030 in the U.S. Fax 599/5-25695. 16 rms, 24 suites. A/C TV TEL. Winter, $170–$290 single or double; $290–$310 suite. Off-season, $120–$190 single or double; $190–$200 suite. (Includes full breakfast.) AE, MC, V. Free parking. Closed Sept.

This small resort lies 8 miles east of Philipsburg and is reached by a twisting, scenic road. On the windward side of the island, on a circular harbor on the eastern shore near the French border, the fortresslike structure stands guard over a 35-acre protected marina and has a private half-moon sandy beach. There is a central courtyard and an al fresco lobby, with white wicker and fine paintings. More than half the units are suites or duplexes, and most have a West Indian decor. The bedrooms have balconies overlooking the pond or sea. The most elegant and expensive accommodation is a tower suite.

Dining/Entertainment: Off the courtyard, and opening onto the sea, is a bar/lounge, as warm and comfortable as a private home. The dining room is exceptional, and the chef turns out a well-prepared continental cuisine intermixed with some Créole dishes. All dining is à la carte.

Services: Laundry.

Facilities: Saltwater swimming pool (22 by 44 feet).

MODERATE

Holland House

Front St. (P.O. Box 393), Philipsburg, St. Maarten, N.A. ☎ **599/5-22572,** or 800/223-9815 in the U.S. Fax 599/5-24673. 54 units, 6 suites. A/C TV TEL. Winter, $145 single; $160 double; $175–$190 suite. Off-season, $84 single; $99 double; $114–$129 suite. AE, DC, MC, V. Free parking.

With an urban-minded location 15 minutes east of the airport in the heart of town, this hotel rents cozy apartments decorated with furnishings from the Netherlands and the United States, with emphasis on rattan. Units have exposure to the street or to the (polluted) beach, and each contains a tiny kitchenette, ideal for light cooking. You're right on the beach, where you can order drinks at the bar, and an open-air dining terrace fronts Great Bay. The hotel is near all the major restaurants and shops of Philipsburg. Even if you're not staying here, you might want to call and reserve a table for dinner; this is one of the few hotels that serves authentic Dutch specialties at its restaurant, the Governor's Restaurant. International and Indonesian specialties are also served.

Mary's Boon

Simpson Bay (P.O. Box 2078, Philipsburg), St. Maarten, N.A. ☎ **599/5-54235.** Fax 599/5-53403. 12 units. Take the first right turn from the airport toward Philipsburg. Winter, $150 double. Off-season, $75–$90 double. Continental breakfast $5 extra. Children under 16 not accepted. No credit cards. Free parking.

This small, casual inn offers oversize stylish apartments with kitchenettes, designed as private villas. They lie directly on a 3-mile sandy beach, just south of the Juliana Airport and 15 minutes from Philipsburg. It's near the airport—but big planes are rare, and only land in the daytime. The rooms are decorated in rattan and wicker, and louvered windows open to sea breezes. Most rooms are in separate cottages, but there are two units in the main house. The efficiencies have ceiling fans.

There's a dining gallery fronting Simpson Bay. The cuisine is French/West Indian/international and is served in a restaurant with a view of the sea. In the bar you fix your own drinks on the honor system. Dinners are not served from August 15 to October 15.

⑤ Pasanggrahan

15 Front St. (P.O. Box 151), Philipsburg, St. Maarten, N.A. ☎ **599/5-23588.** Fax 599/5-22885. 24 rms. Winter, $114–$148 single or double. Off-season, $68–$88 single or double. Breakfast from $4.95 extra AE, MC, V. Free parking. Closed Sept.

Pasanggrahan is the Indonesian word for guesthouse, and this one is West Indian in style. A small, informal guesthouse, it's right on the busy, narrow main street of Philipsburg, toward the end of the mountain side of Front Street. It's set back under tall trees, with a white wooden veranda. The interior has peacock bamboo chairs, Indian spool tables, and a gilt-framed oil portrait of Queen Wilhelmina. So many guests asked to see the bedroom where the queen and her daughter, Juliana, stayed in World War II that the management turned it into the Sydney Greenstreet Bar. The renovated bedrooms have king-size beds and in some cases Saban bedspreads; some are in the main building, and others are in an adjoining annex. All accommodations have ceiling fans, and all but six are air-conditioned.

Set among the wild jungle of palms and shrubbery is the dining area, the Pasanggrahan Restaurant. Service is from noon to 3pm and 6 to 10pm daily. A two-course dinner costs $14.95. The private beach is only 50 feet away.

CONDOS & GUESTHOUSES

The Beach House

160 Front St. (P.O. Box 211), Philipsburg, St. Maarten, N.A. ☎ **599/5-22456.** Fax 599/5-30308. 8 studios. A/C TV. Winter, $78 studio for one; $88 studio for two. Off-season, $48 studio for one; $58 studio for two. AE, MC, V. Free parking.

This little guesthouse sits on Windward Beach at Great Bay, 6 miles east of the airport. One-bedroom studios, with fully equipped kitchenettes, daily maid service, and private balconies, are furnished in a simple Caribbean motif. Several of the best restaurants of St. Maarten are virtually at your doorstep.

Town House Villas

175 Front St. (P.O. Box 347), Philipsburg, St. Maarten, N.A. ☎ **599/5-22898,** 212/545-8469 in New York City, or 800/223-9815 in the U.S. Fax 599/5-22418. 11 apartments. A/C TV. Winter, $250 apartment for one or two; $300 apartment for three or four. Off-season, $125 all apartments. No credit cards. Free parking.

This group of duplex villas lies at the edge of the restaurant and shopping district of Philipsburg. At your doorstep is Great Bay Beach, dotted with palms—it's all shut off from the main street by a rugged stone wall and a wrought-iron gate. The town houses are handsome, rather formal with slanted shingled mansard roofs. Each apartment has two large bedrooms and $1^{1}/_{2}$ baths. There's a completely equipped kitchen, plus raised dining area in the long and well-furnished living room. Wide glass doors open onto ocean-view patios. You can enjoy a view of the bay from your living room or your terrace.

WHERE TO DINE
EXPENSIVE

✪ Antoine's

49 Front St., Philipsburg. ☎ **599/5-22964.** Reservations recommended, especially in season. Appetizers $5.75–$15; main courses $13.75–$36. AE, MC, V. Lunch Mon–Sat 11:30am–5pm; dinner Mon–Sat 5–10pm. Closed Aug–Oct. FRENCH/CREOLE.

Antoine's offers *la belle cuisine* in an atmospheric building next to the Little Pier in the center of Philipsburg. You can enjoy an apéritif in the cocktail bar. If the crowd is right (usually in winter), Antoine's takes on worldly sophistication, with impressive wines, top-quality service, and a long list of Gallic specialties. Fresh local fish is always available, but well-sauced beef and chicken dishes are also served. The spiny Caribbean langouste is regularly featured and prepared very well indeed. Soups are likely to range from vichyssoise to gazpacho; main dishes, from roast duckling in brandy sauce to filet mignon béarnaise.

Felix Restaurant

Pelican Bay. ☎ **599/5-42797.** Reservations recommended. Appetizers $7–$16; main courses $20–$30; lunch platters $4–$16. AE, MC, V. Lunch daily 11:30am–3pm; dinner Thurs–Tues 6:30–10pm. Closed Aug–Oct. FRENCH.

One of the island's best choices for an al fresco meal, this place is at its most romantic during candlelit dinners when seating choices range from intimate sheltered booths to outdoor tables set within sight and sound of the sea. Many of the seafood specialties come from the lobster tank. Choices might include chateaubriand for two, rack of lamb, and fish caught locally. Other specialties include lobster pasta, veal filets served Viennese style, duck breast with orange sauce, and filet mignon with your choice of three sauces. The restaurant, on the road to the Pelican Resort & Casino, also has a lounge. Margaret and Richard (Felix) Ducrot are the owners.

La Terrasse

In the Sheraton Port de Plaisance, Union Rd., Cole Bay. ☎ **599/5-45222.** Reservations required. Appetizers $6–$14; main courses $21–$35. AE, DC, MC, V. Lunch Mon–Sat 11:30am–3pm; dinner Mon–Sat 7–10:30pm; brunch Sun 11am–3pm. FRENCH/ INTERNATIONAL.

This hotel restaurant on St. Maarten was launched by chefs who have apprenticed with some of the three-star chefs of France, including Michel Guérard, Paul Bocuse, and Alain Senderens. Sunday brunch is a self-service American-style buffet with smoked salmon, pancakes, and the works.

The major talent of the kitchen emerges in the evening, however, tempting diners with such appetizers as a natural duck-liver terrine, warm sea-scallop salad, and marinated shrimps in pastry. The fish and seafood range from salmon with sautéed endives to monkfish medallions with spices. Exceptional meat and poultry dishes include roast duckling from Challans in a black-olive sauce and rack of lamb roasted with garlic and fresh rosemary. For dessert, one of the most popular items is a soufflé made with the "fruit of the day."

Le Bec Fin

119 Front St., Philipsburg, ☎ **599/5-22976.** Reservations required. Appetizers 7–10; main courses $16–$31. AE, MC, V. Lunch daily 11:30am–2:30pm; dinner daily 6–10pm. FRENCH.

Le Bec Fin, in Museum Arcade, is one of the best restaurants on St. Maarten, on either the Dutch or the French side. It has hosted the Dutch royal family. You walk across a courtyard and ascend a flight of steps to reach this restaurant, which has a view over the harbor. You might start with seafood tagliatelli in a fresh ginger sauce, then follow with either peppersteak flambé or grilled red snapper. Grilled lobster is also regularly featured.

✪ Le Perroquet

72 Airport Rd. ☎ **599/5-54339.** Reservations required. Appetizers $6.50–$10; main courses $18–$26. AE, MC, V. Dinner only. Tues–Sun 6–10pm. Closed June and Sept. FRENCH.

Only a short walk from the airport sits the domain of M. Pierre Castagne, a French chef of exceptional ability. The name of this restaurant comes from the famed Chicago restaurant. The St. Maarten version is in a typical West Indian house with shutters open to the trade winds blowing around Simpson Bay Lagoon. Monsieur Castagne offers such dishes as ostrich breast (yes, that's right) in a bordelaise sauce and filet of boar, but you can also order more familiar fare, beginning with a savory fish soup or a fresh mâché salad, and moving on to mussels marinara, duck with a Grand Marnier orange sauce, or red snapper in a garlic sauce. Some of the specialties are wheeled in on a table so you can make a visual selection—a nice touch.

Pelican Reef Restaurant and Seafood House

Waterfront Marina, at the Pelican Resort & Casino, Simpson Bay. ☎ **599/5-42503,** ext. 1578. Reservations recommended. Appetizers $6.25–$11.95; main courses $14.50–$27.95; fixed price meals $20.95–$21.95. AE, MC, V. Dinner only, daily 6–10:30pm. STEAK/ SEAFOOD.

This American steakhouse not only serves what are reputed to be the island's best steaks, but also offers tasty chops and seafood. The hosts, Marvin and Jean Rich, offer fine, friendly service, and present an array of good-quality ingredients, art-fully served with a view over Simpson Bay. Signature dishes include a hearty slab of prime rib on the bone, grilled Argentinian style on a charcoal grill; whole Caribbean lobster, baked and stuffed; grilled filet of fish, perhaps red snapper, from local waters; rack of baby lamb; or a thick veal chop. Save room for the conch fritters with two sauces, and follow with a "chocolate island" or their frozen fantasy dessert. A special feature of the wine list is a "tasting" of fine armagnacs, unique because they are from single estates and both are made from 100% ugni blanc, a rare grape used only in the making of armagnacs and cognacs.

Spartaco

Almond Grove Plantation Estate, Cole Bay. ☎ **599/5-45379.** Reservations recommended. Appetizers $12–$18; main courses $20–$24. AE, MC, V. Dinner only, Tues–Sun 6–11pm. Closed June–Oct. ITALIAN.

Spartaco lies in a residential suburb midway between Philipsburg and the airport. Its limestone walls were originally built in 1803 as part of the West Indian manor house, but the decor today includes strong doses of 1930s art deco and some high-tech design. Guests sit in the main dining room or on a breeze-filled wrap-around veranda. The menu includes fresh black tagliolini (angel-hair pasta flavored with squid ink, served with shrimp, parsley, and garlic sauce) and swordfish Mediterranean (composed of parsley, garlic, capers, and an olive oil that owner Spartaco Sargentoni imports from his relatives who produce it on a farm outside Florence). The antipasti, from squid and mussels to eggplant and carpaccio, make a fine beginning.

MODERATE

Alba

Lowlands, Cupecoy. ☎ **599/5-52100.** Reservations recommended. Appetizers $6.75–$12.75; main courses $9–$19.75. AE, MC, V. Dinner only, daily 6pm–midnight. Closed June–Sept. ITALIAN.

Overlooking the Treasure Island Casino, this restaurant is known for its tender filet mignon, thick-crust pizza, and candlelit dinners. A full array of familiar and classic Italian fare, from both the north and south of Italy, is featured. In the prominent bar, a wide-screen TV shows sporting events and easy-listening videos. Dress ranges from relatively formal to casual, and sometimes there's dancing. Every afternoon from 4:30 to 6:30pm there's a two-for-one happy hour.

Chesterfields

Great Bay Marina, Pointe Blanche. ☎ **599/5-23484.** Reservations recommended. Appetizers $5.50–$7.50; main courses $7.95–$18. No credit cards. Breakfast daily 7:30–10:30am; lunch Mon–Sat 11:30am–2:30pm; dinner daily 5:30–10pm; brunch Sun 10:30am–2:30pm. AMERICAN/CARIBBEAN.

Chesterfield's has a special attraction other than its good food. It offers pier-side dining with a view of the harbor, on a trade wind–swept veranda near Great Bay Marina, east of Philipsburg. The yachting set gathers here, and everybody seems to know everybody else. The setting and the dress are both casual, and you dine on several international specialties, with fresh seafood and French-inspired cookery a highlight. On Wednesday night try the prime rib served with sautéed mushrooms, or at any time, red snapper Créole or broiled, duck Chesterfield, or seafood pasta. In season, there's always some lively activity going on, such as champagne Sunday brunches with eggs Benedict or Florentine, or seafood omelets.

The Wajang Doll

137 Front St., Philipsburg. ☎ **599/5-22687.** Reservations required. Dinner $18.90 for 14 dishes, $24.90 for 19 dishes. AE, MC, V. Dinner only. Mon–Sat 6:45–10pm. Closed Sept. INDONESIAN.

Housed in a wooden West Indian building on the main street of town, the Wajang Doll is one of the best Indonesian restaurants in the Caribbean. There's a low-slung front porch where you can watch the pedestrian traffic outside, and big windows in back overlook the sea. The restaurant is best known for its 19-dish dinner, known as a rijstaffel (rice table). The cuisine varies from West Java to East Java, and the chef crushes his spices every day for maximum pungency, according to an ancient craft. Other specialties include fried snapper in a chili sauce, marinated pork on a bamboo stick, and Javanese chicken dishes.

INEXPENSIVE

Don Carlos Restaurant

Airport Rd., Simpson Bay. ☎ **599/5-53112.** Reservations not required. Appetizers $2.50–$6.50; main courses $9.50–$28.50. AE, DC, MC, V. Daily 7:30am–10pm. MEXICAN/CARIBBEAN/INTERNATIONAL.

The restaurant is located just five minutes east of the airport with a view of arriving and departing planes from the floor-to-ceiling windows surrounded by international flags. The place serves breakfast, lunch, and dinner. Owners Shenny and Carl Wagner invite you for a drink in their Pancho Villa Bar before your meal in their hacienda-style dining room with a multilingual staff.

The Greenhouse

Bobby's Marina, Philipsburg. ☎ **599/5-22941.** Reservations not required. Appetizers $3–$5; main courses $9–$18; lunch from $8. AE, MC, V. Lunch Mon–Fri 11am–5pm; dinner Tues–Sun 5:30–11pm. AMERICAN.

Open to a view of the harbor, off Front Street, the Greenhouse is filled with plants, as befits its name. As you dine, breezes filter through the open-air eatery. Lunches include the catch of the day, a wide selection of burgers, and conch chowder. Dinners might feature chunks of lobster in wine sauce or a whole red snapper. On "Fabulous Friday," for only $10.95 you can eat unlimited ribs and chicken. Happy Hour from 4:30 to 7pm features a free buffet. Some guests not only enjoy half-price drinks but get their fill of food for the evening.

⑤ The Italian Connection

Waterfront Marina, at the Pelican Resort & Casino, Simpson Bay. ☎ **599/5-42503,** ext. 1072. Reservations not required. Appetizers $2.75–$7.95; pizza $7.95–$15.50; pasta $6.95–$15.50; main courses $12.95–$15.95. AE, MC, V. Daily noon–10pm. ITALIAN.

This pasta house and pizzeria offers tropical fresh-air Italian dining at the marina on Simpson Bay. The chef makes pizzas, such as "The Mama Mia," from scratch and loads them with flavorful ingredients. Lunch and dinner specials—changed daily—are likely to feature breast of chicken or filets of local fish. The sauces over the pastas are richly flavored. Try, for example, tender filet of red snapper topped with plum tomatoes or loin of pork cacciatore from an ancient Florentine recipe. You might begin with antipasto, finishing with a homemade Italian ice cream for dessert. Special nights include a "Taste of St. Maarten," on Tuesday, a Caribbean dinner and show that costs $16.95 and offers calypso, reggae, and soca. On "Golden Oldies Night," Thursday, a DJ entertains with music from the 1950s, 1960s, and 1970s. The lights are turned down low so guests can dance under the stars. A special dinner costs $15.95.

SPORTS & OUTDOOR ACTIVITIES

BEACHES   St. Maarten has 36 beautiful white sand beaches, and it's comparatively easy to find a part of the beach for yourself. *Warning:* If it's too secluded, be careful. Don't carry valuables to the beach; there have been reports of robberies on some remote beaches.

Regardless of where you stay, you're never far from the water. If you're a beach-sampler, you can often use the changing facilities at some of the bigger resorts for a small fee. (Nudists should head for the French side of the island, although the Dutch side is getting more liberal about such things.)

On the west side of the island, west of the airport, **Mullet Bay Beach** is shaded by palm trees and can get crowded on weekends. Water-sports equipment rentals can be arranged through the hotel.

Great Bay Beach is preferred if you're staying along Front Street in Philipsburg. This mile-long beach is sandy, but since it borders the busy capital it may not be as clean as some of the more remote beaches. Immediately to the west, at the foot of Fort Amsterdam, **Little Bay Beach** looks like a Caribbean postcard, but it, too, can be overrun with visitors from Little Bay Resort and Casino and Belair Beach Hotel.

Stretching the length of Simpson Bay Village, **Simpson Bay Beach** is shaped like a half moon with white sands. It lies west of Philipsburg before you reach the airport. Water-sports equipment rentals are available here.

North of the airport, **Maho Bay Beach,** at the Maho Beach Hotel and Casino, is shaded by palms and is ideal in many ways, if you don't mind the planes taking off and landing. Palms provide shade, and food and drink can be purchased at the hotel.

The sands are pearly white at **Oyster Pond Beach,** near the Oyster Pond Hotel northeast of Philipsburg. Bodysurfers like the rolling waves here. In the same location, **Dawn Beach** is noted for its underwater tropical beauty (reefs lie offshore). The approach is through the Dawn Beach Hotel.

DEEP-SEA FISHING   Half-day or full-day deep-sea fishing excursions are offered aboard a 31-foot Bertram named *Sea Brat* (☎ 599/5-24096), which berths at Bobby's Marina in Philipsburg. The vessel departs from the marina (at the foot of Front Street) upon prior reservation and includes all bait and tackle, instruction for novices, an open bar, and (for the full-day excursion) lunch. The cost is $375 for a half-day and $650 for a full-day outing, for up to six passengers. A two-day advance reservation is recommended.

GOLF   The **Mullet Bay Resort** (☎ 599/5-52801, ext. 1851) has an 18-hole course, one of the most challenging in the Caribbean, designed by Joseph Lee. Mullet Pond and Simpson Bay Lagoon provide both beauty and hazards. For Mullet Bay guests, greens fees are $40 for 9 holes or $65 for 18 holes. Nonresidents pay $55 for 9 holes, $95 for 18 holes. Prices include use of a cart.

HORSEBACK RIDING   At **Crazy Acres,** Wathey Estate, Cole Bay (☎ 599/5-42793), riding expeditions invariably end on an isolated beach where the horses, with or without their riders, enjoy the cool waters in an after-ride romp. Two experienced escorts accompany a maximum of eight people on the outings, which begin at 9:30am and 2:30pm Monday through Saturday and last 2¹/₂ hours. The price is $50 per person. Riders of all levels of experience are welcome, with the single provision that they wear bathing suits under their riding clothes for the grand finale on the beach. It's recommended that reservations be made at least two days in advance. Riding lessons are available.

PICNIC SAILS   A popular pastime is to sign up for a day of picnicking, sailing, snorkeling, and sightseeing aboard one of several boats providing this service. The sleek sailboats usually pack large wicker hampers full of victuals and stretch tarpaulins over sections of the deck to protect sun-shy sailors.

The *Gabrielle* (☎ 599/5-23170) sails from Bobby's Marina in Philipsburg year round and offers either a full-day or half-day trip—both of which include lunch, beer, French wine, and use of all equipment. The *Gabrielle* is a 46-foot ketch with a spacious shaded cockpit and large decks. A maximum of 14 people are taken to a secluded cove or small island where you can sunbathe, swim, and snorkel. You can make reservations at your hotel or by phone. The price is $65 per person for a full day sail. A shorter sail is also offered, a coastal sail with lunch, priced at $45 per person, and held on designated days from 10:30am to 3pm. There's also a sunset sail, on designated days, priced at $27.50 per person, with drinks, from 5 to 7pm.

A REVITALIZATION CENTER   **L'Aqualigne,** Pelican Resort and Casino, Simpson Bay (☎ 599/5-42426), is a world-class European health, fitness, and beauty spa that offers services ranging from aqua-aerobics to massages, from cellulite therapy to body sculpting, and from holistic rejuvenation to diagnosing the hormonal system metabolism. As well as spa vacations, L'Aqualigne offers recuperative vacations for guests wishing reconstructive surgery performed by specialists from Europe and the United States. Spa services include waxing, massages, medical pedicures, manicures, body peelings, facials, and beauty treatments. Spa facilities include eight separate treatment rooms, saunas, steam room, and ice plunge and therapy pool. Consultation in fitness and beauty, anticellulite treatment, nutrition, weight control, antiwrinkle treatment, and reconstruction surgery are offered. The center will send you full details. It's open daily from 9am to 6pm.

SAILING TO OTHER ISLAND COUNTRIES   Experienced skippers make one-day voyages to St. Barts in the French West Indies and to Saba, another of the Dutch Windwards in the Leewards; they stop long enough for passengers to familiarize themselves with the island ports, shop, and have lunch. To arrange a trip, ask at your hotel or at the **St. Maarten Tourist Bureau,** 23 Walter Nisbeth Rd. in Philipsburg (☎ 599/5-22337).

The *Quicksilver* (☎ 599/5-24697), a 61-foot motor-sailing catamaran, leaves from Great Bay Marina daily at 9am and returns around 5pm. It makes a 1¹/₂-hour run to the French island of St. Barts, where you can visit the little capital of Gustavia, shop, and tour the island at your leisure. The $55 fare includes an open bar. You can visit the *Quicksilver* at the dock.

Also available is *The Falcon* (☎ 599/5-22167), a catamaran which moors in the Great Bay Marina, and sails Monday through Saturday to St. Bart's. The cost is $60 per person, including an open bar.

The *White Octopus* (☎ 599/5-24096 during the day, 599/5-23170 in the evening), a 75-foot motor catamaran, offers spacious upper and lower decks for passengers on the 1¹/₂-hour trip from St. Maarten to St. Barts. The boat leaves Philipsburg on Monday, Tuesday, Thursday, Friday, and Saturday at 9am and returns at 5pm. On Wednesday the boat departs from Captain Oliver's Marina, Oyster Pond, at 8:30am and returns at 5:30pm. The cost is $60 per person. For another $25 you're granted an island tour and lunch at a St. Bart's restaurant.

TENNIS You can try the courts at most of the large hotels, but Tennis Village at **Mullet Bay Resort** (☎ **599/5-52801,** ext. 1860) is the undisputed champion of both the Dutch and French sides of the island, with 10 tennis courts, two of which are lit at night. Residents of Mullet Bay pay $18 per hour for a singles game or $28 per hour for a doubles game. Nonresidents pay $25 per hour for singles or $35 per hour for doubles. There's a nighttime surcharge after 6pm of $20 per hour for illumination. Private lessons go for $45 for one hour or $30 for a half hour.

WATER SPORTS **Windsurfing** and **jet-skiing** are especially popular on St. Maarten. The unruffled waters of Simpson Bay Lagoon, the largest in the West Indies, are ideal for these sports, as well as for **waterskiing.**

St. Maarten's crystal-clear bays and the countless coves make for good **snorkeling** and **scuba diving.** Underwater visibility reportedly runs from 75 to 125 feet. The biggest attraction for scuba divers is the 1801 British man-of-war, HMS *Proselyte*, which came to a watery grave on a reef a mile off the coast. Most of the big resort hotels have facilities for scuba diving, and their staff can provide information about underwater tours, for photography as well as night diving.

One of the major water-sports centers, **Maho Bay Watersports,** in the Mullet Bay Resort, Mullet Bay (☎ **599/5-52801,** ext. 1871), is the longest-established diving operation on the island, and it provides scuba lessons. A resort course—including beach instruction, all equipment, and a beach dive—costs $50. PADI or SSI certification is available for $350, including 40 hours of instruction. A one-tank dive for certified divers is priced at $50. Dive packages are available on request. You can rent snorkel equipment and other dive items. The center is open daily from 8:30am to 5pm.

SHOPPING

St. Maarten is not only a free port, but there are no local sales taxes. Prices are sometimes lower here than anywhere else in the Caribbean; however, you must be familiar with the prices of what you're looking for to know what actually *is* a bargain. Many well-known shops on Curaçao have branches here, in case you're not going on to the ABC islands (Aruba, Bonaire, and Curaçao).

Except for the boutiques at resort hotels, the main shopping area is in the center of Philipsburg. Most of the shops are on two leading streets, Front Street (called Voorstraat in Dutch), which is closer to the bay, and Back Street (Achterstraat), which runs parallel. Shopping hours in general are 8am to noon and 2 to 6pm Monday through Saturday. If a cruise ship is in port, many shops are also open on Sunday.

SHOPPING CENTERS

Museum Arcade
119 Front St., with an entrance on Great Bay Beach.

This gallery of specialty shops is designed in an authentic old West Indian style and was built around St. Maarten's first museum. The museum is part of a foundation designed to promote excavations and other explorations on the island, as well as to carry out other projects related to the island's history and its cultural and artistic past. The museum is housed in a cottage on Front Street that dates from 1888 and was built in the West Indian gingerbread style. The museum is open Monday through Friday from 10am to 4pm and charges an admission of $1.

The Museum Arcade features six shops, a French café, and a French restaurant. The variety of items available ranges from Italian leather goods to French perfumes to novelty souvenirs. Visitors can enjoy the open-air terrace, breezy courtyard, and, perhaps more important, the public bathrooms.

Old Street Shopping Center

With entrances on Front St. and Back St. ☎ **599/5-24712.**

The Old Street Shopping Center lies 170 yards east of the courthouse. Its lion's-head fountain is the most photographed spot on St. Maarten. Built in a West Indian-Dutch style, it features more than two dozen shops and boutiques, including branches of such famous stores as Columbian Emeralds. Dining facilities include the Philipsburg Grill and Ribs Co. and Pizza Hut. The stores are open Monday through Saturday from 9:30am to 6pm, but the Philipsburg Grill and Ribs Co. is open on Sunday as well, to 11pm.

SPECIALTY STORES

Antillean Liquors

Juliana Airport. ☎ **599/5-54267.**

This duty-free shop attracts the last-minute shopper and is open daily 365 days a year, from 7am to 7:30pm. It has a complete assortment of all the leading brands of liquor and liqueurs, as well as cigarettes and cigars.

Caribbean Camera Centre

79 Front St. ☎ **599/5-25259.**

The Caribbean Camera Centre has a wide range of merchandise, but it's always wise to know the prices charged back home.

Colombian Emeralds International

Front St. ☎ **599/5-22438.**

Here you'll find stones from collector to investment quality. Unmounted duty-free emeralds from Colombia, as well as emerald, gold, diamond, ruby, and sapphire jewelry, will tempt you. Another branch is in the Old Street Arcade.

Guavaberry Company

10 Front St. ☎ **599/5-24497.**

This place sells the rare island folk liqueur of St. Maarten that for centuries was made in private homes but is now available to everyone. Sold in square bottles, the product is made from rum that's given a unique flavor by use of rare, local berries usually grown in the hills in the center of the island. Don't confuse guavaberries with guavas—they're very different. The liqueur is aged and has a fruity, woody, almost bittersweet flavor, and you can blend it with coconut for a unique guavaberry colada or pour a splash into a glass of icy champagne. Stop in at their shop and free-tasting house, which is open daily from 9am to 5pm.

H. Stern Jewellers

56 Front St. ☎ **599/5-23328.**

This is the Philipsburg branch of a worldwide firm that engages in mining, designing, manufacturing, exporting, and retailing jewelry in all price ranges. They use precious gems to create pieces in contemporary and traditional designs.

La Romana

Royal Palm Plaza, 61 Front St. ☎ **599/5-22181.**

Arguably the most interesting international specialty boutique on the island, this shop offers an excellent selection of the famous line of La Perla swimwear/beachwear for men and women, the La Perla fine lingerie collection, and the latest Fendi bags, luggage, accessories, and perfume. The management states that prices are sometimes up to 40% less than U.S. prices.

Little Switzerland
42 Front St. ☎ **599/5-23530.**

These fine-quality European imports are made even more attractive by the prices charged here. Elegant famous-name watches, china, crystal, and jewelry are for sale, plus perfume and accessories.

Loulian's Boutique
4 Hendrikstraat. ☎ **599/5-22169.**

This shop is in a historic West Indian house, renovated and preserved in its original gingerbread-style architecture—a first in St. Maarten. You'll find shoes for both men and women, and handbags for women as well. A number of leather items are also sold, including wallets, belts, and traveling bags. Most of the merchandise is made in Colombia.

New Amsterdam Store
54 Front St. ☎ **599/5-22787.**

A tradition in the islands since 1925, this store on St. Maarten opened in 1967 on Front Street. Purveyors of fine linen, it features no fewer than eight distinct boutiques under one roof, represented by Polo by Ralph Lauren, Perry Ellis, Regatta, Givenchy, and J'aime Ça by Bettina. The footwear boutique carries such brands as Bally, Sebago, and Birkenstock. Gottex, Israel's finest swimwear, is also sold.

Shipwreck Shop
Front St. ☎ **599/5-22962.**

Here you'll find West Indian hammocks, beach towels, steak plates, salad bowls, baskets, handmade jewelry, T-shirts, postcards, stamps, books, and much more. It's the home of wood carvings, native art, sea salt, cane sugar, and spices—in all, a treasure trove of Caribbean handcrafts.

Yellow House (Casa Amarilla)
Wilhelminastraat. ☎ **599/5-23438.**

Residents of the Dutch-speaking islands know this shop as a branch of a century-old establishment on Curaçao. All kinds of perfumes and luxury items are sold including Christian Dior cosmetics. Everything is sold at duty-free prices.

ST. MAARTEN AFTER DARK

On the Dutch side of St. Maarten there are few real nightclubs. After-dark activities begin early here, as guests select their favorite nook for a sundowner—perhaps the garden patio of **Pasanggrahan** (see "Where to Stay," above).

Visitors watch for the legendary **"green flash,"** an atmospheric phenomenon written about by Hemingway that sometimes occurs in these latitudes just as the sun drops below the horizon. Each evening guests wait expectantly, and have been known to break into a round of applause at a particularly spectacular sunset.

Many hotels sponsor **beachside barbecues** (particularly in season) with steel bands and native music and folk dancing. Outsiders are welcomed at most of these events, but call ahead to see if it's a private affair.

DISCOS & NIGHT CLUBS

Cheri's Café

In the Cinnamon Grove Shopping Center, Maho Beach. ☎ **599/5-53361.**

This island hot spot won the *Caribbean Travel and Life* readers' pick for best bar in the Caribbean. Known for its inexpensive food and live bands, it's an island institution. American expatriate Cheri Baston is the duenna of this open-air café serving some 400 meals a night. The place is really only a roof without walls, and it's not on a beach. But people flock to it anyway, devouring 16-ounce steaks at $16.75 or a simple burger at $5.50. It's also possible to get grilled fish beginning at $12.25 a platter. You can dine under the canopy or on a terrace under the stars. Everyone from movie stars to beach bums comprise the clientele. Some come for the inexpensive food, others for the potent drinks, and some to dance to the music.

Coconuts Comedy Club

In the Maho Beach Hotel and Casino, Maho Plaza ☎ **599/5-52115.** Admission $10.

On the upper lobby of this previously recommended hotel, the comedy club presents shows Sunday through Friday at 9:30pm and again at 11:30pm. Management promises "the best young comedians from the United States." Beer begins at $3.

Studio 7

In the Mullet Bay Resort and Casino, Mullet Bay. ☎ **599/5-52801.** Admission $8.

One of the busiest watering holes in this sprawling resort lies adjacent to one of the island's largest casinos. It's open Tuesday through Sunday night, with lots of glitter and recently released electronic music from the recording centers of the world. Drinks begin at $4. Open from 11pm to 4am only on Friday and Saturday nights.

Turtle Pier Bar

Airport Rd., Simpson Bay. ☎ **599/5-52230.**

One of the most frequented watering holes on St. Maarten, this restaurant-bar features live music several nights a week. Throughout the week, it's a special favorite among visitors and locals alike. A sun deck with lounge chairs is ideal for lazing around with a planter's punch. Boaters often come here for a shower; this pier bar has its own dock and a menagerie of chattering monkeys and squawking parrots—in all, some 200 animals. Sid Wathey and his American-born wife, Lorraine, are the hosts at this funky place. Cheap beer on draft packs them in, as does the all-you-can-eat ribs dinners for $9.95. The day begins at 8am when large American breakfasts are served, and the action lasts at least until midnight daily.

CASINOS

Most of the casinos are in the big hotels, such as the **Mullet Bay Resort and Casino,** the **Maho Beach Hotel and Casino** (with its glittering Casino Royale), and the **Great Bay Beach Hotel and Casino** (see "Where to Stay," above, for descriptions and locations).

The **Casino Royale,** at the Maho Beach Hotel on Maho Bay, opened in 1975. It has 16 blackjack tables, six roulette wheels, and three craps and three Caribbean stud-poker tables. The casino offers baccarat, mini-baccarat, and a large collection of more than 250 slot machines. It's open daily from 1pm to 4am. The Casino

Royale Piano Bar is open nightly from 9:30pm, featuring the best of jazz, pop, and Caribbean music. There's no admission, and a snack buffet is complimentary.

Located at the Mullet Bay Resort, the **Grand Casino,** one of the Caribbean's largest, offers both Atlantic City– and Las Vegas–style rules and features a wide range of games, including baccarat, craps, double-deck 21, and progressive slots. The Grand is open daily from 1pm until 3am.

A popular casino is at the previously recommended **Pelican Resort and Casino** (☎ **599/5-42503**), built to a Swiss design incorporating a panoramic view of Simpson Bay. The Las Vegas–style casino has two craps tables, three roulette tables, nine blackjack tables, five stud-poker tables, and 120 slot machines. It's open daily from 1pm to 3am.

The Roman-themed **Coliseum Casino,** on Front Street in Philipsburg (☎ **599/5-32102**), which opened in 1990, has taken several steps to attract gaming enthusiasts, especially "high rollers," and has the highest table limits on St. Maarten— $1,000 maximum. Upon the management's approval, the Coliseum also offers credit lines for clients with a good credit rating at any U.S. casino. The Coliseum features about 200 slot machines, four blackjack tables, three poker tables, and two roulette wheels. Several times a year the Coliseum holds special slot machine and blackjack tournaments. The Coliseum is open daily from 11am to 3am.

One of the Caribbean's most spectacular casinos is the $20-million **Mont Fortune Casino,** Union Road (☎ **599/5-45222**), a popular attraction at Port de Plaisance, ITT Sheraton's luxurious resort overlooking Simpson Bay. You'll be in the company of gaming devotees from across North and Latin America who are drawn to Mont Fortune as much for the ambience as for what the casino has to offer. This opulent gamer's paradise boasts 35,000 square feet of entertainment and gaming space (12,500 dedicated solely to gaming) and 153 state-of-the-art slot and video-slot machines. The casino is open daily from noon to 3:30am, and although the setting of Mont Fortune is elegant, casual dress is the rule. If blackjack is your passion, you'll want to take advantage of the 18 tables in the main casino and two tables in the private high-stakes' room (one of the largest on the island). Or try Caribbean Stud, baccarat, mini-baccarat, and craps. The casino has eight Keno machines, four blackjack tables, and 42 poker machines. For some hot jazz and reggae, you can head for La Belle Vie, a nightclub in the casino building open only on Friday and Saturday.

2 St. Eustatius

Called "Statia," this Dutch-held island is just an 8-square-mile pinpoint in the Netherlands Antilles, still basking in its 18th-century heritage as the "Golden Rock." One of the true backwaters of the West Indies, it's just awakening to tourism.

Perhaps the island might best be visited on a day trip from St. Maarten to see if you like it for an extended stay. As Caribbean islands go, it's rather dull here, and its beaches of volcanic black sand aren't especially alluring. Some pleasant strips of beach exist on the Atlantic side, but the surf there is dangerous for swimming.

If you're a hiker or a diver, the outlook improves considerably. Hikes are possible around the base of the Quill, an extinct volcano on the southern end of the island. Wandering through a tropical forest, you encounter wild orchids, philodendron, heliconia, anthurium, fruit trees, ferns, wildlife, and birds, with the inevitable oleander, hibiscus, and bougainvillea.

The island's reefs are covered with corals and enveloped by marine life. At one dive site, known as Crack in the Wall, or sometimes "the Grand Canyon," pinnacle coral shoots up from the floor of the ocean. Living among the reefs are barracudas, eagle rays, black-tip sharks, and other large ocean fish.

If you want to relax, not worry about nightlife, and aren't too demanding when you go to a restaurant, then seek out Statia at a point 150 miles east of Puerto Rico, 90 miles east of St. Croix, 38 miles due south of St. Maarten, and 17 miles southeast of Saba.

Two extinct volcanoes, the Quill and "Little Mountain," are linked by a sloping agricultural plain known as De Cultuurvlakte, where yams and sweet potatoes grow.

Overlooking the Caribbean on the western edge of the plain, **Oranjestad** (Orange City) is the capital and the only village, consisting of both an Upper and Lower Town, connected by stone-paved, dogleg Fort Road.

Statia was sighted by Columbus in 1493, on his second voyage, and the island was claimed for Holland by Jan Snouck in 1640. The island's history was turbulent before it settled down to peaceful slumber under Dutch protection. From 1650 to 1816 Statia changed flags 22 times!

Once the trading hub of the Caribbean, Statia was a thriving market, both for goods and for slaves.

Before the American Revolution the population of Statia did not exceed 1,200, most of whom were slaves engaged in raising sugarcane. When war came and Britain blockaded the North American coast, Europe's trade was diverted to the Caribbean. Dutch neutrality lured many traders, which led to the construction of a mile and a half of warehouses in Lower Town. The Americans obtained gunpowder and ammunition through Statia.

ORIENTATION
GETTING THERE

St. Eustatius can be reached from Dutch St. Maarten's Juliana Airport via **Windward Islands Airways International (Winair)** (☎ **599/5-52568** on St. Maarten). The flying time to Statia's Franklin Delano Roosevelt Airport is only 20 minutes from St. Maarten, with flights six times a day. Once on Statia, connections can also be made for flights to either Saba or St. Kitts. There are two flights a day to Saba and two flights a week to St. Kitts.

The little airline, launched in 1961, has an excellent safety record and has flown such passengers as David Rockefeller. The plane has 20 seats and is called a STOL (short takeoff and landing). You can visit just for the day, but I recommend spending more time here. Always reconfirm your return passage once you're on Statia.

GETTING AROUND

BY TAXI   Taxis are your best bet. They meet all incoming flights, and on the way to the hotel, I assure you that your driver will offer himself as a guide during your stay on the island. Taxi rates are low, probably no more than $3 to $5 to your hotel from the airport. If you book a two- to three-hour tour (and in that time you should be able to cover all the sights on Statia), the cost is about $35 per vehicle.

BY RENTAL CAR   Avis (☎ **800/331-1212** in the U.S.) is your best bet if you want to reserve a car in advance. With unlimited mileage included, it rents a Honda Excel or similar vehicle for $50 a day or $300 a week, with a collision-damage waiver

St. Eustatius

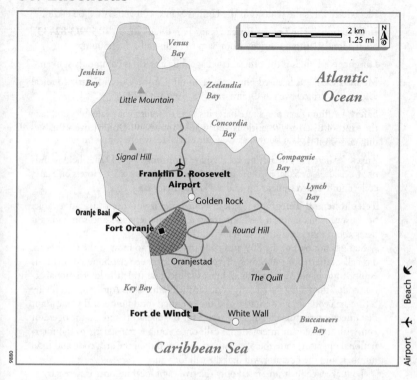

costing $8 a day. Drivers must be 21 years old and present a valid license and credit or charge card. Avis is at the airport (☎ **599/3-82421**) and in the center of Oranjestad at Lampeweg Building no. 1 (☎ **599/3-82421**).

FAST FACTS: St. Eustatius

Area Code   St. Eustatius is *not* part of the Caribbean's 809 area code. For information on calling St. Eustatius, see "Telephone and Telegraph," below.

Banks   Barclay's Bank, Wilhelminastraat, Oranjestad (☎ **599/3-82392**), the only bank on the island, is open from 8:30am to 1pm Monday through Friday and also from 4 to 5pm on Friday. On weekends, most hotels will exchange money.

Currency   The official unit of currency is the **Netherlands Antilles guilder (NAf)**, at 1.77 NAf to each $1 U.S., but nearly all places will quote you prices in U.S. dollars.

Customs   There are no Customs duties since the island is a free port.

Documents   U.S. and Canadian citizens need proof of citizenship, such as a passport, voter registration card, or a birth certificate, along with an ongoing ticket. If you're using a birth certificate or voter registration card, you'll also need some photo ID. British subjects need a valid passport.

Electricity   It's the same as in the United States, 100 volts A.C., 60 cycles.

Information   The **Tourist Bureau** is at 3 Fort Oranjestraat (☎ **599/3-82433**), open Monday through Friday from 8am to noon and 1 to 4:30pm.

Language   Dutch is the official language, but English is commonly spoken.

Medical Care   A licensed physician is on duty at the Queen Beatrix Medical Center, 25 Princessweg in Oranjestad (☎ **599/3-82211**).

Safety   Although crime is rare here, it's wise to secure your valuables and take the kind of discreet precautions you would anywhere. Don't leave valuables unguarded on the beach.

Taxes   There is no departure tax if you're returning to the Dutch-held islands of St. Maarten or Saba; if you're going elsewhere, the tax is $5. Hotels on Statia collect an 8% government tax and a 5% electricity tax.

Telephone and Telegraph   Ask at your hotel if you need to send a cable. St. Eustatius maintains a 24-hour-a-day telephone service—and sometimes it takes about that much time to get a call through!

Statia is not part of the 809 area code that applies to most of the Caribbean. To call Statia from the States, if your long-distance telephone company is equipped to handle international direct dialing, dial 011 (the international access code), then 599 (the country code for the Netherlands Antilles), and finally 3 (the area code for all of Statia) and the five-digit local number. If you cannot dial direct internationally, dial 0 ("zero," for the operator) and tell the operator you wish to make an international call; once you are transferred to the international operator, state the 599 country code and then the area code and local number, and the operator will dial the call for you.

To make a call within Statia, only the five-digit local number is necessary.

Time   St. Eustatius operates on Atlantic standard time year round. Thus in winter, when the United States is on standard time, if it's 6pm in Oranjestad it's 5pm in New York. During daylight saving time in the United States the island keeps the same time as the U.S. East Coast.

Tipping and Service   Tipping is at the visitor's discretion, and most hotels, guesthouses, and restaurants include a 10% service charge.

Water   The water here is safe to drink.

Weather   The average daytime temperature ranges from 78° to 82° Fahrenheit. The annual rainfall is only 45 inches.

WHERE TO STAY

Don't expect deluxe hotels or high-rises—Statia is strictly for escapists. Sometimes guests are placed in private homes. A 15% service charge and 8% government tax are added to hotel bills. The Talk of the Town Bar & Restaurant, listed under "Where to Dine," below, also rents rooms.

Airport Apartments View

Golden Rock, St. Eustatius, N.A. ☎ **599/3-82474.** Fax 599/3-82517. 9 apartment. A/C TV TEL. $55 apartment for two; $70 apartment for one. Breakfast $5 extra. AE, MC, V. Free parking.

Airport Apartments View has two locations: Most units are in the Golden Rock area near the airport and four others are in Upper Town, Oranjestad, Princessweg.

The accommodations in the Golden Rock area all have compact refrigerators, coffee makers, and private baths. They consist of five one-bed apartments for one or two people and four two-bed units for up to four guests. On the premises are a bar/restaurant and an outdoor patio with a swimming pool and barbecue facilities.

In Upper Town, the accommodations consist of two three-bedroom units holding up to nine guests and two two-bedroom apartments for up to four people. They all have kitchens, living rooms, cable television, dining rooms, and baths.

✪ Golden Era Hotel

Lower Town, St. Eustatius, N.A. ☎ **599/3-82345.** Fax 599/3-82445. 20 rms. Winter, $70 single; $88 double; $104 triple. Off-season, $60 single; $75 double; $90 triple. MAP $30 per person extra. AE, DC, MC, V. Free parking.

Set directly on the water, this modern hotel is clean, serviceable, and comfortable. Built in stages between 1968 and 1975, the establishment, including its simply decorated bar and dining room, is operated by Hubert Lijfrock. Eight of the accommodations don't have a water view, but the remaining rooms offer a full or partial exposure to the sea; all are tasteful and spacious. Lunch is served daily from noon to 2pm, with courses costing $3.75 to $10. Dinner, offered nightly from 6:30 to 9:30pm, features such dishes as lobster, filet of beef, shrimp, chicken, snapper, and grouper. The fruit punch, with or without the rum, is delectable. The hotel also has a swimming pool.

La Maison Sur La Plage

Zeelandia Beach. St. Eustatius, N.A. ☎ **599/3-82256.** 10 cottages. TV $75 cottage for one or two; $105 cottage for three. Breakfast $6 extra. AE, MC, V. Free parking.

On the Atlantic side of the island, fronting Zeelandia Beach, this beachfront hostelry lies only a mile from the airport. The waters of the Atlantic here can have an undertow, so swimming is risky. Severely damaged by hurricanes, the property hasn't quite bounced back yet. Guests are housed in a series of sparsely furnished cottages, each with two bedrooms and a little private porch where a continental breakfast is served. The place is simply furnished and clean, with no air conditioning. Facilities include a pool. Many visitors are drawn to the hotel's charming French restaurant. With ocean views, it serves a classic French cuisine including such dishes as escargots, steak with pepper sauce, and duck breast with a green-peppercorn sauce.

Old Gin House and Mooshay Bay Publick House

Bay Rd. (P.O. Box 172), Lower Town, St. Eustatius, N.A. ☎ **599/3-82319.** Fax 599/3-82555. 20 rms. Winter, $85 single; $115 double; $135 triple. Off-season, $65 single; $85 double; $115 triple. Breakfast $8 extra. AE, DC, MC, V. Free parking.

This two-in-one hotel, which has known better days, has six rooms facing the beach in Oranjestad; the others are across the street, opening onto a pool. Run by John May, an expatriate American, the inn sports antiques mixed with practical pieces; an old cannon discovered while digging the swimming hole has been retired to a peaceful nook.

The Publick House is brick and has a double row of balconies. An overseer's gallery has been turned into a library and backgammon room. Cooled by overhead fans and sea breezes, each accommodation has paintings and wrought-iron wall hangings from Haiti.

Across the street, the Old Gin House originally began as a hot-dog stand in 1972, but it grew and grew, and is now a six-room inn of character, small but special. A two-story unit faces the sea and the rooms are cooled by breezes. The ceilings are high and balconies open onto the waterfront.

WHERE TO DINE

L'Etoile

6 Van Rheeweg, northeast of Upper Town. ☎ **599/3-82299.** Reservations required. Appetizers $4.50–$5.50; main courses $6.50–$20. No credit cards. Mon–Sat noon–10pm. Sun noon–6pm. CREOLE.

Caren Henríquez has had this second-floor restaurant with a few simple tables for some time. She is well known in Statia for her local cuisine, but you don't run into too many tourists here. Favored main dishes include the ubiquitous "goat water" (a stew), stewed whelks, mountain crab, and tasty spareribs. She also prepares Caribbean-style lobster. Caren is also known for her pastechis—deep-fried turnovers stuffed with meat. Expect a complete and very filling meal.

Old Gin House and Mooshay Bay Publick House

Lower Town. ☎ **599/3-82319.** Reservations not required. Appetizers $2.75–$8.75; main courses $10–$22. AE, DC, MC, V. Lunch daily noon–2pm; dinner daily 6:30–8pm. CONTINENTAL.

Overlooking the beach, the Old Gin House and Mooshay Bay Publick House provide a nostalgic atmosphere where lunch guests can enjoy a shady treillage terrace. You might begin with a daiquiri before going on to order a luncheon special, perhaps lobster Newbury crêpes or a hamburger. Lunches begin at $5.50.

At the Old Mooshay Bay dining room, continental cuisine is served poolside with candlelight and pewter. Sample the grapefruit soup, snapper mousse, or rack of lamb. Try to arrive before the dinner hour so you can enjoy a drink in the pub, a structure of wooden beams and old ship-ballast bricks.

Talk of the Town Bar & Restaurant

L. E. Sadlerweg, Golden Rock, St. Eustatius, N.A. ☎ **599/3-82236.** Reservations not required. Appetizers $4.80–$10.90; main courses $10.90–$14.10. AE, MC, V. Lunch daily 11:30am–2pm; dinner daily 7–10pm. (Bar stays open later.) AMERICAN/CREOLE.

In the Golden Rock area on the edge of town, about a five-minute walk from the airport, this spot is owned by Nora and Koos Sneek, who serve red snapper, steaks, chicken cutlet, and spareribs. The bar is open from 11am "until."

The 18 bedrooms above the restaurant are rented at $54 for a single, $68 to $83 for a double, year round. Prices include breakfast. All the rooms are air-conditioned and have private baths, phones, and TVs. There is a swimming pool.

WHAT TO SEE & DO

The capital, **Oranjestad,** stands on a cliff looking out on a beach and the island's calm anchorage, where in the 18th century you might have seen 200 vessels offshore. **Fort Oranje** was built in 1636 and restored in honor of the U.S. Bicentennial celebration of 1976. Today, perched atop the cliffs, its terraced rampart is lined with the old cannons. As mentioned, this fort may have been the first in the world to acknowledge the Stars and Stripes of the newly created republic of the United States of America. You'll see a bronze plaque honoring the fact that "Here the sovereignty of the United States of America was first formally acknowledged to a national vessel by a foreign official." The plaque was presented by Franklin D. Roosevelt. The fort is now used for government offices.

St. Eustatius Historical Foundation Museum, Upper Town (☎ **599/ 3-82288**), is also called the de Graaff House in honor of its former tenant,

Johannes de Graaff, who ordered the first-ever foreign salute to the Stars and Stripes at Fort Oranje (see above). After British Admiral Rodney sacked Statia for its tribute to the United States, he installed his own headquarters in this 18th-century house. Today a museum, the former governor's house stands in a garden, with a 20th-century wing crafted from 17th-century bricks. Exhibits demonstrate the process of sugar refining, shipping and commerce, defense, archeological artifacts from the colonial period, and a pair of elegantly beautiful 18th-century antique furnished rooms. There is a section devoted to the pre-Columbian period. In the wing annex is a massive piece of needlework by an American, Catherine Mary Williams, showing the flowers of Statia. The museum is open Monday through Friday from 9am to 5pm and on Saturday and Sunday from 9am to noon; admission costs $2 for adults, $1 for children.

A few steps away, a cluster of 18th-century buildings surrounding a quiet courtyard is called **Three Widows' Corner.**

Nearby are the ruins of the first **Dutch Reformed church.** To reach it, turn west from Three Widows' Corner onto Kerkweg. Tilting headstones record the names of the characters in the island's past. The St. Eustatius Historical Foundation recently completed restoration of the church. Visitors may climb to the top level of the tower and see the bay as lookouts did many years before.

Once Statia had a large colony of Jewish traders, and **Honen Dalim,** the second Jewish synagogue in the western hemisphere, can be explored, although it's in ruins. It was begun about 1740 and was damaged by a hurricane in 1772; it fell into disuse at the dawn of the 19th century. The synagogue stands beside Synagogpad, a narrow lane whose entrance faces Madam Theatre on the square.

The walls of a *mikvah* (ritual bath) rise beside the **Jewish burial ground** on the edge of town. The oldest stone in the cemetery is that of Abraham Hisquiau de la Motta, who died in 1742. The inscription is in both Portuguese and Hebrew. The most recent marker is that of Moses Waag, who died February 25, 1825. Most poignant is the memorial of David Haim Hezeciah de Lion, who died in 1760 at the age of two years, eight months, 26 days; carved into the baroque surface is an angel releasing a tiny songbird from its cage.

In addition, a short ride from Oranjestad takes you to the road's end at White Wall. There on your left is **Sugarloaf,** a minireplica of Rio's famed cone. On the right is a panoramic view of St. Kitts.

At the base of the pink-gray cliff beneath Fort Oranje, **Lower Town** was the mercantile center of Statia in the 18th century. Bulging with sugar, rum, and tobacco, Lower Town was once filled with row upon row of brick warehouses. In some of these warehouses, slaves were held in bondage awaiting shipment to other islands in the Caribbean. You can wander at leisure through the ruins, and stop later at the Old Gin House for a drink (see "Where to Dine," above).

The Quill, an extinct volcano, called "the most perfect" in the Caribbean, shelters a lush tropical rain forest—a botanical wonderland—in its deep, wide crater. The Quill rises to 1,960 feet on the southern edge of the island. Hikers climb it, and birdwatchers come here for a glimpse of the blue pigeon, a rare bird known to frequent the breadfruit and cottonwood trees in the mountains. See "Hiking" in "Sports & Outdoor Activities" below.

SPORTS & OUTDOOR ACTIVITIES

BEACHES Miles of golden sandy beaches are not the reason most visitors come to Statia. However, there are some, notably **Oranje Baai,** which has lots of black sand and fronts the Caribbean side of the island, off Lower Town. Other beaches include **Zeelandia** and **Lynch.** On the southwestern shore of Statia are the best volcanic beaches for swimming. Ask a taxi driver to take you to what he or she thinks is the best spot.

CRAB CATCHING   I'm perfectly serious. If you're interested, you can join Statians in a crab hunt. The Quill's crater is the breeding ground for these large crustaceans. At night they emerge from their holes to forage, and that's when they're caught. Either with flashlights or relying on moonlight, the "hunters" climb the Quill, catch a crab, and take the local delicacy home to prepare stuffed crab back.

HIKING   Perhaps this is the most popular sporting activity. Those with the stamina can climb the slopes of the Quill. The highest point on the island, the Quill may be young in terms of geology (meaning 4,000 years old), but it's is already extinct. Its volcanic cone harbors a crater filled with a dense tropical rain forest, containing towering kapok trees among other vegetation. A dozen or more species of wild orchids—some quite rare—grow here, and some 50 species of birdlife call it home. Islanders once grew cocoa, coffee, and cinnamon in the crater's soil, but today bananas are the only crop. The tourist office will supply you with a list of a dozen trails with varying degrees of difficulty and can also arrange for you to go with a guide whose fee is $20 or more (that has to be negotiated, of course).

TENNIS   Tennis can be played at the **Community Center** on Rosemary Lane (☎ 599/3-82249). The court has a concrete surface and is lit for night games. Changing rooms are available. The court costs $2.80, and you must bring your own equipment.

WATER SPORTS   On the Atlantic side of the island, at Concordia Bay, the **surfing** is best. However, there is no lifeguard protection.

Snorkeling is available through the Caribbean Sea to explore the remnants of an 18th-century man-of-war and the walls of warehouses, taverns, and ships that sank below the surface of Oranje Bay more than 200 years ago.

Dive Statia is a full PADI diving center on Fishermen's Beach in Lower Town (☎ 599/3-82435), offering beginning instruction to divemaster certifications. Its professional staff guides divers of all levels of experience to spectacular walls, untouched coral reefs, and historic shipwrecks. Dive Statia offers one- and two-tank boat dives, costing $40 to $72. Night dives and snorkel trips are also available.

SHOPPING

Merchandise is very limited. Most shops, what few there are, are open Monday through Friday from 8am to noon and 1:30 to 5:30pm, and on Saturday from 10am to noon and 2:30 to 5:30pm; however, hours depend on local whims that day.

The Hole in the Wall
Upper Town. ☎ 599/3-82265.

This shop is literally built into a wall adjacent to the Catholic church grounds. It features local handcrafts, designed and hand-sketched by the owner, Mary Ann Wichmann. Available are hand-painted cotton resortwear (painted and designed on the premises), postcards, and jewelry made from natural local plants and some from "blue slave beads" from the 18th century. Also stocked are authentic

17th-century clay pipe-stem earrings. Open Monday through Friday from 9am to 12:30pm.

Mazinga Giftshop

Fort Oranje Straat, Upper Town. ☎ **599/3-82245.**

Here you'll find an array of souvenirs—T-shirts, liquor, costume jewelry, 14-karat-gold jewelry, cards, drugstore items, beachwear, children's books, handbags, Delft from Holland, and paperback romances. You may have seen more exciting stores in your life, but this is without parallel the best Statia offers.

The Park Place (St. Eustatius Arts Gallery)

Upper Town. ☎ **599/3-82452.**

Across from Kool Korner and the tourist office is an art gallery carrying the works of many local artists. Original watercolors, ceramics, textile art, and carved-wood and hand-painted items are all for sale. In addition, Park Place sells genuine locally made steel drums in regular and mini-sized tenor pans; embroidered items such as napkins, placemats, and bun warmers, straw items; watercolors; and reproductions of antique Caribbean art.

ST. EUSTATIUS AFTER DARK

Stone Oven

15 Faeschweg, Upper Town. ☎ **599/3-82543.** Admission $3.

Although it functions from time to time as a simple restaurant, this place is best known as a bar where people sometimes dance when the mood and music are right. A small house with a garden patio and a cozy Caribbean decor, it's especially animated after 9pm on Friday and Saturday, when it hosts a recurring party for virtually anyone who shows up. It's open Wednesday through Sunday from 9pm to 1am. Beer costs $2.50 and up.

3 Saba

An extinct volcano, with no beaches or flat land, exotic cone-shaped Saba is 5 square miles of rock carpeted with such lush foliage as orchids, giant elephant ear, and Eucharist lilies. At its zenith it measures 2,900 feet at Mount Scenery, which the locals call simply "The Mountain." Under the sea the volcanic walls that form Saba continue a sheer drop to great depths, making for some of the most wonderful dives in the Caribbean. Divers and hikers are increasingly attracted to the island.

Unless you're a serious hiker or diver, you might confine your look at Saba to a day-trip from St. Maarten (and flee as the sun sets). If you're a self-sufficient type who demands almost no artificial amusement, then sleepy Saba might be your hideaway.

Saba is 150 miles east of Puerto Rico and 90 miles east of St. Croix. Most visitors fly from St. Maarten, 28 miles to the north.

Columbus is credited with sighting Saba in 1493. Before it became permanently Dutch, it was passed back and forth among Europeans 12 times.

Sabans were known to take advantage of their special topography—they pelted invaders from above with rocks and boulders. Because of the influence of English missionaries and Scottish seamen from the remote Shetland Islands who settled on the island, Saba has always been English speaking. The official language, however, is Dutch. Also, because of those early settlers from Europe, 60% of the population is Caucasian, many with red hair and freckled fair skin.

ORIENTATION
GETTING THERE

By Plane   You can leave New York's JFK Airport in the morning and be at Captain's Quarters on Saba for dinner that night by taking a direct flight on either of the two airlines that currently fly from the United States to St. Maarten. From Juliana Airport there, you can fly to Saba on **Winair (Windward Islands Airways International)** (☎ **599/4-62255** on Saba or **599/5-52568** on St. Maarten). Flying time is 12 minutes, and the round-trip fare is $60.

Arriving by air from St. Maarten, the traveler steps from Winair's 20-passenger STOL (short takeoff and landing) plane onto the tarmac runway of the **Juancho Yrausquin Airport.** The airstrip is famous as one of the shortest (if not *the* shortest) landing strips in the world, stretching only 1,312 feet along the aptly named Flat Point, one of the few level areas on the island.

Many guests at hotels on St. Maarten fly over to Saba on the morning flight, spend the day sightseeing, then return to St. Maarten on the afternoon flight. Winair connections can also be made on Saba to both St. Kitts and Statia.

GETTING AROUND

BY TAXI   Taxis meet every flight. The cost of a two-hour tour is about $10 per person if there are at least four passengers making the trip.

BY RENTAL CAR   None of the "big three" car-rental companies maintains a branch on Saba, partly because most visitors opt to get around by taxi. In the unlikely event that you should dare to drive a car on Saba, locally operated companies include **Doc's Car Rentals,** Windwardside (☎ **599/4-62271**), and **Johnson's Rental,** Windwardside (☎ **599/4-62269**). Both rent about six Mazdas, and both charge around $45 per day. Some insurance is included in the rates, but you might be held partly responsible for any financial costs in the event of an accident. Because of the very narrow roads and dozens of cliffs, it is crucial to exercise caution when driving in Saba. And don't drink and drive!

BY HITCHHIKING   Now frowned upon in much of the world, hitchhiking has long been an acceptable means of transport on Saba, where everybody seemingly knows everybody else. On recent rounds, my taxi rushed a sick child to the plane and picked up an old man to take him up the hill because he'd fallen and hurt himself—all on my sightseeing tour! (I didn't mind.) By hitchhiking, you'll probably get to know everybody else, too.

ON FOOT   The traditional means of getting around on Saba is still much in evidence. But I suggest that only the sturdy in heart and limb walk from the Bottom up to Windwardside. Many do, but you'd better have some shoes that grip the ground, particularly after a recent rain.

FAST FACTS: Saba

Area Code   Saba is not part of the Caribbean's 809 area code. For information on calling Saba, see "Telephone and Telegraph," below.

Banks   The main bank on the island is Barclays, Windwardside (☎ **599/4-62216**), open Monday through Friday from 8:30am to 2pm.

Currency   Saba, like the other islands of the Netherlands Antilles, uses the **Netherlands Antilles guilder (NAf),** valued at 1.77 NAf to $1 U.S. However, prices given here are in U.S. currency unless otherwise designated, since U.S. money is accepted by almost everybody here.

Customs   You don't have to go through Customs when you land at Juancho E. Yrausquin Airport, as this is a free port.

Documents   The government requires that all U.S. and Canadian citizens show proof of citizenship, such as a passport or voter registration card with photo ID. A return or ongoing ticket must also be provided. Britishers must have a valid passport.

Drugstore   Try The Pharmacy, The Bottom (☎ **599/4-63289**).

Electricity   Saba uses 110 volts A.C., 60 cycles, so most U.S.–made appliances don't need transformers or adapters.

Information   The **Saba Tourist Board,** run by Glenn C. Holm, is at Lambees Place in the heart of Windwardside (☎ **599/4-62231**). It's open Monday through Friday from 8am to noon and 1 to 5pm, and on Sunday from 10am to 2pm.

Medical Care   Saba's hospital complex is the A.M. Edwards Medical Centre, The Bottom (☎ **599/4-63289**).

Police   Call **599/4-63237.**

Safety   Crime on this island, where everyone knows everyone else, is practically nonexistent. But who knows? A tourist might rob you. It would be wise to safeguard your valuables.

Taxes   The government imposes a 5% tourist tax on hotel rooms. If you're returning to St. Maarten or flying over to Statia, you must pay a $2 departure tax. If you're going anywhere else, however, a $5 tax is imposed.

Telephone and Telegraph   Cables and international telephone calls can be placed at Lands Radio Office, The Bottom (☎ **599/4-63211**).

Saba is not part of the 809 area code that applies to most of the Caribbean. To call Saba from the United States, if your long-distance telephone company is equipped to handle international direct dialing, dial 011 (the international access code), then 599 (the country code for the Netherlands Antilles), and finally 4 (the area code for all of Saba) and the five-digit local number. If you cannot direct-dial internationally, dial 0 ("zero," for the operator) and tell the operator you wish to make an international call; once you are transferred to the international operator, state the 599 country code and then the area code and local number, and the operator will dial the call for you.

To make a call within Saba, only the five-digit local number is necessary.

Time   Saba is on Atlantic standard time year round, one hour earlier than eastern standard time. When the United States is on daylight saving time, clocks on Saba and the U.S. East Coast read the same.

Tips and Service   Most restaurants and hotels add a 10% or 15% service charge to your bills to cover tipping.

Weather   You'll encounter a temperature of 78° to 82° Fahrenheit. The annual rainfall is 42 inches.

WHERE TO STAY

Captain's Quarters

Windwardside, Saba, N.A. ☎ **599/4-62377**, or 212/289-6031 in New York. Fax 599/4-62377, or 212/289-1931 in New York. 18 rms. MINIBAR TV TEL. Winter, $125 single; $145 double. Off-season, $105 single; $135 double. Additional person $45 extra. (Include American breakfast.) MC, V. Free parking.

A restored circa 1850s sea captain's house has been converted into a guesthouse where many visitors, including royalty and celebrities, spend hideaway holidays. Just off the village center of Windwardside, it's a complex of several guesthouses surrounding the main house with its traditional verandas and covered porches. You make your way here by going down a narrow, steep lane. Thrust out toward the water is a freshwater swimming pool surrounded by a terrace, where you can sunbathe or order refreshments from an open-air bar. The cool and refreshing dining room is nestled behind the main house amid a screen of plants. Service is polite and formal at the candlelit dinners.

The main house serves as office, library, sitting room, and kitchen on the first floor, with two private accommodations above (one is a honeymoon haven). The house is furnished with antiques gathered from many ports of the world. About half the bedrooms contain four-poster beds, and each has a balcony overlooking the sea and Mount Scenery; TV and air conditioning are available in some rooms. Well-designed and cozy studio rooms are in the garden. Everything is a quaint reminder of New England.

Cranston's Antique Inn

The Bottom, Saba, N.A. ☎ **599/4-63203**. 6 rms. $44 single; $57.50 double; $69 triple. (Rates include breakfast.) No credit cards.

Everyone congregates for rum drinks and gossip on the front terrace of this inn near the village roadway, on the west coast north of Fort Bay. It's an old-fashioned house, more than 100 years old at least, and every bedroom has antique four-poster beds. Mr. Cranston, the owner, will gladly rent you the same room where Queen Juliana once spent a holiday. Aside from the impressive wooden beds, the furnishings are mostly hit or miss.

Mr. Cranston has a good island cook, who makes use of locally grown spices. Local dishes are offered, such as goat meat, roast pork from island pigs, red snapper, and broiled grouper. Meals begin at $12 and are served on a covered terrace in the garden or inside. The house is within walking distance of Ladder Bay.

Juliana's Apartments

Windwardside, Saba, N.A. ☎ **599/4-62269**. Fax 599/4-62389. 7 rms, 1 apartment, 1 cottage. Transportation: Take a taxi from the center (a 10-minute ride). Winter, $90 single; $115 double; $135 apartment or cottage. Off-season, $60 single; $75 double; $100 apartment or cottage. Additional person $20 extra. Dive packages available. Breakfast $5–$8 extra. AE, MC, V. Free parking.

Near Captain's Quarters, this hostelry is set on a hillside. Modern and immaculate, the accommodations have balconies and access to a sun deck for lounging. Each unit is simply but comfortably furnished and contains a radio. Juliana's offers a 2^{1}/$_{2}$-room apartment complete with kitchenette, and Flossie's Cottage, a two-bedroom home with a spacious living room, a dining room, a color TV, and a fully equipped kitchen. There's also a recreation room and a swimming pool. The complex contains a simple restaurant, Tropics Café.

Saba

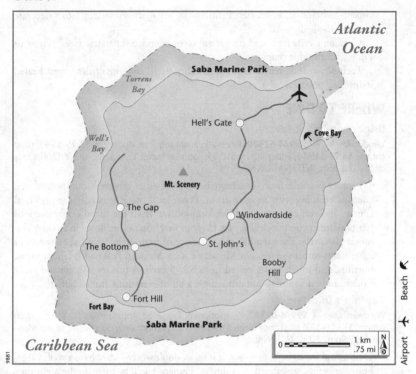

Atlantic Ocean

Saba Marine Park

Torrens Bay

Well's Bay

Hell's Gate

Cove Bay

Mt. Scenery

The Gap

Windwardside

The Bottom

St. John's

Booby Hill

Fort Hill

Fort Bay

Saba Marine Park

Caribbean Sea

0   1 km
     .75 mi

N

Beach   Airport

9881

Scout's Place

Windwardside, Saba, N.A. ☎ **599/4-62205.** Fax 599/4-62388. 15 rms, 1 apartment. Year-round, $35–$65 single; $55–$85 double; $100 apartment for two. (Includes continental breakfast.) MC, V. Free parking.

Right in the center of the village, Scout's Place is hidden from the street. Set on the ledge of a hill, the place is owned by Diana Medora, who makes guests feel right at home. With only 16 accommodations, it's still the second-largest inn on the island. The old house has a large covered but open-walled dining room, where every table has a view of the sea. It's an informal place, with an individual decor that might include Surinam hand-carvings, peacock chairs in red-and-black wicker, and silver samovars. The rooms open onto an interior courtyard filled with flowers, and each unit has a view of the sea. The apartment with kitchenette is suitable for up to five occupants; an extra person is charged $20.

Willards of Saba

Booby Hill, Saba, N.A. ☎ **599/4-62498.** Fax 599/4-62482. 5 rms, 3 bungalows, 1 suite. Winter, $150 single; $180 double; $250 bungalow for two; $300 honeymoon suite. Summer discounts of around 20%. Breakfast $7.50 extra. AE, DC, MC, V.

Developed by Brad Willard, this is the newest upscale hotel on Saba. Opened in 1994, it contains only nine accommodations, five of which are in a concrete building designed in the island's distinctive style of red roofs, white walls, and green shutters. Because of its position in a garden high on a hill overlooking the island's southeastern coastline, each accommodation has sweeping views and access to almost-constant ocean breezes. Paintings by expatriate American artists decorate many of the bedrooms.

Corazon's restaurant and its bar are recommended separately (see "Where to Dine," later in this chapter).

Facilities include tennis courts, hot tub/jacuzzi, and one of the largest heated swimming pools on Saba.

WHERE TO DINE

Brigadoon Pub & Eatery

Windwardside. ☎ **599/4-62380.** Reservations not required. Appetizers $3.95–$5.95; main courses $8.95–$19.95; Friday fish fry $10.95; Saturday buffet $12.95. AE, MC, V. Dinner only daily 6–9:30pm. INTERNATIONAL.

Whenever possible, fresh local ingredients are used at this restaurant housed in a colonial building with an open front. Fresh local fish is generally the preferred course, and you can also order live local lobster, from the island's only live lobster tank (prices on this delicacy are likely to vary). Steaks are flown in weekly. You might also prefer the Saba fish pot, a variety of fresh catch from Saba's waters in a basil-and-tomato sauce. On Monday's it's a Mexican fiesta with fajitas, tacos, burritos, and much more, priced from $2.95 each. A fish fry is presented every Friday, and on Saturday you can sample a bit of everything from a buffet.

Captain's Quarters

Windwardside. ☎ **599/4-62377.** Reservations not required. Appetizers $3.50–$10.50; main courses $13.50–$22; fixed price meals $18–$20. MC, V. Lunch daily noon–2pm; dinner Mon–Sat 6:30–9pm. INTERNATIONAL.

Dining is al fresco here; however, if it rains, don't worry—they have a roof. Large, hearty appetites are catered to at dinner. Perhaps you'll be there on the night they have fresh grouper or lobster. The food here is better than ever. Soups are homemade and good. Fresh vegetables are regularly available, and the wine list has been extended. The cuisine has Dutch, French, Créole, and Indonesian accents.

Corazon

In Willard's Hotel, Booby Hill. ☎ **599/4-62498.** Reservations required. Appetizers $7.50; main courses $22.50–$35. AE, DC, MC, V. Lunch daily 11:30am–3pm; dinner daily 6–9pm. ANTILLEAN.

Set in a previously recommended hotel (the newest and one of the most interesting on Saba), this restaurant features a breezy island decor, a sweeping, high-altitude view of the island's southeastern coastline, and some of the freshest fish and lobster on the island. Most of the catch featured on the "island-inspired" menu comes from the boats of local fisherfolk. Menu items change with the availability of the ingredients, although grouper, snapper Florentine, and lobster thermidor are usually featured on the menu. There's a pleasant bar on the premises where you might enjoy a round of before-dinner drinks.

Saba Chinese Bar & Restaurant (Moo Goo Gai Pan)

Windwardside. ☎ **599/4-62268.** Reservations not required. Appetizers $3–$6; main courses $4–$17. No credit cards. Tues–Sun 11am–midnight. CHINESE.

Amid a cluster of residential buildings on a hillside above Windwardside, this place is operated by a family from Hong Kong. It offers some 120 dishes, an unpretentious decor of plastic tablecloths and folding chairs, and a cookery so popular that many residents claim this to be their most frequented restaurant. Meals include an array of Cantonese and Indonesian specialties—lobster Cantonese, Chinese chicken with mushrooms, sweet-and-sour fish, chicken with cashew nuts, conch chop suey, several curry dishes, roast duck, and nasi goreng.

Scout's Place

Windwardside. ☎ **599/4-62205.** Reservations required two to three hours in advance. Lunches $12; fixed-price dinner $16.50–$25. MC, V. Lunch daily at 12:30pm; dinner daily at 7:30pm. INTERNATIONAL.

For visitors over for the day, Scout's Place is a popular dining spot, but you should have your driver stop by early and make a reservation for lunch for you. Food at Scout's is simple and good, rewarding and filling, and the price is low too. Dinner is more elaborate, with tables placed on an open-side terrace, the ideal spot for a drink at sundown. Fresh seafood is a specialty, as is curried goat.

WHAT TO SEE & DO

Tidy white houses cling to the mountainside, and small family cemeteries adjoin each dwelling. Lace-curtained gingerbread-trimmed cottages give a Disneyland aura.

The first Jeep arrived on Saba in 1947. Before that, Sabans went about on foot, climbing from village to village. Hundreds of steps had been chiseled out of rock by the early Dutch settlers in 1640.

Engineers told them it was impossible, but Sabans built a single cross-island road by hand. Filled with hairpin turns, it zigzags from Fort Bay, where a deep-water pier accommodates large tenders from cruise ships, to a height of 1,600 feet. Along the way it has fortresslike supporting walls.

Past storybook villages, the road goes over the crest to **the Bottom.** Derived from the Dutch word *botte,* which means "bowl-shaped," this village is nestled on a plateau and surrounded by rocky volcanic domes. It occupies about the only bit of ground, 800 feet above the sea. It's also the official capital of Saba, a Dutch village of charm, with chimneys, gabled roofs, and gardens.

From the Bottom you can take a taxi up the hill to the mountain village of **Windwardside,** perched on the crest of two ravines at about 1,500 feet above sea level. This village of red-roofed houses, the second most important on Saba, is the site of the two biggest inns and most of the shops. From Windwardside you can climb steep steps cut in the rock to yet another village, **Hell's Gate,** teetering on the edge of a mountain. However, there's a serpentine road from the airport to Hell's Gate, where you'll find the island's largest church. Only the most athletic climb from here to the lip of the volcanic crater.

In Windwardside, the **Harry L. Johnson Memorial Museum** is in an old sea captain's home, with antique furnishings, evoking an 1890s aura. Filled with family memorabilia, the house can be visited for an admission of $2. The surprise visit of the late Jacqueline Kennedy Onassis is still vividly recalled. It's open Monday through Friday from 10am to noon and 1 to 4pm.

SPORTS & OUTDOOR ACTIVITIES

HIKING   The island is as beautiful above the water as it is below. Mountain walking is the major sport, and the top of **Mount Scenery,** a volcano that erupted 5,000 years ago, is a wildlife reserve. Allow more than a day and take your time climbing the 1,064 sometimes slippery concrete steps up to the cloud-reefed mountain. You'll pass along a lush rain forest with palms, bromeliads, elephant ears, heliconia, mountain raspberries, lianas, and tree ferns. In her pumps, Queen Beatrix of the Netherlands climbed these steps and, upon reaching the summit, declared: "This is the smallest and highest place in my kingdom." One of the inns will pack you a picnic lunch. The higher you climb, the cooler it grows, about a drop of 1° Fahrenheit every 328 feet; on a hot day this can be an incentive. The peak is 2,855 feet high.

If you don't want to set out on your own, **botanical tours** are offered, as well as other hikes with your special interests in mind, arranged by the Saba Tourist Bureau (☎ **599/4-62231**) or Captain's Quarters (☎ **599/4-62377**), costing $50 for a party of four to eight people. The botanical tour takes you to the top of Mount Scenery into the tropical rain forest where orchids bloom in winter and golden heliconia in spring. A shorter hike is possible to Maskehorne Hill, where huge rock formations covered with orchids and bromeliads lead to a view of Windwardside. You can walk up the steps and cut through the terraced fields and forest of Big Rendezvous to an overlook of Crispeen. For a different view of the island, hike along Sandy Cruz, starting at Upper Hell's Gate and walking along the Deep Gut, with its blend of cultivated fields and windswept forest.

TENNIS   Tennis buffs will find a free concrete **public court** in the Bottom.

WATER SPORTS   Don't come here for beaches—Saba has only one sand beach, and it's about 20 feet long. Sports here are mostly do-it-yourself. Visitors, such as John F. Kennedy, Jr., enjoy the underwater scenery and dark, volcanic sands and coral formations.

   Saba Deep Dive Center, P.O. Box 22, Fort Bay, Saba, N.A. (☎ **599/4-63347**), is a full-service dive center that offers scuba diving, snorkeling, equipment rental/repair, and tank fills. Whether 1 diver or 20, novice or experienced, Mike Myers and his staff of NAUI/PADI/ACUC/CMAS instructors/divemasters are concerned with personalized service and great diving. Dive sites around Saba, all protected by the Saba Marine Park, have permanent moorings and range from shallow to deep. Divers see pinnacles, walls, ledges, overhangs, and reefs—all with abundant coral and sponge formations and a wide variety of both reef and pelagic marine life. There is also a fully operational recompression chamber/hyperbaric facility located in the Fort Bay Harbor. The In Two Deep Restaurant and the Deep Bou-

---

The Coral Gardens

Circling the entire island and including four offshore underwater mountains (seamounts), the Saba Marine Park, Fort Bay (☎ **599/4-63295**), preserves the island's coral reefs and marine life. The park is zoned for various pursuits. The all-purpose recreational zone includes Wells Bay Beach, Saba's only beach, but it's seasonal—it disappears with the winter seas, only to reappear in late spring. There are two anchorage zones for visiting yachts and Saba's only harbor. The five dive zones include a coastal area and four seamounts, a mile offshore. In these zones are more than two dozen marked and buoyed dive sites and a snorkeling trail. You plunge into a world of coral and sponges, swimming with parrotfish, doctorfish, and damselfish. The snorkel trail, however, is not for the neophyte. It can be approached from Wells Bay Beach but only from May through October. Depths of more than 1,500 feet are found between the island and seamounts, which reach a minimum depth of 90 feet. There's a $2-per-dive visitor fee and a $2-per-person, per week, yacht visitor fee. Funds are also raised through souvenir sales and donations. The park office at Fort Bay is open Monday through Friday from 8am to 5pm.

tique offer air-conditioned comfort, a view of the harbor area and the Caribbean Sea, good food and drink, and a wide selection of clothes, swimwear, lotions, and sunglasses. A certification course goes for $375. A single-tank dive costs $45; a two-tank dive, $80. Night dives are $60. The center is open daily from 8am to 6pm, with Saturday-night dinners.

Sea Saba Dive Center, Windwardside (☎ **599/4-62246**), has seven experienced instructors eager to share their knowledge of Saba Marine Park: famous deep and medium-depth pinnacles, walls, spur-and-groove formations, and giant boulder gardens. Their two 40-foot uncrowded boats are best suited for a comfortable day on Saba's waters. Daily boat dives are made between 10am and 2pm, allowing a relaxing interval for snorkeling. Courses range from resort through divemaster. Extra day and night dives can be arranged. A two-tank dive costs $80; package prices are available with advance booking.

Wilson's Dive Shop, Fort Bay Harbour, Windwardside (☎ **599/4-62541**), is operated by Bill "Wilson" McQueen, who pioneered sport diving in Saba. He charted the majority of shoals, walls, shelves, reefs, pinnacles, and seamounts, and now shares them with divers, giving a personal touch. He takes divers to the "Pinnacles" where they encounter big pelagics and reef sharks at 90 feet. Divers wind their way around Diamond Rock, spying barracuda, stingrays, grouper, and snapper in lush, gently sloping walls. Divers also explore Tent Reef, a long underwater fault with crevasses, ledges, overhangs, and drop-offs, with depths ranging from 40 to 130 feet. Wilson's boat *Mama* is a spacious 40-foot vessel with plenty of shade. This full-service dive center has both PADI and NAUI instructors, and the dive shop offers packages. Otherwise, a single-tank dive goes for $45; a two-tank dive, for $80.

SHOPPING

After lunch you can go for a stroll in Windwardside and stop at the boutiques, which often look like someone's living room—and sometimes they are. Most stores are open Monday through Saturday from 9am to noon and 2 to around 5:30pm.

The traditional **drawn threadwork** of the island is famous. Sometimes this work, introduced by a local woman named Gertrude Johnson in the 1870s, is called Spanish work, because it was believed to have been perfected by nuns in Caracas. Selected threads are drawn and tied in a piece of linen to produce an ornamental pattern. It can be expensive if a quality linen has been used.

Try to come home with some **"Saba Spice,"** an aromatic blend of 150-proof cask rum, with such spices as fennel seed, cinnamon, cloves, and nutmeg, straight from someone's home brew. It's not for everyone (too sweet), but it will make an exotic bottle to show off at home.

Around the Bend
At Scout's Place, Windwardside. ☎ **599/4-62519.**

Housed in a charming little Saba cottage, this store is run by ex-Manhattanite Jean Macbeth, whose taste is reflected in her hand-painted tops, hand-batiked casual wear, jewelry, tote bags, and a collection of amusing, locally made oddments. Open Monday through Saturday from 10am to 4pm and on Sunday from 11am to 2pm.

Saba Artisan Foundation
The Bottom. ☎ **599/4-63260.**

In recent years, the foundation has made a name for itself in the world of fashion with hand-screened resort fashions. The clothes are casual and colorful. Among the items sold are men's bush-jacket shirts, numerous styles of dresses and skirts, napkins, and placemats, as well as yard goods. Island motifs are used in many designs. Also popular are the famous Saba drawn-lace patterns. The fashions are designed, printed, sewn, and marketed by Sabans. Mail-order as well as wholesale distributorship inquiries are invited. Open Monday through Friday from 8am to noon and 1 to 5pm, and on Saturday and Sunday from 9:30 to 11:30am.

Jamaica 11

Most visitors already have opinions of this English-speaking nation before they arrive. They know of its boisterous culture of reggae and rastafarianism, and that it contains white sandy beaches, jungles, rivers, mountains, and clear waterfalls. The art and cuisine of the country are also potent lures.

Jamaica can be a tranquil island, but it can also be affected by crime, drugs, and muggings. There is racial tension here. But those visitors who are escorted from the airport to their heavily patrolled hotel grounds and who venture out into Jamaica only on expensive organized tours are largely sheltered from the more unpredictable and sometimes dangerous side of Jamaica. Those who want to see "the real Jamaica," or at least the island in greater depth, had better be prepared for some hassle. Vendors on the beaches and in the markets can be particularly aggressive. Most Jamaicans, in spite of their hard times, have unrelenting good humor, welcoming visitors to their islands. Others, certainly a minority, harm the tourism business, so that many visitors vow "never to return." The hypnotic, haunting seduction of Jamaica remains in spite of the traumatic political upheavals that have characterized Jamaica in the past decades, beginning in the 1970s.

Should you go? By all means, "yes." Jamaica is worth it! But be prudent, be cautious, the same way you would if visiting New York, Miami, or Los Angeles. Whatever you do, don't call the locals "natives." They feel it's insulting, and are proud of just being called Jamaicans.

This country, which lies 90 miles south of Cuba, with which it was chummy in the 1970s when much of the world feared that Jamaica was going Communist, is the third largest of the Caribbean islands, with some 4,400 square miles of predominantly green land, a mountain ridge peaking at 7,400 feet above sea level, and on the north coast, many beautiful white sand beaches with clear blue sea.

GETTING THERE

There are two **international airports** on Jamaica: Donald Sangster in Montego Bay and Norman Manley in Kingston. The most popular routings to Jamaica are from New York and Miami. Remember to reconfirm all flights, going and returning, no later than 72 hours before departure. Flying time from Miami is 1¼ hours; from Los

Angeles, $5^1/_2$ hours; from Atlanta, $2^1/_2$ hours; from Dallas, 3 hours; from Chicago and New York, $3^1/_2$ hours; and from Toronto, 4 hours.

Some of the most convenient and popular services to Jamaica are provided by **American Airlines** (☎ 800/433-7300 in the U.S.) through its hubs in New York and Miami. Throughout the year, a daily nonstop flight departs from New York's Kennedy Airport at 8:45am. Touching down in Montego Bay, it continues on without a change of aircraft to Kingston. Return flights to New York from Jamaica usually depart from Montego Bay, touch down briefly in either Miami or Kingston, then continue nonstop back to Kennedy. From Miami, at least four daily flights depart for Kingston, and four daily flights for Montego Bay.

Air Jamaica (☎ 800/523-5585 in the U.S.), the national carrier, operates about 13 flights a week from New York's JFK, most of which stop at both Montego Bay and Kingston. More frequent are the flights that the airline operates to Jamaica from Miami. Three fly nonstop to Kingston and two fly nonstop to Montego Bay. The airline offers connecting service within Jamaica through its reservations network to a small independent airline, **Trans-Jamaican**, whose planes usually hold between 10 and 17 passengers. Trans-Jamaican's flights fly from the country's international airports at Montego Bay and Kingston to small airports, including Port Antonio, Boscobel (near Ocho Rios), Negril, and Tinson Pen (a small airport near Kingston).

Continental (☎ 800/525-0280 in the U.S.) offers daily nonstop service from its hub at Newark, New Jersey, to Montego Bay, at least in winter. Check with the airline.

Air Canada (☎ 800/363-5440 in Canada, ☎ 800/776-3000 in the U.S.) flies to Jamaica from Toronto, Montréal, Halifax, and Winnipeg in winter. Flights from Toronto depart year-round on a daily basis to Montego Bay and Kingston.

Travelers based in Britain usually opt for one of the flights operated by the country's premier airline, **British Airways** (☎ 800/247-9297). Aircraft fly Wednesday, Friday, and Sunday nonstop between London's Gatwick and Montego Bay, touching down briefly in Kingston before continuing back to London.

GETTING AROUND

BY PLANE   The majority of travelers to Jamaica, particularly tourists, enter the country via Montego Bay. The island's domestic air service is provided by **Trans-Jamaican Airlines** (☎ 809/923-8680 in Kingston, **809/952-5401** in Montego Bay, **809/975-3254** in Ocho Rios, **809/993-2405** in Port Antonio, or **809/957-4251** in Negril), which offers 30 scheduled flights daily, covering all the major resort areas. For example, there are 11 flights a day between Kingston and Montego Bay, and three flights a day between Negril and Port Antonio. Reservations can be made through overseas travel agents or through Air Jamaica. Incidentally, Tinson Pen Airport in the heart of downtown Kingston is for domestic flights only. Car-rental facilities are available only at the international airports at Kingston and Montego Bay.

BY TAXI & BUS   Kingston has no city taxis with meters, so agree on a price before you get in. In Kingston and the rest of the island, special taxis and buses for visitors are operated by JUTA (Jamaica Union of Travellers Association) and have the union's emblem on the side of the vehicle. All prices are controlled, and any local JUTA office will supply a list of rates. JUTA drivers do nearly all the ground transfers, and some offer sightseeing tours. There are many companies offering sightseeing tours on the island.

BY RENTAL CAR   Jamaica is big enough, and public transportation is unreliable enough, that a car is a necessity if you plan to do much independent sightseeing. (In lieu of this, you can always take an organized tour to the major sights and spend the rest of the time on the beaches near your hotel.) Subject to many variations depending on the road conditions, driving time for the 50 miles from Montego Bay to Negril is 1 $1/2$ hours; from Montego Bay to Ocho Rios, 62 miles and 1 $1/2$ hours; from Ocho Rios to Port Antonio, 60 miles and 2 $1/2$ hours; from Ocho Rios to Kingston, 60 miles and 2 hours; from Kingston to Mandeville, 65 miles and 1 $1/2$ hours; and from Kingston to Port Antonio, 68 miles and 2 hours.

For resolution of any accident claims that may result, and for the ease of any billing irregularities, it's best to stick to branches of U.S.–based rental outfits. Unfortunately, prices of car rentals in Jamaica have skyrocketed recently, making it one of the most expensive rental scenes in the Caribbean. Equally unfortunate are the unfavorable insurance policies that apply to virtually every car-rental agency in Jamaica.

Avis (☎ **800/331-1084** in the U.S.) maintains offices at the international airports in both Montego Bay (☎ **952-4543**) and Kingston (☎ **809/924-8013**). The company's least expensive car requires a two-day advance booking and costs $385 per week, plus 12 $1/2$% tax. The company's collision-damage waiver (CDW) costs another $12.50 per day. If you choose not to accept it, you'll be responsible for up to the full cost of the damage to your car, unless other insurance policies you already own become activated. Even if you accept the CDW, you'll still be responsible for the first $1,000 worth of damage to the car. Renters must be 25 years old.

Budget Rent-a-Car (☎ **809/952-3838** at the Montego Bay Airport, or **809/938-2189** in Kingston) requires renters to be 25 to 65 years old for its regular rates; otherwise, drivers 18 to 24 pay an extra $7.50 a day. Cars such as a Suzuki Alto rent for $209 and up per week with unlimited mileage, plus 12 $1/2$% government tax. A daily CDW costs another $15 and is mandatory. In the event of an accident, renters are still responsible for the first $1,500 worth of damages.

Hertz (☎ **800/654-3001** in the U.S.) operates branches at the airports at both Montego Bay (☎ **809/979-0438**) and Kingston (☎ **809/924-8028**). Its least expensive subcompact car rents for a surprisingly pricey $456 per week, plus 12 $1/2$% tax, with unlimited mileage included. A CDW costs $15 extra per day, and reduces (but does not eliminate) the customer's responsibility for accident damage to the car. (Without the waiver, you'll be liable for $3,000 worth of damage, depending on where you rent it; with the waiver, the amount of your liability is reduced to between $750 and $1,000.) Drivers must be 25 years old.

At most companies, you'll be required to leave an imprint of a valid credit or charge card before you can drive away in a rental car. In rare instances, an exception might be made which allows you to leave a substantial cash deposit of around $1,000 instead. You'll also face a sometimes rigorous background check of your credit record and employment history.

Be forewarned that in Jamaica *driving is on the left,* and you should exercise more than your usual caution here because of the unfamiliar terrain. Don't drink and

Jamaica

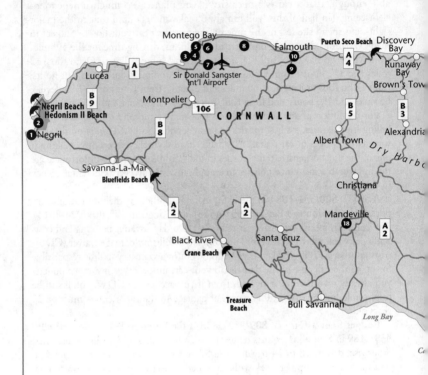

Montego Bay
Falmouth
Puerto Seco Beach
Discovery Bay
Runaway Bay
Brown's Tow
Lucea
Negril Beach
Hedonism II Beach
Negril
Montpelier
CORNWALL
Albert Town
Alexandri
Dry Harbo
Savanna-La-Mar
Bluefields Beach
Christiana
Mandeville
Black River
Santa Cruz
Crane Beach
Treasure Beach
Bull Savannah
Long Bay
Ce

Caribbean Sea

Cornwall Beach ❸
Doctor's Cave Beach ❻
Dunn's River Falls ⑪
Falmouth ⑩
Kingston ⑮
Mandeville ⑱
Martha Brae's Rafters Village ❾

Montego Bay ❺
Negril ❶
Negril Beach ❷
Norman Manley
  International Airport ⑭
Ocho Rios ⑫
Port Antonio ⑬

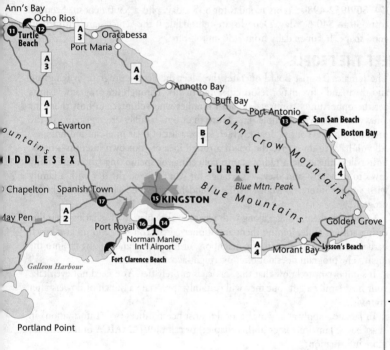

Caribbean Sea

Ann's Bay
Ocho Rios
11 **12** Turtle Beach
A3 Oracabessa
Port Maria
A3
A4
A1
Ewarton
ountains
MIDDLESEX

Annotto Bay
Buff Bay
Port Antonio **13** San San Beach
Boston Bay

John Crow Mountains

B1

SURREY
Blue Mtn. Peak
Blue Mountains

Chapelton
Spanish Town
17
15 KINGSTON
A4

May Pen
A2
Port Royal **16** **14**
Norman Manley Int'l Airport
Fort Clarence Beach

Galleon Harbour

Golden Grove

A4 Morant Bay Lysson's Beach

Portland Point

0 ━━━ 6.5 mi
10.4 km
N

Airport ✈
Beach ⛱

Port Royal **16**
Rose Hall **8**
Sir Donald Sangster
  International Airport **7**
Spanish Town **17**
Walter Fletcher Beach **4**

drive, and be especially cautious at night. Speed limits in town are 30 m.p.h., and 50 m.p.h. outside towns. Gas is measured by the Imperial gallon (a British unit of measurement that will give you 25% more than a U.S. gallon), and the charge is payable only in Jamaican dollars—most stations don't accept credit or charge cards. Your own valid driver's license from back home is acceptable for short-term visits to Jamaica.

BY BIKE & SCOOTER   These can be rented in Montego Bay, and you'll need your valid driver's license. **Montego Honda/Bike Rentals,** 21 Gloucester Ave. (☎ **809/952-4984**), rents Hondas for $35 a day, plus a $300 deposit. Scooters cost $30 to $40 per day. Deposits are refundable if the vehicles are returned in good shape. It's open daily from 7:30am to 5pm.

MEET THE PEOPLE

The Jamaica Tourist Board operates the Meet the People program in Kingston and the island's five major resort cities and towns. Through the program, visitors get the opportunity to meet Jamaican families who volunteer to host them for a few hours or even a whole day. More than 650 families are registered in the project with the Tourist Board, which keeps a list of their interests and hobbies. All you have to do is give the board a rough idea of your own interests—birds, butterflies, music, ham radio, stamp collecting, or spelunking (there are many caves to explore)—and they will arrange for you to spend the day with a family with similar interests. Many lasting friendships have developed through this program.

Once with them, you go along with whatever they plan to do, sharing their life, eating at their table, joining them at a dinner party. You may end up at a beach barbecue, afternoon tea with the neighbors, or just sitting and talking far into the night. The program does not offer overnight accommodation.

It's important to know that this service is entirely free. You need not even take your host family a gift, but they will certainly appreciate a bunch of flowers after your visit.

In Jamaica, apply at any of the local tourist board offices (see "Information" in "Fast Facts: Jamaica," later in this chapter) or call **800/JAMAICA** in the U.S. for more information.

REGGAE FESTIVALS

Kingston comes alive to the pulsating sounds of reggae during **Reggae Sunsplash '96,** the world's largest annual reggae festival, taking place at Jamworld Festival Village the first week in August. This week-long music extravaganza features some of the most prominent reggae groups and artists, including Ziggy Marley, Cocoa Tea, and the Melody Makers.

Some time during the second week of August a **Reggae Sunfest** takes place at the Bob Marley Performing Center in Montego Bay. Usually this is a four-day musical event. Some of the biggest names in reggae, both from Jamaica and worldwide, usually perform. Many local hotels are fully booked for the festival, so advance reservations are necessary. The Jamaican Tourist Board's U.S. and Canadian offices (see "Information" in "Fast Facts: Jamaica," later in this chapter) can give you information about packages and group rates for the festivals. Other reggae concerts and festivals featuring top performers are held throughout the year in Jamaica. Ask the tourist board.

SPORTS & OUTDOOR ACTIVITIES
BEACHES

Of course, many visitors will want to do nothing more "sporting" than lie on the beach. For specific recommendations of the best beaches in Jamaica, see the "What to See and Do" sections in the writeups of the individual resort areas.

DEEP-SEA FISHING

Northern Jamaican waters are world renowned for their gamefish, including dolphin, wahoo, blue and white marlin, sailfish, tarpon, Allison tuna, barracuda, and bonito. The Jamaica International Fishing Tournament and Jamaica International Blue Marlin Team Tournaments run concurrently at Port Antonio every September or October. Most major hotels from Port Antonio to Montego Bay have deep-sea fishing facilities, and there are many charter boats.

At **Port Antonio,** a 30-foot-long sport-fishing boat with a tournament rig is available for rental. Taking out up to six passengers at a time, it charges $150 per half day or $280 per day, with crew, bait, tackle, and soft drinks included. It docks at Port Antonio's International Marina, off West Palm Avenue, in the center of town. Call **809/993-3086** for bookings.

Seaworld Resorts Ltd., whose main office lies near the Cariblue Hotel, at Rose Hall, just east of Montego Bay (☎ **809/953-2180**), operates flying-bridge cruisers, with deck lines and outriggers, for fishing expeditions. A half-day fishing trip costs $330 for up to four participants.

GOLF

Jamaica has the best courses in all the West Indies. Montego Bay alone has four championship courses. Here's a sampling:

The one at the **Wyndham Rose Hall Resort,** Rose Hall (☎ **809/953-2650**), called "one of the top five courses in the world," is an unusual and challenging seaside and mountain course built on the shores of the Caribbean. Its eighth hole skirts the water, then doglegs onto a promontory and a green thrusting 200 yards into the sea. The back nine is the most scenic and interesting, rising into steep slopes and deep ravines on Mount Zion. The 10th fairway abuts the family burial grounds of the Barretts of Wimpole Street, and the 14th passes the vacation home of singer Johnny Cash. The 300-foot-high 13th tee offers a rare panoramic view of the sea and the roof of the hotel, and the 15th green is next to a 40-foot waterfall, once featured in a James Bond movie. A fully stocked pro shop, a clubhouse, and a professional staff are among the amenities. Nonresidents of the Wyndham pay $50 for 18 holes and $30 for nine holes. Guests at the Wyndham are charged $40 for 18 holes, $20 for 9 holes. Mandatory cart rental costs $36 for 18 holes, and the use of a caddy—also mandatory—is another $12 for 18 holes.

The excellent course of **Tryall** (☎ **809/956-5660**), 12 miles from Montego Bay, is the site of the Jamaica Classic Annual, first played in 1939, and the home of the Johnnie Walker Tournament with the biggest golf purse in the world. For 18 holes, guests of Tryall are charged $40 in spring, summer, and fall, $60 in winter. Nonresidents of Tryall pay $75 from mid-April to mid-December and $125 in winter.

The **Half Moon,** at Rose Hall (☎ **809/953-2560**), features a championship course, designed by Robert Trent Jones, which opened in 1961. The course has manicured and diversely shaped greens. For 18 holes nonresidents pay $45 in summer, $85 in winter. Hotel guests receive a 50% discount. Carts in any season cost $25 for 18 holes, and caddies (mandatory in any season) are hired for $12 in any season.

The **Ironshore Golf & Country Club,** Ironshore, St. James, Montego Bay (☎ **809/953-2800**), another well-known 18-hole golf course with a 72 par, is privately owned. It is, however, open to all golfers who show up. In winter, greens fees for 18 holes are $45, dropping in summer to $30.

Super Club's Runaway Golf Club, at Runaway Bay near Ocho Rios on the north coast (☎ **809/973-2561**), charges no admission for residents who stay at any of Jamaica's affiliated Super Clubs. For nonresidents, the price is $51 for 18 holes in summer, rising to $56 in winter. Players can rent carts and clubs.

Sandals Golf & Country Club, at Ocho Rios (☎ **809/974-0119**), is free to residents of Sandals properties. If you're not staying at Sandals, you can still play for $25 for 9 holes or $35 for 18 holes year round. The golf course lies about 700 feet above sea level, a five-minute drive from Ocho Rios.

Manchester Country Club, Brumalia Road (☎ **809/962-2403**), is Jamaica's oldest golf course, but has only nine greens. Beautiful vistas unfold from 2,201 feet above sea level. Greens fees are J$250 ($8), and caddy fees run J$100 ($3.20) for 18 holes. The course has a clubhouse and restaurant.

HORSEBACK RIDING

The best riding is in the Ocho Rios area. Jamaica's most complete equestrian center is the **Chukka Cove Farm and Resort,** at Richmond Llandovery, St. Ann (☎ **809/972-2506**), located less than 4 miles east of Runaway Bay. A one-hour trail ride costs $23, and a two-hour mountain ride costs $35. The most popular ride is a three-hour beach jaunt where, after riding over trails to the sea, you can unpack your horse and swim in the surf. Refreshments are served as part of the $50 charge. A six-hour beach ride, complete with picnic lunch, goes for $90 to $100. Polo lessons are also available, costing $40 for 30 minutes.

Another good program for equestrians is offered at the **Rocky Point Riding Stables,** at the Half Moon Club, Rose Hall, Montego Bay (☎ **809/953-2286**). Housed in what's probably the most beautiful barn and stables on Jamaica, built in the colonial Caribbean style in 1992, it offers around 30 horses and a helpful staff. A 90-minute beach or mountain ride costs $30, while a 2$^{1}/_{2}$-hour combination ride (including treks along hillsides, forest trails, and beaches, and ending with a saltwater swim) goes for $40.

TENNIS

Most hotels have their own courts, many floodlit for night games. If your hotel does not have a court, expect to pay around $10 to $12 per hour at another hotel.

WATER SPORTS

Water options for the sports-lover proliferate throughout Jamaica, with many activities offered as part of all-inclusive packages by the island's major hotels. However, there are other well-maintained facilities for water sports not connected to the hotel offerings.

Jamaica has some of the finest diving waters in the world, with an average diving depth of 35 to 95 feet. Visibility is usually 60 to 120 feet. Most of the diving is done on coral reefs, which are protected by underwater parks where fish, shells, coral, and sponges are plentiful. Experienced divers can also see wrecks, hedges, caves, dropoffs, and tunnels.

In Falmouth, ✪ **Seaworld,** at the Trelawny Beach Hotel (☎ **809/954-2450**), offers scuba-diving programs to the offshore coral reefs that are considered some of the most spectacular of the Caribbean. There are three PAIC-certified dive guides, one dive boat, and all the necessary equipment for either inexperienced or already-certified divers. Guests of the Trelawny benefit from free introductory lessons and the availability of a free daily dive; nonresidents are charged $30 per dive. Transportation is provided to all dive sites, and night dives are offered for around $50 each. The Trelawny Beach also offers free snorkeling, waterskiing, Sunfish sailing, windsurfing, and glass-bottom-boat rides to hotel guests; for others, various fees are charged.

Negril Scuba Centre, in the Negril Beach Club Hotel, Norman Manley Boulevard (☎ **809/957-4425**), is the most modern, best-equipped scuba facility in Negril. A professional staff of internationally certified scuba instructors and divemasters teach and guide divers to several of Negril's colorful coral reefs. Beginner's dive lessons are offered daily, as well as multiple-dive packages for certified divers. Full scuba certifications and specialty courses are also available.

A resort course, designed for first-time divers with basic swimming abilities, includes all instruction, equipment, a lecture on water and diving safety, and one open-water dive. It begins at 10am daily and ends at 2pm. Its price is $75. A one-tank dive costs $30 per dive plus $20 for the rental of equipment (not necessary if divers bring their own gear). More economical is a two-tank dive, which includes lunch. It costs $55, plus the (optional) $20 rental of all equipment. This organization is PADI-registered, although it accepts all recognized certification cards.

One of the best-recommended dive facilities in Negril is **Sundivers, Inc.,** a PADI-approved five-star dive shop located on the premises of the Poinciana Beach Hotel (☎ **809/957-4069**), on Norman Manley Boulevard, near Sandals Negril. A four-day certification course costs $330, a resort course for beginners costs $75, and a one-tank dive for already-certified divers costs $35, plus $10 for the rental of the necessary equipment. More than 20 dive sites, including coral reefs, caves, and hedges, are located at Poinciana.

Snorkeling   Equipment is available in many places for $15 per day.

Sunfish Sailing   Many hotels and some public beaches have Sunfish sailboats for rent at about $10 to $15 per hour. Hotels with their own fleets will charge less.

Waterskiing   It costs $15 for a 15-minute ski run, and many hotels offer training facilities. Doctor's Cave Beach in Montego Bay and the Blue Lagoon in Port Antonio are the best venues for this sport.

Windsurfing   Some hotels have boards for windsurfing available. Rentals usually cost about $15 per hour.

FAST FACTS: Jamaica

Area Code   To call Jamaica direct from North America, dial area code **809,** then the local number. The area code is not needed for calls on the island.

Banks   Banks islandwide are open Monday through Friday from 9am to 5pm. There are Bank of Jamaica exchange bureaus at both international airports (Montego Bay and Kingston), at cruise-ship piers, and in most hotels.

Currency   The unit of currency in Jamaica is the **Jamaican dollar,** and it uses the same symbol as the U.S. dollar, "$." There is no fixed rate of exchange for the Jamaican dollar. Subject to market fluctuations, it's traded publicly. Visitors to Jamaica can pay for any goods in U.S. dollars. *Be careful!* Unless it is clearly stated, always insist on knowing whether a price is being quoted in Jamaican or U.S. dollars.

In this guide I've generally followed the price-quotation policy of the establishment, whether in Jamaican dollars or U.S. dollars. For clarity, I have used the symbol "J$" to denote prices in Jamaican dollars; the conversion into U.S. dollars follows in parentheses. When dollar figures stand alone, they are always U.S. currency.

Jamaican currency is issued in banknotes of J$1, J$2, J$5, J$10, J$20, J$50, and J$100. Coins are 1¢, 5¢, 10¢, 20¢, 25¢, and 50¢. At press time (but subject to change), the exchange rate of Jamaican currency is J$31 to $1 U.S. (J$1 equals about 3¢ U.S.).

Customs   Do not bring in (or take out) illegal drugs from Jamaica. Your luggage is searched. *Ganja*-sniffing police dogs are stationed at the airport. Otherwise, you can bring in most items intended for personal use.

Documents   U.S. and Canadian residents do not need passports, but must have proof of citizenship (or permanent residency) and a return or ongoing ticket. Other visitors, including Britishers, need passports, good for a maximum stay of six months.

Immigration cards, needed for bank transactions and currency exchange, are given to visitors at the airport arrivals desks.

Drugs   Although drugs are commonly sold on Jamaica, hard drugs and *ganja* (marijuana) are illegal and imprisonment is the penalty for possession. Some tourists have even attempted to bring *ganja* back into the United States, but U.S. Customs agents, well aware of the drug situation in Jamaica, have easily caught and arrested many chance-takers.

As to medications, prescriptions are accepted by local pharmacies only if issued by a Jamaican doctor. Hotels have doctors on call. If you need any particular medicine or treatment, bring evidence, such as a letter from your own doctor.

Drugstores   In Montego Bay, try McKenzie's Drug Store, 16 Strand St. (☎ **809/952-2467**); in Ocho Rios, Great House Pharmacy, Brown's Plaza (☎ **809/974-2352**); and in Kingston, Moodie's Pharmacy, in the New Kingston Shopping Centre (☎ **809/926-4174**).

Electricity   Most places have the standard electrical voltage of 110, as in the United States. However, some establishments operate on 220 volts, 50 cycles. If your hotel is on a different current from your U.S.–made appliance, ask for a transformer and adapter.

Embassies   The **U.S. Embassy** is at the Jamaica Mutual Life Centre, 2 Oxford Rd., Kingston 5 (☎ **809/929-4850**). The **Canada High Commission** is at Mutual Security Bank Building, 30–36 Knutsford Blvd., Kingston 5 (☎ **809/926-1500**), and there's a Canadian Consulate at 29 Gloucester Ave.,

Montego Bay (☎ **809/952-6198**). The **United Kingdom High Commission** is at 28 Trafalgar Rd., Kingston 10 (☎ **809/926-9050**).

Emergencies For the **police** and **air rescue,** dial **119;** to report a **fire** or call an **ambulance,** dial **110.**

Etiquette For various reasons, some Jamaicans dislike having their pictures taken, so ask permission first. Don't call the locals "natives"; "Jamaicans" will do.

Hospitals In Kingston, the University Hospital is at Mona (☎ **809/ 927-1620**); in Montego Bay, the Cornwall Regional Hospital is at Mount Salem (☎ **809/952-5100**); and in Port Antonio, the Port Antonio General Hospital is at Naylor's Hill (☎ **809/993-2646**).

Information Before you go, you can obtain information from the **Jamaica Tourist Board** at the following U.S. addresses: 300 W. Wienca Rd., Suite 100A, Atlanta, GA 30342 (☎ **404/250-9971**); 500 N. Michigan Ave., Suite 1030, Chicago, IL 60611 (☎ **312/527-4800**); 1320 S. Dixie Hwy., Suite 1100, Coral Gables, FL 33146 (☎ **305/665-0557**); 8214 Westchester, Suite 500, Dallas, TX 75225 (☎ **214/361-8778**); 3440 Wilshire Blvd., Suite 1207, Los Angeles, CA 90010 (☎ **213/384-1123**); 866 Second Ave., New York, NY 10017 (☎ **212/856-9727**); and 1315 Walnut St., Suite 918, Philadelphia, PA 19107 (☎ **215/545-1061**). In Canada, go to 1 Eglinton Ave. E., Suite 616, Toronto, ON M4P 3A1 (☎ **416/482-7850**). Britishers can go to the London office: 1–2 Prince Consort Rd., London SW7 4BZ (☎ **0171/224-0505**).

Once on Jamaica, you'll find tourist board offices at 2 St. Lucia Ave., Kingston (☎ **809/929-9200**); Cornwall Beach, St. James, Montego Bay (☎ **809/952-4425**); Shop no. 20, Adrija Place, Negril, Westmoreland (☎ **809/957-4243**); in the Ocean Village Shopping Centre, Ocho Rios, St. Ann (☎ **809/974-2582**); and in City Centre Plaza, Port Antonio (☎ **809/993-3051**).

Marrying You can get a marriage license after 24 hours' residence on the island, and then marry as soon as it can be arranged. You will need your birth certificate, and; where applicable, divorce documents or death certificates. All documents must be properly certified—ordinary photostat copies will not be accepted. Most Jamaican hotels will make arrangements for your wedding and license. Otherwise, one of the headquarters of the Jamaica Tourist Board can assist you in meeting and making arrangements with a government marriage officer.

Nudity Nude bathing is allowed at a number of hotels, clubs, and beaches (especially in Negril), but only where there are signs stating SWIMSUITS OPTIONAL. Elsewhere, the law will not even allow topless sunbathing.

Safety You can get into a lot of trouble in Jamaica or you can have a care-free vacation—much depends on what you do and where you go. Major hotels have security guards who protect the grounds. Under no circumstances should you accept an invitation to see "the real Jamaica" from some stranger you meet on the beach. Exercise caution when traveling around Jamaica. Safeguard your valuables and never leave them unattended on a beach. Likewise, never leave luggage or other valuables in a car, or even the trunk of a car. The U.S. State Department, in a travel advisory, stated: "Crime in Kingston, Jamaica's capital, exceeds the level of criminal activity elsewhere in the Caribbean." Visitors are warned not to walk around at night. Caution is also advisable in many north-coast tourist areas, especially remote houses and isolated villas that can't afford to employ security forces. For the latest advisories, call the U.S. State Department (☎ **202/647-5225**).

Shopping Hours   Hours vary widely, but as a general rule most business establishments are open Monday through Friday from 8:30am to 5pm (or in some places, earlier at 4:30pm). Some shops are open on Saturday until noon.

Taxes   The government imposes a 12% per night room tax. You will be charged a J$200 ($6.40) departure tax at the airport, payable in either Jamaican or U.S. dollars.

Telephone   All overseas telephone calls incur a government tax of 15%.

Time   Jamaica is on eastern standard time year round. However, when the United States is on daylight saving time, at 6am in Miami it's 5am in Kingston.

Tips and Service   Tipping is customary. A general 10% or 15% is expected in hotels and restaurants on occasions when you would normally tip. Some places add a service charge to the bill. Tipping is not allowed in the all-inclusive hotels.

Water   It's usually safe to drink piped-in water, islandwide, as it is filtered and chlorinated; however, it's more prudent to drink bottled water, if available.

Weather   Expect temperatures around 80° to 90° Fahrenheit on the coast. Winter is a little cooler. In the mountains it can get as low as 40°. There is generally a breeze, which in winter is noticeably cool. The rainy periods in general are October through November (although it can extend into December) and from May through June. Normally rain comes in short, sharp showers; then the sun shines.

1 Kingston

Kingston, the largest English-speaking city in the Caribbean, is the capital of Jamaica, with a population of more than 650,000 people living on the plains between Blue Mountain and the sea.

The buildings are a mixture of very modern, graceful old, and plain ramshackle. It's a busy city, as you might expect, with a natural harbor that's the seventh largest in the world. The University of the West Indies has its campus on the edge of the city. The cultural center of Jamaica is here, along with industry, finance, and government. Now covering some 40 square miles, the city was founded by the survivors of the 1692 Port Royal earthquake, and in 1872 it became the capital, superseding Spanish Town.

WHERE TO STAY

Remember to ask if the 12% room tax is included in the rate quoted when you make your reservation. The rates listed below are year round, unless otherwise noted.

All leading hotels in security-conscious Kingston have guards.

Terra Nova Hotel

17 Waterloo Rd., Kingston 10, Jamaica, W.I. ☎ **809/926-2211.** Fax 809/929-4933. 21 rms. A/C TV TEL. $165 single or double. Breakfast $6–$10 extra. AE, DC, MC, V. Free parking.

A gem among small, independently run hotels, this house is on the western edge of New Kingston, near West Kings House Road. Built in 1924 as a wedding present for a young bride, it has had a varied career. It was once the family seat of the Myers rum dynasty, and the birthplace and home of Christopher Blackwell, promoter of many Jamaican singers and musical groups, including Bob Marley and the Wailers. In 1959 the house was converted into a hotel, and, set in 2¹/₂ acres of gardens with a backdrop of greenery and mountains, it is now considered one of the best small Jamaican hotels.

Most of the bedrooms are in a new wing. Above the portico is a balcony coffee terrace. The Spanish-style El Dorado Room, with a marble floor, wide windows, and spotless linen, offers local and international food. Your à la carte breakfast is served on the balcony or in the dining room, and there's a swimming pool behind the hotel.

A HOTEL AT NEARBY PORT ROYAL

Morgan's Harbour Hotel & Beach Club

Port Royal, Kingston 1, Jamaica, W.I. ☎ **809/924-8464.** Fax 809/924-8464. 50 rms, 6 suites. A/C MINIBAR TV TEL. Transportation: A public ferryboat departs every two hours from near Victoria Pier on Ocean Boulevard. Many visitors arrive by car or taxi, or else by the hotel's private boat from Victoria Pier. $129 single; $159 double; $184 suite. Breakfast $8– $10. AE, MC, V. Free parking.

This is the most visible building within the historic ruin of what was once believed to be the wickedest city on earth, Port Royal. Rebuilt after 1988's Hurricane Gilbert, Morgan's lies near the end of a long sandspit whose rocky and scrub-covered length shelters the harbor of Kingston. On the premises is a 200-year-old redbrick building originally constructed to melt pitch for the sailing ships of His Majesty's navy, a swimming area defined by docks and buoys, and a series of wings whose eaves are accented with hints of gingerbread. Set on 22 acres of flat and rock-studded seashore, the resort contains a breezy waterfront restaurant called Henry Morgan's and a popular bar (where ghost stories about the old Port Royal seem especially lurid as the liquor flows on Friday night), plus the largest marina facility in Kingston. Longtime residents quietly claim that the ghosts of those soldiers killed by a long-ago earthquake are especially visible on hot and very calm days, when British formations seem to march out of the sea accompanied by the jangling of keys.

The hotel rents well-furnished bedrooms, each furnished in an 18th-century Chippendale-Jamaican motif.

WHERE TO DINE

✪ Blue Mountain Inn

Gordon Town Rd. ☎ **809/927-1700.** Reservations required. Head north on Old Hope Road into the mountains. Appetizers $4–$6; main courses $17.60–$41.60. AE, DC, MC, V. Dinner only, daily 7–11pm. CARIBBEAN/SEAFOOD/STEAK.

About a 20-minute drive north from downtown Kingston is an 18th-century coffee plantation house set high on the slopes of Blue Mountain, surrounded by trees and flowers on the bank of the Mammee River. On cold nights, log fires blaze, and the dining room gleams with silver and sparkling glass. The inn is one of Jamaica's most famous restaurants, not only for food but also for atmosphere and service. Men are required to wear jackets (ties are optional), but the effort is worth it and the cool night air justifies it. Women are advised to take a wrap.

Menus change monthly and feature Caribbean dishes, fresh seafood, and U.S. steaks, all served with a selection of fresh vegetables; examples might include New Orleans bourbon-and-garlic shrimp, chicken Kiev, or an array of lobster dishes. Top off your meal with tropical fruit salad and ice cream, Tía Maria parfait, baked

Alaska, or a more ambitious banana or pineapple flambé. The wine list includes European varieties together with local beverages.

WHAT TO SEE & DO

Even if you're staying at one of the resorts at Ocho Rios or Port Antonio, you may want to visit Kingston for brief sightseeing, and for trips to nearby Port Royal and Spanish Town.

IN TOWN

One of the major attractions, **Devon House,** 26 Hope Rd. (☎ **809/929-7029**), was built in 1881 by George Stiebel, a Jamaican who, after mining in South America, became one of the first black millionaires in the Caribbean. A striking classical building, the house has been restored to its original beauty by the Jamaican National Trust. The grounds contain craft shops, boutiques, two restaurants (see "Where to Dine," above), and shops that sell the best ice cream in Jamaica in exotic fruit flavors, and a bakery and pastry shop with Jamaican puddings and desserts. The main house also displays furniture of various periods and styles. Admission to Devon House is $2, and it's open Tuesday through Saturday from 9:30am to 5pm.

Almost next door to Devon House are the sentried gates of **Jamaica House,** residence of the prime minister, a fine, white-columned building set well back from the road.

Continuing along Hope Road, at the crossroads of Lady Musgrave and King's House roads, turn left and you'll see a gate on the left with its own personal traffic light. This leads to **King's House,** the official residence of the governor-general of Jamaica, the queen's representative on the island. The outside and front lawn of the gracious residence, set in 200 acres of well-tended parkland, is sometimes open to view Monday through Friday from 10am to 5pm. The secretarial offices are housed next door in an old wooden building set on brick arches. In front of the house is a gigantic banyan tree in whose roots, legend says, duppies (as ghosts are called in Jamaica) take refuge when they're not living in the cotton trees.

Between Old Hope and Mona roads, a short distance from the Botanical Gardens, is the **University of the West Indies,** built in 1948 on the Mona Sugar Estate, the third of the large estates in this area. Ruins of old mills, storehouses, and aqueducts are juxtaposed with modern buildings on what must be the most beautifully situated campus in the world. The chapel, an old sugar factory building, was transported stone by stone from Trelawny and rebuilt on the campus close to the old sugar factory, the remains of which are well preserved and give a good idea of how sugar was made in slave days.

The **National Library of Jamaica** (formerly the West India Reference Library), Institute of Jamaica, 12 East St. (☎ **809/922-0620**), a storehouse of the history, culture, and traditions of Jamaica and the Caribbean, is the finest working library for West Indian studies in the world. It has the most comprehensive, up-to-date, and balanced collection of materials—including books, newspapers, photographs, maps, and prints—to be found anywhere in the Caribbean. Of special interest to visitors are the regular exhibitions that attractively and professionally highlight different aspects of Jamaica and West Indian life. September to June, it's open Monday through Thursday 9:30am to 4:30pm and on Friday from 9:30am to 4pm.

The **Bob Marley Museum** (formerly Tuff Gong Studio), 56 Hope Rd. (☎ **809/927-9152**), is said to be the most-visited sight in Kingston, although unless you're a Bob Marley fan it may not mean much to you. The clapboard house with its garden and high surrounding wall was the famous reggae singer's home and recording studio until his death. The museum is open on Monday, Tuesday, Thursday, and Friday from 9am to 5pm and on Wednesday and Saturday from noon to 6pm. Admission is $4 for adults, $1 for children 4 to 12, free for children under 4. It's reached by bus no. 14.

PORT ROYAL

From West Beach Dock, Kingston, a ferry ride of 20 to 30 minutes will take you to Port Royal, which conjures up pictures of swashbuckling pirates led by Henry Morgan, swilling grog in harbor taverns. This was once one of the largest trading centers of the New World, with a reputation for being the wickedest city on earth (Blackbeard stopped here regularly on his Caribbean trips). But the whole thing came to an end at 11:43am on June 7, 1692, when a third of the town disappeared under water as the result of a devastating earthquake. Nowadays, Port Royal, with its memories of the past, has been designated by the government for redevelopment as a tourist destination.

As you drive along the Palisades, you arrive first at **St. Peter's Church.** It's usually closed, but you may persuade the caretaker, who lives opposite, to open it if you want to see the silver plate, said to be spoils captured by Henry Morgan from the cathedral in Panama. In the ill-kept graveyard is the tomb of Lewis Galdy, a Frenchman swallowed up and subsequently regurgitated by the 1692 earthquake.

Fort Charles, the only one remaining of Port Royal's six forts, has withstood attack, earthquake, fire, and hurricane. Built in 1656 and later strengthened by Morgan for his own purposes, the fort was expanded and further armed in the 1700s, until its firepower boasted more than 100 cannons, covering both the land and the sea approaches. After subsequent earthquakes and tremors, the fort ceased to be at the water's edge and is now well inland. In 1779 Britain's naval hero, Horatio Lord Nelson, was commander of the fort and trod the wooden walkway inside the western parapet as he kept watch for the French invasion fleet. It is administered by the Institute of Jamaica (☎ **809/922-0620**).

The **Fort Charles Maritime Museum** is in the former British naval headquarters where Nelson served. Scale models of the fort and ships of past eras are to be seen in the small museum. It's open from 10am to 4pm Monday through Friday, to 5pm on Saturday and Sunday. Admission is $1 for adults, free for children.

Part of the complex, **Giddy House,** once the Royal Artillery storehouse, is another example of what the earth's movements can do. Walking across the tilted floor is an eerie and strangely disorienting experience.

SPANISH TOWN

From 1662 to 1872 Spanish Town was the capital of the island. Originally founded by the Spaniards as Villa de la Vega, it was sacked by Cromwell's men in 1655 and all traces of Roman Catholicism were obliterated. The English cathedral, surprisingly retaining a Spanish name, **St. Jago de la Vega,** was built in 1666 and rebuilt after being destroyed by a hurricane in 1712. As you drive into the town from Kingston, the ancient cathedral, rebuilt in 1714, catches your eye with its brick tower and two-tiered wooden steeple, which was not added until 1831. As the cathedral was built on the foundation and remains of the old Spanish church, it is half-English, half-Spanish, showing two definite styles, one romanesque, the other gothic.

Of cruciform design and built mostly of brick, the cathedral is historically one of the most interesting buildings on the island. The black and white marble stones of the aisles are interspersed with ancient tombstones, and the walls are heavy with marble memorials that are almost a chronicle of Jamaica's history, dating back as far as 1662. Episcopalian services are held regularly on Sunday at 7 and 11am and at 6:30pm, sometimes conducted by the bishop of Jamaica, whose see this is.

Beyond the cathedral, turn right and two blocks along you'll reach Constitution Street and the **Town Square.** This little square is surrounded by towering royal palms.

On the west side is old **King's House,** gutted by fire in 1925, though the facade has been restored. This was the residence of Jamaica's British governors until 1972 when the capital was transferred to Kingston, and many celebrated guests—among them Lord Nelson, Admiral Rodney, Captain Bligh of HMS *Bounty* fame, and King William IV—stayed here.

Beyond the house is the **Jamaica People's Museum of Craft & Technology,** Old King's House, Constitution Square (☎ **809/922-0620**), open Monday through Friday from 9:30am to 4pm. Admission is $1. The garden contains examples of old farm machinery, an old water mill wheel, a hand-turned sugar mill, a coffee pulper, an old hearse, and a fire engine. An outbuilding contains a museum of crafts and technology, together with a number of smaller agricultural implements. In the small archeological museum are old prints, models (including one of King's House based on a written description), and maps of the town's grid layout from the 1700s.

The streets around the old Town Square contain many fine Georgian town houses intermixed with tin-roofed shacks. Nearby is the **market,** so busy in the morning that you'll find it difficult, almost dangerous, to drive through. It provides, however, a bustling scene of Jamaican life.

Driving to Spanish Town from Kingston on the A1 (Washington Boulevard), at Central Village you come to the **Arawak Museum,** on the right. It lies in the hamlet of White Marl, just outside Spanish Town, and is run by the Institute of Jamaica (☎ **809/922-0620**). The entrance appears to lead to a quarry, but don't be put off. Drive down to the museum, a hexagonal building on the site of one of the largest Arawak settlements on the island. It's open Monday through Thursday from 9:30am to 4:30pm and on Friday from 9:30am to 4pm. The small museum contains drawings, pictures, and diagrams of Arawak life, plus old flints and other artifacts that help you to understand the early history or prehistoric period of Jamaica. Smoking of tobacco seems to have been a habit even in 1518, when Arawaks were recorded as lighting hollow tubes at one end and sucking the other. The visitor can also see signs of an original Arawak settlement at White Marl, around the museum's main building. Admission is free but contributions are appreciated as the museum is in bad shape and in dire need of restoration.

2 Port Antonio

Port Antonio is a verdant and sleepy seaport on the northeast coast of Jamaica, 63 miles northeast of Kingston. It has been called the Jamaica of 100 years ago. Port Antonio is the mecca of the titled and the wealthy, including European royalty and stars like Whoopi Goldberg, Peter O'Toole, and Tommy Tune.

The small, bustling town of Port Antonio is like many on the island: clean and untidy, with sidewalks around a market filled with vendors; tin-roofed shacks competing with old Georgian and modern brick and concrete buildings. The market is a place to browse local craftwork, spices, and fruits.

In other days visitors arrived by banana boat and stayed at the Titchfield Hotel (which burned down) in a lush, tropical, unspoiled part of the island. Captain Bligh landed here in 1793 with the first breadfruit plants, and Port Antonio claims that the ones grown in this area are the best on the island. Visitors still arrive by water—but now it's in cruise ships that moor close to Navy Island, and the passengers come ashore just for the day.

Navy Island and the long-gone Titchfield Hotel were owned for a short time by film star Errol Flynn. The story is that after suffering damage to his yacht, he put into Kingston for repairs, visited Port Antonio by motorbike, fell in love with the area, and in due course acquired Navy Island, some say in a gambling game. Later, he either lost or sold it and bought a nearby plantation, Comfort Castle, still owned by his widow, Patrice Wymore Flynn, who spends most of her time there. He was much loved and admired by the Jamaicans and was totally integrated into the community. They still talk of him in Port Antonio—his reputation for womanizing and drinking lives on.

GETTING THERE   To reach Port Antonio from the capital, you can take the A4 through Port Morant and up the east coast, or drive north on the A3 through Castleton and travel east along the north coast.

WHERE TO STAY
VERY EXPENSIVE

✪ Trident Villas & Hotel

Rte. A4 (P.O. Box 119), Port Antonio, Jamaica, W.I. ☎ **809/993-2602,** or 800/237-3237 in the U.S. Fax 809/993-2590. 8 rms, 18 suites. TEL. Winter, $275 single; $350 double; $620 suite. Off-season, $160 single; $220 double; $340 suite. MAP $65 per person extra. AE, MC, V. Free parking.

About 2¹/₂ miles east along Allan Avenue on the coast toward Frenchman's Cove stands an elegant rendezvous of the rich and famous. This deluxe hotel complex is one of the most tasteful and refined on the north shore. Sitting regally above jagged coral cliffs with a seaside panorama, the hotel is the personal and creative statement of Earl Levy, scion of a prominent Kingston family. Nearby he has erected a multimillion-dollar replica of a European château, known as Trident Castle, which can be rented as one unit. Here, guests are grandly housed in eight large bedrooms beautifully furnished in plantation style.

The hotel's main building is furnished with antiques, and flowers decorate the sea breeze–cooled lobby. Your accommodations will be a studio cottage or tower, reached by a pathway through the gardens. In a cottage, a large bedroom with ample sitting area opens onto a private patio with a view of the sea. All cottages and tower rooms have baths with tubs and showers, plus ceiling fans and plenty of storage space. Jugs of ice and water are constantly replenished. Solo travelers are accommodated in either junior or deluxe villa suites, while two or three guests are lodged in junior, deluxe villa, prime minister's, or imperial suites. There's a small private sand beach, and the gardens embrace a pool and a gingerbread gazebo. Lounges, tables, chairs, and bar service add to your pleasure.

Dining/Entertainment: The main building has two patios, one covered, where breakfast and lunch are served. You can also have breakfast on your private patio, served by your own butler. At dinner, when men are required to wear jackets and ties, silver service, crystal, and Port Royal pewter sparkle on the tables. Dinner is a multicourse fixed-price meal, so if you're concerned with dietary restrictions, you should make your requirements known early so that alternative food can be served.

Services: Room service, laundry, babysitting.

Facilities: Swimming pool, tennis, horseback riding, and such water sports as sailing and snorkeling (included in the tariffs).

EXPENSIVE

Fern Hill Club

Mile Gully Rd., San San (P.O. Box 100), Port Antonio, Jamaica, W.I. ☎ **809/993-3222;** for information and reservations, call 416/620-4666 in Toronto. Fax 809/993-2257. 31 rms and suites. A/C TV. **Directions:** Drive eastward along Allan Avenue and watch for the signs. Winter, $300 double; $380 suite for two. Off-season, $210 double; $300 suite for two. Single supplement $60 in winter, $50 in summer. (Rates all-inclusive.) AE, MC, V. Free parking.

Attractive, airy, and panoramic, Fern Hill occupies 45 forested acres high above the coastline, attracting primarily a British or Canadian clientele. Technically classified as a private club, the establishment is comprised of a colonial-style clubhouse and three outlying villas, plus a comfortable annex at the bottom of the hill. The accommodations are highly private, drawing a large patronage among honeymooners.

Dining/Entertainment: There is the Blue Mahoe Bar (named after the wood that sheathes it) and a patio for dining. The hotel restaurant offers an international menu (see "Where to Dine," below).

Services: A shuttle bus making daily trips down the steep hillside to the beach.

Facilities: Three swimming pools, tennis court.

Goblin Hill Villas at San San

San San (P.O. Box 26), Port Antonio, Jamaica, W.I. ☎ **809/993-3286,** or 809/925-8108 in Kingston for reservations. Fax 809/925-6248. 28 villas. A/C. Winter, $1,850 per week one-bedroom villa; $2,130 per week two-bedroom villa for four. Off-season, $1,710 per week one-bedroom villa; $1,885 per week two-bedroom villa for four. (Rates include transfers and rental car.) AE, MC, V. Free parking.

This green and sun-washed hillside once reputed to shelter goblins is now filled with vacation homes on San San Estate. The swimming pool is surrounded by a vine-laced arbor, which lies just a stone's throw from an almost-impenetrable forest. A long flight of steps leads down to the crescent-shaped sands of San San beach. The accommodations are town-house style against the landscape, and some units have ceiling fans and king-size beds.

Dining/Entertainment: In the villas, housekeepers prepare and serve meals.

Services: Housekeepers attend to chores in villas.

Facilities: Two Laykold tennis courts, beach, swimming pool, snorkeling, windsurfing, scuba diving.

MODERATE

Jamaica Palace

Williamsfield (P.O. Box 277), Port Antonio, Jamaica, W.I. ☎ **809/2020,** or 800/423-4095 in the U.S. Fax 809/993-3459. 21 rms, 59 suites. A/C TEL. **Directions:** Head 1 mile east on Allan Avenue. Winter, $130–$160 single or double; $190–$325 suite. Off-season, $115–$145 single or double; $170–$290 suite. MAP $45 per person extra. AE, MC, V. Free parking.

Rising like a stately mansion from a hillock surrounded by 5 tropically land-scaped acres, this hotel opened in 1989. Its owner, German-born Siglinde von Stephani-Fahmi, set out to combine the elegance of a European hotel with the relaxed atmosphere of a Jamaican resort. The public rooms are filled with furnishings and art from Europe, including a 6-foot Baccarat crystal candelabra, and a pair of Italian ebony-and-ivory chairs from the 15th century. Outside, the Palace offers white marble columns (Tara style), sun-filled patios and balconies, and an unusual 114-foot swimming pool shaped like the island of Jamaica.

Accommodations include 21 deluxe rooms, 52 junior suites, six full suites, and an imperial suite. All rooms are large, with 12$^{1}/_{2}$-foot ceilings and oversize marble bathrooms. Suites are individually furnished with crystal chandeliers, Persian rugs, and original works of art. TV is available upon request.

Dining/Entertainment: Both continental and Jamaican food are served in the main dining room with its lighted "waterwall" sculpted from Jamaican cave stones, where men are requested to wear jackets and ties. There's also a poolside café with a barbecue area. Live dance music and calypso bands are featured.

Services: Room service, laundry, babysitting, massage facilities, fashion boutique (operated by Patrice Wymore Flynn, widow of Errol Flynn), complimentary shuttle service and admission to three nearby white sandy beaches.

Facilities: Swimming pool.

Navy Island Marina Resort

Navy Island (P.O. Box 188), Port Antonio, Jamaica, W.I. ☎ **809/993-2667.** Fax 809/993-2667. 1 rm, 10 villas. $80 single or double; $110 one-bedroom villa for one, $140 one-bedroom villa for two; $180 two-bedroom villa for three, $220 two-bedroom villa for four. Additional person (maximum of six in a unit) $20 extra. (Rates include breakfast.) AE, MC, V. Transportation: Private ferry (see below).

Jamaica's only private island getaway, this resort and marina is on that "bit of paradise" once owned by actor Errol Flynn. Today this cottage colony and yacht club is one of the best-kept travel secrets in the Caribbean. To reach the resort, you'll have to take a ferry from the dockyards of Port Antonio on West Street for a short ride across one of the most beautiful and convoluted harbors of Jamaica. Guests of the hotel travel free, but temporary visitors pay J$50 ($1.60) for the round-trip. The ferry travels daily from 7am to 10pm.

Each accommodation is designed as a studio cottage or villa branching out from the main club. Ceiling fans and trade winds keep the cottages cool, and mosquito netting over the beds adds a plantation touch. There is only one hotel room, which can be rented as a single or double.

One of the resort's beaches is a secluded clothing-optional stretch of sand known as Trembly Knee Cove. You can leisurely explore the island, whose grounds are dotted with hybrid hibiscus, bougainvillea, and palms (many of which were originally ordered planted by Flynn himself).

Dining/Entertainment: At night, after enjoying drinks in the HMS Bounty Bar, guests can dine in the Navy Island Restaurant. A five-course dinner is served nightly from 7 to 10pm and costs $10 to $25.

Services: Free ferry service.

Facilities: Swimming pool, two beaches, water sports (including scuba diving and windsurfing).

WHERE TO DINE

All hotels welcome outside guests for dinner, but reservations are required.

Fern Hill Club

Mile Gully Rd. ☎ **809/993-3222.** Reservations required. Directions: Head east on Allan Avenue. Fixed-price meal $10 at lunch, $30 at dinner. AE, MC, V. Lunch daily 1–2pm; dinner daily 7:30–9:30pm. INTERNATIONAL/JAMAICAN.

One of the finest dining spots in Port Antonio has a sweeping view of the rugged coastline; sunset watching here is said to be the best at the resort. Well-prepared specialties are served: jerk chicken, jerk pork, grilled lobster, and Créole fish. Beach barbecues are staged on Monday night, and a folkloric dinner-dance is presented on Friday.

Rafter's Restaurant

St. Margaret's Bay. ☎ **809/993-2778.** Reservations not required. Appetizers $3–$5; main courses $9–$20. AE, MC, V. Daily 8am–6pm. JAMAICAN.

Rafter's Restaurant lies at the edge of the river at the point where still waters provided a convenient resting point for the commercial raft operators who used to float goods downstream. Jean McGill and Beverley Dixon are the managers of this establishment. The neoclassical pavilion housing the establishment was built in 1954 by a local architect for the earl of Mansfield. Food includes sandwiches, burgers, an array of salads, steak or chicken, as well as grilled lobster. Fresh fish is served grilled, steamed, or pan-fried. The turnoff leading to this place is about 5 miles west of Port Antonio; follow the signs.

✪ Trident Hotel Restaurant

Rte. A4. ☎ **809/993-2602.** Reservations required. Directions: Head east on Allan Avenue. Lunch $15–$25; fixed-price dinner $45. AE, MC, V. Lunch daily noon–4pm; dinner daily 8–10pm. INTERNATIONAL.

The Trident Hotel Restaurant has for a long time been frequented by those seeking a high-level cuisine. Part of the main hotel building, the restaurant has an air of elegance. The high-pitched wooden roof set on white stone walls holds several ceiling fans that gently stir the air. The antique tables are set with old china, English silver, and Port Royal pewter. The formally dressed waiters will help you choose your wine and whisper the name of each course as they serve it: Jamaican salad, coconut soup, dolphin (fish) with mayonnaise-and-mustard sauce, steak with broccoli and sautéed potatoes, and peach Melba and Blue Mountain coffee with Tía Maria, a Jamaican liqueur. The six-course dinner menu is changed every day. Tip at your discretion. Men are required to wear jackets and ties.

Yachtsman's Wharf

16 West St. ☎ **809/993-3053.** Reservations not required. Main courses $6–$13. No credit cards. Daily 7:30am–10pm. INTERNATIONAL.

Beneath a thatch-covered roof at the end of an industrial pier near the departure point for the ferries to Navy Island, this rustic bar and restaurant is a favorite of the expatriate yachting set. Crews from many of the ultra-expensive yachts have dined here and have pinned their ensigns on the roughly textured planks and posts. It opens for breakfast, which costs $3 to $4, and stays open all day. Menu items include the usual array of tropical drinks, burgers, seafood ceviche, curried chicken, and ackee with saltfish. Main dishes include vegetables.

WHAT TO SEE & DO

Athenry Gardens and Cave of Nonsuch

Portland. ☎ **809/993-3740.** Admission (including guide for gardens and cave) $5 adults, $2.50 children under 12. Open daily 9am–5pm (last tour at 4:30pm).

These sights are south-southeast from Port Antonio: From Harbour Street in Port Antonio, turn south in front of the Anglican church onto Red Hassel Road and proceed approximately a mile to Breastworks community (fork in road). Take the left fork, cross a narrow bridge, go immediately left after the bridge, and proceed approximately 3¹/₂ miles to the village of Nonsuch. Twenty minutes from Port Antonio, it's an easy drive and an easy walk to see the stalagmites, stalactites, fossilized marine life, and evidence of Arawak civilization. The cave is 1¹/₂ million years old. From the Athenry Gardens, there are panoramic views over the island and the sea. The gardens are filled with coconut palms, flowers, and trees. Complete guided tours are given.

Crystal Springs

Buff Bay, Portland. ☎ **809/929-6280.** Admission J$100 ($3.20) adults, J$50 ($1.60) children. Daily 9am–5:30pm.

Crystal Springs is a tract of forested land whose borders were originally recorded in 1655. Then, it was attached to a nearby plantation whose Great House is now under separate (and private) ownership. Visitors, however, can trek through the organization's 156 acres of forest whose shelter is much beloved by bird-and wildlife. A simple restaurant, usually open daily from 8am to 5pm, is on the premises, as well as a series of cottages erected in the early 1990s. These are usually rented to visiting ornithologists who don't care for the amenities or distractions of a traditional resort.

Folly Great House

On the outskirts of Port Antonio on the way to Trident Village, going east along the A4. Admission free.

This house was built, it is said, in 1905 by Arthur Mitchell, an American millionaire, for his wife, Annie, daughter of Charles Tiffany, founder of the famous New York store. Sea water was used in the concrete mixtures of its foundations and mortar, and the house began to collapse only 11 years after they moved in. Because of the beautiful location, it's easy to see what a fine Great House it must have been, but the years and vandals have not added to its attractiveness; decay and graffiti mar the remains of the two-story mansion.

Somerset Falls

8 miles west of Port Antonio, just past Hope Bay on the A4. Tour, $2. Daily 9am–5pm.

The waters of the Daniels River pour down a deep gorge through the rain forest, with waterfalls and foaming cascades. You can take a short ride in an electric gondola to the hidden falls. A stop on the daily Grand Jamaica Tour from Ocho Rios, this is one of Jamaica's most historic sites; the falls were used by the Spanish before the English captured the island. At the falls, you can swim in the deep rock pools and buy sandwiches, light meals, soft drinks, beer, and liquor at the snack bar. The guided tour includes the gondola ride, a visit to a cave, and a visit to the freshwater fish farm.

SPORTS & OUTDOOR ACTIVITIES

BEACHES

Port Antonio has several white sand beaches, including the famous **San San Beach,** open to the public. Some are free and others charge for use of facilities. **Boston Beach** is free, and often has light surfing, and there are picnic tables as well as a restaurant and snack bar. Before heading to this beach, stop nearby and get the makings for a picnic lunch at the most famous center for peppery jerk pork and chicken in Jamaica. These rustic shacks also sell the much rarer jerk sausage. The dish was said to originate with the Maroons who lived in the hills beyond and occasionally ventured out to harass plantation owners. The location is east of Port Antonio and the Blue Lagoon.

Also free is **Fairy Hill Beach** (Winnifred), with no changing rooms or showers. **Frenchman's Cove Beach** attracts a chic crowd to its white sand beach combined with a freshwater stream. Nonhotel guests are charged a fee.

Navy Island, once Errol Flynn's personal hideaway, is a fine choice for swimming (one beach is clothing optional) and snorkeling (at **Crusoe's Beach**). Take the boat from the Navy Island dock on West Street across from the Exxon station. It's a seven-minute ride to the island, and a round-trip costs J$50 ($1.60). The ferry runs 24 hours a day. The island is the setting for the Navy Island Marina Resort (see "Where to Stay," above).

✪ RAFTING

Rafting started on the Río Grande as a means of transporting bananas from the plantations to the waiting freighters. In 1871 a Yankee skipper, Lorenzo Dow Baker, decided that a seat on one of the rafts was better than walking, but it was not until Errol Flynn arrived that the rafts became popular as a tourist attraction. Flynn used to hire the craft for his friends, and he encouraged the drivers to race down the Río Grande, and bets were placed on the winner. Now that bananas are transported by road, the raft skipper makes one or maybe two trips a day down the waterway. If you want to take a raft trip, **Río Grande Attractions Limited,** c/o Rafter's Restaurant, St. Margaret's Bay (☎ **809/993-2778**), can arrange it for you.

The rafts, some 33 feet long and only 4 feet wide, are propelled by stout bamboo poles. There is a raised double seat about two-thirds of the way back for the two passengers. The skipper stands in the front, trousers rolled up to his knees, the water washing his feet, and guides the lively craft down the river, about 8 miles between steep hills covered with coconut palms, banana plantations, and flowers through limestone cliffs pitted with caves, through the Tunnel of Love, a narrow cleft in the rocks, then on to wider, gentler water.

The day starts at the Rafter's Restaurant, west of Port Antonio at Burlington on St. Margaret's Bay. Trips last 2 to 2¹/₂ hours and are offered from 8am to 4pm daily at a cost of $40 per raft, which is suitable for two people. From the Rafter's Restaurant, a fully insured driver will take you in your rented car to the starting point at Grants Level or Berrydale, where you board your raft. The trip ends at the Rafter's Restaurant, where you collect your car, which has been returned by the driver. If you feel like it, take a picnic lunch, but bring enough for the skipper too, who will regale you with lively stories of life on the river.

3 Ocho Rios

This north-coast resort is a two-hour drive east of Montego Bay or west of Port Antonio. Ocho Rios was once a small banana and fishing port, but tourism became the leading industry long ago. This resort, short on charm, is now Jamaica's cruise-ship capital. The bay is dominated on one side by a bauxite-loading terminal and on the other by a range of hotels with sandy beaches fringed by palm trees. Runaway Bay, once only a satellite of Ocho Rios but now a resort area in its own right, is presented in the next section.

Ocho Rios and neighboring Port Antonio have long been associated with celebrities. Its two most famous writers are Sir Noel Coward (who invited the world to his doorstep), and Ian Fleming, creator of James Bond (see "What to See

Ocho Rios

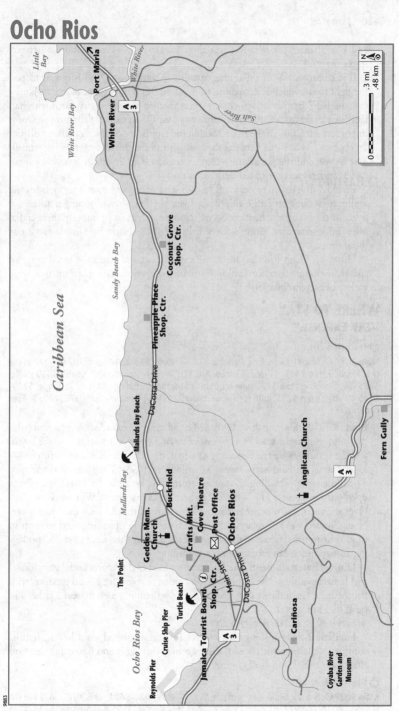

Caribbean Sea

Little Bay

Port Maria

White River

White River

A 3

White River

Salt River

White River Bay

Sandy Beach Bay

Coconut Grove Shop. Ctr.

Pineapple Place Shop. Ctr.

DaCosta Drive

Mallards Bay Beach

Mallards Bay

Buckfield

The Point

Geddes Mem. Church

Crafts Mkt.

Cove Theatre

Post Office

Ochos Rios

Anglican Church

A 3

Fern Gully

Jamaica Tourist Board

Turtle Beach

Shop. Ctr.

Main Street

DaCosta Drive

A 3

Cruise Ship Pier

Reynolds Pier

Ocho Rios Bay

Cariñosa

Coyaba River Garden and Museum

N

0   .3 mi
    .48 km

9983

and Do," below, for details about their homes here—Firefly and Goldeneye, respectively).

It is commonly assumed among Spanish-speakers that Ocho Rios was named for eight rivers, which is its Spanish translation. But it doesn't mean that in Jamaican. In 1657 British troops chased off a Spanish expeditionary force who had launched a raid from Cuba. The battle was near Dunn's River Falls, now the most important attraction of the resort. Seeing the rapids, the Spanish called the district *las chorreros.* That battle between the Spanish and the British forces was so named. The British and the Jamaicans weren't too good with Spanish names back then, so *las chorreros* was corrupted into "ocho rios."

Frankly, unless you're on a cruise ship, you may want to stay away from the major attractions on cruise-ship days. Even the duty-free shopping markets are overrun then, and the hustlers become more strident in promoting their crafts, often junk souvenirs. Dunn's River Falls becomes almost impossible to visit at those times.

However, Ocho Rios has its own unique flavor and offers the usual range of sports, including a major fishing tournament every fall, in addition to a wide variety of accommodations.

WHERE TO STAY
VERY EXPENSIVE

✪ Jamaica Inn
Main St. (P.O. Box 1), Ocho Rios, Jamaica, W.I. ☎ **809/974-2514,** or 800/243-9420 in the U.S. Fax 809/974-2449. 41 rms. 4 suites. A/C TEL. Winter (including all meals), $340 single; $385–$435 double; from $475 suite for two. Off-season (including MAP), $175 single; $220–$245 double; from $275 suite for two. Children under 14 not accepted. AE, MC, V. Free parking.

Built in 1950, this long, low, U-shaped building is surrounded by grass and palm trees and set near the sea 1¹/₂ miles east of town. Lovely patios open onto the lawns, and the bedrooms are reached along garden paths. This gracious, family-run inn—long a Jamaican landmark—spent $4 million in 1993 to upgrade all the rooms. The old charm, including the antique furniture, remains, however. The rooms open onto balconies. The White Suite here was a favorite of Winston Churchill. Over the years, many other celebrities have favored the inn with their patronage. Noel Coward was a regular, and Erroll Flynn and Ian Fleming used to drop in from time to time. Close to the shore the sea is almost too clear to make snorkeling an adventure, but farther out it's rewarding.

Dining/Entertainment: The European-trained chef prepares both international and Jamaican dishes. The emphasis is on cuisine that uses fresh local produce, with lighter dishes, including pasta. The management requires men to wear a jacket and tie at night in winter.

Services: Room service, laundry.

Facilities: Swimming pool, wide champagne-colored sand beach, tennis, comfortable lounge with books, games room with cards and jigsaw puzzles; golf close by at the Upton Golf Course.

✪ Plantation Inn
Main St. (P.O. Box 2), Ocho Rios, Jamaica, W.I. ☎ **809/974-5601,** or 800/752-6224 in the U.S. Fax 809/974-5912. 61 rms, 15 suites. A/C TEL. Winter, $155–$185 single; $195–$225 double; $235–$265 triple; from $295 suite for two. Off-season, $90–$110 single; $130–$150

double; $170–$190 triple; from $180 suite for two. MAP $55 per person extra. AE, DC, MC, V. Free parking.

Opened in 1955, this hotel evokes a southern antebellum mansion. It is reached by a sweeping driveway and entered through a colonnaded portico, set above the beach in gardens 1$^1/_2$ miles east of town. At any moment, you expect Vivien Leigh as Scarlett to come rushing down to greet you. All bedrooms open off balconies and have their own patios overlooking the sea. The double rooms are attractively decorated with chintz and comfortable furnishings, and there are also junior suites. Apart from the regular hotel, there are two units that provide lodgings: Plantana Villa above the eastern beach sleeps two to six people; Blue Shadow Villa on the west side accommodates up to eight guests.

Dining/Entertainment: There's an inside dining room, but most of the action takes place under the tropical sky. You can have breakfast on your balcony and lunch is served outdoors. English tea is served on the terrace every afternoon. On Thursday guests can enjoy a cultural folk show while dining.

Services: Room service, facials, massages, waxing.

Facilities: Two private beaches (36 steps down from the garden; seats on the way provide resting spots), jungle gym with exercise equipment, sauna, two tennis courts, snorkeling, Sunfish sailing, windsurfing, scuba diving, kayaking, glass-bottom boat; golf available at an 18-hole course a 15-minute drive away.

INEXPENSIVE

Hibiscus Lodge Hotel

87 Main St. (P.O. Box 52), Ocho Rios, Jamaica, W.I. ☎ **809/974-2676.** Fax 809/974-1874. 27 rms. Winter, $76 double; $113 triple. Off-season, $66 double; $95 triple. American breakfast $6 extra. AE, DC, MC, V. Free parking.

The Hibiscus Lodge Hotel offers more value for your money than any resort at Ocho Rios. It's an intimate little inn with character and charm, perched precariously on a cliffside three blocks from the Ocho Rios Mall, along the shore. All bedrooms, either doubles or triples, have private baths, ceiling fans, and verandas opening to the sea. Singles can be rented for the double rate.

After a day spent swimming in a pool suspended over the cliffs, with a large sun deck, guests can enjoy a drink in the unique swinging bar. On the 3-acre site are a Jacuzzi and tennis court, along with conference facilities. The owners, Richard Powell and Alfred Doswald, also provide dining at the Almond Tree (see "Where to Dine," below). The Grotto is a piano bar open daily from 5pm to 2am.

🔵 Family-Friendly Accommodations

Trelawny Beach Hotel   *(see p. 501)* Outside Falmouth, this resort is known for its Children's Fun Centre, featuring a playground, arts and crafts activities, sandcastle building, tennis clinics, and reggae dance contests.

Boscobel Beach   *(see p. 488)* The best place on the island for families with children is outside Ocho Rios. There's a children's center and a mini-zoo, and special deals exist for single parents. There's also a special program for grandparents and their grandchildren.

FDR (Franklyn D. Resort)   *(see p. 499)* At Runaway Bay, this all-inclusive resort caters to families and features a Kiddies' Centre. There's even a disco for tots. Special children's meals are served.

All-Inclusive Resorts

Boscobel Beach

P.O. Box 63, Ocho Rios, Jamaica, W.I. ☎ **809/974-3331,** or 800/859-7873 in the U.S. Fax 809/975-7370. 196 rms, 11 suites. A/C TV TEL. Winter, $855–$920 single; $1,560–$1,690 double; from $1,830 suite for two. Off-season, $610–$785 single; $1,070–$1,420 double; from $1,560 suite for two. One child under 14 per paying adult stays free in parents' room; second child under 14 $50 extra. (Rates for all-inclusive three-day package.) AE, MC, V. Free parking.

The name of this resort is old Spanish for "beautiful gardens by the sea"—it's that and more. Set on 14½ acres of prime seafront property, it stands 10 miles east of Ocho Rios. Children are encouraged and welcomed, with a big program set aside for them, including a children's center, a mini-zoo, and other activities. The resort also makes special rates for single parents traveling with children and is unique in promoting a special program for grandparents and their grandchildren. All the well-furnished and attractively decorated rooms are equipped with radios and refrigerators. Some of them feature large balconies and sunken bathtubs. A series of 44 refurbished lanai rooms (these are smaller) open right onto the beach.

Dining/Entertainment: Dinner is offered in an open-air dining room (a special children's meal is served earlier). The Barbecue Pit is decorated with a children's theme and is promoted as a "kids only" restaurant. There are also five bars on the property, including one at the beach that serves snacks throughout the day. A disco opens at 11pm. Live local entertainment is a nightly feature.

Services: Transfers to and from the airport, transfers to the golf course, babysitting, laundry.

Facilities: Children's facilities (see above), four tennis courts (lit for night play), fully equipped gym, exercise classes, aerobics, two Jacuzzis, reggae dance classes, windsurfing, sailing, waterskiing, scuba diving; golf nearby.

✪ Ciboney Ocho Rios

Main St. (P.O. Box 728), Ocho Rios, St. Ann, Jamaica, W.I. ☎ **809/974-1036,** or 800/333-3333 in the U.S. and Canada. Fax 809/974-5838. Winter, $325–$340 single; $450–$480 double; $520 junior villa suite for two; $660 one-bedroom villa suite for two; $790 honeymoon villa suite; $260 per person two–bedroom villa suite for four; $255 per person three-bedroom villa suite for six. Off-season, $310–$325 single; $420–$450 double; $480 junior villa suite for two; $510 one-bedroom villa suite for two; $760 honeymoon villa suite; $240 per person two-bedroom villa suite for four; $240 per person three-bedroom villa suite for six. (Rates include all meals and drinks, most spa facilities, in-room video movies, land and some water sports, and nightly entertainment.) AE, DC, MC, V. Free parking.

Opened in 1990, this all-inclusive resort is a Radisson-hotel franchise. It's a short drive (1½ miles) southeast of town on 45 acres of private estate dotted with red-tile villas and a Great House in the hills overlooking the Caribbean Sea. Across from the imposing gate near the entrance to the resort are the white sands of a private beach. All but a handful of the accommodations are in one-, two-, or three-bedroom villas, each of which offers a pool, fully equipped kitchen, and shaded terrace. Honeymoon villas have their own whirlpools. Thirty-six of the accommodations are traditional single or double rooms on the third floor of the Great House. Regardless of their location, accommodations are high-ceilinged, airy, and decorated in Caribbean colors. Throughout the property, a series of stone retaining walls hold the sloping grounds into carefully landscaped beds of flowering trees and vines.

Dining/Entertainment: The Manor Restaurant & Bar offers both indoor and outdoor patio dining for dinner and entertainment, with classic Jamaican food.

The Marketplace Restaurant has a contemporary menu of both American and Jamaican foods, and Alfresco Casa Nina, in a seaside setting, highlights Italian cuisine. Orchids is a restaurant developed in collaboration with the Culinary Institute of America, with a menu based on haute cuisine combined with the concept of healthy foods. Finally, late-night entertainment and dancing are featured at Nicole.

Services: Complimentary manicure and pedicure, choice of 25-minute massages.

Facilities: European-inspired beauty spa with its own health-and-fitness center, several different conference rooms, six tennis courts (lit for night play), beach club offering an array of water sports, two main swimming pools with swim-up bars (plus 90 other semiprivate swimming pools on the grounds), spa with 20 Jacuzzis; golf nearby.

Couples Ocho Rios

Tower Isle, along the A3 (P.O. Box 330), Ocho Rios, Jamaica, W.I. ☎ **809/975-4271**, or 800/268-7537 in the U.S. Fax 809/975-4439. 172 rms, 6 suites. A/C TEL. Winter, $1,346–$1,486 per couple. Off-season, $1,294–$1,430 per couple. No one 17 or under accepted. (Rates for three nights include all meals, drinks, cigarettes, activities, and airport transfers.) AE, MC, V. Free parking.

Don't come here alone—you won't get in! The management defines couples as "any man and woman in love." (I've been told that most couples are married, many on their honeymoons.) Everything is in pairs—even the chairs by the moon-drenched beach. Some couples slip away from the resort, which is an 18-minute drive (5 miles) east of town, to Couples' private island to bask in the buff.

Once you've paid the initial fee, you're free to use all the facilities—there will be no more bills. Even the cigarettes and whiskey are free. You get three meals a day, including all the wine you want; breakfast is bountiful. And tips aren't permitted!

The bedrooms have either a king-size bed or two doubles and pleasantly traditional furnishings. Each has a patio, fronting either the sea or the mountains. The hotel usually accepts bookings for a minimum of any three nights of the week, but most guests book in here on weekly terms. A four-day stay is required at certain peak periods, such as over the Christmas holidays.

Dining/Entertainment: Dinners are five courses, and afterward there's dancing on the terrace every evening, with entertainment. Guests have a choice of four restaurants.

Services: Room service (for breakfast only), laundry.

Facilities: Five tennis courts (three lit at night), Nautilus gym, scuba diving, snorkeling, windsurfing, sailing, waterskiing.

✪ The Enchanted Garden

Main Rd. (P.O. Box 284), Ocho Rios, Jamaica, W.I. ☎ **809/974-1400**, or 800/847-2535 in the U.S. Fax 809/974-5823. 72 rms, 40 suites. A/C TV TEL. Winter, $175–$220 single; $300–$380 double; $420–$500 suite for two. Off-season, $150–$190 single; $250–$330 double; $360–$460 suite for two. (Rates include meals, snacks, and bar drinks; house wines at lunch and dinner; aerobics, yoga, and meditation classes; all nonmotorized water sports; entertainment; daily shuttle to private beach club, taxes, round-trip transfers to airport at Montego Bay.) AE, DC, MC, V. Free parking.

The most verdant of Jamaican resorts opened in 1991 on a secluded hilltop high above the commercial center of town. Owned and developed by Edward Seaga, former Jamaican prime minister, the land includes 20 acres of rare botanical specimens, a serpentine mass of nature trails, and 14 cascading waterfalls much beloved by such former visitors as Mick Jagger. The resort's lobby is a pink-with-white-gingerbread tower accented with marble floors, big windows, and enormous potted palms. From its upper floors, views stretch to the seacoast and beyond, while from its base a network of paths leads to the outbuildings that contain the other elements of the resort. Bisected by the Turtle River, whose 14 waterfalls are highlighted with garden paths and spotlights, the place is of particular interest to botanists and birdwatchers.

The bedrooms have sturdy rattan furniture and are contained in eight different low-rise buildings set amid the resort's carefully conceived landscaping. Each has a private patio or balcony, and some contain kitchens.

Dining/Entertainment: The resort's restaurants include L'Eau Mirage (continental food), including Thai, Japanese, Indonesian, and regional Chinese food. The Pasta Bar, designed like a treehouse amid the leaves of a tropical forest, offers pastas, salad bar, and jerk chicken at the edge of the swimming pool. Guests may also dine at the Seaquarium, offering a cold buffet in a setting surrounded by tropical fish. The Beach Club, set a minivan ride from the hotel, accommodates guests with its own grill, snack bar, and water sports. Annabella's nightclub provides a variety of after-dinner entertainment amid a decor like something out of the *Arabian Nights.*

Services: Daily transportation to the Beach Club, shuttle for shopping, horseback riding, golf, massage, facial, manicure and pedicure, concierge.

Facilities: Spa, beauty salon, two lighted tennis courts, walk-in aviary featuring hundreds of exotic birds (feeding time is every afternoon around 4pm), fitness center. There's also a Seaquarium with 15 aquaria for marine-life exotica, exposed to the view of guests who dine or drink at the nearby bar, and hammock gardens that offer snooze spots and shrubberies and flowers.

Jamaica Grande Renaissance Resort

Main St. (P.O. Box 100), Ocho Rios, St. Ann, Jamaica. ☎ **809/974-2201,** or 800/228-9898 in the U.S. and Canada. Fax 809/974-5378. 705 rms, 15 suites. A/C TV TEL. Winter, $255–$275 single; $340–$360 double; $560–$800 suite. Off-season, $195–$215 single; $280–$300 double; $440–$800 suite. (Rates include meals, drinks, and water sports.) AE, DC, MC, V. Free parking.

This is the largest hotel in Jamaica, the much-publicized combination of two high-rise beachfront hostelries constructed in 1975 and 1976. In 1992 the hotel was reorganized by the Jamaican government, under the management of Ramada Hotels and Go-Go Tours. In 1993 a breezeway and an elaborate cluster of waterfalls and swimming pools were inserted into what had been parking lots between the towers, and the entire complex was unified into a coherent whole. Today the end result contains more beachfront than any other hotel in Ocho Rios, a comfortably accessorized array of public rooms often filled with members of tour groups from around the world, and the largest conference facilities on Jamaica. The bedrooms are tile-floored and blandly furnished with Caribbean furniture. Each opens onto a private balcony.

Dining/Entertainment: The establishment's restaurants include the Dragon (Chinese) and L'Allegro (Italian), and the less formal Café Jamique and Mallard's Court (international). There's also a beachfront grill and a total of eight bars scattered throughout the premises. The hotel operates the Jamaic'N Me Crazy Disco and a casino, with only slot machines.

Services: Daily activities programs.

Facilities: Tennis courts lit for nighttime play, year-round children's program, a full range of water sports.

Sandals Dunn's River

Along the A3 (P.O. Box 51), Ocho Rios, Jamaica, W.I. ☎ **809/972-1610,** or 800/ SANDALS in the U.S. and Canada. Fax 809/972-1611. 246 rms, 10 suites. TV TEL. Winter, $1,640–$2,140 double; $2,460 suite for two. Off-season, $1,540–$2,040 double; $2,340 suite for two. (Rates for three days/three nights, the minimum allowable stay, include all meals, "anytime" snacks, unlimited wine and drinks, airport transfers, tax, and services.) AE, MC, V. Free parking.

Having known various incarnations as the Jamaica Hilton and Eden II, this luxury, all-inclusive resort has now found its latest identity as a member of Butch Stewart's rapidly expanding Sandals empire. Opened in 1991, this is probably the finest of the Sandals resorts, at least in the opinion of some guests who have sampled them all. Only male-female couples are allowed.

Set on the seafront between Ocho Rios and St. Ann's Bay, the resort is very sports oriented. It occupies 25 well-landscaped acres, offering attractively furnished and often quite spacious accommodations. All the rooms were reconstructed architecturally after the Sandals takeover. An Italianate/Mediterranean styling was followed, and in some respects the hotel is the most Europeanized in aura of all the Ocho Rios hostelries. The guest rooms are scattered among the six-story main building, two lanai buildings, and a five-story west wing.

Dining/Entertainment: Before retreating to the disco, guests choose among several dining options. The International Room is elegant, with emerald and rose fabric-covered walls and rosewood furniture. West Indian Windies serves Caribbean specialties. D'Amore offers Italian cuisine, and Restaurant Teppanyaki serves Chinese, Polynesian, and Japanese dishes.

Services: Tours to Dunn's River Falls, shuttles to Sandals Ocho Rios, massages—all complimentary.

Facilities: Three Jacuzzis, two whirlpool baths, fitness center, jogging course, beach bar, pitch-and-putt golf course, one of the most spectacular swim-up bars on Jamaica in the lagoon-shaped pool; transport to the Sandals Golf and Country Club.

Sandals Ocho Rios

Main St. (P.O. Box 771), Ocho Rios, Jamaica, W.I. ☎ **809/974-5691,** or 800/SANDALS in the U.S. and Canada. Fax 809/974-5700. 237 rms. TV TEL. Winter, $1,440–$1,760 double. Off-season, $1,360–$1,700 double. (Rates for four days/three nights include all meals, "anytime" snacks, unlimited wine and drinks, airport transfers, and the services and facilities listed below.) Six-day minimum stay required at Christmas. AE, MC, V. Free parking.

Another Jamaican addition to the ever-expanding "couples only" empire of Gordon (Butch) Stewart, who pioneered similar properties in Montego Bay and Negril, Sandals Ocho Rios attracts a mix of coupled singles and married folk, including honeymooners. The resort uses the same formula: one price per male-female couple, including everything. This is the most discreet of the Sandals resorts, romantic and low-key. On 13 well-landscaped acres, it offers comfortably furnished rooms with either ocean or garden views, and there are some cottage units, too. All rooms are reasonably large, with king-size beds, hairdryers, and radios. The resort is 1 mile west of the town center.

Dining/Entertainment: You can drink your free drinks at an oceanside swim-up bar, and nightly theme parties and live entertainment take place in a modern amphitheater. A unique feature of the resort is an open-air disco. For dining, the resort's main dining room is St. Anne's. There's also Michelle's for Italian food and the Reef Terrace Grill for a gourmet Jamaican cuisine and fresh seafood.

Services: Round-trip transfers from the airport, tours to Dunn's River Falls, massages, laundry.

Facilities: Three freshwater pools, private artificial beach, sporting equipment and instruction (including waterskiing, windsurfing, sailing, snorkeling, and scuba diving), paddleboats, kayaks, glass-bottom boat, Jacuzzi, saunas, fully equipped fitness center, two tennis courts.

Sans Souci Lido

On the A3 (P.O. Box 103), Ocho Rios, Jamaica, W.I. ☎ **809/974-2353,** or 800/859-7873 in the U.S. Fax 809/974-2544. 12 rms, 90 suites, 9 penthouses. A/C MINIBAR TV TEL. Winter, $1,035 single; $1,970 double; from $2,410 suite for two; from $3,350 penthouse for two. Off-season, $895 single; $1,590 double; from $1,870 suite for two; from $2,730 penthouse for two. (Rates for all inclusive three-night package.) AE, DC, MC, V. Free parking.

Sans Souci, French for "without a care," a pink cliffside fantasy, recently completed a $7-million renovation, turning it into an all-inclusive Jamaica SuperClub, accepting couples or singles age 16 and over. It's 3 miles east of town on a forested plot of land whose rocky border abuts the sea. Erected, demolished, and erected again, the resort witnessed the visits of some gilt-edged titles of Britain in the 1960s when the premises were leased as private apartments. In 1984, after a financial shuffle, it reopened as a deluxe resort terraced into a hillside. A cliffside elevator brings guests to an outdoor bar. There's a freshwater pool, plus a mineral bath big enough for an elephant, and a labyrinth of catwalks and bridges stretching over rocky chasms filled with surging water.

Each accommodation features a veranda or patio, copies of Chippendale furniture, plush upholstery, and subdued colonial elegance. Some contain Jacuzzis.

Dining/Entertainment: The resort offers guests the Casanova (see "Where to Dine," below). In addition, Ristorante Palazzina by the beach is open from 7:30 to 10:30am and 12:30 to 3pm. In addition, the Balloon Bar tries to bring back some of the 1920s art of "cocktailing." There are also several terraces for drinking.

Services: Room service, laundry/valet, massages, babysitting.

Facilities: Established in 1987, the resort's spa (known in Jamaica as Charlie's Spa) grew out of the hotel's mineral springs, frequented for medicinal benefits since the 1700s. Considered effective for treating certain skin disorders, arthritis, and rheumatism, the spa is considered the finest place on Jamaica for a health-and-fitness vacation, and one of the finest in the entire Caribbean. The spa program also includes workouts (low-impact aerobics), weight training, "aquacize" classes in the mineral pools, massages, facials, and other invigorating body treatments. At night, spa clients can order low-calorie bar cocktails. The restaurant features a special spa menu, although since this is laid-back Jamaica, no one will insist that you stick to it. The ultimate spa package features four massages and one body treatment, plus an array of other offerings such as a facial, a manicure, a pedicure, and a personal fitness consultation.

Sports-lovers appreciate the hotel's three Laykold tennis courts (two lighted) and the nearby croquet lawn. Scuba diving, snorkeling, windsurfing, deep-sea fishing, and Sunfish and catamaran sailing are available at the beach. Guests can golf on an 18-hole course and watch polo matches while they take afternoon tea at the St. Ann Polo Club, Drax Hall.

WHERE TO DINE
EXPENSIVE

The Casanova

In the Sans Souci Lido, along the A3, 3 miles east of Ocho Rios. ☎ **809/974-2353.** Reservations recommended. Fixed-price dinner $32; lunch from $20. AE, DC, MC, V. Lunch daily 12:30–3pm; dinner daily 7–9:30pm. INTERNATIONAL.

In the main building of this previously recommended hotel, the Casanova is one of the most elegant dining enclaves along the north coast of Jamaica. In the late 1960s Harry Cipriani (of Harry's Bar fame in Venice) taught the staff some of his culinary techniques. The pasta is made fresh daily, along with many of the other staples. Jazz from a lattice-roofed gazebo might accompany your meal. Typical dishes include smoked chicken breast in a continental berry sauce as an appetizer, or a small vegetable mousse with a fontina cheese sauce. For your main course, you might prefer osso buco (braised veal shanks) or roasted Cornish hen with citrus and mild spice. Desserts are sumptuous, and might be followed by one of the house's four special coffees.

Ruins Restaurant, Gift Shop, and Boutique

Turtle River, DaCosta Dr. ☎ **809/974-2442.** Reservations required. Appetizers $2–$8; main courses $12–$35. AE, DC, MC, V. Lunch Mon–Sat noon–2:30pm; dinner daily 6–9:30pm. CHINESE/INTERNATIONAL.

Here you dine at the foot of a series of waterfalls in the center of town that can be considered a tourist attraction in their own right. In 1831 a British entrepreneur constructed a sugar mill on the site, using the powerful stream to drive his water wheels. Today, all that remains is a jumble of ruins, hence the restaurant's name. After you cross a covered bridge, perhaps stopping off for a drink at the bar in the outbuilding first, you find yourself in a fairyland where the only sounds come from the tree frogs, the falling water from about a dozen cascades, and the discreet clink of silver and china. Tables are set on a wooden deck leading all the way up to the pool at the foot of the falls, where moss and other vegetation line the stones at the base. At some point you may want to climb a flight of stairs to the top of the falls, where bobbing lanterns and the illuminated waters below afford one of the most delightful experiences on the island. Menu items include a wide range of Chinese food, such as sweet-and-sour pork or chicken, several kinds of chow mein or chop suey, and a house specialty—lobster sautéed in a special sauce. International dishes include lamb or pork chops, chicken Kiev, steaks, and an array of fish.

MODERATE

✪ Almond Tree Restaurant

In the Hibiscus Lodge Hotel, 87 Main St. ☎ **809/974-2813.** Reservations recommended. Appetizers $1.50–$8.60; main courses $12–$36. AE, DC, MC, V. Lunch daily noon–2:30pm; dinner daily 6–9:30pm. INTERNATIONAL.

The Almond Tree is a two-tiered patio restaurant, with a tree growing through the roof, overlooking the Caribbean at this previously recommended resort three blocks from the Ocho Rios Mall. Lobster thermidor is the most expensive item on the menu, but I prefer their bouillabaisse (made with conch and lobster). Also excellent are the roast suckling pig, medallions of beef Anne Palmer, and a fondue bourguignonne. Jamaican plantation rice is a local specialty. The wine list offers a variety of vintages, including Spanish and Jamaican. Have an apéritif in the unique "swinging bar" (swinging chairs, that is).

Dock "On the Bay"

Fisherman's Point. ☎ **809/974-7168.** Reservations recommended. Appetizers $3–$5; main courses $13–$27. AE, MC, V. Lunch daily 11am–2:30pm; dinner daily 3–11pm. JAMAICAN/INTERNATIONAL.

Part of a complex of rental units (Fisherman's Point), "On the Bay" lies in the heart of Ocho Rios, in the vicinity of Turtle Beach. The rather elegant dining spot was launched in 1987. For dinner, you can always count on "today's catch," perhaps Caribbean lobster, and certainly seafood chowder and shrimp in garlic butter. One section of the menu is devoted to Jamaican specialties, including curried goat. You can also order such international dishes as paella, beef Stroganoff, and chicken Cordon Bleu. Dock "On the Bay" occupies a point near the end of the peninsula jutting seaward. It's the closest restaurant to the cruise-ship pier. Its most attractive feature is a sun-flooded garden-style patio.

✪ Evita's Italian Restaurant

Eden Bower Rd. ☎ **809/974-2333.** Reservations recommended. Appetizers $3–$5.50; main courses $7.50–$20. AE, MC, V. Daily 11am–11pm. ITALIAN.

Located a five-minute drive south of the commercial heart of Ocho Rios, in a hillside residential neighborhood that enjoys a panoramic view over the city's harbor and beachfronts, this is the premier Italian restaurant of Ocho Rios and is one of the most fun restaurants along the north coast of Jamaica. Its soul and artistic flair come from Eva Myers, convivial former owner of some of the most legendary bars of Montego Bay, who established her culinary headquarters in this white, gingerbread Jamaican house in 1990. An outdoor terrace adds additional seating and enhanced views. More than half the menu is devoted to pastas, and the selection includes almost every variety known in northern and southern Italy. Other dishes include heartier fare, such as grilled steaks. Italian (or other) wines by the bottle might accompany your menu choice. The restaurant lies a few steps from Enchanted Gardens, an all-inclusive resort.

INEXPENSIVE

Little Pub Restaurant

59 Main St. ☎ **809/974-2324.** Reservations recommended. Appetizers $2.50–$7.50; main courses $13–$28. AE, MC, V. Breakfast daily 7–11am; lunch daily 11am–4:30pm; dinner daily 6pm–midnight. JAMAICAN/INTERNATIONAL.

Located in a redbrick courtyard with a fountain and a waterfall surrounded by souvenir shops in the center of town, this indoor-outdoor pub's centerpiece is a restaurant in the dinner-theater style. Top local and international artists are featured, as are Jamaican musical plays. No one will mind if you just enjoy a drink while seated on one of the pub's barrel chairs. But if you want dinner, proceed to one of the linen-covered tables capped with cut flowers and candlelight. Menu items include barbecued chicken, stewed snapper, grilled kingfish, and lobster specialties.

ⓢ Parkway Restaurant

60 DaCosta Dr. ☎ **809/974-2667.** Reservations not required. Appetizers $1.75–$5; main courses $8–$20. AE, MC, V. Daily 8am–11pm. JAMAICAN.

This popular establishment in the commercial center of town couldn't have a plainer facade. Inside, it continues to be unpretentious, but many local families and members of the business community know that they can get some of the best-tasting and least expensive local dishes here of any place in Ocho Rios. On clean napery, amid a serviceable decor, hungry diners are fed Jamaican-style chicken, curried goat, and filet of red snapper, and to top it off, banana-cream pie. Lobster and fresh fish are usually featured.

WHAT TO SEE & DO

BEACHES

Most visitors head for the beach. The most visited is the often-overcrowded **Mallards Beach** shared by hotel guests and cruise-ship passengers, but locals may steer you to **Turtle Beach** in the south.

ATTRACTIONS

A pleasant drive south of Ocho Rios along the A3 will take you inland through **Fern Gully.** This was originally a riverbed, but now the main road winds up some 700 feet among a profusion of wild ferns, a tall rain forest, hardwood trees, and lianas. For the botanist, there are hundreds of varieties of ferns, and for the less plant-minded, roadside stands offer fruit and vegetables, carved-wood souvenirs, and basketwork. The road runs for about 4 miles, and then at the top of the hill you come to a right-hand turn onto a narrow road leading to Golden Grove.

Head west when you see the signs pointing to Lydford. You'll pass the remains of **Edinburgh Castle,** built in 1763, the lair of one of Jamaica's most infamous murderers, a Scot named Lewis Hutchinson, who used to shoot passersby and toss their bodies into a deep pit built for the purpose. The authorities got wind of his activities, and although he tried to escape by canoe, he was captured by the navy under the command of Admiral Rodney and was hanged. Rather proud of his achievements (evidence of at least 43 murders was found), he left £100 and instructions for a memorial to be built. It never was, but the castle ruins remain.

Continue north on the A1 to **St. Ann's Bay,** the site of the first Spanish settlement on the island, where you can see the **Statue of Christopher Columbus,** cast in his hometown of Genoa, erected near St. Ann's Hospital on the west side of town, close to the coast road. There are a number of Georgian buildings in the town. The **Court House** near the parish church, built in 1866, is most interesting.

Brimmer Hall Estate

Port Maria, St. Mary's. ☎ **809/974-2244.** Tours, $15. Tours given Thurs at 2pm.

Some 21 miles east from Ocho Rios, in the hills 2 miles from Port Maria, this 1817 estate is an ideal place to spend a day. You can relax beside the pool and sample a wide variety of brews and concoctions, including an interesting one called "Wow!" The Plantation Tour Eating House offers typical Jamaican dishes for lunch, and there is a souvenir shop with a good selection of ceramics, art, straw goods, wood carvings, rums, liqueurs, and cigars. All this is on a working plantation where you are driven around in a tractor-drawn jitney to see the tropical fruit trees and coffee plants, and learn from the knowledgeable guides about the various processes necessary to produce the fine fruits of the island.

Columbus Park Museum

Queens Hwy., Discovery Bay. ☎ **809/973-2135.** Admission free. Open daily 9am–5pm.

This is a large, open area between the main coast road and the sea at Discovery Bay. You just pull off the road and then walk among the fantastic collection of exhibits, which range from a canoe made of a solid piece of cottonwood in the same way the Arawaks did it more than five centuries ago, to a stone cross, a monument originally placed on the Barrett estate at Retreat by Edward Barrett, brother of poet Elizabeth Barrett Browning. You'll see a tally, used to count bananas carried on men's heads from plantation to ship, as well as a planter's strongbox with a weighted lead base to prevent its theft. Also among the exhibits are 18th-century cannons, a Spanish water cooler and calcifier, a fish pot made from bamboo, a corn husker, and a water wheel of the type used on the sugar estates in the mid-19th century for all motive power. You can follow the history of sugar since its introduction in 1495 by Columbus, who brought canes from Gomera in the Canary Islands, and see how Khus Khus, a Jamaican perfume, is made from the roots of a plant, and how black dye is extracted from logwood. Pimento trees, from which allspice is produced, dominate the park. A large mural by Eugene S. Hyde depicts the first landing of Columbus at Puerto Bueno (Discovery Bay) on May 4, 1494. The museum is well worth a visit to learn of the varied cultures that have influenced Jamaica's development.

Coyaba River Garden and Museum

Shaw Park. ☎ **809/974-6235.** Admission $4.50 for those age 13 and up, $2.25 children 6–12, free for children 5 and under. Open daily 8am–5pm. Take the Fern Gully/Kingston Road, turn left at St. John's Anglican Church, and follow the signs to Coyaba, just half a mile farther away.

A mile from the center of Ocho Rios, at an elevation of 420 feet, this park and museum were built on the grounds of the former Shaw Park plantation. The name *coyaba* comes from the Arawak name for paradise. Coyaba is a Spanish-style museum with a river and gardens filled with native flora, a cut-stone courtyard, fountains, an art gallery, and a crafts shop and bar. The museum boasts a collection of artifacts from the Arawak, Spanish, and English settlements in the area.

✪ Dunn's River Falls

On the A3. ☎ **809/974-2857.** Admission $5 adults, $2 children 2–12, free for children under 2. Open daily 9am–5pm (8am–5pm on cruise-ship-arrival days).

From St. Ann's Bay, follow the A3 east back to Ocho Rios and you'll pass Dunn's River Falls. There is plenty of parking space, and for a charge, you can relax on the beach or climb with a guide to the top of the 600-foot falls. You can splash in the waters at the bottom of the falls or drop into the cool pools higher up between the cascades of water. The beach restaurant provides snacks and drinks, and dressing rooms are available. If you're planning to climb the falls, wear old tennis shoes to protect your feet from the sharp rocks and to prevent slipping.

Firefly

Grants Pen, in St. Mary, 20 miles east of Ocho Rios above Oracabessa. ☎ **809/997-7201.** Admission $10. Open daily 9am–5pm.

Firefly was the home of Sir Noel Coward and his longtime companion, Graham Payn, who, as executor of Coward's estate, donated it to the Jamaica National Heritage Trust. The recently restored house is as it was on the day Sir Noel died in 1973, even to the clothes, including Hawaiian print shirts hanging in the closet in his austere bedroom with its heavy mahogany four-poster. The library contains a collection of his books, and the living room is warm and comfortable with big armchairs and two grand pianos where he composed several famous tunes. When the English Queen Mother was entertained here, the lobster mousse Coward was serving melted, so he opened a can of pea soup. Guests were housed in Blue Harbour, a villa nearer Port Maria where Sir Noel lived before building Firefly, and included Evelyn Waugh, Sir Winston Churchill, Errol Flynn and his wife (Patrice Wymore), Sir Laurence Olivier, Vivien Leigh, Claudette Colbert, Katharine Hepburn, and Mary Martin. Paintings by the noted playwright, actor, author, and composer adorn the walls. An open patio looks out over the pool and the sea, and across the lawn, on his plain, flat white marble grave is inscribed simply: "Sir Noel Coward, born December 16, 1899, died March 26, 1973."

Goldeneye

Oracabessa, 13 miles east of Ocho Rios. ☎ **809/974-5833.**

Noel Coward was a frequent guest of Ian Fleming at Goldeneye, made fashionable in the 1950s. It was here that the most famous secret agent in the world, 007, was born in 1952. Fleming built the house in 1946, and wrote each of the 13 original Bond books here. Through the large gates, with bronze pineapples on the top, came a host of international celebrities: Evelyn Waugh, Truman Capote, Graham Greene. The house was closed and dilapidated for some time after the writer's death, but its present owner, British music publisher Christopher Blackwell, has restored the property. Although Fleming kept the place "just back to the basics," Blackwell sought the help of a designer to revamp the interior. Fleming's original desk, where 007 was born, remains, however. Unless you're a guest of the tenant, you aren't allowed to visit as it is private property. However, all 007 fans in this part of the world like to go by, hoping for a look. Look for the Esso sign and take the narrow lane nearby going to the sea.

Harmony Hall

Tower Isle, on the A3, 4 miles east of Ocho Rios. ☎ **809/974-2870.** Admission free. Gallery open daily 10am–6pm.

Harmony Hall was built near the end of the 19th century as another one of the Great Houses of Jamaica, and was connected with a pimento estate. Today, after a restoration, it's a center for a gallery selling paintings and other works by Jamaican artists. High-quality arts and crafts are also sold—not the usual junky assortment you might find at the beach. Watson's shopping shuttle stops at various hotels and makes a lunchtime trip Monday through Saturday.

Prospect Plantation

On the A3, St. Ann. ☎ **809/974-2058.** Tours, $12 adults, free for children under 12; one-hour horseback ride, $20. Tours given Mon–Sat at 10:30am, 2pm, and 3:30pm; Sun at 11am, 1:30pm, and 3pm.

Three miles east of Ocho Rios along the A3, adjoining the 18-hole Prospect Mini Golf Course, is a working plantation. A visit to this property combines the opportunity to take an educational, relaxing, and enjoyable tour. On your leisurely ride by covered jitney through the scenic beauty of Prospect, you'll readily see why this section of Jamaica is called "the garden parish of the island." You can view the many trees planted by such visitors as Sir Winston Churchill, Dr. Henry Kissinger, Charlie Chaplin, Pierre Trudeau, Sir Noel Coward, and many others. You will learn about and see growing pimento (allspice), bananas, cassava, sugarcane, coffee, cocoa, coconut, pineapple, and the famous leucaena "Tree of Life." You'll see Jamaica's first hydroelectric plant and sample some of the exotic fruit and drinks.

Horseback riding is available on three scenic trails at Prospect. The rides vary from 1 to $2^1/_4$ hours. Advance booking of 1 hour is necessary to reserve horses.

SHOPPING
SHOPPING CENTERS

There are seven main shopping plazas. The originals are Ocean Village, Pineapple Place, and Coconut Grove. Newer ones include the New Ocho Rios Plaza, in the center of town, with some 60 shops. Island Plaza is another major shopping complex, as is the Mutual Security Plaza with some 30 shops. Opposite the New Ocho Rios Plaza is the Taj Mahal, with 26 duty-free stores.

OCEAN VILLAGE SHOPPING CENTRE   Here are numerous boutiques, food stores, a bank, sundries purveyors, travel agencies, service facilities—what have you. The **Ocho Rios Pharmacy** (☎ 809/974-2398) sells most proprietary brands, perfumes, plasters for sore heels, and suntan lotions, among its many wares. You can call the shopping center at 974-2683.

PINEAPPLE PLACE SHOPPING CENTRE   Just east of Ocho Rios, this is a collection of shops in cedar-shingle-roofed cottages set amid tropical flowers.

OCHO RIOS CRAFT PARK   This is a complex of some 150 stalls through which to browse. An eager seller will weave you a hat or a basket while you wait, or you can buy from the mixture of ready-made hats, hampers, handbags, placemats, and lampshades. Other stands stock hand-embroidered goods and will make up small items while you wait. Wood carvers work on bowls, ashtrays, wooden-head carvings, and statues chipped from lignum vitae, and make cups from local bamboo. Even if you don't want to buy, this lively and colorful park is worth a visit.

COCONUT GROVE SHOPPING PLAZA   This collection of low-lying shops is linked by walkways and shrubs. The merchandise consists mainly of local craft items. Many of your fellow shoppers may be cruise-ship passengers.

ISLAND PLAZA   This shopping complex is right in the heart of Ocho Rios. Some of the best Jamaican art is to be found here, all paintings by local artists. You can also purchase local handmade crafts (be prepared to do some haggling over price and quality), carvings, ceramics, even kitchenware, and most definitely the inevitable T-shirts.

SPECIALTY SHOPS

In general, the shopping is better at Montego Bay if you're going there. If not, wander the Ocho Rios crafts markets, although much of the merchandise has the same monotony. Among the few places that deserve special mention are the following: **Casa de Oro,** Pineapple Place (☎ **809/974-2577**), which specializes in selling duty-free watches, fine jewelry, and the classic perfumes; **Caribbean Camera Centre,** Pineapple Place (☎ **809/974-2421**), the best place for cameras and photographic supplies; **Ruth Clarage,** Pineapple Place (☎ **809/974-2658**), offering women's clothing in original prints and designs, often florid, with costume jewelry and accessories as well; and, finally, **Swiss Stores,** in the Ocean Village Shopping Centre (☎ **809/974-2519**), selling all the big names in Swiss watches, including Juvenia, Tissot, Omega, Rolex, Patek Philippe, and Piaget—and here the Rolex watches are real, not those fakes touted by hustlers on the streets of Ocho Rios. The Swiss outlet also sells duty-free handcrafted jewelry, some of dubious taste but some really exquisite jewelry as well.

OCHO RICOS AFTER DARK

Boonoonoonoos is Jamaican for "very nice" or "super," and also stands for a "happening" in Jamaica.

Hotels often provide live entertainment to which nonresidents are invited. Ask at your hotel desk where "the action" is on any given night. Otherwise, you may want to look in on **Silks Nightclub,** in the Shaw Park Hotel, Cutlass Bay (☎ **809/974-2552**), which has a smallish dance floor and a sometimes-animated crowd of drinkers and dancers. Nonresidents of this well-known hotel can enter for J$70 ($2.20) each. The club is open Wednesday through Monday from 10pm until 3am.

4 Runaway Bay

Once this resort was a mere western satellite of Ocho Rios. However, with the opening of some large resort hotels, plus a colony of smaller hostelries, Runaway Bay is now a destination in its own right.

This part of Jamaica's north coast has several distinctions: It was the first part of the island seen by Columbus, the site of the first Spanish settlement on the island, and the point of departure of the last Spaniards leaving Jamaica following their defeat by the British. Columbus landed at Discovery Bay on his second voyage of exploration in 1494, and in 1509 Spaniards established a settlement called Sevilla Nueva (New Seville) near what is now St. Ann's Bay, about 10 miles east of the present Runaway Bay village. Sevilla Nueva was later abandoned when the inhabitants moved to the southern part of the island.

WHERE TO STAY & DINE

EXPENSIVE

FDR (Franklyn D. Resort)
Main St. (P.O. Box 201), Runaway Bay, St. Ann, Jamaica, W.I. ☎ **809/973-4591,** or 800/654-1FDR in the U.S. Fax 809/973-3071. 76 suites. A/C TV TEL. Winter, $259–$273 per person. Off-season, $229–$236 per person. Children under 16 stay free in parents' suite. (Rates include all meals, bar drinks, beer, cigarettes, sports, and entertainment.) AE, DC, MC, V. Free parking.

An all-inclusive resort, FDR is geared to families with children and is dedicated to including all meals and activities in a net price. The resort, named after its Jamaican-born owner and developer (Franklyn David Rance), is on 6 acres of flat, sandy land dotted with flowering shrubs and trees, on the main seaside highway (the A1), 17 miles west of Ocho Rios. Each of the Mediterranean-inspired buildings has a terra-cotta roof, a loggia or outdoor terrace, Spanish marble in the bathroom, and a personal attendant whose cooking, cleaning, child-caring, and miscellaneous services come with each of the units. Although neither its narrow beach nor its modest swimming pools are the most desirable on the island, many visitors appreciate the spacious units and the wholehearted concern of the resort for the amusement of its resident children. Each unit contains a kitchenette where, if you want, meals can be prepared by the personal attendant.

Dining/Entertainment: Two restaurants on the property serve free wine with lunch and dinner, a piano bar provides music every evening, and a handful of bars keeps the drinks flowing whenever you're ready for them. Live music is provided nightly.

Services: A "Girl Friday" babysits for free every day between 8am and 5pm, after which she can be engaged privately for $3 an hour. There's a children's supervisor in attendance at "Kiddies' Centre" (where a computer center, a kiddies' disco, and even kiddies' dinners are regular features). Adults appreciate the scuba lessons, picnics, photography lessons, arts and crafts lessons, and donkey rides.

Facilities: Water sports, illuminated tennis courts, satellite TV room, disco, exercise gym, free use of bicycles for getting around the neighborhood; free tours to Dunn's River Falls and Ocho Rios shopping are included.

Jamaica, Jamaica

P.O. Box 58, Runaway Bay, Jamaica, W.I. ☎ **809/973-2436**, or 800/859-7873 in the U.S. Fax 809/973-2352. 234 rms, 4 suites. A/C TEL. Winter, $675–$725 per person. Off-season, $535–$625 per person. Children under 16 not accepted. (Rates all-inclusive for three nights) AE, DC, MC, V. Free parking.

Six miles west of Ocho Rios, this stylish incarnation of a resort that has known several identities since it was built operates on a price plan including three meals a day, all free drinks, and a galaxy of other benefits. It's long, low-lying clubhouse is approached by passing through a park filled with tropical trees and shrubbery. Inside the lobby is the best re-creation of the South Seas on Jamaica, with hanging wicker chairs and totemic columns. Each of the rooms has a view of a well-landscaped courtyard, with a private balcony overlooking the sea. Near the wide sandy beach is a mini-jungle with dangling hammocks, a swimming pool is nearby, and there's even a nearby nude beach.

Dining/Entertainment: Live music emanates from the stylish Terrace every evening at 7pm, and a nightclub offers live shows six nights a week at 10pm. You dine either in the beachside restaurant or in the more formal Italian restaurant, Martino's.

Services: Reggae exercise classes held twice daily.

Facilities: Gym filled with Nautilus equipment, swimming pool, sports activities center (featuring scuba diving, windsurfing, and a golf school), 18-hole championship golf course.

MODERATE

Ⓢ Eaton Hall Beach Hotel

P.O. Box 112, Runaway Bay, St. Ann, Jamaica, W.I. ☎ **809/973-3503**, or 800/972-2158 in the U.S. Fax 809/973-2432. 52 rms. A/C. Winter, $195–$215 single; $214–$254 double. Off-season, $130–$165 single; $180–$196 double. Children under 12 not accepted. (Rates include three meals a day, taxes, tips, and use of facilities and services mentioned below.) AE, DC, MC, V. Free parking.

An original plantation Great House has been restored and turned into this small hotel of charm and character, two blocks east of the town's main square. The brick foundation walls are probably those of an English fort dating from the 17th or 18th century. A subterranean passage, now bricked up, leads from the living room to the coral cliffs behind the house. The property is a successful coordination of old blended with new. Some of the bedrooms of the Great House open onto an arched portico, and four units in the main house front the sea. On each side of the hall are bedroom wings with ocean views furnished with tropical designs and older mahogany pieces. Carved mahogany four-poster beds are found in some of the rooms. Many of the accommodations lie in a handful of modern villas set on a low and rocky ledge about 6 feet above the sea. Some rooms have phones.

Dining/Entertainment: Entertainment, weekly floor shows, and a Jamaican buffet two or three times a week are also part of the all-inclusive plan. There is one restaurant that offers American, Jamaican, and continental foods, and there are two bars.

Services: Laundry.

Facilities: Sunfish sailing, snorkeling equipment, scuba diving.

INEXPENSIVE

⑤ Runaway H.E.A.R.T. Country Club

P.O. Box 98, Runaway Bay, St. Ann, Jamaica, W.I. ☎ **809/973-2671,** or 800/526-2422 in the U.S. Fax 809/973-2693. 20 rms. A/C TV TEL. Winter, $55 single; $100 double. Off-season, $50 single; $80 double. AE, MC, V. Five-day/four-night MAP package $489 per person. AE, MC, V. Free parking.

Called "the best-kept secret in Jamaica," this place is located on the main road, and it practically wins hands down as the bargain of the north coast. One of Jamaica's few training and service institutions, the club and its adjacent academy are operated by the government to provide a high level of training for young Jamaicans interested in the hotel trade. The hotel is very well run with a professional staff intermixed with trainees who are helpful and eager to please, and offer perhaps the finest service of any hotel in the area.

The rooms are bright and airy and have either a king-size bed, a double bed, or twin beds. Accommodations open onto private balconies with views of well-manicured tropical gardens or vistas of the bay and golf course.

Dining/Entertainment: Guests enjoy having a drink in the piano bar (ever had a cucumber daiquiri?) before heading for the dining room, the Cardiff Hall Restaurant, which has a combination of Jamaican and continental dishes. Nonresidents can also enjoy dinner, served nightly from 7 to 10pm; a well-prepared meal costs around $25. The academy has won awards for some of its dishes, including "go-go banana chicken" and curried codfish.

Services: Laundry.

Facilities: Swimming pool, golf course.

5 Falmouth

This port town lies on the north coast about 23 miles east of Montego Bay. Trelawny (see "Where to Stay," below) put it on the tourist map. The town in itself is interesting but ramshackle. There is talk about fixing it up for visitors, but no one has done it yet. If you leave your car at Water Square, you can explore the town in about an hour or so. The present Courthouse was reconstructed from the early 19th-century building, and fisherfolk still congregate on Seaboard Street. You'll pass the Customs Office and a parish church dating from the closing years of the 18th century. Later, you can go on a shopping expedition outside town to Caribatik (see "Shopping," below).

WHERE TO STAY

Trelawny Beach Hotel

Rte. A1 (P.O. Box 54), Falmouth, Jamaica, W.I. ☎ **809/954-2450,** or 800/336-1435 in the U.S. Fax 809/954-2173. 317 rms, 33 bungalows. TEL. Winter, $229 single; $338 double. Off-season, $189 single; $258 double. (Rates all-inclusive) AE, DC, MC, V. Free parking.

This self-contained resort on 8 acres is about a 45-minute drive (30 miles) east of Sangster International Airport in Montego Bay, along the A1. Locally made materials, in keeping with the policy of the "New Jamaica," were used when possible, including wicker furniture along with floral fabrics. The 1,400-foot beach area was achieved with the leasing of 1,100 feet of adjacent frontage. Bohíos (open-sided huts) were built around the pool area, and many trees and flowers planted.'

Accommodations are in rooms with private balconies and an ocean or mountain view. Bungalows by the pool area are also available at additional charges (these are more suited to families). Rates include the services and facilities listed below.

Dining/Entertainment: There is live entertainment nightly, and parties are often held for the guests. A Jamaican Night poolside barbecue is held on Tuesday and a Beach Party Spectacular on Thursday with food, bonfires, music, and dancing. A la carte dinners are served in the Jamaican Room and buffets on the Palm Terrace the rest of the week.

Services: Shuttle-bus service to and from Montego Bay; lessons in scuba diving, snorkeling, Sunfish sailing, windsurfing, waterskiing, and reggae dancing.

Facilities: Four lit Laykold tennis courts, swimming pool, children's activity center that offers supervised activities daily, water sports.

WHERE TO DINE

⑤ Glistening Waters Inn and Marina
Rock Falmouth, between Falmouth and the Trelawny Beach Hotel. ☎ **809/954-3229.** Reservations not required. Main courses J$155–J$450 ($5–$14.40). MC, V. Lunch daily 11am–2:30pm; dinner daily 6–9:30pm. SEAFOOD.

Residents of Montego Bay often make the 22-mile drive out here, along the A1, just to sample an ambience of the almost-forgotten Jamaica of another era. The well-recommended restaurant with a veranda overlooking the lagoon is housed in what was originally a private clubhouse of the aristocrats of nearby Trelawny. The furniture here may remind you of a stage set for *Night of the Iguana.* Menu items may include local fish dishes, such as snapper or kingfish, served with bammy (a form of cassava bread). Other specialties are three different lobster dishes, three different preparations of shrimp, three different conch viands, fried rice, and pork served as chops or in a stew. The waters of the lagoon contain a rare form of phosphorescent microbes which, when the waters are agitated, glow in the dark. Ask about "Evening Booze cruises," which cost $3 per person for diners. Departures are nightly at about 6:30pm.

SHOPPING

Two miles east of Falmouth on the north-coast road is **Caribatik Island Fabrics,** at Rock Wharf on the Luminous Lagoon (☎ 809/954-3314). You'll recognize the place easily, as it has a huge sign painted across the building's side. This is the private living and work domain of Keith Chandler, who established the place with his late wife, Muriel, in 1970. Today the batiks created by Muriel Chandler before her death in 1990 are viewed as stylish and sensual garments by the chic boutiques in the States.

In the shop is a full range of fabrics, scarves, garments, and wall hangings, some patterned after such themes as Jamaica's "Doctor Bird" and various endangered animal species of the world. Muriel's Gallery continues to sell a selection of her original batik paintings. Either Keith or a member of the staff will be glad to describe the intricate process of batiking during their open hours: 9am to 4pm Tuesday through Saturday. They're closed in September.

6 Montego Bay

Montego Bay first attracted tourists in the 1940s when Doctor's Cave Beach was popular with the wealthy who bathed in the warm water fed by mineral springs. The town, now Jamaica's second-largest city, is on the northwestern coast of the island. In spite of the large influx of visitors, it still retains its own identity with a thriving business and commercial center, and it functions as the market town for most of western Jamaica. It has cruise-ship piers and a growing industrial center at the free port. The history of Mo Bay, as the islanders call it, goes back to 1494 when it was discovered as an Arawak settlement.

As Montego Bay has its own airport, the Donald Sangster International Airport, those who vacation here have little need to visit Kingston, the island's capital, unless they are seeking its cultural pleasures. Otherwise, you have everything in Mo Bay, the most cosmopolitan of Jamaica's resorts.

WHERE TO STAY
VERY EXPENSIVE

✪ Half Moon Golf, Tennis & Beach Club

Rose Hall (P.O. Box 80), Montego Bay, Jamaica, W.I. ☎ **809/953-2211,** or 800/626-0592 in the U.S. Fax 809/953-2731. 50 rms, 170 suites and villas. A/C TEL. Winter, $250–$340 single; $300–$480 double; $530–$900 suite or villa. Off-season, $145–$185 single; $190–$270 double; $300–$500 suite or villa. MAP $65 per person extra. AE, DC, MC, V. Free parking.

Located about 8 miles east of Montego Bay's city center and some 6 miles from the international airport, the Half Moon Club is considered one of the 300 best hotels in the world. Attracting distinguished guests over the years, such as former President George Bush, the resort complex consists of spacious hotel rooms, suites, and private one- to three-bedroom villas scattered over 400 acres of fertile land-scapes carefully arranged to provide maximum privacy. Each accommodation is comfortably furnished in an English colonial/Caribbean motif, including some mahogany four-poster beds, and many of the private villas have private swimming pools.

Dining/Entertainment: The Sugar Mill restaurant is set beside a working water wheel from a bygone sugar estate (see "Where to Dine," below). The Seagrape Terrace (named after the 80-year-old seagrape trees that push up from the pavement surrounding them) offers meals served outdoors. Il Giardino is an Italian restaurant serving a savory cuisine. Nightly entertainment includes music from a resident band, and nightly folklore and musical shows. You can also easily taxi into Montego Bay to sample the nightlife there.

Services: Room service (7am to midnight), laundry, babysitting, lessons in various water sports.

Facilities: Shopping arcade (with a pharmacy and boutiques), beauty salon, sauna and massage facilities, a mile-long beach, sailing, windsurfing, snorkeling, scuba diving, deep-sea fishing, two freshwater swimming pools, 13 tennis courts (7 floodlit at night), four lit squash courts, 18-hole Robert Trent Jones–designed golf course; horseback riding can be arranged.

✪ Round Hill Hotel and Villas

On the A1 (P.O. Box 64), Montego Bay, Jamaica, W.I. ☎ **809/952-5150**, or 800/972-2159 in the U.S. Fax 809/952-2505. 36 rms, 27 villas. A/C TEL. Winter, $250–$330 single; $300–$380 double; $470–$690 villa. Off-season, $140–$280 single; $190–$230 double; $260–$360 villa. Additional person $50 extra. MAP $65 per person extra in winter, $60 extra in summer. AE, DC, MC, V. Free parking.

Opened in 1954 and now a Caribbean legend, this is one of the most distinguished hotels in the West Indies. It stands on a lushly landscaped 98-acre peninsula 8 miles west of town, once part of Lord Monson's sugar plantation, which slopes gracefully down to a sheltered cove whose edges house the establishment's elegant reception area and social center. Guests have included the Kennedys, Cole Porter, and more recently Paul McCartney. Many evenings are defined as "informal," except Saturday, when a jacket and tie or black tie is required for men. Likewise, it's preferred that tennis players wear all white on the tennis courts.

Surrounded by landscaped tropical gardens, Round Hill accommodates some 200 guests, who enjoy its private beach, the views of Jamaica's north shore and the mountains, and the colonial elegance of the resort. Deluxe hotel accommodations are in a richly appointed seaside building known as the Pineapple House. Each opens onto views of the water and beach.

There are also privately owned villas dotted over the hillside, most available for private rental when the owners are not in residence. Each contains two, three, or four individual suites with a private living area and/or patio; 17 of the villas have their own swimming pools. Each villa is individually decorated, sometimes lavishly so, and includes the services of a uniformed maid, a cook, and a gardener.

Dining/Entertainment: At a little sandy bay is an intimate straw hut and an open terrace where guests congregate for informal luncheons. Jamaican and continental dishes are served on a candlelit terrace or in the Georgian colonial room overlooking the sea. The entertainment is varied—a bonfire beach picnic on Monday, a Jamaican night on Friday, and Round Hill's gala night every Saturday. Designer Ralph Lauren, who owns one of the Round Hill villas, decorated the cocktail bar with white sailcloth, gleaming brass, cane-backed mahogany furniture, and navy-blue-and-white–striped cotton upholstery.

Services: Room service (10am to 9:30pm), concierge, laundry, babysitting, valet service, in-villa preparations of meals.

Facilities: Swimming pool, top-quality tennis courts (lit at night), safety-deposit boxes, windsurfing, glass-bottomed-boat rides, scuba diving, horseback riding, sailing, paddleboats, rubber-sided inflatable boats, waterskiing. The hotel also has a full spa regime—private, low key, and personally geared to the client, with classes ranging from yoga to aerobics.

✪ Tryall Golf, Tennis, and Beach Club

P.O. Box 1206, St. James, Montego Bay, Jamaica, W.I. ☎ **809/956-5660**, or 800/238-5290 in the U.S. Fax 809/956-5673. 47 rms, 45 villas. A/C TEL. Winter, $245–$360 single; $295–$395 double; $480–$490 villa. Off-season, $150–$180 single; $185–$215 double; $235–$260 villa. Additional person $70 extra in winter, $55 extra off-season. MAP $66 per person extra. AE, DC, MC, V. Free parking.

Comprising more acreage than almost any hotel on Jamaica, this stylish and upscale resort sits on the site of a 2,200-acre former sugar plantation about 12 miles west of the heart of town. Known as one of the grandest resorts of Jamaica, the property lies along a 1½-mile seafront and is presided over by a 160-year-old Georgian-style Great House. The accommodations are either in modern wings or luxurious villas scattered throughout the surrounding acreage. The bedrooms are decorated in cool pastels with an English colonial decor. All contain ceiling fans, along with picture windows framing sea and mountain views. The resort's famous villas are set amid lush foliage and are designed for privacy. Each villa comes with a full-time staff, including a cook, maid, laundress, and gardener. All have private swimming pools.

Dining/Entertainment: The more formal of the resort's eating areas is in the Great House, where antiques evoke the grandeur and power of the plantation era. Less formal meals are served in a beachside café. A resident band plays everything from reggae to slow-dance music every night during dinner. Afternoon tea is served in the Great House every afternoon from 4 to 6pm.

Services: 24-hour room service, babysitting, laundry, massage; lessons given in golf, tennis, and water sports.

Facilities: Championship 18-hole par-71 golf course (site of many world-class golf competitions and the pride of this elegant property), seven Laykold tennis courts, 2-mile jogging trail, swimming pool with a swim-up bar, windsurfing, snorkeling, deep-sea fishing, paddleboats, glass-bottom boats.

EXPENSIVE

Seacastles

Rose Hall (P.O. Box 1), Montego Bay, St. James, Jamaica, W.I. ☎ **809/953-3250**, or 305/ 667-8860 for reservations. Fax 809/953-3062. 198 suites. A/C TEL. Winter, $138–$156 suite for one; $150–$234 suite for two; $291–$330 suite for four; $390 suite for six. Off-season, $90–$108 suite for one; $102–$186 suite for two; $246–$282 suite for four; $342 suite for six. Additional person $24 extra. MAP $42 per person extra. AE, DC, MC, V. Free parking.

One of the most architecturally dramatic hotels in the region was built 11 miles east of Montego Bay along the A1 on a grassy and isolated seafront acreage in 1991, on what had once been sugarcane fields. Its development included at least a 50% participation by the Jamaican government, which helped to market many of the units as privately owned condominiums. The result was an airy, widely separated compound of postmodern buildings vaguely influenced by English colonial models in Newport, Rhode Island. The resort contains only suites, each with kitchen or kitchenette, and each scattered among half a dozen imposing outbuildings ringed with greenery and capped with cedar-shingled roofs. Lawns slope down to the beach, past arbors, gazebos, bars, and water-sports kiosks.

Dining/Entertainment: The main restaurant, the Castles Restaurant, is a second-floor enclave overlooking the graceful symmetry of the swimming pool. Less formal meals and drinks are offered in the Clifftop Bar.

Services: Laundry, babysitting, a staff that organizes such activities as beer-drinking contests, volleyball on the beach, show times with staff and guests, Bingo, and diving contests.

Facilities: Freshwater pool, water-sports facilities, tour desk for island tours.

Wyndham Rose Hall Resort

Rose Hall (P.O. Box 999), Montego Bay, Jamaica, W.I. ☎ **809/953-2650**, or 800/822-4200 in the U.S. Fax 809/953-2617. 452 rms, 19 suites. A/C TEL. Winter, $165–$205 single or double; from $400 suite. Off-season, $115–$145 single or double; from $300 suite. MAP $48.40 per person extra. AE, DC, MC, V. Free parking.

Just 9 miles east of the Montego Bay airport, Wyndham Rose Hall is at the bottom of a rolling 30-acre site along the north-coast highway. On a former sugar plantation that once covered 7,000 acres, the hotel abuts the 200-year-old home of the legendary "White Witch of Rose Hall," now a historic site. Although it's popular as a convention site, the hotel also caters to a family market where children are considered an important part of the clientele. The seven-story H-shaped structure features numerous rooms with a sea view. Most units have two queen-size beds, and each accommodation has a private balcony.

Dining/Entertainment: There are three restaurants and a busy staff of social organizers. It's never more than a short walk to one of the many bars scattered around the hotel property.

Services: Room service (7am to 11pm), babysitting, laundry, massage.

Facilities: Two pools (one for wading, one for swimming), sandy beach, complimentary sailboats, top-rated golf course meandering over part of the hotel grounds, tennis complex (with six lit all-weather Laykold courts) headed by pros who offer a complete tennis program, air-conditioned fitness center.

MODERATE

ⓢ Doctor's Cave Beach Hotel

Gloucester Ave. (P.O. Box 94), Montego Bay, Jamaica, W.I. ☎ **809/952-4355.** Fax 809/952-5204. 80 rms, 10 suites. A/C TEL. Winter, $110–$120 single; $130–$140 double; $160 suite for two. Off-season, $80–$90 single; $105–$115 double; $140 suite for two. Additional person $30 extra. Breakfast from $10 extra. AE, DC, MC, V. Free parking.

Across the street from the well-known Doctor's Cave Beach in the bustle of the town's commercial zone, this hostelry has its own gardens, a swimming pool, a Jacuzzi, and a small gymnasium. The rooms are simply but comfortably furnished, and suites have kitchenettes. The establishment's two restaurants include the Coconut Grove, whose outdoor terrace is floodlit at night, and the less formal Greenhouse. In the Cascade Bar, where a waterfall tumbles down a stone wall, you can listen to a piano duo during cocktail hours.

Holiday Inn

Rose Hall (P.O. Box 480), Montego Bay, Jamaica, W.I. ☎ **809/953-2485,** or 800/HOLIDAY in the U.S. Fax 809/953-2840. 516 rms, 5 suites. A/C TV TEL. Winter, $150–$200 single or double; $280–$385 suite. Off-season, $106–$135 single or double; $224–$336 suite. Children under 19 stay free in parents' room; children under 12 eat free. MAP $39 per person extra. AE, DC, MC, V. Free parking.

This oceanside stone hotel is separated from the busy street by a screen of palm trees. Located 7 miles northeast of Sangster International Airport (and 8 miles east of Montego Bay's center), the hotel ensures its guests' privacy by having a guard at the entrance to screen those coming in. Numerous amenities include a free-form pool whose narrowest section is spanned by an arched footbridge.

There are four bars, three restaurants, the Rhythm Disco, and live entertainment by the pool nightly. Laundry, room service (from 7am to 10pm), and babysitting are available. Facilities include a swimming pool, a sandy beach, water sports (glass-bottom boats, sailboats, and scuba and skin diving), tennis courts, a children's playground, a fitness center, and a gaming room with both slot machines and electronic games.

ⓢ Reading Reef Club

The A1, on Bogue Lagoon, at the bottom of Long Hill (P.O. Box 225), Reading, Montego Bay, Jamaica, W.I. ☎ **809/952-5909,** or 800/223-6510 in the U.S. Fax 809/952-7217. 30 rms, 4 suites. A/C. Winter, $75 single; $125–$165 double; $250 two-bedroom suite; $325 three-bedroom suite. Off-season, $60 single; $120–$130 double; $200 two-bedroom suite; $275 three-bedroom suite. MAP $35 per person extra. AE, MC, V. Free parking.

This pocket of posh was created by an American, JoAnne Rowe. JoAnne, a former fashion designer whose hobby is cooking, has a sense of style and a flair for cuisine that are reflected in the running of this hotel. Located on $2^1/_2$ acres at the bottom of Long Hill Road, a 15-minute drive west of Montego Bay, the hotel opened in 1986 on a 350-foot sandy beach where people relax in comfort, unmolested by beach vendors. The complex of four buildings overlooks beautiful reefs praised for their aquatic life by Jacques Cousteau.

The accommodations, which include two- and three-bedroom suites, open onto a sea view. All have ceiling fans and a light Caribbean motif. The luxury rooms have minibars, and the three-bedroom suites offer kitchenettes. See "Where to Dine," below, for the restaurant recommendation. There is also a bar lounge and a beachside luncheon barbecue specializing in Jamaican (jerk) sausages, English sausages, and Tex-Mex food. Services include laundry, valet, drivers for island tours, and massages. Guests also enjoy the freshwater swimming pool, a boutique selling gift items and T-shirts, a private beach, and free water sports including snorkeling on the Reading Reef, windsurfing, and sailing in a 12-foot sailboat. Scuba diving costs extra.

Wexford Court Hotel

Gloucester Ave. (P.O. Box 108), Montego Bay, Jamaica, W.I. ☎ **809/952-2854,** or 800/237-3421 in the U.S. Fax 809/952-3637. 61 rms, 6 one-bedroom apartments. A/C TV TEL. Winter, $110–$115 single; $120–$125 double; $130 apartment. Off-season, $80–$85 single; $90–$95 double; $100 apartment. MAP $30 per person extra. AE, DC, MC, V. Free parking.

On the main road about 10 minutes from downtown Mo Bay and close to Doctor's Cave Beach, this hotel has a pleasant pool and a patio where calypso is enjoyed in season. The apartments have living/dining areas and kitchenettes, so you can cook for yourself. All rooms have patios shaded by gables and Swiss chalet–style roofs. The Wexford Grill includes a good selection of Jamaican dishes, such as chicken deep-fried with honey. Guests can enjoy drinks in a bar nearby. The hotel is owned and operated by Godfrey G. Dyer, who has led an interesting life—he has been a policeman, a detective, and a taxi business entrepreneur.

Winged Victory Hotel

5 Queen's Dr., Montego Bay, Jamaica, W.I. ☎ **809/952-3892.** Fax 809/952-5986. 16 rms, 8 suites. A/C. Winter, $90–$110 single or double; $175–$225 suite. Off-season, $70–$90 single or double; $110–$150 suite. MAP $35 per person extra. AE, MC, V. Free parking.

On the hillside road in Montego Bay, in the Miranda Hill District, this tall and modern hotel delays revealing its true beauty until you pass through its comfortable public rooms into a Mediterranean-style courtyard in back. There, urn-shaped balustrades enclose a terraced garden, a pool, and a veranda looking over the faraway crescent of Montego Bay. The veranda's best feature is the Calabash Restaurant. The dignified owner, Roma Chin Sue, added hotel rooms to her already well-known restaurant in 1985. All but five have a private balcony or veranda, along with an attractively eclectic decor that is part Chinese, part colonial, and part Iberian.

INEXPENSIVE

⑤ Coral Cliff Hotel

165 Gloucester Ave. (P.O. Box 253), Montego Bay, Jamaica, W.I. ☎ **809/952-4130.** Fax 809/952-6532. 32 rms. A/C TEL. Winter, $57–$64 single; $59–$66 double; $65–$67 triple. Off-season, $49–$60 single; $53–$64 double; $62–$68 triple. Breakfast $5–$10 extra. MC, V. Free parking.

Montego Bay

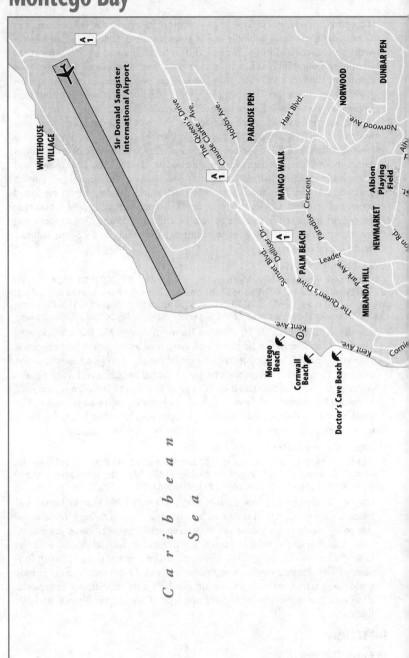

A1
Sir Donald Sangster International Airport
WHITEHOUSE VILLAGE
The Queen's Drive
Claude Clarke Ave.
Hobbs Ave.
PARADISE PEN
A1
MANGO WALK
Hart Blvd.
NORWOOD
DUNBAR PEN
Norwood Ave.
Paradise Crescent
Albion
Albion Playing Field
NEWMARKET
A1
Sunset Blvd.
Delisser D.
PALM BEACH
Leader
Park Ave.
MIRANDA HILL
The Queen's Drive
Kent Ave.
Montego Beach
Cornwall Beach
Doctor's Cave Beach
Kent Ave.
Cornie

Caribbean Sea

9884

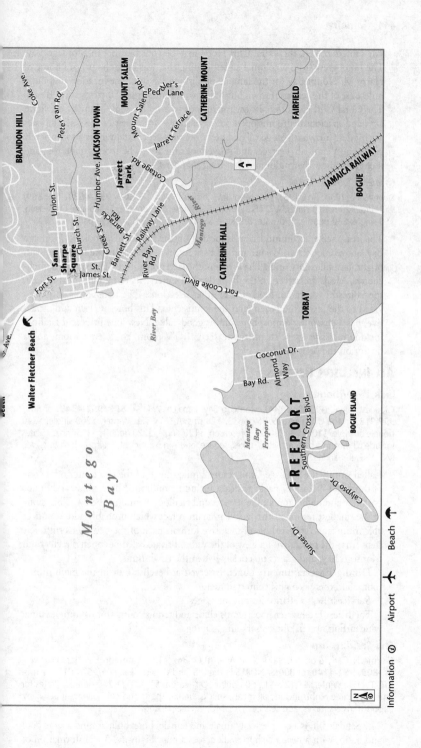

Montego Bay

Walter Fletcher Beach

BRANDON HILL

Coke Ave.

Peter Pan Rd.

Union St.

JACKSON TOWN
Humber Ave.

MOUNT SALEM

Mount Salem Rd.

Peddler's Lane

Jarrett
Park

Jarrett Terrace

CATHERINE MOUNT

FAIRFIELD

Fort St.

Sam
Sharpe
Square

Church St.

Creek St.

St. James St.

Barracks Rd.

Barnett St.

Railway Lane

Cottage Rd.

Montego River

River Bay Rd.

River Bay

Fort Cooke Blvd.

CATHERINE HALL

A
1

JAMAICA RAILWAY

BOGUE

TORBAY

Coconut Dr.

Bay Rd.

Almond Way

FREEPORT

Montego
Bay
Freeport

Southern Cross Blvd.

BOGUE ISLAND

Calypso Dr.

Sunset Dr.

Information ⊙   Airport ✈   Beach ⬆

N

For value received, the Coral Cliff Hotel may be your best bet in Montego Bay. The hotel grew from a colonial-style building that was once the private home of Harry M. Doubleday (of the famous publishing family). The location is about a mile west of the center of town but only two minutes from Doctor's Cave Beach. The Coral Cliff also offers its own luxurious swimming pool. Many of the light, airy, and spacious bedrooms open onto a balcony with a view of the sea. The rates are modest for what you get. The hotel's breeze-swept restaurant is appropriately called the Verandah Terrace, and it overlooks the bay. The food is good too, and includes lobster thermidor and pan-fried snapper.

🄢 Royal Court Hotel

Sewell Ave. (P.O. Box 195), Montego Bay, Jamaica, W.I. ☎ **809/952-4531.** Fax 809/952-4532. 20 rms, 3 suites. A/C TEL. Winter, $60 single; $80 double; $120 suite. Off-season, $50 single; $60 double; $90 suite. Breakfast $5–$7 extra. AE, MC, V. Free parking.

This reasonable accommodation is located on the hillside overlooking Montego Bay, above Gloucester Avenue and off Park Avenue. The rooms are furnished with bright, tasteful colors, and all have patios; the larger ones have fully equipped kitchenettes. Meals are served in the Pool Bar and Eatery. Its restaurant, Leaf of Life, specializes in vegetarian food among other selections. Free transportation is provided to the town, the beach, and the tennis club. This hotel is clean and attractive, has a charming atmosphere, and is good value. New amenities and facilities include massage, gym, steam room, Jacuzzi, TV room, conference room, and a doctor on the premises.

ALL-INCLUSIVE RESORTS

Jack Tar Village

Gloucester Ave. (P.O. Box 144), Montego Bay, Jamaica, W.I. ☎ **809/952-4340,** or 800/999-9182 in the U.S. Fax 809/952-6633. 128 rms. A/C TV TEL. Winter, $200 single; $340 double or triple. $100 child (2–12). Off-season, $120 single; $220 double; $315 triple. (Rates include all meals, drinks, activities, taxes, service, and—in winter only—airport transfers.) AE, MC, V. Free parking.

Called simply the "Village," this resort 2 miles north of the city center offers one of those "all-inclusive" package deals, including unlimited beer, wine, and liquor both day and night, and all the services and facilities mentioned below. This is one of the smallest resorts in the Jack Tar chain, a fact which probably adds a noticeable intimacy to its bustling all-inclusive format. Each of the bedrooms sits a few steps from the beach, with a view of the water. Private balconies open directly onto Montego Bay, and guests practically live in their swimsuits.

Dining/Entertainment: Lunch is served at beachside or in the main dining room, and there is nightly entertainment.

Services: Reggae dance lessons, massages.

Facilities: Freshwater pool, tennis clinic and tennis courts (for daytime), sauna, windsurfing, waterskiing, snorkeling, sailing.

The Sandals Inn

(Formerly Carlyle on the Bay), Kent Ave. (P.O. Box 412), Montego Bay, Jamaica, W.I. ☎ **809/952-4140,** or 800/SANDALS in the U.S. and Canada. Fax 809/952-6913. 52 rms. A/C TV TEL. Winter, $1,120–$1,265 double. Off-season, $1,080–$1,200 double. (Rates for four days/three nights include all meals, snacks, drinks, sports and entertainment activities, airport transfers, taxes, and services.) AE, MC, V. Free parking.

The Sandals Inn is a couples-only (male and female) hotel built around a large pool and patio, with a beach a short walk across a busy highway. A transformation of an older hotel, this is the least expensive, least glamorous, least accessorized, least spacious, and least attractive of the Sandals all-inclusive resorts scattered across Jamaica. The relative lack of plushness, however, is compensated by the nearby attractions of downtown Montego Bay, by the reasonable cost, and by the ability of any guest to enter with free day passes (including free transportation) either of the other two Sandals resorts of Montego Bay. Thirty-eight rooms open onto the swimming pool. All the accommodations contain king-size beds, hairdryers, and clock radios. The rates are all-inclusive, which means three meals a day, "anytime" snacks, unlimited drinks both day and night, even tips.

Dining/Entertainment: Food is served in bountiful portions in the resort's only dining room, and there is nightly entertainment.

Services: 24-hour room service, free round-trip airport transfers.

Facilities: Recreational and sports program, exercise room, saunas, Jacuzzi, tennis courts, swimming pool, room safes.

Sandals Montego Bay

Kent Ave. (P.O. Box 100), Montego Bay, Jamaica, W.I. ☎ **809/952-5510,** or 800/SANDALS in the U.S. and Canada. Fax 809/952-0816. 211 rms, 32 suites. A/C TV TEL. Winter, $1,320–$1,580 double; $1,700–$2,960 suite for two. Off-season, $1,320–$1,540 double; $1,670–$2,900 suite for two. (Rates for four days/three nights include all meals, drinks, activities, service, taxes, and airport transfers.) AE, MC, V. Free parking.

Located five minutes northeast of the airport, next to Whitehouse Village, this honeymoon haven may have the highest occupancy rate of all resorts in the Caribbean. The 19-acre site is a couples-only (male and female), all-inclusive resort, where everything—all meals, snacks, nightly entertainment (including those notorious toga parties), unlimited drinks night or day at one of four bars, tips, and round-trip airport transfers and baggage handling from the Montego Bay airport—is covered in the price.

In contrast to its somewhat more laid-back nearby counterpart (the Sandals Royal Caribbean; see below), this resort offers many different "fun in the sun" participatory activities for a clientele and staff who tend to be extroverted and gregarious; the Playmakers, as staff members are called, keep everybody amused and the joint jumping.

Accommodations are either in villas spread along 1,700 feet of white sandy beach or in the main house where all bedrooms face the sea and contain private balconies. All units are well furnished, with king-size beds, hairdryers, and radios. Reserve as far ahead as possible.

Dining/Entertainment: In addition to its main dining room, the resort concentrates on a number of specialty restaurants, including Tokyo Joe's, serving six-course Oriental meals; the Beach Grill; and the Oleander Deck, with "white glove service," featuring a Jamaican and Caribbean cuisine. Those who haven't tired themselves can head for the late-night disco, which often has rum and reggae nights.

Services: Free shuttle bus to the resort's twin, the Sandals Royal Caribbean, whose facilities are open without charge to residents here.

Facilities: Waterskiing, snorkeling, sailing, scuba diving, windsurfing, paddleboats and a glass-bottom boat, two freshwater pools, three Jacuzzis, tennis (available day or night), fully equipped fitness center.

Sandals Royal Caribbean

Mahoe Bay (P.O. Box 167), Montego Bay, Jamaica, W.I. ☎ **809/953-2231,** or 800/SANDALS in the U.S. and Canada. Fax 809/953-2788. 176 rms. 14 suites. A/C TV TEL.

Winter, $1,400–$1,600 per couple; $1,960 suite for two. Off-season, $1,340–$1,520 per couple; $1,860 suite for two. (Rates for four days/three nights include all meals, snacks, drinks, taxes, service, activities, and airport transfers.) AE, MC, V. Free parking.

Four miles east of town, this all-inclusive couples-only (male and female) resort is a reincarnation of what was once a prestigious Montego Bay hotel constructed in the Jamaican colonial style. The earlier hotel was once patronized by Queen Elizabeth and Prince Philip. The building lies on its own private beach (which, frankly, isn't as good as the one at the Sandals Montego Bay). Some of the British colonial atmosphere remains, as reflected by a formal tea in the afternoon, but there are modern touches as well, such as a private island reached by boat where clothing is optional.

The spacious rooms range from standard to superior to deluxe. Even higher in price are the deluxe beachfront accommodations or a junior suite. Amenities include hairdryers and radios.

Dining/Entertainment: Regency Suite and Deck is the Jamaican-inspired main dining room. Specialty restaurants include Bali Hai, an Indonesian restaurant built on the previously mentioned offshore island, and the Courtyard Grill, with such specialties as grilled sirloin, grilled snapper, and smoked marlin. There are four bars, plus food and drink available throughout the day. Live music by a local reggae band is presented.

Services: Laundry, massage, free shuttle bus to the resort's twin Sandals (whose facilities are available without charge to any resident). If you're not married to your companion when you arrive here, management can arrange (if you wish) for the wedding before you leave.

Facilities: Scuba diving, windsurfing, sailing, three tennis courts, swimming pool.

Sea Garden Beach Resort
Kent Ave. (P.O. Box 300), Montego Bay, Jamaica, W.I. ☎ **809/952-4780,** or 800/545-9001 in the U.S. Fax 809/952-7543. 97 rms. A/C. Winter, $690–$738 single; $483–$528 per person double. Off-season, $624–$666 single; $438–$456 per person double. (Rates for four days/three nights include all meals, snacks, drinks, activities, service, taxes, and airport transfers.) AE, MC, V. Free parking.

About 1¹/₂ miles east of Montego Bay, five minutes from the airport, this resort stands near some of the most popular public beaches. Designed in a British colonial style of neo-Victorian gingerbread, tall columns, and white lattices, it is airy, comfortable, and stylish. A dining room is under a high arched ceiling sheathed in mahogany whose view opens onto a flagstone-covered courtyard. The accommodations lie in sprawling motel-like units built around the pool in back. Each unit contains a private balcony or patio and simple mahogany furniture.

Dining/Entertainment: One main dining room is the venue for international meals. There are four bars, and a resident band plays six nights a week.

Services: Babysitting, laundry, free transportation to and from the airport.

Facilities: Two lit tennis courts, water sports (such as sailing, snorkeling, and windsurfing).

Vista Ambassador
Gloucester Ave. (P.O. Box 262), Montego Bay, Jamaica, W.I. ☎ **809/952-4703,** or 800/JAMAICA in the U.S. Fax 809/952-6810. 116 units. A/C TEL. $1,250–$1,530 single; $1,730–$1,930 double; from $2,060 villa suite for two. Children 1–12 (one per adult)

sharing parents' room free; children 13–17 are charged 50% of the adult rate. (Five-night package includes all meals, drinks, and airport transfers.) AE, MC, V. Free parking.

Set on landscaped grounds adjacent to the Montego Bay Craft Market, this hotel was once known as Lifestyles. But in January 1995 it transformed itself into the first all-inclusive family resort spa on Jamaica, set on 10 acres of tropical gardens. From the hotel, panoramic views of Montego Bay and the Caribbean are possible. Originally the hotel was created when an older hotel mushroomed with a series of modern wings and upgraded accommodations. Although it stands on a hillside with no beach of its own (it does have a swimming pool), it lies a five-minute walk from the white sands of Walter Fletcher Beach.

Contemporary tropical furnishings decorate the bedrooms, which can be adjusted to accommodate various family sizes, with standard and deluxe rooms as well as junior, one-bedroom, and two-bedroom villa suites. Each is equipped with a cable TV, safe, radio, clock, and ironing board. Each suite also has a private terrace with a Jacuzzi and wet bar.

Dining/Entertainment: The Island Verandah offers breakfast and casual dining, whereas the Blue Horizon is more elegant, featuring à la carte selections at dinner. Three conveniently located lounges are Dolphins, a pool and juice bar; Expressions, a karaoke bar; and Rhapsody, a piano lounge.

Facilities: Spa and gym (with sauna, steam room, Jacuzzi, wet rooms, and many spa services, including massages, facials, body scrubs, and herbal wraps), adult swimming pool and children's pool, tennis court, private beach club.

WHERE TO DINE

The resort area has some of the finest—and most expensive—dining on the island. But if you're watching your wallet, you'll find that food is often sold right on the street. For example, on Kent Avenue you might try jerk pork, a delicacy peculiar to Jamaica. Seasoned spareribs are also grilled over charcoal fires and sold with extra-hot sauce, and you'll want to order a Red Stripe beer to go with it. Cooked shrimp are also sold on the streets of Mo Bay; they don't look it, but they're very hotly spiced, so be warned. If you have an efficiency unit with a kitchenette, you can cook fresh lobster or the "catch of the day" bought from Mo Bay fishers.

EXPENSIVE

The Diplomat

9 Queen's Dr. ☎ **809/952-3353.** Reservations recommended. Appetizers $6.50–$8; main courses $21–$28; fixed–price seven-course Jamaican dinner $30. AE, DC, MC, V. Dinner only, Mon–Sat 6:30–9:15pm. Transportation: Private restaurant van. CONTINENTAL/JAMAICAN.

The Diplomat offers a delightful, informal, yet elegant evening. Hidden in a long white wall, gates lead to a sweeping driveway through clipped lawns, old trees, and colorful flower beds to a gracious house. Georg Kahl, your host, does not require ties and jackets for men, but shorts and T-shirts are frowned upon. Guests dine on the terrace overlooking a floodlit ornamental pool with fountains playing and trees silhouetted with lights leading down toward the sea. Dishes might be grilled rib lamb chops, boneless chicken sautéed or grilled, steaks, veal, filet of fish, or grilled Jamaican lobster in a butter sauce. Liqueurs are served at your table or in the drawing room. This is a good place from which to watch Mo Bay's famous sunsets, and arrangements can be made for a van to pick you up when you make your reservation.

Georgian House

2 Orange St. ☎ **809/952-0632.** Reservations recommended. Appetizers $4.50–$7.50; main courses $25–$33. AE, MC, V. Lunch Mon–Sat noon–3pm; dinner daily 6–11pm. Transportation: Private restaurant van. INTERNATIONAL.

The Georgian House brings a grand cuisine and an elegant setting to the heart of town. The 18th-century buildings were constructed by an English gentleman for his mistress, or so it is said. You can select either the upstairs room, which is more formal, or the garden terrace, with its fountains, statues, lanterns, and cut-stone exterior. The international cuisine is backed by a fine wine list. You might begin with a typically Jamaican appetizer such as ackee and bacon, then follow with pan-barbecued shrimp (you peel the shrimp yourself, but are given a scented fingerbowl). Baked spiny lobster is another specialty. Continental dishes, such as tournedos Rossini, are also prepared with flair. For dessert, try chocolate cake or crème caramel. When you make reservations, ask for the restaurant's round-trip transportation provided to and from most hotels.

Julia's

Julia's Estate, Bogue Hill. ☎ **809/952-1772.** Reservations required. Fixed-price dinner $33. AE, MC, V. Dinner only, daily 5:30–10:30pm. Transportation: Private restaurant van. ITALIAN.

The winding jungle road you take to reach this place is part of the before-dinner entertainment. After a jolting ride to a site high above the city and its bay, you pass through a walled-in park which long ago was the site of a private home built in 1840 for the duke of Sutherland. Today the building that is the land's focal point is a long, low-slung modern house whose fresh decor encompasses sweeping views. When you make your reservation, you can ask for a van to come to your hotel and pick you up. Raimondo and Julia Meglio, drawing on the cuisine of their native Italy, prepare chicken cacciatore, breaded milanese cutlet with tomato sauce and mozzarella cheese, filet of fresh fish with lime juice and butter, and 10 different kinds of pasta. Lobster, veal, and shrimp are regularly featured.

◌ Norma at the Wharfhouse

Reading Rd. ☎ **809/979-2745.** Reservations recommended. Directions: Drive 15 minutes west of the town center along the A1. Appetizers $4–$8; main courses $20–$30. MC, V. Lunch Thurs–Sun 11am–3pm; dinner Tues–Sun 6:30–10pm. NOUVELLE JAMAICAN.

Set in a coral-stone warehouse whose 2-foot-thick walls are bound together with molasses and lime, this is the finest restaurant in Montego Bay, a favorite of many of Jamaica's visiting celebrities. Originally built in 1780, it was restored by Millicent Rogers, heiress of the Standard Oil fortune, and now serves as the north-shore domain of Norma Shirley, one of Jamaica's foremost restaurateurs. You can request a table either on the large pier built on stilts over the coral reef (where a view of Montego Bay glitters in the distance) or in an elegantly formal early 19th-century dining room illuminated only with flickering candles. Before- or after-dinner drinks are served either in the restaurant or in an informal bar in a separate building, much favored by local clients, the Wharf Rat. Service in the restaurant is impeccable and the food is praised throughout the island.

Menu specialties include grilled deviled crab backs, smoked marlin with papaya sauce, chicken breast with callaloo, nuggets of lobster in a mild curry sauce, and chateaubriand larded with pâté in a peppercorn sauce. Dessert might be a rum-and-raisin cheesecake or a piña-colada mousse.

Richmond Hill Inn

45 Union St., Montego Bay, Jamaica, W.I. ☎ **809/952-3859.** Reservations recommended. Appetizers $2.50–$9; all main courses (with soup, salad, garlic bread, and dessert) $35. AE, MC, V. Lunch daily 11am–3pm; dinner daily 5–10pm.Take a taxi (a four-minute ride uphill, east of the town's main square). INTERNATIONAL/CONTINENTAL.

This plantation-style house was originally built in 1806 by members of the Dewar's whiskey distillery, who happened to be distantly related to Annie Palmer, the "White Witch of Rose Hall." Today it's run by an Austrian-derived mother-daughter team, who prepare well-flavored food for an appreciative clientele. Lunches are simple affairs featuring club sandwiches, salads, and if anyone asks for it, a lobster platter. Dinners are more substantial, and include a shrimp-and-lobster cocktail, an excellent house salad, different preparations of dolphin, breaded breast of chicken, surf and turf, wienerschnitzel, filet mignon, and a choice of dessert cakes. Usually, a pianist performs six days a week during the dinner hour. Arrangements can be made for you to be picked up at your hotel.

✪ Round Hill Dining Room

In the Round Hill Hotel and Villas, along the A1, 8 miles west of the center of Montego Bay. ☎ **809/952-5150.** Reservations required. Appetizers $3.50–$9; main courses $18–$39. AE, DC, MC, V. Lunch daily 12:30–2:30pm; dinner daily 7–9:30pm. INTERNATIONAL.

Considered the most prestigious dining room in Montego Bay, this is the culinary retreat of some of the western hemisphere's most discreetly renowned personalities. To reach the dining room, you'll have to pass through the resort's open-air reception area and proceed through a garden. Many visitors opt for a drink in the large and high-ceilinged bar area before moving on to their dinner, which is served either on a terrace perched above the surf or (during inclement weather) under an open-sided breezeway.

Although many dishes are classic, others more innovative reflect a taste of Jamaica. For example, shrimp and pasta Caribe is sautéed with chopped herbs, cream, and wine and rasta pasta is tossed with vegetables and basil. Caribbean veal is stuffed with spicy crab meat and seared, and the catch of the day is served jerked, broiled, or steamed with butter, herbs, and ginger. Herb-roasted Calypso chicken is slow roasted with aromatic herbs, chunks of tomatoes, and served with natural jus. Of course, you can also order more classic dishes, including rack of lamb and prime rib of beef along with a medallion of lobster sautéed with cream and served over fettuccine.

✪ Sugar Mill Restaurant

At the Half Moon Club, Half Moon Golf Course, Rose Hall, along the A1. ☎ **809/953-2228.** Reservations required. Appetizers $5–$11; main courses $15–$30. AE, MC, V. Lunch daily noon–2:30pm; dinner daily 7:30–10pm. INTERNATIONAL/CARIBBEAN.

After a drive through rolling landscape, you arrive at a stone ruin of what used to be a water wheel for a sugar plantation 8 miles east of Montego Bay. Guests dine on an open terrace by candlelight, with a view of a pond, the water wheel, and plenty of greenery. You can also dine inside.

Although he came from Switzerland, it was in the Caribbean that chef Hans Schenk blossomed as a culinary artist. He has entertained everybody from the British royal family to Farouk, the former king of Egypt. Lunch, beginning at $7, can be a relatively simple affair, perhaps an ackee burger with bacon, preceded by Mama's pumpkin soup and followed with a homemade rum-and-raisin ice cream. Smoked north-coast marlin is a specialty. The chef is said to make the most elegant Jamaican bouillabaisse on the island, or elegant "jerk" versions of pork, fish, or chicken. He also prepares today's catch. You top your meal with a cup of Blue Mountain coffee. A minivan will be sent to most hotels to pick you up.

Taste Jamaica Ltd.

In the Half Moon Plaza. ☎ **809/953-9688.** Reservations not required. Appetizers $3.50–$5.50; main courses $7.50–$18. AE, DC, MC, V. Breakfast daily 9am–noon; lunch daily 12:30–3pm; dinner daily 7:30–10pm. CARIBBEAN/INTERNATIONAL.

One of the island's newest restaurants is the focal point of an upscale shopping complex that opened in 1994. Set on the main coastal road about 8 miles east of Montego Bay, it caters to the culinary needs of about 45 upscale villas, administered by the Half Moon Club Hotel. It's usually filled with an appealing mix of local residents, sunseeking expatriates, and passing motorists. With a Caribbean-marketplace theme, the restaurant displays fresh fish, meats, tropical fruits, and freshly baked baguettes and pastries. Choices include fish escovitch, several kinds of pasta, chicken fricassée, curried conch, mango roast pork, and jerked fish or chicken. The most expensive main course allows you a selection of virtually everything available that day at "the market." There's also a deli section for sandwiches and a host of take-away dishes. Don't overlook this place as an option for midmorning coffee and pastries. An on-site pastry chef prepares a comforting array of French and Antillean pastries.

MODERATE

Ambrosia

Across from the Wyndham Rose Hall Resort, Rose Hall. ☎ **809/953-2650.** Reservations recommended. Appetizers $4–$10; main courses $13–$29. AE, MC, V. Dinner only, daily 6:30–10pm. MEDITERRANEAN.

This restaurant sits across from one of the largest hotels in Montego Bay, 9 miles east of the airport. Its cedar-shingled design and its trio of steeply pointed roofs give the impression that the place is a clubhouse for some neocolonial country club. Once you enter the courtyard, complete with a set of cannons, you find yourself in one of the loveliest restaurants in the area. You'll enjoy a sweeping view over the rolling lawns leading past the hotel and down to the sea, interrupted only by Doric columns. The menu includes pasta, seafood, and such Mediterranean favorites as shrimp scampi, herb-crusted rack of lamb, and lobster tail provençal.

Calabash Restaurant

In the Winged Victory Hotel, 5 Queen's Dr. ☎ **809/952-3892.** Reservations recommended. Appetizers $4–$7; main courses $10–$35. AE, MC, V. Lunch daily noon–2:30pm; dinner daily 6–10pm. INTERNATIONAL/JAMAICAN.

Perched on the hillside road in Montego Bay 500 feet above the distant sea, this well-established restaurant has amused and entertained Peter O'Toole, Francis Ford Coppola, and Roger Moore. It was originally built as a private villa by a doctor in the 1920s. More than 25 years ago owner Roma Chin Sue established its Mediterranean-style courtyard and its elegantly simple eagle's-nest patio as a well-managed restaurant. The seafood, Jamaican classics, and international favorites include curried goat, lobster dishes, the house specialty of mixed seafood en coquille (served with a cheese-and-brandy sauce), and a year-round version of a Jamaican Christmas cake.

Cascade Room

At the Pelican Restaurant, Gloucester Ave. ☎ **809/952-3171.** Reservations recommended. Appetizers $3–$5; main courses $12–$25. AE, DC, MC, V. Dinner only, daily 6–10pm. SEAFOOD/JAMAICAN.

With an intimate setting and relaxing atmosphere, the Cascade Room is one of Montego Bay's best seafood restaurants. It's a hideaway within a larger and less elegant restaurant known as the Pelican. Rushing waterfalls and cool tropical foliage blend with the natural cedar of the interior to make dining an enjoyable experience. Excellent service combines with the finest of seafood, such as lobster in the shell, shrimp Créole, filet of red snapper, and ackee and codfish. A salad bar is offered nightly. There is bar service and an adequate choice of wines.

Marguerite's By the Sea

Gloucester Ave. ☎ **809/952-4777.** Reservations required for the dining room. Beer garden, sandwiches, snacks, and platters $5–$10. Dining room, appetizers $4.50–$6; main courses $18–$30. AE, DC, MC, V. Dining room, dinner only daily 6–10:30pm. Beer garden, daily 11:30am–10:30pm. INTERNATIONAL/SEAFOOD.

This two-in-one restaurant and beer garden—called "Margueritaville"—across from Coral Cliff offers an international cuisine specializing in seafood. The beer garden is ideal for lunch, as it's on a breeze-swept terrace overlooking the sea. The menu includes sandwiches, salads, and hot food, such as pepper shrimp.

But at night the magic of the place comes alive next door in the dining room. The changing menu is often based on fresh produce, including a catch of the day—you can ask the chef to steam it in coconut milk if you prefer—with grilled New York sirloin steaks also available. You can finish with the house specialty, a coffee ice-box cake. This is one of the more popular Mo Bay restaurants.

Pier 1

Howard Cooke Blvd. ☎ **809/952-2452.** Reservations not required. Appetizers $3–$6; main courses $15–$25. AE, MC, V. Mon–Fri 9:30am–11pm, Sat 1pm–midnight, Sun 2pm–midnight. Transportation: Private minivan. SEAFOOD.

One of the major dining and entertainment hubs of Mo Bay was built on landfill in the bay. Fisherfolk bring fresh lobster to the restaurant, which the chef prepares in a number of ways, including Créole style or curried. You might begin with one of the typically Jamaican soups such as conch chowder or red pea (which is actually red bean). At lunch their hamburgers are said to be the juiciest in town, or you might find their quarter-decker steak sandwich with mushrooms equally tempting. The chef also prepares such famous island dishes as jerk pork or chicken, and Jamaican red snapper. Finish your meal with a slice of moist rum cake. You can drink or dine on the ground floor, open to the sea breezes, but most guests seem to prefer the more formal second floor. If you call, the staff can arrange to have you picked up in a minivan at most hotels (you're also returned).

✪ Reading Reef Club Restaurant

Bogue Lagoon, on the A1 at the bottom of Long Hill Rd. ☎ **809/952-5909.** Reservations required. Appetizers $3–$8; pastas $10–$11; main courses $14–$24. AE, DC, MC, V. Lunch daily noon–3pm; dinner daily 7:30–10pm. ITALIAN/CONTINENTAL/CARIBBEAN.

There are those, and perhaps Lady Sarah Churchill was among them, who claim that the food served in this second-floor terrace overlooking the bay is among the finest—perhaps *the* finest—in Montego Bay. The menu is the creative statement of JoAnne Rowe (see "Where to Stay," above), who has a passion for cooking and menu planning, a skill she perfected while entertaining prominent people in Montego Bay at her private dinner parties. Today her cook specializes in seafood, Italian, continental, and Caribbean recipes, such as perfectly prepared scampi, along with imaginative pasta dishes, such as spaghetti with fresh ginger, garlic, and parmesan. Her food is excellent, including a catch of the day, perhaps snapper, yellowtail, kingfish, or dolphin. She also imports quality New York sirloin steaks, but whenever possible likes to use local produce. Dinner might begin with Jamaican soup, such as pepperpot or pumpkin, and the restaurant is known for its lime pie. Lunches are low profile with a more limited menu. The restaurant is 4 miles west of the town center along the main seafront road (the A1), opening onto beautiful Bogue Lagoon.

Town House

16 Church St. ☎ **809/952-2660.** Reservations recommended. Appetizers $2.50–$6; main courses $14–$30. AE, DC, MC, V. Lunch Mon–Sat 11:30am–3:30pm; dinner daily 6–10:30pm. Transportation: Free limousine service. JAMAICAN/INTERNATIONAL.

Housed in a redbrick building from 1765, the Town House is a tranquil luncheon choice, offering sandwiches and salads, or more elaborate fare if your appetite demands it. At night it's floodlit, with outdoor dining on a veranda overlooking an 18th-century parish church. You can also dine in what used to be the cellars, where old ship lanterns give a warm light. The chef offers a wide selection of main courses, including the local favorite, red snapper en papillote (baked in a paper bag). I'm fond of the chef's large rack of barbecued spareribs, with the owners' special Tennessee sauce. Their pasta and steak dishes are also good. The restaurant often attracts the rich and famous, including Marlon Brando and Sean Connery. Free limousine service is offered to and from many hotels in the Montego Bay area.

INEXPENSIVE

⑤ The Native Restaurant

Queens Dr. ☎ **809/979-2769.** Reservations recommended. Appetizers $2–$5; main courses $9–$18. AE, MC, V. Tues–Sun 11:30am–10pm. JAMAICAN.

Open to the breezes, this casual restaurant with panoramic views serves some of the finest Jamaican dishes in the area. You can have a drink at the bamboo bar, with its extensive collection of international wines, and perhaps go for a swim in the restaurant pool between courses. Appetizers include jerk reggae chicken and ackee and saltfish, or perhaps smoked marlin. This can be followed by such old favorites as steamed fish, or fried or jerk chicken. One of the most expensive items is lobster with garlic butter, or you may prefer the curried shrimp. Perhaps the most tropical offering is "goat in a boat" (that is, a pineapple shell). Although fresh desserts are prepared daily, you may choose just a Jamaican Blue Mountain coffee.

The Pelican

At the Pelican, Gloucester Ave. ☎ **809/952-3171.** Reservations recommended. Appetizers $1.50–$3; main courses $8–$15. AE, DC, MC, V. Daily 7am–11pm. Transportation: Free hotel pickup in the restaurant's van. JAMAICAN.

A Montego Bay landmark, the Pelican has been serving good food at reasonable prices for more than a quarter of a century. It's ideal for families, as it keeps long hours, breakfast flowing into lunch and lunch into dinner. Many diners come here at lunch for one of the well-stuffed sandwiches, or they may order juicy burgers and barbecue chicken. You can also select from a wide array of Jamaican dishes, including stew peas and rice, curried goat, Caribbean fish, fried chicken, and curried lobster. A "meatless menu" including such dishes as a vegetable plate or vegetable chili is also featured. Sirloin and seafood are also available, and the soda fountain serves old-fashioned sundaes with real whipped cream, making it about the best "cool for kids" recommendation at the resort.

⑤ Pork Pit

27 Gloucester Ave. ☎ **809/952-1046.** Reservations not required. One pound of jerk pork J$260 ($8.30). No credit cards. Daily 11am–11:30pm. JAMAICAN.

The Pork Pit is the best place to go for the famous Jamaican jerk pork and jerk chicken, and the location is right in the heart of Montego Bay, near Walter Fletcher Beach. In fact, many beach buffs come over here for a big lunch. Prices are reasonable. Picnic tables encircle the building, and everything is open-air and informal. The menu also includes steamed roast fish. Half a pound of jerk meat, served with a baked yam or baked potato and a bottle of Red Stripe—which costs J$40 ($1.30) per bottle—is usually sufficient for a meal.

WHAT TO SEE & DO
VISITING WITH THE ANIMALS

Jamaica Safari Village

Outside Falmouth. ☎ **809/954-3065** for reservations. Walking tours, $6.50 adults, $3 children. Open daily 8:30am–5pm.

Continual conducted tours are offered through a petting-zoo area and breeding centers, and alongside crocodile ponds. (Did you know that a 750-pound adult croc can move at 40 miles per hour?) You may get to hear the crocodile love call, which is original to say the least. Safari Village served as a film set for the James Bond thriller *Live and Let Die.* You can also enjoy rafting through a mangrove while poled by a guide. On the grounds is a Jerk Food Centre.

Rocklands Wildlife Station

Anchovy, St. James. ☎ **809/952-2009.** Admission J$150 ($4.80). Open daily 2–5pm.

This sanctuary was established by Lisa Salmon, known as the Bird Lady of Anchovy, and it attracts nature-lovers and birdwatchers. It's a unique experience to have a Jamaican doctor bird perch on your finger to drink syrup, to feed small doves and finches millet from your hand, and to watch dozens of other birds flying in for their evening meal. Don't take children five and under, as they tend to worry the birds. Smoking and playing transistor radios are forbidden. Rocklands is about a mile outside Anchovy on the road from Montego Bay.

THE GREAT HOUSES

Occupied by plantation owners, the Great Houses of Jamaica were always built on high ground so that they overlooked the plantation itself and could see the next house in the distance. It was the custom for the owners to offer hospitality to travelers crossing the island by road. Travelers were spotted by the lookout, who noted the rising dust, and bed and food were then made ready for the traveler's arrival.

Greenwood Great House

On the A1. ☎ **809/953-1077.** Admission $10 adults, $5 children. Open daily 9am–6pm.

Greenwood is even more interesting to some house tourers than Rose Hall. On its hillside perch, it lies 14 miles east of Montego Bay and 7 miles west of Falmouth. Erected in the early 19th century, the Georgian-style building was the residence of Richard Barrett between 1780 and 1800, who was of the same family as Elizabeth Barrett Browning. On display is the original library of the Barrett family, with rare books dating from 1697, along with oil paintings of the Barrett family, china made by Wedgwood for the family, and a rare exhibition of musical instruments in working order, plus a fine collection of antique furniture. The house today is privately owned but open to the public.

✪ Rose Hall Great House

Rose Hall Hwy. ☎ **809/953-2323.** Admission $10 adults, $6 children. Open daily 9am–6pm.

The most famous Great House in Jamaica is the legendary Rose Hall, a 9-mile jaunt east from Montego Bay along the coast road. The subject of at least a dozen gothic novels, Rose Hall was immortalized in the H. G. deLisser book *White Witch of Rosehall.* The house was built about two centuries ago by John Palmer. However, it was Annie Palmer, wife of the builder's grandnephew, who became the focal point of fiction and fact. Called "Infamous Annie," she was said to have dabbled in witchcraft. She took slaves as lovers, and then killed them off when they bored her. Servants called her "the Obeah woman" (*Obeah* is Jamaican for "voodoo"). Annie was said to have murdered several of her coterie of husbands while they slept, and eventually suffered the same fate herself in a kind of poetic justice. Long in ruins, the house has now been restored and can be visited by the public. Annie's Pub lies on the ground floor.

ORGANIZED TOURS & EVENTS

The **Croydon Plantation,** Catadupa, St. James (☎ **809/979-8267**), is a 25-mile ride from Montego Bay. It can be visited on a half-day tour from Montego Bay on Tuesday, Wednesday, and Friday. Included in the $45 price are round-trip transportation from your hotel, a tour of the plantation, a tasting of varieties of pineapple and tropical fruits in season, and a barbecued chicken lunch. Most hotel tour desks can arrange this tour.

For a plantation tour, go on a **Hilton High Day Tour,** with an office on Beach View Plaza (☎ **952-3343**). Round-trip transportation on a scenic drive through historic plantation areas is included. Your day starts at the plantation with a continental breakfast served at the old plantation house. You can roam around the 100 acres of the plantation and visit the German village of Seaford town or St. Leonards village nearby. A Jamaican lunch of roast suckling pig with rum punch is served at 1pm. The charge for the day is $50 per person for the plantation tour, breakfast, lunch, and transportation. There's an additional charge of $10 for 30 minutes of horseback riding. Tour days are Tuesday, Wednesday, Friday, and Sunday.

SPORTS & OUTDOOR ACTIVITIES

BEACHES   Cornwall Beach (☎ **809/952-3463**) is a long stretch of white sand beach with dressing cabañas. Admission to the beach is J$15 (50¢) for adults, J$10 (30¢) for children, for the entire day. A bar and cafeteria offer refreshment. Hours are 9am to 5pm daily.

Across from the Doctor's Cave Beach Hotel (see "Where to Stay," above), **Doctor's Cave Beach** on Gloucester Avenue (☎ **809/952-2566**), helped launch Mo Bay as a resort in the 1940s. Admission to the beach is J$22 (70¢) for adults, half price for children. Dressing rooms, chairs, umbrellas, and rafts are available from 9am to 5pm daily.

One of the premier beaches of Jamaica, **Walter Fletcher Beach** (☎ **809/952-5783**), in the heart of Mo Bay, is noted for its tranquil waters, which makes it a particular favorite for families with children. Changing rooms are available, as is lifeguard service. You can have lunch here in a restaurant. The beach is open daily from 10am to 6pm, with an admission charge of J$20 (60¢) for adults, half price for children.

BOAT CRUISES   Day and evening cruises are offered aboard the *Calico,* a 55-foot gaff-rigged wooden ketch that sails from Pier 1 on the Montego Bay waterfront. An additional vessel, *Calico B,* also carries another 40 passengers per boat ride. You can be transported to and from your hotel for either cruise. The day voyage, which departs at 10am and returns at 3pm, provides a day of sailing, sunning, and snorkeling (with equipment supplied), plus a Jamaican buffet lunch served on the beach, all to the sound of reggae and other music. The cruise costs $50 per person and is offered daily. On the *Calico*'s evening voyage, which costs $25 per person and is offered Wednesday through Saturday from 5 to 7pm, cocktails and wine are served as you sail through sunset. For information and reservations, call Capt. Bryan Langford, North Coast Cruises Ltd. (☎ **809/952-5860**). A three-day notice is recommended.

RAFTING   Rafting on the Martha Brae is an exciting adventure. To reach the starting point, drive east to Falmouth and turn approximately 3 miles inland to **Martha Brae's Rafters Village.** The rafts are similar to those on the Río Grande, and cost $34 per raft, with two riders allowed on a raft, plus a small child if accompanied by an adult. The trips last $1^{1}/_{4}$ hours and operate daily from 8:30am to 4:30pm. You sit on a raised dais on bamboo logs. The rafters supplement their incomes by selling carved gourds. Along the way you can stop and order cool drinks or beer along the banks of the river. There's a bar, a restaurant, and a souvenir shop in the village. Call **809/952-0889** for more information.

   Mountain Valley Rafting offers rafting excursions on the Great River which depart from the Lethe Plantation, about 10 miles south of Montego Bay. Rafts are available for $34 for up to two participants as part of trips that last about an hour and operate daily from 8:30am to 4:30pm. Rafts are composed of bamboo trunks with a raised dais to sit on. In some cases, a small child can accompany two adults on the same raft, although due caution should be exercised if you choose to do this. Ask about pickup by taxi at the end of the rafting run to return you to your rented car. Another option is available for residents of local hotels who want to be picked up by van at their hotels. For $40 per person, a half-day experience will include transportation to and from your hotel, an hour's rafting, lunch, a garden tour of the Lethe property, and a taste of Jamaican liqueur. These tours are operated by Mountain Valley, 31 Gloucester Ave. (☎ **809/952-0527**).

SHOPPING

You can find good duty-free items here, including Swiss watches, Irish crystal, French perfumes, English china, Danish silverware, Portuguese linens, Italian handbags, Scottish cashmeres, Indian silks, and liquors and liqueurs. Appleton's overproof, special, and punch rums are excellent value. Tía Maria and Rumona (the one coffee-, the other rum-flavored) are the best liqueurs. Khus Khus is the local perfume. Jamaican arts and crafts are available throughout the resort and at the Crafts Market (see below).

   The main shopping areas are at **Montego Freeport,** within easy walking distance of the pier; **City Centre** (where most of the in-bond shops are, aside from at the large hotels); and **Holiday Village Shopping Centre.**

   The **Old Fort Craft Park,** a shopping complex with 180 vendors (all licensed by the Jamaica Tourist Board), fronts Howard Cooke Boulevard up from Gloucester Avenue in the heart of Montego Bay on the site of Fort Montego. A market with a varied assortment of handcrafts, it's ideal browsing country for both souvenirs and more serious purchases. You'll see a selection of wall hangings, hand-woven straw items, and hand-carved wood sculpture, and you can even get your hair braided. Fort Montego, now long gone, was constructed by the British in the mid-18th century as part of their defense of "fortress Jamaica." But it never saw much action, except for firing its cannons every year to salute the monarch's birthday.

At the **Crafts Market,** near Harbour Street in downtown Montego Bay, you can find a wide selection of handmade souvenirs of Jamaica, including straw hats and bags, wooden platters, straw baskets, musical instruments, beads, carved objects, and toys. That "jipijapa" hat is important if you're going to be out in the island sun.

One of the newest and most intriguing places for shopping is a mall, **Half Moon Plaza,** set on the coastal road about 8 miles east of the commercial center of Montego Bay. This upscale minimall caters to the shopping and gastronomic needs of residents of one of the region's most elegant hotels, the Half Moon Club. (Residents of the 45 private villas that the hotel administers consider it a convenient boon to the success of their vacations.) In the mall is a well-recommended restaurant, Taste Jamaica Ltd. (☎ 809/953-9688), and at least two other restaurants. Also on the premises are a bank and about 25 shops, each arranged around a central courtyard, each selling a wide choice of carefully selected merchandise.

ARTS & CRAFTS

Ambiente Art Gallery
9 Fort St. ☎ **809/952-7919.**

A 100-year-old clapboard cottage set close to the road houses this gallery. The Austrian-born owner, Maria Hitchins, is considered one of the doyennes of the Montego Bay art scene. She has personally encouraged and developed scores of local fine art works and prints by local artists. Open Monday through Saturday from 9am to 6pm.

Bay Gallery
St. James Place. ☎ **809/952-7668.**

The Bay Gallery lies on the upper floor of this airy shopping complex near the tourist office. Gilou Bauer always presents an interesting selection of Jamaican artists. Open Monday through Saturday from 10am to 6pm, on Sunday by appointment only.

Blue Mountain Gems Workshop
at the Holiday Village Shopping Centre. ☎ **809/953-2338.**

Here you can take a tour of the workshops to see the process from raw stone to the finished product you can buy later. Wooden jewelry, local carvings, and one-of-a-kind ceramic figurines are also sold. Hours are 9am to 5:30pm Monday through Saturday.

Neville Budhai Paintings
Budhai's Art Gallery, Reading Main Rd., Reading. ☎ **809/979-2568.**

This is the art center of a distinguished artist, Neville Budhai, the president and co-founder of the Western Jamaica Society of Fine Arts. He has a distinct style and is said to capture the special flavor of the island and its people in his artworks. The artist may sometimes be seen sketching or painting in Montego Bay or along the highways of rural Jamaica. His studio is 5 miles east of Montego Bay on the way to Negril. Open daily from 9am to 5 or 6pm.

Things Jamaican
44 Fort St. ☎ **809/952-5605.**

This is a showcase for the talents of the artisans of Jamaica. Here is displayed a wealth of products, even food and drink, including rums and liqueurs along with jerk seasoning orange-pepper jelly. Look for Busha Browne's fine Jamaican sauces, especially spicy chutneys or planters spicy piquant sauce. These recipes are prepared and bottled by the Busha Browne Company in Jamaica just as they were 100 years ago. Many items for sale are carved from wood, including sculpture, salad bowls, and trays. You'll also find large hand-woven Jamaican baskets. Also look for reproductions of the Port Royal collection. Port Royal was buried by an earthquake and tidal wave in 1692. After resting underwater for 275 years, beautiful pewter items were recovered and are living again in reproductions. They include Rat-tail spoons, a spoon with the heads of the monarchs William and Mary, Splay-Footed Lion Rampant spoons, and spoons with Pied-de-Biche handles. Many items were reproduced faithfully, right down to the pit marks and scratches. To complement this pewter assortment, Things Jamaican created the Port Royal Bristol-Delft Ceramic Collection, based on original pieces of ceramics found in the underwater digs. Open Monday through Friday from 9am to 5pm and on Saturday from 9am to 4pm.

FASHION

Jolie Madame Fashions
30 City Centre Bldg. ☎ **809/952-3126.**

Its racks of clothing for women and girls might contain evening dresses, casual clothes, and beach attire. Many garments range from $50 to $200. Norma McLeod, the establishment's overseer, designer, coordinator, and founder, is always on hand to arrange custom-made garments. Open Monday through Saturday from 8:30am to 7pm.

Klass Kraft Leather Sandals
44 Fort St. ☎ **809/952-5782.**

Next door to Things Jamaican, this store offers sandals and leather accessories made on location by a team of Jamaican craftspeople. All sandals cost less than $30. Open Monday through Friday from 9am to 5pm and on Saturday from 10am to 3pm.

JEWELRY

Golden Nugget
8 St. James Shopping Centre, Gloucester Ave. ☎ **809/952-7707.**

The Golden Nugget is a duty-free shop with an impressive collection of watches for both women and men, and a fine assortment of jewelry, especially gold chains. The shop also carries leading brand-name cameras and a wide assortment of French perfumes. Set in the manicured confines of one of Montego Bay's most modern shopping compounds, it's run by India-born Sheila Mulchandani. Open Monday through Saturday from 9am to 6pm, on Sunday by appointment only.

MONTEGO BAY AFTER DARK

There are a lot more activities to pursue in Montego Bay in the evenings than going to the discos, but the resort area certainly has those, too. Much of the entertainment is offered at the various hotels.

Pier 1, Howard Cooke Boulevard (☎ **809/952-2452**), already previewed as a selection for Jamaican cookery (see "Where to Dine," above), might also be your entertainment choice for a night on the town. Friday night sees disco action from 10pm to 5am and a J$100 ($3.20) cover charge is assessed. Red Stripe beer costs J$50 ($1.60).

Every Sunday, Tuesday, and Thursday from 7 to 11pm there's an **Evening on the Great River,** during which you ride in a fishing canoe up the river 10 miles west of Montego Bay. A torchlit path leads to a re-created Arawak village, where you eat, drink as much as you like at the open bar, and watch a floor show of live reggae music. The Country Store offers jackass rope (tobacco by the yard), nutmeg, cinnamon, brown sugar, and all sorts of country items for sale. The cost, with transportation, is $55 per person; children under 12 go for half price. The operator is Great River Productions, 42 Gloucester Ave., Reading, St. James (☎ **809/952-5047**).

An interesting Jamaican experience is **Combo at Lollypop on the Beach,** at Sandy Bay, Hanover, half a mile west of Tryall, held every Wednesday from 7:30 to 11pm (also on Saturday if the demand is heavy). Your $55 includes round-trip transport to the beach from Mo Bay hotels; a glass-bottom-boat ride with a calypso band; dinner of seafood and jerk meats; traditional dance groups performing Kumina, reggae, the basket dance, the bamboo dance, and the limbo; and dancing on the beach. Children go for half price. The festivities are run by Resort Tours and Travel Ltd. 5 Queen's Dr., Montego Bay (☎ **809/952-4121**).

Boonoonoonoos Beach Party is held on Friday from 7 to 11pm on Walter Fletcher Beach, Montego Bay, costing $48. A live band, three-course Jamaican dinner, open Jamaican bar, and a floor show make for a festive evening. For information, call the Coconut Grove Great House, Ocho Rios (☎ **809/974-2619**). It's not recommended for children.

The **Cricket Club** at the Wyndham Rose Hall (☎ **809/953-2650**) is more than just a sports bar. It's a place where people go to meet and mingle with an international crowd. Televised sports, karaoke sing-alongs, tournament darts, and backgammon are all part of the fun. Drinks begin at $3, and the club is open daily from 7pm to 1am. There's no cover charge.

7 Negril

Jamaica's hedonistic resort, on the western tip of the island, is famed for its 7-mile beach. Negril is 50 miles and about a two-hour drive from Montego Bay's airport, along a winding road and past ruins of sugar estates and Great Houses. From Kingston, it's about a four-hour drive, a distance of 150 miles.

This once-sleepy village has turned into a tourist mecca, with visitors drawn to its beaches along three well-protected bays—Long Bay, Bloody Bay (now Negril Harbour), and Orange Bay. Negril became famous in the late 1960s when it attracted laidback American and Canadian youth, who liked the idea of a place with no phones and no electricity; they rented modest digs in little houses on the West End where the local people extended their hospitality. But those days are long gone. Today a "new Negril," with its new, more sophisticated hotels and all-inclusive resorts such as Hedonism II and Sandals Negril, draws a better-heeled and less rowdy crowd, including hundreds of European visitors.

At some point you'll want to explore Booby Key (or Cay), a tiny islet off the Negril coast. Once it was featured in the Walt Disney film *20,000 Leagues Under the Sea,* but now it's overrun with nudists from Hedonism II.

Chances are, however, you'll stake out your own favorite spot along Negril's 7-mile beach. You don't need to get up for anything, as somebody will be along to serve you. Perhaps it'll be the "banana lady," with a basket of fruit perched on her head. Maybe the "ice cream man" will set up a stand right under a coconut palm. Surely the "beer lady" will find you as she strolls along the beach with a carton of Jamaican beer on her head, and hordes of young men will peddle illegal *ganja* whether you smoke it or not.

There are really two Negrils: The West End is the site of many little eateries, such as Chicken Lavish, and cottages that still receive visitors. The other Negril is on the east end, the first you approach on the road coming in from Montego Bay. Here the best hotels, enjoying some of the most panoramic beachfronts, such as Negril Gardens, are giving Negril a touch of class.

WHERE TO STAY

In addition to the following, the Café au Lait/Mirage Cottages (listed under "Where to Dine," below) has accommodations for rent.

EXPENSIVE

Poinciana Beach Hotel

Norman Manley Blvd. (P.O. Box 44), Negril, Jamaica, W.I. ☎ **809/957-4256,** or 800/468-6728 in the U.S. Fax 809/957-4229. 90 rms, 6 studios, 12 suites, 22 villas. A/C TV. Winter, $307 single; $198 double; $202 studio for two; $280 suite for two; $208–$215 villa for two. Off-season, $249 single; $165 double; $169 studio for two; $212 suite for two; $174–$180 villa for two. (Rates all-inclusive per person.) AE, MC, V. Free parking.

Set on 6 acres of land, this hotel and villa vacation resort operates only on the full-board, attracting couples, singles, and families with a variety of accommodations and an extensive sports program. It's a mixture of both contemporary and colonial design, with tile floors, rattan and wood furnishings, and private balconies and ocean views. On Seven Mile Beach, it opened in the 1980s with just two private accommodations and has grown considerably. Superior rooms consist of one bedroom and bath and a private balcony or patio, and suites are furnished with a kitchenette and a large wraparound balcony. Some suites offer Jacuzzi-type tubs. Studios are similar to the living/dining area of the suites, and villas consist of one or two bedrooms, a living/dining area with kitchenette, and a private balcony or patio. Villa guests can enjoy a personal housekeeper and cook.

Dining/Entertainment: A poolside restaurant, the Captain's Table, serves breakfast and dinner daily, with both Jamaican dishes and international specialties. The Upper Deck Café offers lunch and after-dinner snacks, and at the Beach Bar a lively native band entertains five evenings a week during happy hour. Other evening entertainment is often staged, including a reggae/soca barbecue night on Saturday.

Service: Beauty salon, babysitting, children's program, massage.

Facilities: Two freshwater swimming pools, heated Jacuzzi, lawn and table tennis, 24-hour exercise gyms, water sports (including windsurfing, snorkeling, kayaks, glass-bottom boat rides, Sunfish and Hobie cat sailing, and scuba diving).

Seasplash Resort

Norman Manley Blvd., Negril, Jamaica, W.I. ☎ **809/957-4041,** or 800/526-2422 in the U.S. Fax 809/957-4049. 15 suites. A/C TV TEL. Winter, $177 suite for one; $220 suite for two; $240 suite for three; $260 suite for four. Off-season, $115 suite for one; $135 suite for two; $155 suite for three; $175 suite for four. Full board $57 per person extra. AE, MC, V. Free parking.

Partly because of its small size, this resort often has a sense of intimacy and personal contact among the staff and the guests. In deliberate contrast to the mega-resorts nearby, it lies on a small but carefully landscaped sliver of beachfront land planted with tropical plants. The suites are spacious and stylishly decorated with wicker furniture and fresh pastel colors. All are the same size and contain the same amenities—a kitchenette, a balcony or patio, large closets, and either a king-size bed or twin beds—although those on the upper floor have higher ceilings and an enhanced feeling of space.

The resort contains two different restaurants, Calico Jack's (a simple lunchtime *bohío*) and the more elaborate Tan-Ya (see "Where to Dine," below). Services include babysitting, laundry, and room service. Guests have use of a small gym, a Jacuzzi, and a swimming pool with a thatch-covered gazebo-style bar at one end, and there is immediate access to the beach.

MODERATE

⑨ Charela Inn

Norman Manley Blvd. (P.O. Box 33), Negril, Jamaica, W.I. ☎ **809/957-4277.** Fax 809/957-4414. 39 rms. A/C TEL. Winter, $125–$150 single; $140–$170 double. Off-season, $80–$100 single; $96–$113 double. MAP $35 per person extra. Five-night minimum stay in winter. MC, V. Free parking.

A seafront inn reminiscent of a Spanish hacienda, this place sits on the main beach strip on 3 acres of landscaped grounds. The building has an inner courtyard with a tropical garden and a round freshwater swimming pool opening onto one of the widest (250-ft.) sandy beaches in Negril. The inn attracts a loyal following of visitors seeking a "home away from home." Its dining room faces both the sea and the garden, and offers both an à la carte menu and a five-course fixed-price meal that is changed daily. Sunsets are toasted on open terraces facing the sea. Simplicity and a quiet kind of elegance are the keynote of the inn.

Negril Beach Club Hotel

Norman Manley Blvd. (P.O. Box 7), Negril, Jamaica, W.I. ☎ **809/957-4220**, or 800/526-2422 in the U.S. and Canada. Fax 809/957-4364. 47 rms, 6 suites. A/C. Winter, $85 single; $95 double; $167 suite for one; $224 suite for two. Off-season, $56 single; $67 double; $122 suite for one; $167 suite for two. MAP $30 per person extra. AE, MC, V. Free parking.

This casual, informal resort is designed around a series of white stucco cottages with exterior stairways and terraces. The entire complex is clustered like a horseshoe around a rectangular garden whose end abuts a sandy beach just north of Negril. There's ample parking on the premises and easy access to a full range of sporting facilities, including snorkeling, a pool, volleyball, table tennis, and windsurfing. Other activities can be organized nearby, and beach barbecues and buffet breakfasts are ample and frequent. Accommodations range from simply furnished rooms, rented either as a single or double, to one- and two-bedroom suites, each with a kitchenette. The well-appointed rooms each have private bath or shower; the less expensive units don't have balconies. The Seething Cauldron Restaurant on the beach serves barbecues, seafood, and such Jamaican specialties as roast suckling pig and ackee and codfish. Because some of this establishment's units are devoted to time-share investors, some of the accommodations are not always available for rentals.

ⓢ Negril Gardens Hotel

Norman Manley Blvd. (P.O. Box 58), Negril, Jamaica, W.I. ☎ **809/957-4408**, or 800/752-6824 in the U.S., 800/567-5327 in Canada. Fax 809/957-4374. 65 rms. A/C TV. Winter, $125–$135 single or double. Off-season, $100–$110 single or double. Additional person $30 extra; two children stay free in parents' room. MAP $40 per person extra. AE, MC, V. Free parking.

Negril Gardens rests amid tropical verdure on the famous 7-mile stretch of beach. The two-story villas are well furnished, and rooms open onto a front veranda or a balcony with either a beach or a garden view. The units on the garden side are cheaper and face the swimming pool with a pool bar and a tennis court.

Directly on the beach is a Tahiti-style bar, and right behind it stands an al fresco restaurant, the Orchid Terrace, serving some of the best food in Negril. Non-residents are also invited to patronize this facility, where they can choose from Jamaican cookery and international dishes, such as various versions of conch, lobster, and other seafood, plus curried goat and stew peas, or chicken fricassée. Dinner is nightly from 7 to 10pm.

Negril Tree House

Norman Manley Blvd. (P.O. Box 29), Negril, Jamaica, W.I. ☎ **809/957-4287**, or 800/NEGRIL-1 in the U.S. Fax 809/957-4386. 55 rms. 12 suites. Winter. $110–$140 single or double: $240–$270 family suite for up to four. Off-season, $80–$110 single or double; $140–$160 family suite for up to four. Breakfast $8 extra. AE, MC, V. Free parking.

Owned by Gail Y. Jackson, the Negril Tree House is a desirable little escapist retreat with an ideal beachfront location. Scattered across the property in 11 octagonal buildings are the simply furnished units, including 12 suites, each with very small tile baths and air conditioning or ceiling fans. Suites also have kitchenettes and TVs. The resort features a number of water sports, including parasailing, snorkeling, and jet-skiing. The Tree House also has a swimming pool and Jacuzzi.

INEXPENSIVE

ⓢ Negril Cabins

Ruthland Point, Negril, Jamaica, W.I. ☎ **809/957-4350**. Fax 809/957-4381. 50 cabins. Winter, $84–$93 cabin for one; $120–$132 cabin for two; $155–$162 cabin for three. Off-season, $64–$71 cabin for one; $92–$109 cabin for two; $122–$139 cabin for three. Children under 16 stay free in parents' room. Breakfast $8 extra. AE, MC, V. Free parking.

Except for the palms and the Caribbean vegetation, you might imagine yourself at a log-cabin complex in the Maine Woods. In many ways, this is the bargain hotel of Negril, suitable for the budget-conscious eager to get away from it all. The cabins are on the easternmost edge of Negril, beside the road leading in from Montego Bay, in a forest across the road from a beach called Bloody Bay, where the infamous 18th-century pirate, Calico Jack, was killed by the British.

The unadorned cabins are really small cottages, none more than two stories high, rising on stilts. Each timber cottage includes a balcony patio, and some are air-conditioned. The hotel's 9-acre garden is planted with royal palms, bull thatch, and a rare variety of mango tree (its fruit is called simply "number eight"). The establishment's bar and restaurant serve tropical punch, a medley of fresh Jamaican fruits, and flavorful but unpretentious Jamaican meals. A children's program is also available and live entertainment is offered on some nights.

ALL-INCLUSIVE RESORTS

☼ Grand Hotel Lido

Bloody Bay (P.O. Box 88), Negril, Jamaica, W.I. ☎ **809/957-4010,** or 800/859-7873 in the U.S., 800/553-4320 in Canada. Fax 809/957-4317. 182 junior suites, 18 one-bedroom suites. A/C MINIBAR TV TEL. Winter, $1,300–$1,390 suite for one; $2,000–$2,180 suite for two. Off-season, $1,145–$1,235 suite for one; $1,690–$1,870 suite for two. (Rates for minimum stay of four days/three nights include all meals, snacks, drinks, enter-tainment, sports activities, taxes, service charges, and airport transfers.) AE, MC, V. Free parking.

Considered the grandest and most architecturally stylish hotel in its chain, the Grand Hotel Lido sits on a flat and lushly landscaped stretch of land adjacent to Hedonism II, at the easternmost end of the beach strip. Regarded as the most upscale and discreetly elegant of the string of resorts known as Jamaica's SuperClubs, it opened in 1989 to fanfare. Each contains a stereo system, lots of space, and either a patio or a balcony that (except for a few) overlooks the beach. The smaller of the resort's two beaches is reserved for nudists. Only adults are welcome, but unlike many other all-inclusive resorts, especially Club Med, there is no resistance here to giving a room to a single occupant. Even after the resort's quartet of restaurants closes, there are three different dining enclaves that remain open throughout the night and are tucked into alluring corners of the resort, each with a bubbling Jacuzzi nearby.

Dining/Entertainment: In addition to the cavernous and airy main dining room, there is a trio of restaurants, including one devoted to nouvelle cuisine, another to continental food, and a third to Italian pasta. Guests also enjoy an all-night disco, the piano bar, and the dozens of pool tables and dart boards of no fewer than nine bars, so getting a drink here is never a problem.

Services: 24-hour room service, concierge, laundry, tour desk that arranges visits to other parts of Jamaica, instructors to teach tennis and sailing.

Facilities: Four tennis courts, two swimming pools, four Jacuzzis, gym/sauna/health club, two fine beaches lined with chaise longues; one of the most glamorous yachts in the West Indies, the M-Y *Zein,* offered long ago by Aristotle Onassis to Prince Rainier and Grace of Monaco as a wedding present.

Hedonism II

Negril Beach Rd. (P.O. Box 25), Negril, Jamaica, W.I. ☎ **809/957-4200,** or 800/859-7873 in the U.S. Fax 809/957-4289. 280 rms. A/C. Winter, $605–$725 per person based on double occupancy. Off-season, $517–$586 per person based on double occupancy. Single-room supplement $75 per day. (Rates for four days/three nights include all meals, drinks, activities, taxes, service charges, and airport transfers.) AE, DC, MC, V. Free parking.

Devoted to the pursuit of pleasure, Hedonism II packs "the works" into a one-package deal, including all the drinks and partying anyone might want. There is no tender of any sort, and tipping is not permitted. Of all the members of its chain, this is the most animated. The rooms are stacked in two-story clusters dotted around a sloping 22-acre site. Most of the guests, who must be at least 18 years of age, are Americans. Closed to the general public, this is not a "couples-only resort," as singles are both accepted and encouraged. There is a daily supplement for single occupancy; otherwise, the hotel will find you a roommate. On one section of this establishment's beach, clothing is optional. The resort also has a secluded beach on nearby Booby Key (originally Cay) where guests are taken twice a week for picnics. The complex is beside Negril's main road stretching east toward Montego Bay, about 2 miles east of the center.

Dining/Entertainment: Nightly entertainment is presented, along with a live band, a high-energy disco with a stage for the presentation of occasional live performers, and a piano bar. Buffets are staged, and the cuisine is international. There is also a clothing-optional bar and grill.

Services: Massage.

Facilities: Sailing, snorkeling, waterskiing, scuba diving, windsurfing, glass-bottom boat, clothing-optional Jacuzzi, swimming pool, six tournament-class tennis courts (lit at night), two badminton courts, basketball court, two indoor squash courts, volleyball, table tennis, Nautilus and free-weight gyms, aerobics, indoor games room.

Negril Inn

Norman Manley Blvd. (P.O. Box 59), Negril, Jamaica, W.I. ☎ **809/957-4209,** or 800/634-7456 in the U.S. Fax 809/957-4365. 46 rms. A/C. Winter, $200 single; $320 double; $450 triple. Off-season, $140 single; $220 double; $270 triple. (Rates include all meals, drinks, activities, taxes, service charges, and airport transfers.) AE, MC, V. Free parking.

Located in the heart of the 7-mile beach stretch, about 3 miles east of the town center, beside the main road leading in from Negril, this is one of the smallest all-inclusive resorts in Negril. Because of its size, the atmosphere is more low-tech, calmer, and less energy-charged than the atmosphere in its larger competitors. The resort, *not* confined to couples only, offers guest rooms with private balconies, spread through a series of two-story structures in a garden setting. The helpful staff offers a host of activities, day and night. Children are not accepted in winter.

Dining/Entertainment: Included in the package are all meals, all alcoholic drinks (except champagne), and nightly entertainment (including a disco). Meals are consumed in the resort's only restaurant, although there are bars in the disco and beside the pool.

Services: Room service (for breakfast only), laundry, round-trip transfers to and from the airport at Montego Bay, filtered water from a 10,000-gallon plant on the premises.

Facilities: Windsurfing, waterskiing, scuba diving, snorkeling, hydrosliding, aqua bikes, glass-bottom boat, two floodlit tennis courts, Jacuzzi, piano room, Universal weight room, freshwater pool.

Sandals Negril

Rutland Point, Negril, Jamaica, W.I. ☎ **809/957-4216,** or 800/SANDALS in the U.S. and Canada. Fax 809/957-4338. 187 rms, 16 suites. A/C TV TEL. Winter, $1,580–$1,940 double; $2,140–$2,360 suite. Off-season, $1,500–$2,360 double; $2,020–$2,220 suite. (Rates for a minimum stay of four days/three nights include all meals, snacks, drinks, activities, taxes, service charges, and airline transfers.) AE, MC, V. Free parking.

Sandals Negril is an all-inclusive, couples-only (male-female) resort, part of the expanding "empire" of the enterprising Gordon "Butch" Stewart, who pioneered similar operations in Montego Bay. The word "Sandals" in Jamaica has come to stand for a "no problem, mon" vacation, as they say locally. The resort occupies some 13 acres of prime beachfront land a short drive east of Negril's center, on the main highway leading in from Montego Bay. It's about a $1^{1}/_{2}$-hour drive (maybe more) from the Montego Bay airport. Round-trip transfers to and from Montego Bay are part of the package deal.

The developers linked two older hotels into a unified whole with very little incentive to ever set foot off the property. The crowd is usually convivial, decidedly informal, and often young. There are five divisions of accommodations, rated standard, superior, deluxe, deluxe beachfront, and one-bedroom suite. The casually well-furnished rooms have a tropical motif, and hairdryers and radios.

Dining/Entertainment: Rates include all meals, even snacks, and unlimited drinks day and night at one of four bars (two swim-up pool bars and add a special feature). Coconut Cove is the main dining room, but guests can also elect to eat at one of the specialty rooms, including the Sundowner, offering white-glove service and a Jamaican cuisine, and the 4 C's, with low-calorie health food served beside the beach. Kimono offers a Japanese cuisine. Nightly entertainment, including theme parties, is also included.

Services: Laundry, massage.

Facilities: Two freshwater swimming pools, tennis courts for day or night, scuba diving, snorkeling, Sunfish sailing, windsurfing, canoeing, aerobics classes, glass-bottom boat, fitness center (with saunas and Universal exercise equipment).

✪ Swept Away

Norman Manley Blvd. (P.O. Box 77), Negril, Jamaica, W.I. ☎ **809/957-4040**, or 800/545-7937 in the U.S. and Canada. Fax 809/957-4060. 134 suites. A/C TEL. Winter $1,275–$1,620 per couple. Off-season, $1,185–$1,500 per couple. (Rates for three nights, include all meals, drinks, activities, taxes, airport transfers, and services.) AE, MC, V. Free parking.

Opened in 1990, this is one of the best-equipped hotels in Negril—it's certainly the one most conscious of sports, emotional relaxation, and physical and mental fitness. All-inclusive, it caters to male-female couples eager for an ambience with all possible diversions but absolutely no organized schedule of when or with whom to play them. The resort occupies 20 flat and sandy acres, which straddle both sides of the highway leading in from Montego Bay, $3^1/_2$ miles east of Negril center.

The accommodations (the hotel defines them as "veranda suites" because of their large balconies) are in 26 two-story villas clustered together and accented with flowering shrubs and vines, a few steps from the 7-mile beachfront. Each accommodation contains a ceiling fan, a king-size bed, and (unless the vegetation obscures it) sea views.

Dining/Entertainment: The resort's social center is its international restaurant, Feathers, which lies inland, across the road from the sea. There's also an informal beachfront restaurant and bar, and four bars scattered throughout the property, including a "veggie bar."

Services: Room service (for continental breakfast only), laundry, tour desk for arranging visits to other parts of Jamaica.

Facilities: Racquetball, squash, and 10 lighted tennis courts; fully equipped gym; aerobics; yoga; massage; steam; sauna; whirlpool; billiards; bicycles; beachside swimming pool; scuba diving; windsurfing; reef snorkeling.

WHERE TO DINE
EXPENSIVE

Rick's Café

West End Rd. ☎ **809/957-4335**. Reservations not required. Appetizers $3–$9; main courses $14–$28. No credit cards. Daily 2–10pm. SEAFOOD/STEAK.

At sundown, everybody in Negril heads toward the lighthouse along the West End strip to Rick's Café—whether or not they want a meal. Of course, the name was inspired by the old watering hole of *Casablanca*. Here the sunset is said to be the most glorious at the resort, and after a few fresh-fruit daiquiris (pineapple, banana, or papaya), you'll give no argument. "Casual" is the word in dress, and reggae and rock are heard on the sound track.

There are several Stateside specialties, including imported steaks along with a complete menu of blackened dishes (Cajun style). The fish is always fresh, including red snapper, fresh lobster, or grouper, and you might begin with a Jamaican fish chowder. You can also buy plastic bar tokens at the door, which you can use instead of money à la Club Med.

MODERATE

Café au Lait/Mirage Cottages

Lighthouse Rd., West End, Negril, Jamaica, W.I. ☎ **809/957-4471.** Fax 809/957-4414. Reservations not required. Appetizers $2.50–$6; main courses $7.50–$26. MC, V. Lunch daily noon–3pm; dinner daily 5–10pm. FRENCH/JAMAICAN.

Daniel and Sylvia Grizzle, a Jamaican/French couple, prepare the cuisine as well as direct the smooth operation of this place, located 2¹/₂ miles from the town center along the West End beach strip. Menu items include quiches, escargots, lobster, and an unusual crêpe made with cheese and callaloo. There are five kinds of pizza, roast lamb, fish steak, and curried shrimp, and there is a wine list stressing French products. Dessert may be lime tart with fresh cream.

Set in 4¹/₂ acres of tropical garden, the property flanks both sides of the road. On the land side, there are two two-bedroom cottages, ideal for four to six people. On the sea side, where high cliffs dominate the coastline, they have one one-bedroom cottage, one duplex, and four large studios with big balconies and views of the coast. All accommodations have private baths and ceiling fans, and all are air-conditioned. Winter rates are $88 to $98 daily for one person and $95 to $110 for two; off-season tariffs range from $45 to $55 daily for one, $55 to $66 for two. There are sunning areas, three access ladders to the sea, and a gazebo for relaxing in the shade.

Le Vendôme

In the Charela Inn, Negril Beach. ☎ **809/957-4277.** Reservations required for Sat dinner. Appetizers $6–$8; main courses $10–$29; fixed-price meal $22.50–$29.50; continental breakfast $4.50; English breakfast $8.50. MC, V. Breakfast daily 7:30–10am; lunch daily 12:30–2:30pm; dinner daily 7–10pm. JAMAICAN/FRENCH.

Some 3¹/₂ miles from the center, this establishment enjoys a good reputation for its food. Nonresidents are invited to sample the cuisine that's a combination of, in the words of owners Daniel and Sylvia Grizzle, a "dash of Jamaican spices" with a "pinch of French flair." Their wine and champagne are imported from France. You dine on a terra-cotta terrace, where you can enjoy a view of the palm-studded beach. You may want to order a homemade pâté, perhaps a vegetable salad to begin with, and then follow with baked snapper, duckling à l'orange, or a seafood platter.

Mariners Inn & Restaurant

West End Rd. ☎ **809/957-4348.** Reservations not required. Appetizers $1.50–$6; pizzas $1.75–$10; main courses $6.50–$18. AE, MC, V. Lunch daily 11am–3pm; dinner daily 6–10pm. JAMAICAN/AMERICAN.

The main reason most guests come here is the boat-shaped bar and the adjoining restaurant, entered through a tropical garden that eventually slopes down to the beach. As you drink or dine, the breezes will waft in, adding to one of the most relaxed experiences in Negril. Curried chop suey and chicken are available, as are cheese omelets, homemade pâté, and—if you really want to dine elegantly—lobster, cooked in white wine. Look also for the chef's specials of the day. The restaurant is along the West End strip.

Negril Tree House

Norman Manley Blvd. ☎ **809/957-4287.** Reservations not required. Appetizers $3.50–$5; main courses $12–$23. AE, MC, V. Daily 7am–11pm. JAMAICAN.

This informal beachfront place takes its name from a mamee tree that grows through the main building of this resort hotel. Dining is on the second floor, but guests can come early and have a drink in the beachfront bar. This is a lively center both day and night. At lunch you can ask for a homemade soup, perhaps pepperpot, a sandwich, or else more elaborate fare, such as a typically Jamaican dish of escovitched fish. Some of the produce comes from the owner's own farm in the country.

At night, Gail Y. Jackson, your hostess, offers her full repertoire of dishes, including a lobster spaghetti "worth a detour." You might begin with a callaloo quiche and later follow with roast chicken (a specialty) or conch steak. Try the Tía Maria parfait for dessert. You can dine both inside and out.

Restaurant Tan-Ya'S/Calico Jack's

In the Seasplash Resort, Norman Manley Blvd. ☎ **809/957-4041.** Reservations recommended. Appetizers $2.50–$6; main courses $6–$23; lunch sandwiches and salads $5–$7; lunch platters $6.50–$7.50. AE, MC, V. Lunch daily 11am–3pm; dinner daily 6:30–10pm. JAMAICAN/INTERNATIONAL.

Set within the thick white walls of a previously recommended resort, these two restaurants provide well-prepared food and the charm of a small, family-run resort. Informal lunchtime food is served at Calico Jack's, whose tables are in an enlarged gazebo, near a bar and the resort's swimming pool. The resort's gastronomic showcase, however, is Tan-Ya's. There, specialties include lemon-flavored shrimp, Tan-Ya's snapper with herb butter, three different preparations of lobster, smoked Jamaican lobster with a fruit salsa, and deviled crab backs sautéed in butter.

BUDGET

ⓢ Chicken Lavish

West End Rd. ☎ **809/957-4410.** Reservations not required. Main courses $3.50–$5.50. MC, V. Daily 9am–10pm. JAMAICAN.

I've found that Chicken Lavish, whose name I love, is the best of the lot. Just show up on the doorstep and see what's cooking. It's located along the West End beach strip. Curried goat is a specialty, as is fresh fried fish. The red snapper is caught in local waters. But the main reason I've recommended the place is because of the namesake. Ask the chef to make his special Jamaican chicken. He'll tell you, and you may agree, that it's the best on the island. What to wear here? Dress as you would to clean up your backyard on a hot August day.

ⓢ Cosmo's Seafood Restaurant & Bar

Norman Manley Blvd. ☎ **809/957-4330.** Reservations not required. Appetizers J$20–J$90 (60¢–$2.90); main courses J$140–J$470 ($4.50–$15). V. Daily 9am–10pm. SEAFOOD.

One of the best places to go for local seafood is centered around a Polynesian thatched bohío open to the sea and bordering the main beachfront. This is the dining spot of Cosmo Brown, who entertains locals as well as visitors. You can order his famous conch soup, or conch in a number of other ways, including steamed or curried. He's also known for his savory kettle of curried goat, or you might order freshly caught seafood or fish, depending on what the catch turned up. It's a rustic establishment, and prices are among the most reasonable at the resort.

⊗ Paradise Yard

Gas Station Rd. ☎ **809/957-4006.** Reservations not required. Appetizers J$50–J$120 ($1.60–$3.80); main courses J$150–J$440 ($4.80–$14.10). V. Daily 8am–10pm. JAMAICAN.

Set on the verdant flatlands of downtown Negril, near the police station and a 10-minute walk from the beach, this simple but welcoming restaurant is the undisputed domain of Jamaican-born chef and owner Lorraine Washington. Meals, served either on the outdoor terrace or in an airy and comfortable interior decorated with roughly textured boards and pink tiles, might include the house specialty, "Rasta Pasta" (defined as red and green "dreadlocks pasta" chosen in honor of the colors of the Jamaican flag, with tomatoes, pepper, and ackee), pasta with lobster, curried chicken, Mexican enchiladas, and some of the best pumpkin soup on Jamaica.

8 Mandeville

The "English Town," Mandeville lies on a plateau more than 2,000 feet above the sea in the tropical highlands. The commercial part of the town is small and is surrounded by a sprawling residential area popular with the large North American expatriate population mostly involved with the bauxite-mining industry. Much cooler than the coastal resorts, it's a possible center from which to explore the entire island.

Shopping in the town is a pleasure, whether in the old center or in one of the modern complexes, such as Grove Court. The market in the center of town teems with life, particularly on weekends when the country folk bus into town for their weekly visit. The town has several interesting old buildings. The square-towered church built in 1820 has fine stained glass, and the little churchyard tells an interesting story of past inhabitants of Mandeville. The Court House, built in 1816, is a fine old Georgian stone-and-wood building with a pillared portico reached by a steep, sweeping double staircase. See "What to See and Do," below, to read about Marshall's Pen, one of the Great Houses in Mandeville.

WHERE TO STAY

Hotel Astra

62 Ward Ave., Mandeville, Jamaica, W.I. ☎ **809/962-3265.** 20 rms, 2 suites. TV TEL. $60–$75 single or double; $150 suite. (Includes continental breakfast.) AE, MC, V. Free parking.

My top choice for a stay in this area is the family-run Hotel Astra, operated by Diana McIntyre-Pike, known to her family and friends as Thunderbird—she's always coming to the rescue of guests, happily picks up people in her own car and takes them around to see the sights, plus organizes introductions to people of the island. The accommodations are mainly in two buildings reached along open walkways.

The Astra, 1 mile west of the town center, along the road (A2) from Kingston, houses a Visitor Information Centre, and guests are offered assistance with tours of Mandeville and throughout Jamaica, especially the south coast. Through her marketing company, Countrystyle, Diana promotes community tourism where travelers meet local people and stay in small communities including bed-and-breakfast homes to get the real "flavor" of Jamaica.

Dining/Entertainment: The Country Fresh Restaurant, entered from the front-desk area, offers excellent meals. Lunch or dinner is a choice of a homemade soup such as red pea or pumpkin, followed by local fish and chicken specialties. The kitchen is under the personal control of Diana, who is always collecting awards in Jamaican culinary competitions. Someone is on hand to explain to you the niceties of any particular Jamaican dish.

A complete meal costs $10 to $20, with some more expensive items such as lobster and steak. Dinner is served from 6 to 9:30pm every day of the week. Thursday is barbecue night, when guests and townsfolk gather around the pool to dine.

The Revival Room is the bar, where everything including the stools is made from rum-soaked barrels. Try the family's own homemade liqueur and "reviver," a pick-me-up concocted from Guinness, rum, egg, condensed milk, and nutmeg. Hours are 11am to 11pm daily.

Facilities: There are a pool and a sauna. The inn also offers a natural health program including physical therapy/therapeutic massages, acupressure/reflexology, electro-muscle stimulation, short-term fast for weight loss and health, and colon therapy headed by a top French-Canadian professional doctor who has a drugless therapy center nearby. You can also spend the afternoon at the Manchester Country Club, where tennis and golf are available. Horses can be provided for cross-country treks.

Mandeville Hotel

4 Hotel St. (P.O. Box 78), Mandeville, Jamaica, W.I. ☎ **809/962-2138.** Fax 809/962-0700. 47 rms, 9 suites. TV TEL. $65–$85 single or double; from $95 suite. Breakfast from $3 extra. AE, MC, V. Free parking.

This ornate hotel with the same name that preceded this modern establishment was established around the turn of the century, and for a while housed part of the British military garrison. In the 1970s the venerable hotel was replaced with this modern peach-colored substitute, which was completely refurbished in 1976. It lies in the heart of Mandeville, across from the police station. Today the hotel has an outdoor and indoor bar and a spacious lounge, and good food and service. Activity centers mainly around the pool and the coffee shop, where substantial meals are served at moderate prices. There are attractive gardens, and golf and tennis can be played at the nearby Manchester Country Club.

WHERE TO DINE

Mandeville Hotel

4 Hotel St. ☎ **809/962-2460.** Reservations recommended. Appetizers J$35–J$40 ($1.10–$1.30); main courses J$140–J$180 ($4.50–$5.80). AE, MC, V. Breakfast daily 6:30–9:30am; lunch daily 12:30–2:30pm; dinner daily 6:30–9:30pm. JAMAICAN.

Close to the city center, near the police station, and popular with local businesspeople who use the coffee shop by the pool for a quick luncheon stop, the Mandeville Hotel offers a wide selection of sandwiches, plus milkshakes, tea, and coffee. In the restaurant the à la carte menu offers Jamaican pepperpot soup, lobster thermidor, fresh snapper, and kingfish. Potatoes and vegetables in season are included in the main-dish prices. A full Jamaican breakfast begins at J$80 ($2.60). From the restaurant's dining room, you'll have a view of the hotel's pool and the green hills of central Jamaica.

WHAT TO SEE & DO

Mandeville is the sort of place where you can become well acquainted with the people and feel like part of the community.

One of the largest and driest **caves** on the island is at Oxford, about 9 miles northwest of Mandeville. Signs direct you to it after you leave Mile Gully, a village dominated by St. George's Church, some 175 years old.

Among the interesting attractions, **Marshall's Pen** is one of the Great Houses, an old coffee plantation home some 200 years old, which has been restored and furnished in traditional style. The house is a history lesson in itself, as in 1795 it was owned by one of the governors of Jamaica—the earl of Balcarres. It has been in the hands of the Sutton family since 1939; they farm the 300 acres and breed Jamaican Red Poll cattle. This is very much a private home and should be treated as such. Guided tours can be arranged. A contribution of $10 per person is requested. For information or an appointment to see the house, contact Ann or Robert Sutton, Marshall's Pen, Great House, P.O. Box 58, Mandeville, Jamaica, W.I. (☎ **809/962-2260**).

At **Marshall's Pen cattle estate and private nature reserve,** near Mandeville, guided birding tours of the scenic property and other outstanding birding spots on Jamaica may be arranged in advance for groups of birdwatchers. Self-catering accommodation is sometimes available for birdwatchers only, but arrangements must be made in advance. Of Jamaica's 256 species of birds, 89 species (including 25 endemics and many North American migrants) may be seen in the wild at Marshall's Pen. For further information, contact Ann or Robert Sutton, Marshall's Pen, P.O. Box 58, Mandeville, Jamaica, W.I. (☎ **809/962-2260**). Sutton is the author of *Birds of Jamaica.*

Milk River Mineral Bath, Milk River, Clarendon (☎ **809/924-9544;** fax 809/986-4962), lies 9 miles south of the Kingston–Mandeville highway. It boasts the world's most radioactive mineral waters, recommended for the treatment of arthritis, rheumatism, lumbago, neuralgia, sciatica, and liver disorders. These mineral-laden waters are available to guests of the Milk River Mineral Spa & Hotel, Milk River, Clarendon, Jamaica, W.I., as well as to casual visitors to the enclosed baths or mineral swimming pool. The baths contain water at approximate body temp (90°) and are channeled into small tubs six feet square by three feet deep, each enclosed in a cubicle where participants undress and dress again after their baths. The cost of a bath is J$40 ($1.30) for adults and J$25 (80¢) for children, and baths usually last about 15 minutes (it isn't good to remain too long in the waters). The restaurant offers fine Jamaican cuisine and health drinks in a relaxed old-world atmosphere. Some guests check into the adjacent hotel, where there are 25 rms (17 with bath), many with air-conditioning, TV, and phone. Six of the rooms are in the main body of the hotel (a century-old Great House that was converted into a hotel in the 1930s). With MAP included, rates for rooms with bath are $62 single and $84 double. Rates for rooms without bath are $57 single and $79 double. American Express, MasterCard, and Visa are accepted.

12

The French West Indies

It's France in the Caribbean, where Gallic charm combines with tropical beauty. For most visitors, that's reason enough to visit. A long way from Europe, France's western border is composed mainly of Guadeloupe and Martinique, with a scattering of tiny offshore dependencies, such as the six little clustered Iles des Saintes.

Martinique is the northernmost of the Windwards, while butterfly-shaped Guadeloupe is near the southern stretch of the Leewards. These are not colonies, as many visitors wrongly assume, but the westernmost *départements* of France, meaning that these *citoyens* are full-fledged citizens of *la belle France,* a status they have enjoyed since 1946.

Martinique has mountains dotted with lush vegetation, rain forests bursting with bamboo and breadfruit trees, and even a patch of desert in the south. But most visitors, including those from France, come just for the white sandy beaches.

In island boutiques you can purchase that Hermès scarf you've always wanted, perhaps a bottle of Chanel perfume, or even some Baccarat crystal. For breakfast, freshly baked croissants will rest on your plate. The French cheese arrived only that morning from Marseilles. In this sensual land the sexy beguine seems timeless, and the Créole cuisine is among the most distinctive in the West Indies.

Volcanic, tropically forested Guadeloupe, Martinique's companion island, is less favored by tourists but has plenty to offer as well. It has perhaps even more recommendable Créole restaurants, and its landscape is stippled with pineapple groves, banana plantations, and sugarcane fields. The surf pounds hard against its Atlantic coast facing east, but the leeward bathing beaches on the west coast offer calmer seas.

Other satellites of the French West Indies include St. Martin (which shares an island with the Dutch-held St. Maarten; see Chapter 10), St. Barthélemy, Marie-Galante, and La Désirade, a former leper colony.

Unlike Barbados and Jamaica, the French West Indies are Johnny-come-latelies to tourism. Although cruise-ship passengers had arrived long before, mass tourism began in these islands only in the 1970s. Créole customs make these islands unique in the Caribbean. The inhabitants also serve some of the best food in the Caribbean, although one irate reader found it a "farcical version" of that offered in New Orleans. Don't be afraid if I've sent you to a dilapidated wooden shack. You may find the *New York Times* food editor there too, sampling a regional meal.

INFORMATION

For more information on these islands before you leave home, contact the **French West Indies Tourist Board,** 610 Fifth Ave., New York, NY 10020 (☎ **900/ 990-0040** for France on Call, with a per-minute charge). You can also contact branch offices at 9454 Wilshire Blvd., Beverly Hills, CA 90212 (☎ **213/ 272-2661**) and 645 N. Michigan Ave., Chicago, IL 60611 (☎ **312/337-6301.** In Canada, visit 1981 avenue McGill College, Suite 490, Montréal, PQ H3A 2W9 (☎ **514/844-8566.**

1 Martinique

France's anchor in the Caribbean world, Martinique was the birthplace of the Empress Joséphine. In her youth, Madame de Maintenon, mistress of Louis XIV, also lived here in the small fishing village of Le Prêcheur.

Columbus first charted Martinique, and the French settled the island when the king's gentleman, Belain d'Esnambuc, took possession in the name of Louis XIII in 1635. In spite of some intrusions by British forces, the French have remained here ever since. So committed were the French to their West Indian colonies that in 1763 (the year of the Empress Joséphine's birth) they relinquished all their political influence in Canada for the right to remain on the island unchallenged by British interlopers. Emigration from France produced sugarcane plantations and rum distilleries.

In the beginning of their colonization, the French imported black slaves from Africa to work the plantations, but at the time of the French Revolution, slavery began to decline on Martinique. It wasn't until the mid-19th century, however, that its abolition was obtained by Victor Schoelcher, a Paris-born deputy from Alsace. Since 1946 Martinique has been a part of France.

Martinique is also part of the Lesser Antilles and lies in the semitropical zone; its western shore faces the Caribbean and its eastern shore faces the more turbulent Atlantic. It's some 4,340 miles from France, 2,000 miles from New York, 2,300 miles from Montréal, and 1,450 miles from Miami.

The surface of the island is only 420 square miles—50 miles at its longest and 21 miles at its widest point.

The ground is mountainous, especially in the rain-forested northern part where Mount Pelée, a volcano, rises to a height of 4,656 feet. In the center of the island the mountains are smaller, with Carbet Peak reaching a 3,960-foot summit. The high hills rising among the peaks or mountains are called *mornes*. The southern part of Martinique has only big hills, reaching peaks of 1,500 feet at Vauclin, 1,400 feet at Diamant. The irregular coastline of the island provides five bays, dozens of coves, and miles of sandy beaches.

The climate is relatively mild, with the average temperature in the 75° to 85° Fahrenheit range. At higher elevations it's considerably cooler. The island is cooled by a wind the French called *alizé,* and rain is frequent but doesn't last very long. From late August to November might be called the rainy season. April to September are the hottest months.

The early Carib peoples, who gave Columbus such a hostile reception, called Martinique "the island of flowers," and indeed it has remained so. The vegetation is lush, and includes hibiscus, poinsettias, bougainvillea, coconut palms, and mango trees. Almost any fruit that can grow in the ground sprouts out of Martinique's soil—pineapples, avocados, bananas, papayas, and custard apples.

Birdwatchers are often pleased at the number of hummingbirds. The mountain whistler, the blackbird, the mongoose, and multicolored butterflies are also spotted. After sunset, there's a permanent concert of grasshoppers, frogs, and crickets.

ORIENTATION
GETTING THERE

BY PLANE   Lamentin International Airport lies outside the village of Lamentin, a 15-minute taxi ride east of Fort-de-France and a 40-minute taxi ride northeast of the island's densest concentration of resort hotels (the Trois Islets peninsula). Most flights to Martinique and Guadeloupe require a transfer on a neighboring island—usually Puerto Rico, but occasionally Antigua. Direct or nonstop flights to the French islands from the U.S. mainland are rare: Air France (see below) offers only one flight per week, on Sunday. From Miami, it stops at each of the two islands.

American Airlines (☎ 800/433-7300) flies into its busy hub in San Juan, and from there, passengers transfer to one of usually two daily **American Eagle** (same phone number) flights heading to both Martinique and Guadeloupe. (American offers flights into San Juan from dozens of points throughout North America.) Taking off between 1:30 and 2pm, late enough to allow connections from virtually anywhere, the Eagle flights usually arrive at their destinations between $1^1/_2$ hours and 2 hours later. During the off-season, the evening flights to both islands are sometimes combined into a single flight, landing first at one island before continuing on to the next. Return flights to San Juan usually depart separately from both islands twice a day.

For passengers originating on the West Coast, American Airlines offers daily direct flights from Los Angeles to San Juan which depart at 7:20am. They touch down briefly in Dallas before continuing on nonstop to Puerto Rico, in time for ongoing connections to Martinique, Guadeloupe, and St. Martin.

Consult an American Airlines reservations clerk about booking your hotel simultaneously with your airfare, since substantial discounts sometimes apply if you handle both tasks at the same time.

Air France (☎ 800/237-2747) flies from Miami to Martinique (with continuing service to Guadeloupe and Guyana) every Sunday. More frequent are the airline's separate four-times-per-week nonstop flights from Paris's Charles-de-Gaulle airport to both Martinique and Guadeloupe.

LIAT (☎ 809/462-0700, or 212/251-1717 in New York City), the Antigua-based carrier, flies from Antigua to both Martinique and Guadeloupe several times a day, sometimes with connections on to Barbados. Both Antigua and Barbados are important air-terminus links for such transcontinental carriers as American Airlines (see above) and British Airways (☎ 800/247-9297), which flies into both Antigua and Barbados from London.

BY FERRY   You can travel between Guadeloupe and Martinique by boat; the sea route provides a leisurely crossing in about $3^3/_4$ hours with an intermediate stop at either Les Saintes or Dominica. The trip is made on modern, comfortable craft operated by **Trans Antilles Caribbean Express,** whose newest addition is a 112-foot catamaran with a capacity of 100 passengers and a capability of 38 knots. The Express schedule lists daily 8am departures from Pointe-à-Pitre and 1 or 2pm

Martinique

N

Atlantic Ocean

Macouba
Basse-Pointe
Grand' Rivière
Leyritz
Montagne Pelée
Le Lorrain
Ajoupa-Bouillon
Le Marigot
Le Prêcheur

Ste-Marie
St-Pierre
Morne des Esses
Madras
Trinité

Le Carbet

Bellefontaine
St-Joseph
Case-Pilote

Fort-de-France
Le François

Pointe du Bout

Anse Mitan

Trois-Ilets
Vauclin
Grande Anse
Anses-d'Arlets
Rivière-Pilote
Le Diamant
Diamant
Ste-Luce
Le Marin

Ste-Anne
Cap Chevalier

Plage des Salines

Caribbean Sea

Beach

departures from Fort-de-France. The fare is 315 F ($59.90) one way per adult, or 450 F ($85.50) round-trip. For details and reservations, contact Trans Antilles Express, 6 Immeuble Darse, quai Gatine, 97110 Pointe-à-Pitre, Guadeloupe (☎ **596/91-13-43**), or Caribbean Express, Terminal Inter-Iles, Bassin de Radoub, Fort-de-France, 97200 Martinique (☎ **596/63-12-11**). Trip time is 2³/₄ hours.

GETTING AROUND

BY BUS AND TAXI COLLECTIF   There are two types of buses operating on Martinique. Regular buses, called *grands busses,* hold about 40 passengers and cost $1 to $5 to go anywhere within the city limits of Fort-de-France. But to travel beyond the city limits, *taxis collectifs* are used. These are privately owned minivans that traverse the island and bear the sign TC. Their routes are flexible and depend on passenger need. A simple one-way fare is 30 F ($5.70) from Fort-de-France to Ste-Anne. Taxis collectifs depart from the heart of Fort-de-France from the parking lot of Pointe Simon. There is no phone number to call for information about this unpredictable means of transport, and there are no set schedules. Traveling in a taxi collectif is for the adventurous tourist—they are crowded and not very comfortable.

BY TAXI   Travel by taxi is popular but expensive. Most of the cabs aren't metered, and you'll have to agree on the price of the ride before getting in. Most visitors arriving at Lamentin Airport head for one of the resorts along the peninsula of Pointe du Bout. To do so costs about 150 F ($28.50) during the day, about 200 F ($38) in the evening. Night fares are in effect from 8pm to 6am, when 40% surcharges are added. For a radio taxi, call **596/63-63-62.**

If you want to rent a taxi for the day, it's better to have a party of at least three or four people to keep costs low. Depending on the size of the car, expect to pay 800 F ($152) and up for a five-hour trip.

BY RENTAL CAR   The scattered nature of Martinique's geography makes renting a car especially tempting. Martinique has several local car-rental agencies, but clients have complained of mechanical difficulties and billing irregularities. I recommend renting from one of America's "big three" (Hertz, Budget, and Avis). A valid driver's license, such as one from the United States or Canada, is needed to rent a car for up to 20 days. After that, an International Driver's License is required.

Most car-rental rates are about $60 a day, including unlimited mileage. **Budget** (☎ **800/527-0700**) has offices at rue Félix-Eboué, 12, in Fort-de-France (☎ **596/63-69-00**); **Avis** (☎ **800/331-2112**), at rue Ernest-Deproge, 4, in Fort-de-France (☎ **596/70-11-60**); and **Hertz** (☎ **800/654-3001**), at rue Ernest-Deproge, 24, in Fort-de-France (☎ **596/60-64-64**). These rental companies also have kiosks at Lamentin Airport.

Remember that regardless of which company you choose, you'll be hit with a whopping 14% value-added tax (VAT) on top of the final bill. Collision-damage waivers (CDWs), an excellent idea in a country where the populace drives somewhat recklessly, cost $12 and up per day.

Each of the companies maintains a kiosk in the arrivals hall of the island's Lamentin Airport, with staffs willing to transport prospective renters to pickup depots a short drive away. Prices are usually lower if you reserve a car in North America at least two business days before your arrival. Renters must be 21 years old at Hertz and Avis, and 23 at Budget.

BY FERRY   The least expensive way to go between quai d'Esnambuc in Fort-de-France and Pointe du Bout is by ferry (*vedette*), costing 13 F ($2.50) per passenger. Ferry schedules are printed in the free visitor's guide *Choubouloute*, which is distributed by the tourist office. However, if the weather is bad, the service may be cancelled.

Ferry service has been expanded between Fort-de-France and the little beach resorts of Anse Mitan and Anse-à-l'Ane, which are across the bay and are home to many small hotels and a multitude of Créole restaurants. A boat departs daily from quai d'Esnambuc in Fort-de-France every 30 minutes from 6am to 7pm. The piers at Anse Mitan and Anse-à-l'Ane are departure points for those areas. The trip takes only about 15 minutes.

BY BICYCLE AND MOTORBIKE   Bicycles and motorbikes are rentable from **Discount** in Pointe du Bout (☎ **596/66-54-37**), as well as **Funny** in Fort-de-France (☎ **596/63-33-05**). The new 18-speed VTT (*velo tout terrain,* or all-terrain bike) is revolutionizing cycling.

For tour information on the "mountain" bike, contact **Jacques-Henry Vartel,** VT Tilt, Anse Mitan (☎ **596/66-01-01**).

CARNIVAL

If you like masquerades and dancing in the streets, you should attend carnival, or "Vaval" as it's known here. The event of the year, carnival begins right after the New Year, as each village prepares costumes and floats. Weekend after weekend, frenzied celebrations take place, reaching fever pitch just before Lent.

Fort-de-France is the focal point, and the spirit of the carnival envelops the island, as narrow streets are jammed with floats. On Ash Wednesday the streets of Fort-de-France are filled with *diablesses,* or she-devils (portrayed by members of both sexes). Costumed in black and white, they crowd the streets to form King Carnival's funeral procession. As devils cavort about and the rum flows, a funeral pyre is built at La Savane. When it's set on fire, the dancing of those "she-devils" becomes frantic (many are thoroughly drunk at this point).

Long past dusk, the cortège takes the coffin to its burial, ending carnival until another year.

FAST FACTS: Martinique

Area Code   Martinique is not part of the Caribbean's 809 area code. For information on telephone calls from North America, see "Telephone," below.

Banking Hours   Banks are open Monday through Friday from 7:30am to noon and 2:30 to 4pm.

Consulate   The nearest U.S. consulate is on Barbados.

Currency   The **French franc (F)** is the legal tender here. Exchange your money at banks because they give much better rates than hotels. Currency quotations in this chapter are in both U.S. dollars and French francs. At press time, 1 franc is exchanged for 19¢ (5.28 F = $1 U.S.). Of course, exchange rates are subject to fluctuations and are quoted only for your general guidelines.

Currency Exchange   A money-exchange service, **Change Caraïbes** (☎ **596/ 51-57-91**), operates daily at the arrivals building at Lamentin Airport.

Customs   Items for personal use, such as tobacco, cameras, and film, are admitted without formalities or tax if not in excessive quantity.

Documents   U.S. and Canadian citizens need proof of identity (a voter registration card or birth certificate, plus a photo ID, or a passport) for stays of less than 21 days. After that, a valid passport is required. A return or ongoing ticket is also necessary. British subjects need a valid passport.

Drugstores   Try the Pharmacie de la Paix, at the corner of rue Perrinon and rue Victor-Schoelcher in Fort-de-France (☎ 596/71-94-83).

Electricity   Electricity here is 220 volts A.C., 50 cycles, the same as that used on the French mainland. However, check with your hotel to see if they have converted the electrical voltage and outlets in the bathrooms (some have). If they haven't, bring your own transformer and adapter for U.S. appliances; don't count on the hotel's.

Emergencies   Call the police at **17,** report a fire at **18,** and summon an ambulance at **596/75-15-75.**

Hospitals   There's a 24-hour emergency room at Hôpital La Meynard, Châteauboeuf, right outside Fort-de-France (☎ 596/55-20-00).

Information   The **Office Départemental du Tourisme** (tourist office) is on boulevard Alfassa in Fort-de-France (☎ 596/63-79-60), open Monday through Friday from 8am to 5pm and on Saturday from 8am to noon. The Information Desk at Lamentin Airport is open daily until the last flight comes in.

Languages   French, the official language, is spoken by almost everyone. The local Créole patois uses words borrowed from France, England, Spain, and Africa. In the wake of increased tourism, English is occasionally spoken in the major hotels, restaurants, and tourist organizations—but don't count on driving around the countryside and asking for directions in English.

Medical Care   Health services and medical equipment are both modern and comprehensive. There are some 18 hospitals and clinics on the island. In an emergency, your hotel can put you in touch with the nearest one.

Safety   Crime is hardly rampant on Martinique, yet there are still those who prey on unsuspecting tourists. Follow the usual precautions here, especially in Fort-de-France (a large Caribbean city) and in the tourist-hotel belt of Pointe du Bout. It's wise to protect your valuables and never leave them unguarded on the beach.

Telephone   To call Martinique from the United States, if your long-distance telephone company is equipped to handle international direct dialing, dial **011** (the international access code), then **596** (the country code for the French West Indies), and finally the six-digit local number. If you cannot direct-dial internationally, dial **0** ("zero," for the operator) and tell the operator you wish to make an international call; once you are transferred to the international operator, state the **596** country code and then the local number, and the operator will dial the call for you. To make a call within Martinique, only the six-digit local number is necessary.

Time   Martinique is on Atlantic standard time year round, one hour later than eastern standard time except when daylight saving time is in effect. Then Martinique time is the same as the East Coast of the United States.

Water   Potable water is found throughout the island.

Weather   The climate is relatively mild—the average temperature is in the 75° to 85° Fahrenheit range.

FORT-DE-FRANCE

A melange of New Orleans and Menton (French Riviera), Fort-de-France is the largest town on Martinique and lies at the end of a large bay surrounded by evergreen hills. Iron-grillwork balconies overflowing with flowers are common-place here.

The proud people of Martinique are even more fascinating than the town. Today the Créole women are likely to be seen in jeans instead of their traditional turbans and Empress Joséphine–style gowns, and they rarely wear those massive earrings that used to jounce and sway as they sauntered along.

Narrow streets climb up the steep hills where houses have been built to catch the overflow of the capital's more than 100,000 inhabitants.

WHERE TO STAY

Rates are sometimes advertised in U.S. dollars, sometimes in French francs, and sometimes in a combination of the two currencies. It depends on the individual hotel.

Hôtel La Batelière

Route 32, 97200 Schoelcher, Martinique, F.W.I. ☎ **596/61-49-49.** Fax 61-70-57. 194 rms, 6 duplexes and suites. A/C MINIBAR TV TEL. Winter, 950–1,700 F ($180.50–$323) single; 1,100–2,100 F ($209–$399) double; from 2,500 F ($475) duplex or suite. Off-season, 670–920 F ($127.30–$174.80) single; 830–1,100 F ($157.70–$209) double; from 1,900 F ($361) duplex or suite. (Rates include buffet breakfast.) AE, DC, MC, V. Free parking.

Built in the late 1960s and renovated in 1991, this waterside French-modern high-rise hotel is a white stucco structure, set back in a garden from its wide private beach. The hotel lacks super-glamour, but successfully offers many social activities and dining choices. Each unit contains a tile bath, but best of all are the roomwide glass doors that open onto your own water-view terrace.

In the Blue Marine dining room, French, international, and Créole cuisine is served, and there's a beach restaurant near the swimming pool. Tennis is free, except at night when there's a surcharge. On the premises are a beauty salon, barbershop, and a handful of boutiques. A casino and disco (the Queen's Club) were added in 1994.

Hôtel L'Impératrice

Place de la Savane, rue de la Liberté, 97200 Fort-de-France, Martinique, F.W.I. ☎ **596/63-06-82,** or 800/223-9815 in the U.S. Fax 72-66-30. 44 rms. A/C TV TEL. 300–400 F ($57–$76) single; 460–560 F ($87.40–$106.40) double. (Rates include breakfast.) AE, DC, MC, V. Free parking.

Favored by businesspeople, this stucco-sided hotel faces a landscaped mall in the heart of town, near the water's edge and close to the tourist office. Originally built in the 1950s and named in honor of one of Martinique's most famous exports (Joséphine), it has encircling balconies overlooking the traffic at the western edge of the sprawling promenade known as the Savane. The lounge has large, white wickerwork chairs and an adjoining bar. Or you may prefer the second-floor bar, whose trademark colors of green and white have been repainted (but never changed) since its original construction. The bedrooms are modern and functional, and many contain TV sets. The front rooms tend to be noisy; yet, to compensate, windows overlook the life along the Savane. The hotel's restaurant, Le Joséphine, does a brisk business with local shoppers in town for the day.

Don't expect too charming, or too articulate, a staff here. Almost no one speaks English, and the staff has seen many a client come and go over the years. Despite the confusion in the very noisy lobby, and the bland decor of the simple bedrooms, you might end up enjoying this place.

Le Lafayette

Rue de la Liberté, 5, 97200 Fort-de-France, Martinique, F.W.I. ☎ **596/73-80-50,** or 800/223-9815 in the U.S. Fax 60-97-75. 24 rms. A/C MINIBAR TV TEL. 300–340 F ($57–$64.60) single; 350–400 F ($66.50–$76) double. Breakfast 35 F ($6.70) extra. AE, DC, MC, V. Free parking.

You'll enter this modern hotel, located right on La Savane, through rue Victor-Hugo; the reception hall is up a few steps of terra-cotta. The dark-brown wooden doors are offset by the soft beige walls. Japanese wall tapestries decorate the bedrooms, and most rooms contain twin beds in a dark-brown wood. The bathrooms are in pure white, and the overall impression is of a neat, but simple hostelry. A Vietnamese restaurant, Le Dragon d'Or, open every day for lunch and dinner, was inaugurated on the hotel's ground floor in 1994.

WHERE TO DINE

La Plantation

In Martinique Cottages, Pays Mélé Jeanne-d'Arc, Lamentin. ☎ **596/50-16-08.** Reservations required. Appetizers 75–150 F ($14.30–28.50); main courses 100–200 F ($19–$38). AE, MC, V. Lunch Mon–Fri noon–2pm; dinner Mon–Sat 7:30–9:30pm. FRENCH.

Near the airport, a 20-minute drive south of Fort-de-France, La Plantation is acclaimed as one of the finest restaurants on the island. In a small French Antillean hotel, the restaurant is run by a dynamic brother and sister, Jean-Marc and Peggy Arnaud. Knowledgeable gourmands flock to their country retreat. An imaginative cuisine is the aim of the chef, Marcel Ravin, who studied in Alsace before returning to his native Martinique. Menu items include foie gras in the style of the French mainland, an assiette gourmande composed of lobster and foie gras, cream of sea urchin soup, white salmon cutlets roasted with olive oil, an émincé of sweetbreads, a traditional version of rack of lamb, and the restaurant's signature dish, a soufflé of lobster served in the lobster's shell.

Le Coq Hardi

Rue Martin-Luther-King, 52. ☎ **596/71-59-64.** Reservations recommended. Appetizers 55–85 F ($10.50–$16.20); main courses 100–200 F ($19–$38). AE, MC, V. Lunch Thurs–Tues noon–2pm; dinner Thurs–Tues 7–10:45pm. Transportation: Take a taxi (two-minute ride) north from the main square (La Savane) of Fort-de-France. STEAK/GRILLS

The premier steakhouse on Martinique is maintained by one of the island's most likable and realistic restaurateurs, Alphonse Sintive. Trained as a master butcher and *charcutier* before World War II on the French mainland, he can regale you with stories of his experiences in the French Foreign Legion in Indochina and Algeria. The juicy steaks and chops are imported from France and grilled over a wood fire. You'll find this restaurant beside a steeply inclined traffic artery, which crisscrosses a residential hillside just outside the center of town. Hearty eaters will appreciate the large portions. A specialty is tournedos Rossini with foie gras. Considered one of the most generous and likable hosts on the island, Mr. Sintive usually offers a free after-dinner drink (*digestif*) to anyone who mentions this guidebook.

WHAT TO SEE & DO

At the center of the town lies a broad garden planted with many palms and mangoes, **La Savane,** a handsome savannah with shops and cafés lining its sides. In the middle of this grand square stands a statue of Joséphine, "Napoleon's little Créole," made of white marble by Vital Debray. With the grace of a Greek goddess, the statue poses in a Regency gown and looks toward Trois-Ilets, where she was born.

After viewing her, you can head for the **St. Louis Roman Catholic Cathedral,** on rue Victor-Schoelcher, built in 1875. It's an extraordinary iron building, which someone once likened to "a sort of Catholic railway station."

A statue in front of the Palais de Justice is of the island's second main historical figure, Victor Schoelcher (you'll see his name a lot on Martinique). As mentioned, he worked to free the slaves more than a century ago.

The **Bibliothèque Schoelcher,** rue de la Liberté (☎ **596/70-26-67**), also honors this popular hero. The elaborate structure was first displayed at the Paris Exposition of 1889. However, the Romanesque portal in red and blue, the Egyptian lotus-petal columns, even the turquoise tiles were imported piece by piece from Paris and reassembled here.

Guarding the port is **Fort St-Louis,** built in the Vauban style on a rocky promontory. In addition, **Fort Tartenson** and **Fort Desaix** stand on hills overlooking the port.

The **Musée Départemental de la Martinique,** rue de la Liberté, 9 (☎ **596/71-57-05**), the one bastion on Martinique that preserves its pre-Columbian past, has relics left from the early settlers, the Arawaks, and the Caribs. The museum faces the Savane and is open Monday through Friday from 8:30am to 1pm and 2:30 to 5pm, and on Saturday from 9am to noon and 2 to 5pm, charging 15 F ($2.90) for adults and 5 F ($1) for children.

Sacré-Coeur de Balata Cathedral, at Balata, overlooking Fort-de-France, is a copy of the one looking down from Montmartre upon Paris—and this one is just as incongruous, maybe more so. It's reached by going along route de la Trace (route N3). Balata is 6 miles north of Fort-de-France.

A few minutes away on route N3, the **Jardin de Balata (Balata Garden)** (☎ **596/64-48-73**) is a tropical botanical park. The park was created by Jean-Philippe Thoze on land the jungle was rapidly reclaiming around a Créole house that belonged to his grandmother. He has also restored the house, furnishing it with antiques and engravings depicting life in other days, and with bouquets and baskets of fruit renewed daily. The garden contains flowers, shrubs, and trees growing in profusion and offering a vision of tropical splendor. Balata is open daily from 9am to 5pm. Admission is 35 F ($6.70) for adults and 15 F ($2.90) for children.

AN EXCURSION TO TROIS-ILETS

Marie-Josèphe-Rose Tascher de la Pagerié was born here in 1763. As Joséphine, she was to become the wife of Napoléon I and empress of France from 1804 to 1809. She'd been married before to Alexandre de Beauharnais, who'd actually wanted to wed either of her two more attractive sisters. Six years older than

Napoléon, she pretended that she'd lost her birth certificate so he wouldn't find out her true age. Although many historians call her ruthless and selfish (certainly unfaithful), she is still revered by some on Martinique as an uncommonly gracious lady. Others have less kind words for her, because Napoléon is said by some historians to have "reinvented" slavery, and blame Joséphine's influence.

After 20 miles of driving south from Fort-de-France, you reach Trois-Ilets, a charming little village. One mile outside the hamlet, turn left to **La Pagerié,** where a small museum (☎ **596/68-34-55**) of mementos relating to Joséphine has been installed in the former estate kitchen. Along with her childhood bed in the kitchen, you'll see a passionate letter from Napoléon. The collection was compiled by Dr. Robert Rose-Rosette. Here Joséphine gossiped with her slaves and played the guitar.

Still remaining are the partially restored ruins of the Pagerié sugar mill and the church (in the village itself) where she was christened in 1763. The plantation was destroyed in a hurricane. The museum is open Tuesday through Friday from 9am to 5pm and on Saturday and Sunday from 9am to 1pm and 2:30 to 5:30pm, charging 20 F ($3.80) for admission.

A botanical garden, the **Parc des Floralies,** is adjacent to the golf course Golf de l'Impératrice Joséphine, as is the museum devoted to Joséphine described above.

Maison de la Canne, Pointe Vatable (☎ **596/68-32-04**), stands on the road to Trois-Ilets. (From Fort-de-France, you can take a taxi or shuttle bus to La Marina, Pointe du Bout; from there, a bus heads for Pointe Vatable.) It was created in 1987 to house a permanent exhibition that tells the story of sugarcane with panels, models, tools, a miniature slave ship, an ancient plow tethered to life-size models of two oxen, a restored carriage, and a copper still. Hostesses guide visitors through the exhibition. It's open Tuesday through Sunday from 9:30am to 5:30pm, with an admission of 15 F ($2.90).

POINTE DU BOUT

Pointe du Bout is a narrow peninsula across the bay from the busy capital of Fort-de-France. It's considered the best-accessorized resort area of Martinique, with at least four of the island's largest hotels, an impressive marina, about a dozen tennis courts, swimming pools, and facilities for horseback riding and all kinds of water sports. There's also a Robert Trent Jones–designed golf course, a handful of independent restaurants, a gambling casino, and boutiques. Except for the hillside that contains the Hôtel Bakoua, most of the hotel district is flat and verdant, with carefully maintained gardens and rigidly monitored parking zones.

GETTING THERE   To drive there from Fort-de-France, leave by route 1, which takes you for a few minutes along the autoroute. You cross the plain of Lamentin, the industrial area of Fort-de-France and the site of the international airport. Very frequently the air is filled with the fragrance of caramel because of the large sugarcane factories in the surrounding area.

After 20 miles of driving, you reach Trois-Ilets, Joséphine's hometown. Three miles farther on your right, take the D38 to Pointe du Bout.

For those who want to reach Pointe du Bout by sea, there's a ferry service (see "Getting Around," above) running all day long (until midnight) from Fort-de-France for a fare of 13 F ($2.50).

WHERE TO STAY

Expensive

❖ Hotel Bakoua-Sofitel

Pointe du Bout, 97229 Trois-Ilets, Martinique, F.W.I. ☎ **596/66-02-02,** 071/730-7144 in London, or 800/221-4542 in the U.S. Fax 66-00-41. 140 rms, 2 suites. A/C MINIBAR TV TEL. Winter, 1,415–1,800 F ($268.90–$342) single; 2,060–2,830 F ($391.40–$537.70) double; 3,500 F ($665) suite. Off-season, 1,000 F ($190) single; 1,500 F ($285) double; 2,800 F ($532) suite. (Rates include continental breakfast.) MAP rates 195–210 F ($37.10–$39.90) per person extra. AE, DC, MC, V. Free parking.

Considered a famous and desirable hotel with a long history of glamour, this hostelry is known for the beauty of its landscaping and its position on a hillside somewhat removed from the bustle of the many hotels that surround it, 17 miles from the airport. Built in 1966, and run by the Sofitel chain, this hotel consists of three low-rise buildings in the center of a garden, plus another, bungalow-type building, right on the beach. Celebrities are often attracted to the hotel. The rooms are generally small and conservatively modern.

Dining/Entertainment: A dramatically engineered bar, crafted into a perfect circle out of exotic Caribbean hardwood, is one of the ideal rendezvous points of Pointe du Bout. The hotel contains a beachside snack bar as well as an upscale and elegant French restaurant, Le Chateaubriand. Dinner is served nightly from 7 to 10pm. Other places to eat include Le Jardin Tropicale and La Sirene, the latter specializing in seafood.

Services: Concierge, laundry, babysitting, free twice-daily shuttle bus to the golf course.

Facilities: Swimming pool, active sports program (including a free golf lesson and a free driving lesson), diving center; waterskiing, jet-skiing, golf, and horseback riding available nearby.

Hôtel Méridien Trois-Ilets

Pointe du Bout, Trois-Ilets (B.P. 894, 97245 Fort-de-France), Martinique, F.W.I. ☎ **596/66-00-00,** or 800/543-4300 in the U.S. and Canada. Fax 66-00-74. 287 rms, 8 suites. A/C TV TEL. Winter, 1,250 F ($237.50) single or double; 3,000 F ($570) suite. Off-season, 950 F ($180.50) single or double; 1,500 F ($285) suite. (Rates include buffet breakfast.) AE, MC, V. Free parking.

This is the largest, most visible, and tallest building in the resort community of Pointe du Bout, with some of the most extensive facilities, although it's definitely not the most desirable place to stay. In spite of that, the largest number of visitors to Martinique end up here. Owned and operated by Air France, it contains a slightly shabby reception area which opens onto the palm-fringed swimming pool, the waters of the bay, and the faraway lights of Fort-de-France. The hotel is slightly angled to follow the contours of the shoreline, so each of its bedrooms overlooks either the Caribbean or the bay. The small bedrooms were renovated late in 1990, and remain a patchwork of hasty repairs. Each contains a private balcony and conservatively modern furnishings with tropical accents. Farther out on the point is an old French colonial fort.

Dining/Entertainment: La Capitane, the best restaurant at the hotel, is open to a view of the sea, which is its best feature, not its "messhall" decor. The casino provides evening amusement every night between 9pm and 3am. Around the huge block of rooms are a waterside garden, a 100-foot marina, and a cabaña bar near the swimming pool. Every Thursday night the hotel hosts the Ballets Martiniquais in a pavilion near the pool. A Créole buffet supper follows this folklore show.

Services: 24-hour room service, laundry, concierge, massage.

Facilities: Swimming pool, two tennis courts, sauna, hairdressing salon, water sports (including scuba diving, sailing, snorkeling, waterskiing, and windsurfing).

Novotel Carayou

Pointe du Bout, 97229 Trois-Ilets, Martinique, F.W.I. ☎ **596/66-04-04**, or 800/221-4542 in the U.S. Fax 66-00-57. 197 rms. A/C MINIBAR TV TEL. Winter, 960 F ($182.40) single; 1,140 F ($216.60) double; 1,370 F ($260.30) triple. Off-season, discounts of around 25%. (Rates include continental breakfast.) AE, DC, MC, V. Free parking.

This hotel has always prided itself on the lushness of its gardens and the low-rise glamour of its garden setting. Radically renovated in late 1994 and early 1995, it reopened with an almost completely rebuilt physical plant. The accommodations are in a series of two-story outbuildings, each is encircled by large lawns dotted with coconut or palm trees and many flowering shrubs. The hotel is a member of France's biggest hotel chain, the Accor Group.

Dining/Entertainment: The establishment contains at least three different dining areas, including a formal French and Créole restaurant and a beachfront grill for sandwiches and salads. Créole cookery, particularly the preparation of fish, has always been done with flair here. One appealing bar, La Paillote, is outfitted with a view of the sea and many nautical accessories.

Services: 24-hour concierge, laundry.

Facilities: Swimming pool, a small beach, water sports (including windsurfing, scuba diving, waterskiing, sailboat rentals, and snorkeling).

Moderate

Hôtel La Pagerié

Pointe du Bout, 97229 Trois-Ilets, Martinique, F.W.I. ☎ **596/66-05-30**, or 800-221-4542 in the U.S. Fax 66-00-99. 98 apartments. A/C TV TEL. Winter, 550–680 F ($104.50–$129.20) apartment for one; 610–935 F ($115.90–$177.70) apartment for two; 795–1,145 F ($151.10–$217.60) apartment for three. Off-season, 483 F ($91.80) apartment for one; 581 F ($110.40) apartment for two; 720 F ($136.80) apartment for three. (Rates include breakfast.) AE, DC, MC, V. Free parking.

The facilities here are relatively modest compared to those in some of the larger and more expensive hotels of Pointe du Bout, but its guests are able to compensate by visiting the many restaurants, bars, and sports facilities that proliferate nearby. Set close to the gardens of the Hôtel Bakoua-Sofitel, a 16-mile drive from the airport, this moderately priced hotel offers you your own personal apartment, although the walls are thin. Accommodations are neat and uncomplicated, with tile floors and splashes of color. Each has a small refrigerator and a balcony with a view opening onto the bay, and about two-thirds of the units contain tiny kitchenettes. (There is no price supplement for units with kitchenette.) The hotel contains a small swimming pool and a small bar, open only in the evening, plus a restaurant, L'Hibiscus. Clients usually walk the short distance to the establishment's neighbor hotel, the Novotel Carayou.

Budget

Auberge de L'Anse Mitan

Anse Mitan, 97229 Trois-Ilets, Martinique, F.W.I. ☎ **596/66-01-12**, or 800/223-9815 in the U.S. Fax 66-01-05. 19 rms, 6 studios. A/C TEL. Winter, 330 F ($62.70) single (including breakfast); 420 F ($79.80) double (including breakfast) 400 F ($76) studio for one or two (without breakfast). Off-season, 280 F ($53.20) single (including breakfast); 330 F ($62.70) double (including breakfast); 300 F ($57) studio for one or two (without breakfast). AE, DC, MC, V. Free parking.

Many guests prefer its location at the isolated end of a road whose more commercial side is laden with restaurants and a bustling nighttime parade. The hotel was originally built in 1930, but it has been renovated several times since then by the hospitable Athanase family. What you see today is a three-story concrete-box-type structure. Six of the units are studios with kitchens and TVs; all have private shower. You don't get a lot that's special here, but few object to the price.

La Petite Louisiane

Anse Mitan, 97229 Trois-Ilets, Martinique, F.W.I. ☎ **596/66-05-36.** Fax 66-07-45. 8 rms. A/C TEL. Winter, 308 F ($58.50) single; 386 F ($73.30) double. Off-season, 210 F ($39.90) single; 210 F ($39.90) double. Breakfast buffet 40 F ($7.60) extra. AE, MC, V. Free parking.

The bedrooms offered by this small inn, beside the main highway about a mile southwest of the tourist complex at Pointe du Bout, are considered a kind of adjunct to the establishment's main focus, which is its Créole restaurant (see "Where to Dine," below). The bedrooms, however, are clean and uncomplicated, decorated almost completely in white, and appropriate for clients who plan to spend lots of time at the local beach, which lies a short drive away. Nightlife, water sports, and the bustle associated with a large resort are at Pointe du Bout, less than a mile away.

WHERE TO DINE

Davidiana

La Marina, Pointe du Bout. ☎ **596/66-09-44.** Reservations usually not required. Appetizers 25–60 F ($4.80–$11.40); main courses 80–150 F ($15.20–$28.50). AE, MC, V. Lunch daily noon–3pm; dinner daily 7–11pm. FRENCH/CREOLE.

This is today's incarnation of the once-famous Chez Sidonie, whose namesake chef was the most acclaimed Créole cook on Martinique. Located beside the marina, across the road from the Hôtel Méridien, the restaurant is the domain of Robert Choucroune, who maintains a boutique below it and has renovated the upstairs dining room. Amid light-colored oil paintings, madras-patterned curtains and napery, and sweeping views over the marina, you can enjoy Créole food. Menu items include such time-tested favorites as fish soup, accras of codfish, fricassée of crayfish, and colombos of lamb, as well as a bistro-inspired array of fish, chicken, and pork dishes. One especially unusual dish here is sharkmeat stew, which the chefs prepare in the Créole style. The flavors are zesty, the ambience restful.

La Mouïna

Route de Redoute, 127. ☎ **596/79-34-57.** Reservations required. Appetizers 50–130 F ($9.50–$24.70); main courses 90–180 F ($17.10–$34.20). MC, V. Lunch Mon–Fri noon–2:30pm; dinner Mon–Fri 7:30–9:30pm. Transportation: Taxi. FRENCH/CREOLE.

La Mouïna, whose name is a Créole word for a meeting house, is a restaurant offering one of the finest luncheons on the island. Sitting next to the police station in the suburb of Redoute, about 1 1/2 miles north of Fort-de-France, this 60-year-old white colonial house shelters the culinary domain of one of the island's most experienced groups of chefs. There's also a garden, which the owners maintain and is better appreciated by daylight. You might begin with crabes farcis (stuffed crabs) or escargots de Bourgogne, then follow with tournedos Rossini, rognon de veau entier grillé (whole grilled kidneys), or duckling in orange sauce. The owners are particularly fond of their version of red snapper en papillotte. Ask at your hotel for good directions before setting out (or even better, take a taxi), because it's hard to find.

La Petite Louisiane

Anse Mitan, Trois-Ilets. ☎ **596/68-05-36.** Reservations recommended. Appetizers 40–80 F ($7.60–$15.20); main courses 70–125 F ($13.30–$23.80). AE, MC, V. Lunch daily noon–3pm; dinner daily 7–10pm. FRENCH/CREOLE.

Set in a much-restored West Indian house, on the main highway beside the entrance road leading into Trois-Ilets, this well-established restaurant acquired a new owner late in 1993. Much patronized by local residents, it features a well-prepared cuisine of French and Créole specialties, which you enjoy in an indoor-outdoor dining room of low-slung, clapboard-sided charm. Menu items include filets of flying fish with curry, stuffed crab backs, filet of John Dory with coconut, blanquette of shellfish, émincé of conch, gratin of crab, whitefish in mustard sauce, salads studded with strips of magret of duckling, stuffed quail with passionfruit sauce, and chicken breasts stuffed with conch.

THE SOUTH LOOP

We now leave Pointe du Bout and head south for more sun and beaches. Resort centers here include Le Diamant and Sainte-Anne.

On the way to them from Trois-Ilets, you can follow a small curved road that brings you to **Anse-à-l'Ane, Grande Anse,** and **Anses d'Arlets.** At any of these places are small beaches, quite safe and usually not crowded.

At Anses d'Arlets the scenery is beautiful. Fishing boats draw up on the beach, and the nets are spread out to dry in the sun.

From Anses d'Arlets, route D37 takes you to Diamant. The road offers much scenery.

LE DIAMANT

Set on the island's southwestern coastline, this village offers a good beach, which is open to the prevailing southern winds. The village is named after one of Martinique's best-known geological oddities, Le Rocher du Diamant (Diamond Rock), a barren offshore island which juts upward from the sea to a height of 573 feet. Sometimes referred to as the Gibraltar of the Caribbean, it figured prominently in a daring British-led invasion in 1804, when British mariners carried a formidable amount of ammunition and 110 sailors to the top. There, despite frequent artillery bombardments from the French-held coastline, the garrison held out for 18 months, completely dominating the passageway between the rock and the coastline of Martinique. Intrepid foreigners sometimes visit Diamond Rock, but the access across the strong currents of the channel is considered risky.

Diamond Beach, on the Martinique "mainland," offers a sandy bottom, verdant groves of swaying palms, and many different surf and bathing possibilities. The entire district has developed in recent years into a resort, scattered with about 10 hotels, most of which consist of simple clusters of low-rise buildings with good landscaping and access to the beach.

Where to Stay & Dine

⑤Hotel Diamant Les Bains

97223 Le Diamant, Martinique. F.W.I. ☎ **596/76-40-14.** Fax 76-27-00. 26 rms. A/C TV TEL. Winter, 380–480 F ($72.20–$91.20) single; 500–600 F ($95–$114) double. Off-season, 310–380 F ($58.90–$72.20) single, 380–450 F ($72.20–$85.50) double. (Rates include continental breakfast.) MC, V. Free parking. Closed 10 days in June, and Sept 1 to mid-Oct.

Originally built in the 1950s, and today capably managed by resident owners Hubert and Marie-Yvonne Andrieu, this is a simple, unpretentious, family-style hotel. Twenty of its 26 accommodations are in a series of outlying motel-style bungalows set either in a garden or beside the beach; another six are in the resort's main building containing the dining and drinking facilities. Two of the rooms are outfitted for handicapped clients. From the edge of the resort's swimming pool you can enjoy a view of the offshore island of Diamond Rock. Most accommodations have white tile floors, small refrigerators, and built-in furniture made from polished fruitwoods.

The main building, whose bedrooms are lined along an upper deck, houses the restaurant, where Mr. Andrieu works as the establishment's chef. Full meals are served at lunch and dinner every day of the week except Wednesday. A fixed-price meal at any time of the day costs 120 F ($22.80), and might include classic Créole specialties such as crab salad, spicy black pudding, and a fish blaff. Dessert might be a coconut flan. The cuisine is for the most part Créole, with some French dishes thrown in. Locally caught fish often appears on the menu.

Novotel Le Diamant

97223 Le Diamant, Martinique, F.W.I. ☎ **596/76-42-42,** or 800/221-4542 in the U.S. Fax 76-22-87. 181 rms, 6 suites. A/C TV TEL. Winter, 1,100–1,550 F ($209–$294.50) single; 1,200–2,000 F ($228–$380) double; from 2,420 F ($459.80) suite. Off-season, 635 F ($120.70) single; 780 F ($148.20) double; 1,280 F ($243.20) suite. (Rates include buffet breakfast.) AE, DC, MC, V. Free parking.

Two miles outside the village and 18 miles south of Fort-de-France on 6 acres of forested land, the Novotel resort is in one of the most beautiful districts on Martinique—on a rock-bordered peninsula that was famous as an 18th-century stronghold of the (eventually defeated) English. A low-rise building fitted into the landscaping around it, this hotel is known for a beautiful setting and a particularly difficult staff. It's the ultimate in laissez-faire, hands-off management, where clients, often tour groups from France, are basically left to fend almost completely for themselves. Even if the staff is not to your liking (and this has been the case year after year at this hotel), you might end up enjoying your holiday here.

From many of the bedrooms, the views are more evocative of the South Pacific than of the Caribbean. Units face either the pool or the coast, with its view of Diamond Rock, and are tropical in their decor. The reception opens onto a large pool which you can cross over on a Chinese-style wooden bridge to connect with the dining facilities. These include Le Flamboyant (dinner only, and the most formal); La Cabaña du Pêcheur (lunch and dinner); and a poolside café. Outside the hotel, the neighboring beaches aren't too crowded, and aren't too good either. Lawns and gardens, as well as tennis courts, surround the hotel. Water sports are also offered. The trip from the airport in a taxi should take about 40 minutes.

SAINTE-ANNE

As you follow the road south to Trois Rivières, you'll come to **Sainte-Luce,** perhaps one of the island's most charming villages. Beaches of varying quality surround the town, and it's the site of the Forêt Montravail. Continuing, you'll reach Rivière-Pilote, quite a large town, and **Le Marin,** at the bottom of a bay of the same name.

From Le Marin, a 5-mile drive brings you to Sainte-Anne, at the extreme southern tip of Martinique. This is a sleepy little village, with white sand beaches. It opens onto views of the Sainte Lucia Canal, and nearby is the site of the Petrified Savannah Forest. The French call it **Savane des Pétrifications.** It's a field of petrified volcanic boulders in the shape of logs. The eerie, desertlike site, no-man's-land, is studded with cacti. The region is so barren you'll not want to linger long.

After passing Le Marin, you reach **Vauclin,** a fishing port and market town that is pre-Columbus. If you have time, stop in at the 18th-century **Chapel of the Holy Virgin.** Visitors like to make an excursion to **Mount Vauclin,** the highest point in southern Martinique. There they are rewarded with one of the most scenic panoramas in the West Indies.

Where to Stay

La Dunette

97227 Sainte-Anne, Martinique, F.W.I. ☎ **596/76-73-90.** Fax 76-76-05. 18 rms. A/C TV TEL. Winter, 550 F ($104.50) single; 650 F ($123.50) double. Off-season, 350 F ($66.50) single; 450 F ($85.50) double. (Rates include continental breakfast.) MC, V. Free parking.

A motel-like stucco structure set directly beside the sea, this hotel appeals to clients who appreciate its simplicity and its isolation from the more built-up resort areas of other parts of Martinique. A three-story building originally built in the late 1960s, it lies near the Club Med and the white sandy beaches of the Salines. Best defined as an unpretentious seaside inn with a simple, summery decor, the hotel is accented with a garden filled with flowers and tropical plants. The furnishings are casual and modern, and although some of the rooms are quite small, each benefitted from a complete renovation in 1994. Drinks are served every night on the terrace above the sea. The on-site restaurant is open year round. Water sports and excursions can be arranged for you, but mostly it attracts do-it-yourself types.

Les Boucaniers [Buccaneer's Creek] Club Mediterranée

Point Marin, 97227 Sainte-Anne, Martinique, F.W.I. ☎ **596/76-76-13,** or 800/CLUB-MED in the U.S. Fax 76-72-02. 313 rms. A/C. Winter, 830–1,550 F ($157.70–$294.50) per person double. Off-season, 760 F ($144.40) per person double. Single occupancy is granted in any season only if space is available, for a supplement of 20%–30% over the going rate for the week of your visit. Children under 12 not accepted. AE, MC, V. (Rates include all meals and sports.) Free parking.

Set on a peaceful cove at the southernmost tip of Martinique, about a 50-minute drive from the airport, this resort offers all-inclusive packages. Designed as a series of scattered outbuildings reminiscent of a Créole village, the club is on the 48-acre site of a former pirate's hideaway at Buccaneer's Creek, amid a forest of coconut palms. The accommodations are in comfortable bungalows with twin beds and private shower baths. Although many Club Meds welcome children, this particular club is most fully geared to single guests or couples, some of which like the *au naturel* beach nearby. The emphasis is often on group activities, with much ado over communal gathers and conviviality, and meals are served at long tables whose seating plans are conducive to meeting other guests, even if you don't want to.

Dining/Entertainment: In a domed two-level building in the heart of the resort, you'll find an amusement center, a theater, dance floor, and bar. A walk along rue du Port (the main street of Club Med) leads to a conically roofed circular Tour du Port, a bar that overlooks the sailboat fleet anchored in the marina. Nonguests on a tour of Martinique are welcome to stop in and enjoy a large buffet with Créole specialties. The resort contains a communal dining room, as well as a pair of dining rooms specializing in beef and seafood, and the somewhat less formal Café du Port. A late-night disco stays open until the wee hours.

Services: Social director, massage.

Facilities: Sailing, waterskiing, snorkeling; part of the beach is reserved for nude sunbathing.

Where to Dine

Aux Filets Bleus

Point Marin, Sainte-Anne. ☎ **596/76-73-42.** Reservations required. Appetizers 35–130F ($6.70–$24.70); main courses 90–210 F ($17.10–$39.90); fixed-price meal 59 F ($11.20), 99 F ($18.80), 120 F ($22.80), 200 F ($38), and 250 F ($47.50). MC, V. Lunch daily 12:30–2:30pm; dinner daily 7:30–9:30pm. CREOLE.

Set on a flat area close to the beach, a 30-minute drive south of the airport, this is a family-run blue-and-white restaurant flanked by canopies and separated from the road by a hedge. Once you've entered, the seaside exposure of the al fresco dining room and its terrace makes you feel as if you're in an isolated tropical retreat, where the only sound is the splash of waves and the tinkling of ice in glasses. What appears to be a glass-covered reflecting pool set into the floor is actually a lobster tank—supposedly one of only a few on the island. Specialties include bouillabaisse de la mer, which is three types of fish covered with a tomato and onion sauce; crabmeat salad with a coulis of tomato, basil, and olive oil; salade "filets bleues," with fresh crayfish, hearts of palm, avocados, fresh tomatoes, and whiskey-laden cocktail sauce; and pavé de daurade aux senteurs des îles (whitefish with a coriander-and-fennel sauce). It's possible to go for a swim before or after your meal.

THE NORTH LOOP

As we swing north from Fort-de-France, our main targets are Le Carbet, St-Pierre, Montagne Pelée, and Leyritz. However, I'll sandwich in many stopovers along the way.

From Fort-de-France there are three ways to head north to Montagne Pelée. The first way is to follow route N4 up to St-Joseph. There you take the left fork for 3 miles after St-Joseph and turn onto the D15 toward Marigot.

Another way to Montagne Pelée is to take the N3 through the vegetation-rich *mornes* until you reach Le Morne Rouge. This road is known as "route de la Trace," and is now the center of the Parc Naturel de la Martinique.

Yet a third route to reach Montagne Pelée is to follow the N2 along the coast. Near Fort-de-France, the first town you reach is Schoelcher.

Farther along the N2 you reach Case-Pilote, and then Bellefontaine. This portion, along the most frequented tourist route in Martinique—that is, Fort-de-France to St-Pierre—will remind many a traveler of the French Riviera. Bellefontaine is a small fishing village, with boats stretched along the beach. Note the many houses also built in the shape of boats.

EN ROUTE AT MORNE DES ESSES

Where to Dine

⑤ Le Colibri (The Hummingbird)

Allée du Colibri. ☎ **596/69-91-95.** Reservations not required. Appetizers 30–120 F ($5.70–$22.80); main courses 100–200 F ($19–$38). AE, DC, MC, V. Lunch daily noon–3pm; dinner daily 7–11pm. CREOLE.

In the hamlet of Morne des Esses, you might want to stop for lunch at Le Colibri, which is the home of Mme Clotilde Paladino and her daughters. If the terrace fills up with weekenders from Fort-de-France, you'll be seated on another smaller veranda where you can survey the cooking. The place is decidedly informal, and it exudes the warmth of madame. The typically Créole cookery is first class. You might begin with a calalou soup with crab or a sea-urchin tart. I recommend a buisson d'ecrevisses (a stew of freshwater crayfish), stuffed pigeon, chicken with coconut, and roast suckling pig. For dessert, try a coconut flan. French wines accompany most meals. It lies on the northeastern coastline, near St. Aubin, about 20 miles from Fort-de-France.

LE CARBET

Leaving Bellefontaine, a 5-mile drive north will deliver you to Le Carbet. Columbus landed here in 1502, and the first French settlers arrived in 1635. In 1887 Gauguin lived here for four months before going on to Tahiti. You can stop for a swim at an Olympic-size pool set into the hills, or watch the locals scrubbing clothes in a stream. The town lies on the bus route from Fort-de-France to St-Pierre.

The **Centre d'Art Musée Paul-Gauguin,** Anse Turin, Le Carbet (☎ **596/ 78-22-66**), is near the beach, represented in the artist's two paintings, *Bord de Mer.* The landscape has not changed in 100 years. The museum, housed in a five-room building, commemorates the French artist's stay on Martinique in 1887, with books, prints, letters, and other memorabilia. There are also paintings by René Corail, sculpture by Hector Charpentier, and examples of the artwork of Zaffanella. Of special interest are faïence mosaics made of once-white pieces that turned pink, maroon, blue, and black in 1902 when the fires of Montagne Pelée devastated St-Pierre. There are also changing exhibits of works by local artists. The museum is open daily from 10am to 5pm, with an admission of 15 F ($2.90).

ST-PIERRE

At the beginning of this century, St-Pierre was known as the "Little Paris of the West Indies." Home to 30,000 inhabitants, it was the cultural and economic capital of Martinique. On May 7, 1902, the citizens read in their daily newspaper that "Montagne Pelée does not present any more risk to the population than Vesuvius does to the Neapolitans."

However, on May 8, at 8am, the southwest side of Montagne Pelée exploded into fire and lava. At 8:02am all 30,000 inhabitants were dead—that is, all except one. A convict in his underground cell was saved by the thickness of the wall. When islanders reached the site, the convict was paroled and left Martinique to tour in Barnum and Bailey's circus.

St-Pierre never recovered its past splendor. Now it could be called the Pompeii of the West Indies. Ruins of the church, the theater, and some other buildings can be seen along the coast. A 50-passenger submarine enables visitors to explore the underwater wrecks of the ships destroyed in 1902 by the eruption of the volcano (until 1994 the wrecks had been accessible only to scuba divers). High-speed quadrimarans bring visitors by water from Fort-de-France to St-Pierre for $14. The cost of the submarine exploration is considerable but worth it to many: $71 for adults, $35 for children.

The **Musée Volcanologique,** rue Victor-Hugo, St-Pierre (☎ **596/78-15-16**), was created by American volcanologist Franck Alvard Perret, who turned the museum over to the city in 1933. Here, in pictures and relics dug from the debris, you can trace the story of what happened to St-Pierre. Dug from the lava is a clock that stopped at the exact moment the volcano erupted. The museum is open daily from 9am to 5pm, with an admission of 10 F ($1.90), free for children under 8.

LE PRÊCHEUR

From St-Pierre, you can continue along the coast north to Le Prêcheur. Once the home of Madame de Maintenon, the mistress of Louis XIV, it's the last village along the northern coast of Martinique. Here you can see hot springs of volcanic origin and the **Tombeau des Caraibes (Tomb of the Caribs),** where, according to legend, the collective suicide of many West Indian natives took place after they returned from a fishing expedition and found their homes pillaged by the French.

MONTAGNE PELEE

A panoramic and winding road (route N2) takes you through a tropical rain forest. The curves are of the hairpin variety, and the road is twisty and not always kept in good shape. However, you're rewarded with tropical flowers, baby ferns, plumed bamboo, and valleys so deeply green you'll think you're wearing cheap sunglasses.

The village of Morne Rouge, right at the foot of Montagne Pelée, is a popular vacation spot for Martiniquais. From there on, a narrow and unreliable road brings you to a level of 2,500 feet above sea level, 1,600 feet under the round summit of the volcano that destroyed St-Pierre. Montagne Pelée itself rises 4,575 feet above sea level.

If you're a trained mountain climber, and you don't mind four or five hours of hiking, you can scale the peak to Grand Rivière. Realize that this is a mountain, that rain is frequent, and that temperatures drop very low. Tropical growth often hides deep crevices in the earth, and there are other dangers. So if you're really serious about this climb, you should hire an experienced guide. As for the volcano, its death-dealing rain in 1902 apparently satisfied it—at least for the time being!

Upon your descent from Montagne Pelée, drive down to **Ajoupa-Bouillon,** which some describe, perhaps with justification, as the most beautiful town on Martinique. Abounding in flowers and shrubbery with bright yellow and red leaves, this little village is the site of the remarkable **Gorges de la Falaise.** These are mini-canyons on the Falaise River up which one can travel to reach a waterfall. Ajoupa-Bouillon also makes a good lunch stop.

Where to Dine

Abri Restaurant

Ajoupa-Bouillon. ☎ **596/53-32-13.** Reservations not required. Appetizers 35–50 F ($6.70–$9.50); main courses 75–130 F ($14.30–$24.70). MC, V. Lunch only, daily noon–3pm. CREOLE.

In the hills, about 7 miles northeast of the village of Lorrain, near Martinique's northern tip, is a large concrete building not unlike an aircraft hangar, whose rough edges are softened by potted plants. Originally a cockfight stadium, this restaurant serves meals that might begin with a glass of freshly squeezed sugarcane juice. The kitchen is known for its fricassée of crayfish, which is served to you and two or three others in a large bowl with herbs. You must shell the fish, then dip it into the sauce. It's a messy—and expensive—affair. You might prefer instead to order fish stuffed with sea urchins and cooked in coconut fronds. To begin, you can order calalou soup with crab or many kinds of accras, ranging from sea urchins to pumpkin.

LEYRITZ

Continue east toward the coast, toward the town of Basse-Pointe in northeastern Martinique. A mile before Basse-Pointe, turn left and follow a road that goes deep into sugarcane country to Leyritz, where you'll find one of the best-restored plantations on Martinique, and perhaps stop by for lunch.

Where to Stay & Dine

✪ Hôtel Plantation de Leyritz

97218 Basse-Pointe, Martinique, F.W.I. ☎ **596/78-53-92.** Fax 78-92-44. 67 rms. A/C TV TEL. Winter, 410–690 F ($77.90–$131.10) single; 510–790 F ($96.90–$150.10) double. Off-season, 330 F ($62.70) single; 430 F ($81.70) double. (Rates include continental breakfast.) MC, V. Free parking.

This hotel, which offers spa facilities, was built around 1700 by a plantation owner, Bordeaux-born Michel de Leyritz. It was the site of the "swimming pool summit meeting" in 1974 between Presidents Gerald Ford and Valéry Giscard d'Estaing. Today, instead of these politicians, you are likely to meet a stampede of cruise-ship passengers. It's still a working banana plantation, which was restored to its original character. There are 16 acres of tropical gardens, and at the core is an 18th-century stone Great House. From the grounds, the view sweeps across the Atlantic and takes in fearsome Montagne Pelée. The owners have kept the best of the old, such as the rugged stone walls (20 inches thick), the beamed ceilings, and the tile and flagstone floors. They have created a cozy setting of mahogany tables, overstuffed sofas, and gilt mirrors. About half the accommodations lie in a series of small outbuildings scattered around the property; others are in a newer annex adjacent to the spa. Don't expect well-polished luxury—that's not the style here. All rooms and public areas here were renovated in 1992.

Dining/Entertainment: The dining room is in a rum distillery, incorporating the fresh spring water running down from the hillside. Eating here is dramatic at night, and the cuisine is authentically Créole. Tour-bus crowds predominate at lunch, which costs 150 F ($28.50) and up. Your Créole lunch might be grilled chicken covered in coconut-milk sauce, along with oussous—a freshwater crayfish that comes in a herb sauce—sautéed breadfruit, and sautéed bananas. Dinner is more elaborate, with both French and Créole dishes, including duck with pineapple, a colombo of lamb, and boudin (blood pudding) Créole. Dinners are fixed-price affairs, costing 150 F ($28.50) each. Lunch is served from 12:30 to 3pm and dinner is from 7:30 to 9pm daily.

Services: Laundry.

Facilities: Outdoor swimming pool.

BASSE-POINTE

At the northernmost point on the island, Basse-Pointe is a land of pineapple and banana plantation fields, covering the Atlantic-side slopes of Mount Pelée volcano.

Where to Dine

⊛ Chez Mally Ebjam

Route de la Côte Atlantique. ☎ **596/78-51-18.** Reservations required. Appetizers 40–105 F ($7.60–$20); main courses 65–165 F ($12.40–$31.40). AE, MC, V. Lunch daily noon– 3pm; dinner by special arrangement only. Closed July. FRENCH/CREOLE.

This local legend operates from a modest house beside the main road in the center of town, 36 miles from Fort-de-France. Appreciating its exotic but genteel charm, many visitors prefer to drive all the way from Pointe du Bout to dine here instead of at the Leyritz Plantation. You sit at one of a handful of tables on the side porch, unless you prefer a seat in the somewhat more formal dining room.

Grandmotherly Mally Edjam (who is ably assisted by France-born Martine Hugé) is busy in the kitchen turning out her Créole delicacies. Both women know how to prepare all the dishes for which the island is known: stuffed land crab with a hot seasoning, small pieces of conch in a tart shell, and a classic colombo de porc (the Créole version of pork curry). Equally acclaimed are the establishment's lobster vinaigrette, the papaya soufflé (which must be ordered in advance), and the highly original confitures, which are tiny portions of fresh island fruits, such as pineapple and guava, that have been preserved in a vanilla syrup.

GRAND' RIVIÈRE

After Basse-Pointe, the town you reach on your northward trek is Grand' Rivière. From there you must turn back, but before doing so you may want to stop at a good restaurant right at the entrance to the town.

Where to Dine

Yva Chez Vava

Boulevard de Gaulle. ☎ **596/55-72-72.** Reservations recommended. Appetizers 25–100 F ($4.80–$19); main courses 80–150 F ($15.20–$28.50). AE, MC, V. Lunch only, daily noon–4pm. FRENCH/CREOLE.

Directly west of Basse-Pointe, in a beige-fronted building beside the main highway, Yva Chez Vava is easy to spot. You'll also find plenty of space to park your car. With a simple country-inn style, it's actually a *maison privée*. A la carte menu items include Créole soup, a blaff of sea urchins, lobster, and various colombos. Local family recipes are the mainstay of this modest bistro. Yva is the daughter of the recently deceased Vava. Yva carries on the preparation of such local delicacies as z'habitants (crayfish), vivaneau (red snapper), tazard (kingfish), and accras (cod fritters).

LE MARIGOT

This small village was relatively ignored by tourists until hotelier Jean-Louis de Lucy used France's tax-shelter laws to restore a landmark plantation (see below) and turn it into one of the finest hotels on the island. True, the nearest good beach is at Trinité, about a 30-minute drive from the hotel, but guests of the Habitation LaGrange don't seem to mind that.

Where to Stay & Dine

Habitation LaGrange

97225 Le Marigot, Martinique, F.W.I. ☎ **596/53-60-60.** Fax 53-50-58. For reservations, contact Caribbean Inns Ltd., P.O. Box 7411, Hilton Head Island, SC 29983 (toll free 800/633-7411 in the U.S.) 11 rms, 1 suite. A/C MINIBAR TEL. Winter, 1,500–1,700 F ($285–$323) single; 1,900–2,600 F ($361–$494) double; 2,500 F ($475) suite. Off-season, 1,400–1,600 F ($266–$304) single; 1,800–2,000 F ($342–$380) double; 2,300 F ($437) suite. (Rates include breakfast.) AE, MC, V. Free parking.

This hotel lies in isolation about a mile north of the village of Le Marigot, on 6 acres of its own land whose edges are engulfed by acreages of banana fields. Set about 1 1/2 miles inland from the coast, it was originally built in 1928 as part of the last sugar plantation and rum distillery established on Martinique. Today the ruins of that distillery rise a short distance from the Louisiana-style main house.

Accommodations lie either in the main house or in a comfortable annex, which was erected in 1990. Each accommodation is different, and each contains antique or reproduction furniture crafted from mahogany, baldaquin-style beds, and accessories steeped in the French colonial style. Each unit contains a veranda or patio, and ample vistas over a tropical landscape of gardens and faraway banana groves.

Dining/Entertainment: Meals are prepared in the Créole style by local chefs and served in an open-sided pavilion, the Ajoupa. Fixed-price dinners cost 250 F ($47.50) for three courses without wine, and simple but elegant lunchtime platters cost around 110 F ($20.90) each.

Services: 24-hour room service, concierge (who can arrange rentals of cars or sailing craft and sports activities around the island), pickup service available from the airport (on request).

Facilities: Swimming pool.

SAINTE-MARIE

Heading south along the coastal road, you'll pass Le Marigot to reach a sightseeing stop in the little town of Sainte-Marie. The **Musée du Rhum Saint-James,** at the Saint James Distillery (☎ **596/69-30-02**), displays engravings, antique tools and machines, and other exhibits tracing the history of sugarcane and rum from 1765 to the present. Guided tours of the museum also include a visit to the distillery and storage area, and a session of rum tasting. Admission free, the museum is open daily from 9am to 6pm.

TRINITÉ

If you head back south along the coastal route (N1) from Ste-Marie, you'll pass through the small village of Trinité on the Atlantic side of Martinique. It would hardly merit a stopover were it not for the Saint-Aubin Hôtel.

Where to Stay

Saint-Aubin Hôtel

97220 Trinité, Martinique, F.W.I. ☎ **596/69-34-77.** Fax 69-41-14. 15 rms. A/C TEL. Winter, 320–360 F ($60.80–$68.40) single; 420–580 F ($79.80–$110.20) double. Off-season, 300 F ($57) single; 360–460 F ($68.40–$87.40) double. AE, DC, MC, V. (Rates include continental breakfast.) Free parking.

A former restaurant owner, Normandy-born Guy Forêt has sunk his fortune into restoring this three-story Victorian house and turning it into a three-star hostelry, one of the loveliest inns in the Caribbean. The house was originally built in 1920 of brick and poured concrete as a replacement for a much older wood-sided house that had served as the seat of a large plantation. It was named after the uninhabited islet of Saint-Aubin, which lies offshore, and which is visible from the hotel. Painted a vivid pink with fancy gingerbread, it was once a plantation house. It sits on a hillside above sugarcane fields and Trinité's bay, 14½ miles from the airport, 19 miles from Fort-de-France, and 2 miles from the seaside village of Trinité itself. There are 800 yards of public beach, plus there's a swimming pool on the grounds. All rooms sport wall-to-wall carpeting and modern (not antique) furniture. There are some family rooms as well. After dinner you can relax on the veranda on the first and second floors. Rooms have a view of either the garden or the sea. The hotel restaurant and bar are reserved for use of hotel guests. Meals are served only at dinnertime, never at lunch, Monday through Saturday. A fixed-price meal is offered for 140 F ($26.60) per person. Meals might include avocado vinaigrette, Créole black pudding, grilled fresh fish, stuffed crab, or fish poached in court bouillon.

Le François

Continuing your exploration of the east coast of Martinique, you can stop over in Le François to visit the **Musée Rhum Clement** at the Domaine de l'Acajou (☎ 596/54-62-07), which is open daily from 9am to 6pm, charging an admission of 30 F ($5.70). This museum is unique because on top of its distillery museum is an 18th-century mansion with period furnishings. The house commemorates the summit meeting of Presidents Mitterand and Bush in 1992. A Christopher Columbus exhibit is set up in caves, and there are other exhibits tracing the arrival of slavery in the islands. The museum is located in a parklike setting and one can easily spend two or three hours exploring the exhibits and grounds.

ACTIVITIES AROUND THE ISLAND
Camping

Camping is permitted in some places, including in the mountains and forests and on many beaches. Check with the local mayor's office or property owner before setting up camp. Campsites are usually basic, although comfortable camps with cold showers and toilets are on the southeast coast at Macabou; at Ste-Luce, Le Marin, and Ste-Anne on the south coast; and Anse-à-l'Ane near Trois-Ilets. Contact the **Office National des Forêts** (☎ 596/60-70-70) for more information.

Sports & Outdoor Activities

The Martiniquais often don't work at their sports as hard as many North Americans do, but they do have an active sports program. Scuba diving, snorkeling, fishing, and waterskiing can be enjoyed all along the coastline. Golf clubs are at your disposal in all the first-class hotels (tariffs vary considerably, depending on the duration and season).

BEACHES   The beaches south of Fort-de-France are white, while the northern strands are composed mostly of gray sand. Outstanding in the south is the 1 1/2-mile **Plage des Salines,** near Ste-Anne, with palm trees and a long stretch of white sand, and the 2 1/2-mile-long **Diamant,** with the landmark Diamond Rock offshore. Swimming on the Atlantic coast is for experts only, except at **Cap Chevalier** and **Presqu'ile de la Caravelle Nature Preserve.**

The clean white sandy beaches of **Pointe du Bout,** site of the major hotels of Martinique, were created by developers. However, to the south the white sand beaches at **Anse Mitan** have always been there welcoming visitors, including many snorkelers. Incidentally, nudist beaches are not officially sanctioned, although topless sunbathing is widely practiced at the big hotels, often around their swimming pools. Public beaches rarely have changing cabins or showers. Some hotels charge nonguests for the use of changing and beach facilities, and request a deposit for rental of towels.

DEEP-SEA FISHING   Increased facilities for deep-sea fishing have been developed in Martinique because of the demand created by the fine catches of tuna, barracuda, dolphin, kingfish, and bonito. Most hotels maintain a list of the yachts and skippers who agree to take groups of fisherfolk out for a day of *la pêche à la ligne* on the wide blue sea. The cost of renting such a boat, in which all equipment is usually included, is around 1,750 F ($332.50) for a half-day fishing expedition. (This cost is usually divided among four to eight participants.) Most game fish tend to be most active very early in the morning, and many fishermen claim that no real benefits exist for fishing after 10am, so departures tend to leave before breakfast, around 6am. One boat which was in demand at press time, and which was in contact with the concierge staffs at most of the island's large hotels, was *Scheherazade,* although any of several boats could be substituted for it a few hours before your departure. Plan on breakfast after your return to port, around 10:30am.

GOLF   The famous golf course designer, Robert Trent Jones, visited Martinique and left behind the 18-hole **Golf de l'Impératrice-Joséphine** at Trois-Ilets (☎ **596/68-32-81**), a five-minute, 1-mile drive from the leading resort area of Pointe du Bout and about 18 miles from Fort-de-France. This, the only golf course on Martinique, unfolds its greens from the birthplace of Empress Joséphine for whom it is named, across rolling hills with scenic vistas down to the sea. Amenities include a pro shop, a bar, a restaurant, and three tennis courts. Greens fees are 250 F ($47.50) per person for 18 holes. Residents of certain hotels (including the Bakoua, the Méridien, and the Novotel Le Diamant) receive discounts on their greens fees, and pay 220 F ($41.80).

HIKING   Inexpensive guided excursions for tourists are organized by the personnel of the **Parc Naturel Régional de la Martinique** year-round. Special excursions can be arranged for small groups by contacting the Parc Naturel Régional de la Martinique, Excollège Agricole de Tivoli, B.P. 437, 97200 Fort-de-France (☎ **596/64-42-59**).

The **Presqu'île de la Caravelle Nature Preserve,** a well-protected peninsula jutting into the Atlantic Ocean, has safe beaches and well-marked trails to the ruins of historic Château Debuc and through tropical wetlands.

Serious hiking excursions to climb Montagne Pelée and explore the Gorges de la Falaise or the thick coastal rain forest between Grand' Rivière and Le Prêcheur are organized with local guides at certain times of the year by the park staff.

HORSEBACK RIDING   The premier riding facility on Martinique, **Ranch Jack,** Thorne Habitué, Trois-Ilets (☎ **596/68-37-69**), offers morning horseback rides for both experienced and novice riders, at a cost of 350 F ($66.50) per person for a $3^1/_2$- to 4-hour ride. Jacques and Marlene Guinchard make daily promenades across the beaches and fields of Martinique, with a running explication of the history, fauna, and botany of the island. Cold drinks are included in the price, and transportation is usually free to and from the hotels of nearby Pointe du Bout. This is an ideal way to discover both botanical and geographical Martinique.

SCUBA DIVING & SNORKELING   Scuba divers come here to explore the St-Pierre shipwrecks sunk in the 1902 volcano eruption and the Diamond Rock caves and walls. Small scuba centers operate at many of the hotels.

Snorkeling equipment is usually available free to hotel guests, who quickly learn that coral, fish, and ferns abound in the waters around the Pointe du Bout hotels.

Across the bay from Fort-de-France, in the Hôtel Méridien, **Bathy's Club** (☎ **596/66-00-00**) is one of the major scuba centers for Pointe du Bout and welcomes anyone who shows up. Daily dive trips, depending on demand, leave from the Méridien Hôtel's pier. Prices include equipment rental, transportation, guide, and drinks on board. Dives are conducted twice daily, from 8am to noon and 2 to 6pm, and full-day charters can be arranged. The dive shop on the Méridien's beach stocks everything from weight belts and tanks to partial wetsuits and underwater cameras. Dives cost 250 F ($47.50) per person. Initial instruction is offered for beginners, free if they're residents of the Hôtel Méridien. Other Martinique hotels also have scuba centers.

MONGOOSE VS. THE SNAKE   Some people say you've not really seen Martinique until you've attended a match between a mongoose and a snake. Said to have been imported by East Indian workers, this is a to-the-death struggle. If you attend such an event, you're to remain deadly still. Even lighting a cigarette is supposed to break the concentration of the combatants. Incidentally, the mongoose almost always wins. Even if the snake should win, the fight is still unfair, because another mongoose will be brought out to do combat with the snake. Some taxi drivers or small innkeepers on the island will tell you where to go to watch this "sport." Frankly, I prefer to skip it.

SAILING   While this is a big pastime in Martinique, it's also a big cost unless there are enough in your party. Only a select few can afford yacht charters, either crewed or bareboat. If you want to see the waters around Martinique, it's better to go on one of the sailboat excursions in the bay of Fort-de-France and on the southeast coast of the island. Ask at your hotel desk what ships are taking passengers on cruises in Martinique waters. These vessels tend to change from season to season.

On a smaller scale, many hotels (including the Méridien at Pointe du Bout) will rent Hobie cats and Sunfish to their guests, but only if sailing competence can be demonstrated.

TENNIS   Each large hotel has courts. Residents play free during the day, and night games usually require a surcharge of around 15 F ($2.90) per hour for illumination. Nonguests are faced with a playing-time charge that's about 50 F ($9.50) per hour, although the tennis pros at Bathy's Club at the Hôtel Méridien in Pointe du Bout usually allow nonresidents to play for free if the courts are otherwise unoccupied—except at night when the charge is almost universally imposed.

Another good choice is to play at one of the three courts on the grounds of **Golf de l'Impératrice-Joséphine** at Trois-Ilets (☎ **596/68-32-81**), a five-minute drive from the major hotels at Pointe du Bout. The setting here is one of the most beautiful on Martinique.

WATERSKIING & WINDSURFING   Waterskiing is available at every beach near the large hotels, and costs about 160 F ($30.40) for a 15-minute ride.

Windsurfing is the most popular sport in the French West Indies. Equipment and lessons are available at all hotel water-sports facilities, especially the Hôtel Méridien, Pointe du Bout (☎ **596/66-00-00**), where 30-minute lessons cost 80 F ($15.20). However, board rentals are only 100 F ($19) per hour.

SHOPPING

In Fort-de-France

Your best buys on Martinique are French luxury imports, such as perfumes, fashions, Vuitton luggage, Lalique crystal, or Limoges dinnerware. Sometimes (but don't count on it) prices are as much as 30% to 40% below those in the United States.

One cautious reader points out that if you pay in dollars, store owners supposedly will give you a 20% discount; however, when you pay in dollars, the exchange rates vary considerably from store to store, and almost invariably they are far less favorable than that offered at one of the local banks. He writes: "The net result is that you received a 20% discount, but then they take away from 9% to 15% on the dollar exchange, giving you a net savings of only 5% to 11%—not 20%." He further notes, "Actually, you're probably better off shopping in the smaller stores where prices are 8% to 12% less on comparable items and paying in francs that you have exchanged at a local bank."

The main shopping street is **rue Victor-Hugo.** The other two leading shopping streets are **rue Schoelcher** and **rue St-Louis.**

Facing the tourist office and alongside **quai d'Esnambuc** is an open market where you can purchase local handcrafts and souvenirs. Many of these are tacky, however.

Far more interesting is the display of vegetables and fruit—quite a show—at the **open-air stalls along rue Isambert.** Don't miss it for its local ambience, and you can't help but smell the **fish market** alongside the Levassor River.

Gourmet chefs will find all sorts of spices in the open-air markets, or such goodies as tinned pâté or canned quail in the local *supermarchés.*

For the ubiquitous local fabric, madras, there are shops on every street with bolts and bolts of it, all colorful and inexpensive. So-called haute couture and resortwear are sold in many boutiques dotting downtown Fort-de-France.

Most shops are open Monday through Friday from 7:30am to 12:30pm and 2:30 to 5:30pm, and on Saturday from 8am to noon; closed Sunday. Try to postpone your shopping trip if a cruise ship is in town.

Cadet-Daniel

Rue Antoine-Siger, 72. ☎ **596/71-41-48.**

Cadet-Daniel, which opened in 1840, sells Christofle silver, Limoges china, and crystal from Daum, Baccarat, Lalique, and Sèvres. Like some nearby stores, it also offers island-made 18-karat-gold baubles, including the beaded *collier chou,* or "darling's necklace," long a required ornament for a Créole costume.

Galeries Lafayette

Rue Victor-Schoelcher, 10, near the cathedral. ☎ **596/71-89-50.**

This is a small-scale branch of what's probably the most famous department store in Paris, the world-class Galeries Lafayette. Specializing in fashion for men, women, and children, it also offers leather goods, jewelry, watches, and all the predictably famous names in French perfume and fashion.

La Bella Matadore

Immeuble Vermeil-Marina, Pointe du Bout. ☎ **596/66-04-88.**

The owner of this shop, Martinique-born Marie-Josée Ravenel, has carefully researched the history and traditions associated with the island's jewelry. Virtually all the merchandise sold here derives from models developed during slave days by the matadores (prostitutes), midwives, and slaves. Designs are vivid and bold, and for the most part crafted on the island from 18-karat gold. Especially popular are the necklaces, brooches, and pendants popularized by some of the island's most evocative women during the 18th and 19th centuries. Set midway between the La Pagerié Hôtel and the Méridien Hôtel, the store carries baubles that range in price from 59 F ($11.20) (for a pendant shaped like the island of Martinique itself) to around 12,000 F ($2,280) for a gold necklace.

La Case à Rhum

In the Galerie Marchande, rue de la Liberté, 5. ☎ **596/73-73-20.**

Before leaving Martinique, you may want to purchase some rum, considered by aficionados to be one of the world's finest distilled drinks. Hemingway in *A Moveable Feast* lauded it as the perfect antidote to a rainy day. This shop is the best place for browsing, offering all the brands of rum manufactured on Martinique (at least 12), as well as several others famous for their age and taste. They offer samples in small cups to prospective buyers. I suggest that you try Vieux Acajou, a dark, mellow Old Mahogany, or a blood-red brown liqueurlike rum bottled by Bally.

La Galleria
Route de Lamentin.

Set midway between Fort-de-France and the Lamentin airport, this is, by anyone's estimate, the most upscale and elegant shopping complex on Martinique. On the premises are purveyors of goods from both France and the Caribbean, with merchandise dispersed among more than 60 different vendors. You'll find a handful of cafés and simple restaurants on site to relieve your hunger pangs as you shop, as well as an outlet or two for the local pastries and sweets for which Martinique is known.

Merlande
Rue Victor-Schoelcher, 10, near the cathedral. ☎ **596/71-89-50.**

One of the finest department stores in the Caribbean, Merlande sells fashions for men, women, and children, along with leather goods, jewelry, watches, and such famous names in perfume as Chanel, Hermès, and Yves Saint-Laurent.

The enterprise also has another store, **Au Sans-Pareil,** rue Blénac, 26 (☎ **71-52-32**), known for its toys, luggage, beauty accessories, china, crystal, and silver, including such famed names as Baccarat.

Nouvelles Galeries
Rue Blénac, 26. ☎ **596/71-52-32.**

This is another of the capital's large department stores. It is known for its toys, luggage, beauty accessories, china, crystal, and silver. The emphasis on both of these stores is French with Caribbean overtures.

Roger Albert
Rue Victor-Hugo, 7. ☎ **596/71-71-71.**

All the big names in perfumes from Paris are here, as well as crystal from Baccarat and Lalique, chinaware from Limoges, figurines by Lladró, and sportswear by Lacoste and Tacchini. The merchandise is of the highest quality and provides one of the finest selections in the Caribbean. Long established, just off the Savane, this is the best-known duty-free store on Martinique.

Elsewhere on the Island

If you're staying at one of the hotels on the peninsula of Pointe du Bout, you'll find that the Marina complex there has a number of interesting boutiques. Several sell handcrafts and curios from Martinique. They are sometimes of good quality, and are quite expensive, regrettably, particularly if you purchase some of their batiks of natural silk and their enameled jewel boxes.

There are the sturdy straw food baskets in the shops of **Morne-des-Esses,** the *vannerie* (basket-making) capital of Martinique.

Poterie de Trois-Ilets
Quartier Poterie, Trois-Ilets. ☎ **596/68-17-12.**

At Christmastime, many of the island's traditional foie gras and pastries are presented in crocks made by Martinique's largest earthenware factories, the Poterie de Trois-Ilets. At least 90% of its production is devoted to brickmaking. However, one small-scale offshoot of the company devotes itself to the production of earth-toned stoneware and pottery whose colors and shapes have contributed to the folklore of Martinique. In theory, the studios are open Monday through Saturday from 7am to 4pm, but call before you set out to make sure they'll accept visitors.

MARTINIQUE AFTER DARK

Everybody who goes to Martinique wants to see the show performed by **Les Grands Ballets Martiniquais,** a bouncy group of about two dozen dancers, along with musicians, singers, and choreographers. This is probably the most interesting program of folk dances in the Caribbean. Launched in the early 1960s, this group performs the traditional dances of Martinique and has been acclaimed in both Europe and the States. With a swoosh of gaily striped skirts and clever acting, the dancers capture all the exuberance of the island's soul. The group has toured abroad with great success, but they perform best on their home ground presenting tableaux that tell of jealous brides and faithless husbands, demanding overseers and toiling cane cutters. Dressed in traditional costumes, the island women and men dance the spirited mazurka, which was brought from the ballrooms of Europe, and the exotic beguine. Cole Porter, incidentally, did not invent the beguine. It's a Martiniquais dance—some would call it a way of life. It's best to see it for yourself, or dance it, if you think you can.

Les Grands Ballets perform Monday at the Hôtel Diamant-Novotel, Wednesday at the Novotel Carayou, Thursday at the Méridien Trois-Ilets, Friday at the Bakoua Beach, and Saturday at Hôtel La Batalière, but this can vary, so check locally. In addition, the troupe gives mini-performances aboard visiting cruise ships. The cost of dinner and the show is usually 225 F ($42.80) per person. Most performances are at 9pm, with dinners at the hotels beginning at 7:30pm.

There's also some nightlife revolving around **the four major hotels** at Pointe du Bout—Bakoua Beach, Novotel Carayou, Méridien Trois-Ilets, and Hôtel La Pagerié. As mentioned, on certain nights you can watch Les Grands Ballets Martiniquais. In addition, musicians, some of them quite young, play nightly in the larger hotels.

The **Casino Trois-Ilets,** on the premises of the Méridien Trois-Ilets, Pointe du Bout (☎ **596/60-00-00**), is open every night from 9pm to 3am. Here you can try to win the cost of your vacation by playing roulette, blackjack, or chemin-de-fer. Some form of photo identification is required at the entrance. You present it along with 70 F ($13.30). The most recent room (to which entrance is free) is devoted entirely to slot machines.

2 Guadeloupe

"The time is near, I believe, when thousands of American tourists will come to spend the winter among the beautiful countryside and friendly people of Guadeloupe." Or so Theodore Roosevelt accurately predicted on February 21, 1916. Guadeloupe isn't the same place it was when the Rough Rider himself rode through, but the natural beauty he witnessed, and certainly the people, are still there to be enjoyed.

Guadeloupe is part of the Lesser Antilles, about 200 miles north of Martinique, closer to the United States than its cousin. In addition to tourism, sugar production and rum beef up the local economy. The total surface of Guadeloupe and its satellite islands is close to 700 square miles. There's a lot of similarity in climate, animals, and vegetation between Martinique and Guadeloupe.

Guadeloupe is, in fact, formed by two different islands, separated by a narrow seawater channel known as the Rivière Salée. **Grande-Terre,** the eastern island, is typical of the charm of the Antilles, with its rolling hills and sugar plantations.

On the other hand, **Basse-Terre,** to the west, is a rugged mountainous island, dominated by the 4,800-foot volcano La Soufrière, which is still alive. Its mountains are covered with tropical forests, impenetrable in many places. Bananas grown on plantations are the main crop. The island is ringed by beautiful beaches, which have attracted much tourism.

ORIENTATION
GETTING THERE

Most flights into Guadeloupe are tied in with air connections to Martinique. See "Getting There" in "Orientation" in the Martinique section, earlier in this chapter.

GETTING AROUND

BY BUS   As on Martinique, there is no rail service. But buses link almost every hamlet to Pointe-à-Pitre. However, you may need to know some French to use the system. From Pointe-à-Pitre you can catch one of these jitney vans, either at the Gare Routière de Bergevin if you're going to Basse-Terre, or the Gare Routière de Mortenol if Grande-Terre is your destination. Service is daily from 5:30am to 7:30pm. The fare from the airport to Pointe-à-Pitre terminal on rue Peynier is 5 F ($1).

BY TAXI   You'll find taxis when you arrive at the airport, but no limousines or buses. From 9pm until 7am, cabbies are legally entitled to charge you 40% more. In practice, either day or night, the taxi drivers charge you whatever they think the market will bear, although technically fares are regulated by the government. Always agree on the price before getting in. Approximate fares are 100 F ($19) from the airport to Gosier hotels, or 60 F ($11.40) from the airport to Pointe-à-Pitre. Radio taxis can be called at **590/90-00-00** or at **590/82-99-88.**

If you're traveling with people or are imaginative in putting a party together, it's possible to sightsee by taxi. Usually the concierge at your hotel will help you make this arrangement. Fares are usually negotiated.

BY RENTAL CAR   Your access to a car enables you to circumnavigate Basse-Terre, which many aficionados claim is one of the loveliest drives in the Caribbean. Car-rental kiosks at the airport are usually open to meet international flights. Rental rates at local companies might appear lower, depending on the agency, but several readers have complained of mechanical problems and billing irregularities, and difficulties in resolving insurance disputes in the event of accidents. If you want to be sure to get a car when you arrive, it's often best to reserve one in advance through the nationwide toll-free numbers of North America's largest car-rental companies: **Hertz** (☎ toll free **800/654-3001**), **Avis** (☎ toll free **800/331-1084**), and **Budget** (☎ toll free **800/527-0700**), each of which is represented on the island.

At all three, the best values are usually offered when you reserve at least two days in advance and keep the car for at least a week. If you decide to rent a car after your arrival on the island, each of the companies maintains its headquarters at the island's Le Raizet airport. For information, contact Avis at **590/82-02-71,** Budget at **590/82-95-58,** or Hertz at **590/82-00-14.** The price of renting a car for a week at all of these companies is, at presstime, about $210 (in high season). Prices are usually 20% to 25% lower between March and early December.

Each of the companies maintains different minimum ages for its renters. Avis requires that its drivers be 25 or older; Budget, that its drivers be 23 or older. Hertz is the least stringent of the three, allowing 21-year-olds (with a valid credit or charge card) to rent one of its vehicles.

All three companies offer additional insurance in the form of a collision-damage waiver, priced at $11 extra per day. Unless you have other forms of insurance, I recommend that you buy the extra coverage. At all three companies, even if you buy the extra coverage you'll still be liable for up to $180 worth of damage to your car. If you don't buy the extra insurance, you'll be liable in some cases for much more money—sometimes up to the full value of the vehicle. In some cases, payment for your rental with certain types of credit or charge cards can eliminate the need for any additional collision-damage waivers, although you should consult directly with your card issuer for details about this.

As in France, *driving is on the right-hand side of the road,* and there are several gas stations along the island's main routes. Because of the distance between gas stations away from the capital, try not to let your gas gauge fall below the halfway mark, and don't drink and drive.

FAST FACTS: Guadeloupe

Area Code   Guadeloupe is not part of the Caribbean's 809 area code. To phone Guadeloupe from the North American mainland, see "Telephone," below.

Currency   The official monetary unit is the **French franc (F),** although some shops will take U.S. dollars. At press time the exchange rate was 5.28 F to $1 U.S. (1 F = 19¢), and this was the rate used to calculate the dollar values given in this chapter. As this is sure to fluctuate a bit, use this rate for guidance only.

Customs   Items for personal use, "in limited quantities," can be brought in tax free.

Documents   For stays of less than 21 days, U.S. or Canadian residents need only proof of identity (a voter registration card or birth certificate with a photo ID, or a passport), plus a return or ongoing plane ticket. For a longer stay, a valid passport is required. British visitors need a valid passport.

Drugstores   The pharmacies carry French medicines, and most over-the-counter American drugs have French equivalents. Prescribed medicines can be purchased if the traveler has a prescription. At least one drugstore is always open, but the schedule is always changing. The tourist office can tell you what pharmacies are open at what time.

Electricity   The local electricity is 220 volts A.C., 50 cycles, which means that you'll need a transformer and an adapter. Some of the big resorts lend these to guests, but don't count on it. One hotel I know had only six in stock, and a long, long waiting list (and of the six, two were broken!). Take your own.

Emergencies Call the police at **17,** report a fire at **18,** and summon an ambulance at **82-89-33,** or if the situation is less urgent, at **82-13-17.**

Information The major tourist office in Guadeloupe is the **Office Départemental du Tourisme,** Square de la Banque, 5, in Pointe-à-Pitre (☎ **590/82-09-30**).

Language The official language is French, and Créole is the unofficial second language. As on Martinique, English is spoken only in the major tourist centers, rarely in the countryside.

Medical Care There are five modern hospitals on Guadeloupe, plus 23 clinics. Hotels and the Guadeloupe tourist office can assist in locating English-speaking doctors. A 24-hour emergency room operates at the Centre Hopitalier de Pointe-à-Pitre, Abymes (☎ **82-98-80**).

Safety Like Martinique, Guadeloupe is relatively free of serious crime. But don't go wandering alone at night on the streets of Pointe-à-Pitre; by nightfall they are relatively deserted and might be dangerous. Purse-snatching by fast-riding motorcyclists has been reported, so exercise caution.

Taxes A departure tax, required on scheduled flights, is included in the airfares. Hotel taxes are included in all room rates.

Telephone Guadeloupe, as a *département* of France, is *not* part of the 809 area code that applies to most of the Caribbean. To call Guadeloupe from the United States, if your long-distance telephone company is equipped to handle international direct dialing, dial **011** (the international access code), then **590** (the country code for Guadeloupe), and finally the six-digit local number. If you cannot direct-dial internationally, dial **0** ("zero," for the operator) and tell the operator you wish to make an international call; once you are transferred to the international operator, state the **590** country code and then the local number, and the operator will dial the call for you. To make a call within Guadeloupe, only the six-digit local number is necessary.

Time Guadeloupe is on Atlantic standard time year round, one hour ahead of eastern standard time (when it's 6am in New York, it's 7am on Guadeloupe). When daylight saving time is in effect in the States, clocks in New York and Guadeloupe show the same time.

Tips and Service Hotels and restaurants usually add a 10% to 15% service charge, and most taxi drivers who own their own cars do not expect a tip.

Tobacco American tobacco and cigarettes are available at hotel shops, and Guadeloupe also has some *café-tabacs* selling foreign cigarettes.

POINTE-À-PITRE

The port and chief city of Guadeloupe, Pointe-à-Pitre lies on Grande-Terre. Unfortunately, it doesn't have the old-world charm of Fort-de-France on Martinique, and what beauty it does possess is often hidden behind closed doors.

Having been burned and rebuilt so many times, the port has emerged as a town lacking in character, with modern apartments and condominiums forming a high-rise backdrop over jerry-built shacks and industrial suburbs. The rather narrow streets are jammed during the day with a colorful crowd creating a permanent traffic tie-up. However, at sunset the town becomes quiet again and almost deserted.

The real point of interest in Pointe-à-Pitre is shopping. It's best to visit the town in the morning—you can easily cover it in half a day—taking in the waterfront and outdoor market (the latter is livelier in the early hours). Be careful about walking alone on the nearly deserted streets of Pointe-à-Pitre at night.

The town center is **place de la Victoire,** a park shaded by palm trees and poincianas. Here you'll see some old sandbox trees said to have been planted by Victor Hugues, the mulatto who organized a revolutionary army of both whites and blacks to establish a dictatorship. In this square he kept a guillotine busy, and the death-dealing instrument stood there (but not in use) until modern times.

With the recent completion of the **Centre St-Jean-Perse,** a $20-million project that had been on the drawing boards for many years, the waterfront of Pointe-à-Pitre has been transformed from a bastion of old warehouses and cruise-terminal buildings into an architectural complex comprising a hotel, three restaurants, 80 shops and boutiques, a bank, and the expanded headquarters of Guadeloupe's Port Authority.

Named for Saint-John Perse, the 20th-century poet and Nobel Laureate who was born just a few blocks away, the center is designed in contemporary French Caribbean style, which blends with the traditional architecture of Pointe-à-Pitre. It offers an array of French Caribbean attractions: duty-free shops selling Guadeloupean rum and French perfume; a renowned restaurant, La Canne à Sucre; small tropical gardens planted around the complex; and a location right near the open-air markets and small shops of this bustling port of call. For brochures, maps, and data on sightseeing, the Guadeloupe tourist office is just minutes away.

WHERE TO STAY

Hôtel Bougainvillée

Angle des rues Delgrès et Frébault, 97110 Pointe-à-Pitre, Guadeloupe, F.W.I. ☎ **590/ 90-14-14.** Fax 91-36-82. 34 rms, 2 suites. A/C TEL. Winter, 450–690 F ($85.50–$131.10) single; 550 F ($104.50) double; from 714 F ($135.70) suite. Off-season, 355 F ($67.50) single; 420 F ($79.80) double; 550 F ($104.50) suite. Breakfast 45 F ($8.60) extra. AE, DC, MC, V. Free parking.

It's concrete and without frills, but the Bougainvillée is clean and serviceable. Its location on a busy street corner guarantees a regular clientele of commercial travelers. Guests register in a wood-trimmed, renovated lobby before taking a cramped elevator to one of the bedrooms. They're all maintained, with white walls and heavy dark furniture like something you'd find in Iberia, and each contains a private bath and shower. Ten rooms have a minibar, and most contain their own TV.

WHERE TO DINE

✪ La Canne à Sucre

Quai no. 1, Port Autonome. ☎ **590/82-10-19.** Reservations recommended. Street-level Brasserie, appetizers 50–70 F ($9.50–$13.30); main courses 60–120 F ($11.40–$22.80). Upstairs restaurant, appetizers 75–140 F ($14.30–$26.60); main courses 100–180 F ($19–$34.20). AE, MC, V. Brasserie, Mon–Sat 8am–midnight. Restaurant, lunch Mon–Fri noon–2:30pm; dinner Mon–Sat 7:30–10:30pm. MODERN FRENCH/CREOLE.

Three feet from the water's edge, beside the quays where the cruise ships deposit their passengers, this is one "sugarcane" that has created a local sensation. It's the most select rendezvous for superbly prepared local cuisine on the island. Gerard

Guadeloupe

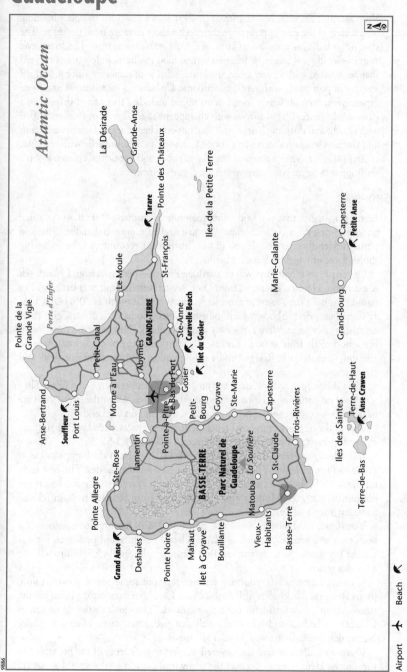

Atlantic Ocean

Pointe de la Grande Vigie

Anse-Bertrand ↖ Souffleur
Port Louis

Pointe Allegre

Ste-Rose

Lamentin

Morne à l'Eau

Petit-Canal

Porte d'Enfer

Le Moule

St-François

GRANDE-TERRE

Abymes

Pointe-à-Pitre

Le Bas del Fort

Gosier

Ste-Anne ↖ Caravelle Beach
↖ Ilet du Gosier

Pointe des Châteaux
↖ Tarare

La Désirade
Grande-Anse

Iles de la Petite Terre

Deshaies

↖ Grand Anse

Pointe Noire

Mahaut

Ilet à Goyave

Bouillante

BASSE-TERRE

Parc Naturel de Guadeloupe

La Soufrière

Matouba

Vieux-Habitants

St-Claude

Basse-Terre

Petit-Bourg

Goyave

Ste-Marie

Capesterre

Trois-Rivières

Marie-Galante

Grand-Bourg

Capesterre ○
↖ Petite Anse

Iles des Saintes

Terre-de-Haut ↖ Anse Crawen

Terre-de-Bas

Airport ✈   Beach ↖

9886

Virginius and his wife, Marie, moved in 1991 into a concrete-and-glass building with a view of the many cruise ships that dock a short distance from the shore. The style of both dining areas is a mixture of Créole with art nouveau. The street level contains an elegant brasserie, where informal food might include a brioche of red snapper covered with lobster sauce, duckmeat salad with raspberry vinegar, and red snapper in puff pastry with exotic mushrooms. Upstairs is a more formal, and more expensive, restaurant where menu items might include a filet of red snapper in a passionfruit sauce, filet of marlin with champagne sauce, breast of chicken stuffed with conch, and duckling basted with starfruit-enriched vinegar. Desserts are lavish and sinful: a soursop sherbet or a coupe Canne à Sucre (a rondelle with old rum, coconut sherbet, whipped cream, banana, caramel, and a touch of cinnamon). It's traditional to begin your meal with a small rum punch.

SHOPPING

Frankly, I suggest that you skip a shopping tour of Pointe-à-Pitre if you're going on to Fort-de-France on Martinique, as you'll find far more merchandise there, and perhaps friendlier service. If you're not, however, I recommend the following shops, some of which line rue Frébault.

Of course, your best buys will be anything French—perfumes from Chanel, silk scarves from Hermès, cosmetics from Dior, crystal from Lalique and Baccarat. I've found (but not often) some of these items discounted as much as 30% below U.S. or Canadian prices. Shops, which most often will accept U.S. dollars, give these discounts only to purchases made by traveler's check. Purchases are duty free if brought directly from store to airplane. In addition to the places below, there are also duty-free shops at Raizet Airport selling liquor, rums, perfumes, crystal, and cigarettes.

Most shops open at 9am, close at 1pm, then reopen between 3 and 6pm. They are closed on Saturday afternoon, Sunday, and holidays. When the cruise ships are in port, many eager shopkeepers stay open longer and on weekends.

One of the best places to buy French perfumes, at prices often lower than those charged in Paris, is **Phoenicia,** rue Frébault, 8 (☎ **590/83-50-36**).

Rosebleu, rue Frébault, 5 (☎ **590/82-93-44**), has one of the biggest stocks in Pointe-à-Pitre of jewelry, perfumes, gifts, and fashion accessories. The best crystal made in France is sold here. If you pay with traveler's checks, you'll get discounts. It's open Monday through Saturday from 9:30am to 6pm (closed Monday from 1 to 2pm).

Vendôme, rue Frébault, 8–10 (☎ **590/83-42-84**), has imported fashions for both men and women, as well as a large selection of gifts and perfumes, including the big names. Usually you can find someone who speaks English to sell you a Cardin watch.

If you're adventurous, you may want to seek out some native goods in little shops along the backstreets of Pointe-à-Pitre. Considered collector's items are the straw hats or salacos made in Les Saintes islands. They look distinctly related to Chinese coolie hats and are usually well designed, often made of split bamboo. Native doudou dolls are also popular gift items.

Open-air stalls surround the **covered market** at the corner of rue Frébault and rue Thiers. Here you can discover the many fruits, spices, and vegetables that are enjoyable just to view if not to taste. In madras turbans, local Créole women make deals over their strings of fire-red pimientos. The bright fabrics they wear compete with the rich tones of oranges, papayas, bananas, mangoes, and pineapples, and the sounds of an African-accented French fill the air.

MOVING ON

Saint-John Perse once wrote about the fine time sailors had when they arrived in Pointe-à-Pitre when it was used as a stopover anchorage on the famous route du Rhum. But since that day is long gone, you may not want to linger; you can take a different route instead, this one to the "South Riviera," from Pointe-à-Pitre to Pointe des Châteaux.

LE BAS DU FORT

The first tourist complex, just 2 miles east of Pointe-à-Pitre, is called Le Bas du Fort, near Gosier.

The **Aquarium de la Guadeloupe,** place Créole, Marina Bas-du-Fort (☎ **590/ 90-92-38**), is rated as one of the three most important of France and is the largest and most modern in the Caribbean. Just off the main highway near Bas-du-Fort Marina, the aquarium is home to tropical fish, coral, underwater plants, and huge sharks and other sea creatures. The exhibits are all clearly labeled. Open daily from 9am to 7pm. Admission is 38 F ($7.20) for adults, 20 F ($3.80) for children 12 and under.

WHERE TO STAY

Fleur d'Epée Novotel

Le Bas du Fort, 97190 Gosier, Guadeloupe, F.W.I. ☎ **590/90-40-00**, or 800/221-4542 in the U.S. Fax 90-99-07. 190 rms. A/C TV TEL. Winter, 680–885 F ($129.20–$168.20) single; 845–1,510 F ($160.60–$286.90) double. Off-season, 600 F ($114) single; 800 F ($152) double. (Rates include continental breakfast.) AE, DC, MC, V. Free parking.

This is the most visible branch on Guadeloupe of a France-based hotel chain whose financial success has inspired feature stories in newspapers around Europe. Built in 1978, it stands beside a pair of crescent-shaped bays whose white sands are shaded by palms and sea-grape trees, near the center of the resort complex of Bas du Fort, about 3 miles south of Pointe-à-Pitre. Geared for the resort market, the hotel has a low-rise design of only three floors; each bedroom is a well-scrubbed, modern, tiled enclave of quiet, with private bath and a simple but functional floor plan that is duplicated in Novotels around the world. There's a breeze-filled restaurant on the premises, as well as about a dozen indoor/outdoor eateries within walking distance, many with views of the beach.

Marissol

Le Bas du Fort, 97190 Gosier, Guadeloupe, F.W.I. ☎ **590/90-84-44,** or 800/221-4542 in the U.S. Fax 90-83-32. 200 rms. A/C TEL. Winter, 775–925 F ($147.30–$175.80) single; 1,040–1,335 F ($197.60–$253.70) double. Off-season, 576–766 F ($109.40–$145.50) single; 768–1,040 F ($145.90–$197.60) double. (Rates include continental breakfast.) AE, DC, MC, V. Free parking.

Near the entrance to the touristic complex of Bas du Fort, about 3 1/2 miles south of Pointe-à-Pitre, is a secluded bungalow colony of two- and three-story structures that were originally built in 1975 and partially renovated in 1989. The Marissol is set away from the main road and occupies the grounds that stretch between a secondary route and the shoreline. In a setting of banana trees and lawns, it offers first-class comfort, with rooms either in bungalows or in the two wings, which open onto a view of the parklike grounds or the water. The furnishings are sober and modern (nothing special), the floors are tiled, the baths have a separate toilet, and all units have either twin or double beds.

Dining/Entertainment: Next to the pool is a circular bar, Le Wahoo. The hotel's deluxe restaurant, Le Grand Baie, opens onto a terrace where you can order Créole specialties or traditional French cuisine. Sicali is an open grill lying halfway between the beach and the pool. The in-house disco, Diapasen, is open Monday through Friday from 9pm until very late, with free admission and a beer priced at 18 F ($3.40).

Services: Laundry, massage, babysitting, concierge.

Facilities: Small beach, large swimming pool, beauty and fitness center known as "Gym-Tropique" (with a "hammam" steam room, exercise lessons called "gymnastique douce," relaxation exercises based on yoga, and hot-water baths with algae or oils), water-sports kiosk (featuring windsurfing, sailing, and snorkeling); scuba diving can be arranged.

WHERE TO DINE

✪ La Plantation

Galerie Commerciale de la Marina, Le Bas du Fort. ☎ **590/90-84-83.** Reservations required. Appetizers 70–160 F ($13.30–$30.40); main courses 110–260 F ($20.90–$49.40). AE, DC, MC, V. Lunch Mon–Fri noon–2:30pm; dinner Mon–Sat 7–10:30pm. MODERN FRENCH.

La Plantation is a stylish pink-toned establishment whose main dining room overlooks the resort's marina complex 3 miles south of Pointe-à-Pitre. In this intimate, air-conditioned setting, modern adaptations of French cuisine are presented by Gianni Ferraris, the Turin, Italy–born owner. He and his French-born chefs turn out delectable meals, which might include a salad of crayfish and foie gras, suprême of salmon with red butter sauce, suprême of steamed fish with baby vegetables, panache of smoked seafish with three sauces, friandises of crayfish à la Mandarin Imperiale, grilled filet of beef with béarnaise sauce, stuffed conch in the Créole style, gratin of oysters, and dorado with basil sauce.

GOSIER

Some of the biggest and most important hotels of Guadeloupe are found at this holiday center, with its nearly 5 miles of beach, stretching east from Pointe-à-Pitre.

For an excursion, you can climb to **Fort Fleur-d'Epée,** dating from the 18th century. Its dungeons and battlements are testaments to the ferocious fighting between the French and British armies in 1794 seeking to control the island. The well-preserved ruins command the crown of a hill. From there you'll have good views over the bay of Pointe-à-Pitre, and on a clear day you can see the neighboring offshore islands of Marie-Galante and Iles des Saintes.

WHERE TO STAY

Archipel Callinago Beach Hotel and Village

Pointe de la Verdure, 35, Gosier, Guadeloupe, F.W.I. ☎ **590/84-25-25,** Fax 84-24-90. 40 rms. 115 studio apartments. A/C MINIBAR TV TEL. Winter, 737–810 F ($140–$153.90) single; 907–1,054 F ($172.30–$200.30) double; 836–983 F ($158.80–$186.80) studio apartment with kitchenette for two. Off-season, 500 F ($95) single; 600 F ($114) double; 475 F ($90.30) studio apartment with kitchenette for two. American buffet breakfast 75 F ($14.30) extra for apartment occupants. AE, DC, MC, V. Free parking.

Named after a Carib military hero, and reminiscent of a small resort along the Mediterranean, this hotel stands along the Gosier beachfront 2 miles east of

Pointe-à-Pitre. The rooms are housed in pink-and-white stucco buildings, and contain private baths and balconies. Most of the accommodations, however, are in a separate compound designed somewhat like a small village. Contained within it are a series of spacious studios and duplex apartments with modern furnishings, a bathroom, and a complete kitchen. A sliding glass wall opens onto a small private balcony overlooking Gosier Bay. Each of the duplexes, suitable for three or four occupants, contains a spiral staircase which leads to an upstairs bedroom, with a private bath and another small terrace.

Dining/Entertainment: Although residents can prepare their meals in their own kitchens, there's a Créole/French restaurant on the premises that serves breakfast and dinner, the Tomaly, whose name is translated from the Arawak as "Meal." A less formal restaurant, Le Sucrier, serves lunch and offers a view of the swimming pool.

Services: Room service (for breakfast), laundry, babysitting.

Facilities: Beach, freshwater swimming pool, two tennis courts, market selling food supplies; waterskiing, sailing, snorkeling, pedalboating, and windsurfing available at an extra cost.

Coralia Auberge de la Vielle Tour

Montauban, 97190 Gosier, Guadeloupe, F.W.I. ☎ **590/84-23-23.** Fax 84-33-43. 153 rms. A/C MINIBAR TV TEL. 1,140–1,385 F ($216.60–$263.20) single; 1,270–1,740 F ($241.30–$330.60) double. (Rates include buffet breakfast.) AE, DC, MC, V. Free parking. Closed Apr–Nov.

Now a large chain hotel, this longtime favorite grew from a family inn that had been built around the shadow of a sugar mill whose thick walls dated from 1835. Today the mill serves as the resort's reception area. The personal service and much of the flavor of the inn of yesterday are now largely gone, but this is still a viable choice. Lying only three blocks from the center of Gosier, the 4-acre estate offers you a series of vintage rooms, short on charm, or more modern accommodations in town houses on the other side of the pool. Decorated with modern, bright colors, these more up-to-date units are more spacious. Balconies sometimes overlook the gardens and a small private beach (which sometimes brims to overflowing).

Dining/Entertainment: The resort contains two restaurants, the more formal of which is discussed in "Where to Dine," below. Breakfast and lunch are served in the poolside Ajoupa Restaurant. Sometimes limbo dancers are brought in, and buffets and barbecues are planned.

Services: Concierge, babysitting, laundry.

Facilities: Water sports from the hotel's small beach (including snorkeling, sailing, windsurfing, and swimming), tennis court (lit at night), swimming pool.

Ecotel Guadeloupe

Route de Gosier, 97190 Gosier, Guadeloupe, F.W.I. ☎ **590/90-60-00.** Fax 90-60-60. 44 rms. A/C MINIBAR TV TEL. Winter, 500 F ($95) single; 650 F ($123.50) double. Off-season, 315 F ($59.90) single; 400 F ($76) double. (Rates include breakfast.) AE, DC, MC, V. Free parking.

A restful retreat surrounded by gardens, an 8-minute drive from the capital and 10 minutes (6 miles) east of the airport, the Ecotel Guadeloupe is now a conventional hotel and no longer a place for training students interested in the hotel business, as its name and original function suggest. It's modern in styling, yet its restaurant (Jardin Gourmand), bar, and the bedrooms are French West Indian in feeling. Each of the simple and slightly battered accommodations open onto a view of the pool, the gardens, or the adjoining forest. The units contain many built-in pieces. Don't expect luxury here—the place is anything but elegant. The air conditioning is occasionally not strong enough for some guests, but it's silent.

Dining/Entertainment: At the restaurant, Le Jardin Gourmand, serving dinner only, you can order such specialties as filet de machoiran, a fleshy fish shipped in from Guyana; the local red snapper done in a variety of ways; and a gâteau de langouste (spiny lobster) with whiskey. Alongside the swimming pool is Pap-Pap, a snack bar. Breakfast is served on an al fresco extension of the reception area.

Services: Room service (for breakfast), laundry, babysitting.

Facilities: Swimming pool, car-rental desk, shopping boutiques.

La Créole Beach Hôtel

Pointe de la Verdure, 97190 Gosier, Guadeloupe, F.W.I. ☎ **590/90-46-46.** Fax 90-46-66. 315 rms, 6 duplexes. A/C MINIBAR TV TEL. Winter, 740–1,000 F ($140.60–$190) single; 900–1,425 F ($171–$270.80) double; from 2,100 F ($399) duplex. Off-season, 740 F ($140.60) single; 900 F ($171) double; from 1,450 F ($275.50) duplex. (Rates include continental breakfast.) AE, DC, MC, V. Free parking.

Sporting the nicest hotel design of any Gosier establishment, half New Orleans and half colonial, La Créole stands alongside two beaches in a setting of lawns and trees, as well as hibiscus and bougainvillea. Renovated in 1994, the bedrooms are traditional in tone, with dark-wood pieces and carpeted floors. Your balcony will be large enough to be your breakfast spot or a perch for your sundowner.

Dining/Entertainment: The hotel restaurant, attractively decorated with plants, serves many local specials along with a more familiar international cuisine. During the day guests enjoy drinks at the poolside bar or a lunch at the beach snack bar. Another restaurant, Le Zawag, lies just on the rocks by the sea, offering fresh fish and seafood along with lobster.

Services: Room service (at mealtimes), laundry, babysitting.

Facilities: Swimming pool, tennis courts, scuba diving, waterskiing, sailboat rentals, deep-sea fishing.

WHERE TO DINE

✪ Auberge de la Vieille Tour

In the Coralia Auberge de la Tour Hôtel, Montauban, Gosier. ☎ **590/84-23-23.** Reservations recommended. Appetizers 55–95 F ($10.50–$18.10); main courses 120–200 F ($22.80–$38); fixed-price meal 200 F ($38). AE, DC, MC, V. Dinner only, daily 7–9:30pm. Closed Apr–Nov. FRENCH/CREOLE.

One of the finest restaurants on the island is in a big-windowed pavilion near the swimming pool of the previously recommended hotel east of Pointe-à-Pitre. The best tables have a view of Ilet du Gosier and naturally are the most requested. Decorated in the French style, the restaurant is staffed with a bevy of islanders dressed in traditional Créole garb. The menu changes but perhaps the fish soup with fennel will get you going, and might be followed by veal sweetbreads braised with honey or roast lamb with a saffron sabayon. The locally caught red snapper is likely to be accompanied by cucumber balls and mango butter (yes, mango butter).

Chez Violetta

Perinette Gosier. ☎ **590/84-10-34.** Reservations not required. Appetizers 35–90 F ($6.70–$17.10); main courses 60–140 F ($11.40–$26.60); fixed-price meal 80–120 F ($15.20–$22.80). AE, DC, MC, V. Lunch daily noon–3:30pm; dinner daily 7:30–11pm. FRENCH/CREOLE.

At the far-eastern end of Gosier village, en route to Ste-Anne, this is the most formally decorated of all the Créole restaurants on the island. It has Louis XIII–style velvet-covered chairs, striped wallpaper in rich but somber colors, and a decor that looks as if it had been transported from Burgundy. In spite of its neocolonial trappings, this was the domain of a high priestess of Créole cookery. Her name was Violetta Chaville, and her skill became almost a legend on the island. Today her brother, Josef Galaya, carries on in her tradition.

On the à la carte menu, try stuffed crabs, blaff of seafood, and fresh fish of the day (perhaps red snapper). For an appetizer, ask for cod fritters or beignets called accra. The classic blood sausage, boudin, is also served here. In addition, the chef does a fine conch ragoût, superb in texture and flavor; it's best when served with hot chiles grown on Guadeloupe. On occasion, he'll even prepare a brochette of shark, if available. Fresh pineapple makes an ideal dessert, or you can try the banana cake.

La Chaubette

Route de Ste-Anne. ☎ **590/84-14-29.** Reservations recommended. Appetizers 15–30 F ($2.90–$5.70); main courses 55–90 F ($10.50–$17.10). MC, V. Lunch Mon–Sat noon–4pm; dinner Mon–Sat 7–11pm. CREOLE.

Begin your meal here with a rum punch, made with white rum and served with a lime wedge and sugar. But don't order too much—it's lethal, and you won't be able to get through the rest of dinner. This is a "front porch" Créole restaurant with lots of local color. About a 12-minute run east of Pointe-à-Pitre, it's almost like the Guadeloupe version of a roadside inn, with its red-checked tablecloths and curtains made of bamboo. Mme Gitane Chavalin is in charge, and she's known in the area for her Créole recipes. She uses the fish and produce of her island whenever possible. When it's available, her langouste is peerless, as is her hog's-head cheese with a minced-onion vinaigrette. Finish with coconut ice cream or a banana flaming with rum.

La Veranda

In the Hôtel/Résidence Canella Beach, Pointe de la Verdure, Gosier. ☎ **590/90-44-00.** Reservations recommended. Appetizers 30–70 F ($5.70–$13.30); main courses 65–105 F ($12.40–$20); lunch salads and platters 25–80 F ($4.80–$15.20). AE, DC, MC, V. Lunch daily noon–3pm; dinner daily 7–10pm. FRENCH/CREOLE.

Set on the grounds of a hotel and apartment complex in Gosier, this restaurant is an indoor/outdoor affair with a view of the nearby beach and a reputation for good food. Decorated in tones of pink and white, with dozens of potted plants, it changes its venue radically from daylight to evening hours. At lunch, the place serves a series of salads, and such cooked dishes as assiettes antillaises (with a selection of Créole delicacies), and fresh fish served as brochettes or as filets. At dinner, the menu is more elaborate and service is deliberately prolonged. Menu items after dark include a predictable array of traditional Créole dishes, as well as such French dishes as a croustillade of sea urchins, a féroces d'avocat (with avocado mousse, codfish, and manioc flour), escalope de mérou with ginger sauce, and a soupière of scallops with freshwater crayfish. One section of the restaurant is air-conditioned, the other open to the sea breezes. A live band plays nightly.

STE-ANNE

About 9 miles east of Gosier, little Ste-Anne is a sugar town and a resort offering many fine beaches and lodging facilities. In many ways, it's the most charming of the villages of Guadeloupe, with its town hall in pastel colors, its church, and its principal square, place de la Victoire, where a statue of Schoelcher commemorates the abolition of slavery in 1848.

WHERE TO STAY & DINE

Club Med–Caravelle

97180 Ste-Anne, Guadeloupe, F.W.I. ☎ **590/88-21-00,** or 800/CLUB-MED in the U.S. Fax 88-06-06. 329 rms. A/C TEL. Winter, $1,050–$1,180 per person double. Off-season, $750 per person double. (Rates include meals and activities.) Children 6–12 are charged 75% of the adult rate; children under 6 not accepted. Single supplements 20%–40% above the per-person double rate, depending on the accommodations. AE, MC, V. Free parking. Transportation: Free hotel shuttle meets passengers at the airport.

Ste-Anne's best-known resort is Club Med–Caravelle, covering 45 acres along a peninsula dotted with palm trees. Its beach is one of the finest in the French West Indies. Beads are legal tender here. Club Med vacations are open to members only, but membership is available. An all-inclusive vacation package is offered at one price, which depends on the time of year, and includes all-you-can-eat meals daily, with unlimited wine at lunch and dinner, plus use of all sports facilities, with expert instruction and equipment.

Note that during the summer (but a bit less so during the winter) this resort, more than any other Club Med in the Caribbean, markets itself almost exclusively to a French clientele through its sales outlets in Paris. Though North Americans are welcome, be warned that almost all midsummer activities here are conducted in French, which may or may not suit your particular vacation plans. Rooms tend to be small, as are the baths.

Dining/Entertainment: Throughout the year, food is a specialty at this resort. The breakfast and lunch buffet tables groan with French, continental, and Créole food. Dinner is served in the main dining room, which has been enlarged and remodeled into a series of small, comfortable sections, or in the candlelit and more romantic La Beguine annex restaurant. There's a weekly folklore night when the dinner features specialties of the region, along with a performance by the Guadeloupe folklore ballet. Also in the evening, guests gather around the bar and dance floor, which becomes the theater for nightly entertainment. Afterward you can dance at the midnight disco.

Services: Laundry.

Facilities: Beach, windsurfing, sailing, snorkeling trips (leaving daily from the dock), sea excursions to explore the island's coastline, six tennis courts, archery, calisthenics, volleyball, basketball, table tennis.

Hotel La Toubana

Durivage (B.P. 63), 97180 Ste-Anne, Guadeloupe, F.W.I. ☎ **590/88-25-70.** Fax 88-38-90. 32 bungalows. A/C MINIBAR TEL. Winter, 680–1,130 F ($129.20–$214.70) bungalow for one; 850–1,400 F ($161.50–$266) bungalow for two. Off-season, 500–600 F ($95–$114) bungalow for one; 620–720 F ($117.80–$136.80) bungalow for two. (Rates include breakfast.) AE, DC, MC, V. Free parking.

The Hôtel La Toubana is centered around a low-lying stone building on a cliff overlooking the bay and Ste-Anne Beach. Many guests come here just for the view, which on a clear day encompasses Marie-Galante, Dominica, La Désirade, and the Iles des Saintes, but you'll quickly learn that there's far more to this charming place that just a panorama. The red-roofed bungalows lie scattered among the tropical shrubs along the adjacent hillsides (*toubana* is the Arawak word for "small house"). Each unit contains a kitchenette.

Dining/Entertainment: The hotel restaurant, Le Baobab, offers both indoor and al fresco dining stretching right up to the edge of the pool.

Services: Room service (for breakfast), laundry, babysitting.

Facilities: Beach (a five-minute walk from any lodging), tennis courts; deep-sea fishing and other water sports can be arranged.

Le Relais du Moulin

Châteaubrun, 97180 Ste-Anne, Guadeloupe, F.W.I. ☎ **590/88-23-96.** Fax 88-03-92. 40 units. A/C MINIBAR TEL. Winter, 468–530 F ($88.90–$100.70) single; 560–624 F ($106.40–$118.60) double. Off-season, 380–450 F ($72.20–$85.50) single; 450–500 F ($85.50–$95) double. (Rates include continental breakfast.) AE, DC, MC, V. Free parking.

The 19th-century stone tower that serves as this establishment's centerpiece was originally built as the headquarters of a prosperous sugar plantation. Today it juts boldly above the hilly countryside on the outskirts of Ste-Anne, and serves as the registration desk and lobby for the resort. About half the units here are private bungalows with red roofs and white walls. The remainder are duplex apartments, grouped into interconnected clusters of four, whose white exterior walls are covered with trumpet vines and bougainvillea. Each unit has a private bath, terrace with a hammock, and refrigerator. Unless you take the initiative to go out exploring on your own, you might follow the examples of many of the other clients of this hotel, who pass their time sunning, reading, and sleeping.

Dining/Entertainment: The resort contains two different eating areas, one of which lies near the swimming pool (Le Restaurant). Another (Le Courcelle) is in an indoor area with a faux–half-timbered look. Lunches and dinners alternate between the two of them, depending on the weather, the season, and the number of guests in residence at the time.

Facilities: Because the resort lies inland, and requires a car or taxi to reach the nearest beach, most clients congregate around the resort's swimming pool. There are also a set of rentable bicycles on site.

ST-FRANÇOIS

Continuing east from Ste-Anne, you'll notice many old round towers named for Father Labat, the Dominican founder of the sugarcane industry. These towers were once used as mills to grind the cane. St-François, 25 miles east of Pointe-à-Pitre, used to be a sleepy fishing village, known for its native Créole restaurants. Then Air France discovered it and opened a Méridien hotel with a casino. That was followed by the promotional activities of J. F. Rozan, a native, who invested heavily to make St-François a jet-set resort. Now the once-sleepy village has first-class accommodations, as well as an airport available to private jets, a golf course, and a marina.

WHERE TO STAY

Hamak

97118 St-François, Guadeloupe, F.W.I. ☎ **590/88-59-99,** or 800/633-7411 in the U.S. Fax 88-41-92. 56 suites. A/C MINIBAR TV TEL Winter, $270–$310 suite for one; $300–$350 suite for two. Off-season, $170–$220 suite for one; $200–$250 suite for two. (Rates include continental breakfast.) AE, MC, V. Free parking. Closed Aug 29–Oct 3.

This resort lies 25 miles east of Pointe-à-Pitre and a quarter of a mile from the Méridien. Its sandy beach along the lagoon and its proximity to golf and a tiny airport once made it the most popular place on the island for what was known then as the "jet set." It was the site of the 1979 international summit that brought

President Carter and Giscard d'Estaing, among others, here. Despite its sometimes-illustrious clientele, it maintains a simple and unpretentious style of management, with few dress-code restrictions, and a friendly, open-handed approach to newcomers. Spread on a 250-acre estate, the accommodations are in villas (each with two individual tropical suites with twin beds opening onto a walled garden patio where you can sunbathe *au naturel*). Each of the beige-sided bungalows houses two visitors comfortably, although some readers have found the rooms quite cramped and simple for the prices charged.

Dining/Entertainment: Hamak maintains a day bar and a night bar, and a dining room which opens onto views of both the beach and the garden. Outsiders can dine here if they reserve in advance.

Services: Room service, laundry, babysitting.

Facilities: The island's most visible golf course, the Robert Trent Jones–designed Golf Municipale de St-François, lies a short walk from the hotel, charging greens fees of 250 F ($47.50) for 18 holes. On the premises of the hotel are tennis courts, a private beach, and facilities for windsurfing and other water sports. The premises does not contain a swimming pool, but few clients seem to mind, in view of the nearby beach.

✪ La Plantation Ste-Marthe

97118 St. François. ☎ **590/88-43-58.** Fax 88-72-47. 96 rms, 24 duplex suites. A/C TEL. Winter, 750–1,210 F ($142.50–$229.90) single; 1,060–1,540 F ($201.40–$292.60) double; 1,360–1,860 F ($258.40–$353.40) duplex suite for two. Off-season, 550–700 F ($104.50–$133) single; 860–1,000 F ($163.40–$190) double; 1,160–1,300 F ($220.40–$247) duplex suite for two. (Rates include breakfast.) AE, MC, V. Free parking.

Built on the site of a 19th-century sugar plantation in 1992, this is Guadeloupe's newest major hotel. Although the manor house that once stood on the premises is now in ruins, vestiges of the 15-acre site's original function are still visible in the stables, the ruined rum distillery, and the molasses factory whose crumbling walls still evoke a sense of the French colonial empire. All buildings that are associated with a holiday-maker, however, are new, scattered amid the vegetation of a landscaped garden whose centerpiece is a large swimming pool. (Beach-lovers are shuttled to and from the nearby seacoast by minivan.)

Accommodations are in a quartet of three-story buildings, the architecture of which was inspired by the Créole buildings of Louisiana. Each unit has lots of exposed wood and boldly patterned tiles, and a large terrace or balcony which many visitors end up using as an extension of their living quarters. The duplex suites feature a sleeping loft designed in a style that might remind you of a big-city apartment. The furnishings are modernized versions of antique French designs, with lots of woven cane.

Dining/Entertainment: The hotel's main restaurant, La Vallée d'Or, has an ambitious menu based on modern French cuisine, and main courses priced at 120 to 200 F ($22.80 to $38) each. It's open daily for both lunch and dinner. The premises also contains two bars, one by the reception area, another (which features a live pianist every evening) in the restaurant.

Services: Concierge, babysitting, minivan transfers to and from the beach (La Plage du Lagon).

Facilities: Two tennis courts, one of the largest swimming pools on the island, health club, water sports.

Le Méridien St-François

97118 St-François, Guadeloupe, F.W.I. ☎ **590/88-51-00**, or 800/543-4300 in the U.S. Fax 88-40-71. 249 rms, 16 suites. A/C TV TEL. Winter, 1,350–1,500 F ($256.50–$285) single or double. Off-season, 950 F ($180.50) single or double. Year round, 2,050–3,100 F ($389.50–$589) suites. (Rates include continental breakfast.) AE, DC, MC, V. Free parking.

With five floors, and a design that was inaugurated as one of the first Méridien hotels ever built for Air France, this is one of the tallest buildings in St-François. It stands alongside one of the best beaches on Guadeloupe on 150 acres of land at the southernmost tip of the island, a 20-minute walk from the village of St-François. The climate, quite dry here, is refreshed by trade winds. The four-star hotel offers rooms overlooking the sea or the Robert Trent Jones–designed golf course with many amenities and furnishings in a modern style combined with Créole overtones. Some rooms are in need of refurbishing.

Dining/Entertainment: Guests dine at Balaou, a terraced restaurant where a fixed-price three-course meal costs 155 to 195 F ($29.50 to $37.10). Other dining choices include the Casa Zomar, serving lunch only, and the Bambou snack bar for sandwiches and salads.

Services: 24-hour room service, massage, babysitting, laundry.

Facilities: Swimming pool, two tennis courts, windsurfers, small airport for anyone wanting to charter flights to neighboring islands; golf available for an extra charge of 250 F ($47.50) at the course next door (☎ **88-41-87** for information), nearby marina, access to additional water sports.

WHERE TO DINE

La Louisiane

Quartier Ste-Marthe, outside St-François. ☎ **590/88-44-34.** Reservations not required. Appetizers 40–95 F ($7.60–$18.10); main courses 70–150 F ($13.30–$28.50). MC, V. Lunch Tues–Sun noon–2pm; dinner Tues–Sun 7–10pm. Closed Two weeks in June and two weeks in Sept. FRENCH/CARIBBEAN.

The oldest building in the neighborhood about 1¹/₂ miles east of St-François, this century-old former plantation house is sheltered from the road by trees and shrubbery. When they emigrated, French owners Daniel and Muriel Hogon brought with them some of the best cuisine of their native regions, Provence and the Vosges. Meals might include a filet of marlin with garlic sauce, sharkmeat with saffron sauce, filet of red snapper with a basil-flavored cream sauce, or veal escalope with shrimp. The establishment manages to convey the nostalgia of France of long ago, in an environment streaming with Caribbean sunlight and vegetation.

Restaurant Les Oiseaux

Anse des Rochers. ☎ **590/88-56-92.** Reservations required. Appetizers 25–70 F ($4.80–$13.30); main courses 80–160 F ($15.20–$30.40). MC, V. Lunch Sat–Sun noon–3pm; dinner daily 6–10:30pm. Closed first two weeks in Sept. FRENCH/ANTILLEAN.

Probably the best imitation of a Provençal farmhouse on the island stands on a seaside road about 3¹/₂ miles west of St-François on a scrub-covered landscape whose focal point is the sea and the island of Marie-Galante. Its walled-in front garden frames a stone-sided, low-slung building that produces an aroma of a southern French and Antillean cuisine worth the detour. This is the domain of Arthur Rollé and his French-born wife, Claudette, originally from Picardy in northern France, who serve dishes like fish mousse, Créole-style beef, a cassoulette of seafood, and a filet en croûte with red-wine sauce. Try also the marmite Robinson, inspired by the tale of Robinson Crusoe, a delectable fondue of fish and vegetables which you cook for yourself in a combination of bubbling coconut and corn oil. Dessert might be a composite of four exotic sherbets or a crêpe.

POINTE DES CHÂTEAUX

Seven miles east of St-François is Pointe des Châteaux, the easternmost tip of Grand-Terre, where the Atlantic meets the Caribbean. Here, where crashing waves sound around you, you'll see a cliff sculpted by the sea into castlelike formations, the erosion typical of France's Brittany coast. The view from here is panoramic. At the top is a cross put there in the 19th century.

You might want to walk to **Pointe des Colibris,** the extreme end of Guadeloupe. From there you'll have a view of the northeastern sector of the island, and to the east a look at La Désirade, another island which has the appearance of a huge vessel anchored far away. Among the coved beaches found around here, **Pointe Tarare** is the *au naturel* one.

LE MOULE

To go back to Pointe-à-Pitre from Pointe des Châteaux, you can use an alternative route, the N5 from St-François. After a 9-mile drive, you reach the village of Le Moule, which was founded at the end of the 17th century, and known long before Pointe-à-Pitre. It used to be a major shipping port for sugar. Now a tiny coastal fishing village, it never regained its importance after it was devastated in the hurricane of 1928, like so many other villages of Grand-Terre. Because of its more than 10-mile-long crescent-shaped beach, it's developing as a holiday center. Modern hotels built along the beaches have opened to accommodate visitors.

Specialties of this Guadeloupian village are palourdes, the clams that thrive in the semisalty mouths of freshwater rivers. Known for being more tender and less "rubbery" than saltwater clams, they often, even when fresh, have a distinct sulfur taste not unlike that of overpoached eggs. Local gastronomes prepare them with saffron and aged rum or cognac.

Nearby, the sea unearthed some skulls, grim reminders of the fierce battles fought among the Caribs, French, and English. It's called "the Beach of Skulls and Bones."

The **Edgar Clerc Archeological Museum La Rosette,** Parc de la Rosette (☎ 590/23-57-43), shows a collection of both Carib and Arawak artifacts gathered from various islands of the Lesser Antilles. The museum is open Monday through Friday from 9am to 12:30pm and 2 to 5:30pm; it closes Wednesday afternoon but is also open on Saturday and Sunday from 9am to 12:30pm and 2 to 6pm. Admission is 15 F ($2.90). The museum lies 3 miles from Le Moule in the direction of Campêche.

To return to Pointe-à-Pitre, I suggest that you use the D3 toward Abymes. The road winds around as you plunge deeply into Grand-Terre. As a curiosity, about halfway along the way, a road will bring you to **Jabrun du Nord** and **Jabrun du Sud.** These two villages are inhabited by Caucasians with blond hair, said to be survivors of aristocrats slaughtered during the Revolution. Those members of their families who escaped found safety by hiding out in Les Grands Fonds. The most important family here is named Matignon, and they gave their name to the colony known as "les Blancs Matignon." These citizens are said to be related to Prince Rainier of Monaco.

Pointe-à-Pitre lies only 10 miles from Les Grands Fonds.

A DRIVING TOUR NORTH FROM POINTE-À-PITRE

From Pointe-à-Pitre, head northeast toward Abymes, passing next through Morne à l'Eau; you'll reach **Petit Canal** after 13 miles. This is Guadeloupe's sugarcane country, and a sweet smell fills the air.

PORT LOUIS

Continuing northwest along the coast from Petit Canal, you come to Port Louis, well known for its beach, La Plage du Souffleur, which I find best in the spring, when the brilliant white sand is effectively shown off against a contrast of the flaming red poinciana. During the week the beach is an especially quiet spot. The little port town is asleep under a heavy sun, and it has some good restaurants.

Where to Dine

Le Poisson d'Or

Rue Sadi-Carnot, 2, Port Louis. ☎ **590/22-88-63.** Reservations required. Appetizers 20–35 F ($3.80–$6.70); main courses 60–130 F ($11.40–$24.70); fixed-price meal 85 F ($16.20). MC, V. Lunch daily 11:30am–3pm; dinner by reservation only. Drive northwest from Petit Canal along the coastal road. CREOLE.

You'll enter this white-sided Antillean house by walking down a narrow corridor and emerging into a rustic dining room lined with varnished pine. Despite the simple setting, the food is well prepared and satisfying. Don't even think of coming here at night without an advance reservation—you might find the place locked up and empty. The establishment's true virtue, however, is evident during the lunch hour, when, depending on the season, it's likely to shelter a mixture of local residents and tourists from the French mainland. Try the stuffed crabs, the court bouillon, topped off by coconut ice cream, which is homemade and tastes it. The place is a fine choice for an experience with Créole cookery, complemented by a bottle of good wine.

ANSE BERTRAND

About 5 miles from Port Louis lies Anse Bertrand, the northernmost village of Guadeloupe. What is now a fishing village was the last refuge of the Carib tribes, and a reserve was once created here. Everything now, however, is sleepy.

Where to Dine

⑤ Chez Prudence (Folie Plage)

Anse Laborde, 97121 Anse Bertrand, Guadeloupe, F.W.I. ☎ **590/22-11-17.** Reservations recommended. Appetizers 25–55 F ($4.75–$10.45); main courses 70–150 F ($13.30–$28.50); fixed-price meal 100–153 F ($19–$29.10). AE, MC, V. Lunch daily noon–3pm; dinner daily 7–10pm. CREOLE.

About a mile north of Anse Bertrand at Anse Laborde, this place is owned by Prudence Marcelin, a *cuisinière patronne* who enjoys much local acclaim for her Créole cookery. She draws people from all over the island, especially on Sunday when this place is its most crowded. Island children frolic in the establishment's saltwater pool, and in between courses diners can shop for handcrafts, clothes, and souvenirs sold by a handful of nearby vendors. Her court bouillon is excellent, as is either her goat or chicken (curried) colombo. The palourdes (clams) are superb, and she makes a zesty sauce to serve with fish. The place is relaxed and casual.

She also rents half a dozen very basic motel-style bungalows priced at 250 F ($47.50) for single or double occupancy, for overnight stays.

✪ Le Château de Feuilles

Campêche, Anse Bertrand. ☎ **590/212-30-30.** Reservations required, especially in summer when meals are prepared only in anticipation of your arrival. Appetizers 68–100 F ($12.90–$19); main courses 100–150 F ($19–$28.50). V. Winter, lunch Tues–Sun 11:30am–4pm. At night, at least 10 diners must reserve before they will open. Closed Sept. FRENCH/CARIBBEAN.

Set inland from the sea, amid 8 rolling acres of greenery and blossoming flowers, this gastronomic hideaway is owned and run by a Norman-born couple, Jean-Pierre and Martine Dubost. To reach their place, which is 9 miles from Le Moule on the Campêche road near the extreme eastern tip of Grande-Terre, motorists must pass the ruins of La Mahaudière, an 18th-century sugar mill. A gifted chef making maximum use of local ingredients, Monsieur Dubost prepares pâté of warm sea urchins, sautéed conch with Créole sauce, a cassoulette of crayfish, gigot of shark with fresh pasta and saffron sauce, and a sauerkraut of fresh fish with papaya and a traditional version of magret of duckling. One unusual taste sensation is a pavé of tazar (a local fish) served with a fresh vanilla sauce.

CONTINUING THE TOUR

From Anse Bertrand, you can drive along a graveled road heading for **Pointe de la Grande Vigie,** the northernmost tip of the island, which you reach after 4 miles of what I hope will be cautious driving. Park your car and walk carefully along a narrow lane which will bring you to the northernmost rock of Guadeloupe. The view of the sweeping Atlantic from the top of rocky cliffs is remarkable—you stand about 280 feet above the sea.

Afterward, a 4-mile drive south on quite a good road will bring you to the **Porte d'Enfer** or "gateway to hell." Once there, you'll find the sea rushing violently against two narrow cliffs.

After this kind of awesome experience in the remote part of the island, you can head back, going either to Morne à l'Eau or Le Moule before connecting to the road taking you back to Pointe-à-Pitre.

AROUND BASSE-TERRE

Leaving Pointe-à-Pitre by the N1, you can explore the lesser windward coast. After a mile and a half you cross the Rivière Salée at Pont de la Gabarre. This narrow strait separates the two islands that form Guadeloupe. For the next 4 miles the road runs straight through sugarcane fields.

At the sign, on a main crossing, turn right on the N2 toward **Bale Mahault.** Leaving that town on the right, head for **Lamentin.** This village was settled by corsairs at the beginning of the 18th century. Scattered about are some colonial mansions.

STE-ROSE

From Lamentin, you can drive for 6¹/₂ miles to Ste-Rose, where you'll find several good beaches. On your left, a small road leads to **Sofaia,** from which you'll have a panoramic view over the coast and forest preserve. The locals claim that a sulfur spring here has curative powers.

Where to Stay

La Sucrerie du Comté

Conté de Lohéac, 97115 Ste-Rose, Guadeloupe, F.W.I. ☎ **590/28-60-17.** Fax 28-65-63. 52 rms. A/C. Winter, 350–420 F ($66.50–$99.80) single; 500–600 F ($95–$114) double.

Off-season, 310 F ($58.90) single; 400 F ($76) double. (Rates include breakfast.) MAP rates 140 F ($26.60) per person extra. MC, V. Free parking.

Set on the west coast of Basse-Terre, on 8 acres of forested land overlooking the sea, this resort opened in 1991. Although the ruins of a 19th-century sugar factory are on the premises, most of the resort is new. There's a restaurant on site, open daily for lunch and dinner, with full meals priced from 150 F ($28.50) each, and a bar set beneath a veranda-style roof near a swimming pool. Accommodations are in 26 rectangular, ocher-colored bungalows, each cramped but cozy, each filled with chunky and rustic furniture handmade from Brazilian hardwoods and a bay window overlooking either the sea or a garden. (Each bungalow contains two units, both with ceiling fans; none has a TV or telephone.) Scuba diving and fishing can be arranged.

Where to Dine

Restaurant Clara

Ste-Rose. ☎ **590/28-72-99.** Reservations recommended. Appetizers 25–50 F ($4.80–$9.50); main courses 50–120 F ($9.50–$22.80). MC, V. Lunch Thurs–Tues noon–2:30pm; dinner Thurs–Tues 7–10pm. CREOLE.

On the waterfront near the center of town is the culinary statement of Clara Lesueur and her talented and charming semiretired mother, Justine. Clara lived for 12 years in Paris as a member of an experimental jazz dance troupe, but she returned to Guadeloupe, her home, and set up her breeze-cooled restaurant. Try for a table on the open patio, where palm trees complement the color scheme.

Clara and Justine artfully meld the French style of fine dining with authentic, spicy Créole cookery. Specialties may include ouassous (freshwater crayfish), brochette of swordfish, palourdes (small clams), several different preparations of conch, sea-urchin omelets, and crabes farcis (red-orange crabs with a spicy filling). The "sauce chien" served with many of the dishes is a blend of hot peppers, garlic, lime juice, and "secret things" that go well with the house drink, made with six local fruits and ample quantities of rum. Your dessert sherbet might be guava, soursop, or passionfruit.

DESHAIES/GRAND ANSE

A few miles farther along, you reach Pointe Allegre, the northernmost point of Basse-Terre. At **Clugny Beach,** you'll be at the site where the first settler landed on Guadeloupe.

A couple of miles farther will bring you to **Grand Anse,** one of the best beaches on Guadeloupe. It's very large and still secluded, sheltered by many tropical trees.

At **Deshaies,** snorkeling and fishing are popular pastimes. The narrow road winds up and down and has a corniche look to it, with the blue sea underneath, the view of green mountains studded with colorful hamlets.

Nine miles from Deshaies, **Pointe Noire** comes into view. Its name comes from black volcanic rocks. Look for the odd polychrome cenotaph in town.

ROUTE DE LA TRAVERSEE

Four miles from Pointe Noire, you reach **Mahaut.** On your left begins the ✪ **route de la Traversée,** the Transcoastal Highway. This is the best way to explore the scenic wonders of **Parc Naturel de Guadeloupe** when traveling between the capital, Basse-Terre, and Pointe-à-Pitre. I recommend going this way, as you pass through a tropical forest.

To preserve the Parc Naturel, Guadeloupe has set aside 74,100 acres, or about one-fifth of its entire terrain. Reached by modern roads, this is a huge tract of mountains, tropical forests, and magnificent scenery.

The park is home to a variety of tame animals, including Titi (a raccoon adopted as its official mascot), and such birds as the wood pigeon, turtledove, and thrush. Small exhibition huts, devoted to the volcano, the forest, or to coffee, sugarcane, and rum, are scattered throughout the park.

The Parc Naturel has no gates, no opening or closing hours, and no admission fee.

From Mahaut you climb slowly in a setting of giant ferns and luxuriant vegetation. Four miles after the fork, you reach **Les Deux Mamelles (The Two Breasts),** where you can park your car and go for a hike. Some of the trails are for experts only; others, such as the Pigeon Trail, will bring you to a summit of about 2,600 feet where the view is impressive. Expect to spend at least three hours going each way. Halfway along the trail you can stop at Forest House. From that point, many lanes, all signposted, branch off on trails that will last anywhere from 20 minutes to two hours. Try to find the **Chute de l'Ecrevisse,** the "Crayfish Waterfall," a little pond of very cold water which you'll discover after a quarter of a mile.

After the hike, the main road descends toward Versailles, a hamlet about 5 miles from Pointe-à-Pitre.

However, before taking this route, while still traveling between Pointe Noire and Mahaut on the west coast, you might consider the following luncheon stop.

Where to Dine

Chez Vaneau

Mahaut/Pointe Noire. ☎ **590/98-01-71.** Reservations not required. Appetizers 25–40 F ($4.80–$7.60); main courses 60–75 F ($11.40–$14.30). AE, MC, V. Lunch daily noon–5pm; dinner daily 7pm–midnight. CREOLE.

Set in an isolated pocket of forest about 18 miles north of Pointe Noire, far from any of its neighbors, Chez Vaneau offers a wide, breeze-filled veranda overlooking a gully, the sight of local neighbors playing cards, and steaming Créole specialties coming from the kitchen. This is the well-established domain of Vaneau Desbonnes, who is assisted by his wife, Marie-Gracieuse, and their children. Specialties include oysters with a piquant sauce, crayfish bisque, ragoût of goat, fricassée of conch, different preparations of octopus, and roast pork.

BOUILLANTE

If you don't take the route de la Traversée at this time but wish to continue exploring the west coast, you can head south from Mahaut until you reach the village of Bouillante, which is exciting for only one reason: You might encounter former French film star Brigitte Bardot, as she's a part-time resident.

Try not to miss seeing the small island called **Ilet à Goyave** or **Ilet du Pigeon.** Jacques Cousteau often explored the silent depths around it.

Facing the islet is the best choice for a luncheon on the whole island. After a meal at La Touna, you can explore around the village of Bouillante, the country known for its thermal springs. In some places if you scratch the ground for only a few inches you'll feel the heat.

Where to Dine near Bouillante

Chez Loulouse

Malendure Plage. ☎ **590/98-70-34.** Reservations not required. Appetizers 25–35 F ($4.80–$6.70); most main courses 50–80 F ($9.50–$15.20). AE, MC, V. Lunch daily noon–3:30pm; dinner daily 7–10pm. CREOLE.

Another good choice for lunch is Chez Loulouse, a staunchly matriarchal establishment with plenty of offhanded charm, beside the sands of the well-known beach, opposite Pigeon Island. Many guests prefer their rum punches on the panoramic veranda, overlooking a scene of loaded boats preparing to depart and merchants hawking their wares. A quieter oasis is the equally colorful dining room inside, just past the bar. There, beneath a ceiling of palm fronds, is a wraparound series of Créole murals that seem to go well with the reggae music emanating loudly from the bar.

This is the creation of one of the most visible and charming Créole matrons on this end of the island, Mme Loulouse Paisley-Carbon. Assisted by her children, she offers house-style Caribbean lobster, spicy versions of conch, octopus, accras, gratin of christophine (squash), and savory colombos (curries) of chicken or pork. Although most of the main courses at this restaurant rarely exceed 80 F ($15.20), lobster and crayfish can sometimes reach as much as 170 F ($32.30) per person.

La Touna

Galet Pigeon, Malendure. ☎ **590/98-70-10.** Reservations recommended on Sun. Appetizers 35–65 F ($6.70–$12.40); main courses 60–150 F ($11.40–$28.50). MC, V. Lunch Tues–Sun noon–3pm; dinner Tues–Sat 7–9:30pm. Closed Sept 15–Oct 15. Directions: In the village of Mahaut, turn left on route 2 and drive south. SEAFOOD/CREOLE.

Built on a narrow strip of sand between the road and the sea, its foundation almost touching the water, this restaurant has a marine panorama, which complements the seafood specialties prepared here. Most of the dining tables are on a side veranda whose ceiling is covered with palm fronds. Many guests delay a meal until after a drink in the sunken bar whose encircling banquettes give the impression of a ship's cabin.

You are brought a tray on which are seven or eight carafes, each filled with a rum-soaked tropical fruit, such as guava, maracoja, pineapple, and passionfruit. You select the ingredients you prefer and mix your own drink. Of course if you prefer the house specialty, you'll have a combination of fruit with or without rum, one of the most refreshing drinks on the island. Menu items make use of the freshest ingredients, many of them brought in daily from local waters. Full meals might include a mousse of smoked swordfish, calamari provençal, stuffed crabs, stuffed sea urchins, kingfish au poivre, or various platters of fish and shellfish from Caribbean waters.

VIEUX HABITANTS

The winding coast road brings you to Vieux Habitants (Old Settlers), one of the oldest villages on the island, founded in 1636. The name comes from the people who settled it. After serving in the employment of the West Indies Company, they retired here. But they preferred to call themselves inhabitants, so as not to be confused with slaves.

BASSE-TERRE

Another 10 miles of winding roads bring you to Basse-Terre, the seat of the government of Guadeloupe, lying between the water and La Soufrière, the volcano. Founded in 1634, it's the oldest town on the island and still has a lot of charm; its market squares are shaded by tamarind and palm trees.

The town suffered heavy destruction at the hands of British troops in 1691 and again in 1702. It was also the center of fierce fighting during the French Revolution, when the political changes that swept across Europe caused explosive tensions on Guadeloupe. (As it did in the mainland of France, the guillotine claimed many lives on Guadeloupe during the infamous Reign of Terror.)

In spite of the town's history, there isn't much to see in Basse-Terre except for a 17th-century cathedral and Fort St-Charles, which has guarded the city (not always well) since it was established.

Where to Stay & Dine en Route

Le Houëlmont

Rue de la République, 34, 97120 Basse-Terre, Guadeloupe, F.W.I. ☎ **590/81-35-96.** Reservations required. Appetizers 25–50 F ($4.80–$9.50); main courses 65–200 F ($12.40–$38); fixed-price meal from 90 F ($17.10). MC, V. Lunch Mon–Sat noon–3pm; dinner Mon–Sat 7–10:30pm. INTERNATIONAL.

Set in the monumental heart of town, near the bus station, across a boulevard from a massive government building called the Conseil Général, is the oldest and best-established restaurant in the island capital, Le Houëlmont. The restaurant is named after an extinct volcano which can be viewed from the windows of the dining room. After climbing a flight of stairs to the paneled second story, diners enjoy a sweeping view over the hillside sloping down to the sea one block away. Madame Boulon, the owner, an old-time Guadeloupienne restaurateur, offers fixed-price and à la carte meals. Specialties include a medley of Créole food, such as accras, court-bouillon of fish, grilled fish, steaks, shellfish, and blood sausage, plus French and international dishes.

It's also possible to rent one of the eight bedrooms here, each with private bath and air conditioning (some units contain TVs). Year round, single rooms cost 280 F ($53.20), doubles are 350 F ($66.50), and breakfast goes for an additional 35 F ($6.70) per person per day.

LA SOUFRIÈRE

The big attraction of Basse-Terre is the famous sulfur-puffing La Soufrière volcano, which is still alive, but dormant—for the moment at least. Rising to a height of some 4,800 feet, it's flanked by banana plantations and lush foliage.

After leaving the capital at Basse-Terre, you can drive to **St-Claude,** a suburb, 4 miles up the mountainside at a height of 1,900 feet. It has an elegant reputation for its perfect climate and tropical gardens.

Instead of going to St-Claude, you can head for **Matouba,** in a country of clear mountain spring water. The only sound you're likely to hear at this idyllic place is of birds and the running water of dozens of springs. The village was settled long ago by Hindus.

From St-Claude, you can begin the climb up the narrow, winding road the Guadeloupeans say leads to hell—that is, ✪ **La Soufrière.** The road ends at a parking area at La Savane à Mulets, at an altitude of 3,300 feet. That is the ultimate point to be reached by car. Hikers are able to climb right to the mouth of the volcano. However, in 1975 the appearance of ashes, mud, billowing smoke, and earthquakelike tremors proved that the old beast was still alive.

In the resettlement process, 75,000 inhabitants were relocated to Grande-Terre. However, no deaths were reported. But the inhabitants of Basse-Terre still keep a watchful eye on the smoking giant.

Even in the parking lot, you can feel the heat of the volcano merely by touching the ground. Steam emerges from fumaroles and sulfurous fumes from the volcano's "burps." Of course, fumes come from its pit and mud cauldrons as well.

Where to Dine En Route

Chez Paul de Matouba

Rivière Rouge. ☎ **590/80-29-20.** Reservations not required. Appetizers 25–35 F ($4.80–$6.70); main courses 65–100 F ($12.40–$19); fixed-price meal 100 F ($19). MC, V. Lunch only, daily noon–4pm. Closed Mon off-season. Directions: Follow the clearly marked signs—it's beside a gully close to the center of the village. CREOLE/INTERNATIONAL.

You'll find good food in this family-run restaurant, which sits beside the banks of the small Rivière Rouge (Red River). The dining room on the second floor is enclosed by windows, allowing you to drink in the surrounding dark-green foliage of the mountains. The cookery is Créole, and crayfish dishes are the specialty. However, because of the influence of the region's early settlers, East Indian meals are also available. By all means, drink the mineral or spring water of Matouba. What one diner called "an honest meal" might include stuffed crab, colombo (curried) chicken, as well as an array of French, Créole, and Hindu specialties. You're likely to find the place overcrowded in the winter season with the tour-bus crowd.

THE WINDWARD COAST

From Basse-Terre to Pointe-à-Pitre, the road follows the east coast, called the Windward Coast. The country here is richer and greener than elsewhere on the island.

To reach **Trois Rivières** you have a choice of two routes: One goes along the coastline, coming eventually to Vieux Fort, from which you can see Les Saintes archipelago. The other heads across the hills, Monts Caraïbes.

Near the pier in Trois Rivières you'll see the pre-Columbian petroglyphs carved by the original inhabitants, the Arawaks. They are called merely Roches Gravées, or "carved rocks." In this archeological park, the rock engravings are of animal and human figures, dating most likely from A.D. 300 or 400. You'll also see specimens of plants, including cocoa, pimento, and banana, that the Arawaks cultivated long before the Europeans set foot on Guadeloupe. From Trois Rivières, you can take boats to Les Saintes.

After leaving Trois Rivières, you continue on route 1. Passing through the village of Banaier, you turn on your left at Anse Saint-Sauveur to reach the famous ✪ **Chutes du Carbet,** a trio of waterfalls. The road to two of them is a narrow, winding one, along many steep hills, passing through banana plantations as you move deeper into a tropical forest.

After 3 miles, a lane, suitable only for hikers, brings you to Zombie Pool. Half a mile farther along, a fork to the left takes you to Grand Etang, or large pool. At a point 6 miles from the main road, a parking area is available and you'll have to walk the rest of the way on an uneasy trail toward the second fall, Le Carbet. Expect to spend around 20 to 30 minutes, depending on how slippery the lane is.

Then you'll be at the foot of this second fall where the water drops from 230 feet. The waters here average 70° Fahrenheit, which is pretty warm for a mountain spring.

The first fall is the most impressive, but it takes two hours of rough hiking to get there. The third fall is reached from Capesterre on the main road by climbing to Routhiers. This fall is less impressive in height, only 70 feet. When the Carbet water runs out of La Soufrière, it's almost boiling.

After Capesterre, you can go along for 4¹/₂ miles to see the statue of the first tourist who landed on Guadeloupe, which stands in the town square of Ste-Marie. The tourist was Christopher Columbus, who anchored a quarter of a mile from Ste-Marie on November 4, 1493. In the journal of his second voyage he wrote, "We arrived, seeing ahead of us a large mountain which seemed to want to rise up to the sky, in the middle of which was a peak higher than all the rest of the mountains from which flowed a living stream."

However, when Caribs started shooting arrows at him, he left quickly.

After Ste-Marie, you pass through Goyave, then Petit-Bourg, seeing on your left the route de la Traversée before reaching Pointe-à-Pitre. You will have just completed the most fascinating scenic tour Guadeloupe has to offer.

SPORTS & OUTDOOR ACTIVITIES AROUND THE ISLAND

BEACHES   Chances are, your hotel will be right on a beach or will lie no more than 20 minutes from a good one. There is a plentitude of natural beaches dotting the island from the surf-brushed dark strands of western Basse-Terre to the long stretches of white sand encircling Grande-Terre. Public beaches are generally free, but some charge for parking. Unlike hotel beaches, they have few facilities. Hotels welcome nonguests, but charge for changing facilities, beach chairs, and towels.

Sunday is family day at the beach. Topless sunbathing is common at hotels, less so on village beaches. Nudist beaches also exist, including at **Ilet du Gosier,** off the shore of Gosier, site of many leading hotels.

Outstanding beaches of Guadeloupe include **Caravelle Beach,** a long, reef-protected stretch of sand outside Ste-Anne, about 9 miles from Gosier.

Another nudist beach, **Plage de Tarare,** lies near the tip of Grand-Terre at Pointe des Châteaux, site of many local restaurants.

On Basse-Terre, one of the best beaches is **Grande Anse,** a palm-sheltered beach north of Deshaies on the northwest coast.

Other good beaches are found on the offshore islands, Iles des Saintes and Marie-Galante (see below).

DEEP-SEA FISHING   The season for barracuda and kingfish is January to May. For tuna, dolphin, and bonito, it's December to March. Hotels will recommend deep-sea-fishing boats. At Marina Bas-du-Fort, **Caraïbe Pêche** (☎ **590/90-97-51**) charters Jeanneaus and Merry Fishers for one-day outings.

GOLF   Guadeloupe's only golf course is the well-known **Golf de St-François** (☎ **590/88-41-87**) at St-François, opposite the Hôtel Méridien, about 22 miles east of Raizet Airport. The golf course runs alongside an 800-acre lagoon where windsurfing, waterskiing, and sailing prevail. The course, designed by Robert Trent Jones, is a 6,755-yard, par-71 course, which presents many challenges to the golfer, with water traps on 6 of the 18 holes, massive bunkers, prevailing trade winds, and a particularly fiendish 400-yard, par-4 ninth hole. The par-5 sixth is the toughest hole on the course; its 450 yards must be negotiated into the constant easterly winds. Greens fees are 250 F ($47.50) per day per person, which allows a full day of playing time. A complete set of golf clubs can be rented for 100 F ($19) for the day.

HIKING The **Parc Naturel de Guadeloupe** is the best hiking grounds in the Caribbean, in my opinion (see the touring notes on route de la Traversée in "Around Basse-Terre," above). Marked trails cut through the deep foliage of rain forests until you come upon a waterfall or perhaps a cool mountain pool. The big excursion country, of course, is around the volcano, La Soufrière. Hiking brochures are available from the tourist office. Hotel tour desks can arrange this activity.

Warning: Hikers may experience heavy downpours. The annual precipitation on the higher slopes is 250 inches per year, so be prepared.

SAILING Sailboats of varying sizes, crewed or bareboat, are plentiful. Information can be secured at any hotel desk. Sunfish sailing can be arranged at almost every beachfront hotel.

SCUBA DIVING Scuba divers seem to be drawn more to the waters off Guadeloupe than to any other point in the French-speaking islands. Its allure derives from its lack of underwater currents, its relatively calm seas, and the establishment of the **Cousteau Underwater Reserve,** a kind of French national park with many attractive dive sites, where the underwater environment is rigidly protected. Jacques Cousteau described the waters off Guadeloupe's Pigeon Island as "one of the world's 10 best diving spots." During a typical dive, sergeant majors become visible at a depth of 30 feet, spiny sea urchins and green parrotfish at 60 feet, and magnificent stands of finger, black, brain, and star coral come into view at depths of 80 feet.

Every year, the specific sites favored by Guadeloupe's many dive aficionados change from one underwater locale to another. At press time, the most popular of these bear such names as Aquarium, Piscine, Jardin de Corail, Pointe Carrangue, Pointe Barracuda, and Jardin Japonais. Although scattered around the periphery of the island, many are in the bay of Petit Cul-de-Sac Marin, south of Rivière Salée, the channel that separates the two halves of Guadeloupe. North of the Salée is another bay, Grand Cul-de-Sac Marin, where the small islets of Fajou and Caret also boast fine diving.

Centre International de la Plongée (C.I.P.), B.P. 4, Malendure Plage, 97125 Pigeon, Bouillante, Guadeloupe, F.W.I. (☎ **590/98-81-72**), is usually acknowledged as one of most businesslike and professional dive operations on the island. In a wood-sided house on Malendure Plage, close to a well-known restaurant, Chez Loulouse, it benefits from a position at the edge of the Cousteau Underwater Reserve. Dive boats depart three times a day, usually at 10am, 12:30pm, and 3pm. A one-tank dive costs 150 F ($28.50), whereas what the Americans refer to as a "resort course" for first-time divers (the French refer to it as a *baptème*) costs 170 F ($32.30) and is usually conducted one-on-one with one participant and an instructor.

TENNIS All the large resort hotels have tennis courts, many of which they light at night for games. The noonday sun is often too hot for most players. If you're a guest, tennis is free at most of these hotels, but you will be charged for night play.

If your hotel doesn't have a court, you might consider an outing to **Le Relais du Moulin,** Châteaubrun, near Ste-Anne (☎ **590/88-23-96**).

WINDSURFING & WATERSKIING Windsurfing is the hottest sport on Guadeloupe today, and it's available with lessons at all the major beach hotels, at a cost of 120 F ($22.80) and up. Most seaside hotels can arrange waterskiing at 100 F ($19) for 15 minutes' boating time.

GUADELOUPE AFTER DARK

Guadeloupeans claim that the beguine was invented here, not on Martinique, and they dance the beguine as if they truly did own it. Of course, calypso and the merengue move rhythmically along—the islanders are known for their dancing.

Ask at your hotel where the folkloric **Ballets Guadeloupeans** will be appearing. This troupe makes frequent appearances at the big hotels, although they don't enjoy the fame of the Ballets Martiniquais, the troupe on the neighbor island already described.

Casino de la Marina, avenue de l'Europe (☎ **590/88-41-44**), stands near the Hotel Méridien St-François. It's open daily from noon to 3am to those age 18 or above with proof of identity—a driver's license or valid passport. Once inside, you can play American roulette and blackjack. Dress is casual. A free buffet is served on Friday night. Drinks begin at 45 F ($8.60), and admission is 69 F ($13.60).

Another casino, **Gosier-les-Bains,** is in the resort community of Gosier (Bas du Fort), on the grounds of the Hôtel Arawak (☎ **590/84-18-33**). Entrance is free, but an ID card with a photo, or a passport, is required for admission. Although dress tends to be casually elegant, coat and tie are not required. The casino is open Sunday through Thursday from 9pm to 3am, and on Friday and Saturday from 9pm to 4am (one room containing slot machines is open every night from 6pm until closing). The most popular games are blackjack, roulette, and chemin-de-fer.

AN EXCURSION TO THE ILES DES SAINTES

A cluster of eight islands off the southern coast of Guadeloupe, the Iles des Saintes are certainly off the beaten track. The two main islands and six rocks are Terre-de-Haut, Terre-de-Bas, Ilet-à-Cabrit, La Coche, Les Augustins, Grand Ilet, Le Redonde, and Le Pâté; only Terre-de-Haut ("land above"), and to a lesser extent Terre-de-Bas ("land below"), attract visitors.

If you're planning a visit, **Terre-de-Haut** is the most interesting Saint to call upon. It's the only one with facilities for overnight guests.

Some claim that Les Saintes has one of the nicest bays in the world, a lilliput Rio de Janeiro with a sugarloaf. The isles, just 6 miles from the main island, were discovered by Columbus on November 4, 1493, who named them "Los Santos."

The history of Les Saintes is very much the history of Guadeloupe itself. In years past, the islands have been heavily fortified, as they were considered Guadeloupe's Gibraltar. The climate is very dry, and until the desalination plant opened, water was often rationed.

The population of Terre-de-Haut is mainly Caucasian, all fisherfolk or sailors and their families who are descended from Breton corsairs. The very skilled sailors maneuver large boats called *saintois* and wear coolielike headgear called a *salaco,* which is shallow and white with sun shades covered in cloth built on radiating ribs of thick bamboo. Frankly, the hats look like small parasols. If you want to take a photograph of these sailors, please make a polite request (in French, no less; otherwise they won't know what you're talking about). Visitors often like to buy these hats (if they can find them) for use as beach wear.

Terre-de-Haut is a place for discovery and lovers of nature, many of whom stake out their exhibitionistic space on the nude beach at Anse Crawen.

ORIENTATION
Getting There

BY PLANE   The fastest way to get there is by plane. The "airport" is a truncated landing strip that accommodates nothing larger than 20-seat Twin Otters. **Air Guadeloupe** (☎ **590/82-47-00** or **82-47-47**) has two round-trips daily from Pointe-à-Pitre, which take 15 minutes.

BY FERRY   Most islanders reach Terre-de-Haut via one of the several ferryboats that travel from Guadeloupe every day. Most visitors opt for one of the two boats that depart every day from Pointe-à-Pitre's Gare Maritime des Iles, on quai Gatine, across the street from the well-known open-air market. The trip requires 50 minutes each way, and costs 160 F ($30.40) for round-trip passage. Three different ferryboats also depart from Trois Rivières, and two other ferryboats leave from the island's capital of Basse-Terre. Transit from either of these last two cities requires 25 minutes each way, and costs 85 F ($16.20) for the round-trip passage.

The most popular departure time for Terre-de-Haut from Pointe-à-Pitre is at 8am Monday through Saturday, and at 7am on Sunday, with return at 4pm. (Be at the ferryboat terminal at least 15 minutes prior to the anticipated departure.) For more information and last-minute departure schedules, contact **Frères Brudey** (☎ **590/83-12-45**) or **Trans Antilles Express,** Gare Maritime, quai Gatine, Pointe-à-Pitre (☎ **590/91-60-87**).

Getting Around

On an island that doesn't have a single car-rental agency, you get about by walking or renting a **bike** or **motorscooter,** which can be rented at hotels and in town near the pier.

There are also minibuses called **Taxis de l'Ile** (eight in all), which take six to eight passengers.

WHERE TO STAY

Bois Joli

97137 Terre-de-Haut, Les Saintes, Guadeloupe, F.W.I. ☎ **590/99-52-53,** or toll free 800/223-9815 in the U.S. Fax 99-55-05. 21 rms, 8 bungalows. Winter, 645 F ($122.60) single; 860 F ($163.40) double; 1,225 F ($232.80) bungalow for two. Off-season, 570 F ($108.30) single; 740 F ($140.60) double; 1,100 F ($209) bungalow for two. (MAP rates.) MC, V. Free parking.

On the western part of the island, 2 miles from the village, overlooking a fine beach, Bois Joli sits in confectionery pink, a stucco block on a palm-studded rise of a slope. Accommodations are in the main house and eight bungalows on the hillside. Bold-patterned fabrics are used on the beds, and the rooms have modern furnishings. All but two of the units are air-conditioned, with various combinations of shower and bath arrangements. Most rooms have private phones. Families might be interested in renting one of the bungalows. The food is good Créole cooking. Mr. Blandin can arrange for waterskiing, sailing, boat trips to some of the islets or rocks that form Les Saintes, and snorkeling. The restaurant is closed every Monday during off-season. In winter, reservations are suggested at least six months in advance.

Hôtel La Saintoise

Place de la Mairie, 97137 Terre-de-Haut, Les Saintes, Guadeloupe, F.W.I. ☎ **590/99-52-50.** 8 rms. A/C. 250 F ($47.50) single; 350 F ($66.50) double. (Rates include continental breakfast.) MC, V.

Originally built in the 1960s, La Saintoise is a modern, two-story building set near the almond trees and widespread poinciana of the town's main square, near the ferryboat dock, across from the town hall. As in a small French village, the inn places tables and chairs on the sidewalk, where you can sit out and observe what action there is. The owner will welcome you and show you through the uncluttered lobby to one of his bedrooms, each of which is outfitted with a tile bath. They're on the second floor, and the furnishings are admittedly modest. The aura throughout is of a small but decent inn in the French Caribbean, with few amenities, the simplest of furnishings, and an ultra-simple physical plant.

Kanaoa

97137 Terre-de-Haut, Les Saintes, Guadeloupe, F.W.I. ☎ **590/99-51-36.** Fax 99-55-04. 19 rms. A/C TEL. Winter, 425 F ($80.80) single; 500 F ($95) double. Off-season, 325 F ($61.80) single; 380 F ($72.20) double. (Rates include continental breakfast.) MC, V.

Named after the open-sided log canoes originally used by the Arawaks, this modern concrete structure erected on a little beach at Pointe Coquelet, north of the town center, is utterly plain. All accommodations have private showers and rather spartan furnishings; five have views of the sea and Anse Mire cove. A very limited amount of English is spoken and the staff might not be able to respond to many of your needs. Despite that, the hotel exerts a powerful allure on escapists of all sorts. The location is 1¼ miles from the airport. A garden with its own swimming pool is near the hotel, and a restaurant serves breakfast, lunch, and dinner on the premises.

Le Village Créole

Point Coquelet, 97137 Terre-de-Haut, Les Saintes, Guadeloupe, F.W.I. ☎ **590/99-53-83.** Fax 99-55-55. 22 rms. A/C MINIBAR TEL. Winter, 640–990 F ($121.60–$188.10) single or double. Off-season, 460–560 F ($87.40–$106.40) single or double. MC, V.

Owned and operated by a family from the French mainland, this hotel was built in 1987 on 3½ acres that border 130 yards of seashore, close to the foundations of Fort Napoléon, on the northern edge of town, at the mouth of the harbor. The buildings reflect the traditional architectural style of the island. Eleven villas are divided into two first-class duplexes, all with a washer-dryer, a flower-filled patio, and summery furniture. Each unit has its own kitchen, and although there's no restaurant on the premises, the owner is very nice about referring guests to about a dozen of the island's 27 eateries. Daily maid service is also included. The owner prefers weekly rentals, but shorter or longer stays are possible. Bicycles can be rented and day trips planned.

WHERE TO DINE

Chez Jeannine (Le Casse-Croûte)

Fond-de-Curé, Terre-de-Haut. ☎ **590/99-53-37.** Reservations recommended for large groups only. Fixed-price meal 70 F ($13.30) for two courses, 85 F ($16.20) for three courses. V. Breakfast/lunch daily 8am–3pm; dinner daily 6:30–9:30pm. CREOLE.

The creative statement of Mme Jeannine Bairtran, originally from Guadeloupe, this restaurant is in a simple Créole house decorated with modern Caribbean accessories, a three-minute walk south of the town center. Only fixed-price meals are served, and they include avocado stuffed with crabmeat, a gâteau de poissons (literally "fish cake"), and several different curry-enhanced stews (including one made with goat). Crayfish and grilled fish (the ubiquitous catch of the day) appear daily on the menu. Local vegetables are used. The ambience is that of a Créole bistro—in other words, a hut with nautical trappings and bright tablecloths.

Les Amandiers

Place de la Mairie. ☎ **590/99-50-06.** Reservations recommended. Main courses 65–90 F ($12.40–$17.10); fixed-price meals 60–80 F ($11.40–$15.20). AE, MC, V. Lunch daily 11am–2:30pm; dinner daily 7–11pm. CREOLE.

Across from the town hall on the main square of Bourg is perhaps the most traditional Créole bistro on Terre-de-Haut. A TV set (at loud volume) might be providing entertainment in the bar at the time of your visit. Monsieur and Madame Charlot Brudey are your hosts in this beige-painted building whose upper balconies sport tables and chairs for open-air dining. Conch (lambi) is prepared either in a fricassée or a colombo, a savory curry stew. Also available is a court bouillon of fish, a gâteau (terrine) of fish, and a seemingly endless supply of grilled crayfish, a staple of the island. The catch of the day is also grilled the way you like it. You'll find an intriguing collection of stews, concocted from fish, bananas, and christophine (chayote, to many readers.) A knowledge of French would be helpful around here.

Relais des Iles

Route de Pompierre. ☎ **590/99-53-04.** Reservations recommended. Fixed-price meal 150–190 F ($28.50–$36.10). MC, V. Lunch Wed–Mon noon–2pm; dinner Wed–Mon 7–8:30pm. Closed May 20–June 30. FRENCH/SEAFOOD.

This restaurant was built in the 1970s as an Antillean adaptation of a Swiss chalet, with a stone base and an upper story of weathered wood. (Its French owners, Bernard and Nanette Mathieu, had lived for several years in Switzerland before coming to the West Indies.) It lies midway between the village and Pompierre Plage, on a hilltop eyrie a five-minute walk from either. Menu items include lobster from the establishment's own holding tank, a spicy version of fish soup, feuilleté of sea urchins, a selection of grilled fresh fish, magret of duckling in orange sauce, white-chocolate mousse in raspberry sauce, and crêpes Alaska.

WHAT TO SEE & DO

On Terre-de-Haut, the main settlement is at **Bourg,** a single street that follows the curve of the fishing harbor. A charming hamlet, it has little houses with red or blue doorways, balconies, and Victorian gingerbread gewgaws. Donkeys are the beasts of burden, and everywhere you look are fish nets drying in the sunshine. You can also explore the ruins of **Fort Napoléon,** which is left over from those 17th-century wars, including the naval encounter known in European history books as "The Battle of the Saints." You can see the barracks and prison cells, as well as the drawbridge and art museum. Occasionally you'll spot an iguana scurrying up the ramparts. Directly across the bay, atop Ilet-à-Cabrit, sits the fort named in honor of Empress Joséphine.

You might also get a sailor to take you on his boat to the other main island, **Terre-de-Bas,** which has no accommodations, incidentally. Or you can stay on Terre-de-Haut and hike to **Le Grand Souffleur** with its beautiful cliffs, and to **Le Chameau,** the highest point on the island, rising to a peak of 1,000 feet.

Scuba-diving centers are not limited to mainland Guadeloupe. The underwater world off Les Saintes has attracted deep-sea divers as renowned as Jacques Cousteau, but even the less experienced may explore its challenging depths and multicolored reefs. Intriguing underwater grottoes found near Fort Napoléon on Terre-de-Haut are also explored.

AN EXCURSION TO MARIE-GALANTE

This offshore dependency of Guadeloupe is an almost-perfect circle of about 60 square miles. Almost exclusively French-speaking, it lies 20 miles south of Guadeloupe's Grand-Terre and is full of rustic charm.

Columbus noticed it before he did Guadeloupe, on November 3, 1493. He named it for his own vessel, but didn't land there. In fact, it was 150 years later that the first European came ashore.

The first French governor of the island was Constant d'Aubigne, father of the marquise de Maintenon. Several captains from the West Indies Company attempted settlement, but none of them succeeded. In 1674 Marie-Galante was given to the Crown, and from that point on its history was closely linked to that of Guadeloupe.

However, after 1816 the island settled down to a quiet slumber. You could hear the sugarcane growing on the plantations—and that was about it. Many windmills were built to crush the cane, and lots of tropical fruits were grown.

Now, some 30,000 inhabitants live here and make their living from sugar and rum, the latter said to be the best in the Caribbean. The island's climate is rather dry, and there are many good beaches. One of these stretches of sand covers at least 5 miles—brilliantly white. However, swimming can be dangerous in some places. The best beach is at **Petite Anse,** 6 ¹/₂ miles from **Grand-Bourg,** the main town, with an 1845 baroque church. The 18th-century Grand Anse rum distillery can be visited, as can the historic fishing hamlet of Vieux Fort.

GETTING THERE & GETTING AROUND

Air Guadeloupe (☎ 590/27-61-90) will bring you to the island in just 20 minutes from Pointe-à-Pitre, landing at Les Basse Airport on Marie-Galante, about 2 miles from Grand-Bourg. Round-trip passage costs 385 F ($73.20).

Antilles Trans Express, Gare Maritime, quai Gatine, Pointe-à-Pitre (☎ 590/91-13-43), operates boat service to the island with three daily round-trips between Pointe-à-Pitre and Grand-Bourg. The round-trip costs 160 F ($30.40). Departures from Pointe-à-Pitre are daily at 8am, with a return from Grand-Bourg at 3:45pm.

A limited number of **taxis** are available at the airport, but the price should be negotiated before you drive off.

WHERE TO STAY & DINE

There are only a few little accommodations on the island, which, even if they aren't very up-to-date in amenities, are clean and hearty. At least the greetings are friendly. They may also be bewildering if you speak no French.

L'Auberge de l'Arbre à Pain

Rue Jeanne-d'Arc, 32, 97112 Grand-Bourg, Marie-Galante, Guadeloupe, F.W.I. ☎ 590/97-73-69. 7 rms. A/C. 200 F ($38) single; 230–250 F ($43.70–$47.50) double; 280–300 F ($53.20–$57) triple. Breakfast 20 F ($3.80) extra. MC, V. Directions: At the harbor, take the first street going toward the church.

Set behind a clapboard facade close to the street, a five-minute stroll from the harborfront, this establishment was named after the half-dozen breadfruit trees (*les arbres à pain*) that shelter it from the sun. Guests will find simple but respectable accommodations here. Each room has uncomplicated furnishings, a private bath, and easy access to nearby beaches.

Meals at the popular restaurant are served daily from noon to 2pm and 7 to 11pm. Main courses cost 60 F to 80 F ($11.40 to $15.20) and include a selection of fresh fish and shellfish. Usually whatever's available includes a court bouillon of fish, a soufflé of sea urchins, and meat dishes. No reservations are required for the restaurant (everyone seems simply to drop in). Because the bedrooms are usually in demand throughout the winter, advance reservations for overnight stays are important.

AN EXCURSION TO LA DÉSIRADE

The ubiquitous Columbus spotted this *terre désirée* or "sought-after land" after his Atlantic crossing in 1493. Named La Désirade, the island, which is less than 7 miles long and about 1¹/₂ miles wide, lies just 5 miles off the eastern tip of Guadeloupe proper. This former leper colony is often visited on a day excursion (Club Med types like it a lot).

The island has fewer than 2,000 inhabitants, including the descendants of Europeans exiled here by royal command. Tourism has hardly touched the place, if you can forget about those "day trippers," and there are almost no facilities for overnighting, with a hardly recommendable exception or two.

The main hamlet is **Grande Anse,** which has a small church with a presbytery and flower garden, and the homes of the local inhabitants. **Le Souffleur** is a village where boats are constructed, and at **Baie Mahault** are the ruins of an old leper colony from the early 18th century.

The best **beaches** are Souffleur, a tranquil oasis near the boat-building hamlet, and Baie Mahault, a small beach that's a Caribbean cliché with white sand and palm trees.

GETTING THERE   From Pointe-à-Pitre, **Air Guadeloupe** (☎ **590/82-47-00**) offers flights to La Désirade three times a week on aircraft containing between 9 and 19 passengers. The round-trip cost is 360 F ($68.40) per person, and trip time is around 20 minutes each way.

Because of the infrequency of flights and the expense, most passengers opt for transit to La Désirade by ferryboat, which leaves at 8am every morning from the wharves at St-François, near Guadeloupe's eastern tip, and returns from La Désirade for St-François every day at 3pm. Trip time is around 50 minutes, depending on conditions at sea.

GETTING AROUND   On La Désirade, three minibuses run between the airport and the towns. To get around, you might negotiate with a local driver. Bicycles are also available.

3 St. Martin

"Why French St. Martin?" you may ask. It hardly has the attractions of St. Thomas, Puerto Rico, or Jamaica. There are no dazzling sights, no spectacular nightlife. Even the sports scene on St. Martin isn't as well organized as on many Caribbean islands, although the Dutch side has golf and other diversions.

Most people visit St. Martin just to relax on its many white sandy beaches. Mostly they come to sample "France in the tropics" on the smallest island in the world to be divided between two sovereign states, France and the Netherlands. France got the larger part, with 21 of the total 37 square miles. The north is French, the south Dutch. The Dutch even spell the name of the island differently: Sint Maarten.

French St. Martin not only has some of the best cuisine in the Caribbean, but is filled with an extraordinary number of bistros and restaurants for such a small place. It has a distinctly French air. Policemen, for example wear *képis.* The towns have names like Colombier and Orléans, the streets are called "rue de la Liberté" and "rue de la République," and the tricolor of France flies over the *gendarmerie* in Marigot, the capital.

Don't come here to escape the crowds, however. From a sleepy backwater in Caribbean tourism in 1970, the place has boomed, with a year-round population of 11,000, plus thousands of tourists, often tour groups and conventioneers, arriving weekly.

The island, both the French and Dutch side, is almost completely devoid of racial tensions, although crime, usually muggings and robberies of tourists, is on the rise.

Both French St. Martin and Dutch Sint Maarten are highly touted for their shopping bargains. Sometimes you can pick up a bargain, perhaps a French or Dutch import, but many goods such as electronics can be purchased much more cheaply on the U.S. mainland.

The island has two jurisdictions, but there is complete freedom of movement between the two sectors. If you arrive on the Dutch side and clear Customs there, there'll be no red-tape formalities when crossing over to the French side—either for shopping, perhaps a hotel, or certainly for eating, as it has the best food (with some notable exceptions).

French St. Martin is governed from Guadeloupe and has direct representation in the government in Paris. Lying between Guadeloupe and Puerto Rico, the tiny island has been half French, half Dutch since 1648.

The principal town on the French side is **Marigot,** the seat of the subprefect and municipal council. Visitors come here not only for shopping, as the island is a free port, but also to enjoy the excellent cookery in the Créole bistros.

Marigot is not quite the same size as its counterpart, Philipsburg, in the Dutch sector. It has none of the frenzied pace of Philipsburg, which is often overrun with cruise-ship passengers. In fact, Marigot looks like a French village transplanted to the Caribbean. If you climb the hill over this tiny port, you'll be rewarded with a view from the old fort there.

About 20 minutes by car beyond Marigot is **Grand-Case,** a small fishing village that is an outpost of French civilization with many good restaurants and a few places to stay.

Note: You'll find the **map of St. Martin** at the beginning of Chapter 9.

For a description of the facilities and attractions of Dutch St. Maarten, refer to Chapter 10.

ORIENTATION
GETTING THERE

Most arrivals are at the Dutch-controlled **Queen Juliana International Airport,** St. Maarten. For a more detailed description of transportation on that side of the island, see "Getting There" in "Orientation" for St. Maarten in Chapter 10.

If you're coming from St. Barts, however, **Air Guadeloupe** (☎ **590/27-61-90** on St. Barts or **590/90-37-37** on St. Martin) has 10-minute flights into French St. Martin's **Espérance Airport** in Grand-Case (☎ **590/87-51-21**), where you clear Customs.

GETTING AROUND

BY BUS   It's much cheaper to get around on one of the island's buses, which run daily from 6am until midnight. One departs from Grand-Case for Marigot every 20 minutes. There's a departure every hour from Marigot to the Dutch side. A sample bus fare from Marigot to Grand-Case is $2.

BY TAXI   For visitors, the most common means of transport is a taxi. A **Taxi Service & Information Center** operates at the port of Marigot (☎ **590/ 87-56-54**). Always agree on the rate before getting into an unmetered cab. Taxi fares from Marigot to Grand-Case, from Juliana airport to Marigot, and from Juliana airport to La Samanna are all about $10. These fares are in effect from 7am to 10pm; after that, they go up by 25% until midnight, rising by 50% after midnight.

You can also book two-hour sightseeing trips around the island, either through the organization listed above or at any hotel desk. The cost is $50 for one or two passengers, plus $10 for each additional.

BY RENTAL CAR   The division of the island into dual political zones used to make car rentals on St. Martin rather complicated. In past years, car-rental companies were unwilling to rent one of their cars to clients staying on the opposite side of the border, preferring that clients in hotels on the French side rent only from agencies on the French side. Fortunately, those rivalries no longer seem to exist, as rental companies on both sides of the Dutch-French border are now cooperating more fully with one another. The main complication you'll face is a local law that forbids clients from picking up a rental car immediately upon arrival at Juliana airport. (This law was instigated by the island's union of taxi drivers, although in recent months, according to some sources, that policy is less strictly enforced than in previous years.)

Because of this law, many visitors hire a taxi to take them directly to their hotels as soon as they arrive at Juliana airport on the Dutch side. After you're settled in, most rental companies (including Avis, Budget, and Hertz) will either deliver a car directly to your hotel, or a van will transport you without charge to a depot where the cars are stored. That depot might lie on either the French or the Dutch side, depending on the location of your hotel and the renting outfit's inventory of cars. Unlike in years past, once a car is rented, no one seems to mind whether you drop it off on the French or the Dutch side on the day of your departure. Of course, it usually pays to ask lots of questions and to communicate your intentions clearly on the first day of your rental.

Each of the largest North American car-rental companies maintains at least one branch on both the French and Dutch sides of the island. (For more information on this, see "Getting Around" in "Orientation" for St. Maarten in Chapter 10). All three charge roughly equivalent rates, which are usually similar to rates at branches of the same company on the Dutch side. **Avis** (☎ toll free **800/ 331-1084**), **Budget** (☎ toll free **800/527-0700**), and **Hertz** (☎ toll free **800/ 654-3001**) each charge between $222 and $228 per week, plus 5% tax, for their least expensive vehicles, with unlimited mileage included. Occasionally, additional discounts are granted for membership in organizations such as the AAA or AARP.

Each company requires that renters be at least 25 years or older, and each charges between $9.50 and $11 a day for a collision-damage waiver (CDW). Even if you buy the waiver, you'll still be responsible for $250 to $600 worth of collision damage to your car. If you don't buy it, and if you don't carry private insurance to protect you, you'll be liable for up to the full value of the car. Use of certain types of credit or charge cards sometimes eliminates the need to pay for a CDW, although you'll have to confirm the details of this directly with your card issuer. For information once you reach the French side of St. Martin, call Avis (☎ 590/87-50-60) and Hertz (590/87-73-01). Budget prefers that clients on the French side call its branch on the Dutch side (☎ 599/5/54030) for deliveries of cars, even though the car a renter gets might derive from a source on the French side.

Regardless of how you negotiate your car rental, you'll probably use very little gasoline driving around the flat landscapes of the island. One tank of gas should last an entire week.

FAST FACTS: St. Martin

Area Code   St. Martin is not part of the Caribbean's 809 area code. For information on telephoning to and on the island, see "Telephone," below.

Banking Hours   Banks are generally open Monday through Thursday from 8:30am to 1pm and on Friday from 8:30am to 1pm and 4 to 5pm.

Currency   The currency, officially at least, is the **French franc (F),** yet U.S. dollars seem to be preferred wherever you go. Canadians should convert their money into U.S. dollars and not into francs. At press time, the exchange rate was 5.28 F to $1 U.S. (1 F = 19¢).

Documents   U.S. and Canadian citizens should have either a passport, a voter registration card, or a birth certificate, plus an ongoing or a return ticket. With a birth certificate or voter registration card, you'll also need photo ID. British subjects need a valid passport.

Electricity   The electricity is 220 volts A.C., 50 cycles. Some hotels have altered the voltage and outlets in the bathrooms, so check. If not, don't count on the hotel; bring your own transformer and adapter if you plan to use appliances.

Information   The tourist board, called the **Office du Tourisme,** is at Mairie de Saint-Martin at Marigot (☎ 590/87-57-21).

Language   English is widely spoken on St. Martin, although this is a French possession. A patois is spoken only by a small segment of the local populace.

Medical Care   There's a hospital in Marigot (☎ 87-87-67), and hotels will help visitors in contacting English-speaking doctors.

Safety   The crime wave hitting Dutch-held St. Maarten also plagues French St. Martin. Travel with extreme caution here, especially at night. Avoid driving at night along the Lowlands road. Armed patrols have helped the situation somewhat, but hotel safes should be used to guard your valuables. You can reach the police by calling **87-50-06.**

Tax   A departure tax of 15 F ($2.90) at Espérance airport is included in Air Guadeloupe's published fare.

Telephone   French St. Martin is linked to the Guadeloupe telephone system, which is *not* a part of the 809 area code that applies to most of the Caribbean.

St. Martin

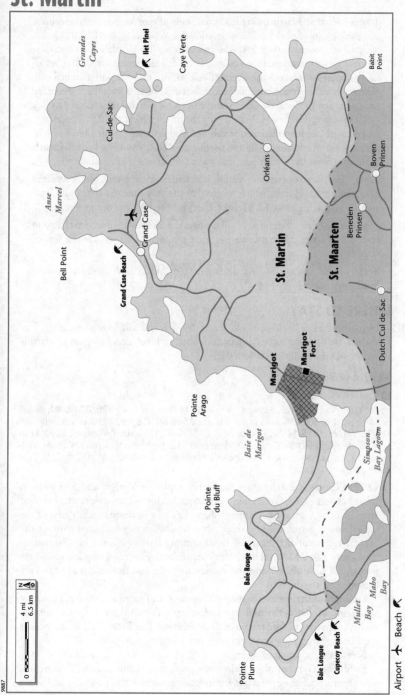

Grandes Cayes

Ilet Pinel

Caye Verte

Babit Point

Cul-de-Sac

Oréans

Boven Prinsen

Anse Marcel

Grand Case

Beneden Prinsen

Bell Point

Grand Case Beach

St. Martin

St. Maarten

Dutch Cul de Sac

Pointe Arago

Marigot

Marigot Fort

Baie de Marigot

Simpson Bay Lagoon

Pointe du Bluff

Baie Rouge

Pointe Plum

Baie Longue

Cupecoy Beach

Mullet Bay

Maho Bay

Airport ✈   Beach ⌐

0   4 mi
    6.5 km
N

9887

To call French St. Martin from the United States, if your long-distance telephone company is equipped to handle international direct-dialing, dial 011 (the international access code), then 590 (the country code for Guadeloupe), and then the six-digit local number. If you cannot direct-dial internationally, dial 0 ("zero," for the operator) and tell the operator you wish to make an international call; once you have been transferred to the international operator, state the 590 country code and then the local number, and the operator will dial the call for you.

To make a call within St. Martin only the six-digit local number is necessary; no codes are needed unless you're calling "long distance" to the Dutch side of the island, in which case dial 93 and the five-digit Dutch number. (To call French St. Martin from the Dutch side, dial 06 and the six-digit local number.)

Time   St. Martin operates on Atlantic standard time year round, one hour ahead of eastern standard time, which means that the only time the U.S. East Coast and St. Martin are in step is during the daylight saving time of summer.

Tips and Service   Your hotel is likely to add a 10% to 15% service charge to your bill to cover tipping. Likewise, most restaurant bills include the service charge.

Water   The water of St. Martin is safe to drink. In fact, most hotels serve desalinated water.

WHERE TO STAY

Hotels on French St. Martin add a *taxe de séjour* and a 10% service charge. The visitors' tax on hotel rooms differs from hotel to hotel, depending on its classification, but the minimum is $3 a day.

VERY EXPENSIVE

✪ La Belle Créole

Pointe du Bluffe (B.P. 4181, Marigot), 97065 St. Martin, F.W.I. ☎ **590/87-66-00,** or toll free 800/HILTONS. 800/268-9275 in Canada. Fax 87-56-66. 138 rms, 18 suites. A/C MINIBAR TV TEL. Winter, $315–$455 single or double; $495–$1,410 suite. Off-season, $230–$280 single or double; $340–$940 suite. Children under 12 stay free in their parents' room. MAP rates $55 per person extra. (Rates include continental breakfast.) AE, DC, MC, V. Free parking.

La Belle Créole is 2 miles from the French capital of Marigot and 5 miles from Juliana airport on the Dutch side. The deluxe Mediterranean-style resort, modeled after a fantasy Côte d'Azur fishing village, lies on a peninsula within view of the capital and is surrounded by three white beaches. Stone walkways connect the central square of the resort to the accommodations housed in 27 separate three-story villas. Most units have private terraces. Five types of guest rooms are rented. All have either king-size or double beds, and five rooms are specially equipped for the disabled.

Dining/Entertainment: Seating 200 patrons, La Provence, the hotel's gourmet restaurant, offers continental and Créole cuisine, plus three different "theme" nights including barbecue and seafood buffets. The Plaza Café is the hotel's inexpensive lunch restaurant, café, and snack bar.

Services: Laundry, babysitting.

Facilities: Gym, outdoor swimming pool, four tennis courts (lit at night), water sports (including parasailing, windsurfing, waterskiing, jet-skiing, and scuba diving), beauty center.

✪ La Samanna

Baie Longue (B.P. 4077), 97064 St. Martin CEDEX, F.W.I. ☎ **590/87-51-22,** or toll free 800/854-2252. Fax 87-87-86. 36 rms. 44 suites. A/C MINIBAR TV TEL. Winter, $490–$750 single or double; $860–$1,200 suite. Off-season, $325–$380 single or double; $625–$900 suite. MAP $65 per person extra. AE, DC, MC, V. Free parking. Closed Sept–Oct.

Sleek, chic, and sexy, La Samanna admits it's "not for everyone." Off-the-record celebrity visits are commonplace around here. However, if you're a person devoted to good, wholehearted, unabashed sybaritism—and have lots of money—you should fit in beautifully here. Set on a landscaped 55-acre piece of choice property northwest of Mullet Bay, La Samanna opens onto a mile and a half of white sandy beach. The resort, like so many places on St. Martin, is more evocative of the Côte d'Azur or Morocco than the Caribbean—it's what the French call *intime, tranquille, et informel.*

The hotel, managed by the ultra-luxurious hotel chain Rosewood Hotels, offers a melange of styles. Arches and balconies in pure "Greek-fishing-village-white" are set off by stunning royal-blue doors and umbrellas. Splashes of bold fabrics are used on the puffy cushions on the Haitian furniture, which is mostly in wicker and rattan. The colors reflect the Caribbean itself: turquoise, corals, soft pinks, and blues. The choice of rooms is complicated. In the main building you'll find twin-bedded rooms with balconies that are screened from the terrace by a thatched ramada roof. Or you can ask for one of the two dozen one-bedroom suites, one of the 16 two-bedroom suites, or one of the six suites with three bedrooms—each with fully equipped kitchen, living room, dining area, and large patio.

Dining/Entertainment: Dining is al fresco with a French cuisine prepared by some of the best chefs in the Caribbean. You dine out on a candlelit terrace overlooking Baie Longue. After dinner, the bar becomes a disco. At the poolside grill, waiters serve food on the beach.

Services: 24-hour room service, laundry, babysitting, massages; a hotel driver meets all guests at the airport.

Facilities: Fitness and activity center with daily aerobics classes, outdoor swimming pool, waterskiing, three tennis courts, library, sailboat rentals, shopping boutique.

Le Méridien L'Habitation/Le Domaine

Anse Marcel (B.P. 581, Marigot), 97106 St. Martin, F.W.I. ☎ **590/87-67-00,** or toll free 800/543-4300 in the U.S. Fax 87-30-38. 314 rms, 82 suites. A/C MINIBAR TV TEL. Winter, $320–$530 single or double; $490–$730 suite. Off-season, $190–$210 single or double; $330 suite. AE, DC, MC, V. Free parking. Closed Sept.

Since its expansion in 1992, this has become the largest resort complex on the French side of St. Martin, and one of its most heavily promoted. It's tucked under Pigeon Pea Hill, opening onto one of the tiny island's most scenic white sandy beaches. Its older section (L'Habitation) was erected in the mid-1980s by a consortium of French insurance companies on a 150-acre tract of scrubland nestled between the sea and an almost impenetrable mountain ridge. (Its position was considered almost inaccessible until a crew of engineers cut a 2-mile road through some of the most rugged terrain on the island, 7 miles from Marigot and a 35-minute drive north of Juliana airport.) In the early 1990s, after the project had been purchased by Air France, work began on Le Domaine, a few steps to the west of the original complex. Today both resorts are fully integrated, sharing all their entertainment, dining, drinking, and recreational facilities.

Accommodations at both resorts are in a string of neo-Victorian two- and three-story buildings ringed with lattices, gingerbread, and verandas. Rooms in Le Domaine for the most part overlook the ocean, and are therefore more expensive. Rooms in L'Habitation for the most part overlook a 120-slip marina and a garden. All rooms and suites are comfortably and stylishly furnished, each with soundproofing, balcony or terrace, two-sink bathroom, radio, and an airy decor of tropical furniture. Each of the suites contains a kitchenette.

Dining/Entertainment: The pool bar (Le Carbet) resembles a tile-sheathed gazebo on stilts at the edge of the water. Breakfast buffets are served in Le Balaou restaurant, while Le BBQ offers grilled meats and seafood. Haute cuisine is available every evening in La Belle France (see "Where to Dine," below), while pastas, grills, and Italian food are served in La Veranda, an Italian bistro.

Services: Room service, laundry, babysitting (7am to 11pm).

Facilities: Three swimming pools, 1,600-foot stretch of white sandy beach, nightclub complex, 100-slip marina. A Pirates' Club offers a wide range of activities for children 2 to 14. Guests have complimentary access to Privilege Resort and Spa, a complex on the hill linked by frequent minibus service from the hotel. Both fitness training and European spa–style treatments are featured, including aerobics classes, tennis, body building, squash, and racquetball—in all, everything geared to give you a complete mental and physical tune-up.

EXPENSIVE

Captain Oliver's Hotel Resort

Oyster Pond (B.P. 645), 97150 St. Martin, F.W.I. ☎ **590/87-40-26.** Fax 87-40-84. 50 bungalows. A/C MINIBAR TV TEL. Winter, $190–$210 bungalow for one or two. Off-season, $114–$130 bungalow for one or two. (Rates include continental breakfast.) AE, MC, V. Free parking.

This hotel is named for Oliver Lange, who was a Paris restaurateur for nearly a quarter of a century before coming here. At the French-Dutch border 10 miles east of Juliana airport, near the prestigious Oyster Pond Hotel on the Dutch side, he constructed pink bungalows in a labyrinth of outlying cottages, each ringed with a suggestion of gingerbread and connected with boardwalks. High on a hill, the cottages command excellent views, and from the large terraces you can gaze over to St. Barts. Each unit is furnished in white rattan and decorated with local prints. The accommodations come with kitchenettes, marble baths, double sinks, large double closets, and many amenities. Each bungalow is provided with two beds, plus a sofa bed, which makes them possible family rentals.

Dining/Entertainment: See "Where to Dine," below. A pool bar is open daily from 2 to 10pm and a breakfast room and snackbar, the Dinghy Duck, serves daily from 7am to midnight.

Services: Room service, laundry, babysitting.

Facilities: Scuba-diving facilities, outdoor swimming pool, private taxi boat to beach, shopping boutiques.

Esmeralda Resort

Baie Orientale (B.P. 541), 97150 St. Martin, F.W.I. ☎ **590/87-36-36,** 203/847-9445 in Connecticut, or toll free 800/622-7836 in the U.S. Fax 87-35-18. 50 rms. 7 suites. A/C TV TEL. Winter, $350–$400 single or double; $500–$800 standard suite; $875–$2,200 deluxe suite. Off-season, $180–$220 single or double; $280–$400 standard suite; $515–$1,180 deluxe suite. (Rates include continental breakfast.) AE, MC, V. Free parking.

Originally conceived as a site for a single private villa, and then for a semiprivate club for like-minded guests of the owner, this hillside housing development a 25-minute taxi ride northeast of Juliana airport has blossomed into a full-scale resort with views over Orient Bay and a decidedly French focus. The landscaping includes palms, cactus, and an array of flowers. Up to a maximum of four separate vaguely Spanish mission–style accommodations are in one of 14 tile-roofed villas whose interior doors can be locked or unlocked as needed to create a variety of different-size units. Each of the units contains a kitchenette, bathroom, private terrace, and a private entrance.

Dining/Entertainment: A bar and grill lie close to the nearby beach, and a more formal lunch and evening restaurant, L'Astrolabe, is on the property, with hot disco action. The hotel maintains cooperative relationships with five local beach bars, any of which allows guests of Esmeralda to sign for drinks throughout the day and evening.

Services: Room service (for dinner), laundry, babysitting, massage.

Facilities: 14 swimming pools, tennis courts, scuba diving, waterskiing.

Grand Case Beach Club

Grand-Case, 97150 St. Martin, F.W.I. ☎ **590/87-51-87**, or toll free 800/447-7462 in the U.S. and Canada. 40 studios, 33 suites. A/C TV TEL. Winter, $210–$260 studio for one or two; $260–$305 one-bedroom suite for two; $425 two-bedroom suite for four. Off-season, $95–$145 studio for one or two: $110–$170 one-bedroom suite for two; $215–$300 two-bedroom suite for four. Additional person $32 extra. (Rates include continental breakfast.) AE, MC, V. Free parking.

Within walking distance of Grand-Case, 7 miles from Juliana airport, this is a beachfront condominium hotel, where most units open onto ocean-view terraces. You have a choice of ocean- or garden-view studios and one- and two-bedroom suites. Each has a fully equipped kitchen and private patio. Units are airy, with tile floors, rattan furnishings, a pale pastel decor, and daily maid service. The ambience at the hotel is informal. This is the type of place where you make friends with other guests and plan to see them "same time next year."

Dining/Entertainment: The Café Panoramique, extending out on a bluff, overlooks Grand-Case and the sunset, and serves three meals (French cuisine) a day. In addition, the club operates an 80-seat restaurant and bar, the Panoramic Beach, overlooking the beach and the ocean. Designed as a French bistro and seafood restaurant, it features such dishes as a sautéed shrimp provençal, snapper with baby shrimp in a cream sauce, grouper, lobster, and other fish dishes, as well as a wide variety of French meat and poultry specialties. A guest lounge contains billiards and a giant TV for movies, news, and sports.

Services: Laundry, babysitting.

Facilities: Two beaches, beach boutique, water sports (including waterskiing, snorkeling, and sailing), free use of the Caribbean's first artificial-grass tennis court, swimming pool, car and Jeep rentals.

Hôtel Anse Margot

Baie Nettle (B.P. 4701, Marigot), 97150 St. Martin, F.W.I. ☎ **590/87-92-01**, Fax 87-92-13. 58 rms, 38 suites. A/C TV TEL. Winter, $138–$159 single; $169–$180 double; from $218 suite. Off-season, $119–$136 single; $143–$167 double; from $201 suite. (Rates include buffet breakfast.) AE, DC, MC, V. Free parking.

This French-owned resort just west of Marigot consists of eight pastel-colored buildings built in 1988 on the narrow strip of scrub-covered sand that separates the ocean from the largest of the island's saltwater lagoons. The site is virtually "hotel row" today. Each of the multistory buildings is adorned with ornate balconies and gingerbread in a stylized version of Créole architecture. The bedrooms are furnished in a French Antillean decor of pastel floral colors, and the many amenities include a small refrigerator.

Dining/Entertainment: The resort's social center rises like a miniature temple, with a pair of swimming pools flanking it on two sides. After dark, a pianist performs live music which might include Piaf or jazz. A French cuisine is served in the hotel's restaurant, Entre Deux Mers.

Services: Room service, laundry, babysitting.

Facilities: Scuba diving, two outdoor swimming pools, waterskiing, sailboat rentals, shopping boutiques.

Hôtel L'Esplanade Caraïbe

B.P. 5007, Grand-Case, 97150 St. Martin. ☎ **590/87-06-55**, or toll free 800/633-7411. Fax 87-29-15. 24 suites. A/C TV TEL. Winter, $135–$215 suite for one; $165–$242 suite for two; $260–$300 suite for four. Off-season, $105–$135 suite for one; $120–$175 suite for two; $180–$200 suite for four. Continental breakfast $8 extra. AE, MC, V. Free parking.

Although the much-weathered hamlet of Grand-Case has always been known as a potpourri of many different restaurants, its hotel choices were always rather limited. In 1992 this changed with the construction of an elegant collection of suites on a steeply sloping hillside above the town's approach road from Marigot. Sheathed with cascades of bougainvillea, and accented with a vaguely Hispanic overlay of white walls, hand-painted tiles, and cream-colored roofs, the resort's various elements are interconnected by a network of concrete stairs that add to the layout's drama. (It might not be a good idea for the infirm or elderly to consider this as their hotel.)

The resort has a swimming pool, a series of terraced gardens, and access to a beach which you'll reach after descending a winding, stair-dotted pathway after a six-minute walk. Views from the bedrooms and their terraces are always angled out toward the sea. At press time, the only on-site dining option was a snack bar (breakfast, lunch, and all-day drinks) beside the pool, open daily from 7am to 7pm.

● Family-Friendly Accommodations

Marissol   *(see p. 505)* Outside Guadeloupe's Gosier, this hotel has an informal atmosphere and a wide range of sporting activities that keeps parents and kids busy from sunrise to sundown.

Hôtel Plantation de Leyritz   *(see p. 490)* On this working banana plantation in the north of Martinique, kids enjoy the tropical gardens and later spend nights with their parents in former slave quarters now converted to comfortable bedrooms.

Mont Vernon   *(see p. 539)* On French St. Martin, this all-suite hotel on the beach at Orient Bay is a resort complex. Children 12 and under stay free in the same suite with their parents, and there's a children's à la carte menu available.

Le Méridien L'Habitation/Le Domaine   *(see p. 535)* The hotel's Pirates' Club is a complimentary activity program for children 2 to 14—everything from pool games to an introduction to canoeing.

No one seems to mind that, as each of the accommodations contains a kitchen with a large refrigerator and up-to-date cookware. The rooms have a blue-and-white color scheme and wicker furniture.

Under the same management, and also in Grand-Case, are two other small, intimate hotels with pretentions of luxury. The more visible of the two is the 17-room Le Pavillon Beach Hotel, whose prices and allure are roughly equivalent to those of the parent hotel.

Mont Vernon

Chevrise Baie Orientale (B.P. 1174, Marigot), 97062 St. Martin, F.W.I. ☎ **590/87-62-00**, or toll free 800/233-0888 in the U.S. Fax 87-37-27. 394 suites. A/C TV TEL. Winter, $215–$390 suite for one; $240–$390 suite for two; $315–$475 suite for three. Off-season, $105–$250 suite for one; $155–$250 suite for two; $185–$310 suite for three. Children under 12 stay free in their parents' suite. (Rates include buffet breakfast.) AE, MC, V. Free parking.

Opened in 1989, this resort complex with a lacy gingerbread architecture on the northeastern coast of the island offers junior suites and two-room suites, with twin or king-size beds and private balconies opening onto the water. Each room has a number of amenities, such as a refrigerator. It's a favorite of many a package-tour group.

Dining/Entertainment: There's a 200-seat main restaurant, Le Créole; a 50-seat main bar and patio; an 80-seat beach bar; and a 100-seat pool snack bar with a barbecue, called Le Sloop. French, Italian, and Créole cuisine are offered.

Services: Laundry, babysitting, massage.

Facilities: Duty-free shopping arcade, large swimming pool with sun deck, tennis courts, archery, water-sports center where deep-sea fishing can be arranged.

MODERATE

Laguna Beach Hotel

Baie Nettle, 97150 St. Martin, F.W.I. ☎ **590/87-91-75.** Fax 87-81-65. 62 rms. A/C TV TEL. Winter, $96–$131 single; $99–$135 double. Off-season, $72–$102 single; $76–$109 double. American buffet breakfast $11 extra. AE, MC, V. Free parking.

On the road between Marigot and the Lowlands, the Laguna Beach Hotel, which opened in 1988, offers accommodations in a pair of two-level buildings, which are not as glamorous as those at Anse Margot. The rooms, for the most part, are spacious and include radios, VCRs, terraces, private safes, refrigerators, and hairdryers. The Laguna has a central freshwater swimming pool and three tennis courts. Its dining room is open to the breezes. The public rooms are furnished in part with rattan and decorated with Haitian art. Laundry service and babysitting are offered.

La Résidence

Rue du Général-de-Gaulle (B.P. 679), Marigot, 97150 St. Martin, F.W.I. ☎ **590/87-70-37.** Fax 87-90-44. 21 rms. A/C MINIBAR TV TEL. $78 single; $98 double. (Rates include continental breakfast.) AE, MC, V. Free parking.

In the commercial center of town, La Résidence has a concrete facade enlivened with neo-Victorian gingerbread fretwork. Because of its location, it is favored by business travelers. The rooms are arranged around a landscaped central courtyard with a fish-shaped fountain. A bar with a soaring tent serves drinks to clients relaxing on wicker and bentwood furniture. Each of the bedrooms contains minimalist decor, and all but a few have sleeping lofts and a duplex design of mahogany-trimmed stairs and balustrades. Room service is available. The hotel is known for its French and Créole restaurant, where meals begin at $28. Lunch and dinner are served in a series of small curtained gazebos, divided by tropical plants that grow from a garden below. Such dishes are served as stuffed sea crab with Créole sauce, and filet of duck with peaches.

Le Pirate

B.P. 677, Marigot, 97150 St. Martin, F.W.I. ☎ **590/87-78-37,** or 800/666-5756. Fax 87-95-67. 55 rms. A/C TV TEL. Winter, $550–$650 F ($104.50–$123.50) single or double; 750 F ($142.50) triple or quad. Off-season, 450–550 F ($85.50–$104.50) single or double; 650 F ($123.50) triple or quad. Continental breakfast 32 F ($6.10) extra. AE, DC, MC, V. Free parking.

Set on a narrow strip of sandy land between the open sea and a salt pond, Le Pirate lies on the main road from Marigot to the Lowlands, a 20-minute taxi ride north of Juliana airport. Its aim, as voiced by the management, is to combine "French savoir-vivre with Créole color." Each of its comfortably furnished bedrooms has a kitchenette and a balcony opening onto views over the harbor or marina. Large rooms, really studios, are rented, suitable for three or four guests. The hotel has a small swimming pool a few paces from the beach. Laundry and babysitting are available.

Marine Hôtel Simson Beach

Baie Nettle (B.P. 172, Marigot), 97150 St. Martin, F.W.I. ☎ **590/87-54-54.** Fax 87-92-11. 120 studios, 45 duplexes. A/C TV TEL. Winter, $131 studio for one; $143 studio for two; $184–$196 duplex. Off-season, $106 studio for one; $118 studio for two; $161 duplex. (Rates include buffet breakfast.) AE, DC, MC, V. Free parking.

One of the most stylish hotels in its price bracket on the French side on the island is operated by the French hotel conglomerate Accor. Considered good value for the money, the Marine occupies a flat, sandy stretch of land between a saltwater lagoon and the beach, 5 miles west of Juliana airport. French travelers on "le budget" flock to this place. Decorated in peach, turquoise, and maize, it was designed with five three-story buildings, each like a large, balconied Antillean house. In its center, two swimming pools serve as the focal point for a bar built out over the lagoon, an indoor/outdoor restaurant, and a flagstone terrace that hosts steel bands and cocktail parties in the evening.

The hotel offers accommodations with ceiling fans, wicker furniture, and kitchenettes set on outdoor patios. The most desirable accommodations, on the third (top) floor, contain sloping ceilings sheltering sleeping lofts as well as two bathrooms. Laundry and babysitting are available.

Résidence Alizéa

Mont Vernon, 97150 St. Martin, F.W.I. ☎ **590/87-33-42.** Fax 87-41-15. 18 rms, 8 bungalows. A/C TV TEL. After passing through Grand-Case, turn left and follow the signs along the cul-de-sac. Winter, $173 single or double; $252 bungalow. Off-season, $126 single or double; $186 bungalow. (Rates include continental breakfast.) AE, MC, V. Free parking.

On the northeastern end of the island, this is the smallest hotel in a district sparsely dotted with some of the biggest blockbusting resorts on the French side. The inn opens onto a panoramic vista of Orient Bay. A swimming pool is on the premises, but the beach is a 10-minute hike through fields and across a road. Each accommodation differs from its neighbors in size, but all contain a kitchenette set on an open-air veranda, a light and airy collection of wooden furniture, and a color scheme of Caribbean pastels.

There are no facilities for lunch in the hotel, because of the five simple beachfront restaurants nearby. Dinner, however, is well known, and is recommended separately (see "Where to Dine," below). The establishment is best known for its restaurant, where trade winds (known in French as *les alizés*), ceiling fans, rose-colored walls, and a two-sided view of the bay are the most important furnishings. Full meals begin at $45 each, and include French and Gallicized Caribbean dishes, such as calalou-and-spinach soup with coconut, and sea scallops in filo pastry on a bed of tomatoes and provençal herbs.

⑤ Sol Hôtel Ambiance

Oyster Pond, 38, 97150 St. Martin, F.W.I. ☎ **590/87-38-10.** Fax 87-32-23. 9 bungalows. A/C. Winter, $115 bungalow for one; $130 bungalow for two; $150 bungalow for three. Off-season, $75 bungalow for one; $90 bungalow for two; $115 bungalow for three. (Rates include continental breakfast and a one-way transfer either to or from the airport.) AE, MC, V. Free parking.

This pastel-ornamented building overlooks the yachts bobbing in the Oyster Pond right at the French-Dutch border 8 miles east of Juliana airport close to Captain Oliver's. Built in 1987 and remodeled in 1994, this remote outpost consists of bungalows done in traditional West Indian style. Although small, it aims to provide all the services of a large hotel, including a good-size pool, daily maid service, and fax. Each unit, offering either a king-size bed or twin beds, has a kitchenette and a private terrace overlooking the ocean.

INEXPENSIVE

Le Royale Louisiana

Rue du Général-de-Gaulle, Marigot, 97150 St. Martin, F.W.I. ☎ **590/87-86-51.** Fax 87-96-49. 54 rms, 14 duplexes. A/C TV TEL. Winter, 330 F ($62.70) single; 410 F ($77.90) double; 690 F ($131.10) duplex. Off-season, 260 F ($49.40) single; 370 F ($70.30) double; 480–600 F ($91.20–$114) duplex. (Rates include continental breakfast.) AE, DC, MC, V. Free parking.

Occupying a prominent position in the center of Marigot, 10 miles north of Juliana airport, this hotel is designed in a hip-roofed French-colonial Louisiana style; its rambling balconies are graced with ornate balustrades. Each accommodation contains big sunny windows and modern furniture. The standard rooms have either king- or queen-size beds. The duplexes, ideal for families, have a bedroom and bath on the upper level and a sitting room with a fold-out sofa on the lower floor. Duplex rates are not based on the number of occupants. A simple menu of breakfasts and lunchtime salads and sandwiches is served in the hotel's restaurant. A bar on the premises is open in the evening, but no meals are served.

WHERE TO DINE
IN BAIE LONGUE

La Samanna

Bale Longue. ☎ **590/87-51-22.** Reservations required for dinner, not for lunch. Appetizers 150–250 F ($28.50–$47.50); main courses 220–325 F ($41.80–$61.80). AE, DC, MC, V. Lunch daily 12:30–2:30pm; dinner daily 7–9:30pm. Closed Sept–Oct. FRENCH.

Even though you may not be staying at La Samanna, northwest of Mullet Bay, you might want to make a reservation to enjoy a meal on the resort's dining terrace. Judges of this cuisine have declared it among the best in the Caribbean, matching the finest world-class restaurants in Paris. The high prices reflect its image. Innovatively prepared and impeccably presented, dishes include lobster risotto, a hot and cold array of California foie gras, and Norwegian salmon with a sauce of red flame seedless grapes. Many dishes are a modernized version of the cuisine of Provence. The Dover sole and the oysters are flown in fresh from France, and the steaks are imported from New York. The al fresco dining terrace's zigzag parapet overlooks the sea, with dinner served by candlelight. Each table is set with Rosenthal china, lit by lamps from the *Orient Express*, and, at lunch, adorned with local flowers. (Lunches, where a theatrically prepared steak tartare is a favorite, are less expensive.)

The Indian Bar, which envelops guests under a billowing canopy of wedding tenting, is a cozy respite for drinks. Located in the main building with a terrace overlooking the pool, the bar has no set hours. La Samanna's underground, air-controlled wine cellar houses more than 25,000 bottles from elite vineyards around the world.

IN & AROUND MARIGOT

Very Expensive

✪ La Vie en Rose

Boulevard de France at rue de la République. ☎ **590/87-54-42.** Reservations required. Appetizers $8.50; main courses $29–$35. AE, MC, V. Lunch daily 11:30am–2:30pm; dinner daily 6:30–10pm. FRENCH.

In this balconied second-floor restaurant, the cozy dining room, with ceiling fans and candlelight, evokes the nostalgia of the 1920s. If you don't like the parlor, you can sit at one of the tables on a little veranda overlooking the harbor, provided you requested one when you made a reservation. The chefs prepare lobster fricassée, entrecôte in red-wine sauce, red snapper bedded in a spinach mousse, breast of chicken stuffed with vegetables and served with truffle sauce, sliced breast of duckling with black-currant sauce, filets of beef with lobster and Nantua sauce, filet of beef with a shallot/red-butter sauce, and filet of red snapper in puff pastry with red-butter sauce. The desserts are some of the best on the island.

Expensive

La Maison sur le Port

Rue de la République. ☎ **590/87-56-38.** Reservations recommended. Appetizers $7–$10; main courses $17–$20; fixed-price dinner $21.50; lunch platters $7–$10. AE, MC, V. Lunch Mon–Sat noon–2:30pm; dinner Mon–Sat 6–10pm. FRENCH.

Christian Verdeau and his staff welcome people to enjoy their French cuisine in a refined atmosphere and elegant surroundings, with a view of three waterfalls in the garden. The tables are dressed with snowy tablecloths and Limoges china. At lunch, when you are seated on the covered terrace, you can choose from a number of salads as well as fish and meat courses. Dinner choices include fresh fish, such as snapper, salmon, or lobster; homemade pâté de foie gras; and filet of lamb, veal, or steak, each with a light sauce. Duck has always been a specialty. You can order from a wine list with an extensive selection of imported French products at moderate prices, or you may want to try the house cocktail, made with blanc de blanc wine, fresh orange juice, Grand Marnier, and a splash of lemon juice. Many guests come here at sundown to enjoy the harbor view.

Le Mini Club

Rue de la Liberté. ☎ **590/87-50-69.** Reservations required. Appetizers $5–$14; main courses $18–$35; fixed-price dinner $25; Wed and Sat dinner buffet $45. AE, MC, V. Lunch Mon–Sat noon–3pm; dinner daily 7–10:30pm. FRENCH/CREOLE.

After you climb a sloped flight of wooden stairs, you'll find yourself in an environment once described as a treehouse built among coconut palms. Suspended on a wooden deck above the sands of the beach, this establishment is filled with

Haitian murals and grass carpeting. The specialties include lobster soufflé (made for two or four people), an array of fish and vegetable terrines, red snapper with Créole sauce, sweetbreads in puff pastry, and many kinds of salad. Dessert might be bananas flambéed with cognac. Lavish buffets are held every Wednesday and Saturday night, with unlimited wine included. The restaurant is along the seafront at Marigot.

Moderate

Ⓢ La Brasserie de Marigot

Rue du Général-de-Gaulle, 11. ☎ **590/87-94-43.** Reservations not required. Appetizers 35–45 F ($6.70–$8.60); main courses 45–85 F ($8.60–$16.20). AE, MC, V. Mon–Sat 7:30am–9pm, Sun 8:30am–3pm. FRENCH/CARIBBEAN.

This is where the real French eat. Opened in a former bank, it has a marble-and-brass decor, a sort of retro 1950s style with green leather banquettes. Meals include pot-au-feu, choucroûte (sauerkraut garni), blanquette de veau, cassoulette, even chicken on a spit and steak tartare. Lobster is the most expensive item on the menu. Naturally, you can order interesting terrines here, and wine is sold by the glass, carafe, or bottle. The kitchen also prepares a handful of Caribbean dishes such as red snapper in lobster sauce. The brasserie, located in the center of town, is air-conditioned, with sidewalk tables overlooking the pedestrian traffic outside. It also features the most glamorous "take-out" service on St. Martin.

Ⓢ Le Pub

Rue de la Liberté. ☎ **590/87-51-58.** Reservations recommended. Appetizers $3–$6; main courses $7–$18. AE, MC, V. Lunch Mon–Sat noon–3pm; dinner daily 6–10pm. (Bar, daily 5pm–midnight.) CONTINENTAL/PUB.

One block from the post office in the center of town, this restaurant attracts visiting yachting people to its casual expatriate ambience. The atmosphere is like a dark-paneled British pub, filled with flags from yachts and nations throughout the world. Appetizers include stuffed mushroom caps, escargots, and good soups—especially fish chowder and baked onion. Their own boat catches the red snapper. The house special is beef Wellington, served with a red wine sauce. The English pies are the choice of the pub crowd who also enjoy the two dart boards.

IN & AROUND GRAND-CASE

This beach town, a scant mile-long brush stroke, has the greatest concentration of fine dining spots in the Caribbean. On the town's one and only street there are more than 18 restaurants serving the cuisines of at least half a dozen cultures.

Expensive

Chez Martine

Boulevard de Grand-Case, 140. ☎ **590/87-51-59.** Reservations required. Appetizers 60–135 F ($11.40–$25.70); main courses 95–195 F ($18.10–$37.10). AE, MC, V. Lunch Mon–Sat noon–3pm; dinner daily 6:30–10:30pm. FRENCH.

Diners sit at a well-set table on a gingerbread terrace overlooking the sea at this very French Antillean place, and the staff gives capable service. You get a number of choices in cuisine. To begin, try uncooked salmon (marinated in a sauce of fresh herbs), snails in garlic butter, or foie gras. The most tempting part of the menu is that listed under "Poissons." You can order grilled island lobster in puff pastry or red snapper soufflé. For dessert, try a French pastry. Read the wine list from both sides of the *carte*: The bottles aren't cheap.

Hévéa

Boulevard de Grand-Case. ☎ **590/87-56-85.** Reservations required. Appetizers $8–$21.50; main courses $22–$38; menu gourmand $55. MC, V. Dinner only, daily 6:30–10pm. Closed Sept and Mon Apr 15–Dec 14. FRENCH.

A small and intimate restaurant, with only 10 tables, Hévéa is owned by Jacqueline Dalbera. Here you can enjoy French cuisine inspired by Nice in pleasant formal surroundings of French furniture. Dishes might include a marinated fresh raw salmon and sea scallops in lime juice and dill, sliced duck breast in a wine sauce with black currants, and a dessert specialty of chocolate marquise.

Il Nettuno

Boulevard de Grand-Case. ☎**590/87-77-38.** Reservations recommended. Appetizers $6–$14; pastas $13–$22; main courses $18–$26; lunch platters $6–$16. AE, MC, V. Lunch daily noon–3pm; dinner daily 6–10:30pm. Closed June 1–15 and Sept. ITALIAN/SEAFOOD.

In a clapboard house, midway along the main street of Grand-Case, adjacent to the town's main pier, II Nettuno is considered one of the best Italian restaurants on either side of the island. It features an interior painted in shades of pink, draped with fish nets, chianti bottles, and memorabilia of the Washington Redskins, home team of the restaurant's owner. Menu items include freshly made pastas such as agnoloti stuffed with escargots, ricotta, and porcini mushrooms; linguine frutte di mare; penne with salmon; and ravioli de magro (stuffed with spinach and ricotta). There's also saltimbocca and a choice of traditional Italian veal and chicken dishes, prepared cacciatore or parmesan style; and fresh fish, which always includes mahi mahi, salmon, tuna, and swordfish. (Ask for these either blackened, served with saffron sauce and saffron pasta, or grilled and served with a tangy gorgonzola and green-peppercorn sauce.) There's an apéritif bar for a before-dinner drink if you want one.

◐ L'Auberge Gourmande

Boulevard de Grand-Case. ☎ **590/87-73-37.** Reservations required. Appetizers $6–$14; main courses $16–$26. AE, MC, V. Dinner only, Thurs–Tues at 7 and 9pm. Closed Sept. FRENCH.

This restaurant is in a century-old typical French Antillean house. Philippe Cassan, the chef, is assisted by his wife, Christine, who also has much experience in running restaurants. If you appreciate good French food and a family ambience, along with professional service, this is the place for you. Begin with vichyssoise, onion soup, or perhaps the mussel soup flavored with orange. Follow with red snapper filet with red sweet peppers, or perhaps the grilled lobster. The stuffed pork with mushrooms is excellent, as is the duck breast with a honey-and-lime sauce. For dessert, try the profiteroles. Ask about *le service au vin*, which allows you to taste several wines.

Moderate

◉ Cha Cha Cha's

Boulevard de Grand-Case, 61. ☎ **590/87-53-63.** Reservations not required. Appetizers $5.50–$12; main courses $14.50–$19.50. MC, V. Dinner only, Mon–Sat 6–11pm. CARIBBEAN.

On the main street of Grand-Case, this increasingly popular eatery is set in a French colonial building. Ceiling fans, local artwork, and trade winds create the atmosphere in this Caribbean-style café with two bars and a tropical garden. At this current island hot spot, the menu might be called *haute Caraíbes* fare. Try steamed snapper in a black-bean sauce, perhaps seared tuna with a passionfruit-and-tomato compote. Blackened shrimp with a spicy mango salad is another pleaser, and grilled meat dishes are a special feature. A selection of tropical tapas—18 different varieties—costs $3.25.

IN COLOMBIER

La Rhumerie

Colombier. ☎ **590/87-56-98.** Reservations required. Appetizers 38–50 F ($7.20–$9.50); main courses 95–250 F ($18.10–$47.50). AE, MC, V. Dinner only, Fri–Wed 7–9:30pm. Closed Sept–Oct. FRENCH/CREOLE.

Minutes from Marigot, in the tiny hamlet of Colombier, West Indies–born owner Fracillette Le Moine continues a tradition established by her late husband, Yannick, from Brittany, in serving fine food. They transformed this private home in a country setting into a restaurant that also serves traditional French dishes, such as stuffed crab back, escargots, and onion soup gratiné. But the place is best known for Créole cuisine, including curried goat, a salad of coffre (a local fish), conch in fresh herbs, and poulet boucanne Créole (home-smoked chicken served with baked green papayas and christophine au gratin).

IN ANSE MARCEL

La Belle France

In the Méridien L'Habitation/Le Domaine, Marcel Cove. ☎ **590/87-67-00.** Reservations required. Appetizers $15–$20; main courses $20–$41. AE, DC, MC, V. Dinner only, daily 7–10pm (last order). FRENCH/SEAFOOD.

This beautifully appointed gourmet restaurant is the culinary showcase of the island's largest resort, the previously recommended Méridien (see "Where to Stay," above). Tucked away in a remote corner of the island, adjacent to the resort's main swimming pool, the restaurant is open on all sides to the tropical breezes, and outfitted in a color scheme of blue, white, and faded pink. Menu items include lobster prepared in at least three different ways, filet of red snapper with anis sauce, pavé of tuna with a red-wine-and-cinnamon sauce, escalopes of mérou with essence of vanilla, rack of lamb with thyme, and duckling roasted in sea salt.

AT ORIENT BAY

❍ Le Restaurant du Résidence Alizéa

Mont Vernon. ☎ **590/87-41-20.** Reservations required. Appetizers $9–$11; main courses $22–$30; fixed-price meal $33; menu gourmet $40. AE, MC, V. Dinner only, daily 6:30–10:30pm. Closed Tues off-season. FRENCH/CREOLE.

This restaurant is considered a little-known culinary gem, not enough appreciated on an island loaded with competitors. In a previously recommended hotel, on the island's northeastern edge, it commands a two-sided view of Orient Bay from its pink-walled premises. The menu changes daily. The chef, Laurent Guyon, has worked with widely acclaimed chef Roger Verger at the Moulin de Mougins along the French Riviera. At the time of your visit you might try such dishes as cream of mahi mahi soup, freshly made tagliatelle with truffles and port-wine sauce, warm oysters with a caviar and champagne-flavored cream sauce, fricassée of conch, colombo of tuna, rack of lamb seasoned with thyme, sautéed filet of veal with basil and black-truffle sauce, and a selection of vegetarian dishes.

In Oyster Pond

Captain Oliver Restaurant

In Captain Oliver's Hotel Resort. ☎ **590/87-30-00.** Reservations recommended. Appetizers $6.50–$19; main courses $16–$24. AE, MC, V. Daily 7am–10pm. FRENCH/CREOLE.

Partially built on piers above the bay right at the Dutch border and overlooking a yacht-filled harbor, Captain Oliver is reached from either Marigot or Philipsburg along a twisting road. Once there, you'll find West Indian conch, "fish soup of the captain," a fisherman's platter, tuna steak grilled with caper sauce, and fresh grilled lobster. This place has been known to island gourmets since it opened in 1983. It adjoins a previously reviewed bungalow colony facing the island of St. Barts, and a marina adds to its appeal, particularly at night.

Specialty Dining

Should the heat of the day get to you, stop in at **Etna Ice Cream Per Dolce Vita,** avenue Kennedy, 4, in Port La Royale (☎ 590/87-72-72). Here, Paolo and Betty Smiroldo operate a gelateria-pasticcieria, with homemade ice creams created from fresh fruit. Ice-cream items range from 5.50 to 35 F ($1 to $6.70). The tartufo is as good as the one served on the piazza Navona in Roma, and they also have spumoni, cassata, and espresso, along with French croissants and pastries. A fresh-fruit drink, frullato, is prepared in front of you, and you can also order homemade frozen yogurt. The "sweet life" holds forth here daily Monday through Saturday from 8am to 6:30pm.

SPORTS & OUTDOOR ACTIVITIES

BEACHES   The island as a whole has 36 perfect white sandy beaches. The hotels, for the most part, have grabbed up the choicest sands, and usually for a small fee nonguests can use hotel beaches and changing facilities. Topless sunbathing is practiced commonly at the beaches on the French side. **Club Orient Naturist Resort** (☎ 590/87-33-85) has the only nudist beach on the island, but nude or mono-kini (as opposed to bikini) is relatively common, even though total nudity is not officially endorsed.

Ilet Pinel, a tiny island off St. Martin, is perfect for beach recluses. You can get there by negotiating with a passing fisherman to provide transport back and forth.

Beyond the sprawling Mullet Beach Resort on the Dutch side, **Cupecoy Bay Beach** lies just north of the Dutch-French border. On the western side of the island, it's a string of three white sandy beaches set against a backdrop of caves and sandstone cliffs that provide morning shade. The beach doesn't have facilities but is very popular. One section of the beach is "clothing optional."

Top rating on St. Martin goes to **Baie Longue,** a long beautiful beach that's rarely overcrowded. Chic La Samanna (see "Where to Stay," above) opens onto this stretch. The location is to the north of Cupecoy Beach, reached by taking the Lowlands road. Don't leave any valuables in your car, as many break-ins have been reported. If you continue north along the highway, you reach the approach to another long and popular stretch of sand, **Baie Rouge.** Snorkelers are drawn to the rock formations at both ends of this beach. There are no changing facilities, but, for some, that doesn't matter as they prefer to get their suntan *au naturel.*

On the north side of the island, to the west of Espérance airport, **Grand-Case Beach** is small but select. The sand is white and clean, but the previously recommended Grand-Case Beach Club takes up a huge hunk of the beach.

For a description of beaches on the Dutch side, see "Sports and Outdoor Activities" in Section 1 on St. Maarten in Chapter 10.

SCUBA DIVING   Scuba diving is excellent around St. Martin, with reef, wreck, night, cave, and drift diving; the depth of dives is 20 to 70 feet. Off the northeastern coast on the French side, dive sites include Ilet Pinel for shallow diving; Green Key, a barrier reef; Flat Island for sheltered coves and geologic faults; and Tintamarre, known for its shipwreck. To the north, Anse Marcel and neighboring Anguilla are good choices. Most hotels will arrange for scuba excursions on request. There is a PADI scuba-dive center, **Lou Scuba Club,** at the Marine Hôtel Simson Beach, Nettle Bay (☎ **590/87-16-61**). Its dives, costing from $45, range from 25 to 70 feet.

You can also try the **Blue Ocean Watersport and Dive Center,** La Belle Creole Hotel, Baie Nettle (**590/87-66-89**). Marigot (☎ **590/87-89-73**). A certified dive costs $45, including equipment. A PADI certification course is available for $350 and takes five days. Both scuba clubs offer 3 dives for $120, 5 dives for $175, and 10 dives for $300.

SNORKELING   The calm waters ringing the shallow reefs and tiny coves found throughout the island make it a snorkeler's heaven. The waters off the northeastern shores of St. Martin have been classified as a regional underwater nature reserve, **Reserve Sous-Marine Régionale.** The area, comprising Flat Island (also known as Tintamarre), Pinel Islet, Green Key, and Petite Clef, is thus protected by official government decree. The use of harpoons is strictly forbidden. Snorkeling can be enjoyed individually or on sailing trips. Equipment can be rented at almost any hotel.

At the **Grand-Case Beach Club** (☎ **590/87-51-87**), a one-hour snorkeling trip costs $20 per person, including masks and fins.

TENNIS   Tennis buffs heading for French St. Martin can play at most hotels. Once a rarity on the French side of the island, tennis is now a regular amenity.

The **Méridien L'Habitation** has six courts, all lit for night play, and **La Belle Créole** has four, also lit. The Omnisport (artificial grass) court at **Grand Anse Beach Club** is also lit. There are three unlit courts at the exclusive **La Samanna.**

WATERSKIING & PARASAILING   Most beachfront hotels have facilities for waterskiing as well as parasailing. Waterskiing averages $40 per half hour, and parasailing costs about $25 to $30 a ride.

WINDSURFING   Almost every beachfront hotel has facilities for this, and lessons average $20 to $25 per hour. Sport Away is a windsurfing school at Orient Bay; it was founded by Nathalie Simon, famous in international championship circles. For information about this sport, contact the **St. Martin Windsurfing Association** in Marigot (☎ **590/87-93-24**).

SHOPPING

Many day-trippers come over to Marigot from the Dutch side just to look at the collection of boutiques and shopping arcades. Because it's a duty-free port, you'll find some of the best shopping in the Caribbean. There is a wide selection of French goods, including crystal, perfumes, jewelry, and fashions, sometimes at 25% to 50% less than in the United States and Canada. There are also fine liqueurs, cognacs, and cigars. Whether you're seeking jewelry, perfume, or St-Tropez bikinis, you'll find it in one of the boutiques along rue de la République and rue de la Liberté in Marigot.

Most of the boutiques on the French side are open Monday through Saturday from 9am to noon or 12:30pm and from 2 to 6pm. When cruise ships are in port on Sunday and holidays, some of the larger shops open again.

Prices are often quoted in U.S. dollars, and salespeople frequently speak English. Credit and charge cards and traveler's checks are generally accepted. Look especially for French luxury items, such as Lalique crystal, Vuitton bags (the real item, not the fake seen worldwide), and Chanel perfume.

IN MARIGOT

At harborside in Marigot there's a frisky **morning market** with vendors selling spices, fruit, shells, and local handcrafts.

At **Port La Royale,** the bustling center of everything, mornings are even more alive: Schooners unload produce from the neighboring islands, boats board guests for picnics on deserted beaches, a brigantine sets out on a sightseeing sail, and the owners of a dozen different little dining spots are getting ready for the lunch crowd. The largest shopping arcade on St. Martin, it has many boutiques, some of which come and go with great rapidity.

Another shopping complex, the **Galerie Périgourdine,** facing the post office, is again a cluster of boutiques. Here you might pick up some designer wear for both men and women, including items from the collection of Ted Lapidus.

Gingerbread Gallery

Marina Royale, 14. ☎ **590/87-73-21.**

Owner Simone Seitre scours Haiti four times a year to secure the best works of a cross section of Haitian artists, both the "old master" and the talented amateur. One of the most knowledgeable purveyors of Haitian art in the Caribbean, this pan-European has promoted Haitian art at exhibits around the world. Even if you're not in the market for an expensive piece of art (the paintings come in all price ranges), you'll find dozens of charming and inexpensive handcrafts. The little gallery is a bit hard to find, on a narrow alleyway at the marina next to the Café de Paris, but it's worth the search.

Havane

Port La Royale. ☎ **590/87-70-39.**

Havane offers exclusive collections of French clothing, both in sports and high-fashion designs for men and women.

La Romana

Rue de la République. ☎ **590/87-88-16.**

In the heart of Marigot, this specialty boutique retails the latest collections of La Perla and Fendi. La Perla lines include swimwear, resortwear for day and evening, perfume, and lingerie. The Fendi collection of bags, luggage, and accessories is one of the largest in the Caribbean.

Lipstick

Port La Royale, rue Kennedy. ☎ **590/87-73-24.**

Try Lipstick for the largest assortment of duty-free fragrances and cosmetics, as well as beauty preparations by such name designers as Dior and Yves St. Laurent. You can also get facials and massages here. There's another branch of Lipstick along rue de la République in Marigot (☎ **87-53-92**).

Little Switzerland

Rue de la République. ☎ **590/87-50-03.**

This is one of the best places on the island if you're seeking European imports at prices lower than in the United States. You get not only name china and crystal, but also precision Swiss watches. The jewelry collection in both its Philipsburg branch and the one at Marigot is perhaps one of the largest in the West Indies. There are many gift items as well, and you can select your favorite fragrance.

Maneks
Rue de la République. ☎ 590/87-54-91.

Worth a stopover, Maneks has a little bit of everything: video cameras, tobacco products, liquors, gifts, souvenirs, radio cassettes, Kodak film, watches, T-shirts, sunglasses, and pearls from Majorca. The shop also carries beach accessories.

Oro de Sol Jewelers
Rue de la République. ☎ 590/87-56-51.

In this well-stocked store is one of the most imaginative selections on St. Martin, including an array of gold watches by Cartier, Ebel, Patek Philippe, and the like, as well as high-fashion jewelry studded with precious stones.

IN ORLEANS

Roland Richardson
Orléans. ☎ 590/87-32-24.

Local artist Roland Richardson welcomes visitors into his house to view and purchase his original watercolors and prints of island vistas on Tuesday and Thursday from 10am to 5pm. The premier local artist on the island, he is a promoter of the island's culture and tradition. In his work he captures and preserves the natural beauty of St. Martin.

ST. MARTIN AFTER DARK

Some St. Martin hotels have dinner-dancing, piano-lounge music, and even discos. But the most popular after-dark pastime is leisurely dining.

Club l'Aventure, rue de la République (☎ 87-13-84), is designed in a waterfront format akin to that of a yacht club. This is the most talked-about nightclub on St. Martin. It contains a restaurant on its street level, where meals cost around $25 per person. Upstairs is a disco, where even 40-year-olds feel comfortable mingling with the island's young and energetic. Entrance is $5, and drinks begin at $5 each. It's open nightly from 10:30pm until the management decides to close some time in the wee hours.

4 St. Barthélemy

For luxury with minimum hassle—although at a high price tag—St. Barts is the most platinum destination in the Caribbean, rivaled only by Anguilla. It's sophistication in the tropics, chic, rich, and so very Parisian. Forget such things as historical sights or ambitious water-sports programs here, and come for the relaxation in ultimate comfort, the French cuisine (often haute), and the white sandy beaches.

New friends call it "St. Barts," while old-time visitors prefer "St. Barths." Either way, it's short for St. Barthélemy—named by its discoverer Columbus in 1493 and pronounced "San Bar-te-le-*mee.*" The uppermost corner of the French West Indies, it's the only Caribbean island with a touch of Sweden in its personality.

For the most part, St. Bartians are descendants of Breton and Norman fisherfolk. Many are long-limbed and attractive, of French and Swedish ancestry, the latter showing in their fair skin, blond hair, and blue eyes. The mostly Caucasian population is small, about 3,500 living in some 8 square miles, 15 miles southeast of St. Martin and 140 miles north of Guadeloupe.

Occasionally you'll see St. Bartians dressed in the provincial costumes of Normandy, and when you hear them speak Norman French, you'll think you're back in the old country—except for the temperature. In little Corossol, more than anywhere else, you can see the people following traditions brought from 17th-century France. You might see elderly women wearing the starched white bonnets. This special headgear, brought from Brittany, was called *quichenotte*, a corruption of "kiss-me-not," and may well have served as protection from the close attentions of Englishmen or Swedes on the island. The bonneted women can also be seen at local celebrations, particularly on August 25, St. Louis's Day. Many of these women are camera-shy, but they offer their homemade baskets and hats for sale to tourists.

For a long time the island was a paradise for a few millionaires, such as David Rockefeller, who has a hideaway on the northwest shore, and Edmond de Rothschild, who occupies some fabulous acres at the "other end" of the island. The Biddles of Philadelphia are in the middle. Nowadays, however, St. Barts is developing a broader base of tourism as it opens more hotels. Nevertheless, the island continues as a celebrity favorite in the Caribbean, attracting the likes of Tom Cruise, Harrison Ford, and Mikhail Baryshnikov. In February, the island guest list often reads like a roster from "Lifestyles of the Rich and Famous."

The island's capital is **Gustavia,** named after a Swedish king; in fact, Gustavia is St. Barts's only town and seaport. It's a landlocked, hurricane-proof harbor, looking like a little dollhouse-scale port.

ORIENTATION
GETTING THERE

BY PLANE   From the United States, the principal gateways are St. Maarten (see Chapter 10), St. Thomas (see Chapter 6), and Guadeloupe (see Section 2 in this chapter). At any of these islands, connections to St. Barts can be made on interisland carriers.

It's just a 10-minute flight from Juliana airport on Dutch-held St. Maarten. From St. Maarten, the best way to go is on a flight of **Windward Islands Airways International (Winair)** (☎ 590/27-61-01). This airline, which has carried such passengers as Queen Beatrix of Holland and Jacqueline Onassis, will fly you over to St. Barts in the morning and back around 5 in the afternoon. But I recommend that you spend more time to savor the special flavor of St. Barts.

If you're on Guadeloupe, you can fly in aboard **Air Guadeloupe** (☎ 590/27-61-90), a one-hour trip. Air Guadeloupe also has regular service to St. Barts from the small Espérance airport on the French side of St. Martin.

It's also possible to fly with **Virgin Air** (toll free 800/522-3084), which has regular service to St. Barts from San Juan and St. Thomas.

Many jokes have been made about the makeshift landing strip on St. Barts. It's short, and accommodates small craft—the biggest plane it can land is a 19-seat STOL (short takeoff and landing craft). As a chilling sight, a cemetery adjoins the strip! Locals pray to the white cross that stands between two hills flanking the field.

St. Barthelemy

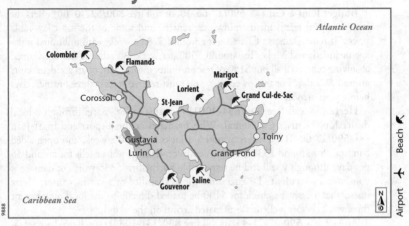

Your plane has to make a curving swoop through a hilltop pass. No matter, everybody seems to arrive in one piece.

Traveler's Advisory: Always reconfirm your return flight from St. Barts with one of the secondary carriers recommended above. If you don't, you'll find that your reservation has been canceled. Also, don't check your luggage all the way through to St. Barts or you may not see your belongings for a few days. Check your bags to your gateway destination, whatever island you are connecting through, most often Dutch St. Maarten. Then take your luggage to whatever carrier you're using and recheck your bags to St. Barts. You'll be glad you did.

BY BOAT OR FERRY   There is a variety of services between St. Maarten and St. Barts, but schedules vary with the season, so it's best to check on the spot. Contact the offices of such vessels as *White Octopus*, which arrives in St. Barts around 10:30am or 11am after a 1¹/₂- to 2-hour crossing from St. Maarten. The vessel de-parts from St. Barts at 3:30pm and arrives back at St. Maarten at 5pm. The price is $50 for the round-trip, plus $5 departure tax. Call **599/5/23170** for more information.

Visitors can also arrive on St. Barts by ferryboat from French St. Martin or Dutch St. Maarten. There are daily round trips on the *Gustavia Express*, a motor-ized catamaran leaving Gustavia several times a day. The vessel then returns from Marina Port la Royale in Marigot on French St. Martin or Bobby's Marina in Philipsburg on Dutch St. Maarten. To reserve, call **590/27-77-24.** A one-way fare is $35: a round-trip, $50.

GETTING AROUND

BY TAXI   Taxis meet all flights and are not very expensive, mostly because no one destination is all that far from any other. Dial **590/27-66-31** for taxi service. A typical rate, St-Jean to Cul-de-Sac, costs $20. Night fares are higher, as are fares on Sunday and holidays.

BY RENTAL CAR   The hilly terrain, and perhaps the sense of adventure of the residents, combine to form a car-rental situation unique in the Caribbean. Never have I seen as many open-sided Mini-Mokes and Suzuki Samurais as I have on St. Barts. Painted in vivid colors, they're fast, fun, and very windy. You'll enjoy driving one too, as long as you're handy with a stick shift and don't care about your coiffure.

Budget Rent-a-Car (☎ **590/27-66-30,** or toll free **800/527-0700**) offers the least stringent terms for its midwinter rentals, and some of the most favorable prices. It rents Daihatsu Charades for around $280 a week, with unlimited mileage included, and Mokes for around $300 per week. A collision-damage waiver, absolving renters of all but $150 of responsibility in the event of an accident, costs around $8 a day. For the lowest rate, you must reserve at least three business days before your arrival.

Hertz (☎ toll free **800/654-3001**) operates on St. Barts through a local dealership, Henry's Car Rental. With branches at the airport and in St-Jean (☎ **590/27-60-21**), it offers Suzuki Sidekicks for $390 a week, and open-sided Samurais for around $330 a week. A collision-damage waiver sells for around $8 per day, although you'll still be responsible for the first $335 worth of damage if you have an accident. To guarantee the availability of a car in winter, Hertz insists that a cashier's check for $100 be mailed directly to the local rental agent three weeks before a client's anticipated arrival on the island.

At **Avis** (☎ **590/27-71-43,** or toll free **800/331-1084**), you'll need a reservation a full month in advance during high season, plus the advance payment of a $100 deposit. The company's Mazda 323s are priced at $330 a week; its VW Golfs (with automatic transmission and air conditioning), also at $330 per week.

Gas is extra. Tanks hold enough to get you to one of the island's two gas stations. Never drive with less than half a tank of gas; you might regret it if you do, especially since the Shell station near the airport is closed from noon on Saturday until Monday morning. The island's only other gas station, near L'Orient, is slightly more accommodating. All valid foreign driver's licenses are honored. No one will mind if you honk your horn furiously while going around the island's blind corners, a practice that avoids many sideswiped fenders. Drive slowly and with consideration, and don't drink and drive.

BY MOTORBIKES & SCOOTERS Denis Dufau operates **Rent Some Fun** in Gustavia (☎ **590/27-70-59**). A helmet is needed, and potential bikers must pay a $100 deposit as well as rental fee of $21 to $26 a day. If renting for a week, one day is free. A driver's license is also required.

BY SIGHTSEEING TOURS Group tours are scaled to the island's size: eight passengers per minibus. If you go by private taxi, of course, it's more expensive. An hour-long tour by minibus costs about $40 for three or $50 for up to eight; prices, naturally, have to be negotiated. The local tourist office can arrange private tours, as can most hotel desks. Or you can call **Hugo Cagan** (☎ **590/27-61-28**) or **Florian La Place** of the Taxi Drivers Group (☎ **590/27-70-79**) and negotiate a price for what you want to do. **St. Barts Voyages** (☎ **590/27-79-23**), a local travel agency, also arranges tours.

FAST FACTS: St. Barthélemy

Area Code   St. Barts is not part of the Caribbean's 809 area code. For details on calling to and on the island, see "Telephone," below.

Banks   There are two banks on the island, both in Gustavia and both open Monday through Friday. The Banque Française Commerciale, rue du Général-de-Gaulle (☎ **590/27-62-62**), is open from 8am to noon and 2 to 4:30pm. The Banque Nationale de Paris, rue du Bord-de-Mer (☎ **590/27-63-70**), is open from 8am to noon and 2 to 3:30pm.

Currency   The official monetary unit is the **French franc (F),** but most stores and restaurants prefer payment in U.S. dollars. Most hotels also quote their rates in American currency at a discount from the rates as quoted in francs. For your reference, at press time the exchange rate was 5.28 F to $1 U.S. (1 F = 19¢), and this is the rate that is used in this chapter. As this is sure to fluctuate a bit, use this rate for guidance only.

Customs   You are allowed to bring in items for personal use, including tobacco, cameras, and film.

Documents   If you're flying in, you'll need to present your return or ongoing ticket. U.S. and Canadian citizens need only photo identification or a passport. Visitors from Britain must have a valid passport.

Drugstores   The Pharmacie de Gustavia is on rue de la République (☎ 590/27-61-82) in Gustavia. It's open Monday through Saturday from 8:30am to 7pm.

Electricity   The electricity is 200 volts A.C., 50 cycles; therefore, U.S.–made appliances require French plugs and transformers.

Information   Go to the **Office du Tourisme,** quai du Général-de-Gaulle, in Gustavia (☎ 590/27-87-27).

Medical Care   St. Barts is not the greatest place to find yourself in a medical emergency. It has two doctors and some on-call specialists. Contact the Hôpital de Bruyne (☎ 27-60-35) for minor cases. Serious medical cases are often flown out to St. Martin.

Safety   Although crime is rare here, it would be wise to protect your valuables. Don't leave them unguarded on the beach or in parked cars, even if locked in the trunk.

Taxes   An airport departure tax of 15 F ($2.90) is assessed. Hotels do not add a room tax.

Telephone   St. Barts is linked to the Guadeloupe telephone system, which is *not* part of the 809 area code that applies to most of the Caribbean. To call St. Barts from the United States, if your long-distance telephone company is equipped to handle international direct dialing, dial 011 (the international access code), then 590 (the country code for the French West Indies), and finally the six-digit local number. If you cannot direct-dial internationally, dial 0 ("zero," for the operator) and tell the operator you wish to make an international call; once you are transferred to the international operator, state the 590 country code and the local number, and the operator will dial the call for you. To make a call within St. Barts, only the six-digit local number is necessary.

Time   When standard time is in effect in the United States and Canada, St. Barts is one hour ahead of the U.S. East Coast. Thus, when it's 7pm on St. Barts, it's only 6pm in New York or Toronto. When daylight saving time is in effect in the United States, clocks in New York and St. Barts show the same time.

Weather   The climate of St. Barts is ideal: It's dry with an average temperature of 72° to 86° Fahrenheit.

WHERE TO STAY

With the exception of a few of the super-priced hotels, most places here are homey, comfortable, and casual. Everything is small, as tiny St. Barts is hardly in the mainstream of tourism. In March it's often hard to get in here unless you've made reservations far in advance. Accommodations throughout the island, with some exceptions, tend to be exceptionally expensive, and a service charge of 15% is added to your bill. Some hotels quote their rates in U.S. dollars, others in French francs.

St. Barts has a sizable number of villas, beach houses, and apartments for rent by the week or month. Villas are dotted around the island's hills—very few are on the beach. Instead of an oceanfront bedroom, you get a spectacular view. One of the best agencies to contact for villa, apartment, or condo rentals is **St. Barth Properties,** 18 Depot St., Franklin, MA 02038 (☎ **508/528-7727,** or **800/421-3396** in the U.S. and Canada). There, Peg Walsh, who believes in "living your dream," will inform you of what's available and at what price, depending on the season. She can also make arrangements for car rentals and air travel to St. Barts, and is very helpful in providing information about the island. Sometimes, for example, you can rent a villa for $980 per week off-season, rising to $2,010 per week in winter. But all sorts of price arrangements are available, ranging from moderate to super-expensive. In addition to villas, Ms. Walsh can also arrange accommodations in all categories of St. Barts's hotels, ranging from the Carl Gustaf to the White Sand Beach cottages.

VERY EXPENSIVE

✪ Carl Gustaf

Rue des Normands, Gustavia 97099 St. Barthélemy. ☎ **590/27-82-83,** or 800/932-3222 in the U.S. Fax 27-82-37. 14 suites. A/C MINIBAR TV. Winter, $770–$920 one-bedroom suite; $1,000–$2,000 two-bedroom suite. Off-season, $500 one-bedroom suite; $660 two-bedroom suite. (Rates include continental breakfast.) AE, MC, V. Free parking.

The most glamorous (and most expensive) hotel in Gustavia rises above the town's harbor from a position on a steeply sloping hillside. It's like a regal eagle's nest. Each accommodation is in one of a dozen pale-pink, red-roofed villas whose facilities include a private kitchenette, two phones, fax machines, two stereo systems, two color TVs, and comfortably plush rattan furniture. Access to each building is via a central staircase, which tests the stamina of even the most active of guests. The wood-frame units are angled for maximum views of the boats bobbing far below in the bay. The allure is French, not unlike what you'd find on the coast of Provence.

Dining/Entertainment: There's a restaurant set on the uppermost level of the hotel, and a small but charming bar. The cuisine is a gastronomic French and Créole interpretation, with lunches costing $30 to $50. Often a well-known chef from Paris appears in winter. There's also a sunset bar with live music, featuring a different cocktail every day.

Services: 24-hour room service, concierge, massage.

Facilities: Sauna, exercise room, 46-foot yacht for excursions.

Christopher Hôtel

Pointe Milou (B.P. 571), 97098 St. Barthélemy, F.W.I. ☎ **590/27-63-63,** or 800/471-9090 in the U.S. Fax 27-92-92. 40 rms. A/C MINIBAR TEL. Winter, $325–$360 single or double. Off-season, $225–$280 single or double. Children under 12 (limit of two) stay free in parents' room. (Rates include American breakfast.) AE, MC, V. Closed Sept.

St. Barts' newest major hotel opened in 1993 on the island's northeastern edge, in a neighborhood of private villas and relative seclusion. Built and managed by Sofitel, the luxury division of the Paris-based hotel giant Accor, it offers a

French-colonial decor, and a low-rise design that incorporates four slate-roofed, white-sided buildings arranged in a semicircle above a rocky coastline. Although the hotel is not adjacent to a sandy beach, clients usually drive about 10 minutes to reach any of at least three different swimming areas nearby. Most of the resort's activities revolve around the swimming pool. Each room has a veranda or balcony overlooking the sea, a ceiling fan, and in some instances, a semiprivate garden.

Dining/Entertainment: Breakfast and gourmet French dinners are served at L'Orchidée, while lunch is a poolside affair, featuring platters, light snacks, and low-calorie or dietetic meals.

Services: Room service (7am to midnight), a concierge (who can arrange horseback riding, scuba diving, or deep-sea fishing).

Facilities: The resort's swimming pool, a 4,500-square-foot pair of interconnected ovals with a bridge, is the largest on the island. Nearby, a fitness center/health club offers nutritional counseling, massage, and relaxation therapy, usually with the supervision of a full-time physiotherapist. A complimentary massage is included in the price of a stay here.

✪ Filao Beach

Baie de St-Jean (B.P. 167), 97099 St. Barthélemy, F.W.I. ☎ **590/27-64-84.** Fax 27-62-24. 30 rms. A/C MINIBAR TV TEL. Winter, 1,750–3,200 F ($332.50–$608) single or double. Off-season, 1,000–1,900 F ($190–$361) single or double. (Rates include continental breakfast and airport transfers.) AE, DC, MC, V. Free parking. Closed Sept 5–Oct 21.

In this crescent-shaped, white stucco beachside bungalow hotel on the main beach, a four-minute drive from the airport, each room is named after a château in France. This is the only Relais & Châteaux in the French Caribbean. Try to reserve Bungalow 10 or 40, near the beach. All rooms are modern and elegantly simple, and well upholstered with large closets, private safes, ceiling fans, and sun-flooded terraces, where you can enjoy a leisurely breakfast.

Dining/Entertainment: A bar and restaurant, open only for lunch, overlooks St. Jean's Beach and serves both a French and international cuisine.

Services: Laundry and babysitting can be arranged.

Facilities: Freshwater swimming pool; scuba diving, snorkeling, windsurfing, and waterskiing can be arranged.

Hôtel Guanahani

Anse de Grand Cul-de-Sac, 97133 St. Barthélemy, F.W.I. ☎ **590/27-66-60,** or 800/223-6800 in the U.S. Fax 27-70-70. 55 rms, 21 suites. A/C MINIBAR TV TEL. Winter, $400–$470 single or double; $640–$710 suite. Off-season, $230–$295 single or double; $440–$510 suite. (Rates include continental breakfast.) AE, DC, MC, V. Free parking.

A member of the prestigious Leading Hotels of the World, an organization representing the finest hotels around the globe, the Hôtel Guanahani, in the northeast part of the island, opened with Gallic fanfare in 1986 and became the largest hotel on the island. Well signposted, this beachfront resort is spread over 7 steeply sloping and well-landscaped acres with pastel-colored cottages trimmed in gingerbread. Its units include doubles, deluxe rooms, spa suites, and one-bedroom suites, all with private patios, refrigerators, ceiling fans, and radios. The spa suites offer small outside spas (cold Jacuzzi), and the one-bedroom suites have their own private splash pools and are equipped with kitchens.

Dining/Entertainment: The Guanahani has two restaurants. The more formal is Bartolomeo (see "Where to Dine," below). Indigo is the poolside café, available for breakfast and lunch.

Services: Room service, laundry, babysitting, massages.

Facilities: Two freshwater swimming pools and a Jacuzzi with a good view of Grand Cul-de-Sac, two hard-surface tennis courts (lit at night), a private white sandy beach on a reef-protected bay, water sports (some at an additional charge).

✪ Hôtel Manapany Cottages

Anse des Cayes (B.P. 114), 97133 St. Barthélemy, F.W.I. ☎ **590/27-66-55**, or 800/ 847-4249 in the U.S. Fax 27-75-28. 32 rms, 20 suites. A/C TV TEL. Winter, $240 single; $390– $430 double; $465–$515 junior suite; $760–$935 club suite. Off-season, $150 single; $240–$430 double; $290–$515 junior suite; $385–$935 club suite. (Rates include continental breakfast.) AE, DC, MC, V. Free parking.

The Hôtel Manapany climbs a steep, well-landscaped hillside on the northwestern side of the island, a 10-minute taxi ride north of the airport. This is one of the most luxurious and stylish hotels in the Caribbean (the name, translated from Malagese, means "small paradise"). It offers a cluster of units on the hillside and another group along the water, all with red roofs and rambling verandas open to the sea. Wicker furniture combines tropical comfort with Gallic style. Behind sliding glass doors, you'll find either one or two bedrooms, a large-screen TV with in-house video movies, ceiling fans, a tile bath, and a kitchenette. You register in a villa at the base of the hill.

Dining/Entertainment: The restaurant, Ouanalao, is a crescent-shaped terrace overlooking the seafeaturing casual dining with light lunches and candlelit romantic dinners. Italian dishes and fresh pastas are the specialties. More formal meals are served in an elegant raftered dining room, the Ballahou (see "Where to Dine," below). The Ouanaloa is open throughout the year; however, the Ballahou gourmet restaurant serves only in winter.

Services: Concierge, room service, laundry, babysitting.

Facilities: Small-scale spa facility for massages and stress reduction.

La Banane

L'Orient, 97133 St. Barthélemy, F.W.I. ☎ **590/27-68-25.** Fax 27-68-44. 9 rms. MINIBAR TV TEL Winter, 1,700–2,500 F ($323–$475) double. Off-season, 860–980 F ($163.40– $186.20) double. MAP 220 F ($41.80) extra. AE, V. Free parking. Closed Sept 8–Oct 20.

About a mile from the airport on the outskirts of the village of L'Orient, off the shore road near Autour de Rocher, is this small, intimate, and well-furnished hotel, filled with some of the most stylish antiques on the island. The complex is ringed by a fence whose boundaries are a three-minute walk from the beach. My favorite accommodation contains a large mahogany four-poster bed whose trim was made from a little-known Central and South American wood called angelique. The other units are less spacious, but each has a VCR, some Haitian art, a mixture of antique and modern designs, a refrigerator, a private terrace, and louvered windows overlooking the garden. Some units are air-conditioned.

Dining/Entertainment: The small inn has a good French restaurant, featuring cabaret. A table d'hôte dinner is served nightly in the French style, with superb duck but also beef and veal dishes. Fresh fish depends on market availability.

Services: Room service.

Facilities: Two freshwater pools; beach nearby.

St. Barth Isle de France

Baie des Flamands, 97133 St. Barthélemy, F.W.I. ☎ **590/27-61-81**, or 800/628-8929 in the U.S. Fax 27-86-83. 17 rms, 6 suites, 7 bungalows. A/C MINIBAR TV TEL. $420–$540 single or double; $550–$700 suite; $290–$380 bungalow. Off-season, $300–$375 single or double; $500 suite; $240–$255 bungalow. (Rates include continental breakfast.) AE, DC, MC, V. Free parking.

Set amid a forest of palm trees immediately adjacent to one of the island's finest beaches, this resort opened in 1992. The hotel, centered around a re-creation of a colonial plantation house, is small and charming, with unusually spacious bedrooms for St. Barts. Each contains a private safe, a coffee maker, a carefully contrived French or English colonial tropical decor (usually with a four-poster bed), and richly textured fabrics from the looms of France. The bathrooms are especially opulent, filled with perfumed accessories.

Dining/Entertainment: There's a simple but agreeable restaurant, which wisely abandons any pretense of gourmet food, and two bars.

Services: 24-hour room service, laundry.

Facilities: Air-conditioned squash court, direct access to an excellent beach, two swimming pools a few steps from the beach, tennis court (illuminated at night), exercise room, gift shop.

EXPENSIVE

Eden Rock

St-Jean, 97133 St. Barthélemy, F.W.I. ☎ **590/27-72-94.** Fax 27-88-37. 6 rms. A/C. Winter, $300 single; $336 double. Off-season, $166 single; $184 double. (Rates include continental breakfast.) MC, V. Free parking. Transportation: Taxi (a three-minute ride from the airport).

When the quartzite promontory this hotel sits on was purchased many years ago by the island's former mayor, Rémy de Haenen, the seller was an old woman who laughed at him for paying too many francs for it. Today it's part of the island lore. The building capping its pinnacle looks like an idealized version of a Provençal farmhouse and offers some of the best panoramas on the island. It's surrounded on three sides by the waters of St. Jean Bay. I prefer the terra-cotta terrace, especially in the glare of noon, when the frigatebirds are wheeling and diving for fish in the turquoise waters. Inside the stone walls is a collection of French antiques and paintings, including a few drawings by Monsieur de Haenen's father, a well-known turn-of-the-century illustrator. The de Haenen family offers six bedrooms, each with a sea view, air conditioning or ceiling fan, and plenty of old-fashioned charm. Today the hotel is managed by Mr. de Haenan's granddaughter. Because of its small size and limited number of bedrooms, it's wise to reserve early at this hotel.

Dining/Entertainment: The hotel has a bar and a well-known restaurant, the Eden Roc. There's also a less expensive on-site eatery, Le Barbecue, which is open daily for lunch and dinner, serving meals priced at around 55 to 170 F ($10.50 to $32.30) per person.

El Sereno Beach Hôtel

Grand Cul-de-Sac (B.P. 19), 97095 St. Barthélemy, F.W.I. ☎ **590/27-64-80,** or 800/742-4276 in the U.S. Fax 27-75-47. 20 rms, 9 villas. A/C MINIBAR TV TEL. Winter, $235–$275 single; $265–$340 double; $1,150–$1,400 villa. Off-season, $140–$160 single; $155–$185 double; $700 villa. Continental breakfast $12 extra. AE, MC, V. Free parking. Closed Sept–Oct 15.

El Sereno's low-slung pastel facade and its isolated location 4 miles east of Gustavia create the aura of St-Tropez in the Antilles. A lot of the Riviera crowd is attracted to it, partly because of its Lyon-born owner, Marc Llepez. On the premises are accommodations with garden views, plus a trio of units overlooking the sea. Each unit contains two beds, an individual safe, a refrigerator, and video movies. In 1991 the hotel opened nine villas, each with a large bedroom, a living room, a kitchen, and a wide terrace.

Dining/Entertainment: The feeling is a bit like a private compound, whose social center is an open-air bar and poolside restaurant, La Toque Lyonnaise (see "Where to Dine," below). In addition, guests and others can also patronize La Lagon Bleu, serving barbecue including both fish and meat. Many dishes taste of Provence. Reservations aren't accepted at this one.

Facilities: Freshwater pool, in the center of which is a verdant island.

François Plantation

Colombier, 97133 St. Barthélemy, F.W.I. ☎ **590/27-78-82,** or 800/932-3222 in the U.S. Fax 27-61-26. 12 bungalows. A/C MINIBAR TV TEL. Winter, $315–$360 bungalow for one; $350–$400 bungalow for two. Off-season, $180–$216 bungalow for one; $200–$240 bungalow for two. (Rates include American breakfast and rental car.) AE, MC, V. Free parking. Closed Aug 15–Oct 20.

This complex 2 miles northwest of Gustavia, a 10-minute ride from the airport, re-creates the plantation era. Set inland in a tropical garden (not on the beach) are 12 bungalows, each decorated in an elegant West Indian style, with reproduction antique four-poster beds. Each has a ceiling fan and safe. Eight of the units open onto sea views, while others front a garden vista. The owners are Françoise and François (you heard right) Beret, longtime residents of St. Barts.

Dining/Entertainment: The hotel has an exceptional restaurant (see "Where to Dine," below).

Services: Laundry.

Facilities: Swimming pool with view.

MODERATE

Castelets

Morne Lurin (B.P. 60), 97133 St. Barthélemy, F.W.I. ☎ **590/27-61-73,** or 800/223-1108 in the U.S. Fax 27-85-27. 6 rms, 2 two-bedroom villas. $120–$295 single or double; $420 villa for two; $650 villa for four. (Rates include continental breakfast.) AE, MC, V. Free parking. Closed Sept–Oct.

This is a discreet, well-entrenched bastion of French culture which reopened in 1993 after a misguided two-year sojourn (and a name change) under an outside management. Reborn under the French-speaking team which helped create it originally, Castelets occupies a hillside perch dotted with trees about three-quarters of a steeply inclined mile from Gustavia. Built of roughly textured stone and thick-timbered verandas in the Provençal style, it contains only eight discreet and private accommodations. Two of the bedrooms are in the hotel's headquarters. Villas contain kitchens and indoor-outdoor terraces; all units have views over the land and sea.

Dining/Entertainment: Even if you don't stay here, you might visit for dinner, as the in-house restaurant is candlelit, elegant, and romantic. Only dinner is served, at two seatings (7 and 9pm daily), but only when the hotel is open (see above). Appetizers cost 50 to 100 F ($9.50 to $19); main courses run 140 to 250 F ($26.60 to $47.50). Reservations are important.

Facilities: Small swimming pool; Grand Saline and Gouverneur beaches are a short hike away.

Ⓢ Le Village Saint-Jean

Baie de Saint-Jean (B.P. 623), 97098 St. Barthélemy CEDEX, F.W.I. ☎ **590/27-61-39,** or 800/633-7411 in the U.S. Fax 27-77-96. 6 rms. 20 cottages. 1 Jacuzzi suite. A/C TEL. Winter, $135 single or double; $165–$399 cottage or suite. Off-season, $85 single or double; $110–$190 cottage or suite. (Rates include continental breakfast in rooms but not in cottages.) AE, MC, V. Free parking.

Over the years, this cottage colony hideaway1 mile from the airport in the direction of St-Jean, has attracted a distinguished clientele, including food critic Craig Claiborne. Lying in the most central part of St. Barts, it offers, in my opinion, the best value on this high-priced resort island. Its cottages, built of stone and wood, contain kitchens, sun decks or gardens, as well as terrace living rooms, plus balconies and ceiling fans. Although the rate structure is modest compared to other places on the island, don't be surprised to see a movie star or a media headliner here; after all, some of them like to save money too.

The complex has an excellent restaurant and bar, Le Patio, with a terrace. The hotel's swimming pool has two decks overlooking the bay, cascading water, and a Jacuzzi. It's also a two-minute walk down to the beach. Founded in the early 1960s, this was the first inn of its kind on St. Barts, and it is still administered by the Charneau family. You will probably be welcomed by the gracious and charming (also English-speaking) Catherine.

Tropical Hôtel

St-Jean (B.P. 147), 97095 St. Barthélemy, F.W.I. ☎ **590/27-64-87.** Fax 27-81-74. 20 rms. A/C TV TEL. Winter, $170–$230 single; $200–$310 double. Off-season, $105 single; $165 double. Minimum stay four days in high season, one week over the Christmas holidays. (Rates include continental breakfast.) AE, MC, V. Free parking.

This little picture-postcard inn, trimmed in gingerbread, offers an intimate and restful atmosphere. It's perched on a hillside about 50 yards above St. Jean Beach (a mile from the airport and a mile and a half from Gustavia). The hotel (almost a bungalow inn) rents rooms with private shower, king-size bed, tile floor, and a refrigerator to cool your tropical drinks. Nine come with a sea view and balcony, and 11 contain a porch opening onto a garden that is so lush it looks like a miniature jungle.

There's a hospitality center, where guests read, listen to music, or order drinks at a paneled, inviting bar ringed with antiques. The freshwater swimming pool is small, but water sports are available on the beach. Breakfast is served at the poolside terrace, and light meals are served throughout the day at the snack bar.

BUDGET

Hôtel Normandie

L'Orient, 97133 St. Barthélemy, F.W.I. ☎ **590/27-61-66.** Fax 27-98-83. 8 rms. 330–430 F ($62.70–$81.70) single or double. Breakfast 42 F ($8) extra. No credit cards. Free parking.

This is what the French call an *auberge antillaise.* Set inland a good haul from the beach, 3 miles east of the airport, it offers bedrooms of casual comfort (some are air-conditioned and others contain ceiling fans). The least expensive rooms are next to the highway without air conditioning, and the most expensive units are those next to the swimming pool with air conditioning. A modest, family-owned hotel, it presents a row of louvered shutters to the street outside. A swimming pool with a terrace is found in the rear. It's one of the least expensive places to stay on St. Barts.

WHERE TO DINE
IN GUSTAVIA
Expensive
Au Port

Rue Sadi-Carnot. ☎ **590/27-62-36.** Reservations recommended, especially for veranda tables. Appetizers 65–135 F ($12.40–$25.70); main courses 95–195 F ($18.10–$37.10); menu Créole 200 F ($38). AE, MC, V. Dinner only, daily 6:30–10pm. Closed Sept–Oct. FRENCH/CREOLE.

From the outside, this looks like a consciously raffish harborfront building, with a narrow veranda jutting above the bumpy road outside. You climb a steep and tiled flight of stairs to reach its second-floor dining room, in the center of town at the waterfront, where a decor of neocolonial charm acts as the appropriate foil for the satisfying classic cuisine. Artifacts decorating the establishment include different sailboat maquettes and antiquities. You might begin with a fish terrine with a herb sauce, crab and conch ravioli, or perhaps a gizzard and duck-liver salad with passion sauce. The partners, Alain Bunel and Fred Diab, prepare excellent fish and meat dishes, including jumbo prawn colombo served with spicy rice and chicken leg with morels. They also prepare duck filet with wine sauce.

La Langouste

Rue Bord-de-la-Mer. ☎ **590/27-69-47.** Reservations required. Appetizers 35–50 F ($6.70–$9.50); main courses 50–180 F ($9.50–$34.20). MC, V. Lunch daily noon–2pm; dinner daily 7–10pm. CREOLE/FRENCH.

La Langouste used to be known as "Annie's." Annie, of the island family of Ange, is still around, but she prefers to name her place in honor of the clawless Caribbean lobster instead of herself. In a century-old building erected during the Swedish domain over the island, her zesty little restaurant is near the Gendarmerie. You get down-to-earth Créole cookery here, and that means stuffed land crabs, conch ragoût, cod fritters (called accra de morue), the namesake langouste, always-fresh fish, and curried chicken. Every Friday fresh red snapper is served. Lunches are light, but dinner is a Créole delight.

Le Clocher

Rue Courbet. ☎ **590/27-96-96.** Reservations recommended. Appetizers 75–120 F ($14.30–$22.80); main courses 100–150 F ($19–$28.50). MC, V. Dinner only, daily 7–10pm. Closed Sept. FRENCH.

This is a popular newcomer to an island whose culinary tastes seem to grow less formal every year. It occupies a rectangular green-and-white clapboard building high on a residential hillside above Gustavia's coastal road. Large windows look to the harbor below. The menu items are straightforward and somewhat standardized, and include foie gras, steaks, and filets of such fish as snapper and daurade, sometimes prepared in a style that the kitchen refers to as "Tahitian."

✪ Le Sapotillier

Rue Sadi-Carnot. ☎ **590/27-60-28.** Reservations required. Appetizers 65–125 F ($12.40–$23.80); main courses 150–200 F ($28.50–$38); fixed-price meals 230–290 F ($43.70–$55.10). MC, V. Dinner only, daily 6:30–11pm. Closed May to mid-Oct, and Sun off-season. FRENCH/SEAFOOD.

This West Indian house is the domain of Austrian-born Adam Rajner, who runs one of the finest restaurants in Gustavia. Set on the innermost embankment of the capital's harbor, Le Sapotillier is at the top of the list for every visiting gourmet. Named after a gnarled and wind-blown sapodilla tree in the courtyard, the restaurant offers diners a choice of seating locations. They can enjoy the candlelit patio or select a table in the old wood-sided Antillean bungalow that was transported to the site from the outlying village of Corossol on the shoulders of local laborers.

Mr. Rajner, in the best tradition of European innkeeping, pays strict attention to the quality and presentation of his food. Your meal might begin with a hot goat-cheese salad with a hazelnut-oil dressing or homemade duck-liver pâté, perhaps homemade fish soup. Among the more interesting meat dishes, a whole young pigeon on spinach is served, as is a filet of young lamb with ratatouille. A couscous is made with large spicy shrimp, or you might order steamed stingray with a horse-radish sauce. A casserole of sea scallops and prawns is flavored with balsamic vinegar and served with Créole sauce.

Moderate

🟊 Eddy's Ghetto

Rue du Général-de-Gaulle. Reservations not required. Appetizers $6.50–$8; main courses $16–$20. No credit cards. Dinner only, Mon–Sat 7–10pm. FRENCH/CREOLE.

Priding itself on its role as the island's most unpretentious restaurant, whose only glamour comes from its simple white walls and open access to the Caribbean breezes, Eddy's Ghetto is in a small Antillean house near the harborfront. Meals, served at simple wooden tables, might include crab salad, ragoût of beef, and grilled filets of fish and chicken. Available wines include an array of passably good French vintages, which seem to go well with an atmosphere best described as laidback and French. The owner is Eddy Stakelborough, who sells T-shirts from behind the establishment's bar.

L'Escale

La Pointe. ☎ **590/27-81-06.** Reservations required in high season. Appetizers 65–90 F ($12.40–$17.10); main courses 80–175 F ($15.20–$33.30). MC, V. Dinner only, daily 6:30pm–midnight. Closed Sept 15–Oct 15. FRENCH/ITALIAN.

Some villa owners cite L'Escale as their favorite restaurant on the island. On the wharf, where yachts tie up, it stands alongside another popular spot, Le Marine Café. Frankly, you can dine lightly and inexpensively here or spend a lot of money, depending on your menu selections and appetite. Typical fare might include one of their excellent salads, pizzas, or pasta dishes. Or at night, sitting on the restaurant's al fresco terrace, you can order one of their grilled-meat specialties or fresh fish "according to arrival."

ANSE DES CAYES

✪ Restaurant Ballahou

In the Hôtel Manapany Cottages, Anse des Cayes. ☎ **590/27-66-55.** Reservations required for non–hotel guests. Appetizers 135–195 F ($25.70–$37.10); main courses 160–275 F ($30.40–$52.30). AE, DC, MC, V. Dinner only, daily 7:30–9:30pm. Closed Apr 15–Nov 15. FRENCH/SEAFOOD.

Named after a small variety of swordfish, this is one of the best and most elegant restaurants on the island, with a sun-flooded pink-and-white interior, a five-minute drive north of the airport. To enter, you pass beneath a portal dripping in fanciful Caribbean gingerbread. Dining is under a high ceiling whose rafters curve around the perimeter of an oval swimming pool. Elaborate dinners are served by candlelight inside and are accompanied by live music. The specialties might include bisque of lobster, braised sweetbreads, duck with a sweet orange sauce, and kidneys cooked with Armagnac. There is a piano bar.

IN THE ST-JEAN BEACH AREA

Chez Francine
Plage de St-Jean. ☎ **590/27-60-49.** Reservations recommended. Appetizers 55–65 F ($10.50–$12.40); main courses 85–150 F ($16.20–$28.50); fixed-price meal 180–280 F ($34.20–$53.20). MC, V. Lunch daily 11:30am–3:30pm; dinner Tues–Sun 6–11pm. FRENCH/CREOLE.

Chez Francine, 1 mile east of the airport, maintains a delightfully informal atmosphere as exemplified by the owners, Alain and Martine Van Dan Hout who have run the place for more than 15 years. People from all over the island come here. The place is really little more than a boardwalk terrace built on top of the sand a few feet from the beach. Its overhead awnings and blackboard menu encourage an attire of bathing suits, or less. Typical meals, often preceded by a frothy piña colada, might include their famous sautéed lobster, shark sushi, grilled chicken or fish, a selection of wine or beer, and a choice of homemade tortes and cakes. The establishment is a busy focal point of beach life during the day.

⑤ Le Patio
Village St-Jean. ☎ **590/27-70-67.** Reservations required. Appetizers 52–85 F ($9.90–$16.20); main courses 52–138 F ($9.90–$26.20). MC, V. Dinner only, Thurs–Tues 6:30–10pm. Closed June and Sept. ITALIAN.

Le Patio, 1 mile from the airport in the direction of St-Jean, enjoys a deserved reputation for offering some of the best food values on the island. A northern Italian cuisine, along with pizza and some French dishes, are featured at this restaurant, which enjoys a panoramic view. For appetizers, both hot and cold antipasti are featured, along with carpaccio made from either beef or salmon. A selection of homemade pasta dishes include the chef's selection of the day. Fish is often grilled, perhaps red snapper, and a wide selection of pizza is also offered. The restaurant features "selections of the week," which are changed every seven days or so but might include such special dishes as grilled local fish in a sauce chien (hot) or escalope parmigiana.

Le Pelican
Plage de St-Jean. ☎ **590/27-64-64.** Reservations recommended, especially for dinner. Appetizers 45–115 F ($8.60–$21.90); main courses 90–500 F ($17.10–$95). AE, MC, V. Lunch daily 11:30am–3pm; dinner Mon–Sat 6:30–10pm. CREOLE/FRENCH.

The ambience and cuisine differ so much here from day to night that you'd almost think you were in two different restaurants. Lunch is served outdoors in the shade of an elongated parasol, within earshot of the nearby surf. While sipping French wine in the Antillean sunshine, you can enjoy fish soup, lobster bisque, and a generously portioned Créole platter laden with accras, shellfish, blood pudding, and grilled fish. Dinners are more elaborate, with lobster salad, green-pepper steak, grilled chicken with mustard, and, one of the most popular items, grilled catch of the day. Cajun-style bouillabaisse is the chef's specialty. The setting, 1 mile east of the airport, incorporates three high-ceilinged dining rooms with pastel colors, a view of the sea, and candlelight. Live music is featured in the piano bar until 1am, where guests dance after dining.

AT MORNE LURIN

Santa Fe Restaurant

Morne Lurin. ☎ **590/27-61-04.** Reservations not required. Appetizers $2.50–$4.50; main courses $11–$22. No credit cards. Lunch Mon–Tues and Thurs–Sat noon–2pm; dinner Thurs–Tues 5–10pm. AMERICAN.

Set inland from the sea, atop one of the highest elevations on the island, this burger house and sports bar has carved out a formidable niche for itself with the island's English-speaking clientele. Located about a mile east of Gustavia, it features wide-screen TVs which show such annual events as the New Year's Day Parade and the American Superbowl to as many as 450 viewers. You can take in the view of the surrounding landscapes for free, although most clients stop for one of the well-recommended hamburger, steak, shrimp, or barbecued chicken dishes. Most checks are under $15, unless you have a lot to drink. Open since 1966, this restaurant is now run by the second generation of the same family, Mary Lynn, along with her husband, Rodney Bryan.

COLOMBIER

✪ François Plantation Restaurant

Colombier. ☎ **590/27-78-82.** Reservations required. Appetizers 110–160 F ($20.90–$30.40); main courses 190–300 F ($36.10–$57). AE, MC, V. Dinner only, daily 6:30–10pm. Closed Aug 15–Oct 20. FRENCH.

Françoise and François Beret take justifiable pride in their traditional cuisine. Their dining room, part of the old plantation that stood here 2 miles northwest of Gustavia, is attractively decorated and inviting. The wine, the service, and the quality of ingredients used in the dishes presented are top-notch. The chef might tempt you with a traditional fish soup or one of the salads, and typical dishes might be a combination of Caribbean fish cooked in a bouillabaisse style, filet of red snapper with a St. Barts hot-pepper sauce, lasagne of sea trout, or duck "cakes" performed with plum honey and ginger.

ANSE DU GRAND CUL-DE-SAC

Bartolomeo

In the Hôtel Guanahani, Anse du Grand Cul-de-Sac. ☎ **590/27-66-60.** Reservations required, especially for non–hotel guests. Appetizers 80–150 F ($15.20–$28.50); main courses 250–400 F ($47.50–$76). AE, DC, MC, V. Dinner only, daily 7:30–9:30pm. Closed Sept–Oct. FRENCH/SEAFOOD.

This is the deluxe dining choice for one of the most exclusive and expensive hotels on the island. The menu selection changes frequently, but always includes a variety of gastronomic specialty dishes, interestingly spiced, sauced, and served. The restaurant, which is a blend of casual and elegant taste in both ambience and cuisine, also offers an outside terrace for drinks and dinner. There is also nightly piano entertainment.

GRANDE SALINE

Le Tamarin

Plage de Saline. ☎ **590/27-72-12.** Reservations required. Appetizers $4.20–$6.70; main courses 22–35 F ($10–$16). MC, V. Lunch daily 12:30–3pm; dinner Thurs–Sat 7–9:30pm. Closed dinner off-season. FRENCH/CREOLE.

The favored place in the sun is Le Tamarin, which picks up the beach traffic—many in revealing bikinis—from the nearby Plage de Saline. It's isolated amid rocky hills and forests east of Gustavia, in a low-slung cottage whose eaves are lined with gingerbread. Inside, a teak-and-bamboo motif prevails. If you have to wait, you can order an apéritif in one of the hammocks stretched under a tamarind tree (hence the name of the restaurant). Fresh fish is invariably featured, but meat dishes and poultry also are cooked well. Service can be hectic, but if you're in a rush you shouldn't be here. It's for a lazy afternoon on the beach, and also serves dinner a few nights a week in season.

GRAND CUL-DE-SAC

Club Lafayette

Grand Cul-de-Sac. ☎ **590/27-62-51.** Reservations required for lunch. Appetizers 85–225 F ($16.20–$42.80); main courses 175–300 F ($33.30–$57). AE, MC, V. Lunch only, daily noon–4pm. Closed May–Nov. FRENCH/CREOLE.

Lunching here, at a cove on the eastern end of the island, east of Marigot, is like taking a meal at your own private beach club. After a dip in the ocean or pool, you can order a *planteur* in the shade of a sea grape, and later proceed to lunch itself: a roquefort-and-walnut salad, charcoaled langouste, grilled fresh fish, or breast of duck. In other words, this is no hamburger fast-food beach joint. Afterward, have a refreshing citrus-flavored sherbet. For dinner, you might begin with a warm goat-cheese salad, then follow with fish filet in a sorrel sauce.

✪ La Toque Lyonnaise

In El Sereno Beach Hôtel ☎ **590/27-64-80.** Reservations recommended. Appetizers 75–160 F ($14.30–$30.40); main courses 155–195 F ($29.50–$37.10); fixed-price dinner 250–350 F ($47.50–$66.50). AE, MC, V. Lunch daily noon–2:30pm; dinner daily 7–10pm. Closed June–Oct. FRENCH.

Four miles east of Gustavia, one of the premier restaurants on the island fronts a swimming pool and is partially open to the sky. Most guests come here for the *menu lyonnais*, reflecting the culinary background of Christine and Marc Llepez, the owners. They invite chefs from Lyon, the gastronomic capital of France, to visit St. Barts. The current chef is Michel Fredric, who trained at some of France's leading three-star restaurants, including Paul Bocuse in Lyon. His menu features seafood, such as marinated salmon in ginger cream, grilled lobster flavored with vanilla beans, and crayfish in pastry with a pistou sauce. The wine list is among the finest on the island. The restaurant is open to sea breezes and contained in an angular modern pavilion decorated in a tropical style with lattices.

✪ Restaurant Flamboyant

Grand Cul-de-Sac. ☎ **590/27-75-65.** Reservations required. Fixed-price dinner 210 F ($39.90). MC, V. Dinner only, Tues–Sun 7–9:30pm. Closed Sept. FRENCH/CREOLE.

On the western edge of the island, directly east of Marigot, this place is on the veranda level of the isolated island home of Albert Balayn, a chef who studied cuisine in France before returning to his native island. The preferred seating is on a panoramic terrace, where the hillside location contributes to a view over fields, forest, and sea. You might begin with eggplant pâté or a stuffed christophine, then follow with small lobster casserole or breast of duck in a cider sauce. Dessert might include a homemade chocolate mousse or coconut flan.

VITET

ⓢ Hostellerie des Trois Forces

Vitet. ☎ **590/27-61-25.** Reservations required. Appetizers 50–120 F ($9.50–$22.80); main courses 45–200 F ($8.60–$38). AE, MC, V. Lunch Mon–Sat noon–3pm; dinner Mon–Sat 7–9:45pm. FRENCH/CREOLE/VEGETARIAN.

This place, 2 miles east of the airport, has a resident astrologer, a French provincial decor, well-scrubbed surfaces, and food with a genuine allure. The food is well prepared and beautifully served, and for dessert you get an astrological forecast thrown in. The heart and soul of the place is Hubert de la Motte, who arrived from Brittany with his wife and sister to create a hotel where happiness, good food, comfort, and conversation are a way of life. Even if you don't stay here, you might want to drive out for a meal. Evening meals are more formal and might include fish pâté, beef shish kebab with curry sauce, grilled fresh lobster, veal kidneys flambé with cognac, a cassolette of snails, and such succulent desserts as crêpes Suzette flambé. "Each dish takes time," in the words of the owner, because it's prepared fresh. Count on a leisurely meal.

PUBLIC

Maya's

Public. ☎ **590/27-75-73.** Reservations required. Appetizers 45–80 F ($8.60–$15.20); main courses 145–165 F ($27.60–$31.40). AE, MC, V. Dinner only, Mon–Sat 6–11pm. Closed June to mid-Oct. CREOLE.

This is the kind of place you might find on Martinique—because that's where its French-Créole chef, Maya Veuzelin-Gurley, is from. You might begin with the salad of tomatoes, arugula, and endive, then follow with grilled fish in sauce chien (hot) or a grilled filet of beef. She also prepares what she calls "sailor's chicken" with soya sauce and coconut milk. For dessert, try the coconut tart. Maya's is directly west of Gustavia.

SPORTS & OUTDOOR ACTIVITIES

BEACHES   There are 14 white sand beaches on St. Barts. Few are ever crowded, even in winter, and all are public and free. Nudism is prohibited, but topless is quite common. The most famous beach is **St-Jean,** which is actually two beaches divided by the Eden Rock promontory. It offers water sports, beach restaurants such as Chez Francine, and a few hotels, as well as some shady areas. **Flamands,** to the west, is a very wide beach with a few small hotels and some areas shaded by lantana palms. For beaches with hotels, restaurants, and water sports, **Grand Cul-de-Sac,** on the northeast shore, fits the bill. This is a narrow beach protected by a reef.

Gouvenor, a beach on the south, can be reached by driving through Gustavia and up to Lurin. Turn at the Santa Fe Bar Restaurant (see "Where to Dine," above) and head down a narrow road. The beach is gorgeous, but wear lots of sunscreen as there is no shade. **Saline,** to the east of Gouvenor, is reached by driving up the road from the commercial center in St-Jean; a short walk over the sand dune and you're there. Like Gouvenor, Saline offers some waves, but again there is no shade. **Lorient,** on the north shore, is quiet and calm, with shady areas. **Marigot,** also on the north shore, is narrow but offers good swimming and snorkeling.

Colombier is a beach difficult to get to but well worth the effort. It can only be reached by boat or by taking a rugged goat path from Petite Anse past Flamands, a 30-minute walk. Shade and snorkeling are found there, and you can pack a lunch and spend the day.

FISHING   People who like fishing are fond of the waters around St. Barts. From March through July, they catch dolphin (the fish, not the mammal); in September, wahoo. Atlantic bonito, barracuda, and marlin also turn up with frequency. **Marine Service,** quai du Yacht-Club (☎ **590/27-70-34**), rents 29- to 37-foot cabin cruisers, which were created for big-game fishing, for 2,500 to 4,000 F ($475 to $760) for the boat. The rate is for four hours, with captain and first mate.

TENNIS   It's mainly for hotel guests. There's a court at the **St. Barths Beach Hotel,** Grand Cul-de-Sac (☎ **590/27-60-70**). One of the best courts is at the **Hôtel Manapany Cottages** (☎ **590/27-66-55**) (see "Where to Stay," above). Use of the court is free to residents both day and night. Nonresidents pay 100 F ($19) per hour during daylight, 150 F ($28.50) for nighttime illumination. It's also possible to play on the courts of the Hôtel Guanahani, at Grand Cul-de-Sac (☎ **590/27-66-60**) (see "Where to Stay," above).

WATERSKIING   Waterskiing is authorized from 9am to 1pm and again from 4:40pm to sundown. Because of the shape of the coastline, skiers must remain at least 80 yards from shore on the windward side of the island and 110 yards off on the leeward side.

Stéphan Jouany, one of the best waterskiers on St. Barts, takes out skiers of all levels of proficiency. Arrangements can be made through **Marine Service,** quai du Yacht-Club (☎ **590/27-70-34**) in Gustavia. The cost is about 210 F ($39.90) per half hour.

WATER SPORTS   **Marine Service,** quai du Yacht-Club (☎ **590/27-70-34**), is the most complete water-sports facility on the island. It operates from a one-story building set directly on the water at the edge of a marina, on the opposite side of the harbor from the more congested part of Gustavia. The outfit offers a series of dives. Programs include exploration for beginners, as well as for certified divers, night dives, PADI certification (within a week), and dives to the wreck of the *Non-stop,* a 210-foot yacht sunk during Hurricane Hugo. An *Aquascope* for 10 passengers is available for a one-hour trip among tropical fish and colorful flora to the wreck *Non-stop.* The rate is 160 F ($30.40) per person. One of the most interesting half-day trips goes to Colombier Beach or Fourchue Island, the best for snorkeling (see below). Trips are daily from 9am to 12:30pm and 1 to 5pm.

Ile Fourchue (Forked Island) is a popular rendezvous point for boats. Named for its configuration, with rocky peaks separated by valleys, Ile Fourchue is horseshoe-shaped, with a protected anchorage. Its only permanent residents are goats, but a few ruins bear witness to the fact that it was once the home of a Breton who lived a Robinson Crusoe–style life here for many years. Another attraction is Colombier Beach (see "Beaches," above). A full day's excursion to both Ile Fourchue and Colombier costs 480 F ($91.20) per person, with lunch included. A half-day excursion to Colombier costs 290 F ($55.10) per person, including a French picnic. Each cruise features an open bar.

WINDSURFING   Windsurfing is one of the most popular sports practiced on St. Barts. Try **St. Barth Wind School,** at the Tom Beach Hotel on Pelican Beach near Chez Francine (☎ **590/27-71-22**). It's open daily from 9am to 5pm.

Windsurfing generally costs 100 to 120 F ($19 to $22.80) per hour. Professional instructors are on hand.

SHOPPING

You don't pay any duty on St. Barts—everything is out-of-bond—so it's a good place to buy liquor and French perfumes, at some of the lowest prices in the Caribbean. Perfume, for example, is cheaper on St. Barts than it is in France itself. Champagne is cheaper than in Epernay, France. St. Barts is the only completely free-trading port in the world, with the exception of French St. Martin and Dutch St. Maarten. Only trouble is, selections are limited. However, you'll find good buys in sportswear, crystal, porcelain, watches, and other luxuries.

If you're in the market for some island crafts, try to find those convertible-brim, fine straw hats St. Bartians like to wear. *Vogue* once featured this high-crown headwear in its fashion pages. They also have some interesting block-printed resort clothes in cotton.

Shopping hours are usually Monday through Friday from 8:30am to noon and from 2 to 5pm, and on Saturday from 8:30am to noon.

La Cave du Port Franc
Quai de la République, Gustavia. ☎ **590/27-86-29.**

For wine devotees, there are two good choices, including La Cave in Marigot (☎ **590/27-63-21**), and the more centrally located one above. Both carry fine French vintages, which are stored in temperature-controlled "cellars."

La Fonda Hermès
Rue de la République, Gustavia. ☎ **590/27-66-15.**

This is the only outlet in the Caribbean of the famous Parisian haberdasher. It stands across the street from the port. Be warned, you'll pay dearly for some French allure.

Little Switzerland
Rue de la France, Gustavia. ☎ **590/27-64-66.**

Behind glass cases is an array of untaxed crystal, china, jewelry, watches, and luxurious merchandise.

Loulou's Marine
Rue de la France, Gustavia. ☎ **590/27-62-74.**

Some of its merchandise could come from any general store in France and some of it is so specialized that only a yacht owner could appreciate it. This is possibly the most gregarious rendezvous point in town, and amid pulleys, coils of rope, and folded sailcloth, you'll find clothing, luggage, shirts, shoes, and beachwear.

Samson & Co.
Quai de la République, Gustavia. ☎ **590/27-60-46.**

Samson & Co. stocks art from the Philippines and Bali and sells batiks and hand-painted clothing for both men and women.

The Shell Shop
Rue du Général-de-Gaulle, Gustavia.

This small shop offers shells, coral, and jewelry made on St. Barts. Shells and coral from all over the world, local handcrafts and block printing, free paperbacks, and U.S. sports information are also available here.

Smoke and Booze

Rue du Général-de-Gaulle, Gustavia. ☎ **590/27-60-24.**

This is the place to go for wine, liquor, liqueurs, and tobacco, as well as for toys and souvenirs. They'll package your beverage purchases for you to take home.

ST. BARTS AFTER DARK

Most guests consider a French Créole dinner under the stars near the sea enough of a nocturnal adventure. After that, there isn't a lot of excitement.

In Gustavia, the most popular gathering place is **Le Select,** rue de la France (☎ **590/27-86-87**), apparently named after its more famous granddaddy in the Montparnasse section of Paris. It's utterly simple, and a game of dominoes might be under way as you walk in. In the open-air café garden, near the port, tables are placed outside on the gravel. The outdoor grill promises a "cheeseburger in Paradise." You never know who might show up here, perhaps Mick Jagger, perhaps Jimmy Buffett. Beer begins at 12 F ($2.30), and the place is open Monday through Saturday from 10am to 11pm. The locals like it a lot, and outsiders are welcomed but not necessarily embraced until they get to know you a bit. If you want to spread a rumor and have it travel fast across the island, start it here.

The British Windwards

13

These windward islands lie in the direct path of the trade winds, which swoop down from the northeast. British affiliated (now independent), they are Gallic in manner, Caribbean in outlook.

French habits can be traced back to early Gallic invaders, as the islands changed hands many times before coming into Britain's orbit. On such islands as St. Lucia, and especially Dominica, you'll hear a Créole patois. English, however, is also spoken.

The British Windwards are made up of four main islands—St. Lucia, St. Vincent, Grenada, and Dominica—along with a scattering of isles or spits of land known as the Grenadines. Truly far-out islands, the Grenadines are a chain stretching from St. Vincent to Grenada. Some people group Barbados and Trinidad and Tobago in the British Windwards, but I have preferred to treat these independent island nations separately in the following chapters.

Topped by mountains and bursting with greenery, the British Windwards in this chapter are still far enough off the mainline tourist circuit to make a visit to them something of an adventure. At some of the more remote oases, you'll have the sand crabs, iguanas, and sea birds to enjoy all by yourself.

For the most part, the islands are small and volcanic in origin. Most of the inhabitants used to live on their crops. There's little or no industry, except for tourism.

1 Dominica

It has been called "the most original island in the Caribbean." What that means is that the meager beaches aren't worth the effort, but natural attractions and river swimming form the allure. What is not often said is that naturalists who make the effort to visit Dominica get to experience not only the feeling of Caribbean nature grown wild but they will also sample the small island rural life that has largely disappeared on the more developed islands. Dominica is, after all, one of the poorest and least developed islands in the Caribbean, where many of its citizens make a subsistence living from fishing or living off the land.

Hiking and mountain climbing are other reasons to visit Dominica, and the flora is extremely lush—and often rare. Covered by a dense tropical rain forest that blankets its mountain slopes, including cloud-wreathed Morne Diablotin at 4,747 feet, it has vegetation unique in the West Indies.

Untamed, unspoiled Dominica (pronounced Dom-in-*ee*-ka, and not to be confused with the Spanish-speaking Dominican Republic) is known for its clear rivers and waterfalls, its hot springs and boiling lakes. According to myth, it has 365 "rivers," one for each day of the year. This is the most rugged of Caribbean islands.

Dominica, with a population of 71,000, lies in the eastern Caribbean, between Guadeloupe to the north and Martinique to the south. English is the official language, but a French patois is widely spoken. The Caribs, the indigenous people of the Caribbean, live as a community on the northeast of the island. The art and craft of traditional basketry is still practiced and is unique to today's Carib community, whose numbers have dwindled to 3,000.

The mountainous island is 29 miles long and 16 miles wide, with a total land area of 290 square miles, many of which have never been seen by explorers other than, presumably, the Caribs.

Because of the pristine coral reefs, dramatic dropoffs, and shipwrecks found in the crystal-clear waters with visibility of 100 feet plus, scuba diving is becoming increasingly popular, particularly off the west coast, site of Dominica's two dive operations.

Rainfall varies from 50 inches along the dry west coast to as much as 350 inches in the tropical rain forests of the mountainous interior, where downpours are not uncommon.

Clothing is casual, including light summer wear for most of the year. However, take along walking shoes for those trips into the mountains and a sweater for cooler evenings. Bikinis and swimwear should not be worn in the streets of the capital city, Roseau, or in the villages.

National Day celebrations on November 3 commemorate Columbus's discovery in 1493 and independence in 1978. Cultural celebrations of Dominica's traditional dance, music, song, and story telling begin in mid-October and continue to Community Day, November 4, when people from different communities undertake community-based projects.

To sum up, come to Dominica for the beauties of nature more than *la dolce vita*.

ORIENTATION
GETTING THERE

BY PLANE   There are two airports on Dominica, neither of which is large enough to handle a jetliner; therefore, there are no direct flights from North America. The **Melville Hall Airport** is on the northeastern coast of the island, almost diagonally across the island from the capital, Roseau, on the southwestern coast. Should you land at Melville Hall, there's a 1 1/2-hour taxi ride into Roseau, a tour across the island through the forest and coastal villages. The fare from Melville Hall to Roseau is $17 per person, and drivers have the right to gather up at least four passengers in their cabs. By private taxi the cost could be $50.

The newer **Canefield Airport** is about a 15-minute taxi ride to the north of Roseau. The 2,000-foot airstrip accommodates smaller planes than those that can land at Melville Hall. From here, the typical taxi fare into town is $8.

For many North Americans, the easiest way to reach Dominica is to take a flight to Antigua (see "Getting There" in Section 1 of Chapter 9). From there, you can

Dominica

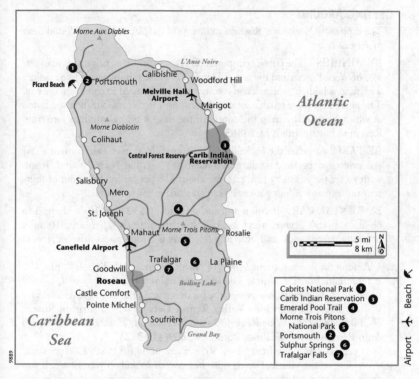

Morne Aux Diables

L'Anse Noire

Calibishie

Woodford Hill

Picard Beach

Portsmouth

Melville Hall
Airport

Marigot

**Atlantic
Ocean**

Morne Diablotin

Colihaut

Central Forest Reserve

Carib Indian
Reservation

Salisbury

Mero

St. Joseph

Mahaut

Morne Trois Pitons

Rosalie

Canefield Airport

Trafalgar

La Plaine

Goodwill

Roseau

Boiling Lake

Castle Comfort

Pointe Michel

Soufrière

**Caribbean
Sea**

Grand Bay

0   5 mi
         8 km

N

Cabrits National Park ❶
Carib Indian Reservation ❸
Emerald Pool Trail ❹
Morne Trois Pitons
   National Park ❺
Portsmouth ❷
Sulphur Springs ❻
Trafalgar Falls ❼

Beach ✖   Airport ✈

9889

take one of the five daily **LIAT** (☎ **809/462-0700**) flights to Dominica. Another possibility would be to fly via St. Maarten. From there, LIAT offers one nonstop flight daily, and two other daily flights with intermediary stops.

It's also possible to fly to Guadeloupe (see "Getting There" in Section 2 of Chapter 12). Once on Guadeloupe, you can make a connection to Dominica on **Air Guadeloupe** (☎ **809/449-1060**). This airline has two flights a day to Dominica except on Sunday when there is no morning flight (flight time: 30 minutes). If you're in Fort-de-France on Martinique, you can take a LIAT flight to Dominica. Many experienced Dominica visitors flying in from neighboring islands ultimately resort to chartering a small plane from such organizations as **Mustique Airways** (☎ **809/458-4380**) or **Air Anguilla** (☎ **809/497-2643**), either of which would arrange a special expedition to Dominica from almost anywhere in the central or southern Caribbean.

BY BOAT   The **Caribbean Express,** sailing from the French West Indies (see Chapter 12), runs between Guadeloupe in the north to Martinique in the south, and Dominica is a port of call along the way. Call **596/60-12-38** for exact schedules. Departures are twice a week.

In addition, *Madikera,* a car ferry, is a competitive service, sailing to Roseau on Wednesday, Friday, Saturday, and Sunday. For information about schedules, contact Trois Pitons Travel, 5 Great Marlborough St. in Roseau (☎ **809/ 448-6977**).

GETTING AROUND

The capital of Dominica is **Roseau,** and many of the places to stay are found there or very close by.

BY MINIBUS The public transportation system consists of private minibus service between Roseau and the rest of Dominica. These minibuses are filled mainly with schoolchildren, workers, and country people who need to come into the city. Taxis may be a more reliable means of transport for visitors, but there are hotels at which buses call during the course of the day. A typical minibus fare from Roseau to Portsmouth is EC$8 ($3).

BY TAXI At either the Melville Hall or Canefield airport, you can rent a taxi and prices are regulated by the government (see "Getting There," above). If you want to see the island by taxi, rates are about $18 per car for each hour of touring, and as many as four passengers can go along at the same time.

BY RENTAL CAR If you rent a car, a fee of EC$30 ($11.10) is charged to obtain a driver's license, which is available at the airports. There are 310 miles of newly paved roads, and only in a few areas is a four-wheel-drive necessary. *Driving is on the left.*

Among the major car-rental firms of North America, only Budget Rent-a-Car is represented on Dominica. The island contains a handful of small, usually family-owned car-rental companies, the condition and price of whose vehicles vary widely. Their ranks include **Valley Rent-a-Car,** Goodwill Road in Roseau (☎ 809/448-3233); **Wide Range,** 79 Bath Rd., Roseau (☎ 809/448-2198); and **Auto Rentals,** Goodwill Road, Roseau (☎ 809/448-3425).

In general, rates range from $45 to $65 per day, or from $234 to $300 per week, depending on the vehicle. Drivers must be between 25 and 65 years of age. If you don't use a credit or charge card, a substantial cash deposit is required for rentals at any of them.

Most U.S.–based renters, however, opt to reserve their car in advance from the local representative of **Budget Rent-a-Car,** whose headquarters are near the island's major airport on the Main Highway, Canefield (☎ 809/449-2080). (For reservations and information before you leave, call toll free 800/527-0700.) Moderate discounts are sometimes available for clients who reserve 24 hours before the anticipated pickup. The establishment's least expensive car rents for $234 per week, with unlimited mileage, plus 5% tax. A car with automatic transmission and air conditioning rents for $318 per week. A seven-day advance notice is required to obtain these rates. A collision-damage waiver (CDW) costs $8 a day, yet you'll still be liable for up to the first $500 of damage to your car.

BY SIGHTSEEING TOUR **Dominica Tours,** in the Anchorage Hotel, Castle Comfort (☎ 809/448-2638), offers some of the best tours on the island, including hiking, birdwatching, and photo safaris. The most popular tour is to Boiling Lake. Other favorite tours are to the Carib Reservation and to Emerald Pool, a grotto in the heart of the rain forest. A two-hour tour to the Sulphur Springs and a visit to the Botanical Gardens is also offered. I also recommend a combined tour of Trafalgar Triple Waterfalls, Sulphur Springs (via the Morne and Botanical Gardens), and Freshwater Lake, including a picnic lunch and rum punch. Tour prices range from $30 to $50, the latter for the more extensive tour taking in the rain forest and the Carib Reservation.

FAST FACTS: Dominica

Area Code To call Dominica from the United States, dial area code 809 and then the seven-digit local number. For information on calling Dominica from other islands in the same area code and on dialing local numbers when on the island, see "Telecommunications," below.

Banking Hours Banks are open Monday through Thursday from 8am to 3pm and on Friday from 8am to 5pm.

Currency Dominica uses the **Eastern Caribbean dollar (EC$),** worth about 37¢ in U.S. currency. Prices in this section are given in U.S. dollars unless otherwise indicated.

Customs Dominica is lenient, allowing you personal and household effects, plus 200 cigarettes, 50 cigars, and 40 ounces of liquor or wine per person.

Documents To enter, U.S. and Canadian citizens must have proof of citizenship, such as a passport, or a voter registration card or birth certificate along with a photo ID. In addition, an ongoing or return ticket must be shown. British visitors should have a valid passport.

Drugstores Try Jolly's Pharmacy, 33 King George St., Roseau (☎ **809/ 448-3388**).

Electricity The electricity is 220–240 volts A.C., 50 cycles, so both adapters and transformers are necessary for U.S.–made appliances. It's advisable to take a flashlight with you to Dominica, in case of power outages.

Emergencies Call the police, report a fire, or summon an ambulance by dialing **999.**

Holidays These include January 1 (New Year's Day), Carnival (Monday and Tuesday before Ash Wednesday), Good Friday, Easter Monday, May 1 (May Day), June 5 (Whit Monday), August Monday (first Monday in August), November 3 (Independence Celebrations), November 4 (Community Service Day), December 25 (Christmas), and December 26 (Boxing Day).

Hospitals The island hospital is Princess Margaret Hospital, Federation Drive, Goodwill (☎ **448-2231**). However, those with serious medical complications may want to forgo a visit to Dominica, as island medical facilities are often inadequate.

Information The **Dominica Tourist Information Office** is on the Old Market Plaza, Roseau, with administrative offices at the National Development Corporation offices, Valley Road (☎ **809/448-2186**); it's open on Monday from 8am to 5pm, and Tuesday through Friday from 8am to 4pm. Also, there are information bureaus at Melville Hall Airport (☎ **809/445-7051**) and Canefield Airport (☎ **809/449-1242**). Before you go, contact the **Caribbean Tourism Association,** 20 E. 46th St., New York, NY 10017 (☎ **212/682-0435**). In Canada, information is available at the OECS Mission in Canada, Suite 1050, 112 Kent St., Ottawa, ON K1P 5P2 (☎ **613/236-8952**), and in England at the Caribbean Tourism Organization, Vigilant House, 120 Wilton Rd., London SW1V 1JZ (☎ **0171/233-8382**).

Language English is the official language. Locals often speak a Créole-French patois.

Safety   Although crime is rare here, it would be wise to safeguard your valuables. Never leave them unattended on the beach or left alone in a locked car.

Taxes   A 5% government room tax is added to every hotel accommodation bill, plus a 3% tax on alcoholic drinks and food items. Anyone who remains on Dominica for more than 24 hours must pay an $8 departure tax.

Telecommunications   Dominica maintains phone, telegraph, teletype, Telex, and telefax connections with the rest of the world. International direct dialing (IDD) is available, as well as U.S. direct service through AT&T. To call Dominica from within the Caribbean's 809 area code, including on the island of Dominica, dial the seven-digit local number.

Time   Dominica is on Atlantic standard time, one hour ahead of eastern standard time in the United States. Dominica does not observe daylight saving time, so when the United States changes to daylight time, clocks in Dominica and the U.S. East Coast tell the same time.

Tips and Service   Most hotels and restaurants add a 10% service charge to all bills. Where this charge has not been included, tipping is up to you.

Water   The water is drinkable from the taps and in the high mountain country. Pollution is hardly a problem here.

Weather   Daytime temperatures average between 70° and 85° Fahrenheit. Nights are much cooler, especially in the mountains. The rainy season is June to October, when there can be warnings of hurricane activity. Regrettably, Dominica lies in the "hurricane path," and fierce storms have taken their toll on the island over the years.

WHERE TO STAY

Don't forget that the government imposes a 5% tax on hotel rooms, and a 3% tax on beverages and food, which will be added to your hotel bill. Unless otherwise noted, the rates given below are year round.

IN ROSEAU & CASTLE COMFORT

Evergreen Hotel

P.O. Box 309, Castle Comfort, Dominica, W.I. ☎ **809/448-3288.** Fax 809/448-6800. 16 rms. A/C TV TEL. $82 single; $113 double; $139 triple. (Includes full breakfast.) AE, DC, MC, V. Free parking.

Built in 1986, this pleasant family-run hotel looks a bit like a Swiss chalet from the outside. A few of the rooms have access to wraparound tile-floored verandas; all have stone accents. It sits amid a cluster of other hotels about a mile south of Roseau. A stony beach is visible a few steps beyond the garden. Inside and out, the airy, spacious, comfortably modern place is trimmed with the richly textured local gommier wood. Mena Winston, the Dominican-born owner, assists in the preparation of each of the well-flavored meals, costing $18. Laundry service and scuba diving can be arranged. The hotel has added a swimming pool.

Fort Young Hotel

Victoria St. (P.O. Box 519), Roseau, Dominica, W.I. ☎ **809/448-5000,** or 800/223-1588, 800/531-6767 in Canada. Fax 809/448-5006. 32 rms, 2 suites. A/C TV TEL. Transportation: Take a taxi (a 15-minute ride from Canefield Airport). $105 single; $125 double; $140–$160 suite. Continental breakfast $8 extra. AE, MC, V. Free parking.

This hotel, which opened in 1989, grew from the ruins of the 1770 Fort Young. Attracting both commercial travelers and tourists, it offers comfortable bedrooms with ceiling fans and balconies. The most desirable units open onto the sea. The modern hotel's core is embraced by the crescent-shaped sweep of the historic walls of the old fort. There is an outdoor pool, a hotel restaurant featuring an international menu, laundry, and room service. Tours of the area can be arranged.

The Garraway Hotel

Place Heritage, The Bayfront (P.O. Box 789), Roseau, Dominica, W.I. ☎ **809/449-8800.** Fax 809/449-8807. 20 rms, 11 suites. A/C TV TEL. $95 single; $105 double; $116–$170 suite. Breakfast $5–$8 extra. AE, MC, V. Free parking.

This hotel opened in 1994 adjacent to the long-established home of its owners, the Garraway family. Rising four pale-green stories above the capital's harborfront, and noticeable as one of the tallest buildings in town, it offers clean bedrooms, usually with views stretching all the way to Dominica's southernmost tip. The bedrooms are outfitted with rattan furniture and pastel-colored fabrics with flowered prints. On the premises is a restaurant, the Balisier (recommended separately in "Where to Dine" below), and, adjacent to the sea, the Pavement Café. Room service and laundry service are available, and babysitting can be arranged.

Reigate Hall Hotel

Mountain Rd. (P.O. Box 200), Reigate, Dominica, W.I. ☎ **809/448-4031.** Fax 809/448-4034. 17 rms, 2 suites. A/C TEL. $55 single; $65 double; $150–$180 (including breakfast) suite. Continental breakfast $5.60 extra. AE, MC, V. Free parking.

On a steep hillside about a mile east of Roseau, this hotel was originally built in the 18th century as a plantation house. Today it's known as the best hotel on the island, its rooms enjoying panoramic views. Some parts of the original structure are left, but the building has been substantially altered. The hotel has a comfortably airy design of hardwood floors and exposed stone. The guest rooms curve around the sides of a rectangular swimming pool. The hotel has an outdoor tennis court, a gym, a good restaurant (see "Where to Dine," below), laundry, babysitting, and room service.

Reigate Waterfront Hotel

Castle Comfort, Roseau, Dominica, W.I. ☎ **809/448-4031.** Fax 809/448-4034. 24 rms. A/C TV TEL. $55 single; $65 double. Continental breakfast $8 extra. AE, MC, V. Free parking.

Set 1 mile south of Roseau, in two-story buildings that formerly belonged to the now-defunct Sissereaux hotel, this beachfront property is owned and managed by the previously recommended Reigate Hall Hotel. Less solidly built than its prestigious partner, but renovated as recently as 1993, it offers airy rooms with balconies, simple furniture, and a beachfront kind of allure that some guests find appealing. There's a bar (the Tibuco) and a restaurant on the premises. Every Wednesday night there's a barbecue with live music from a local band. A minibus is available, on request and after a bit of a delay, to shuttle passengers between the two properties, a seven-minute drive apart.

ALONG THE BEACHFRONT

Castaways Beach Hotel

P.O. Box 5, Mero, Dominica, W.I. ☎ **809/449-6244,** or 800/223-9815 in the U.S. Fax 809/449-6246. 27 rms. $72 single; $86 double; $106 triple. MAP $30 per person extra. MC, V. Free parking.

The island's first major resort along the coast north of Roseau lies some 13 miles north of the capital, 8 miles north of Canefield Airport on the west coast. Nestled between the tropical forest and a mile-long black sand beach and ringed on the inland side with huge tamarind trees, the hotel has rooms shaded by tall coconut palms. Each of the spacious accommodations has a private bath or shower and is filled with simple contemporary furniture. Some of the rooms are air-conditioned; others are cooled by ceiling fans. Many units also contain phone and TV.

The hotel dining room is recommended separately (see "Where to Dine," below). On the beach is an open-air bar built in a fashion similar to the chikees of the Seminole people in the Florida Everglades, thatched with palmetto fronds. Water sports can be arranged through the reception desk, as can guided excursions to the island's principal sights. There's a dive shop on the premises.

AT SALISBURY

Lauro Club

P.O. Box 483, Roseau, Dominica. ☎ **809/449-6602.** Fax 809/449-6603. 10 apartments. $73 studio apartment for one; $86–$100 studio apartment for two; $105 one-bedroom apartment for one; $122–$140 one-bedroom apartment for two. Breakfast $8 extra. AE, DC, MC, V. Free parking.

One of the newest hotels in Dominica was built in 1991, a short walk uphill from the island's west coast, about half a mile from the town of Salisbury (pop. 2,000), midway between Roseau and Portsmouth. Owned and operated by a married pair of Swiss expatriates (Roland and Laurence Pralong), it's a simple but neat compound of white-sided concrete buildings with either green, red, or gray roofs, depending on the building materials available at the time. While the studios share a cottage with another studio, the one-bedroom units are independent unto themselves. None has TV or telephone, but each has a covered veranda crafted from brown-stained wood, flower-patterned draperies and upholsteries, and views angled toward the water. Although the sea is nearby, a beach suitable for swimming requires a five-minute walk and the use of a long, serpentine staircase which descends down to the sea. On the premises is a restaurant (the Sea Breeze), serving breakfast ($8) and dinner ($21), and a poolside snack bar serving sandwiches and burgers throughout the day. Table tennis, scuba diving, snorkeling, and guided tours of Dominica are available through the reception desk.

IN THE RAIN FOREST

Papillote Wilderness Retreat

Trafalgar Falls Rd. (P.O. Box 2287), Roseau, Dominica, W.I. ☎ **809/448-2287.** Fax 809/448-2285. 8 rms, 1 suite. $60 single; $65 double; $75 suite. Continental breakfast $5 extra. AE, MC, V. Free parking. Closed Sept.

This hotel and restaurant is run by the Jean-Baptistes: Cuthbert handles the restaurant, and his wife, Anne Grey, was a marine scientist. Their place, 4 miles east of Roseau, stands right in the middle of Papillote Forest, at the foothills of Morne Macaque. In this remote setting, they have created a unique rain-forest resort; you can lead an Adam and Eve life here, surrounded by exotic fruits, flowers, and herb gardens. Laundry and room service are available.

Don't expect constantly sunny weather, since this part of the jungle is known for its downpours; their effect, however, keeps the orchids, begonias, and brilliantly colored bromeliads lush. The 12 acres of sloping and forested land are pierced with a labyrinth of stone walls and trails, beside which flows a network of freshwater streams, a few of which come from hot mineral springs. Natural hot mineral baths are available, and you'll be directed to a secluded waterfall where you can swim in the river. The Jean-Baptistes also run a boutique in which they sell Dominican products, including appliquéed quilts made by local artisans. Even if you don't stay here, it's an experience to dine on the thatch-roofed terrace (see "Where to Dine," below).

WHERE TO DINE

It's customary to eat at your hotel, although Dominica has a string of independent eateries. Dress is casual. If you're going out in the evening, always call to make sure your dining choice is actually open and also that you have proper transportation there and back.

IN ROSEAU

Balisier

In the Garraway Hotel, The Bayfront. ☎ **809/449-8800.** Reservations required. Appetizers $3–$4; main courses $16–$25; lunch from $15; Fri buffet lunch $16.70. AE, MC, V. Lunch daily noon–2:30pm; dinner daily 6:30–9:30pm. INTERNATIONAL.

Named after a local species of banana famed for its beautiful flowers, this restaurant occupies the ground floor of a previously recommended hotel. Designed for maximum exposure to a view over Roseau's harbor, it serves well-recommended food which might include shrimp mousse; chicken Garraway (breast of chicken stuffed with plantain and sweet corn); roulade of flying fish served with a tomato-peanut sauce; loin of pork with pineapple, mushrooms, and onions; and a choice of steak, vegetarian, or lobster dishes. Any of these might be followed with a slice of the establishment's homemade coconut-cream pie. Lunches are simpler than dinners, and might include West Indian curries, fish Créole, or several kinds of salad.

Ⓢ Guiyave

15 Cork St. ☎ **809/448-2930.** Reservations recommended. Appetizers EC$5–EC$7 ($1.90–$2.60); main courses EC$22–EC$30 ($8.10–$11.10). AE, MC, V. Mon–Fri 8:30am–3pm, Sat 9am–2:30pm. CREOLE.

 Family-Friendly Accommodations

Windjammer Landing Villa Beach Resort   *(see p. 588)* This St. Lucia resort complex offers a "Golden Family Plan." It features a personal nanny for five days, supervised children's activities, a kiddies' cocktail party, and a villa food pack (soft drinks, cereals, whatever) on arrival.

Club Med   *(see p. 589)* One of the most children-oriented chain members in the Caribbean, the Club Med on St. Lucia has separate playtime facilities for children and offers babysitting. Children under 5 often stay free during off-peak promotional weeks.

Calabash   *(see p. 634)* Children 12 and under are welcome at this Grenada hostelry in summer and housed for $35 a day, including all meals, in rooms with their parents. Only children over 12 are welcome in winter.

This airy restaurant occupies the second floor of a wood-frame West Indian house. Rows of tables almost completely fill the narrow balcony overlooking the street outside. You can enjoy a drink at the stand-up bar on the second floor. The establishment is open only for breakfast and lunch. Specialties include different preparations of conch and rabbit, octopus and lobster, spareribs, chicken, crab backs, and mountain chicken. On Saturday they prepare rôtis and "goat water." The place is known for its juices, including refreshing glasses of soursop, tamarind, sorrel, cherry, and strawberry. One part of the establishment is a pâtisserie specializing in French pastries.

☼ La Robe Créole

3 Victoria St. ☎ **809/448-2896.** Reservations required. Appetizers $4–$5; main courses $20–$25. MC, V. Mon–Sat noon–9:30pm. CREOLE/SEAFOOD.

Considered the most important independent restaurant in the capital, La Robe Créole sits in a low-slung colonial house, beside a sunny plaza on a slope above the sea, behind a facade draped with flowering vines. The staff, dressed in madras Créole costumes, serves food in a long and narrow dining room capped with heavy beams and filled with relics from the 19th century. You can enjoy pumpkin-pimiento soup, callaloo with cream of coconut soup, crab back, pizzas, mountain chicken in beer batter, and shrimp in coconut with garlic sauce. For dessert, try banana or coconut cake or ice cream.

A section of the restaurant, **The Mouse Hole,** is a good place for food on the run. You can take out freshly made sandwiches and salads, and light meals start at $6. They make good Trinidad-inspired rotis here—wheat pancakes wrapping beef, chicken, or vegetables. On Dominica, these rotis are often flavored with curry. The Mouse Hole is open Monday through Saturday from 8am to 9:30pm.

Orchard Restaurant

31 King George St. ☎ **809/448-3051.** Reservations required. Appetizers EC$4–EC$10 ($1.50–$3.70); main courses EC$20–EC$50 ($7.40–$18.50). AE, MC, V. Lunch Mon–Sat noon–2:30pm; dinner Mon–Fri 7–10pm. CREOLE.

Late in 1986, this restaurant opened in its new home—a clean, wood-lined oasis of calm on a busy street in the capital, a 10-minute drive south of Canefield Airport. There's a bar, as well as a large dining room and a lattice-covered courtyard to one side. You can order take-out food here, but most clients come for the bar and the sit-down meals. Meals include mountain chicken, callaloo soup with crabmeat, coconut shrimp, black pudding, blood sausage, goat water, several pumpkin dishes, and breadfruit puffs. Friday night features barbecued meat dishes.

Reigate Hall Restaurant

In the Reigate Hall Hotel, Mountain Rd. ☎ **809/448-4031.** Reservations recommended, especially if you're not a hotel guest. Appetizers $3.50–$8.50; main courses $15–$28. AE, MC, V. Lunch daily 1–3pm; dinner daily 7–10:30pm. FRENCH/CREOLE.

Reigate Hall lies only a mile east of the center of Roseau, but it seems so much longer because of the tortuous road leading up to it. On the second story of this previously recommended hotel (see "Where to Stay," above), the restaurant is an intimately lit enclave of polished tropical hardwoods and exposed stone. A masonry spillway splashing water onto the paddles of a water wheel adds an old-fashioned accent. Menu items are derived from both French and Créole recipes and might include fish soup, beef curry, coq au vin, prawns in garlic sauce, seafood au gratin, and mountain chicken in a champagne sauce.

ⓢ World of Food Restaurant and Bar

In Vena's Hotel, 48 Cork St. ☎ **809/448-3286.** Reservations not required. Appetizers EC$20–EC$45 ($7.40–$16.70); main courses EC$25–EC$58 ($9.30–$21.50). No credit cards. Lunch daily noon–2:30pm; dinner daily 6–10:30pm. CREOLE.

In the 1930s, the garden containing this restaurant belonged to a well-known novelist, Jean Rhys. Today it's the patio for one of the most charming Créole restaurants in Roseau. Some say that its owner, Vena McDougal, is the best Créole cook in town. You can have a drink at the stone-walled building at the far end of the garden if you want, but many guests select one of the tables in the shadow of a large mango tree. Specialties include steamed fish or fish steak, curried goat, chicken-filled roti, black pudding, mountain chicken, breadfruit puffs, callaloo-and-watercress soup, crab backs, conch, and tee-tee-ree (fried fish cakes). She's said to make the best rum punches on the island as well. The restaurant is attached to Vena's Hotel (really a guesthouse). If you want to reach the restaurant without passing through Vena's, its entrance is on Field's Lane.

ALONG THE BEACHFRONT

Castaways Beach Hotel

Mero. ☎ **809/449-6244.** Reservations not required. Appetizers EC$6–EC$20 ($2.20–$7.40); main courses EC$25–EC$70 ($9.30–$25.90). AE, MC, V. Lunch daily noon–2pm; dinner daily 7–9pm. CREOLE.

If you're touring north along the coast, consider stopping in for a meal at the Castaways, 13 miles north of Roseau. In this resort setting, managing director Linda Harris welcomes nonguests to her hotel dining room with its waterfront setting. Guests dress in casual resortwear, dine informally, and enjoy the hospitality of the staff. Here you get the cuisine for which Dominica is known, including the crapaud or mountain chicken. They have a delicacy most often compared to quail. You can also get lambi (conch), as well as island crab mixed with a savory Créole stuffing. All dishes are garnished with the fruits and vegetables of Dominica's rich soil, such as passionfruit. Before dining, try a rum punch in the lounge or beach bar.

IN THE RAIN FOREST

ⓢ Papillote Wilderness Retreat

Trafalgar Falls Rd. ☎ **809/448-2287.** Reservations recommended for lunch, required for dinner. Appetizers EC$10–EC$12 ($3.70–$4.45); main courses EC$20–EC$50 ($7.40–$18.50); fixed-price dinner EC$50 ($18.50). AE, MC, V. Lunch Mon–Sat 11:30am–2pm; dinner Mon–Sat 7–9pm. CREOLE/CARIBBEAN.

Previously recommended for its lodgings (see "Where to Stay," above), this is also one of the most alluringly located restaurants in Dominica. Even if you're not staying here, come by taxi for lunch or dinner; it's only 4 miles east of Roseau. Amid nature trails rife with exotic flowers, century-old trees, and filtered sunlight, you dine on a masonry terrace a few steps from a sociable bar topped with a slab of samaan wood. The array of healthful food includes flying fish, river shrimp, mountain chicken, dolphin, kingfish, breadfruit puffs, and tropical salads. Don't forget to bring sturdy walking shoes and a bathing suit. Non-guests may use the pool for EC$5 ($1.90). Near the dining terrace, Cuthbert built a Jacuzzi-size pool, which is constantly filled with the mineral-rich waters of a hot spring.

WHAT TO SEE & DO

Those making day trips to Dominica from other Caribbean islands will want to see the ✪ **Carib Indian Reservation,** in the northeast. In 1903 Britain got the Caribs to agree to accept boundaries on 3,700 acres of land set aside for them. Hence, this is the last remaining domain of this once-hostile tribe who gave their name to the archipelago—Caribbean. Their look is Mongolian, and they are no longer "pure-blooded," as they have married outside of their tribe. Today they survive by fishing, growing food, and weaving baskets and vertivert grass mats, which they sell to the outside world. They still make dugout canoes too.

It's like going back in time when you explore ✪ **Morne Trois Pitons National Park,** a primordial rain forest, "me Tarzan, you Jane" country. Mists rise gently over lush, dark-green growth, drifting up to blue-green peaks that have earned for Dominica the title of "Switzerland of the Caribbean." Framed by banks of giant ferns, rivers rush and tumble. Trees sprout orchids, and everything seems blanketed with some type of parasitic growth. Green sunlight filters down through timeless trees, and the roar of a waterfall creates a blue mist.

One of the best starting points for a visit to the park is the village of Laudat, 7 miles from Roseau. Exploring this green heart of Dominica is for serious botanists and only the most skilled hikers, who should never penetrate unmarked trails without a very experienced guide.

Deep in the park is the **Emerald Pool Trail,** a half-mile nature trail that forms a circuit loop on a footpath passing through the forest to a pool with a beautiful waterfall. Downpours are frequent in the rain forest, and at high elevations cold winds blow. It lies 3¹/₂ miles northeast of Pont Casse.

Five miles up from the **Roseau River Valley,** in the south-central sector of Dominica, **Trafalgar Falls** can be reached after you drive through the village of Trafalgar. There, however, you have to approach by foot, as the slopes are too steep for vehicles. After a 20-minute walk past growths of ginger plants and vanilla orchids, you arrive at the base, where a trio of falls converge into a rock-strewn pool. Boulders sprout vegetation and tree ferns encircle the flowing water.

The **Sulphur Springs** are evidence of the island's volcanic past. Jeeps or Land Rovers get quite near. Not only Sulphur Springs but also the Boiling Lake are bubbling evidence of underground volcanic activity, north and east of Roseau. This seemingly bubbling pool of gray mud sometimes belches smelly sulfurous fumes—the odor is like a rotten egg. Only the very fit should attempt the six-hour round-trip to **Boiling Lake,** the world's second-largest boiling lake. Go only with an experienced guide, as, according to reports, some tourists lost their lives in the **Valley of Desolation**—they stumbled and fell into the boiling waters.

Finally, consider a visit to **Titou Gorge,** a deep and narrow gorge where it's possible to swim under a waterfall. Later you can get warm again in a hot sulfur spring close by. One reader compared swimming here to "adventure fantasies, dreams, or Indiana Jones movies." However, you should only do this with an experienced guide (arranged at the tourist office). The guide will transport you to the gorge and will know if swimming is dangerous, which it is after heavy rainfall.

On the northwestern coast, **Portsmouth** is Dominica's second-largest settlement. Once there, you can row up the Indian River in native canoes, visit the ruins of old Fort Shirley in Cabrits National Park, and bathe at Sandy Beach on Douglas Bay and Prince Rupert Bay.

Cabrits National Park, on the northwestern coast, 2 miles south of Douglas Bay ☎ **809/448-2401,** ext. 415), is a 1,313-acre protected site containing mountain scenery, tropical forests, swampland, volcanic sand beaches, coral reefs, and the ruins of a fortified 18th-century garrison of British, then French construction. The park's land area is a panoramic promontory formed by twin peaks of extinct volcanoes, overlooking fine beaches, with Douglas Bay on one side and Prince Rupert Bay across the headland. Part of Douglas Bay forms the marine section of the park. Fort Shirley, the large garrison last used as a military post in 1854, is being wrested from encroaching vegetation. A small museum highlights the natural and historic aspects of the park. The name Cabrits comes from the Spanish-Portuguese-French word for goat, because of the animals left there by early sailors to provide fresh meat on future visits.

Stranger Than Paradise

Wild and untamed Dominica offers very experienced and physically fit hikers some of the most bizarre geological oddities in the Caribbean. Sights include scalding lava covered with a hot, thin, and not-very-stable crust; a boiling lake where mountain streams turn to vapor as they come into contact with superheated volcanic fissures; and a barren wasteland known as the Valley of Desolation.

All these attractions are in the 16,000 heavily forested acres of the **Morne des Trois Pitons National Park,** in the island's south-central region. Hiking tours should be conducted only if accompanied by a guide, who usually appears mysteriously in the village of Laudat. Few markers appear en route, but the trek, which includes one of the worthiest assortments of geological oddities, stretches 6 miles in both directions from Laudat to the Boiling Lake. Bring lunch and a guide, and walk cautiously, particularly in districts peppered with bubbling hot springs. Regardless of where you turn, you'll run into streams and waterfalls, the inevitable result of an island whose mountaintops receive up to 400 inches of rainfall a year. (Winds on the summits are strong enough to have pushed one recreational climber to her death several years ago—proceed with caution.) Ferns, orchids, trees, and epiphytes create a tangle of underbrush, and insect, bird, and reptilian life is profuse.

Your trek should include a visit to the **Titou Gorge,** a deep and very narrow ravine whose depths were created as lava floes cooled and contracted. En route, there might be views of rare Sisserou and Jacquot parrots, monkeys, and vines whose growth seems to visibly increase on an hourly basis. The hill treks of Dominica have been described as "sometimes easy, sometimes hellish," and if it should happen to rain during your climb (and it rains very frequently on Dominica), your path is likely to become very slippery. But botanists and geologists agree with the assessment of experienced hikers, that climbs through the jungles of Dominica are some of the most rewarding in the Caribbean.

Be warned that to proceed along the island's badly marked trails into areas that can be physically treacherous is not a good idea, and climbing alone or even in pairs is not advisable. Forestry officials recommend **Ken's Hinterland Adventure Tours & Taxi Service,** in the island capital of Roseau (☎ **809/448-4850**). Depending on their destination and the oddities they feature, treks cost $100 to around $150 for up to four participants, and require five to eight hours round-trip. Transportation from Roseau in a minivan to the starting point of your hillclimb is usually included in the price.

SPORTS & OUTDOOR ACTIVITIES

BEACHES   True beach buffs who demand great beaches as part of their Caribbean holiday will look elsewhere for a good time. Dominica has some of the worst beaches in the Caribbean. Some beaches are in the northwest part of the island, around Portsmouth, and there are also secluded beaches in the northeast, along with spectacular coastal scenery. But all of these are hard to reach, and you might settle instead for a freshwater swimming pool or river swimming.

The finest beach, lying on the northwestern coast, is **Picard.** It stretches for about 2 miles, a strip of grayish sand with palm trees in the background. The previously recommended Castaways Beach Hotel opens onto this beach. Snorkelers like it a lot, and windsurfing is another sport practiced here. The finest swimming, however, is said to be along the banks of the **Layou River.**

HIKING   Serious hikers find Dominica a major challenge. Guides should be used for all unmarked trails. You can arrange for a guide by going to the office of the **Dominica National Park** in the Botanical Gardens in Roseau (☎ **448-2732**) or the Dominica Tourist Board.

SCUBA DIVING   You can discover diving on the island with **Dive Dominica Ltd.,** in the Castle Comfort Diving Lodge, P.O. Box 2253, Castle Comfort, Dominica, W.I. (☎ **809/448-2188,** or toll free **800/544-7631**). Open-water certification (both NAUI and PADI) instruction is given, costing $400 for five or six days of instruction. A 36-foot diving catamaran gets you to the dive sites in comfort. There are 11 rooms available at the diving lodge, where a seven-night dive package costs $799.

Divers from all over the world patronize the **Dive Centre** at the Anchorage Hotel in Castle Comfort (☎ **809/448-2638**). A fully qualified PADI staff awaits divers there. A single-tank dive costs $40; a double-tank dive, $60; and a night dive, $50. A unique whale and dolphin watch from 3pm to sunset is a popular feature, costing $50 for $3^{1}/_{2}$ hours of fun. Author Peter Benchley once went whale-watching with this group. With a pool, classrooms, private dock, and a well-trained staff, this is considered the most complete dive resort on Dominica.

SHOPPING

Store hours are usually 8am to 5pm Monday through Friday and 9am to 1pm on Saturday. In Roseau, near the Old Market Plaza, of historical significance as a former slave-trading market and more recently the Wednesday-, Friday-, and Saturday-morning vegetable market, now houses three craft shops, each specializing in coconut, straw, and Carib craft products.

Tropicrafts Island Mats, at Queen Mary Street and Turkey Lane (☎ **809/ 448-2747**), offers the well-known grass rugs handmade and woven in several intricate patterns at Tropicrafts' factory. They also have for sale handmade bags, shopping bags, and placemats, all appliquéed by hand. The handmade dolls are popular with doll collectors. The Dominican vertivert-grass mats are known throughout the world. There's another outlet on Bay Street opposite Burroughs Square in Portsmouth (☎ **809/445-5956**).

Caribana, 31 Cork St. (☎ **809/448-2761**), displays Dominica's art, craft, and culture. This is the latest manifestation of the old Caribana Handicrafts, established by the late Iris Joseph, who is credited with creating the straw-weaving industry on the island. Caribana is operated by her granddaughter. The staff is usually pleased to explain the dyeing processes that turn the straw into one of three different earth-related tones. When straw is buried in the earth, it turns black; when it's soaked in saffron, it turns yellow; and when it's boiled with the bark of a tang tree, it turns purple. The premises also contains a small café housed in the Irish Dangleben Gallery.

DOMINICA AFTER DARK

It's not very developed, but there is some. A couple of the major hotels, such as the **Castaways Beach Hotel** (☎ 809-449-6244) and **Reigate Hall Hotel** (☎ 809-448-4031), have entertainment on weekends, usually a combo or "jing ping" (traditional local music). In the winter season, the Castaways sponsors a barbecue on the beach on the weekends with live music. The **Anchorage Hotel** at Castle Comfort (☎ 809/448-2638) also has live entertainment and a good buffet on Thursday. Call for details.

The Warehouse, Checkhall Estate (☎ 809/449-1303), a five-minute drive north of Roseau, adjacent to Canefield Airport, is the island's only disco, a social magnet open on Friday and Saturday for the island's night owls and disco lovers. It's owned and operated by Rosie and Cleve Royer, who converted a 200-year-old stone building, once used to store rum. Recorded disco, reggae, and other music is played at loud volumes from 11pm to 4am. Entrance costs EC$10 ($3.70), and beer costs EC$4 ($1.50).

2 St. Lucia

In very recent years St. Lucia (pronounced *Loo*-sha)—second largest of the Windward Islands—has become one of the most popular tourist destinations in the Caribbean, with some of its finest resorts, both chain and independent. The heaviest tourist development is concentrated in the northwest, between the capital of Castries and the northern end of the island. This is the site of a string of white sandy beaches that put St. Lucia on world tourist maps.

The rest of the island remains relatively unspoiled, a checkerboard of green-mantled mountains, gentle valleys, banana plantations, a bubbling volcano, giant tree ferns, wild orchids, and fishing villages. There's a hint of the South Pacific about it, and a mixed French and British heritage.

A mountainous island of some 240 square miles, St. Lucia has about 120,000 inhabitants. The capital, **Castries,** is built on the southern shore of a large, almost-landlocked harbor surrounded by hills. The approach to the airport is almost a path between hills, and it's very impressive.

Famous native son Derek Walcott, called "one of the greatest English-language poets alive today," was born in Castries. His father was an unpublished poet who died when Walcott was just a year old, and his mother was a former headmistress at the Methodist school on St. Lucia. In 1992 Walcott won the Nobel Prize for literature from the Swedish Academy of Letters in Stockholm. He prefers, however, not to tout the charms of St. Lucia too warmly, and told the press, "I don't want everyone to go there and overrun the place."

ORIENTATION
GETTING THERE

Most airline routings require at least a touchdown in one or another Caribbean island before continuing on to St. Lucia.

BY PLANE   Both **American Airlines** and **American Eagle** (☎ 800/433-7300) service St. Lucia's two widely separated airports (see below) with one daily non-stop flight to each airport from its hub in San Juan, Puerto Rico.

Air Canada (☎ 800/363-5440 in Canada, or (☎ toll free **800/776-3000** in the U.S.) has two nonstop flights that depart on Saturday and Sunday from Toronto in winter.

If you're already on the islands and plan to visit St. Lucia, **LIAT** (☎ 809/462-3142) has small planes flying into Vigie Airport from such international hubs as Antigua and Barbados. Be warned that LIAT flights tend to island-hop through many different islands en route to St. Lucia, although some readers consider this part of the adventure.

British Airways (☎ 800/247-9297) offers three flights a week from London's Gatwick airport to St. Lucia's Hewanorra airport. All of these touch down briefly on Antigua before continuing to St. Lucia. Service is available on Tuesday, Friday, and Sunday.

The island maintains two separate **airports** whose different locations cause end-less confusion to most newcomers. Most international long-distance flights land at **Hewanorra International Airport** in the south, 45 miles from Castries. If you fly in here and you're booked into a hotel in the north, you'll have to spend about an hour and a half going along the potholed East Coast Highway. The average taxi ride costs $60 for up to four passengers. Once this airport was known as "Beane Field," when Roosevelt and Churchill agreed to construct a big air base here dur-ing the depths of World War II.

However, flights from other parts of the Caribbean usually land at the somewhat-antiquated **Vigie Field** in the island's northeast, whose location just outside Castries is much more convenient to the capital and most of the island's hotels.

GETTING AROUND

BY LOCAL BUS   Minibuses (with names like "Lucian Love") and jitneys connect Castries with such main towns as Soufrière and Vieux Fort. They are generally overcrowded and often filled with produce on the way to market. However, since taxis are expensive, it might be a "last resort" means of transport. At least it's cheap. Buses for Cap Estate, in the northern part of the island, leave from Jeremy Street in Castries, near the market. Buses going to Vieux Fort and Soufrière leave from Bridge Street in front of the department store.

BY TAXI   Taxis are ubiquitous on the island, and most drivers are eager to please. The drivers have to be quite experienced to cope with the narrow, hilly, switchback roads outside the capital. Special programs have trained them to serve as guides. Their cars are unmetered, but tariffs for all standard trips are fixed by the government. Make sure you determine if the driver is quoting a rate in U.S. dol-lars or the EC$.

BY RENTAL CAR   First, *remember to drive on the left*, and try to avoid some of the island's more obvious potholes. You'll need a St. Lucia driver's license, which can easily be purchased at either airport when you arrive, or at the car-rental kiosks when you pick up your car. Present a valid driver's license from home to the counter attendant or government official and pay a fee of $16.

All three of the big U.S.–based car-rental companies maintain offices on St. Lucia.

St. Lucia

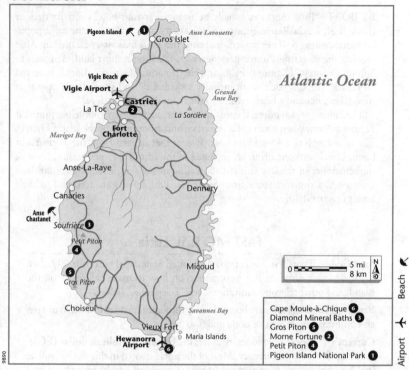

Budget (☎ 809/452-8021, or 800/527-0700) rents to motorists ages 25 to 65. It charges $300 weekly for its cheapest vehicle, with a $5 daily collision-damage waiver (with a $200 deductible clause). It grants unlimited mileage.

Its competitor Avis (☎ 809/454-2046, or 800/331-2112) rents to motorists 25 years of age or more. Its cheapest vehicle goes for $360 weekly, with an expensive $17 daily collision-damage waiver (no deductible). The first 600 miles are free.

Hertz (☎ 809/452-0679, or 800/654-3001) rents to motorists age 25 or more, charging $330 weekly for its cheapest car, with a $12 collision-damage waiver. There's a $400 deductible clause, and you're granted unlimited mileage.

All three companies maintain offices at (or will deliver cars to) both of the island's airports. (Each also has an office in Castries and, in some cases, at some of the island's major hotels.)

Drive carefully, honk your horn while going around the island's blind hairpin turns, and don't drink and drive.

BY SIGHTSEEING TOUR Most hotel front desks will make arrangements for tours that take in all the major sights of St. Lucia. For example, **St. Lucia Representative Services,** Reduit (☎ 809/452-8232), offers many island tours, such as a shopping tour Monday through Friday at $15; and a Rain Forest Walk at $40 on Monday and Wednesday. Or you can take full-day boat trips along the west coast to the volcano for $70 per person. Tours to neighboring islands can also be arranged. Tours operate only if enough passengers are booked to satisfy minimum requirements. The company has representatives making stops at most of the major hotels.

BY BOAT   Boat tours can usually be arranged at your hotel's activity desk or through **St. Lucia Representative Services** (see above). One of the most popular tours, costing $70 per person, is aboard the *Endless Summer* catamaran. After viewing the towering Pitons, passengers are taken on a short land excursion to Sulphur Springs, Diamond Falls, and the Botanical Gardens. Lunch is served on board. The trip back north includes a swimming and snorkeling stopover at Anse Chastanet and a brief cruise into the natural bay of Marigot.

The company also offers, if demand warrants it, a full-day snorkeling tour that departs at 9am, when a van collects participants from many of the island's hotels. The tour involves a 45-minute boat transfer that departs from the Vigie Yacht basin. Lunch and one drink are included in the cost of $45 per person. Most of the remainder of the day is spent snorkeling in the translucent waters off Anse Chastenet, a short distance from Soufrière. Participants are returned to their hotels at around 4pm.

FAST FACTS: St. Lucia

Area Code   To call St. Lucia from the United States, dial area code 809, then the seven-digit number. For information on how to make calls once on the island, and other telecommunications, see "Telephone," below.

Banking Hours   Banks are open Monday through Thursday from 8am to 1pm and on Friday from 8am to noon and 3 to 5pm.

Currency   The official monetary unit is the **Eastern Caribbean dollar (EC$)**. It's about 37¢ in U.S. currency. Most of the prices quoted in this section will be in American dollars, as they are accepted by nearly all hotels, restaurants, and shops.

Customs   At either airport, Customs may be a hassle if there is the slightest suspicion, regardless of how ill-founded, that you are carrying illegal drugs.

Documents   U.S., British, and Canadian citizens need a valid passport, plus an ongoing or return ticket.

Drugstore   The best is William Pharmacy, Williams Building, Bridge Street, in Castries (☎ **809/452-2797**).

Electricity   Bring an adapter and transformer, as St. Lucia runs on 220–230 volts A.C., 50 cycles.

Emergency   Call the police at **999**.

Hospitals   There are 24-hour emergency rooms at St. Jude's Hospital, Vieux Fort (☎ **809/454-6041**), and Victoria Hospital, Hospital Road, Castries (☎ **809/452-2421**).

Information   The **St. Lucia Tourist Board** is at Point Seraphine, Castries (☎ **809/452-5968**); in the United States, the office is at 820 Second Ave., New York, NY 10017 (☎ **212/867-2950,** or toll free **800/456-3984**). In Canada, information is available at Suite 457, Islington, ON M9A 4X4 (☎ **416/236-0936,** or toll free **800/456-3984**). In the United Kingdom, information is available at 421A Finchley Rd., London NW3 6HJ (☎ **0171/431-4045**).

Language   With its mixed French and British heritage, St. Lucia has interesting speech patterns. Although English is the official tongue, St. Lucians probably don't speak it as you do. Islanders also speak a French-Créole patois, similar to that heard on Martinique.

Post Office   The General Post Office is on Bridge Street in Castries. It's open Monday through Friday from 8:30am to 4pm.

Safety   St. Lucia has its share of crime, like everyplace else these days. Use common sense and protect yourself and your valuables. If you've got it, don't flaunt it! Don't pick up hitchhikers if you're driving around the island. Of course, the use of narcotic drugs is illegal, and possession or sale of such could lead to stiff fines or jail.

Service   Most hotels and restaurants add a 10% service charge.

Taxes   The government imposes an 8% occupancy tax on hotel-room rentals, and there's an $11 departure tax.

Telephone   On the island, dial all seven digits of the local number. Faxes may be handed in at hotel desks or at the offices of Cable & Wireless in the George Gordon Building on Bridge Street in Castries (☎ **809/452-3301**).

Time   St. Lucia is on Atlantic standard time year round, placing it one hour ahead of New York or Miami. However, when the United States is on daylight saving time, St. Lucia matches the clocks of the U.S. East Coast.

Weather   This little island, lying in the path of the trade winds, has year-round temperatures of 70° to 90° Fahrenheit.

WHERE TO STAY

Most of the leading hotels on this island are in the same price range—you have to seek out the bargains (begin at the end of this section). Once you reach your hotel, chances are you'll feel pretty isolated, but that's what many guests want. Many St. Lucian hostelries have kitchenettes where you can prepare simple meals. Prices are usually quoted in U.S. dollars. Don't forget the 8% hotel tax and the 10% service charge added to your bill.

VERY EXPENSIVE

✪ Ladera Resort

P.O. Box 225, Soufrière, St. Lucia, W.I. ☎ **809/459-7323,** or 800/841-4145 in the U.S. and Canada. Fax 809/459-5156. 13 suites, 6 villas. Winter, $330–$450 suite for one or two; $500 suite for three; $550 suite for four; $475–$650 villa for one or two; $600–$700 villa for three; $575–$750 villa for four. Off-season, $195–$350 suite for one or two; $295–$375 suite for three; $320–$400 suite for four; $295–$525 villa for one or two; $320–$500 villa for three; $345–$575 villa for four. Honeymoon packages available. MAP $40 per person extra. AE, MC, V. Free parking.

Outside the town of Soufrière, in the southern tier of St. Lucia, this luxury hideaway is perched on a hillside 1,000 feet above sea level. It's sandwiched between the Pitons, opening onto the Caribbean Sea. Opened in 1992, the villas and suites are all "open air," with only three walls—the west side of each unit is exposed to the view.

Villas and suites are constructed of tropical hardwoods, stone, and tile, and are furnished with 19th-century French furniture, wicker, and accessories built by local craftspeople. All units are decorated with local artwork and have indoor gardens.

Certain villas and suites have plunge pools as well. To get in here in winter, reserve four months in advance.

Dining/Entertainment: The Dasheene Restaurant & Bar offers fine dining, specializing in a local Créole and continental cuisine. The seafood served is caught fresh daily, and is most often preferred grilled. Guests enjoy high tea in Ladera's botanical garden.

Services: Shuttle service to the beach at Anse de Pitons, complimentary transportation to and from the town of Soufrière and Hewanorra International Airport.

Facilities: Large swimming pool and deck lying below the restaurant and bar with a view of the Pitons (used in the filming of the movie *Superman II*), horseback riding, scuba diving and snorkel trips, sailboating, fishing charters.

EXPENSIVE

✪ Anse Chastanet

Anse Chastanet Beach (P.O. Box 7000, Soufrière), St. Lucia, W.I. ☎ **809/459-7000,** or 800/223-1108 in the U.S. Fax 809/459-7700. 48 rms. Winter, $240–$390 single; $330–$450 double; $420–$675 triple. Off-season, $100–$265 single; $140–$356 double; $180–$450 triple. (MAP rates.) AE, DC, MC, V. Free parking.

One of the few places that merits the cliché "tropical paradise," this is not only St. Lucia's premier dive resort but also an exceptional Caribbean inn, combining warm service, excellent food, a beach location, and first-class facilities. It lies 18 miles north of Hewanorra International Airport (a 50-minute taxi ride), 2 miles north of Soufrière on a forested hill, a 103-step climb above palm-fringed Anse Chastanet Beach. You're surrounded by coffee trees, mangoes, papayas, banana plants, breadfruit, grapefruit, coconut palms, flamboyants, and hibiscus. The core of the house is a main building decorated in a typical island style, with a relaxing bar and dining room.

Guests can stay on the beach in spacious accommodations styled like West Indian plantation villas, with four rooms each, two up and two down. Other units, constructed like octagonal gazebos, cooled by ceiling fans, have views of the Pitons, St. Lucia's famous twin peaks. Each accommodation is large and comfortably appointed with locally made furniture crafted from island woods.

Dining/Entertainment: You can dine or drink on a wind-cooled terrace built like a treehouse over the tropical landscape in the Pitons Bar and Restaurant. Even if you're not a guest of the hotel, but are in the area touring for the day, consider a stopover at the beachside restaurant, Trou au Diable, offering a West Indian cuisine and a barbecue grill, plus a Créole dinner buffet twice weekly. The rotis are served with a mango chutney, and you can also order beef or chicken satays with a peanut sauce.

Services: Laundry, babysitting, transfers from the airport (available with advance notification).

Facilities: Five-star PADI dive operation, waterskiing, sailboat rentals.

✪ Windjammer Landing Villa Beach Resort

Labrelotte Bay (P.O. Box 1504, Castries), St. Lucia, W.I. ☎ **809/452-0913,** or 800/743-9609 in the U.S., 800/267-7600 in Canada, 800/373-742 in the United Kingdom. Fax 809/452-0907. 114 villas and suites. A/C TEL. Winter, $200–$270 suite for one or two; $280–$375 villa for two; $435–$485 villa for four; $500–$560 villa for six. Off-season, $140–$180 suite for one or two; $205–$260 villa for two; $340 villa for four; $425 villa for six. Additional person $45 extra. MAP $54 per person extra. AE, DC, MC, V. Free parking.

About a 15-minute drive from the capital, north of Reduit Beach, the Windjammer is set on 55 tropical acres. The resort was designed with a vaguely Moorish motif heavily influenced by Caribbean themes; pastel colors of pinks, blues, and greens predominate. It is composed of a cluster of white villas climbing a forested hillside above a desirable beach. This is an all-suite or all-villa resort (the larger villas have private plunge pools). The good-size interiors offer separate living and dining rooms, fully equipped kitchens, ceiling fans, cassette players, clocks, and VCRs upon request. All bedrooms adjoin private baths and open onto sun terraces.

Dining/Entertainment: A housekeeper/cook arrives daily, or you can choose from the Windjammer's three restaurants and two bars. The main restaurant, the breezy Jammers, features all-day dining. Try the mango and papaya pancakes for breakfast. At night, the restaurant offers a French/Caribbean cuisine, such as fresh lobster and shrimp Créole.

Facilities: Water sports, horseback riding, greens fees, and tennis (included in the rates); largest freshwater pool on the island, with built-in waterfalls; guests are taken out on the 44-foot cabin cruiser *Columbus*. Fitness center, children's program, health and beauty club.

All-Inclusive Resorts

Club Med

Savannes Bay, St. Lucia, W.I. ☎ **809/454-6546,** or 800/CLUB-MED in the U.S. Fax 809/454-6017. 256 rms. A/C. Dec–Apr, $950–$1,300 per person double. May–Nov, $780 per person double. $505 single surcharge 20%–30%. Children 2–11 in parents' room $620–$845 Dec–Apr, $505 May–Nov. During certain off-peak promotional weeks (usually spring or fall), children under 5 stay free in parents' room. (Rates per week include all meals and use of most facilities.) AE, MC, V. Free parking.

Club Med is a resort set on a 95-acre property near a black sand beach. The carefree lifestyle holds forth on the southernmost tip of St. Lucia, opening onto Savannes Bay, just five minutes from the international airport at Hewanorra. Completely refurbished, the club offers beachside living in four-story buildings in a coconut grove. Each room contains a private shower. This Club Med caters to children and has separate children's facilities.

Dining/Entertainment: In the heart of the complex is an open-air bar and a dance and theater area. Meals are served in the second-floor dining room with a panoramic view, and guests enjoy unlimited wine at lunch and dinner. Guests also have a choice of two other restaurants.

Services: Laundry, babysitting.

Facilities: Freshwater swimming pool, eight tennis courts, volleyball, archery, soccer, basketball, calisthenics, softball, Sailing Center with two large sailboats that take about two dozen sailors on full-day or overnight sailing trips; well-equipped Workout Center. Facilities (some of which cost extra) for horseback riding, windsurfing, and scuba diving; separate facilities for children.

✪ Club St. Lucia

Smugglers Village (P.O. Box 915), St. Lucia, W.I. ☎ **809/450-0551.** Fax 809/450-0281. 372 rms, 16 suites. Winter, $220–$270 single; $290–$386 double; $364 suite for two. Off-season, $190–$215 single; $254–$286 double; $320 suite for two. (Rates include all meals, drinks, and use of facilities.) AE, DC, MC, V. Free parking.

The most economical but also the least luxurious all-inclusive resort on the island sits in Cap Estate on a 50-acre site, an area near Le Sport, 8 miles north of Vigie airport at the northern tip of the island. It opens onto a curved bay where smugglers of yore used to bring in brandies, cognacs, and cigars from Martinique. The club's core is a wooden building with decks from which you can look down on a free-form pool. Accommodations are in bungalows scattered over landscaped grounds and feature one king-size or two twin beds, air conditioning or ceiling fans, and patios or terraces. Your fellow guests are likely to be vacationing Brits.

Dining/Entertainment: The emphasis is on sports and entertainment, and the inclusive package the resort puts together is an impressive one, offering all meals, even snacks, along with unlimited beer, wine, and mixed drinks both day and night. Guests have a choice of dining in the club's regular restaurant, Lakatan, or of sampling the seafood at Lambi's. The food is standard resort fare. A pizza parlor is one of the attractions. To break the monotony, guests are often transported to a restaurant, the Great House, where they receive a discount on meals ordered. This restaurant at Cap Estate offers a view of Anse Becune Bay and Martinique. Other activities include free movies and nightly entertainment.

Services: Laundry, babysitting, shuttle bus to Rodney Bay and Reduit Beach.

Facilities: Day or night tennis, unlimited water sports (waterskiing, Sunfish sailing, windsurfing, snorkeling, and pedalboats), three swimming pools, two beaches, children's Mini Club with a playground and a supervised activities program.

Jalousie Plantation

P.O. Box 251, Soufrière, St. Lucia. ☎ **809/459-7566**, or 800/877-3643. Fax 809/459-7667. 103 cottages, 12 suites. A/C MINIBAR TV TEL. Winter, $450 suite for one; $700 suite for two; $750–$950 cottage for two. Off-season, $385–$425 suite for one; $570–$650 suite for two; $610–$850 cottage for two. Children 5–15 in the parents' room $125 each, children under 5 free. (Rates all-inclusive.) AE, DC, MC, V. Free parking.

After a series of embarrassing false starts, this hotel is up, running, and proud of its new competitive edge on the touristic marketplace. It lies on 325 acres of what is probably the most sought-after piece of real estate on St. Lucia—the lush amphitheater formed by the twin bulks of St. Lucia's most memorable geological feature, the Gros Pitons. Built on land originally owned by Lord Glenconnor (the British beer baron responsible for the establishment of Mustique as a rarefied hideaway during the 1970s), it retains the architectural inspiration of the Créole plantation houses that originally peppered the landscape of this fertile terrain. Great efforts are spent in preserving the ecosystems of the land around Jalousie, justifying its reputation as one of the most environmentally friendly resorts anywhere. The staff includes 22 gardeners whose duties include protecting the offshore reefs, coaxing hydroponic gardens into high-yield crops (which appear on the resort's dining table out of season), and operating one of the most environmentally friendly sewage-treatment plants in the Caribbean.

The accommodations are in big-windowed, brown-sided cottages that nestle (sometimes a bit too close together) amid the verdant landscaping of the sloping terrain. Each contains a private safe, a private veranda, and furnishings evocative of the plantation era. Many have private plunge pools. Public areas mingle rustic chic (vaulted and timbered ceilings, rambling verandas loaded with wicker) with such stylish antiques and accessories as Venetian glass mirrors, Persian carpets, and Turkish and Indian inlaid furniture that appear to have been assembled by some of the most sophisticated decorators of Europe.

Dining/Entertainment: The resort's four restaurants include the Pier Restaurant (seafood and Créole cuisine serving only dinner, with live music twice a week), the Plantation Room (set on the upper level of the resort's centerpiece, the Great House), the Verandah (for breakfast buffets), and the Bayside Bar and Grill (for grilled meats, salads, and sandwiches served beside the pool). There are also at least four bars of various degrees of formality scattered over the premises.

Services: Room service (7am to 11pm), guided nature and strength-building walks, services for the planning of virtually any kind of wedding, a staff who can obtain or arrange tours or rental cars.

Facilities: High- and low-impact aerobics, stretch and Aquacise classes, Jacuzzis, complete array of spa facilities and treatments, men's and women's saunas, squash courts, four "Plexicushion" tennis courts (three lit for night play), beauty salon, swimming pool, a complete array of water sports (which includes facilities for scuba); a gray sand beach beckons swimmers to enjoy the surf.

Le Sport

P.O. Box 437, Cariblue Beach, St. Lucia, W.I. ☎ **809/450-8551,** or 800/544-2883 in the U.S. and Canada. Fax 809/450-0368. 100 rms, 2 suites. A/C TEL. Winter, $400–$530 double; $540–$900 suite. Off-season, $410–$470 double; $560–$840 suite. Single supplement $40. 75% discount for children 2–6 and 50% discount for children 7–12 sharing parents' room. (Rates all-inclusive.) AE, DC, MC, V. Free parking.

Le Sport "cares for your body." An all-inclusive resort, Le Sport is a citadel of first-class living and pampering, on a 1,500-acre estate at the northernmost tip of the island. You're an 8-mile run from Castries, and guests seem to prefer this isolation.

The resort makes a promise faithfully kept: Everything "you do, see, enjoy, drink, eat, and feel" is included in the price. That means not only accommodation, three meals a day, all refreshments, and bar drinks, but also use of all sports equipment, facilities, and instruction, plus airport transfers. The bedrooms, all overlooking the sea, contain a private bath with a shower and hairdryer. The cheapest time to book in here is from January 7 through the 20th, when rates may be lower than they are off-season.

Dining/Entertainment: Breakfast and lunch are buffet style. Dinner offers a choice of a lighter fixed-price menu or an à la carte menu. Non–hotel guests are welcome to dine here, and meals are served in an open-air restaurant overlooking the Caribbean. The food served here is arguably the best of that offered by the all-inclusive resorts. Live entertainment is provided, and a piano bar is popular until late at night.

Services: Room service (for breakfast), transfers to and from the airport, laundry, babysitting.

Facilities: Full program of daily scuba diving, windsurfing, waterskiing, snorkeling, sailing, pool swimming, use of a floodlit tennis court, fencing, archery, and riding. Emphasis on European body tonics based on Thalassotherapy, involving the healthful pampering of seawater massage, thermal jet baths, toning, physical culture, and beauty treatments for both sexes. Rather basic exercise room.

Rendezvous

P.O. Box 190, Malabar Beach, St. Lucia, W.I. ☎ **809/452-4211,** or 800/544-2883 in the U.S. and Canada. 89 rms, 11 suites. A/C TEL. Winter, $370–$430 double; $445–$490 suite for two. Off-season, $370–$420 double; $435–475 suite for two. (Rates all-inclusive.) AE, DC, MC, V. Free parking.

Rendezvous (formerly Couples, St. Lucia) is an unusual hotel, where all meals, drinks, entertainment, and most incidental expenses are included in the initial price. There are several price categories, depending on the season and the accommodation; top prices are charged for oceanfront luxury suites for two. The resort lies in a 7-acre tropical garden north of Vigie airport, near Castries. The center of the complex is under a gridwork of peaked roofs floored with terra-cotta tiles. Set on the edge of a beach bordered by palm trees, the hotel has a garden centered around a 150-year-old samaan tree. No children are allowed, and only couples are accepted. The hotel provides a $309 rebate toward the accommodation with a minimum stay of six nights.

Dining/Entertainment: The resort offers a choice of restaurants. A classical colonial-styled dining room called the Trysting Place is highlighted by polished brass chandeliers and wainscoting paneling at chair height. Sand and pale-pink walls with gilded sconces, carved cherubs, and terra-cotta brackets support vases and urns. Air conditioning is provided in this enclosed restaurant. The Pasta Terrace is an informal open-air restaurant featuring pastas as well as traditional favorites. Each Wednesday night a barbecue dinner offers steak, ribs, chicken, and fish to the beat of steel-band music. Following the meal is a beach party. For live entertainment six nights a week, guests frequent the Piano Bar, which stays open until the last couple retires. The resort's own pianist, choosing from a vast repertoire, plays a variety of tunes ranging from soft ballads to upbeat medleys. After a round of sing-alongs, dance enthusiasts can visit the Terrace Bar for dancing until 1am. Guests are also invited to the manager's rum punch party on Tuesday night and the weekly staff and guest show on Thursday.

Services: A member of the staff will meet your plane at the airport.

Facilities: Two freshwater outdoor swimming pools, swim-up bar at the free-form pool with landscaped island, fitness center, sauna, scuba-diving facilities, waterskiing, tennis courts, golf lessons, catamaran cruises, windsurfing, sailing, beach volleyball, fitness classes, bicycle tours.

Sandals Halcyon

Choc Bay (P.O. Box GM 910, Castries), St. Lucia, W.I. ☎ **809/453-0222,** or 800/SANDALS. Fax 809/451-8435. 170 rms. TV TEL. Winter, $1,607–$2,025 per person double. Off-season, $1,520–$1,925 per person double. (Rates all-inclusive for seven days.) AE, DC, MC, V. Free parking.

This is the smaller and less well accessorized of the two Sandals properties on St. Lucia. Many cost-conscious guests select this 22-acre resort with the understanding that free 15-minute minibus transfers are offered between it and its larger twin, Sandals St. Lucia. The combination allows some cost savings, plus free access to the nine-hole golf course and enlarged amenities of the larger resort. In keeping with Sandals' admission policies, only male-female couples are welcome at this resort. It's a 15-minute drive northeast of Castries, and contains three pools (one with a swim-up bar), a piano bar, a wide array of water sports and diversionary activities, and a firm commitment to providing all food, drink, and diversions for one all-inclusive price.

Sandals St. Lucia at La Toc

La Toc Rd. (P.O. Box 399, Castries), St. Lucia, W.I. ☎ **809/452-3081,** or 800/SANDALS in the U.S. and Canada. Fax 809/452-1012. 219 rms, 54 suites. A/C TV TEL. $1,775–$2,250 double; $2,395–$2,875 suites. (Rates all-inclusive for four days/three nights.) AE, DC, MC, V. Free parking.

It was widely viewed as a coup when the Jamaica-based Sandals chain acquired the sprawling acreage of a defunct hotel originally managed by Cunard. In 1993, a new incarnation of the old resort opened on a forested 155-acre site which slopes steeply down to the sea on the island's northwestern coast, a 10-minute drive west of Castries. Centered around a gazebo-capped swimming pool which incorporates an artificial waterfall, a swim-up bar, and a dining pavilion, the resort offers larger-than-expected bedrooms where each unit contains a king-size four-poster bed with mahogany headboard, a balcony or patio, a safe, a hairdryer, and a pastel-colored tropical decor. Consistent with policies at Sandals throughout the Caribbean, only couples (male-female) without children are admitted. The minimum stay in any season is three nights/four days.

Dining/Entertainment: The resort contains five food outlets. French food is offered in the resort's most upscale eatery, La Toc. Japanese food is served at Kimono's, where food is cooked on a heated table top, teppanyaki style. (There's also the main dining room for continental food, and Les Pitons, serving St. Lucian specialties.) The Arizona Restaurant, as befits its name, offers the cuisine of the American Southwest. After dark, guests gravitate to Jaime's, the on-site nightclub/disco, for late-night diversions or to Herbie's Piano Bar.

Services: Massage, hairdresser/manicure, currency exchange, tour desk.

Facilities: Nine-hole golf course, five tennis courts (lit for night play), health club, a series of "neighborhood Jacuzzis" which appear unexpectedly in different areas of the resort.

Wyndham Morgan Bay Resort

Choc Bay (P.O. Box 2167, Gros Islet), St. Lucia, W.I. ☎ **809/450-2511**, or 800/822-4200 in the U.S. Fax 809/450-1050. 240 rms, 2 suites. A/C TV TEL. Winter, $280–$315 single; $410–$480 double. Off-season, $245–$275 single; $340–$400 double. Year round, $550 suite for two. In winter, children 13–18 staying in parents' room $70, children 3–12 $50, children under 3 free; off-season, children under 18 stay free in parents' room. (Rates all-inclusive.) AE, DC, MC, V. Free parking.

Set a 10-minute drive north of Castries, on 45 landscaped acres partially shaded with trees and flowering shrubs, this all-inclusive resort draws more Europeans than Americans. Opened in 1992, and operated by the Dallas-based Wyndham chain, it offers accommodations in six different annexes, each painted in Wyndham's distinctive shade of peach-pink. The accommodations contain marble-trimmed bathrooms and are outfitted with patios or verandas and furniture crafted from rattan or wicker. Unlike some other all-inclusive hostelries on the island, this one welcomes children, providing a Kids Club for them (ages 4 to 12).

Dining/Entertainment: The resort's premier restaurant is the Palm Grill, which faces the beach, for candlelit lunches and dinners. Less formal meals are served overlooking the garden in the Trade Winds snack bar and grill. The cuisine is resort standard, nothing more. Local musicians, steel bands and calypso, often perform live in the Sundowner Bar.

Services: Car-rental kiosk on site, tour desk.

Facilities: A heart-shaped freshwater swimming pool, four tennis courts (two lit for night play), fitness center (with saunas, Jacuzzis, and steam room), archery, croquet, water sports, day-care center outfitted like a summer camp for children of guests; the beach is small with unclear water.

MODERATE

⑤ Harmony Marina Suites

Rodney Bay Lagoon (P.O. Box 155, Castries), St. Lucia, W.I. ☎ **809/452-8756.** Fax 809/452-8677. 30 one-bedroom suites. A/C TV TEL. Winter, $147–$246 suite for one or two. Off-season, $82–$163 suite for one or two. Additional person $30 extra in winter, $21 extra off-season. MAP $30–$45 per person extra. AE, MC, V. Free parking.

Between 1992 and 1993 this cream-colored set of two-story buildings, a short walk from one of the island's finest beaches, was renovated and upgraded. Originally built in 1980, the complex now offers well-maintained accommodations. Four of the suites contain kitchenettes—ideal for families on a budget—and complete with coffee makers, refrigerators, and a wet bar. The suites sit adjacent to a saltwater lagoon where boats find refuge from the rough waters of the open sea. Each of the units offers a patio or balcony with views of moored yachts, the lagoon, and surrounding hills. The suites are decorated in rattan, wicker, and florals. All suites, except the VIP/honeymoon units (eight of these) have sofa sleepers folding out to make a double bed in the living room. The VIP suites feature a double Jacuzzi, four-poster queen-size bed on a pedestal, and a sun deck, bidet, and white rattan furnishings. The establishment's restaurant, the Mortar & Pestle, is recommended separately (see "Where to Dine," below).

⑤ The Islander

Rodney Bay (P.O. Box 907, Castries), St. Lucia, W.I. ☎ **809/452-8757,** 212/545-8469 in New York City, or 800/223-9815 in the U.S., 800/468-0023 in Canada. Fax 809/452-0958. 40 rms, 20 studios, 4 two-bedroom apartments. A/C TV TEL. Winter, $110 single; $120 double; $120 studio for one; $130 studio for two; $240 two-bedroom apartment for six. Off-season, $75 single; $85 double; $80 studio for one; $90 studio for two; $175 two- bedroom apartment for six. Additional person $25 extra in winter, $20 extra off-season. MAP $28 per person extra. AE, DC, MC, V. Free parking.

North of Castries, near the St. Lucian Hotel and Reduit Beach, this well-recommended hotel has an entrance whose walls are festooned with hanging flowers. A brightly painted fishing boat serves as a buffet table near the pool, and there's a spacious covered bar area perfect for socializing with the owner, Greg Glace. Twenty of the accommodations are studios, with kitchenettes and private baths or showers, while the rooms have private showers and small bars with mini-refrigerators; the studios are slightly more expensive. Four two-bedroom apartments are in an annex across the street. Overlooking a grassy courtyard sheltered with vines and flowers, all rooms also have radios. A network of walkways lead to a convivial restaurant. Guests walk a few hundred feet to the beach or take a courtesy bus.

Moorings Marigot Bay Resort

Marigot Bay (P.O. Box 101, Castries), St. Lucia, W.I. ☎ **809/451-4357,** or 800/334-2435 in the U.S. Fax 809/451-4353. 16 cottages. Winter, $130 one-bedroom cottage for two. Off-season, $80 one-bedroom cottage for two. Additional person $15 extra. MAP $49 per person extra. AE, MC, V. Free parking.

Operated by a company famous for chartering yachts, this resort lies at the southern edge of a symmetrically shaped lagoon which author James Michener described as "the most beautiful bay in the Caribbean." The resort consists of a wood-sided, heavily timbered main building and a series of veranda-fronted accommodations that extend over a steeply sloping hillside above the bay. A ferryboat makes frequent runs across the bay to a neighboring resort, Doolittle's Inn (see "Where to Dine," below).

Well known in yachting circles for the safe haven provided by Marigot Bay, the Moorings offers an opportunity to do very little except relax amid the palm and banana groves, to swim and sail, perhaps to read. Some of the accommodations in the hotel are privately owned and rented while the owners are away. The decor varies according to the individual tastes of the owners, but are usually inspired by the West Indian style, with lots of rattan, pastel colors, and open-sided verandas.

Dining/Entertainment: The Hurricane Hole (part of the Moorings) and Doolittle's Pub & Restaurant (part of Doolittle's Inn, on the bay's north side and interconnected to the Moorings with a cable-ferry) are both recommended separately (see "Where to Dine," below).

Services: Laundry, babysitting.

Facilities: Swimming pool, PADI-approved scuba center, base for the Moorings Yacht Charter fleet.

Rex St. Lucian

P.O. Box 512, Reduit Beach, St. Lucia, W.I. ☎ **809/452-8351**, 305/471-6170 in Miami. 0181/741-5333 in London, or toll free 800/255-5859 in the U.S. Fax 809/452-8331. 260 rms. TEL. Winter, $165–$245 single or double; $230–$350 triple. Off-season, $135 single or double; $185 triple. MAP $46 per person extra. AE, DC, MC, V. Free parking.

Some 6¹/₂ miles north of Castries, the St. Lucian not only has one of the best programs of water sports on the island, but it also opens onto the most panoramic beachfront, Reduit Beach. One of the largest hotels on St. Lucia, it has well-landscaped grounds, with swaying palms, latticed breezeways, and flowering shrubs. The bedrooms are a bit tired after hosting too many tour groups, but this is an action-oriented hotel where guests spend little time in the rooms. Almost all the rooms are air-conditioned. Some guests find the activities and food here so rich and varied that they never leave the grounds, although I recommend that you do.

Dining/Entertainment: Many clients book in on the MAP and take their meals in the Hummingbird Restaurant. However, if you wish to partake of an à la carte selection from both Caribbean and international food, you can head for the Flamingo. You'll also be on the doorstep of some of the finest independent restaurants on the island, including Capone's. The St. Lucian has the best disco on the island, plus entertainment almost nightly, including floor shows, limbo dancing, fire-eaters, and a steel band.

Services: Room service, laundry, babysitting, doctor on 24-hour call.

Facilities: Beach and water sports, including scuba diving and windsurfing (some free to guests, but nonresidents can also participate; see "Sports and Recreation," below).

WHERE TO DINE

As virtually every hotel on St. Lucia seems to be going all-inclusive, the independent restaurants have had to sail through rough waters. But there are quite a few, nevertheless, of varying quality. Most restaurants are open for lunch and dinner, unless otherwise noted. The big problem about dining out at night, as it is on nearly all Caribbean islands, is getting to that special hideaway and back again with adequate transportation across the dark, potholed roads.

EXPENSIVE

In Castries

Green Parrot

Red Tape Lane, Morne Fortune, St. Lucia, W.I. ☎ **809/452-3399.** Reservations recommended. Fixed-price dinner EC$90–EC$110 ($33.30–$40.70); lunch appetizers EC$8 ($3) each; lunch main courses EC$40–EC$110 ($14.80–$40.70). AE, MC, V. Lunch daily noon–3pm; dinner daily 7pm–midnight. AMERICAN/CARIBBEAN.

About a mile and a half east of the center, the Green Parrot overlooks Castries Harbour. It will take about 12 minutes to walk from downtown, and the effort will be worth it, as this is an elegant choice for dining. It's the home of its chef, Harry, who got his long years of training in prestigious restaurants and hotels in London, including Claridges. Guests take their time and make an evening of it. Many enjoy a before-dinner drink in the Victorian-style salon, such as a Grass Parrot (made from coconut cream, crème de menthe, bananas, white rum, and sugar).

The price of a meal in the English-colonial dining room usually includes entertainment: Harry is not only a cook, but also an entertainer of some note. Folkloric shows (with limbo dancers and fire eaters, followed by music for dancing) are pre-sented on Wednesday and Saturday, while Tuesday is a barbecue and Monday is "ladies' night." Then, any woman who wears a flower in her hair, when accom-panied by a man in a coat and tie, receives a free dinner.

All this may sound gimmicky, but the food doesn't suffer because of all the activity. There's an emphasis on St. Lucian specialties, using home-grown produce when it's available. Try the christophine au gratin (a Caribbean squash with cheese) or the Créole soup made with callaloo and pumpkin. There are also five kinds of curry with chutney, as well as a selection of omelets and sandwiches at lunchtime. Steak Pussy Galore is a specialty.

The Green Parrot also offers some of the island's least expensive lodgings, each room with air conditioning and telephone. In winter, singles cost $90 and doubles are $110, lowered in off-season to $68 single or $80 double. Breakfast costs $5 to $6 extra.

At Marigot Bay

Hurricane Hole

In the Moorings Marigot Bay Resorts, Marigot Bay. ☎ **809/451-4357.** Reservations recom-mended for nonresidents. Appetizers EC$8.50–EC$22 ($3.10–$8.10); main courses EC$43–EC$67 ($15.90–$24.80). AE, MC, V. Lunch daily noon–3pm; dinner daily 6:30–10pm. INTERNATIONAL/ST. LUCIAN.

Cozy, candlelit, and nautical, this is the restaurant maintained at the Moorings Marigot Bay Resort, an establishment that charters yachts to clients from around the hemisphere. The congenial bar does a brisk business before dinner, when the Marigot Hurricane (rum, banana, grenadine, apricot brandy) is especially popular. Specialties include callaloo soup studded with seafood, conch chowder, stuffed crab backs, shrimp calypso, curried chicken, grilled breast of chicken with peppercorns, pork chops, grilled sirloin or filet mignon, at least two different preparations of lobster, and surf and turf. Ceiling fans spin languidly as you dine.

MODERATE

In Castries

Jimmie's

Vigie Cove Marina. ☎ **809/452-5142.** Reservations not accepted. Appetizers EC$6–EC$12.50 ($2.20–$4.60); main courses EC$36–EC$65 ($13.30–$24.10). AE, MC, V. Mon–Sat 9am–10:30pm, Sun 6–10:30pm. Closed Mid-July to Aug. CREOLE.

Near Vigie airport, with a view of Castries Harbour and the Morne, Jimmie's is known for its fish menu and tasty Créole cookery prepared with fresh ingredients daily. Jimmie is a native St. Lucian, and after training in England, he returned to his homeland to open this spot popular with visitors and locals alike. Its bar is con-sidered a prime rendezvous point. Guests like the open-air terrace dining and dishes that taste just like "mama made," provided your mother came from the islands and learned secret Créole spices. Try the conch, octopus, or kingfish in Créole sauce.

San Antoine

Morne Fortune. ☎ **809/452-4660.** Reservations recommended. Appetizers EC$12–EC$30 ($4.40–$11.10); main courses EC$50–EC$100 ($18.50–$37). AE, MC, V. Lunch Mon–Fri noon–2:30pm; dinner Mon–Sat 6:30–10:30pm. CONTINENTAL/WEST INDIAN.

Constructed in the 19th century as a Great House, this restaurant lies up the Morne and offers vistas over the capital and the water. Sometime in the 1920s it was turned into the first hotel on St. Lucia by Aubrey Davidson-Houston, the British portrait painter whose subjects have included W. Somerset Maugham. However, in 1970 it was destroyed by fire. When it was restored in 1984, whatever could be retained, including the original stonework, was given a new lease on life, cleaned, and repaired. You might begin with the classic callaloo soup of the island, then follow with fettuccine Alfredo, or perhaps fresh fish en papillote. Lobster thermidor might also be featured. Frankly, many readers have found the view and ambience far more stunning than the cuisine.

At Marigot Bay

Doolittle's Inn/Doolittle's Pub & Restaurant

Marigot Bay. (P.O. Box 523, Castries), St. Lucia, W.I. ☎ **809/451-4761.** Reservations not required. Appetizers EC$6–EC$20 ($2.20–$7.40); hamburgers and rotis EC$14–EC$25 ($5.20–$9.30); main courses EC$22–EC$48 ($8.10–$17.80). AE, MC, V. Daily 10:30am–11pm. AMERICAN SNACKS.

Named after the big-budget Rex Harrison film (a flop) shot in the nearby bay, this restaurant and pub rises from a grove of coconut palms at the northern edge of the bay, adjacent to a small marina. Doolittle's Pub is a favorite watering hole of locals, tourists, and yachties. Known for its excellent hamburgers and rotis—the most popular lunchtime fare—it also offers such intriguing dishes as chicken and lobster quesadillas. At dinner you may prefer the fisherman's catch, prepared according to your wishes—grilled, pan-fried in butter, poached, or Créole style. Fish and chips St. Lucian style is regularly offered, as is a docksider New York strip dinner with fresh local vegetables. The open-air waterfront pub sets the stage for various forms of entertainment, including reggae on Saturday night. In winter, there is live musical entertainment most nights, ranging from country to folk, from soca to reggae.

Note that Doolittle's clientele usually arrives via the inn's ferryboat. Attached with a cable to either end of Marigot Bay, it makes the short run from its base at the Moorings Marigot Bay Resort about every 10 minutes throughout the day and evening.

There are also various accommodations to rent, including eight suites with a screened-in balcony, king-size bed, shower, refrigerator, and hotplate. You can also rent one-, two-, and three-bedroom villas on a hillside reached via a tram ride. These villas are self-contained, with a full kitchen, separate bedrooms, screened balcony, and some with sitting areas. In winter, suites cost $85 and villas rent for $125 to $225; off-season, suites are $70 for two and villas run $100 to $200. Scuba-diving packages are also offered.

In Gros Islet

⑤ Banana Split

St. George's St., Gros Islet. ☎ **809/450-8125.** Reservations recommended. Appetizers EC$5–EC$7 ($1.90–$2.60); main courses EC$25–EC$75 ($9.30–$27.80). No credit cards. Lunch Mon–Sat noon–2pm; dinner Mon–Sat 6:30–10pm. CREOLE.

Between Castries and Cap Estate is a huge barnlike wooden building with its sides open to a view of the sea. One diner suggested that it's "not unlike an American Legion hall set up for a Sunday chicken dinner." Read that, rowdy American Legion hall. Actually the building was copied from dance-hall models that the owner saw when touring Austria. He is Cletus Hippolyte, a St. Lucia–born artist and musician who toured Europe as a jazz player. Dining at a simply set, long wooden table, you might begin with one of the soups made with local ingredients, such as lobster, pumpkin, or callaloo. Or perhaps you'd prefer a crab-back appetizer, followed by chicken Créole. Lobster also appears as a main dish, either boiled and served with lime butter or curried or offered thermidor style. For dessert, order the namesake banana split. On Friday from 11pm, there are jump-up and reggae shows, when a band arrives.

In Rodney Bay

The Bistro (On the Waterfront)

Rodney Bay. ☎ 809/452-9494. Reservations recommended. Appetizers EC$12–EC$25 ($4.40–$9.30); main courses EC$25–EC$64 ($9.30–$23.70). AE, MC, V. Dinner only, daily 5:30–10:30pm. Closed Thurs May–Nov. SEAFOOD/INTERNATIONAL.

Operated by Nick and Pat Bowden, a husband-and-wife team of English expatriates, this always-popular restaurant was designed as a long, thin veranda which offers more waterfront tables than any other restaurant on the island. The bistro features a comfortable bar area where drinks begin at EC$5 ($1.90) and a flavorful array of seafood and pasta dishes. Menu items include seafood cannelloni stuffed with lobster and crabmeat and served with a parmesan-cream sauce; filets of red snapper layered with shrimp mousse and served in puff pastry; seafood Créole studded with conch, snapper, and shrimp; breast of chicken sautéed with lobster tails and served with lobster sauce; and an agliata of fresh calamari prepared with garlic, olive oil, and Italian herbs.

Capone's

Rodney Bay. ☎ **809/452-0284.** Reservations required. Appetizers EC$12.50–EC$22 ($4.60–$8.10); main courses EC$28–EC$60 ($10.40–$22.20). AE, MC, V. Tues–Sun 11am–10:30pm. ITALIAN.

In pink and black, Capone's could have been inspired by the old Billy Wilder film *Some Like It Hot*, starring Marilyn Monroe. Actually, this is an art deco rendition of a speakeasy along Miami Beach in the 1930s. North of Reduit Beach, near the lagoon, it's brightly lit at night.

At the entrance is a self-service pizza parlor that also serves burgers and well-stuffed pita-bread sandwiches. However, I recommend that you go into the back for a really superb Italian meal, beginning with a drink, perhaps "Prohibition Punch" or a "St. Valentine's Day Massacre," served by "gangster" barmen. A player piano enlivens the atmosphere. You might begin with a pasta (the lasagne is a favorite, especially when accompanied by a "Little Caesar" salad). For your main course, try flame-grilled chicken breast with Dijon mustard (with ham and cream cheese), fresh local charcoal-grilled fish, or some of the best steaks on the island. Finish with an Italian espresso.

Charthouse

Rodney Bay. ☎ **809/452-8115.** Reservations recommended. Appetizers $3–$7; main courses $11–$30. AE, MC, V. Dinner only. Mon–Sat 6–10:30pm. Closed: Sept. AMERICAN/CREOLE.

In a large grangelike building with a skylit ceiling and mahogany bar, the Charthouse, one of the oldest restaurants in the area, is built several feet above the bobbing yachts of the lagoon, without walls, to allow an optimum view of the water. The restaurant serves good food in large portions and, combined with helpful staff virtually unchanged since its inception, the Charthouse continues to enjoy its reputation as one of the island's most popular dining venues. The specialties might include callaloo soup, St. Lucian crab backs, "meat-falling-off-the-bone" baby back spareribs, and fresh local lobster (from September to April you can often witness the live lobster being delivered from the boat at around 5pm). If you fancy a well-cooked charcoal-broiled steak, you'll see why this dish made the restaurant famous.

Ⓢ The Lime

Rodney Bay. ☎ **809/452-0761.** Reservations recommended for dinner. Appetizers EC$6.50–EC$16 ($2.40–$5.90); main courses EC$29–EC$70 ($10.70–$25.90). MC, V. Lunch Wed–Mon 11am–2pm; dinner Wed–Mon 6:30–11pm. Closed Mid-June to July 7. AMERICAN/CREOLE.

The Lime stands north of Reduit Beach in an area that's becoming known as restaurant row. Some of these places are rather expensive, but the Lime continues to keep its prices low, its food good and plentiful, and its service and welcome among the finest on the island, all of which attract both locals and visitors. West Indian in feeling, the Lime has an open-air setting. In honor of its namesake, the restaurant features a lime special as a drink. Specialties are stuffed crab backs and fish steak Créole, and they also serve shrimp, steaks, lamb and pork chops, and roti. The steaks are done over a charcoal grill.

Mortar & Pestle

In the Harmony Marina Suites, Rodney Bay Lagoon. ☎ **809/452-8756.** Reservations recommended, especially for dinner. Appetizers EC$8–EC$25 ($3–$9.30); main courses EC$45–EC$90 ($16.70–$33.30). AE, MC, V. Lunch daily noon–3pm; dinner daily 7–10pm. CARIBBEAN/INTERNATIONAL.

Set on the waterfront of Rodney Bay Lagoon, in a previously recommended hotel, this restaurant offers indoor-outdoor dining overlooking a view of boats which moor at the nearby marina. The menu features a selection of dishes derived from St. Lucia and the neighboring islands. These include filets of fish martiniquais (usually red snapper sautéed in garlic butter with onions and mushrooms and simmered in a white-wine-and-cream sauce), filets of pan-fried Barbados flying fish (in season), loin of pork with ginger sauce, and Trinidad-style calypso chicken. Several preparations of lobster are also available, along with an international selection of wines. Music from a steel band or some other local band sometimes accompanies the meals here.

IN SOUFRIÈRE

Ⓢ The Still

Soufriére. ☎ **809/459-7224.** Reservations not required. Appetizers EC$5–EC$9 ($1.90–$3.30); main courses EC$15–EC$60 ($5.60–$22.20). AE, MC, V. Breakfast daily 8–10:30am; lunch daily 11am–5pm. CREOLE.

The first thing you'll see as you drive up the hill from the harbor is a very old rum distillery set on a platform of thick timbers. The restaurant lies less than a mile east of Soufrière. The site is a working cocoa, copra, and citrus plantation that has been in the same St. Lucian family for four generations. The front blossoms with avocado and breadfruit trees, and a mahogany forest is a few steps away. The bar near the front veranda is furnished with glossy tables cut from cross sections of mahogany tree trunks. A more formal and spacious dining room is nearby.

WHAT TO SEE & DO

Lovely little towns, beautiful beaches and bays, mineral baths, banana plantations—even a volcano is here to visit.

CASTRIES

The capital city has grown up around its harbor, which occupies the crater of an extinct volcano. Charter captains and the yachting set drift in here, and large cruise-ship wharfs welcome vessels from around the world. Because of those devastating fires mentioned earlier, the town today has a look of newness, with glass-and-concrete (or steel) buildings replacing the French colonial or Victorian look typical of many West Indian capitals.

The **Saturday-morning market** in the old tin-roofed building on Jeremy Street in Castries is my favorite "people-watching" site on the island. The country women dress up in their traditional garb of cotton headdress; the number of knotted points on top reveals their marital status (ask one of the locals to explain it to you). The luscious fresh fruits and vegetables of St. Lucia are sold as weather-beaten men sit close by playing *warrie*, which is a fast game played with pebbles on a carved board. You can also pick up such St. Lucia handcrafts as baskets and unglazed pottery.

Government House is a late Victorian building. A **Roman Catholic cathedral** stands on Columbus Square, which has a few restored buildings.

Beyond Government House lies **Morne Fortune**, which means "Hill of Good Luck." No one had much luck here, certainly not the battling French and British fighting for Fort Charlotte. The barracks and guard rooms changed nationalities many times. You can visit the 18th-century barracks complete with a military cemetery, a small museum, the Old Powder Magazine, and the "Four Apostles Battery" (the apostles being a quartet of grim muzzle-loading cannons). The view of the harbor of Castries is panoramic. You can see north to Pigeon Island or south to the Pitons. To reach Morne Fortune, head east on Bridge Street.

PIGEON ISLAND NATIONAL LANDMARK ·

St. Lucia's first national park was originally an island flanked on one side by the Caribbean and on the other by the Atlantic. It is now joined to the mainland island by a causeway. On its west coast are two white sand beaches. There's also a restaurant, Jambe de Bois, named after a wooden-legged pirate who once used the island as a hideout for his men.

Pigeon Island also offers an Interpretation Centre, equipped with artifacts and a multimedia display of local history, ranging from the Amerindian occupation of A.D. 1,000 to the Battle of Saints, when Admiral Rodney's fleet set out from Pigeon Island and defeated Admiral De Grasse in 1782.

The Captain's Cellar Olde English Pub lies under the center and is evocative of an 18th-century English bar. Pigeon Island, only 44 acres in size, got its name from the red-neck pigeon or ramier which once made this island home. It is ideal for picnics, weddings, and nature walks. The park is open daily from 9am to 5pm, charging an entrance fee of EC$5 ($1.90). For more information, call the St. Lucia National Trust (☎ 809/452-5005).

✪ MARIGOT BAY

Movie crews, formerly those for Rex Harrison's *Dr. Doolittle* and Sophia Loren's *Fire Power*, like to use this bay, one of the most beautiful in the Caribbean, for background shots. Lying 8 miles south of Castries, it's narrow yet navigable by yachts of any size. Here Admiral Rodney camouflaged his ships with palm leaves while lying in wait for French frigates. The shore, lined with palm trees, remains relatively unspoiled, but some building sites have been sold. Again, it's a delightful spot for a picnic if you didn't take your food basket to Pigeon Island.

SOUFRIERE

This little fishing port, St. Lucia's second-largest settlement, is dominated by two pointed hills called ✪ **Petit Piton** and **Gros Piton.** These two hills, "The Pitons," have become the very symbol of St. Lucia. They are two volcanic cones rising to 2,460 and 2,619 feet. Formed of lava and rock, and once actively volcanic, they are now clothed in green vegetation. Their sheer rise from the sea makes them a landmark visible for miles around. Waves crash around their bases.

Near Soufrière lies the famous "drive-in" volcano. Called ✪ **Mount Soufrière,** it's a rocky lunar landscape of bubbling mud and craters seething with fuming sulfur. You literally drive your car into an old (millions of years) crater and walk between the sulfur springs and pools of hissing steam. A local guide is usually waiting beside them, shrouded in sulfurous fumes that are said to have medicinal properties. For a fee, he'll point out the blackened waters, among the few of their kind in the Caribbean. If you do hire a guide, agree—then doubly agree—on what that fee will be.

Nearby are the ✪ **Diamond Mineral Baths,** surrounded by a tropical arboretum. Constructed on orders of Louis XVI in 1784, whose doctors told him that these waters were similar in mineral content to the waters at Aix-les-Bains, they were intended for recuperative effects for French soldiers fighting in the West Indies. Later destroyed, they were rebuilt after World War II. They have an average temperature of 106°F and lie near one of the geological attractions of the island, a waterfall that changes colors (from yellow to black to green to gray) several times a day. For EC$5 ($1.85), you can bathe and benefit from the recuperative effects yourself.

From Soufrière in the southwest, the road winds toward Fond St-Jacques where you'll have a good view of mountains and villages as you cut through St. Lucia's Cape Moule-à-Chique tropical rain forest. You'll also see the Barre de l'Isle divide.

CAPE MOULE-A-CHIQUE

At the southern tip of the island, Cape Moule-à-Chique is where the Caribbean Sea merges with the Atlantic. Here the town of Vieux Fort can be seen, as can the neighboring island of St. Vincent, 26 miles away.

BANANA PLANTATIONS

Bananas are the island's leading export. As you're being hauled around the island by taxi drivers, ask them to take you to one of the huge plantations that allow visitors to come on the grounds. I suggest a sightseeing look at one of the trio of big ones—the Cul-de-Sac, just north of Marigot Bay; La Caya, in Dennery on the east coast; and the Roseau Estate, south of Marigot Bay.

SPORTS & OUTDOOR ACTIVITIES

BEACHES   Since most of the island hotels are built right on the beach, you won't have far to go for swimming. All beaches are open to the public, even those along hotel properties. However, if you use any of the hotel's beach equipment, you must pay for it, of course. I prefer the beaches along the western coast, because a rough surf on the windward side makes swimming there potentially dangerous.

Leading beaches include **Pigeon Island,** off the northern shore, with white sand and picnic facilities. **Vigie Beach,** north of Castries Harbour, is one of the most popular on St. Lucia. It has fine sands, often a light beige in color. But for a novelty, you might try the black volcanic sand at Soufrière. The beach there is called **La Toc.**

Just north of Soufrière is that beach connoisseur's delight, the white sands of **Anse Chastanet,** set at the foothills of lush, green mountains. While here, you

---

Rare Creatures

The fertile volcanic soil of St. Lucia sustains a rich diversity of bird and animal life. Some of the richest troves for ornithologists are in protected precincts off the St. Lucian coast, in either of two national parks (Frigate Islands Nature Reserve and the Maria Islands Nature Reserve).

The **Frigate Islands** are a cluster of rocks set a short distance offshore from Praslin Bay, midway up St. Lucia's eastern coastline. Barren except for tall grasses that seem to thrive in the salt spray, the islands were named after the scissor-tailed frigate birds (*Fregata magnificens*), which breed there every year between May and July. Then, large colonies of the graceful birds float in well-choreographed formations over islands that are visited only under the closely supervised permission of government authorities. Many visitors believe that the least controversial way to admire the Frigate Islands (and to respect their fragile ecosystems) is to walk along the nature trail that the St. Lucian government has hacked along the clifftop of the St. Lucian mainland, about 150 feet inland from the shoreline. Even without binoculars, you'll be able to see the frigates wheeling overhead. You'll also enjoy eagle's-eye views of the unusual geology of the St. Lucian coast, which includes sea caves, dry ravines, a waterfall (which flows only during rainy season), and a strip of mangrove swamp.

The **Maria Islands** are larger and more arid, and are exposed almost constantly to salt-laden winds blowing up from the equator. Set to the east of the island's southernmost tip, offshore from the town of Vieux Fort, they contain a strictly protected biodiversity which can be visited. The approximately 30 acres of cactus-dotted land comprising the two largest islands (Maria Major and Maria Minor) include over 120 species of plant life, lizards, butterflies, and snakes that are believed to be extinct in other parts of the world. These include the large ground lizard (*Zandolite*), and the nocturnal, nonvenomous kouwes (*Dromicus ornatus*) snake.

The Marias are also a bird refuge, populated by such species as the sooty tern, the bridled tern, the Caribbean martin, the red-billed tropicbird, and the brown noddy, which usually builds its nest under the protective thorns of prickly pear cactus.

If permission is granted, visitors will set foot on either parks only as part of groups who arrive by boat under the supervision of a qualified guide. The cost is around $60 per person for the Frigates, and around $80 per person for the Marias, for guided tours that last a full day. These must be arranged through the staff of the St. Lucia National Trust (☎ **809/452-5005**), who will supply further details.

might want to patronize the facilities of the previously recommended Anse Chastanet Hotel. Reduit Beach with its fine brown sands lies between Choc Bay and Pigeon Point.

DEEP-SEA FISHING   The waters around St. Lucia are known for their gamefish, including blue marlin, sailfish, mako sharks, and barracuda, with tuna and kingfish among the edible catches. Most hotels can arrange for fishing expeditions. Call **Mako Watersports** (☎ **809/452-0412**) or **Captain Mike's** (☎ **809/452-7044**) for information about fishing trips.

GOLF   St. Lucia has a nine-hole golf course at the **Cap Estate Golf Club,** at the northern end of the island (☎ **809/450-8523**). Greens fees are $25 for 18 holes and there are no caddies. Hours are 8am to sunset daily. Another nine-hole course is now called **St. Lucia Sandals** (☎ **809/452-3081**), although preference is given to the all-inclusive guests of the hotel.

HORSEBACK RIDING   North of Castries, you can rent a horse at **Cas-En-Bas and Cap Estate Stables** (to make arrangements, call René Trim (☎ **809/ 450-8273**). The cost is $30 for one hour; a two-hour ride costs $50. Ask about a picnic trip to the Atlantic, with a barbecue lunch and drink included, for $50. Departures are on horseback at 8:30am. Nonriders can be included; they are transported to the site in a van and pay half price.

SCUBA DIVING   In Soufrière, **Scuba St. Lucia,** in the Anse Chastanet Hotel (☎ **809/459-7000**), established in 1981, offers one of the world's top dive locations at a five-star PADI dive center. At the southern end of Anse Chastanet's quarter-mile-long, soft, secluded beach, it offers great diving and comprehensive facilities for divers of all levels. Some of the most spectacular coral reefs of St. Lucia—many only 10 to 20 feet below the surface of the water—lie a short distance from the beach and provide shelter for many denizens and a backdrop for schools of reef fish.

Many professional PADI instructors offer dive programs two or three times a day. Photographic equipment is available for rent (film can be processed on the premises), and instruction is offered in picture taking, the price depending on the time and equipment involved. Experienced divers can rent the equipment they need on a per-item basis. The packages include tanks, backpacks, and weightbelts. Through participation in the establishment's "specialty" courses, divers can obtain PADI certification. A two- to three-hour introductory lesson, including a short theory session, equipment familiarization, development of skills in shallow water, and a tour of the reef, with all equipment included, costs $75. Single dives cost $30. Hours are 8am to 5:45pm daily.

TENNIS   Most of the big hotels have their own courts. If yours doesn't, ask at the front desk for the nearest one. Some of the courts on St. Lucia are lit for night games.

WATER SPORTS   Unless you're interested in scuba (in which case you should head for the facilities at the Anse Chastenet Hotel), the best all-around watersports center is **St. Lucian Watersports,** at the Rex St. Lucian Hotel (☎ **809/ 452-8351**). Waterskiing costs about $15 for a 10-minute ride. Windsurfers can be rented for $25 an hour; lessons cost $30 per person for a three-hour course. Snorkeling is free for guests of the hotel; nonresidents pay $25, including equipment.

SHOPPING

Stores are generally open Monday through Friday from 8am to 4pm and on Saturday from 8am to noon—but watch those early closings at some shops on Wednesday. Most of the shopping is in Castries, where the principal streets are William Peter Boulevard and Bridge Street. Many stores will sell you goods at duty-free prices (providing you don't take the merchandise with you but have it delivered to the airport or cruise dock). There are some good buys—not remarkable—in bone china, jewelry, perfume, watches, liquor, and crystal. Souvenir items include bags and mats, local pottery, and straw hats—again, nothing remarkable.

Built with an eye to the cruise-ship passenger, **Pointe Seraphine** has the best collection of shops on the island, together with offices for car rentals, organized taxi service (for sightseeing), a bureau de change, Philatelic Bureau, Information Centre, and international telephones. Cruise ships berth right at the shopping center. Under red roofs in a Spanish-style setting, the complex requires the presentation of a cruise pass or an airline ticket to the shopkeeper when purchasing goods. Visitors can take away their purchases, except liquor and tobacco, which will be delivered to the airport. The center is open in season, Monday through Friday from 8am to 5pm and on Saturday from 8am to 2pm; off-season, Monday through Friday from 9am to 4pm and on Saturday from 9am to 4pm. It is also open when cruise ships are in port.

Among the shops represented, **Studio Images** (☎ 809/452-6883) offers a wide selection of perfumes, including such brand names as Estée Lauder, Oscar de la Renta, and Yves St. Laurent. **J. Q. Charles** (☎ 809/452-7591) offers china, crystal, glassware, jewelry, perfumes, liquor, and local arts and crafts.

Gablewoods Mall, on Gros Islet Highway 2 miles north of Castries, contains three restaurants and one of the densest concentrations of shops on the island. Some visitors consider the best clothing and sundry shop to be **Top Banana** (☎ 809/451-6389). Inventory includes beachwear, scuba equipment, gifts, and casual resortwear. Other branches of this store can be found at both the Rex St. Lucian Hotel and the Windjammer Hotel.

Bagshaws
La Toc. ☎ **809/452-2139.**

Just outside Castries, this is the leading island hand-printer of silk-screen designs. An American, Sydney Bagshaw, founded the operation in the mid-1960s, and today it is operated by his daughter-in-law, Alice Bagshaw. The family has devoted their considerable skills to turning out a high-quality line of fabric as colorful as the Caribbean. The birds (look for the St. Lucia parrot), butterflies, and flowers of St. Lucia are incorporated into their original designs. The highlights are an extensive household line in vibrant prints on linen, as well as clothing and beachwear for both men and women, and the best T-shirt collection on St. Lucia. At La Toc Studios, the printing process can be viewed seven days a week.

There are four other retail outlets: in the Pointe Seraphine Duty Free Shopping Mall (☎ 809/452-7570), in Marigot Bay (☎ 809/451-4378), in Rodney Bay (☎ 809/452-8831), and at the "Best of St. Lucia" at Hewanorra International Airport, Vieux Fort (☎ 809/454-8874).

Caribelle Batik
Howelton House, Old Victoria Rd., The Morne. ☎ **809/452-3785.**

In this workshop, just five minutes' drive from Castries, you can watch St. Lucian artists creating intricate patterns and colors for the ancient art of making batik. You can also purchase batik in cotton and silk, made up in casual and beach clothing, plus wall hangings and other gift items reflecting the Caribbean. Drinks are served in the Dyehouse Bar and Terrace in the renovated Victorian-era building.

Eudovic Art Studio

Goodlands, Morne Fortune. ☎ 809/452-2747.

Vincent Joseph Eudovic is a master artist and wood carver whose sculptures have been exhibited in the O.A.S. headquarters in Washington, D.C., and have gained an increasing fame. He usually carves his imaginative free-form sculptures from local tree roots, such as teak, mahogany, and red cedar, and follows the natural pattern, sanding the grain until it's of almost satin smoothness. Some of his carvings are from Laurier Cannelle trees, which have disappeared from the island, although their roots often remain in a well-preserved state. Native to St. Lucia, he teaches pupils the art of wood carving. In the main studio, much of the work of his pupils is on display. However, ask to be taken to his private studio, where you'll see his remarkable work. Open Monday through Friday from 7:30am to 6pm and on Saturday from 8am to 3pm.

While at Eudovic's Studio, you could pop into the bar for a drink. It's open Monday through Saturday from 8am to 4:30pm.

Noah's Arkade

Jeremie St. ☎ 809/452-2523.

Many of the Caribbean handcrafts and gifts here are routine tourist items, yet you'll often find something interesting if you browse around. They sell local straw placemats and rugs, wall hangings, sandals, maracas, steel drums, shell necklaces, and warri boards. Branches are found at Hewanorra International Airport and the Pointe Seraphine Duty Free Shopping Mall.

Sea Island Cotton Shop

Bridge St. ☎ 809/452-3674.

Catering almost exclusively to tourists, this is the largest shop in the center of Castries. It carries T-shirts, Sunny Caribbee herbs and spices, hand-painted souvenirs, and beach- and swimwear. There are other locations in Gableswood Mall, the Rex St. Lucian Hotel, and the Windjammer Landing Villa Beach Resort.

ST. LUCIA AFTER DARK

There isn't much except the entertainment offered by hotels. In the winter months, at least one hotel offers a steel band or calypso music every night of the week. Otherwise, check to see what's happening at **Capone's** (☎ 809/452-0284) and **The Green Parrot** (☎ 809/452-3167)—see "Where to Dine," above.

Splash, in the St. Lucian Hotel, Reduit Beach (☎ 809/452-8351), is the best disco on the island, with a large dance floor in a roomy air-conditioned area. The club plays an assortment of music from local reggae and calypso to American and European disco. You must be 18 or over to enter. Hotel guests are admitted free; others pay EC$25 ($9.30). Splash is open Wednesday through Saturday from 9pm until all the patrons depart. Beer costs EC$7 ($2.60).

The Lime (see "Where to Dine," above) also operates **The Late Lime Night Club,** offering entertainment Wednesday through Monday, beginning at 10pm and lasting until the crowd folds. Jazz, reggae, golden oldies—it's all here, even easy-listening music on Sunday. Wednesday and Saturday are disco nights, and on Friday live jazz entertainment is a feature. Admission is EC$15 ($5.60).

3 St. Vincent

One of the major Windward Islands, sleepy St. Vincent is only now awakening to tourism, which hasn't yet reached massive dimensions here. Sailors and the yachting set have long known of St. Vincent and its satellite bays and beaches in the Grenadines.

Visit St. Vincent for its botanical beauty and the Grenadines for the best sailing waters in the Caribbean. Don't come for nightlife, grand cuisine, and fabled beaches. There are some white sand beaches near Kingstown on St. Vincent, but most of the other beaches ringing the island are of black sand. The yachting crowd seems to view St. Vincent merely as a launching pad for the 60-mile string of the Grenadines, but there are enough attractions on the island to merit an exploration all on its own.

Unspoiled by the worst fallout that mass tourism sometimes brings, the people actually treat visitors like people: Met with courtesy, they respond with courtesy. British customs predominate, along with traces of Gallic cultural influences, but all with a distinct West Indian flair.

ORIENTATION
GETTING THERE

In the eastern Caribbean, St. Vincent—the "gateway to the Grenadines" (see Section 4)—lies 100 miles west of Barbados, where most visitors from North America fly first, and then make connections that will take them on to St. Vincent's **E. T. Joshua Airport** and the Grenadines. For transportation from North America to Barbados, see "Getting There" in "Orientation," in Chapter 14.

From Barbados, you can connect with one of five daily **LIAT** (☎ **809/ 458-4841**) flights to St. Vincent. The flight from Barbados takes just 35 minutes. LIAT also flies in from Trinidad, St. Lucia, and Grenada.

Air Martinique (☎ **809/458-4528**) runs twice daily service between Martinique, St. Lucia, St. Vincent, and Union Island.

Increasing numbers of visitors to St. Vincent prefer the dependable service of one of the best-managed charter airlines in the Caribbean, **Mustique Airways.** For reservations, contact Mustique Airways/Grenadine Travel Company, P.O. Box 1232, St. Vincent, W.I. (☎ **809/458-4380**), or their representative at the Mustique Airport (☎ **809/458-4621**). The airline makes frequent runs from St. Vincent to the major airports of the Grenadines. With advance warning, Mustique Airways will arrange a specially chartered (and reasonably priced) transport for you and your party to and from many of the surrounding islands (including Grenada, Aruba, St. Lucia, Antigua, Barbados, Trinidad, and any other in the southern Caribbean). The price of these chartered flights is less than you might expect, and often matches the fares on conventional Caribbean airlines. Currently the airline owns seven small aircraft, none of which carries more than nine passengers.

GETTING AROUND

BY BUS Flamboyantly painted "al fresco" buses travel the principal arteries of St. Vincent, linking the major towns and villages. The price is low, depending on where you're going, and the experience will connect you with the people of the island. The central departure point is the bus terminal at the New Kingstown Fish Market. Fares range from EC$1 to EC$6 (40¢ to $2.20).

BY TAXI   The government sets the rates for fares, but taxis are unmetered; the wise passenger will always ask the fare and agree on the charge before getting in. Figure on spending about $7 to go from the E. T. Joshua Airport to your hotel, maybe more. You should tip about 12% of the fare.

If you don't want to drive yourself, you can also hire taxis to take you to the island's major attractions. Most drivers seem to be well-informed guides (it won't take you long to learn everything you need to know about St. Vincent). You'll spend EC$40 to EC$50 ($14.80 to $18.50) per hour for a car holding two to four passengers.

BY RENTAL CAR   Driving on St. Vincent is a bit of an adventure because of the narrow, twisting roads and the *drive-on-the-left requirement.* To drive like a Vincentian, you'll soon learn to sound your horn a lot as you make the sharp curves and turns. If you present your valid U.S. or Canadian driver's license at the police department on Bay Street in Kingstown, and pay an EC$40 ($14.80) fee, you'll obtain a temporary permit to drive.

The major car-rental companies do not have branches on St. Vincent. Rental cars cost EC$120 to EC$185 ($44.40 to $68.50) a day, but that must be determined on the spot. Contact **Kim's Rentals,** on Grenville Street in Kingstown (☎ **809/456-1884**), or **Star Garage,** also on Grenville Street in Kingstown (☎ **809/456-1743**).

FAST FACTS: St. Vincent

Area Code   St. Vincent can be dialed directly from the United States by using the Caribbean area code, 809, and the seven-digit number. For information on dialing once on the island, see "Telephone," below.

Banking Hours   Most banks are open Monday through Thursday from 8am to either 1 or 3pm and on Friday from either 8am to 5pm or from 8am to 1pm and 3 to 5pm, depending on the bank.

Currency   The official currency of St. Vincent is the **Eastern Caribbean dollar (EC$),** worth about 37¢ in U.S. money. Most of the quotations in this chapter appear in the U.S. dollars unless marked EC$. Most restaurants, shops, and hotels will accept payment in U.S. dollars or traveler's checks.

Documents   British, Canadian, or U.S. citizens should have proof of identity and a return or ongoing airplane ticket. Passports, voter registration cards, or birth certificates are sufficient.

Drugstore   Try Deane's Pharmacy, Middle Street, Kingstown (☎ **809/ 457-2056**), open Monday through Saturday from 8:30am to 4pm.

Electricity   Electricity is 220 volts A.C., 50 cycles, so you'll need an adapter and a transformer. Some hotels have transformers, but it's best to bring your own.

Holidays   These include January 1 (New Year's Day), January 22 (St. Vincent and Grenadines Day), Good Friday, Easter Monday, May 2 (Labour Day), Whit Monday, July 1 (Caricom Day), July 2 (Carnival Tuesday), August Monday (dates vary), October 27 (Independence Day), December 25 (Christmas Day), and December 26 (Boxing Day).

Information   The local **Department of Tourism** is on Bay Street, Government Administrative Centre, Kingstown (☎ **809/457-1502**). Inquiries in the

United States can be made to the **St. Vincent and Grenadines Tourist Office,** 801 Second Ave., 21st Floor, New York, NY 10017 (☎ **212/687-4981,** or toll free **800/729-1726**), and 6505 Cove Creek Place, Dallas, TX 75240 (☎ **214/236-6451,** or toll free **800/235-3029**).

Language   English is the official language.

Medical Care   There are two hospitals on St. Vincent, Kingstown General Hospital, Kingstown (☎ **809/456-1185**), and Medical Associates Clinic, Kingstown (☎ **809/457-2598**).

Post Office   The General Post Office on Halifax Street in Kingstown is open Monday through Friday from 8:30am to 3pm and on Saturday from 8:30 to 11:30am. There are sub-post offices in 56 districts throughout the state, and these include offices on the Grenadine islands of Bequia, Mustique, Canouan, Mayreau, and Union Island.

Safety   St. Vincent and its neighboring islands of the Grenadines are still considered safe islands to visit. In Kingstown, the capital of St. Vincent, chances are you'll encounter little serious crime. However, take the usual precautions and never leave valuables unguarded.

Taxes and Service   The government imposes an airport departure tax of EC$20 ($7.40) per person. A 5% government occupancy tax is charged for all hotel accommodations, and hotels and restaurants add a 10% to 15% service charge.

Telephone   Once on the island, dial all seven digits of the local number (not the 809 area code). The same is true for the Grenadines.

Time   Both St. Vincent and the Grenadines operate on Atlantic standard time year round: When it's 6am on St. Vincent, it's 5am in Miami. During daylight saving time in the United States, St. Vincent keeps the same time as the U.S. East Coast.

Weather   The climate of St. Vincent is pleasantly cooled by the trade winds all year. The tropical temperature is in the 78° to 82° Fahrenheit range. The rainy season is May to November.

WHERE TO STAY

Don't expect high-rise resorts here, as everything is kept small. The places are comfortable, not fancy, and you usually get a lot of personal attention from the staff. Remember that most hotels and restaurants add a 5% government tax and a 10% to 15% service charge to your bill; ask about this when you register.

VERY EXPENSIVE

Young Island

P.O. Box 211, Young Island, St. Vincent, W.I. ☎ **809/458-4826,** or 800/223-1108 in the U.S. and Canada. Fax 809/457-4567. 29 cottages. Winter, $340–$500 cottage for one; $430–$590 cottage for two. Off-season, $185–$405 cottage for one; $275–$495 cottage for two. Additional person $90 extra. "Lovers' packages" available. (MAP rates.) AE, MC, V. Free parking.

This 32-acre resort, which might have attracted Gauguin, is supposedly where a Carib tribal chieftain kept his harem. It lies just 200 yards off the south shore of St. Vincent, to which it is linked by a ferry from the pier right on Villa Beach, a five-minute ride. Wooden and stone bungalows are set in a tropical garden, and the beach is of brilliant white sand. Hammocks are hung under thatched roofs.

You're housed in Tahitian cottages—all for couples—with a bamboo decor and outdoor showers. Floors are of seashells and terrazzo, covered with rush rugs. Many readers, however, have complained of hearing "domestic noises" in the rooms adjoining them. Ask about package rates, under the category of "young lovers"; these are bargain deals offered during off-season periods.

Dining/Entertainment: Food and service are not always of a high standard, in spite of the longtime fame of this hotel. Dining is by candlelight, and dress is informal. Sometimes a steel band plays for dancing after dinner, and you're serenaded by strolling singers. On some nights the hotel transports guests over to the rock on its other island, Fort Duvernette, for a cocktail party. There, hors d'oeuvres are cooked over charcoal pits, and a local band plays under torchlight. Island specials are served at the Coconut Bar, a thatched bohío on stilts that actually serves many of its drinks in fresh coconuts.

Services: Room service (for breakfast), babysitting.

Facilities: Swimming pool (modeled on a tropical lagoon and set into landscaped grounds) and a saltwater lagoonlike pool (at the far end of the beach, where you can hear parrots and macaws chattering), tennis court (lit for night games), Carib canoes and Sailfish. All water sports (such as scuba diving and waterskiing) are available.

EXPENSIVE

Grand View Beach Hotel

P.O. Box 173, Villa Point, St. Vincent, W.I. ☎ **809/458-4811,** or 800/223-6510 in the U.S. Fax 809/457-4174. 19 rms, 2 honeymoon suites. MINIBAR TV TEL. Winter, $150 single; $210 double; from $270 suite. Off-season, $95 single; $130 double; from $190 suite. MAP $25 per person extra. AE, DC, MC, V. Free parking.

Owner-manager F. A. (Tony) Sardine named this place well: The "grand view" promised is of islets, bays, yachts, Young Island, headlands, lagoons, and sailing craft. Villa Point lies just 5 minutes from the airport and 10 minutes from Kingstown. On well-manicured grounds, this resort is set on 8 acres of gardens. The converted plantation house is a large, white, two-story mansion. Twelve rooms are air-conditioned.

Dining/Entertainment: In spite of the good local reputation of this hotel, the food served here continues to draw complaints from some readers, although others have praised it. One cited a "fish appetizer" that was a small spoonful of tuna straight from the can, and another wrote of the distasteful frozen fish and bland vegetables. The service here has won no praise.

Services: Room service, laundry, babysitting.

Facilities: Swimming pool, tennis and squash courts, fitness club with a range of exercise options and sauna and massage.

MODERATE

The Lagoon Marina & Hotel

P.O. Box 133, Blue Lagoon, St. Vincent, W.I. ☎ **809/458-4308.** Fax 809/457-4716. 19 rms. Winter, $95–$100 single or double. Off-season, $80–$90 single or double. Breakfast $3.70–$7.40 extra. AE, MC, V. Free parking.

A two-story grouping of rambling modern buildings crafted from local wood and stone, this hotel lies 4 miles from the airport on the main island road. There's a pleasantly breezy bar with open walls and lots of exposed planking. As you relax, you'll overlook a moored armada of boats tied up at a nearby marina. A two-tiered swimming pool, terraced into a nearby hillside, offers two lagoon-shaped places to swim. Snorkeling, windsurfing, and daily departures on sailboats to Mustique and Bequia can be arranged through the hotel. Each of the high-ceilinged accommodations has a balcony; eight are air-conditioned. Room service, laundry, and babysitting are provided. A dive shop is on the premises.

Villa Lodge Hotel

P.O. Box 1191, Villa Point, St. Vincent, W.I. ☎ **809/458-4641,** or 800/742-4276 in the U.S. Fax 809/457-4468. 10 rms. A/C TV TEL. Winter, $140 single; $185 double. Off-season, $120 single; $165 double. (MAP rates.) AE, MC, V. Free parking.

Set at the side of a residential hillside a few minutes southeast of the center of Kingstown and E. T. Joshua Airport, this is a favorite of visiting businesspeople. Because of its access to the beach and its well-mannered staff, it still evokes in residents the feeling of being lodged in a well-proportioned, conservatively modern villa. It's ringed with tropical, flowering trees and shrubs growing in the gardens. The air-conditioned rooms have ceiling fans, king-size beds, mini-refrigerators, hairdryers, and comfortable rattan and local mahogany furniture.

Dining/Entertainment: There's a wood-sheathed bar on the second floor with a view of Young Island and the Grenadines, and a dining room where good food is served, usually from a fixed-price menu.

Services: Room service, laundry, babysitting.

Facilities: Swimming pool.

BUDGET

Ⓢ Cobblestone Inn

P.O. Box 867, Kingstown, St. Vincent, W.I. ☎ **809/456-1937.** Fax 809/456-1938. 19 rms. A/C TEL. $60 single; $72 double. (Rates include breakfast.) AE, MC, V. Free parking. Transportation: Take a taxi (a 10-minute ride south of the airport).

Originally built as a warehouse for sugar and arrowroot in 1814, the core of this historic hotel is made of stone and brick. Today it's one of the most famous hotels of St. Vincent, known for its labyrinth of passages, arches, and upper hallways. To reach the high-ceilinged reception area, you pass from the waterfront through a stone tunnel into a chiseled courtyard. At the top of a massive sloping stone staircase you are shown to one of the simple old-fashioned bedrooms. Some units have a TV, and some have windows opening over the rooftops of town. Meals are served on a third-floor eagle's eyrie high above the hotel's central courtyard. Rows of windows and thick mahogany tables in its adjacent bar create one of the most unusual hideaways in town. The hotel is convenient for town; however, you'll have to drive about 3 miles to the nearest beach.

Coconut Beach Inn

P.O. Box 355, Indian Bay, St. Vincent, W.I. ☎ **809/457-4900.** Fax 809/457-4900. 10 rms. $45–$55 single; $75 double. (Rates include continental breakfast.) AE, MC, V. Free parking.

This owner-occupied inn, restaurant, and bar lies five minutes (2 miles) south of the airport and a five-minute drive from Kingstown. The hotel, which grew out of a villa constructed in the 1930s by one of the region's noted eccentrics, lies across the channel from the much more expensive Young Island. Its seaside setting makes it a choice for swimming and sunbathing. Island tours, such as sailing the Grenadines, can be arranged, as can diving, snorkeling, and mountain climbing. Each unit is furnished in a straightforward modern style, though the bedrooms vary widely from one another. A beach bar at water's edge serves tropical drinks, and an open-air restaurant opens onto a view of Indian Bay and features West Indian and Vincentian cooking prepared from local foods. Steaks, Cornish game hens, and hamburgers round out the fare.

$ Heron Hotel

P.O. Box 226, Kingstown, St. Vincent, W.I. ☎ **809/457-1631.** Fax 809/457-1189. 14 rms, 1 suite. A/C TEL. Transportation: Take a taxi (a 15-minute ride north of the airport). $44 single; $55 double; $60 suite. (Rates include full breakfast.) MC, V. Free parking.

One of those enduring favorites with people who like a guesthouse with a lot of West Indian flavor sits in a bustling location in town. The hotel is in a wood-frame warehouse that a century ago stored vast quantities of copra (dried coconut) before it was shipped to Europe. Today its big-windowed premises is a hotel that's more like a guesthouse from long ago or at least 40 years ago. Nothing much has changed or been improved upon here since then. You can always read quietly in an elegantly sparse living room. American and Créole meals are served beneath the soaring ceiling of a room whose view encompasses a private courtyard encircled by some of the simple but comfortable accommodations. Room 15 is particularly spacious. Lunch is served daily from 11:30am to 1:30pm and dinner daily from 7:30 to 8:30pm.

Petit Byahaut

Petit Byahaut Bay, St. Vincent, W.I. ☎ **809/457-7008.** Fax 809/457-7008. 7 tents. $125–$145 per person per day or $595–$695 per person for five days/five nights. Single supplement $35 daily. (Rates include all meals, snorkeling, beach items, sailboats, and rowboats.) Scuba packages available. MC, V.

This most adventurous accommodation on the island for those who like eco-tourism lies $4^1/2$ miles north of Kingstown on the leeward coast and is accessible only by boat. Snorkelers, scuba divers, hikers, and nature lovers are attracted to it. It accepts no more than 14 guests at a time. They're housed in roomy tents with "solar showers" and large roofed decks. A house-party atmosphere prevails. Opening onto a horseshoe-shaped bay, the complex stands in a 50-acre private valley. Foliage between the tents provides privacy. A seaside bar and restaurant offer wholesome meals. Picnics are prepared during the day, and dinner is by candlelight. The snorkeling and scuba diving right off the beach are excellent, and water-sports equipment is provided.

WHERE TO DINE

Most guests eat at their hotels on the Modified American Plan (half board). Unlike the situation on many Caribbean islands, many Vincentian hostelries serve an authentic West Indian cuisine. There are also a few independent eateries as well, but not many.

Basil's Bar & Restaurant

Bay St. Kingstown. ☎ **809/457-2713.** Reservations recommended. Appetizers EC$10–EC$20 ($3.70–$7.40); main courses EC$30–$55 ($11.10–$20.40); lunch buffet EC$30 ($11.10). AE, MC, V. Daily 8am–10pm. SEAFOOD/INTERNATIONAL.

This brick-lined enclave is a less famous annex of the legendary Basil's Beach Bar on Mustique. It lies in the early 19th-century walls of an old sugar warehouse, on the waterfront in Kingstown beneath the previously recommended Cobblestone Inn. The air-conditioned interior is accented with exposed stone and brick, soaring arches, and a rambling mahogany bar, which remains open throughout the day. The menu could include lobster salad, shrimp in garlic butter, sandwiches, hamburgers, and barbecued chicken. Dinners feature grilled lobster, escargots, shrimp cocktail, grilled red snapper, and grilled filet mignon. You can order meals here throughout the day and late into the evening—until the last satisfied customer leaves. The lunch buffet is available daily from noon to 2pm.

⑤ Bounty

Halifax St., Kingstown. ☎ **809/456-1776.** Reservations not required. Snacks and sandwiches EC$3.85–EC$6 ($1.40–$2.20); main courses EC$10–EC$13 ($3.70–$4.80). No credit cards. Mon–Fri 8:30am–5pm, Sat 8:30am–1:30pm. AMERICAN/CREOLE.

Opposite Barclay's Bank in the center of Kingstown, you'll find Bounty behind a green-and-white facade. A friendly local staff greets you, and people who work nearby frequent the place, making it their "second home." An art gallery offers a variety of local works. Fill up on pastries of all kinds, rotis, hot dogs, hamburgers, and sandwiches, along with homemade soups. Fish and chips are also served. The interesting collection of drinks includes passionfruit and golden apple.

✪ French Restaurant

Villa Beach. ☎ **809/458-4972.** Reservations required. Appetizers EC$18–EC$45 ($6.70–$16.70); main courses EC$40–EC$80 ($14.80–$29.60). AE, MC, V. Lunch daily noon–2pm; dinner daily 7–9:30pm. Closed Sept. FRENCH/SEAFOOD.

In a clapboard house 2 miles from the airport, near the pier where the ferry from Young Island docks, this is one of the most consistently good restaurants on the island. It offers a long, semishadowed bar, which you pass on your way to the rear veranda. There, overlooking the moored yachts off the coast of Young Island, you can enjoy well-seasoned, Gallic-inspired food. Surrounded with vine-laced lattices, you may order seafood casserole, curried conch, stuffed crab back, or lobster crêpes. This is the only restaurant on St. Vincent that offers fresh lobster from a tank. Finish off with a chocolate mousse. Lunch is simpler, with fresh fish, beef kebab, spicy chicken, lobster Créole, quiche Lorraine, omelets, or tunafish salads.

Juliette's Restaurant

Egmont St. ☎ **809/457-1645.** Reservations not required. Appetizers EC$4–EC$6 ($1.50–$2.20); breakfast and lunch platters EC$10–EC$16 ($3.70–$5.90). No credit cards. Breakfast Mon–Fri 8:30–9:30am; lunch Mon–Fri 11am–4pm, Sat 8:30am–2pm. AMERICAN/CREOLE.

Set amid the capital's cluster of administrative buildings, across from the National Commercial Bank, this red-and-white concrete building probably dispenses more lunches to more office workers than any other establishment in town. Only breakfast and lunch are served, amid clean and respectable surroundings which are headed by a 20-year veteran of the restaurant trade, Juliette Campbell. (Ms. Campbell's husband is the island's well-known attorney general.) Menu items include soups, curried mutton, an array of fish, stewed chicken, stewed beef, and sandwiches. Many of the platters are garnished with fried plantains and rice. The restaurant is never open for dinner.

Rooftop Restaurant & Bar

Bay St., Kingstown. ☎ **809/457-2845.** Reservations not required for lunch, recommended for dinner. Appetizers EC$8–EC$15 ($3–$5.60); main courses EC$20–EC$35 ($7.40–$13); lunch platters EC$18 ($6.70). AE, MC, V. Lunch Mon–Sat 11:30am–3pm; dinner Mon–Sat 6:30–10pm. WEST INDIAN/INTERNATIONAL.

This restaurant does a thriving business because of its well-prepared food and its location three stories above the center of Kingstown. After you climb some flights of stairs, you'll see a bar near the entrance, an indoor area decorated in earth tones, and a patio open to the prevailing breezes. Lunches stress traditional Créole recipes using fish, chicken, mutton, beef, and goat. Dinners are more international, and include lobster, snapper with lemon-butter and garlic sauce, steaks with onions and mushrooms, and several preparations of pork. Every Friday a karaoke sing-along setup is featured, and on Saturday evening there's a steel band in attendance after 6pm. Beer at the bar costs EC$3.50 ($1.30). In addition, 55 different drinks are featured at the bar.

WHAT TO SEE & DO

Special events include the week-long **Carnival** in early July, one of the largest in the eastern Caribbean, with steel-band and calypso competitions, along with the crowning of the king and queen of the carnival.

KINGSTOWN

Lushly tropical, the capital isn't as architecturally fascinating as St. George's on Grenada. Some English-style houses do exist, many of them looking as if they belonged in Penzance, Cornwall, instead of the Caribbean. However, you can still meet old-time beachcombers if you stroll on Upper Bay Street. White-haired and bearded, they can be seen loading their boats with produce grown on the mountain, before heading to some secluded beach in the Grenadines. This is a chief port and gateway to the Grenadines, and you can also view the small boats and yachts that have dropped anchor here. The place is a magnet for charter sailors.

At the top of a winding road on the north side of Kingstown, **Fort Charlotte** (☎ 809/456-1165) was built on Johnson Point, enclosing one side of the bay. Constructed about the time of the American Revolution, it was named after Queen Charlotte, the German consort of George III. The ruins aren't much to inspect; the reason to come here is the view. The fort sits atop a steep promontory some 640 feet above the sea. From its citadel, you'll have a commanding sweep of the leeward shores to the north, Kingstown to the south, and the Grenadines beyond. On a clear day you can even see Grenada. A trio of cannons used to fight off French troops are still in place. You'll see a series of oil murals depicting the history of black Caribs. Admission is free, and it's open daily from 6am to 6pm.

The second major sight is the ✪ **Botanic Gardens** (☎ 809/457-1003), on the north side of Kingstown about a mile from the center. Founded in 1765 by Gov. George Melville, they are the oldest botanic gardens in the West Indies. In this Windward Eden, you'll see 20 acres of such tropical exotics as teak, almond, cinnamon, nutmeg, cannonball, and mahogany; some of the trees are more than two centuries old. One of the breadfruit trees was reputedly among those original seedlings brought to this island by Captain Bligh in 1793. There is also a large *Spachea perforata* (the Soufrière tree), a species believed to be unique to St. Vincent and not found in the wild since 1812. The gardens are open Monday through Friday from 7am to 4pm, on Saturday from 7 to 11am, and on Sunday from 7am to 6pm. No admission is charged.

✪ THE LEEWARD HIGHWAY

The leeward or west side of the island has the most dramatic scenery. North from Kingstown, you rise into lofty terrain before descending to the water again. There are views in all directions. On your right you'll pass the Aqueduct Golf Course before reaching Layou. If you want to play golf, check its status, as it often opens and closes. Here you can see the massive **Carib Rock,** with a human face carving dating back to A.D. 600. This is considered one of the finest petroglyphs in the Caribbean.

Continuing north you reach **Barrouallie,** where there's another Carib stone altar. Even if you're not into fishing, you might want to spend some time in this whaling village, where some still occasionally set out in brightly painted boats armed with harpoons, Moby-Dick style, to seek the elusive whale. However, "Save the Whale" devotees need not harpoon their way here in anger. Barrouallie may be one of the last few outposts in the world where such whale-hunting is carried on, but Vincentians point out that it doesn't endanger an already endangered species since so few are caught each year. If one is caught, it's an occasion for festivities.

The leeward highway continues to **Chateaubelair,** the end of the line. There you can swim at the attractive **Richmond Beach** before heading back to Kingstown. In the distance, the volcano, La Soufrière, looms menacingly in the mountains.

The adventurous set out from here to see the **Falls of Baleine,** $7^1/_2$ miles north of Richmond Beach on the northern tip of the island, accessible only by boat. Coming from a stream in the volcanic hills, Baleine is a freshwater fall. If you're interested in making the trip, check with the tourist office in Kingstown about a tour there.

THE WINDWARD HIGHWAY

This road runs along the eastern Atlantic coast from Kingstown. Waves pound the surf, and all along the rocky shores are splendid seascapes. If you want to go swimming along this often-dangerous coast, stick to the sandy spots, as they offer safer shores. Along this road you'll pass coconut and banana plantations and fields of arrowroot.

North of Georgetown lies the **Rabacca Dry River,** which was the flow of lava from the volcano at its eruption at the beginning of the 20th century. The journey from Kingstown to here is only 24 miles, but it will seem like much longer. For those who want to go the final 11 miles along a rugged road to **Fancy,** the northern tip of the island, a Land Rover, Jeep, or Moke will be needed.

MARRIQUA VALLEY

Sometimes known as the Mesopotamia Valley, this area is considered one of the lushest cultivated valleys in the eastern Caribbean. Surrounded by mountain ridges, the drive takes you through a landscape planted with nutmeg, cocoa, coconut, breadfruit, and bananas. The road begins at Vigie Highway, to the east of the E. T. Joshua Airport runway. At Montréal you'll come upon natural mineral springs. Only rugged vehicles should make this trip.

Around Kingstown, you can also enjoy the **Queen's Drive,** a scenic loop into the high hills to the east of the capital. From there, the view is magnificent over Kingstown and its yacht-clogged harbor to the Grenadines in the distance.

SPORTS & OUTDOOR ACTIVITIES

BEACHES   All beaches on St. Vincent are public, and many of the best ones border hotel properties, which you can patronize for drinks or luncheons. Most of the resorts are in the south, where the beaches have white or golden-yellow sand. However, many of the beaches in the north have sands that look like lava ash in color. The safest swimming is on the leeward beaches; the windward beaches can be dangerous.

Some of the best beaches are the white sands of **Villa Beach** or the black sands of **Buccament Bay** or **Questelle's Bay,** all west-coast sites.

FISHING It's best to go to a local fisherman for advice if you're interested in this sport, which your hotel will usually arrange for you. The government of St. Vincent doesn't require visitors to take out a license. If you arrange things in time, it's sometimes possible to accompany the fishermen on one of their trips, perhaps 4 or 5 miles from shore. A modest fee should suffice. The fishing fleet leaves from the leeward coast at Barrouallie. They've been known to return to shore with everything from a 6-inch redfish to a 20-foot pilot whale.

SAILING & YACHTING St. Vincent and the Grenadines are one of the great sailing centers of the Caribbean. Here you can obtain yachts that are fully provisioned if you want to go bareboating, or if you're a well-heeled novice, you can hire a captain and a crew. Hotels can recommend charter yachts.

Volcano Safaris

A safari to St. Vincent's hot volcano, **Soufrière,** is an intriguing adventure. As you travel the island, you can't miss its cloud-capped splendor. This volcano has occasionally captured the attention of the world. The most recent eruption was in 1979, when the volcano spewed ashes, lava, and hot mud that covered the vegetation on its slopes and forced thousands of Vincentians to flee its fury. Belching rocks and black curling smoke filled the blue Caribbean sky. Jets of steam spouted 20,000 feet into the air. About 17,000 people were evacuated from a 10-mile ring around the volcano.

Fortunately, the eruption was in the sparsely settled northern part of the island. The volcano lies away from most of the tourism and commercial centers of St. Vincent, and even if it should erupt again, volcanologists do not consider it a danger to visitors lodged at beachside hotels along the leeward coast. The last major eruption of the volcano occurred in 1902, when 2,000 people were killed. Prior to its 1979 eruption, the volcano had been quiet since 1972. The activity that year produced a 324-foot-long island of lava rock jutting up from the water of Crater Lake.

At the rim of the crater you'll be rewarded with one of the most panoramic views in the Caribbean. That is, if the wind doesn't blow too hard and make you topple over into the crater itself! Extreme caution is emphasized. Inside, you can see the steam rising from the crater.

The trail back down is much easier, I assure you.

Even if you're an experienced hiker, don't attempt to explore this volcano without an experienced guide. Also, wear suitable hiking clothes and be sure that you're in the best of health before making the arduous journey. The easiest route is the 3-mile-long eastern route leaving from Rabacca. Some people attempt this on their own. The more arduous trail—longer by half a mile—is the western trail from Chateaubelair, which definitely requires a guide. The round-trip to the crater takes about five hours.

The St. Vincent Forestry Headquarters (☎ **809/457-8594**), in the village of Campden Park, about 3 miles from Kingstown along the west coast, offers a pamphlet giving hiking data to Soufrière. It's open Monday through Saturday from 8am to noon and 1 to 4pm. Sam's Taxi Tours (☎ **809/456-4338**) offers guided hikes up to La Soufrière, costing $100 for up to six people.

SNORKELING & SCUBA DIVING   The best area for snorkeling and scuba diving is the Villa/Young Island section on the southern end of the island.

Dive St. Vincent, on the Young Island Cut (☎ **809/457-4928**), has been owned and operated by a transplanted Texan, Bill Tewes, for more than 10 years. The oldest dive company in the country, Dive St. Vincent now has two additional dive shops: Dive Canouan, at the Canouan Beach Hotel on Canouan Island, and Grenadines Dive, on Union Island at the Sunny Grenadines Hotel. The shops have a total of six instructors and three divemasters, as well as seven dive boats. The chain of dive shops allows visitors to dive or be certified while sailing throughout St. Vincent and the Grenadines with a consistency of quality. All shops offer dive/ snorkel trips as well as sightseeing day trips, and complete dive instruction. Single-tank dives cost $50 and two-tank dives cost $90, including all equipment and instructors and/or divemaster guides. Dive packages are available.

TENNIS   Young Island and the **Grand View Beach Hotel** (see "Where to Stay," above) have tennis courts.

SHOPPING

You don't come to St. Vincent to shop, but once here, you might pick up some items in the Sea Island cotton fabrics and clothing that are specialties here. In addition, Vincentian artisans make pottery, jewelry, and baskets that have souvenir value at least. Most shops are open Monday through Friday from 8am to 4pm. Stores generally close from noon to 1pm for lunch. Saturday hours are 8am to noon.

Since Kingstown consists of about 12 small blocks, you can walk and browse and see about everything in a morning's shopping jaunt. Try to be in town for the colorful, noisy **Friday-morning market.** You might not purchase anything, but you'll surely enjoy the riot of color.

Juliette's Fashions
Middle St. ☎ **809/456-1143.**

Owned and operated by the same entrepreneur as Juliette's Restaurant (see "Where to Dine," above), this is probably the best-stocked women's clothing store on St. Vincent. Beneficiary of its owner's frequent buying trips to New York and Miami, it sells women's sportswear, evening wear, beachwear, and costume jewelry.

Noah's Arkade
Bay St., Kingstown. ☎ **809/457-1513.**

Noah's sells handcrafts from the West Indies, including wood carvings, T-shirts, and a wide range of books and souvenirs. Noah's has shops at the Frangipani Hotel, Bequia, St. Vincent, and the Grenadines.

St. Vincent Handicraft Centre
Franches St. ☎ **809/457-2516.**

Here you'll see a large display of the handcrafts of the island. On the site of an old cotton gin, this shop offers you a chance to see craftspeople at work, perhaps on macramé, pottery, textiles, or metalwork jewelry. Grass floor mats are a popular item.

St. Vincent Philatelic Services Ltd.
Lower Bay St., Kingstown. ☎ **809/457-1911.**

This is the largest operating bureau in the Caribbean, and its issues are highly acclaimed around the world by stamp collectors. Stamp enthusiasts can visit or order by mail.

Stecher's Jewelry Ltd.

Lot 19, Lane Bay St., Kingstown. ☎ **809/457-1142.**

In the Cobblestone Arcade, this long-established store offers a good selection of quality watches, china, porcelain, and jewelry. Waterford crystal is also sold as well as Lladrò figures. The entrance is through the courtyard of the Cobblestone Inn.

Y. de Lima Ltd.

Bay and Egmont sts., Kingstown. ☎ **809/457-1681.**

The familiar Y. de Lima Ltd. is well stocked with cameras, stereo equipment, clocks, binoculars, and jewelry. Paragon bone china is sold, along with a selection of gift items. Caribbean gold and silver jewelry are also featured.

ST. VINCENT AFTER DARK

The focus is mainly on the hotels, and activities are likely to include nighttime barbecues and dancing to steel bands. In season, at least one hotel seems to have something planned every night during the week. Inquire locally.

The Aquatic Club

Next to the Young Island landing pier. ☎ **809/458-4205.**

The best-known spot for entertainment is still this raucous club, which "jumps up" with action on Saturday night. Guests from all the hotels come here to enjoy the music and sing-alongs. Drinks begin at EC$3 ($1.10). Hours are 11pm to 4am daily.

The Attic

In the Kentucky Bldg., at Melville and Back sts., Kingstown. ☎ **809/457-2558.** Cover EC$5–EC$50 ($1.90–$18.50), depending on the entertainment.

The Attic features jazz and easy-listening music. Music is live only on Friday and Saturday; Tuesday and Thursday it's recorded. Wednesday is karaoke night. A beer costs EC$4 ($1.50). Open Monday through Saturday from 9am "until."

Touch Entertainment Centre (TEC)

Back St., Kingstown. ☎ **809/457-1825.**

Opposite Kentucky Fried Chicken on the top floor of the Cambridge Building, this is the best-known nightspot in the region. With advanced lighting, it's a soundproof (from the outside) air-conditioned environment, suitable for visitors. Every Wednesday night is disco night, especially for the "young and restless." Thursday night is "Oldies Goldies" night, often attracting couples. Friday is party night, and Saturday is devoted to live entertainment. Drinks begin at EC$2 (70¢), and the premises are open nightly from 9:30pm until 10 the following morning.

4 The Grenadines

South of St. Vincent, which administers them, this small chain of islands extends for more than 40 miles and offers the finest yachting area in the eastern Caribbean. The islands are strung like a necklace of precious stones, and have such romantic-sounding names as Bequia, Mustique, Canouan, and Petit St. Vincent. We'll explore Union and Palm Islands, and Mayreau as well.

A few of the islands have accommodations, which we'll visit, but many are so small and so completely undeveloped and unspoiled that they attract only beach-combers and stray boaters.

Populated by the descendants of African slaves, the Grenadines collectively add up to a land mass of 30 square miles. No one has been able to ascertain why the chain of islands is called the Grenadines, but at least two main reasons are given. It was the custom of the Spaniards to name newly discovered lands after cities, towns, or villages back home, so it may well be that when they discovered Grenada (and named it after the city in southern Spain), they also found the little islands nearby, calling them Grenadines, as the plural diminutive of Granada (that is, "the little Grenadas").

It is also reported that the early roving French called the islands Grenadilles or Grenadines mainly because the islands had an abundance of wild passionfruit. The passionfruit flower is known to the French as *grenadine*.

These bits of land, often dots on nautical charts, may lack natural resources, yet they're blessed with white sandy beaches, coral reefs, and their own kind of sleepy beauty. If you don't spend the night in the Grenadines, you should at least go over for the day to visit one of them and enjoy a picnic lunch (which your hotel will pack for you) on one of the long stretches of beach.

GETTING THERE

BY PLANE Four of the Grenadines—Bequia, Mustique, Union Island, and Canouan—have small airports, the landing spots for flights on **Mustique Airways** (☎ 809/458-4380 on St. Vincent). Planes are technically considered charters, although flights depart St. Vincent for Bequia daily at 8am and 5pm. The cost is EC$70 ($25.90) round-trip if passengers return the same day; otherwise the charge is EC$80 ($29.60) if one overnights on Bequia.

BY BOAT The ideal way to go, of course, is to rent your own yacht, as many wealthy visitors do. But a far less expensive method of transport is to go on a mail, cargo, or passenger boat as the locals do—but you'll need time and patience. However, boats do run on schedules, and generally are punctual. The **government mail boat,** M.V. *Snapper,* leaves St. Vincent on Monday and Thursday at 10:30am, stops at Bequia, Canouan, and Mayreau, and arrives at Union Island at about 3:30pm. On Tuesday and Friday, the boat leaves Union Island at about 6:30am, stops at Mayreau and Canouan, reaches Bequia at about 11am, and makes port at St. Vincent at noon. One-way fares from St. Vincent are: to Bequia, EC$10 ($3.70) Monday through Saturday and EC$12 ($4.45) on Sunday; to Canouan, EC$13 ($4.80); to Mayreau, EC$15 ($5.55); and to Union Island, EC$20 ($7.40).

You can also reach Bequia daily on the *Admiral I* and *II*. For information on these sea trips, inquire at the **Tourist Board,** Bay Street, in Kingstown (☎ 809/457-1502).

BEQUIA

Only 7 square miles of land, Bequia (pronounced "*Beck*-wee") is the largest of St. Vincent's Grenadines. It's the northernmost island in the Grenadines, offering quiet lagoons, reefs, and long stretches of nearly deserted beaches. Descended from seafarers and other early adventurers, its population of some 6,000 Bequians will probably give you a friendly greeting if you pass them along the road. Of the inhabitants, 10% are of Scottish ancestry, who live mostly in the Mount Pleasant region. A feeling of relaxation and informality prevails on Bequia.

The island lies 9 miles south of St. Vincent. There is a small airport, and you can also travel here by boat (see "Getting There," above).

St. Vincent and the Grenadines

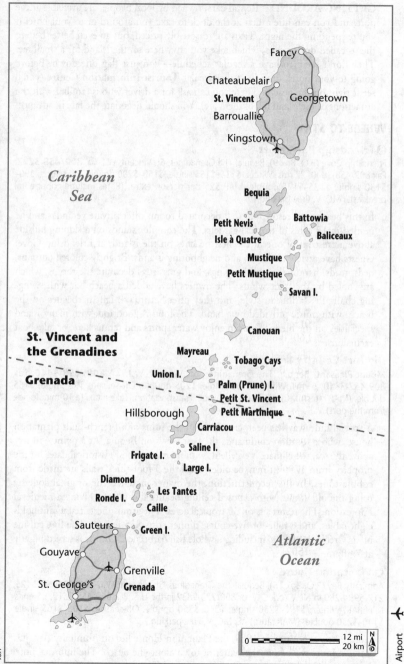

Fancy

Chateaubelair

St. Vincent

Georgetown

Barrouallie

Kingstown ✈

Caribbean Sea

Bequia

Petit Nevis

Battowia

Isle à Quatre

Baliceaux

Mustique

Petit Mustique

Savan I.

Canouan

Mayreau

Tobago Cays

Union I.

Palm (Prune) I.

St. Vincent and the Grenadines

Petit St. Vincent

Grenada

Petit Martinique

Hillsborough

Carriacou

Saline I.

Frigate I.

Large I.

Diamond

Les Tantes

Ronde I.

Caille

Sauteurs

Green I.

Gouyave

Atlantic Ocean

✈ Grenville

St. George's ✈

Grenada

0   12 mi
        20 km

N

✈ Airport

9891

GETTING AROUND   Rental cars, owned by local people, are available at the port, and you can hire a **taxi** at the dock to take you around or to your hotel if you're spending the night. Taxis are reasonably priced, but an even better bet are the so-called **dollar cabs,** which take you anywhere on the island for a small fee. They don't seem to have a regular schedule—you just flag one down. Before going to your hotel, drop in at the circular **Tourist Information Centre** (you'll see it right on the beach). There you can ask for a driver who is familiar with the attractions of the island (all of them are). You should negotiate the fare in advance.

WHERE TO STAY

❸ Friendship Bay Resort

Friendship Cove (P.O. Box 9), Bequia, The Grenadines, St. Vincent, W.I. ☎ **809/458-3222.** Fax 809/458-3840. 27 rms. Winter, $115–$155 single; $150–$200 double. Off-season, $90–$130 single; $125–$175 double. MAP $25 per person extra. (Rates include continental breakfast.) MC, V. Free parking.

In this beachfront resort, the well-decorated rooms offer private verandas and lie nestled in 12 acres of tropical gardens. The complex stands on a sloping hillside above a crescent of one of the best beaches on the island, at Friendship Cove. Guests have a view of the sea and neighboring islands. Brightly colored curtains, bedspreads, handmade wall hangings, and grass rugs decorate the rooms, which are cooled by the trade winds. The owners have added a beach bar with swinging chairs in Caribbean style, and they offer Saturday-night barbecues on the beach, with music provided by a band. The food is good too, with many island specialties on the menu. You can enjoy water sports and tennis here, or take boat excursions.

Old Fort Country Inn

Mount Pleasant, Bequia, The Grenadines, St. Vincent, W.I. ☎ **809/458-3440.** Fax 809/457-3340. 6 rms. Winter, $130 single; $205 double. Off-season, $95 single; $165 double. (MAP rates.) MC, V. Closed Aug–Sept. Transportation: Take a taxi (a 10-minute ride from the port).

A special hideaway has been created from the ruins of a French-built plantation house, whose location commands the best views on Bequia. At a point 450 feet above the sea, the climate is excellent, with no mosquitoes. Historical dates list the property from 1756 (it may be older), and the 3-foot-thick walls are made from cobblestones. In the reconstruction, the owner matched the original style by using the old stones with exposed ceiling beams and rafters, giving a medieval impression. The resort sits on 30 tropical acres. The atmospheric restaurant holds eight tables, and a four- or five-course dinner costs $35 to $45. The fine cuisine offers Créole specialties, including a whole fish barbecued. Dinner is served nightly at 7:30pm.

✪ Plantation House

Admiralty Bay (P.O. Box 16), Bequia, The Grenadines, St. Vincent, W.I. ☎ **809/458-3425,** 212/599-8280 in New York City, or 800/223-9832 in the U.S. Fax 809/458-3612. 25 units. MINIBAR. Winter, $190–$250 single; $260–$350 double. Off-season, $105–$165 single; $140–$230 double. (MAP rates.) AE, MC, V. Free parking.

Completely renovated in 1989, the Plantation House lies on Admiralty Bay, just a five-minute walk from the center of town along the beach. The informal hotel has what is known as "new Caribbean style." The accommodations consist of 17 West Indian "superior" cottages, painted in peach and white, each with its own private porch, plus three luxury beachfront units with fans, and five deluxe rooms with air conditioning in the main house. Facilities include a dining room, a bar, a beach-bar grill, and a kidney-shaped beachside pool, all set in 10 acres of tropical gardens. The excellent cuisine is continental, and barbecues, tennis, and scuba diving are offered.

Spring on Bequia

Spring Bay, Bequia, The Grenadines, St. Vincent, W.I. ☎ **809/458-3414,** or 612/823-1202 in Minneapolis. Fax 809/457-3305. 10 rms. Dec. 15–Apr 14, $90–$155 single; $120–$195 double. Nov–Dec 14 and Apr 15–June 15, $60–$120 single; $80–$140 double. MAP $40 per person extra. AE, MC, V. Free parking. Closed June 16–Oct. Transportation: Take a taxi (a 1-mile ride from Port Elizabeth).

In the late 1960s the avant-garde design of this hotel won an award from the American Institute of Architects. Fashioned from beautifully textured honey-colored stone, it combines design elements from both Japan and Scandinavia; however, its flattened hip roof was inspired by the old plantation houses of Martinique. Constructed on the 18th-century foundations of a West Indian homestead, it sits in the middle of 28 acres of hillside orchards, producing oranges, grapefruit, bananas, breadfruit, plums, and mangoes.Because of the almost-constant blossoming of one crop or another, you get the feeling of springtime (hence the name of the establishment). Candy Leslie, the Minnesota-born owner, will welcome you. From the main building's stone bar and open-air dining room, you might hear the bellowing of a herd of cows. On the premises is a swimming pool and a tennis court. Each of the units is ringed with stone and contains Japanese-style screens to filter the sun. Access to the sandy beach is through a coconut grove.

WHERE TO DINE

The food is good and healthful here—lobster, chicken, and steaks from such fish as dolphin, kingfish, and grouper, plus tropical fruits, fried plaintain, and coconut and guava puddings made fresh daily. Even the beach bars are kept spotless.

Frangipani

in the Hotel Frangipani, Port Elizabeth. ☎ **809/458-3255.** Reservations required for dinner. Appetizers EC$6–EC$18 ($2.20–$6.70); main courses EC$35–EC$70 ($13–$25.90); fixed-price meal EC$42–EC$80 ($15.50–$29.60); Thurs barbecue EC$65 ($24.10). MC, V. Breakfast daily 7:30–10am; lunch daily 10am–5pm; dinner daily 7–9pm. Closed Sept to mid-Oct. Transportation: Dollar cab to the harbor. CARIBBEAN.

This waterside dining room is one of the best restaurants on the island. The yachting crowd often comes ashore to dine here. With the exception of the juicy steaks imported for barbecues, only local food is used in the succulent specialties. Lunches, served throughout the day, include sandwiches, salads, and seafood platters. Dinner specialties include conch chowder, baked chicken with rice-and-coconut stuffing, lobster, and an array of fresh fish. A fixed-price menu is available, or you can order à la carte. A Thursday-night barbecue with live entertainment is an island event.

Friendship Bay Resort

Port Elizabeth. ☎ **809/458-3222.** Reservations required for dinner. Appetizers EC$12–EC$20 ($4.40–$7.40); main courses EC$32–EC$65 ($11.80–$24.10). MC, V. Lunch daily 11:30am–3pm; dinner daily 7:30–10pm. Closed Sept–Oct 15. INTERNATIONAL/WEST INDIAN.

You'll find this dining room in the welcoming precincts of this previously recommended hotel. Guests dine in a candlelit room high above a sweeping expanse of seafront on a hillside rich with the scent of frangipani and hibiscus. Lunch is served at the beach bar, but dinner is more elaborate. It might include grilled lobster in season, curried beef, grilled or broiled fish (served Créole style with a spicy sauce), shrimp curry, and charcoal-grilled steak flambé. An island highlight is the Friday- and Saturday-night jump-up and barbecue. The Swedish owners also present a combination Swedish smörgåsbord and West Indian Créole buffet on Sunday at the beach, complete with a steel band.

Whaleboner Inn

Admiralty Bay, Port Elizabeth. ☎ **809/458-3233.** Reservations required for dinner. Appetizers $8–$17; main courses $20–$30; lunch from $12. AE, MC, V. Daily 8am–10:30pm. CARIBBEAN/SEAFOOD.

An enduring favorite, the Whaleboner is still going strong. It's next to the Hotel Frangipani, directly south of Port Elizabeth. Inside, the bar is carved from the jawbone of a giant whale, and the bar stools are made from the vertebrae. Dinner is served only from 7 to 10:30pm, although the bar often stays open later, depending on the crowd. The owners offer the best pizza on the island, along with a selection of fish and chips or well-made sandwiches for lunch. At night you may want one of the wholesome dinners prepared by a West Indian cook, including a choice of lobster, fish, chicken, or steak. Favored by the yachting set, the restaurant has full bar service. The Whaleboner Boutique adjoins the restaurant and offers a variety of holiday items made from batik and silk-screen-print Sea Island cotton, souvenirs, model whaling boats, and T-shirts.

WHAT TO SEE & DO

The main harbor village, **Port Elizabeth,** is known for its safe anchorage, Admiralty Bay. The bay was a haven in the 17th century for the British, French, and Spanish navies, as well as for pirates. Descendants of Captain Kydd (a.k.a. Kidd) still live on the island. Today the yachting set "from anywhere" puts in here, often bringing a kind of excitement to the locals.

If you want to see boats, just walk along the beach. There, craftspeople construct vessels by hand, a method they learned from their ancestors. Whalers sometimes still set out from here in wooden boats with hand harpoons, just as they do from a port village on St. Vincent.

Frankly, after you leave Port Elizabeth there aren't many sights, and you'll probably have your driver, booked for the day, drop you off for a long, leisurely lunch and some time on a beach. However, you'll pass a fort with a harbor view, and drive on to Industry Estates, which has a Beach House restaurant serving a fair lunch. At **Paget Farm,** you can wander into an old whaling village, and maybe inspect a few jawbones left over from the catches of yesterday.

At Moonhole, there's a vacation and retirement community built into the cliffs, really free-form sculpture. These are private homes, of course, and you're not to enter without permission. For a final look at Bequia, head up an 800-foot hill that the local people call **"The Mountain."** From that perch, you'll have a 360° view of St. Vincent and the Grenadines to the south.

SPORTS & OUTDOOR ACTIVITIES

Dive Bequia, Plantation House, Admiralty Bay (P.O. Box 16), Bequia, St. Vincent, W.I. (☎ **809/458-3504**), specializes in diving and snorkeling.

Scuba dives cost $50 for one, $85 for two in the same day, and $400 for a 10-dive package. Introductory lessons cost $15 each per person. A six-dive open-water certification course is $400. A snorkeling trip is $20 per person. Prices include all the necessary equipment.

SHOPPING

This is not a particularly good reason to come to Bequia, but there is some.

The Crab Hole
Next door to the Plantation House. ☎ 809/458-3290.

At shops scattered along the water you can buy hand-screened cotton made by Bequians. The best of these is the Crab Hole, where they invite guests to visit their silk-screen factory in back. Later you can make purchases at their shop in front, including sterling silver and 14-karat jewelry.

Noah's Arkade
In the Frangipani Hotel, Port Elizabeth. ☎ 809/458-3424.

Island entrepreneur Lavinia Gunn sells Vincentian and Bequian batiks, scarves, hats, T-shirts, dresses, and a scattering of pottery. There are also dolls, placemats, baskets, and homemade jellies concocted from grapefruit, mango, and guava, plus West Indian cookbooks and books on tropical flowers and reef fish. This place stands a few steps from the terrace bar of the Frangipani Hotel.

Sargeant's Model Boatshop Bequia
Front St., Port Elizabeth. ☎ 809/458-3344.

Anyone on the island can show you the way to the workshops of Sargeant's Model Boatshop Bequia, lying west of the pier past the oil-storage facility. Sought out by yacht owners looking for a scale-model reproduction of their favorite vessel, Lawson Sargeant is the self-taught wood carver who established this business. Models are carved from a soft local wood called gumwood, then painted in brilliant colors of red, green, gray, or blue, whatever your fancy dictates. When a scale model of the royal family's yacht, *Britannia*, was commissioned in 1985, it required five weeks of work, meticulous blueprints, and cost $10,000. You can pick up a model of a Bequia whaling boat for much less. The Sargeant family usually keeps 100 model boats in many shapes and sizes in inventory.

MUSTIQUE

This island of luxury villas, which someone once called "Georgian West Indian," 15 miles south of St. Vincent, is so remote and small it almost deserves to be unknown, and it would be if it weren't for Princess Margaret and other world-class celebrities who have cottages here.

The island is privately owned by a consortium of businesspeople. When word of Princess Margaret's retreat splashed on front pages in London, it was owned by beer baron Colin Tennant, a millionaire Scottish nobleman, now Lord Glenconner. An eccentric dandy, he was often photographed in silk scarfs and Panama hats. On the trail of Margaret and her cousin, the earl of Lichfield, came a host of celebrities, including Truman Capote, Paul Newman, Mick Jagger, Raquel Welch, Richard Avedon, and Prince Andrew.

The island is only 3 miles long and 1 mile wide, and it has only one major hotel (see below). After settling in, you'll find many good white sandy beaches against a backdrop of luxuriant foliage. My favorite is Macaroni Beach, where the water is turquoise.

On the northern reef of Mustique lies the wreck of the French liner *Antilles*, which went aground on the Pillories in 1971. Today its massive hulk, now gutted, can be seen cracked and rusting a few yards offshore, an eerie sight.

If you wish to tour the small island, you can rent a Mini-Moke to see some of the most elegant homes in the Caribbean. You can even rent Les Jolies Eaux (Pretty Waters)—that is, if you can afford it. This is the Caribbean home of Princess Margaret. A five-bedroom/five-bath house, it has a large swimming pool, naturally. Accommodating 10 guests, it's available only when HRH is not in residence. If you rent it, the princess will require references.

GETTING THERE & GETTING AROUND   The best way to go to Mustique is by air charter on **Mustique Airways** (☎ 809/458-4380 in St. Vincent), which maintains two daily commuter flights between St. Vincent and Mustique. Flights depart St. Vincent daily at 7am and 4pm, and land on Mustique about 10 minutes later. Flights then head immediately back to St. Vincent. Chartered planes arrive on Mustique on the small airstrip in the middle of the bird sanctuary. The airport closes at dusk, because there are no landing lights. The cost is EC$110 ($40.70), and there's no discount for same-day returns. Once there, you can call **Michael's Taxi** (☎ **809/458-4621,** ext. 448). But chances are, someone at Cotton House will already have seen you land.

WHERE TO STAY

✪ The Cotton House

Mustique, The Grenadines, St. Vincent, W.I. ☎ **809/456-4777,** or 800/447-7462 in the U.S. Fax 809/456-4777. 20 rms and suites. MINIBAR TEL. Winter (AP), $550–$575 deluxe double; $630–$660 junior suite for two; $730–$760 deluxe suite for two. Off-season (MAP), $325 deluxe double; $450 junior suite for two; $550 deluxe suite for two. AE, MC, V. Free parking.

This exclusive hotel, once operated as a private club, is now as casually elegant as is its clientele. The 18th-century main house is built of coral and stone and was painstakingly restored, rebuilt, and redecorated by Oliver Messel, uncle by marriage to Princess Margaret. The entire property was again renovated in 1994. The design of the hotel is characterized by arched louvered doors and cedar shutters. The antique loggia sets the style—everything from Lady Bateman's steamer trunks to a scallop-shell fountain on a quartz base. Guests sit here and enjoy their sundowners, perhaps after a game on the tennis court, a swim in the pool surrounded by Messel's "Roman ruins," and a buffet lunch at poolside. Some of the establishment's rooms were also designed by Messel. Units are in two fully restored Georgian houses, a trio of cottages, a newer block of four rooms, and a five-room beach house, all of which open onto windswept balconies or patios.

Dining/Entertainment: The hotel enjoys an outstanding reputation for its West Indian/continental food and service. Nonresidents are welcome to dine here, but they must make a reservation. The hotel also has three bars.

Services: Room service, laundry, babysitting.

Facilities: Two tennis courts, deep-sea fishing, sailboats, horseback riding.

⑤ Firefly

Mustique, The Grenadines, St. Vincent, W.I. ☎ **809/456-3414.** Fax 809/456-3510. 4 rms. TEL. Winter, $95 single; $110 double. Off-season, $60 single; $80 double. (Rates include full breakfast.) AE, MC, V. Free parking.

Firefly attracts those who aren't necessarily rich and famous but would still like to soak up the beauty and ambience of Mustique. Ms. Billy Mitchell rents rooms with balconies overlooking Britannia Bay and the Lower Grenadines. The location is about two minutes from the beach. It's a homelike British sort of place, nothing plastic, a hospitable guesthouse with an informal nonchalance. The rooms are somewhat open-air, with walls extending halfway up. The place is built with local wood and roughly hewn stone, with a high-vaulted ceiling. It has somewhat the feel of a small castle. There's a small refrigerator in the rooms. Evening meals can be served by special arrangement, and tennis, horseback riding, and scuba diving can be arranged.

WHERE TO DINE

Basil's Beach Bar

13 Britannia Bay. ☎ **809/458-4621.** Reservations not required. Appetizers EC$12–EC$35 ($4.40–$13); main courses EC$45–EC$75 ($16.70–$27.80); fixed-price meal EC$65 ($24.10) at lunch, EC$85 ($31.50) at dinner. AE, MC, V. Lunch daily 11am–3pm; dinner daily 7:30–10:30pm. (Bar, daily 8am "until very late.") SEAFOOD.

Nobody ever goes to this island of indigenous farmers and fisherfolk without spending a night drinking at Basil's, a "South Seas island"–type establishment more authentic than any reproduction in an old Dorothy Lamour flick. It's the gathering place for yachters, as well as owners of those luxurious villas. Who knows who might be at the next table? Princess Margaret, Spike Lee, Mick Jagger, Jerry Hall, David Bowie, Stephen Segal, and Michael Caine, or an array of fashion models, princes, filmmakers, and most definitely royal photographer Lord Lichfield. The bar, but mainly its owner, has received a lot of newspaper publicity. Its greeter, Basil S. Charles, is a 6-foot 4-inch heavily muscled charmer whom *Esquire* magazine called "the island's most famous product after its sandy beaches."

Some people come here to drink and watch a beautiful view, but Basil's is also, by reputation, one of the finest seafood restaurants in the Caribbean. Both lunch and dinner are served daily at this establishment built on piers above the sea. You can dine under the open-air sun screens or with the sun blazing down on you. On Wednesday night you can "jump-up" at a barbecue, and on Friday night there's limbo dancing, fire-eating, and folk dancing. A boutique is also on the premises. On nights when there's a live band, a cover charge of $8 is imposed.

CANOUAN

In the shape of a half circle, Canouan is surrounded by coral reefs and blue lagoons. The island is only 3¹/₂ miles by 1¹/₂ miles in size, and is visited mainly by those who want to enjoy its splendid long beaches. Canouan has a population of fewer than 1,000 people, many of whom fish for a living.

The governing island, St. Vincent, lies 14 miles to the north and Grenada 20 miles to the south. Canouan rises from its sandy beaches to the 800-foot-high peak of Mount Royal in the north. There you'll find unspoiled forests of white cedar.

GETTING THERE   You can only reach Canouan by taking a charter flight on **Mustique Airways** (☎ 809/458-4380 in St. Vincent). The cost from St. Vincent to Canouan is $175 per airplane each way; the aircraft carries only five passengers. You can also reach Canouan from St. Vincent by boat (see "Getting There," in the introduction to the Grenadines, above).

WHERE TO STAY & DINE

Canouan Beach Hotel

South Glossy Bay (P.O. Box 530, Kingstown, St. Vincent, W.I.), Canouan, The Grenadines, St. Vincent, W.I. ☎ **809/458-8888,** or 212/545-8469 in New York City. Fax 809/458-8885. 32 rms. A/C. Winter, $233–$379 single; $312–$506 double. Off-season, $140–$220 single; $216–$336 double. (Rates all-inclusive.) AE, MC, V. Free parking. Transportation: Take a taxi (a five-minute ride from the airport).

By far the best place to stay on Canouan, this hotel opened in 1984 and offers attractive accommodations on its 7 acres of beachfront. The location is about an eighth of a mile from the island's airport on a periwinkle-studded peninsula jutting out between the Atlantic and the Caribbean. This resort is a sort of expatriate French fantasy of a Gauguinesque tropical retreat. Each of the stone accommodations has sliding glass doors and comfortable furnishings. The resort's social center lies beneath the sun screen of a mahogany-trussed parapet whose sides are open to a water view. A pair of lush but uninhabited islands lie offshore. Snorkeling, windsurfing, small sailboats, and a catamaran are available without charge to guests. All water sports, buffet lunches, barbecue suppers, and drinks are included. Guests are booked in here for one week. The resort maintains a rather glamorous 36-foot catamaran, which departs six afternoons a week for neighboring islands and seabourne jaunts. This seems to be the main organized activity of the resort, which attracts a predominantly French clientele.

UNION ISLAND

Midway between Grenada and St. Vincent, Union Island is the southernmost of the Grenadines. It's known for its dramatic 900-foot peak, Mount Parnassus, which is seen by yachting people from miles away. For those cruising in the area, Union is the port of entry for St. Vincent. Yachters are required to check with Customs upon entry.

Perhaps you'll sail into Union on a night when the locals are having a "big drum" dance—costumed islanders dance and chant to the beat of drums made of goatskin.

GETTING THERE   The island is reached either by chartered or scheduled aircraft, by cargo boat, by private yacht, or by mail boat (see "Getting There" in Section 3 on St. Vincent and at the beginning of this section). Both **Air Martinique** (☎ 809/458-4528) and **LIAT** (☎ 809/457-1821) fly into Union Island.

WHERE TO STAY & DINE

Anchorage Yacht Club

Clifton, Union Island, The Grenadines, St. Vincent, W.I. ☎ **809/458-8221.** Fax 809/458-8365. 9 rms, 4 bungalows. A/C Winter, $70 single; $100 double; $160 bungalow. Off-season, $63 single; $90 double; $140 bungalow. Additional person $35 extra. (Rates include continental breakfast.) MC, V. Free parking.

The leading hotel on the island occupies a prominent position a few steps from the bumpy landing strip near a cluster of boutiques and shops. It combines a three-fold function as a hotel, a restaurant and bar, and a marine-service facility. Each of the bedrooms is set between a pair of airy verandas and has white tile floors and modern furniture. The most expensive units are the bungalows along the beach.

The yachting club meets in the wood-and-stone bar, where you can order meals for EC$80 ($29.60). The menu might include fish soup, a wide array of fresh fish, and Créole versions of lamb, pork, and beef. Try the mango daiquiri. The bar is open all day and into the night, but meals are served daily: breakfast from 7 to 10am, lunch from noon to 2:30pm, and dinner from 7 to 10:30pm.

One of the most unusual holding pens in the Caribbean lies a few steps from the marina. A handful of ferocious-looking (but reputedly harmless) nurse sharks are penned into a holding tank as a kind of zoological exhibition.

PALM ISLAND

Is this island a resort or is the resort the island? Casual elegance and privacy prevail on these 100 acres in the southern Grenadines. Surrounded by five white sand beaches, the island is sometimes called "Prune," so one can easily understand the more appealing name change. A little islet in the sun, it offers complete peace and quiet with plenty of sea, sand, sun, and sailing.

GETTING THERE   To get to Palm Island, you must first fly to Union Island (see "Getting There" in "Orientation," in Section 3 on St. Vincent for details). From Union Island, a hotel launch will take you to Palm Island.

WHERE TO STAY & DINE

Palm Island Beach Club

Palm Island, The Grenadines, St. Vincent, W.I. ☎ **809/458-8824,** or 800/776-PALM in the U.S. Fax 809/458-8804. 24 rms. Winter, $230 single; $345 double. Off-season, $165 single; $245 double. (Rates include all meals, afternoon tea, use of snorkeling gear, and airport transfers.) AE, MC, V.

The club is the fulfillment of a long-cherished wish held by John and Mary Caldwell to establish a hotel on an idyllic and isolated island. That dream came true, and in time such celebs as Ted Kennedy, Barbra Streisand, Donald Trump, and Françoise Sagan showed up. John is nicknamed "Coconut Johnny," because of his reforestation hobby of planting palms. At Prune Island, he planted hundreds upon hundreds of trees until its name was changed to Palm Island. An adventurer, this Texan once set out to sail by himself across the Pacific, coming to rest off the coast of Fiji. He made it to Australia, where he constructed his own ketch, *Outward Bound*, loaded his family aboard, and took off again. Eventually he made it to the Grenadines, where he operated a charter business. His exploits, including getting embroiled in a hurricane, were documented in the autobiographical book *Desperate Voyage*, an account of his 106-day, 8,500-mile journey at sea.

Just right for the Grenadine frame of mind, he eventually built this cottage colony with enough room for 50 guests spaced under palms on the white sandy beach. Accommodations are in the Beach Club duplex bungalows or in one of the villas, which are equipped for housekeeping, and are built of stone and wood, with louvered walls as well as sliding glass doors that open onto terraces. The furniture was built by the Caldwells. All rooms are superior, with ceiling fans, window screens, rattan furniture, beach lounges, private showers, small refrigerators, and outdoor walled patios on the oceanfront. Rates include afternoon tea served on the patio, a welcome drink, the manager's weekly punch party, airport transfers, tennis, and snorkel gear.

Dining is in a "South Seas island"–style pavilion where the food is good and plentiful. The nautically oriented guests like to have tall drinks at the sunset beach bar or at the nearby Yacht Club Bar and Restaurant.

The Caldwells still maintain a small charter fleet of yachts for day sails, with one of their amiable West Indian crewmembers aboard to assist. These natives are experts on local history, customs and tall tales, and safe sailing.

PETIT ST. VINCENT

A private island 4 miles from Union in the southern Grenadines, this speck of land is rimmed with white sandy beaches. On 113 acres, it's an out-of-this-world corner of the Caribbean that's only for self-sufficient types, who want to be away from just about everything.

GETTING THERE   The easiest way to get to Petit St. Vincent is to fly to Union Island via St. Vincent (see "Getting There" in "Orientation," in Section 3 on St. Vincent for details). Make arrangements with the hotel to have its "PVS boat" pick you up on Union Island.

WHERE TO STAY & DINE

Petit St. Vincent Resort

Petit St. Vincent, The Grenadines, St. Vincent, W.I. ☎ **809/458-8801,** or 800/654-9326 in the U.S. Fax 809/458-8428. 22 cottages. MINIBAR. Dec 19–Mar 12, $555 cottage for one; $710 cottage for two. Mar 13–Apr 10, $450 cottage for one; $580 cottage for two. Apr 11–Aug and Nov–Dec 18, $350 cottage for one; $450 cottage for two. (Rates all-inclusive.) AE, V (personal checks accepted and preferred). Closed Sept–Oct.

On this offbeat island oasis there exists the Petit St. Vincent Resort, which has a kind of nautical chic. It was conceived by Hazen Richardson, who had to do everything from planting trees to laying cables. The property was once owned by the archbishop of Trinidad. Open to the trade winds, this self-contained cottage colony was designed by a Swedish architect, Arne Hasselquist, who used purpleheart wood and the local stone, called blue bitch (yes, that's right), for the walls. This is the only place to stay on the island, and if you don't like it and want to check out, you'd better have a yacht waiting; but, chances are, you'll be pleased.

The cottages are built on a hillside or set close to the beach, in a 113-acre setting. The cottages open onto big outdoor patios, all with views. Each is cooled by trade winds and paddle-style ceiling fans. Wicker and rattan along with khuskhus rugs set the Caribbean tone of the place. When you need something, write out your request, place it in a slot in a bamboo flagpole, and run up the yellow flag. One of the waiters will arrive on a motorized cart to collect your order.

To make reservations, contact Petit St. Vincent, P.O. Box 12506, Cincinnati, OH 45212 (☎ **513/242-1333,** or **800/654-9326**).

MAYREAU

A tiny cay, 1¹/₂ square miles of land in the Grenadines, Mayreau is a privately owned island shared by a hotel and a little hilltop village of about 170 inhabitants. It's on the route of the mail boat that plies the seas to and from St. Vincent, visiting also Canouan and Union Island.

WHERE TO STAY & DINE

Saltwhistle Bay Club

Mayreau, The Grenadines, St. Vincent, W.I. ☎ **809/458-8444,** or toll free 800/561-7258 in the U.S. and Canada. Fax 809/458-8944. 10 rms. Winter, $330 single; $490 double. Off-season, $200 single; $300 double. Children under 18 granted 50% discounts. (MAP rates.) AE. Closed Sept. Transportation: Private hotel launch from the airport on Union Island, costing $50 per person round-trip.

This is a last frontier for people seeking a tropical island paradise. A Canadian-German couple, Tom and Undine Potter, who for several years operated a beachside restaurant here catering to yachting visitors, have expanded their operation into a hotel complex. The accommodations were built by local craftspeople, using local stone, floor tiles, and such tropical woods as purpleheart and greenheart. All units are cooled by ceiling fans. Slightly less formal and less expensive than the Petit St. Vincent Resort on Petit St. Vincent (see above), to which it is frequently compared, the place is appropriate for escapists unwilling to spend stratospheric sums for their seclusion.

The dining room at the hotel is made up of circular stone booths topped by thatch canopies, and you can enjoy seafood fresh from the waters around Mayreau—lobster, curried conch, and grouper. Guests can get acquainted at the bar. By day you can go snorkeling, fishing, windsurfing, cruising on a yacht, or just lolling in one of the hammocks strung among the trees in the 20-acre tropical garden, perhaps taking a swim along the expanse of white sand beaches that curve along both the leeward and windward sides of the island. One of the enjoyable excursions arranged by the Potters is a "Robinson Crusoe" picnic on a little uninhabited island nearby. Scuba divers will be glad to know that there's a shipwreck to explore, a 1912 gunboat lying in 40 feet of water a few hundred feet offshore.

For correspondence, send inquiries to the Saltwhistle Bay Club, 1020 Bay Ridge Dr., Kingston, ON K7P 2S2, Canada (☎ **613/634-7108,** or toll free **800/ 561-7258**).

5 Grenada

Its political troubles now over, this sleepy island offers fairly friendly people and the lovely and popular white sands of Grand Anse Beach. Exploring the lush interior, especially Grand Etang National Park, is a worthwhile diversion. Crisscrossed by nature trails and filled with dozens of secluded coves and sandy beaches, Grenada is a safe and secure place to visit, unlike its status in the 1980s. Grenada is not necessarily for the serious partier—and definitely not for those seeking action at the casino. Instead, it attracts visitors who like snorkeling, sailing, fishing, and doing nothing more invigorating than lolling on a beach under the sun.

The "Spice Island," Grenada is an independent three-island nation that includes Carriacou, the largest of the Grenadines, and Petit Martinique. The air on Grenada is full of the fragrance of spice and exotic fruits; the island has more spices per square mile than any other place in the world—cloves, cinnamon, mace, cocoa, tonka beans, ginger, and a third of the world's supply of nutmeg. "Drop a few seeds anywhere," the locals will tell you, "and you have an instant garden." The central area is like a jungle of palms, oleander, bougainvillea, purple and red hibiscus, crimson anthurium, bananas, breadfruit, birdsong, ferns, and palms.

Beefed up by financial aid from the United States, Grenada has revived a sagging tourist industry. Following the election of Nicholas Braithwaite as prime minister in 1990, the present government of Grenada is regarded as "U.S. friendly." Much improvement to the island, including a workable phone system and better roads, has been made with the benefit of U.S. aid.

Carnival time on Grenada is the second weekend of August, with colorful parades, music, dancing—what have you. The festivities begin on a Friday, continuing practically nonstop to Tuesday. Steel bands and calypso groups perform at Queen's Park. Jouvert, one of the highlights of the festival, begins at 5am on Monday with a parade of Djab Djab/Djab Molassi, devil-costumed figures daubed with a black substance. (*Be warned:* Don't wear your good clothes to attend this event—you may get sticky from close body contact.) The carnival finale, a gigantic "jump-up," ends with a parade of bands from Tanteen through the Carenage into town.

Grenada has a **People to People** program that allows you to meet the doctor, the waiter, or the spice-basket maker. This free program matches visitors to the island with Grenadians who share similar interests. Just write to New Trends Tours (see below), requesting an introduction. Be sure to specify your interests and what you'd like to do on the island—play golf, have lunch, go to church—or specify the profession of the person you'd like to meet. If you're already on Grenada, stop by the New Trends Tours office. For more information on Grenada's "People to People" program, contact New Trends Tours, P.O. Box 797, St. George's, Grenada, W.I. (☎ 809/444-1236).

ORIENTATION
GETTING THERE

The **Point Salines International Airport**—financed in part by Cuba (and finished by the United States)—opened with much fanfare in October 1984, on the anniversary of the U.S. rescue mission of the island. At the southwestern toe of Grenada, the airport not only makes it possible for jumbo jets to land, but it also makes most of the major hotels accessible in only 5 to 15 minutes by taxi.

In 1990, **American Airlines** (☎ 800/433-7300) became the first U.S.–based carrier to fly to Grenada with regularly scheduled flights. Service is via American's hub in San Juan. Using a Boeing 727 "stretch" aircraft, which accommodates 145 passengers, the daily flight departs San Juan at 1:35pm and arrives on Grenada around 3pm. The daily return flight departs Grenada around 4pm and arrives in San Juan at 5:25pm.

BWIA (☎ 800/327-7401) has a daily morning flight (hours vary) leaving Kennedy airport in New York, with a stopover on Barbados or in Port-of-Spain (Trinidad). BWIA's return flight to Kennedy arrives in the evening in New York. Schedules are subject to change.

LIAT (☎ 809/462-0700) also has regularly scheduled service between Barbados and Grenada, as well as to the smaller neighboring island of Carriacou (see below). There are at least two flights daily between Barbados and Grenada, although flights are sometimes cancelled with little notice. I've often spent hours and hours waiting in the Barbados airport for a plane. Through either LIAT or BWIA, you can connect on Barbados with several international airlines, including British Airways, Air Canada, American Airlines, and Air France.

In addition, **British Airways** (☎ 800/247-9297) flies to Grenada every Thursday and Saturday from London's Gatwick airport, making a single stop at Antigua en route.

GETTING AROUND

BY BUS   Minivans, charging EC$1 to EC$6 (40¢ to $2.20), are the most economical means of transport. The most popular run is between St. George's and Grand Anse Beach. Most minivans depart from Market Square or from the Esplanade area of St. George's.

BY TAXI   Rates are set by the government. Most arriving visitors take a cab at the Point Salines International Airport to one of the hotels near St. George's, at a cost of about $15. Add 33¹/₃% to the fare from 6pm to 6am. You can also use most taxi drivers as a guide for a day's sightseeing, and the cost can be divided

Grenada

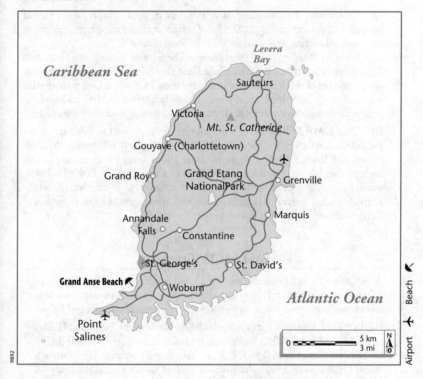

Caribbean Sea

Levera Bay

Sauteurs

Victoria

Mt. St. Catherine

Gouyave (Charlottetown)

Grand Roy

Grand Etang National Park

Grenville

Annandale Falls

Constantine

Marquis

St. George's

St. David's

Grand Anse Beach

Woburn

Atlantic Ocean

Point Salines

0   5 km
     3 mi

N

Beach

Airport

9892

among three or four passengers. If so, count on paying about $15 per hour. Again, this figure is to be negotiated.

BY RENTAL CAR   First, you must remember to *drive on the left*. A U.S., British, or Canadian driver's license is valid on Grenada; however, you must obtain a local permit costing EC$30 ($11.10), before getting onto the roads. These permits can be obtained either from the car-rental companies or from the traffic department on the Carenage in St. George's.

Among the major U.S.–based car-rental firms, only **Avis** (☎ **800/331-2112**) is represented. Operating out of a Shell gasoline station on Lagoon Road, on the southern outskirts of Saint George's, Avis will sometimes agree to meet at the airport anyone who reserves a car, but requires at least four days' delay before its toll-free reservations service will guarantee the availability of a car. (To avoid this four-day delay, many renters choose to call Avis directly at their Grenada headquarters; ☎ **809/440-3946.** Prices tend to be lower, however, if you use the toll-free number in the States and maintain the designated four-day waiting period.) Renters are required to be between 25 and 65 years old, and to present a valid credit or charge card and driver's license when picking up their car.

At press time, Avis's cheapest car was better accessorized than you might have expected: a Mitsubishi Lancer with automatic transmission and air conditioning. Its rental costs around $300 a week, with unlimited mileage included. Additional insurance in the form of a collision-damage waiver (CDW) is available for EC$16 ($5.90) per day. If you don't buy it, you'll be liable for up to the full value of the car in the event of an accident. If you do buy it, your liability won't extend beyond a maximum cost of $300. Use of certain credit or charge cards might in some cases eliminate your need for the additional insurance.

A Word of Warning About Local Drivers: There's such a thing as a Grenadian driving machismo where the drivers take blind corners with abandon. An extraordinary number of accidents are reported in the lively local paper. Gird yourself with nerves of steel, don't drink and drive, and be extra alert for children and roadside pedestrians while driving at night. In fact, try to avoid night driving if possible.

BY LOCAL AIR SERVICES Many visitors like to fly over to Grenada's satellite island, Carriacou, for the day. **LIAT** (☎ **809/462-0700**) makes the short takeoff and landing (STOL) flight in about 20 minutes. There are one or two flights a day. It's also possible to fly **Airlines of Carriacou** (☎ **809/444-3549**), which has daily scheduled service not only to Carriacou but to St. Vincent and the Grenadines. For reservations, you can contact a travel agent, LIAT, or Airlines of Carriacou itself at the Point Salines airport.

FAST FACTS: Grenada

Area Code To call Grenada from the United States, dial area code 809, then a three-digit city code, and then a four-digit number. For information about telecommunications once you're on the island, see "Telecommunications," below.

Banks In St. George's, the capital, you'll find Barclays, at Church and Halifax streets (☎ **809/440-3232**); Scotiabank, on Halifax Street (☎ **809/440-3274**); the National Commercial Bank (NCB), at the corner of Halifax and Hillsborough streets (☎ **809/440-3566**); the Grenada Bank of Commerce, at the corner of Halifax and Cross streets (☎ **809/440-3521**); and the Grenada Cooperative Bank, on Church Street (☎ **809/440-2111**).

Currency The official currency is the **Eastern Caribbean dollar (EC$),** worth about 37¢. Always determine which dollars—EC or U.S.—you're talking about when someone on Grenada quotes you a price.

Documents Proof of citizenship is needed to enter the country. A passport is preferred, but a birth certificate or voter registration card is accepted for American, British, and Canadian citizens, providing they also have photo ID.

Electricity Electricity is supplied on the island by Grenada Electricity Services. It's 220–240 volts A.C., 50 cycles, so transformers and adapters will be needed for U.S.–made appliances.

Embassies and High Commissions Grenada, unlike many of its neighbors, has a **U.S. Embassy** at St. George's (☎ **809/444-1173**). It also has a **British High Commission,** on Church Street, St. George's (☎ **809/440-3536**).

Emergencies Dial **911** to summon the police, report a fire, or call an ambulance.

Holidays Holidays include New Year's Day, Independence Day (February 7), National Day (March 13), Carnival (Saturday before Ash Wednesday to Ash Wednesday), Easter, Labour Day (first Monday in May), Emancipation Day (first Monday in August), October 25 (Thanksgiving Day), Christmas, and Boxing Day (December 26).

Information   Go to the **Grenada Board of Tourism,** The Carenage, in St. George's (☎ **809/440-2279**), open Monday through Friday from 8am to 4pm. Maps, guides, and general information are available. In the United States, the **Grenada Tourist Office** is at 820 Second Ave., Suite 900D, New York, NY 10017 (☎ **212/687-9554,** or toll free **800/927-9554**). In Canada, contact the **Grenada Board of Tourism,** 439 University Ave., Suite 820, Toronto, ON M5G 1Y8 (☎ **416/595-1339**); and in London, contact the **Grenada Board of Tourism,** 1 Collingham Gardens, London, SW5 0HW (☎ **0171/370-5164**).

Language   English is commonly spoken on this island of some 100,000 people because of the long years of British influence. However, now and then you'll hear people speaking in a French-African patios handed down from long ago.

Medical Care   There is a general hospital, St. George's Hospital (☎ **809/440-2051**), with an x-ray department and operating theater. Private doctors and nurses are available on call.

Pharmacies   Try Gittens Pharmacy, Halifax Street, St. George's (☎ **809/440-2165**).

Post Office   The General Post Office in St. George's is open Monday through Thursday from 8am to 4pm, with a lunch break from 11:45am to 1pm. On Friday hours are 8am to 5pm. It's closed on Saturday and Sunday.

Radio   The tri-island state boasts four radio stations, two on the medium-wave band and two on the FM band.

Safety   Although crime is rare here, it would be wise to safeguard your valuables. Never leave them unprotected on the beach.

Service   A 10% service charge is added to most restaurant and hotel bills.

Taxes   A 10% VAT (value-added tax) is imposed on food and beverages, and there's an 8% room tax. Upon leaving Grenada, you must fill out an immigration card and pay a departure tax of EC$35 ($13).

Telecommunications   International telephone service is available 24 hours a day from pay phones. Public telegraph, Telex, and fax services are also provided from the Carenage offices of Grenada Telecommunications Ltd. (Grentel) in St. George's (☎ **809/440-1000** for all Grentel offices), open Monday through Friday from 7am to 7pm, on Saturday from 7am to 1pm, and on Sunday and holidays from 10am to noon. To call another number on Grenada, dial all seven digits, as the island is divided among four area codes: 440, 442, 443, and 444. The most commonly used is 440.

Weather   Grenada has two distinct seasons, dry and rainy. The dry season is from January through May; the rest of the year is the rainy season, although the rainfall doesn't last long. The average temperature is 80° Fahrenheit. Because of constant trade winds, there is little humidity.

WHERE TO STAY

Many of Grenada's hostelries evoke the Mediterranean more than the Caribbean in their architecture. Don't forget that your hotel or inn will probably add a service charge to your bill—ask in advance about this. Also, there's an 8% government tax on food and beverage tabs.

VERY EXPENSIVE

✪ Calabash

L'Anse aux Epines (P.O. Box 382, St. George's), Grenada, W.I. ☎ **809/444-4334,** or 800/528-5835 in the U.S. and Canada. Fax 809/444-5050. 30 suites. A/C TEL. Winter, $365–$495 suite for two. Off-season, $255–$335 suite for two. Single occupancy $30 less; additional person $140–$155 extra in winter, $115–$125 extra off-season. (MAP rates.) AE, MC, V. Free parking.

Built in the early 1960s, the Calabash is today the best-established resort, and perhaps the most venerated hotel, on Grenada. Five miles south of St. George's and only minutes from the Point Salines International Airport, it occupies a landscaped 8-acre beach plot along an isolated section of Prickly Bay (L'Anse aux Epines). Many of the shrubs on the grounds make some of the stone outbuildings look diminutive. Foremost among the plants are the scores of beautiful calabashes (gourds) for which the resort was named. The social center of the place is a low-slung, rambling building whose walls are chiseled from blocks of dark-gray stone. The accommodations consist of eight private pool suites (for two) and 22 whirlpool bath suites (for two)—all with a veranda.

Dining/Entertainment: The hotel's restaurant serves a West Indian and continental menu. Entertainment, ranging from piano music to steel bands, is provided four or five nights a week.

Services: Room service, laundry, babysitting.

Facilities: Tennis court, outdoor swimming pool, sailboat rentals.

✪ La Source

Pink Gin Beach (P.O. Box 852, St. George's), Grenada, W.I. ☎ **809/444-2556,** or 800/544-2883 in the U.S. and Canada. Fax 809/444-2561. 90 rms, 10 suites. A/C TV TEL. Winter, $240–$305 single; $400–$530 double; $490–$590 suite for two. Off-season, $260–$275 single; $410–$470 double; $510–$530 suite for two. (Rates all-inclusive.) AE, MC, V. Free parking.

Noted as the first completely all-inclusive hotel on Grenada, this retreat, opened late in 1993, covers 40 acres of what had previously been a cocoa and nutmeg plantation. Within a minute's drive of the island's international airport, and associated with two St. Lucian resorts known for their allegiance to the concept of total body fitness, La Source stresses revitalization of the body and mind through spa treatments and exposure to the glories of nature. Meals, drinks, water sports, entertainment, and most (but not all) spa treatments are included in one all-inclusive price.

In a hillside compound of white-walled, terra-cotta-roofed buildings vaguely inspired by the colonial plantation houses of the West Indies, the resort is floored with multicolored marble tiles and furnished for the most part with mahogany and greenheart furniture imported from Venezuela. Adding visual interest are handfuls of exotic furnishings and artworks from India, Pakistan, Morocco, and Thailand. The bedrooms evoke accommodations in a dignified colonial plantation house, each with mahogany four-poster beds, hairdryers, and radios.

Dining/Entertainment: The Great Room is the resort's main dining room. Less formal is the open-sided Garden Restaurant. Live piano music is presented during the cocktail hour in one bar, while a small stage in the other offers live bands for dancing.

Services: Concierge, and instruction in such pastimes as cycling, fencing, windsurfing, calypso dancing, drink mixing, weight training, and each of the sports activities offered on site.

Facilities: Two free-form swimming pools whose waters are interconnected by a stream of flowing water, two white sand beaches separated from one another by a rocky knoll, a nonregulation "mashie" golf course—with very short distances between the holes (outings to a regulation nine-hole golf course in the area can be arranged). The resort's architectural centerpiece is the Oasis Spa, which offers massages, saunas, land and water aerobics classes, yoga, stress-management treatments, salt loofah rubs, and honeymoon massage instruction teaching couples the intricacies of mutual massage.

✪ Spice Island Inn

Grand Anse (P.O. Box 6, St. George's), Grenada, W.I. ☎ **809/444-4258,** 212/251-1800 in New York City, or toll free 800/223-9815 in the U.S. Fax 809/444-4807. 56 suites. A/C MINIBAR TEL. Winter, $270–$425 suite for one; $320–$475 suite for two. Off-season, $215–$310 suite for one; $250–$345 suite for two. (MAP rates.) AE, MC, V. Free parking.

On an estate overlooking the Caribbean, this inn is built along 1,200 feet of Grand Anse beach, directly north of the airport. The main house, reserved for dining and dancing, has a tropical aura and lots of nice touches, showing that taste and concern went into the design of the place. A total of 32 units are beach suites, and these are preferred by many visitors. Second-floor suites have terraces overlooking the ocean and the garden. Seventeen units have their own private plunge pools where guests can go skinny-dipping if desired. Furnishings in the rooms are not elaborate, with outdoorsy-type pieces such as wicker chairs. The bathrooms are the largest and most luxurious on Grenada, with fluffy white towels (enough to please Frank Sinatra) and spa-Jacuzzis.

Dining/Entertainment: The waiter will arrive with your breakfast (a just-plucked red hibiscus resting on the tray), and you'll enjoy it on a shaded patio, your very own. Hotel chefs not only prepare an international cuisine but also deftly turn out good Grenadian food, including soursop ice cream (nutmeg is also a specialty), breadfruit vichyssoise, and Caribbean lobster. Sometimes a combo plays for dancing.

Services: Room service for all three meals.

Facilities: Beach, private swimming pools, fitness center, day and night tennis.

EXPENSIVE

Grenada Renaissance Resort

P.O. Box 441, Grand Anse Beach, Grenada, W.I. ☎ **809/444-4371,** or 800/228-9898 in the U.S. Fax 809/444-4800. 184 rms, 2 suites. A/C TV TEL. Winter, $180–$240 single or double; $360 suite. Off-season, $127–$175 single or double; $320 suite. MAP $50 per person extra. AE, DC, MC, V. Free parking.

Renovated in 1991, this hotel stands 3 miles north of the airport on a desirable stretch of beachfront, behind a cedar-shingled facade whose design might have been inspired by an 18th-century plantation house. Any comparison with another century, however, ends when visitors see the interior. Guests register beneath an octagonal roof of the entrance hall, then are ushered between a pair of manicured formal gardens to their (often-small) rooms, which are furnished with a formal blend of English reproduction pieces, carpeting, and clock radios. Each has a balcony or veranda, some of which open onto sun-flooded views of the beach.

Dining/Entertainment: Traditionally, everyone, at some point in a visit to Grenada, has dropped in here for a drink, although there are now many other places to patronize. Guests or nonresidents can dine both in or out of doors in the Greenery restaurant. Entertainment is usually offered at night.

Services: Room service, laundry, babysitting.

Facilities: Beach, swimming pool, water-sports kiosk (for the rental of sailboats, windsurfers, and snorkeling equipment).

Rex Grenadian

Point Salines (P.O. Box 893, St. George's), Grenada, W.I. ☎ **809/444-3333,** or 800/255-5859 in the U.S. and Canada. Fax 809/444-1111. 192 rms. 20 suites. A/C TEL. Winter, $175–$260 single or double; $360 suite. Off-season, $115–$200 single or double; $300 suite. MAP $49 per person extra. AE, DC, MC, V. Free parking.

Opened late in 1993, this is the largest and most important hotel on the island. It's set on 12 rocky, partially forested acres which slope steeply down to a pair of white-sand beaches, about a quarter of a mile from the island's international airport. Arranged roughly into a hexagon around a landscaped core, each of the wintergreen and pale-blue units is configured differently from its neighbor, and each is outfitted in rattan, wicker, and muted tropical fabrics. Many (but not all) offer sea views. Adjacent to the accommodations is a 2-acre artificial lake strewn with islands that are connected to the "mainland" with footbridges and paddle boats.

Dining/Entertainment: Drinking and dining options include the International, specializing in buffets with foods from around the world; and the canopy-covered Courtyard Café, for lunches, drinks, and snacks. The Oriental offers Asian cuisine. Spicers Bar and Restaurant serves lunches, salads, and fast food, whereas Traders Beach Bar whips up tropical drinks. In the evenings, the Tamarind Lounge offers cabaret singing and disco music. The Verandah Bar in the sports Pavilion gives you a chance to sip a cold beer while enjoying a game of pool.

Services: Room service, babysitting, laundry.

Facilities: Water-sports options include scuba, snorkeling, sailing, and deep-sea fishing; other diversions can be arranged. There's a fitness center in an outlying annex (the Pavilion), two beaches, and what is probably the most dramatic swimming pool on the island. Graced with a water cascade and its own bar and restaurant, it was drilled and blasted directly into the volcanic rock of a stony promontory jutting out toward the open ocean.

✪ Secret Harbour

Mount Hartman Bay, L'Anse aux Epines (P.O. Box 11, St. George's), Grenada, W.I. ☎ **809/444-4439,** or 800/334-2435 in the U.S. and Canada. Fax 809/444-2090. 20 suites. A/C TEL. Winter, $225 suite for one or two; $245 suite for three; $265 suite for four. Off-season, $125 suite for one or two; $165 suite for four. Additional person $20 extra. MAP $49 per person extra. AE, MC, V. Free parking.

Seen from the water of Mount Hartman Bay, Secret Harbour reminds one of a Mediterranean complex on Spain's Costa del Sol—a tasteful one, that is, with white stucco arches, red-tile roofs, and wrought-iron light fixtures. From all over Grenada, including some island plantation homes, antiques were purchased, restored, and installed here. The bathrooms are also luxurious, with sunken tubs lined with Italian tiles and lighting from unglazed medallion windows. Each of the suites has a dressing room, living area, and patio overlooking the water. Steps lead down to the beach. Units also have small refrigerators.

Secret Harbour is a favorite of the yachting set. While many guests stay at the hotel, others stay on yachts anchored off the property. Owned by the Moorings, an international hotel and yacht-charter company based in Clearwater, Florida, Secret Harbour is located about 20 minutes from Point Salines International Airport and 15 minutes from St. George's.

Dining/Entertainment: The antiques-filled Mariners Restaurant features an international menu, often prepared with fresh produce from Grenada. Guests enjoy the lobby/bar/terrace in the evening, savoring the tranquility with no loud, aggressive entertainment. The restaurant, which is open daily from 7am to 10pm, overlooks Mount Hartman Bay. Nonresidents should make dinner reservations if they want to come here in the evening.

Services: Room service, laundry.

Facilities: Marina; wide range of water sports (including snorkeling and windsurfing), sailing, and boating programs (including bareboat charters and "Learn to Cruise" lessons), tennis court, swimming pool, beach.

Twelve Degrees North

L'Anse aux Epines (P.O. Box 241, St. George's), Grenada, W.I. ☎ **809/444-4580;** call collect for reservations. Fax 809/444-4580. 8 apartments. Winter. $185 one-bedroom apartment for two: from $300 two-bedroom apartment for four. Off-season, $130 one-bedroom apartment for two: $220 two-bedroom apartment for four. Additional person $60–$70 extra. Children under 15 not accepted. No credit cards. Free parking.

On a very private beach, this complex is operated by Joseph Gaylord, a former commercial real-estate broker from New York, who greets visitors in front of a large flame tree on his front lawn. He owns this cluster of spotlessly clean efficiency apartments, 3 miles east of the airport at Point Salines.

Many of the staff members have been with Mr. Gaylord since he opened the place many years ago. They'll cook breakfast, prepare lunch (perhaps pumpkin soup and flying fish), do the cleaning and laundry, and fix regional specialties for dinner (which you heat up for yourself later). A grass-roofed beach bar faces the water. Each unit (two with two bedrooms and six with one bedroom) comes with an individual uniformed housekeeper/cook, who arrives at 8 o'clock each morning to perform the thousand small kindnesses that make Twelve Degrees North a favorite lair for returning guests from America and Europe. Each unit is equipped with an efficiency kitchen with a 16-cubic-foot refrigerator. The large beds can be separated or pushed together. The owner prefers to rent by the week, because, as he says, "a few days aren't enough to get to know Grenada."

Facilities: Beach, windsurfers, double-seated kayak, swimming pool, snorkeling equipment, tennis court, two Sunfish—all free.

MODERATE

⑤ Blue Horizons Cottage Hotel

P.O. Box 41, Grand Anse, Grenada, W.I. ☎ **809/444-4316.** Fax 809/444-4807. 36 cottages. A/C TV TEL. Winter, $140–$155 cottage for one; $145–$165 cottage for two. Off-season, $95–$105 cottage for one; $100–$110 cottage for two. AE, DC, MC, V. Free Parking.

Co-owners Royston and Arnold Hopkin purchased this place from a bankrupt estate. Sons of the famous Grenadian hotelkeepers Audrey and Curtis Hopkin, they transformed the neglected property into one of the finest on the island. The units are spread throughout a flowering garden of 6$^1/_4$ acres. Rates depend on the category of the cottage: superior or deluxe. Each has an efficiency kitchen and comfortable solid mahogany furniture. Children are welcome, and they can watch the 21 varieties of native birds said to inhabit the grounds.

Guests who prefer to cook in their rooms can buy supplies from a Food Fair at Grand Anse, a 10-minute walk away. Most important, Grand Anse Beach is only 5 minutes away by foot. On the grounds is one of the best restaurants on the island, La Belle Créole (see "Where to Dine," below). Lunch is served around a pool bar. Laundry, babysitting, and room service are provided.

Coyaba Beach Resort

Grand Anse Beach (P.O. Box 336, St. George's), Grenada, W.I. ☎ **809/444-4129.** Fax 809/444-4808. 40 rms. A/C TV TEL. Winter, $115 single; $165 double. Off-season, $75 single; $95 double. Additional person $40 extra in winter, $20 extra off-season. MAP $35 per person extra. AE, DC, MC, V. Free parking.

On a 2½-acre site on Grand Anse Beach next to the medical school, this resort is 6 miles from St. George's and 3 miles north of Point Salines International Airport. Opened in 1987, the hotel has views of the town and of St. George's harbor. All units have double beds, plus verandas and patios, spacious baths, and hairdryers. Laundry service is available, as are room service and babysitting. The hotel offers two open-air restaurants, the main dining room, Pepperpot, and the less formal El Cabana, at poolside. There are two bars as well, one at poolside. Activities include tennis on a Laykold court, volleyball, and water sports offered by Grenada Aquatic Ltd. on the premises.

⊛ Horse Shoe Beach Hotel

L'Anse aux Epines (P.O. Box 174, St. George's), Grenada, W.I. ☎ **809/444-4244,** or 718/726-8600 in New York City. Fax 809/444-4844. 4 rms, 6 suites, 12 villas. A/C TEL. Winter, $85 single; $100 double; $130–$150 suite for two; $120 villa for one; $130 villa for two. Extra person $20. Off-season, $70 single; $80 double; $110–$115 suite for two; $90 villa for one; $100 villa for two. Additional person $20 extra in winter, $15 extra off-season. MAP $40 per person extra. AE, DC, MC, V. Free parking.

This small Mediterranean-style hotel with vintage charm is set on a hilltop on the south coast of the island 3 miles east of the airport. Constructed on a small promontory, the complex captures the sea breezes at night, and you'll hear the rustling sound of wind blowing through the acres of tropical gardens. The doorway to the Spanish stucco building is almost hidden by the foliage. The Grenadian-Iberian dining room and red-tile lounge has cozy nooks and original oil paintings. The restaurant frames views of the beach and swimming pool, as well as of the gardens. Guests are so well coddled here that they keep returning to the appealing rooms furnished with antiques from old island-family houses.

A dozen accommodations are in six terra-cotta–roofed villas. Each shares a kitchenette with its neighbor, and each has a canopied four-poster bed and a private terrace. In the main building are six suites, more modern in concept and slightly larger than the outlying villas. The beach requires a stroll down a carefully landscaped hillside. Guests are also transported to Grand Anse Beach.

WHERE TO DINE
EXPENSIVE

✪ Canbouley

Morne Rouge. ☎ **809/444-4401.** Reservations recommended. Appetizers EC$10–EC$20 ($3.70–$7.40) at lunch, EC$14–EC$30 ($5.20–$11.10) at dinner (off-season); main courses EC$22–EC$30 ($8.10–$11.10) at lunch, EC$38–EC$55 ($14.10–$20.40) at dinner (off-season); five-course fixed-price meal (in winter) EC$80–EC$100 ($29.60–$37). AE, DC, MC, V. Lunch Mon–Sat 11:30am–2:30pm; dinner Mon–Sat 7pm–9:30pm. Closed Sept. CARIBBEAN.

This restaurant manages to instill a gracious kind of West Indian formality with an elegant Caribbean-colonial decor and some of the most unusual Antillean food on Grenada. Set beside Grand Anse Beach, it occupies a clapboard house painted in vibrant Caribbean colors of orange, blue, and green. (Even the staff is neatly dressed in white and a shade of blue matching that of the decor.) Menu items are more intensely original at night than at lunchtime, and throughout the winter the only evening option available is a fixed-price menu with five courses. Specialties include coconut crêpes stuffed with crabmeat and served with callaloo relish, cornmeal baked or fried in coconut milk (the result is a traditional starch known as "cuckoo"), blackened flying fish, fried conch served with a local citrus sauce, deep-fried shrimp served with a guava-lime coulis, grilled or baked chicken served with a sauce of tomatoes and local herbs, and many kinds of steak. The owners are Eric and Gina Lee Johnson.

○ Coconut's Beach Restaurant

Grand Anse Beach. ☎ **809/444-4644.** Reservations recommended. Appetizers EC$7–EC$25 ($2.60–$9.30); main courses EC$35–EC$75 ($13–$27.80); lunch platters EC$15–EC$35 ($5.60–$13). AE, MC, V. Lunch daily 10am–6pm; dinner daily 6:30–10pm. Closed Mon off-season. FRENCH/CREOLE.

Because of its location within a 10-minute ramble from at least four major hotels, many of its clients opt to walk along the beach to reach it. (Others take a taxi along a sloping, winding road; others arrive by yacht.) Raffish and informal, the restaurant occupies a pink-and-green clapboard house set directly on the sands of the beach, about half a mile north of St. George's. In the dining room you can watch the staff at work in the exposed kitchen. Meals might include the catch of the day with a variety of sauces, curried conch, T-bone steaks, grilled lobster, lobster gratin, or fisherman's platter.

○ La Belle Créole

At Blue Horizons, Grand Anse Beach. ☎ **809/444-4316.** Reservations required for non-hotel guests. Appetizers $5–$7; main courses $22–$28; five-course dinner $40. AE, DC, MC, V. Lunch daily 12:30–2pm; dinner daily 7–9pm. CREOLE/SEAFOOD.

One of the best restaurants on Grenada, a five-minute walk from Grand Anse Beach, is run by Arnold and Royston Hopkin, sons of "Mama" Audrey Hopkin, long considered the best cook on the island if you're seeking West Indian specialties. Archways frame views of the mountains and the beach. The walls and ceilings are covered with a type of island reed called roseau (which, strangely enough, must be cut only during a certain phase of the moon to provide a durable, long-lasting building surface; if cut at any other time of the month, the covering, experience has taught, disintegrates into a powder within six months).

Lunch, which can be taken poolside, features soup and chicken, fish, or lobster salad. Dinner features a fixed-price menu, with a variety of choices from continental recipes with West Indian substitutions for ingredients not available on the island. A typical dinner might begin with dolphin (fish) mousse with callaloo; then conch chowder; followed by a main course, such as Créole veal roll stuffed with ham, chicken livers, onions, and seasonings, baked in a wine sauce; and served with local vegetables, such as a dasheen soufflé and christophines, along with candied plaintain; and the meal might end with a "mango delight." Guests can also order à la carte.

MODERATE

Bird's Nest

Grand Anse. ☎ **809/444-4264.** Reservations recommended. Appetizers EC$8–EC$15 ($3–$5.60); main courses EC$20–EC$50 ($7.40–$18.50). AE, MC, V. Mon–Sat 9am–11pm; Sun 6–11pm. CHINESE/CREOLE.

For change-of-pace dining, I suggest the Bird's Nest, in its own building with three palm trees at the entrance, opposite the Grenada Renaissance, 3 miles north of the airport. This family business offers Chinese food, mainly Szechuan and Cantonese, along with seafood and Caribbean cuisine. The most expensive main courses, of course, are those with a lobster base. You'll see the familiar shrimp eggrolls along with eight different chow meins. Sweet-and-sour fish is a favorite, and daily specials are posted. A take-out service is available.

$ Morne Fendue

St. Patrick's. ☎ **809/442-9330.** Reservations required. Fixed-price lunch EC$40 ($14.80). No credit cards. Lunch only. Mon–Sat 12:30–3pm. CREOLE.

As you're touring north from the beach at Grand Anse, one place is memorable. It's Betty Mascoll's Morne Fendue, 25 miles north of St. George's. This 1912 plantation house, constructed the year she was born, is her ancestral home. It was built of carefully chiseled river rocks held together with a mixture of lime and molasses, as was the custom in that day. Mrs. Mascoll and her loyal staff, two of whom have been with her for many, many years, always need time to prepare for the arrival of guests, so it's imperative to call ahead. Lunch is likely to include yam and sweet-potato casserole, curried chicken with lots of hot spices, and a hotpot of pork and oxtail. Because this is very much a private home, tipping should be performed with the greatest tact. Nonetheless, the hardworking cook and maid seem genuinely appreciative of a gratuity. Mrs. Mascoll is now in her 80s and struggling to continue her long tradition of hospitality.

The Nutmeg

The Carenage, St. George's. ☎ **809/440-2539.** Reservations not required. Appetizers EC$15–EC$25 ($5.60–$9.30); main courses EC$15–EC$55 ($5.60–$20.40). AE, MC, V. Mon–Sat 8am–11pm, Sun 5–11pm. SEAFOOD.

Right on the harbor, the Nutmeg is over the Sea Change Shop where you can pick up paperbacks and souvenirs. It's another rendezvous point for the yachting set and a favorite with just about everybody, both expatriates living on the island and visitors. It is suitable for a snack or a full-fledged dinner, and its drinks are very good. Try one of the Grenadian rum punches made with Angostura bitters, grated nutmeg, rum, lime juice, and syrup. An informal atmosphere prevails, as you're served your filet of fish with potato croquettes and string beans. There's always fresh fish, and usually callaloo soup. Lambi (that ubiquitous conch) is also done very well here. Lobster thermidor is the most expensive food item on the menu. There's a small wine list with some California and German selections, and you can drop in for just a glass of beer to enjoy the sea view. Sometimes, however, you'll be asked to share a table.

The Red Crab

L'Anse aux Epines. ☎ **809/444-4424.** Reservations required in winter. Appetizers EC$15–EC$28 ($5.60–$10.40); main courses EC$30–EC$85 ($11.10–$31.50). AE, MC, V. Lunch Mon–Sat 11am–2pm; dinner Mon–Sat 6–10:30pm. Transportation: Take a taxi (a five-minute ride from the Grand Anse Beach resorts). WEST INDIAN/INTERNATIONAL.

The Red Crab, a popular eating place for visitors and locals alike, is only a short taxi ride from the major hotels. Specialties include local lobster tail, lambi (conch), locally caught fish (snapper, dolphin, grouper), pepper steaks, and garlic shrimp. Dessert might be a homemade cheesecake. The owner-chef once worked as the executive chef of the Trinidad Hilton.

Rudolf's

The Carenage, St. George's. ☎ **809/440-2241.** Reservations recommended. Appetizers EC$10.50–EC$18.50 ($3.90–$6.80); main courses EC$26–EC$55 ($9.60–$20.40). MC, V. Mon–Sat 10am–midnight. INTERNATIONAL.

This long-established restaurant overlooks a deep, U-shaped harbor lined with commercial establishments in St. George's. On the north center of the Carenage, it's also a good spot for drinks in the late afternoon if you want to join the yachting machismo set. If you stick around for dinner, you'll find that the food is well prepared, with more choices offered than in most places on Grenada. The menu includes about 13 different steak dishes, and if you're dining lighter, you're faced with a selection of some eight different omelets. Soups are both hot and cold, ranging from French onion to gazpacho. Try the lobster, fish, or conch. Specials are posted daily.

Spice Island Inn

Grand Anse Beach. ☎ **809/444-4258.** Reservations required. Fixed-price dinner $40; breakfast/lunch from $12. AE, MC, V. Breakfast daily 7:30–9:30am; lunch daily 12:30–2:30pm; dinner daily 7–9pm. CREOLE/SEAFOOD.

A favorite way to enjoy a meal on Grenada is on an uncrowded beachfront in the full outdoors, with only a parapet over your head to protect you from sudden tropical showers. The parapet here, built of imported pine and cedar, looks like a Le Corbusier rooftop. At this inn, located directly north of the airport, the view is of one of the best beaches in the Caribbean—miles of white sand sprouting an occasional grove of sea grape or almond trees. You can eat lunch in a swimsuit. Dinner menus change frequently and can be cooked to your specifications. Local seafood is featured on the constantly changing menu. Friday is barbecue night, Saturday a local band plays, and a Grenadian barbecue is presented Wednesday night.

BUDGET

⑤ Mamma's

Lagoon Rd., St. George's. ☎ **809/440-1459.** Reservations required a day in advance. Fixed-price meal EC$50 ($18.50). No credit cards. Lunch daily 11am–1:30pm; dinner daily 7:30–9:30pm. CREOLE.

Mamma's lies on the road leading to Grenada Yacht Services. Every trip to the Caribbean should include a visit to an establishment like this. Serving copious meals, this Mamma became particularly famous during the U.S. intervention in Grenada, as U.S. servicepeople adopted her as their own island mama. Mamma (alias Insley Wardally) is now deceased, but her daughter, Cleo, carries on.

Meals, I was told, come in two sizes: "the usual" and "the special." (But I was later told that "the usual" and "the special" were the same.) Either way, meals include such dishes as callaloo soup with coconut cream, shredded cold crab with lime juice, freshwater crayfish, fried conch, and a casserole of cooked bananas, yams, and dasheen, along with ripe baked plantain, and rotis made of curry and yellow chickpeas, followed by sugar-apple ice cream. Mamma's seafoods are likely to include crab backs, octopus in a hot-and-spicy sauce, and even turtle steak, although the latter could be an endangered species. Mamma is also known for her "wild meats," including armadillo, opossum, monkey (yes, that's right), game birds, and even the endangered iguana. Gourmets flock to this restaurant to sample these delicacies, and the unusual menu has been widely written about in U.S. media.

However, "wild things" are only available when Cleo can obtain them. The specialty drink of the house is rum punch—the ingredients are a secret. Dinner here must be reserved a day in advance so you'll be sure of having a choice of 22 different foods from Grenada.

Portofino

The Carenage, St. George's. ☎ **809/440-3986.** Reservations recommended. Appetizers EC$10.50–EC$18.50 ($3.90–$6.80); main courses EC$26–EC$55 ($9.60–$20.40). AE. Mon–Fri 11am–11pm, Sat–Sun 6–11pm. ITALIAN.

In the geographical center of town, in a pleasant Italian terrace garden-style restaurant on the second floor of a waterfront building, this place offers a beautiful view of the inner harbor. The menu lists 12 varieties of pizza, costing EC$14 to EC$35 ($5.20 to $13). Other offerings include five types of spaghetti, other kinds of pasta, eggplant parmigiana, veal milanese, and lobster. There's also a take-out service.

WHAT TO SEE & DO
St. George's

The capital city of Grenada, St. George's is one of the most attractive ports in the West Indies. Its landlocked inner harbor is actually the deep crater of a long-dead volcano, or so one is told.

In the town you'll see some of the most charming Georgian colonial buildings to be found in the Caribbean, still standing in spite of a devastating hurricane in 1955. The streets are mostly steep and narrow, which enhances the attractiveness of the ballast bricks, wrought-iron balconies, and red tiles of the sloping roofs. Many of the pastel warehouses date back to the 18th century. Frangipani and flamboyant trees add to the palette of color.

The port, which some have compared to Portofino, Italy, is flanked by old forts and bold headlands. Among the town's attractions is an 18th-century, pink, Anglican **church,** on Church Street, and the **Market Square** where colorfully attired farm women offer even more colorful produce for sale.

Fort George, on Church Street, built by the French, stands at the entrance to the bay, with subterranean passageways and old guardrooms and cells.

Everyone strolls along the waterfront of **The Carenage** or relaxes on its Pedestrian Plaza, with seats and hanging planters providing shade from the sun.

On this side of town, the **Grenada National Museum,** at the corner of Young and Monckton streets (☎ **809/440-3725**), is set in the foundations of an old French army barracks and prison built in 1704. Small but interesting, it houses finds from archeological digs, including the petroglyphs, native fauna, the first telegraph installed on the island, a rum still, and memorabilia depicting Grenada's history. The most comprehensive exhibit traces the native culture of Grenada. One of the exhibits shows two bathtubs—the wooden barrel used by the fort's prisoners and the carved marble tub used by Joséphine Bonaparte during her adolescence on Martinique. The museum is open Monday through Friday from 9am to 4:30pm and on Saturday from 10am to 1pm. Admission is EC$2.50 (90¢).

The Outer Harbour is also called the **Esplanade.** It's connected to the Carenage by the Sendall Tunnel, which is cut through the promontory known as St. George's Point, dividing the two bodies of water.

You can take a drive up to Richmond Hill where **Fort Frederick** stands. The French began construction on the fort in 1779; however, after Grenada was returned to Britain, following the Treaty of Versailles in 1783, the English carried on the work until its completion in 1791. From its battlements you'll have a superb view of the harbor and of the yacht marina.

An afternoon tour of St. George's and its environs takes you into the mountains northeast of the capital. About a 15-minute drive takes you to ✪ **Annandale Falls,** a tropical wonderland, where a cascade about 50 feet high falls into a basin. The overall beauty is almost Tahitian, and you can have a picnic surrounded by liana vines, elephant ears, and other tropical flora and spices. The **Annandale Falls Centre** (☎ **809/440-2452**) houses gift items, handcrafts, and samples of the indigenous spices of Grenada. Nearby, an improved trail leads to the falls where you can enjoy a refreshing swim. Swimmers can use the changing cubicles at the falls free. The center is open daily from 8am to 4pm.

AROUND THE ISLAND

The next day you can head north out of St. George's along the western coast, taking in beaches, spice plantations, and the fishing villages that are so typical of Grenada.

You pass through **Gouyave,** a spice town, the center of the nutmeg and mace industry. Both spices are produced from a single fruit. Before reaching the village, you can stop at the Dougaldston Estate, where you'll witness the processing of nutmeg and mace.

Proceeding along the coast, you reach **Sauteurs,** at the northern tip of Grenada. This is the third-largest town on the island. It was from this great cliff that the Caribs leaped to their deaths instead of facing enslavement by the French.

To the east of Sauteurs is the palm-lined **Levera Beach,** an idyll of sand where the Atlantic meets the Caribbean. This is a great spot for a picnic lunch, but

---

Of Cuckoos and Hummingbirds

In the center of the island, reached along the major interior road between Grenville and St. George's, is ✪ **Grand Etang National Park,** containing the island's spectacular rain forest, which has been made more accessible by hiking trails. Beginning at the park's forest center, the Morne LeBaye Trail affords a short hike along which you can see to the 2,309-foot Mount Sinai and the east coast. Down the Grand Etang Road trails lead to the 2,373-foot summit of Mount Qua Qua and the Ridge and Lake Circle Trail, taking hikers on a 30-minute trek along **Grand Etang Lake,** the crater of an extinct volcano lying in the midst of a forest preserve and bird sanctuary. Among the birds you are likely to see are the yellow-billed cuckoo and the emerald-throated hummingbird. The park is also a playground for Mona monkeys—those that didn't end up in Mamma's stewpot. Covering 13 acres, the water is a cobalt blue. All three trails offer the opportunity to see a wide variety of Grenada's flora and fauna. Guides for the park trails are available, but they must be arranged for in advance. After a rainfall, the trails can be very slippery; hikers should wear sneakers or jogging shoes, and carry drinking water as well. Much of the rain falls on Grenada between June and November. The park's **Grand Etang Interpretation (Nature) Centre,** on the shores of Grand Etang Lake, is open daily from 8am to 4pm, featuring a video show about the park. An admission of $1 is charged.

swimming can sometimes be dangerous. On the distant horizon you'll see some of the Grenadines.

Opened in 1994, the 450-acre **Levera National Park** has several white sandy beaches for swimming and snorkeling, although the surf is rough here where the Atlantic meets the Caribbean. It's also a hiker's paradise, and offshore are coral reefs and seagrass beds. The park contains a mangrove swamp, a lake, and a bird sanctuary—perhaps you'll see a rare tropical parrot. Its interpretation center (☎ 809/442-1018) is open Monday through Friday from 8am to 4pm, on Saturday from 10am to 4pm, and on Sunday from 10am to 5pm.

Heading down the east coast of Grenada, you reach **Grenville,** the island's second city. If possible, pass through here on a Saturday morning when you'll enjoy the hubbub of the native fruit-and-vegetable market. There is also a fish market along the waterfront. A nutmeg factory here welcomes visitors.

From Grenville, you can cut inland into the heart of Grenada. Here you're in a world of luxuriant foliage, passing along nutmeg, banana, and cocoa plantations up to Grand Etang, previously mentioned. You will then begin your descent from the mountains. Along the way you'll pass hanging carpets of mountain ferns. Going through the tiny hamlets of Snug Corner and Beaulieu, you eventually come back to the capital.

On yet another day, you can drive south from St. George's to the beaches and resorts spread along the already much-mentioned **Grand Anse,** which many people consider one of the most beautiful beaches in the West Indies. Water-taxis can also take you from the Carenage in St. George's to Grand Anse.

Point Salines, where the airport is now located, is at the southwestern tip of the island, where a lighthouse stood for 56 years. However, a sculpture of the lighthouse has been constructed on the grounds just outside the airport terminal building. A panoramic view ranging from the northwest side of Grenada to the green hills in the east to the undulating plains in the south can be seen from a nearby hill.

Along the way you'll pass through the village of **Woburn,** which was featured in the film *Island in the Sun,* and go through the sugar belt of **Woodlands,** with its tiny sugarcane factory.

SPORTS & OUTDOOR ACTIVITIES

BEACHES One of the best beaches in the Caribbean is ✪ **Grand Anse,** 2 miles of sugar-white sands extending into deep waters far offshore. Most of Grenada's best hotels are within walking distance of Grand Anse. You can also take off and discover dozens more beaches on your own, as they're all public.

BOAT EXCURSIONS *Rhum Runner* and *Rhum Runner II* are metal-hulled catamarans that operate out of St. George's Harbour. They're available for reef viewing, cocktail cruises, barbecue evenings, moonlight cruises, and snorkeling tours. The ships cruise Grenada's coast, with all-you-can-drink punch parties, live music, steel bands, and limbo parties. The average price of a cruise is $20 per person. For more information, contact **Best of Grenada,** The Carenage (☎ 809/440-2198).

DEEP-SEA-FISHING Fisherfolk come here from November to March in pursuit of both blue and white marlin, yellowfin tuna, wahoo, sailfish, and other catches. Most of the bigger hotels have a sports desk that will arrange fishing trips for you. The **Annual Game Fishing Tournament,** held in January, attracts a number of regional and international participants.

Havadu is a 32-foot ocean-going pirogue, available for deep-sea-fishing offshore excursions, and snorkeling. Various prices depend on the size of the group. For more information, contact **Best of Grenada,** The Carenage (☎ **809/440-2198**).

GOLF   At the **Grenada Golf Course and Country Club,** Woodlands (☎ **809/444-4128**), you'll find a nine-hole course, with greens fees of $12 for nine holes. The course is open Monday through Saturday from 8am to sunset and on Sunday from 8am to noon. The course offers a view of both the Caribbean Sea and the Atlantic.

SCUBA DIVING & SNORKELING   Along with many other water sports, Grenada offers the diver an underwater world, rich in submarine gardens, exotic fish, and coral formations, sometimes with underwater visibility stretching to 120 feet. Off the coast is the wreck of the ocean liner *Bianca C,* which is nearly 600 feet long. Novice divers might want to stick to the west coast of Grenada, while more experienced divers might search out the sights along the rougher Atlantic side.

Scuba World, in the Grenada Renaissance, Grand Anse Beach (☎ **809/444-4371,** ext. 638), is directly on the beach. Considered the premier dive outfit on the island, it offers single-tank dives for $40 or night dives for $45. A two-tank dive costs $75, and PADI instructors will offer an open-water certification program for $375 per person.

In addition, Scuba World is the best center for water sports, offering snorkeling trips for $18 (1¹/₂ to 2 hours) or windsurfing with board rentals for $15 per half hour. Sunfish rentals are $10 per half hour, parasailing is $30 per 10 minutes, and waterskiing is $15 per run. Even deep-sea-fishing arrangements can be made.

If you'd rather strike out on your own, take a drive to Woburn and negotiate with a fisherman for a ride to **Glovers Island,** an old whaling station, and snorkel away. Glovers Island is an uninhabited rock spit lying a few hundred yards offshore from the hamlet of Woburn.

Warning: Divers should know that Grenada doesn't have a decompression chamber for the relief of the bends. Should this happen to you, it would require an excruciatingly painful air trip to Trinidad.

TENNIS   Tennis, like cricket and football, is a popular everyday sport in Grenada. Guests at the Secret Harbour, Grenada Renaissance, Calabash, Coyaba Beach Resort, and Twelve Degrees North can avail themselves of those well-kept courts.

SHOPPING

Everybody who visits Grenada comes home with a basket of spices, better than any you're likely to find in your local supermarket. These hand-woven panniers of palm leaf or straw are full of items grown on the island, including the inevitable nutmeg, as well as mace, cloves, cinnamon, bay leaf, vanilla, and ginger. The local stores also sell a lot of luxury-item imports, mainly from England, at prices that are almost (not quite) duty free. Store hours, in general, are 8 to 11:45am and 1 to 3:45pm Monday through Saturday.

Gift Remembered
Cross St., St. George's. ☎ **809/440-2482.**

In the center of town a block from the water, Gift Remembered sells handcrafts, straw articles, jewelry, stamps, film, postcards, books, and magazines.

Huggins
Grand Etang Rd. ☎ **809/440-2031.**

Huggins deals in diamonds, precious stones, and gold and silver jewelry, plus china and crystal that includes such world-renowned names as Wedgwood, Aynsley, Blue Delft, Royal Doulton, Royal Brierley, and Coalport. They also have designer sunglasses, scarves, and accessories.

Imagine
Grand Anse Shopping Centre. ☎ **809/444-4028.**

Imagine offers an excellent line of Caribbean handcrafts in natural materials, including dolls, ceramics, straw items, clothing, and a good gift selection. It also features resortwear.

Spice Island Perfumes Ltd.
The Carenage. ☎ **809/440-2006.**

One of the most interesting shops in St. George's is this small store and workshop. It produces and sells perfumes, potpourri, and teas made from the locally grown flowers and spices. If you like, they'll spray you with a number of desired scents, including island flower, spice, frangipani, jasmine, patchouli, and wild orchid. The shop stands near the harbor entrance, close to the Ministry of Tourism, post office, and public library. Open Monday through Friday from 8:30am to 4:30pm and on Saturday from 9am to 1pm.

Tikal
Young St., St. George's. ☎ **809/440-2310.**

This early 18th-century brick building is off the Carenage, next to the museum. You'll find a potpourri of tastefully chosen handcrafts from around the world as well as the finest crafts made on Grenada, including batiks, ceramics, wood carvings, paintings, straw work, and clothing.

Yellow Poui Art Gallery
Cross St., St. George's. ☎ **809/440-3001.**

A two-minute walk from Market Square, this is the most interesting shop for souvenirs and artistic items. Here you can see oil paintings and watercolors, sculpture, prints, photography, rare antique maps, engravings, and woodcuts, with prices beginning at $10 and going up. There's also a comprehensive display of newly acquired works from Grenada, the Caribbean area, and other sources, shown in three rooms. A continuous photo exhibition is also seen. Open Monday through Friday from 9:15am to 3:15pm and on Saturday from 9:15am to 12:15pm.

GRENADA AFTER DARK

Regular evening entertainment is provided by the resort hotels and includes steel bands, calypso, reggae, folk dancing, and limbo, even crab racing. Ask at your hotel desk to find out what's happening at the time of your visit.

For those seeking culture, the 200-seat **Marryshow Folk Theatre,** Herbert Blaize Street near Bain Alley, St. George's (☎ **809/440-2451**), offers performances of Grenadian, American, and European folk music, drama, and West Indian interpretative folk dance. This is a project of the University of the West Indies School of Continuing Studies. Check with the Marryshow Theatre or the tourist office to see what's on. Tickets cost EC$15 to EC$20 ($5.60 to $7.40).

The island's most popular nightspot is **Fantazia 2001,** at the Gem Holiday Beach Resort, Morne Rouge Bay, St. George's (☎ **809/444-2288**). It's air-conditioned, with state-of-the-art equipment, good acoustics, and fantastic disco lights. The best in regional and international sounds is heard. Theme nights are frequent, ranging from "Oldie Goldies" to reggae nights. Live shows are presented on Friday and Saturday. Admission to the club costs $3.70 to $7.40 per person, depending on the entertainment, and drinks range from $1 to $3.

AN EXCURSION TO CARRIACOU

Largest of the Grenadines, Carriacou, "land of many reefs," is populated by about 8,000 inhabitants, mainly of African descent, who are scattered over its 13 square miles of mountains, plains, and white sand beaches. There's also a Scottish colony, and you'll see such names as MacFarland. In the hamlet of Windward, on the east coast, villagers of mixed Scottish and African descent carry on the tradition of building wooden schooners. Large skeletons of boats in various stages of readiness line the beach where workers labor with the most rudimentary of tools, building the West Indian trade schooner fleet. If you stop for a visit, a master boatbuilder will let you climb the ladder and peer inside the shell, and will explain which wood came from which island, and why the boat was designed in its particular way. Much of the population, according to reputation, is involved in smuggling; otherwise, they are sailors, fisherfolk, shipwrights, and farmers.

GETTING THERE   The fastest method of transport is on a 19-seat plane, which takes just 25 minutes from the Point Salines International Airport on Grenada to Carriacou's **Lauriston Airport.** For information on air service between Carriacou and Grenada, see "By Local Air Services" in "Getting Around" in the "Orientation" section on Grenada, above.

Boats leave from Grenada for Carriacou at 9am on Tuesday, Wednesday, Friday, Saturday, and Sunday, charging $7.50 for a one-way ticket or $12 round-trip. On Sunday there's a round-trip excursion boat. Otherwise, boats return from Carriacou to Grenada on Monday and Thursday. The tourist office will have the latest details. From Hillsborough, you can sail on to Petit Martinique (see below). Carriacou has recommendable accommodations; Petit Martinique does not.

WHERE TO STAY & DINE

Caribbee Inn at Prospect

Prospect, Carriacou, Grenada, W.I. ☎ **809/443-7380.** Fax 809/443-8142. 8 rms, 5 suites. Winter, $120 single or double; $170 suite. Off-season, $90 single or double; $130 suite. MAP $35 per person extra. Free parking.

Set on the rolling hills at the northern edge of the island, this inn stands on its own secluded cove with a view of a scattering of offshore islands. On the premises are a small library and a cultivated garden with a small swimming pool. Each accommodation is cooled by trade winds. The hotel's restaurant serves a combination of French and Créole cuisine (also to nonresidents who phone ahead) every evening at a single sitting, around 7pm, for a fixed price of around $30. Hiking, snorkeling, and boating are among the several popular daytime activities.

Cassada Bay Hotel

Belmont, Carriacou, Grenada, W.I. ☎ **809/443-7494.** Fax 809/443-7672. 16 cabins. Winter, $75 cabin for one; $90 cabin for two. Off-season, $65 cabin for one; $80 cabin for two. Continental breakfast $5 extra. MC, V. Free parking. Transportation: Guests are met at the airport (a five-minute ride).

Formerly a research study center for a university marine biology department, this property has now been comfortably converted into a secluded hotel. It occupies a prime hillside with panoramic views of uninhabited islands. The cabins of two units are made of rough-cut timber and have all-white paneled rooms with simple furniture, double bedrooms, living rooms, and verandas, all serviced by a maid. The bedrooms have insect screens, white louvered windows, and ceiling fans. The restaurant serves traditional West Indian food, and there's an open-air bar terrace to watch the sun go down with a rum punch made with local limes and flavored with freshly ground nutmeg. The area is ideal for beach buffs and snorkelers, and local boats take picnic-bound passengers for trips to nearby islands. There are two dive operations within easy reach, and Jeep rentals can be arranged.

Silver Beach Resort

Silver Beach, Beauséjour Bay, Carriacou, Grenada, W.I ☎ **809/443-7337,** 212/545-8469 in New York City, or 800/223-9815 in the U.S. Fax 809/443-7165. 10 rms, 5 cottages. Winter, $85–$100 single; $100–$120 double; from $85 cottage. Off-season, $75–$85 single; $90–$105 double; from $75 cottage. Continental breakfast $6 extra. AE, MC, V. Free parking. Transportation: Take a taxi (a five-minute ride north of the airport).

This small hotel is about a five-minute walk north of Hillsborough on a mile-long white sand beach. Accommodations include spacious cottages, with bedrooms, living rooms, fully equipped kitchenettes, and patios; there are also bedrooms, each with a sea view from its own patio. The charges include gas, electricity, linen, cutlery, and crockery. The bar and dining pavilion is found between the cottages and the beach. At dinner you can sample some good Carriacouan dishes prepared by local cooks, including lobster, conch, and fresh fish. Locally grown vegetables and fruits are served. Fishing, snorkeling, scuba diving, windsurfing, and boating to nearby islands can be arranged, including trips to World's End Reef in the Tobago Cays. Tennis is also available.

WHAT TO SEE & DO

The best time to visit Carriacou is in August in time for its **regatta,** which was begun by J. Linton Rigg in 1965 with the work boats and schooners for which the Grenadines are famous. Now work boats, three-masted schooners, and miniature "sailboats" propelled by hand join the festivities. Banana boats docking at the pier are filled with people rather than bananas, and sailors from Bequia and Union Island camp on tiny Jack-a-Dan and Sandy Isle, only 20 minutes away by outboard motor from Hillsborough. The people of the Grenadines try their luck at the greased pole, foot races, and, of course, the sailing races. Music fills the air day and night, and impromptu parties are held. At the three-day celebration, Big Drum dancers perform in the Market Square.

The **Big Drum dance** is part of the heritage of Carriacou brought from Africa and nurtured here more purely than perhaps on any other Caribbean island. The "Go Tambo," or Big Drum, is an integral part of such traditional events as stone feasts (marking the setting of a tombstone) and the accompanying rites. The feast, called saraca, and setting of the tombstone may be as long as 20 years after a death. Another event involving the Big Drum and saracas is the *maroon.* This can involve a dream interpretation, but it seems actually to be just a regular festivity, held in various places during the dry season, with dancing and feasting. A boat launching may also be accompanied by the Big Drum and the saraca and usually draws crowds of participants.

The **Carriacou Parang Festival** is usually held on the weekend closest to December 25. The festival serves to maintain the indigenous culture of the people of Carriacou. Bands are formed out of guitar, cuatro, bass drum, and violin. No electronics are needed.

Hillsborough is the chief port and administrative center, handling the commerce of the little island, which is based mainly on growing limes and cotton. The capital bustles on Monday when the produce arrives, then settles down again until "mail day" on Saturday. The capital is nestled in a mile-long crescent of white sand.

The **Carriacou Museum,** in Hillsborough on Paterson Street ☎ **809/ 443-8280),** opposite Grentel, has a display of Amerindian artifacts, European china, glass shards, and exhibits of African culture. In two small rooms, it preserves the history of Carriacou which parallels that of its neighbor island, Grenada. It's open Monday through Friday from 9:30am to 3:45pm.

Also on Carriacou is the **Sea Life Centre,** created by the North American Environmental Research Products organization and designed to educate both the islanders and visitors about sea life, especially the lambi (conch) and turtle. It features native paintings of fishermen at work, drawings of the life cycles of the sea's inhabitants, and microscopes and incubators set up for visitors to view the baby conch and turtles that the center breeds.

PETIT MARTINIQUE

The only inhabited one of Carriacou's offshore islands, and also the largest, is 486-acre Petit (pronounced "pitty") Martinique, with a population of about 600. The chief occupation is listed as building and sailing fishing boats, but it's also infamous as the (reputed) center of the smuggling trade among the islands. Cigarettes and liquor from St. Barts' and St. Maarten's duty-free ports are popular smuggled goods.

14 Barbados

Barbados has many attractions and some Bajans like to think of it as "an England in the tropics," but what put the island on the map is its seemingly endless pink and white sandy beaches. Rich in tradition, Barbados has one of the grandest array of hotels—many of them super-expensive—in the Caribbean. Although it doesn't offer casinos, it has more than beach life for those travelers interested in learning about the culture of another people. It has more sightseeing attractions than most islands of the West Indies.

Afternoon tea remains a tradition at many places, cricket is still the national sport, and many Bajans speak with a British accent. Crime has been on the rise in recent years, although Barbados is still viewed as a safe destination. The difference between the haves and the have-nots doesn't cause the sometimes-violent clash of culture here that it does on some other islands, such as Jamaica.

Don't rule out Barbados if you're seeking an island getaway. Although the south coast is known for its nightlife and is filled with often-inexpensive hotels, and its west-coast beach strip is completely built up, some of the island remains undeveloped. The east coast is fairly tranquil and you can often be alone here, but since it faces the Atlantic the waters aren't tranquil as they are on the Caribbean side. Nevertheless, many escapists, especially Canadians seeking a low-cost place to stay in the winter, don't seem to mind.

Because it's so built up with hotels and condos, Barbados offers more package deals than most islands. "Steals" are possible in the off-season, which lasts from April until mid-December. You don't necessarily have to pay the "rack rate" (walk-in rate for individual bookings) if you'll take the time to shop for a deal. Barbados is filled with bargains, especially along its southern coast directly below Bridgetown. This strip of beachfront, isn't the most glamorous, but it's the most reasonable in price.

ORIENTATION
GETTING THERE

More than 20 daily flights arrive on Barbados from all over the world. **Grantley Adams International Airport** is on Highway 7, on the southern tip of the island at Long Bay, between Oistins and The Crane (a village). From North America, the four major gateways to Barbados are New York, Miami, Toronto, and San Juan. Flying time to Barbados from New York is 4¹/₂ hours, from Miami it's 3¹/₂ hours, from Toronto it's 5 hours, and from San Juan, 1¹/₂ hours.

American Airlines (☎ 800/433-7300) has dozens of connections passing through San Juan. One flight departs New York's JFK at 9:30am and flies non-stop to Barbados, arriving at 3:06pm local time. Another flight departs JFK at 8am and flies to San Juan, connecting to another American flight departing San Juan at 1:30pm and arriving in Barbados at 2:58pm. A daily direct flight departs Miami at 9am and arrives in Barbados at 1:55pm local time. A nonstop Airbus 300 departs Barbados at 4:06pm on the return flight heading for San Juan. Passengers can usually speed through U.S. Customs clearance in San Juan rather than in their home cities, saving time and inconvenience.

Travelers via New York and Miami can opt for nonstop flights offered daily by **BWIA** (☎ 800/327-7401), the national airline of Trinidad and Tobago. BWIA also offers many flights from Barbados to Trinidad.

Canadians sometimes select nonstop flights to Barbados from Toronto. **Air Canada** (☎ 800/363-5440 in Canada, or 800/776-3000 in the U.S.) operates daily flights from Toronto to Barbados in winter, plus an additional flight on Sunday from Montréal.

Barbados is a major hub of the Caribbean-based airline known as **LIAT** (☎ 809/434-5428 for reservations, or 809/428-0986 at the Barbados airport), which provides service from Barbados to a handful of neighboring islands, including St. Vincent and the Grenadines, Antigua, and Dominica.

British Airways (☎ 800/247-9297) offers nonstop service to Barbados from both of London's major airports (Heathrow and Gatwick). In winter BA flies a Concorde once a week from Heathrow to Barbados. Check with BA or a travel agent about the possibility of a once-a-week two-hour Concorde flight from New York to Barbados.

GETTING AROUND

BY BUS Unlike most of the British Windwards, Barbados has a reliable bus system fanning out from Bridgetown to almost every part of the island. On most major routes, there are buses running every 20 minutes or so. Bus fares are BD$1.75 (90¢) wherever you go. Exact change is required.

The nationally owned **buses** of Barbados are blue with yellow stripes. They're not numbered, but their destinations are marked on the front. Departures are from Bridgetown, leaving from Fairchild Street for the south and east; from Lower Green and the Princess Alice Highway for the north going along the west coast. Call the Barbados Tourist Board (☎ 809/436-6820) for bus schedules and information.

Privately operated **minibuses** run shorter distances and travel more frequently. They are bright yellow, with their destinations displayed on the bottom left corner of the windshield. Minibuses in Bridgetown are boarded at River Road, Temple Yard, and Probyn Street. They, too, cost BD$1.75 (90¢).

BY TAXI Typical of this part of the world, taxis aren't metered, but their rates are fixed by the government. Taxis on the island are identified by the letter Z on the license plates. One to five passengers can be transported at the same time, and can share the fare. Overcharging is infrequent; most drivers have a reputation for courtesy and honesty. Taxis are plentiful, and drivers will produce a list of standard rates, which is $16 per hour.

Barbados

Maycock's Bay

ST. LUCY

Fairfield

1B

1C

Ga

Colleton

Charles Duncan O'Neale Hwy

Six Men's Bay

ST. PETER

Gre

Heywoods Beach

SCOTLA

Speightstown

Mullins Bay

2A

Mount

1

Caribbean Sea

ST. JAMES

1A

Welchman Hall

Holetown

Sunset Crest

ST. THO

Paynes Bay

2

2A

To

Warrens

Paradise Beach

Cumming Hwy

ST. MICH

Black Rock

2

Errol Barrow

Brighton Beach

Spring Garden Hwy

3

Deep Water Harbour

Queen's Park

Pine

6

Blv

BRIDGETOWN

Carlisle Bay

Worthin

Hastings

St. La

Rockley Beach

9893

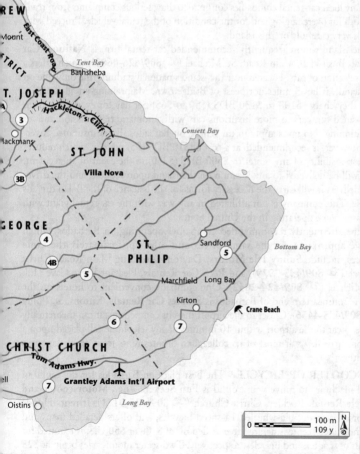

Atlantic
Ocean

organ Lewis Beach

REW

Mount

T. JOSEPH

3

lackmans

3B

GEORGE

4

4B

5

CHRIST CHURCH

7

ell

Oistins

RICT

Tent Bay
Bathsheba

East Coast Road

Hackleton's Cliff

Consett Bay

ST. JOHN

Villa Nova

ST.
PHILIP

Sandford

5

Bottom Bay

Marchfield   Long Bay

Kirton

Crane Beach

6

7

Tom Adams Hwy.

Grantley Adams Int'l Airport

Long Bay

0 ▬▬▬ 100 m
        109 y

N

Beach   Airport   Lighthouse

BY RENTAL CAR   If you don't mind *driving on the left*, you may find a rental car ideal for a Bajan holiday. A temporary permit is needed if you don't have an International Driver's License. The rental agencies listed below will all issue you a visitor's permit or you can go to the police desk upon your arrival at the airport. You're charged a registration fee of $10 BDS ($5), and you must have your own license. The speed limit is 20 m.p.h. inside city limits, 30 m.p.h. elsewhere on the island.

None of the major U.S.–based car-rental companies maintains affiliates on Barbados, but a host of local companies rent vehicles, many of which are in bad shape. Except in the peak of the midwinter season, cars are usually readily available without a prior reservation.

Because of the complicated navigation of Bajan roads, most renters pay for a taxi from the airport to their hotel and then call for the delivery of a rental car. This is especially advisable because of the delay that's sometimes experienced waiting for a rental car to become available upon your arrival at the Barbados airport.

Many local car-rental companies continue to draw serious complaints from readers, both for overcharging and for the condition of the rental vehicle. Proceed with rentals very carefully on this island.

The island's most frequently recommended car-rental firm is **National Car Rental,** Bush Hall, Main Road, St. Michael (☎ **809/426-0603**), which offers a wide selection of cars. Located near the island's national stadium (the only one on the island), it lies 3 miles northeast of Bridgetown. Maintaining an all-Japanese fleet, they charge $100 to $130 BDS ($50 to $65) per day for everything from open-sided fun cars to more luxurious cars with automatic transmission and air conditioning. No taxes apply to car rentals on Barbados. Extra insurance coverage, however, is recommended, at a cost of $10 BDS ($5) per day, which reduces the responsibility of any renter to $500 BDS ($250) in the event of an accident. Cars will be delivered to any location on the island upon request, and the driver who delivers it will carry the necessary forms for the issuance of the Bajan driver's license. This company is not affiliated in any way with the car-rental giant with the same name operating in the United States.

Other frequently recommended companies operating on Barbados, which charge approximately the same prices and offer approximately the same services, include **Sunny Isle Motors,** Dayton, Worthing Main Road, Christ Church (☎ **809/435-7979**), and **P&S Car Rentals,** Pleasant View, Cave Hill, St. Michael (☎ **809/424-2052**). One company convenient to hotels on the remote southeastern end of Barbados is **Stoutes Car Rentals,** Kirtons, St. Philip (☎ **809/435-4456**). Closer to the airport than its competitors, it can theoretically deliver a car to the airport within 10 minutes of any telephone call placed upon a visitor's arrival. As at most of its colleagues, Stoutes rents from an all-Japanese inventory.

BY SCOOTER OR BICYCLE   The best place on Barbados for the rental of small machines to move you around is **Fun Seekers, Inc., Motorscooter and Bicycle Rental,** Rockley, Christ Church (☎ **809/435-9171**). It rents Honda motorscooters and big-wheeled 14-speed bicycles, and offers detailed maps and recommended scenic itineraries free. A deposit of $100 or $50 U.S. is required for rentals of scooters and bicycles, respectively. Two-seater motorcycles begin at $28 per day, and bicycles rent for $20 per day. Discounts are offered for seven-day rentals. Rental of a motorscooter requires the presentation of a valid driver's license issued from your state or country of residence, and the issuance (by Fun Seekers) of a Bajan driver's license, priced at $10 BDS ($5).

BY SIGHTSEEING TOUR   Nearly all Bajan taxi drivers are familiar with the entire island, and usually like to show it off to visitors. If you can afford it, touring by taxi is far more relaxing than—and preferable to—taking a standardized bus tour.

One company that offers an alternative to the usual taxi tour of the island is **Limbo Lady Tours,** 78 Old Chancery Lane, Christ Church (☎ **809/435-8206**). This company offers a comprehensive land and sea tour called "The Best of Both." Their minivans collect participants at most of the island's hotels, then carry a maximum of 14 guests on a 6-hour experience that combines a $2^{1}/_{2}$-hour island tour, with lunch at one of Bridgetown's restaurants. This is followed by a $2^{1}/_{2}$-hour cruise (with drinks and snorkeling gear provided) on a classically elegant 44-foot CSY yacht named *Limbo Lady.* The all-inclusive price for this sea-and-land tour is $120 BDS ($60). Patrick Gonsalves (a former resident of Florida) is the skipper, who usually ensures the easy transmission of both island information and a good time.

FAST FACTS: Barbados

American Express   The island's American Express affiliate is Barbados International Travel Services, Inc., Horizon House, McGregor Street (P.O. Box 605C), Bridgetown, Barbados, W.I. (☎ **809/431-2423**), located in the heart of Bridgetown.

Area Code   To phone Barbados from mainland North America, dial area code 809 and the seven-digit local number.

Business Hours   Most banks on Barbados are open Monday through Thursday from 9am to 3pm and on Friday from 9am to 1pm and 3 to 5pm. Stores are open Monday through Friday from 8am to 4pm and on Saturday from 8am to noon. Most government offices are open Monday through Friday from 8:30am to 4:30pm.

Consulate   Contact the **U.S. Consulate,** in the ALICO Building, Lower Broad Street, Cheapside, in Bridgetown (☎ **809/431-0225**); the **Canadian High Commission,** Bishop Court, Hill Pine Road (☎ **809/429-3550**); or the **British High Commission,** Lower Collymore Rock, St. Michael (☎ **809/436-6694**).

Currency   The **Barbados dollar (BDS)** is the official currency, available in $100, $20, $10, and $5 notes, as well as $1, 25¢, and 10¢ silver coins, plus 5¢ and 1¢ copper coins. The Bajan dollar is worth 50¢ in U.S. currency. Unless otherwise specified, currency quotations in this chapter are in U.S. dollars. Most stores take traveler's checks or U.S. dollars. However, it's best to convert your money at banks and pay in Bajan dollars.

Dentist   Because of the density of its population, Barbados might have more dentists than any other Caribbean island. One who is particularly well recommended is Dr. Derek Golding, who, with two other colleagues, maintains one of the busiest practices on Barbados. Located at the Beckwith Shopping Mall in Bridgetown (☎ **809/426-3001**), he accepts most of the emergency dental problems from the many cruise ships that dock in the waters off Barbados. This practice will accept any emergency and often remains open late for last-minute problems. All members of this dental team received their training in the United States, Britain, Canada, or New Zealand.

Doctor Take your pick—there are dozens on Barbados. Your hotel might have a list of doctors on call, although some of the best recommended are Dr. J. D. Gibling (☎ 809/432-1772), and Dr. Adrian Lorde or his colleague Dr. Ahmed Mohamad (☎ 809/424-8236), any of whom will pay house calls to patients unable or unwilling to leave their hotel rooms.

Documents A U.S. or Canadian citizen coming directly from America to Barbados for a period not exceeding three months must have proof of identity and national status, such as an original birth certificate, citizenship papers, a driver's license with photograph, university or school ID card with photograph, job ID with photograph, or senior-citizen card with photograph. For stays longer than three months, a passport is required. An ongoing or return ticket is also necessary. British subjects need a valid passport.

Electricity The electricity is 110 volts A.C., 50 cycles, so at most establishments recommended you can use your U.S.–made appliances.

Emergencies In an emergency, call **119**. Other important numbers include the police at **112**, the fire department at **113**, and an ambulance at **115**.

Holidays Public holidays are January 1, January 21, Good Friday, Easter Monday, May 1 (May Day), Whit Monday (seven weeks after Easter), Kadooment Day (first Monday in August), United Nations Day (first Monday in October), Independence Day (November 30), Christmas Day (December 25), and Boxing Day (December 26).

Hospitals A 600-bed facility, the Queen Elizabeth Hospital (☎ 809/436-6450) is on Martinsdale Road in Bridgetown. There are several private clinics as well, one of the most expensive and best recommended of which is the Bayview Hospital, St. Paul's Avenue, Bayville, St. Michael (☎ 809/436-5446).

Information The **Barbados Tourism Authority** is on Harbour Road (P.O. Box 242), Bridgetown, Barbados, W.I. (☎ 809/427-2623), which you can call or write for information. In the United States, you can obtain information before you go at the following offices: 800 Second Ave., New York, NY 10017 (☎ 212/986-6516), or 3440 Wilshire Blvd., Suite 1215, Los Angeles, CA 90010 (☎ 213/380-2198; the toll free number is 800/221-9831). In Canada, offices are at 5160 Yonge St., Suite 1800, North York, ON M2N 6L9 (☎ 416/512-6569), and 615 René Lévesque Blvd. W., Suite 460, Montréal, PQ H3B 1P5 (☎ 514/861-0085, or 800/268-9122). In the United Kingdom, the Barbados Tourism Authority is at 263 Tottenham Court Rd., London W1P 9AA (☎ 0171/636-9448).

Language The Barbadians, or Bajans, as they're called, speak English, but with their own island lilt.

Mail Most hotel desks can attend to your mailing. Otherwise, the Main Post Office is at Cheapside, St. Michael's (☎ 809/436-4800), on the outskirts of Bridgetown.

Safety Crimes against tourists used to be rare, but the U.S. State Department reports rising crime, such as purse snatching, pickpocketing, armed robbery, and even sexual assault upon women. The department advises that you don't leave cash or valuables in your hotel room, beware of purse snatchers when walking, exercise caution when walking on the beach or visiting tourist attractions, and be wary of driving in isolated areas of Barbados.

Taxes and Service   When you leave, you'll have to pay a $25-BDS ($12.50) departure tax. When you go to pay your hotel bill, you'll find that you've been charged a 5% government sales tax. And while I'm on the subject, most hotels and restaurants add at least a 10% service charge to your bill.

Telecommunications   You should have no trouble with telecommunications out of Barbados. Telegrams may be sent at your hotel front desk or at the Barbados External Telecommunications Ltd. office, The Wharf, Bridgetown, which is open Monday through Friday from 8am to 5pm and on Saturday from 8am to 1pm. International telephone, fax, Telex, and data-access services are also available.

Water   Barbados has a pure water supply. It's pumped from underground sources in the coral rock that covers six-sevenths of the island, and it's safe to drink.

Weather   Daytime temperatures are in the 75° to 85° Fahrenheit range throughout the year.

1 Where to Stay

Per square inch, Barbados has the best hotels in the Caribbean. Many are small and personally run. Most of my recommendations are sited on St. James Beach, the fashionable sector. However, you'll have to head south from Bridgetown to such places as Hastings and Worthing for the best bargains, often in self-contained efficiencies or studio apartments where you can do your own cooking.

Here's the bad news: Because of Barbados's long and continuing popularity, nowadays with back-to-back charter groups these hotels often are extremely expensive in high season. Many hotels will also insist that you take two meals at their establishments if you're there in the winter. However, Barbados has some bargains, and I've surveyed the best of these as well.

Prices cited in this section, unless otherwise indicated, are in U.S. dollars. Remember that the government hotel tax and a 10% service charge will be added to your final bill.

ON THE WEST COAST
VERY EXPENSIVE

✪ Cobblers Cove Hotel

Road View, St. Peter, Barbados, W.I. ☎ **809/422-2291,** 0181/367-5175 in London, or toll free 800/223-6510 in the U.S., 800/424-5500 in Canada. Fax 809/422-1460. 39 suites. A/C MINIBAR TEL. (MAP rates.) Winter, $490–$820 standard suite for two; $1,200 Camelot Suite for two. Off-season, $300–$440 standard suite for two; $630 Camelot Suite for two. AE, MC, V. Free parking. Closed late Aug to late Sept.

Considered one of the small, exclusive hotels of Barbados, Cobblers Cove grew out of a beachfront mansion built like a fort—with crenellations in a mock-medieval style. The home, now a member of Relais & Châteaux, was erected over the site of a former British fort that used to protect vessels going into the harbor at nearby Speightstown, a 10-minute walk away. Today, after an exhaustive overhaul, the hotel is a favorite honeymoon retreat offering first-class suites in a phalanx of 10 Iberian-style villas placed throughout the gardens.

Overlooking a white sand beach, each unit has a spacious living room, private balcony or patio, and a kitchenette. One of the most exclusive accommodations you can rent on all of Barbados is the Camelot Suite on the rooftop of the original mansion; it's beautifully decorated and offers panoramic views of both the beach and the garden. Meals can be delivered to your suite and consumed in privacy. The resort contains many acres of well-developed tropical gardens and lawns.

Dining/Entertainment: The open-air dining room overlooks the sea. The cuisine has won many awards and has an emphasis on Caribbean specialties from the sea. These might include a fish of the day grilled or poached with Bajan seasoning, or shrimp flavored with ginger. Nearby is the resort's social center, its bar.

Services: Laundry, babysitting, arrangements for island tours, car rentals.

Facilities: Complimentary tennis day or night, swimming pool, water sports (including waterskiing, Sunfish sailing, snorkeling, and windsurfing).

✪ Glitter Bay

Porters, St. James, Barbados, W.I. ☎ **809/422-5555**, 0181/367-5175 in London, or 800/283-8666 in the U.S., 800/567-5327 in Canada. Fax 809/422-3940. 83 units. A/C MINIBAR TEL. Winter, $375–$395 double; $470–$555 one-bedroom suite for two; $845–$995 two-bedroom suite for four. Off-season, $195–$285 double; $220–$405 one-bedroom suite for two; $415–$675 two-bedroom suite for four. MAP $60 per person extra. AE, DC, MC, V. Free parking.

This carefully maintained resort has discreet charm and Mediterranean allure. Built in 1981 by a small Barbados-based hotel chain (the Pemberton Group), it lies on a 10-acre plot of manicured lowlands near a sandy beachfront a mile north of Holetown. In the 1930s this property was owned by Sir Edward Cunard of shipbuilding fame. The parties he gave here in the Great House were so famous that it helped make Barbados synonymous with glitter and glamour back in England. The accommodations are in a white mini-village of Iberian inspiration, whose patios, thick beams, and red terra-cotta tiles surround a garden whose centerpiece is a swimming pool, an artificial waterfall, and a simulated lagoon. Often the accommodations are privately owned by absentee investors, many of them British, who use them during annual holidays on Barbados; otherwise, the units are available to renters. Most units contain unusual artworks, built-in furniture, louvered doors, and spacious outdoor patios or balconies ringed with shrubbery. The larger units contain small kitchenettes, and some of the biggest accommodations are suitable for four to six people.

Dining/Entertainment: The hotel's social center is the Piperade Restaurant, beneath a terra-cotta roof amid a garden. Offering classical, modern, and West Indian cuisine, it contains its own bar. On Monday a gala Bajan buffet is presented, and Friday is barbecue night. The Sunset Beach Bar is a popular rendezvous spot. Sheltered by shrubbery and tropical trees, guests can dance on an outdoor patio and enjoy local entertainment, such as a steel band or calypso.

Services: 24-hour room service, concierge, laundry, babysitting, business services, limousine service.

Facilities: Fitness and massage center, two tennis courts (complimentary for guests day and night), and complimentary water sports (including waterskiing, windsurfing, snorkeling, and catamaran sailing), two swimming pools (one a shallow children's pool); golf at nearby Royal Westmoreland (a Pemberton associated company); horseback riding, scuba diving, and motor boating can be arranged.

✪ Royal Pavilion

Porters, St. James, Barbados, W.I. ☎ **809/422-5555**, 0181/367-5175 in London, or 800/283-8666 in the U.S., 800/567-5327 in Canada. 72 junior suites, 3 villas. A/C MINIBAR TEL. Winter, $475–$520 suite for two; $895–$995 villa for four; $1,250–$1,375 villa for six. Off-season, $230–$350 suite for two; $445–$675 villa for four; $675–$745 villa for six. MAP $60 per person extra. Children under 12 not accepted in winter. AE, DC, MC, V. Free parking.

A spectacular place to stay, this Pemberton hotel a mile north of Holetown is next door to Glitter Bay, part of the same chain, whose gardens it shares. The lush resort was built on the site of the former Miramar Hotel, which was radically re-designed in 1987 into a new pink-walled format with lily ponds and splashing fountains. British grace and Bajan hospitality blend happily in this aristocratic property, which became one of the finest resorts on Barbados the moment it opened. The architects created a California-hacienda style for their 72 waterfront junior suites and a villa consisting of three suites in 8 acres of beautifully landscaped gardens. Television sets are available in any room upon request. Guests staying here can visit the drinking, dining, and sports facilities at Glitter Bay (and vice versa).

Dining/Entertainment: There are two oceanfront restaurants. Tabora's serves breakfast and lunch. The more formal Palm Terrace, set below the seaside columns of an open-air loggia, is open only for dinner. Both restaurants offer an à la carte menu of Caribbean and international fare. The chef specializes in flambé dishes, and on Wednesday night in winter an international buffet is presented.

Services: 24-hour room service, concierge, laundry, babysitting, business service, limousine service.

Facilities: Freshwater swimming pool overlooking ocean, massage center, two tennis courts (complimentary for guests day and night), water-sports program (including complimentary snorkeling, waterskiing, sailing, and windsurfing), duty-free shops, beauty shop with hairdresser; guests also enjoy privileged tee times at nearby Royal Westmoreland, an affiliated Pemberton company.

✪ Sandy Lane

St. James, Barbados, W.I. ☎ **809/432-1311**, or 800/225-5843 in the U.S. and Canada. Fax 809/432-2954. 96 rms, 24 suites. A/C MINIBAR TEL. (Map rates.) Winter, $720–$850 double; from $1,000 suite. Off-season, $545–$595 double; $645 suite. AE, DC, MC, V. Free parking.

Originally established in 1961, on the 380-acre site of a bankrupt sugar plantation less than a mile south of Holetown, this hotel once attracted many of the grand-est names in Britain. In 1991, after a period of much-publicized decline, the hotel received a multi-million-dollar infusion of cash from the Forte chain, its present owners. Today the place represents luxury, with beautiful suites and rooms (all doubles), a private beach, and one of the most prestigious golf courses on Barbados. The swimming pool is surrounded by Italianate gardens, Roman fountains, and colonnaded verandas; the overall effect is one of neo-Palladian gran-deur. The buildings are made of cut coral, with shingle roofs, baronial arches, high ceilings, and a porte-cochère—in all, estatelike with tall gates, a driveway, and ornamental steps. All rooms and suites have refrigerators.

Dining/Entertainment: You can order a cool salad at the pool at lunch, and later enjoy a continental-inspired candlelight dinner. Buffet tables are frequent, as is regular native entertainment, such as calypso. You can also dine on Italian cuisine in the Seashell Restaurant, or at the Sandy Bay Restaurant (the resort's culinary showcase), or munch on club sandwiches and hamburgers at either the Oasis Beach Bar or an informal bar/restaurant beside the golf course. Scattered in various corners of the place, you'll find five different bars. Live entertainment (usually from a dance band) is presented nightly, and a Bajan floor show and cabaret is presented once a week.

Services: 24-hour room service, laundry and dry cleaning, concierge.

Facilities: 18-hole golf course, swimming pool, five all-weather tennis courts (two lit for night play), water sports (including scuba diving, windsurfing, sailboat rentals, and snorkeling), Tree House Club, an activities center for children two to seven.

Settlers Beach

St. James, Barbados, W.I. ☎ **809/422-3052,** or 800/223-1108. Fax 809/422-1937. 22 villas. A/C TEL. Winter, $550–$600 villa for two; $600–$650 villa for three; $650–$700 villa for four. Off-season, $240 villa for two; $260 villa for three; $280 villa for four. MAP $50 per person extra. AE, MC, V. Free parking.

This seaside collection of comfortable villas is located on 4 acres of beachfront property 8 miles from Bridgetown, north of Holetown. Each unit has two bedrooms, two bathrooms, a spacious tile-floored lounge and dining room, and a fully equipped kitchen. The apartments are decorated in sunny colors.

Dining/Entertainment: The square-roofed restaurant has won awards and is considered one of the finer ones on the island. A bar lies nearby.

Services: 24-hour room service, laundry, babysitting.

Facilities: Swimming pool, two tennis courts, sandy beach.

✿ Treasure Beach

Payne's Bay, St. James, Barbados, W.I. ☎ **809/432-1346,** or 800/223-6510 in the U.S., 800/424-5500 in Canada. Fax 809/432-1094. 24 suites. A/C TEL. Winter, $275–$460 one-bedroom suite for one or two; $550–$700 two-bedroom penthouse suite. Off-season, $140–$215 one-bedroom suite for one or two; $280–$320 two-bedroom penthouse suite. MAP $45 per person extra. AE, DC, MC, V. Free parking.

Set on about an acre of sandy beachfront land, in a mini-village of two-story buildings arranged into a horseshoe pattern around a swimming pool and garden, Treasure Beach has one of the most loyal clienteles of any hotel on the island. It's small but choice, known for its well-prepared food and the comfort and style of its amenities. The atmosphere is both intimate and relaxed, with personalized service a mark of the well-trained staff. The hotel is set in tropical gardens in St. James in the glitter "hotel belt" of Barbados, about half a mile south of Holetown. The accommodations are beautifully furnished in a tropical motif and open onto private balconies or patios. The clientele is about evenly divided between North American and British clients. Children under 12 are accepted only upon "special request."

Dining/Entertainment: Even if you aren't staying here, try to sample some of the culinary specialties at the Treasure Beach Restaurant, including freshly caught seafood and favorites from the Bajan culinary repertoire. Lunch is served daily from noon to 2pm and dinner is from 7 to 9:30pm. The bar is open to the gardens, and it's here that you can order tropical fruit drinks or whatever.

Services: Room service (7:30am to 9:30pm), valet and laundry service, safety-deposit boxes, concierge available to arrange for car rentals and island tours.

Facilities: Rental of sailboats, access to nearby golf and tennis courts.

EXPENSIVE

Almond Beach Club

Vauxhall, St. James, Barbados, W.I. ☎ **809/432-7840,** or 800/4-ALMOND in the U.S. Fax 809/432-2115. 95 rms, 65 suites. A/C TV TEL. Winter, $310–$390 single; $410–$490 double; $455–$530 suite for two. Off-season, $250–$310 single; $315–$410 double; $380–$450 suite for two. (Rates include all meals.) AE, DC, MC, V. Children under six not accepted. Free parking.

Set on flat and sandy acreage about a two-minute walk from its more famous neighbor, Sandy Lane, this hotel lies on the island's west coast, south of Holetown, opening onto Payne's Bay. An overhauled restoration of an older property, it was the first of Barbados's all-inclusive resorts, established in 1991 as part of a $2-million refurbishment. It was known then as the Pineapple Beach Hotel, later changing its name to the Almond Beach Club. Accommodations are spread among seven low-rise three-story buildings (no elevators). Pool-view units open onto three freshwater swimming pools and the gardens, planted with frangipani trees and palms; beachfront units open onto the Caribbean. Island motifs form the room decor, with tropical fabrics and tile floors.

Dining/Entertainment: The all-inclusive program offers a dine-around option allowing guests to consume one lunch and one dinner per week-long stay at one of three neighboring hotels. On the premises is a continental restaurant (the Almond Beach), a West Indian/Bajan restaurant (Enid's), and a beachfront snack bar. The Rum Shop Bar evokes 19th-century colonial days and offers a sampling of virtually every kind of distilled rum on Barbados. Lively nightly entertainment—jazz bands, steel-drum bands, Bajan folk dancing, and up-to-date music, as well as piano bar entertainment—until 2am.

Services: Laundry, babysitting, guest services department (organizing island tours).

Facilities: Three freshwater swimming pools, tennis and squash courts, fitness center with sauna, fishing, windsurfing, waterskiing, reef fishing, kayaking, and "banana boating."

Almond Beach Village

Speightstown, St. Peter, Barbados, W.I. ☎ **809/422-4900,** or 800/4-ALMOND in the U.S. Fax 809/422-1581. 292 rms, 23 suites. A/C TV TEL. Winter, $310–$390 single; $410–$490 double; $355–$530 suite. Off-season, $250–$310 single; $315–$410 double; $280–$450 suite. (Rates all-inclusive.) AE, MC, V. Free parking.

Set on 30 acres of prime beachfront property along Highway 2A, 15 miles north of Bridgetown, this is a companion resort to the all-inclusive Almond Beach Club (see above). Formerly known as Heywoods, this resort continues the policy of bringing "all-inclusive" resorts to Barbados. The rooms are spread among seven three- and four-story buildings (no elevators). Pool-view rooms have views of the swimming pools and gardens, and beach rooms lie along the beach with views of the Caribbean. All accommodations have been restored in a classic tropical style, featuring a balcony or patio, air conditioning, private bath and shower, safety-deposit box, direct-dial phone, color TV, radio, hairdryer, and coffee maker.

Dining/Entertainment: So you won't feel trapped at the hotel for all your meals, the resort offers a choice of four different restaurants and five bars, including Enid's for Bajun cuisine, the Family Restaurant, the Continental Restaurant, and the Italian Restaurant. A dine-around program is also possible. There's disco action three nights a week with live music on weekends. A piano bar, sing-alongs, and laser karaoke complement the three floor shows weekly.

Services: Room service (at lunch and dinner), medical center, laundry.

Facilities: Five hard-surface tennis courts, par-3 nine-hole golf course, two air-conditioned squash courts, nine freshwater swimming pools plus Jacuzzis, water-sports center, fitness center, 1 mile of beachfront, children's program.

Buccaneer Bay Hotel

Paynes Bay, St. James, Barbados, W.I. ☎ **809/432-7981.** Fax 809/432-7230. 30 rms, 4 suites. A/C. Winter, $156–$252 single; $222–$300 double; $330–$408 suite. Off-season, $90–$144 single; $132–$174 double; $240 suite. Children under 12 stay free in parents' room. Dinner $32.50 per person extra. (Rates include English breakfast.) AE, MC, V. Free parking.

This hotel is small and intimate, run with a casual kind of elegance by Val and Richard Richings, who also operate the Bagatelle Restaurant (see "Where to Dine," below). Many of the bedrooms, all overlooking one of the best sandy beaches along the west coast, are of generous size, as they were originally constructed as apartments or condos for a consortium of doctors. Some of the bedrooms contain balconies with an ocean view. Ice water is also always available, and the accommodations contain small refrigerators. TV is also available upon request.

Dining/Entertainment: Guests have a choice of three options for dining, all under the same management. The British-born managers operate a house taxi to take guests to the Bagatelle Restaurant or they can dine at the Bamboo Beach Bar, one of the best beach bars along the west coast. The hotel also operates its own in-house dining room, serving international food with a West Indian flavor. Once a week guests are taken on a "rum cruise." Local combos and a piano player entertain several times a week.

Services: Room service, babysitting, valet, laundry.

Facilities: Freshwater swimming pool and sit-in pool bar; Sunfish, windsurfing, snorkeling, scuba diving, and horseback riding all arranged nearby.

Coconut Creek Club

Derricks, St. James, Barbados, W.I. ☎ **809/432-0803.** Fax 809/438-4697. 53 rms. A/C TEL. Winter, $255–$305 single; $295–$345 double. Off-season, $165–$215 single; $205–$255 double. (MAP rates.) AE, MC, V. Free parking.

Small, intimate, and known as an escape for publicity-shy European celebrities, this is an elegantly informal and landscaped retreat on the West Coast, about a mile south of Holetown. It resembles an exclusive country retreat in Devon, England. About half the accommodations lie atop a low bluff overlooking what might be the two most secluded beaches on the island's west coast. (Because of the configuration of the nearby coastline, access to these beaches is possible only by boat, from a handful of nearby privately owned villas, and from the gardens of the hotel.) Many of the bedrooms are built on the low cliff edge overlooking the ocean, while others open onto the pool or the flat, tropical garden. Each bedroom has a veranda or balcony where breakfast can be served.

Dining/Entertainment: The establishment's only restaurant, Cricketers, was modeled after an upscale English pub. Bajan buffets and barbecues are served on the restaurant's vine-covered open pergola, overlooking the gardens and the sea. (The inn's food has been praised by *Gourmet* magazine.) There's dancing to West Indian calypso and steel bands almost every night. Clients on the MAP are encouraged to dine at the restaurants connected to this chain's two other properties, the Tamarind Cove Hotel and the Colony Club, for no additional charge.

Services: Room service (7:30am to 10pm), babysitting, arrangements for island tours and rental cars.

Facilities: Freshwater swimming pool, complimentary water sports (including waterskiing, windsurfing, snorkeling, and Hobie cat sailing); scuba diving can be arranged for an extra charge; tennis available nearby.

Colony Club

Porters, St. James Beach, Barbados, W.I. ☎ **809/422-2335.** Fax 809/438-4697. 64 rms, 34 suites. A/C TEL. Winter, $285–$410 single; $325–$450 double; $395–$510 suite. Off-season, $185–$245 single; $225–$285 double; $260–$295 suite. (MAP rates.) AE, DC, MC, V. Free parking.

Originally established by an English expatriate in the 1950s, this establishment is considered one of the discreetly elegant hotels of the island's western coast. Set behind an entrance lined with Australian pines, it occupies a site a mile north of Holetown beside one of the island's best beaches. The Colony has grown from a small "English country house party"–type place to a complex of restored rooms that look out over shaded verandas and landscaped grounds. About a third of the establishment's rooms lie beside the sea; the others are scattered throughout the gardens. On 7 acres of tropical gardens, the grounds contain free-form lagoon rock pools. The rooms and suites are all air-conditioned with bath, shower, phone, radio, and bar. All have either a patio or a balcony, with some extending up to the lagoon rock pools.

Dining/Entertainment: Set between the beachside freshwater pool and the main building is the open-sided Laguna Restaurant. Orchids, the hotel's formal restaurant, offers an international cuisine. The dance floor, on an "island" in the middle of the pool, is accessed by a footbridge. Most evenings there's live entertainment and dancing; once a week a floor show is presented.

Services: Room service (7:30am to 9:30pm), laundry, babysitting, arrangements for outings and excursions.

Facilities: Freshwater swimming pool, hairdressing/beauty salon, water sports, chauffeured speedboat and catamaran rides, air-conditioned fitness center, two floodlit tennis courts.

Coral Reef Club

St. James Beach, Barbados, W.I. ☎ **809/422-2372,** or 800/223-1108. Fax 809/422-1776. 39 rms, 30 cottages. A/C TEL. Winter, $205–$315 single; $310–$595 double; $405–$595 cottage for two. Off-season, $125–$170 single; $150–$330 double; $190–$330 cottage for two. (MAP rates.) AE, MC, V. Free parking.

The innkeepers of this small luxury hotel set standards that are hard for their competitors to attain, as this is one of the best and most respected establishments on the island. Set on elegantly landscaped and flat land beside the sea, about a five-minute drive north of Holetown, it devotes most of its efforts to maintaining a collection of veranda-fronted private cottages that surround a main building and clubhouse. This contains the reception area, a reading room, a dining area and bar, and a quartet of deluxe bedrooms on the second floor. The cottages are scattered about a dozen landscaped acres, fronting a long strip of white sandy beach, ideal for swimming. The cottages open onto private patios, and some of the rooms have separate dressing rooms.

Dining/Entertainment: You can enjoy lunch in an open-air area. Dining and wining in the evening is in an attractive room overlooking the ocean. A first-class chef is in the kitchen. There's a weekly folklore show and barbecue every Thursday, and a Bajan buffet on Monday evening, featuring an array of food, along with whole baked fish and lots of local entertainment.

Services: Room service (during restaurant hours), laundry, massage, a helpful reception staff.

Facilities: Freshwater swimming pool, tennis court (floodlit at night), water sports (including windsurfing, snorkeling, scuba diving, and use of a minifleet of small sailboats).

Sandpiper Inn

Holetown, St. James, Barbados, W.I. ☎ **809/422-2251,** or 800/223-1108. Fax 809/422- 1776. 21 rms, 24 suites. A/C TEL. Winter, $295–$350 single or double; $420–$835 suite. Off-season, $125–$170 single or double; $220–$380 suite. MAP $45 per person extra. AE, MC, V. Free parking.

The Sandpiper has more of a South Seas look than most of the hotels of Barbados. Affiliated with the Coral Reef Club (see above), it's a self-contained, intimate resort on the waterside. The resort maintains a Bajan flavor and stands in a small grove of coconut palms and flowering trees right on the beach, a three-minute walk north of Holetown. This cluster of rustic-chic units surrounds the swimming pool, and some have a fine sea view. The rooms open onto little terraces that stretch along the second story, where you can order drinks or have breakfast. Each unit contains a small refrigerator.

Dining/Entertainment: Dining is under a wooden ceiling, and the cuisine is both continental and West Indian. Once a week in winter, big buffets are spread out for you, with white-capped chefs in attendance. There are two bars, one of which sits a few paces from the surf.

Services: Room service (7am to 10:30pm), laundry, babysitting.

Facilities: Swimming pool, two lighted tennis courts.

Tamarind Cove

Paynes Bay, St. James Beach (P.O. Box 429, Bridgetown), Barbados, W.I. ☎ **809/432-1332.** Fax 809/432-6317. 37 rms, 80 suites. A/C TEL. Winter, $305–$470 single; $345–$410

 Family-Friendly Accommodations

Glitter Bay *(see p. 658)* "If your daddy's rich and your mama's good lookin'," as the song goes, the best place is Glitter Bay with its cottagelike suites and kitchenettes. Children are charged $35 to $55 per day when sharing a suite with their parents.

Divi Southwinds Beach Resort *(see p. 666)* On 20 acres, this modern resort offers two-bedroom suites with full kitchens. A swimming pool is reserved for children.

Sandy Beach Hotel *(see p. 667)* Children get reduced rates at this south-coast beach resort, with its one- and two-bedroom suites with fully equipped kitchenettes.

Casuarina Beach Club *(see p. 668)* Family run, it also caters to families with reasonably priced suites offering kitchenettes and a pair of swimming pools.

Almond Beach Village *(see p. 661)* This all-inclusive resort maintains one of the best children's programs on the island. It has a club just for children (with videos, Nintendo, computer lab, books, and board games), two children's playgrounds, kiddies' pool, activity center, pool and beach games, nature walks, water sports, treasure hunts, storytime, arts and crafts, and evening entertainment.

double; $395–$570 suite. Off-season, $205–$290 single; $245–$275 double; $295–$355 suite. (MAP rates.) AE, DC, MC, V. Free parking.

This place was originally launched in 1969, when the daughter (Janet Kidd) of British newspaper magnate Lord Beaverbrook established a hotel on her land to accommodate her friends who flew in for polo matches on her world-class polo grounds. Shortly after its construction, it was acquired by a British-based hotel chain (St. James Beach Properties Ltd.), which soon transformed it into the flagship of their chain. In 1990, an $8-million restoration expanded it into one of the most noteworthy hotels on Barbados.

Designed in an Iberian style, with pale-pink walls and red terra-cotta roofs, it occupies a desirable site beside St. James Beach 1 1/2 miles south of Holetown. Its name derives from the presence near one of its restaurants of the largest tamarind tree on Barbados. The stylish and comfortable accommodations are in a series of hacienda-style buildings interspersed with vegetation. Each unit has a patio or balcony overlooking the gardens or ocean.

Dining/Entertainment: In addition to an informal beachfront eatery, Tamarind contains two elegant restaurants, the more memorable of which is Neptune's, specializing in sophisticated preparations of seafood. The Flamingo is the main restaurant. A handful of bars are scattered throughout the property, and there's some kind of musical entertainment every night.

Services: Room service, babysitting, laundry, massage, concierge staff.

Facilities: Immediately adjacent white-sand beach, three freshwater swimming pools, complimentary water sports (including waterskiing, windsurfing, catamaran sailing, and snorkeling); golf, tennis, horseback riding, and polo available nearby.

BUDGET

Traveller's Palm

265 Palm Ave., Sunset Crest, St. James, Barbados, W.I. ☎ **809/432-7722.** 16 apartments. A/C. Winter, $70 apartment for two. Off-season, $45 apartment for two. MC, V. Free parking.

Designed for those who want to be independent, this is a choice collection of well-furnished apartments with fully equipped kitchens, a five-minute drive south of Holetown. The apartments have a spacious living- and dining-room area, as well as a patio where you can have breakfast or a candlelit dinner you've prepared yourself (no meals are served here). The apartments are filled with bright colors and handcrafted furniture, and they open onto a well-kept lawn with a swimming pool. Serviced by maids, the apartments contain one bedroom. A handful of beaches are within a five-minute walk. There is a snack bar beside the establishment's pool.

SOUTH OF BRIDGETOWN

Barbados Hilton

Needham's Point (P.O. Box 510), St. Michael's, Barbados, W.I. ☎ **809/426-0200,** or 800/HILTONS in the U.S., 800/268-9275 in Canada. Fax 809/436-8946. 182 rms, 2 suites. A/C MINIBAR TV TEL. Winter, $235–$278 single; $310–$346 double; $530–$576 suite. Off-season, $171–$193 single; $229–$251 double; $312–$358 suite. (Map rates.) AE, DC, MC, V. Free parking.

On more than 14 acres of landscaped gardens, this is a self-contained resort, although it lies on the heavily populated southern edge of Bridgetown near an oil refinery. Built in 1966, and overhauled and redecorated several times since then, it occupies the rugged peninsula where in the 18th century the English navy built Fort Charles. The Hilton's architecture incorporates bleached coral interspersed with jutting balconies and wide expanses of glass. The bedrooms are arranged around a central courtyard filled with tropical gardens, and vines cascade from the skylit roof. Each of the comfortable units has a balcony with a view of Carlisle Bay on the north side or the Atlantic on the south. Several kinds of water sports are offered on the nearby beach, whose outermost edge is protected from storm damage by a massive breakwater of giant rocks.

Dining/Entertainment: The Verandah restaurant, whose backdrop is a row of diminutive clapboard Bajan houses, serves island and international specialties to the accompaniment of live music. The hotel has a gaming room with slot machines and both a beachfront daytime bar and snack restaurant and a nighttime bar.

Services: Room service (7am to midnight), concierge, laundry, massage.

Facilities: Four tennis courts (lit at night), in-house sauna and health club; access to horseback riding and golf.

Grand Barbados Beach Resort

Aquatic Gap, Bay St. (P.O. Box 639), Bridgetown, St. Michael's, Barbados, W.I. ☎ **809/ 426-0890.** Fax 809/436-9823. 128 rms, 5 suites. A/C MINIBAR TV TEL. Winter, $200–$235 single; $220–$260 double; $450 suite. Off-season, $130–$175 single; $145–$190 double; $300 suite. MAP $47 per person extra. AE, DC, MC, V. Free parking.

About a mile southeast of Bridgetown on scenic Carlisle Bay, this well-designed resort incorporates an older hostelry dating from 1969 that was massively overhauled in 1986. Set on 4 acres of grounds, it offers well-furnished bedrooms with many amenities, including a mini-safe and eight-channel satellite TV. The two top floors are devoted to executive rooms, including a lounge where a complimentary continental breakfast is served along with hot beverages from 7 to 10am and 6 to 10pm.

Dining/Entertainment: At the end of a 260-foot historic pier is the Schooner Restaurant, specializing in seafood and buffet lunches. The Boardwalk Café is an informal al fresco dining area open from 7am to 10pm daily. It's also the hotel's entertainment center, where live shows are often presented.

Services: Room service (7am to 10pm), laundry, activity coordinator arranging tours and rentals.

Facilities: Water sports, outdoor swimming pool, Jacuzzi, sauna, Sunfish sailing, free use of the hotel's fitness center; complimentary day/night tennis nearby; sports, such as golf, waterskiing, and horseback riding, can be arranged.

ON THE SOUTH COAST
MODERATE

Divi Southwinds Beach Resort

St. Lawrence Gap, Christ Church, Barbados, W.I. ☎ **809/428-7181,** or 800/367-3484. Fax 809/428-4674. 33 studios, 127 suites. A/C TV TEL. Winter, $185–$215 studio for one or two; $205–$245 one-bedroom suite for one or two; $330–$355 two-bedroom suite for four. Off-season, $110–$125 studio for one or two; $140–$155 one-bedroom suite for one or two; $200 two-bedroom suite for four. MAP $40 per person extra. AE, MC, V. Free parking.

Midway between Bridgetown and the hamlet of Oistins, this resort was created when two distinctly different resorts were combined into a single coherent whole. Scattered over sandy flatlands of about 20 acres, the resorts were built in 1975 and 1986, respectively. Each enjoys a loyal clientele. The showplace of the present resort are the newer (inland) buildings consisting of one- and two-bedroom suites

with full kitchens ideal for families. This section looks like a tastefully interconnected series of town houses, with spacious wooden balconies and views of a large
L-shaped swimming pool. From these buildings, visitors need only cross through
two groves of palm trees and a narrow lane to reach the beach. The older, more
modest (but fully renovated) units lie directly on the beachfront, ringed with palm
trees, near an oval swimming pool of their own.

Dining/Entertainment: The Aquarius Restaurant, which rises above the largest of the resort's swimming pools, is the resort's main dining and drinking
emporium. A satellite snack bar/drink bar lies beside the beach, near the older
units.

Services: Laundry, island tours.

Facilities: Three swimming pools (one a wading pool reserved for children),
sailboat rentals, snorkeling equipment.

Sandy Beach Hotel

Worthing, Christ Church, Barbados, W.I. ☎ **809/435-8000.** Fax 809/435-8053. 89 units.
A/C TV TEL. Winter, $95 single or double; $190–$265 one-bedroom suite; $285–$375
two-bedroom suite. Off-season, $60 single or double; $100–$150 one-bedroom suite;
$175–$225 two-bedroom suite. Additional person $30 extra in winter, $25 extra off-season.
Children under 12 stay free in parents' room. MAP $40 per adult extra. AE, MC, V. Free
parking.

Originally established in 1980 and renovated in 1994 on 2 acres of beachfront land
4 miles southeast of Bridgetown, this Barbadian-owned hotel rises around its
architectural centerpiece, a soaring conical cedar-sheathed structure known
locally as a *palapa*. Suitable for families with children, the resort contains only
one- and two-bedroom suites, plus 16 honeymoon suites with queen-size beds
and completely private patios. All the tastefully decorated and spacious accommodations have fully equipped kitchenettes and private balconies or patios, and
all the furniture at this informal place is locally made. Facilities for the disabled
are provided in some of the ground-floor suites.

Dining/Entertainment: The Beachfront Restaurant, specializing in seafood and
steaks, is under the palapa and opens onto a view of the beach and swimming pool.
Every Tuesday the resort sponsors a rum-punch party, a Trinidad-style steel band,
and a Bajan buffet. Then, outsiders are welcome. Caribbean specialties, such as flying fish, cou-cou, curries, and pepperpot, are served. Entertainment is presented
three nights a week.

Services: Room service (7:30am to 10pm), laundry, dry cleaning, activities desk
to arrange island tours.

Facilities: Swimming pool with tropical waterfall, children's play area, wading
pool. Water sports, which cost extra, include three-hour snorkeling trips, windsurfing, paddleboats, Sailfish, scuba lessons, and use of air mattresses, snorkels, fins,
and masks.

Southern Palms

St. Lawrence, Christ Church, Barbados, W.I. ☎ **809/428-7171,** or 800/424-5500 in the U.S.
Fax 809/428-7175. 73 rms, 20 suites. A/C TEL. Winter, $170–$205 double; $260 suite.
Off-season, $95–$115 double; $150 suite. MAP $40 per person extra. AE, DC, MC, V. Free
parking.

A seafront club with a distinct personality, Southern Palms lies on the Pink Beach
of Barbados, midway between the airport and Bridgetown. The core of the resort
is a pink-and-white manor house built in the Dutch style, with a garden-level
colonnade of arches. Spread along the sands are multiarched two- and three-story

buildings. Italian fountains and statues add to the Mediterranean feeling. In its more modern block, an eclectic mixture of rooms includes some with kitchenettes, some facing the ocean, others opening onto the garden, and some with penthouse luxury. Each room is a double, and suites have small kitchenettes. A cluster of straw-roofed buildings, the drinking and dining facilities, link the accommodations together.

Dining/Entertainment: The Khus-Khus Bar and Restaurant serves both a West Indian and a continental cuisine. A local orchestra often entertains by providing merengue and steel-band music.

Services: Room service (7am to 11pm), laundry, tour desk.

Facilities: Terrace for sunning, two beachside freshwater swimming pools, sailboat rentals, two tennis courts; snorkeling and scuba diving available.

INEXPENSIVE

⑤ Bagshot House Hotel

St. Lawrence, Christ Church, Barbados, W.I. ☎ **809/435-6956.** 16 rms. TEL. Winter, $80 single; $130 double. Off-season, $50 single; $80 double. (Rates include breakfast.) No credit cards. Free parking.

Custom-built in 1956 as a small, family-managed hotel, the Bagshot House has flowering vines tumbling over the railing of the balconies and an old-fashioned and unhurried kind of charm. The hotel was named after the early 19th-century manor house that once stood on this site, which was willed to the hotel's present owner, Mrs. Eileen Robinson. In 1955 the house was demolished and this concrete hotel built in its place. In front, the beach stretches out before you. Some of the well-kept, simply furnished units boast views of the water. Only two units are air-conditioned. For an extra charge, a TV can be placed in your room. A sunbathing deck, which doubles as a kind of living room for the resort, is perched at the edge of a lagoon. A deckside lounge is decorated with paintings by local artists, and an à la carte restaurant, Secrets, is on the premises (see "Where to Dine,") later in this chapter.

Casuarina Beach Club

St. Lawrence Gap, Christ Church, Barbados, W.I. ☎ **809/428-3600,** or 800/223-9815 in the U.S. Fax 809/428-1970. 123 studios, 20 one-bedroom suites, 14 two-bedroom suites. A/C TEL. Winter, $160–$170 studio for one or two; $190 one-bedroom suite; $320 two-bedroom suite. Off-season, $80–$100 studio for one or two; $115–$120 one-bedroom suite; $160–$180 two-bedroom suite. Children under 12 stay free in parents' room. MAP $35 per person extra. AE, MC, V. Free parking.

You'll approach this resort, located midway between Bridgetown and Oistins, through a forest of palm trees swaying above a well-maintained lawn. Originally established in 1981, with substantial additions and improvements completed in 1991, the resort is pleasant, family run, and unpretentious. Designed with red-tile roofs and white walls, the main building has a series of arched windows leading onto verandas, although to get to your accommodation you pass through the outlying reception building and beside the pair of swimming pools. These are separated from the wide sandy beach by a lawn area dotted with casuarina and bougainvillea. On the premises is an octagonal roofed open-air bar and restaurant, two floodlit tennis courts, a gift shop, a tiny store for the purchase of foodstuffs, and a fitness room. The front desk can arrange most seaside activities through outside agencies. Each accommodation is equipped with a ceiling fan and rattan furniture, and each suite contains a kitchenette for preparing snacks and meals.

The hotel is decorated with local artwork, including paintings, terra-cotta pots, and sculptures.

⑤ Ocean View

Hastings, Christ Church, Barbados, W.I. ☎ **809/427-7821.** Fax 809/427-7826. 28 rms, 4 suites. TEL. Winter, $75–$110 single; $95–$145 double; $220 suite. Off-season, $55–$65 single; $55–$75 double; $120 suite. MAP $40 per person extra. AE, MC, V. Free parking.

This is the oldest hotel on Barbados, founded in 1901. Built between the busy road and the beach, 4 miles southeast of Bridgetown, the pink-and-white Ocean View has some of the graciousness of a colonial English house, including an open staircase and a seaside porch that's good for lounging. Every bedroom is different—some large, some small and cozy—and has island antiques. Most rooms have air conditioning, and all have ceiling fans.

This vintage hostelry also serves good food. You can dine at a table overlooking the sea, helping yourself at the well-known Sunday planters' buffet lunch in winter for $27.50—as in the olden days, there's a big spread of Bajan specialties. Ernest Hemingway attended some buffets here, enjoying especially the callaloo soup, flying fish, and pepperpot, according to local legend.

⑤ Woodville Beach Apartments

Hastings, Christ Church, Barbados, W.I. ☎ **809/435-6694.** Fax 809/435-9211. 28 apartments. TEL. Winter, $76–$80 studio apartment for one or two; $95 one-bedroom apartment for one or two; $135 two-bedroom apartment for up to four. Off-season, $45–$56 studio apartment for one or two; $60 one-bedroom apartment for one or two; $90 two-bedroom apartment for up to four. No credit cards. Free parking.

These apartments represent one of the best bargains on Barbados and are ideal for families on a budget holiday. Set directly on a rocky shoreline $2^1/2$ miles southeast of Bridgetown, in the heart of the village of Hastings, on slightly less than an acre of land, this is a U-shaped apartment complex built around a pool terrace overlooking the sea. Functional and minimalist in decor, it is nevertheless clean and comfortable. The tiny kitchenettes in each accommodation are fully equipped, and a variety of rental units are offered. All have balconies or decks, and about 13 of the units contain air conditioning. There are supermarkets, stores, and banks within easy walking distance. Although a handful of athletic guests attempt to swim off the nearby rocks, most opt for a five-minute walk to the white sands of nearby Rockley (Accra) Beach. No meals are served.

BUDGET

⑤ Fairholme

Maxwell, Christ Church, Barbados, W.I. ☎ **809/428-9425.** 11 rms, 20 studio apartments. A/C. Winter, $28 single; $30 double; $55 studio apartment. Off-season, $25 single; $28 double; $35 studio apartment. Breakfast $6 extra. No credit cards. Free parking.

Fairholme is a converted plantation house whose sleeping quarters have been enlarged during the past 20 years with a handful of interconnected annexes. The main house and its original gardens are just off a major road 6 miles southeast of Bridgetown, a five-minute walk to the beach and across from its neighbor hotel, the Sea Breeze, which has a waterfront café and bar that Fairholme guests are allowed to use. The older part has 11 double rooms, each of which has a living-room area and a patio overlooking an orchard and swimming pool. Beside the pool is a lawn for sunbathing and a bar for island beverages. More recently added are 20 Spanish-style studio apartments, all with balcony or patio, built in the old plantation, with high cathedral ceilings, dark beams, and traditional furnishings. The restaurant has a reputation for home-cooking—wholesome, nothing fancy, but the ingredients are fresh. On the premises are the remnants of a very old wall, part of the ruined foundation of the original plantation complex. A note about this establishment's air conditioning: At the reception desk you buy a brass token for $3 that you insert into your air conditioner for around eight hours of cooling-off time.

ON THE EAST COAST
MODERATE

Crane Beach Hotel
Crane Bay, St. Philip, Barbados, W.I. ☎ **809/423-6220.** Fax 809/423-5343. 14 rms, 4 suites. TEL. Winter, $160 single or double; $270–$295 suite. Off-season, $100 single or double; $150–$175 suite. MAP $35 per person extra. AE, DC, MC, V. Free parking.

Near the easternmost end of the island about 14 miles from Bridgetown, a 15-minute drive northeast of the airport via Highway 7, this remote hilltop hostelry stands on a cliff overlooking the Atlantic. Crane Beach was called by one writer "the most beautiful spot on earth." At least Prince Andrew thought so when he built his clearly visible house on a nearby cliff. In the vicinity of Marriott's Sam Lord's Castle, the hotel opens onto one of the best beaches on Barbados, and is reached by walking down some 200 steps. Canopied beds and antique furnishings grace many of the bedrooms, and often the views are panoramic. Some units are air-conditioned, and a few have kitchenettes.

Dining/Entertainment: Many visitors for the day head here just to have a drink on the panoramic terrace or to order a meal. An international cuisine is served with West Indian flair. At night the tables are candlelit. Its Sunday brunch is a well-attended event.

Services: Room service, babysitting, laundry.

Facilities: The Roman-style swimming pool with columns, separating the main house from the dining room, has perhaps been used as a backdrop for more fashion layouts than any other place in the Caribbean. The resort also has tennis courts.

Marriott's Sam Lord's Castle
Long Bay, St. Philip, Barbados, W.I. ☎ **809/423-7350,** or 800/223-6388 in the U.S. Fax 809/423-5918. 234 rms. A/C MINIBAR TEL. Winter, $194–$240 single or double. Off-season, $94–$119 single or double. MAP $44 per person extra. AE, DC, MC, V. Free parking.

Today this resort is a smoothly operated compound maintained by the Marriott chain, but its architecturally acclaimed centerpiece was originally built in 1820 by one of Barbados's most notorious scoundrels. According to legend, Samuel Hall Lord (the "Regency Rascal") built the estate with money acquired by luring ships to their wreck on the jagged but hard-to-detect rocks of Cobbler's Reef. This he accomplished by placing lanterns along the trees of the island's relentlessly windy east coast in patterns that imitated the lights of safe harbors in other parts of the maritime world. As the ships were bashed to pieces on the rocks, Lord and his cohorts would loot them and then sell their cargoes at high (and tax-free) profits.

The Great House, near the easternmost end of the island, about 14 miles from Bridgetown, a 15-minute drive northeast of the airport, was built in the pirate's more mellow "golden years," and craftspeople were imported from England to reproduce sections of the queen's castle at Windsor. The decor includes the dubiously acquired but nonetheless beautiful art of Reynolds, Raeburn, and Chippendale.

Amid 72 landscaped acres, the estate has a wide, lengthy private sandy beach edged by tall coconut trees. Accommodations are comfortable and stylish, in a series of modern wings which ramble throughout the surrounding gardens.

Dining/Entertainment: Three meals a day are served in the Wanderer Restaurant, and you can order a hamburger at Oceanus Café, right on the beach. There are many bars as well. A fiesta night in the hotel's Bajan Village is offered once a week, as is a shipwreck barbecue and beach party with a steel-drum band, a limbo show, and fire-eaters on South Beach.

Services: Beauty/barber shop, laundry, babysitting, concierge to arrange island tours and whatever.

Facilities: Three swimming pools, exercise room, shuffleboard, table tennis, library; sailing, horseback riding, snorkeling, fishing, and other activities can be arranged.

INEXPENSIVE

⑤ Kingsley Club

Cattlewash-on-Sea, near Bathsheba, St. Joseph, Barbados, W.I. ☎ **809/433-9422.** Fax 809/433-9226. 7 rms. Winter, $92 single; $101 double. Off-season, $79 single; $84 double. MAP $43 per person extra. Take Hwy. 3 north of Bathsheba. AE, MC, V. Free parking.

This hidden-away little West Indian inn is far removed from the bustle of the tourist-ridden west coast. In the foothills of Bathsheba, opening onto the often-turbulent Atlantic, the Kingsley Club lies on the northeast coast. A historic inn with many associations, it offers simply furnished but clean and comfortable bedrooms. At night, you can sit back and enjoy a rum punch made from an old planter's recipe. The club enjoys a reputation for good cooking, and its Bajan food will be recommended later for those traveling to the east coast just for the day. Cattlewash Beach is one of the longest, widest, and least crowded in Barbados. But be aware that swimming here can be extremely dangerous.

2 Where to Dine

ON THE WEST COAST
EXPENSIVE

✪ Bagatelle Restaurant

Hwy. 2A, St. Thomas. ☎ **809/421-6767.** Reservations recommended. Fixed-price dinner $42.50. AE, MC, V. Dinner only, daily 7–9:30pm. Closed Sun May–Oct. Cut inland near Paynes Bay north of Bridgetown, 3 miles from both Sunset Crest and the Sandy Lane Hotel. FRENCH/CARIBBEAN.

This restaurant is housed in one of the most historic and impressive buildings on the island. Set a 15-minute drive north of Bridgetown, and originally built in 1645 as the residence of the island's first governor (Lord Willoughby), it lies on 5 acres of forest whose trees are uplit with some of the best lighting in the Caribbean. The sylvan retreat lies in the cool uplands, just south of the island's center, and retains the allure of its original buildings.

The Bagatelle is one of the island's finest and most elegant choices for dining on a French cuisine with a Caribbean flavor. Candles and lanterns illuminate the old archways and the ancient trees. Service is among the best I found on Barbados. Try homemade duck-liver pâté, deviled Caribbean crab backs, or smoked flying fish mousse with horseradish mayonnaise. The beef Wellington Bagatelle style with a chasseur sauce is a favorite, as is the crisp roast duckling with an orange-and-brandy sauce. The local catch of the day—perhaps the most popular item on the menu—can be prepared grilled, barbecued, or in the style of Baxters Road (that is, spicily seasoned and sautéed in deep oil). A different list of home-made desserts is featured nightly, and coffee can be served on the terrace.

✪ Carambola

Derricks, St. James. ☎ **809/432-0832.** Reservations recommended. Appetizers $5.50–$12; main courses $19–$45. AE, MC, V. Dinner only, Mon–Sat 6:30–9:30pm. Closed Aug. FRENCH/THAI.

Built beside the road that parallels the island's western coastline, 1 1/2 miles south of Holetown, atop the upper edge of a 20-foot seaside cliff, Carambola offers one of the most panoramic terraces for dining in the Caribbean. In the shadow of a much-enlarged Bajan house that was originally built during the 1950s as a private home, the restaurant quickly moved to the forefront of island dining experiences. The cuisine is creative, with modern French-inspired touches. Owner Robin Walcott has decided to blend two of the world's most famous cuisines, from Thailand and France, on one menu. You might begin with hot-and-sour prawn soup and follow with green-curry chicken and Thai eggplant. Or you can enjoy a more French selection, perhaps dolphin with a Dijon-mustard sauce. Red curry of duck is another delectable item, as is the jumbo shrimp with shellfish sauce.

La Cage aux Folles

Summerland Great House, Prospect, St. James. ☎ **809/424-2424.** Reservations recommended, especially in winter. Appetizers $12.50–$14; main courses $20–$45. MC, V. Dinner only, Wed–Mon 7–10:30pm. Closed June. ASIAN/INTERNATIONAL.

This restaurant is the statement of a pair of entrepreneurs who have established several other restaurants both in London and on Barbados. It's located between Batts Rock and Tamarind Cove in an island house, where the decor is evocative of an old-fashioned plantation house, with tall ceilings, crystal chandeliers, and a balcony for sundowners. The most impressive room (reserved for groups and wedding receptions) centers around a reflecting pool and is lined with Bajan antiques or antique reproductions.

Try the sesame prawn pâté, sweet-and-sour shrimp, or Créole fish soup. Other courses include crispy aromatic duck and a dish inspired by the cuisine of India: tikka makhani, a creamy and spicy chicken cooked slowly in a tandoori and served with stir-fried vegetables. For dessert, perhaps profiteroles with chocolate sauce and an old-fashioned English syllabub are the best choices.

La Maison

Holetown, St. James. ☎ **809/432-1156.** Reservations recommended. Appetizers $6–$14; main courses $22.50–$40. MC, V. Dinner only, Tues–Sun 6:30–10pm. FRENCH/CARIBBEAN.

Located on the beach south of Holetown, this restaurant was established in 1990 in a coral-sided building that was constructed in the 1970s as a copy of an older Barbadian home for members of the Cunard family. Open on two sides to the sea and to a flowering courtyard (whose centerpiece is a mermaid-capped fountain), the restaurant derives most of its decor from the exposed coral of its walls and the glow of its intricate ceiling, crafted solely of a Guyanan hardwood called greenheart. Intriguing appetizers are likely to include blackened flying fish filets set on a sweet-potato salad. The main courses are wide-ranging in appeal, everything from caramelized honey-glazed duck breast with Oriental spices to squid with a Caribbean sand crab filling. Marinated filet of lamb is served with roasted peppers and a herb pomme purée. Desserts aren't neglected either, and a delectable one is spicy tropical fruits in phyllo pastry with cinnamon ice cream.

✪ Neptune's

In the Tamarind Cove Beach Resort, Paynes Bay, St. James. ☎ **809/432-1332.** Reservations recommended. Appetizers $6.50–$10; main courses $20–$40. AE, DC, MC, V. Dinner only, daily 6:30–9pm. Closed Tues off-season. SEAFOOD.

By anyone's standards, this is the most desirable seafood restaurant on Barbados. Located south of Holetown, within the pink hacienda-inspired walls of one of the island's most respected resorts, it abandons completely the "ocean breezes blowing through the hibiscus blossoms" mode that permeates most of the island's other restaurants. Instead, you'll find a stylish octagonal room sheathed in *faux* malachite, whose emerald-green tones reflect the colors of an illuminated aquarium in the room's center. Service is impeccable.

Appetizers range from smoked-salmon mousse to an Oistins fish gumbo (seafood, okra, and greens). Stuffed flying fish is also served as an appetizer, flavored with an orange-and-turmeric sauce. The chef's blackened fish is the eternal favorite, or you can order garlic shrimp, lobster thermidor, or even breast of chicken Caribee (served with a green-peppercorn and guava sauce). The dessert menu is one of the most elaborate on Barbados, ranging from the chef's favorite cheesecake recipes to a harvest of fresh fruit in a light orange-and-mango sauce.

Many visitors opt for a before-dinner drink in a coral-sided bar adjacent to the restaurant, where a polite staff serves lethal rum sours.

The Palm Terrace

In the Royal Pavilion Hotel, Porters, St. James. ☎ **809/422-4444.** Reservations required. Appetizers $15–$40; main dishes $25–$45. AE, DC, MC, V. Dinner only, daily 7–9:30pm. CARIBBEAN/FRENCH.

North of Bridgetown between Sunset Crest and Gibbs Beach, in an elegant setting on a pink-marble terrace evocative of the Mediterranean, this dramatic restaurant opens onto the oceanfront. In a previously recommended luxurious hotel, the Palm Terrace has a French chef who oversees a Bajan staff. Together they turn out some of the more delectable cuisine offered at any west-coast hotel. To the sounds of music, with the trade winds sweeping in, you can sample such dishes as charcoal-grilled local lobster with a choron sauce, roast rack of lamb with hazelnuts, filet of beef au jus, terrine of confit of duck, and an array of other dishes such as sautéed fish filet in a cream-and-jelly sauce, or blackened fish in a spicy marinade. Desserts feature tarts, crème caramel, chocolate fantasy, and a cinnamon soufflé. Many desserts are flambéed.

MODERATE

⑤ Bamboo Beach Bar

Paynes Bay, St. James. ☎ **809/432-0910.** Reservations not required. Appetizers $4–$9; main courses $12.50–$20; lunch from $8. AE, MC, V. Lunch daily noon–6:30pm; snacks daily 3–6pm; dinner daily 7–10pm. BAJAN/INTERNATIONAL.

The most famous beach bar along the west coast, 6 miles north of Bridgetown along Highway 1, the Bamboo Beach Bar stands next door to the previously recommended Buccaneer Bay Hotel and is under the same management. Its open and airy setting is both cheery and intimate, and it makes an ideal venue for drinks, snacks, or full meals. Entertainment, such as a steel drum, is often featured. For a beach bar, the menu is surprisingly sophisticated, including appetizers such as lobster cocktail and escargots in a creamy garlic-and-herb sauce. There's also a choice of evening soups, each homemade. For your main course you can roam the world, ordering the Bamboo fish pie from the Caribbean, or such dishes as shrimp kebabs, skewered swordfish, or pork sate with pilaf rice. Lunch always features a selection of salads and soup, along with Baxters Road cutter (flying fish in a salt bun), burgers, Bajan fried chicken, Caribbean "firehouse" chili and rice, or a steakfish of the day (dolphin or kingfish). Homemade dessert and cakes follow. A special part of the menu is reserved for kids.

Château Créole

Porters, St. James. ☎ **809/422-4116.** Reservations recommended. Appetizers $5–$8; main courses $14–$31. AE, MC, V. Dinner only, Mon–Sat 7–9:30pm (last seating). BAJAN/CREOLE.

Built around 1975, this stucco-and-tile house is set 2 miles north of Holetown in a tropical garden dotted with a trio of gazebos. After passing under an arbor, you'll be invited to order a drink, served on one of the flowered banquettes that fill various parts of the house. Meals are taken on the rear terrace, al fresco style, by candlelight. Menu specialties include Créole dishes such as stuffed crab backs. You might like Créole red-bean soup, a succulent version of fish chowder, baked white-fish stuffed with crabmeat and herbs, or chicken with fresh mangoes and ginger.

✪ The Fathoms

Paynes Bay, St. James. ☎ **809/432-2568.** Reservations recommended for dinner. Appetizers $3.50–$6; main courses $6–$8 at lunch, $15–$32 at dinner. AE, MC, V. Lunch daily 11am–3pm; dinner daily 6:30–10pm (last order). INTERNATIONAL.

Housed in a red-roofed stucco house close to the surf of the island's western coastline, south of Holetown near one of the island's fish markets, this pleasant restaurant serves meals on an outdoor terrace shaded by a mahogany tree and in an interior decorated with accents of terra-cotta, wood, and pottery.

The restaurant serves a fairly ambitious luncheon menu, ranging from octopus ceviche to shrimp and crab étouffée for appetizers, followed by main courses of everything from burgers to spicy pork crêpes. At night you might begin with cashew-crusted calamari (with a lime-and-mango dip) or pork and crab spring rolls. Main dishes range from pan-fried barracuda with a dill-and-mustard sauce to dolphin with a chive beurre blanc. Upstairs is a Santa Fe–style tapas bar, primarily for drinks, wines, and finger foods. A pool table and board games help you pass the evening away at this attractive watering hole open daily from 5pm until the crowd finally departs for the night.

Koko's

Prospect, St. James. ☎ **809/424-4557.** Reservations recommended. Appetizers $3.50–$8; main courses $12–$22. MC, V. Dinner only, daily 6:30–9:30pm (last seating). Closed Mon May–Nov. BAJAN.

Koko's is an award-winning restaurant, known for its excellent Caribbean cookery, a kind of Bajan *cuisine moderne.* The location alone is appealing: It's in a charming once-private house, built on coral blocks on a terrace overlooking the sea. You might begin with a homemade local soup, perhaps pepperpot, made with "roots of the Caribbean," or stir-fried squid with lime-and-mayonnaise sauce as an appetizer. Shrimp and crab fritters are served with a fiery dip. Main dishes include the chef's "ketch of de day," as well as barracuda teriyaki, roast pork calypso, or steamed or pan-fried flying fish. Each dessert is homemade and luscious.

Legend Restaurant

Mullins Bay, St. Peter. ☎ **809/422-0631.** Reservations recommended. Appetizers $2.50–$7.50; main courses $9–$24. AE, MC, V. Dinner only, daily 6–11pm. CARIBBEAN.

Designed as the centerpiece of a 12-unit condominium complex on the northwestern side of the island, about a 15-minute drive south of Speightstown, this restaurant occupies a plantation Great House originally built in 1806 of coral limestone blocks by British sugar barons known as the Edmonds family. Separated from the sea by a road and a pleasant garden, the restaurant offers dining amid a maze of arches composed of chiseled blocks of coral. Selections from one of the most imaginative menus on the island include fluffy jumbo shrimp dipped in a coconut/beer-batter sauce and served with a tamarind sauce; chicken and banana wrap-around, with spicy peanut-and-coconut sauce; cream of field mushroom soup; a galaxy of jumbo curried shrimp, served on a ribbon of grilled plantain and accompanied with a jewel center of mango chutney; or lemon fettuccine in a creamy cheese sauce surrounded by a variety of grilled fish.

✪ Raffles

First St., Holetown. ☎ **809/432-6557.** Reservations recommended. Appetizers $12–$20 BDS ($6–$10); main courses $40–$65 BDS ($20–$32.50). AE, DC, MC, V. Dinner only, daily 7–10pm (last order). CARIBBEAN.

Set amid the weatherbeaten buildings along the main street of Holetown, in a pink-and-white, much-renovated older building, this cozy enclave has a relatively unusual list of gastronomic specialties. A decor of *faux* leopardskin and safari-derived artifacts adds to the exotic atmosphere. Menu items include spicy shrimp salad on a bed of local greens, Bajan saltfish cakes, Jamaican ackee with saltfish, African babouttie (ground and heavily curried beef baked with custard and served with sliced bananas), barbecued pork, tenderloin steaks, and a changing array of local fish. These include dolphin, barracuda, kingfish, flying fish, and sea trout, prepared in any of at least three different methods (blackened, grilled, sautéed, or whatever).

SPEIGHTSTOWN

Mango Café

2 West End, Queen St. ☎ **809/422-0704.** Reservations recommended. Appetizers $3–$7; main courses $11–$37.50. AE, MC, V. Dinner only, Sun–Thurs 6pm–late (no set closing time). INTERNATIONAL.

Speightstown was never noted for its dining choices until the opening of this café, restaurant, and bar overlooking the water. Run by a couple from New Orleans, the restaurant offers entertainment on some nights, and features daily specials. It's best known for its seafood, and the owners buy the catch of the day directly from the fishermen's boats. You might begin with a soup of the day or a green-peppercorn pâté, followed by today's catch, which might be anything from grouper to red snapper to barracuda. Smoked salmon and seafood crêpes are also featured regularly. If you don't like fish, you'll find such fare as U.S. tenderloin steak, chicken in orange sauce, or barbecued spareribs.

SOUTH OF BRIDGETOWN

Brown Sugar

Aquatic Gap, St. Michael. ☎ **809/426-7684.** Reservations recommended. Appetizers $4–$8; main courses $11–$20; fixed-price buffet lunch $14. AE, DC, MC, V. Lunch Sun–Fri noon–2:30pm; dinner daily 6–9:30pm (last order). BAJAN.

Hidden behind lush foliage, Brown Sugar is an al fresco restaurant in a turn-of-the-century coral limestone bungalow south of Bridgetown. The ceiling is latticed, with slow-turning fans, and there's an open veranda for dining by candlelight in a setting of hanging plants. The chefs prepare some of the tastiest Bajan specialties on the island. Among the soups, I suggest hot gungo-pea soup (pigeon peas cooked in chicken broth and zested with fresh coconut milk, herbs, and a touch of white wine). Of the main dishes, Créole orange chicken is popular, or perhaps you'd like stuffed crab backs. Conch fritters and garlic pork are also spicy. A selection of locally grown vegetables is also offered. For dessert, I recommend the walnut-rum pie with rum sauce. The restaurant is known for its lunches, which are served buffet style to local businesspeople.

ON THE SOUTH COAST
MODERATE

⑤ David's Place

St. Lawrence Main Rd., Christ Church. ☎ **809/435-6550.** Reservations recommended. Appetizers $4–$7; main courses $14–$30; combination platters $25–$40. AE, MC, V. Lunch Tues–Fri 11am–3pm; dinner daily 6–10pm (last order). BAJAN/INTERNATIONAL.

Owner-operator Jay Milne promises that in his restaurant you'll sample "Barbadian dining at its best," and he delivers on that promise. The establishment is south of Bridgetown between Rockley Beach and Worthing, in an old-fashioned Bajan house with strongly contrasting tones of black and white both inside and outside. It has a seaside location on St. Lawrence Bay. Tables are positioned so that diners get a view of the Caribbean. You might begin with a hot-and-creamy pumpkin soup, then follow with a Bajan pepperpot or such freshly caught fish of the day as dolphin, kingfish, or red snapper. The chef might even prepare "Baxters Road chicken" marinated in lime, salt, and herbs. Desserts include coconut-cream pie.

Ile de France

In the Windsor Arms Hotel, Hastings, Christ Church. ☎ **809/435-6869.** Reservations recommended. Appetizers $4–$12; main courses $19–$33. AE, MC, V. Dinner only, Tues–Sun 6:30–9:30pm (last order). CLASSIC FRENCH.

A 12-minute drive southeast of the center of Bridgetown, this restaurant presents the finest and most authentic French cuisine on Barbados. Place yourself in the capable hands of Michel and Martine Gramaglia, two French-born *expatriés* who handle their kitchen and dining room etiquette with an enviable savoir-faire. Meals are served on a candlelit outdoor terrace overlooking a manicured garden, beside one of the oldest and most venerable hotels on the island. Ingredients are either flown in from France (or Martinique) or obtained fresh on Barbados. Specialties might include escargots de Bourgogne, a flavorful version of soupe de poissons avec langoustines, or a marinade aux trois poissons whose exact composition depends on the catch of the day. Other classic dishes include tournedos with a béarnaise sauce, roast lobster, rack of lamb, and a fisherman's plate with the catch of the day, shrimp, and lobster. For dessert try the tart tatin or banana terrine. The atmosphere is charming and traditional.

Luigi's Restaurant

Dover Woods, St. Lawrence Gap, Christ Church. ☎ **809/428-9218.** Reservations recommended. Appetizers $4–$8.50; main courses $12.50–$16.50. MC, V. Dinner only, daily 6–10:30pm (last order). ITALIAN.

Since 1963 this open-air Italian trattoria has operated in a green-and-white build-ing built as a private house. The feeling is contemporary, airy, and comfortable. Miles and Lisa Needham are the owners/managers.Pizzas are offered as appetizers, along with more classic choices such as half a dozen escargots or a Caesar salad (when available). Half orders of many pastas are also available as starters. The baked pastas, such as a creamy lasagne, are delectable, and you can also order the fresh fish or veal special of the day, among other dishes. For dessert, try the zabaglione or one of the wide selections of coffee, ranging from Italian to Russian or Turkish.

Pisces

St. Lawrence Gap, Christ Church. ☎ **809/435-6564.** Reservations recommended. Appe-tizers $3.50–$8; main courses $14–$30. AE, DC, MC, V. Dinner only, daily 6–9:30pm (last order). From Bridgetown, take Hwy. 7 south for about 4 miles; then turn right at the sign toward St. Lawrence Gap. BAJAN.

Pisces offers al fresco dining at water's edge. A beautiful restaurant with a tropi-cal decor, it serves primarily a Caribbean seafood menu. You might begin with one of the soups, perhaps a crab and pigeon pea or "tropical gazpacho." A Guava chicken kebab is another temptation. Seafood fanciers enjoy the Pisces platter, consisting of charcoal-broiled dolphin, fried flying fish, broiled kingfish, and butter-fried prawns. You might also be drawn to seasonal Caribbean fish, which can be broiled, blackened, or pan-fried before it's served with lime-herb butter. Another seasonal delight is snapper Caribe, which is stuffed with shrimp, tomato, and herbs, then baked and served with a white-wine sauce. A limited but good selection of poultry and meat is offered, including roast pork Barbados with a traditional Bajan stuffing.

Secrets

In Bagshot House, St. Lawrence Coast Rd., Christ Church. ☎ **809/428-9525.** Reservations recommended. Appetizers $14–$20 BDS ($7–$14); main courses $32–$60 BDS ($16–$30). AE, MC, V. Dinner only, Mon–Sat 6–10pm (last order). Closed Sept. INTERNATIONAL.

Set behind the pink facade of one of the island's most historic hotels, this is one of the newest (founded 1992) and best restaurants of Barbados's southwestern coast. Its owners are the Bajan-British husband-and-wife team of Mark and Amanda Evelyn, who maintain an elegant dining room outfitted with lattices, a beachfront terrace, and lots of potted plants. Service and accessories are relatively formal, although the only dress code is that visitors shouldn't wear shorts. Many dishes are based on fresh seafood, and include at least three different preparations (blackened, Créole, provençal, or grilled) of such fish as grouper, flying fish, snap-per, and dolphin. Also available are at least three different preparations of lobster, and an array of chicken dishes. A beef specialty is beef Armand, which is prepared in a style similar to beef Wellington.

Virginian Restaurant

In the Seaview Hotel, Hastings Main Rd., Christ Church. ☎ **809/427-7963.** Reservations recommended. Appetizers $3–$7; main courses $12–$27.50. AE, MC, V. Dinner only, daily 6–10pm. BAJAN/INTERNATIONAL.

The Virginian Restaurant is known for its home-cookery served in a much-restored 18th-century manor house. Guests climb a flight of exterior steps to reach the high-ceilinged dining room, housed in an unpretentious and time-worn hotel. Meals might include shrimp Suzannah, stuffed flying fish, and U.S. steaks. You might begin with Bajan ceviche.

Witch Doctor

St. Lawrence Gap, Christ Church. ☎ **809/435-6581.** Reservations recommended. Appetizers $3.50–$6.50; main courses $11–$30. MC, V. Dinner only, daily 6:15–9:45pm. BAJAN/AFRICAN.

The Witch Doctor hides behind a screen of thick foliage in the heart of the southern coast. The decor, in honor of its name, features African and island wood carvings of witch doctors. The place purveys a fascinating cuisine with some unusual concoctions that are tasty and well prepared, a big change from a lot of the bland hotel fare. For an appetizer, try the split-pea and pumpkin soup. You'll also be offered ceviche (cold, soused in lime). Chef's specialties include various flambé dishes such as steak, shrimp Créole, fried flying fish, and chicken piri-piri (inspired by Mozambique).

INEXPENSIVE

⑤ The Ship Inn

St. Lawrence Gap, Christ Church. ☎ **809/435-6961.** Reservations recommended for the Captain's Carvery only. Appetizers $3–$6; main courses $8–$13; all-you-can-eat carvery meal $10.50 at lunch, $20 at dinner, plus $7.50 for appetizer and dessert. AE, MC, V. Lunch Sun–Fri noon–3pm; dinner daily 6–10:30pm (last order). ENGLISH PUB/BAJAN.

South of Bridgetown between Rockley Beach and Worthing, the Ship Inn is a traditional English-style pub with an attractive, rustic decor of nautical memorabilia. As an alternative, patrons may wish to drink and enjoy a tropical atmosphere in a garden bar. Many guests come for darts and to meet friends, and certainly to listen to the live music presented nightly by some of the island's top bands (see "Barbados After Dark," later in this chapter). The Ship Inn serves substantial bar food, such as homemade steak-and-kidney pie, shepherd's pie, and chicken, shrimp, and fish dishes. For more formal dining, visit the Captain's Carvery, where you can have your fill of succulent cuts from prime roasts on a nighttime buffet table, and an array of traditional Bajan food (filets of flying fish). Diners can enjoy their repast in a tropical garden. An additional attraction to dining at the Carvery is that after dinner guests can listen to top local bands performing in the pub at no extra charge. The establishment stocks beers from Jamaica, Trinidad, and Europe.

⑤ T.G.I. Boomers

St. Lawrence Gap, Christ Church. ☎ **809/428-8439.** Reservations not required. Appetizers $3.50–$7; main courses $9–$22.50; lunch specials $3.50–$7; American breakfast $6.50; daiquiris $3–$5. AE, MC, V. Daily 7:30am–11:30pm. AMERICAN/BAJAN.

Four miles south of Bridgetown near Rockley Beach along Highway 7, T.G.I. Boomers offers some of the best bargain meals on the island. An American/Bajan operation, it has an active bar and a row of tables where food is served, usually along with frothy pastel-colored drinks. The cook prepares a special catch of the day, and the fish is served with soup or salad, rice or baked potato, and a vegetable. You can always count on seafood, steaks, and hamburgers. For breakfast, you might want two eggs with bacon, toast, and coffee. For lunch, try a daily Bajan special or a jumbo sandwich. Be sure to try one of the 16-ounce daiquiris.

ON THE EAST COAST

⑤ Atlantis Hotel

Bathsheba, St. Joseph. ☎ **809/433-9445.** Reservations required for the Sun buffet and the 7pm dinner, recommended at all other times. Two-course fixed-price lunch or dinner $16.50;

Sun buffet $17.25. AE. Lunch daily 11:30am–3pm; dinner daily at 7pm (and don't be late). BAJAN.

Considered useful for an insight into the old-fashioned Barbados of several years ago, the slightly run-down Atlantis Hotel is often filled with both Bajans and visitors. It's located between Cattlewash-on-Sea and Tent Bay on the east coast (Atlantic Ocean). In the sunny, breeze-filled interior, with a sweeping view of the turbulent ocean, Enid I. Maxwell has been welcoming visitors from all over the world ever since she opened the place in 1945. Her copious buffets are considered one of the best food values on the island. From loaded tables, you can sample such Bajan foods as pumpkin fritters, peas and rice, macaroni and cheese, chow mein, souse, and/or a Bajan pepperpot. No one ever leaves here hungry.

Kingsley Club
Cattlewash-on-Sea, near Bathsheba, St. Joseph. ☎ 809/433-9422. Reservations required for dinner, recommended for lunch. Appetizers $3.50; main courses $8–$16; fixed-price four-course meal $25–$35. AE, MC, V. Lunch daily noon–3pm; dinner daily 6:30–7:30pm (last order). BAJAN.

A historic inn recommended previously for its rooms, the Kingsley Club also serves some of the best Bajan food on the island in a turn-of-the-century house cooled by Atlantic breezes. You're invited to "come tuck in" and enjoy your fill of split-pea-and-pumpkin soup, dolphin meunière, or planters fried chicken, followed by one of their homemade desserts, perhaps coconut pie. The inn lies amid the rolling hills of the northeastern coast of Barbados in an area called the Scotland district, a quarter mile northeast of Bathsheba, about 15 miles from Bridgetown.

3 What to See & Do

Barbados is worth exploring, either in your own car or with a taxidriver guide. Unlike on so many islands of the Caribbean, the roads are fair and quite passable. If you get lost, the people in the countryside are generally helpful and speak English.

EXPLORING BRIDGETOWN

Often hot and traffic clogged, the capital, Bridgetown, merits no more than a morning's shopping jaunt. An architectural hodgepodge, it was founded by 64 settlers sent out by the earl of Carlisle in 1628.

Since some half million visitors arrive on Barbados by cruise ship, the government has opened a $6-million terminal for them. It offers a variety of shopping options, including 20 duty-free shops, 13 local retail stores, and scads of vendors. Many of these reflect the arts and crafts of Barbados, or cruise passengers can choose among a range of products, including jewelry, liquor, china, crystal, electronics, perfume, and leather goods. Some shops sell Barbadian wood carvings and art, as well as locally made fashions. The interior was designed to re-create an island street scene, including storefronts appearing as traditional chattel houses in brilliant island colors with street lights, tropical landscaping, benches, and push carts.

Begin your tour at **The Careenage,** from the French word meaning to turn vessels over on their side for cleaning. This was a haven for the clipper ship, and even though today it doesn't have its yesteryear color, it's still worth exploring.

At **Trafalgar Square,** the long tradition of British colonization is perhaps immortalized. The monument here, honoring Lord Nelson, was executed by Sir

Richard Westmacott and erected in 1813. The **Public Buildings** on the square are of the great, gray Victorian gothic variety that you might expect to find in South Kensington, London. The east wing contains the meeting halls of the Senate and the House of Assembly, with some stained-glass windows representing the sovereigns of England. Look for the Great Protector himself, Oliver Cromwell.

Behind the Financial Building, **St. Michael's Cathedral,** east of Trafalgar Square, is the symbol of the Church of England transplanted. This Anglican church was built in 1655, but was completely destroyed in a 1780 hurricane. Reconstructed in 1789, it was also damaged by a hurricane in 1831, but was not completely demolished as before. George Washington is said to have worshipped here on his Barbados visit.

For years, guides pointed out a house on Upper Bay Street where Washington allegedly slept during his only visit outside the United States. Beginning in 1910, the building was called "The Washington House," although historians seriously doubted the claim. Now, after a careful investigation, the house where Washington slept has been identified by historians as the **Codd House** in Bush Hill, which lies about half a mile south of the Upper Bay Street location. The building is privately owned and is not open to the public.

The **Synagogue,** Synagogue Lane (☎ **809/432-0840**), is one of the oldest in the western hemisphere and is surrounded by a burial ground of early Jewish settlers. The present building dates from 1833. It was constructed on the site of an even older synagogue, erected by Jews from Brazil in 1654. Sometime in the early 20th century the synagogue was deconsecrated, and the structure has since served various roles. In 1983, the government of Barbados seized the deteriorating building, intending to raze it and build a courthouse on the site. An outcry went up from the small Jewish community on the island; money was raised for its restoration, and the building was saved and is now part of the National Trust of Barbados and a synagogue once again.

At this point, you can hail a taxi if you don't have a car and visit **Garrison Savannah,** just south of the capital. Cricket matches and other games are played in this open-air space of some 50 acres. Horse races are often held here.

The **Barbados Museum,** St. Ann's Garrison, St. Michael (☎ **809/427-0201**), is housed in a former military prison. In the exhibition "In Search of Bim," extensive collections show the island's development from prehistoric to modern times. "Born of the Sea" gives fascinating glimpses into the natural environment. There are also fine collections of West Indian maps, decorative arts, and fine arts. The museum sells a variety of quality publications, reproductions (maps, cards, prints), and handcrafts. Its Courtyard Café is a good place for a snack or light lunch. The museum is open Monday through Saturday from 9am to 5pm and on Sunday from 2 to 6pm. Admission is $5 for adults, $2.50 for children.

Nearby, the russet-red **St. Ann's Fort,** on the fringe of the Savannah, garrisoned British soldiers in 1694. The fort wasn't completed until 1703. The Clock House survived the hurricane of 1831.

SIGHTSEEING INLAND

Take Highway 2 from Bridgetown and follow it to **Welchman Hall Gully,** in St. Thomas (☎ **809/438-6671**), a lush tropical garden owned by the Barbados National Trust. You'll see some specimens of plants that were here when the English settlers landed in 1627. Many of the plants are labeled—clove, nutmeg, tree fern, and cocoa, among others—and occasionally you'll spot a wild monkey.

You'll also see a ravine and limestone stalactites and stalagmites, as well as breadfruit trees that are claimed to be descended from the seedlings brought ashore by Captain Bligh of the *Bounty*. Admission is $5, half price for children 6 to 12, and kids 5 and under enter free. It's open daily from 9am to 5pm.

Also at Welchman Hall, St. Thomas, ✪ **Harrison's Cave** is the No. 1 tourist attraction of Barbados, and visitors have the chance to view this beautiful, natural, underground world from aboard an electric tram and trailer. Before the tour, a video show of the cave is shown in the presentation hall. During the tour, visitors see bubbling streams, tumbling cascades, and deep pools, which are subtly lit, while all around stalactites hang overhead like icicles. Stalagmites rise from the floor. Visitors may disembark and get a closer look at this natural phenomenon at the Rotunda Room and the Cascade Pool. Tours are conducted daily from 9am to 4pm (closed Good Friday, Easter Sunday, and Christmas Day). You should reserve by calling **809/438-6640.** Admission is $10 for adults and $5 for children.

Flower Forest, St. Joseph (☎ **809/433-8152**), at Richmond Plantation (an old sugar plantation), stands 850 feet above sea level near the western edge of the "Scotland district," a mile from Harrison's Cave. Set in one of the most scenic parts of Barbados, it's more than just a botanical garden; it's where people and nature came together to create something beautiful. After viewing the grounds, visitors can purchase handcrafts at Best of Barbados. It's open from 9am to 5pm daily, and admission is $6 BDS ($3) for adults and $3 BDS ($1.50) for children.

HISTORICAL SIGHTS

Francia Plantation

St. George, Barbados. ☎ **809/429-0474.** Admission $4. Mon–Fri 10am–4pm. On the airport/West Coast Highway, turn east onto Hwy. 4 at the Norma A. Niles Roundabout (signposted to Hwy. X). After going half a mile, turn left onto Hwy. X (signposted to Gun Hill). After another mile, turn right at the Mobil gas station and follow Hwy. X past St. George's Parish Church and up the hill for a mile, turning left at the sign to Francia.

A fine family home, this house stands on a wooded hillside overlooking the St. George Valley and is still owned and occupied by descendants of the original owner. You can explore several rooms, including the dining room with family silver and an 18th-century James McCabe bracket clock. On the walls are antique maps and prints, including a map of the West Indies printed in 1522.

Gun Hill Signal Station

Hwy. 4. ☎ **809/429-1358.** Admission $4 adults, $2 children under 14. Mon–Sat 9am–5pm. Take Hwy. 3 from Bridgetown and then go inland from Hwy. 4 toward St. George Church.

One of two such stations owned and operated by the Barbados National Trust, the Gun Hill Signal Station is strategically placed on the highland of St. George and commands a panoramic view from the east to the west. Built in 1818, it was the finest of a chain of signal stations and was also used as an outpost for the British army stationed here at the time. The old military cookhouse has been restored and houses a snack bar and gift shop.

Morgan Lewis Sugar Windmill

St. Andrew. ☎ **809/426-2421.** Admission $2.50 adults, $1.25 children under 14. Mon–Fri 9am–5pm. Follow Hwy. 1 past Farley Hill National Park to Hwy. 2.

This is typical of the wind-driven mills that crushed the juice from the sugarcane from the 17th to the 19th century, producing sugar that made Barbados Britain's most valuable possession in the Americas. It was from the Barbados sugarcane that rum was first produced. The mill is on the northeastern coast of the island, overlooking the "Scotland district."

Sunbury Plantation House

6 Cross Roads, St. Philip. ☎ **809/423-6270.** Admission $8 BDS ($4), $4 BDS ($2) children. Daily 10am–4:30pm.

This 300-year-old plantation house is steeped in history, featuring mahogany antiques, old prints, and a unique collection of horse-drawn carriages. This is the only Great House on Barbados where all the rooms are open for viewing. An informative tour is given, and later guests can patronize the Courtyard Restaurant and Bar for meals or drinks. There's also a gift shop on site. Twice a week Sunbury offers a planter's candlelight dinner, a four-course meal served at a 200-year-old mahogany table, the same one where Sam Lord dined. The price is $60 per person and transportation can be arranged. Call the number above for reservations or more information.

SUBMERGED SIGHTSEEING

You no longer have to be an experienced diver to see what lives 150 feet below the surface of the sea around Barbados. Now all visitors can view the wonders that lie beneath the sea aboard *Atlantis II*, a submarine for sightseeing. The air-conditioned submersible seats 28 passengers, and, with two crew members, makes several dives daily from 9am to 6pm. Passengers are transported aboard a ferry boat from the Careenage in downtown Bridgetown to the submarine site, about a mile from the west coast of Barbados. The ride offers a view of the west coast of the island.

The submarine has 16 two-foot-wide viewing ports, 8 on either side of the vessel, plus a 52-inch port at the front. Beside the rainbow of colors, tropical fish, and plants, you'll see a shipwreck that lies upright and intact below the surface. The total time of the trip is about two hours. The price is $69.50 for adults, or $39.75 for children (who must be 3 feet tall). For reservations, contact **Atlantis Submarines (Barbados), Inc.,** Horizon House, McGregor Street, Bridgetown (☎ **809/436-8929**). It's also possible to go cruising over one of the shore reefs observing marine life without getting wet. You sit in air-conditioned comfort aboard the *Atlantis Seatrec*, a semi-submersible boat, which gives you a chance to get a snorkeler's view of the reef through large viewing windows. You can also relax on deck as you take in the scenic coastline before or after the aquatic encounter. The tour costs $29.50 for adults; children 4 to 12 are charged half fare (not suitable for those 3 or under). For reservations, call the same number given above.

WALKING TOURS

The **Barbados National Trust** offers Sunday-morning hikes throughout the year. The program, which gives participants an opportunity to learn about the natural beauty of Barbados, is co-sponsored by the duke of Edinburgh's Award Scheme and the Barbados Heart Foundation and attracts more than 300 participants weekly.

Led by young Barbadians and members of the National Trust, the hikes cover a different area of the island each week. Tour escorts also give brief educational talks on various aspects of the hikes, such as geography, history, geology, and agriculture. The hikes, free and open to participants of all ages, are divided into three categories: fast, for those who wish to hike for the exercise; medium, for those wishing exercise but at a slower pace than the fast walk; and slow, or fondly known as the "stop and stare" hike, for those wishing to walk at a leisurely pace.

All the hikes leave promptly at 6am and begin and end in the same place, where parking is available. Each hike is about 5 miles long and takes about three hours to complete. Visitors needing transportation should contact the Barbados National Trust (☎ **809/426-2421**). The staff there will tell you where to meet for the hike.

DRIVING TOUR
Around Barbados

Start: Bridgetown.
Finish: Bridgetown.
Time: Six hours, excluding stopovers.
Best Time: Any sunny day.
Worst Times: When cruise ships are in the harbor, as roads and attractions are at their most congested then.

If you can afford it, the ideal way to take this tour is with a local taxi driver, who will generally negotiate a fair rate. Of course, you can tour on your own, although you'll have to rent an expensive car. Locals know the roads, which are often unmarked; visitors don't. If you do explore on your own, you can count on getting lost, at least several times. Although Barbados contains many direction signs, highway authorities will often leave you "stranded" at strategic junctions, and it's very easy to take a wrong turn if you don't know the way. Even people who live on Barbados often get confused. No clear, concise map of Barbados has yet been devised. Maps only help you as regards general directions; when you're looking for the route to a specific destination, they can often be most unhelpful.

Having said that, know that part of the fun of exploring Barbados is the discovery of the island. So if you do get lost a few times, and miss an attraction or two, no great harm should befall you if that happens.

After leaving Bridgetown (see above), head south along Highway 7, passing through the resorts of Hastings, Rockley, Worthing, and St. Lawrence.

After going through Worthing, and providing you can find this madly badly marked road, turn right along:

1. **St. Lawrence Gap,** which is a virtual "restaurant row" of Barbados, including such well-established places as the Witch Doctor and the Ship Inn (see "Where to Dine," earlier in this chapter). There are also several budget- and medium-priced hotels located along this "strip," which is generally lively both day and night.

At the end of St. Lawrence Gap, resume your journey along Highway 7 by taking a right turn. You'll bypass the town of:

2. **Oistins,** a former shipping port that today is a fishing village. Here the Charter of Barbados was signed at the Mermaid in 1652, as the island surrendered to Commonwealth forces. (The Mermaid Inn, incidentally, was owned by a cousin of John Turner, who built the House of the Seven Gables in Salem, Massachusetts.)

At the sign, take a left for Providence and the Grantley Adams Airport, a continuation of Highway 7. You'll pass the airport on your right. After bypassing the airport, follow the signs to Sam Lord's Castle. At the hamlet of Spencers, leave Highway 7 and turn onto Rock Hall Road, going through the villages of St. Martins and Heddings until you come to the Crane Beach Hotel.

☕ **TAKE A BREAK** Virtually everyone touring the south coast makes the remote hilltop **Crane Beach Hotel,** Crane Bay, St. Philip Parish (☎ **809/ 423-6220**), their stopover point. Its view of the Atlantic and its much-photographed Roman-style swimming pool are beloved of all visiting cruise-ship passengers.

After leaving the hotel, follow Crane Road east. Turn right at the sign and continue to the end of the road and:

3. **Sam Lord's Castle** (see "Where to Stay," earlier in this chapter). Although this is a hotel, it's also one of the major sightseeing attractions of Barbados and can serve as a refueling stop if you didn't already stop at the Crane Beach Hotel. Built by slaves in 1820, and furnished in part with Regency pieces, the house is like a Georgian plantation mansion. Take note of the ornate ceilings, said to be the finest example of stucco work in the western hemisphere. At the entrance to the hotel are shops selling handcrafts and souvenirs. If you're not a guest, you'll have to pay $2.50 to enter.

After leaving Sam Lord's Castle, take a right onto Long Bay Road and continue east. Go right via the village of Wellhouse and continue along the main road, which skirts the coastline but does not touch the coast. On your right you'll see:

4. **Ragged Point Lighthouse.** Turn right down a narrow road to the easternmost point of Barbados. Built in 1885, the lighthouse stands on a rugged cliff. Since that time, its beacon has gone out as a warning to ships approaching the dangerous reef, called The Cobblers. The view from here is panoramic.

After leaving the lighthouse, continue straight along Marley Vale Road (although don't expect proper signs). At the sign to Bayfield, go right and pass Three Houses Park. Take a right at the sign to Bridgetown onto Thickets Road. Take a right again at the sign to Bathsheba. When you come to another signpost, turn left toward Bathsheba and follow the signs to:

5. **Codrington College,** which opened in 1745. A cabbage-palm–lined avenue leads to old coral-block buildings. Today the college is a training school for men and women from the entire Caribbean to enter the ordained ministry of the Anglican church. The college is under the auspices of the Dioceses of the West Indies. Entrance is $2.50.

After leaving the college, go right, then take the next left up the steep Coach Hill Road where you'll see excellent views of the east coast and the lighthouse just visited. At the top of the hill, continue right and follow the signs to:

6. **St. John's Church,** perched on the edge of a cliff opening on the east coast some 825 feet above sea level. The church dates from 1836 and in its graveyard in the rear rests a descendant of Emperor Constantine the Great, whose family was driven from the throne in Constantinople (Istanbul) by the Turks. Ferdinando Paleologus, the royal relative, died on Barbados in 1678.

After leaving the church, go left and then take the next right onto Gall Hill Road. Stay on this road until you reach Four Roads Junction, go along Wakefield Road, and at the sign, turn left and then take the next right into the grounds of:

7. **Villa Nova,** in St. John (☎ **809/433-1524**). Built in 1834 as a fine sugar-plantation Great House, it's furnished with period antiques in Barbadian mahogany and surrounded by 6¹⁄₂ acres of landscaped gardens and trees. Its most famous association was with Sir Anthony Eden, former prime minister of

Driving Tour—Around Barbados

0 ━━━━ 100 m
      109 y

N

Atlantic Ocean

North Point

Cuckold Point

Harrison Point

Fairfield

Pico Teneriffe
St. Nicholas Abbey

Half Moon Fort

Colleton

Cherry Tree Hill
Wildlife Preserve
Greenland

Morgan Lewis Beach

Farley Hill

Morgan Lewis
Sugar Windmill

St. Andrew's
Church

Speightstown

Barclays Park

Gibbs Beach

Turner's Hall Woods

Chalky Mount Potteries
Chalky Mount

Mount Hillaby

Flower Forest

Bathsheba

Andromeda Botanic Gardens

Folkestone
Underwater Park

St. James
Church

Welchman
Hall Gully

Congor Rocks

St. John's
Church

Holetown

Welchman Hall

Blackmans

Harrison's
Cave

Sunset Crest

Codrington
College

Culpepper Island

Villa Nova

Ragged Point
Lighthouse
Three Houses
Kitridge Point

Locust Hall

Warrens

Bushy Park
Sandford

Black Rock

Sunbury
Plantation House
Long Bay

Marchfield

Marriott's Sam
Lord's Castle
Beachy Head
Crane Beach

Kirton

BRIDGETOWN

Queen's Park

Garrison Savannah
Needham's Point

Worthing

Hastings
Rockley Beach

St. Lawrence

Maxwell

Grantley Adams Int'l Airport

Oistins

South Point

*Caribbean
Sea*

SCOTLAND DISTRICT

Hackleton's Cliff

Spring Garden Hwy.

Errol Barrow Hwy.

Tom Adams Hwy.

1 St. Lawrence Gap
2 Oistins
3 Sam Lord's Castle
4 Ragged Point Lighthouse
5 Codrington College
6 St. John's Church
7 Villa Nova
8 Andromeda Botanical Gardens
9 Bathsheba

10 East Coast Road
11 Cherry Tree Hill
12 St. Nicholas Abbey
13 Farley Hill National Park
14 Barbados Wildlife Reserve
15 Speightstown
16 Gold Coast
17 St. James Church
18 Holetown

✝ Church

✈ Airport

Lighthouse

Great Britain, who purchased it from the government in 1965. In 1966 the earl and countess of Avon entertained Queen Elizabeth II and Prince Philip at the Great House. It has since been sold to private owners. Visiting hours are Monday through Friday from 9am to 4pm, and the admission is $4 per person.

After leaving Villa Nova, turn left and pass through the hamlet of Venture. At the next intersection, continue left until you see the sign pointing right toward Easy Hall, another east-coast hamlet. At the next sign, pointing in the direction of Flower Forest, go left along Buckden House Road. Take the next right and head down Highway 3, a steep, curvy road toward the ocean. Turn right in the direction of Bathsheba and follow the signs to the:

8. **Andromeda Botanical Gardens,** Bathsheba, St. Joseph (☎ **809/433-9384**). On a cliff overlooking Bathsheba on the rugged east coast, limestone boulders make for a natural 8-acre rock-garden setting, where thousands of orchids are in bloom every day of the year along with hundreds of hibiscus and heliconia. Many varieties of ferns, bromeliads, and other species that are house plants in temperate climates grow here in splendid profusion. A section is a palm garden, with more than 100 species. A simple guide helps visitors to identify many of the plants. The garden was started in 1954 by the late Mrs. Iris Bannochie, on land that had belonged to her family for more than 200 years and is now managed by the National Trust. On the grounds you'll occasionally see frogs, herons, guppies, and sometimes a mongoose or a monkey. With an admission of $10 BDS ($5), the gardens are open daily from 9am to 5pm; children under 12 enter free.

After leaving the gardens, turn right and follow the signs to something you may badly need at this point, a:

☕ **TAKE A BREAK** The **Atlantis Hotel,** Bathsheba, St. Joseph Parish (☎ **809/433-9445**), one of the oldest hotels on Barbados, is where Enid Maxwell has been serving her favorite Bajan dishes, including flying fish and pickled breadfruit, for longer than she cares to remember. Tattered but respectable, this hotel was once a villa built by a wealthy planter in 1882. It's directly on the seacoast, just south of the "Scotland District." It offers a fixed-price menu at lunch and features a well-attended Sunday buffet (see "Where to Dine," earlier in this chapter, for more details).

After refueling, continue north along the coast road to the town of:

9. **Bathsheba,** where ocean rollers break, forming cascades of white foam. This place has been called "Cornwall (England) in miniature." Today the old fishing village is a favorite low-cost resort for Bajans, although the waters of the Atlantic Ocean are considered dangerous for swimmers.

The trail north from Bathsheba takes you along the:

10. **East Coast Road,** which runs for many miles, opening onto dramatic views of the Atlantic. Chalky Mount rises from the beach to a height of 500 feet, forming a trio of peaks, and a little to the south, Barclays Park is a 15-acre natural wonder presented as a gift to the people of Barbados by the British banking family. There's a snack bar and a place to picnic here.

Climb Morgan Lewis Hill to reach one of the breathtaking sights of Barbados:

11. **Cherry Tree Hill,** on Highway 1, offering one of the finest views on Barbados. You can look right down the eastern shore past Bathsheba to the lighthouse at

Ragged Point, already described. The place is about 850 feet above sea level, and from its precincts you'll see out over the "Scotland district." The cherry trees from which the hill got its name no longer stand here, having given way to mahogany.

On Cherry Tree Hill, signs point the way to:

12. St. Nicholas Abbey (☎ **809/422-8725**), a Jacobean plantation Great House and sugarcane fields that have been around since about 1650. It was never an abbey—an ambitious owner in about 1820 simply christened it as such. More than 200 acres are still cultivated each year. In the parish of St. Peter, the structure—at least the ground floor—is open to the public Monday through Friday from 10am to 3:30pm, charging an admission of $2.50; children under 13 enter free. The house is believed to be one of three Jacobean houses in the western hemisphere, and is characterized by curved gables. Lt.-Col. Stephen Cave, the owner, is descended from the family that purchased the sugar plantation and Great House in 1810. Light refreshments are offered for sale.

After leaving the abbey, follow the road to Diamond Corner, where you go left. Take another left onto the Charles Duncan O'Neal Highway to:

13. Farley Hill National Park, in northern St. Peter Parish. It was used in filming the 1950s film *Island in the Sun,* starring Harry Belafonte. The park, dedicated by Queen Elizabeth in 1966, is open daily from 8:30am to 6pm. You pay a vehicular entrance fee of $1.50 for cars. After disembarking in the parking area, you can walk the grounds and enjoy the tropical flowers and lush vegetation.

Across the road from the park lies the:

14. Barbados Wildlife Reserve (☎ **809/422-8826**), a project operated by the Barbados Primate Research Center in St. Peter, standing in a mahogany forest. From 10am to 5pm daily, for an admission charge of $10 BDS ($5) for adults (half price for children), you stroll through what is primarily a monkey sanctuary. Aside from the uncaged monkeys, you can see wild hares, deer, tortoises, otters, wallabies, and a variety of tropical birds. Another attraction of the Wildlife Reserve is the Grenade Hall Signal Station & Forest. The signal station, which has been renovated from the original built in 1819, offers the most panoramic view of the east, west, and north coasts. Housed in the signal station are archeological findings accompanied by a recorded commentary. Next to the signal station are 5 acres of indigenous woodland of whitewood, inkberry, liana vines, and other species. The forest is open to the public from 10am to 5pm daily.

From Farley Hill Park and the Wildlife Reserve, backtrack to the junction of Highways 1 and 2. From here, head west along Highway 1 and follow the signs to:

15. Speightstown, which was founded around 1635 and for a time was a whaling port. The "second city" of Barbados, the town has some colonial buildings constructed after the devastating hurricane of 1831. The parish church, rebuilt in a half-Grecian style after the hurricane, is one of the places of interest.

After exploring Speightstown, if you have time, turn left in the direction of the:

16. Gold Coast, the protected western shoreline that opens onto the gentler Caribbean. Along the shoreline of the parishes of St. James and St. Peter are the island's plushest hotels (see "Where to Stay," earlier in this chapter).

On Highway 1, directly north of Holetown, lies:

17. St. James Church, St. James, an Anglican church rebuilt in 1872 on the site of the early settlers' church of 1660. On the southern porch is an old bell, bearing the inscription "God Bless King William, 1696." Locals still recall the 1982 visit of Ronald and Nancy Reagan.

Continue south on Highway 1 to:

18. Holetown, the main center of the west coast; it takes its name from the town of Hole on the Thames River. Here the first English settlers landed in the winter of 1627. An obelisk marks the spot where the *Olive Blossom* landed the first Europeans. The monument, for some reason, lists the date erroneously as 1605.

After Holetown, Highway 1 continues south to Bridgetown, the end of your driving tour.

4 Sports & Outdoor Activities

The principal activities are swimming and sunning, which are far preferable on the western coast in the clear, buoyant waters, though you may also want to visit the surf-pounded Atlantic waters on the east, which are better for viewing than swimming.

BEACHES Barbadians will tell you that their island has a beach for every day of the year. If you're only visiting for a short time, however, you'll probably be happy with the ones that are easy to find. They're all open to the public, even those in front of the big resort hotels and private homes, and the government requires that there be access to all beaches, via roads along the property line or through the hotel entrance. The beaches on the west, the so-called **Gold Coast,** are the most popular. These include Paradise Beach, Paynes Bay and Sandy Lane Bay, Treasure Beach, Gibbs Bay, Heywoods Beach, Rockley, and Bentson Beach. To reach the ones on the east, drive through the cane fields to **North Point, Cove Bay,** or **Archer's Bay,** or head down to the beautiful but more perilous one at **Bathsheba.** I could go on and on, but perhaps you'll try them all and then find your own.

BOAT TRIPS Largest of the coastal cruising vessels, the *Bajan Queen* is modeled after a Mississippi riverboat and is the only cruise ship offering table seating and dining on local fare produced fresh from the on-board galley. There is also cover available from too much sun or rain. The *Bajan Queen* becomes a showboat by night, with local bands providing music for dancing under the stars. You are treated to a dinner of roast chicken, barbecued steak, and seasoned flying fish with a buffet of fresh side dishes and salads. Cruises are usually sold out, so you should book early to avoid disappointment. Each cruise costs $105 BDS ($52.50) and includes transportation to and from your hotel. For reservations, contact Jolly Roger Cruises, Shallow Draft, Bridgetown Harbour (☎ **809/436-6424**).

The same company also owns two motorized replicas of pirate frigates, the *Jolly Roger I* and the *Jolly Roger II,* both of which use the skull and crossbones as a decorative motif. One or both of these, depending on demand, departs five mornings a week for daytime snorkeling cruises from 10am to 2pm. Included in the price of $105 BDS ($52.50) is an all-you-can-eat buffet, complimentary drinks, and free use of snorkeling equipment. There's an on-board boutique on both of these boats, and lots of ho-ho-ho-ing. For information, telephone **809/436-6424,** or visit the berth at Bridgetown Harbour.

Limbo Lady Sailing Cruises, 78 Old Chancery Lane, Christ Church (☎ **809/ 420-5418**). Patrick Gonsalves himself skippers his classic 44-foot CSY yacht,

Limbo Lady, and his wife, Yvonne, a singer and guitarist, serenades you on a sunset cruise. Daily lunch cruises are also possible, with a stop for swimming and snorkeling (equipment provided). Both lunch and sunset cruises offer a complimentary open bar and transportation to and from your hotel. Lunch cruises lasting 4¹/₂ hours cost $50, and three-hour sunset cruises, including a glass of champagne, go for $42. Moonlight dinner cruises can also be arranged (call the number above for more information).

CRICKET   First made popular in 1870, this is the national pastime on Barbados. Matches can last from a day for one inning to five days for two innings. The late Sir Frank Worrell became the first nonpolitical national hero after he scored 3,860 runs in 51 tests at an average of 49.48 runs. If you'd like to see a local match, watch for announcements in the newspapers or ask at the Tourist Board.

DEEP-SEA FISHING   The fishing is first-rate in the waters around Barbados, where fishers pursue dolphin, marlin, wahoo, barracuda, and sailfish, to name only the most popular catches. There's also an occasional cobia.

   The Dive Shop, Pebbles Beach, Aquatic Gap, St. Michael (☎ **809/426-9947**), can arrange half-day charters for one to six people (all equipment and drinks included), costing $300 per boat. Under the same arrangement, the whole-day jaunt goes for $600. In other words, no discount.

GOLF   The island's best-maintained and most prestigious links are the 18-hole championship golf course of the **Sandy Lane Hotel,** St. James (☎ **809/ 432-1311**), on the west coast. Greens fees are $85 in winter and $60 in summer for 18 holes, or $55 in winter and $40 in summer for 9 holes.

HORSEBACK RIDING   A different view of Barbados is offered by the **Caribbean International Riding Centre,** c/o the Roachford family, Auburn, St. Joseph's (☎ **809/433-1453**). Maintained by Swedish-born Elizabeth Roachford and her four daughters, it boards nearly 40 horses. Mrs. Roachford or one of her daughters (each of whom was trained in the standards of the Swedish equestrian traditions) offer a variety of trail rides for horse enthusiasts of any level of experience. Their shortest ride provides a 75-minute escorted trek through tropical forests, followed by relaxation over a cool drink in the clubroom. The price, which includes transportation to and from your hotel and a complimentary drink, is $28. Longest of all is a three- to four-hour equestrian tour of the historic Villa Nova Plantation, which includes a tour of the famous Great House and the countryside around it and lunch, all at a cost of $88. Advance reservations are strongly advised.

SNORKELING & SCUBA DIVING   The clear waters off Barbados have a visibility of more than 100 feet most of the year. More than 50 varieties of fish are found on the shallow inside reefs. On night dives, sleeping fish, night anemones, lobsters, moray eels, and octopuses can be seen. On a mile-long coral reef two minutes by boat from **Sandy Beach,** sea fans, corals, gorgonias, and reef fish are plentiful. *J.R.,* a dredge barge sunk as an artificial reef in 1983, is popular with beginners for its coral, fish life, and 20-foot depth. The *Berwyn,* a coral-encrusted tugboat that sank in Carlisle Bay in 1916, attracts photographers because of its variety of reef fish, shallow depth, good light, and visibility.

   The **Asta Reef,** with a drop of 80 feet, has coral, sea fans, and reef fish in abundance. It's the site of a Barbados wreck sunk in 1986 as an artificial reef. **Dottins,** the most beautiful reef on the west coast, stretches 5 miles from Holetown to Bridgetown and has numerous dive sites at an average depth of 40 feet and

Touring the Green Hills

Unless visitors made special efforts to explore the lush interior of this former British colony, most of their time on Barbados might be confined to the island's densely populated coastal plain. Much of Barbados's true beauty can only be appreciated through treks, tours, or hillclimbs through such rarely visited parishes as St. Thomas and St. George (both of which are landlocked) and the Atlantic-coast parishes of St. Andrews and St. John (where the rough surf of the Atlantic usually discourages the embarkation of sailing vessels). Until recently, most visitors were requested to restrict their sightseeing in these relatively undeveloped parishes to the sides of the highways and roads. But a locally owned tour operator, Highland Outdoor Tours, conducts a series of tours across privately owned land. With its verdant, rolling hills and many dramatic rock outcroppings, much of the terrain might remind you of a windswept but balmy version of Scotland.

You'll have the option of conducting your tour on horseback, on foot, or as a passenger in a tractor-drawn jitney. Horseback rides and walking tours last anywhere from two to five hours. As you traverse what used to be some of the most productive sugar plantations in the British Empire, your guide will describe the geology, architecture, and historical references you'll see en route. A wide range of add-ons can be arranged as part of your experience, including barbecued dinners and/or picnic lunches prepared over the open hearth of a historic Bajan home.

All tours depart from the Highland Outdoor Tour Center in the parish of St. Thomas (in north-central Barbados). Transportation to and from your hotel is included in the price of horseback tours (from $50), hiking tours (from $70), and tractor-drawn jitney tours (from $25). For more information, contact **Highland Outdoor Tours,** Canefield, St. Thomas Parish, Barbados, W.I. (☎ **809/438-8069**).

---

dropoffs of 100 feet. The S.S. *Stavronika*, a Greek freighter, is a popular dive site for advanced divers. Crippled by fire in 1976, the 360-foot freighter was sunk a quarter mile off the west coast to become an artificial reef in **Folkestone Underwater Park.** The mast is at 40 feet, the deck at 80 feet, and the keel at 140 feet. It's encrusted with coral.

The Dive Shop, Pebbles Beach, Aquatic Gap, St. Michael (☎ **809/426-9947**), offers some of the best scuba diving on Barbados (charging $40 per one-tank dive or $55 for a two-tank dive). Every day, two dive trips go out to the nearby reefs and wrecks. In addition, snorkeling trips and equipment rentals are possible. Visitors with reasonable swimming skills who have never dived before can sign up for a resort course. Priced at $50, it includes pool training, safety instructions, and a one-tank open-water dive. The establishment is NAUI and PADI certified. It's open daily from 9am to 5pm.

TENNIS   Most major hotels have their own tennis courts, some of which are lit for night games. Generally, if you're not a guest the hotels charge $16 to $20 BDS ($8 to $10) per hour of court time.

WINDSURFING   Experts say that the windsurfing off Barbados is as good as any this side of Hawaii. Judging from the crowds of 20- to 35-year-olds who flock here, it's probably true. Windsurfing on Barbados has turned into a very big business between November and April. Thousands of windsurfers from all over the world now come here from as far away as Finland, Argentina, and Japan. The shifting of the trade winds between November and May and the shallow offshore reef off Silver Sands create unique conditions of wind and wave swells. This allows windsurfers to reach speeds of up to 50 knots and do complete loops off the waves. **Silver Sands** is rated the best spot in the Caribbean for advanced windsurfing (skill rating five to six). In other words, one needs the skills similar to a professional downhill skier to master these conditions.

An establishment set up especially to handle the demand is the **Barbados Windsurfing Club,** Silver Sands Hotel, Christ Church (☎ **809/428-6001**). It rents boards and gives lessons. Club Mistral, a company run by Mistral A.G. of Germany, manufacturer of fine windsurfing boards, provides the rental fleet for the Barbados facility. Board rentals cost $20 per hour, or $40 for a half day.

5 Shopping

Barbados merchants can sometimes treat you to duty-free merchandise at prices 20% to 40% lower than in the United States and Canada. Duty-free shops have two prices listed on items of merchandise, the local retail price and the local retail price less the government-imposed tax.

Some of the best duty-free buys include cameras (Leica, Rolex, and Fuji), watches (Omega, Piaget, Seiko), crystal (Waterford and Lalique), gold (especially jewelry), bone china (Wedgwood and Royal Doulton), cosmetics and perfumes, and liquor (including Barbados rum and liqueurs), along with tobacco products and cashmere sweaters, tweeds, and sportswear from Britain.

If you purchase items made on the island of Barbados, you don't have to pay duty if you're a citizen.

The outstanding item in Barbados handcrafts is black-coral jewelry. Clay pottery is another Bajan craft. I recommend a visit to Chalky Mount Potteries, where this special craft originated. Potters turn out different products, some based on designs centuries old. In the shops, you'll also find a selection of locally made vases, pots, pottery mugs, glazed plates, and ornaments.

From local grasses and dried flowers, wall hangings are made, and island craftspeople also turn out straw mats, baskets, and bags with raffia embroidery. Still in its infant stage, leatherwork is also found now on Barbados, particularly handbags, belts, and sandals.

Cruise passengers generally head for the previously mentioned **Shopping Terminal** at Bridgetown Harbour, with some 20 duty-free shops, 13 local and regional merchandise shops, and several vendors.

Shopping hours, in general, are 8am to 4pm Monday through Friday and 8am to noon on Saturday.

Best of Barbados

In the Southern Palms, St. Lawrence Gap, Christ Church. ☎ **809/428-7171.**

Part of an islandwide chain of seven stores, Best of Barbados sells only products designed and/or made on Barbados. It was established in 1975 by an English-born painter, Jill Walker, whose prints are bestsellers, and her husband, Jimmy. They sell articles celebrating aspects of island life, including coasters, mats, T-shirts, pottery, dolls and games, and cookbooks, among other items. This tasteful shop is in a pink-and-white building around the corner from the entrance to Southern Palms.

Cave Shepherd
Broad St., Bridgetown. ☎ **809/431-2121.**

The best place to shop for duty-free merchandise on Barbados is Cave Shepherd, which has branches at Sunset Crest in Holetown, Speightstown, Grantley Adams International Airport, and the Bridgetown Harbour. Cave Shepherd is the largest department store on Barbados and one of the most modern in the Caribbean. It was established in 1906, when the Cave family were the sole owners, but after a disastrous fire in 1969, it was rebuilt with the financial assistance of more than 2,000 Barbadians and went public. The store offers perfumes, cosmetics from the world's leading houses, fine full lead crystal and English bone china, sweaters, cameras, gold and silver jewelry, swimwear, leather goods, and batik, handcrafts, and souvenirs. More than 70 brands of liqueurs are sold as well as other spirits. After you finish shopping, relax on the top floor in the cool comfort of the Ideal Restaurant. Cave Shepherd has another restaurant, the Balcony, overlooking the street.

Cotton Days
Bay St., St. Michael. ☎ **809/427-7191.**

Boutiques abound on Barbados, and Cotton Days is one of the the best known and most stylish. It inventories a wide array of casually elegant one-of-a-kind garments suitable for cool nights and hot climates. For inspiration, the in-house designers turn to the flora and fauna of the island and the underwater world. The sales staff is skilled at selecting whimsical accessories to accompany the dresses, blouses, and shifts sold here. Magazines such as *Vogue* and *Glamour* have praised this establishment's collections.

Da Costas Louis Bayley Shops
In the Da Costas Mall, Broad St., Bridgetown. ☎ **809/431-0029.**

At this outlet you'll find a wide selection of fragrances and cosmetics from such famous houses as Giorgio, Chanel, Guerlain, Yves St. Laurent, La Prairie, and more. Fine china and crystal from European manufacturers such as Lladró are also sold, as is an array of goodies from Waterford, Lalique, Swarovski, Baccarat, and others. The shop also specializes in watches and jewelry, offering a wide range of 14- and 18-karat-gold jewelry, with both precious and semiprecious stones. Watches include Rolex, Swatch, Omega, Raymond Weil, Tag Heuer, Ebel, and others. The store also stocks the distinctive Mont Blanc pens.

Earthworks Pottery / The Potter's House Gallery
Edgehill Heights 2, St. Thomas Parish. ☎ **809/425-0223.**

Some serious shoppers consider this one of the artistic highlights of Barbados. Deep in the island's central highlands, its modern building was erected in the 1970s by American-born Goldie Spieler. Trained as an art teacher and ceramic artist, Ms. Spieler and her son, David, create whimsical plates, cups, saucers, and serving vessels whose blue and green colors emulate the color of the Bajan sea and sky. (Some of their fans claim that a breakfast of corn flakes in a cerulean-blue porringer on a snowy Stateside morning re-creates the warmth of a Caribbean holiday.) Many objects are decorated with the Antillean-inspired swirls and zigzags, and can be shipped virtually anywhere. On the premises is the studio where the objects are crafted, and a showroom that sells the output of at least half a dozen other island potters. (These include works by local ceramic artists Maggie Bell, Bill Grace, Susan Beale, and a community of Bajan artists known as the Chalky Mount Cooperative.) Prices per piece range from $3 to $400.

The Great House Gallery
At the Bagatelle Restaurant, Hwy. 2A, St. Thomas. ☎ **809/421-6767.**

On the airy upper floor of one of the most historic Great Houses on Barbados, this art gallery combines an inventory of artworks with West Indian graciousness. Displayed on high white walls amid the reflected glow of an antique mahogany floor, the gallery maintains the same hours as the restaurant downstairs (see "Where to Dine," earlier in this chapter), adding a cultivated gloss to the rituals of dining and drinking. Established by Richard and Valerie Richings, the gallery sells oils and watercolors by Caribbean, South American, and British artists priced at $20 to $2,000. Among them are included the award-winning works of the owners themselves.

Harrison's
1 Broad St., Bridgetown, ☎ **809/431-5500.**

In addition to this main shop, Harrison's has 14 branch stores, all selling a wide variety of duty-free merchandise, including china, crystal, jewelry, leather goods, sweaters, and perfumes—all at fair prices. They've been in business since the 19th century.

Mall 34
Broad St. ☎ **809/429-9235.**

One of Bridgetown's most modern shopping complex offers duty-free shopping in air-conditioned comfort. You can find watches, clocks, china, jewelry, crystal, linens, sweaters, and liquor, together with souvenir items and tropical fashions. A restaurant is on the top floor of the building and there's a little café downstairs.

Pelican Village
Princess Alice Hwy., Bridgetown. ☎ **809/426-1966.**

While in Bridgetown, go down to the Pelican Village on Princess Alice Highway leading down to the city's Deep Water Harbour. A collection of island-made crafts and souvenirs is sold here in a tiny colony of thatch-roofed shops, and you can wander from one to the other. Sometimes you can see craftspeople at work. Some of the shops to be found here are gimmicky and repetitive, although interesting items can be found.

Walker's Caribbean World
St. Lawrence Gap. ☎ **809/428-1183.**

Close to the Southern Palms, it also offers many locally made items for sale, as well as handcrafts from the Caribbean Basin. Here you can buy the famous Jill Walker prints. If you purchase items made on the island of Barbados, you don't have to pay U.S. Customs duties if you're a citizen of the United States.

6 Barbados After Dark

Most of the big resort hotels feature entertainment nightly, often dancing to steel bands and occasional Bajan floor shows. Sometimes beach barbecues are staged.

For the most authentic Bajan evening possible, head for **Baxters Road** in Bridgetown, a street that reaches its peak of liveliness on Friday and Saturday after 11pm. In fact, if you stick around until dawn, the joints are still jumping. The street is safer than it looks, because Bajans come here to have fun, not to make trouble. Entertainment tends to be spontaneous. Some old-time visitors have compared Baxters Road to the backstreets of New Orleans in the 1930s. If you fall in love with the place, you can "caf crawl" up and down the street, where nearly every bar is run by a Bajan mama. Each place has its own atmosphere.

The most popular "caf" on Baxters Road is **Enid's** (she has a phone, "but it doesn't work"), a little ramshackle establishment where Bajans come to devour fried chicken at 3 in the morning. Her place is open daily from 8:30pm to 8:30am, when the last satisfied customer departs into the blazing morning sun and Enid heads home to get some sleep before the new night begins. You can also stop in for a Banks beer.

Beach Club

Sunset Crest, St. James. ☎ **809/432-1309.** Admission free Sun–Fri; free Sat for diners, $5 for nondiners. Open daily from 11am to 2am.

This bar and restaurant serves as a social focal point for Sunset Crest, with many island residents happily hobnobbing with their friends and colleagues. Happy hour at the Beach Bar is from 5 to 6pm nightly, when drinks are half price. Fish fries, barbecues, or buffets are offered from 7 to 10pm daily, priced from $10 to $17.50. There's live entertainment every night, including bands and amateur talent shows. Sunday night is show night, when the entertainment is bigger and more theatrical than usual.

Club Xanadu

In the Ocean View, Hastings, Christ Church. ☎ **809/427-7821.** Admission $42.50 for dinner and the show, $12.50 for the show only. The dinner buffet is at 7pm, the show at 9pm.

In this previously recommended small hotel, musical revues are presented, written, and choreographed by an American, David McCarthy. Call to inquire about the shows, as they are different every year. One successful one was called *Shout*, based on a high school setting in the 1950s. It's open on Thursday, Friday, and Saturday only.

Coach House

Paynes Bay, St. James. ☎ **809/432-1163.** Cover charge of $4.50 (although as soon as you pay it, you'll be given coupons worth $3 for drinks at the bar). Open daily from noon to 2am.

The Coach House, named after a pair of antique coaches that sometimes stand outside, is a green-and-white house said to be 200 years old. The atmosphere is a Bajan version of an English pub, with an outdoor garden bar. Businesspeople and habitués of nearby beaches come here to order buffet lunches, where Bajan food is served Sunday through Friday from noon to 3pm. The price is $10.50 for an all-you-can-eat lunchtime assortment that includes local vegetables and salads prepared fresh daily. If you visit from 6 to 10:30pm, you can order bar meals, including flying-fish burgers, priced at $8 and up. Live music is presented most nights, featuring everything from steel bands to jazz, pop, and rock. The pub is on the main Bridgetown–Holetown road, just south of Sandy Lane, about 6 miles north of Bridgetown. Live music and an attentive crowd assemble together here nightly from 9pm to closing.

Harbour Lights

Marine's Villa, Upper Bay St., Bridgetown. ☎ **809/436-7225.** Admission $6–$9, depending on the performers. Open every night from 9:30pm to 4:30am, with live music Friday through Monday.

This is probably the most popular weekend venue for dancing, drinking, flirting, and "jiving to the music" on all of Barbados. In a modern seafront building whose oceanfront patio allows dancers the chance to cool off, the place plays reggae, soca, and just about anything else that happens to be popular in the Caribbean at the time. No one under 18 is admitted. Grilled meats and hamburgers are available from a barbecue pit/kiosk on the premises. Drinks begin at $1.75. The location is beside the seacoast, about a mile southeast of Bridgetown.

John Moore Bar

On the waterfront, Weston, St. James Parish. ☎ **809/422-2258.** Open daily from 9am until the last patron leaves.

Some visitors consider this the most atmospheric and least pretentious bar on Barbados. Established in 1958 in what had been a storefront, it was rebuilt in 1970 about 100 yards northwest of the town's only fire station. Although its namesake (John Moore) died in 1987, the place is owned and managed by Mr. Lamont (Breedy) Addison, whose tenure here began as a teenager, working as an employee of Mr. Moore almost since the bar's original opening. If you think this bar functions only as a watering hole, think again: It's probably the most influential nerve center in this waterfront town, filled throughout the day and evening with the widest and most congenial group of residents in the neighborhood. Most visitors opt for a rum punch or beer, but if you're hungry, platters of local fish can be prepared, after a moderate delay, for between $5 and $7 each. Beer costs $1.50 BDS (75¢); rum punch, around $3 BDS ($1.50).

✪ Plantation Restaurant and Garden Theatre

Main Rd. (Hwy. 7), St. Lawrence, Christ Church. ☎ **809/428-5048.** Admission (including unlimited drinks) $50 for dinner and the show, $25 for the show only.

This is the island's most visible showcase for evening dinner theater and Caribbean cabaret. Dinner and a show are presented every Wednesday, Thursday, Friday, and Saturday. Dinner is served at 6:30pm, and one of two different shows (either *Barbados by Night* or the *Plantation Tropical Spectacular II*) is presented at 8:15pm. Both involve plenty of exotic costumes and lots of reggae, calypso, limbo, and Caribbean exoticism. Reservations in advance are recommended.

The Ship Inn

St. Lawrence Gap, Christ Church. ☎ **809/435-6961.** Cover $4.50 after 8:30pm. Admission daily from noon to 2am.

Previously recommended as a drinking and dining venue (see "Where to Dine," earlier in this chapter), this inn is now among the leading dining and entertainment centers on the south coast. The pub is the "hot spot." Top local bands perform every night of the week, and patrons gather to listen to live reggae, calypso, and Top-40 music. The entrance fee (see below) to the Ship Inn complex is redeemable in food or drink at any of the other bars or restaurants in the complex. That means that guests are actually only paying $1.50 for the live entertainment.

Trouble in Paradise

In the Barbados Museum, St. Ann's Garrison, St. Michael. ☎ **809/420-3409.** Admission $40 for the show, drinks, and transport; $20 for the show and drinks only.

At this previously recommended museum, a theatrical presentation combines intrigue and mystery in a show presented every Thursday night at 7pm. The museum that contains all this (and whose exhibits you are invited to inspect) was originally built as a British military garrison and lies close to the island's largest horseracing track, the Garrison Savannah. Advance reservations are necessary.

Waterfront Café

Cavan's Lane, The Careenage, Bridgetown. ☎ **809/427-0093.** No cover. Bar service from 10am to midnight.

By anyone's estimate, this is the busiest, most interesting, and most animated nighttime watering hole in Bridgetown. In a turn-of-the-century warehouse originally built to store bananas and freeze fish, it welcomes both diners and drinkers to its reverberating walls for Créole food, beer, and pastel-colored drinks. Live music (reggae, ragtime, rock 'n' roll, or jazz) is presented Monday through Saturday from 8 to 11:30pm. Hamburgers cost $8, full Créole meals average $22.50, and rum punch goes for $3.25. Careenage Coffee, laced with various after-dinner potions, is an enduring favorite. Food is served Monday through Saturday from noon to midnight.

Trinidad & Tobago

Chartered by Columbus on his third voyage in 1498, Trinidad has been peopled by immigrants from almost every corner of the world—Africa, the Middle East, Europe, India, China, and the Americas. It is against such a background that the island has become the fascinating mixture of cultures, races, and creeds that it is today.

Trinidad, which is about the size of Delaware, and its neighbor island, tiny Tobago, 20 miles to the northeast, together form a nation popularly known as "T&T." The islands of the new country are the southernmost outposts of the West Indies. Trinidad lies only 7 miles from the Paria Peninsula of Venezuela, to which in prehistoric times it was once connected.

The Spanish settled the island, which the Native Amerindians had called Iere, or "land of the hummingbird." The Spaniards made their first permanent settlement in 1592 and held onto it longer than they did any of their other real estate in the Caribbean. The English captured Trinidad in 1797, and it remained British until the two-island nation declared its independence in 1962. The Republic of Trinidad and Tobago is a parliamentary democracy, with a president and a prime minister.

FAST FACTS: Trinidad & Tobago

Area Code   To call Trinidad or Tobago from the United States, dial area code 809 and then the local number. For information on making local calls on the islands, see "Telecommunications," below.

Banking Hours   Most banks are open Monday through Thursday from 8am to 2pm and on Friday from 9am to noon and 3 to 5pm.

Currency   The **Trinidad and Tobago dollar (TT)** is loosely pegged to the U.S. dollar at an exchange rate of $5.65 TT = $1 U.S. ($1 TT = $17^1/2$¢). Ask what currency is being referred to when rates are quoted. I've used a combination of both in this chapter, depending on the establishment. U.S. and Canadian dollars are accepted in exchange for payment, particularly in Port-of-Spain. However, you'll do better by converting your Canadian or U.S. dollars into local currency. British pounds should be converted into the local currency. Unless otherwise specified, dollar quotations appearing in this chapter are in U.S. currency.

Customs Readers have reported long delays in clearing Customs on Trinidad. Personal effects are duty free, and visitors may bring in 200 cigarettes or 50 cigars plus one quart of "spirits."

Documents Visitors arriving in Trinidad and Tobago should have an on-going or return ticket from their point of embarkation. You'll be asked to fill out an immigration card upon your arrival, and the carbon copy of this should be saved, as it must be returned to immigration officials when you depart. Citizens of the United States, Britain, and Canada need passports to enter Trinidad and Tobago.

Electricity The electricity is 110 or 220 volts A.C., 60 cycles, but ask when making your hotel reservations so you'll know if you'll need transformers and/or adapters.

Embassies and High Commissions In Port-of-Spain on Trinidad, the **U.S. Embassy** is at 19 Queen's Park West (☎ **809/622-6371**); the **Canadian High Commission** is at 72 South Quay (☎ **809/623-7254**); and the **British High Commission** is at 19 St. Clair Ave., St. Clair (☎ **809/622-2748**).

Emergency Call the **police** at **999.** To report a **fire** or summon an **ambulance,** dial **990.**

Holidays These include January 1 (New Year's Day), Good Friday, Easter Monday, June 7 (Whit Monday), June 18 (Corpus Christi), June 19 (Labour Day), August 1 (Emancipation Day), August 31 (Independence Day), September 24 (Republic Day), December 25 (Christmas Day), and December 26 (Boxing Day).

Information Before you go, write or call the **Trinidad & Tobago Tourism Development Authority,** 25 W. 43rd St., Suite 1508, New York, NY 10036 (☎ **212/719-0540**). Locally, contact the board at 10–14 Philip St., Port-of-Spain (☎ **809/623-1932**).

Language English is the official language, although you'll hear it spoken with many different accents, including cultured British. Hindi, Chinese, French, and Spanish are also spoken.

Safety As a general rule, Tobago is safer than its larger neighbor, Trinidad. Crime does exist, but it's not of raging dimensions. If you can, avoid the downtown streets of Port-of-Spain at night, especially those around Independence Square where muggings have been reported. It would also be wise to safeguard your valuables and never leave them unattended at the beach or even in a locked car.

Taxes and Service The big hotels and restaurants add a 10% to 15% service charge to your final tab. In addition, the government imposes a 15% Value-Added Tax (VAT) on room rates. It also imposes a departure tax of $75 TT ($13.30) on every passenger more than five years old.

Telecommunications On the islands, you don't need to dial the 809 area code, just the seven-digit number. Cables and faxes may be handed in at a hotel desk.

Time Trinidad and Tobago time is the same as the U.S. East Coast. But when the States go on daylight saving time, Trinidad and Tobago does not; so when it's 6am in Miami, it's 7am in T&T.

Weather Trinidad has a tropical climate all year, with constant trade winds maintaining mean temperatures of 84° Fahrenheit during the day, 74° at night, with a range of 70° to 90°. The rainy season runs from May to November, but it shouldn't deter a visit at that time; the rain usually lasts no more than two hours before the sun comes out again. However, carry along plenty of insect repellent for visits during those times.

1 Trinidad

Trinidad is completely different from the other islands of the Caribbean, and that forms part of its charm and appeal. Visitors in increasing numbers are drawn to this island of many rhythms, where the swinging sounds of calypso, limbo, and steel-drum bands all began. However, it's not for everyone. Because Port-of-Spain is one of the most bustling commercial centers in the Caribbean, more business travelers than tourists are drawn here. Although the island has beaches, the best of them are far away from the capital.

For those seeking a more Robinson Crusoe beach holiday, Tobago (coming up) would be a more ideal choice. Although Port-of-Spain, with its shopping centers, fast-food joints, modern hotels, and active nightlife, draws mixed reviews from readers, the island itself is lush. Far removed from the traffic jams of the capital, you can explore the lush fauna and flora of the island. It's estimated that there are some 700 varieties of orchids alone, plus 400 species of birds.

The people are part of the attraction on this island, the most cosmopolitan in the Caribbean. Its polyglot population includes Syrians, Chinese, Americans, Europeans, East Indians, Parsees, Madrasis, Venezuelans, and the last of the original Amerindians, the early settlers of the island. You'll also find Hindustanis, Javanese, Lebanese, African descendants, and Créole mixtures. The main religions are Christianity, Hinduism, and Islam. In all there are about 1.2 million inhabitants, whose language is English, although you may hear speech in a strange argot, Trinibagianese.

Port-of-Spain, in the northwestern corner of the island, is the capital, with the largest concentration of the population, about 120,000. With the opening of its $2-million cruise-ship complex in Port-of-Spain, Trinidad now has become a major port of call for Caribbean cruise lines. Many craft shops operate in the complex.

One of the most industrialized nations in the Caribbean, and the third-largest exporter of oil in the western hemisphere, Trinidad, measuring 50 by 38 miles, is also blessed with the huge 114-acre Pitch Lake from which comes most of the world's asphalt. Further, it's also the home of Angostura Bitters, the recipe for which is a guarded secret.

ORIENTATION
GETTING THERE

From North America, Trinidad is one of the most distant islands in the Caribbean. Because of the legendary toughness of Trinidadian Customs, it's preferable to arrive during the day (presumably when your stamina might be at its peak) if you can schedule it.

Trinidad is the transfer point for many passengers heading on to the beaches of Tobago. For information about getting to Tobago, refer to Section 2 of this chapter.

Most passengers from the eastern half of North America opt for transit on **American Airlines** (☎ 800/433-7300), which has connections through New York. American also offers a daily nonstop flight to Trinidad from Miami, which is especially useful for transfers from the Middle West and the West Coast.

From New York, **BWIA** (☎ 800/538-2942) offers between one and four daily flights into Port-of-Spain, depending on the day of the week and the season. Only a handful of these are nonstop; most of them touch down en route, usually in Barbados, Antigua, or Guyana (and sometimes at all three) before continuing without a change of aircraft on to Trinidad, the airline's home base. From Miami, BWIA offers a daily nonstop flight to Port-of-Spain which departs every afternoon at 2:30pm and arrives in Trinidad in the early evening.

Air Canada (☎ 800/363-5440 in Canada, or **800/776-3000** in the U.S.), makes two weekly nonstop flights from Toronto to Port-of-Spain (on Friday and Saturday) plus one additional flight from Toronto that stops in Barbados on its way to Port-of-Spain.

GETTING AROUND

BY BUS   All the cities of Trinidad are linked by regular bus service from Port-of-Spain. Fares are low: from $1 (for runs within the capital). However, the old buses are likely to be very overcrowded. Always try to avoid them at rush hours. Beware of pickpockets.

BY TAXI   There are only unmetered taxis on Trinidad, and they're identified by their license plates, beginning with the letter H. There are also "pirate taxis" as well—private cars that cruise around and pick up passengers like a regular taxi. Maxi Taxis or vans can also be hailed on the street. A taxi ride from Piarco Airport into Port-of-Spain generally costs about $25.

Most drivers also serve as guides. Their rates, however, are based on route distances, so get an overall quotation and agree on the actual fare before setting off. All fares are subject to 50% increases after midnight.

BY RENTAL CAR   There are some 4,500 miles of good roads, but whereas touring outside Port-of-Spain goes quickly, the fierce traffic jams of the capital are legendary. And although your rental car will probably have a right-hand-mounted steering wheel, *you'll be required to drive on the left.* You'll also need a good map.

The major U.S.–based car-rental firms currently have no franchises on the island, so you have to make arrangements with a local firm (go over the terms and insurance agreements carefully). Count on spending about $50 per day or more, with unlimited mileage included. In theory you should have an international driver's license, but a valid U.S., British, or Canadian license will do for stays of up to two months.

One of the island's leading local car-rental firms is **Bacchus Taxi & Car Rental Service,** 37 Tragarete Rd., Port-of-Spain (☎ 809/622-5588). With unlimited mileage, plus all insurance included, a functional but peppy Nissan, Sunny, or Charmant rents for $200 TT ($35.40) per day.

To avoid the anxiety of driving, you can rent taxis and local drivers for your sightseeing jaunts. Although it costs more, it alleviates the hassles of badly marked (or unmarked roads) and contact with the sometimes bizarre local driving patterns; if a rented taxi and driver is too expensive, you can take an organized tour. Night driving is especially hazardous.

Trinidad

BY ORGANIZED TOUR   Sightseeing tours are offered by **The Travel Centre,** Uptown Mall, Edward Street, Port-of-Spain (☎ **809/623-5096**). The tours are made in late-model sedans, with a trained driver-guide. Prices are quoted on a seat-in-car basis. Private arrangements will cost more.

A city tour, lasting two hours and costing $16 per person for three or more, will take you past the main points of interest of Port-of-Spain: Whitehall, the President's House, Queen's Park Savannah, the Botanical Gardens, the National Museum and Art Gallery, the Emperor Valley Zoo, cathedrals, a mosque, temples, and through the commercial and residential centers, then to Lady Young Lookout for a view of the city. This trip leaves daily at 9am, costing $16 per person for three or more.

You'll see tropical splendor at its best on a Port-of-Spain/Maracas Bay/Saddle Road jaunt leaving at 1pm daily, lasting 3¹/₂ hours. The tour begins with a drive around Port-of-Spain, passing the main points of interest listed above and then going on through the mountain scenery over the "Saddle" of the northern range to Maracas Bay, a popular beach. You return via Saddle Road, Santa Cruz Valley, the village of San Juan, and the Lady Young Road for the view of Port-of-Spain.

An Island Circle Tour is a 9- to 10-hour journey that includes lunch and a welcome drink. Leaving at 9am daily, your car goes south along the west coast with a view of the Gulf of Paria, across the central plains, through Pointe-à-Pierre and San Fernando, and on eastward into rolling country overlooking sugarcane fields.

Then you go down into the coconut plantations along the 14-mile-long Mayaro Beach for a swim and lunch before returning along Manzanilla Beach and back to the city. The cost is $55 per person for three or more.

An especially interesting trip is to the Caroni Swamp and Bird Sanctuary, a four-hour trek by car and boat into the sanctuary where you'll see rich Trinidad birdlife. The cost is $30 per person for three or more.

ESSENTIALS

The **Port-of-Spain General Hospital** is on Charlotte Street (☎ **809/623-2951**). The main **post office** is on Wrightson Road, Port-of-Spain, and is open Monday through Friday from 7am to 5pm. You can send a cable or fax at the offices of **Textel,** 1 Edward St., Port-of-Spain.

WHERE TO STAY

The number of hotels is limited, and don't expect your Port-of-Spain room to open directly on a white sandy beach—the nearest beach is a long, costly taxi ride away. Don't forget that 15% tax and 10% service charge will be added to your hotel and restaurant bills. All hotels raise their rates at Carnival.

EXPENSIVE

✪ Trinidad Hilton

Lady Young Rd. (P.O. Box 442), Port-of-Spain, Trinidad, W.I. ☎ **809/624-3211**, or 800/HILTONS in the U.S., 800/268-9275 in Canada. Fax 809/624-4485. 394 rms, 25 suites. A/C TV TEL. $133–$155 single; $156–$175 double; from $275 suite. Breakfast from $11 extra. DC, MC, V. Free parking.

This is the most dramatic and architecturally sophisticated hotel on Trinidad. Because of its position on some of the steepest terrain in Port-of-Spain, the building's lobby lies on its uppermost floor, and the rooms are staggered in rocky but verdant terraces that sweep down the hillside. Its location just above Queen's Park Savannah provides most of its rooms with a view of the sea and mountains.

The hotel offers a wide range of accommodations, from standard rooms through rooms with minibars; the more expensive rooms, on the Executive Floor, have upgraded services and amenities and complimentary continental breakfast. Regardless of their comfort levels, all units have balconies and a comfortably neutral international decor. One of the benefits of a stay here is that some of the most sought-after musical entertainment on Trinidad appears as a standard part of the hotel's many offerings. And for the business traveler, the Hilton is the best choice of the island.

Dining/Entertainment: The main dining room, La Boucan (see "Where to Dine," below), contains museum-quality murals by one of the island's best-known artists (Geoffrey Holder). Less formal are the Pool Terrace and the Gazebo, both of which serve Caribbean and international food and colorful drinks in sun-flooded settings. Live music is played every evening in the Carnival Bar until 1 or 2am. The cover charge is $15 TT ($2.70). The hotel always books plenty of activities, with pool barbecues featuring roast suckling pig, weekly fiestas, sometimes extraordinarily talented steel-band concerts, and limbo concerts. The Lobby Bar offers snacks and beverages from 4pm to 6:30am.

Services: Room service (6am to 11:30pm), concierge, babysitting, travel agency, laundry.

Facilities: Swimming pool with a refreshment bar (the Gazebo), pharmacy, bank, two all-weather tennis courts (lit at night), two-story arcade with boutiques, business center (with 24-hour Telex, fax, and cable facilities; worldwide courier service for documents; and secretarial and translation services).

MODERATE

Trinidad Holiday Inn

Wrightson Rd. at London Rd. (P.O. Box 1017), Port-of-Spain, Trinidad, W.I. ☎ **809/ 624-3366,** or 800/HOLIDAY in the U.S. and Canada. Fax 809/625-4166. 230 rms, 9 suites. A/C TV TEL. $95 single; $105 double; $115 triple; from $185 suite. MAP $25 per person extra. AE, MC, V. Free parking.

Originally built during the 1960s in an international modern style, and proud of its role as the second-largest hotel on Trinidad, the Holiday Inn lies on the northern perimeter of the city's commercial zone, a five-minute walk from the center. The bedrooms have been renovated and contain private balconies along with two double beds. The hotel has added two executive floors and such room amenities as trouser pressers, magnifying mirrors, hairdryers, mahogany furniture, and brass lamps. The rooms have been furnished with a tasteful Caribbean pastel theme.

Carnival & Calypso

Called "the world's most colorful festival," the Carnival of Trinidad is a spectacle of dazzling costumes and gaiety. Hundreds of bands of masqueraders parade through the cities on the Monday and Tuesday preceding Ash Wednesday, bringing traffic to a standstill. The island seems to explode with music, fun, and dancing.

Hotel accommodations are booked months in advance, and most inns raise their prices at the time.

Some of the carnival costumes cost hundreds of dollars. For example, "bands" might depict the birds of Trinidad, such as the scarlet ibis and the keskidee; or a bevy of women might come out in the streets dressed as cats. Costumes are also satirical and comical.

Trinidad, of course, is the land of calypso, which grew out of the folksong of the African–West Indian immigrants. The lyrics command great attention, as they're rich in satire and innuendo. The calypsonian is considered a poet-musician, and lyrics have often been capable of toppling politicians from office. In banter and bravado, the calypsonian gives voice to the sufferings and aspirations of his people. At carnival time the artist sings his compositions to spectators in tents. There is one show a night at each of the calypso tents around town, from 8pm to midnight. Tickets for these are sold in the afternoon at most record shops.

Carnival parties, or fêtes, with three or four orchestras at each one, are public and are advertised in the newspaper. For a really wild time, attend a party on Sunday night before Carnival Monday. To reserve tickets, contact the National Carnival Committee, 82–84 Frederick St., Port-of-Spain, Trinidad (☎ **809/ 623-8867**).

You can attend rehearsals of steel bands at their headquarters, called *panyards*, beginning about 7pm. Preliminary band competitions are held at the grandstand of the Queen's Park Savannah in Port-of-Spain and at Skinner Park in San Fernando, beginning two weeks before Carnival.

Dining/Entertainment: The main dining room, the Olympia Restaurant, is adorned with Roman-style pillars, with plants cascading over the top. It has a definite European aura. In addition, La Ronde Restaurant, with a classical French decor, is the only revolving restaurant in the Caribbean, and serves an international cuisine. A bar just above the lobby offers nightly taped indigenous island music.

Services: Room service, laundry, babysitting.

Facilities: Hair salon, gift shops, full gym, exotic pool with "sunken" bar, a pool for children, business center.

INEXPENSIVE

Asa Wright Nature Centre and Lodge

Spring Hill Estate, Arima, Trinidad, W.I. ☎ **809/667-4655,** or 800/426-7781 in the U.S. Fax 809/667-4655. 23 rms. Winter, $139 single; $210 double. Off-season, $106 single; $160 double. (Rates include all meals, afternoon tea, and a welcoming rum punch.) No credit cards. Free parking.

There really isn't anything else like it in the Caribbean. Known to birdwatchers throughout the world, this center sits on 196 acres of protected land at an elevation of 1,800 feet in the rain-forested northern mountain range of Trinidad, 10 miles north of Arima, beside Blanchisseuse Road. Hummingbirds, toucans, bellbirds, manakins, several varieties of tanagers, and the rare oilbird are all on the property. It's not uncommon for a guest who has not previously visited the South American tropics to record 30 "lifebirds" before breakfast, and this without leaving the veranda of the main house. Accommodations are available in the lodge's self-contained rooms, in guest bedrooms in the Edwardian main house, or in one of the cottages built on elevated ground above the main house; all have private baths.

Guided tours are available on the nature center's grounds, which contain several well-maintained trails. The center also offers guided bird tours to a variety of different wildlife habitats.

For more information or to make reservations, call the above toll-free number or write Caligo Ventures, 156 Bedford Rd., Armonk, NY 10504.

Ⓢ Chaconia Inn

106 Saddle Rd. (P.O. Box 3340), Maraval, Trinidad, W.I. ☎ **809/628-8603**. Fax 809/628-3214. 27 rms, 4 apartments. A/C TV TEL. $65–$75 single; $75–$85 double or twin; $110–$120 two-bedroom apartment. MAP $30 per person extra. AE, DC, MC, V. Free parking.

 Family-Friendly Accommodations

Holiday Inn *(see p. 703)* Trinidad's Port-of-Spain is not the best place for a holiday with the family, but if you're there, the Holiday Inn is a good, clean, safe haven. It has a swimming pool reserved just for children, and kids like to dine in the revolving restaurant overhead.

Blue Waters Inn *(see p. 717)* Tobago's haven for nature-lovers is also a haven for families who can rent self-catering facilities (suitable for two adults and two children). Children also get a 50% reduction on meals.

Richmond Great House *(see p. 719)* Families seeking a bargain gravitate to this former 18th-century Great House set on a cocoa- and coconut-growing plantation on Tobago. The grounds have a pool and a barbecue.

Named for the country's scarlet national flower, the Chaconia is a miniature self-contained resort 3 miles north of Port-of-Spain in the cool mountain residential valley of Maraval. Its buildings are simple, and its furnishings are in a contemporary motel idiom. You'll be housed in one of three different types of accommodations, including two-bedroom apartments, superior rooms, and standard rooms. All are equipped with private baths and radios, and the superior rooms and apartments also have kitchenette facilities. The hotel restaurant (referred to as the Lounge) is recommended separately (see "Where to Dine," below).

⑤ Kapok Hotel and Restaurant

16–18 Cotton Hill, St. Clair, Trinidad, W.I. ☎ **809/622-6441.** Fax 809/622-9677. 65 rms, 6 suites. A/C TV TEL. $69 single; $82 double; from $135 suite. Continental breakfast from $4 extra. AE, DC, MC, V. Free parking.

The Kapok is a modern nine-floor hotel located in the pleasant residential suburb of St. Clair, a minute's drive from the city's biggest park, the Savannah. From its lounge, you have a panoramic view not only of the Savannah, but also of the Gulf of Paria. Guests who prefer small to medium-size hotels feel at home here, and appreciate the slick neatness, the comfortably appointed bedrooms, and the rooftop restaurant serving Chinese and Polynesian food. On the ground floor of the hotel is the Café Savanna, one of the better-known restaurants of Trinidad. In the back is an expanded pool area with a waterfall, garden, menagerie, and sun deck. The well-furnished, spacious rooms have private baths and are decorated with wicker furniture.

The Normandie Hotel and Restaurant

10 Nook Ave., St. Ann's (P.O. Box 851), Port-of-Spain, Trinidad, W.I. ☎ **809/624-1181.** Fax 809/624-1181. 53 units. A/C TV TEL. $77.15–$96.15 single; $89.80–$108.80 double; $108.80 loft studio for one; $121.45 loft studio for two; $134.10 loft studio for three. Breakfast $3–$5 extra. AE, DC, MC, V. Free parking.

Originally built in the 1920s by two French brothers, this was already a well-established hotel when its owners modernized it in 1986. It rises around a banyan- and banana-filled courtyard that surrounds a swimming pool accented with a jet of water. Inside, each room has a balcony or patio, and the beds in some rooms are set onto minilofts arranged in a small-scale but serviceable duplex format. The cheaper rooms here have drawn fire from readers, especially the noisy air conditioning.

Calm and cosmopolitan, the hotel sits $3^1/_2$ miles northwest of the city center, next to one of the best art galleries on Trinidad, a skylight-covered shopping center, an attractive restaurant (La Fantasie), the botanical gardens of Port-of-Spain, and the official residence of the prime minister of Trinidad and Tobago.

Valley Vue Hotel

Ariapita Rd., St. Ann's, Trinidad, W.I. ☎ **809/624-0940.** Fax 809/627-8046. 56 rms, 12 suites. A/C MINIBAR TV TEL. $70–$90 single; $80–$100 double; $100–$120 suite for two. Full breakfast $7 extra. AE, DC, MC, V. Free parking.

Originally built in 1986, this modern hotel about 5 miles northwest of the center of Port-of-Spain maintains a vaguely English kind of decor, lots of wicker furniture, and occasional use of marble in its floors and walls. Each of the pleasant bedrooms contains two telephones, a balcony, and comfortably unpretentious furniture. Because of the view, deluxe doubles cost as much as suites. On the premises is an oval swimming pool with a "swim-through" bar and a water slide, two squash courts, gym, and an airy restaurant serving an American-Créole cuisine. It's open daily from 7am to 11pm.

WHERE TO DINE

The food probably should be better than it is, considering all the different culinary backgrounds that shaped the island, including West Indian, Chinese, French, and Indian.

Stick to local specials such as stuffed crabs or chip-chip (tiny clamlike shellfish), but skip the armadillo or opossum stewpots. Spicy Indian rôtis filled with vegetables or ground meat seem to be everyone's favorite lunch, and everyone's favorite drink is a fresh rum punch flavored with the home-produced Angostura bitters. Except for a few fancy places, dress tends to be very casual.

MODERATE

✪ Café Savanna

In the Kapok Hotel, 16–18 Cotton Hill, St. Clair. ☎ **809/622-6441.** Reservations recommended. Appetizers $8.50–$23 TT ($1.50–$4.10); main courses $38–$98 TT ($6.70–$17.30). AE, DC, MC, V. Mon–Fri 11:45am–10pm, Sat 6:45–10:30pm. CARIBBEAN.

On the ground floor of a previously recommended hotel, a minute's drive from the Savannah, Café Savanna serves an excellent Caribbean cuisine that's known throughout the island. The specialties change seasonally, but sizzling steaks are always offered and lobster is often available. Begin perhaps with a pâté Café Savanna, which is chicken-liver pâté with rum served on toast with a boat of pepper jelly. Or try "Tassa Fever," boned chicken simmered in a tasty curry with local spices. "Woman Soca" is a medley of shrimp, lobster, and fish simmered with tomatoes, mushrooms, paprika, and cream; and "Mille Fleurs" is filet of fish marinated in fresh herbs and folded into a banana leaf. Meat and poultry selections might include grilled medallions of pork stuffed with a medley of vegetables and served with a mustard sauce, or skewered chicken marinated in olive oil, tequila, and garlic, then grilled. The café is known for its locally homemade ice creams, in such flavors as coconut, passionfruit, soursop, piña colada, and mocha. The warmly accented haven of the dining room is embellished with slabs of opaque glass. Also in the same hotel is the popular Tiki Village Restaurant, which serves Chinese and Polynesian food (see below).

✪ La Boucan

In the Trinidad Hilton, Lady Young Rd. ☎ **809/624-3211.** Reservations required. Appetizers $21–$30 TT ($3.70–$5.30); main courses $59–$125 TT ($10.40–$22.10); lunch buffet $66 TT ($11.70). AE, DC, MC, V. Lunch Mon–Sat noon–2:30pm; dinner Mon–Sat 7–11:30pm. INTERNATIONAL.

Considered the finest restaurant on Trinidad, with some of the most sumptuous buffets, this establishment satisfies the eye as well as the palate. Against one of its longest walls stretches a graceful, museum-quality mural by Geoffrey Holder, one of the most famous artists of the Caribbean. (Born on Trinidad, although living in New York most of his life, he painted this mural to honor the social gatherings that used to take place in Port-of-Spain's central park, the Savannah. Today, it's considered one of the island's most famous works of art.)

Typical dishes include sirloin or tenderloin steaks; a daily selection of fish (usually grouper or snapper), which is grilled, poached, or pan-fried according to your wishes and served with herb-butter sauce; pasta primavera with pesto sauce; at least four kinds of local curries (including lamb, chicken, fish, or shrimp); Créole-style shrimp; and chateaubriand for two. Desserts are sumptuous. Live music from a lacquered piano (and on weekends from a dance band) provides entertainment.

La Fantasie

In the Normandie Hotel and Restaurant, 10 Nook Ave., St. Ann's Village. ☎ **809/624-1181,** ext. 2306. Reservations recommended. Appetizers $10–$25 TT ($1.80–$4.40); main courses $40–$100 TT ($7.10–$17.70). AE, DC, MC, V. Lunch daily noon–2pm; dinner daily 6–10pm. FRENCH/CREOLE.

Off Queen's Park Savannah, and named after the 18th-century plantation that once stood here, La Fantasie is loaded with style and features a tempting modern Créole cuisine. The changing menu might include filet mignon with a tamarind-flavored sauce, chicken curry, locally caught Trinidadian salmon in a wine-based sauce with sultana raisins and bananas, and shrimp with Créole sauce in a pastry shell flavored with cheese. "Fish walk up the hill" is grilled fish with chopped herbs. Meals might follow with a Trinidadian fruitcake with a rum-flavored custard.

The Lounge

In the Chaconia Inn, 106 Saddle Rd., Maraval. ☎ **809/628-8603.** Reservations recommended. Appetizers $12–$26 TT ($2.10–$4.60); main courses $45–$100 TT ($8–$17.70). AE, DC, MC, V. Lunch daily 11am–2pm; dinner daily 7–11pm. INTERNATIONAL.

On the street level of the previously recommended hotel, this conservatively decorated, modern dining room offers international cuisine to a busy crowd of lunch and dinnertime clients, most of whom appreciate its straightforward, uncomplicated cuisine. Menu items include several different preparations of fish, steak, shrimp, pork, and pasta dishes, as well as salads and a small choice of vegetarian dishes. On Saturday night the establishment's facilities are supplemented with those of the Roof Garden Restaurant, on the hotel's uppermost floor, where barbecued meals are featured once a week.

⑤ Rafters

6A Warner St., Newtown. ☎ **809/628-9258.** Reservations required. Appetizers $25–$35 TT ($4.40–$6.20); main courses $35–$125 TT ($6.20–$22.10); buffets from $85 TT ($15). AE, DC, MC, V. Mon–Thurs 11:30am–midnight, Fri 11am–3am, Sat 7pm–3am. SEAFOOD.

Rafters is housed in a century-old grocery shop in the central business district of a suburb of Port-of-Spain, a short walk off the Savannah. Four nights a week there are buffets, and you can also order from an à la carte menu devoted mainly to local seafood items. Buffets begin at 7:30pm. On Wednesday there's a seafood buffet, and on Thursday, Friday, and Saturday there are carvery buffets. On the regular menu, house specialties include seafood Créole, filet Oscar (the day's fresh catch broiled in lemon butter and topped with a seasoned crabmeat). You can also order boneless breast of chicken wrapped around a cheese-and-vegetable stuffing, then oven-baked and served under a blanket of spicy Créole sauce. In the lounge, a snack-and-sandwich menu is offered daily, attracting clients of all ages and occupations. Busy crowds congregate on Friday and Saturday nights to listen to the sounds of the DJ or live local bands. Entrance is free, except during live performances when a $10-TT ($1.80) cover charge is levied.

✪ Solimar

6 Nook Ave., St. Ann's. ☎ **809/624-6267.** Reservations recommended. Appetizers $9–$39 TT ($1.60–$6.90); main courses $51–$145 TT ($9–$25.70). AE, MC, V. Dinner only, Mon–Sat 6:30–10:30pm. (Bar, Mon–Sat 5–10:30pm.) Closed one week in mid-May, two weeks in mid-Aug (exact dates vary). INTERNATIONAL.

By some estimates, this restaurant offers the most creative cuisine and most original format in Trinidad and Tobago. Established by an English-born chef (Joe Brown) who worked for many years in the kitchens of Hilton hotels around the world, it occupies a garden-style building whose open walls are cooled by ceiling fans. As you dine, you'll hear the sound of an artificial waterfall which cascades into a series of fish ponds. The restaurant is opposite the Normandie Hotel and Restaurant, 3½ miles northwest of the city center.

The menu, which changes every six weeks, presents local ingredients inspired by the cuisines of the world. Dishes might include a Singapore-derived specialty of beef serondeng (cooked with tamarind, cilantro, and coconut), an English-inspired combination of grilled breast of chicken and jumbo shrimp dressed with a lobster sauce, and a Sri Lankan dish of herb-flavored chicken vindaloo. Choice aged U.S. meats such as rib eye are grilled.

Tiki Village

In the Kapok Hotel, 16–18 Cotton Hill, St. Clair. ☎ **809/622-6441.** Reservations recommended, especially for dinner. Appetizers $5–$15 TT (90¢–$2.70); main courses $35–$82 TT ($6.20–$14.50). AE, DC, MC, V. Lunch daily 11:30am–7pm; dinner daily at 7:30 and 9pm. POLYNESIAN/CHINESE.

The Tiki Village, named after and inspired by a South Seas theme, perches on the top floor of a previously recommended hotel and has a panoramic view of the nearby Queen's Park Savannah. Decorated in a medley of sunset colors, the restaurant prides itself on an assortment of hors d'oeuvres (which arrives flaming at your table) known as a Polynesian delight. The eggroll is among the best I've ever ordered in the West Indies. Among the main courses, I'd recommend the Hawaiian luau fish—a whole fish coated with water-chestnut flour and fried crisply before it's engulfed in a sweet-and-pungent sauce. Chicken provincial is boneless cubes sautéed in a black-bean sauce. Desserts include a Polynesian cheesecake, followed by Chinese tea. Especially charming is the assortment of dim sum (delicately fashioned Chinese versions of ravioli), which appear on the lunchtime menu only on Saturday and Sunday.

INEXPENSIVE

Restaurant Singho

Long Circular Mall, Port-of-Spain. ☎ **809/628-2077.** Reservations not required. Appetizers $3–$30 TT (50¢–$5.30); main courses $30–$200 TT ($5.30–$35.40). AE, DC, MC, V. Daily 11am–11pm. CHINESE.

Lined with planks of cedar, this restaurant contains an almost mystically illuminated bar and aquarium. The restaurant is on the second floor of one of the capital's largest shopping malls, midway between the commercial center of Port-of-Spain and the Queen's Park Savannah. A la carte dishes include shrimp with oyster sauce, shark-fin soup, stewed or curried beef, almond pork, and spareribs with black-bean sauce. A large percentage of this establishment's business derives from its take-away service, which is one of the best known in town.

✪ Veni Mangé

13 Lucknow St. ☎ **809/622-7533.** Reservations recommended for lunch groups over six and always for Wednesday-night dinners. Appetizers $6–$12 TT ($1.10–$2.10); main courses $22–$38 TT ($3.90–$6.70). AE, MC, V. Lunch Mon–Fri 11:30am–2:30pm, dinner Wed 7:30–10pm. CREOLE.

Built in the 1950s of ocher stucco, Veni Mangé (which translates from the Créole argot as "come and eat") lies on a tranquil residential street right off Western Main Road, 3 miles west of the city center, on the opposite edge of the Savannah from the Hilton Hotel. If you can find this tiny home, you'll get a warm welcome from

Allyson Hennessy and her sister, Rosemary Hezekiah. (Allyson hosts a daily television talk show that's broadcast throughout Trinidad.) Best described as a new generation of Créole women, both Allyson and Rosemary (whose parents were English/Venezuelan and African-Caribbean/Chinese) entertain with their humor and charm.

Start with the bartender's special, a coral-colored fruit punch, which is a rich, luscious mixture of the golden papaya and a banana whose skin is allowed to turn black so that its taste is most flavorsome. On some days they do an authentic callaloo soup, which, according to Trinidadian legend, can make a man propose marriage. Save room for one of the main courses, such as curried crab or West Indian hotpot (a variety of meat cooked Créole style), perhaps a vegetable lentil loaf. The helpings are large, and if you still have room, order their pineapple upside-down cake, unless you prefer a homemade version of soursop ice cream or a coconut mousse.

Dinner—a "Caribbean Night"—is only served on Wednesday nights ($12 per person). On Friday the place stays open until 10pm as a bar and rendezvous point.

WHAT TO SEE & DO
IN PORT-OF-SPAIN

One of the busiest harbors in the Caribbean, Trinidad's capital, Port-of-Spain, can be explored on foot. Most tours begin at ✪ **Queen's Park Savannah,** on the northern edge of the city. Called "The Savannah," it consists of 199 acres, complete with a race course, cricket fields, and vendors hawking coconut water. What is now the park was once a sugar plantation until it was swept by a fire in 1808 that destroyed hundreds of homes.

Among the Savannah's outstanding buildings is the pink-and-blue **Queen's Royal College,** containing a clock tower with Westminster chimes. Today a school for boys, it stands on Maraval Road at the corner of St. Clair Avenue. On the same road, the family home of the Roodal clan is affectionately called **"the gingerbread house"** by Trinidadians. It was built in the baroque style of the French Second Empire.

In contrast, the family residence of the Strollmeyers was built in 1905 and is a copy of a German Rhenish castle. Nearby stands **Whitehall,** which was once a private mansion but today has been turned into the office of the prime minister of Trinidad and Tobago. In the Moorish style, it was erected in 1905 and served as the U.S. Army headquarters in World War II. These houses, including Hayes Court, the residence of the Anglican bishop of Trinidad, and others form what is known as **"the magnificent seven"** big mansions standing in a row.

On the south side of the Memorial Park, a short distance from the Savannah and within walking distance of the major hotels, stands the **National Museum and Art Gallery,** 117 Frederick St. (☎ **809/623-5941**), open Tuesday through Saturday from 10am to 6pm. The museum contains a representative exhibition of Trinidad artists, including an entire gallery devoted to Michel Jean Cazabon (1813–88), permanent collections of historical artifacts giving a general overview of the island's history and culture, Amerindian archeology, British historical documents, and a small natural-history exhibition including geology, corals, and insect collections.

At the southern end of Frederick Street, the main artery of Port-of-Spain's shopping district, stands **Woodford Square.** The gaudy **Red House,** a large neo-Renaissance building built in 1906, is the seat of the government of Trinidad and Tobago. Nearby stands **Holy Trinity Cathedral,** whose gothic look may remind you of the churches of England. Inside, look for the marble monument to Sir Ralph Woodford made by the sculptor of Chantry.

Another of the town's important landmarks is **Independence Square,** dating from Spanish days. Now mainly a parking lot, it stretches across the southern part of the capital from the **Cathedral of the Immaculate Conception** to Wrightson Road. The Roman Catholic church was built in 1815 in the neo-gothic style and consecrated in 1832.

The cathedral has an outlet that leads to the **Central Market,** on Beetham Highway on the outskirts of Port-of-Spain. Here you can see all the spices and fruits for which Trinidad is known. It's one of the island's most colorful sights, made all the more so by the wide diversity of people who sell their wares here.

At the north of the Savannah, the **Royal Botanical Gardens** (☎ 809/ 622-1221) cover 70 acres and is open daily from 6am to 6pm. Once part of a sugar plantation, the park is filled with flowering plants, shrubs, and rare and beautiful trees, including an orchid house. Seek out also the raw beef tree—an incision made in its bark is said to resemble rare, bleeding roast beef. Licensed guides will take you through and explain the luxuriant foliage to you. In the garden is the **President's House,** official residence of the president of Trinidad and Tobago. Victorian in style, it was built in 1875. Part of the gardens is the **Emperor Valley Zoo,** Royal Botanical Gardens (☎ 809/622-3530), in St. Clair, which shows a good selection of the fauna of Trinidad as well as some of the usual exotic animals from around the world. The star attractions are a family of mandrills, a reptile house, and open bird parks. You can take shady jungle walks through tropical vegetation. Adults pay $4 TT (70¢); children 3 to 12, $2 TT (40¢); and children under 3 are admitted free. It's open from 9:30am to 5:30pm daily.

AROUND THE ISLAND

For one of the most popular attractions in the area, the **Asa Wright Nature Centre,** see "Where to Stay," above.

On a peak 1,100 feet above Port-of-Spain, **Fort George** was built by Gov. Sir Thomas Hislop in 1804 as a signal station in the days of the sailing ships. Once it could be reached only by hikers, but today it's accessible by an asphalt road. From its citadel, you can see the mountains of Venezuela. The drive is only 10 miles, but to play it safe, allow about two hours for the excursion.

At sundown, clouds of scarlet ibis, the national bird of Trinidad and Tobago, fly in from their feeding grounds to roost at the ✪ **Caroni Bird Sanctuary.** The 40-square-mile sanctuary couldn't be more idyllic, with blue, mauve, and white lilies, oysters growing on mangrove roots, and caimans resting on mudbanks. The sanctuary lies about a half-hour drive (7 miles) south of Port-of-Spain.

The sanctuary is a big mangrove swamp interlaced with waterways. Visitors are taken on a launch through these swamps to see the birds (bring along some insect repellent). Most visitors leave their hotels at 3pm for a 4pm departure. There are also departures at 5am for early, early risers. Count on spending about $25 for the tour, which includes a pickup at your hotel. A reliable boat operator is **Winston Nanan's Bird Sanctuary Tours,** 38 Bamboo Grove Sett, no. 1 Butler Highway (☎ 809/645-1305). The sanctuary is open all year, but its innermost core can be visited only from August to April.

The ✪ **Pitch Lake** lies on the west coast of Trinidad with the village of Le Brea on its north shore. To reach the Pitch Lake from Port-of-Spain, take the Solomon Hocoy Highway. It's about a two-hour drive, depending on traffic (which can be heavy around Port-of-Spain). At Le Brea, you'll find some bars and restaurants.

One of the wonders of the world, its surface like elephant skin, the lake is 300 feet deep at its center. It's possible to walk on its rough hide, but I don't recommend that you proceed far. Legend has it that the lake devoured a tribe of Chayma Amerindians, punishing them for eating hummingbirds in which the souls of their ancestors reposed. The bitumen mined here has been used for paving highways throughout the world. This lake was formed millions of years ago, and it is believed that at one time it was a huge mud volcano into which muddy asphaltic oil seeped. Churned up and down by underground gases, the oil and mud eventually formed asphalt. According to legend, Sir Walter Raleigh discovered the lake in 1595 and used the asphalt to caulk his ships. Some say that no matter how much is dug out the lake is fully replenished in a day, but actually the level of the lake drops at the rate of about 6 inches a year. A tour of 120 miles around the lake lasts five hours.

The ✪ **Saddle** is a humped pass on a ridge dividing the Maraval Valley and the Santa Cruz Valley. Along this circular run you'll see the luxuriant growth of the island, as reflected by grapefruit, papaya, cassava, and cocoa. Leaving Port-of-Spain by Saddle Road, going past the Trinidad Country Club, you pass through Maraval Village with its St. Andrew's Golf Course. The road rises to cross the ridge at the spot from which the Saddle gets its name. After going over the hump, you descend through Santa Cruz Valley, rich with giant bamboo, into San Juan and back to the capital along Eastern Main Road or via Beetham Highway. You'll see panoramic views in every direction. This tour takes about two hours and covers 18 miles.

Nearly all cruise-ship passengers are hauled along Trinidad's "Skyline Highway," the **North Coast Road.** Starting at the Saddle, it wends for 7 miles across the Northern Range and down to Maracas Bay. At one point, 100 feet above the Caribbean, you'll see on a clear day as far away as Venezuela in the west or Tobago in the east, a sweep of some 100 miles.

Most visitors take this route to ✪ **Maracas Beach,** one of the most splendid on Trinidad. Enclosed by mountains, it has the cliché charm of a Caribbean fantasy—white sands, swaying coconut palms, and crystal-clear water.

SPORTS & OUTDOOR ACTIVITIES

For golf and tennis holidays, you should read some of the previous chapters.

BEACHES   Trinidad isn't thought of as beach country, yet, surprisingly, it has more beach frontage than any other island in the West Indies. The only problem is that most of its beaches are undeveloped and found in distant, remote places, far removed from Port-of-Spain. The closest of the better beaches, **Maracas** (see the North Coast Road, in the previous section), is a full 18 miles from Port-of-Spain. (For lovely, inviting, and more accessible beaches, see Section 2 on Tobago.)

GOLF   The oldest golf club on the island, **Moka** (☎ **809/629-2314**) is in Maraval, about 2 miles from Port-of-Spain. This 18-hole course has a clubhouse that offers every facility to all visitors, and the course has been internationally acclaimed since it was the setting for the 1976 Hoerman Cup Golf Tournament.

TENNIS   The **Trinidad Hilton,** Lady Young Road (☎ **809/624-3111**), has the best courts. These are two chevron courts lit for night play. There are public courts in Port-of-Spain on the grounds of the Prince's Building (ask at your hotel for directions to these).

SHOPPING

One of the large bazaars of the Caribbean, Port-of-Spain has luxury items from all over the globe, including Irish linens, English china, Scandinavian crystal, French perfumes, Swiss watches, and Japanese cameras. More interesting than these usual items are the Asian bazaars where you can pick up items in brass. Reflecting the island's culture are calypso shirts (or dresses), sisal goods, woodwork, cascadura bracelets, silver jewelry in local motifs, and saris. For souvenir items, visitors often like to bring back figurines of limbo dancers, carnival masqueraders, or calypso singers.

Most stores are open Monday through Friday from 8am to 4pm (some shops remain open until 5pm). Liquor and food stores close at noon on Thursday, and nearly all shops, except liquor and food, close at noon on Saturday.

Art Creators and Suppliers
Apt. 402, Aldegonda Park, 7 St. Ann's Rd., St. Ann's. ☎ **809/624-4369**.

It's in a banal apartment complex, but the paintings and sculptures sold inside are among the finest in the Caribbean. Clara Rosa De Lima and Stella Beaubrun, the creative forces behind the gallery, are recognized for their knowledge of Trinidadian art. The works sold here are fairly priced examples of the best on Trinidad. Among the artistic giants are Glasgow, Robert Mackie, Noel Vaucrosson, Sundiata, Keith Ward, Jackie Hinkson, and many others. Ms. De Lima and Mrs. Beaubrun are usually candid about the relative merits of the artists they represent and maintain dialogue with a handful of artists from different countries. Open Monday through Friday from 10am to 1pm and 4 to 7pm, and on Saturday from 10am to noon.

Gallery 1-2-3-4
St. Ann's Village. ☎ **809/625-5502**.

Probably more iconoclastic and less conservative than any other gallery on the island, this art center displays its paintings in a space of minimalist walls and careful lighting. The gallery opened in 1985, and since then has attracted the attention of the art world because of its wide selection of Caribbean artists. Open Monday through Friday from 9am to 5pm and on Saturday from 8:30am to noon.

The Market
10 Nook Ave., St. Ann's. ☎ **809/624-1181**.

One of the most fashionable shopping complexes on Trinidad contains some 20 boutiques that represent some of the best jewelers, designers, and art dealers on the island. At this complex, you'll find a wide assortment of merchandise to buy, including clothing, cosmetics, bags, shoes, china, decorative tableware, handcrafts, and designer jewelry and accessories. The complex forms an interconnected bridge among three previously recommended establishments: the Normandie Hotel and Restaurant, the restaurant La Fantasie, and a top-notch art emporium, Gallery 1-2-3-4.

Stecher's
27 Frederick St. ☎ **809/623-5912.**

For those luxury items I mentioned above, visit Stecher's, which sells crystal, watches, jewelry, perfumes, Georg Jensen silver, Lladró, Wedgwood, Royal Doulton, Royal Albert, Aynsley, Hutschenreuther china, and other in-bond items that can be delivered to Piarco International Airport upon your departure. If you don't want to go downtown, you'll be glad there's a branch at the Hilton. Among the other famous names represented here are Patek-Philippe, Cartier, Girard Perregaux, Royal Crown Derby, Bing & Grøndahl, Lalique, Baccarat, Orrefors, Kosta-Boda, and Swarovski. If you miss both shops, you can always pay a last-minute call at their tax-free airport branch, where they sell famous brands of sunglasses, perfume, Cartier watches, lighters and pens, leather goods, Swarovski crystal, local ceramics, cigarettes and cigars, and pens by Mont Blanc, Waterman, and others. There's also a branch at the Cruise Ship Complex at the Port-of-Spain docks.

Y. De Lima
83 Queen St. ☎ **809/623-1364.**

This is another good store for duty-free cameras, watches, and local jewelry. Its third-floor workroom will make whatever you want in goldwork. You may emerge with everything from steel-drum earrings to a hibiscus-blossom brooch.

TRINIDAD AFTER DARK

Chaconia Inn
106 Saddle Rd., Maraval. ☎ **809/628-8603.** Admission free Sun–Fri, $10 Sat.

This place becomes a "hot spot" on Friday and Saturday night when a Trinidadian band is brought in from 10pm to 3am. Drinks begin at $3.50.

Mascamp Pub
French St. at Ariapata Ave. ☎ **809/623-3745.** Admission $2–$5.

This is the only venue on Trinidad where calypso music from the island's greatest bands is presented continually throughout the year. (Many similar establishments offer the art form only during Carnival.) Set on the western outskirts of Port-of-Spain, it promotes a "rootsy," sometimes raucous, and generally high-energy format that's recommended only to adventurous readers who happen to love live musical performances with an ethnic slant. Styled like a large American bar with an open stage against one wall, it charges between $2 and $5 (U.S.) for one of the array of drinks.

Although simple lunches are served here every weekday from 11am to around 3pm, for a cost of around $7 (U.S.), the establishment is far more recommendable (and exciting) as a nightspot. Live music begins every night at 9pm and continues until as late as 4am, but calypso and its modern variations are the almost exclusive format every Friday, Saturday, and Sunday.

Trinidad Hilton
Lady Young Rd. ☎ **809/624-3211.** Admission (including a buffet dinner with grills) $104 TT ($18.40).

The Hilton stages a Poolside Fiesta show, which happens every Tuesday night, with a folkloric performance beginning at 9pm and continuing live until 11pm.

It features lots of live music from calypso and steel bands after that. It's probably the most spectacular on Trinidad.

2 Tobago

Unlike bustling Trinidad, Tobago is sleepy, and Trinidadians come there, especially on weekends, to enjoy its wide sandy beaches. The legendary home of Robinson Crusoe, Tobago is only 27 miles long and 7 1/2 miles wide. The people are hospitable, and their villages are so tiny they seem to blend with the landscape.

Safe, serene, and tranquil, Tobago is reached after some transportation hassles from North America, especially for those who have to go through the airport at Trinidad. Once there, Tobago is one of the greatest escapes in the Caribbean. It's for those who like a generous dose of sand and sun in an atmosphere not especially lively.

Tobago, called "the land of the hummingbird," lies 20 miles northeast of Trinidad, to which it's connected by frequent flights. It has long been known as a honeymooner's paradise. The physical beauty of Tobago is stunning, with its forests of breadfruit, mango, cocoa, and citrus, through which a chartreuse-colored iguana will suddenly dart.

Fish-shaped Tobago was probably sighted by Columbus in 1498 when he charted Trinidad, but the island was so tiny he paid no attention to it in his log. For the next 100 years it lay almost unexplored. In 1628 when Charles I of England gave it to one of his nobles, the earl of Pembroke, the maritime countries of Europe suddenly showed a belated interest. From then on, Tobago was fought over no fewer than 31 times by the Spanish, French, Dutch, and English, as well as marauding pirates and privateers.

After 1803 the island settled down to enjoy a sugar monopoly unbroken for decades. Great Houses were built, and in London it used to be said of a wealthy man that he was "as rich as a Tobago planter." The island's economy collapsed in 1884 and Tobago entered an acute depression. The ruling monopoly, Gillespie Brothers, declared itself bankrupt and went out of business. The British government made Tobago a ward of Trinidad in 1889, and sugar was never revived.

The island's villagelike capital is **Scarborough,** which is also the main port. Most of the shops are clustered in streets around the market. From Scarborough one can either go cross-country toward Plymouth or head toward the southwestern part of Tobago.

ORIENTATION
GETTING THERE

BY PLANE   BWIA (☎ 800/538-2942), the national airline of Trinidad and Tobago, links the two islands with shuttles, which run on Monday and Thursday. The flights are mainly in the afternoon and evening, but there is one that leaves on those days at 6:30am. The flight lasts 20 minutes, and the cost of a round-trip is $40 per person.

A more convenient alternative is one of the many daily flights on a recently established Trinidad-based airline, **Air Caribbean** (☎ 809/623-2500). It maintains popular shuttle flights between Trinidad and Tobago, departing from Port-of-Spain every two hours daily between 6am and 8pm. The final return to Trinidad departs from Tobago daily at 9pm. A round-trip ticket costs $50. Know in advance that since the beaches of Tobago are a favorite of vacationing Trinidadians, shuttle flights on any airline between the two islands are almost always crowded, and, on weekends, sometimes impossibly overbooked. Air Caribbean, however, operates extra flights on Friday, Sunday, and public holidays to meet traffic demands.

LIAT (☎ 809/462-0701) maintains one daily flight from Trinidad to Tobago. From Barbados, St. Vincent, and most other islands which require inconvenient and expensive transfers through other hubs, many passengers opt for a specifically chartered aircraft from such operators as **Mustique Airways** (☎ 809/458-4380). On special request, it services virtually anywhere in the southern Caribbean from its base on St. Vincent.

Tobago's small airport lies at Crown Point, near the island's southwestern tip.

BY BOAT   It's possible to travel between Trinidad and Tobago by ferry service managed and operated by the **Port Authority of Trinidad and Tobago.** Call either the office in Port-of-Spain (☎ **809/625-3055**) or in Scarborough, Tobago (☎ **809/639-2181**), for departure times and more details. Ferries leave once a day (trip time is five hours). The round-trip fare is $60 TT ($10.60) in tourist class and $50 TT ($8.90) in economy class. Cabins are also available for $80 TT ($14.20).

GETTING AROUND

BY BUS   Inexpensive public buses travel from one end of the island to the other several times a day. Of course, expect an unscheduled stop at any passenger's doorstep, and never, never, be in a hurry.

BY TAXI   From the airport to your hotel, take an unmetered taxi, which will cost $6 to $20, depending on the location of your hotel. You can also arrange (or have your hotel do it for you) a sightseeing tour by taxi. Rates must be negotiated on an individual basis.

BY RENTAL CAR   Contact **Tobago Travel,** Milford Road, Store Bay (☎ 809/639-8778), where the average cost of a vehicle begins at $50 per day, with unlimited mileage. An international driver's license or your valid license from home entitles you to drive on the roads of Tobago. Don't forget to *drive on the left.*

ESSENTIALS

Nearly all passengers arrive from Trinidad, where they have already cleared Customs. The **Tobago Tourist Bureau,** Scarborough Hall, Scarborough (☎ 809/639-2125), provides general information about the island. There's a **pharmacy** at Scarborough Drugs, Wilson Road in Scarborough (☎ 809/639-4161). The **Tobago County Hospital** is on Fort Street, Scarborough (☎ 809/639-2551).

WHERE TO STAY

The hotels of Tobago attract those who seek hideaways instead of action at high-rise resorts. Sometimes to save money, it's best to take the MAP (breakfast and dinner) plan when reserving a room. Don't forget to ask if the 15% VAT on hotel rates and a service charge is included in the prices quoted to you.

EXPENSIVE

✪ Grafton Beach Resort

Black Rock (P.O. Box 25), Tobago, W.I. ☎ **809/639-0191,** or 800/223-6510 in the U.S., 800/424-5500 in Canada. Fax 809/639-0030. 112 rms. 2 suites. A/C MINIBAR TV, TEL. Winter, $225 single; $252 double; $600 suite. Off-season, $162 single; $225 double; $550 suite. Breakfast $12 extra. AE, DC, MC, V. Free parking.

One of the best resorts on the island, this luxurious complex of stone-and-stucco buildings lies on 5 acres 4 miles south of Scarborough, between a low-rising hill and the pale-dotted stretch of a white sand beach, 4 miles from the airport, on Grafton Road. Each accommodation contains a ceiling fan and a sliding glass door opening onto a balcony. In addition to such amenities as a hairdryer, rooms often contain teak furnishings and terra-cotta tiles along with marble baths.

Dining/Entertainment: The resort's swimming pool, traversed by an ornamental bridge, is ringed with café/restaurant tables, and there are several different bars (including a swim-up bar). Both a regional and international cuisine are served in the Ocean View and Neptunes restaurants. Limbo dancing and calypso, or some other form of entertainment, are featured nightly.

Services: 18-hour room service, laundry, babysitting, massages.

Facilities: Two squash courts, gym, dive shop, outdoor swimming pool; access to a nearby golf course.

Mount Irvine Bay Hotel and Golf Club

Mount Irvine (P.O. Box 222, Scarborough), Tobago, W.I. ☎ **809/639-8871,** or 800/74-CHARMS in the U.S. Fax 809/639-8800. 99 rms, 6 suites. A/C TV TEL. Winter, $205–$360 single; $215–$360 double; $720 suite. Off-season, $130–$275 single; $150–$275 double; $510 suite. One child under 12 stays free in parents' room. AE, DC, MC, V. Free parking.

Originally established in 1972 on the grounds of an 18th-century sugar plantation, Tobago's most exclusive resort occupies 16 acres of a recreational complex that totals more than 150 acres, about a 5-mile drive northwest of the airport. Most of this acreage is devoted to the Mount Irvine Golf Course, one of the finest in the Caribbean. The remainder is filled with sprawling lawns and tropical gardens, in the center of which rise the ruins of a stone sugar mill and a luxurious oval swimming pool. The grounds slope down to a lovely beach. Most accommodations are in a two-story hacienda-inspired wing of guest rooms, each of which opens toward a view of green lawns and flowering shrubbery. The remainder of the accommodations are in small cottages or villas covered with heliconia. Each cottage or villa has two rooms (rented separately) with a private bath and patio and a view of the fairways or the water.

Dining/Entertainment: The hotel features three top-class restaurants, including the Sugar Mill, built around the circular core of a 200-year-old stone mill under a shingled, raftered conical roof. It serves breakfast, lunch, and dinner. The hotel also offers dining at Le Beau Rivage at the golf course, and at the Jacaranda, which has a high standard of international cuisine. You can relax in the air-conditioned Cocrico Lounge, or enjoy exotic drinks on the Sugar Mill Terrace. There's dancing about every evening, and calypso singers are often brought in to entertain guests. Barbecues are a regular feature, as are limbo dancers and occasional shows.

Services: Room service (7am to 10pm), babysitting, laundry, massage.

Facilities: Tennis courts, swimming pool with swim-up bar, beauty salon, barbershop; boat rentals, windsurfers, and snorkeling equipment available at the

Tobago

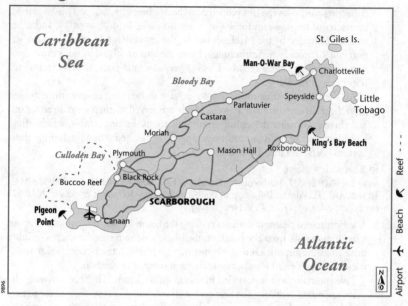

beach. Guests become temporary members of the golf club (see "Sports & Outdoor Activities," below) and receive complimentary greens fees.

Plantation Beach Villas

Stonehaven Bay, Blackrock, Tobago, W.I. ☎ **809/639-0455.** Fax 809/639-0455. 6 villas. A/C TEL. Winter, $380 villa for one to four; $442 villa for five or six. Off-season, $255 villa for one to four; $317 villa for five or six. AE, DC, MC, V. Free parking.

This is a pink-sided compound of two-story villas set near the island's southwestern tip, on a forested hillside adjacent to Tobago's nature reserve. Its verdant setting and cool, white-painted verandas evoke the age of British colonization of Tobago, a feeling enhanced by their traditional design and their touches of gingerbread. Each villa contains three bedrooms (each with its own bathroom), a kitchen, white-tiled floors, a wide teak-floored veranda, and a somewhat more narrow veranda servicing the bedrooms of the second floor. Furnishings include rattan and wicker pieces, as well as reproductions of mahogany furniture evocative of Tobago's plantation era. There's a small rectangular swimming pool on the lawn, which is shared by all six villas. The villas' management can arrange to provide a cook or childminder, and water sports can be arranged on site. Although most occupants of these buildings prefer to stay in for their meals, several restaurants are close at hand. Budgeteers appreciate the self-service washing machines and dryers on-site.

MODERATE

Blue Waters Inn

Batteaux Bay, Speyside, Tobago, W.I. ☎ **809/660-4341,** or 800/744-4000 in the U.S. Fax 809/660-5195. 31 rms, 4 efficiencies, 3 suites. Winter, $80 single; $90 double; $106 efficiency; $178 one-bedroom suite; $186–$268 two-bedroom suite. Off-season, $48 single; $56 double; $72 efficiency; $100 one-bedroom suite; $120–$152 two-bedroom suite. Breakfast $7.20 extra. AE, DC, MC, V. Free parking.

Attracting nature-lovers, this property on the northeastern coast of Tobago extends into acres of tropical rain forests with myriad exotic birds, butterflies, and other wildlife. Managed by the MacLean family, the inn is about 24 miles from the airport and 20 miles from Scarborough. From the airport, it's a 1 1/4-hour drive along narrow, winding country roads. This is a very informal place, so leave your fancy resortwear at home.

All the basic no-frills rooms have a private shower and ceiling fan, although several are air-conditioned as well. Meals are served in their casual restaurant, and there's also a bar dispensing tropical libations. Fishing, tennis, windsurfing, kayaking, and skin diving can be arranged, as can boat trips (including glass-bottom boats) to Little Tobago.

⑤ Kariwak Village

Store Bay (P.O. Box 27, Scarborough), Tobago, W.I. ☎ **809/639-8545.** Fax 809/639-8441. 18 rms. A/C TEL. Winter, $90 single or double. Off-season, $60 single or double. MAP $25 per person extra. AE, DC, MC, V. Free parking.

A self-contained cluster of cottages evoking the South Pacific, this complex is about a six-minute walk from the beach on the island's western shoreline, a two-minute drive from the airport. During its construction in 1982, the builders made much use of Tobago's palm fronds, raw teak, coral stone, and bamboo.

Live entertainment is provided in season on weekends. The food served in the main restaurant is among the best on the island, and you may want to come here for a meal even if you aren't staying here. A fixed-price meal, either à la carte or in the form of one of the weekend buffets, ranges from $18 to $20 per person. The establishment's name is a combination of the two native tribes that originally inhabited Tobago, the Caribs and the Arawaks.

Palm Tree Village

Milford Rd. (P.O. Box 327); Little Rockley Bay, Milford, Tobago, W.I. ☎ **809/639-4347.** Fax 809/639-4180. 20 rms, 18 villas. A/C TEL. Winter, $120 single or double; $240 villa. Off-season, $75 single or double; $150 villa. Children under 13 stay free in parents' room. Breakfast $10 extra. AE, MC, V. Free parking.

Favored by families with children, this hotel and villa complex occupies 5 1/2 acres of landscaped grounds on the island's southwestern coast. Opened in 1991, it's arranged into a dignified compound of cream-colored, tile-roofed buildings set adjacent to a narrow beach and a pair of swimming pools. Each unit opens onto a view of the ocean, and has either a patio or a balcony and an attractive collection of simple furniture. All are comfortably furnished in a tropical motif of pastel colors, and contain satellite TV and a safe; the villas also have a fully equipped kitchen. Entertainment is occasionally presented in the establishment's beachfront bar and restaurant, the Carambeau. Facilities include a pool bar, a fitness center, a beach bar, and a daily minivan shuttle from the hotel to four of Tobago's most popular beaches.

⑤ Turtle Beach

Courland Bay (P.O. Box 201, Scarborough), Tobago, W.I. ☎ **809/639-2851.** Fax 809/639-1495. 125 rms. A/C TEL. Winter, $145 single or double; $200 triple. Off-season, $110 single or double; $150 triple. MAP $45 per person extra. AE, MC, V. Free parking.

Standing directly on a mile of sandy beach on Courland Bay, Turtle Beach sits on the leeward shore in the midst of a 600-acre coconut plantation. It's 8 miles from the airport and 5 miles from Scarborough. The entrance loggia is a long covered terrace where you can enjoy the relaxed, casual lifestyle of the hotel while seated on sofas and in armchairs with a tall fruit-and-rum drink. Lunches are served around the garden pool or at the beach. Three times a week calypso music can be heard in the evening; perhaps a steel band will be brought in. If you don't want the beach, you can swim in a freshwater pool. Fishing can be arranged, as can snorkeling at Buccoo Reef. A water-sports shop is on the hotel premises.

Accommodations lie in an interconnected series of white two-story bungalows, between beds of hibiscus and oleander. All rooms are oceanfront and have a bathroom with both tub and shower, a patio or balcony, and smartly tailored furnishings. Rooms on the second floor have sloped open-beamed ceilings, with white walls and shuttered doors that can be pushed back to enlarge the living areas.

INEXPENSIVE

⊛ Richmond Great House

Belle Garden, Tobago, W.I. ☎ **809/660-4467.** 6 rms, 3 suites. $80 single or double; $130 suite. (Rates include American breakfast.) No credit cards. Free parking.

One of the most charming accommodations on the island is an 18th-century Great House set on 6 acres, part of a cocoa- and coconut-growing estate. Near Richmond Beach, it's owned by Dr. Hollis R. Lynch, who is a Tobago-born professor of African history at Columbia. As befits his profession, he has decorated the mansion with African art along with a collection of island antiques. Guests are free to explore the garden and grounds and to enjoy the pool and the barbecue. On the premises are two 19th-century tombs containing the remains of the original English founders of the plantation. All accommodations have a private bathroom and an individualized decor. The hotel lies on the southern (windward) coast of Tobago, and the airport is within a 45-minute drive. Both a regional and international cuisine is served. Since it's such a small place, the cook talks to guests about their culinary preferences. Lunch begins at $10, with a dinner going for $17.50.

Sandy Point Beach Village

Crown Point, Tobago, W.I. ☎ **809/639-8533.** Fax 809/639-8495. 9 studios, 35 suites. A/C TV TEL. Winter, $60 studio for one or two; $70–$80 suite. Off-season, $35 studio for one or two; $45–$55 suite. Additional adult $10 extra; children under 12 $5 in room shared with parents. MAP $15 per person extra. MC, V. Free parking.

Built in two different sections in 1977 and 1991, this miniature vacation village somewhat resembles a Riviera condominium. All but six of the units (those at poolside) contain a kitchenette. It's just a three-minute run from the airport, but its shoreside position on the island's southwestern coast makes it seem remote. The little village of peaked and gabled roofs is landscaped all the way down to the sandy beach, where there's a rustic Steak Hut, which serves meals throughout the day and evening. The units are fully equipped, and each opens onto a patio, toward the sea, or onto a covered loggia. The studios contain living and dining areas with Jamaican wicker furniture, plus satellite color TV. Some of the studios have a rustic open stairway leading to a loft room with bunk beds, although there's a twin-bedded room on the lower level as well. On the premises are two different swimming pools, plus a small gym and a disco in the basement.

WHERE TO DINE
EXPENSIVE
✪ Le Beau Rivage

In the Mount Irvine Bay Hotel, Tobago Golf Course, Buccoo Bay. ☎ **809/639-8871.**
Reservations required. Appetizers $30–$70 TT ($5.30–$12.40); main courses $85–$145 TT
($15–$25.70). AE, DC, MC, V. Dinner only, daily 7–10pm. FRENCH/CARIBBEAN.

Run by the previously recommended hotel, this restaurant is in a clubhouse built
in 1968, which once served as the headquarters of the golf course that surrounds
it on every side. From its windows you'll have a sweeping view of one of Tobago's
most historic inlets, Mount Irvine Bay. Menu choices include combinations of
local ingredients with continental inspirations of *cuisine moderne*, such as grilled
Caribbean lobster, grilled filet of red snapper in a tomato purée, chicken Cordon
Bleu (stuffed with ham and cheese and wrapped in bacon), and roast duckling
stuffed with tropical fruits. Dessert might include a fresh mango flan floating on
a coulis of tropical fruits. The restaurant is a five-minute drive northwest of the
airport.

MODERATE
✪ The Blue Crab

Robinson St., Scarborough. ☎ **809/639-2737.** Reservations recommended for lunch,
required for dinner. Appetizers $8–$12 TT ($1.40–$2.10); main courses $50–$110 TT ($8.90–
$19.50); lunch platters $29–$35 TT ($5.10–$6.20). AE, MC, V. Lunch daily 11am–3pm;
dinner Fri–Wed by advance reservation only. CARIBBEAN/INTERNATIONAL.

One of my favorite restaurants in the capital, adjacent to the town's only Methodist church, this family-run establishment occupies an Edwardian-era house with
an oversize veranda. This is the domain of the Sardinha family, who returned to
their native country after a sojourn in New York. Keeping their establishment
together with "spit and love" after setting it up in 1984, they learned to make the
most of local ingredients and regional spices. Dinners might not always be available; when they are served, the menu will be dictated by whatever is available that
day in the marketplace. Menu items include fresh conch, stuffed crab backs,
shrimp, an array of Créole meat dishes grilled over coconut husks, flying fish in a
mild curry-flavored batter, shrimp with garlic butter or cream, and a vegetable-
laced rice dish of the day. Lobster is, of course, the most expensive item on
the menu.

Kiskadee Restaurant

In the Turtle Beach Hotel, Courland Bay. ☎ **809/639-2851.** Reservations recommended
for those not staying in the hotel. Appetizers $40–$45 TT ($7.10–$8); main courses $65–$90
TT ($11.50–$15.90). AE, DC, MC, V. Lunch daily 1–2:30pm; dinner daily 7–9:30pm.
CREOLE/CARIBBEAN.

Five miles from Scarborough, the Kiskadee is informally casual; its tables sit on an
outdoor veranda whose edges overlook a tropical garden and the sea. *Cuisine
minceur* is sometimes available as a low-calorie alternative to the other specialties,
which include pumpkin and coconut-cream soup, fresh fish filet served on a
banana leaf, roast duckling with a soy and golden-apple sauce, and rosette of plantain and island crab Créole, or freshwater crayfish served in a mixture of citrus
sauce. Another specialty is chicken suprême Angostura (breast stuffed with banana,
smoked ham, a dash of bitters, and shredded coconut).

Old Donkey Cart House

Bacolet St., Scarborough, Tobago, W.I. ☎ **809/639-3551.** Reservations recommended. Appetizers $18–$48 TT ($3.20–$8.50); main courses $45–$115 TT ($8–$20.40). AE, MC, V. Lunch Thurs–Tues noon–3pm; dinner Thurs–Tues 6:30pm–midnight. INTERNATIONAL.

An unusual and noteworthy restaurant occupies a green-and-white Edwardian house about half a mile south of Scarborough. Its entrepreneurial owner, Gloria Jones-Knapp, sometimes works as a fashion model in Europe. "Born, bred, and dragged up" on Tobago, she is today the island's leading authority on selected European wines, which she purchases with her husband. These selections include Italian, French, Austrian, and German wines. Her restaurant also serves freshly made fruit drinks laced with the local rum. Meals might include stuffed crab back, homemade pasta, shrimp and crabmeat cocktail, fresh fish, beef Stroganoff, salads, homemade garlic bread, and callaloo soup with crab. Dining can be enjoyed either in the palm garden or on the verandas of the Hibiscus Bar while seated in rattan chairs. If you're interested, ask about the apartment suites for rent, costing $70 to $140 daily, double occupancy, including breakfast and taxes.

The Steak Hut

In the Sandy Point Beach Village, Crown Point. ☎ **809/639-8533.** Reservations recommended. Appetizers $15 TT ($2.70); main courses $75–$90 TT ($13.50–$15.90). MC, V. Breakfast daily 7:30–10am; lunch daily noon–3pm; dinner daily 7–9pm. STEAK.

On the island's southwestern side, the Steak Hut serves the best meat on the island, specializing in U.S. sirloin, T-bone, porterhouse, and tenderloin. The location, near the beach and swimming pool of this previously recommended hotel, is ideal, especially in the evening. The seafront restaurant also features local fish steaks—shark, flying fish, grouper, dolphin, barracuda, and kingfish. A steel band plays most Saturday nights.

✪ Sugar Mill Restaurant

In the Mount Irvine Bay Hotel, Buccoo Bay. ☎ **809/639-8871.** Reservations required for those not staying at the hotel. Appetizers $20–$30 TT ($3.50–$5.30); main courses $35–$120 TT ($6.20–$21.20); fixed-price meal $140 TT ($24.80). AE, DC, MC, V. Lunch daily noon–3pm; dinner daily 7–10pm. INTERNATIONAL.

About a 5-mile drive northwest of the island's airport, this restaurant has at its core a 200-year-old sugar mill whose walls were fashioned from chiseled blocks of coral. Out of it radiate the spidery arms of a beamed ceiling, the shingles of which protect the dozens of tables from the direct sunlight. Open-air, breezy, casually elegant, and permeated with the scent from nearby jasmine, this is probably the best restaurant on Tobago.

Lunch includes everything from salads and sandwiches to lamb chops provençal or sirloin steak. Dinner might include lobster bisque, a carbonade of beef, shrimp Newburg with rice pilaf, marinated grilled chicken, lobster sautéed in ginger, and filet of dolphin. Meals are usually accompanied by live music and entertainment, at least in season.

INEXPENSIVE

Jemma's Seaview Kitchen

Speyside. ☎ **809/660-4066.** Reservations required. Appetizers $35–$50 TT ($6.20–$8.90); main courses $50–$120 TT ($8.90–$21.20). No credit cards. Mon–Thurs 9am–9pm, Fri 9am–5pm. Sun by appointment only. WEST INDIAN.

A short walk north of the hamlet of Speyside, on Tobago's northeastern coast, this is one of the very few restaurants in the Caribbean designed as a treehouse. Although the establishment's simple kitchen is firmly anchored to the shoreline, the dining area is set on a platform nailed to the massive branches of a 200-year-old almond tree that leans out over the water. Some 50 tables are available on a wooden deck which even provides a rooflike structure for shelter from the rain.

The establishment's owner is Mrs. Jemma Sealey, whose charming staff provides fixed-price meals where soup or salad is usually included in the price of a main course. Lunch platters include shrimp, fish, and chicken, while dinners feature more elaborate portions of each of those, as well as steaks, curried lamb, grilled or curried kingfish, lamb chops, and lobster served grilled or thermidor style. No liquor is served (only soft drinks), but no one will mind if you bring your own beer, wine, or spirits.

WHAT TO SEE & DO

In Tobago's capital, **Scarborough,** you can visit the local market Monday through Saturday morning and listen to the sounds of a Créole patois.

The town need claim your attention only briefly before you climb up the hill to **Fort King George,** about 430 feet above the town. Built by the English in 1779, it was later captured by the French. After that it jockeyed back and forth among various conquerors until nature decided to end it all in 1847, blowing off the roofs of its buildings. The cannons still mounted had a 3-mile range, and one is believed to have come from one of the ships of Sir Francis Drake (you can still see a replica of the *Tudor Rose*). One building used to house a powder magazine, and you can see the ruins of a military hospital. Artifacts are displayed in a gallery on the grounds.

The **Tobago Museum,** Barrack Guard House, 84 Fort King George (☎ **809/ 639-3970**), on the grounds of the fort, displays numerous artifacts of the Amerindian culture, relics of the people who inhabited the island before the arrival of Columbus. There are original maps and documents, some going back as far as the 1600s. Also presented are documents related to the slave trade and military relics of the men who occupied the fortress in the 18th and 19th centuries. It's open Monday through Friday from 9am to 5pm, costing $3 for adults and $1 for children.

From Scarborough, you can drive northwest to **Plymouth,** Tobago's other town. In the graveyard of the little church is a tombstone dating from 1783 with a mysterious inscription: "She was a mother without knowing it, and a wife, without letting her husband know it, except by her kind indulgences to him."

Perched on a point at Plymouth is **Fort James,** which dates from 1768 when it was built by the British as a barracks. Now it's mainly in ruins.

From Speyside, you can make arrangements with a local fisherman to go to **Little Tobago,** a 450-acre offshore island where a bird sanctuary attracts ornithologists. Threatened with extinction in New Guinea, many birds, perhaps 50 species in all, were brought over to this little island in the early part of this century.

Off Pigeon Point lies **Buccoo Reef** (see "Sports & Outdoor Activities," below) where sea gardens of coral and hundreds of fish can be seen in waist-deep water. This is the natural aquarium of Tobago. Nearly all the major hotels arrange boat trips to these acres of submarine gardens, which offer the best scuba diving and snorkeling. Even nonswimmers can wade knee-deep in the waters. Remember to protect your head and body from the tropical heat and to guard your feet against the sharp coral.

After about half an hour at the reef, passengers reboard their boats and go over to **Nylon Pool,** with its crystal-clear waters. Here in this white sand bottom, about a mile offshore, you can enjoy water only 3 or 4 feet deep. After a swim, you'll be returned to Buccoo Village jetty in time for a goat and crab race.

SPORTS & OUTDOOR ACTIVITIES

BEACHES   If beach-fringed Tobago wasn't in fact the alleged location of Daniel Defoe's immortal story, the visitors who enjoy its superb beaches hardly seem to care. On Tobago sands you can still feel like Robinson Crusoe in a solitary cove, at least for most of the week before the Trinidadians fly over to sample the sands on a Saturday.

A good beach, **Back Bay,** is within an eight-minute walk of the Mount Irvine Bay Hotel. Along the way you'll pass a coconut plantation and an old cannon emplacement. Sometimes there can be dangerous currents here, but you can always enjoy exploring Rocky Point with its brilliantly colored parrot fish.

Try also **Man-O-War Bay,** one of the finest natural harbors in the West Indies, at the opposite end of the island. Once there, you'll come to a long sandy beach, and you can also enjoy a picnic at a government-run rest house.

The finest for last, **Pigeon Point,** on the island's northwestern coast, is the best-known bathing area with a long coral beach. Thatched shelters provide havens for changing into bathing attire, as well as tables and benches for picnics.

BOATING   The **Turtle Beach Hotel,** Courland Bay (☎ 809/639-2851), rents Aqua-finn sailboats and is a registered Mistral Sailing Centre.

FIELD TRIPS   Four different field trips offer closeup views of Tobago's exotic and often-rare tropical birds, as well as a range of other island wildlife and lush tropical flora. Naturalists of the Trinidad-Tobago area guide these excursions. The trips lead you to forest trails, coconut plantations, along rivers, and past waterfalls. Each trip lasts about two to three hours, so you can take at least two per day if you like. One excursion goes to two nearby islands. The price per trip is $48 to $55 per person. For details, contact **Pat Turpin,** Man-O-War Bay Cottages, Charlottesville (☎ 809/660-4327).

GOLF   Tobago is the proud possessor of an 18-hole, 6,800-yard golf course at Mount Irvine. Called the **Tobago Golf Club** (☎ 809/639-8871), it covers 150 breeze-swept acres and was featured in the "Wonderful World of Golf" TV series. The course—and even beginners agree—is considered "friendly" to golfers. As a guest of the Mount Irvine Bay Hotel you are granted temporary membership and use of the clubhouse and facilities. All serious golfers should stay at the Mount Irvine. Nonresidents pay $35 to $40 for 18 holes, and residents play for free.

TENNIS   The **Turtle Beach Hotel** (☎ 809/639-2851) has courts. The best courts, however, are at the **Mount Irvine Bay Hotel** (☎ 809/639-8871), where two good courts are available free to guests. Night tennis costs $5.

WATER SPORTS   Unspoiled reefs off Tobago teem with a great variety of marine life. Divers can swim through rocky canyons 60 to 130 feet deep, and underwater photographers can shoot pictures they won't find anywhere else. Snorkeling over the celebrated Buccoo Reef is one of the specialties of Tobago. Hotels arrange for their guests to visit this underwater wonderland. (See "What to See and Do," above.)

The **Turtle Beach Hotel,** Courland Bay (☎ 809/639-2851), is the best equipped for water sports. Sailing and windsurfing are available free, and waterskiing is offered at reasonable rates.

Dive Tobago Ltd., Pigeon Point (P.O. Box 53, Scarborough), Tobago, W.I. (☎ 809/639-2150), is the oldest and most established dive operation on Tobago, operated by James Young. It caters to the beginner as well as to the experienced diver. A basic resort course, taking half a day and ending in a 30-foot dive, costs $55. Young is a certified PADI diver.

Tobago Dive Experience, Grafton Beach Resort, Black Rock (☎ 809/ 639-0191), offers scuba dives, snorkeling, and boat trips. All dives are guided, with a boat following. Exciting drift dives are available for experienced divers. Manta rays are frequently seen five minutes from the shore, and there is rich marine life with zonal compaction. A one-tank dive costs $35 with no equipment or $42 with equipment.

Man Friday Diving, Charlotteville (☎ 809/660-4676), is a Danish-owned dive center with certified PADI and CMAS instructors along with PADI divemasters. The location is right on the beach of Man-O-War Bay at the northernmost tip of Tobago. With more than 40 different dive sites, they are always able to find suitable locations for diving, no matter what the water conditions are. Guided boat trips for certified divers go out twice a day, at 9:30am and at 2pm. A resort course costs $75; a PADI open-water certification, $375. A two-tank dive costs $70, with a night dive going for $50.

SHOPPING

Scarborough's stores have a limited range of merchandise, more to tempt the browser than the serious shopper.

Cotton House Fashion Studio

Old Windward Rd., Bacolet. ☎ 809/639-2727.

This is one of the island's best choices for "hands-on" appreciation of the fine art of batik. (Batik is an Indonesian tradition where melted wax, brushed onto fabric, resists the impregnation of dyes into selected parts of the cloth, thereby creating unusual colors and designs.) It contains one of the largest collections of batik clothing (for men and women) and wall hangings on Tobago, many suitable for resortwear. Dying techniques are demonstrated to clients, who can try their skills at the art form.

TOBAGO AFTER DARK

Hotels with nightlife include the **Mount Irvine Bay Hotel** (☎ 809/639-8871) and the **Turtle Beach Hotel** (☎ 809/639-2851), both previously recommended. The Turtle Beach has a popular barbecue on Saturday night from 7 to 9:30pm, with poolside dancing to a steel band, continuing until late. The price is $278 TT ($49.20). At the Mount Irvine you might find disco action, or you can listen to the music of a steel band.

Formerly Dutch possessions, the so-called ABC group of islands—Aruba, Bonaire, and Curaçao—lie just off the northern coast of Venezuela. The islands cover only 363 square miles, with a widely diversified population of some 225,000 people, many of whom speak Papiamento, a patois language, although Dutch is the official tongue.

Duty-free shopping and gambling are promoted by the governments on all three islands. Curaçao has the most Dutch atmosphere, with a number of 18th-century buildings. Curaçao, along with Aruba, also has the most developed tourist centers, while Bonaire attracts the most dedicated scuba divers. Someone once said that there are more flamingos than people on Bonaire. Aruba has the best beaches and the most hotel accommodations.

The canny Dutch emerged from the European power struggle in the West Indies with these tiny specks of land, arid and for all appearances inconsequential. But they proceeded to turn these ugly-duckling properties into some of the most valuable real estate in the Caribbean. These spotless islands still retain old-world charm and are clean and thriving.

On January 1, 1986, Aruba became a separate entity within the Kingdom of the Netherlands under a political arrangement called Status Aparte. Before that date, it was a member of the Netherlands Antilles, consisting of six Dutch Caribbean islands. With Aruba's new status, the Kingdom of the Netherlands has three separate components: the Netherlands, the Netherlands Antilles, and Aruba. The government of the Netherlands is responsible for the defense and foreign affairs of the kingdom, but other government tasks are carried out by each island country for itself.

In addition to Bonaire and Curaçao, the Netherlands Antilles encompasses Saba, St. Eustatius (Statia), and St. Maarten, already discussed in Chapter 10, "The Dutch Windwards in the Leewards."

Cactus fences surround pastel-washed houses, divi-divi trees with their windblown look stud the barren countryside, free-form boulders are scattered about, and on occasion you'll come across an abandoned gold mine.

1 Aruba

Forget lush vegetation on Aruba—that's impossible with only 17 inches of rainfall annually. Aruba is dry and sunny almost year round, with clean, exhilarating air like that found in the desert of Palm Springs, California. Its own Palm Beach, one of the best in the world, draws tourists in droves, as do its glittering casinos.

Aruba is not a chic address like St. Barts or Anguilla, but honeymooners, sun worshippers, snorkelers, sailors, weekend gamblers and find it suits their needs just fine. As you lie back along the 7-mile stretch of white sand beach, enjoying a daytime 82° weather, you are not harassed by the locals peddling wares you don't want, there is almost no racial tension, and, chances are, you won't get mugged. Trade winds keep the island from becoming uncomfortably hot, and there is very low humidity.

Aruba stands outside the hurricane path. Its coastline on the leeward side is smooth and serene, with white sandy beaches; but on the eastern coast, the windward side, the look is rugged and wild, typical of the windswept Atlantic.

Many visitors come here for the annual pre-Lenten **Carnival,** a month-long festival with events day and night. With music, dancing, parades, costumes, and "jump-ups," Carnival is the highlight of Aruba's winter season.

ORIENTATION
GETTING THERE

On **American Airlines** (☎ 800/433-7300), Aruba-bound passengers can catch a daily nonstop 4$\frac{1}{2}$-hour flight departing New York's JFK airport at 10:45am. The nonstop return flight leaves Aruba between 4 and 5pm every day. From American's hub in San Juan, Puerto Rico, two daily nonstop flights depart every day for Aruba. American also offers a daily nonstop flight from Miami to Aruba. This service enables vacationers from Chicago, Los Angeles, San Francisco, and Seattle to fly directly to Aruba via the American Airlines Miami hub.

American's lowest fare is included in their "land package," whereby prearranged and prepaid accommodations at selected hotels (recommended in this guide) are booked at the same time as the airfare through American's tour department. Contact an American Airlines reservations clerk or a travel agent for details.

For clients who prefer to make their own hotel arrangements, American offers its least expensive tickets to those who can reserve at least 14 days in advance. Weekday travel—that is, Monday through Thursday—is usually cheaper than travel in any direction on a Friday, Saturday, or Sunday.

ALM (☎ toll free 800/327-7230) has good connections into Aruba from certain parts of the United States. On Friday, Saturday, and Sunday there is nonstop service from Miami, and on Monday, Wednesday, and Thursday there is also service from Miami but with a stopover on Curaçao. There is no direct flight from Atlanta, but there is one flight a week from Atlanta to Aruba with a stopover on Curaçao. The Atlanta flight usually arrives early enough in the day to allow a late-afternoon visit to the beach.

Tiny **Air Aruba** (☎ 800/88-ARUBA), the country's national carrier, boasts Newark (N.J.), Baltimore, and Miami as North American gateways. Air Aruba offers daily nonstop flights from Miami, daily flights from Newark, and twice-weekly (Wednesday and Saturday) nonstop flights from Baltimore. Air Aruba also has links to Bonaire and Curaçao.

Air Canada (☎ 800/363-5440 in Canada, 800/776-3000 in the U.S.) operates a directl weekly flight in winter from Toronto to Aruba on Saturday. Travelers can also take advantage of good connections from Canada to Miami on Air Canada, and then on to Air Aruba from Miami to Aruba.

GETTING AROUND

BY BUS   Aruba has an excellent bus service, with a round-trip fare between the beach hotels and Oranjestad of $1.75. Bus schedules are available at the Arubus Office at the central bus station on Zoutmanstraat. Your hotel reception desk will also know the approximate times the buses pass by where you're staying. There is regular daily service from 6am to midnight. Try to have the exact change.

BY TAXI   In Aruba, the taxis are unmetered but rates are fixed, so tell the driver your destination and ask the fare before getting in. A ride from the airport to most of the hotels, including those at Palm Beach, costs about $15 per car, and a maximum of four passengers is allowed. Some of the local people don't tip, although it's good to give something extra, especially if the driver has helped you with luggage.

BY RENTAL CAR   Unlike most Caribbean islands, Aruba makes it easy to rent a car and explore independently. The roads connecting the major tourist attractions are excellent, and a valid U.S. or Canadian driver's license is accepted by each of the major car-rental companies. Most of the big hotels have desks that will rent cars to you. Ask them a day in advance and you'll have a better chance of getting the car you want.

Three major U.S. car-rental companies maintain offices on Aruba, and a quick comparison of prices before you leave the United States will reveal current price differences. Many of the companies have both airport branches and kiosks at the major hotels. No taxes are imposed on car rentals on Aruba, but insurance can be tricky. Even with the purchase of a collision-damage waiver (from $8 per day), a driver is still responsible for between $300 and $500 worth of damage. (Avis doesn't even offer this waiver, so in the event of an accident—unless you have private insurance—you'll be liable for up to the full value of damage to your car.)

Budget Rent-a-Car (☎ **800/472-3325**) consistently offers the lowest rates. A car with manual transmission and no air conditioning rents for $222 per week in high season, with unlimited mileage. All the rentals at **Hertz** (☎ toll free **800/654-3001**) and most of the rentals at **Avis** (☎ toll free **800/331-1084**) have automatic transmission and air conditioning, which tend to raise the rental price. The lowest weekly rate at Hertz is $282; at Avis, $276 per week. Budget requires that renters be at least 25; Avis, 23; and Hertz, 21. For rental information, call Budget at **297/8/28600,** Avis at **297/8/24800,** and Hertz at **297/8/24886.**

BY MOTORCYCLE AND MOPED   Since the roads of Aruba are good and the terrain flat, many visitors prefer this form of transport. Mopeds and motorcycles cost an average of $37 to $40 per day, respectively. They're available at **George's Scooter Rental,** L. G. Smith Blvd. 136, Oranjestad (☎ **297/8/25975**).

BY SIGHTSEEING TOUR   You'll find **taxis** with English-speaking drivers available as guides. Most of them seem well informed about their island and are eager to share it with you. A one-hour tour (and you don't need much more than that) is offered at $30 per hour for a maximum of four passengers.

De Palm Tours, L. G. Smith Blvd. 142, Oranjestad (☎ **297/8/24400**), has desks at all the major hotels. Their latest attraction is De Palm Island, a complete entertainment facility built on a private island just five minutes by ferry from Aruba. Their tours include a wide range of activities, featuring snorkeling, beach barbecues, and folklore shows. Their office is open Monday through Saturday from 8:30am to noon and 1pm to 5pm. The cost of their organized jaunts range upward from $17.50, depending on what activity you select.

FAST FACTS: Aruba

Area Code   Aruba is not part of the Caribbean 809 area-code system. See "Tele-communications," below, for information on making calls to and on this island.

Banking Hours   Banks are open Monday through Friday from 8am to noon and 1:30 to 3:45pm.

Currency   The currency is the **Aruba florin (AFl),** which is divided into 100 cents. Silver coins are in denominations of 5, 10, 25, and 50 cents and 1 and $2^{1}/_{2}$ florins. The 50-cent piece, the square "yotin," is probably Aruba's best-known coin. The current exchange rate is 1.77 AFl to $1 U.S. (1 AFl is worth about 56¢). U.S. dollars are accepted throughout the island. Unless otherwise stated, prices quoted in this chapter are in U.S. dollars.

Documents   To enter Aruba, U.S., British, and Canadian citizens may submit a valid passport or a birth certificate (or, for U.S. citizens only, a voter registration card with a photo ID).

Electricity   The electricity is 110 volts A.C., 60 cycles, the same as in the United States.

Emergencies   For the police, dial **11100.** For a medical emergency, dial **74300.** For the fire department, call **115.**

Holidays   Aruba celebrates January 1 (New Year's Day), Carnival Monday, Good Friday, Easter Monday, March 18 (National Anthem and Flag Day), April 30 (Queen's Birthday), May 1 (Labor Day), Ascension Day, and December 25–26 (Christmas Day and second Christmas Day).

Information   For information, go to the **Aruba Tourism Authority,** L. G. Smith Boulevard (☎ **297/8/23777**). Before leaving home, you can also contact the Aruba Tourism Authority at the following locations: 1000 Harbor Blvd., Weehawken, NJ 07087 (☎ toll free **800/TO-ARUBA**); 2344 Salzedo St., Miami, FL 33144 (☎ **305/567-2720**); 199 14th St. NE, Suite 1506, Atlanta, GA 30309 (☎ **404/892-7822**); or 86 Bloor St. W., Suite 204, Toronto, ON M5S 1M5, Canada (☎ **416/975-1950**).

Language   The official language is Dutch, but nearly everybody speaks English. The language of the street is often Papiamento. Spanish is also widely spoken.

Medical Care   To receive medical care, go to the Horacio Oduber Hospital (☎ **297/8/74300**). It's a modern building near Eagle Beach, with excellent medical facilities. Hotels also have medical doctors on call, and there are good dental facilities as well (appointments can be made through your hotel).

Safety   Aruba is one of the Caribbean's safer destinations, in spite of its numerous hotels and gambling casinos. Of course, pickpockets and purse-snatchers are around, but in no great numbers. However, it would be wise to guard your valuables. Never leave them unattended on the beach or even in a locked car.

Taxes and Service   The government of Aruba imposes a 5% room tax, as well as a $10 airport departure tax. At your hotel, you'll have an 11% to 15% service charge added to charges for room, food, and beverages.

Telecommunications   Telegrams and Telexes can be sent from the Government Telegraph and Radio Office, at the Post Office Building in Oranjestad, or

Aruba

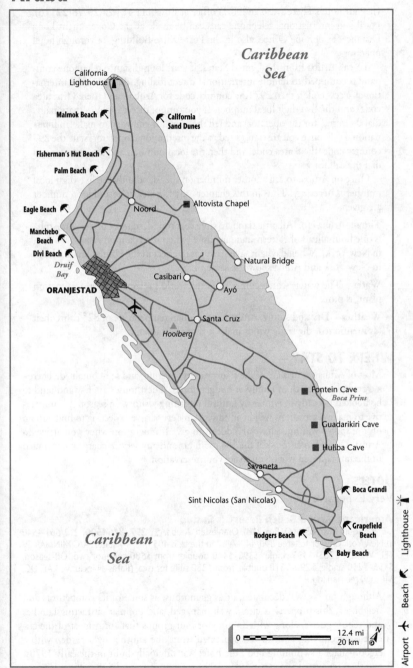

via your hotel. There's also an I.T.T. office at Bosabora 41 (☎ **297/8/22116**). Local and international telephone calls can be made at the Government Long Distance Telephone Office, also in the Post Office Building, or through hotel operators.

To call Aruba from the United States, if your long-distance telephone company is equipped to handle international direct dialing, dial **011** (the international access code), then 297 (the country code for Aruba), and then 8 (the area code) and the five-digit local number. If you cannot direct-dial internationally, dial **0** ("zero," for the operator) and tell the operator you wish to make an international call; once you are transferred to the international operator, state the 297 country code, the 8 area code, and then the local number, and the operator will dial the call for you.

Once on Aruba, to call another number on the island only the five-digit local number is necessary. Thus in this chapter only the area code and local number are given.

Time   Aruba is on Atlantic standard time year round, so most of the year Aruba is one hour ahead of eastern standard time (when it's 10am on Aruba, it's 9am in New York). When daylight saving time is in effect in the United States, clocks in New York and Aruba show the same time.

Water   The water, which comes from the world's second-largest desalination plant, is pure.

Weather   Dry and sunny, Aruba has a median temperature of 82° Fahrenheit (as mentioned, the trade winds make it more bearable).

WHERE TO STAY

Most of Aruba's hotels are of the resort variety, bustling and self-contained. There's a tremendous dearth of family or budget hotels. Guesthouses are few and tend to be booked up early in winter by faithful returning visitors. In season, it's imperative to make reservations well in advance; don't ever arrive expecting to find a room on the spot—you must have an address to give Immigration when you arrive on Aruba. Don't forget to ask if the 5% room tax and any service charge are included in the rates quoted when you make your reservation.

HOTELS
Very Expensive

Americana Aruba Beach Resort & Casino
J. E. Irausquin Blvd. 83 (P.O. Box 218), Oranjestad, Aruba. ☎ **297/8/64500**, 212/661-4540 in New York City, or toll free 800/447-7462 in the U.S. 405 rms, 14 suites. A/C MINIBAR TV TEL. Winter, $285–335 single; $390–$440 double; from $580 suite for two. Off-season, $195–$210 single; $290–$310 double; from $380 suite for two. (Rates all-inclusive.) AE, DC, MC, V. Free parking.

Although not as well decorated, or as glamorous, as some of its competitors and neighbors, this property is clean, well managed, and popular, attracting families and repeat guests, along with an array of tour groups that form most of the clientele. Occupying twin towers separated from one another by a garden with a lagoon-shaped swimming pool, the hotel was originally built in the early 1970s, and then renovated and expanded in 1990 at a cost of around $25 million. It seems to need constant refurbishment, however. Each of the bedrooms is comfortably furnished with conservatively contemporary upholstered furniture in pastel colors.

Dining/Entertainment: Le Petit Café is the establishment's most formal restaurant. Other choices include the Trade Winds. My favorite spot for a quiet drink is Jardin Brezilien, a second-floor veranda filled with plants and wicker settees overlooking the splashing fountains of the resort's swimming pool. There's also an in-house casino.

Services: Room service, laundry, massages, babysitting.

Facilities: White strip of palm-dotted beach, lagoon-shaped pool, two tennis courts, health club.

Aruba Hilton and Casino

J. E. Irausquin Blvd. 77, Palm Beach, Aruba. ☎ **297/8/64466,** or 800/HILTONS in the U.S., 800/445-8667 in Canada. Fax 297/8/68217. 231 rms, 40 suites. A/C MINIBAR TV TEL. Winter, $240–$340 single; $250–$350 double; $530–$1,500 suite. Off-season, $155–$175 single; $165–$185 double; $385–$1,300 suite. Breakfast from $13.50. AE, DC, MC, V. Free parking.

Originally built in the 1980s under the management of another chain, this 14-story skyscraper rises beside a white sand beach in a cluster of other high-rise hotels north of Oranjestad. Reopened as a Hilton late in 1993, after millions of dollars' worth of renovations, its lobby is sheathed in layers of stucco tinted in South American desert-inspired colors of terra-cotta and cerulean blue. Each of the bedrooms offers a balcony, an ocean view, comfortable furniture designed in Caribbean themes and colors such as sea-foam green, and lots of electronic amenities. The three uppermost floors are entirely devoted to suites.

Dining/Entertainment: The Casablanca Casino occupies a large room adjacent to the lobby. Adjacent to it are the Casablanca Casino Bar and Rick's Café, serving Mediterranean and Provençal cuisine, and Las Antillas Grill Restaurant, serving steaks and salads. Other eateries include at least four other drinking and dining areas. There's also a Music Hall offering cabaret and nightclub acts.

Services: 24-hour room service, laundry, babysitting, concierge.

Facilities: Fitness center, water-sports facilities, one tennis court, free-form Olympic-size swimming pool (on three different levels, whose waters are rippled by half a dozen waterspouts and fountains).

Divi Aruba Beach Resort

J. E. Irausquin Blvd. 45, Oranjestad, Aruba. ☎ **297/8/23300,** or 800/22-DORAL in the U.S. Fax 8/31940. 202 rms, 1 suite. A/C MINIBAR TV TEL. Winter, $250–$375 single or double; $400 junior suite; $600 one-bedroom suite. Off-season, $160–$200 single or double; $200 junior suite; $375 one-bedroom suite. MAP $50 per person extra. Honeymoon and windsurfing packages available. AE, DC, MC, V. Free parking.

Near the largest beach on the island, north of Oranjestad and 6 miles northwest of the airport, this casual, comfortable Doral-managed resort dating from 1969 is one of the island's friendliest oases. A rambling, low-rise structure, it has Iberian architectural accents, offering some rooms in the bungalow style, others in two- and three-story buildings or lanais. Each unit has a bath with tub and shower and a private terrace or balcony.

Dining/Entertainment: Meals are served on the casual Pelican Terrace or in the Red Parrot dining room. All year, dancing and entertainment are offered nightly. The Alhambra Casino stands across the road from the resort.

Services: Laundry, babysitting.

Facilities: Two freshwater swimming pools, tennis court, water-sports center.

✪ Hyatt Regency Aruba

L. G. Smith Blvd. 85, Palm Beach, Aruba. ☎ **297/8/61234,** or 800/233-1234 in the U.S. and Canada. Fax 8/61682. 340 rms, 20 suites. A/C MINIBAR TV TEL. Winter, $295–$400 single or double; $455 single or double Regency Club; from $880 suite. Off-season, $155–$250 single or double; $305 single or double Regency Club; from $880 suite. Additional person $45 extra, $75 extra in Regency Club. MAP $62 per person. AE, DC, MC, V. Free parking.

The most glamorous resort on Aruba lies on 12 landscaped acres about 2 miles north of Oranjestad. Built in the early 1990s at a cost exceeding $57 million, it offers a gracefully decorated series of public rooms reminiscent of a large-scale South American hacienda, with soaring ceilings, paneling, ceiling beams, and a postmodern Caribbean facade with art deco touches. The finest gardens on Aruba are dotted with waterfalls and reflecting pools, exotic birds, and stonework. The bedrooms are luxurious in their appointments, filled with many amenities, including original artworks commissioned from around the Americas. Furniture in the guest rooms and public areas is of wicker, rattan, and bleached ash, sometimes carved by Mexican or Guatemalan artisans. Guests in the hotel's 29 Regency Club rooms, located on the ninth floor, receive the special features of a private concierge, upgraded linens, and other amenities. There's a lounge where daily complimentary continental breakfast and evening hors d'oeuvres and cocktails are served.

Dining/Entertainment: Situated throughout the property are several restaurants and lounges, including the indoor/outdoor Ruinas Del Mar restaurant, with decor reminiscent of Aruba's gold-mining past. Fashioned out of native island stone, it's positioned on the edge of the lagoon and offers scenic ocean views; the cuisine is Mediterranean. For more casual dining, the beachfront Palms Restaurant presents an open-air Caribbean-style seafood grill. The Balashi Bar, accented by a swim-up bar, is conveniently located for guests lounging either poolside or on the beach. Al Fresco, an outdoor lounge of the main lobby, overlooks the courtyard, pool area, and beach. Other dining choices include the Olé Restaurant, serving Spanish tapas with singing waiters and other live entertainment, and Café Piccolo, an Italian-style café and bistro. The Casino Copacabana with its entertainment and gaming tables evokes the Côte d'Azur.

Services: 24-hour room service, laundry, massages, babysitting.

Facilities: A $2.5-million multilevel pool complex and lagoon (with waterfalls, tropical gardens, and slides), health and fitness facilities (including exercise room, saunas, massage, steam rooms, outdoor whirlpool, and sun-aerobics deck), two tennis courts (lit at night); scuba diving can be arranged.

Tamarijn Aruba Beach Resort

J. E. Irausquin Blvd. 41, Palm Beach, Aruba. ☎ **297/8/24150,** or toll free 800/22-DORAL in the U.S. Fax 8/31940. 236 rms. A/C TV TEL. Winter, $265–$350 single; $400–$500 double. Off-season, $185 single; $280 double. (Rates all-inclusive.) AE, DC, MC, V. Free parking.

The center of a trio of hostelries owned and managed by the Doral chain, this resort 6 miles northwest of the airport enjoys one of the longest beachfronts on Aruba. Built in a Dutch style of two-story units, it resembles a collection of connected waterfront town houses. The narrow strip of sandy turf between the accommodations and the beach is planted with copses of almonds, palms, and sea grapes. Each of the sunny rooms contains a radio and big glass doors that slide open to accept the breezes from the beach.

Dining/Entertainment: At one end of the long and narrow property, the open-air Bunker Bar is perched, as its name suggests, on stilts above a lopsided fortification remaining intact from World War II. On the premises are several drinking spots, including the Palm Court, Cunucu Terrace, and the Pizza Bar.

Services: Laundry, babysitting. Electric carts transport visitors to the Alhambra Casino and the Divi Aruba Beach Resort, where admission to the casino and use of the facilities are free.

Facilities: Swimming pool, two hard-surface tennis courts (lit at night), water sports (including scuba diving and waterskiing).

Expensive

Aruba Palm Beach Resort and Casino

J. E. Irausquin Blvd. 79, Oranjestad, Aruba. ☎ **297/8/23900,** or toll free 800/345-2782 in the U.S. and Canada. Fax 8/621941. 176 rms, 20 cabañas, 4 suites. A/C TV TEL. Winter, $179–$221 single or double; $215–$236 cabaña; $231–$263 suite. Off-season, $103–$126 single or double; $131–$142 cabaña; $147–$158 suite. Additional person $15 extra. MAP $33 per person extra. AE, DC, MC, V. Free parking.

Originally built in 1966 during the earliest stages of Aruba's hotel boom, this seashell-pink high-rise palazzo stands in a choice location, in a beachside palm grove 6 miles north of the airport. Accented with coral stone and Moorish arches both inside and out, the place is sleek, stylish, and comfortable, with a polite staff and rooms that benefited from a complete overhaul in 1988. Every unit has quality and character, with all the modern amenities, including small refrigerators.

Dining/Entertainment: You can enjoy the Las Vegas–inspired Palm Casino, nightly entertainment in the Oasis Lounge, fine dining in the Palm Garden Café, or cozy outdoor dining in the nautically inspired Seawatch Restaurant, which features U.S. beef and seafood. Live music is offered in the Players Club, which remains open nightly until 3am.

Services: Room service, laundry, babysitting, beauty salon.

Facilities: Olympic-size freshwater swimming pool (probably the best on the island for swimming laps), children's pool, two tennis courts, an array of shops; excursions include scuba diving and windsurfing.

Aruba Sonesta Resort & Casino

L. G. Smith Blvd. 82, Oranjestad, Aruba. ☎ **297/8/36000,** or toll free 800/SONESTA in the U.S. and Canada. Fax 8/34389. 275 rms, 23 suites. A/C MINIBAR TV TEL. Winter, $225–$325 single or double; $400–$600 suite. Off-season, $160–$210 single or double; $310–$535 suite. Additional person $30 extra. MAP $39 per person extra. AE, DC, MC, V. Free parking.

Launched in 1991, this hotel rises from a position in the busy heart of Oranjestad, and combines a shopping mall with its reception facilities to create one of the best-designed urban complexes on Aruba. It compensates for its lack of on-site beach facilities by ferrying its clients by motor launch to a private island a seven-minute boat ride offshore. Boats depart at 20-minute intervals throughout the day from a canal that bisects the hotel lobby. The bedrooms are comfortable and well upholstered, offering easy access to the casino and restaurant facilities of the island's busy waterfront. This hotel is no longer owned or managed by the U.S.–based Sonesta Group, although it retains its original name and access to Sonesta's reservations network.

Dining/Entertainment: The top restaurant is L'Escale, specializing in French cuisine and interconnected to the largest casino in downtown Oranjestad, the Crystal Casino. There's also a simpler eatery, the Brasserie, near the reception area. About half a dozen other restaurants, under separate management, are within a few minutes' walk. Desires Nightclub, off the main lobby, offers nightly entertainment, music for listening, or dancing. It's open Monday through Thursday from 9pm to 1am and on Friday and Saturday from 9pm to 3am.

Services: Room service (7am to 3am), laundry, babysitting; "A Just Us Kids" program (complimentary for guests) is offered year round, with counselor-supervised activities for kids ages 5 through 12.

Facilities: Swimming pool; nearby tennis courts, fitness center, and downtown Oranjestad. There's a 40-acre offshore island with many different water sports and a restaurant and bar.

CONDOS & TIME-SHARE PROPERTIES

Time-sharing and condos have become a major vacation investment on Aruba. Even if you're not interested for yourself, you may want to consider renting a unit as a one-time vacationer.

Amsterdam Manor Beach Resort

J. E. Irausquin Blvd. 252 (P.O. Box 1302), Oranjestad, Aruba. ☎ **297/8/71492.** Fax 8/71463. 73 units. A/C TV TEL. Winter, $140–$290 unit for one or two. Off-season, $90–$220 unit for one or two. Additional person $20 extra. AE, DC, MC, V. Free parking.

Opened in 1991, this hotel sports one of the two or three most interesting facades on the island. Inspired by the interconnected rows of canalfront houses in Amsterdam (or by a sprawling manor house on Curaçao), it lies amid an arid landscape across the street from Eagle Beach. Owned by a trio of Dutch investors, it has a series of inner courtyards, a vivid sense of colonial Dutch life, a swimming pool fed by a pair of splashing waterfalls, and a simple bar and restaurant. More than in any other hotel on the island, accommodations draw from 19th-century Dutch models, and contain pinewood furniture, country-rustic colors of dull reds, blues, and greens, and in some cases, high ceilings leading to gable-capped peaks. Units contain fully equipped kitchens, and come as studios and one- or two-bedroom units.

La Cabana All Suite Beach Resort & Casino

J. E. Irausquin Blvd. 250 (P.O. Box 672), Oranjestad, Aruba. ☎ **297/8/79000,** 212/251-1710 in New York City, or toll free 800/835-7193 in the U.S. and Canada. Fax 8/75474. 803 studios and suites. A/C MINIBAR TV TEL. Winter, $200–$240 studio; $230–$280 one-bedroom suite; $395–$485 two-bedroom suite; $605–$755 three-bedroom suite. Off-season, $105–$140 studio; $130–$160 one-bedroom suite; $210–$275 two-bedroom suite; $325–$425 three-bedroom suite. AE, DC, MC, V. Free parking.

 Family-Friendly Accommodations

Divi Aruba Beach Resort *(see p. 731)* This Aruba resort gives substantial food and lodging discounts to children 3 to 12. Children 12 and under sharing a room with two adults stay free.

Hyatt Regency Aruba *(see p. 732)* This deluxe resort features supervised activities and special programs for children 3 to 15 on weekends and holidays throughout the summer. There's also a program of activities for teens 13 to 17, including Jeep excursions. Snorkeling trips. "Rock Out," barbecues, dances, and sunset sails.

Avila Beach Hotel *(see p. 770)* A unique choice on Curaçao, this hotel is built right on the beach, and it's a safe haven in which kids can frolic. Baby cots can be provided.

Originally conceived in 1991 as a 441-unit all-suite resort, this establishment was almost doubled in size in 1993 when another 362 units were built on the flatlands in back. Today, La Cabana is the largest and most ambitiously marketed hotel on Aruba (and also the third-largest hotel in the Caribbean) catering to a clientele who appreciate all the facilities of a private apartment in their hotel accommodation. The centerpiece of the older section is a free-form pool sunk into a landscaped courtyard, across the coastal road from the beach. The four-story, pink-sided accommodations in the newer section are angled around a lavishly landscaped courtyard of their own, in the center of which are two pools, rows of mature palm trees, and an artificial waterfall.

Regardless of their location, the studios and suites are carefully engineered cocoons of pink or blue, each with richly furnished kitchens and a patio or veranda, and, in all cases, Jacuzzis, mini-safes, and alarm clocks. Ground-floor rooms afford less privacy. Suites can be combined through interconnecting doors to create accommodations suitable for up to ten occupants.

Dining/Entertainment: In a separate outbuilding, the hotel maintains its Royal Cabana Casino, reportedly the third largest in the Bahama-Caribbean region. The Tropicana theater presents a changing cast of female impersonators who add a Las Vegas–style glitter. Scattered around the premises are five different bars, snack kiosks, and restaurants, specializing in either Italian cuisine, steaks, or seafood. Different bars cater to cravings for frozen yogurt, chocolates, espresso, or tropical drinks. Buffet-style barbecues or Mexican barbecues are featured during the several-times-a-week theme parties.

Services: The hotel provides an on-site child-care center, the Club Cabana Nana, which supervises and amuses children 5 to 12 for a cost of $80 a week; it's open daily except Saturday. There's also an intricately scheduled array of daily activities (beach tennis, aerobics, billiards for kids, etc.).

Facilities: Health club (with squash and racquetball courts and a limited array of spa treatments), several specialty stores selling everything from groceries to luxury goods, five tennis courts (illuminated for night play), water-sports facilities (including scuba, windsurfing, sailing, and snorkeling).

Playa Linda Beach Resort

J. E. Irausquin Blvd. 87 (P.O. Box 235, Oranjestad), Palm Beach, Aruba. ☎ **297/8/61000,** or toll free 800/223-6510 in the U.S., 800/424-5500 in Canada. Fax 8/63479. 194 studios and suites. A/C TV TEL. Winter. $220 studio for one or two; $330 one-bedroom suite; $650 two-bedroom suite. Off-season, $170 studio for one or two; $220 one-bedroom suite; $420 two-bedroom suite. Additional person $30 extra. (Rates include continental breakfast.) AE, DC, MC, V. Free parking.

Designed in an M shape of receding balconies, this salmon-colored time-share complex sits amid tropical foliage and native Aruban flora on a desirable stretch of white sandy beachfront 6 miles northwest of the airport. The units offer kitchens and private verandas, and contain foldaway couch beds suitable for children. Amenities and facilities at Playa Linda include a large lagoon-shaped swimming pool, outdoor whirlpool baths, tennis courts, and a shopping arcade featuring a beauty parlor, perfumery, and souvenir and gift shop. The Linda Vista Restaurant serves international food. Laundry and babysitting are available.

WHERE TO DINE

Sometimes, at least on off-season package deals, visitors on the MAP (breakfast and dinner) are allowed to dine around on an exchange plan with other hotels.

In Oranjestad
Expensive
✪ Chez Mathilde
Havenstraat 23. ☎ **297/8/34968.** Reservations recommended. Appetizers $7.50–$16; main courses $18.50–$32. AE, DC, MC, V. Lunch Mon–Sat 11:30am–2:30pm; dinner daily 6–11pm. FRENCH.

The *restaurant français* at Oranjestad is expensive, but most satisfied customers agree that it's worth the price, especially those diners who order the chef's bouillabaisse, made with more than a dozen different sea creatures. You might also want to try the tournedos au poivre. Other well-recommended dishes include rack of lamb chops with fine French herbs, a juicy grilled veal chop topped with a slice of goose-liver filet, and filet of red snapper topped with a blend of onions, tomatoes, green peppers, fresh herbs, and a dash of rum—baked in parchment paper. Not only do you get distinguished food and service, including a haute-cuisine classic French repertoire, but you can enjoy your repast in an elegant setting. The structure housing the restaurant, near the Sonesta Hotel, Beach Club & Casino Aruba, a five-minute drive north of the airport, was built in the 1800s, and it has been preserved more or less as it was originally. The restaurant is named after Mathilde Oduber, the last member of the family to live in this house (she died here in 1978). The intimate dining rooms contain beautifully set tables and a restrained but romantic decor. Enjoy an apéritif while you peruse the comparatively large wine list. Live piano music enhances the total experience.

Escale
In the Sonesta Hotel, Beach Club & Casino Aruba, L. G. Smith Blvd. 82. ☎ **297/8/36000.** Reservations recommended in winter. Appetizers $5–$12; main courses $20–$32. AE, DC, MC, V. Dinner only, daily 6:30–11pm. FRENCH/INTERNATIONAL.

Although it features a direct access to the noise and bustle of Oranjestad's Crystal Casino, this restaurant is calm, elegant, and peaceful, thanks to a raised bar area which separates it from the action nearby. Designed in the style of the French Empire, it offers panoramic views of the harborfront, formal service, and well-prepared French cuisine. Menu choices might include lobster bisque with Alaska crabmeat, marinated slices of quail, pan-fried crabcakes, crêpes stuffed with smoked salmon, rack of lamb provençal, pasta primavera with shredded breast of duck, grilled veal chop, peppery grouper, and butterfly scampi with Texas goat cheese.

Gasparito
Gasparito 3. ☎ **297/8/67144.** Reservations recommended. Appetizers $3.95–$7.25; main courses $17.50–$37.50; AE, MC, V. Dinner only, Mon–Sat 5–11pm. ARUBAN/INTERNATIONAL.

This bright, upbeat restaurant is set in a traditional Aruban-style house with green napery and yellow walls adorned with local art. The atmosphere is lively and the food varied. Diners can enjoy such dishes as baked chicken stuffed with a peach, filet mignon served with either sautéed mushroom or black-pepper sauce, or a variety of keshi yena (Dutch cheese stuffed with a choice of beef, chicken, or seafood). The menu also features an array of fresh seafood, including lobster served with a garlic-butter sauce or sautéed with onions, green peppers, tomatoes, and a multitude of spices. If there's any room left at the end of the meal, you can finish with a bowl of ice cream of your choosing served with bananas and cinnamon.

Moderate

La Dolce Vita

Palm Beach 39. ☎ **297/8/65241.** Reservations recommended, especially in high season. Appetizers $4.95–$8.25; main courses $10.95–$25.95. AE, MC, V. Dinner only, Thurs–Tues 6–11pm. ITALIAN.

Since 1980 La Dolce Vita has been among the most acclaimed Italian restaurants on Aruba. It wasn't long before it was discovered by the food and wine critics of such prestigious Stateside magazines as *Gourmet.* In an arid neighborhood inland from the sea, it's a rustic-style restaurant ringed with a cactus garden. Menu items are creatively Italian, and include most of the usual favorites as well as a scattering of unusual dishes. A meal might include slices of veal served parmesan style, with marsala sauce, Cordon Bleu style, a la Florio (with artichokes), or a la Bartolucci (with ricotta, spinach, and mozzarella). Snapper can be prepared in three ways: simmered with clams and mussels, broiled with lemon or wine, or stuffed with pulverized shrimp. Also available is a stewpot of fish, and linguine with either red or white clam sauce. Finish with an espresso, a zabaglione, or perhaps some Italian ice cream.

The Waterfront Crabhouse

Seaport Market, L. G. Smith Blvd. ☎ **297/8/35858.** Reservations recommended. Appetizers $3.95–$7.95; main courses $13.95–$24.95; continental breakfast $5.95; lunch from $12. AE, MC, V. Breakfast daily 8–11am; lunch daily noon–4pm; dinner daily 5:30–11pm. SEAFOOD.

Set at the most desirable end of a shopping mall in downtown Oranjestad, overlooking a manicured lawn, this restaurant evokes a dining room on the coast of California. Amid a decor of painted murals showing underwater life and rattan furniture, and tables placed both indoors and on a garden-terrace, you can enjoy well-prepared seafood. Menu items include such appetizers as stuffed clams and fried squid with a marinara sauce, and linguine with white or red clam sauce, which can be ordered on the side or as a main course. The chef lists "crabs, crabs, crabs" as his specialty, including garlic crabs, Alaska crab legs, and (in season) soft-shell crabs. Other items include stuffed Maine lobster and Cajun grilled shrimp, blackened and cooked over an open fire. A wide range of other fish dishes, including yellowfin tuna or swordfish are also grilled over an open fire. Ecologists will appreciate that all fish served are hook-and-line caught, never from drift nets.

Inexpensive

Bali Floating Restaurant

L. G. Smith Blvd. ☎ **297/8/20680.** Reservations required. Appetizers $3.50–$8; main courses $10.50–$22; $45 Indonesian rice table for two; $45 Chinese rice table for two. AE, MC, V. Lunch Mon–Sat noon–2:30pm; dinner daily 6–10:30pm. CHINESE/INDONESIAN.

Housed in an Asian houseboat decorated with bamboo and Indonesian art, the Bali Floating Restaurant is moored in Oranjestad's harbor. Diners are treated to the popular Chinese or Indonesian rijstaffel (rice table), a complete meal of rice surrounded by 21 different dishes, served at your table in individual portions. The rijstaffel is not spicy, but the sambal (hot, hot) is served on the side for the more adventurous to try. A mini-version is served for lunch, as well as sandwiches and snacks. The rijstaffel may be ordered per person, but try to go with a group, since it's a fun meal that everyone will enjoy. The menu also offers such dishes as fried squid in garlic with hot chili peppers, the fresh catch of the day in a sweet-and-sour sauce, and shrimp in hot ginger sauce.

⑤ Boonoonoonoos

Wiihelminastraat 18. ☎ **297/8/31888.** Reservations recommended for dinner in winter. Appetizers $3.50–$9.75; main courses $12.50–$28.75. AE, DC, MC, V. Daily 11:30am–10:30pm. CARIBBEAN/INTERNATIONAL.

Named after the legendary beach parties of Jamaica (Boonoonoonoos), this restaurant in an old-fashioned Aruban house on the capital's main shopping street celebrates the widely divergent traditions of Caribbean cuisine. It offers a confectionary decor of blues, greens, and pinks, a bar outfitted with rows of hard-bottomed benches, and a crew of waiters in striped vests and bow ties. Even if you're not visiting the rest of the Caribbean, you can go on a culinary tour by wandering across the menu. Try, for example, an appetizer known as ajaka, which is an Aruban dish seasoned with chicken and wrapped in banana leaves. Soups also make good appetizers, including a local pumpkin soup and a homemade fish soup. For a main dish, the most popular is actually Aruban: keshi yena (Aruban chicken casserole). You can also order Jamaican jerk ribs, based on a recipe dating back three centuries. You might also try a Bajan pepperpot or curried chicken Trinidad style. A small section of the menu is devoted to a French cuisine, including filet mignon and Dover sole meunière. This place continues to draw mixed reactions from readers, everything from raves to attacks. Slow service seems to be one of the major complaints.

NEAR PALM BEACH

Moderate

Chalet Suisse

J. E. Irausquin Blvd. 246. ☎ **297/8/75054.** Reservations recommended. Appetizers $4–$10; main courses $13–$25. AE, DC, MC, V. Dinner only, Mon–Sat 6–10:30pm. SWISS/INTERNATIONAL.

Designed like an alpine chalet, and set beside the highway close to La Cabana Hotel, this restaurant is probably the closest replica of an old-fashioned Swiss dining room in the entire Caribbean. In deliberate contrast to the arid scrublands that surround it, the restaurant is an air-conditioned refuge of thick plaster walls and roughly textured pinewood panels crafted into octagonal ceiling medallions infused with a kind of ersatz *gemütlich*. Menu items include lobster bisque or Dutch pea soup, beef Stroganoff, pasta of the day, wienerschnitzel, roast duckling with orange sauce, broiled breast of capon with herbs, red snapper with Créole sauce, and an array of high-calorie desserts.

De Olde Molen (The Old Mill)

L. G. Smith Blvd. 330, Palm Beach. ☎ **297/8/62060.** Reservations recommended. Appetizers $2.75–$7.50; main courses $14–$26.50. AE, DC, MC, V. Dinner only, Mon–Sat 6–11pm. INTERNATIONAL.

This landmark structure is just across the street from the Hilton Hotel and within walking distance of a number of other Palm Beach hotels. The windmill housing the restaurant was built in 1804 in Holland, but it was torn down, shipped to Aruba, and reconstructed piece by piece, a gift of the queen of the Netherlands. Since 1960 it has been a tourist-focused destination for dinner. An international and regional cuisine is served, including thick Dutch split-pea soup, Chateaubriand for two people, veal Cordon Bleu, shrimp provençal, and red snapper arubiano (with a Créole sauce). You might want to finish your meal with an Irish coffee.

⑤ The Old Cunucu House

Palm Beach 150. ☎ **297/8/61666.** Reservations recommended. Appetizers $3.95–$6.95; main courses $13.95–$26.95. AE, DC, MC, V. Dinner only, Mon–Sat 6–10:30pm. ARUBAN/ INTERNATIONAL.

When it was originally built as a private house in the 1920s, this was the only building in its neighborhood. Today, although other buildings and restaurants have sprouted up nearby, it retains its deliberately understated original decor of very thick plaster-coated walls, ultra-simple furniture, and tile floors. Many visitors appreciate a before-dinner drink under a shed-style roof in front, where chairs and tables overlook a well-kept garden studded with desert plants. The restaurant maintains a warm, traditional feeling. It focuses on local and international recipes, including fish soup, fried squid, coconut fried shrimp, and broiled swordfish. Several dishes are served with funchi (cornmeal) and pan bati (a local pancake).

Sandra's

J. E. Irausquin Blvd. 224. ☎ **297/8/71517.** Reservations recommended. Appetizers $3.75– $6.75; main courses $11–$37.50. AE, MC, V. Dinner only, Tues–Sun 5:30–10:30pm. Closed first two weeks in Sept. INTERNATIONAL.

In a one-story green-and-white building beside the highway between Oranjestad and the island's high-rise hotels, this is a comfortable and unpretentious restaurant that serves well-prepared food. There's an air-conditioned interior, as well as wrap-around terraces for anyone who wants to dine outside. All main courses include a complimentary visit to the salad bar. Menu items include lobster bisque, several kinds of pastas, chicken parmigiana, seafood Newburg, and jumbo shrimp in either garlic or Créole sauce. A meat combo for two diners features portions of filet mignon, pork chops, chicken breast, and sausages, all of which are cooked on a hot stone placed on your table. Also popular is broiled seafood pasta à la Sandra's, with fettuccine and mushrooms.

Inexpensive

⑤ Steamboat Buffet & Deli

J. E. Irausquin Blvd. 370. ☎ **297/8/66700.** Reservations not accepted. Breakfast buffet $8.80 per person; lunch sandwiches $8 each; dinner buffet $16 per person. AE, MC, V. Breakfast daily 7am–noon; lunch daily noon–4pm; dinner daily 6–10:30pm. INTERNATIONAL BUFFETS/SANDWICHES.

In a miniature shopping center across from the Americana Aruba Hotel, this is the most famous and popular buffet restaurant on the island. Decorated in a nautically inspired theme of marine blue and white, with lots of varnished pine and shining brass, it presents copious breakfast and dinner buffets from tables crafted from the bows of well-scrubbed rowboats. (Even the staff dresses up as officers and deckhands on an oceangoing vessel.) During breakfast a chef will prepare omelets any way you want, and at dinner the place fills up with extended local families and their children who appreciate the low prices. Be warned that at lunchtime the only thing on the menu is an uncomplicated selection of overstuffed deli-style sandwiches, although the bar area won't refrain from serving you a drink if you ask for it.

AT OR NEAR NOORD
Expensive

❂ Valentino's

In the Caribbean Palm Village, Noord 43-E. ☎ **297/8/62700.** Reservations recommended. Appetizers $6.25–$8.75; main courses $11–$25.75. AE, DC, MC, V. Dinner only, Mon–Sat 6–11pm. ITALIAN.

Many visitors consider this the most elegant Italian restaurant on Aruba. Nestled in the central courtyard of an upscale condominium complex, it offers the possibility of a before-dinner apéritif near the entrance, then invites guests to climb a flight of stairs to reach the peak-ceilinged dining room. There, amid a color scheme of soft pinks and grays, you'll have a glassed-in view of a well-designed kitchen, views over the palms and pools of the condominium complex, and the attentions of the youthful but well-trained staff who hail from around the world. Menu items usually indicate which region of Italy they originated in, and might include panzerotti Valdostana (crêpes stuffed with cheese, chicken, ham, and mushrooms, and baked with tomato sauce), mozzarella in carrozza (cheese bread topped with fried mozzarella and served with tomato sauce), fettuccine with salmon, penne del pastor (a Sardinian dish with chicken, ricotta, parmesan, and bolognese sauce), veal scaloppine with zucchini in cream sauce, tenderloin pepper steak, rack of lamb in rosemary sauce with mint jelly, and a selection of fish dishes.

Moderate
The Buccaneer

Gasparito 11-C. ☎ **297/8/66172.** Reservations not accepted. Appetizers $4.75–$6; main courses $12–$23. AE, MC, V. Dinner only, Mon–Sat 5:30–10pm. SEAFOOD/INTERNATIONAL.

In a rustic-looking building near the hamlet of Noord, close to many of the island's biggest high-rise hotels, this is one of the most reasonably priced and popular seafood restaurants on Aruba. Inside, you'll find a decor of varnished pine, nautical accessories, and bubbling aquariums, many of them positioned immediately adjacent to some of the dining tables. Menu items include crabmeat cocktail, shrimp in Pernod sauce, paella arubiana, broiled frogs' legs, lobster thermidor, and a land-and-sea platter containing portions of fish, shrimp, and tenderloin. A simple dessert menu contains peach Melba. A commodious bar area is on the premises for anyone interested in lingering over drinks.

La Paloma

Noord 39. ☎ **297/8/74611.** Reservations recommended. Appetizers $2.50–$7; main courses $10–$26. AE, MC, V. Dinner only, Wed–Mon 6–11pm. ITALIAN/INTERNATIONAL.

Established in 1983 in a low-slung Mediterranean-inspired villa, this was one of the first restaurants along a road that later sprouted with less-desirable competitors. A 10-minute drive north of Oranjestad, it contains a semicircular bar area and a crowded but convivial dining area filled with bamboo and rattan furniture. The menu is devoted to international and Italian cuisine. Italian choices include gamberoni parmigiani, linguine scampi marinari, and frittata stuffed eggplant; international selections include lobster provençal, red snapper in papillotte, a seafood platter, a 12-ounce filet mignon, and a 14-ounce strip loin steak.

Papiamento

Washington 61. ☎ **297/8/24544.** Reservations recommended, especially on weekends. Appetizers $3–$16; main courses $18.50–$35. AE, MC, V. Dinner only, Tues–Sun 6:30–10:30pm. CONTINENTAL.

One of the most popular independent restaurants on Aruba occupies a stone farm-house whose foundations are probably about 200 years old. Transformed into a stylish hideaway, and named after Aruba's distinctive patois, it boasts a collection of modern paintings, and such old-world touches as massive brass chandeliers. A distinguishing culinary feature is the way fresh meat or seafood is served raw on sizzling marble slabs so that your dinner is cooked in front of you the way you like. Meals might include chicken parmesan, snapper provençal, lamb chops or snapper cooked on a hot stone at table, filet mignon, surf and turf, lobster, sirloin, and a combination platter of shrimp and scallops.

EAST OF ORANJESTAD

Moderate

⑤ Brisas del Mar

Savaneta 222A. ☎ **297/8/47718.** Reservations required. Appetizers $4.50–$6.30; main courses $10.50–$32. AE, MC, V. Lunch Tues–Sun noon–2:30pm: dinner daily 6:30–9:30pm. SEAFOOD.

A 15-minute drive east of Oranjestad, near the police station, Brisas del Mar is like a place you might encounter in some outpost in Australia. Here, in very simple surroundings right at water's edge, Lucia Rasmijn opened this little hut with an air-conditioned bar in front of which the locals gather to drink the day away. The place is often jammed on weekends with many of the same local people, who come here to drink and dance. In back the tables are open to the sea breezes, and nearby you can see the catch of the day, perhaps wahoo, being sliced up and sold to local buyers. Specialties include mixed seafood platter, baby shark, and broiled lobster; you can order meat and poultry dishes as well, including tenderloin steak and broiled chicken.

Charlie's Bar and Restaurant

B. v/d Veen Zeppenveldstraat 56 (Main St.), San Nicolas. ☎ **297/8/45086.** Reservations not required. Daily soup $4.75; main courses $15–$18. No credit cards. Mon–Sat noon–9:30pm. (Bar, Mon–Sat noon–10pm.) SEAFOOD/INTERNATIONAL.

A 25-minute drive east of Oranjestad, Charlie's, dating from 1941, qualifies through its decor and history as the most interesting reason to visit San Nicolas; it's the most overly decorated bar in the West Indies, sporting an array of memorabilia and local souvenirs. Where roustabouts and roughnecks once brawled, you'll find tables filled with contented tourists admiring thousands of pennants, banners, and trophies dangling from the high ceiling. Two-fisted drinks are still served, but the menu has improved since the good old days, when San Nicolas was one of the toughest towns in the Caribbean. You can now enjoy freshly made soup, grilled scampi, Créole-style squid, and churrasco. Sirloin steak and red snapper are usually featured.

⑤ Mi Cushina

Cura Cabai. ☎ **297/8/48335.** Reservations recommended. Appetizers $3–$9; main courses $10–$24. AE, DC, MC, V. Lunch Fri–Wed noon–2pm; dinner Fri–Wed 6–10pm. ARUBAN/INTERNATIONAL.

On the main road about a mile before San Nicolas, Mi Cushina serves up fried fish with funchi (cornmeal), stewed lamb with pan bati (a local pancake), and other tasty dishes. A selection of international food is also served. The decor includes a ceiling made of coffee bags, light fixtures on old wagon wheels, and family photographs, along with tools and utensils used in the past. There's a display of musical instruments used by Arubans long ago.

WHAT TO SEE & DO

The capital of Aruba, **Oranjestad,** attracts shoppers rather than sightseers. The bustling city has a very Caribbean flavor, and it's part Spanish, part Dutch in architecture. Cutting in from the airport, the main thoroughfare, Lloyd G. Smith Boulevard, goes along the waterfront and on to Palm Beach, changing its name along the way to J. E. Irausquin Boulevard. But most visitors cross it heading for Caya G. F. Betico Croes, where they find the best free-port shopping.

After a shopping trip, you might return to the harbor where fishing boats and schooners, many from Venezuela, are moored. Nearly all newcomers to Aruba like to take a picture of the **Schooner Harbor.** Not only does it have colorful boats docked along the quay, but boatpeople display their wares in open stalls. The local patois predominates. A little farther along, at the fish market, fresh fish is sold directly from the boats. Also on the sea side of Oranjestad, **Wilhelmina Park** was named after Queen Wilhelmina of the Netherlands. A tropical garden has been planted along the water, and there's a sculpture of the Queen Mother.

Aside from shopping, the major attractions of Aruba are ✪ **Eagle Beach** and ✪ **Palm Beach,** considered along the finest in the Caribbean. Most of Aruba's high-rise hotels are stretched Las Vegas–strip style along these pure-white sand stretches on the leeward coast.

MUSEUMS

I know you didn't come to Aruba to look at museums, but just in case . . .

Archeological Museum

Zoutmanstraat 1. ☎ **297/8/28979.** Admission free. Daily 8am–noon and 1–4pm.

Diagonally across the street from the Sonesta Hotel, Beach Club & Casino Aruba, the Archeological Museum contains on its first floor pre-Columbian artifacts found at numerous places on the island. You'll see agricultural and home equipment dating back 1,000 years, and even skeletons of people who were buried in big earthenware urns. In addition, there's a collection of skeletons and tools dating back 2,000 years.

Museo Arubano

Oranjestraat, just off L. G. Smith Blvd. behind the government buildings. ☎ **297/8/26099.** Admission $1.15. Mon–Fri 9am–noon and 1–4pm.

In the restored Fort Zoutman, the Museo Arubano (also called the King Willem III Tower and Fort Zoutman Museum) contains material on the culture and history of Aruba, with artifacts dating from the earliest times of the island through colonial days and up to the present. The 18th-century fort, the oldest building on Aruba, has at its entrance the King Willem III Tower, which served as a lighthouse for almost 100 years.

OUT IN THE COUNTRY

If you can lift yourselves from the sands for one afternoon, you might like to drive into the *cunucu,* which in Papiamento means "the countryside." Here Arubans live in very modest but colorful pastel-washed houses decorated with tropical plants, which require expensive desalinated water to grow. Of course, all visitors venturing into the center of Aruba want to see the strangely shaped divi-divi tree with its trade-wind–blown coiffure.

Rocks stud Aruba, and the most impressive ones are those found at **Ayo** and **Casibari,** northeast of Hooiberg. These stacks of diorite boulders are the size of buildings. The rocks, weighing several thousand tons, are a puzzle to geologists. On the rocks at Ayo are ancient Amerindian drawings. At Casibari, you can climb the boulder-strewn terrain to the top for a panoramic view of the island or wander around lower down looking at rocks nature has carved into seats and likenesses of prehistoric birds and animals. Casibari is open daily from 9am to 5pm. No admission is charged. There's a lodge at Casibari where you can buy souvenirs, snacks, soft drinks, and beer.

Guides can also point out drawings on the walls and ceiling of the **Caves of Canashito,** south of Hooiberg. While there, you may get to see the giant green parakeets.

Hooiberg is affectionately known as "The Haystack." It's Aruba's most outstanding landmark, and anybody with the stamina can take the steps all the way to the top of this 541-foot-high hill. One Aruban jogs up there every morning. From its precincts in the center of the island you can see Venezuela on a clear day.

On the jagged, windswept northern coast, the **Natural Bridge** has been carved out of the coral rock by the relentless surf. In a little café overlooking the coast you can order snacks. There you'll also find a souvenir shop with a large selection of trinkets, T-shirts, and wall hangings, all for reasonable prices.

You turn inland for the short trip to **Pirate's Castle** at Bushiribana, which stands on a cliff on the island's windward coast. This is actually a deserted gold mill from the island's now-defunct industry. Another gold mill is in the old ghost town on the west coast, Balashi.

You can continue to the village of Noord, known for its **St. Anne's Church,** with a hand-carved, 17th-century Dutch altar.

EAST TO SAN NICOLAS

Driving along the highway more or less paralleling the south coast of Aruba toward the island's southernmost section, you may want to stop at the **Spaans Lagoen (Spanish Lagoon),** where legend says pirates used to hide out as they waited to plunder rich cargo ships in the Caribbean. Today this is an ideal place for snorkeling, and you can picnic at tables under the mangrove trees.

On to the east, you'll pass an area called **Savaneta,** where some of the most ancient traces of human habitation have been unearthed. You'll see along here the first oil tanks marking the position of the Lago Oil & Transport Company Ltd., the Exxon subsidiary around which the town of San Nicolas developed, although it had been an industrial center since the days of phosphate mining in the late 19th century. A "company town" until the refinery was closed in 1985, San Nicolas, 12 miles from Oranjestad, is called the Aruba Sunrise Side, and tourism has become its main economic factor. The town has a blend of cultures—customs, style, languages, color, and tastes. In the area are caves with Arawak artwork on the walls and a modern innovation, a PGA-approved golf course with sand "greens" and cactus traps.

Boca Grandi, on the windward side of the island, is a favorite windsurfing location; or if you prefer quieter waters, you'll find them at **Baby Beach** and **Rodgers Beach,** on Aruba's lee side. Overlooking the latter two beaches is **Seroe Colorado (Colorado Point),** from which it's possible to see the coastline of Venezuela as well as the pounding surf on the windward side. You can climb down the cliffs, and perhaps spot an iguana here and there; protected by law, the once-endangered saurians now proliferate in peace.

Other sights in the San Nicolas area are the **Guadarikiri Cave** and **Fontein Cave,** where you can see the wall drawings, plus the **Huliba** and **Tunnel of Love caves,** with guides and refreshment stands. Guadarikiri Cave is a haven for wild parrots.

AN UNDERWATER JOURNEY

One of the island's most diverting pastimes involves an underwater journey on one of the world's few passenger submarines, operated by ✪ **Atlantis Submarines,** Seaport Village Marina (opposite the Sonesta Hotel, Beach Club & Casino Aruba), Oranjestad (☎ **297/8/36090**). An underwater ride offers one of the Caribbean's best opportunities for nondivers to witness firsthand the underwater life of a coral reef, with fewer obstacles and dangers than posed by a scuba expedition. Carrying 46 passengers to a depth of up to 150 feet, the submarine organizes departures from the Oranjestad harborfront every hour on the hour, Tuesday through Sunday from 10am to 2pm (there are no departures on Monday). Each tour includes a 25-minute transit by catamaran to Barcadera Reef, 2 miles southeast of Aruba, a site chosen for the huge variety of its underwater flora and fauna. At the reef, participants transfer to the submarine for a one-hour underwater lecture and tour.

Allow two hours for the complete experience. The cost is $62 for adults and $29 for children 4 to 16 (no children under 4 are admitted). Advance reservations are essential, either through the concierge of one of the island's hotels or via the telephone number listed above. In either event, a staff member will ask for a credit- or charge-card number (and give you a confirmation number) to hold the booking for you.

SPORTS & OUTDOOR ACTIVITIES

BEACHES   The western and southern shore, called the **Turquoise Coast,** attracts sun seekers to Aruba. **Palm Beach** and **Eagle Beach** (the latter closer to Oranjestad) are the best beaches. No hotel along the strip owns the beaches, all of which are open to the public (if you use any of the hotel's facilities, however, you'll be charged, of course). You can also spread your towel on **Manchebo Beach** or **Druif Bay Beach**—in fact, anywhere along 7 miles of uninterrupted sugar-white sands. In total contrast to the leeward side, the north or windward shore is rugged and wild.

CRUISES   Visitors interested in combining a boat ride with a few hours of snorkeling should contact **De Palm Tours,** which has offices in eight of the island's hotels and its main office at L. G. Smith Blvd. 142, in Oranjestad (☎ **297/ 8/24400**). For $38 per person, they'll take you on a "fun cruise" aboard a catamaran. After a cruise of 1¹/₂ hours, passengers stop for 3 hours at their private De Palm island for snorkeling. Lunch and an open bar aboard are included in the price. The tour, if participation warrants it, departs daily at 10am and returns at 4pm.

DEEP-SEA FISHING   In the deep waters off the coast of Aruba you can test your skill and wits against the big ones—wahoo, marlin, tuna, bonito, and sailfish. **De Palm Tours,** L. G. Smith Blvd. 142, in Oranjestad (☎ **297/8/24400**), takes out a maximum of six people (four of whom can fish at the same time) on one of its four boats, which range in length from 29 to 38 feet. Half-day tours, with all equipment included, begin at $250 for two people, and $270 for six. The prices are doubled for full-day trips. Boats leave from the docks in Oranjestad. De Palm maintains 11 branches, most of which are in Aruba's major hotels.

GOLF   Visitors can play at the **Aruba Golf Club,** Golfweg 82 (☎ **297/ 8/42006**) near San Nicolas, on the southeastern end of the island. Although it has only 10 greens, they are played from different tees to simulate an 18-hole play. Twenty-five different sand traps add an extra challenge. Greens fees are $10 for 18 holes and $7.50 for 9 holes. The course is open daily from 7:30am to 5pm, although anyone wishing to play 18 holes must begin the rounds before 1:30pm. Golf carts and clubs can be rented on site in the pro shop. On the premises is an air-conditioned restaurant and changing rooms with showers.

By the time you read this, Aruba's long-awaited **Tierra del Sol golf course** (☎ **297/8/37800**) should be open. Designed by the Robert Trent Jones II Group, the course is on the northwest coast, near the California Lighthouse. The 18-hole, par-71 golf course was designed to combine the beauty of the island's indigenous flora, such as the swaying divi-divi tree, with lush greens. Facilities include a restaurant and lounge in the clubhouse, two swimming pools, and eight tennis courts. The course is managed by Hyatt Resorts Caribbean.

SCUBA DIVING, SNORKELING & OTHER WATER SPORTS   You can snorkel in rather shallow waters, and scuba divers find stunning marine life with endless varieties of coral as well as tropical fish in infinite hues; at some points visibility is up to 90 feet. The goal of most divers is the German freighter *Antilia,* which was scuttled in the early years of World War II off the northwestern tip of Aruba, not too far from Palm Beach.

Red Sails Sports, Palm Beach. (☎ **297/8/161603**), is the best water-sports center on the island. The center has an extensive variety of activities, including sailing, windsurfing, waterskiing, and scuba diving. Scuba diving can be experienced in one day with Red Sail dive packages, including shipwreck dives as well as exploration of marine reefs. Guests are first given a poolside resort course where Red Sail's certified instructors teach procedures that ensure safety during dives. For those who wish to become certified, full PADI certification can be achieved in as little as four days. One-tank dives cost $30 and up.

Divi Winds Center, J. E. Irausquin Blvd. 41 (☎ **297/8/23300,** ext. 623), near the Tamarind Aruba Beach Resort, is the windsurfing headquarters of the island. Equipment is made by Fanatic, Inc., and is rented for $18 per hour or $35 per half day. The resort is on the quiet (Caribbean) side of the island, and doesn't face the fierce Atlantic waves. Sunfish lessons can be arranged, and snorkeling gear can be rented. There's another location at the Hyatt.

TENNIS   Most of the island's beachfront hotels have tennis courts, often swept by trade winds, and some have top pros on hand to give instruction. Many of the courts can also be lit for night games (I don't advise playing in Aruba's noonday sun), usually with a surcharge. Some hotels restrict their courts to use by guests.

By the time you read this, the best tennis should be at the **Aruba Racket Club** (☎ **297/8/37800**), the island's first world-class tennis facility, with eight courts, an exhibition center court, a pro shop, a swimming pool, an aerobics center, a fitness center, and a shopping center. The location is part of the Tierra del Sol complex on Aruba's northwest coast, near the California Lighthouse.

SHOPPING

Aruba manages to compress six continents into the half-mile-long Caya G. F. Betico Croes in Oranjestad, the main shopping street of the capital. While this is not technically a free port, the duty is so low (3.3%) that articles are attractively priced—and Aruba has no sales tax. You'll find the usual array of Swiss watches;

German and Japanese cameras; jewelry; liquor; English bone china and porcelain; Dutch, Swedish, and Danish silver and pewter; French perfume; British woolens; Indonesian specialties; and Madeira embroidery. Delft blue pottery is an especially good buy. More good buys include Holland cheese (Edam and Gouda), as well as Holland chocolate and English cigarettes in the airport departure area.

Philatelists interested in the wealth of colorful and artistic stamps issued in honor of the changed government status of Aruba can purchase a complete assortment, as well as other special issues, at the post office in Oranjestad.

In general, shops are open Monday through Saturday from 8am to noon and 2 to 6pm. Many stores are closed on Tuesday afternoon and some seem to keep irregular hours off-reason, especially in the fall and spring.

SHOPPING CENTERS

Alhambra Moonlight Shopping Center
Adjacent to the Alhambra Casino, L. G. Smith Blvd. ☎ **297/8/35000.**

This is a blend of international shops, outdoor marketplaces, and cafés and restaurants. Merchandise ranges from fine jewelry, chocolates, and perfume to imported craft items, leather goods, clothing, and lingerie. The shopping bazaar is open daily from 5pm to midnight.

Seaport Mall
L. G. Smith Blvd. 82. ☎ **297/8/24622.**

Comprising Seaport Village Mall, the Crystal Casino, and the Aruba Sonesta Resort & Casino, this complex is landmarked by the Crystal tower and is located across from the harbor at the "entrance" of the center of downtown, only 5 miles from the cruise terminal. Here are more than 120 stores, boutiques, and eateries, carrying a wide selection of merchandise to meet everyone's taste and budget—fashions, gifts, souvenirs, sporting goods, liquors, and fragrances. Top brands are featured, such as Gucci, Escada, Ralph Lauren Polo, Givenchy, Paloma Picasso, Lancôme, Baccarat, Lalique, Fendi, Movado, Valentino, Christofle, and many others known internationally. Most shops are open Monday through Saturday from 9am to 6pm.

One of the shops, the **Boulevard Book & Drugstore** (☎ 297/8/27358) has a complete range of goods from the latest paperback books to cosmetics, candies, gifts, toys, better-quality T-shirts and sweatshirts, sportswear, and souvenirs. You can also buy stamps, roadmaps, current magazines, and newspapers.

SPECIALTY SHOPS

Artistic Boutique
Caya G. F. Betico Croes 25. ☎ **297/8/23142.**

This boutique carries 14- and 18-karat fine gold jewelry set with precious or semiprecious stones, as well as porcelain figurines from well-known companies. It also sells Oriental antiques, handmade dhurries and rugs, plus a wide variety of Madeira fine linens and organdy tablecloths.

Aruba Trading Company
Caya G. F. Betico Croes 14. ☎ **297/8/22602.**

The Aruba Trading Company offers a complete range of tourist items: perfumes; cosmetics; souvenirs; gift items of porcelain, Delft, Hummel, and crystal ware; liquor; and cigarettes (the last two purchases can be delivered to your plane).

Ciro

In the Sonesta Seaport Village Mall. ☎ **297/8/36045.**

This popular international costume jewelry store is found at Sonesta's Seaport Village Mall near the center of Oranjestad. It carries a complete line of rings, brooches, earrings, and bracelets. It's estimated that savings on some items range from 20% to 30% off Stateside prices.

D'Orsy's

In the Oranjestad Strada Complex II. ☎ **297/8/31233.**

At this parfumerie, Ralph Lauren's Safari fragrance is the best-selling item. But many other fragrances are also sold, including Lancôme, Cartier, Tiffany, and Estée Lauder.

Gandelman Jewelers

Main St. 5A. ☎ **297/8/32121.**

Gandelman offers an extensive collection of fine gold jewelry and famous-name timepieces at duty-free prices. They also have stores in the Americana Hotel, Airport Departure Hall, Aruba Hilton, and Hyatt Regency Hotel.

La Pomme

In the Seaport Village Mall. ☎ **297/8/38180.**

A designer boutique, this outlet features the couture line, Escada. A typical day suit for Escada costs about $900, with evening ensembles priced at $1,400. Other Escada lines include shoes, bags, accessories, sportswear, and fragrance. La Pomme also showcases the Louis Feraud collection.

Les Accessories

In the Seaport Village Mall. ☎ **297/8/37965.**

Agatha Brown, an award-winning American designer, operates this shop, selling her exclusive designs in quality leather purses handmade in Florence, Italy. More than 70 designs are found in this Aruba boutique, where prices range from $85 to $600. Brown designs, imports, and retails her bags directly from her shop, eliminating markup and duty costs. She also offers assorted designer sportswear collections, including hand-woven rayon shawls from Venezuela, handy as swimsuit cover-ups.

Little Switzerland Jewelers

Caya G. F. Betico Croes 47. ☎ **297/8/21192.**

Famous for its duty-free 14- and 18-karat-gold jewelry and watches, Little Switzerland also carries a big variety of famous-name Swiss watches. There are branches at most of the large hotels in Aruba.

New Amsterdam Store

Caya G. F. Betico Croes 50. ☎ **297/8/21152.**

Aruba's leading department store is best for linens, with its selection of napkins, placemats, and embroidered tablecloths with sources that range all the way from China. It has an extensive line of other merchandise as well, from Delft blue pottery to beachwear and boutique items, along with assorted gift items, porcelain figures by Hummel, watches, French and Italian women's wear, and leather bags and shoes.

Penha

Caya G. F. Betico Croes 11–13. ☎ **297/8/24161.**

Penha offers one of the largest selections of top-name perfumes and cosmetics on the island.

ARUBA AFTER DARK
The Club & Bar Scene

Nongamblers or those who grow tired of the casinos can patronize a hotel's cocktail lounges and supper clubs. You don't have to be a guest of the hotel to visit to see the shows, but you should make a reservation. Tables at the big shows, especially in season, are likely to be booked early in the day. Usually you can go to one of the major hotel supper clubs and only order drinks.

The Alhambra
L. G. Smith Blvd. 47. ☎ **297/8/35000.**

Designed like a neon-swathed update of a moghul's palace, this complex of buildings and courtyards contains about a dozen shops selling souvenirs, leather goods, jewelry, and beachwear. On the premises you'll find a casino and at least three restaurants, which usually become animated at night. These include Munchies, for steak sandwiches, pizzas, and tacos; and there's also a New York–style deli for sandwiches. Liu's Place serves a wide range of frozen tropical cocktails. One of the best dining values on the island is offered at Roseland, which serves an all-you-can-eat dinner buffet, costing $12.95 between 6 and 7:30pm and $14.95 from 7:30 to 10pm. It's open nightly. Most popular of all is Cleo's Lounge (The Sports Bar), which offers live music and dancing daily from 8pm to 2am. As the music plays, you can order draft beer, priced at $2 a glass, and watch sports events from North America on several large-screen TVs. No one will mind if you ramble over to the in-house casino for a late-night roll of the slots.

Casinos

The casinos of the big hotels along Palm Beach are the liveliest nighttime destinations, and they stay open as long as business demands, often into the wee hours. In plush gaming parlors, guests try their luck at roulette, craps, blackjack, and of course the one-armed bandits. The **Americana Aruba Beach Resort** (☎ 297/8/24500) opens daily at noon for slots, blackjack, and roulette, and at 8pm for all games. The **Holiday Inn Aruba Beach Resort** (☎ 297/8/67777) wins the prize for all-around action. Its casino doors are open from 9am to 4pm. The **Aruba Palm Beach Resort & Casino** (☎ 297/8/23900) opens its slots at 9am and its other games at 1pm.

One of the island's best casinos is the **Crystal Casino** at the Aruba Sonesta Resort & Casino (☎ 297/8/36000), open daily from 8am to 4am. The 14,000-square-foot casino offers 11 blackjack tables, 270 slot machines, four roulette tables, three Caribbean stud-poker tables, two craps tables, one mini-baccarat table, and three baccarat tables. The casino evokes European casinos with its luxurious furnishings, ornate moldings, marble, brass, gold-leaf, and crystal chandeliers.

Visitors have a tendency to flock to the newest casinos on the island, and these include those at the **Aruba Hilton and Casino** (☎ 297/8/64466) and at the **Hyatt Regency Aruba** (☎ 297/8/61234). But outdrawing them all is the **Royal Cabana Casino** (☎ 297/8/39000), at the previously recommended La Cabana All Suite Beach Resort & Casino. It's known for its multitheme three-in-one restaurant, but mainly for its showcase cabaret theater and nightclub, which features everything from Las Vegas–style revues to female impersonators to comedy series on the weekend. You should call to find out what's happening here at the time of your visit and to reserve a table if the action interests you. The largest casino on Aruba, it offers 33 tables and games, plus 320 slot machines.

One of the busiest casinos on Aruba is the **Alhambra,** L. G. Smith Blvd. 47 (☎ **297/8/35000**). More than just a casino, it offers a collection of restaurants and boutiques, along with an inner courtyard designed like an 18th-century Dutch village. From the outside the complex looks Moorish, with serpentine mahogany columns and repeating arches rising to a pinnacle defined by a duet of sea-green domes; the desert setting of Aruba seems appropriate. The casino and its satellites are open daily from 10am till very late at night. Dress is informal.

2   Bonaire

Although it has other attractions, Bonaire seems at times to exist solely for scuba divers. Unspoiled Bonaire offers some of the best scuba and snorkeling grounds in the Caribbean. A beachcomber's retreat, it's also known for its powdery white sands and turquoise waters, where underwater photographers find a visibility of 100 feet or more.

It's also a birdwatcher's haven, with 135 different species—not only the flamingo, but also the big-billed pelican, as well as parrots, snipes, terns, parakeets, herons, and hummingbirds. Bring a pair of binoculars.

Bonaireans zealously want to protect their environment. Even though they eagerly seek tourism, they aren't interested in creating "another Aruba," with its high-rise hotel blocks. Spearfishing isn't allowed in its waters, nor is the taking or destruction of any coral or other living animal from the sea. Unlike some islands, Bonaire isn't just surrounded by coral reefs—it *is* the reef, sitting on the top of a dry, sunny underwater mountain. And its shores are thick with rainbow-hued fish. Only 5 miles wide and 24 miles long, Bonaire is poised in the Caribbean close to the coast of South America, known for many generations as the Spanish Main. It's just 50 miles north of Venezuela. The island, whose name in Amerindian means "low country," attracts those seeking that out-of-the-way spot, that uncrowded shore.

Part of the Netherlands Antilles (an autonomous part of the Netherlands), Bonaire has a population of about 10,000. Its capital is **Kralendijk.** It's most often reached from its neighbor island of Curaçao, 30 miles to the west. Like Curaçao, it's desertlike, with a dry and brilliant atmosphere. Often it's visited by "day trippers," who rush through here in pursuit of the shy, elusive flamingo.

Boomerang-shaped Bonaire comprises about 112 square miles, making it the second largest of the ABC Dutch-affiliated grouping. Its northern sector is hilly, tapering up to Mount Brandaris, all of 788 feet. However, the southern half, flat as a flapjack, is given over to bays, reefs, beaches, and a salt lake that attracts the flamingos.

The big annual event is the **October Sailing Regatta,** a five-day festival of racing sponsored by the local tourist bureau. Now an international affair, the event attracts sailors and spectators from around the world, as a flotilla of sailboats and yachts anchor in Kralendijk Bay. If you're planning to visit during regatta days, make sure you have an iron-clad hotel reservation.

ORIENTATION
GETTING THERE

The only nonstop flights to Bonaire from North America are offered on **ALM** (☎ toll free 800/327-7230). These fly only twice a week from Atlanta and once daily from Miami. There are also three weekly direct flights to Bonaire (through Aruba) from Newark, New Jersey, on Air Aruba (☎ toll free 800/882-7822). After a touchdown on Aruba, these flights then continue on to Bonaire.

Convenient for many travelers are the daily **American Airlines** (☎ 800/433-7300) flights in Curaçao from Miami. These depart late enough in the day (11am) to allow easy transfers from anywhere on North America's east coast. They reach Curaçao early enough to allow immediate transfers on to Bonaire. These are usually accomplished on any of ALM's four or five daily nonstop flights between Curaçao (ALM's corporate headquarters) and Bonaire.

Other routings to Bonaire are possible on any of American's daily nonstop flights to Aruba through American's hubs in New York, Miami, and San Juan, Puerto Rico. Once on Aruba, ALM will transfer passengers on to Bonaire, usually after a brief touchdown (or change of equipment) in Curaçao. Although these transfers are somewhat complicated, American will set up any of them, and will also offer reduced rates at some Bonairean hotels if you book your reservation simultaneously with your air passage.

GETTING AROUND

Even though the island is flat, renting Mopeds or motor scooters is not always a good idea. The roads are often unpaved, pitted, and peppered with rocks. Touring through Washington National Park, for example, is best done by van, Jeep, or automobile.

BY TAXI Taxis are unmetered, but the government has established rates. All licensed taxicabs carry a license plate with the letters TX. Each driver should have a list of prices to be produced upon request. As many as four passengers can go along for the ride unless they have too much luggage. As examples of what rates to expect, a trip from the airport to your hotel should cost about $10 to $12. From 8pm to midnight, fares are increased by 25%, and from 11pm to 6am they go up by 50%.

BY RENTAL CAR I recommend **Budget Rent-a-Car,** Kaya Lodewijk D. Gerharts 22, in Kralendijk (☎ 599/7-8300, ext. 225, or **800/472-3325** in the U.S.) and at the airport (☎ **599/7-8315**). This firm rents vehicles for $44 to $60 per day with unlimited mileage. Your valid U.S., British, or Canadian driver's license is acceptable for driving on Bonaire. *Driving on Bonaire is on the right.*

Avis (☎ **800/331-1084**) is also represented on Bonaire, with offices at J. A. Abraham Blvd. 67 (☎ **599/7-5795**) in Kralendijk. Weekly arrangements are cheaper, but daily rates, depending on the car (usually a Toyota), range from $39 to $69, with unlimited mileage.

Finally, **Dollar Rent a Car,** Kaya Grandi 86 (☎ **599/7-8888**), in Kralendijk, is also represented on Bonaire, with a kiosk at the airport for your convenience. Its stock of Japanese-made cars, usually a type of Nissan, costs $28 to $44 daily.

BY SIGHTSEEING TOUR **Bonaire Sightseeing Tours** (☎ **599/7-8778**) transports you on tours of the island, both north and south, taking in the flamingos, slave huts, conch shells, Goto Lake, the Amerindian inscriptions, and other sights. Each of these tours lasts two hours and costs $15 per person. You can take a half-day "City and Country Tour," lasting three hours and costing from $20 per person, allowing you to see the entire northern section and the southern part as far as the slave huts. A special four-hour tour of Washington/Slagbaai National Park can be booked at a cost of $35 per person for a minimum of four. An all-day tour of the national park begins at $55 per person.

Most taxi drivers are informed about the sights of Bonaire and will take you on a tour. You must negotiate the price according to how long a trip you want and what you want to see.

FAST FACTS: Bonaire

Area Code   Bonaire is not part of the Caribbean 809 area code. See "Telecommunications," below, for complete information on making calls to and on this island.

Banking Hours   Banks are usually open Monday through Friday from 8:30am to noon and 2 to 4pm.

Currency   Like the other islands of the Netherlands Antilles (Curaçao, St. Maarten, St. Eustatius, and Saba), Bonaire's coin of the realm is the **Netherlands Antillean florin (NAf),** sometimes called a guilder, equal to 56¢ in U.S. currency. However, mainly U.S. dollars are accepted.

Customs   There are no Customs requirements for Bonaire.

Documents   U.S. and Canadian citizens do not need a passport to enter Bonaire, although a birth or naturalization certificate, alien registration card, or a voter's registration card will be required, plus a return ticket. British citizens may carry a British Visitor's Passport, obtainable at post offices on Bonaire, although a valid passport issued in the United Kingdom is preferred, especially if they plan to visit other countries in the area.

Electricity   The electricity on Bonaire is slightly different from that used in North America (127 volts, 56 cycles, as opposed to U.S. and Canadian voltages of 110 volts, 60 cycles). It's sometimes suitable for any simple North American appliance, including a hairdryer, a small TV, or contact lens sterilizer, with no need for an electric transformer or adapter. However, it's possible to burn out an appliance such as an electric typewriter. Proceed with caution in using any appliance on Bonaire and try to avoid usage if possible because of the erratic current. Be warned, further, that electrical current used to feed or recharge finely calibrated diving equipment should be stabilized with a specially engineered electrical stabilizer. Every dive operation on the island has one of these as part of its standard equipment for visiting divers to use.

Information   For tourist information on Bonaire, go to the **Bonaire Government Tourist Bureau,** Kaya Libertad Simon Bolivar 12, Kralendijk (☎ 599/7-8322), open Monday through Friday from 7:30am to noon and 1:30 to 5pm. Before you go, you can contact the **Bonaire Tourist Office** at Adams Unlimited, 10 Rockefeller Plaza, Suite 900, New York, NY 10020 (☎ 212/956-5911, or toll free **800/U-BONAIR**). In Canada, contact RMR Group, Inc., Taurus House, 512 Duplex Ave., Toronto, ON M4R 2E3 (☎ 416/484-4864).

Language   English is widely spoken, but you'll hear Dutch, Spanish, and Papiamento.

Medical Care   The St. Francis Hospital is in Kralendijk (☎ **599/7-8900**). A plane on standby at the airport takes seriously ill patients to Curaçao for treatment.

Police   Call **8000.**

Safety   "Safe, safe Bonaire" might be the island's motto in this crime-infested world. But remember, any place that attracts tourists also attracts people who prey on them. Safeguard your valuables.

Taxes and Service   The government requires a $4.10-per-person daily room tax on all hotel rooms. Most hotels and guesthouses add a 10% service charge in lieu of tipping. Restaurants generally add a service charge of 15% to the bill. Upon leaving Bonaire, you'll be charged an airport departure tax of $10, so don't spend every penny. There is also an inter-island departure tax of $5.75.

Telecommunications   Service for telephone, Telex, telegraph, radio, and TV is available in English. Bonaire is *not* a part of the 809 area code that applies to most of the Caribbean. To call Bonaire from the United States, if your long-distance telephone company is equipped to handle international direct dialing, dial 011 (the international access code), then 599 (the country code for Bonaire), and then 7 (the area code) and the four-digit local number. If you cannot direct-dial internationally, dial 0 ("zero," for the operator) and tell the operator you wish to make an international call; once you are transferred to the international operator, state the 599 country code, the 7 area code, and then the local number, and the operator will dial the call for you.

Once on Bonaire, to call another number on the island only the four-digit local number is necessary.

Time   Bonaire is on Atlantic standard time year round, one hour ahead of eastern standard time (when it's noon on Bonaire, it's 11am in Miami). When daylight saving time is in effect in the United States, clocks in Miami and on Bonaire show the same time.

Water   Drinking water is pure and safe. It comes from distilled seawater.

Weather   Bonaire is known for its climate, with temperatures hovering at 82° Fahrenheit. The water temperature averages 80°. It's warmest in August and September, coolest in January and February. The average rainfall is 22 inches, and December through March are the rainiest months.

WHERE TO STAY

Hotels, all facing the sea, are low-key, hassle-free, and personally run operations where everybody gets to know everybody else rather fast.

A *Reminder:* Taxes and service charges are seldom included in the prices you are quoted, so ask about them when making your reservations.

VERY EXPENSIVE

Harbour Village Beach Resort

Kaya Gobernador N. Debrot, Playa Lechi (P.O. Box 312), Bonaire, N.A. ☎ **599/7-7500,** or toll free 800/424-0004 in the U.S. and Canada. Fax 599/7-7507. 30 rms, 40 suites. A/C TV TEL. $265–$295 single or double; $395–$695 suite. MAP $40 per person extra. (Rates include breakfast.) AE, DC, MC, V. Free parking.

Bonaire

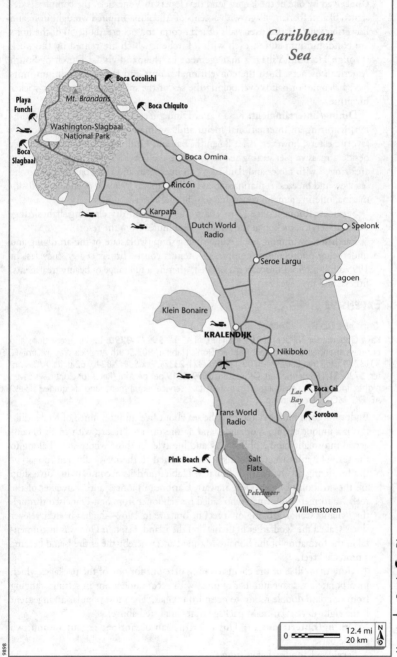

Caribbean
Sea

Boca Cocolishi

Playa
Funchi

Mt. Brandaris

Boca Chiquito

Washington-Slagbaai
National Park

Boca
Slagbaai

Boca Omina

Rincón

Karpata

Dutch World
Radio

Spelonk

Seroe Largu

Lagoen

Klein Bonaire

KRALENDIJK

Nikiboko

*Lac
Bay*

Boca Cai

Sorobon

Trans World
Radio

Pink Beach

Salt
Flats

Pekelmeer

Willemstoren

0   12.4 mi
     20 km

N

Airport   Beach   Diver

9898

Conceived by one of the largest land developers in Venezuela, the complex is designed like an Iberian village, with accents of Andalusia-inspired wrought iron, and flowering vines draped over walls of terra-cotta and ocher. About 50 of the units are condominium suites, each with a kitchen, which are rented by the week through Harbour Village's management by their individual Dutch or South American owners. Both the conventional rooms and the condominium units have balconies or patios overlooking the sea or the marina, and rattan or wicker furniture.

Dining/Entertainment: Kasa Coral Dining Terrace offers breakfast and dinner, featuring an international menu and, on many evenings, live music. My favorite eatery, however, is La Balandra Bar and Grill, a gazebolike structure set beside a massive pier jutting seaward, beside the beach. There, an octagonal bar area ringed with tables and flanked by an open grill and salad bar is open to the sea view and breezes. A marina bar and grill, Captain Wook's, overlooks a 60-slip marina, offering a menu consisting of grill specialties.

Services: Room service (7 to 10am), laundry and dry cleaning, babysitting, wake-up service, pickup at the airport (10 minutes from the resort).

Facilities: Swimming pool, scuba-diving shop (with state-of-the-art diving and underwater photographic equipment), tennis courts, fitness center, bicycles. In 1995 a full-service European spa opened, offering a full range of beauty treatments, fitness, and massage.

EXPENSIVE

Captain Don's Habitat

Kaya Gobernador N. Debrot 103, Bonaire, N.A. ☎ **599/7-8290;** for all reservations and business arrangements, contact Captain Don's Habitat, 903 South America Way, Miami, FL 33132 (☎ toll free 800/327-6709; fax 305/371-2337). Fax 599/7-8240. 62 units. A/C. Winter, $720–$1,163 per person. Off-season, $609–$919 per person. (Rates for eight days/seven nights, include breakfast, airport transfers, tax, service, equipment, and six guided dives.) AE, DC, MC, V. Free parking.

Built on a coral bluff overlooking the sea about five minutes north of Kralendijk, this is a unique diving, snorkeling, and nature-oriented resort, with an air of congenial informality and a philosophy and lifestyle for those whose souls belong to the sea. The infrastructure and staff are devoted to the many different possibilities for diving off the coast of Bonaire. Habitat and its accompanying dive shop are the creation of Capt. Don Stewart, Caribbean pioneer and "caretaker of the reefs," a former Californian who sailed his schooner from San Francisco through the Panama Canal, arriving on a reef in Bonaire in 1962—he has been here ever since. Called the "godfather of diving" on the island, Captain Don was instrumental in the formation of the Bonaire Marine Park, whereby the entire island became a protected reef.

More than 90% of the clients coming here opt for one of the packages which incorporate a variable number of dives with accommodations in settings ranging from standard double rooms to oceanfront villas. The most popular arrangement is the eight-day/seven-night package (rates are listed above).

Dining/Entertainment: This resort has an oceanfront restaurant and two seaside bars.

Services: Laundry, babysitting.

Facilities: Boutique, ocean-bordering pool, complete diving program.

MODERATE

Divi Flamingo Beach Resort & Casino
J. A. Abraham Blvd., Bonaire, N.A. ☎ **599/7-8285, 919/419-3484** in Chapel Hill, N.C., or toll free 0800/373742 in the U.K. Fax 7/8238. 100 rms, 40 studios. A/C. Mid-Dec to Mar, $125–$185 single or double (prices about 10% higher between Christmas and New Year's); from $195 studio. Apr to mid-Dec, $84–$115 single or double; from $125 studio. MAP $42 per person extra. AE, DC, MC, V. Free parking.

North of Kralendijk, this complete beachfront resort, with its water-sports facilities and comfortable bedrooms, was once a neglected, gone-to-seed hotel with a cluster of flimsy wooden bungalows that had been used as an internment camp for German prisoners in World War II. With foresight and taste, the owners turned it into a top-notch resort, offering individual cottages and modern seafront rooms with private balconies resting on piers above the surf, so you can stand out and watch rainbow-hued tropical fish in the water below.

The resort's original rooms were supplemented in 1986 with the addition of time-sharing units, forming Club Flamingo. Each of the units is rentable by the day or week. Accommodations in both sections are spacious and sunny, with ceiling fans and a selection of Mexican accessories. The newer units are clustered into a green-and-white neo-Victorian pavilion facing its own curving swimming pool. Each contains a kitchenette with carved cupboards and cabinets of pickled hardwoods. Both sections benefit from the attentions of a pair of social hostesses and the proximity of a good dive operation and a beautiful beach. A pair of restaurants, the Chibi-Chibi and the Calabase Terrace, provide satisfying meals.

Sand Dollar Condominiums & Beach Club
Kaya Gobernador N. Debrot 79, Bonaire, N.A. ☎ **599/7-8738,** or toll free 800/288-4773 in the U.S. Fax 7/8760. 85 units. A/C TV. Winter, $160 studio for two; $210 one-bedroom unit for two; $240 two-bedroom unit for four; $350 three-bedroom unit for six. Off-season, $150 studio for two; $175 one-bedroom unit for two; $190 two-bedroom unit for four; $300 three-bedroom unit for six. MAP $38.50 per person extra. AE, MC, V. Free parking.

On the beachfront, just 1½ miles north of Kralendijk and 3 miles north of the airport, the Sand Dollar offers studio apartments and one-, two-, and three-bedroom units with all the style, comfort, and convenience of a full-service hotel. All accommodations are equipped with electric ranges, ovens, dishwashers, refrigerators, custom cabinets, and modern furnishings, with decks or balconies facing the ocean. For more information, consult Travel Marketing Services, 343 Neponset St., Canton, MA 02021 (☎ **617/821-1012;** fax 617/821-1568).

Dining/Entertainment: On the grounds is the Green Parrot Restaurant and Bar (see "Where to Dine," below).

Facilities: Two lighted tennis courts, freshwater swimming pool with bar and cabaña, Sand Dollar Dive and Photo (see "Sports & Outdoor Activities," below).

INEXPENSIVE

Carib Inn
J. A. Abraham Blvd. (P.O. Box 68), Kralendijk, Bonaire, N.A. ☎ **599/7-8819.** Fax 599/7-5295. 9 rms. A/C TV. Winter, $69–$99 single or double; $119 two-bedroom unit for four. Off-season, $59–$89 single or double; $109 two-bedroom unit for four. AE, MC, V. Free parking.

On the water, this hotel—owned and managed by American diver Bruce Bowker—is occupied by dedicated scuba divers drawn to its five-star PADI dive facility. This is considered the most intimate little dive resort on Bonaire. Seven of its nine rooms have kitchens where guests can prepare their own meals. All units are equipped with refrigerators, and maid service is provided daily. Accommodations are furnished in a tropical rattan. The baths have been enlarged and refurbished. There is no restaurant or bar, although Richard's Waterfront Dining is close at hand (see "Where to Dine," below). Repeat guests are likely to book this place far in advance in winter.

WHERE TO DINE

Dress is casual and conservative. Food is not the reason to come to Bonaire, although there has been a notable improvement in the cuisine beginning in the late 1980s. Virtually everything is imported. Stick to fresh fish if available. The meats and poultry were shipped frozen to the island.

EXPENSIVE

Chibi-Chibi

In the Divi Flamingo Beach Resort & Casino, J. A. Abraham Blvd. ☎ **599/7-8285.** Reservations recommended. Appetizers $3.95–$8.95; main courses $14.25–$20.25. AE, DC, MC, V. Dinner only, daily 6–10pm. CONTINENTAL.

On the sea on the periphery of Kralendijk, this restaurant is named after the yellow-breasted tropical birds that can be observed from your dining table. An imposing two-tier edifice of exposed planking and wooden balustrades, the restaurant is perched over a coral-encrusted sea bottom, and you can see schools of multicolored fish in the illuminated waters. The chef prepares a continental menu, which also includes Antillean onion soup, veal piccata, fettuccine Flamingo, keshi yena (Edam cheese stuffed with meat and then baked), and some of the freshest fish on the island.

Den Laman Restaurant

Kaya Gobernador N. Debrot 77. ☎ **599/7-8955.** Reservations not required. Appetizers $3.50–$7.75; main courses $12–$29.45. AE, MC, V. Dinner only, Wed–Mon 6–11pm. Closed Sept. SEAFOOD.

Located between the Sunset Beach Hotel and the Sand Dollar Condominiums & Beach Club, Den Laman serves some of the best seafood on Bonaire. An excellent beginning is the fish soup, the chef's special. The fresh fish of the day depends on what was caught, of course. Perhaps you'll order conch Flamingo, a local favorite, or lobster from the tank. Other dishes include grouper Créole or New York sirloin steak. When it's featured, I always go for the red snapper Créole. It's easy to spend $35 here, but it's also possible to dine for less.

✪ Raffle's Seaside Restaurant

Kaya Hellmund 5. ☎ **599/7-8617.** Reservations recommended. Appetizers $3–$5; main courses $16–$20. AE, MC, V. Dinner only, Sun–Fri 6:30pm–midnight. CARIBBEAN/ CONTINENTAL.

Named after Sir Thomas Raffles, founder of Singapore, this sea-bordering restaurant near the Divi Flamingo is in one of the island's oldest houses. Intimate tables, soft jazz music, and candlelight create a romantic ambience in the main air-conditioned restaurant, although you can dine less formally outside on the terrace overlooking the harbor. Nice and Peter Lensvelt, the Dutch-born owners, offer seafood soup made with seven different kinds of fish, and also fish pâté. The locally born chef is known for a specialty, stuffed chicken. The menu always features the catch of the day as well as steak dishes. Another specialty is a South American–style bouillabaisse. The luscious desserts include a dark-chocolate mousse and several different kinds of fresh-fruit sorbets.

MODERATE

⑤ Mona Lisa

Kaya Grandi 15. ☎ **599/7-8718.** Reservations recommended. Appetizers $5–$11; main courses $14.50–$23. AE, MC, V. Dinner only, Mon–Fri 6–10pm. CONTINENTAL.

A local favorite, this is one of the best places in town to get typically Dutch fare, although the offering is continental. There are even Indonesian dishes, and the prices are some of the best around, considering the quality of the food served and the generous portions. Although many regulars come to patronize the Dutch bar and catch up on the latest gossip, the old-fashioned dining room deserves serious attention. On the main street of town, in an old building, guests enjoy the fresh fish of the day (often wahoo) or such meat dishes as lamb filet, tournedos, and sirloin steak. The most-ordered appetizers are onion soup and shrimp cocktail. It's known for serving the freshest vegetables on an island where nearly everything is imported.

⑤ Richard's Waterfront Dining

J. A. Abraham Blvd. 60. ☎ **599/7-5263.** Reservations recommended for groups of five or more. Appetizers $3.50–$5.70; main courses $12.50–$19.90. AE, MC, V. Dinner only, daily 6:30–10:30pm. INTERNATIONAL.

On the airport side of Kralendijk, within walking distance of the Divi Flamingo, this restaurant with its large covered terrace was converted from a former private home. Although reasonable in price, it's the preferred favorite of many locals who have sampled every restaurant on the island. Boston-born Richard Beady and his partner, Mario, from Aruba, operate a welcoming oasis and begin a happy hour at 5:30pm, one hour before dinner. Gathered around the coral bar, guests speculate on the offerings that night. From a chalkboard menu, you're likely to be offered grilled wahoo or the fresh catch of the day, filet mignon béarnaise, U.S. sirloin with green-peppercorn sauce, or shrimp scampi. It's best to begin with the fish soup, if featured. Pastas are also an item here. Seating is on a first-come, first served basis, although groups of five or more should alert the restaurant.

⑤ Zeezicht Restaurant

Kaya Corsow 10. ☎ **599/7-8434.** Reservations not required. Appetizers $8; main courses $8–$26. AE, MC, V. Daily 8am–midnight. INTERNATIONAL.

This is the best place in the capital to go for a sundowner. You join the old salts or the people who live on boats to watch the sun go down, and you try to see the "green flash" that Hemingway wrote about. Pronounced "*Zay*-zict" and meaning "sea view," this place has long been popular for its excellent local cookery. A two-story operation, the restaurant offers a small rijstaffel as well as fresh fish from the nearby fish market. Lobster is occasionally offered, and there's always steak.

INEXPENSIVE

⑤ China Garden

Kaya Grandi 47. ☎ **599/7-8480.** Reservations recommended. Appetizers $1–$16; main courses $4.50–$22. AE, MC, V. Lunch Wed–Mon 11:30am–2pm; dinner Wed–Mon 4:30–10pm. ASIAN.

Good-tasting Eastern dishes, with some Indonesian specialties, are served to West Indians and visitors in this restored Bonairean mansion between the Divi Flamingo and Sunset Beach hotels. Portions are enormous, and prices are low considering what you get. The chefs from Hong Kong also cook Chinese, American, and local dishes, including a variety of curries ranging from beef to lobster. Seafood dishes, prepared in a variety of styles, including lobster in black-bean sauce, are also served. Special culinary features include a Java rijstaffel and the nasi goreng special. The place is air-conditioned and seats 60 guests.

⊖ Green Parrot Restaurant

In the Sand Dollar Condominiums & Beach Club, Kaya Gobernador N. Debrot 79. ☎ **599/ 7-5454.** Reservations recommended. Appetizers $2–$6.75; main courses $13–$20; lunch $4.75–$9. AE, MC, V. Breakfast daily 8–10:30am; lunch daily 11:30am–3pm; dinner daily 3:30–10pm. CONTINENTAL.

Set on a breeze-filled pier, this place is part of the complex of this previously recommended resort, a 15-minute drive from airport. It serves burgers, pasta, sandwiches, and seafood dishes. You can gaze at the waves, enjoy a frozen tropical fruit drink, and watch the sunset. On Saturday night there's a barbecue buffet with entertainment. The food consistently ranks as some of the best on the island, especially the charcoal-grilled fish (based on the catch of the day). You might also try the barbecued chicken and ribs, and various U.S. beef cuts (from T-bone to filet mignon), as well as garlic shrimp and the highly favored onion strings (like an onion loaf).

WHAT TO SEE & DO
KRALENDIJK

The capital, Kralendijk, means "coral dike" and is pronounced "*Kroll*-en-dike," although most denizens refer to it as Playa, Spanish for "beach." A dollhouse town of some 2,500 residents, it's small, neat, pretty, and Dutch-clean, and its stucco buildings are painted pink and orange, with an occasional lime green. The capital's jetty is lined with island sloops and fishing boats.

Kralendijk nestles in a bay on the west coast, opposite **Klein Bonaire,** or Little Bonaire, an uninhabited, low-lying islet a 10-minute boat ride from the capital.

The main street of town leads along the beachfront on the harbor. A Protestant church was built in 1834, and St. Bernard's Roman Catholic Church has some stained-glass windows.

At **Fort Oranje** you'll see a lone cannon dating from the days of Napoleon. If possible, try to get up early to see the **Fish Market** on the waterfront, where you'll see a variety of strange and brilliantly colored fish.

THE TOUR NORTH

The road north is one of the most beautiful stretches in the Antilles, with turquoise waters on your left, coral cliffs on your right. You can stop at several points along this road where you'll find paved paths for strolling or bicycling.

After leaving Kralendijk and passing the Sunset Beach Hotel and the desalination plant, you'll come to **Radio Nederland Wereld Omroep (Dutch World Radio).** It's a 13-tower, 300,000-watter. Opposite the transmitting station is a lovers' promenade, built by nature and an ideal spot for a picnic.

Continuing, you'll pass the storage tanks of the Bonaire Petroleum Corporation, the road heading to **Gotomeer,** the island's inland sector, with a saltwater lake. Several flamingos prefer this spot to the salt flats in the south.

Down the hill the road leads to a section called **"Dos Pos"** or *two wells*, which has palm trees and vegetation in contrast to the rest of the island, where only the drought-resistant kibraacha and divi-divi trees, tilted before the constant wind, can grow, along with forests of cacti.

Bonaire's oldest village is **Rincón.** Slaves who used to work in the salt flats in the south once lived here. There are a couple of bars, including the Amstel and the Tropicana, and the Rincón Ice Cream Parlour makes homemade ice cream in a variety of interesting flavors. Above the bright roofs of the village is the crest of a hill called Para Mira or "stop and look."

A side path outside Rincón takes you to some Arawak inscriptions supposedly 500 years old. The petroglyph designs are in pink-red dye. At nearby **Boca Onima,** you'll find grotesque grottoes of coral.

Before going back to the capital, you might take a short bypass to **Seroe Largu,** which has a good view of Kralendijk and the sea. Lovers frequent the spot at night.

✪ WASHINGTON/SLAGBAAI NATIONAL PARK

Washington/Slagbaai National Park (☎ 599/7-8444) is concerned with the conservation of the island's fauna, flora, and landscape, and is a changing vista highlighted by desertlike terrain, secluded beaches, caverns, and a bird sanctuary. Occupying 15,000 acres of Bonaire's northwesternmost territory, the park was once plantation land, producing divi-divi, aloe, charcoal, and goats. It was purchased by the Netherlands Antilles government, and since 1967 part of the land, formerly the Washington plantation, has been a wildlife sanctuary. The southern part of the park, the Slagbaai plantation, was added in 1978.

The park can be seen in a few hours, although it takes days to appreciate it fully. Touring the park is easy, with two routes: a 15-mile "short" route, marked by green arrows, and a 22-mile "long" route, marked by yellow arrows. The roads are well

---

Coastal Diving

The ✪ **Bonaire Marine Park** was created to protect the coral-reef ecosystem off Bonaire. The park incorporates the entire coastline of Bonaire and neighboring Klein Bonaire. Scuba diving and snorkeling are all popular here. The park is policed, and services and facilities include a Visitor Information Center at the Karpata Ecological Center, lectures, slide presentations, films, and permanent dive-site moorings.

Visitors are asked to respect the marine environment and to refrain from activities that may damage it, such as sitting or walking on the coral. All marine life is completely protected. This means no fishing or collecting fish, shells, or corals—dead or alive. Spearfishing is forbidden. Anchoring is not permitted—all craft must use permanent moorings, except for emergency stops (boats shorter than 12 feet may use a stone anchor). Most recreational activity in the marine park takes place on the island's leeward side and among the reefs surrounding uninhabited Klein Bonaire.

The reefs are home to various coral formations that grow at different depths, ranging from the knobby brain coral at 3 feet to staghorn and elkhorn up to about 10 feet deeper, and gorgonians, giant brain, and others all the way to 40 to 83 feet. Many species of fish inhabit the reefs, and the deep reef slope is home to a range of sponges, groupers, and moray eels.

marked and safe, but somewhat rugged, although they're gradually being improved. Tickets cost $5 for adults and 75¢ for children under 12, and can be purchased at the gate.

Whichever route you take, there are a few important stops you should make. Just past the gate is **Salina Mathijs,** a salt flat that's home to flamingos during the rainy season. Beyond the salt flat on the road to the right is **Boca Chikitu,** a white sand beach and bay. A few miles up the beach lies **Boca Cocolishi,** a two-part black sand beach. Its deep, rough seaward side is separated from the calm, shallow basin by a ridge of coralline algae. Hermit crabs walk the beach and shallow water.

The main road leads to **Boca Bartol,** a bay full of living and dead elkhorn coral, seafans, and reef fish. A popular watering hole good for birdwatching is **Poosdi Mangel. Wajaca** is a remote reef where many sea creatures live, including turtles, octopuses, and trigger-fish. Immediately inland towers 788-foot **Mount Brandaris,** Bonaire's highest peak, at whose foot is **Bronswinkel Well,** a watering spot for pigeons and parakeets. Some 130 species of birds live in the park, many with such exotic names as banana quit and black-faced grassquit. Bonaire has few mammals, but you'll see goats and donkeys, perhaps even a wild bull.

HEADING SOUTH

Leaving the capital again, you pass the **Trans World Radio antennas,** towering 500 feet in the air, transmitting with 810,000 watts. This is one of the hemisphere's most powerful medium-wave radio stations, the loudest voice in Christendom and the most powerful nongovernmental broadcast station in the world. It sends out interdenominational Gospel messages and hymns in 20 languages to places as far away as eastern Europe and the Middle East.

Later, you come on the ✪ **salt flats,** where the brilliantly colored pink flamingos live. Bonaire shelters the largest accessible nesting and breeding grounds in the world. The flamingos build high mud mounds to hold their eggs. The birds are best viewed in spring when they're usually nesting and tending their young. The salt flats were once worked by slaves, and the government has rebuilt some primitive stone huts, bare shelters little more than waist high. The slaves slept in these huts, and returned to their homes in Rincón in the north on weekends. The centuries-old salt pans have been reactivated by the International Salt Company. Near the salt pans you'll see some 30-foot obelisks in white, blue, and orange built in 1838 to help mariners locate their proper anchorages.

Farther down the coast is the island's oldest lighthouse, **Willemstoren,** built in 1837. Still farther along, **Sorobon Beach** and **Boca Cai** come into view. They're at landlocked Lac Bay, which is ideal for swimming and snorkeling. Conch shells are stacked up on the beach. The water here is so vivid and clear you can see coral 65 to 120 feet down in the reef-protected waters.

SPORTS & OUTDOOR ACTIVITIES

The true beauty on Bonaire is under the sea, where visibility is 100 feet 365 days of the year, and the water temperatures range from 78° to 82° Fahrenheit. Many dive sites can be reached directly from the beach, and sailing is another pastime. Birdwatching is among the best in the Caribbean, and for beachcombers there are acres and acres of driftwood, found along the shore from the salt flats to Lac.

BEACHES Bonaire has some of the whitest sand beaches in the West Indies. The major hotels have beaches, but you may want to wander down to the southeast coast for a swim at the "clothes-optional" **Sorobon** or **Boca Cai** on Lac Bay. In the north, you may want to swim at **Playa Funchi,** on the coastline of Washington/Slagbaai National Park.

BOATING   Every visitor to Bonaire wants to take a trip to uninhabited Klein Bonaire. The **Flamingo Beach Hotel** (☎ 599/7-8285) and **Sunset Beach Hotel** at Playa Lechi (☎ 599/7-8448) offer trips daily. You'll be left in the morning for a day of snorkeling, beachcombing, and picnicking, then picked up later that afternoon. Other hotels will also arrange a trip to the islet for you, perhaps including a barbecue.

FISHING   The island's offshore fishing grounds offer some of the best fishing in the Caribbean. A good day's catch might include mackerel, tuna, and wahoo, among the many species out there.

Your best bet is Chris Morkos, **Piscatur Fishing Supplies,** Kaya Herman 4, Playa Pabao (☎ 599/7-8774). A native Bonairean, he has been fishing almost since he was born. A maximum of six people are taken out on a 42-foot boat with a guide and captain, at a cost of $300 for a half day or $500 for a whole day, including all tackle and bait. Reef fishing is another popular sport, in boats averaging 15 and 21 feet. A maximum of two people can go out for a half day at $200 or a whole day at $300. For the same price, a maximum of four people can fish for bonefish and tarpon on the island's large salt flats.

SNORKELING   Snorkeling equipment can be rented at such previously recommended establishments as **Harbour Village Beach Resort,** the **Carib Inn,** or at any of the scuba centers (see above), including **Sand Dollar Dive and Photo, Bonaire Scuba Center,** or **Captain Don's Habitat Dive Shop.**

✪ SCUBA DIVING   One of the richest reef communities in the entire West Indies, Bonaire has plunging walls that descend to a sand bottom at 130 or so feet, abounding in hard corals, numerous seawhips, black-coral trees, basket sponges, gorgonia, and swarms of rainbow-hued tropical fish. Most of the diving is done on the leeward side where the ocean is lake flat. There are more than 40 dive sites on sharply sloping reefs.

The waters off the coast of Bonaire received an additional attraction in 1984. A rust-bottomed general cargo ship, 80 feet long, was confiscated by the police along with its contraband cargo, about 25,000 pounds of marijuana. Known as the *Hilma Hooker* (familiarly dubbed "The Hooker" by everyone on the island), it sank unclaimed (obviously) and without fanfare one calm day in 90 feet of water. Lying just off the southern shore near the capital, its wreck is now a popular dive site.

Bonaire has a unique program for divers in that the major hotels offer personalized, closeup encounters with the island's fish and other marine life under the expertise of Bonaire's dive guides.

Dive I and **Dive II,** at opposite ends of the beachfront of the Divi Flamingo Beach Resort & Casino, J. A. Abraham Boulevard (☎ 599/7-8285), north of Kralendijk, are among the island's most complete scuba facilities. Both operate out of well-stocked beachfront buildings, rent diving equipment, charge the same prices, and offer the same type of expeditions. A resort course for first-time divers costs $88; for experienced divers, a one-tank dive goes for $38.50.

Captain Don's Habitat Dive Shop, Kaya Gobernador N. Debrot 103 (☎ 599/7-8290), is a PADI five-star training facility. The open-air, full-service dive shop includes a classroom, photo/video lab, camera-rental facility, equipment repair, and compressor rooms grouped around spacious seafront patios. Habitat's slogan is "Diving Freedom," and divers can take their tanks and dive anywhere any time of day or night, most often along "The Pike," half a mile of protected reef right in front of the property. The highly qualified staff is there to assist and advise but not to police or dictate dive plans. Diving packages include boat dives, unlimited offshore diving (24 hours a day), unlimited air, tanks, backpack, weights, and belt. Some dive packages also include accommodations and meals (see "Where to Stay," above).

At the **Bonaire Scuba Center,** in the Black Durgon Inn, Playa Lechi (☎ **599/ 7-8846**), some of the island's best diving is available from the doorstep of this seven-room inn. A living reef just 50 feet from shore quickly drops to 150 feet. Snorkeling is also possible from the property. The center caters to both novice and advanced divers, and offers both resort courses and certification courses.

Eco-Adventure Vacations

From the rugged hills and Prickly Candle cacti of the north to the sands of Pink Beach in the south, nature has provided Bonaire with the ecological diversity to offer the best of adventure and eco-tours.

1. **Birdwatching.** Bonaire is home to 190 species of birds, 80 of which are indigenous to the island. But most famous are its flamingos, which can number 15,000 during the mating season.

2. **Diving/Snorkeling.** A visitor can wade right from the shore to the reef to snorkel or dive at any of 80 sites with a colorful array of coral formations and abundant marine life, day or night.

3. **Eco-touring.** Drive or hike through the varied terrain of the island's 13,500-acre Washington Slagbaai National Park, a wildlife sanctuary, where birds, lizards, goats, and iguanas are found in their natural habitat.

4. **Fishing.** Wahoo, tuna, dolphin, blue marlin, Amber Jack, grouper, sailfish, and snapper can be found off the coast of Bonaire. The abundance and variety of fish make the island home to some of the best deep-sea fishing. Bonaire is also one of the best-kept secrets of bone-fishing enthusiasts.

5. **Horseback Riding.** Spend part or all day at one of Bonaire's fine horse ranches, where private lessons and trail rides are available.

6. **Mountain Biking.** Explore more than 186 miles of trails and dirt roads where you can venture off the beaten path to enjoy the scenery and contrasting geography.

7. **Sea Kayaking.** Paddle the protected waters of Lac Bay, or head for the miles of flats and mangroves in the south (the island's nursery) where baby fish and wildlife can be viewed. Kayak rentals are available at Windsurfing Bonaire, Lac Bay (☎ **599/7-5555**), costing $15 per hour or $25 per half day.

8. **Windsurfing.** Consistent conditions—enjoyed by windsurfers with a wide range of skill levels—make the shallow, calm waters of Lac Bay the island's home to the sport. Call Windsurfing Bonaire (☎ **599/7-5555**) for details.

Sand Dollar Dive and Photo, at the Sand Dollar Condominiums & Beach Club, Kaya Gobernador N. Debrot (☎ 599/7-5252), offers dive packages, PADI and NAUI instruction, equipment rental and repairs, and boat, land, and deep-dive trips. The photo shop offers underwater photo and video shoots, PADI specialty courses, E-6 processing, print developing, and equipment rental and repair.

TENNIS   The **Sunset Beach Hotel** at Playa Lechi (☎ 599/7-8448) has two good tennis courts, illuminated for night play. Use of the courts is free to guests of the hotel. A tennis instructor is available, and racquets and balls can be borrowed without charge.

In addition, there are two courts at the **Sand Dollar Condominiums & Beach Club** and **Divi Flamingo Beach Resort** (see "Where to Stay," above); all the courts are lit for night play.

SHOPPING

Kralendijk features an assortment of goods, including gemstone jewelry, wood, leather, sterling, ceramics, liquors, and tobacco at 25% to 50% less than in the United States and Canada. Prices are often quoted in U.S. dollars, and major credit and charge cards and traveler's checks are usually accepted. Most shops are open Monday through Saturday from 8am to noon and 2 to 6pm; they might open for a few hours on Sunday if a cruise ship is in port. Walk along Kaya Grandi in Kralendijk to sample the merchandise.

Ki Bo Ke Pakus ("What Do You Want")
In the Divi Flamingo Beach Resort & Casino, J. A. Abraham Blvd. ☎ **599/7-8239.**

This place has some of the most popular merchandise on the island—T-shirts, handbags, dashikis, locally made jewelry, batiks from Indonesia, and Delft blue items.

Littman Jewelers
Kaya Grandi 35. ☎ **599/7-8160.**

Steve and Esther Littman have restored this old house to its original state. They sell Tag-Heuer dive watches. The shop also carries Daum French crystal and Lladró Spanish porcelain. Next door, the Littmans have a shop called **Littman's Gifts,** selling T-shirts from standard to hand-painted, plus Dutch cheeses, chocolates, fine wines, gift items, costume jewelry, toys, imported crackers, and other food items.

United Colors of Benetton
Kaya Grandi 49. ☎ **599/7-5107.**

This worldwide chain with its multicolored clothing and controversial (to some) ads has invaded Bonaire. Directly imported from Italy, the clothing is often priced 30% lower than in Europe or the United States—or so they claim.

Things Bonaire
Kaya Grandi 38C. ☎ **599/7-8423.**

Things Bonaire has an additional branch at the Sunset Beach Hotel (☎ 599/7-8190). Both shops carry many gift items, including black coral jewelry, sunglasses, postcards, and locally made shell and driftwood items. They also carry men's and women's swimsuits, shorts, T-shirts, beach towels, guayaberas, caps, hats, and visors. Things Bonaire is also the exclusive outlet for "Amazon Lily's" men's and women's wear, jewelry, and souvenirs from Bali.

BONAIRE AFTER DARK

Underwater **slide shows** provide entertainment for both divers and nondivers in the evening. The best shows are at **Captain Don's Habitat** (☎ 599/7-8290) (see "Outdoor Activities," above). Check when you get to Bonaire about times.

Divi Flamingo Beach Resort & Casino

J. A. Abraham Blvd. ☎ **599/7-8285.** Open Monday through Saturday from 8pm to 2am.

A casino opened here in 1984 in a former residence adjoining the property. Promoted as "The World's First Barefoot Casino," it offers blackjack, roulette, poker, wheel of fortune, video games, and slot machines. Gambling on the island is regulated by the government. Entrance is free.

E Wowo

Kaya Grandi 38, at the corner of Kaya L. D. Gerharts. ☎ **599/7-8998.** Admission $6. Open Wednesday through Sunday from 9pm until the early hours.

Outside the hotels, check out the dance floor at E Wowo ("The Eye" in Papiamento), which lies right in the heart of town. Distinguished by two flashing op art eyes, the club occupies the second floor of one of the island's oldest Dutch colonial buildings. The club caters to members, but if you ask at your hotel desk you'll usually be granted an admission pass.

Karel's Beach Bar

On the waterfront. ☎ **599/7-8434.** Open Tuesday through Sunday from 5pm to 2am.

Almost Tahitian in its high-ceilinged, open-walled design, this popular bar is perched above the sea on stilts. You can sit at the long rectangular bar with many of the island's dive and boating professionals or select a table near the balustrades overlooking the illuminated surf. On weekends, local bands entertain. Drinks begin at $4 each.

3 Curaçao

Just 35 miles north of the coast of Venezuela, Curaçao, the "C" of the Dutch ABC islands of the Caribbean, is the most populous in the Netherlands Antilles. It attracts visitors because of its people, who extend a big welcome, as well as its duty-free shopping, lively casinos, water sports, and international cuisine. Fleets of tankers head out from its harbor to bring refined oil to all parts of the world.

Now a peaceful, self-governing part of the Netherlands, Curaçao was discovered not by Columbus, but by one of his lieutenants, Alonso de Ojeda, as well as Amerigo Vespucci, in 1499. The Spaniards exterminated all but 75 members of a branch of the peaceful Arawaks. However, they in turn were ousted by the Dutch in 1634, who also had to fight off French and English invasions.

The Dutch made the island a tropical Holland in miniature. Pieter Stuyvesant, stomping on his pegleg, ruled Curaçao in 1644. The island was turned into a Dutch Gibraltar, bristling with forts. Thick ramparts guarded the harbor's narrow entrance; the hilltop forts (many now converted into restaurants) protected the coastal approaches.

In this century, it remained sleepy until 1915 when the Royal Dutch/Shell Company built one of the world's largest oil refineries to process crude from Venezuela. Workers from some 50 countries poured onto the island, turning Curaçao into a polyglot, cosmopolitan community.

The largest of the Netherlands Antilles, Curaçao is 37 miles long and 7 miles across at its widest point. Because of all that early Dutch building, Curaçao is the most important island architecturally in the entire West Indies, with more European flavor than anywhere else in the Caribbean. After leaving the capital, **Willemstad,** you plunge into a strange, desertlike countryside that may remind you of the American Southwest. The landscape is an amalgam of browns and russets, studded with three-pronged cactus, spiny-leafed aloes, and the divi-divi trees, with their coiffures bent by centuries of trade winds. Classic Dutch-style windmills are in and around Willemstad and in some parts of the countryside. These standard farm models pump water from wells to irrigate vegetation.

Curaçao, together with Bonaire, St. Maarten, St. Eustatius, and Saba, is in the Kingdom of the Netherlands as part of the Netherlands Antilles. Curaçao has its own governmental authority, relying on the Netherlands only for defense and foreign affairs, and a population of 171,000 representing more than 50 nationalities.

ORIENTATION
GETTING THERE

The air routes to **Curaçao International Airport,** Plaza Margareth Abraham (☎ 599/9-682288), are still firmly linked to those leading to nearby Aruba. In recent years, however, developments at such airlines as American (see below) have initiated direct or nonstop routings into Curaçao from such international hubs as Miami.

American Airlines (☎ 800/433-7300) offers a daily nonstop flight to Curaçao from its hub in Miami which departs late enough in the day (11:05am) to permit easy connections from cities all over the Northeast. Fortunately, it arrives early enough in the day (around 3pm) to allow guests to unpack and enjoy a leisurely dinner the same evening. American also offers flights to Curaçao's neighbor, Aruba, from New York, Miami, and San Juan, Puerto Rico. Once on Aruba, many clients transfer on to Curaçao on any of ALM's many shuttle flights. An American Airlines sales representative can also sell discounted hotel packages to clients who book their airfare and overnight accommodations simultaneously.

Air Aruba (☎ 800/882-7822) offers eight flights a week from Newark, N.J., to Aruba (six of these are nonstop; the eighth touches down briefly in Baltimore before continuing on nonstop to Aruba). The same airline also offers daily nonstop flights to Aruba from Miami. There is also direct service from Baltimore to Aruba. In Aruba, regardless of their points of origin, Curaçao-bound passengers either remain on the same plane for its continuation on to Curaçao, or transfer to another aircraft after a brief delay.

Another choice is **ALM** (☎ 800/327-7230), Curaçao's national carrier, independent since 1966, which was established in 1934 as the Caribbean branch of KLM Royal Dutch Airlines. It flies 15 times a week from Miami to Curaçao. Although 10 of these flights stop in either Aruba, Bonaire, or Haiti, three are nonstop. ALM also flies twice a week to Curaçao from Atlanta, usually with a stop in Bonaire en route.

GETTING AROUND

BY BUS Some of the hotels operate a free bus shuttle that will take you from the suburbs to the shopping district of Willemstad. A fleet of DAF yellow buses operates from Wilhelmina Plein, near the shopping center, to most parts of

Curaçao. Some limousines function as "C" buses. When you see one listing the destination you're heading for, you can hail it at any of the designated bus stops.

BY TAXI   Since taxis don't have meters, ask your driver to quote you the rate before getting in. Drivers are supposed to carry an official tariff sheet, which they'll produce upon request. Charges go up by 25% after 11pm. Generally there is no need to tip, unless a driver helped you with your luggage. The charge from the airport to Willemstad is about $15, and the cost can be split among four passengers. If a piece of luggage is so big that the trunk lid won't close, you'll be assessed a surcharge of $1.

In town, the best place to get a taxi is on the Otrabanda side of the floating bridge. To summon a cab, call **648087.**

BY RENTAL CAR   Since all points of touristic interest on Curaçao are easily accessible by paved roads, you may want to rent a car. U.S., British, and Canadian citizens can use their own licenses, if valid, and *traffic moves on the right.* International road signs are observed.

Three of the largest car-rental companies in North America are represented on Curaçao. **Avis** (☎ toll free **800/331-2112**) and **Budget** (☎ toll free **800/527-0700**) offer some of the lowest rates. Compact cars with manual transmission begin at $253 per week at both Avis and Budget, both with unlimited mileage included. The cheapest car at **Hertz** (☎ toll free **800/654-3001**) rents for $258 per week, and represents especially good value because it includes air conditioning. A renter's membership in certain organizations, such as the AAA, or access to a corporate account, might reduce the prices a bit.

At Budget and Hertz, renters must be 25 years old, although at Budget, renters aged 23 or 24 could pay a $3 daily supplement and circumvent that rule. Avis requires a minimum age of only 21. Purchase of a collision-damage waiver (priced at $10 a day at all three companies for their least expensive cars) reduces a renter's liability in case of an accident to between $280 and $300. Use of certain types of credit or charge cards eliminates the need to pay for this extra insurance, although anyone thinking of taking advantage of those benefits must check directly with the issuer of the card to check the details. At least a week before your anticipated arrival on Curaçao, you should phone all three companies for a comparison of their latest prices and promotional offerings. In almost every case, rentals are cheaper for clients who reserve their car from North America before their departure. Once you're on the island, however, call Avis at **599/9-681163,** Budget at **599/9-683420,** and Hertz at **59/9-681182.**

BY SIGHTSEEING TOUR   A tour by **taxi** costs about $20 per hour, and up to four passengers can go on the jaunt.

Taber Tours, Dokweg (☎ **599/9-376637**), offers several tours, both day and night, to points of interest on Curaçao. The tour through Willemstad, to the Curaçao Liqueur distillery, through the residential area and the Bloempot shopping center, and to the Curaçao Museum (admission fee included in the tour price) costs $12.50 for adults, $6.25 for children under 12.

FAST FACTS: Curaçao

Area Code   Curaçao is *not* part of the Caribbean 809 area code. See "Telecommunications," below, for complete information on making calls to and on this island.

Curaçao

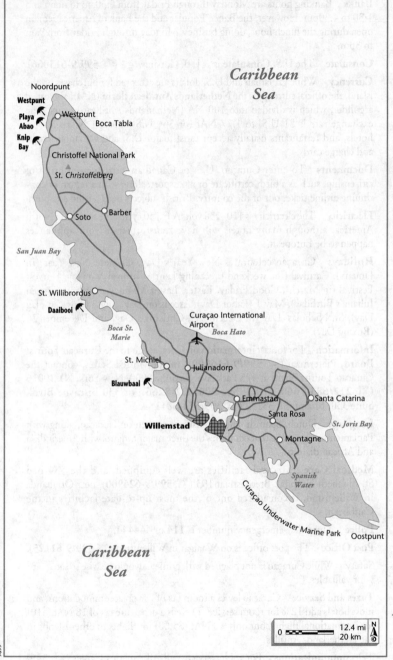

Caribbean Sea

Noordpunt

Westpunt
○ Westpunt
Playa Abao
Knip Bay
Boca Tabla

Christoffel National Park
▲ *St. Christoffelberg*

○ Soto   ○ Barber

San Juan Bay

○ St. Willibrordus
Daaibooi

Boca St. Marie

Curaçao International Airport
✈ *Boca Hato*

St. Michiel ○
○ Julianadorp
Blauwbaai

Emmastad ○   ○ Santa Catarina
Santa Rosa
Willemstad ○   *St. Joris Bay*
○ Montagne

Spanish Water

Curaçao Underwater Marine Park

Oostpunt

Caribbean Sea

Beach ↖   Airport ✈

0 ▭▭▭ 12.4 mi / 20 km   N ↑

9899

Banks   Banking hours are Monday through Friday from 8:30am to noon and 1:30 to 4:30pm. However, the Banco Popular and the Bank of America remain open during the lunch hour, doing business Monday through Friday from 9am to 3pm.

Consulate   The **U.S. Consulate** is at J. B. Gorsiraweg 1 (☎ **599/9-613066**).

Currency   While Canadian and U.S. dollars are accepted for purchases on the island, the official currency is the **Netherlands Antillean florin (NAf),** also called a guilder, which is divided into 100 NA (Netherlands Antillean) cents. The exchange rate is $1 U.S. to 1.77 NAf (or 56¢ U.S. equals 1 NAf). Shops, hotels, and restaurants usually accept most major U.S. and Canadian credit and charge cards.

Documents   To enter Curaçao, U.S. or Canadian citizens need proof of citizenship, such as a birth certificate or a passport, along with a return or continuing airline ticket out of the country. British subjects need a valid passport.

Electricity   The electricity is 110–130 volts A.C., 50 cycles, the same as in North America, although many hotels will have transformers if your appliances happen to be European.

Holidays   Curaçao celebrates New Year's Day, Chinese New Year (in January), Carnival (the weekend preceding Lent), Carnival Monday, Harvest Festival (in March), Good Friday, Easter, Easter Monday, April 30 (Queen Juliana's Birthday), May 1 (Labor Day), Ascension Day, July 2 (Curaçao Flag Day), St. Nicholas' Day (in December), Christmas Day, and December 26 (Boxing Day).

Information   For tourist information on Curaçao, go to the **Curaçao Tourist Board,** Pietermaai (☎ **599/9-616000**). In the United States, contact the Curaçao Tourist Board at 475 Park Ave. S., Suite 2000, New York, NY 10016 (☎ **212/683-7660,** or toll free **800/332-8266**); or 330 Biscayne Blvd., Suite 330, Miami, FL 33132 (☎ **305/374-5811**).

Language   Dutch, Spanish, and English are spoken on Curaçao, along with Papiamento, a language that combines the three major tongues with Amerindian and African dialects.

Medical Care   Medical facilities are well equipped, and the 534-bed St. Elisabeth Hospital, Breedestraat 193 (☎ **599/9-624900**), near Otrabanda in Willemstad, is considered one of the most up-to-date facilities in the Caribbean.

Police   The police emergency number is **114** or **444444.**

Post Office   The post office is on Waaigat in Willemstad (☎ **599/9-61125**).

Safety   While Curaçao is not plagued with crime, it would be wise to safeguard your valuables.

Taxes and Service   Curaçao levies a room tax of 7% on accommodations, and most hotels add 12% for room service. There is a departure tax of 18 NAf ($10) for international flights, but only 10 NAf ($5.60) for flights to other islands in the Netherlands Antilles.

Telecommunications   For cable service, call All America Cables (☎ **599/ 9-611433**) or Landsradio (☎ **599/9-613500**).

Curaçao is not part of the 809 area code that applies to most of the Caribbean. To call Curaçao from the United States, if your long-distance telephone company is equipped to handle international direct dialing, dial 011 (the international access code), then 599 (the country code for Curaçao), and then 9 (the area code) and the local number (the number of digits in the local number varies). If you cannot direct-dial internationally, dial 0 ("zero," for the operator) and tell the operator you wish to make an international call; once you are transferred to the international operator, state the 599 country code, the 9 area code, and then the local number, and the operator will dial the call for you.

Once on Curaçao, to call another number on the island only the local number is necessary; to make calls to an off-island destination, dial 021 and then the area code and number.

Time   Curaçao is on Atlantic standard time year round, one hour ahead of eastern standard time and the same as eastern daylight saving time.

Water   The water comes from a modern desalination plant and is safe to drink.

Weather   Curaçao has an average temperature of 81° Fahrenheit. Trade winds keep the island fairly cool, and it is flat and arid, with an average rainfall of only 22 inches per year—hardly your idea of a lush, palm-studded tropical island.

WHERE TO STAY

Your hotel will be in Willemstad or in one of the suburbs, which lie only 10 to 15 minutes from the shopping center. The bigger hotels often have free shuttle buses running into town, and most of them have their own beaches and pools.

Remember that Curaçao is a bustling commercial center, and the downtown hotels often fill up fast with business travelers and visitors from neighboring countries on a shopping holiday. Therefore, reservations are always important.

When making reservations, ask if the 7% room tax and 12% service charge are included in the price you're quoted.

VERY EXPENSIVE

✪ Sonesta Beach Hotel & Casino Curaçao

Piscadera Bay (P.O. Box 6003, Willemstad), Curaçao, N.A. ☎ **599/9-368800,** or toll free 800/SONESTA in the U.S. Fax 9/627502. 214 rms, 34 suites. A/C MINIBAR TV TEL. Winter, $230–$290 single or double; $330–$850 suite. Off-season, $160–$220 single or double; $240–$610 suite. Additional, person $30 extra. MAP $55 per person extra. AE, DC, MC, V. Free parking.

This is the most glamorous and most visible hotel on the island. Operated by Boston-based Sonesta Hotels, a chain known for its devotion to original artworks throughout its hotels, it opened in 1992 beside the longest and most popular beach on Curaçao, 10 minutes from both the airport and the capital of Willemstad. Its architects, who spent years researching the 18th-century *landhuis* of Curaçao, arranged it into a low-lying cluster of three-story buildings whose distinctive shape and ocher color were adapted directly from the traditional Dutch colonial architecture that permeates the rest of the island. The open-sided lobby was designed for maximum panoramas of the resort's beach and the many fountains that punctuate its landscaping. Scattered throughout the property are unusual, often monumental, artworks by local and international artists, and a collection of unfussy, overstuffed furniture.

Each of the accommodations offers tropical accessories, a view of the ocean, and color schemes of fuchsia and turquoise whose cool tones contrast with the glaring sunlight outside.

Dining/Entertainment: The Palm Café, an American and Caribbean restaurant, is an open-air resting point serving breakfast and lunch. The Emerald Bar & Grill serves grilled continental specialties and light appetizers in an atmosphere similar to that of an upscale private club. The Portofino, open for dinner only, features northern Italian specialties in an airy setting inspired by a resort along the Mediterranean. There's also an in-house casino, with at least six kinds of gambling-related activities.

Services: Concierge, massage, room service (6am to midnight), children's program for kids 5 to 12.

Facilities: Two tennis courts lit at night, lagoon-shaped swimming pool with swim-up bar, two open-air Jacuzzis patterned on Roman models, duty-free shopping arcade, a variety of land and water sports, the largest hotel beach on the island.

EXPENSIVE

✪ Avila Beach Hotel

Penstraat 130 (P.O. Box 791), Willemstad, Curaçao, N.A. ☎ **599/9-614377.** Fax 599/9/611493. 80 rms, 7 suites. A/C TV TEL. Winter, $90–$175 single; $100–$185 double; $240 suite. Off-season, $85–$145 single; $95–$155 double; $220 suite. MAP $45 per person extra. AE, DC, MC, V. Free parking.

This historic hotel consists of both a beautifully restored 200-year-old mansion and a large extension—called La Belle Alliance—completed in 1992, which added 40 deluxe rooms and seven suites. All the new rooms have an ocean view and balcony, and some also contain a kitchenette. The hostelry lies on the shore road leading east out of the city from the shopping center. It's the only beachfront hotel in Willemstad proper, set on its own private beach. The core of the hotel remains the historic mansion, which was built by the English governor of Curaçao during the British occupation of the island at the time of the Napoleonic wars. The mansion was converted into a hotel in 1949, and today attracts the royals of the Netherlands.

Dining/Entertainment: The hotel offers three restaurants: the Belle Terrace (see "Where to Dine," below), the Avila Café, and the pier restaurant, Blues. Blues is open from 5pm to 1am, catering to a crowd with a taste for jazz, swing, and, of course, blues. Antillean nights with local cuisine and live music are featured, as are Saturday-night barbecues.

Services: Babysitting, laundry.

Facilities: Tennis court (available daytime and evening), year-round ocean swimming from private sandy beach, terrace overlooking the ocean.

Curaçao Caribbean Hotel & Casino

Piscadera Bay (P.O. Box 2133, Willemstad), Curaçao, N.A. ☎ **599/9-625000**, or 800/344-1212 in the U.S. Fax 9/625846. 196 rms, 15 suites. A/C TV TEL. Winter, $170–$190 single or double; $225–$235 suite. Off-season, $170–$180 single or double; $190 suite. Buffet breakfast $12 extra. AE, DC, MC, V. Free parking.

This "honeycomb-on-stilts" high-rise resort on the outskirts of Willemstad has a free bus service to take you shopping in town. It's a self-contained complex, with a little beach and cove set among rocky bluffs. The structure is a block of rooms encased in a concrete facade. Glass-enclosed elevators clinging to the exterior walls of the hotel offer a panoramic view as you're whisked to your room. The bedrooms have baths with big towels, traditional furnishings, and private balconies; there's an ice machine on each floor. Many of the rooms appear tired and worn.

Dining/Entertainment: Most impressive to me is the wide-open lower lounge area, giving everyone a trade-wind–swept view of Piscadera Bay. Furnished in wicker, the Pisca Terrace bar and restaurant opens onto an eight-pointed-star–shaped pool and the ruins of a fort two centuries old. You can enjoy a buffet breakfast on this terrace. Other dining choices include La Garuda, serving Indonesian food, and Pirates Restaurant for seafood. Mexican nights are popular, as are Antillean nights with folklore shows. Of course, the casino is a major attraction.

Services: Room service (7am to 11pm), laundry, babysitting, free bus service to town.

Facilities: A dive shop offering the best water-sports program on the island (including skin diving, sailing, deep-sea fishing, and sea Jeeps), two Grasstex tennis courts (lit at night), well-stocked shopping complex.

Princess Beach Resort & Casino

Dr. Martin Luther King Blvd., Willemstad, Curaçao, N.A. ☎ **599/9-367888**, or toll free 800/ 327-3286 in the U.S. and Canada. Fax 599/9/614131. 341 rms, 8 suites. A/C MINIBAR TV TEL. Winter, $135–$220 single; $150–$235 double; from $260 suite. Off-season, $90–$150 single; $105–$165 double; from $190 suite. MAP $35 per person extra. AE, DC, MC, V. Free parking.

A modern, low-rise condominium-style beachfront resort lies in front of the Curaçao Underwater Park and close to the Seaquarium (just a complimentary shuttle ride away from Willemstad). The hotel has the only half-kilometer-long beach on the island. It's a haven for water-sports enthusiasts, with docking facilities for deep-sea fishing and a windsurfing center. Other facilities include two tennis courts, two freshwater pools (one with a swim-up bar), and in the vicinity, a nine-hole golf course. Many of the refurbished bedrooms look out over the beach, and all have hairdryers and either balconies or patios shielded by tropical plants. The most modern rooms are in a wing completed in 1993. A casino— perhaps the best on Curaçao—and nightly entertainment are an added feature. The hotel offers laundry, dry cleaning, room service, and babysitting.

MODERATE

Coral Cliff Resort & Casino

Santa Martha Bay (P.O. Box 3782), Curaçao, N.A. ☎ **599/9-641610.** Fax 599/9/641781. 42 rms. A/C TV TEL. Winter, $150 single; $240 double. Off-season, $130 single; $218 double. (Rates all–inclusive.) AE, MC, V. Free parking.

On the western part of the island, surrounded by 18 acres of grounds, cliffs, mountains, and bays, this is one of the few all-inclusive resorts in the ABC islands. Renovated in 1994, it offers rooms overlooking the Caribbean Sea, each well furnished (but not overly decorated). The location is on a natural beach attracting scuba divers and snorkelers. Water-sports equipment is available at the hotel's beachside water-sports center.

Dining/Entertainment: Guests relax at the beach bar and have a drink as they watch the sun set over the open-air Cliffhanger Bar. Later, they go to the open-air Terrace Restaurant, overlooking the water, for international-style meals. A casino also overlooks the sea.

Services: Complimentary transportation to and from the airport, minibus shuttle into town, laundry, babysitting on request.

Facilities: Day and night tennis, minigolf, volleyball, children's playground; horseback riding and waterskiing arranged.

⑤ Holiday Beach Hotel & Casino

Pater Euwensweg 31 (P.O. Box 2178), Willemstad, Curaçao, N.A. ☎ **599/9-625400.** Fax 599/9/624397. 200 rms. A/C TV TEL. Winter, $132–$147 single; $147–$163 double. Off-season, $90–$100 single; $105–$110 double. MAP $33 per person extra. AE, DC, MC, V. Free parking.

Along a sandy beach dotted with palm trees, this establishment sits near a grassy peninsula jutting out to sea about a mile from the capital and boasts all the facilities of a resort hotel. The main part of the complex houses the Casino Royale, one of the largest casinos on the island, and the premises contains a handful of tennis courts. Local entertainment is offered in the hotel's nightclub. After dinner, you can enjoy a drink in the Tropic Lounge, perhaps before heading to the roulette tables.

The sleeping quarters are in two four-story wings, centering around a U-shaped garden with a large freshwater swimming pool. The modern bedrooms have been recently refurbished, opening onto private balconies. A few open onto the water; others face the parking lot or pool. Wall-to-wall carpeting and big tile baths are just part of the comforts. Laundry, babysitting, and room service are available.

Lion's Dive Hotel & Marina

Bapor Kibrá, Willemstad, Curaçao, N.A. ☎ **599/9-618100.** Fax 599/9/618200. 72 rms. A/C TV TEL. Winter, $100 single; $110 double. Off-season, $90 single; $100 double. Breakfast $8.60 extra. AE, DC, MC, V. Free parking.

On the island's largest white sandy beach, a 30-minute taxi ride southeast of the airport, is a complete dive resort with programs supervised by the Underwater Curaçao staff. Each of its comfortable accommodations has a sea view, as well as a balcony or terrace, and two queen-size beds. Other facilities include a freshwater pool and three restaurants specializing in Italian and American cuisine plus seafood. Introductory dives and resort and certification courses are offered, and on the premises is a fully equipped rental dive shop. Two boat dives are conducted daily. Waterskiing, windsurfing, and sailing can also be arranged. Massage facilities are available, as are laundry and babysitting services. The hotel also has a health club.

INEXPENSIVE

⑤ Hotel Holland

F. D. Rooseveltweg 524, Curaçao, N.A. ☎ **599/9-688044.** Fax 599/9/688114. 40 rms, 5 suites. A/C TV TEL. $66 single; $79 double; from $117 suite. Continental breakfast from $4 extra. AE, DC, MC, V. Free parking.

A five-minute drive from the airport, the Hotel Holland contains the Flying Dutchman Bar, which is a popular gathering place, plus a small casino that opened in 1991. For a few brief minutes of every day, you can see airplanes landing from your perch at the edge of the poolside terrace, where well-prepared meals are served during good weather. This property is the domain of ex-navy frogman Hans Vrolijk and his family. Hans still retains his interest in scuba and arranges dive packages for his guests. The comfortably furnished accommodations have VCRs, refrigerators, and balconies. Laundry, babysitting, and room service are available.

⑤ Plaza Hotel

Plaza Pier (P.O. Box 229), Willemstad, Curaçao, N.A. ☎ **599/9-612500.** Fax 599/9/618347. 232 rms, 18 suites. A/C TV TEL. Rates (including American breakfast): $100 single or double; $140–$300 suite. AE, MC, V. Free parking.

Standing guard over the Punda side of St. Anna Bay, the Plaza is nestled in the ramparts of an 18th-century waterside fort on the eastern tip of the entrance to the harbor, a 20-minute drive south of the airport. In fact, it's one of the harbor's two "lighthouses." (The hotel has to carry marine collision insurance, the only hostelry in the Caribbean with that distinction.) The original part of the hotel followed the style of the arcaded fort. However, now there is a tower of rooms stacked 15 stories high. Each of the bedrooms—your own crow's nest—is comfortably furnished and contains a personal safe, although the room decor strikes many as garish. The pool, with a bar and suntanning area, is placed inches away from the parapet of the fort. In the hotel's Waterfort Grill, you can order American and continental dishes. The hotel offers laundry, babysitting, and room service (from 7:30am to 11pm), and has a small casino.

WHERE TO DINE
EXPENSIVE

✪ Bistro Le Clochard

Riffort, on the Otrabanda side of the pontoon bridge. ☎ **599/9-625666.** Reservations recommended. Appetizers $5.50–$14; main courses $21.30–$29.30. AE, DC, MC, V. Lunch Mon–Fri noon–2pm; dinner Mon–Sat 6:30–11pm. Harborside Terrace, dinner only, Mon–Sat 6–11pm. FRENCH/SWISS.

Bistro Le Clochard has been snugly fitted into the northwestern corner of the grim ramparts of Fort Rif at the gateway to the harbor. Its entrance is marked with a canopy, which leads to a series of rooms, each built under the 19th-century vaulting of the old Dutch fort. Several tables have a view of the Caribbean Sea. More panoramic is the establishment's outdoor terrace (the Harborside Terrace), built directly at the edge of the water, with a view over the harbor and the sparkling lights of the nearby town.

To begin, you might order bouillabaisse à notre façon, a fresh local fish soup, or the chef's own smoked dolphin served with a horseradish sauce. Among the alpine specialties are raclette (melted Swiss cheese served with boiled potato, onions, and pickles), or a fondue bourguignonne. One section of the menu is called "Romancing the Stone." The stone is heated in the oven and remains at a constant temperature. It's brought directly to the table, and, without using oil or fat, your choice from the menu is cooked on the stone—tournedos, sirloin, T-bone, boneless chicken breast, or fresh fish.

✪ De Taveerne

Landhuis Groot Davelaar, Silena. ☎ **599/9-370669.** Reservations required. Appetizers $6–$12; main courses $16–$33. AE, DC, MC, V. Lunch Mon–Fri noon–2pm; dinner Mon–Sat 7–11pm. FRENCH/SEAFOOD.

A red-brick octagonal cupola rises over the roof of this country manor house in a residential neighborhood, inland on the east side of St. Anna Bay. Inside, where the cows used to be sheltered, the owner has created a tavern atmosphere with an antique decor, including furnishings from Curaçao's old homes. The charming restaurant, bar, and wine cellar are enhanced by burnished copper, white stucco walls, dark woods, and terra-cotta tiles. Specialties change frequently, but perhaps you'll start with smoked Dutch eel, lobster soup, or snails bourguignon. Other recommendable dishes include shrimp thermidor, sole meunière, and a salmon gratinée.

Fort Nassau

Near Point Juliana. ☎ **599/9-613086.** Reservations recommended. Appetizers $9.40–$11; main courses $19.80–$27.40. AE, DC, MC, V. Lunch Mon–Fri noon–3pm; dinner daily 7–10pm. INTERNATIONAL.

This restored restaurant and bar is built on a hilltop overlooking Willemstad in the ruins of a formidably buttressed fort dating from 1792, and it has retained an 18th-century decor. From its Battery Terrace, a 360° panorama unfolds of the sea, the harbor, and Willemstad, just a five-minute drive away. You'll even have a faraway view of the island's vast oil refinery. A signal tower on the cliff sends out beacons to approaching ships. You can visit the fashionably decorated bar just to have a drink and watch the sunset; happy hour is 6 to 7pm daily.

An array of appetizers awaits you, including a combination terrine made from layers of both marinated salmon and smoked salmon and served with a vegetable ratatouille and a caviar of salmon. A main-dish specialty is Fort Nassau smoked salmon with sautéed black linguine and leek or a Thai seafood pot. You can also order filet of hare roasted in sesame oil or roast New Zealand lamb.

Wine Cellar

Ooststraat/Concordiastraat. ☎ **599/9-612178.** Reservations required. Appetizers $5.25–$16; main courses $18–$35. AE, MC, V. Lunch Tues–Fri noon–2pm; dinner Tues–Sun 6–11pm. INTERNATIONAL.

Opposite the cathedral in the center of town is the domain of Nico and Angela Cornelisse and their son, Ivo, who offer one of the most extensive wine cartes on the island. You are welcomed into air-conditioned comfort into a Victorian atmosphere, much like an old-fashioned Dutch home, in tones of red and brown. The kitchen turns out an excellent lobster salad and a sole meunière in a butter-and-herb sauce. You might also try, if featured, fresh red snapper or U.S. tenderloin of beef with goat-cheese sauce. Game dishes are imported throughout the year from Holland and are likely to include venison roasted with mushrooms, hare, or roast goose.

MODERATE

Belle Terrace

In the Avila Beach Hotel, Penstraat 130. ☎ **599/9-614377.** Reservations required. Appetizers $7–$14.50; main courses $14–$24.60; menu dégustation $27.20 for two courses, $32.20 for three courses. AE, DC, MC, V. Lunch daily noon–2:30pm; dinner daily 7–10:30pm. INTERNATIONAL/DANISH.

You'll find this open-air restaurant in a 200-year-old mansion on the beachfront of Willemstad. In a relaxed and informal atmosphere, it offers split-level dining. The Schooner Bar, where you can enjoy a rum punch, is shaped like a weather-beaten ship's prow looking out to sea. The restaurant, sheltered by an arbor of flamboyant branches, features Scandinavian, continental, and local cuisine with such specialties as pickled herring, smoked salmon, barracuda, and a Danish lunch platter. Local dishes, such as keshi yena, are on the menu. On Saturday night the chef has a beef-tenderloin barbecue and a help-yourself salad bar. Fish is always fresh at Belle Terrace, and the chef prepares the catch of the day to perfection:

grilled, poached, or meunière. Desserts include Danish pastry and cakes, as well as a large selection of homemade ice creams.

From the airport, follow the signs to Punda. Turn left after the second traffic light in town. Stay on the right side of that road (Plaza Smeets) and go straight ahead. If you keep to the right side of the road you'll enter Penstraat, where you'll find the Avila Beach Hotel on the right-hand side.

Fort Waakzaamheid Bistro

Seru di Domi, Otrabanda. ☎ **599/9-623633.** Reservations recommended. Appetizers $4.60–$11.25; main courses $18–$22; three-course "early bird" dinner (at 5pm) $14.30. AE, MC, V. Dinner only, Wed–Mon 5–11pm. (Bar, open until 1am, later on weekends.) INTERNATIONAL.

Captain Bligh, of *Bounty* fame, captured this old fort in 1804 and laid siege to Willemstad for almost a month. A stone-and-hardwood tavern and restaurant have been installed in the fort, which opens onto a view of the Otrabanda and the harbor entrance. The atmosphere is that of a country tavern. Start with the fish soup and follow with conch, duck, surf and turf, prime rib, or garlic shrimp. Lobster is the most expensive item on the menu, or you may settle instead for Curaçao snapper. A fresh fish is offered each day, with a salad.

⑤ Pisces Seafood

Caracasbaaiweg 476. ☎ **599/9-672181.** Reservations recommended. Appetizers $4.30–$10; main courses $15.75–$34.30. AE, DC, MC, V. Dinner only, Fri–Wed 6–10:15pm. Closed last two weeks in Aug. CREOLE/SEAFOOD.

This West Indian restaurant may be difficult to find, as it's on a flat industrial coastline near a marina and an oil refinery, about 20 minutes from the capital on the island's southernmost tip. There has been a restaurant here since the 1930s, when sailors and workers from the oil refinery came for home-cooked meals. Today the simple frame building offers seating near the rough-hewn bar or in a breeze-swept inner room. Pisces serves combinations of seafood that depend on the catch of the day. Main courses, served with rice, vegetables, and plantains, might include sopi, "seacat" (squid), mula (similar to kingfish), red snapper, or any of these served, if you wish, in copious quantities for two or more people in the Pisces platter. Shrimp and conch are each prepared three different ways; with garlic, with curry, or Creóle style.

Rijstaffel Restaurant Indonesia and Holland Club Bar

Mercuriusstraat 13, Salinja. ☎ **599/9-612999.** Reservations recommended. Appetizers $3.95–$9.90; main courses $12.70–$21.20; rijstaffel $18.90 for 16 dishes, $21.75 for 20 dishes, $29.40 for 25 dishes; all vegetarian rijstaffel $21.20 for 16 dishes. AE, DC, MC, V. Lunch Mon–Sat noon–2pm; dinner daily 6–9:30pm. INDONESIAN.

This is the best place on the island to sample the Indonesian rijstaffel, the traditional rice table with all the zesty side dishes. You must ask a taxi to take you to this villa in the suburbs near Salinja, near the Princess Beach Resort & Casino southeast of Willemstad. You're allowed to season your plate with peppers rated hot, very hot, and palate-melting. At lunchtime, the selection of dishes is more modest, but for dinner, Javanese cooks prepare the specialty of the house, a rijstaffel consisting of 16, 20, or 25 dishes. There's even an all-vegetarian rijstaffel. Warming trays are placed on your table, and the service is buffet style. It's best to go with a party so that all of you can share in the feast.

INEXPENSIVE

The Cockpit

In the Hotel Holland, F. D. Rooseveltweg 524. ☎ **599/9-688044.** Reservations required. Appetizers $4–$9.50; main courses $7.50–$21. AE, DC, MC, V. Daily 7–1am. DUTCH/INTERNATIONAL.

The decor of this restaurant has an aeronautical flavor with the nose of an airplane cockpit the main focal point. Located on the scrub-bordered road leading to the airport, a few minutes from the landing strips, this restaurant serves up international cuisine with an emphasis on Dutch and Antillean specialties. Guests enjoy such dishes as fresh fish in season (served Curaçao style), Dutch-style steak, Caribbean curried chicken, split-pea soup, and various pasta dishes such as the shrimp linguine della mama served in a lobster sauce and topped with melted cheese. All dishes are accompanied by fresh vegetables and Dutch-style potatoes. Guests can enjoy their meals outside around the pool or in the cockpit-inspired dining room.

⑤ Golden Star

Socratesstraat 2. ☎ **599/9-654795.** Reservations not required. Appetizers $4.30–$7.70; main courses $7.50–$25.70. AE, DC, MC, V. Daily 9am–1am. CREOLE.

The best place to go on the island for "criollo," or local food, is inland from the coast road leading southeast from St. Anna Bay, at the corner of Dr. Hugenholtzweg and Dr. Maalweg, southeast of Willemstad. Evoking a roadside diner, the air-conditioned restaurant is very simple, but it has a large menu of very tasty Antillean dishes, such as carco stoba (conch stew), bestia chiki (goat-meat stew), bakijauw (salted cod), and concomber stoba (stewed meat and marble-size spiny cucumbers). Other specialties include criollo shrimp (kiwa) and sopi carni. Everything is served with a side order of funchi, the cornmeal staple. The place has a large local following with an occasional tourist dropping in.

Pinocchio

Schottegatweg 82. ☎ **599/9-376784.** Reservations not required. Appetizers $3.50–$8.50; main courses $12.30–$21.50. AE, DC, MC, V. Mon–Sat 11am–11pm, Sun 8am–11pm. INTERNATIONAL.

Set in the suburb of Salinja, a short drive south of Willemstad, this is a plant- and panel-filled restaurant which caters to couples and families. Decorated in a tropical medley of bright colors, it maintains an active bar area, where drinks cost $2 to $4 each. Menu items are simple and flavorful, including burgers, sandwiches, salads, steaks, fish dishes, buffalo-style chicken wings, and pita pockets filled, Lebanese style, with spiced lamb (shoarma).

Playa Forti

Westpunt. ☎ **599/9-640273.** Reservations not required. Appetizers $3.50–$5; main courses $6–$16. AE, DC, MC, V. Daily 10am–7pm. CREOLE.

A good address to know if you're touring the island, Playa Forti is built on the foundation of a fortress dating from Bonaparte's day; it's near North Point, the extreme northwestern end of Curaçao. Not only do you get good local food here, but you also get one of the most panoramic sea views on the island. If you're touring, drop in for drinks in the afternoon. The waters of Westpunt are ideal for snorkeling and scuba diving if you want to bring your own equipment.

International dishes are presented, but it would be wiser to order some of the Antillean specialties, such as cabrito, a succulent goat stew which tastes a bit like veal. Try also keshi yena, a tasty mixture of beef and chicken that has been pickled and cooked with tomatoes and onions, then wrapped in Edam cheese. Ayaca is a combination of chicken and beef, with olives, raisins, nuts, and spices wrapped in a soft corndough tortilla (it's packed and cooked in banana leaves). Sopidi plata, the fish soup, makes a zesty opening. Or try the fried red snapper Curaçao style—fried a golden brown, then covered in a sauce of tomatoes, onions, and green peppers. It's served with fried plantains and funchi, the local cornmeal preparation.

WHAT TO SEE & DO

Most cruise-ship passengers see only Willemstad—or, more accurately, the shops—but you may want to get out into the *cunucu,* or countryside, and explore the towering cacti and rolling hills topped by *landhuizen* (plantation houses) built more than three centuries ago.

✪ WILLEMSTAD

In Willemstad, the Dutch found a vast natural harbor, a perfect hideaway along the Spanish Main. Not only is Willemstad the capital of Curaçao, it's also the seat of government for the Netherlands Antilles.

The city grew up on both sides of the canal. Today it's divided into the **Punda** and the **Otrabanda,** the latter literally meaning "the other side." Both sections are connected by the **Queen Emma Pontoon Bridge,** a pedestrian walkway. Powered by a diesel engine, it swings open many times every day to let ships from all over the globe pass in and out of the harbor.

The view from the bridge is of the old **gabled houses** in harmonized pastel shades, such as deep earth-toned golds, mustards, and greens. The bright pastel colors, according to legend, are a holdover from the time when one of the island's early governors is said to have had eye trouble and flat white gave him headaches.

The colonial-style architecture, reflecting the Dutch influence, gives the town a "storybook" look. The houses, built three or four stories high, are crowned by "step" gables and roofed with orange Spanish tiles. Hemmed in by the sea, a tiny canal, and an inlet, the streets are narrow, and they're crosshatched by still narrower alleyways.

Except for the pastel colors, Willemstad may remind you of old Amsterdam. It has one of the most intriguing townscapes in the Caribbean.

A **statue of Pedro Luis Brion** dominates the square known as Brionplein right at the Otrabanda end of the pontoon bridge. Born in Curaçao in 1782, he became the island's favorite son and best-known war hero. Under Simón Bolívar, he was an admiral of the fleet and fought for the independence of Venezuela and Colombia.

In addition to the pontoon bridge, the **Queen Juliana Bridge** opened to vehicular traffic in 1973. Spanning the harbor, it rises 195 feet, which makes it the highest bridge in the Caribbean and one of the tallest in the world.

The Waterfront originally guarded the mouth of the canal on the eastern or Punda side, but now it has been incorporated into the Plaza Hotel. The task of standing guard has been taken over by **Fort Amsterdam,** site of the Governor's Palace and the 1769 Dutch Reformed church. The church still has a British cannonball embedded in it. The arches leading to the fort were tunneled under the official residence of the governor.

A corner of the fort stands at the intersection of Breedestraat and Handelskade, the starting point for a plunge into the island's major shopping district.

A few minutes' walk from the pontoon bridge, at the north end of Handelskade, is the **Floating Market,** where scores of schooners tie up alongside the canal, a few yards from the main shopping section. Docked boats arrive from Venezuela and Colombia, as well as other West Indian islands, to sell tropical fruits and vegetables—a little bit of everything, in fact. The modern market under its vast concrete cap has not replaced this unique shopping expedition, which is fun to watch.

Between the I. H. (Sha) Capriles Kade and Fort Amsterdam, at the corner of Columbusstraat and Kerkstraat, stands the **Mikve Israel–Emanuel Synagogue,** one of the oldest synagogue buildings in the western hemisphere. Consecrated on the eve of Passover in 1732, it antedates the first U.S. synagogue (in Newport, Rhode Island) by 31 years and houses the oldest Jewish congregation in the New World, dating from 1651. A fine example of Dutch colonial architecture, covering about a square block in the heart of Willemstad, it was built in a Spanish-style walled courtyard, with four large portals. Sand covers the sanctuary floor following a Portuguese Sephardic custom, representing the desert where Israelites camped when the Jews passed from slavery to freedom. The *theba* (pulpit) is in the center, and the congregation surrounds it. The highlight of the east wall is the Holy Ark, rising 17 feet, and a raised banca, canopied in mahogany, is on the north wall.

Joáo d'Illan led the first Jewish settlers (13 families) to the island in 1651, almost half a century after their expulsion from Portugal by the Inquisition. The settlers came via Amsterdam to Curaçao. The first Jew to arrive on Curaçao (although he stayed less than a year) was Samuel Coheno, an interpreter for the Dutch naval commander, Johan van Walbeck, who conquered Curaçao from the Spaniards in 1634.

The synagogue has services every Friday at 6:30pm and Saturday at 10am, as well as similar holiday service times. Visitors are welcome to all services, with appropriate dress required.

Adjacent to the synagogue courtyard is the **Jewish Cultural Historical Museum,** Kuiperstraat 26–28, housed in two buildings dating back to 1728. They were originally the rabbi's residence and the bathhouse. The $2^1/_2$-centuries-old mikvah, or bath for religious purification purposes, was in constant use until around 1850 when this practice was discontinued and the buildings sold. They have been reacquired through the Foundation for the Preservation of Historic Monuments and turned into the present museum. On display are a great many ritual, ceremonial, and cultural objects, many of which date back to the 17th and 18th centuries and are still in use by the congregation for holidays and life-cycle events.

The synagogue and museum are open to visitors Monday through Friday from 9 to 11:45am and 2:30 to 5pm; if there's a cruise ship in port, also on Sunday from 9am to noon. There's a $2 entrance fee to the museum. The gift shop is in the synagogue office (☎ **599/9-611633**).

WEST OF WILLEMSTAD

The **Curaçao Museum,** Van Leeuwenhoekstraat (☎ **599/9-6238873**), can be walked to from the Queen Emma Pontoon Bridge. It was built in 1853 by the Royal Dutch Army Corps of Engineers as a military quarantine hospital for yellow fever victims and was carefully restored in 1946–48 as a fine example of 19th-century Dutch architecture. Furnished with paintings, objets d'art, and antique furniture made in the 19th century by local cabinetmakers, it re-creates the atmosphere of an era gone by. A novelty is the polka-dot kitchen. The museum contains a large collection from the Caiquetio tribes, the early inhabitants described by Amerigo Vespucci as giants 7 feet tall. There's a modest Children's Museum of Science in the basement, with hands-on exhibits. In the gardens are specimens of the island's trees and plants. There is also a reconstruction of a traditional music pavilion in the garden where Curaçao musicians give regular performances. It's open Monday through Friday from 9am to noon and 2 to 5pm, and on Sunday from 10am to 4pm. Admission is $2 for adults, $1 for children under 14.

The **Curaçao Seaquarium,** off Martin Luther King Boulevard at a site called Bapor Kibrá (☎ **594/9-616666**), has more than 400 species of fish, crabs, anemones, and other invertebrates, sponges, and coral displayed and growing in a natural environment. A rustic boardwalk connects the low-lying hexagonal buildings comprising the Seaquarium complex, which sits on a point off which the *Oranje Nassau* broke up on the rocks and sank in 1906 (the name of the site, Bapor Kibrá, mean "sunken ship"). Located a few minutes' walk along the rocky coast from the Princess Beach Resort & Casino, the Seaquarium is open daily from 8:30am to 10pm. Admission to the Seaquarium is $12.50 for adults, $7 for children under 15.

A special feature of the aquarium is a "shark and animal encounter." Divers, snorkelers, and experienced swimmers are able to feed, film, and photograph sharks, which are separated from them by a large window with feeding holes. In the animal encounter section, swimmers are able to swim among stingrays, lobsters, sabalo, parrotfish, and other marine life, feeding and photographing these creatures in a controlled environment where safety is always a consideration. For the nonswimmer, a 46-foot semi-submarine (underwater observation tower) is in the middle. Sharks as well as other species are "called" to the windows of the semi-submarine for a close-up view. The Seaquarium is also home to Curaçao's only full facility, white sandy, palm-shaded beach.

The **Curaçao Underwater Marine Park** (☎ **599/9-624242**), established in 1983 with the financial aid of the World Wildlife Fund, stretches from the Princess Beach Resort & Casino to the east point of the island, a strip of about 12¹/₂ miles of untouched coral reefs. For information on snorkeling, scuba diving, and trips in a glass-bottom boat to view the park, see "Sports & Outdoor Activities," below.

Also en route to Westpunt, you'll come across a seaside cavern known as **Boca Tabla,** one of many such grottoes on this rugged, uninhabited northwest coast.

In the Westpunt area, a 45-minute ride from Punda in Willemstad, **Playa Forti** is a stark region characterized by soaring hills and towering cacti, along with 200-year-old Dutch land houses, the former mansions that housed the slaveowner plantation heads. For a dining suggestion, see my recommendation of the Playa Forti Restaurant in "Where to Dine," above.

Out toward the western tip of Curaçao, a high wire fence surrounds the entrance to the 4,500-acre ✪ **Christoffel National Park,** Savonet (☎ **599/9-640363**), about a 45-minute drive from the capital. A macadam road gives way to dirt, surrounded on all sides by abundant cactus and bromeliads. In the higher regions you can spot rare orchids. Rising from flat, arid countryside, 1,230-foot-high St. Christoffelberg is the highest point in the Dutch Leewards. Donkeys, wild goats, iguanas, the Curaçao deer, and many species of birds thrive in this preserve, and there are some Arawak paintings on a coral cliff near the two caves. A folk legend surrounds Piedra di Monton, a rockheap accumulated by African slaves who worked on the former plantations. According to the legend passed down through the generations, any worker would be able to climb to the top of the rockpile, jump off, and fly back home across the Atlantic. If, however, the slave had at any time in his life tasted a grain of salt, the magic would not work and he would crash to his death below. The park has 20 miles of one-way trail-like roads, with lots of flora and fauna along the way. The shortest trail is about 5 miles long, and because of the rough terrain, takes about 40 minutes to drive through. Various walking trails are available also. One of them will take you to the top of St. Christoffelberg in about 1½ hours. (Come early in the morning when it isn't so hot.) The park is open Monday through Saturday from 8am to 4pm and on Sunday from 6am to 3pm. Admission is $9 for adults, $3 for children. The park also has a museum with varying exhibitions year round set in an old storehouse left over from plantation days. Guided tours are available by calling **599/9-640363.**

NORTH & EAST OF WILLEMSTAD

Just northeast of the capital, **Fort Nassau** was completed in 1797 and christened by the Dutch as Fort Republic. Built high on a hill overlooking the harbor entrance to the south and St. Anna Bay to the north, it was fortified as a second line of defense in case Waterfront gave way. When the British invaded in 1807, they renamed it Fort George in honor of their own king. Later, when the Dutch regained control, they renamed it Orange Nassau in honor of the Dutch royal family. Today diners have replaced soldiers (see "Where to Dine," above).

Along the coast to the southeast of town, the oddly shaped **Octagon House** on Penstraat was where the liberator, Simón Bolívar, used to visit his two sisters during the wars for Venezuelan independence. This landmark used to be a museum, but it is currently closed.

In the area, the **Amstel Brewery** (☎ **599/9-612944**) allows visitors to tour its plant where Curaçao beer is brewed from desalinated seawater. Tours are given only on Tuesday and Thursday at 9:30am.

In addition, the **Curaçao Liqueur Distillery,** in the Salinja area (☎ **599/ 9-613526**), offers free tours and tastes at Chobolobo, the 17th-century landhuis where the famous liqueur is made. The cordial, named after the region where it originated, is a distillate of dried peel of a particular strain of orange found only on Curaçao. Several herbs are added to give it an aromatic bouquet. It's made by a secret formula handed down through generations. One of the rewards of a visit here is a free snifter of the liqueur at the culmination of the guided tours, offered Monday through Friday from 8am to noon and 1 to 5pm.

On Schottegatweg West, Northwest of Willemstad, past the oil refineries, lies the **Beth Haim Cemetery,** the oldest Caucasian burial site still in use in the western hemisphere. Meaning "House of Life," the cemetery was consecrated before 1659. On about 3 acres are some 2,500 graves. The carving on some of the 17th- and 18th-century tombstones is exceptional.

Landhuis Brievengat, Brienvengat (☎ **599/9-378344**), gives visitors a chance to visit a Dutch version of an 18th-century West Indian plantation house. This stately building, in a scrub-dotted landscape on the eastern side of the island, contains a few antiques, high ceilings, and a frontal gallery facing two entrance towers, said to have been used to imprison slaves and even for romantic trysts. The plantation was originally used for the cultivation of aloe and cattle, but an 1877 hurricane caused the plantation to cease operation. The building was pulled down, but around 1925 the remains of the structure were donated to the Society for the Preservation of Monuments, which rebuilt and restored it. It's open daily from 9:30am to noon and 3 to 9pm; admission is $1.

The **Hato Caves,** F.D. Rosseveltweg (☎ **599/9-680379**), have been called "mystical." Every hour, professional local guides take visitors through this Curaçao world of stalagmites and stalactites, found in the highest limestone terrace of the island. Actually, they were once old coral reefs, which were formed when the ocean water fell and the land mass was uplifted over the years. Over thousands of years, limestone formations were created, some mirrored in an underground lake. After crossing the lake, you enter the "Cathedral," an underground cavern. The largest hall of the cave is called La Ventana or "The Window." Also displayed are samples of ancient Indian petroglyph drawings. The caves are open Tuesday through Sunday from 10am to 5pm, charging $4.25 for adults and $3 for children.

SPORTS & OUTDOOR ACTIVITIES

BEACHES   Its beaches are not as good as Aruba's 7-mile strip of sand, but Curaçao does have some 38 of them, ranging from hotel sands to secluded coves. About 30 minutes from town, in the Willibrordus area on the west side of Curaçao, **Daaibooi** is a good beach. It's free, but there are no changing facilities. A good private beach on the eastern side of the island is **Santa Barbara Beach,** on land owned by a mining company between the open sea and the island's primary water-sports and recreational area known as Spanish Water. On the same land are Table Mountain, a remarkable landmark, and an old phosphate mine. The natural beach has pure-white sand and calm water. A buoy line protects swimmers from boats. Restrooms, changing rooms, a snack bar, and a terrace are among the amenities. You can rent water bicycles and small motorboats. The beach, open daily from 8am to 6pm, has access to the Curaçao Underwater Park.

Blauwbaai (blue Bay) is the largest and most frequented beach on Curaçao, with enough white sand for everybody. Along with showers and changing facilities, there are plenty of shady places to retreat from the noonday sun. To reach it, follow the road that goes past the Holiday Beach Hotel, heading in the direction of Juliandorp. Follow the sign that tells you to bear left for Blauwbaai and the fishing village of San Michiel.

Other beaches include: **Westpunt,** known for the gigantic cliffs that frame it and the Sunday divers who jump from the cliffs into the ocean below. The public beach is located on the northwestern tip of the island. **Knip Bay,** just south of Westpunt, is a beach at the foot of beautiful turquoise waters. On weekends, live music and dancing make the beach a lively place. Changing facilities and refreshments are available. **Playa Abao,** with crystal turquoise water, is a beach at the northern tip of the island.

A *Word of Caution to Swimmers:* The sea water remains an almost-constant 76° Fahrenheit year round, with good underwater visibility, but beware of stepping on spines of the sea urchins that sometimes abound in these waters. To give temporary first aid for an embedded urchin's spine, try the local remedies of vinegar or lime juice, or as the natives advise, a burning match if you are tough. While the urchin spines are not fatal, they can cause several days of real discomfort.

BOATING TOURS   Taber Tours, Dokweg (☎ **599/9-376637**), offers a handful of seagoing tours, such as a snorkel/barbecue trip to Port Marie, which includes round-trip transportation to excellent reef sites, use of snorkeling equipment, and a barbecue, for a cost of $50 per person. No children under 10 are allowed.

A less ambitious tour involves a sunset cruise with wine, cheese, and French bread served on board, and a two-hour sailing trip at dusk, for a cost of $30 per adult and $20 for children under 12.

Travelers looking for a seagoing experience similar to the sailing days of yore should book a trip on the *Insulinde,* Handelskade (☎ **599/9-601340**). this 120-foot traditionally rigged sail logger is available for day trips sunset sails, and chartering. Every Thursday (or by special arrangement), the ship sails north from its berth beside Willemstad's main pier to the island's northwestern shore. There, at Porto Marie (also refered to as Boca St. Marie), guests disembark onto the white sands of a beach, beside a complex of barbecue pits and huts which give a welcome protection from the sun. Included in the $45-per-person charge is an open bar, a barbecued lunch with three kinds of meat and four kinds of salads, and free use of snorkeling equipment. Round-trip transport from some of the island's hotels is also included in the price. Advance reservations are necessary. Outbound transit is by sail; the return is by the ship's engines. Departure from the pier is at 9am every Thursday; return to the pier is around 6pm the same day. Weekend trips to Bonaire are possible for $195 per person round-trip.

GOLF   The **Curaçao Golf and Squash Club,** Wilhelminalaan, in Emmastad (☎ **599/9-373590**), is open to the general public by arrangement only—telephone the day before you wish to play. Greens fees are $15, and both clubs and carts can be rented upon demand. The nine-hole course (the only one on the island) is open to nonmembers Friday through Wednesday only in the morning, from 8am to 12:30pm. (Afternoon tee-offs are reserved for members and for tournaments.) Thursday hours for nonmembers are 10am until sundown.

TENNIS   There are tennis courts at the Curaçao Caribbean Hotel & Casino, Princess Beach Resort & Casino, and Holiday Beach Hotel & Casino.

WATER SPORTS   Most hotels offer their own programs of water sports. However, if your hotel isn't equipped, I suggest that you head for one of the most complete water-sports facilities on Curaçao, **Seascape Dive and Watersports,** at the Curaçao Caribbean Hotel (☎ **599/9-625000,** ext 6056). Specializing in snorkeling and scuba-diving to reefs and underwater wrecks, it operates from a hexagonal kiosk set on stilts above the water, just offshore from the hotel's beach.

Open from 8am to 5pm daily, the company offers snorkeling excursions for $18 per person in an underwater park offshore from the hotel, glass-bottom-boat rides for $10, waterskiing for $45 per half hour, and rental of jet-skis for $34 per half hour. A Sunfish rents for $20, and an introductory scuba lesson, conducted by a competent dive instructor with PADI certification, goes for $45; packages of four dives cost $124. Bottom fishing, with all equipment included, aboard a 38-foot Delta suitable for up to six passengers, costs $180 for a half day and $300 for a full day.

One trip enthusiastically endorsed by some readers departs from the hotel at 7am (when participation warrants). The destination is Little Curaçao, midway between Curaçao and Bonaire. Clothes are optional once you get to the sugar-white sands of the island. Fishing, snorkeling, and the acquisition of an "overall tan" are highlights. The price is $55 per person, and the excursion lasts all day. Another possibility is a boat ride to one of Curaçao's more isolated beaches, Santa Barbara Beach. A full day's outing is $30 per person.

They can also arrange deep-sea fishing for $336 for a half-day tour carrying a maximum of six people, $560 for a full-day tour. Drinks and equipment are included, but you'll have to get your hotel to pack your lunch.

Underwater Curaçao, in Bapor Kibrá (☎ **599/9-618131**), has a complete PADI-accredited underwater sports program. A fully stocked modern dive shop has retail and rental equipment. Individual dives and dive packages are offered, costing $33 per dive for experienced divers. An introductory dive for novices is priced at $65 and a snorkel trip costs only $20, including equipment.

Scuba divers and snorkelers can expect spectacular scenery in waters with visibility often exceeding 100 feet at the **Curaçao Underwater Park,** which stretches along 12½ miles of Curaçao southern coastlines. (Although its premises technically begin at Princess Beach and extend all the way to East Point, the island's most southeasterly tip, some scuba aficionados and island dive operators are aware of other, excellent dive sites outside the official boundaries of this park.) Lying beneath the surface of the water are steep walls, at least two shallow wrecks, gardens of soft corals, and more than 30 species of hard corals. Although access from shore is possible at Jan Thiel Bay an Santa Barbara Beach, most people visit the park by boat. For easy and safe mooring, the park has 16 mooring buoys, placed at the best dive and snorkel sites. A snorkel trail with underwater interpretive markers is laid out just east of the Princess Beach Resort & Casino and is accessible from shore. Spearfishing, anchoring in the coral, and taking anything from the reefs except photographs are strictly prohibited.

SHOPPING

Curaçao is a shopper's paradise. Some 200 shops line the major shopping malls of such wooden-shoe-named streets as Heerenstraat and Breedestraat. Right in the heart of Willemstad, the Punda shopping area is a five-block district. Most stores are open Monday through Saturday from 8am to noon and 2 to 6pm (some from 8am to 6pm). When cruise ships are in port, stores are also open for a few hours on Sunday and holidays. To avoid the cruise-ship crowds, do your shopping in the morning.

Look for good buys in French perfumes, Dutch Delft blue souvenirs, finely woven Italian silks, Japanese and German cameras, jewelry, silver, Swiss watches, linens, leather goods, liquor, and island-made rum and liqueurs, especially Curaçao.

Incidentally, Curaçao is not technically a free port, but its prices are low because of its low import duty.

Benetton
Madurostraat 4. ☎ **599/9-614619.**

This member of a worldwide chain based in Italy has invaded Curaçao with all its many colors. In July you can stock up on winter wear, and in December make summer purchases. Some prices are said to be 20% off Stateside charges.

Bert Knubben Black Koral Shop
In the Princess Beach Resort & Casino, Dr. Martin Luther King Blvd. ☎ **599/9-367888,** ext. 1200.

Bert Knubben is a name synonymous with craftsmanship and quality. Although collection of black coral has been made illegal by the Curaçao government, an exception was made for Bert, a diver who has been harvesting corals from the sea and fashioning them into the fine jewelry and objets d'art for more than 35 years. The jewelry is finished with 14-karat gold.

Boolchand's

Heerenstraat 4B, Punda. ☎ **599/9-612262.**

In business since 1930, Boolchand's features Seiko and Citizen watches and a complete line of cameras, photo, audio and video equipment. A branch store, La Fortunata, has clothing for men, women, and children.

Gandelman Jewelers

Breedestraat 35, Punda. ☎ **599/9-611854.**

This store has a large selection of fine jewelry set with diamonds, rubies, emeralds, sapphires, and other gemstones. Here you'll find timepieces by Piaget, Ebel, Corum, Concord, Baume & Mercier, Movado, Tag-Heuer, Gucci, Fendi, Seiko, Swatch, and many others. Exclusive here is the unique line of Prima Classe leathergoods with the world map. Gandelman Jewelers has eight other stores in the Dutch Caribbean.

Obra Di Man

Bargestraat 57. ☎ **599/9-612413.**

Filled with authentic local handcraft items, including printed T-shirts, handmade dolls, hand-screened fabrics, carved driftwood, and filigree jewelry.

Palais Hindu

Heerenstraat 17. ☎ **599/9-616897.**

To satisfy your audio and video needs, Palais Hindi sells a wide range of video and cassette recorders. They also stock a lot of photographic equipment, along with cameras and watches.

Penha & Sons

Heerenstraat 1. ☎ **599/9-612266.**

Penha & Sons occupies the oldest building in town, built in 1708. Established in 1865, it's the distributor of such names as Boucheron, Jean Patou, Liz Claiborne, Yves Saint Laurent, and other perfumes and cosmetics of Elizabeth Arden, Clinique, Clarins, and Estée Lauder, among others. The collection of merchandise at this prestigious store is quite varied—Hummel figurines and Delft blue souvenirs. Don't miss their men's and women's boutiques, where they feature travel and sportswear. The firm has 12 other stores in the Caribbean.

The Yellow House (La Casa Amarilla)

Breedestraat 46. ☎ **599/9-613222.**

Housed in a yellow-and-white 19th-century building, and operating since 1887, this place sells an intriguing collection of perfume from all over the world, and is the exclusive agent of Christian Dior, Guerlain, and Van Cleef & Arpels.

CURAÇAO AFTER DARK

Most of the action spins around the island's **casinos:** at the Sonesta Beach Hotel & Casino Curaçao, the Curaçao Caribbean Hotel & Casino, the Holiday Beach Hotel & Casino, and the Princess Beach Resort & Casino—all hotels previously recommended. The Emerald Casino at the Sonesta is especially popular, designed to resemble an open-air courtyard. It features 143 slot machines, six blackjack tables, two roulette wheels, two Caribbean stud poker tables, one craps table, one baccarat table, and one mini-baccarat table. The casino at the Princess Beach Hotel is perhaps the liveliest on the island. These hotel gaming houses usually start their action at 2pm, and some of them remain open until 4am. The Princess Beach serves complimentary drinks.

The landlocked, flat, and somewhat dusty neighborhood of **Salinja** is now the nightlife capital of Curaçao, with many drinking and dancing outlets. Among the best of them are:

Club Facade
Lindbergweg 8. ☎ **599/9-614640.** Admission $8.

In the Salinja district, this is one of the most popular discos on the island. Spread over several different levels of a modern building, it has a huge bar and three dance floors, and is sometimes filled with balloons. Beer begins at $2, and there's live music daily. Open Wednesday through Sunday from 8pm to 2am.

L'Aristocrat
Salinja. ☎ **599/9-614353.** Admission $6.

In a sprawling and much-renovated building in the heart of the Salinja district, this is the leading and most attractive disco on Curaçao. Much of the music is live, and much of the preferred taste is for both merengue and salsa. Whenever one of the local bands get tired, recorded disco takes over, albeit briefly. Beer begins at $3. Open on Wednesday, Thursday, and Sunday from 10pm to 3am; on Friday and Saturday from 10pm to 4am.

NOTES

Now Save Money on All Your Travels by Joining

Frommer's
T R A V E L   B O O K   C L U B

The Advantages of Membership:
1. Your choice of any **TWO FREE BOOKS.**

2. Your own subscription to the **TRIPS & TRAVEL** quarterly newsletter, where you'll discover the best buys in travel, the hottest vacation spots, the latest travel trends, world-class events and festivals, and much more.

3. A **30% DISCOUNT** on any additional books you order through the club.

4. **DOMESTIC TRIP-ROUTING KITS** (available for a small additional fee). We'll send you a detailed map highlighting the most direct or scenic route to your destination, anywhere in North America.

Here's all you have to do to join:
Send in your annual membership fee of $25.00 ($35.00 Canada/Foreign) with your name, address, and selections on the form below. Or call 815/734-1104 to use your credit card.

Send all orders to:

--- ✂

FROMMER'S TRAVEL BOOK CLUB
P.O. Box 473 • Mt. Morris, IL 61054-0473 • ☎ 815/734-1104

YES! I want to take advantage of this opportunity to join Frommer's Travel Book Club.

[ ] My check for $25.00 ($35.00 for Canadian or foreign orders) is enclosed.
   All orders must be prepaid in U.S. funds only. Please make checks payable to Frommer's Travel Book Club.

[ ] Please charge my credit card: [ ] Visa or [ ] Mastercard

   Credit card number: _____

   Expiration date: ___ / ___ / ___

   Signature: _____

   Or call 815/734-1104 to use your credit card by phone.

Name: _____

Address: _____

City: _____   State: _____   Zip code: _____

Phone number (in case we have a question regarding your order): _____

Please indicate your choices for TWO FREE books (*see following pages*):

   Book 1 - Code: _____ Title: _____

   Book 2 - Code: _____ Title: _____

For information on ordering additional titles, see your first issue of the *Trips & Travel* newsletter.

Allow 4–6 weeks for delivery for all items. Prices of books, membership fee, and publication dates are subject to change without notice. All orders are subject to acceptance and availability.

AC1

The following Frommer's guides are available from your favorite bookstore, or you can use the order form on the preceding page to request them as part of your membership in Frommer's Travel Book Club.

FROMMER'S COMPLETE TRAVEL GUIDES

(Comprehensive guides to sightseeing, dining and accommodations, with selections in all price ranges—from deluxe to budget)

FROMMER'S $-A-DAY GUIDES

(Dream Vacations at Down-to-Earth Prices)

FROMMER'S COMPLETE CITY GUIDES

(Comprehensive guides to sightseeing, dining, and accommodations in all price ranges)

Amsterdam, 8th Ed.	S176	Minneapolis/St. Paul, 4th Ed.	S159
Athens, 10th Ed.	S174	Montréal/Québec City '95	S166
Atlanta & the Summer Olympic		Nashville/Memphis, 1st Ed.	S141
Games '96 (avail. 11/95)	S181	New Orleans '96 (avail. 10/95)	S182
Atlantic City/Cape May, 5th Ed.	S130	New York City '96 (avail. 11/95)	S183
Bangkok, 2nd Ed.	S147	Paris '96 (avail. 9/95)	S180
Barcelona '93-'94	S115	Philadelphia, 8th Ed.	S167
Berlin, 3rd Ed.	S162	Prague, 1st Ed.	S143
Boston '95	S160	Rome, 10th Ed.	S168
Budapest, 1st Ed.	S139	St. Louis/Kansas City, 2nd Ed.	S127
Chicago '95	S169	San Antonio/Austin, 1st Ed.	S177
Denver/Boulder/Colorado Springs,		San Diego '95	S158
3rd Ed.	S154	San Francisco '96 (avail. 10/95)	S184
Disney World/Orlando '96 (avail. 9/95)	S178	Santa Fe/Taos/Albuquerque '95	S172
Dublin, 2nd Ed.	S157	Seattle/Portland '94-'95	S137
Hong Kong '94-'95	S140	Sydney, 4th Ed.	S171
Las Vegas '95	S163	Tampa/St. Petersburg, 3rd Ed.	S146
London '96 (avail. 9/95)	S179	Tokyo '94-'95	S144
Los Angeles '95	S164	Toronto, 3rd Ed.	S173
Madrid/Costa del Sol, 2nd Ed.	S165	Vancouver/Victoria '94-'95	S142
Mexico City, 1st Ed.	S175	Washington, D.C. '95	S153
Miami '95-'96	S149		

FROMMER'S FAMILY GUIDES

(Guides to family-friendly hotels, restaurants, activities, and attractions)

California with Kids	F105	San Francisco with Kids	F104
Los Angeles with Kids	F103	Washington, D.C. with Kids	F102
New York City with Kids	F101		

FROMMER'S WALKING TOURS

*(Memorable strolls through colorful and historic neighborhoods,
accompanied by detailed directions and maps)*

Berlin	W100	Paris, 2nd Ed.	W112
Chicago	W107	San Francisco, 2nd Ed.	W115
England's Favorite Cities	W108	Spain's Favorite Cities (avail. 9/95)	W116
London, 2nd Ed.	W111	Tokyo	W109
Montréal/Québec City	W106	Venice	W110
New York, 2nd Ed.	W113	Washington, D.C., 2nd Ed.	W114

FROMMER'S AMERICA ON WHEELS

*(Guides for travelers who are exploring the U.S.A. by car, featuring a brand-new
rating system for accommodations and full-color road maps)*

Arizona/New Mexico	A100	Florida	A102
California/Nevada	A101	Mid-Atlantic	A103

FROMMER'S SPECIAL-INTEREST TITLES

Arthur Frommer's Branson!	P107	Frommer's Where to Stay U.S.A.,	
Arthur Frommer's New World		11th Ed.	P102
of Travel (avail. 11/95)	P112	National Park Guide, 29th Ed.	P106
Frommer's Caribbean Hideaways		USA Today Golf Tournament Guide	P113
(avail. 9/95)	P110	USA Today Minor League	
Frommer's America's 100 Best-Loved		Baseball Book	P111
State Parks	P109		

FROMMER'S BEST BEACH VACATIONS
(The top places to sun, stroll, shop, stay, play, party, and swim—with each beach rated for beauty, swimming, sand, and amenities)

California (avail. 10/95)	G100	Hawaii (avail. 10/95)	G102
Florida (avail. 10/95)	G101		

FROMMER'S BED & BREAKFAST GUIDES
(Selective guides with four-color photos and full descriptions of the best inns in each region)

California	B100	Hawaii	B105
Caribbean	B101	Pacific Northwest	B106
East Coast	B102	Rockies	B107
Eastern United States	B103	Southwest	B108
Great American Cities	B104		

FROMMER'S IRREVERENT GUIDES
(Wickedly honest guides for sophisticated travelers and those who want to be)

Chicago (avail. 11/95)	I100	New Orleans (avail. 11/95)	I103
London (avail. 11/95)	I101	San Francisco (avail. 11/95)	I104
Manhattan (avail. 11/95)	I102	Virgin Islands (avail. 11/95)	I105

FROMMER'S DRIVING TOURS
(Four-color photos and detailed maps outlining spectacular scenic driving routes)

Australia	Y100	Italy	Y108
Austria	Y101	Mexico	Y109
Britain	Y102	Scandinavia	Y110
Canada	Y103	Scotland	Y111
Florida	Y104	Spain	Y112
France	Y105	Switzerland	Y113
Germany	Y106	U.S.A.	Y114
Ireland	Y107		

FROMMER'S BORN TO SHOP
(The ultimate travel guides for discriminating shoppers—from cut-rate to couture)

Hong Kong (avail. 11/95)	Z100	London (avail. 11/95)	Z101